THE WAITE GROUP®

WINDOWS 95 COMMON CONTROLS & MESSAGES API BIBLE

RICHARD J. SIMON

WAITE GROUP PRESS™
A Division of
Sams Publishing
Corte Madera, CA

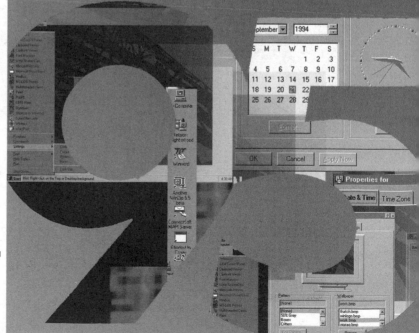

PUBLISHER: Mitchell Waite
EDITOR-IN-CHIEF: Charles Drucker

ACQUISITIONS EDITOR: Jill Pisoni

EDITORIAL DIRECTOR: John Crudo
MANAGING EDITOR: Laura E. Brown
CONTENT EDITOR: Harry Henderson
COPY EDITOR: Merrilee Eggleston
TECHNICAL REVIEWER: Branko Zurkovich

PRODUCTION DIRECTOR: Julianne Ososke
PRODUCTION MANAGER: Cecile Kaufman
PRODUCTION EDITOR: Mark Nigara
DESIGN: Sestina Quarequio, Michele Cuneo
PRODUCTION: Christi Fryday, Jude Levinson, Tom Debolski
COVER DESIGN: Cecile Kaufman and Sestina Quarequio

© 1996 by The Waite Group, Inc.
Published by Waite Group Press™, 200 Tamal Plaza, Corte Madera, CA 94925.

Waite Group Press™ is a division of Sams Publishing.

Waite Group Press is distributed to bookstores and book wholesalers by Publishers Group West, Box 8843, Emeryville, CA 94662, 1-800-788-3123 (in California 1-510-658-3453).

Printed in the United States of America
96 97 98 99 • 10 9 8 7 6 5 4 3 2 1

Library of Congress Cataloging-in-Publication Data
Simon, Richard J.
        Windows 95 common controls and messages API Bible / Richard J. Simon.
            p. cm.
        Includes index.
        ISBN 1-57169-010-7
            1. Microsoft Windows (Computer file)   2. Operating systems (Computers)   I. Title
    QA76.76.063S5586   1996
005.26--dc20

                                                                                    95-5165
                                                                                    CIP

Dedication

To my two children, Alex and Ashley.
—Richard J. Simon

Message from the
Publisher

WELCOME TO OUR NERVOUS SYSTEM

Some people say that the World Wide Web is a graphical extension of the information superhighway, just a network of humans and machines sending each other long lists of the equivalent of digital junk mail.

I think it is much more than that. To me, the Web is nothing less than the nervous system of the entire planet—not just a collection of computer brains connected together, but more like a billion silicon neurons entangled and recirculating electro-chemical signals of information and data, each contributing to the birth of another CPU and another Web site.

Think of each person's hard disk connected at once to every other hard disk on earth, driven by human navigators searching like Columbus for the New World. Seen this way, the Web is more of a super entity, a growing, living thing, controlled by the universal human will to expand, to be more. Yet, unlike a purposeful business plan with rigid rules, the Web expands in a nonlinear, unpredictable, creative way that echoes natural evolution.

We created our Web site not just to extend the reach of our computer book products but to be part of this synaptic neural network, to experience, like a nerve in the body, the flow of ideas, and then to pass those ideas up the food chain of the mind. Your mind. Even more, we wanted to pump some of our own creative juices into this rich wine of technology.

TASTE OUR DIGITAL WINE

And so we ask you to taste our wine by visiting the body of our business. Begin by understanding the metaphor we have created for our Web site—a universal learning center, situated in outer space in the form of a space station. A place where you can journey to study any topic from the convenience of your own screen. Right now we are focusing on computer topics, but the stars are the limit on the Web.

If you are interested in discussing this Web site or finding out more about the Waite Group, please send me e-mail with your comments and I will be happy to respond. Being a programmer myself, I love to talk about technology and find out what our readers are looking for.

Sincerely,

Mitchell Waite

Mitchell Waite, C.E.O. and Publisher

200 Tamal Plaza
Corte Madera CA 94925
415-924-2575
415-924-2576 fax

Internet e-mail:
support@waite.com

Website:
http://www.waite.com/waite

CREATING THE HIGHEST QUALITY COMPUTER BOOKS IN THE INDUSTRY

Waite Group Press
Waite Group New Media

About the Author

Richard J. Simon is the vice president of Development/Information Systems at a software development company in Irving, Texas. Richard manages both the development and the information systems groups, and he is also an active member in the development group where he specializes in client server Windows development in C/C++.

Acknowledgments

I would like to thank Laura Brown for her persistence and dedication to producing a quality book, Jill Pisoni for involving me in this project, and Mitchell Waite for his commitment to publishing the best books on the market. I would also like to thank Harry Henderson, Branko Zurkovich, Merrilee Eggleston, Mark Nigara, and the whole team of people at the Waite Group for all their hard work in publishing this book. Finally, I would like to thank my wife Jinjer, who worked as hard on this book as I did.

—Richard J. Simon

Contents

Table of Contents

Introduction

This is the second book in a series of three books designed and written to save programmers time in developing Windows 95 applications. The main focus of this book is the new Common Control Library and the updated common dialogs. With the use of the common controls and the common dialogs, the Windows 95 interface is more user friendly and standardized than previous versions of Windows.

Because the common controls are new to Windows 95, they are not well documented, and the number of examples available is limited. The purpose of this book is to be the complete reference for the Common Control Library and the updated common dialogs and to answer the questions that many programmers have about these powerful tools. Each of the common controls and common dialogs is fully documented using the familiar *API Bible* format, and each is used in working examples. Some of the examples show advanced features, such as implementing drag-and-drop in list views and tree views using image lists.

This book also covers the Dynamic Data Exchange Management Library (DDEML), messages, and common macros. Chapter 10, the DDEML chapter, covers the APIs for building client and server DDE applications. Chapter 11, the messages chapter, covers most of the messages the Win32 API and other APIs, such as the multimedia API, use in an application. Finally, Chapter 12, the macros chapter, covers the common macros that are used throughout Windows applications. The more specific macros, such as those in the Common Control Library, are defined in their appropriate chapter.

Each chapter covers a particular subject. For example, Chapter 7, Tree View, covers the functions, macros, and messages for the tree view control. Each chapter starts out with a short overview of the subject of the chapter, along with some background. This is followed by a summary table of the pertinent functions, macros, or messages, and finally the detailed descriptions with examples.

The examples show all appropriate variable declarations and usage of the function, macro, or message, along with required supporting source code. The purpose of the examples is not to provide tutorials but to demonstrate the function, macro, or message in a working program. In the interest of keeping the examples clear and concise, some shortcuts are taken that would not be used in a standard application.

All the chapters contain examples, except Chapters 11 and 12, Messages and Macros. These are for reference only. However, you can find examples for most of the messages and macros throughout this book and the other two books in the series, *Windows 95 WIN 32 Programming API Bible,* and *Windows 95 Multimedia & ODBC API Bible.*

Some chapters contain references to functions not covered in this book. You can find the descriptions for these functions in one of the other two books. For example, the CreateWindowEx() function is referenced in this book but is described in Chapter 3 of the Win32 API Bible.

This book was completed with the released version of Windows 95 and Windows NT 3.51. All the source code and projects were built using Microsoft's Visual C++ 2.2, which easily converts to Visual C++ 4.x. Other compilers capable of building Win32 applications should also work; however, you will need to build a project file specific to that compiler.

Originally, this book was going to document all the data structures in a manner similar to the way the messages are documented. As the project evolved, it became obvious that the structures were already defined in the chapters where they were needed, and the value of a summary chapter was not enough to justify the massive number of pages it would take to cover them. Therefore, some structures are not described in full in this book. They are, however, defined when referenced throughout this book and the other books in the places where they are most useful.

I hope you enjoy this book and that it makes your life easier!

Richard J. Simon

Installation

The CD included with this book contains the source code for the example programs featured herein. The code is organized according to chapter; for each chapter of the book, you'll find a corresponding directory on the CD containing the chapter projects. It is in an uncompressed format and can be copied directly from the CD. Be sure to check the README file for updates.

Copying the Source Code with Windows 95

When you are in the Windows 95 desktop, you can copy the source code to your computer's hard disk, using the following steps:

1. Double click on the My Computer icon to open the My Computer window.

2. Double click on the icon for your hard drive in the My Computer window.

3. Click on File in the menu bar.

4. Click on New, then on Folder. This will create a new directory on your hard disk into which you can copy the source code.

5. Type in a name for the new directory (such as Win95 CCM API Bible).

6. Click on My Computer in the chooser bar at the bottom of the Windows 95 desktop to bring up the My Computer dialog box.

7. Double click on the CD icon to view the CD's contents; you can open any subdirectories by clicking on them. These files can now be moved from the CD to the hard drive.

8. Drag the icon for the files into the new directory you created in Step 5. (If you cannot see the new directory, try dragging the My Computer window to a corner of the screen.)

9. Windows 95 will copy the contents of the CD to the new directory, maintaining the same organization as on the CD.

Assistance

If you have difficulty copying the source code from the CD, technical assistance can be obtained from Waite Group Press through these channels:

Phone: (415) 924-8102
E-mail: support@waite.com
Mail: 200 Tamal Plaza, Suite 101
Corte Madera, CA 94925

COMMON CONTROLS AND DIALOGS

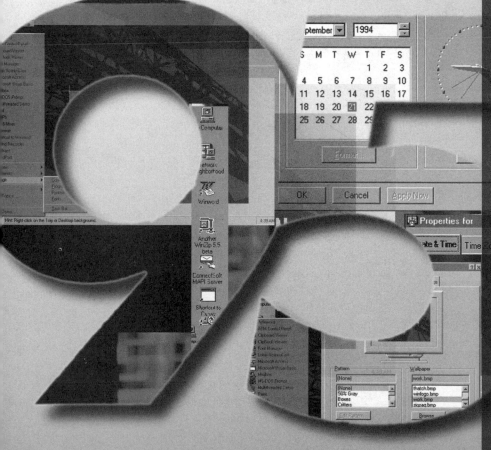

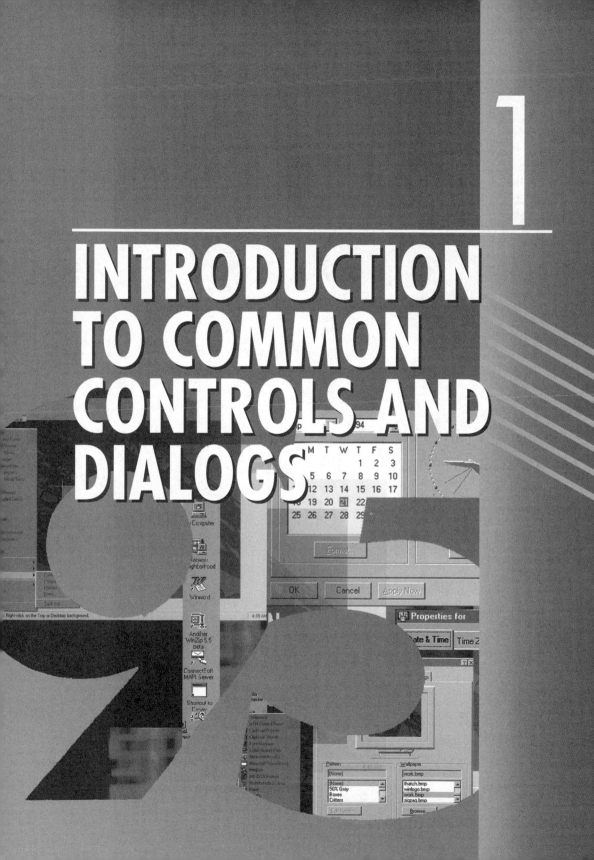

1

INTRODUCTION TO COMMON CONTROLS AND DIALOGS

1

INTRODUCTION TO COMMON CONTROLS AND DIALOGS

The Windows 95 operating system presents the user with a whole new look and feel that is more document-oriented than previous versions of Windows. A lot of the new look is automatically given to Windows 3.x applications, which were developed using the standard Windows controls. However, many of the new user interface features are exclusive to Win32 applications designed for Windows 95. Most of the functionality that was developed to achieve the new look and feel is available to the application developer.

Windows 95 includes updated common dialogs and a new library of common controls, which provides many of the controls that make up a major portion of the new user interface. Many of the traditional third party controls are replaced with the Common Control Library, which includes the following controls:

- Toolbar and status window

- Property sheet, wizard, and tab control

- Image list

- List view and drag list box

- Tree view

- Rich edit control

- Tooltip control, up-down control, hot-key control, trackbar, progress bar, header control, and animation control

Besides the updated look of the common dialogs, a new Page Setup common dialog has been added, which provides the user with a uniform look for applications that print to a printer and allow the user to change page characteristics. The following common dialogs are available:

- Color Selection

- Font Selection

- File Open and Save As

- Find Text and Find/Replace Text

- Print and Page Setup

This chapter gives a general overview of the common controls and dialogs available in Windows 95 and Windows NT. The functions and messages that are universal for common controls are also covered later in this chapter.

Common Controls

Most of the common controls are implemented in a dynamic-link library (COMCTL32.DLL) known as the Common Control Library. The rich edit control is implemented in another DLL (RICHED32.DLL) but is also included as part of the Common Control Library.

The Common Control Library is available in Windows 95 and Windows NT (3.51 and above), so you can develop Win32 applications that take advantage of the new controls on both operating systems.

Using Common Controls

The common controls, with the exception of image lists, are window classes that are registered when the common control DLLs are loaded. Applications then create the controls by specifying the appropriate window class with the CreateWindowEx() function. As with other window class types, you must use messages, or equivalent macros, to work with the common control.

An image list is not an actual control, but a storage container for images that are used in other common controls such as the tree view and list view. The API for image list is unique from the other common controls because it does not use messages. See Chapter 5, Image Lists, for more information about image lists.

An application can use the common controls in the COMCTL32.DLL by linking to the COMCTL32.LIB included in the Win32 SDK. You then need to include a call to the InitCommonControls() function to initialize the DLL prior to using the common controls within your application. The InitCommonControls() function does not take any parameters and its only purpose is to make sure the COMCTL32.DLL gets loaded into memory, which causes the common control window classes to be registered.

If an application requires the rich edit control, the application must use the LoadLibrary() function to load the RICHED32.DLL prior to creating the rich edit control.

The details of creating and using the common controls will not be discussed in this chapter; however, you can get detailed information for each of the common controls in Chapters 3–9.

Toolbars and Status Windows

Toolbars and status windows have been part of most Windows applications for the past few years, with each application using its own implementation of these controls. Now these controls are supported by the Common Control Library, giving all applications that use them a uniform look and feel. Figure 1-1 shows the Windows 95 Explorer with the toolbar, status window, and other common controls pointed out.

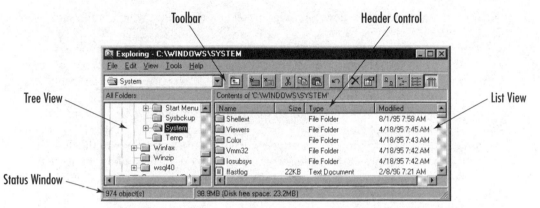

Figure 1-1 Common controls in Windows 95 Explorer

A toolbar is a window that contains other controls, such as buttons and combo boxes. The controls allow the user quick access to common application commands and provide feedback for current settings, such as the current font characteristics. Most applications provide a toolbar at the top of the client area of the main application window.

A status window is a small window that usually resides at the bottom of the client area of the main application window. The status window can display text and graphical information about the current status. The status window commonly displays menu item help as the user highlights different menu items. You can also use the status window to display the current cursor position, the state of the keyboard state keys (CAPS LOCK, NUM LOCK, SCROLL LOCK), and other information that is relevant to the current context of the application.

Property Sheets, Wizards, and Tab Controls

Tab controls provide a user interface that allows the user to switch between different pages of information. The appearance and operation is what you would expect, with a stack of file folders with the tabs showing. When the user selects a tab, the page (file

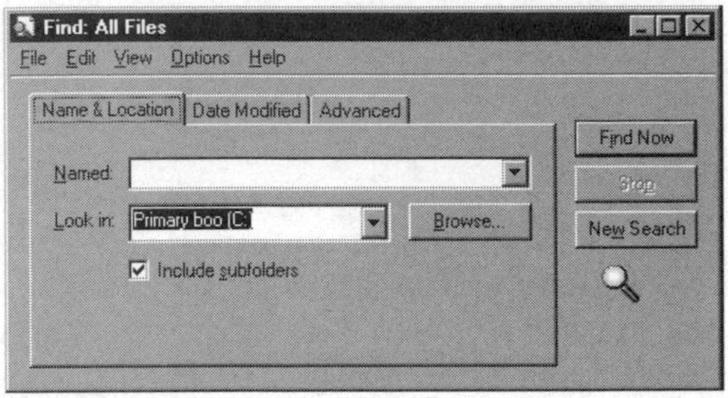

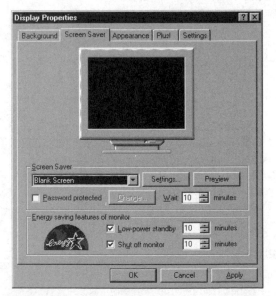

Figure 1-2 Tab control in Windows 95 Find window

folder) is opened. Figure 1-2 shows the Windows 95 Find window, which is an example of a tab control within a window.

An application can use tab controls in situations where not all the information easily fits within a window. The information can be grouped into related pieces of information and placed on individual pages (file folders). Each page is given an identifying name that is displayed on the tab.

A property sheet is a dialog that provides a consistent user interface for viewing and changing the properties of an item such as a file, graphical image, or even the Windows 95 desktop. The property sheet uses the tab control as the body of the dialog box with an OK, Apply, Cancel, and sometimes a Help button at the bottom of the dialog. Just like dialog boxes, property sheets can be modal or modeless in operation. Figure 1-3 shows the property sheet for the Windows 95 desktop.

Figure 1-3 Property sheet for Windows 95 desktop

Property sheets have another option that does not use the tab control: the wizard. Instead of showing the pages as tabs within the tab control, a wizard leads the user through the pages sequentially. Wizards are commonly used to lead the user through a process that requires steps to be performed in a particular order. Figure 1-4 shows the wizard that Windows 95 uses to set up a new printer.

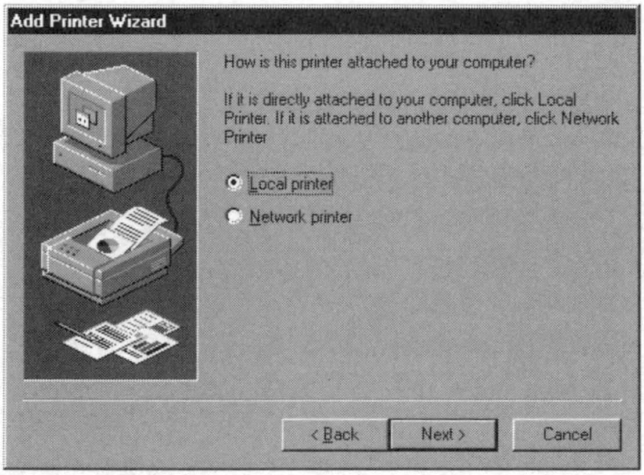

Figure 1-4 Add Printer Wizard for Windows 95

Image Lists

The image list is not a control, even though it is packaged as a common control. Instead it is a storage container for images used in the list view, tree view, and any other use that requires multiple same-sized images.

The image list also implements drag functions that allow you to easily drag full-color images on the screen without flicker. These are the same routines that Windows 95 uses to perform all drag-and-drop operations throughout the operating system.

For more information on the image list and how to use it, see Chapter 5, Image Lists.

List Views and Drag List Boxes

A list view is a control that is similar to a list box in that it maintains a collection of items and can display them in a list. Beyond this similarity, the list view is completely different from the list box. The list view allows each item to have an associated icon. The items can be viewed in four different views: icon, small icon, list, and report.

All the views, except report, display a small or large icon and the name of the item. Report view can also show additional information for the item in separate columns, as seen in Figure 1-1. When the list view is in the icon or small icon view mode, you can also move the items to new locations and reorganize the list view items into a custom view.

If the list view control is more than what is required, and all you need is a simple list box with drag-and-drop capabilities, the Common Control Library also implements an API that easily converts a standard list box into a drag list box. The API subclasses an existing list box to convert it to a drag list box. Once the drag list box is initialized, the user can then drag list box items to new locations.

The drag-and-drop operations for the list view and drag list box do not happen by default. The controls only provide notifications to the application of events that indicate a drag operation. It is up to the application to implement that actual drag operation.

For more information on the list view and drag list box and how to implement the drag-and-drop operation, see Chapter 6, List View and Drag List.

Tree Views

The tree view allows you to present information to the user in a hierarchical tree. Similar third party controls have been used for a few years in Windows applications; however, they haven't looked the same in all applications and each has had its own user interface. The tree view control allows you to easily develop Win32 applications that have a consistent look and feel.

Tree view controls are used liberally throughout the Windows 95 interface. As seen in Figure 1-1, the Windows 95 Explorer uses a tree view to show the directory structure of the computer.

The tree view also allows you to specify an icon based on an item type, not the level within the tree, as with most third party controls. You can then provide a different icon based on the item type that is in the tree and have multiple item types within the same tree. The Windows 95 Explorer does this by placing not just drives and folders in the tree but also the control panel, printers, dial-up networking, the recycle bin, and other item types.

Like the list view, the tree view supports drag-and-drop operations. Again, they don't come by default; the application must process the appropriate notification messages.

For more information on the tree view, see Chapter 7, Tree View.

Rich Edit Controls

The rich edit control is the answer to one of the most common user interface problems a Windows application developer has: The edit control doesn't support what is needed, so it is subclassed. The rich edit control does not have the size limitations of the standard edit control (under Windows 95, the standard edit control has the same 32K limitation as under Windows 3.x). The rich edit control fully supports multiple fonts and font sizes within the same edit control. Advanced formatting, such as paragraphs and tabs, is also supported.

The rich edit control is created and used similarly to the standard edit control. In fact, most of the standard edit control messages work with the rich edit control. Along with the standard edit control messages, the rich edit control has many specific messages to control the advanced features.

The rich edit control is so powerful, you can easily develop an advanced, full-featured editor. The WordPad editor shipped with Windows 95, shown in Figure 1-5, is an example of what you can do with the rich edit control.

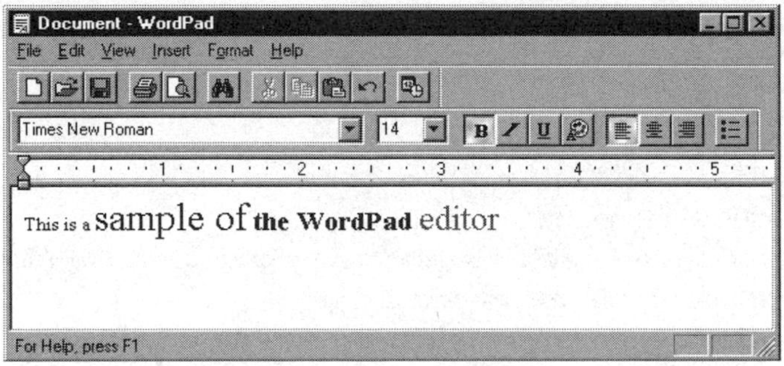

Figure 1-5 Rich edit control in Windows 95 WordPad editor

For more information on the rich edit control and an example of an editor, see Chapter 8, Rich-Text Edit Controls.

Other Common Controls

The remaining common controls (tooltip control, up-down control, hot-key control, trackbar, progress bar, header control, and animation control) go a long way toward providing the final touches on the overall user interface. Some of these controls, such as the tooltip in toolbars, are used as parts of other common controls. Another example is the header control, which is used for the column headers in a list view while in report view.

For a complete description of each of these controls and examples, see Chapter 9, Miscellaneous Controls.

Notification Messages

Most of the common controls notify the parent window of events through notification messages. Many of the controls have special notification codes that are specific to that control. These are covered in the chapters that cover the control. There are also notification codes that are general to almost all of the common controls.

These general notification messages cover events such as clicking the mouse buttons, focus changes, and out of memory situations. They are sent to the parent window through the WM_NOTIFY message, with the *lParam* containing a pointer to an NMHDR structure, which contains the notification code and other information about the event. For the definition of the NMHDR structure, see Chapter 3, Toolbars and Status Windows, under the TBN_BEGINADJUST notification message.

The common notification codes are listed in Table 1-1, along with a description of the notification.

Table 1-1 Common notification codes

Value	Meaning
NM_CLICK	The user has clicked the left mouse button within the control.
NM_DBLCLK	The user has double-clicked the left mouse button within the control.
NM_KILLFOCUS	The control has lost the input focus.
NM_OUTOFMEMORY	The control could not complete an operation because there was not enough memory available.
NM_RCLICK	The user has clicked the right mouse button within the control.
NM_RDBLCLK	The user has double-clicked the right mouse button within the control.
NM_RETURN	The control has the input focus, and the user has pressed the ENTER key.
NM_SETFOCUS	The control has received the input focus.

Common Dialogs

The common dialogs are nothing new to Windows developers. They have been around since Windows 3.1 was introduced, and most Windows developers have incorporated them into their applications.

The purpose of the common dialogs is to provide a consistent user interface for common tasks, such as File Open, Save As, Find/Replace, etc., within a Windows application. An advantage that is not as clear but is equally important is the common API. With the new user interface in Windows 95, the user interface for the common dialogs has also changed. However, the API remains basically the same, with some added functionality. So with little work, your application now has a new look and feel that is consistent with other Windows 95 applications.

Given that a Windows 95 application should also work with Windows NT 3.51, and the Windows NT user interface is the older Windows 3.1, the common dialogs will automatically *downgrade* themselves when running on Windows NT 3.51. However, if the application does not use the default functionality of the common dialogs and changes their look and behavior, the application must handle both operating systems.

For more information, descriptions, and examples of each common dialog, see Chapter 2, Common Dialogs.

2

COMMON DIALOGS

2

COMMON DIALOGS

Common dialog boxes are the standard file, print, page setup, color, font, and search dialog boxes used by Windows applications. They provide a uniform user interface that lets users perform common tasks, such as opening files and printing documents, without learning a new interface for each application. This chapter describes the various common dialog boxes and the related functions.

Dialog Box Types

All of the common dialog boxes are created in essentially the same manner; the application fills a structure and passes it to a function that creates the dialog box. The different common dialog box types have different structures and functions that correspond to the type. Table 2-1 summarizes the different common dialog box types and the related functions and structures.

Table 2-1 Common dialog box types

Type	Description
Color	A dialog box with basic colors that lets the user select a basic color or create and select a custom color. Use the ChooseColor() function and CHOOSECOLOR structure.
Find	A modeless dialog box that lets the user enter a search string and search options. Use the FindText() function and FINDREPLACE structure.
Font	Displays a dialog box with a list of font face names, point sizes, and other font attributes the user can select from. Use the ChooseFont() function and CHOOSEFONT structure.

continued on next page

continued from previous page

Type	Description
Open	A dialog box with a list of file names, directories, and drives. The user can select the directory and file name of a file to be opened. Use the GetOpenFileName() function and OPENFILENAME structure.
Page Setup	A dialog box that lets the user select page configuration options, such as paper orientation, size, source, and margins. Use the PageSetupDlg() function and PAGESETUPDLG structure. This dialog box replaces the Print Setup common dialog box that was used in previous versions of Windows.
Print	A dialog box that lets the user select print job options, such as the printer, the range of pages to print, and the number of copies. Use the PrintDlg() function and PRINTDLG structure.
Replace	A modeless dialog box that lets the user select search and replacement strings and replacement options. Use the ReplaceText() function and FINDREPLACE structure.
Save As	A dialog box with a list of file names, directories, and drives. The user can select the directory and file name or enter the file name of a file to be saved. Use the GetSaveFileName() function and OPENFILENAME structure.

All the common dialog boxes are modal except the Find and Replace dialog boxes. This means that the function that creates the dialog box, such as the PrintDlg() function, does not return until the user has closed the dialog box. The FindText() and ReplaceText() functions, which create the Find and Replace dialog boxes, return before the dialog box closes. The application must use the window handle of the dialog box with the IsDialogMessage() function in the message loop to ensure that the special dialog box keys, such as [TAB] and [ESC], work correctly.

Customizing Common Dialogs

All common dialog boxes are customizable through the flags specified in the structure related to the dialog. Options can be disabled and even controls hidden in some cases. However, the common dialog performs default processing in the same manner and always has the same basic appearance. If an application has a special need that is not supported through the option flags, the common dialog can be further customized by using a custom dialog template and/or a hook function that monitors and responds to messages sent to the default dialog box procedure.

Hook Function

The hook function for a common dialog is enabled by setting an ENABLEHOOK value in the *Flags* member and putting the address of the hook function in an *lpfnHook* member of the structure for the dialog box. The hook function is essentially a DlgProc() function. Listing 2-1 shows the basic form of a hook function.

Listing 2-1 Hook Function

```
UINT APIENTRY MyHook( HWND hdlg, UINT msg, WPARAM wParam, LPARAM lParam )
{
    switch ( msg )
    {
    case WM_*:
```

```
        // process the message
        return TRUE;

    default:
        return FALSE; // Default processing
    }
}
```

The hook function receives messages and notifications before they are dispatched to the dialog box procedure. The exception is the WM_INITDIALOG message, which the hook function receives after the dialog box procedure returns. The hook function can process a message and return TRUE, or let the dialog box procedure process it by returning FALSE.

If the hook function processes the WM_CTLCOLORDLG message, it must return a valid brush handle for painting the background of the dialog box. It must also return a valid brush handle for other WM_CTLCOLOR* messages.

A hook function should never terminate the dialog box by calling the EndDialog() function or the DestroyWindow() function. Instead, use the PostMessage() function to post a WM_COMMAND message with the IDABORT value to the dialog box procedure. When a hook function posts the IDABORT value, the common dialog box function returns the value contained in the low-order word of the *lParam* parameter.

Dialog Template

All common dialog box functions use default dialog templates. If an application requires additional controls that are unique to that application, a custom dialog box template can be substituted for the default template, or in some cases added to the default template. In most cases, when a custom dialog template is used, a hook function is also defined to handle the new controls added to the dialog box.

Enable the custom template by setting an ENABLETEMPLATE or ENABLETEMPLATEHANDLE value in the *Flags* member of the corresponding structure for the dialog box. If the template is a resource in an application or dynamic-link library, set the *hInstance* and *lpTemplateName* members of the structure. If the template is already in memory, the member you set depends on the specific structure.

The purpose of the common dialog boxes is to provide a consistent user interface for common tasks. Custom templates should not be used unless absolutely necessary. If a custom dialog template must be used, care should be taken when designing the new dialog template to maintain the original controls and to place new controls in an empty space without moving existing controls. Also make sure the identifiers for the new controls are unique and do not conflict with existing controls. The default templates and identifiers are available in resource scripts (.DLG) and header (.H) files. Use these as the basis for the new dialog template.

Messages

Common dialog boxes send registered messages to either the window procedure of the *hwndOwner* member of the corresponding structure of the common dialog box or to the hook function. These messages notify the application of events and request responses. Before an application can process a registered message, it must retrieve the message identifier by passing the predefined message string to the RegisterWindow-Message() function. Table 2-2 lists the predefined message strings.

Table 2-2 Registered message strings

Message String	Meaning	
COLOROKSTRING	Approves or rejects a color selection. The *lParam* contains a pointer to the CHOOSECOLOR structure. Use the *lpCustColors* member to check the current color.	
FILEOKSTRING	Approves or rejects a file name. The *lParam* contains a pointer to the OPENFILENAME structure.	
FINDMSGSTRING	Finds or replaces a given string. The *lParam* contains a pointer to the FINDREPLACE structure.	
HELPMSGSTRING	Displays help for a dialog box.	
LBSELCHSTRING	Selection in a list box has changed. The *wParam* parameter is the window handle in which the selection occurred. The low-order word of the *lParam* parameter is the list box item. The high-order word of the *lParam* parameter is one of the following values:	
	Value	**Meaning**
	CD_LBSELADD	The item was selected in a multiple-selection list box.
	CD_LBSELCHANGE	The item was selected in a single-selection list box.
	CD_LBSELNOITEMS	No items exist in a multiple-selection list box.
	CD_LBSELSUB	The item is no longer selected in a multiple-selection list box.
SETRGBSTRING	Sets the current color selection. Sent from the hook procedure to the dialog box. The *lParam* parameter contains the RGB color value.	
SHAREVISTRING	Opening a file causes a sharing violation. The *lParam* parameter is a pointer to the OPENFILENAME structure.	

The Find and Replace dialog boxes send their registered message, FINDMSGSTRING, to the window procedure. Other common dialog boxes send their registered messages to the hook function. The registered message, SETRGBSTRING, is intended to be sent to the common dialog box from the hook function.

The hook function receives a variety of other messages while the dialog box is created and eventually destroyed. For example, the hook function receives a WM_INITDIALOG message with the *lParam* parameter set to the address of the structure used to initialize the dialog box. Most messages are WM_NOTIFY notification messages indicating actions taken by the user in the dialog box. For a detailed discussion of the individual messages a common dialog uses, see the description of the functions later in this chapter.

Help Support

Common dialog boxes provide online help by default. The user can display help for individual controls by selecting the control and pressing the F1 key or by selecting the ? button in the title bar and clicking on a control.

If an application customizes a dialog box by adding new controls, it should extend help support for these controls by processing requests for help in the hook function.

The hook function receives WM_HELP or WM_CONTEXTMENU messages when the user requests help by pressing the [F1] key, using the ? button, or clicking the right mouse button. The application should process these messages for the controls that it added, but let the default dialog box procedure process the messages for the original controls.

Although it is not recommended for Windows 95, you can supplement the default help by adding and supporting a Help button in the dialog box. The Help button is useful for describing the general purpose of the dialog box as it applies to the application. Add the Help button by setting a SHOWHELP value in the *Flags* member of the structure for the dialog box. The application supports the Help button by processing the registered message associated with the HELPMSGSTRING message string. The common dialog box sends this message to the window procedure of the owner window whenever the user selects the Help button.

Function Summary

Table 2-3 summarizes the common dialog functions. The detailed function descriptions follow immediately after the table.

Table 2-3 Common dialog function summary

Function	Meaning
ChooseColor	Uses the color selection common dialog.
ChooseFont	Uses the font selection common dialog.
CommDlgExtendedError	Returns the most recent common dialog extended error code.
FindText	Uses the find text common dialog.
GetFileTitle	Returns a display-only file name from a complete file name.
GetOpenFileName	Uses the file open common dialog.
GetSaveFileName	Uses the file save common dialog.
PageSetupDlg	Uses the page setup common dialog.
PrintDlg	Uses the print common dialog.
ReplaceText	Uses the find and replace text common dialog.

CHOOSECOLOR   ■ Win32s ■ Windows 95 ■ Windows NT

Description   ChooseColor() creates a Choose Color common dialog the user can use to select a color for text, background, or some application-specific purpose. Because palettes are not supported, the color choices offered by the dialog box are limited to the system colors and dithered versions of those colors.

Syntax   BOOL **ChooseColor**(LPCHOOSECOLOR *lpcc*)

Parameters

lpcc   LPCHOOSECOLOR: A pointer to a CHOOSECOLOR structure that, when the function is called, contains information necessary to initialize the dialog box. When ChooseColor() returns, this structure contains information about the user's color selection. See the definition of the CHOOSECOLOR structure below.

Returns   BOOL: If the user selects a color, TRUE is returned. If the user chooses the Cancel button, the Close command on the system menu, or an error occurs, FALSE is returned. Use the CommDlgExtendedError() function to retrieve extended error information. One of the errors listed in Table 2-4 can be returned.

Table 2-4 ChooseColor() extended errors

Value	Meaning
CDERR_FINDRESFAILURE	A specified resource could not be found.
CDERR_INITIALIZATION	Failed during initialization.
CDERR_LOADRESFAILURE	A specified resource could not be loaded.
CDERR_LOADSTRFAILURE	A specified string could not be loaded.
CDERR_LOCKRESFAILURE	A specified resource could not be locked.
CDERR_MEMALLOCFAILURE	Unable to allocate memory for internal structures.
CDERR_MEMLOCKFAILURE	Unable to lock the memory associated with a handle.
CDERR_NOHINSTANCE	The CC_ENABLETEMPLATE flag was specified without providing an instance handle in the *hInstance* member.
CDERR_NOHOOK	The CC_ENABLEHOOK flag was specified without providing a pointer to a hook function in the *lpfnHook* member.
CDERR_NOTEMPLATE	The CC_ENABLETEMPLATE flag was specified without providing a template in the *lpstrTemplateName* member.
CDERR_STRUCTSIZE	The *lStructSize* member of a CHOOSECOLOR structure is invalid.

Include File   commdlg.h

See Also   CommDlgExtendedError()

Related Messages COLOROKSTRING, SETRGBSTRING, HELPMSGSTRING

CHOOSECOLOR Definition

```
typedef struct
{
    DWORD        lStructSize;
    HWND         hwndOwner;
    HWND         hInstance;
    COLORREF     rgbResult;
    COLORREF*    lpCustColors;
    DWORD        Flags;
    LPARAM       lCustData;
    LPCCHOOKPROC lpfnHook;
    LPCTSTR      lpTemplateName;
} CHOOSECOLOR;
```

Members

lStructSize	DWORD: The length, in bytes, of the structure.
hwndOwner	HWND: The window that owns the dialog box. This member can be any valid window handle, or set to NULL if the dialog box has no owner.
hInstance	HWND: The instance handle of the module that contains the dialog box template specified by the *lpTemplateName* member. If the CC_ENABLETEMPLATEHANDLE flag is specified, this member identifies the memory block with a preloaded dialog template.
rgbResult	COLORREF: The color initially selected when the dialog box is created, and contains the user's color selection when the dialog box is closed. When the dialog box is created, the system selects the nearest solid color available if the CC_RGBINIT flag is specified in the *Flags* member and the value of this member is not among the colors available.
lpCustColors	COLORREF*: A pointer to an array of 16 COLORREF variables that contain red, green, blue (RGB) values for the custom color boxes in the dialog box. If the user modifies these colors, the system updates the array with the new RGB values.
Flags	DWORD: The dialog box initialization flags. This member may be a combination of the flags in Table 2-5.

Table 2-5 CHOOSECOLOR *Flags* values

Value	Meaning
CC_ENABLEHOOK	Enables the hook function specified in the *lpfnHook* member.
CC_ENABLETEMPLATE	Causes the system to create the dialog box by using the dialog box template identified by the *hInstance* and *lpTemplateName* members.
CC_ENABLETEMPLATEHANDLE	Indicates that the *hInstance* member identifies a memory block containing a preloaded dialog box template. The system ignores the *lpTemplateName* member if this flag is specified.
CC_FULLOPEN	Causes the entire dialog box to appear when the dialog box is created, including the portion that allows the user to create custom colors. If this flag is not specified, the user must choose the Define Custom Colors button to see this portion of the dialog box.
CC_PREVENTFULLOPEN	Disables the Define Custom Colors button, preventing the user from creating custom colors.
CC_RGBINIT	Causes the dialog box to use the color specified in the *rgbResult* member as the initial color selection.
CC_SHOWHELP	Causes the dialog box to show the Help button. The *hwndOwner* member must not be NULL if this option is specified.

lCustData	LPARAM: Application-defined data the system passes to the hook function identified by the *lpfnHook* member. The system passes the data in the *lParam* parameter of the WM_INITDIALOG message.

lpfnHook

LPCCHOOKPROC: A pointer to a hook function that processes messages intended for the dialog box. An application must specify the CC_ENABLEHOOK flag in the *Flags* member to enable the function; otherwise, the system ignores this member. The hook function must return FALSE to pass a message to the standard color dialog box procedure or TRUE to discard the message.

lpstrTemplateName

LPCTSTR: A pointer to a null-terminated string that names the dialog box template to be substituted for the standard dialog box template. An application can use the MAKEINTRESOURCE macro for numbered dialog box resources. This member is used only if *Flags* specifies the CC_ENABLETEMPLATE flag; otherwise, it is ignored.

Example

This example, shown in Figure 2-1 and Listing 2-2, uses the Choose Color common dialog to allow the user to select the color used as the client area background color. When the user selects the Test! menu item, the Choose Color common dialog is displayed. If the user selects a new color, the window is updated to show that color.

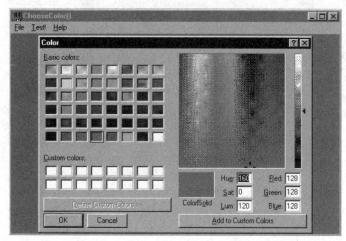

Figure 2-1 ChooseColor() example

Listing 2-2 *Using the ChooseColor() common dialog*

```
#define CUSTCOLORS 16

LRESULT CALLBACK WndProc( HWND hWnd, UINT uMsg, WPARAM wParam, LPARAM lParam )
{
static DWORD dwCustColors[CUSTCOLORS];
static DWORD dwColor = 0;

   switch( uMsg )
   {
```

```
case WM_CREATE :
        // Default the colors to white.
        //.............................
        memset( dwCustColors, 255, sizeof( DWORD )*CUSTCOLORS );
        break;

case WM_PAINT :
        {
            PAINTSTRUCT ps;
            HBRUSH      hBrush;
            RECT        rect;

            // Get the client rect and create a brush.
            //........................................
            GetClientRect( hWnd, &rect );
            hBrush = CreateSolidBrush( dwColor );

            // Paint the client area of the window.
            //.....................................
            BeginPaint( hWnd, &ps );
            FillRect( ps.hdc, &rect, hBrush );
            EndPaint( hWnd, &ps );

            // Delete the brush.
            //..................
            DeleteObject( hBrush );
        }
        break;

case WM_COMMAND :
        switch( LOWORD( wParam ) )
        {
        case IDM_TEST :
            {
                CHOOSECOLOR cc;

                // Initialize the CHOOSECOLOR structure.
                //......................................
                memset( &cc, 0, sizeof( CHOOSECOLOR ) );
                cc.lStructSize  = sizeof( CHOOSECOLOR );
                cc.hwndOwner    = hWnd;
                cc.lpCustColors = dwCustColors;
                cc.rgbResult    = dwColor;
                cc.Flags        = CC_RGBINIT;

                // Create the choose color dialog.
                //................................
                if ( ChooseColor( &cc ) )
                {
                    // If the user chooses a color,
                    // set the selected color as the new color.
                    //.........................................
                    dwColor = cc.rgbResult;
                    InvalidateRect( hWnd, NULL, TRUE );
                }
            }
            break;
```

continued on next page

continued from previous page

```
                case IDM_EXIT :
                        DestroyWindow( hWnd );
                        break;
                }
                break;

        case WM_DESTROY :
                PostQuitMessage(0);
                break;

        default :
                return( DefWindowProc( hWnd, uMsg, wParam, lParam ) );
        }

        return( 0L );
}
```

CHOOSEFONT   ■ Win32s   ■ Windows 95   ■ Windows NT

Description	ChooseFont() creates a Choose Font common dialog box from which the user can select a font, a font style (such as bold or italic), a point size, an effect (such as strikeout or underline), and a text color.
Syntax	BOOL **ChooseFont**(LPCHOOSEFONT *lpcf*)
Parameters	
lpcf	LPCHOOSEFONT: A pointer to a CHOOSEFONT structure that, when the function is called, contains information necessary to initialize the dialog box. When ChooseFont() returns, this structure contains information about the user's font selection. See the definition of the CHOOSEFONT structure below.
Returns	BOOL: If the user selects a font, TRUE is returned. If the user chooses the Cancel button, the Close command on the system menu, or an error occurs, FALSE is returned. Use the CommDlgExtendedError() function to retrieve extended error information. One of the errors listed in Table 2-6 can be returned.

Table 2-6 ChooseFont() extended errors

Value	Meaning
CDERR_FINDRESFAILURE	A specified resource could not be found.
CDERR_INITIALIZATION	Failed during initialization.
CDERR_LOADRESFAILURE	A specified resource could not be loaded.
CDERR_LOADSTRFAILURE	A specified string could not be loaded.
CDERR_LOCKRESFAILURE	A specified resource could not be locked.
CDERR_MEMALLOCFAILURE	Unable to allocate memory for internal structures.
CDERR_MEMLOCKFAILURE	Unable to lock the memory associated with a handle.
CDERR_NOHINSTANCE	The CF_ENABLETEMPLATE flag was specified without providing an instance handle in the *hInstance* member.

Value	Meaning
CDERR_NOHOOK	The CF_ENABLEHOOK flag was specified without providing a pointer to a hook function in the *lpfnHook* member.
CDERR_NOTEMPLATE	The CF_ENABLETEMPLATE flag was specified without providing a template in the *lpTemplateName* member.
CDERR_STRUCTSIZE	The *lStructSize* member of a CHOOSECOLOR structure is invalid.
CFERR_MAXLESSTHANMIN	The value of the *nSizeMax* member is less than the value of the *nSizeMin* member.
CFERR_NOFONTS	No fonts were found.

Include File	commdlg.h
See Also	CommDlgExtendedError()
Related Messages	HELPMSGSTRING

CHOOSEFONT Definition

```
typedef struct
{
    DWORD         lStructSize;
    HWND          hwndOwner;
    HDC           hDC;
    LPLOGFONT     lpLogFont;
    INT           iPointSize;
    DWORD         Flags;
    DWORD         rgbColors;
    LPARAM        lCustData;
    LPCFHOOKPROC  lpfnHook;
    LPCTSTR       lpTemplateName;
    HINSTANCE     hInstance;
    LPTSTR        lpszStyle;
    WORD          nFontType;
    WORD          ___MISSING_ALIGNMENT__;
    INT           nSizeMin;
    INT           nSizeMax;
} CHOOSEFONT;
```

Members

lStructSize   DWORD: The length, in bytes, of the structure.

hwndOwner   HWND: The window that owns the dialog box. This member can be any valid window handle. Set to NULL if the dialog box has no owner.

hDC   HDC: The device context (or information context) of the printer whose fonts will be listed in the dialog box. This member is used only if the *Flags* member specifies the CF_PRINTERFONTS flag; otherwise, this member is ignored.

lpLogFont   LPLOGFONT: A pointer to a LOGFONT structure. If an application initializes the members of this structure before calling the ChooseFont() function and also sets the CF_INITTOLOGFONTSTRUCT flag, ChooseFont() initializes the dialog box with a font that is the closest possible match. After the user closes the dialog box, ChooseFont() sets the members of the LOGFONT structure based on the user's final selection. See the definition of the LOGFONT structure below.

iPointSize	INT: The size of the selected font, in units of 1/10 of a point. ChooseFont() sets this value after the user closes the dialog box.
Flags	DWORD: The dialog box initialization flags. This member may be a combination of the flags in Table 2-7.

Table 2-7 CHOOSEFONT *Flag* values

Value	Meaning
CF_ANSIONLY	In Windows NT, this flag specifies that ChooseFont() should allow the selection of all fonts that use the Windows and Unicode character sets. The user will not be able to select fonts that use the OEM or Symbol character sets. This flag is equivalent to the Windows 95 CF_SCRIPTSONLY flag. This flag is obsolete in Windows 95.
CF_APPLY	Enables the Apply button.
CF_BOTH	Lists the available printer and screen fonts. The *hDC* member identifies the device context (or information context) associated with the printer.
CF_EFFECTS	Enables strikeout, underline, and color effects. If this flag is specified, use the *rgbColors* member of this structure and the *lfStrikeOut* and *lfUnderline* members of the LOGFONT structure pointed to by *lpLogFont* to set the initial effects. ChooseFont() uses these members to store the user's selections after the user closes the dialog box.
CF_ENABLEHOOK	Enables the hook function specified in the *lpfnHook* member of this structure.
CF_ENABLETEMPLATE	Indicates that the *hInstance* member identifies a resource instance that contains the dialog box template identified by the *lpTemplateName* member.
CF_ENABLETEMPLATEHANDLE	Indicates that the *hInstance* member identifies a data block that contains a preloaded dialog box template. The system ignores the *lpTemplateName* member if this flag is specified.
CF_FIXEDPITCHONLY	Selects only fixed-pitch fonts.
CF_FORCEFONTEXIST	Forces the font and style the user selects to exist; otherwise, an error condition occurs.
CF_INITTOLOGFONTSTRUCT	Uses the LOGFONT structure pointed to by the *lpLogFont* member to initialize the dialog box controls.
CF_LIMITSIZE	Selects only font sizes within the range specified by the *nSizeMin* and *nSizeMax* members.
CF_NOFACESEL	Specifies not to make an initial face name selection, because there is no one single face name that applies to the text selection. Set this flag if the text selection contains multiple face names.
CF_NOOEMFONTS	See the CF_NOVECTORFONTS description.
CF_NOSCRIPTSEL	Specifies that there is no selection in the character set combo box. Applications use this flag to support multiple character set selections. This flag is set on input only. When it is set, the script combo box is disabled and the *lfCharSet* member of the LOGFONT structure is set to DEFAULT_CHARSET. This flag is valid only for Windows 95.
CF_NOSIMULATIONS	Does not allow graphics device interface (GDI) font simulations.
CF_NOSIZESEL	Specifies no initial size selection, because there is no one single size that applies to the text selection. Set this flag if the text selection contains multiple sizes.
CF_NOSTYLESEL	Specifies no initial style selection, because there is no one single style that applies to the text selection. Set this flag if the text selection contains multiple styles.

Value	Meaning
CF_NOVECTORFONTS	Does not allow vector font selections.
CF_NOVERTFONTS	Lists only horizontally oriented fonts. This flag is valid only for Windows 95.
CF_PRINTERFONTS	Lists only the fonts supported by the printer associated with the device context (or information context) identified by the *hDC* member.
CF_SCALABLEONLY	Allows only the selection of scalable fonts.
CF_SCREENFONTS	Lists only the screen fonts supported by the system.
CF_SCRIPTSONLY	Allows selection of fonts for all non-OEM and Symbol character sets, as well as the ANSI character set. This supersedes the CF_ANSIONLY value. This flag is valid only for Windows 95.
CF_SELECTSCRIPT	Displays only fonts with the character set identified in the *lfCharSet* member of the LOGFONT structure. The user will not be allowed to change the character set combo box. This flag is valid only for Windows 95.
CF_SHOWHELP	Shows the Help button. The *hwndOwner* member must not be NULL if this option is specified.
CF_TTONLY	Enumerates and allows only the selection of TrueType fonts.
CF_USESTYLE	Specifies that the *lpszStyle* member points to a buffer that contains style data that ChooseFont() should use to initialize the Font Style selection. When the user closes the dialog box, ChooseFont() copies style data for the user's selection to this buffer.
CF_WYSIWYG	Allows only the selection of fonts available on both the printer and the display. If this flag is specified, the CF_BOTH and CF_SCALABLEONLY flags should also be specified.

rgbColors	DWORD: If the CF_EFFECTS flag is specified, this member contains an RGB value that ChooseFont() should use to specify the text color. After the user closes the dialog box, this member contains the RGB value of the color the user selected.
lCustData	LPARAM: Application-defined data the application passes to the hook function. The system passes the data in the *lParam* parameter of the WM_INITDIALOG message.
lpfnHook	LPCFHOOKPROC: A pointer to a hook function that processes messages intended for the dialog box. An application must specify the CF_ENABLE-HOOK flag in the *Flags* member to enable the function; otherwise, the system ignores this member. The hook function must return FALSE to pass a message to the standard dialog box procedure or TRUE to discard the message.
lpTemplateName	LPCTSTR: A pointer to a null-terminated string that names the dialog box template to be substituted for the standard dialog box template. An application can use the MAKEINTRESOURCE macro for numbered dialog box resources. This member is used only if *Flags* specifies the CF_ENABLETEMPLATE flag; otherwise, this member is ignored.
hInstance	HINSTANCE: The instance handle of the module that contains the dialog box template specified by the *lpTemplateName* member. If the

CF_ENABLETEMPLATEHANDLE flag is specified, this member identifies the memory block with a preloaded dialog template.

lpszStyle   LPTSTR: A pointer to a buffer that contains style data. If the CF_USESTYLE flag is specified, ChooseFont() uses the data in this buffer to initialize the style control. When the user closes the dialog box, ChooseFont() copies the string in the style control into this buffer.

nFontType   WORD: The type of the selected font. This member may contain one of the values in Table 2-8.

Table 2-8 CHOOSEFONT *nFontType* values

Value	Meaning
PRINTER_FONTTYPE	The font is a printer font.
SCREEN_FONTTYPE	The font is a screen font.
SIMULATED_FONTTYPE	The font is simulated by the graphics device interface (GDI).

nSizeMin   INT: The minimum point size a user can select. ChooseFont() recognizes this member only if the CF_LIMITSIZE flag is specified.

nSizeMax   INT: The maximum point size a user can select. ChooseFont() recognizes this member only if the CF_LIMITSIZE flag is specified.

LOGFONT Definition

```
typedef struct tagLOGFONT
{
    LONG   lfHeight;
    LONG   lfWidth;
    LONG   lfEscapement;
    LONG   lfOrientation;
    LONG   lfWeight;
    BYTE   lfItalic;
    BYTE   lfUnderline;
    BYTE   lfStrikeOut;
    BYTE   lfCharSet;
    BYTE   lfOutPrecision;
    BYTE   lfClipPrecision;
    BYTE   lfQuality;
    BYTE   lfPitchAndFamily;
    TCHAR  lfFaceName[LF_FACESIZE];
} LOGFONT;
```

Members

lfHeight   LONG: The desired height, in logical units, of the requested font's character cell or character. If *lfHeight* is greater than zero, it specifies the character cell height. If *lfHeight* is less than zero, the absolute value specifies the character height. If set to zero, the default height is used. To specify a height in points, use the following formula:

lfHeight = —MulDiv(*PointSize*, GetDeviceCaps(hDC, LOGPIXELSY), 72);

lfWidth	LONG: The average width, in logical units, of characters in the requested font. If set to zero, the font mapper chooses a *closest match* value. The closest match value is determined by comparing the absolute values of the difference between the current device's aspect ratio and the digitized aspect ratio of available fonts.
lfEscapement	LONG: The angle, in tenths of degrees, between the escapement vector and the x-axis of the device. The escapement vector is parallel to the baseline of a row of text.
lfOrientation	LONG: The angle, in tenths of degrees, between each character's baseline and the x-axis of the device.
lfWeight	LONG: The desired weight of the font. If set to zero, a default weight is used. This parameter can be one of the values in Table 2-9.

Table 2-9 LOGFONT *lfWeight* values

Value	Weight
FW_DONTCARE	0
FW_THIN	100
FW_EXTRALIGHT	200
FW_LIGHT	300
FW_NORMAL	400
FW_MEDIUM	500
FW_SEMIBOLD	600
FW_BOLD	700
FW_EXTRABOLD	800
FW_HEAVY	900

lfItalic	BYTE: Set to TRUE for italics.
lfUnderline	BYTE: Set to TRUE for underline.
lfStrikeOut	BYTE: Set to TRUE for strikeout.
lfCharSet	BYTE: The desired character set. The OEM character set is operating-system dependent. This parameter is important in the font mapping process. To ensure consistent results, specify a specific character set. If a typeface name in the *lfFaceName* parameter is specified, make sure that the *lfCharSet* value matches the character set of the typeface specified in *lfFaceName*. The following values are predefined: ANSI_CHARSET ARABIC_CHARSET BALTIC_CHARSET CHINESEBIG5_CHARSET DEFAULT_CHARSET

continued on next page

continued from previous page

	EASTEUROPE_CHARSET
	GB2312_CHARSET
	GREEK_CHARSET
	HANGEUL_CHARSET
	HEBREW_CHARSET
	JOHAB_CHARSET
	MAC_CHARSET
	OEM_CHARSET
	RUSSIAN_CHARSET
	SHIFTJIS_CHARSET
	SYMBOL_CHARSET
	THAI_CHARSET
	TURKISH_CHARSET
lfOutPrecision	BYTE: The desired output precision. The output precision defines how closely the output must match the requested font's height, width, character orientation, escapement, and pitch. Applications can use the OUT_DEVICE_PRECIS, OUT_RASTER_PRECIS, and OUT_TT_PRECIS values to control which font to use when the system contains more than one font with a given name. *lfOutPrecision* can be one of the following values:

OUT_CHARACTER_PRECIS
OUT_DEFAULT_PRECIS
OUT_DEVICE_PRECIS
OUT_OUTLINE_PRECIS
OUT_RASTER_PRECIS
OUT_STRING_PRECIS
OUT_STROKE_PRECIS
OUT_TT_ONLY_PRECIS
OUT_TT_PRECIS

lfClipPrecision	BYTE: The desired clipping precision. The clipping precision defines how to clip characters that are partially outside the clipping region. To use an embedded read-only font, applications must specify CLIP_EMBEDDED. *lfClipPrecision* can be one or more of the following values:

CLIP_CHARACTER_PRECIS
CLIP_DEFAULT_PRECIS
CLIP_EMBEDDED
CLIP_LH_ANGLES
CLIP_MASK
CLIP_STROKE_PRECIS
CLIP_TT_ALWAYS

lfQuality	BYTE: The desired output quality. The output quality determines how closely GDI attempts to match the logical-font attributes. *lfQuality* can be one of the values in Table 2-10.

Table 2-10 LOGFONT *lfQuality* values

Value	Meaning
DEFAULT_QUALITY	Appearance of the font does not matter.
DRAFT_QUALITY	Appearance of the font is less important than when the PROOF_QUALITY value is used. For GDI raster fonts, scaling is enabled.
PROOF_QUALITY	Character quality of the font is more important than exact matching of the logical-font attributes. For GDI raster fonts, scaling is disabled and the font closest in size is chosen.

lfPitchAndFamily   BYTE: The pitch and family of the font. Use one of the following values to
specify the pitch of the font:
DEFAULT_PITCH
FIXED_PITCH
VARIABLE_PITCH
Combine with one of the values in Table 2-11 using the binary OR (|)
operator to specify the font family.

Table 2-11 LOGFONT *lfPitchAndFamily* values

Value	Description
FF_DECORATIVE	Decorative fonts. Old English is an example.
FF_DONTCARE	Don't care or don't know.
FF_MODERN	Fonts with constant stroke width, with or without serifs. Pica, Elite, and Courier New are examples.
FF_ROMAN	Fonts with variable stroke width and with serifs. MS Serif is an example.
FF_SCRIPT	Fonts designed to look like handwriting. Script and Cursive are examples.
FF_SWISS	Fonts with variable stroke width and without serifs. MS Sans Serif is an example.

lfFaceName   TCHAR[LF_FACESIZE]: A null-terminated string, up to LF_FACESIZE-1
characters, that specifies the typeface name of the font. If *lfFaceName* is
empty, GDI uses a default typeface.

Example   This example displays a sample text string in the font and color the user
selects using the ChooseFont common dialog box (shown in Figure 2-2
and Listing 2-3). When the user selects the Test! menu item, the
ChooseFont common dialog box is displayed. If the user selects a new
font, the sample text string is updated using the new font.

Listing 2-3 Using the ChooseFont() common dialog

```
LRESULT CALLBACK WndProc( HWND hWnd, UINT uMsg, WPARAM wParam, LPARAM lParam )
{
static LOGFONT lf;
static DWORD   dwColor = 0;
```

continued on next page

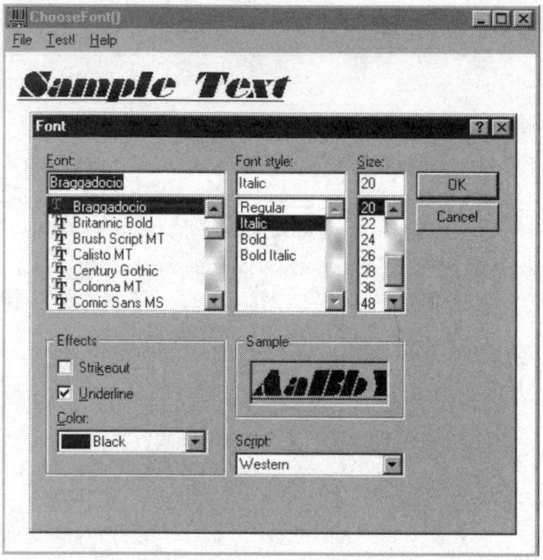

Figure 2-2 ChooseFont() example

continued from previous page

```
switch( uMsg )
{
    case WM_CREATE :
            memset( &lf, 0, sizeof( LOGFONT ) );
            break;

    case WM_PAINT :
            if ( lf.lfFaceName[0] )
            {
                PAINTSTRUCT ps;
                HFONT       hFont, hOldFont;
                DWORD       dwOldColor;

                // Create the font to use.
                //......................
                hFont = CreateFontIndirect( &lf );

                // Display sample text using the font.
                //....................................
                BeginPaint( hWnd, &ps );
                hOldFont   = SelectObject( ps.hdc, hFont );
                dwOldColor = SetTextColor( ps.hdc, dwColor );

                TextOut( ps.hdc, 10, 10, "Sample Text", 11 );

                SelectObject( ps.hdc, hOldFont );
                SetTextColor( ps.hdc, dwOldColor );
                EndPaint( hWnd, &ps );
```

```
                     // Delete the hFont.
                     //..................
                     DeleteObject( hFont );
                 }
                 else
                     return( DefWindowProc( hWnd, uMsg, wParam, lParam ) );

                 break;

        case WM_COMMAND :
                 switch( LOWORD( wParam ) )
                 {
                     case IDM_TEST :
                             {
                                 CHOOSEFONT cf;

                                 // Initialize the CHOOSEFONT structure.
                                 //......................................
                                 memset( &cf, 0, sizeof( CHOOSEFONT ) );
                                 cf.lStructSize  = sizeof( CHOOSEFONT );
                                 cf.hwndOwner    = hWnd;
                                 cf.lpLogFont    = &lf;
                                 cf.Flags        = CF_SCREENFONTS | CF_EFFECTS;
                                 cf.rgbColors    = dwColor;

                                 if ( lf.lfFaceName[0] )
                                     cf.Flags |= CF_INITTOLOGFONTSTRUCT;

                                 // Create the choose font dialog.
                                 //..............................
                                 if ( ChooseFont( &cf ) )
                                 {
                                     // If the user chooses a font,
                                     // repaint the sample text.
                                     //............................
                                     dwColor = cf.rgbColors;
                                     InvalidateRect( hWnd, NULL, TRUE );
                                 }
                             }
                             break;

                     case IDM_EXIT :
                             DestroyWindow( hWnd );
                             break;
                 }
                 break;

        case WM_DESTROY :
                 PostQuitMessage(0);
                 break;

        default :
                 return( DefWindowProc( hWnd, uMsg, wParam, lParam ) );
    }

    return( 0L );
}
```

CommDlgExtendedError ■ Win32s ■ Windows 95 ■ Windows NT

Description	CommDlgExtendedError() returns the most recent error that has occurred during the execution of a common dialog.
Syntax	DWORD **CommDlgExtendedError**(VOID)
Parameters	This function has no parameters.
Returns	DWORD: If the previous call to a common dialog box procedure succeeds, the return value is zero. The return value is CDERR_DIALOGFAILURE if the dialog box could not be created. Otherwise, the return value is a nonzero integer that identifies an error condition from Table 2-12.

Table 2-12 CommDlgExtendedError() error codes

Value	Meaning
CDERR_DIALOGFAILURE	The common dialog box procedure's call to the DialogBox() function failed. For example, this error occurs if the common dialog box call specifies an invalid window handle.
CDERR_FINDRESFAILURE	The common dialog box procedure failed to find a specified resource.
CDERR_INITIALIZATION	The common dialog box procedure failed during initialization. This error often occurs when insufficient memory is available.
CDERR_LOADRESFAILURE	The common dialog box procedure failed to load a specified resource.
CDERR_LOADSTRFAILURE	The common dialog box procedure failed to load a specified string.
CDERR_LOCKRESFAILURE	The common dialog box procedure failed to lock a specified resource.
CDERR_MEMALLOCFAILURE	The common dialog box procedure was unable to allocate memory for internal structures.
CDERR_MEMLOCKFAILURE	The common dialog box procedure was unable to lock the memory associated with a handle.
CDERR_NOHINSTANCE	The ENABLETEMPLATE flag was specified in the *Flags* member of a structure for the corresponding common dialog box, but the application failed to provide a corresponding instance handle.
CDERR_NOHOOK	The ENABLEHOOK flag was specified in the *Flags* member of a structure for the corresponding common dialog box, but the application failed to provide a pointer to a corresponding hook function.
CDERR_NOTEMPLATE	The ENABLETEMPLATE flag was specified in the *Flags* member of a structure for the corresponding common dialog box, but the application failed to provide a corresponding template.
CDERR_REGISTERMSGFAIL	The RegisterWindowMessage() function returned an error value when it was called by the common dialog box procedure.
CDERR_STRUCTSIZE	The *lStructSize* member of a structure for the corresponding common dialog box is invalid.
CFERR_MAXLESSTHANMIN	The size specified in the *nSizeMax* member of the CHOOSEFONT structure is less than the size specified in the *nSizeMin* member.
CFERR_NOFONTS	No fonts exist.
FNERR_BUFFERTOOSMALL	The buffer for a file name is too small. (This buffer is pointed to by the *lpstrFile* member of the structure for a common dialog box.)
FNERR_INVALIDFILENAME	A file name is invalid.
FNERR_SUBCLASSFAILURE	An attempt to subclass a list box failed because insufficient memory was available.

Value	Meaning
FRERR_BUFFERLENGTHZERO	A member in a structure for the corresponding common dialog box points to an invalid buffer.
PDERR_CREATEICFAILURE	The PrintDlg() function failed when it attempted to create an information context.
PDERR_DEFAULTDIFFERENT	An application called the PrintDlg() function with the DN_DEFAULTPRN flag specified in the *wDefault* member of the DEVNAMES structure, but the printer described by the other structure members did not match the current default printer. (This error happens when an application stores the DEVNAMES structure and the user changes the default printer by using Control Panel.) To use the printer described by the DEVNAMES structure, the application should clear the DN_DEFAULTPRN flag and call the PrintDlg() function again. To use the default printer, the application should replace the DEVNAMES structure (and the DEVMODE structure, if one exists) with NULL; this sets the default printer automatically.
PDERR_DNDMMISMATCH	The data in the DEVMODE and DEVNAMES structures describe two different printers.
PDERR_GETDEVMODEFAIL	The printer driver failed to initialize a DEVMODE structure. (This error value applies only to printer drivers written for Windows versions 3.0 and later.)
PDERR_INITFAILURE	The PrintDlg() function failed during initialization, and there is no more specific extended error code to describe the failure. This is the generic default error code for the function.
PDERR_LOADDRVFAILURE	The PrintDlg() function failed to load the device driver for the specified printer.
PDERR_NODEFAULTPRN	A default printer does not exist.
PDERR_NODEVICES	No printer drivers were found.
PDERR_PARSEFAILURE	The PrintDlg() function failed to parse the strings in the [devices] section of the WIN.INI file.
PDERR_PRINTERNOTFOUND	The [devices] section of the WIN.INI file did not contain an entry for the requested printer.
PDERR_RETDEFFAILURE	The PD_RETURNDEFAULT flag was specified in the *Flags* member of the PRINTDLG structure, but the *hDevMode* or *hDevNames* member was nonzero.
PDERR_SETUPFAILURE	The PrintDlg() function failed to load the required resources.

Include File	commdlg.h
See Also	ChooseColor(), ChooseFont(), FindText(), GetFileTitle(), GetOpenFileName(), GetSaveFileName(), PrintDlg(), ReplaceText()
Example	See the example for the PrintDlg() function.

FINDTEXT   ■ Win32s   ■ Windows 95   ■ Windows NT

Description   FindText() creates a Find Text common dialog box that enables the user to find text within a document. The Find Text common dialog box is a modeless dialog that allows the user to place the cursor within the document while the Find Text dialog box remains visible. The user can then go back to the Find Text dialog and continue the search. The application must use the IsDialogMessage() function in the main message loop with the returned window handle to process the Find Text dialog box messages.

FindText() does not perform a search operation; it returns a string typed by the user with other related information. The application must perform the search using the provided information.

The dialog box procedure for the Find Text dialog box passes user requests to the application by sending special messages. The *lParam* parameter of each of these messages contains a pointer to a FINDREPLACE structure. The procedure sends the messages to the window identified by the *hwndOwner* member of the FINDREPLACE structure. An application can use the RegisterWindowMessage() function and the "commdlg_FindReplace" (FINDMSGSTRING) string to register the identifier for these messages.

Syntax   HWND **FindText**(LPFINDREPLACE *lpfr*)

Parameters

lpfr   LPFINDREPLACE: A pointer to a FINDREPLACE structure that contains information used to initialize the dialog box. When the user makes a selection in the dialog box, the system fills this structure with data that describes the user's selection and then sends a message to the application. This message contains a pointer to the FINDREPLACE structure. See the definition of the FINDREPLACE structure below.

Returns   HWND: If successful, the window handle of the dialog box is returned; otherwise, NULL is returned. Use the CommDlgExtendedError() function to retrieve extended error information. One of the errors listed in Table 2-13 can be returned.

Table 2-13 FindText() extended errors

Value	Meaning
CDERR_FINDRESFAILURE	A specified resource could not be found.
CDERR_INITIALIZATION	Failed during initialization.
CDERR_LOADRESFAILURE	A specified resource could not be loaded.
CDERR_LOADSTRFAILURE	A specified string could not be loaded.
CDERR_LOCKRESFAILURE	A specified resource could not be locked.
CDERR_MEMALLOCFAILURE	Unable to allocate memory for internal structures.
CDERR_MEMLOCKFAILURE	Unable to lock the memory associated with a handle.
CDERR_NOHINSTANCE	The FR_ENABLETEMPLATE flag was specified without providing an instance handle in the *hInstance* member.
CDERR_NOHOOK	The FR_ENABLEHOOK flag was specified without providing a pointer to a hook function in the *lpfnHook* member.
CDERR_NOTEMPLATE	The FR_ENABLETEMPLATE flag was specified without providing a template in the *lpstrTemplateName* member.
CDERR_STRUCTSIZE	The *lStructSize* member of a FINDREPLACE structure is invalid.
FRERR_BUFFERLENGTHZERO	A member in FINDREPLACE structure points to an invalid buffer.

Include File	commdlg.h
Related Messages	FINDMSGSTRING, HELPMSGSTRING
See Also	ReplaceText(), CommDlgExtendedError(), IsDialogMessage(), RegisterWindowMessage()

FINDREPLACE Definition

```
typedef struct
{
    DWORD           lStructSize;
    HWND            hwndOwner;
    HINSTANCE       hInstance;
    DWORD           Flags;
    LPTSTR          lpstrFindWhat;
    LPTSTR          lpstrReplaceWith;
    WORD            wFindWhatLen;
    WORD            wReplaceWithLen;
    LPARAM          lCustData;
    LPFRHOOKPROC    lpfnHook;
    LPCTSTR         lpTemplateName;
} FINDREPLACE;
```

Members

lStructSize   DWORD: The length, in bytes, of the structure.

hwndOwner   HWND: The window that owns the dialog box. This member must be a valid window handle and cannot be NULL.

hInstance   HINSTANCE: The instance handle of the module that contains the dialog box template specified by the *lpTemplateName* member. If the FR_ENABLETEMPLATEHANDLE flag is specified, this member identifies the memory block with a preloaded dialog template.

Flags   DWORD: The dialog box initialization flags. This member may be a combination of the flags in Table 2-14.

Table 2-14 FINDREPLACE *Flag* values

Value	Meaning
FR_DIALOGTERM	Indicates that the dialog box is closing. The window handle returned by the FindText() function is not valid if this flag is specified.
FR_DOWN	Determines the direction of searches through a document. If this flag is used, the search direction is down; if the flag is not used, the search direction is up. Initially, this flag specifies the state of the Up and Down controls; afterwards, this flag specifies the user's selection.
FR_ENABLEHOOK	Enables the hook function specified in the *lpfnHook* member of this structure. This flag is used only to initialize the dialog box.
FR_ENABLETEMPLATE	Creates the dialog box by using the dialog box template identified by the *hInstance* and *lpTemplateName* members. This flag is used only to initialize the dialog box.
FR_ENABLETEMPLATEHANDLE	Indicates that the *hInstance* member identifies a data block that contains a preloaded dialog box template. The system ignores the *lpTemplateName* member if this flag is specified.

continued on next page

continued from previous page

Value	Meaning
FR_FINDNEXT	Indicates that the application should search for the next occurrence of the string specified by the *lpstrFindWhat* member.
FR_HIDEMATCHCASE	Causes the system to hide the Match Case check box.
FR_HIDEUPDOWN	Causes the system to hide the Direction check box and the Up and Down controls.
FR_HIDEWHOLEWORD	Causes the system to hide the Match Whole Word Only check box.
FR_MATCHCASE	Indicates case-sensitive searches.
FR_NOMATCHCASE	Disables the Match Case check box. This flag is used only to initialize the dialog box.
FR_NOUPDOWN	Disables the direction radio buttons. This flag is used only to initialize the dialog box.
FR_NOWHOLEWORD	Disables the Whole Word check box. This flag is used only to initialize the dialog box.
FR_REPLACE	Indicates that the application should replace the current occurrence of the string specified in the *lpstrFindWhat* member with the string specified in the *lpstrReplaceWith* member.
FR_REPLACEALL	Indicates that the application should replace all occurrences of the string specified in the *lpstrFindWhat* member with the string specified in the *lpstrReplaceWith* member.
FR_SHOWHELP	Shows the Help button.
FR_WHOLEWORD	Checks the Whole Word check box. Only whole words matching the search string will be considered.

lpstrFindWhat   LPTSTR: A pointer to a buffer, at least 80 characters long, that contains the string to search for. If there is a string specified when the dialog box starts, the dialog box initializes the Find What: text control with this string.

lpstrReplaceWith   LPTSTR: A pointer to a buffer, at least 80 characters long, that contains the replacement string for replace operations. The FindText() function ignores this member.

wFindWhatLen   WORD: The length, in bytes, of the buffer pointed to by the *lpstrFindWhat* member.

wReplaceWithLen   WORD: The length, in bytes, of the buffer pointed to by the *lpstrReplaceWith* member.

lCustData   LPARAM: Application-defined data the system passes to the hook function identified by the *lpfnHook* member. The system passes the data in the *lParam* parameter of the WM_INITDIALOG message.

lpfnHook   LPFRHOOKPROC: A pointer to a hook function that processes messages intended for the dialog box. An application must specify the FR_ENABLEHOOK flag in the *Flags* member to enable the function; otherwise, the system ignores this member. The hook function should return FALSE to pass a message on to the standard dialog box procedure or TRUE to discard the message.

    If the hook function returns FALSE in response to the WM_INITDIALOG message, it is responsible for displaying the dialog box, which is done by calling the ShowWindow() and UpdateWindow() functions. If the application does not call these functions, the dialog box will not be shown.

lpTemplateName	LPCTSTR: A pointer to a null-terminated string that names the dialog box template resource to be substituted for the standard dialog box template. An application can use the MAKEINTRESOURCE macro for numbered dialog resources. This member is used only if the *Flags* member specifies the FR_ENABLETEMPLATE flag; otherwise, this member is ignored.
Example	This example creates a multiline edit control as the client area of the window and places a text string in it. When the user selects the Edit↓Find menu item, the Find common dialog box, shown in Figure 2-3, is displayed and allows the user to search for text within the edit control. When a text string is found, it is selected to show the found text. When the user selects the Edit↓Replace menu item, the Find and Replace common dialog box is displayed and the user is allowed to enter a replacement text string. When the user selects the Replace button on the Find and Replace common dialog box, the selected text is replaced with the new text. The find and replace actions in this example are minimal and should be expanded on for a complete implementation.

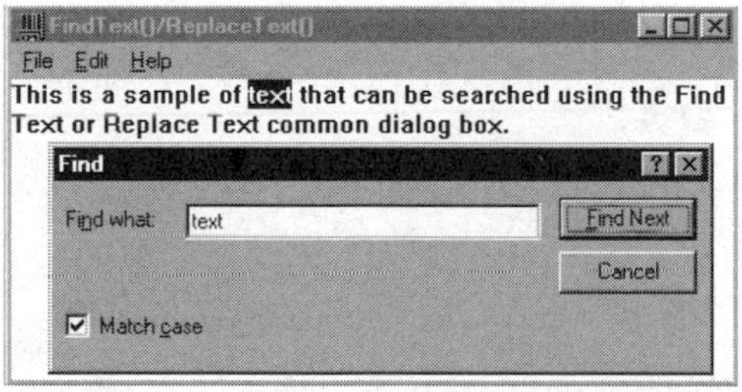

Figure 2-3 FindText() and ReplaceText() example

Listing 2-4 *Using the FindText() and ReplaceText() common dialogs*

```
#define MAX_FIND_LEN   80

LPCTSTR lpszText = "This is a sample of text that can be searched using the"\
                   " Find Text or Replace Text common dialog box.";

LRESULT CALLBACK WndProc( HWND hWnd, UINT uMsg, WPARAM wParam, LPARAM lParam )
{
static FINDREPLACE  fr;
static char         szFind[MAX_FIND_LEN+1];
static char         szReplace[MAX_FIND_LEN+1];
static char         szBuf[512];
static char         szNewBuf[512];

static UINT         uFindMessage = 0;
static HWND         hEdit        = NULL;
static DWORD        dwPos        = 0;


   // Handle Find and Replace common dialog message.
```

continued on next page

continued from previous page

```
//...............................................
if ( uMsg == uFindMessage )
{
    LPFINDREPLACE lpfr = (LPFINDREPLACE)lParam;

    // Handle the Find Next command.
    //.............................
    if ( lpfr->Flags & FR_FINDNEXT )
    {
        LPTSTR lpFound;
        DWORD  dwCurPos = SendMessage( hEdit, EM_GETSEL, 0, 0 );

        // If the position is the same as where we were,
        // increment the position so we find the next string.
        //.....................................................
        if ( LOWORD(dwCurPos) == dwPos && dwPos > 0 )
            dwPos++;
        else
            dwPos = LOWORD( dwCurPos );

        SendMessage( hEdit, WM_GETTEXT, sizeof( szBuf ), (LPARAM)szBuf );

        // Find the search string within the text starting at the
        // current cursor position within the edit control.
        //.........................................................
        lpFound = strstr( &szBuf[ LOWORD(dwPos) ], lpfr->lpstrFindWhat );

        // If the text was found, highlight it.
        //......................................
        if ( lpFound )
        {
            dwPos = lpFound-&szBuf[0];
            SendMessage( hEdit, EM_SETSEL, dwPos,
                        strlen( lpfr->lpstrFindWhat )+dwPos );
        }
        else
            MessageBox( hWnd, "The string was not found.",
                            "Find", MB_OK | MB_ICONINFORMATION );
    }

    // Handle the Replace command.
    //............................
    if ( lpfr->Flags & FR_REPLACE )
    {
        SendMessage( hEdit, WM_GETTEXT, sizeof( szBuf ), (LPARAM)szBuf );

        szBuf[dwPos] = 0;
        strcpy( szNewBuf, szBuf );
        strcat( szNewBuf, lpfr->lpstrReplaceWith );
        strcat( szNewBuf, &szBuf[strlen( lpfr->lpstrFindWhat )+dwPos] );

        SendMessage( hEdit, WM_SETTEXT, 0, (LPARAM)szNewBuf );
        SendMessage( hEdit, EM_SETSEL, dwPos,
                    strlen( lpfr->lpstrReplaceWith )+dwPos );
    }

    // Handle the Replace All command.
    //................................
    if ( lpfr->Flags & FR_REPLACEALL )
```

```
            MessageBox( hWnd, "Replace All is not implemented.",
                             "Replace", MB_OK | MB_ICONINFORMATION );

    // If the dialog is terminating, set the handle to NULL.
    //......................................................
    if ( lpfr->Flags & FR_DIALOGTERM )
        hwndFind = NULL;
}

switch( uMsg )
{
    case WM_CREATE :
            memset( &fr, 0, sizeof( FINDREPLACE ) );

            uFindMessage = RegisterWindowMessage( FINDMSGSTRING );

            hEdit = CreateWindow( "EDIT", "",
                                  WS_CHILD | ES_LEFT |
                                  WS_VISIBLE | ES_MULTILINE | ES_NOHIDESEL,
                                  0, 0,
                                  0, 0,
                                  hWnd,
                                  (HMENU)101,
                                  hInst,
                                  NULL
                                );

            SendMessage( hEdit, WM_SETTEXT, 0, (LPARAM)lpszText );
            break;

    case WM_SIZE :
            MoveWindow( hEdit, 0, 0, LOWORD( lParam ),
                               HIWORD( lParam ), TRUE );
            break;

    case WM_COMMAND :
            switch( LOWORD( wParam ) )
            {
                case IDM_FIND :
                        fr.lStructSize   = sizeof( FINDREPLACE );
                        fr.hwndOwner     = hWnd;
                        fr.lpstrFindWhat = szFind;
                        fr.wFindWhatLen  = MAX_FIND_LEN;
                        fr.Flags         = FR_MATCHCASE |
                                           FR_HIDEUPDOWN | FR_HIDEWHOLEWORD;

                        hwndFind = FindText( &fr );
                        break;

                case IDM_REPLACE :
                        fr.lStructSize     = sizeof( FINDREPLACE );
                        fr.hwndOwner       = hWnd;
                        fr.lpstrFindWhat   = szFind;
                        fr.lpstrReplaceWith = szReplace;
                        fr.wFindWhatLen    = MAX_FIND_LEN;
                        fr.wReplaceWithLen = MAX_FIND_LEN;
                        fr.Flags           = FR_MATCHCASE |
                                             FR_HIDEUPDOWN | FR_HIDEWHOLEWORD;
```

continued on next page

continued from previous page

```
                              hwndFind = ReplaceText( &fr );
                              break;

                 case IDM_EXIT :
                              DestroyWindow( hWnd );
                              break;
            }
            break;

    case WM_DESTROY :
            PostQuitMessage(0);
            break;

    default :
            return( DefWindowProc( hWnd, uMsg, wParam, lParam ) );
    }

    return( OL );
}
```

GETFILETITLE   ■ Win32s ■ Windows 95 ■ Windows NT

Description	GetFileTitle() returns the name of the file identified by the *lpszFile* parameter. In Windows 95, this function retrieves the same text that the system would use in displaying a file name to the user. This text is intended to be used only for display and is in accordance with the user's preferences. Do not use this function to retrieve a file name to use in a file function.

GetFileTitle() returns an error value if the buffer pointed to by the *lpszFile* parameter contains any of the following elements:

■ An empty string

■ A string that contains a wildcard, opening bracket, or closing bracket

■ A string that ends with a colon, forward slash, or backslash

■ A string whose length exceeded the length of the buffer

Syntax	SHORT **GetFileTitle**(LPCTSTR *lpszFile*, LPTSTR *lpszTitle*, WORD *cbBuf*)
Parameters	
lpszFile	LPCTSTR: A pointer to the name and location of a file.
lpszTitle	LPTSTR: A pointer to a buffer that receives the name of the file.
cbBuf	WORD: The length, in characters, of the buffer pointed to by the *lpszTitle* parameter.
Returns	SHORT: If successful, zero is returned. If the file name is invalid, a negative value is returned. If the buffer pointed to by the *lpszTitle* parameter is too small, a positive number that specifies the required buffer size, in characters, is returned.
Include File	commdlg.h
See Also	GetOpenFileName(), GetSaveFileName()
Example	See the example for the GetOpenFileName() function.

GETOPENFILENAME ■ Win32s ■ Windows 95 ■ Windows NT

Description

GetOpenFileName() creates an Open File common dialog box that enables the user to select a file to open. If the application provides a hook function, it should not use the EndDialog() function within the hook function. This prevents the COMDLG32.DLL from properly exiting its worker thread.

The hook function receives WM_NOTIFY notification messages indicating actions taken by the user in the dialog box. The *lParam* parameter for each WM_NOTIFY message is the address of an OFNOTIFY structure that defines the action. The *code* member in the header for the OFNOTIFY structure contains one of the notification values listed in Table 2-18. See the definition of the OFNOTIFY structure below.

An application can send messages to the dialog box from the hook function to retrieve information about the status of the dialog box. Table 2-15 lists the valid message values.

Table 2-15 GetOpenFileName() messages

Value	Description
CDM_GETFILEPATH	Retrieves the path and file name of the selected file.
CDM_GETFOLDERIDLIST	Retrieves the address of the item identifier list corresponding to the folder that the dialog box currently has open.
CDM_GETFOLDERPATH	Retrieves the path and name of the currently open folder or directory for the dialog box.
CDM_GETSPEC	Retrieves the file name, without path, of the currently selected file in the dialog box.
CDM_HIDECONTROL	Hides a specific control.
CDM_SETCONTROLTEXT	Sets the text in a specific control.
CDM_SETDEFEXT	Sets the default file name extension for the dialog box.

Syntax

BOOL **GetOpenFileName**(LPOPENFILENAME *lpofn*)

Parameters

lpofn

LPOPENFILENAME: A pointer to an OPENFILENAME structure that contains information used to initialize the dialog box. When GetOpenFileName() returns, this structure contains information about the user's file selection. See the definition of the OPENFILENAME structure below.

Returns

BOOL: If the user selects a file to open, TRUE is returned. If an error occurs, the user chooses the Cancel button or the Close command on the System menu, or if the buffer identified by the *lpstrFile* member of the OPENFILENAME structure is too small to contain the string that specifies the selected file, FALSE is returned. Use the CommDlgExtendedError() function to retrieve extended error information. One of the errors listed in Table 2-16 can be returned.

Table 2-16 GetOpenFileName() extended errors

Value	Meaning
CDERR_FINDRESFAILURE	A specified resource could not be found.
CDERR_INITIALIZATION	Failed during initialization.
CDERR_LOADRESFAILURE	A specified resource could not be loaded.
CDERR_LOADSTRFAILURE	A specified string could not be loaded.
CDERR_LOCKRESFAILURE	A specified resource could not be locked.
CDERR_MEMALLOCFAILURE	Unable to allocate memory for internal structures.
CDERR_MEMLOCKFAILURE	Unable to lock the memory associated with a handle.
CDERR_NOHINSTANCE	The OFN_ENABLETEMPLATE flag was specified without providing an instance handle in the *hInstance* member.
CDERR_NOHOOK	The OFN_ENABLEHOOK flag was specified without providing a pointer to a hook function in the *lpfnHook* member.
CDERR_NOTEMPLATE	The OFN_ENABLETEMPLATE flag was specified without providing a template in the *lpstrTemplateName* member.
CDERR_STRUCTSIZE	The *lStructSize* member of a OPENFILENAME structure is invalid.
FNERR_BUFFERTOOSMALL	The buffer pointed to by the *lpstrFile* member of the structure is too small.
FNERR_INVALIDFILENAME	A file name is invalid.
FNERR_SUBCLASSFAILURE	An attempt to subclass a list box failed because of insufficient memory.

Include File	commdlg.h
See Also	CommDlgExtendedError(), GetSaveFileName()
Related Messages	FILEOKSTRING, LBSELCHSTRING, SHAREVISTRING, HELPMSGSTRING, WM_NOTIFY

OPENFILENAME Definition

```
typedef struct tagOFN
{
    DWORD           lStructSize;
    HWND            hwndOwner;
    HINSTANCE       hInstance;
    LPCTSTR         lpstrFilter;
    LPTSTR          lpstrCustomFilter;
    DWORD           nMaxCustFilter;
    DWORD           nFilterIndex;
    LPTSTR          lpstrFile;
    DWORD           nMaxFile;
    LPTSTR          lpstrFileTitle;
    DWORD           nMaxFileTitle;
    LPCTSTR         lpstrInitialDir;
    LPCTSTR         lpstrTitle;
    DWORD           Flags;
    WORD            nFileOffset;
    WORD            nFileExtension;
    LPCTSTR         lpstrDefExt;
    DWORD           lCustData;
```

```
LPOFNHOOKPROC  lpfnHook;
LPCTSTR        lpTemplateName;
} OPENFILENAME;
```

Members

lStructSize   DWORD: The length, in bytes, of the structure.

hwndOwner   HWND: The handle of the window that owns the dialog box. This member can be any valid window handle, or set to NULL if the dialog box has no owner.

hInstance   HINSTANCE: The instance handle of the module that contains the dialog box template specified by the *lpTemplateName* member. If the OFN_ENABLETEMPLATEHANDLE flag is specified, this member identifies the memory block with a preloaded dialog template.

lpstrFilter   LPCTSTR: A pointer to a buffer containing pairs of null-terminated filter strings. The first string in each pair describes a filter (for example, "Text Files"), and the second specifies the filter pattern (for example, "*.TXT"). Multiple filters can be specified for a single item by separating the filter pattern strings with a semicolon (for example, "*.TXT;*.DOC;*.BAK"). The last string in the buffer must be terminated by two NULL characters. If this member is set to NULL, the dialog box will not display any filters.

lpstrCustomFilter   LPTSTR: A pointer to a buffer containing a pair of user-defined filter strings. The first string describes the filter, and the second specifies the filter pattern (for example, "WinWord, *.docnn"). The buffer is terminated by two NULL characters. The operating system copies the strings to the buffer when the user closes the dialog box. The system uses the strings to initialize the user-defined file filter the next time the dialog box is created. If this member is NULL, the dialog box lists but does not save user-defined filter strings. If this member is not NULL, the value of the *nMaxCustFilter* member is used to determine the length of the corresponding string in Windows 95.

nMaxCustFilter   DWORD: The size, in characters, of the buffer identified by *lpstrCustomFilter*. This buffer should be at least 40 characters long. This member is ignored if *lpstrCustomFilter* is NULL or points to a NULL string. On Windows 95, the value of *nMaxcustFilter* is used whenever *lpstrCustomFilter* is defined.

nFilterIndex   DWORD: An index into the buffer pointed to by *lpstrFilter*. The system uses the index value to obtain a pair of strings to use as the initial filter description and filter pattern for the dialog box. The first pair of strings has an index value of 1. When the user closes the dialog box, the system copies the index of the selected filter strings into this location. If *nFilterIndex* is zero, the custom filter is used. If *nFilterIndex* is zero and *lpstrCustomFilter* is NULL, the system uses the first filter in the buffer identified by *lpstrFilter*. If all three members are zero or NULL, the system does not use any filters and does not show any files in the file list control of the dialog box.

lpstrFile	LPTSTR: A pointer to a buffer, at least 256 characters long, that contains a file name used to initialize the File Name edit control. If initialization is not necessary, set the first character of this buffer to NULL. When the GetOpenFileName() or GetSaveFileName() function returns, this buffer contains the drive designator, path, file name, and extension of the selected file. If this buffer is too small, the required size is copied into this member.
nMaxFile	DWORD: The size, in characters, of the buffer pointed to by *lpstrFile*. The GetOpenFileName() and GetSaveFileName() functions return FALSE if the buffer is too small to contain the file information. This member is ignored if *lpstrFile* is set to NULL.
lpstrFileTitle	LPTSTR: A pointer to a buffer that receives the title of the selected file. The application should use this string to display the file title. If this member is NULL, the function does not copy the file title.
nMaxFileTitle	DWORD: The maximum length of the string that can be copied into the *lpstrFileTitle* buffer. This member is ignored if *lpstrFileTitle* is set to NULL.
lpstrInitialDir	LPCTSTR: A pointer to a string that specifies the initial file directory. If set to NULL, the system uses the current directory as the initial directory.
lpstrTitle	LPCTSTR: A pointer to a string to be placed in the title bar of the dialog box. If this member is NULL, the system uses the default title (that is, Save As or Open).
Flags	DWORD: The dialog box creation flags. This member may be a combination of the flags listed in Table 2-17.

Table 2-17 OPENFILENAME *Flag* values

Value	Meaning
OFN_ALLOWMULTISELECT	Allows multiple selections in the File Name list box. If the dialog box is created by using a private template, the definition of the File Name list box must contain the LBS_EXTENDEDSEL value. When this flag is set, the *lpstrFile* member points to a buffer containing the path to the current directory and all file names in the selection. The first file name is separated from the path by a space. Each subsequent file name is separated by one space from the preceding file name. With Explorer-style dialogs (dialogs that have the OFN_EXPLORER flag set), a single null character, \0, separates the file names, and two null characters, \0\0, terminate the entire string.
OFN_CREATEPROMPT	The dialog box function should ask whether the user wants to create a file that does not currently exist. This flag automatically uses the OFN_PATHMUSTEXIST and OFN_FILEMUSTEXIST flags.
OFN_ENABLEHOOK	Enables the hook function specified in the *lpfnHook* member.
OFN_ENABLETEMPLATE	Creates the dialog box by using the dialog box template identified by *hInstance* and *lpTemplateName*.

Value	Meaning
OFN_ENABLETEMPLATEHANDLE	Indicates that *hInstance* identifies a data block that contains a preloaded dialog box template. The *lpTemplateName* member is ignored if this flag is specified.
OFN_EXTENSIONDIFFERENT	The file name extension differs from the extension specified by *lpstrDefExt*. The function does not use this flag if *lpstrDefExt* is NULL.
OFN_FILEMUSTEXIST	The user can type only names of existing files in the File Name entry field. If this flag is specified and the user enters an invalid name, the dialog box procedure displays a warning in a message box. If this flag is specified, the OFN_PATHMUSTEXIST flag is also used.
OFN_HIDEREADONLY	Hides the Read Only check box.
OFN_NOCHANGEDIR	The dialog box sets the current directory back to what it was when the dialog box was called.
OFN_NOLONGNAMES	Long file names are not displayed in the File Name list box.
OFN_NONETWORKBUTTON	Hides and disables the Network button.
OFN_NOREADONLYRETURN	The returned file does not have the Read Only check box checked and is not in a write-protected directory.
OFN_NOTESTFILECREATE	The file is not created before the dialog box is closed. This flag should be specified if the application saves the file on a create-nonmodify network sharepoint. When an application specifies this flag, the library does not check for write protection, a full disk, an open drive door, or network protection. Applications using this flag must perform file operations carefully, because a file cannot be reopened once it is closed.
OFN_NOVALIDATE	The common dialog boxes allow invalid characters in the returned file name. Typically, the calling application uses a hook function that checks the file name by using the FILEOKSTRING message. If the text box in the edit control is empty or contains nothing but spaces, the lists of files and directories are updated. If the text box in the edit control contains anything else, *nFileOffset* and *nFileExtension* are set to values generated by parsing the text. No default extension is added to the text, nor is text copied to the buffer specified by *lpstrFileTitle*. If the value specified by *nFileOffset* is less than zero, the file name is invalid. Otherwise, the file name is valid, and *nFileExtension* and *nFileOffset* can be used as if the OFN_NOVALIDATE flag had not been specified.
OFN_OVERWRITEPROMPT	The Save As dialog box generates a message box if the selected file already exists. The user must confirm whether to overwrite the file.
OFN_PATHMUSTEXIST	The user can type only valid paths and file names. If this flag is used and the user types an invalid path and file name in the File Name entry field, the dialog box function displays a warning in a message box.
OFN_READONLY	The Read Only check box is initially checked when the dialog box is created. This flag indicates the state of the Read Only check box when the dialog box is closed.
OFN_SHAREAWARE	If a call to the OpenFile() function fails because of a network sharing violation, the error is ignored and the dialog box returns the given file name. If this flag is not specified, the registered message for SHAREVISTRING is sent to the hook function with a pointer to a null-terminated string for the path and file name in the *lParam* parameter. The hook function responds with one of the following flags:

continued on next page

continued from previous page

Value	Meaning
OFN_SHAREFALLTHROUGH	The file name is returned by the dialog box.
OFN_SHARENOWARN	No further action.
OFN_SHAREWARN	The user receives the standard warning message for this error (the same result as if there were no hook function).
OFN_SHOWHELP	The dialog box shows the Help button. The hwndOwner member must not be NULL if this option is specified.

nFileOffset WORD: A zero-based offset from the beginning of the path to the file name in the string pointed to by *lpstrFile*.

nFileExtension WORD: A zero-based offset from the beginning of the path to the file name extension in the string pointed to by *lpstrFile*. If the user did not type an extension and *lpstrDefExt* is NULL, this member specifies an offset to the terminating null character. If the user typed "." as the last character in the file name, this member is set to zero.

lpstrDefExt LPCTSTR: A pointer to a buffer that contains the default extension. GetOpenFileName() and GetSaveFileName() append this extension to the file name if the user fails to type an extension. This string can be any length, but only the first three characters are appended. The string should not contain a period (.). If this member is set to NULL and the user fails to type an extension, no extension is appended.

lCustData DWORD: Application-defined data that the operating system passes to the hook function identified by *lpfnHook*. The system passes the data in the *lParam* parameter of the WM_INITDIALOG message.

lpfnHook LPOFNHOOKPROC: A pointer to a hook function that processes messages intended for the dialog box. An application must specify the OFN_ENABLEHOOK flag in the *Flags* member to enable the function; otherwise, the operating system ignores this member. The hook function should return FALSE to pass a message to the standard dialog box procedure or TRUE to discard the message.

lpTemplateName LPCTSTR: A pointer to a null-terminated string that names the dialog box template to be substituted for the standard dialog box template. An application can use the MAKEINTRESOURCE macro for numbered dialog box resources. This member is only used if *Flags* specifies the OFN_ENABLETEMPLATE flag; otherwise, this member is ignored.

OFNOTIFY Definition

```
typedef struct _OFNOTIFY
{
    NMHDR            hdr;
    LPOPENFILENAME   lpOFN;
    LPTSTR           pszFile;
} OFNOTIFY;
```

Members

hdr	NMHDR: An NMHDR structure that defines the notification information. See the definition of the NMHDR structure below.
lpOFN	LPOPENFILENAME: A pointer to the OPENFILENAME structure.
pszFile	LPTSTR: A pointer to the file name. This member may be set to NULL.

NMHDR Definition

```
typedef struct tagNMHDR
{
    HWND hwndFrom;
    UINT idFrom;
    UINT code;
} NMHDR;
```

Members

hwndFrom	HWND: The window handle to control sending the message.
idFrom	UINT: The identifier of control sending message.
code	UINT: The notification code. This can be one of the values in Table 2-18.

Table 2-18 NMHDR code values

Value	Meaning
CDN_FILEOK	The user selected the Open or Save button; the dialog box is about to close.
CDN_FOLDERCHANGE	A new folder has been opened in the Open or Save As dialog box.
CDN_HELP	The user selected the Help button.
CDN_INITDONE	The system has finished initializing the dialog box, and the dialog box has finished processing the WM_INITDIALOG message. Also, the system has finished arranging controls in the common dialog box to make room for the controls of the child dialog box (if any).
CDN_SELCHANGE	The user has selected a new file or folder from the file list.
CDN_SHAREVIOLATION	The common dialog box encountered a sharing violation on the file about to be returned.
CDN_TYPECHANGE	The user selected a new file type from the Files of type combo box.

Example   This example, shown in Figure 2-4 and Listing 2-5, uses the GetOpenFileName() function when the user selects the File↓Open menu item to allow the user to select a file name. The filters are set up to allow Text {*.txt} files and All Files {*.*}. Once the user has selected a file name, the file title is retrieved with the GetFileTitle() function and displayed on the client area of the window.

Listing 2-5 Using the GetOpenFileName() function

```
LRESULT CALLBACK WndProc( HWND hWnd, UINT uMsg, WPARAM wParam, LPARAM lParam )
{
static char szFileName[MAX_PATH];

   switch( uMsg )
   {
```

continued on next page

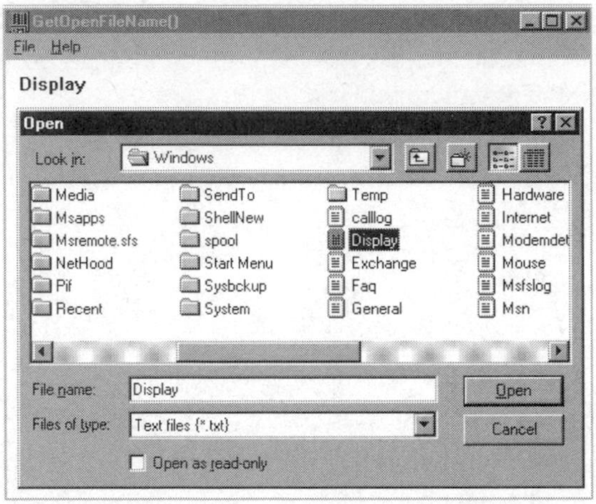

Figure 2-4 GetOpenFileName() example

continued from previous page

```
case WM_CREATE :
        memset( szFileName, 0, sizeof( szFileName ) );
        break;

case WM_PAINT :
        {
            PAINTSTRUCT ps;
            char        szTitle[128];

            // Display the file name.
            //.......................
            BeginPaint( hWnd, &ps );
            if ( szFileName[0] )
            {
                // Get the file title to display.
                //................................
                GetFileTitle( szFileName, szTitle, sizeof( szTitle ) );
                TextOut( ps.hdc, 10, 10, szTitle, strlen( szTitle ) );
            }
            EndPaint( hWnd, &ps );
        }
        break;

case WM_COMMAND :
        switch( LOWORD( wParam ) )
        {
            case IDM_OPENFILE :
                    {
                        OPENFILENAME ofn;

                        // Initialize the OPENFILENAME structure.
                        //........................................
                        memset( &ofn, 0, sizeof( OPENFILENAME ) );
                        ofn.lStructSize = sizeof( OPENFILENAME );
                        ofn.hwndOwner   = hWnd;
                        ofn.lpstrFilter = "Text files {*.txt}\0*.txt\0"\
```

```
                                    "All files {*.*}\0*.*\0\0";
                ofn.lpstrFile     = szFileName;
                ofn.nMaxFile      = MAX_PATH;
                ofn.Flags         = OFN_FILEMUSTEXIST;
                ofn.lpstrDefExt   = "txt";

                // Create the open file dialog.
                //...........................
                if ( GetOpenFileName( &ofn ) )
                    InvalidateRect( hWnd, NULL, TRUE );
            }
            break;

        case IDM_EXIT :
                DestroyWindow( hWnd );
                break;
        }
        break;

    case WM_DESTROY :
            PostQuitMessage(0);
            break;

    default :
            return( DefWindowProc( hWnd, uMsg, wParam, lParam ) );
    }

    return( 0L );
}
```

GetSaveFileName
■ Win32s   ■ Windows 95   ■ Windows NT

Description	GetSaveFileName() creates a Save File common dialog box that enables the user to select a file to save. If the application provides a hook function, it should not use the EndDialog() function within the hook function. This prevents the COMDLG32.DLL from properly exiting its worker thread.

See the description under the GetOpenFileName() function of the related messages and structures.

Syntax   BOOL **GetSaveFileName**(LPOPENFILENAME *lpofn*)

Parameters

lpofn   LPOPENFILENAME: A pointer to an OPENFILENAME structure that contains information used to initialize the dialog box. When GetSaveFileName() returns, this structure contains information about the user's file selection. See the definition of the OPENFILENAME structure under the GetOpenFileName() function.

Returns   BOOL: If the user selects a file to save, TRUE is returned. If an error occurs, the user chooses the Cancel button or the Close command on the System menu, or if the buffer identified by the *lpstrFile* member of the OPENFILENAME structure is too small to contain the string that specifies the selected file, FALSE is returned. Use the CommDlgExtendedError()

function to retrieve extended error information. One of the errors listed in Table 2-19 can be returned.

Table 2-19 GetSaveFileName() extended errors

Value	Meaning
CDERR_FINDRESFAILURE	A specified resource could not be found.
CDERR_INITIALIZATION	Failed during initialization.
CDERR_LOADRESFAILURE	A specified resource could not be loaded.
CDERR_LOADSTRFAILURE	A specified string could not be loaded.
CDERR_LOCKRESFAILURE	A specified resource could not be locked.
CDERR_MEMALLOCFAILURE	Unable to allocate memory for internal structures.
CDERR_MEMLOCKFAILURE	Unable to lock the memory associated with a handle.
CDERR_NOHINSTANCE	The OFN_ENABLETEMPLATE flag was specified without providing an instance handle in the *hInstance* member.
CDERR_NOHOOK	The OFN_ENABLEHOOK flag was specified without providing a pointer to a hook function in the *lpfnHook* member.
CDERR_NOTEMPLATE	The OFN_ENABLETEMPLATE flag was specified without providing a template in the *lpstrTemplateName* member.
CDERR_STRUCTSIZE	The *lStructSize* member of a OPENFILENAME structure is invalid.
FNERR_BUFFERTOOSMALL	The buffer pointed to by the *lpstrFile* member of the structure is too small.
FNERR_INVALIDFILENAME	A file name is invalid.
FNERR_SUBCLASSFAILURE	An attempt to subclass a list box failed because of insufficient memory.

Include File	commdlg.h
See Also	CommDlgExtendedError(), GetOpenFilename()
Related Messages	FILEOKSTRING, LBSELCHSTRING, SHAREVISTRING, HELPMSGSTRING, WM_NOTIFY
Example	This example (Listing 2-6) is similar to the one for the GetOpenFileName() function except that when the user selects the File↓Save As menu item, the GetSaveFileName() function is used to display the Save As common dialog box as shown in Figure 2-5. When the user selects the file name, it is displayed in the client area of the window.

Listing 2-6 Using the GetSaveFileName common dialog

```
LRESULT CALLBACK WndProc( HWND hWnd, UINT uMsg, WPARAM wParam, LPARAM lParam )
{
static char szFileName[MAX_PATH];
static char szFileTitle[MAX_PATH];

   switch( uMsg )
   {
```

```
case WM_CREATE :
        memset( szFileName, O, sizeof( szFileName ) );
        memset( szFileTitle, O, sizeof( szFileTitle ) );
        break;

case WM_PAINT :
        {
            PAINTSTRUCT ps;

            // Display the file name.
            //......................
            BeginPaint( hWnd, &ps );

            if ( szFileTitle[O] )
               TextOut( ps.hdc, 10, 10, szFileTitle,
                        strlen( szFileTitle ) );

            EndPaint( hWnd, &ps );
        }
        break;

case WM_COMMAND :
        switch( LOWORD( wParam ) )
        {
            case IDM_SAVEFILE :
                   {
                       OPENFILENAME ofn;

                       // Initialize the OPENFILENAME structure.
                       //.......................................
                       memset( &ofn, O, sizeof( OPENFILENAME ) );
                       ofn.lStructSize   = sizeof( OPENFILENAME );
                       ofn.hwndOwner     = hWnd;
                       ofn.lpstrFilter   = "Text files {*.txt}\0*.txt\0"\
                                           "All files {*.*}\0*.*\0\0";
```

continued on next page

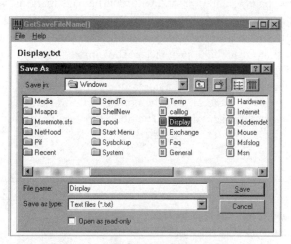

Figure 2-5 GetSaveFileName() example

continued from previous page

```
                    ofn.lpstrFile      = szFileName;
                    ofn.nMaxFile       = MAX_PATH;
                    ofn.lpstrFileTitle = szFileTitle;
                    ofn.nMaxFileTitle  = MAX_PATH;
                    ofn.Flags          = OFN_FILEMUSTEXIST;
                    ofn.lpstrDefExt    = "txt";

                    // Create the save file dialog.
                    //.............................
                    if ( GetSaveFileName( &ofn ) )
                        InvalidateRect( hWnd, NULL, TRUE );
                }
                break;

            case IDM_EXIT :
                    DestroyWindow( hWnd );
                    break;
            }
            break;

    case WM_DESTROY :
            PostQuitMessage(0);
            break;

    default :
            return( DefWindowProc( hWnd, uMsg, wParam, lParam ) );
    }

    return( OL );
}
```

PageSetupDlg   ■ Win32s ■ Windows 95 ■ Windows NT

Description   PageSetupDlg() displays a Page Setup common dialog box. The Page Setup
dialog box lets the user set the attributes of the printed page, such as the
paper type, paper source, page orientation, and width of the page margins.

The Page Setup dialog box includes an image of a sample page that
shows how the user's selections affect the appearance of the printed output. An application can customize the appearance of the sample page by
using the PSD_ENABLEPAGEPAINTHOOK value and setting the
lpfnPagePaintHook member to the address of a hook function. The dialog
box sends the paint messages in Table 2-20 to the hook function whenever
it needs a portion of the sample page redrawn. The hook function receives
these messages in the order in which they are listed.

Table 2-20 PrintSetupDlg() paint messages

Message	Meaning
WM_PSD_PAGESETUPDLG	Notifies the hook function to carry out initialization tasks.
WM_PSD_FULLPAGERECT	Specifies the bounding rectangle of the sample page.
WM_PSD_MINMARGINRECT	Specifies the minimum margin rectangle.

Message	Meaning
WM_PSD_MARGINRECT	Specifies the margin rectangle.
WM_PSD_GREEKTEXTRECT	Specifies the greek-text rectangle.
WM_PSD_ENVSTAMPRECT	Specifies the envelope-stamp rectangle (envelopes only).
WM_PSD_YAFULLPAGERECT	Specifies the bounding rectangle of the sample page.

Syntax	BOOL **PageSetupDlg**(LPPAGESETUPDLG *lppsd*)
Parameters	
lppsd	LPPAGESETUPDLG: A pointer to a PAGESETUPDLG structure that contains information used to intialize the dialog box. When PageSetupDlg() returns, this structure contains information about the user's selections. See the definition of the PAGESETUPDLG structure below.
Returns	BOOL: If the user selects the OK button, TRUE is returned. If the user cancels the Page Setup dialog box or an error occurs, FALSE is returned. Use the CommDlgExtendedError() function to retrieve extended error information. One of the errors listed in Table 2-21 can be returned.

Table 2-21 PageSetupDlg() extended errors

Value	Meaning
CDERR_FINDRESFAILURE	A specified resource could not be found.
CDERR_INITIALIZATION	Failed during initialization.
CDERR_LOADRESFAILURE	A specified resource could not be loaded.
CDERR_LOADSTRFAILURE	A specified string could not be loaded.
CDERR_LOCKRESFAILURE	A specified resource could not be locked.
CDERR_MEMALLOCFAILURE	Unable to allocate memory for internal structures.
CDERR_MEMLOCKFAILURE	Unable to lock the memory associated with a handle.
CDERR_NOHINSTANCE	The PSD_ENABLETEMPLATE flag was specified without providing an instance handle in the *hInstance* member.
CDERR_NOHOOK	The PSD_ENABLEPAGESETUPHOOK flag was specified without providing a pointer to a hook function in the *lpfnPageSetupHook* member, or the PSD_ENABLEPAGEPAINTHOOK flag was specified without providing a pointer to a hook function in the *lpfnPagePaintHook*.
CDERR_NOTEMPLATE	The PSD_ENABLETEMPLATE flag was specified without providing a template in the *lpPageSetupTemplateName* member.
CDERR_STRUCTSIZE	The *lStructSize* member of a PAGESETUPDLG structure is invalid.

Include File	commdlg.h
See Also	CommDlgExtendedError(), PrintDlg()
Related Messages	HELPMSGSTRING

PAGESETUPDLG Definition

```
typedef struct tagPSD
{
    DWORD             lStructSize;
    HWND              hwndOwner;
    HGLOBAL           hDevMode;
    HGLOBAL           hDevNames;
    DWORD             Flags;
    POINT             ptPaperSize;
    RECT              rtMinMargin;
    RECT              rtMargin;
    HINSTANCE         hInstance;
    LPARAM            lCustData;
    LPPAGESETUPHOOK   lpfnPageSetupHook;
    LPPAGEPAINTHOOK   lpfnPagePaintHook;
    LPCTSTR           lpPageSetupTemplateName;
    HGLOBAL           hPageSetupTemplate;
} PAGESETUPDLG;
```

Members

lStructureSize DWORD: The size, in bytes, of the structure.

hwndOwner HWND: The handle of the window that owns the dialog box. This member can be any valid window handle, or set to NULL if the dialog box has no owner.

hDevMode HGLOBAL: Identifies a memory object that contains a DEVMODE structure. Before a call to the PageSetupDlg() function, the structure members may contain data used to initialize the dialog controls. When PageSetupDlg() returns, the structure members specify the state of the dialog box controls. See the definition of the DEVMODE structure in Chapter 11, Messages.

 If the application uses the structure to initialize the dialog box controls, it must allocate space for and create the DEVMODE structure. If the application does not use the structure to initialize the dialog box controls, *hDevMode* may be set to NULL. In this case, PageSetupDlg() allocates memory for the structure, initializes its members, and returns a handle that identifies it. If the device driver for the specified printer does not support extended device modes, *hDevMode* is NULL when PageSetupDlg() returns.

hDevNames HGLOBAL: Identifies a memory object that contains a DEVNAMES structure. This structure contains three strings that specify the driver name, the printer name, and the output port name. Before the call to PageSetupDlg(), the structure members contain strings used to initialize dialog box controls. When PageSetupDlg() returns, the structure members contain the strings selected by the user. The calling application uses these strings to create a device context or an information context. See the definition of the DEVNAMES structure under the PrintDlg function on page 63.

 If the application uses the structure to initialize the dialog box controls, it must allocate space for and create the DEVNAMES structure. If the application does not use the structure to initialize the dialog box controls, *hDevNames* may be set to NULL. In this case, PageSetupDlg() allocates memory for the structure, initializes its members, and returns a handle that identifies it.

If both *hDevMode* and *hDevNames* are set to NULL, PageSetupDlg() initializes *hDevNames* using the current default printer.

Flags   DWORD: The dialog box initialization flags. This member may be a combination of the flags in Table 2-22.

Table 2-22 PAGESETUPDLG *Flag* values

Value	Meaning
PSD_DEFAULTMINMARGINS	Uses the default minimum margin values.
PSD_DISABLEMARGINS	Disables the margins so the user cannot change them.
PSD_DISABLEORIENTATION	Disables the paper orientation.
PSD_DISABLEPAGEPAINTING	Disables the page setup preview.
PSD_DISABLEPAPER	Disables the paper selection.
PSD_DISABLEPRINTER	Disables the Printer button.
PSD_ENABLEPAGEPAINTHOOK	Enables the hook function spec specified in *lpfnPagePaintHook*.
PSD_ENABLEPAGESETUPHOOK	Enables the hook function spec specified in *lpfnPageSetupHook*.
PSD_ENABLEPAGESETUPTEMPLATE	Causes the system to create the dialog box by using the dialog box template identified by *hInstance* and *lpPageSetupTemplateName*.
PSD_ENABLEPAGESETUPTEMPLATEHANDLE	Indicates that *hPageSetupTemplate* identifies a data block that contains a preloaded dialog box template. The system ignores *lpPageSetupTemplateName* if this flag is specified.
PSD_INHUNDREDTHSOFMILLIMETERS	Uses 1/100 of a millimeter as the unit of measure.
PSD_INTHOUSANDTHSOFINCHES	Uses 1/1000 of an inch as the unit of measure.
PSD_INWININIINTLMEASURE	Uses the international preference for the units of measure.
PSD_MARGINS	Sets the initial margin values to the values in the *rtMargin* member.
PSD_MINMARGINS	Sets the minimum margin values to the values in the *rtMinMargin* member.
PSD_NOWARNING	Prevents error messages.
PSD_RETURNDEFAULT	Retrieves information about the default printer without displaying the Page Setup dialog box.
PSD_SHOWHELP	Shows the Help button. The *hwndOwner* member must be a valid window handle.

ptPaperSize   POINT: A POINT structure that contains the width and height of the printer page.

rtMinMargin   RECT: A RECT structure that contains the minimum top, left, bottom, and right margin values. This value is ignored if the PSD_MINMARGINS flag is not specified.

rtMargin   RECT: A RECT structure that contains the top, left, bottom, and right margin values with which to initialize the Page Setup dialog box. When the dialog box closes, this structure contains the user selected margin values.

hInstance	HINSTANCE: The instance handle of the module that contains the dialog box template specified by the *lpPageSetupTemplateName*.
lCustData	LPARAM: Application-defined data that the operating system passes to the hook function pointed to by *lpfnPageSetupHook* and *lpfnPagePaintHook*. The system passes the data in the *lParam* parameter of the WM_INITDIALOG message.
lpfnPageSetupHook	LPPAGESETUPHOOK: A pointer to the function that hooks dialog messages if the application alters the Page Setup dialog box. This member is ignored unless the *Flags* member specifies the PSD_ENABLEPAGESETUPHOOK flag.
lpfnPagePaintHook	LPPAGEPAINTHOOK: A pointer to the function that hooks painting of the page preview of the Page Setup dialog box. This member is ignored unless the *Flags* member specifies the PSD_ENABLEPAGEPAINTHOOK flag.
lpPageSetupTemplateName	LPCTSTR: The name of the Page Setup dialog box template identified by *hInstance*.
hPageSetupTemplate	HGLOBAL: A memory object that contains the preloaded dialog box template to be used instead of the default Page Setup dialog box.
Example	See the example for the PrintDlg() function.

PRINTDLG   ■ Win32s   ■ Windows 95   ■ Windows NT

Description	PrintDlg() displays a Print common dialog box or a Print Setup common dialog box. The Print dialog box enables the user to specify the properties of a particular print job. The Print Setup dialog box allows the user to select additional job properties and to configure the printer.
Syntax	BOOL **PrintDlg**(LPPRINTDLG *lppd*)
Parameters	
lppd	LPPRINTDLG: A pointer to a PRINTDLG structure that contains information used to initialize the dialog box. When PrintDlg() returns, this structure contains information about the user's selections. See the definition of the PRINTDLG structure below.
Returns	BOOL: If the function succeeds in configuring the printer, TRUE is returned. FALSE is returned if an error occurs, the user chooses the Cancel button, or the user chooses the Close command on the System menu. The return value is also FALSE if the user chooses the Setup button to display the Print Setup dialog box, chooses the OK button in the Print Setup dialog box, and then chooses the Cancel button in the Print dialog box. Use the CommDlgExtendedError() function to retrieve extended error information. One of the errors listed in Table 2-23 can be returned.

Table 2-23 PringDlg() extended errors

Value	Meaning
CDERR_FINDRESFAILURE	A specified resource could not be found.
CDERR_INITIALIZATION	Failed during initialization.
CDERR_LOADRESFAILURE	A specified resource could not be loaded.
CDERR_LOADSTRFAILURE	A specified string could not be loaded.
CDERR_LOCKRESFAILURE	A specified resource could not be locked.
CDERR_MEMALLOCFAILURE	Unable to allocate memory for internal structures.
CDERR_MEMLOCKFAILURE	Unable to lock the memory associated with a handle.
CDERR_NOHINSTANCE	The PD_ENABLETEMPLATE flag was specified without providing an instance handle in the *hInstance* member.
CDERR_NOHOOK	The PD_ENABLEHOOK flag was specified without providing a pointer to a hook function in the *lpfnHook* member.
CDERR_NOTEMPLATE	The PD_ENABLETEMPLATE flag was specified without providing a template in the *lpstrTemplateName* member.
CDERR_STRUCTSIZE	The *lStructSize* member of a PRINTDLG structure is invalid.
PDERR_CREATEICFAILURE	The PrintDlg() function failed to create an information context.
PDERR_DEFAULTDIFFERENT	An application called the PrintDlg() function with the DN_DEFAULTPRN flag specified in the *wDefault* member of the DEVNAMES structure, but the printer described by the other structure members did not match the current default printer. (This error happens when an application stores the DEVNAMES structure and the user changes the default printer by using Control Panel.) To use the printer described by the DEVNAMES structure, the application should clear the DN_DEFAULTPRN flag and call the PrintDlg() function again. To use the default printer, the application should replace the DEVNAMES structure (and the DEVMODE structure, if one exists) with NULL; this sets the default printer automatically.
PDERR_DNDMMISMATCH	The data in the DEVMODE and DEVNAMES structures describes two different printers.
PDERR_GETDEVMODEFAIL	The printer driver failed to initialize a DEVMODE structure. (This error value applies only to printer drivers written for Windows versions 3.0 and later.)
PDERR_INITFAILURE	The PrintDlg() function failed during initialization, and there is no more specific extended error code to describe the failure. This is the generic default error code for the function.
PDERR_LOADDRVFAILURE	The PrintDlg() function failed to load the device driver for the specified printer.
PDERR_NODEFAULTPRN	A default printer does not exist.
PDERR_NODEVICES	No printer drivers were found.
PDERR_PARSEFAILURE	The PrintDlg() function failed to parse the strings in the [devices] section of the WIN.INI file.
PDERR_PRINTERNOTFOUND	The [devices] section of the WIN.INI file did not contain an entry for the requested printer.
PDERR_RETDEFFAILURE	The PD_RETURNDEFAULT flag was specified in the *Flags* member of the PRINTDLG structure, but the *hDevMode* or *hDevNames* member was nonzero.

Include File   commdlg.h

See Also   CommDlgExtendedError(), PageSetupDlg(), CreateDC(), StartDoc()

Related Messages   HELPMSGSTRING

PRINTDLG Definition

```
typedef struct tagPD
{
    DWORD             lStructSize;
    HWND              hwndOwner;
    HGLOBAL           hDevMode;
    HGLOBAL           hDevNames;
    HDC               hDC;
    DWORD             Flags;
    WORD              nFromPage;
    WORD              nToPage;
    WORD              nMinPage;
    WORD              nMaxPage;
    WORD              nCopies;
    HINSTANCE         hInstance;
    LPARAM            lCustData;
    LPPRINTHOOKPROC   lpfnPrintHook;
    LPSETUPHOOKPROC   lpfnSetupHook;
    LPCTSTR           lpPrintTemplateName;
    LPCTSTR           lpSetupTemplateName;
    HGLOBAL           hPrintTemplate;
    HGLOBAL           hSetupTemplate;
} PRINTDLG;
```

Members

lStructSize   DWORD: The size, in bytes, of the structure.

hwndOwner   HWND: The handle of the window that owns the dialog box. This member can be any valid window handle, or set to NULL if the dialog box has no owner.

hDevMode   HGLOBAL: Identifies a memory object that contains a DEVMODE structure. Before a call to the PrintDlg() function, the structure members may contain data used to initialize the dialog controls. When PrintDlg() returns, the structure members specify the state of the dialog box controls. See the definition of the DEVMODE structure in Chapter 11, Messages.

        If the application uses the structure to initialize the dialog box controls, it must allocate space for and create the DEVMODE structure. If the application does not use the structure to initialize the dialog box controls, *hDevMode* may be set to NULL. In this case, PrintDlg() allocates memory for the structure, initializes its members, and returns a handle that identifies it. If the device driver for the specified printer does not support extended device modes, *hDevMode* is NULL when PrintDlg() returns.

hDevNames   HGLOBAL: Identifies a memory object that contains a DEVNAMES structure. This structure contains three strings that specify the driver name, the printer name, and the output port name. Before the call to PrintDlg(), the structure members contain strings used to initialize dialog box controls. When PrintDlg() returns, the structure members contain the strings selected by the user. The calling application uses these strings to create a device context or an information context. See the definition of the DEVNAMES structure below.

If the application uses the structure to initialize the dialog box controls, it must allocate space for and create the DEVNAMES structure. If the application does not use the structure to initialize the dialog box controls, *hDevNames* may be set to NULL. In this case, PrintDlg() allocates memory for the structure, initializes its members, and returns a handle that identifies it.

If both *hDevMode* and *hDevNames* are set to NULL, PrintDlg() initializes *hDevNames* using the current default printer.

hDC   HDC: A device context or an information context for the selected printer, depending on whether the *Flags* member specifies the PD_RETURNDC or PC_RETURNIC flag. If neither flag is specified, the value of this member is undefined. If both flags are specified, PD_RETURNDC has priority.

Flags   DWORD: The dialog box initialization flags. This member may be a combination of the flags in Table 2-24.

Table 2-24 PRINTDLG *Flag* values

Value	Meaning
PD_ALLPAGES	The All radio button is selected.
PD_COLLATE	The Collate check box is set on input. When the PrintDlg() function returns, this value indicates that the user selected the Collate option and the printer driver does not support collation. In this case, the application must provide collation. If PrintDlg() sets the PD_COLLATE value on return, it also sets *dmCollate* in the DEVMODE structure to COLLATE_TRUE.
PD_DISABLEPRINTTOFILE	Disables the Print to File check box.
PD_ENABLEPRINTHOOK	Enables the hook function specified in *lpfnPrintHook*.
PD_ENABLEPRINTTEMPLATE	Causes the system to create the dialog box by using the dialog box template identified by *hInstance* and *lpPrintTemplateName*.
PD_ENABLEPRINTTEMPLATEHANDLE	Indicates that *hPrintTemplate* identifies a data block that contains a preloaded dialog box template. The system ignores *lpPrintTemplateName* if this flag is specified.
PD_ENABLESETUPHOOK	Enables the hook function specified in *lpfnSetupHook*.
PD_ENABLESETUPTEMPLATE	Causes the operating system to create the dialog box by using the dialog template box identified by *hInstance* and *lpSetupTemplateName*.
PD_ENABLESETUPTEMPLATEHANDLE	Indicates that *hSetupTemplate* identifies a data block that contains a preloaded dialog box template. The system ignores *lpSetupTemplateName* if this flag is specified.
PD_HIDEPRINTTOFILE	Hides and disables the Print to File check box.
PD_NOPAGENUMS	Disables the Pages radio button and the associated edit control.
PD_NOSELECTION	Disables the Selection radio button.
PD_NOWARNING	Prevents the warning message from being displayed when there is no default printer.

continued on next page

continued from previous page

Value	Meaning
PD_PAGENUMS	Causes the Pages radio button to be in the selected state when the dialog box is created. When PrintDlg() returns, this flag is specified if the Pages radio button is in the selected state.
PD_PRINTSETUP	Causes the system to display the Print Setup dialog box rather than the Print dialog box.
PD_PRINTTOFILE	Causes the Print to File check box to be in the checked state when the dialog box is created. When PrintDlg() returns, the *pOutput* member of the DEVNAMES structure points to the "FILE:" string.
PD_RETURNDC	Causes PrintDlg() to return a device context matching the selections the user made in the dialog box. The device context is returned in *hDC*.
PD_RETURNDEFAULT	Causes PrintDlg() to return DEVMODE and DEVNAMES structures that are initialized for the system default printer without displaying a dialog box. It is assumed that both *hDevNames* and *hDevMode* are set to NULL; otherwise, the function returns an error.
PD_RETURNIC	Similar to the PD_RETURNDC flag except that this flag returns an information context rather than a device context. If neither PD_RETURNDC nor PD_RETURNIC is specified, *hDC* is undefined on output.
PD_SELECTION	Causes the Selection radio button to be in the selected state when the dialog box is created. When PrintDlg() returns, this flag is specified if the Selection radio button is in the selected state. If neither PD_PAGENUMS nor PD_SELECTION is specified, the All radio button is in the selected state.
PD_SHOWHELP	Shows the Help button. The *hwndOwner* member must not be NULL if this flag is specified.
PD_USEDEVMODECOPIES	Same as PD_USEDEVMODECOPIESANDCOLLATE.
PD_USEDEVMODECOPIESANDCOLLATE	Disables the Copies edit control if the printer driver does not support multiple copies and disables the Collate check box if the printer driver does not support collation. Otherwise, directs PrintDlg() to store the user selections for the Copies and Collate options in the *dmCopies* and *dmCollate* members of the DEVMODE structure.
	If the driver supports multiple copies, PrintDlg() stores the requested number of copies in the *dmCopies* member of the DEVMODE structure and stores the value 1 in the *nCopies* member of the PRINTDLG structure. If this flag is not specified, *dmCopies* receives 1 and *nCopies* receives the requested number of copies.
	If the driver supports collation, PrintDlg() sets the *dmCollate* member of the DEVMODE structure to DMCOLLATE_TRUE or DMCOLLATE_FALSE, depending on the user selection. If this flag is not specified, *dmCollate* is ignored and the *Flags* member of PRINTDLG is set to PD_COLLATE only if the user selects the Collate option.

nFromPage   WORD: The starting page number. This value is the initial value for the starting page edit control. When the PrintDlg() function returns, this member specifies the page at which to begin printing. This value is valid only if the PD_PAGENUMS flag is specified.

nToPage   WORD: The ending page number. This value is the initial value for the ending page edit control. When the PrintDlg() function returns, this member

	specifies the last page to print. This value is valid only if the PD_PAGENUMS flag is specified.
nMinPage	WORD: The minimum value for the range of pages specified in the From and To page edit controls.
nMaxPage	WORD: The maximum value for the range of pages specified in the From and To page edit controls.
nCopies	WORD: The initial number of copies for the Copies edit control if *hDevMode* is NULL; otherwise, the *dmCopies* member of the DEVMODE structure contains the initial value. When PrintDlg() returns, this member contains the actual number of copies to print. If the printer driver does not support multiple copies, this value may be greater than one and the application must print all requested copies. If the PD_USEDEVMODECOPIESANDCOLLATE value is set in the *Flags* member, *nCopies* is always set to 1 on return and the *dmCopies* member in the DEVMODE receives the actual number of copies to print.
hInstance	HINSTANCE: The instance handle of the module that contains the dialog box template specified by the *lpTemplateName* or the *lpSetupTemplateName* member.
lCustData	LPARAM: Application-defined data that the operating system passes to the hook function pointed to by *lpfnPrintHook* or *lpfnSetupHook*. The system passes the data in the *lParam* parameter of the WM_INITDIALOG message.
lpfnPrintHook	LPPRINTHOOKPROC: A pointer to the function that hooks dialog messages if the application alters the Print dialog box. This member is ignored unless the *Flags* member specifies the PD_ENABLEPRINTHOOK flag.
lpfnSetupHook	LPSETUPHOOKPROC: A pointer to the function that hooks dialog messages if the application alters the Print Setup dialog box. This member is ignored unless the *Flags* member specifies the PD_ENABLESETUPHOOK flag.
lpPrintTemplateName	LPCTSTR: The name of the Print dialog box template identified by *hInstance*.
lpSetupTemplateName	LPCTSTR: The name of the Print Setup dialog box identified by *hInstance*.
hPrintTemplate	HGLOBAL: A memory object that contains the preloaded dialog box template to be used instead of the default Print Dialog box.
hSetupTemplate	HGLOBAL: A memory object that contains the preloaded dialog box template to be used instead of the default Setup dialog box.

DEVNAMES Definition

```
typedef struct tagDEVNAMES
{
    WORD wDriverOffset;
    WORD wDeviceOffset;
    WORD wOutputOffset;
    WORD wDefault;
    // driver, device, and port name strings follow wDefault
} DEVNAMES;
```

Members

wDriverOffset WORD: The offset in characters from the beginning of this structure to a null-terminated string that contains the file name (without the extension) of the device driver. On input, this string is used to determine the printer to display initially in the dialog box.

wDeviceOffset WORD: The offset in characters from the beginning of this structure to the null-terminated string (maximum of 32 bytes including the null) that contains the name of the device. This string must be identical to the *dmDeviceName* member of the DEVMODE structure.

wOutputOffset WORD: The offset in characters from the beginning of this structure to the null-terminated string that contains the device name for the physical output medium (output port).

wDefault WORD: Specifies whether the strings contained in the DEVNAMES structure identify the default printer. This string is used to verify that the default printer has not changed since the last print operation. On input, if the DN_DEFAULTPRN flag is specified, the other values in the DEVNAMES structure are checked against the current default printer. If any of the strings do not match, a warning message is displayed informing the user that the document may need to be reformatted.

On output, the *wDefault* member is changed only if the Print Setup dialog box was displayed and the user chose the OK button. The DN_DEFAULTPRN flag is used if the default printer was selected. If a specific printer is selected, the flag is not used. All other flags in this member are reserved for internal use by the Print Dialog box procedure.

Example This example (Listing 2-7) creates a multiline edit control as the client area of the window and places a sample text string into it. When the user selects the File ↓Page Setup menu item, the user is presented with the Page Setup common dialog and allowed to set the margins, paper size, and orientation that will be used to print the text in the edit control. When the user selects the File ↓Print menu item, the Print common dialog, shown in Figure 2-6, is displayed. If the user selects a printer and presses the OK button, the text is printed to that printer.

Listing 2-7 Using the PrintDlg common dialog

```
LPCTSTR lpszText = "This sample text will be printed to the printer.";

LRESULT CALLBACK WndProc( HWND hWnd, UINT uMsg, WPARAM wParam, LPARAM lParam )
{
static PAGESETUPDLG psd;
static HWND          hEdit = NULL;

   switch( uMsg )
   {
      case WM_CREATE :
              // Initialize the PAGESETUPDLG structure.
              //.............................................
```

```
            psd.lStructSize       = sizeof( PAGESETUPDLG );
            psd.hwndOwner         = hWnd;
            psd.rtMargin.top      = 1000;
            psd.rtMargin.left     = 1000;
            psd.rtMargin.bottom   = 1000;
            psd.rtMargin.right    = 1000;
            psd.hDevMode          = GlobalAlloc( GHND, sizeof( DEVMODE ) );
            psd.hDevNames         = GlobalAlloc( GHND, sizeof( DEVNAMES ) );
            psd.Flags             = PSD_MARGINS | PSD_INTHOUSANDTHSOFINCHES;

            hEdit = CreateWindow( "EDIT", "",
                                  WS_CHILD | ES_LEFT |
                                  WS_VISIBLE | ES_MULTILINE | ES_NOHIDESEL,
                                  0, 0,
                                  0, 0,
                                  hWnd,
                                  (HMENU)101,
                                  hInst,
                                  NULL
                                );

            SendMessage( hEdit, WM_SETTEXT, 0, (LPARAM)lpszText );
            break;

    case WM_SIZE :
            MoveWindow( hEdit, 0, 0,
                        LOWORD( lParam ),
                        HIWORD( lParam ), TRUE );
            break;

    case WM_COMMAND :
            switch( LOWORD( wParam ) )
            {
                case IDM_PAGESETUP :
                        PageSetupDlg( &psd );
                        break;
```

continued on next page

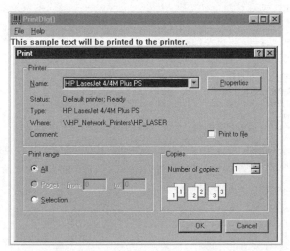

Figure 2-6 PrintDlg() example

continued from previous page

```
case IDM_PRINT :
    {
        PRINTDLG pd;

        // Initialize the PRINTDLG structure.
        //..................................
        memset( &pd, 0, sizeof( PRINTDLG ) );
        pd.lStructSize   = sizeof( PRINTDLG );
        pd.hwndOwner     = hWnd;
        pd.Flags         = PD_RETURNDC;
        pd.hDevMode      = psd.hDevMode;
        pd.hDevNames     = psd.hDevNames;

        // Create the print dialog.
        //........................
        if ( PrintDlg( &pd ) )
        {
            WORD        wCopies;
            char        szBuf[512];
            RECT        rect;
            DOCINFO     di;
            LPDEVMODE   lpDevMode;

            lpDevMode = (LPDEVMODE)GlobalLock( pd.hDevMode );
            memset( &di, 0, sizeof( DOCINFO ) );

            // Initialize rect to size of page.
            //.................................
            rect.top =
                    ( GetDeviceCaps( pd.hDC, LOGPIXELSY )*
                    (psd.rtMargin.top/1000 ))-
                    GetDeviceCaps( pd.hDC, PHYSICALOFFSETY );

            rect.left =
                    ( GetDeviceCaps( pd.hDC, LOGPIXELSX )*
                    (psd.rtMargin.left/1000 ))-
                    GetDeviceCaps( pd.hDC, PHYSICALOFFSETX );

            rect.right =
                    lpDevMode->dmPelsWidth -
                    ( GetDeviceCaps( pd.hDC, LOGPIXELSX )*
                    (psd.rtMargin.right/1000 ))-
                    GetDeviceCaps( pd.hDC, PHYSICALOFFSETX );

            rect.bottom =
                    lpDevMode->dmPelsHeight -
                    ( GetDeviceCaps( pd.hDC, LOGPIXELSY )*
                    (psd.rtMargin.bottom/1000 ))-
                    GetDeviceCaps( pd.hDC, PHYSICALOFFSETY );

            // Initialize di with the document title.
            //.......................................
            di.cbSize      = sizeof( DOCINFO );
            di.lpszDocName = lpszTitle;

            // Retrieve the text from the edit control.
            //.........................................
```

```
                        SendMessage( hEdit, WM_GETTEXT,
                                 sizeof( szBuf ), (LPARAM)szBuf );

                        // Print the text.
                        //................
                        if ( StartDoc( pd.hDC, &di ) > 0 )
                        {
                            for( wCopies = 0;
                                 wCopies < pd.nCopies; wCopies++ )
                            {
                                StartPage( pd.hDC );
                                DrawText( pd.hDC, szBuf, strlen( szBuf ),
                                        &rect, DT_LEFT | DT_WORDBREAK );
                                EndPage( pd.hDC );
                            }

                            EndDoc( pd.hDC );
                        }

                        // Unlock and free resources.
                        //..........................
                        GlobalUnlock( pd.hDevMode );
                        DeleteDC( pd.hDC );
                    }
                    else if ( CommDlgExtendedError() ==
                              PDERR_NODEFAULTPRN )
                    {
                        MessageBox( hWnd, "No default printer selected.",
                                    "Print", MB_OK | MB_ICONSTOP );
                    }
                }
                break;

            case IDM_ABOUT :
                    DialogBox( hInst, "AboutBox", hWnd, (DLGPROC)About );
                    break;

            case IDM_EXIT :
                    DestroyWindow( hWnd );
                    break;
        }
        break;

    case WM_DESTROY :
            GlobalFree( psd.hDevMode );
            GlobalFree( psd.hDevNames );

            PostQuitMessage(0);
            break;

    default :
            return( DefWindowProc( hWnd, uMsg, wParam, lParam ) );
    }

    return( 0L );
}
```

REPLACETEXT

■ Win32s ■ Windows 95 ■ Windows NT

Description   ReplaceText() creates a Find and Replace common modeless dialog box that enables the user to find and replace text within a document. This function does not perform the text replacement operation. The application must perform the replacement using the information entered by the user.

The Find and Replace common dialog uses special messages to pass user requests to the application. The *lParam* of each of these messages contains a pointer to a FINDREPLACE structure. The procedure sends the messages to the window identified by the *hwndOwner* member of the FINDREPLACE structure pointed to by the *lpfr* parameter. An application can register the identifier for these messages by specifying the "commdlg_FindReplace" (FINDMSGSTRING) string with the RegisterWindowMessage() function.

The application must use the IsDialogMessage() function in its main message loop to process dialog messages for the Find and Replace dialog.

Syntax   HWND **ReplaceText**(LPFINDREPLACE *lpfr*)

Parameters

lpfr   LPFINDREPLACE: A pointer to a FINDREPLACE structure that contains information used to initialize the dialog box. When the user makes a selection in the dialog box, the system fills this structure with information about the user's selection and then sends a message to the application. This message contains a pointer to the FINDREPLACE structure. See the definition of the FINDREPLACE structure under the FindText() function.

Returns   HWND: If successful, the window handle of the dialog box; otherwise, NULL is returned. Use the CommDlgExtendedError() function to retrieve extended error information. One of the errors listed in Table 2-25 can be returned.

Table 2-25 ReplaceText() extended errors

Value	Meaning
CDERR_FINDRESFAILURE	A specified resource could not be found.
CDERR_INITIALIZATION	Failed during initialization.
CDERR_LOADRESFAILURE	A specified resource could not be loaded.
CDERR_LOADSTRFAILURE	A specified string could not be loaded.
CDERR_LOCKRESFAILURE	A specified resource could not be locked.
CDERR_MEMALLOCFAILURE	Unable to allocate memory for internal structures.
CDERR_MEMLOCKFAILURE	Unable to lock the memory associated with a handle.
CDERR_NOHINSTANCE	The FR_ENABLETEMPLATE flag was specified without providing an instance handle in the *hInstance* member.

Value	Meaning
CDERR_NOHOOK	The FR_ENABLEHOOK flag was specified without providing a pointer to a hook function in the *lpfnHook* member.
CDERR_NOTEMPLATE	The FR_ENABLETEMPLATE flag was specified without providing a template in the *lpstrTemplateName* member.
CDERR_STRUCTSIZE	The *lStructSize* member of a FINDREPLACE structure is invalid.
FRERR_BUFFERLENGTHZERO	A member in FINDREPLACE structure points to an invalid buffer.

Include File	commdlg.h
See Also	CommDlgExtendedError(), IsDialogMessage(), RegisterWindowMessage(), FindText()
Related Messages	FINDMSGSTRING, HELPMSGSTRING
Example	See the example for the FindText() function.

3

TOOLBARS AND STATUS WINDOWS

TOOLBARS AND STATUS WINDOWS

Virtually all modern Windows applications contain at least one toolbar and a status window (status bar). The toolbar provides an easy method for visual selection of common program commands or functions, while the status window keeps the user informed about program operations. In the past, there was virtually no standard for how toolbars and status windows appeared and were implemented. Every application had its own method and appearance. Windows 95 and the Common Control Library has finally introduced a standard that all applications can easily use to implement toolbars and status windows.

One potential problem with the proliferation of toolbars is that the user may not be able to easily figure out what all the icon symbols mean. To provide an additional means of helping the user navigate, the Common Control Library implements a new control, the tooltip, that allows applications to provide context-sensitive feedback to the user as the mouse cursor passes over objects such as toolbars and dialog controls. The tooltip control gained popularity when it appeared as part of toolbars. With the tooltip control, applications can use tooltips to provide context-sensitive feedback throughout an application. The user need only point at an icon or control to learn its purpose.

Toolbars

Toolbars are control windows that contain one or more buttons. The toolbar sends commands to the parent window when the user selects a button in the same manner as messages are sent when the user selects a menu item. Toolbars provide the user with fast access to frequently used commands. An application can also give the user the ability to customize the toolbars with the built-in customization features. These include the ability to drag buttons on the toolbar to new locations and to display a system-defined dialog box that allows the user to add, delete, and move buttons on the toolbar.

Creating a Toolbar

Toolbar controls can be created in two ways. The easiest way is to use the provided function, CreateToolbarEx(), which allows you to also add an initial set of buttons. The other method is to use the CreateWindowEx() function using the defined value TOOLBARCLASSNAME as the class name. This creates a toolbar that initially does not contain any buttons. The application can add buttons to the toolbar using the TB_INSERTBUTTON and TB_ADDBUTTONS message. The TOOLBARCLASSNAME value is defined in the COMMCTRL.H file and is registered when the Common Control dynamic-link library (DLL) is loaded. An application must use the InitCommonControls() function before attempting to use any of the common control functions or messages. Figure 3-1 shows the toolbar from the Microsoft Windows 95 Explorer. See Chapter 1, Introduction to Common Controls and Dialogs, for more information on the InitCommonControls() function.

Toolbars must be created with the WS_CHILD style. This style is automatically used when the toolbar is created with the CreateToolbarEx() function and must be specified with the CreateWindowEx() function. The initial parent window of the toolbar must also be specified when creating the toolbar. If the parent window changes during execution, it can be changed by using the TB_SETPARENT message. See the CreateToolbarEx() function later in this chapter for an example of how to create a toolbar. For an example of how to create a toolbar with the CreateWindowEx() function, see the TB_BUTTONSTRUCTSIZE message later in this chapter.

The size of the toolbar is handled by the toolbar's window procedure. The size is based on the size of the toolbar buttons and the size of the parent window. The size of the toolbar is automatically adjusted to the appropriate size whenever the toolbar window procedure receives the WM_SIZE or TB_AUTOSIZE message. An application should send either of these messages when the parent window size changes or the button size of the toolbar changes. For example, after sending the TB_SETBUTTONSIZE message to change the button size of the toolbar, send the TB_AUTOSIZE message to force the toolbar to recalculate its size to accommodate the new button size.

When creating a toolbar with the CreateToolbarEx() function, an initial set of buttons can be added to the toolbar. Additional buttons can be added to the toolbar with the TB_ADDBUTTONS or TB_INSERTBUTTON message. If the toolbar is created with the CreateWindowEx() function, the TB_BUTTONSTRUCTSIZE message must be sent prior to using the TB_ADDBUTTONS or TB_INSERTBUTTON message to set the size of the TBBUTTON structure.

Figure 3-1 Windows Explorer toolbar

Toolbar Buttons

Toolbar buttons work similarly to push buttons on a dialog box, with the added ability to have a *checked* state and an *indeterminate* state. These states are the same as the standard check box control states. Using these states, toolbar buttons can toggle between the checked state and the normal state to indicate that an option is turned on or off. For example, the bold toolbar button in an editor application is checked if the bold attribute is turned on, and not checked if the bold attribute is turned off. Toolbar buttons can also be grouped together in the same way that radio buttons are grouped together. In toolbar button groups, only one button can be checked at a time. Tables 3-4 and 3-5 list the different button states and styles for a toolbar button.

Normally, toolbar buttons relate directly to menu items in the main menu of the application. Each toolbar button has a command identifier associated with it. When the user selects the toolbar button, the command identifier for the button is sent in the form of a WM_COMMAND message in the same manner as when the user selects a menu item. It is a good practice to keep the command identifiers the same for the menu item and the toolbar button to simplify handling of the WM_COMMAND message. In some cases, such as when the application needs to know if the user selected an option from the menu or from the toolbar, the command identifier for the toolbar button and menu item may be different.

Button Images

A toolbar button can contain a bitmapped image that identifies its function to the user. A toolbar internally stores an image list for the toolbar buttons. When a toolbar button is added, the index to the image in the internal image list is referenced to give the button a specific image. Each image has a zero-based index. The first image that is added has an index of zero, and subsequent images have an index of one, two, three, etc. When using the CreateToolbarEx() function, an initial image list is specified for the toolbar. Additional images can be added by sending the TB_ADDBITMAP message. The TB_ADDBITMAP message adds the images to the end of the image list and returns the index of the first added image.

The images for a toolbar must be the same size. The default size for each toolbar button image is 16 by 15 pixels. This size can be changed with the TB_SETBITMAPSIZE message; however, it must be changed prior to adding any bitmap images. Figure 3-2 shows a bitmap with four button images.

Button Text

Toolbar buttons can display a text string with the image or in place of the image. Strings are added to the toolbar with the TB_ADDSTRING message and are maintained in the

Figure 3-2 Toolbar image bitmap

same manner as the button images. Each string is given a zero-based index that can be assigned to a button or buttons. The text for the button is displayed below the bitmap image. The application should use the TB_AUTOSIZE message after adding buttons with associated text. This ensures that the buttons are sized to allow room for the text. Figure 3-12, later in this chapter, shows an example of how the text appears on a toolbar button with a button image.

Toolbar Tooltips

The toolbar control has automatic support for tooltips for the buttons on the toolbar. When the user places the cursor on a toolbar button and leaves it there for about one second, the tooltip control is displayed near the cursor. To create a toolbar with tooltips, use the TBSTYLE_TOOLTIPS style with the CreateToolbarEx() or CreateWindowEx() function.

Once a toolbar is created with tooltips, the application must also process the TTN_NEEDTEXT notification. When the application receives this notification, it must provide the tooltip text for the toolbar button.

If the application needs to send messages directly to the tooltip control, use the TB_GETTOOLTIPS message to retrieve the handle of the tooltip control. An application can associate a tooltip control with a toolbar with the TB_SETTOOLTIPS message. For more information on tooltips, see the description later in this chapter.

Customization

Toolbars have the built-in capability to allow the user to customize the buttons. If the application creates the toolbar with the CCS_ADJUSTABLE style, the customization features are enabled for the toolbar. The user can customize the toolbar by dragging buttons to new locations or remove buttons by dragging them off the toolbar. If the user double-clicks the toolbar or the application sends the TB_CUSTOMIZE message, the system-supplied customize dialog box is displayed. This dialog allows the user to move, delete, and add buttons on the toolbar.

The toolbar customization is managed by a series of notification messages (TBN_), described later in this chapter, that the application must process in order for the customization to work. To see how this works, see the example for the TB_CUSTOMIZE message later in this chapter.

The application can save the toolbar's state once the user has finished customizing it by sending the TB_SAVERESTORE message. This message saves the state information in the registry under the specified key and value names. The application can also save the state information before the user begins customization in case the user wants to restore the toolbar to its original state.

Tooltip Controls

Tooltip controls are small pop-up windows that display a single line of descriptive text that gives the user an indication of the purpose for a specific tool. A tooltip can manage several *tools* within an application. Tools are either windows, such as child windows and controls, or an application-defined rectangular area within a window's client area. One of the most common uses for tooltip controls is for toolbar buttons for which users have come to expect tooltips. However, an application is not limited in the use of tooltips. Even dialog box controls can have tooltips to help the user understand a dialog control's purpose. Figure 3-3 shows the Windows Explorer toolbar with a tooltip displayed.

Tooltip controls are hidden most of the time; they only appear when the user pauses the mouse cursor over a tool for a duration of time. By default this duration of time is about one second; however, an application can change this time with the TTM_SETDELAYTIME message. If the user moves the mouse off of the tool or clicks a mouse button, the tooltip is hidden again.

Creating a Tooltip

Tooltip controls are created with the CreateWindowEx() function by specifying the TOOLTIPS_CLASS for the window class. This class is registered when the application calls the InitCommonControls() function to initialize the Common Control DLL. The size, color, and position of the tooltip control are automatically set by the default tooltip window procedure. An application could subclass the tooltip control to change the appearance of the tooltip; however, this is not recommended because the application would not reflect the user's system preferences.

There are two styles specific to the tooltip control, the TTS_ALWAYSTIP and TTS_NOPREFIX. The TTS_ALWAYSTIP style forces a tooltip to appear even if the window that owns the tooltip is not active. The TTS_NOPREFIX style prevents the system from stripping the ampersand (&) character from the tip text. Use this style if the tooltip text contains ampersand characters that should not be stripped. The default action of a tooltip is to strip the ampersand characters so the same text can be used for the menu item and the tool text. A tooltip control has by default the WS_POPUP and WS_EX_TOOLWINDOW styles, even if they are not specified in the CreateWindowEx() function.

Defining Tools

A tooltip control, when created, does not have any tools associated with it. Before the tooltip will begin to show for a tool, it must be added to the list of tools that the tooltip control maintains. This is accomplished by sending the TTM_ADDTOOL message to the tooltip control. A tooltip control supports tools defined as windows, such as child windows or controls, and rectangular areas within a window's client area. See

Figure 3-3 Windows Explorer tooltip

the description for the TTM_ADDTOOL message later in this chapter for more information on how to add the different types of tools.

When adding a tool, it must either have a pointer to a text string, a string resource identifier, or the LPSTR_TEXTCALLBACK value associated with the tool. The first two methods will automatically display the appropriate tooltip text when the mouse is over the tool. The last method will send the TTN_NEEDTEXT notification before the tooltip is displayed. The application must then provide the text for that tool. This is useful when the text for a tool can change during the operation of the application. See the example for the TTN_NEEDTEXT notification message later in this chapter for an example of providing text to the tooltip control.

Relaying Mouse Events

A tooltip control needs to receive mouse events or messages to determine when to display the tooltip window. The easiest way to get the messages to the tooltip control is to add the tools with the TTF_SUBCLASS flag. The tooltip will then subclass the window that contains the tool and intercept the needed messages. In some cases, such as with dialog boxes, it may be preferable for the application to pass the messages to the tooltip control. This is accomplished by sending the TTM_RELAYEVENT message when a window procedure receives the following messages: WM_LBUTTONDOWN, WM_LBUTTONUP, WM_MBUTTONDOWN, WM_MBUTTONUP, WM_MOUSEMOVE, WM_RBUTTONDOWN, and WM_RBUTTONUP. See the example for the TTM_ENUMTOOLS message for how to use the TTM_RELAYEVENT message.

Status Windows

Status windows are windows that typically reside at the bottom of the client area of a window and display context-sensitive information to the user, such as menu item help and cursor position. The status window can be divided into parts to display more than one type of information. Figure 3-4 shows the status window from the Microsoft Windows 95 Explorer application. Here, the status window shows the number of files within the selected disk, the total size of the files in the root directory of the disk, and the amount of free space on the disk.

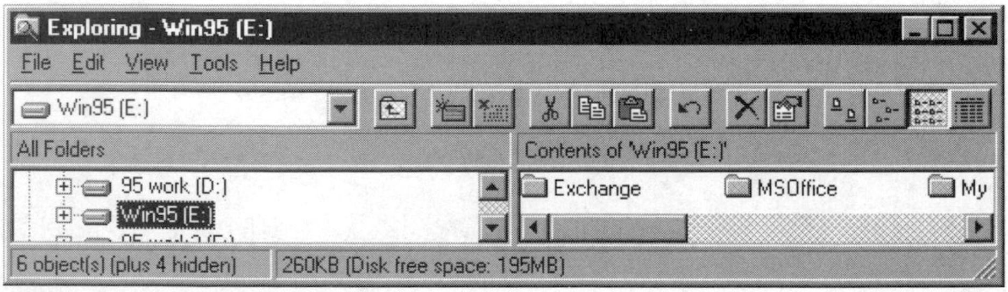

Figure 3-4 Windows Explorer with status window

Creating Status Windows

An application can create a status window by using the CreateStatusWindow() function or the CreateWindowEx() function with the STATUSCLASSNAME window class. This class is registered when the application calls the InitCommonControls() function described in Chapter 1, Introduction to Common Controls and Dialogs. After the status window is created, the application can divide it into separate parts by sending the SB_SETPARTS message. A status window can have a maximum of 255 parts, although it is not practical to have that many in an application.

The default position of a status window is at the bottom of the parent window; however, the CCS_TOP style can be used to have it appear at the top of the parent window's client area. Use the SBARS_SIZEGRIP style to include a sizing grip at the right end of the status window. Even though the SBARS_SIZEGRIP style and the CCS_TOP style can be combined, the size grip will not be functional on the status window.

The initial size of the status window is set by the default window procedure for the status window. The width is the same as the width of the parent window's client area and the height is based on the metrics of the currently selected font. The status window is automatically resized when the window procedure receives the WM_SIZE message. The parent window should pass this message to the status window when it receives the WM_SIZE message. If the default status window height is not appropriate, the application can set the minimum height of a status window's drawing area by sending the SB_SETMINHEIGHT message.

Status Window Text

Any part of a status window can contain text. The application can set the text of a status window part by sending the SB_SETTEXT message. This message also allows the application to specify the drawing method for the text, which determines whether the text has a border and the style of the border. It also determines whether the parent is responsible for drawing the text. This is known as an *owner-drawn* part. By default, the text is left-aligned within the status window part.

Individual parts of a status window can bet set to owner drawn. This gives the application more control over the appearance of the status window part. Owner-drawn parts can be used to display bitmaps or status bars. To define a window part as owner drawn, send the SB_SETTEXT message to the status window with the SBT_OWNERDRAW drawing technique. When the status window part needs to be drawn, the parent window receives the WM_DRAWITEM message with the *wParam* parameter containing the control identifier of the status window.

If a status window only contains one part, the WM_SETTEXT message can be used to change the text of the status window. This will only deal with the text in part zero of the status window.

The Common Control DLL also provides a function, DrawStatusText(), to draw status text without having a status window. This function gives the application the ability to draw text with a sunken or raised border that appears the same as the text that would normally be displayed in a status window.

Simple Status Windows

A status window can be set to *simple mode* by sending a SB_SIMPLE message to the status window. A simple mode status window displays only one part. The simple mode of a status window is often used when displaying menu item help. See the example for the SB_SIMPLE message later in this chapter for how to use this mode and how the status window appears.

The string that the simple mode displays is independent of the text that is displayed in normal mode. Because of this, the simple mode text can be set and the status window mode set back to normal without the text being overwritten in either mode. Any drawing technique can be used when setting text in the simple mode except owner drawn. This is because a simple status window does not support owner drawing.

Function Summary

Table 3-1 summarizes the toolbar, tooltip, and status window functions and messages. The detailed function and message descriptions follow immediately after the table.

Table 3-1 Toolbar, tooltip, status window function and message summary

Function	Meaning
CreateMappedBitmap	Creates a bitmap for use in a toolbar.
CreateStatusWindow	Creates a status window.
CreateToolbarEx	Creates a toolbar window.
DrawStatusText	Draws status text with borders in the style of a status window.
MenuHelp	Displays help text about the current menu in the specified status window.
Message	
SB_GETBORDERS	Retrieves the current widths of the horizontal and vertical borders of a status window.
SB_GETPARTS	Retrieves a count of the parts in a status window.
SB_GETRECT	Retrieves the bounding rectangle of a part in a status window.
SB_GETTEXT	Retrieves the text from a part of a status window.
SB_GETTEXTLENGTH	Retrieves the length, in characters, of the text from a part of a status window.
SB_SETMINHEIGHT	Sets the minimum height of a status window's drawing area.
SB_SETPARTS	Sets the number of parts in a status window and the coordinate of the right edge of each part.
SB_SETTEXT	Sets the text in the specified part of a status window.
SB_SIMPLE	Specifies whether a status window displays simple text or displays all window parts set by a previous SB_SETPARTS message.
TB_ADDBITMAP	Adds one or more images to the list of images for a toolbar.
TB_ADDBUTTONS	Adds one or more buttons to a toolbar.
TB_ADDSTRING	Adds a new string to the list of strings associated with a toolbar.
TB_AUTOSIZE	Causes a toolbar to be resized.
TB_BUTTONCOUNT	Retrieves the number of buttons within a toolbar.
TB_BUTTONSTRUCTSIZE	Sets the size of the TBUTTON structure.

Message	Meaning
TB_CHANGEBITMAP	Changes the bitmap for a button in a toolbar.
TB_CHECKBUTTON	Checks or unchecks a toolbar button.
TB_COMMANDTOINDEX	Retrieves the zero-based index for the button associated with a command identifier.
TB_CUSTOMIZE	Displays the Customize Toolbar dialog box.
TB_DELETEBUTTON	Deletes a button from a toolbar.
TB_ENABLEBUTTON	Enables or disables a button in a toolbar.
TB_GETBITMAP	Retrieves the index of a bitmap associated with a button in a toolbar.
TB_GETBITMAPFLAGS	Retrieves the bitmap flags.
TB_GETBUTTON	Retrieves information about a button in a toolbar.
TB_GETBUTTONTEXT	Retrieves the text of a button in a toolbar.
TB_GETITEMRECT	Retrieves the bounding rectangle of a button in a toolbar.
TB_GETROWS	Retrieves the number of rows of buttons in a toolbar.
TB_GETSTATE	Retrieves information about the state of a button in a toolbar.
TB_GETTOOLTIPS	Retrieves the handle of the tooltip control associated with a toolbar.
TB_HIDEBUTTON	Hides or shows a button in a toolbar.
TB_INDETERMINATE	Sets or clears the indeterminate state of a button in a toolbar.
TB_INSERTBUTTON	Inserts a button in a toolbar.
TB_ISBUTTONCHECKED	Determines whether a button in a toolbar is checked.
TB_ISBUTTONENABLED	Determines whether a button in a toolbar is enabled.
TB_ISBUTTONHIDDEN	Determines whether a button in a toolbar is hidden.
TB_ISBUTTONINDETERMINATE	Determines whether a button in a toolbar is indeterminate.
TB_ISBUTTONPRESSED	Determines whether a button in a toolbar is pressed.
TB_PRESSBUTTON	Presses or releases a button in a toolbar.
TB_SAVERESTORE	Saves or restores the state of the toolbar.
TB_SETBITMAPSIZE	Sets the size of the bitmapped images for a toolbar.
TB_SETBUTTONSIZE	Sets the size of the toolbar buttons.
TB_SETCMDID	Sets the command identifier of a toolbar button.
TB_SETPARENT	Sets the parent window for the toolbar.
TB_SETROWS	Sets the number of rows of buttons in a toolbar.
TB_SETSTATE	Sets the state for the specified button in a toolbar.
TB_SETTOOLTIPS	Associates a tooltip control with a toolbar.
TTM_ACTIVATE	Activates or deactivates a tooltip control.
TTM_ADDTOOL	Registers a tool with a tooltip control.
TTM_DELTOOL	Removes a tool from a tooltip control.
TTM_ENUMTOOLS	Retrieves the information that a tooltip control maintains about a tool.
TTM_GETCURRENTTOOL	Retrieves the information that a tooltip control maintains about the current tool.
TTM_GETTEXT	Retrieves the text that a tooltip control maintains for a tool.
TTM_GETTOOLCOUNT	Retrieves a count of the tools maintained by a tooltip control.
TTM_GETTOOLINFO	Retrieves the information that a tooltip control maintains about a tool.
TTM_HITTEST	Performs a hit test on a tool.

continued on next page

continued from previous page

Message	Meaning
TTM_NEWTOOLRECT	Sets a new bounding rectangle for a tool.
TTM_RELAYEVENT	Passes a mouse message to a tooltip control for processing.
TTM_SETDELAYTIME	Sets the initial, reshow, and autopop-up durations for a tooltip control.
TTM_SETTOOLINFO	Sets the information that a tooltip control maintains for a tool.
TTM_UPDATETIPTEXT	Sets the tooltip text for a tool.
TTM_WINDOWFROMPOINT	Allows a subclass procedure to cause a tooltip to display text for a window other than the one beneath the mouse cursor.

Notification Messages

Message	Meaning
TBN_BEGINADJUST	Indicates that the user has begun customizing a toolbar.
TBN_BEGINDRAG	Indicates that the user has begun dragging a button in a toolbar.
TBN_CUSTHELP	Indicates that the user has chosen the Help button in the Customize Toolbar dialog box.
TBN_ENDADJUST	Indicates that the user has stopped customizing a toolbar.
TBN_ENDDRAG	Indicates that the user has stopped dragging a button in a toolbar.
TBN_GETBUTTONINFO	Retrieves toolbar customization information and notifies the toolbar's parent window of any changes being made to the toolbar.
TBN_QUERYDELETE	Queries the toolbar's parent window as to whether a button may be deleted from a toolbar while the user is customizing a toolbar.
TBN_QUERYINSERT	Queries the toolbar's parent window as to whether a button may be inserted to the left of a button while the user is customizing a toolbar.
TBN_RESET	Indicates that the user has reset the content of the Customize Toolbar dialog box.
TBN_TOOLBARCHANGE	Indicates that the user has customized a toolbar.
TTN_NEEDTEXT	Retrieves the text for a tool.
TTN_POP	Indicates that a tooltip is about to be hidden.
TTN_SHOW	Indicates that a tooltip is about to be shown.

CREATEMAPPEDBITMAP   ■ WIN32S   ■ WINDOWS 95   ■ WINDOWS NT

Description	CreateMappedBitmap() creates a bitmap for use in a toolbar. Use this function to create a new color-mapped bitmap using the bitmap data and colors specified by a given bitmap resource and color mapping information.
Syntax	HBITMAP **CreateMappedBitmap**(HINSTANCE *hInstance*, int *idBitmap*, UINT *wFlags*, LPCOLORMAP *lpColorMap*, int *iNumMaps*)
Parameters	
hInstance	HINSTANCE: The instance handle of the module that contains the bitmap resource.
idBitmap	int: The resource identifier of the bitmap resource.
wFlags	UINT: The bitmap flag. This parameter can be set to zero or CMB_MASKED. The CMB_MASKED value specifies to use the bitmap as a mask.

lpColorMap	LPCOLORMAP: A pointer to a COLORMAP structure that contains the color information needed to map the bitmap. If this parameter is NULL, the function uses the default color map. See the definition of the COLORMAP structure below.
iNumMaps	int: The number of color maps pointed to by the *lpColorMap* parameter.
Returns	HBITMAP: If successful, the handle of the new bitmap; otherwise, NULL is returned.
Include File	commctrl.h
See Also	CreateToolBarEx()

COLORMAP Definition

```
typedef struct _COLORMAP
{
    COLORREF from;
    COLORREF to;
} COLORMAP, *LPCOLORMAP;
```

Members

from	COLORREF: The color to map from.
to	COLORREF: The color to map to.
Example	See the example for the CreateToolbarEx() function.

CREATESTATUSWINDOW

■ WIN32S   ■ WINDOWS 95   ■ WINDOWS NT

Description	CreateStatusWindow() creates a status window. The default is for the status window to be created at the bottom of the client area of the parent window. Use the status window to display information about the current context of the application, such as the currently selected menu item description.
	The application must call the InitCommonControls() function before using this function to make sure that the Common Controls dynamic-link library (DLL) is loaded.
	CreateStatusWindow() calls the CreateWindowEx() function with the STATUSCLASSNAME class name to create the window. It passes the parameters to CreateWindowEx() without modification and sets the position, width, and height parameters to default values.
Syntax	HWND **CreateStatusWindow**(LONG *style*, LPCTSTR *lpszText*, HWND *hwndParent*, UINT *wID*)
Parameters	
style	LONG: The window style for the status window. This parameter must include the WS_CHILD style and should also include the WS_VISIBLE style. Table 3-2 lists the styles that can be combined with the standard window styles.

Table 3-2 CreateStatusWindow() *style* values

Value	Meaning
CCS_BOTTOM	Places the status window at the bottom of the client area (default).
CCS_TOP	Places the status window at the top of the client area.
SBARS_SIZEGRIP	Includes a sizing grip at the right end of the status window. Combining this style with the CCS_TOP produces a nonfunctional sizing grip and is not recommended.

lpszText	LPCTSTR: A pointer to a null-terminated string that contains the status text for the first section of the status window.
hwndParent	HWND: The handle of the parent window to associate with the status window.
wID	UINT: The control identifier for the status window. The window procedure uses this value to identify messages it sends to the parent window.
Returns	HWND: If successful, the handle of the status window; otherwise, NULL is returned.
Include File	commctrl.h
See Also	InitCommonControls(), CreateWindowEx()
Related Messages	SB_GETBORDERS, SB_GETPARTS, SB_GETRECT, SB_GETTEXT, SB_GETTEXTLENGTH, SB_SETMINHEIGHT, SB_SETPARTS, SB_SETTEXT, SB_SIMPLE
Example	This example, shown in Listing 3-1, demonstrates how to create a status window using the CreateStatusWindow() function. The status window has a sizing grip and is attached to the bottom of the window as shown in Figure 3-5. The WM_SIZE message is handled to size the status window when the size of the main window changes.

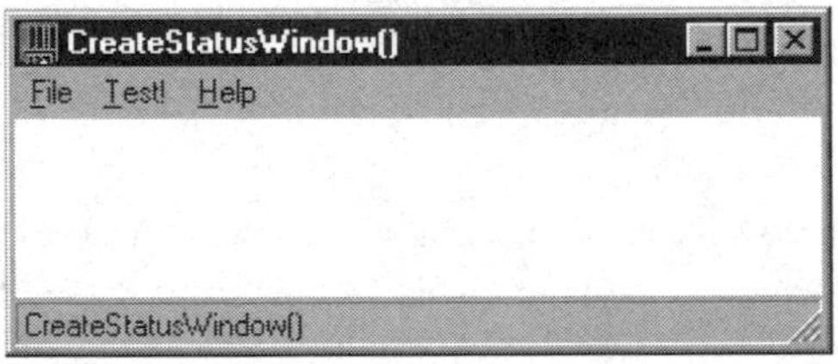

Figure 3-5 CreateStatusWindow() example

Listing 3-1 *Using the CreateStatusWindow() function*

```
LRESULT CALLBACK WndProc( HWND hWnd, UINT uMsg, WPARAM wParam, LPARAM lParam )
{
static HWND hStatusWnd = NULL;

   switch( uMsg )
   {
```

```
    case WM_CREATE :
            // Initialize the common control library
            // and create the status window.
            //.....................................
            InitCommonControls();
            hStatusWnd = CreateStatusWindow(
                            WS_CHILD | WS_VISIBLE |
                            CCS_BOTTOM | SBARS_SIZEGRIP,
                            lpszTitle, hWnd, 101 );
            break;

    case WM_SIZE :
            {
                RECT clrect, strect;

                // Size the status window when the main
                // window is sized.
                //..................................
                GetClientRect( hWnd, &clrect );
                GetClientRect( hStatusWnd, &strect );

                MoveWindow( hStatusWnd, 0, clrect.bottom-strect.bottom,
                        LOWORD( lParam ), HIWORD( lParam ), TRUE );
            }
            break;
        .
        .
        .
```

CREATETOOLBAREX   ■ WIN32S   ■ WINDOWS 95   ■ WINDOWS NT

Description   CreateToolBarEx() creates a toolbar window and adds the specified buttons to the toolbar. The toolbar is associated with the specified parent window. An application can also use the CreateWindowEx() function, specifying the TOOLBARCLASSNAME window class to create a toolbar; however, this method creates a toolbar that initially contains no buttons.

The TOOLBARCLASSNAME window class is registered when the Common Controls dynamic-link library (DLL) is loaded. The application must call the InitCommonControls() function to ensure that this DLL is loaded.

Syntax   HWND **CreateToolbarEx**(HWND *hwnd*, DWORD *style*, UINT *wID*, int *nBitmaps*, HINSTANCE *hBMInst*, UINT *wBMID*, LPCTBBUTTON *lpButtons*, int *iNumButtons*, int *dxButton*, int *dyButton*, int *dxBitmap*, int *dyBitmap*, UINT *uStructSize*)

Parameters

hwnd   HWND: A handle to the parent window for the toolbar.

style   DWORD: The window styles for the toolbar. This parameter must specify at least the WS_CHILD style. It can also include a combination of styles listed in Table 3-3.

Table 3-3 CreateToolbarEx() *style* values

Value	Meaning
CCS_ADJUSTABLE	Enables the built-in customization features for the toolbar. This allows the user to drag a button to a new position or to remove a button by dragging it off the toolbar. In addition, the user can double-click the toolbar to display the Customize Toolbar dialog box, allowing the user to add, delete, and rearrange toolbar buttons.
TBSTYLE_ALTDRAG	Allows the user to change the position of a toolbar button by dragging it while holding down the ALT key. If this style is not specified, the user must hold down the SHIFT key while dragging a button. Note that the CCS_ADJUSTABLE style must be specified to enable toolbar buttons to be dragged.
TBSTYLE_TOOLTIPS	Creates a tooltip control that an application can use to display descriptive text for the buttons in the toolbar.
TBSTYLE_WRAPABLE	Creates a toolbar that can have multiple lines of buttons. Toolbar buttons can "wrap" to the next line when the toolbar becomes too narrow to include all buttons on the same line. Wrapping occurs on separation and nongroup boundaries.

wID	UINT: The control identifier for the toolbar.
nBitmaps	int: The number of button images contained in the bitmap specified by *hBMInst* and *wBMID*.
hBMInst	HINSTANCE: The module instance handle that contains the bitmap resource. Use HINST_COMMCTRL to use the common toolbar bitmaps.
wBMID	UINT: The resource identifier for the bitmap resource. If *hBMInst* is NULL, this parameter must be a valid bitmap handle. When using common toolbar bitmaps, set this parameter to one of the values in Table 3-11.
lpButtons	LPCTBBUTTON: A pointer to an array of TBBUTTON structures that contains information about the buttons to add to the toolbar. See the definition of the TBBUTTON structure below.
iNumButtons	int: The number of buttons to add to the toolbar.
dxButton	int: The width, in pixels, of the buttons to add to the toolbar.
dyButton	int: The height, in pixels, of the buttons to add to the toolbar.
dxBitmap	int: The width, in pixels, of the button images to add to the buttons in the toolbar.
dyBitmap	int: The height, in pixels, of the button images to add to the buttons in the toolbar.
uStructSize	UINT: The size of the TBBUTTON structure.
Returns	HWND: If successful, the window handle of the toolbar; otherwise, NULL is returned.
Include File	commctrl.h
See Also	CreateMappedBitmap(), CreateWindowEx(), InitCommonControls()

Related Messages TB_ADDBITMAP, TB_ADDBUTTONS, TB_ADDSTRING, TB_AUTOSIZE, TB_BUTTONCOUNT, TB_BUTTONSTRUCTSIZE, TB_CHANGEBITMAP, TB_CHECKBUTTON, TB_COMMANDTOINDEX, TB_CUSTOMIZE, TB_DELETEBUTTON, TB_ENABLEBUTTON, TB_GETBITMAP, TB_GETBITMAPFLAGS, TB_GETBUTTON, TB_GETBUTTONTEXT, TB_GETITEMRECT, TB_GETROWS, TB_GETSTATE, TB_GETTOOLTIPS, TB_HIDEBUTTON, TB_INDETERMINATE, TB_INSERTBUTTON, TB_ISBUTTONCHECKED, TB_ISBUTTONENABLED, TB_ISBUTTONHIDDEN, TB_ISBUTTONINDETERMINATE, TB_ISBUTTONPRESSED, TB_PRESSBUTTON, TB_SAVERESTORE, TB_SETBITMAPSIZE, TB_SETBUTTONSIZE, TB_SETCMID, TB_SETPARENT, TB_SETROWS, TB_SETSTATE, TB_SETTOOLTIPS

TBBUTTON Definition

```
{
    int    iBitmap;
    int    idCommand;
    BYTE   fsState;
    BYTE   fsStyle;
    BYTE   bReserved[2];
    DWORD  dwData;
    int    iString;
} TBBUTTON, *LPTBBUTTON;
typedef const TBBUTTON* LPCTBBUTTON;
```

Members

iBitmap   int: Zero-based index of button image.

idCommand   int: The command identifier associated with the button. This identifier is used in a WM_COMMAND message when the button is chosen. If the *fsStyle* member is the TBSTYLE_SEP value, this member must be set to zero.

fsState   BYTE: The button state flags. This member can be a combination of the values listed in Table 3-4.

Table 3-4 TBBUTTON *fsState* values

Value	Meaning
TBSTATE_CHECKED	The button has the TBSTYLE_CHECKED style and is pressed.
TBSTATE_ENABLED	The button is enabled.
TBSTATE_HIDDEN	The button is hidden.
TBSTATE_INDETERMINATE	The button is grayed.
TBSTATE_PRESSED	The button is pressed.
TBSTATE_WRAP	A line break follows the button. The button must also have the TBSTATE_ENABLED state.

fsStyle   BYTE: The button style. This member can be a combination of values listed in Table 3-5.

Table 3-5 TBBUTTON *fsStyle* values

Value	Meaning
TBSTYLE_BUTTON	Creates a standard push button.
TBSTYLE_CHECK	Creates a button that toggles between the pressed and not pressed states, similar to a check box, each time the user clicks it. The button has a different background color when it is in the pressed state.
TBSTYLE_CHECKGROUP	Creates a check button that stays pressed until another button in the group is pressed. This style is used with a group of buttons in the same way a group of radio buttons is used.
TBSTYLE_GROUP	Creates a standard button that stays pressed until another button in the group is pressed. This style is used with a group of buttons in the same way a group of radio buttons is used.
TBSTYLE_SEP	Creates a separator, providing a small gap between button groups. A button that has this style does not receive user input.

bReserved	BYTE[2]: This member is reserved and only defined for Win32.
dwData	DWORD: An application-defined value to associate to the button.
iString	int: The zero-based index of the button string. This can be the return value of the TB_ADDSTRING message.
Example	This example, shown in Figure 3-6 and Listing 3-2, creates a toolbar using the CreateToolbarEx() function. The toolbar initially includes the first three standard New, Open, and Save buttons. The next four buttons are the standard Large Icon, Small Icon, List, and Report view icons. These are added with the TB_ADDBUTTONS message after the TB_ADDBITMAP message is used to add the standard view bitmap to the toolbar. The final four buttons are application defined. The bitmap is loaded with the CreateMappedBitmap() function and added to the toolbar with the TB_ADDBITMAP message. The buttons are then added with the TB_ADDBUTTONS message. A status window is also created on the window in the same manner as in the example for the CreateStatusWindow() function.

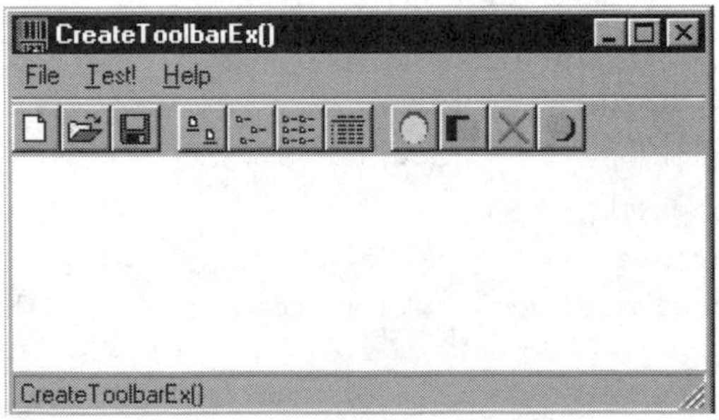

Figure 3-6 CreateToolbarEx() example

Listing 3-2 Using the CreateToolbarEx() function

```
// Toolbar buttons.
//.................
TBBUTTON tbButtons[] =
{
  { STD_FILENEW,  IDM_NEW, TBSTATE_ENABLED, TBSTYLE_BUTTON, 0, 0L, 0},
  { STD_FILEOPEN, IDM_OPEN, TBSTATE_ENABLED, TBSTYLE_BUTTON, 0, 0L, 0},
  { STD_FILESAVE, IDM_SAVE, TBSTATE_ENABLED, TBSTYLE_BUTTON, 0, 0L, 0},
  { 0, 0, TBSTATE_ENABLED, TBSTYLE_SEP, 0, 0L, 0},
  { VIEW_LARGEICONS, IDM_LARGEICON, TBSTATE_ENABLED, TBSTYLE_BUTTON, 0, 0L, 0},
  { VIEW_SMALLICONS, IDM_SMALLICON, TBSTATE_ENABLED, TBSTYLE_BUTTON, 0, 0L, 0},
  { VIEW_LIST, IDM_LISTVIEW, TBSTATE_ENABLED, TBSTYLE_BUTTON, 0, 0L, 0},
  { VIEW_DETAILS, IDM_REPORTVIEW, TBSTATE_ENABLED, TBSTYLE_BUTTON, 0, 0L, 0},
  { 0, 0, TBSTATE_ENABLED, TBSTYLE_SEP, 0, 0L, 0},
  { 0, IDM_TEST1, TBSTATE_ENABLED, TBSTYLE_BUTTON, 0, 0L, 0},
  { 1, IDM_TEST2, TBSTATE_ENABLED, TBSTYLE_BUTTON, 0, 0L, 0},
  { 2, IDM_TEST3, TBSTATE_ENABLED, TBSTYLE_BUTTON, 0, 0L, 0},
  { 3, IDM_TEST4, TBSTATE_ENABLED, TBSTYLE_BUTTON, 0, 0L, 0},
};


LRESULT CALLBACK WndProc( HWND hWnd, UINT uMsg, WPARAM wParam, LPARAM lParam )
{
static HWND hToolWnd   = NULL;
static HWND hStatusWnd = NULL;

   switch( uMsg )
   {
     case WM_CREATE :
             // Initialize the common control library
             // and create the status window and toolbar.
             //........................................
             InitCommonControls();
             hStatusWnd = CreateStatusWindow(
                          WS_CHILD | WS_VISIBLE |
                          CCS_BOTTOM | SBARS_SIZEGRIP,
                          lpszTitle, hWnd, 101 );

             hToolWnd = CreateToolbarEx( hWnd,
                          WS_CHILD | WS_BORDER | WS_VISIBLE,
                          102,
                          11,
                          (HINSTANCE)HINST_COMMCTRL,
                          IDB_STD_SMALL_COLOR,
                          tbButtons, 4,
                          0, 0, 100, 30, sizeof(TBBUTTON) );

             if ( hToolWnd )
             {
                 HBITMAP     hBmp;
                 TBADDBITMAP tb;
                 int index, stdidx;

                 // Add the system-defined view bitmaps.
                 //.....................................
```

continued on next page

continued from previous page

```
            tb.hInst = HINST_COMMCTRL;
            tb.nID = IDB_VIEW_SMALL_COLOR;
            stdidx = SendMessage(hToolWnd, TB_ADDBITMAP, 12, (LPARAM)&tb);

            // Update the indices to the bitmaps.
            //....................................
            for (index = 4; index < 8; index++)
                tbButtons[index].iBitmap += stdidx;

            // Add the view buttons.
            //.......................
            SendMessage(hToolWnd, TB_ADDBUTTONS, 4, (LONG) &tbButtons[4]);

            // Load bitmap to add to the toolbar.
            //....................................
            hBmp = CreateMappedBitmap( hInst, 100, 0, NULL, 0 );

            tb.hInst = NULL;
            tb.nID   = (UINT) hBmp;
            stdidx = SendMessage(hToolWnd, TB_ADDBITMAP, 4, (LPARAM)&tb);

            for (index = 9; index < 13; index++)
                tbButtons[index].iBitmap += stdidx;

            SendMessage(hToolWnd, TB_ADDBUTTONS, 5, (LONG) &tbButtons[8]);
        }
        break;

    case WM_SIZE :
        {
            RECT clrect, strect;

            // Size the status window when the main
            // window is sized.
            //....................................
            GetClientRect( hWnd, &clrect );
            GetClientRect( hStatusWnd, &strect );

            MoveWindow( hStatusWnd, 0, clrect.bottom-strect.bottom,
                        LOWORD( lParam ), HIWORD( lParam ), TRUE );
        }
        break;
```

·
·
·

DrawStatusText   ■ Win32s   ■ Windows 95   ■ Windows NT

Description	DrawStatusText() draws text in the style of a status window with borders. Use this function for displaying status text without the use of a status window.
Syntax	VOID **DrawStatusText**(HDC *hdc*, LPRECT *lprc*, LPCTSTR *pszText*, UINT *uFlags*)
Parameters	
hdc	HDC: The display context for the window.

lprc	LPRECT: A pointer to a RECT structure that contains the position, in client coordinates, of the rectangle in which the text is drawn. The function draws the borders just inside of the edges of the specified rectangle.
pszText	LPCTSTR: A pointer to a null-terminated string that specifies the text to display. Tab characters in the string determine whether the string is left-aligned, right-aligned, or centered.
uFlags	UINT: Text drawing flags. This parameter can be a combination of the values in Table 3-6 or set to zero. If set to zero, the text is drawn with a sunken border.

Table 3-6 DrawStatusText() *uFlags* values

Value	Meaning
SBT_NOBORDERS	Prevents borders from being drawn around the specified text.
SBT_POPOUT	Draws highlighted borders that make the text stand out.
SBT_RTLREADING	Displays text using right-to-left reading order on Hebrew or Arabic systems. This flag is only valid in Windows 95.

Include File	commctrl.h
See Also	CreateStatusWindow()
Example	This example uses the the DrawStatusText() function to display a sample of each text style on the client area of the window (Listing 3-3). Figure 3-7 shows how the different border styles appear on a gray background.

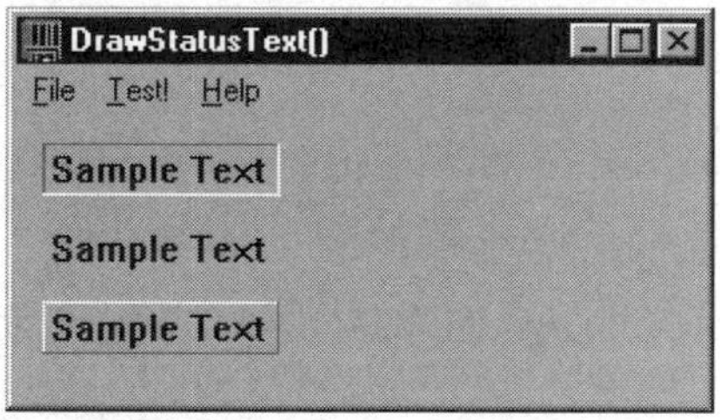

Figure 3-7 DrawStatusText() example

Listing 3-3 Using the DrawStatusText() function

```
LRESULT CALLBACK WndProc( HWND hWnd, UINT uMsg, WPARAM wParam, LPARAM lParam )
{
   switch( uMsg )
   {
   case WM_CREATE :
           // Initialize the common control library.
           //........................................
```

continued on next page

continued from previous page

```
            InitCommonControls();
            break;

    case WM_COMMAND :
            switch( LOWORD( wParam ) )
            {
                case IDM_TEST :
                    {
                        RECT rect;
                        HDC   dc = GetDC( hWnd );

                        GetClientRect( hWnd, &rect );
                        FillRect( dc, &rect, GetStockObject(LTGRAY_BRUSH) );

                        // Paint the different samples of status text.
                        //............................................
                        rect.top    = 10;
                        rect.left   = 10;
                        rect.bottom = 30;
                        rect.right  = 100;
                        DrawStatusText( dc, &rect, "Sample Text", 0 );

                        rect.top    = 40;
                        rect.bottom = 60;
                        DrawStatusText( dc, &rect, "Sample Text",
                                    SBT_NOBORDERS );

                        rect.top    = 70;
                        rect.bottom = 90;
                        DrawStatusText( dc, &rect, "Sample Text",
                                    SBT_POPOUT );

                        ReleaseDC( hWnd, dc );
                    }
                    break;

                    .
                    .
                    .
```

MenuHelp   ■ Win32s   ■ Windows 95   ■ Windows NT

Description	MenuHelp() displays help text about the current menu item in a given status window. Use this function to process the WM_MENUSELECT and WM_COMMAND messages so that help is displayed when the user highlights a menu item.
Syntax	VOID **MenuHelp**(UINT *uMsg*, WPARAM *wParam*, LPARAM *lParam*, HMENU *hMainMenu*, HINSTANCE *hInst*, HWND *hwndStatus*, UINT* *lpwIDs*)
Parameters	
uMsg	UINT: The message value (WM_MENUSELECT or WM_COMMAND).
wParam	WPARAM: The first message parameter.

lParam	LPARAM: The second message parameter.
hMainMenu	HMENU: The handle of the application's main menu.
hInst	HINSTANCE: The instance handle of the module that contains the string resources.
hwndStatus	HWND: The window handle of the status window.
lpwIDs	UINT*: A pointer to an array that contains pairs of string resource identifiers and menu handles. The function searches the array for the handle to the selected menu and, if found, uses the corresponding resource identifier to load the appropriate help string.
Include File	commctrl.h
See Also	CreateStatusWindow(), InitCommonControls()
Related Messages	WM_MENUSELECT, WM_COMMAND
Example	This example, shown in Listings 3-4 and 3-5, demonstrates how to use the MenuHelp() function to process the WM_MENUSELECT message. As the user selects a menu item, the descriptive menu help text is displayed in the status window as shown in Figure 3-8.

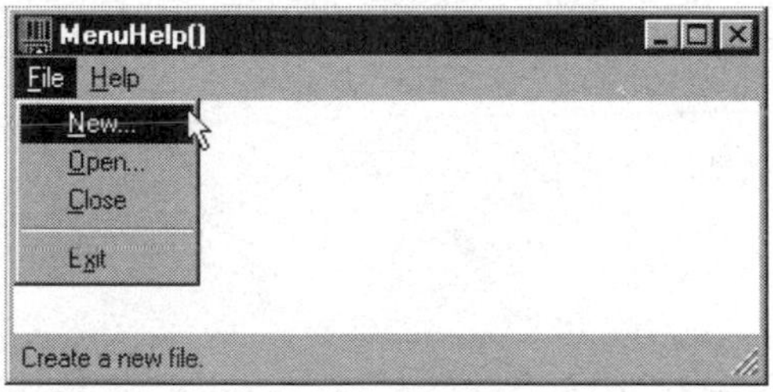

Figure 3-8 MenuHelp() example

Listing 3-4 *Menu and String Table in MENUHELP.RC*

```
MYAPP MENU DISCARDABLE
BEGIN
    POPUP "&File"
    BEGIN
        MENUITEM "&New...",                 IDM_NEW
        MENUITEM "&Open...",                IDM_OPEN
        MENUITEM "&Close",                  IDM_CLOSE
        MENUITEM SEPARATOR
        MENUITEM "E&xit",                   IDM_EXIT
    END
    POPUP "&Help"
    BEGIN
        MENUITEM "&About MenuHelp()...",   IDM_ABOUT
    END
END


STRINGTABLE
BEGIN
```

continued on next page

continued from previous page

```
    IDM_NEW     "Create a new file."
    IDM_OPEN    "Open a file."
    IDM_CLOSE   "Close the current file."
    IDM_EXIT    "Exit the application."
    IDM_ABOUT   "Display the about box."
END
```

Listing 3-5 WndProc() in MENUHELP.C

```
typedef struct
{
   HMENU   hMenuItem;
   UINT    uID;
} MENUPAIRS;

MENUPAIRS Ids[] =
{
   { NULL, 0 },
   { NULL, IDM_NEW },
   { NULL, IDM_OPEN },
   { NULL, IDM_CLOSE },
   { NULL, IDM_EXIT },
   { NULL, IDM_ABOUT },
};

LRESULT CALLBACK WndProc( HWND hWnd, UINT uMsg, WPARAM wParam, LPARAM lParam )
{
static HWND   hStatusWnd = NULL;
static HMENU  hMenu      = NULL;

   switch( uMsg )
   {
      case WM_CREATE :
              // Initialize the common control library
              // and create the status window.
              //.......................................
              InitCommonControls();
              hStatusWnd = CreateStatusWindow(
                                  WS_CHILD | WS_VISIBLE |
                                  CCS_BOTTOM | SBARS_SIZEGRIP,
                                  lpszTitle, hWnd, 101 );

              hMenu = GetMenu( hWnd );
              break;

      case WM_SIZE :
              {
                  RECT clrect, strect;

                  // Size the status window when the main
                  // window is sized.
                  //.......................................
                  GetClientRect( hWnd, &clrect );
                  GetClientRect( hStatusWnd, &strect );

                  MoveWindow( hStatusWnd, 0, clrect.bottom-strect.bottom,
                          LOWORD( lParam ), HIWORD( lParam ), TRUE );
              }
```

```
        break;

case WM_MENUSELECT :
        MenuHelp( uMsg, wParam, lParam, hMenu, hInst,
                  hStatusWnd, (UINT*)&Ids[0] );
        break;
        .
        .
        .
```

SB_GETBORDERS
■ WIN32S   ■ WINDOWS 95   ■ WINDOWS NT

Description	SB_GETBORDERS is a status window message that retrieves the current widths of the horizontal and vertical borders of a status window and places them into a given array of integers. The borders determine the spacing between the outside edge of the window and the rectangles within the window that contain text. The borders also determine the spacing between the rectangles.
Parameters	
wParam	WPARAM: Set to zero.
lParam	LPINT: A pointer to an integer array that has three elements that receive the width of the vertical border, the width of the horizontal border, and the width of the border between rectangles.
Returns	BOOL: If successful, TRUE is returned; otherwise, FALSE is returned.
Include File	commctrl.h
See Also	CreateStatusWindow()
Related Messages	SB_GETPARTS, SB_GETRECT
Example	See example for the SB_GETPARTS message.

SB_GETPARTS
■ WIN32S   ■ WINDOWS 95   ■ WINDOWS NT

Description	SB_GETPARTS is a status window message that retrieves the number of *parts* in a status window. A part is a section within the status window that can contain text or other information. The message also retrieves the coordinate of the right edge for each part up to the specified number of parts.
Parameters	
wParam	WPARAM: The number of parts for which to retrieve coordinates.
lParam	LPINT: A pointer to an integer array that has the same number of elements as the number of parts specified by the *wParam* parameter. Each element in the array receives the client coordinate of the right edge of the corresponding part. If an element is set to -1, the position of the right edge for that part extends to the right edge of the window. Set this parameter to zero to retrieve only the current number of parts in the status window.

Returns	int: If successful, the number of parts in the window is returned; otherwise, zero is returned.
Include File	commctrl.h
See Also	CreateStatusWindow()
Related Messages	SB_SETPARTS, SB_GETBORDERS, SB_GETRECT
Example	This example creates a status window with five parts (shown in Listing 3-6). The first part is sizable and the rest are static. When the user selects the Test! menu item, the SB_GETPARTS message is used to retrieve the number of parts. The SB_GETBORDERS and SB_GETRECT message is used to retrieve the border widths and the size of the first part of the status window. The result is shown in the status window as shown in Figure 3-9.

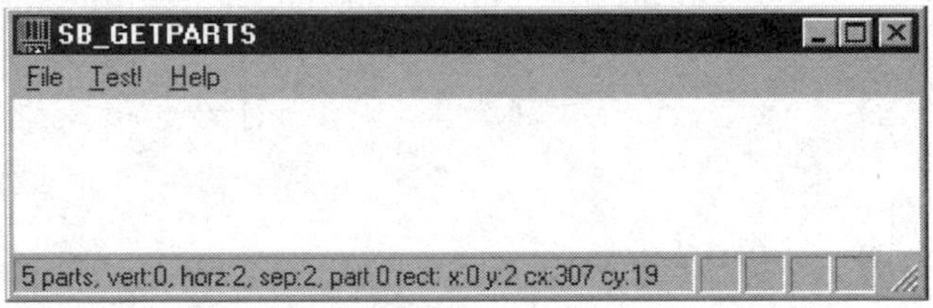

Figure 3-9 SB_GETPARTS example

Listing 3-6 *Using the SB_GETPARTS message*

```
LRESULT CALLBACK WndProc( HWND hWnd, UINT uMsg, WPARAM wParam, LPARAM lParam )
{
static HWND   hStatusWnd = NULL;

   switch( uMsg )
   {
      case WM_CREATE :
               // Initialize the common control library
               // and create the status window.
               //.....................................
               InitCommonControls();
               hStatusWnd = CreateStatusWindow(
                              WS_CHILD | WS_VISIBLE |
                              CCS_BOTTOM | SBARS_SIZEGRIP,
                              "", hWnd, 101 );
               break;

      case WM_SIZE :
               {
               RECT clrect, strect;
               int  i, parts[5];

               GetClientRect( hWnd, &clrect );
               GetClientRect( hStatusWnd, &strect );

               for( i=0; i < 5; i++ )
                  parts[i] = (LOWORD( lParam ) - 100) + i*20;
```

```
            SendMessage( hStatusWnd, SB_SETPARTS, 5, (LPARAM)&parts[0] );

            MoveWindow( hStatusWnd, 0, clrect.bottom-strect.bottom,
                    LOWORD( lParam ), HIWORD( lParam ), TRUE );
        }
        break;

case WM_COMMAND :
        switch( LOWORD( wParam ) )
        {
            case IDM_TEST :
                {
                    RECT rect;
                    char szMsg[128];
                    int  nBorders[3];
                    int  nNumParts = SendMessage( hStatusWnd,
                                            SB_GETPARTS, 0, 0 );

                    SendMessage( hStatusWnd, SB_GETBORDERS, 0,
                                            (LPARAM)nBorders );
                    SendMessage( hStatusWnd, SB_GETRECT, 0,
                                            (LPARAM)&rect );

                    // Build the string to put on the status window.
                    //.............................................
                    wsprintf( szMsg,
                            "%d parts, vert:%d, horz:%d, sep:%d,"\
                            " part 0 rect: x:%d y:%d cx:%d cy:%d",
                            nNumParts,
                            nBorders[0], nBorders[1], nBorders[2],
                            rect.left, rect.top,
                            rect.right, rect.bottom );

                    SendMessage( hStatusWnd, SB_SETTEXT, 0,
                                            (LPARAM)szMsg );
                }
                break;
        .
        .
        .
```

SB_GETRECT   ■ Win32s ■ Windows 95 ■ Windows NT

Description	SB_GETRECT is a status window message that retrieves the bounding rectangle of a part in a status window.
Parameters	
wParam	WPARAM: The zero-based index of the status window part whose bounding rectangle is to be retrieved.
lParam	LPRECT: A pointer to a RECT structure that receives the bounding rectangle coordinates.
Returns	BOOL: If successful, TRUE is returned; otherwise; FALSE is returned.
Include File	commctrl.h

See Also	CreateStatusWindow()
Related Messages	SB_GETPARTS, SB_GETBORDERS
Example	See example for the SB_GETPARTS message.

SB_GETTEXT ■ Win32s ■ Windows 95 ■ Windows NT

Description	SB_GETTEXT is a status window message that retrieves the text from a given part of a status window.
Parameters	
wParam	WPARAM: The zero-based index of the status window part from which to retrieve text.
lParam	LPTSTR: A pointer to the buffer large enough to receive the text. This parameter receives a null-terminated string.
Returns	LRESULT: If successful, a 32-bit value that consists of two 16-bit values is returned. The low word specifies the length, in characters, of the text. The high word specifies the type of operation used to draw the text. This can be one of the values in Table 3-7. If the text has the SBT_OWNERDRAW drawing type, this message returns the 32-bit value associated with the text instead of the length and operation type.

Table 3-7 SB_GETTEXT return values

Value	Meaning
0	The text is drawn with a sunken border to appear lower than the plane of the window.
SBT_NOBORDERS	The text is drawn without borders.
SBT_POPOUT	The text is drawn with a raised border to appear higher than the plane of window.
SBT_RTLREADING	Displays text using right-to-left reading order on Hebrew or Arabic systems. This value is only valid in Windows 95.

Include File	commctrl.h
See Also	CreateStatusWindow()
Related Messages	SB_SETTEXT, SB_GETTEXTLENGTH
Example	This example (shown in Listing 3-7) creates a status window and sets the text to "This is a sample text string." with the SB_SETTEXT message. When the user selects the Test! menu item, the SB_GETTEXTLENGTH message is used to determine the length of the text string contained in the status window. A buffer is allocated that is large enough to hold the string, and the string is retrieved with the SB_GETTEXT message.

Listing 3-7 Using the SB_GETTEXT message

```
LRESULT CALLBACK WndProc( HWND hWnd, UINT uMsg, WPARAM wParam, LPARAM lParam )
{
static HWND  hStatusWnd = NULL;

   switch( uMsg )
   {
      case WM_CREATE :
              // Initialize the common control library
              // and create the status window.
              //.......................................
              InitCommonControls();
              hStatusWnd = CreateStatusWindow(
                                 WS_CHILD | WS_VISIBLE |
                                 CCS_BOTTOM | SBARS_SIZEGRIP,
                                 "", hWnd, 101 );

              SendMessage( hStatusWnd, SB_SETTEXT, 0,
                           (LPARAM)"This is a sample text string." );

              break;

      case WM_SIZE :
              {
                  RECT clrect, strect;

                  // Size the status window when the main
                  // window is sized.
                  //.......................................
                  GetClientRect( hWnd, &clrect );
                  GetClientRect( hStatusWnd, &strect );

                  MoveWindow( hStatusWnd, 0, clrect.bottom-strect.bottom,
                          LOWORD( lParam ), HIWORD( lParam ), TRUE );
              }
              break;

      case WM_COMMAND :
              switch( LOWORD( wParam ) )
              {
                  case IDM_TEST :
                      {
                          DWORD  dwLength;
                          LPTSTR lpString;

                          // Retrieve the length of the string.
                          //.......................................
                          dwLength = SendMessage( hStatusWnd,
                                         SB_GETTEXTLENGTH, 0, 0 );

                          // Allocate a buffer to hold the string.
                          //.......................................
                          lpString = HeapAlloc( GetProcessHeap(),
                                         HEAP_ZERO_MEMORY,
                                         LOWORD( dwLength )+1 );
```

continued on next page

continued from previous page

```
                                    // Retrieve the actual string from the status window.
                                    //........................................................
                                    SendMessage( hStatusWnd, SB_GETTEXT, 0,
                                                            (LPARAM)lpString );

                                    // Display the string.
                                    //....................
                                    MessageBox( hWnd, lpString, lpszTitle,
                                                MB_OK | MB_ICONINFORMATION );

                                    // Free the memory.
                                    //..................
                                    HeapFree( GetProcessHeap(), 0, lpString );
                                }
                                break;
```

SB_GETTEXTLENGTH   ■ WIN32s   ■ WINDOWS 95   ■ WINDOWS NT

Description	SB_GETTEXTLENGTH is a status window message that retrieves the length, in characters, of the text from a given part of a status window.
Parameters	
wParam	WPARAM: The zero-based index of the status window part from which to retrieve text length.
lParam	LPARAM: Set to zero.
Returns	DWORD: If successful, a 32-bit value that consists of two 16-bit values. The low word specifies the length, in characters, of the text. The high word specifies the type of operation used to draw the text. The type can be one of the values in Table 3-8.
Include File	commctrl.h
See Also	CreateStatusWindow()
Related Messages	SB_GETTEXT
Example	See the example for the SB_GETTEXT message.

SB_SETMINHEIGHT   ■ WIN32s   ■ WINDOWS 95   ■ WINDOWS NT

Description	SB_SETMINHEIGHT is a status window message that sets the minimum height of a status window's drawing area. The minimum height is the sum of the *wParam* parameter and twice the width, in pixels, of the horizontal border of the status window. After sending this message, an application must send the WM_SIZE message to the status window to redraw the window. The *wParam* and *lParam* parameters of the WM_SIZE message should be set to zero.

Parameters

wParam　　　　　　　WPARAM: The minimum height, in pixels, of the status window.

lParam　　　　　　　LPARAM: Set to zero.

Include File　　　　commctrl.h

See Also　　　　　CreateStatusWindow()

Example　　　　　This example (shown in Listing 3-8) demonstrates how to use the SB_SETMINHEIGHT to set the minimum height of a status window. When the user selects the Test! menu item, the minimum height is set to 50. The WM_SIZE message is sent to the status window to force it to resize.

Listing 3-8 Using the SB_SETMINHEIGHT message

```
LRESULT CALLBACK WndProc( HWND hWnd, UINT uMsg, WPARAM wParam, LPARAM lParam )
{
static HWND  hStatusWnd = NULL;

   switch( uMsg )
   {
      case WM_CREATE :
              // Initialize the common control library
              // and create the status window.
              //.....................................
              InitCommonControls();
              hStatusWnd = CreateStatusWindow(
                             WS_CHILD | WS_VISIBLE |
                             CCS_BOTTOM | SBARS_SIZEGRIP,
                             "", hWnd, 101 );

              break;

      case WM_SIZE :
              {
                 RECT clrect, strect;

                 // Size the status window when the main
                 // window is sized.
                 //.....................................
                 GetClientRect( hWnd, &clrect );
                 GetClientRect( hStatusWnd, &strect );

                 MoveWindow( hStatusWnd, 0, clrect.bottom-strect.bottom,
                         LOWORD( lParam ), HIWORD( lParam ), TRUE );
              }
              break;

      case WM_COMMAND :
              switch( LOWORD( wParam ) )
              {
                 case IDM_TEST :
                         // Set the minimum height.
                         //......................
```

continued on next page

continued from previous page

```
SendMessage( hStatusWnd, SB_SETMINHEIGHT, 50, 0 );
SendMessage( hStatusWnd, WM_SIZE, 0, 0 );
break;
```

.
.
.

SB_SETPARTS   ■ Win32s   ■ Windows 95   ■ Windows NT

Description	SB_SETPARTS is a status window message that sets the number of parts in a status window and the coordinate of the right edge of each part.
Parameters	
wParam	WPARAM: The number of parts to set. This number cannot be greater than 255.
lParam	LPINT: A pointer to an integer array that has the same number of elements as parts specified by the *wParam* parameter. Each element in the array specifies the position, in client coordinates, of the right edge of the corresponding part. If an element is -1, the position of the right edge for that part extends to the right edge of the window.
Returns	BOOL: If successful, TRUE is returned; otherwise, FALSE is returned.
Include File	commctrl.h
See Also	CreateStatusWindow()
Related Messages	SB_GETPARTS
Example	This example shows how to use the SB_SETPARTS message to create a status window with five separate parts (shown in Listing 3-9). The WM_SIZE message is processed to resize the status window. The first part of the status window has a variable size, depending on the size of the main window, while the other parts are fixed. When the user selects the Test! menu item, a string is set in the first part, shown in Figure 3-10, of the status window using the SB_SETTEXT message.

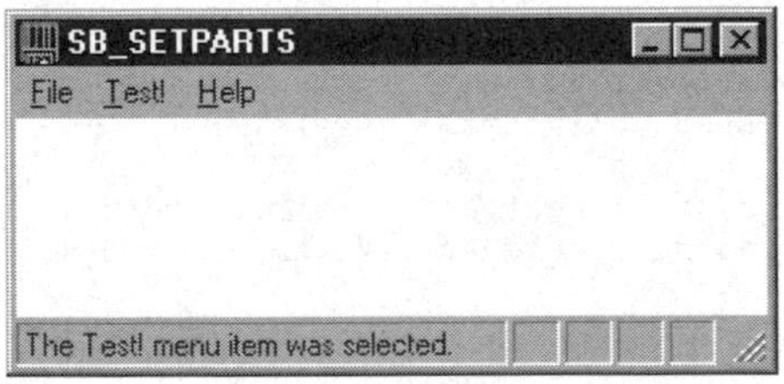

Figure 3-10 SB_SETPARTS example

Listing 3-9 Using the SB_SETPARTS message

```
LRESULT CALLBACK WndProc( HWND hWnd, UINT uMsg, WPARAM wParam, LPARAM lParam )
{
static HWND  hStatusWnd = NULL;
```

```
switch( uMsg )
{
   case WM_CREATE :
            // Initialize the common control library
            // and create the status window.
            //.....................................
            InitCommonControls();
            hStatusWnd = CreateStatusWindow(
                              WS_CHILD | WS_VISIBLE |
                              CCS_BOTTOM | SBARS_SIZEGRIP,
                              "", hWnd, 101 );
            break;

   case WM_SIZE :
            {
               RECT clrect, strect;
               int  i, parts[5];

               // Size the status window when the main
               // window is sized.
               //.................................
               GetClientRect( hWnd, &clrect );
               GetClientRect( hStatusWnd, &strect );

               // Set the arrays up for the parts.
               //.................................
               for( i=0; i < 5; i++ )
                  parts[i] = (LOWORD( lParam ) - 100) + i*20;

               // Send the message to the status window
               // to set up the status window parts.
               //.....................................
               SendMessage( hStatusWnd, SB_SETPARTS, 5, (LPARAM)&parts[0] );

               MoveWindow( hStatusWnd, 0, clrect.bottom-strect.bottom,
                           LOWORD( lParam ), HIWORD( lParam ), TRUE );
            }
            break;

   case WM_COMMAND :
            switch( LOWORD( wParam ) )
            {
               case IDM_TEST :
                     SendMessage( hStatusWnd, SB_SETTEXT, 0,
                        (LPARAM)"The Test! menu item was selected." );
                     break;
               .
               .
               .
```

SB_SETTEXT

■ WIN32S   ■ WINDOWS 95   ■ WINDOWS NT

Description   SB_SETTEXT is a status window message that sets the text in a given part
of a status window. This message invalidates the portion of the window
that has changed, causing it to display the new text when the window next
receives the WM_PAINT message.

Parameters

wParam   WPARAM: The zero-based index of the part to set. If this value is 255, the status window is assumed to be a simple window having only one part. This value can be combined with one of the values from Table 3-8 using the binary OR (|) operator to specify the type of drawing to use for the text.

Table 3-8 SB_SETTEXT text drawing types

Value	Meaning
0	The text is drawn with a sunken border to appear lower than the plane of the window.
SBT_NOBORDERS	The text is drawn without borders.
SBT_OWNERDRAW	The text is drawn by the parent window.
SBT_POPOUT	The text is drawn with a raised border to appear higher than the plane of window.
SBT_RTLREADING	Displays text using right-to-left reading order on Hebrew or Arabic systems. This value is only valid in Windows 95.

lParam   LPCTSTR: A pointer to a null-terminated string that specifies the text to set. If the SBT_OWNERDRAW flag is set in the *wParam* parameter, this parameter is an application-defined 32-bit value to associate with the part. The parent window must interpret the data and draw the text when it receives the WM_DRAWITEM message.

Returns   BOOL: If successful, TRUE is returned; otherwise, FALSE is returned.

Include File   commctrl.h

See Also   CreateStatusWindow()

Related Messages SB_GETTEXT, SB_GETTEXTLENGTH

Example   See the example for the SB_SETPARTS message.

SB_SIMPLE   ■ WIN32S   ■ WINDOWS 95   ■ WINDOWS NT

Description   SB_SIMPLE is a status window message that specifies whether a status window displays simple text or displays all window parts set by a previous SB_SETPARTS message. The window is immediately redrawn when changing from nonsimple to simple, or vice versa.

Parameters

wParam   BOOL: If this parameter is TRUE, the status window displays simple text. If it is FALSE, it displays multiple parts.

lParam   LPARAM: Set to zero.

Returns   BOOL: If the message fails, FALSE is returned.

Include File   commctrl.h

See Also   CreateStatusWindow()

Example

This example, shown in Listing 3-10, demonstrates the SB_SIMPLE message by creating a status window with five parts and switching between simple mode and normal mode, shown in Figure 3-11, when the user selects the Test! menu item.

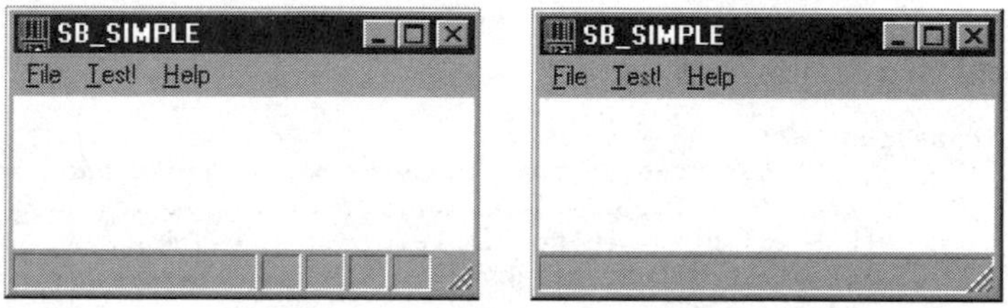

Figure 3-11 SB_SIMPLE example

Listing 3-10 Using the SB_SIMPLE message

```
LRESULT CALLBACK WndProc( HWND hWnd, UINT uMsg, WPARAM wParam, LPARAM lParam )
{
static HWND  hStatusWnd  = NULL;
static BOOL  bShowSimple = FALSE;

    switch( uMsg )
    {
      case WM_CREATE :
              // Initialize the common control library
              // and create the status window.
              //.....................................
              InitCommonControls();
              hStatusWnd = CreateStatusWindow(
                             WS_CHILD | WS_VISIBLE |
                             CCS_BOTTOM | SBARS_SIZEGRIP,
                             "", hWnd, 101 );
              break;

      case WM_SIZE :
              {
                RECT clrect, strect;
                int  i, parts[5];

                // Size the status window when the main
                // window is sized.
                //.................................
                GetClientRect( hWnd, &clrect );
                GetClientRect( hStatusWnd, &strect );

                // Set the arrays up for the parts.
                //.................................
                for( i=0; i < 5; i++ )
                   parts[i] = (LOWORD( lParam ) - 100) + i*20;

                // Send the message to the status window
                // to set up the status window parts.
                //.................................
```

continued on next page

continued from previous page

```
                    SendMessage( hStatusWnd, SB_SETPARTS, 5, (LPARAM)&parts[0] );

                    MoveWindow( hStatusWnd, 0, clrect.bottom-strect.bottom,
                            LOWORD( lParam ), HIWORD( lParam ), TRUE );
                }
                break;

        case WM_COMMAND :
                switch( LOWORD( wParam ) )
                {
                    case IDM_TEST :
                        // Toggle the status window between simple and normal.
                        //...................................................
                        bShowSimple = !bShowSimple;
                        SendMessage( hStatusWnd, SB_SIMPLE, bShowSimple, 0 );
                        break;

                    case IDM_EXIT :
                        DestroyWindow( hWnd );
                        break;
                }
                break;

        case WM_DESTROY :
                PostQuitMessage(0);
                break;

        default :
                return( DefWindowProc( hWnd, uMsg, wParam, lParam ) );
    }

    return( 0L );
}
```

TB_ADDBITMAP   ■ WIN32S   ■ WINDOWS 95   ■ WINDOWS NT

Description	TB_ADDBITMAP is a toolbar message that adds one or more images to the list of button images available for a toolbar. If the toolbar was created by using the CreateWindowEx() function, the application must send the TB_BUTTONSTRUCTSIZE message to the toolbar before sending the TB_ADDBITMAP message.
Parameters	
nButtons	WPARAM: The number of button images in the bitmap.
lptbab	LPTBADDBITMAP: A pointer to a TBADDBITMAP structure that contains the identifier of a bitmap resource and the instance handle to the module that contains the bitmap resource. See the definition of the TBADDBITMAP structure below.
Returns	int: If successful, the index of the first new image is returned; otherwise, -1 is returned.
Include File	commctrl.h
See Also	CreateToolbarEx(), CreateWindowEx()

Related Messages   TB_BUTTONSTRUCTSIZE, TB_ADDBUTTONS

TBADDBITMAP Definition

```
typedef struct
{
    HINSTANCE hInst;
    UINT      nID;
} TBADDBITMAP, *LPTBADDBITMAP;
```

Members

hInst   HINSTANCE: The instance handle to the module that contains a bitmap resource. An application can add the system-defined button bitmaps to the list by specifying HINST_COMMCTRL as the *hInst* member and one of the values listed in Table 3-10 as the *nID* member. Use the values in Table 3-9 to index the standard and view bitmaps.

Table 3-9 System-defined buttons

Index Value	Small	Large	Meaning
STD_COPY			Copy
STD_CUT			Cut
STD_DELETE			Delete
STD_FILENEW			New
STD_FILEOPEN			Open
STD_FILESAVE			Save
STD_FIND			Find
STD_HELP			What's This? (context-sensitive Help mode)
STD_PASTE			Paste
STD_PRINT			Print
STD_PRINTPRE			Print Preview
STD_PROPERTIES			Properties
STD_REDOW			Redo
STD_REPLACE			Replace
STD_UNDO			Undo
VIEW_DETAILS			View as details

continued on next page

continued from previous page

Index Value	Small	Large	Meaning
VIEW_LARGEICONS			View as large icons
VIEW_LIST			View as list
VIEW_NETCONNECT			View map network drive dialog
VIEW_NETDISCONNECT			View network drive disconnect dialog
VIEW_NEWFOLDER			Create new folder
VIEW_PARENTFOLDER			Open parent folder
VIEW_SMALLICONS			View as small icons
VIEW_SORTDATE			View list sorted by date
VIEW_SORTNAME			View list sorted by name
VIEW_SORTSIZE			View list sorted by size
VIEW_SORTTYPE			View list sorted by type

nID   UINT: The resource identifier of the bitmap resource that contains the button images. If *hInst* is NULL, this member must be set to the handle of a bitmap that contains the button images. If *hInst* is HINST_COMMCTRL, this parameter is set to one of the values in Table 3-10.

Table 3-10 TBADDBITMAP system *nID* values

Value	Meaning
IDB_STD_LARGE_COLOR	Adds large, color standard bitmaps
IDB_STD_SMALL_COLOR	Adds small, color standard bitmaps
IDB_VIEW_LARGE_COLOR	Adds large, color view bitmaps
IDB_VIEW_SMALL_COLOR	Adds small, color view bitmaps

Example   See the example for the CreateToolbarEx() function.

TB_ADDBUTTONS   ■ Win32s ■ Windows 95 ■ Windows NT

Description   TB_ADDBUTTONS is a toolbar message that adds one or more buttons to a toolbar. If the toolbar was created by using the CreateWindowEx() function, the application must send the TB_BUTTONSTRUCTSIZE message to the toolbar before sending the TB_ADDBUTTONS message. The application must also add bitmaps to the toolbar with the TB_ADDBITMAP before adding the buttons, because the bitmaps are the images from which the buttons are made.

Parameters

wParam   UINT: The number of buttons to add.

lParam   LPTBBUTTON: A pointer to an array of TBBUTTON structures that contains information about the buttons to add. There must be the same number of elements in the array as buttons specified by *uNumButtons*. See the definition of the TBBUTTON structure under the CreateToolbarEx() function.

Returns   BOOL: If successful, TRUE is returned; otherwise, FALSE is returned.

Include File   commctrl.h

See Also   CreateToolbarEx()

Related Messages TB_BUTTONSTRUCTSIZE, TB_ADDBITMAP

Example   See the example for the CreateToolbarEx() function.

TB_ADDSTRING   ■ Win32s   ■ Windows 95   ■ Windows NT

Description   TB_ADDSTRING is a toolbar message that adds a new string to the list of strings associated with a toolbar. The text is associated with toolbar buttons and displayed on the toolbar button as seen in Figure 3-12 in the example below.

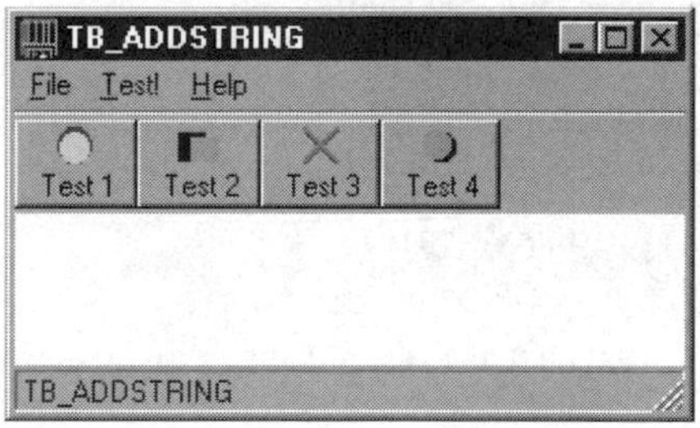

Figure 3-12 TB_ADDSTRING example

Parameters

wParam   HINSTANCE: The instance handle of the module that contains the string resource. If the *lParam* parameter is a pointer to one or more strings to add, this parameter is set to zero.

lParam   LPARAM: The resource identifier for the string resource, or the pointer to a buffer that contains one or more null-terminated strings to add to the list, depending on the value of the *wParam* parameter. If this parameter is a list of strings, the last string must be terminated with two null characters.

Returns	int: If successful, the index of the newly added string is returned; otherwise, -1 is returned.
Include File	commctrl.h
See Also	CreateToolbarEx()
Example	This example, shown in Figure 3-12 and Listing 3-11, creates a toolbar and associates text with each button with the TB_ADDSTRING message. The TB_AUTOSIZE message is used to force the toolbar to resize the buttons to accommodate the text.

Listing 3-11 Using the TB_ADDSTRING message

```c
// Toolbar buttons.
//................
TBBUTTON tbButtons[] =
{
    { 0, IDM_TEST1, TBSTATE_ENABLED, TBSTYLE_BUTTON, 0, 0L, 0},
    { 1, IDM_TEST2, TBSTATE_ENABLED, TBSTYLE_BUTTON, 0, 0L, 0},
    { 2, IDM_TEST3, TBSTATE_ENABLED, TBSTYLE_BUTTON, 0, 0L, 0},
    { 3, IDM_TEST4, TBSTATE_ENABLED, TBSTYLE_BUTTON, 0, 0L, 0},
};

LRESULT CALLBACK WndProc( HWND hWnd, UINT uMsg, WPARAM wParam, LPARAM lParam )
{
static HWND hToolWnd   = NULL;
static HWND hStatusWnd = NULL;

    switch( uMsg )
    {
        case WM_CREATE :
                // Initialize the common control library
                // and create the status window and toolbar.
                //.........................................
                InitCommonControls();
                hStatusWnd = CreateStatusWindow(
                                WS_CHILD | WS_VISIBLE |
                                CCS_BOTTOM | SBARS_SIZEGRIP,
                                lpszTitle, hWnd, 101 );

                hToolWnd = CreateToolbarEx( hWnd,
                                WS_CHILD | WS_BORDER | WS_VISIBLE,
                                102,
                                4,
                                hInst,
                                100,
                                NULL, 0,
                                0, 0, 0, 0, sizeof(TBBUTTON) );

                if ( hToolWnd )
                {
                    char   szText[64];
                    int    index;

                    // Associate strings with each of the buttons.
                    //............................................
                    for (index = 0; index < 4; index++)
```

```
        {
            LoadString( hInst, tbButtons[index].idCommand,
                      szText, sizeof( szText )-1 );

            tbButtons[index].iString = SendMessage( hToolWnd,
                                                   TB_ADDSTRING,
                                                   0, (LPARAM)szText);
        }

        // Add the buttons to the toolbar.
        //...............................
        SendMessage(hToolWnd, TB_ADDBUTTONS, 4, (LONG) &tbButtons[0]);

        // Resize the toolbar.
        //....................
        SendMessage(hToolWnd, TB_AUTOSIZE, 0, 0 );
    }
    break;

case WM_COMMAND :
    switch( LOWORD( wParam ) )
    {
    case IDM_TEST1 :
    case IDM_TEST2 :
    case IDM_TEST3 :
    case IDM_TEST4 :
        {
            char szText[64];

            // Retrieve the text from the button.
            //...................................
            SendMessage(hToolWnd, TB_GETBUTTONTEXT,
                      LOWORD( wParam ),
                      (LPARAM)szText );

            // Place the text on the status window.
            //.....................................
            SendMessage(hStatusWnd, SB_SETTEXT, 0,
                      (LPARAM)szText );
        }
        break;
    .
    .
    .
```

TB_AUTOSIZE   ■ Win32s   ■ Windows 95   ■ Windows NT

Description	TB_AUTOSIZE is a toolbar message that causes a toolbar to be resized. An application should send the TB_AUTOSIZE message after changing the size of a toolbar either by setting the button or bitmap size or by adding strings for the first time.
Parameters	
wParam	WPARAM: Set to zero.
lParam	LPARAM: Set to zero.

Include File	commctrl.h
See Also	CreateToolbarEx()
Related Messages	TB_ADDSTRING, TB_SETBUTTONSIZE
Example	See the example for the TB_ADDSTRING message.

TB_BUTTONCOUNT   ■ Win32s ■ Windows 95 ■ Windows NT

Description	TB_BUTTONCOUNT is a toolbar message that retrieves the number of buttons currently in the toolbar.
Parameters	
wParam	WPARAM: Set to zero.
lParam	LPARAM: Set to zero.
Returns	int: The number of buttons.
Include File	commctrl.h
See Also	CreateToolbarEx()
Example	When the user selects the Test! menu item, this example, shown in Listing 3-12, retrieves the number of buttons with the TB_BUTTONCOUNT message and displays the number in a message box.

Listing 3-12 Using the TB_BUTTONCOUNT message

```
LRESULT CALLBACK WndProc( HWND hWnd, UINT uMsg, WPARAM wParam, LPARAM lParam )
{
static HWND hToolWnd   = NULL;
static HWND hStatusWnd = NULL;

   switch( uMsg )
   {
      case WM_CREATE :
              // Initialize the common control library
              // and create the status window and toolbar.
              //.........................................
              InitCommonControls();
              hStatusWnd = CreateStatusWindow(
                              WS_CHILD | WS_VISIBLE |
                              CCS_BOTTOM | SBARS_SIZEGRIP,
                              lpszTitle, hWnd, 101 );

              hToolWnd = CreateToolbarEx( hWnd,
                              WS_CHILD | WS_BORDER | WS_VISIBLE,
                              102,
                              4,
                              hInst,
                              100,
                              tbButtons, 4,
                              0, 0, 0, 0, sizeof(TBBUTTON) );
              break;

      case WM_SIZE :
              {
```

```
            RECT clrect, strect;

            // Size the status window when the main
            // window is sized.
            //.................................
            GetClientRect( hWnd, &clrect );
            GetClientRect( hStatusWnd, &strect );

            MoveWindow( hStatusWnd, 0, clrect.bottom-strect.bottom,
                        LOWORD( lParam ), HIWORD( lParam ), TRUE );
        }
        break;

    case WM_COMMAND :
        switch( LOWORD( wParam ) )
        {
            case IDM_TEST :
                {
                    char szMsg[40];
                    int  nNum = SendMessage( hToolWnd, TB_BUTTONCOUNT,
                                             0, 0 );

                    wsprintf( szMsg,
                            "There are %d buttons on the toolbar.",
                            nNum );

                    MessageBox( hWnd, szMsg, lpszTitle,
                            MB_OK | MB_ICONINFORMATION );
                }
                break;
        .
        .
        .
```

TB_BUTTONSTRUCTSIZE   ■ WIN32S   ■ WINDOWS 95   ■ WINDOWS NT

Description	TB_BUTTONSTRUCTSIZE is a toolbar message that specifies the size of the TBBUTTON structure the toolbar should expect. If an application uses the CreateWindowEx() function to create the toolbar, the application must send this message to the toolbar before sending the TB_ADDBITMAP or TB_ADDBUTTONS message. The CreateToolBarEx() function automatically sends the TB_BUTTONSTRUCTSIZE message.
Parameters	
wParam	DWORD: The size, in bytes, of the TBBUTTON structure. See the definition of the TBBUTTON structure under the CreateToolbarEx() function.
lParam	LPARAM: Set to zero.
Include File	commctrl.h
See Also	CreateWindowEx(), CreateToolbarEx()
Related Messages	TB_ADDBITMAP, TB_ADDBUTTONS
Example	This example, shown in Listing 3-13, creates a toolbar with the CreateWindowEx() function. Once the toolbar is created, the TB_BUT-

TONSTRUCTSIZE message is sent to the new toolbar before buttons can
be added to it.

Listing 3-13 Using the TB_BUTTONSTRUCTSIZE message

```
// Toolbar buttons.
//................
TBBUTTON tbButtons[] =
{
    { 0, IDM_TEST1, TBSTATE_ENABLED, TBSTYLE_BUTTON, 0, 0L, 0},
    { 1, IDM_TEST2, TBSTATE_ENABLED, TBSTYLE_BUTTON, 0, 0L, 0},
    { 2, IDM_TEST3, TBSTATE_ENABLED, TBSTYLE_BUTTON, 0, 0L, 0},
    { 3, IDM_TEST4, TBSTATE_ENABLED, TBSTYLE_BUTTON, 0, 0L, 0},
};

LRESULT CALLBACK WndProc( HWND hWnd, UINT uMsg, WPARAM wParam, LPARAM lParam )
{
static HWND hToolWnd   = NULL;

   switch( uMsg )
   {
      case WM_CREATE :
              // Initialize the common control library
              // and create the toolbar.
              //.......................................
              InitCommonControls();

              hToolWnd = CreateWindowEx( 0, TOOLBARCLASSNAME, NULL,
                                  WS_CHILD | WS_BORDER | WS_VISIBLE,
                                  0, 0, 0, 0, hWnd, (HMENU)101, hInst,
                                  NULL);

              if ( hToolWnd )
              {
                  HBITMAP      hBmp;
                  TBADDBITMAP tb;
                  int index, stdidx;

                  // Set the size of the TBBUTTON structure.
                  //........................................
                  SendMessage(hToolWnd, TB_BUTTONSTRUCTSIZE,
                              sizeof(TBBUTTON), 0);

                  // Load bitmap to add to the toolbar.
                  //...................................
                  hBmp = CreateMappedBitmap( hInst, 100, 0, NULL, 0 );

                  tb.hInst = NULL;
                  tb.nID   = (UINT) hBmp;
                  stdidx = SendMessage(hToolWnd, TB_ADDBITMAP, 4, (LPARAM)&tb);

                  for (index = 0; index < 4; index++)
                     tbButtons[index].iBitmap += stdidx;

                  // Add the buttons to the toolbar.
                  //...............................
```

```
                SendMessage(hToolWnd, TB_ADDBUTTONS, 4, (LONG) &tbButtons[0]);
        }
        break;
    .
    .
    .
```

TB_CHANGEBITMAP   ■ WIN32s   ■ WINDOWS 95   ■ WINDOWS NT

Description	TB_CHANGEBITMAP is a toolbar message that changes the bitmap for a button in a toolbar.
Parameters	
wParam	UINT: The command identifier of the button that is to receive a new bitmap.
lParam	UINT: The zero-based index of an image in the toolbar's image list to use as the new image for the button. Use the TB_ADDBITMAP message to add new images to the toolbar's image list.
Returns	BOOL: If successful, TRUE is returned; otherwise, FALSE is returned.
Include File	commctrl.h
See Also	CreateToolbarEx()
Related Messages	TB_ADDBITMAP
Example	When the user selects a button on the toolbar, this example uses the TB_CHANGEBITMAP message to change the bitmap of the pressed button to the same bitmap as the third toolbar button (shown in Listing 3-14).

Listing 3-14 Using the TB_CHANGEBITMAP message

```
// Toolbar buttons.
//................
TBBUTTON tbButtons[] =
{
    { 0, IDM_TEST1, TBSTATE_ENABLED, TBSTYLE_BUTTON, 0, 0L, 0},
    { 1, IDM_TEST2, TBSTATE_ENABLED, TBSTYLE_BUTTON, 0, 0L, 0},
    { 2, IDM_TEST3, TBSTATE_ENABLED, TBSTYLE_BUTTON, 0, 0L, 0},
    { 3, IDM_TEST4, TBSTATE_ENABLED, TBSTYLE_BUTTON, 0, 0L, 0},
};

LRESULT CALLBACK WndProc( HWND hWnd, UINT uMsg, WPARAM wParam, LPARAM lParam )
{
static HWND hToolWnd   = NULL;

    switch( uMsg )
    {
        case WM_CREATE :
                // Initialize the common control library
                // and create the toolbar.
                //.......................................
                InitCommonControls();
```

continued on next page

continued from previous page

```
        hToolWnd = CreateWindowEx( 0, TOOLBARCLASSNAME, NULL,
                        WS_CHILD | WS_BORDER | WS_VISIBLE,
                        0, 0, 0, 0, hWnd, (HMENU)101,
                        hInst, NULL);

    if ( hToolWnd )
    {
        HBITMAP     hBmp;
        TBADDBITMAP tb;
        int index, stdidx;

        // Set the size of the TBBUTTON structure.
        //.................................
        SendMessage(hToolWnd, TB_BUTTONSTRUCTSIZE,
                    sizeof(TBBUTTON), 0);

        // Load bitmap to add to the toolbar.
        //.................................
        hBmp = CreateMappedBitmap( hInst, 100, 0, NULL, 0 );

        tb.hInst = NULL;
        tb.nID   = (UINT) hBmp;
        stdidx = SendMessage(hToolWnd, TB_ADDBITMAP, 4, (LPARAM)&tb);

        for (index = 0; index < 4; index++)
            tbButtons[index].iBitmap += stdidx;

        // Add the buttons to the toolbar.
        //.................................
        SendMessage(hToolWnd, TB_ADDBUTTONS, 4, (LONG) &tbButtons[0]);
    }
    break;

case WM_COMMAND :
        switch( LOWORD( wParam ) )
        {
            case IDM_TEST1 :
            case IDM_TEST2 :
            case IDM_TEST3 :
            case IDM_TEST4 :
                    // As a button is selected, change it to a X bitmap.
                    //.................................................
                    SendMessage(hToolWnd, TB_CHANGEBITMAP,
                                LOWORD( wParam ), 2 );
                    break;
    .
    .
    .
```

TB_CHECKBUTTON ■ WIN32S ■ WINDOWS 95 ■ WINDOWS NT

Description	TB_CHECKBUTTON is a toolbar message that checks or unchecks a given button in a toolbar.
Parameters	
wParam	UINT: The command identifier of the button to check.

lParam	BOOL: When this parameter is TRUE, the button is checked. If it is FALSE, the check is removed.
Returns	BOOL: If successful, TRUE is returned; otherwise, FALSE is returned.
Include File	commctrl.h
See Also	CreateToolbarEx()
Related Messages	TB_ISBUTTONCHECKED, TB_GETSTATE
Example	This example, shown in Figure 3-13 and Listing 3-15, uses the TB_CHECKBUTTON and TB_ISBUTTONCHECKED messages to toggle the states of the toolbar buttons as the corresponding menu options are selected by the user.

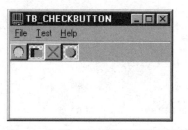

Figure 3-13 TB_CHECKBUTTON
example

Listing 3-15 Using the TB_CHECKBUTTON message

```
// Toolbar buttons.
//................
TBBUTTON tbButtons[] =
{
    { 0, IDM_TEST1, TBSTATE_ENABLED, TBSTYLE_CHECK, 0, 0L, 0},
    { 1, IDM_TEST2, TBSTATE_ENABLED, TBSTYLE_CHECK, 0, 0L, 0},
    { 2, IDM_TEST3, TBSTATE_ENABLED, TBSTYLE_CHECK, 0, 0L, 0},
    { 3, IDM_TEST4, TBSTATE_ENABLED, TBSTYLE_CHECK, 0, 0L, 0},
};

LRESULT CALLBACK WndProc( HWND hWnd, UINT uMsg, WPARAM wParam, LPARAM lParam )
{
static HWND hToolWnd   = NULL;

    switch( uMsg )
    {
       case WM_CREATE :
               // Initialize the common control library
               // and create the toolbar.
               //.........................................
               InitCommonControls();

               hToolWnd = CreateWindowEx( 0, TOOLBARCLASSNAME, NULL,
                                        WS_CHILD | WS_BORDER | WS_VISIBLE,
                                        0, 0, 0, 0, hWnd, (HMENU)101,
                                        hInst, NULL);
```

continued on next page

continued from previous page

```
              if ( hToolWnd )
              {
                  HBITMAP     hBmp;
                  TBADDBITMAP tb;
                  int index, stdidx;

                  // Set the size of the TBBUTTON structure.
                  //........................................
                  SendMessage(hToolWnd, TB_BUTTONSTRUCTSIZE,
                              sizeof(TBBUTTON), 0);

                  // Load bitmap to add to the toolbar.
                  //...................................
                  hBmp = CreateMappedBitmap( hInst, 100, 0, NULL, 0 );

                  tb.hInst = NULL;
                  tb.nID   = (UINT) hBmp;
                  stdidx = SendMessage(hToolWnd, TB_ADDBITMAP, 4, (LPARAM)&tb);

                  for (index = 0; index < 4; index++)
                      tbButtons[index].iBitmap += stdidx;

                  // Add the buttons to the toolbar.
                  //...............................
                  SendMessage(hToolWnd, TB_ADDBUTTONS, 4, (LONG) &tbButtons[0]);
              }
              break;

      case WM_COMMAND :
              switch( LOWORD( wParam ) )
              {
                  // A menu item was selected,
                  // Check the corresponding toolbar button.
                  //........................................
                  case IDM_TESTMENU1 :
                  case IDM_TESTMENU2 :
                  case IDM_TESTMENU3 :
                  case IDM_TESTMENU4 :
                          {
                              BOOL bChecked;

                              bChecked = SendMessage( hToolWnd,
                                                  TB_ISBUTTONCHECKED,
                                                  LOWORD( wParam )-IDM_TOOLBASE,
                                                  0 );

                              // Toggle the toolbar button.
                              //...........................
                              SendMessage(hToolWnd, TB_CHECKBUTTON,
                                          LOWORD( wParam )-IDM_TOOLBASE,
                                          !bChecked );
                          }
                          break;
                  .
                  .
                  .
```

TB_COMMANDTOINDEX   ■ WIN32S   ■ WINDOWS 95   ■ WINDOWS NT

Description	TB_COMMANDTOINDEX is a toolbar message that retrieves the zero-based index for the button associated with a given command identifier.
Parameters	
wParam	UINT: The command identifier associated with the button when the button was added to the toolbar.
lParam	LPARAM: Set to zero.
Returns	int: The zero-based index for the button.
Include File	commctrl.h
See Also	CreateToolbarEx()
Example	See the example for the TB_GETBUTTON message.

TB_CUSTOMIZE   ■ WIN32S   ■ WINDOWS 95   ■ WINDOWS NT

Description	TB_CUSTOMIZE is a toolbar message that displays the Customize Toolbar dialog box. Use this dialog to allow the user to customize the toolbar by adding, removing, and moving buttons.
Parameters	
wParam	WPARAM: Set to zero.
lParam	LPARAM: Set to zero.
Include File	commctrl.h
See Also	CreateToolbarEx()
Example	This example, shown in Figure 3-14 and Listing 3-16, demonstrates how to use the TB_CUSTOMIZE message to allow the user to customize the toolbar. When the user selects the Customize menu item, the Customize

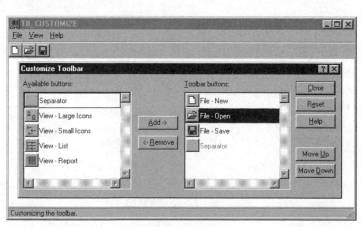

Figure 3-14 TB_CUSTOMIZE example

Toolbar dialog box is displayed by sending the TB_CUSTOMIZE message to the toolbar. The WM_NOTIFY message is used to respond to the customization notification messages for the toolbar. Note how only three buttons are initially displayed on the toolbar. When the application handles the TBN_GETBUTTONINFO notification, text is returned for all the buttons. This example allows all buttons to be moved, added, and deleted from the toolbar. When the application closes, the toolbar's state is saved to the registry with the TB_SAVERESTORE message. The state of the toolbar is restored on startup of the application.

Listing 3-16 Using the TB_CUSTOMIZE message

```
#define IDC_STATBAR    101
#define IDC_TOOLBAR    102

// Toolbar buttons.
//.................
TBBUTTON tbButtons[] =
{
  { STD_FILENEW,  IDM_NEW, TBSTATE_ENABLED, TBSTYLE_BUTTON, 0, 0L, 0},
  { STD_FILEOPEN, IDM_OPEN, TBSTATE_ENABLED, TBSTYLE_BUTTON, 0, 0L, 0},
  { STD_FILESAVE, IDM_SAVE, TBSTATE_ENABLED, TBSTYLE_BUTTON, 0, 0L, 0},
  { VIEW_LARGEICONS, IDM_LARGEICON, TBSTATE_ENABLED, TBSTYLE_BUTTON, 0, 0L, 0},
  { VIEW_SMALLICONS, IDM_SMALLICON, TBSTATE_ENABLED, TBSTYLE_BUTTON, 0, 0L, 0},
  { VIEW_LIST, IDM_LISTVIEW, TBSTATE_ENABLED, TBSTYLE_BUTTON, 0, 0L, 0},
  { VIEW_DETAILS, IDM_REPORTVIEW, TBSTATE_ENABLED, TBSTYLE_BUTTON, 0, 0L, 0},
};


LRESULT CALLBACK WndProc( HWND hWnd, UINT uMsg, WPARAM wParam, LPARAM lParam )
{
static char szTemp[128];
static HWND hToolWnd   = NULL;
static HWND hStatusWnd = NULL;
static BOOL bNeedSave   = FALSE;

   switch( uMsg )
   {
      case WM_CREATE :
              // Initialize the common control library
              // and create the status window and toolbar.
              //.........................................
              InitCommonControls();
              hStatusWnd = CreateStatusWindow(
                              WS_CHILD | WS_VISIBLE |
                              CCS_BOTTOM | SBARS_SIZEGRIP,
                              "", hWnd, IDC_STATBAR );

              hToolWnd = CreateToolbarEx( hWnd,
                              WS_CHILD | WS_BORDER |
                              WS_VISIBLE | CCS_ADJUSTABLE,
                              IDC_TOOLBAR,
                              11,
                              (HINSTANCE)HINST_COMMCTRL,
```

```
                                        IDB_STD_SMALL_COLOR,
                                        tbButtons, 3,
                                        0, 0, 100, 30, sizeof(TBBUTTON) );

            if ( hToolWnd )
            {
                TBADDBITMAP  tb;
                TBSAVEPARAMS tbsp;
                int  index, stdidx;

                // Add the system-defined view bitmaps.
                //......................................
                tb.hInst = HINST_COMMCTRL;
                tb.nID = IDB_VIEW_SMALL_COLOR;
                stdidx = SendMessage(hToolWnd, TB_ADDBITMAP, 12, (LPARAM)&tb);

                // Update the indices to the bitmaps.
                //...................................
                for (index = 3; index < 7; index++)
                    tbButtons[index].iBitmap += stdidx;

                // Restore the toolbar settings.
                //..............................
                tbsp.hkr          = HKEY_CURRENT_USER;
                tbsp.pszSubKey    = "Software\\Waite\\TB_CUSTOMIZE";
                tbsp.pszValueName = "Toolbar";

                SendMessage(hToolWnd, TB_SAVERESTORE, FALSE, (LPARAM)&tbsp);
            }
            break;

    case WM_SIZE :
            {
                RECT clrect, strect;

                // Size the status window when the main
                // window is sized.
                //.....................................
                GetClientRect( hWnd, &clrect );
                GetClientRect( hStatusWnd, &strect );

                MoveWindow( hStatusWnd, 0, clrect.bottom-strect.bottom,
                            LOWORD( lParam ), HIWORD( lParam ), TRUE );
            }
            break;

    case WM_NOTIFY :
            if ( ((LPNMHDR)lParam)->idFrom == IDC_TOOLBAR )
            {
                LPTBNOTIFY lpTBNotify = (LPTBNOTIFY)lParam;

                switch( lpTBNotify->hdr.code )
                {
                    case TBN_QUERYINSERT :
                        return( TRUE );

                    case TBN_QUERYDELETE :
                        return( TRUE );
```

continued on next page

continued from previous page

```
case TBN_GETBUTTONINFO :
    if ( lpTBNotify->iItem < 7 )
    {
        lpTBNotify->tbButton = tbButtons[lpTBNotify->iItem];

        // Load the description for the button.
        //...................................
        if ( lpTBNotify->pszText )
        {
            LoadString( hInst,
                    tbButtons[lpTBNotify->iItem].idCommand,
                    szTemp, sizeof( szTemp )-1 );

            strcpy( lpTBNotify->pszText, szTemp );
            lpTBNotify->cchText = strlen( szTemp );
        }
        return( TRUE );
    }
    break;

case TBN_RESET : // Reset the toolbar.
    {
        int nButtons, i;

        nButtons = SendMessage(hToolWnd, TB_BUTTONCOUNT,
                            0, 0);
        for( i=0; i < nButtons; i++ )
            SendMessage(hToolWnd, TB_DELETEBUTTON, 0, 0);

        SendMessage(hToolWnd, TB_ADDBUTTONS,
                    3, (LPARAM)tbButtons);
    }
    break;

case TBN_CUSTHELP : // Display custom help file.

    WinHelp( hWnd, "CUSTOMIZ.HLP", HELP_CONTEXT, 1 );
    break;

case TBN_BEGINADJUST :
    SendMessage(hStatusWnd, SB_SETTEXT, 0,
                (LPARAM)"Customizing the toolbar." );
    break;

case TBN_BEGINDRAG :
    SendMessage(hStatusWnd, SB_SETTEXT, 0,
                (LPARAM)"Dragging a toolbar button." );
    break;

case TBN_ENDDRAG :
case TBN_ENDADJUST :
    SendMessage(hStatusWnd, SB_SETTEXT, 0,
                (LPARAM)"" );
    break;

case TBN_TOOLBARCHANGE :
    SendMessage(hStatusWnd, SB_SETTEXT, 0,
            (LPARAM)"The toolbar has changed." );
```

```
                            bNeedSave = TRUE;
                            break;
                    }
            }
            break;

    case WM_COMMAND :
            switch( LOWORD( wParam ) )
            {
                case IDM_CUSTOMIZE :
                        SendMessage(hToolWnd, TB_CUSTOMIZE, 0, 0);
                        break;

                case IDM_EXIT :
                        DestroyWindow( hWnd );
                        break;
            }
            break;

    case WM_DESTROY :
            // Save the toolbar settings.
            //.........................
            if ( bNeedSave )
            {
                TBSAVEPARAMS tbsp;

                tbsp.hkr           = HKEY_CURRENT_USER;
                tbsp.pszSubKey     = "Software\\Waite\\TB_CUSTOMIZE";
                tbsp.pszValueName  = "Toolbar";

                SendMessage(hToolWnd, TB_SAVERESTORE, TRUE, (LPARAM)&tbsp );
            }

            WinHelp( hWnd, "CUSTOMIZ.HLP", HELP_QUIT, 0 );

            PostQuitMessage(0);
            break;

    default :
            return( DefWindowProc( hWnd, uMsg, wParam, lParam ) );
    }

    return( 0L );
}
```

TB_DELETEBUTTON ■ WIN32s ■ WINDOWS 95 ■ WINDOWS NT

Description   TB_DELETEBUTTON is a toolbar message that deletes a button from a toolbar.

Parameters

wParam   UINT: The zero-based index of the button to delete.

lParam   LPARAM: Set to zero.

Returns   BOOL: If successful, TRUE is returned; otherwise, FALSE is returned.

Include File commctrl.h
See Also CreateToolbarEx()
Related Messages TB_COMMANDTOINDEX, TB_ADDBUTTONS, TB_INSERTBUTTON
Example See the example for the TB_CUSTOMIZE message.

TB_ENABLEBUTTON ■ WIN32s ■ WINDOWS 95 ■ WINDOWS NT

Description TB_ENABLEBUTTON is a toolbar message that enables or disables a given button in a toolbar.

Parameters
wParam UINT: The command identifier of the button to enable or disable.
lParam BOOL: If set to TRUE, the button is enabled. If set to FALSE, the button is disabled.
Returns BOOL: If successful, TRUE is returned; otherwise, FALSE is returned.
Include File commctrl.h
See Also CreateToolbarEx()
Related Messages TB_ISBUTTONENABLED, TB_GETSTATE
Example This example, shown in Figure 3-15 and Listing 3-17, demonstrates the usage of the TB_ENABLEBUTTON and TB_ISBUTTONENABLED messages to toggle a toolbar button between enabled and disabled as the user selects the corresponding menu item for the button.

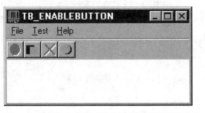

Figure 3-15 TB_ENABLEBUTTON example

Listing 3-17 Using the TB_ENABLEBUTTON message

```
// Toolbar buttons.
//................
TBBUTTON tbButtons[] =
{
    { 0, IDM_TEST1, TBSTATE_ENABLED, TBSTYLE_BUTTON, 0, 0L, 0},
    { 1, IDM_TEST2, TBSTATE_ENABLED, TBSTYLE_BUTTON, 0, 0L, 0},
    { 2, IDM_TEST3, TBSTATE_ENABLED, TBSTYLE_BUTTON, 0, 0L, 0},
    { 3, IDM_TEST4, TBSTATE_ENABLED, TBSTYLE_BUTTON, 0, 0L, 0},
};
```

```
LRESULT CALLBACK WndProc( HWND hWnd, UINT uMsg, WPARAM wParam, LPARAM lParam )
{
static HWND hToolWnd    = NULL;

    switch( uMsg )
    {
        case WM_CREATE :
                // Initialize the common control library
                // and create the toolbar.
                //.......................................
                InitCommonControls();

                hToolWnd = CreateWindowEx( 0, TOOLBARCLASSNAME, NULL,
                                    WS_CHILD | WS_BORDER | WS_VISIBLE,
                                    0, 0, 0, 0, hWnd,
                                    (HMENU)101, hInst, NULL);

                if ( hToolWnd )
                {
                    HBITMAP      hBmp;
                    TBADDBITMAP tb;
                    int index, stdidx;

                    SendMessage(hToolWnd, TB_BUTTONSTRUCTSIZE,
                                sizeof(TBBUTTON), 0);

                    hBmp = CreateMappedBitmap( hInst, 100, 0, NULL, 0 );

                    tb.hInst = NULL;
                    tb.nID   = (UINT) hBmp;
                    stdidx = SendMessage(hToolWnd, TB_ADDBITMAP, 4, (LPARAM)&tb);

                    for (index = 0; index < 4; index++)
                        tbButtons[index].iBitmap += stdidx;

                    SendMessage(hToolWnd, TB_ADDBUTTONS, 4, (LONG) &tbButtons[0]);
                }
                break;

        case WM_COMMAND :
                switch( LOWORD( wParam ) )
                {
                    case IDM_TESTMENU1 :
                    case IDM_TESTMENU2 :
                    case IDM_TESTMENU3 :
                    case IDM_TESTMENU4 :
                            {
                                BOOL bEnabled;

                                // Check if a button is enabled or disabled.
                                //.........................................
                                bEnabled = SendMessage( hToolWnd,
                                            TB_ISBUTTONENABLED,
                                            LOWORD( wParam )-IDM_TOOLBASE,
                                            0 );

                                // Enable/Disable the toolbar button.
                                //..................................
```

continued on next page

continued from previous page

```
            SendMessage(hToolWnd, TB_ENABLEBUTTON,
                        LOWORD( wParam )-IDM_TOOLBASE,
                        !bEnabled );
        }
        break;
```

.
.
.

TB_GETBITMAP   ■ WIN32S   ■ WINDOWS 95   ■ WINDOWS NT

Description	TB_GETBITMAP is a toolbar message that retrieves the index of the bitmap associated with a button in a toolbar.
Parameters	
wParam	UINT: The command identifier of the button whose bitmap index is to be retrieved.
lParam	LPARAM: Set to zero.
Returns	int: If successful, the index of the bitmap is returned; otherwise, zero is returned.
Include File	commctrl.h
See Also	CreateToolbarEx()
Related Messages	TB_CHANGEBITMAP
Example	This example, shown in Listing 3-18, demonstrates how the TB_GETBITMAP message can retrieve the bitmap for a button and how the TB_CHANGEBITMAP message changes a button's bitmap. As the user selects one of the first seven buttons, the bitmap is retrieved and set as the bitmap for the last button on the toolbar as shown in Figure 3-16.

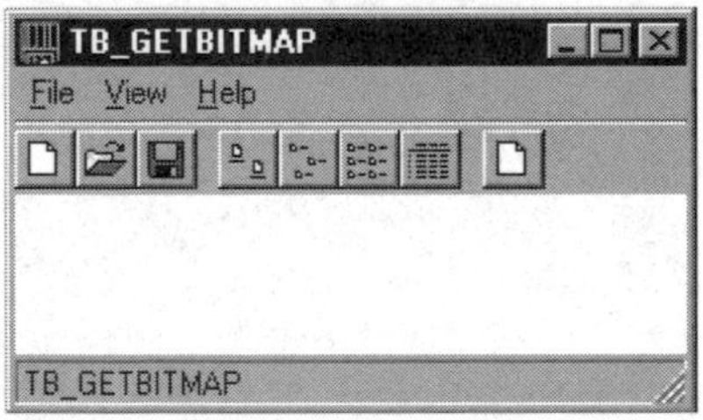

Figure 3-16 TB_GETBITMAP example

Listing 3-18 Using the TB_GETBITMAP message

```
// Toolbar buttons.
//.................
TBBUTTON tbButtons[] =
{
  { STD_FILENEW,  IDM_NEW, TBSTATE_ENABLED, TBSTYLE_BUTTON, 0, OL, O},
```

```
    { STD_FILEOPEN, IDM_OPEN, TBSTATE_ENABLED, TBSTYLE_BUTTON, 0, 0L, 0},
    { STD_FILESAVE, IDM_SAVE, TBSTATE_ENABLED, TBSTYLE_BUTTON, 0, 0L, 0},
    { 0, 0, TBSTATE_ENABLED, TBSTYLE_SEP, 0, 0L, 0},
    { VIEW_LARGEICONS, IDM_LARGEICON, TBSTATE_ENABLED, TBSTYLE_BUTTON, 0, 0L, 0},
    { VIEW_SMALLICONS, IDM_SMALLICON, TBSTATE_ENABLED, TBSTYLE_BUTTON, 0, 0L, 0},
    { VIEW_LIST, IDM_LISTVIEW, TBSTATE_ENABLED, TBSTYLE_BUTTON, 0, 0L, 0},
    { VIEW_DETAILS, IDM_REPORTVIEW, TBSTATE_ENABLED, TBSTYLE_BUTTON, 0, 0L, 0},
    { 0, 0, TBSTATE_ENABLED, TBSTYLE_SEP, 0, 0L, 0},
    { 0, IDM_TEST, TBSTATE_ENABLED, TBSTYLE_BUTTON, 0, 0L, 0},
};


LRESULT CALLBACK WndProc( HWND hWnd, UINT uMsg, WPARAM wParam, LPARAM lParam )
{
static HWND hToolWnd   = NULL;
static HWND hStatusWnd = NULL;

    switch( uMsg )
    {
       case WM_CREATE :
                // Initialize the common control library
                // and create the status window and toolbar.
                //........................................
                InitCommonControls();
                hStatusWnd = CreateStatusWindow(
                                  WS_CHILD | WS_VISIBLE |
                                  CCS_BOTTOM | SBARS_SIZEGRIP,
                                  lpszTitle, hWnd, 101 );

                hToolWnd = CreateToolbarEx( hWnd,
                                  WS_CHILD | WS_BORDER | WS_VISIBLE,
                                  102,
                                  11,
                                  (HINSTANCE)HINST_COMMCTRL,
                                  IDB_STD_SMALL_COLOR,
                                  tbButtons, 4,
                                  0, 0, 100, 30, sizeof(TBBUTTON) );

                if ( hToolWnd )
                {
                    HBITMAP      hBmp;
                    TBADDBITMAP tb;
                    int index, stdidx;

                    // Add the system-defined view bitmaps.
                    //........................................
                    tb.hInst = HINST_COMMCTRL;
                    tb.nID = IDB_VIEW_SMALL_COLOR;
                    stdidx = SendMessage(hToolWnd, TB_ADDBITMAP, 12, (LPARAM)&tb);

                    for (index = 4; index < 8; index++)
                        tbButtons[index].iBitmap += stdidx;

                    SendMessage(hToolWnd, TB_ADDBUTTONS, 4, (LONG) &tbButtons[4]);

                    // Load bitmap to add to the toolbar.
                    //........................................
                    hBmp = CreateMappedBitmap( hInst, 100, 0, NULL, 0 );
```

continued on next page

127

continued from previous page

```
            tb.hInst = NULL;
            tb.nID   = (UINT) hBmp;
            stdidx = SendMessage(hToolWnd, TB_ADDBITMAP, 1, (LPARAM)&tb);

            tbButtons[9].iBitmap += stdidx;

            SendMessage(hToolWnd, TB_ADDBUTTONS, 2, (LONG) &tbButtons[8]);
        }
        break;

    case WM_COMMAND :
        switch( LOWORD( wParam ) )
        {
            case IDM_NEW :
            case IDM_OPEN :
            case IDM_SAVE :
            case IDM_LARGEICON :
            case IDM_SMALLICON :
            case IDM_LISTVIEW :
            case IDM_REPORTVIEW :
                {
                    // Get the bitmap of the selected button.
                    //.....................................
                    int nIdx = SendMessage(hToolWnd, TB_GETBITMAP,
                                         LOWORD( wParam ), 0 );

                    // Change the IDM_TEST
                    // bitmap to the selected one.
                    //..........................
                    SendMessage(hToolWnd, TB_CHANGEBITMAP,
                            IDM_TEST, nIdx );
                }
                break;
```

.
.
.

TB_GETBITMAPFLAGS   ■ Win32s   ■ Windows 95   ■ Windows NT

Description	TB_GETBITMAPFLAGS is a toolbar message that retrieves the bitmap flags for a toolbar.
Parameters	
wParam	WPARAM: Set to zero.
lParam	LPARAM: Set to zero.
Returns	int: If the width of the display has at least 120 pixels per logical inch and can handle large bitmaps, the TBBF_LARGE value is returned; otherwise, zero is returned.
Include File	commctrl.h
See Also	CreateToolbarEx()
Example	This example, shown in Listing 3-19, demonstrates how to use the TB_GETBITMAPFLAGS message to determine if large bitmaps should be used before buttons are added to the toolbar.

Listing 3-19 Using the TB_GETBITMAPFLAGS message

```
// Toolbar buttons.
//..................
TBBUTTON tbButtons[] =
{
    { STD_FILENEW,  IDM_NEW, TBSTATE_ENABLED, TBSTYLE_BUTTON, 0, 0L, 0},
    { STD_FILEOPEN, IDM_OPEN, TBSTATE_ENABLED, TBSTYLE_BUTTON, 0, 0L, 0},
    { STD_FILESAVE, IDM_SAVE, TBSTATE_ENABLED, TBSTYLE_BUTTON, 0, 0L, 0},
};


LRESULT CALLBACK WndProc( HWND hWnd, UINT uMsg, WPARAM wParam, LPARAM lParam )
{
static HWND hToolWnd   = NULL;

    switch( uMsg )
    {
        case WM_CREATE :
                // Initialize the common control library
                // and create the toolbar.
                //.......................................
                InitCommonControls();

                hToolWnd = CreateWindowEx( 0, TOOLBARCLASSNAME, NULL,
                                    WS_CHILD | WS_BORDER | WS_VISIBLE,
                                    0, 0, 0, 0, hWnd, (HMENU)101,
                                    hInst, NULL);

                if ( hToolWnd )
                {
                    BOOL        bLargeButtons;
                    TBADDBITMAP tb;
                    int index, stdidx;

                    // Determine if large buttons should be used.
                    //............................................
                    bLargeButtons = (SendMessage(hToolWnd, TB_GETBITMAPFLAGS,
                                            0, 0 ) == TBBF_LARGE);

                    // Set the size of the TBBUTTON structure.
                    //.........................................
                    SendMessage(hToolWnd, TB_BUTTONSTRUCTSIZE,
                                sizeof(TBBUTTON), 0);

                    // Add the bitmap to the toolbar.
                    //...............................
                    tb.hInst = HINST_COMMCTRL;
                    tb.nID   = bLargeButtons ? IDB_STD_LARGE_COLOR :
                                            IDB_STD_SMALL_COLOR;
                    stdidx = SendMessage(hToolWnd, TB_ADDBITMAP, 11, (LPARAM)&tb);

                    for (index = 0; index < 3; index++)
                        tbButtons[index].iBitmap += stdidx;

                    // Add the buttons to the toolbar.
                    //................................
                    SendMessage(hToolWnd, TB_ADDBUTTONS, 3, (LONG) &tbButtons[0]);
```

continued on next page

continued from previous page

```
                SendMessage(hToolWnd, TB_AUTOSIZE, 0, 0);
        }
        break;
          .
          .
          .
```

TB_GETBUTTON   ■ Win32s   ■ Windows 95   ■ Windows NT

Description	TB_GETBUTTON is a toolbar message that retrieves information about a given button in a toolbar. A TBBUTTON structure is filled with the values stored in the toolbar for the button.
Parameters	
wParam	UINT: The zero-based index of the button for which to retrieve information.
lParam	LPTBBUTTON: A pointer to a TBBUTTON structure that receives the button information. See the definition of the TBBUTTON structure under the CreateToolbarEx() function.
Returns	BOOL: If successful, TRUE is returned; otherwise, FALSE is returned.
Include File	commctrl.h
See Also	CreateToolbarEx()
Related Messages	TB_COMMANDTOINDEX
Example	This example, shown in Listing 3-20, uses the TB_GETBUTTON, TB_COMMANDTOINDEX, and TB_GETITEMRECT messages to retrieve information about a button as the user presses the buttons on the toolbar. The TB_COMMANDTOINDEX message is used to determine the index of the button the user pressed. The TB_GETBUTTON and TB_GETITEMRECT messages retrieve information about the button that is displayed on the client area of the window.

Listing 3-20 Using the TB_GETBUTTON message

```
// Toolbar buttons.
//.................
TBBUTTON tbButtons[] =
{
  { STD_FILENEW,  IDM_NEW, TBSTATE_ENABLED, TBSTYLE_BUTTON, 0, 0L, 0},
  { STD_FILEOPEN, IDM_OPEN, TBSTATE_ENABLED, TBSTYLE_BUTTON, 0, 0L, 0},
  { STD_FILESAVE, IDM_SAVE, TBSTATE_ENABLED, TBSTYLE_BUTTON, 0, 0L, 0},
  { 0, 0, TBSTATE_ENABLED, TBSTYLE_SEP, 0, 0L, 0},
  { VIEW_LARGEICONS, IDM_LARGEICON, TBSTATE_ENABLED, TBSTYLE_BUTTON, 0, 0L, 0},
  { VIEW_SMALLICONS, IDM_SMALLICON, TBSTATE_ENABLED, TBSTYLE_BUTTON, 0, 0L, 0},
  { VIEW_LIST, IDM_LISTVIEW, TBSTATE_ENABLED, TBSTYLE_BUTTON, 0, 0L, 0},
  { VIEW_DETAILS, IDM_REPORTVIEW, TBSTATE_ENABLED, TBSTYLE_BUTTON, 0, 0L, 0},
};

LRESULT CALLBACK WndProc( HWND hWnd, UINT uMsg, WPARAM wParam, LPARAM lParam )
```

```
{
static HWND hToolWnd   = NULL;

   switch( uMsg )
   {
      case WM_CREATE :
               // Initialize the common control library
               // and create the status window and toolbar.
               //.........................................
               InitCommonControls();

               hToolWnd = CreateToolbarEx( hWnd,
                                           WS_CHILD | WS_BORDER | WS_VISIBLE,
                                           102,
                                           11,
                                           (HINSTANCE)HINST_COMMCTRL,
                                           IDB_STD_SMALL_COLOR,
                                           tbButtons, 4,
                                           0, 0, 100, 30, sizeof(TBBUTTON) );

               if ( hToolWnd )
               {
                  TBADDBITMAP tb;
                  int index, stdidx;

                  // Add the system-defined view bitmaps.
                  //....................................
                  tb.hInst = HINST_COMMCTRL;
                  tb.nID = IDB_VIEW_SMALL_COLOR;
                  stdidx = SendMessage(hToolWnd, TB_ADDBITMAP, 12, (LPARAM)&tb);

                  for (index = 4; index < 8; index++)
                     tbButtons[index].iBitmap += stdidx;

                  SendMessage(hToolWnd, TB_ADDBUTTONS, 4, (LONG) &tbButtons[4]);
               }
               break;


      case WM_COMMAND :
               switch( LOWORD( wParam ) )
               {
                  case IDM_NEW :
                  case IDM_OPEN :
                  case IDM_SAVE :
                  case IDM_LARGEICON :
                  case IDM_SMALLICON :
                  case IDM_LISTVIEW :
                  case IDM_REPORTVIEW :
                        {
                           TBBUTTON tb;
                           RECT     rect;
                           HDC      hdc;
                           char     szTmp[64];

                           // Get the index of the button.
                           //............................
                           int nIdx = SendMessage(hToolWnd, TB_COMMANDTOINDEX,
                                          LOWORD( wParam ), 0 );
```

continued on next page

continued from previous page

```
                              // Get the button information.
                              //...........................
                              SendMessage(hToolWnd, TB_GETBUTTON,
                                        nIdx, (LPARAM)&tb );

                              // Get the rect of the button.
                              //...........................
                              SendMessage(hToolWnd, TB_GETITEMRECT,
                                        nIdx, (LPARAM)&rect );

                              // Output button information.
                              //...........................
                              hdc = GetDC( hWnd );

                              wsprintf(szTmp, "Button index: %d", tb.iBitmap );
                              TextOut( hdc, 10, 40, szTmp, strlen( szTmp ) );

                              wsprintf(szTmp, "Button command: %d", tb.idCommand );
                              TextOut( hdc, 10, 60, szTmp, strlen( szTmp ) );

                              wsprintf(szTmp,
                                      "Button rect: left=%d"\
                                      " top=%d right=%d bottom=%d",
                                  rect.left, rect.top, rect.right, rect.bottom );
                              TextOut( hdc, 10, 80, szTmp, strlen( szTmp ) );

                              ReleaseDC( hWnd, hdc );
                          }
                          break;
```

TB_GETBUTTONTEXT ■ WIN32s ■ WINDOWS 95 ■ WINDOWS NT

Description	TB_GETBUTTONTEXT is a toolbar message that retrieves the text of a button in a toolbar.
Parameters	
wParam	UINT: The command identifier of the button whose text is to be retrieved.
lParam	LPTSTR: A pointer to a buffer large enough to receive the button text.
Returns	int: If successful, the length, in characters, of the string copied to the buffer not including the null terminator; otherwise, -1 is returned.
Include File	commctrl.h
See Also	CreateToolbarEx()
Example	See the example for the TB_ADDSTRING message.

TB_GETITEMRECT ■ WIN32s ■ WINDOWS 95 ■ WINDOWS NT

Description	TB_GETITEMRECT is a toolbar message that retrieves the bounding rectangle of a button in a toolbar.

Parameters

wParam	UINT: The zero-based index of the button for which to retrieve the bounding rectangle.
lParam	LPRECT: A pointer to a RECT structure that receives the coordinates of the bounding rectangle.
Returns	BOOL: If successful, TRUE is returned; otherwise, FALSE is returned.
Include File	commctrl.h
See Also	CreateToolbarEx()
Example	See the example for the TB_GETBUTTON message.

TB_GETROWS   ■ Win32s   ■ Windows 95   ■ Windows NT

Description	TB_GETROWS is a toolbar message that retrieves the number of button rows in a toolbar with the TBSTYLE_WRAPABLE style.

Parameters

wParam	WPARAM: Set to zero.
lParam	LPARAM: Set to zero.
Returns	int: The number of rows is returned.
Include File	commctrl.h
See Also	CreateToolbarEx()
Example	See the example for the TB_SETROWS message.

TB_GETSTATE   ■ Win32s   ■ Windows 95   ■ Windows NT

Description	TB_GETSTATE is a toolbar message that retrieves information about the state of a button in a toolbar, such as whether it is enabled, pressed, or checked.

Parameters

wParam	UINT: The command identifier of the button for which to retrieve the button state.
lParam	LPARAM: Set to zero.
Returns	int: If successful, the button state information; otherwise, -1 is returned. The button state can be a combination of the values listed in Table 3-11.

Table 3-11 Toolbar button states

Value	Meaning
TBSTATE_CHECKED	The button has the TBSTYLE_CHECKED style and is pressed.
TBSTATE_ENABLED	The button is enabled.
TBSTATE_HIDDEN	The button is hidden.

continued on next page

continued from previous page

Value	Meaning
TBSTATE_INDETERMINATE	The button is grayed.
TBSTATE_PRESSED	The button is pressed.
TBSTATE_WRAP	A line break follows the button.

Include File   commctrl.h

See Also   CreateToolbarEx()

Related Messages   TB_ISBUTTONCHECKED, TB_ISBUTTONENABLED, TB_ISBUTTON-
HIDDEN, TB_ISBUTTONINDETERMINATE, TB_ISBUTTONPRESSED

Example   This example has a group of radio button style buttons for the View command. As the user selects a menu item from the View menu, it checks the
menu item and the corresponding toolbar button as shown in Figure 3-17.
If the user selects a toolbar button, the corresponding menu item is selected. The TB_GETSTATE message is used to determine the state of the
buttons when the WM_INITMENUPOPUP message is processed.

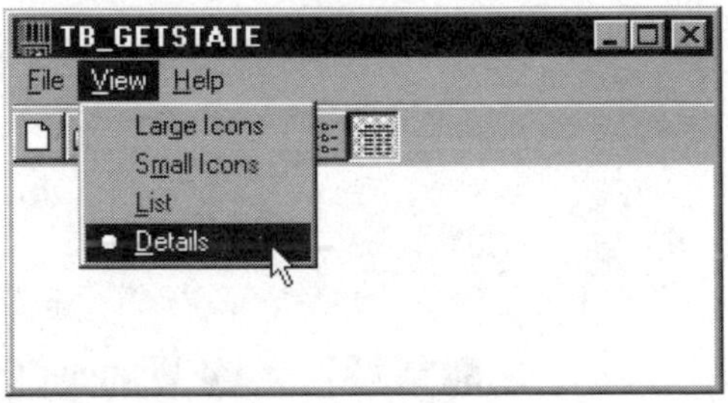

Figure 3-17 TB_GETSTATE example

Listing 3-21 Using the TB_GETSTATE message

```
LRESULT CALLBACK WndProc( HWND hWnd, UINT uMsg, WPARAM wParam, LPARAM lParam )
{
static HWND hToolWnd   = NULL;

   switch( uMsg )
   {
      case WM_INITMENUPOPUP :
             if ( LOWORD( lParam ) == 1 )
             {
             UINT nCmd;

             for ( nCmd = IDM_LARGEICON; nCmd <= IDM_REPORTVIEW; nCmd++ )
             {
                if ( SendMessage(hToolWnd, TB_GETSTATE,
                             nCmd, 0 ) & TBSTATE_CHECKED )
                {
                    CheckMenuRadioItem((HMENU)wParam, IDM_LARGEICON,
                                                 IDM_REPORTVIEW,
```

```
                                              nCmd,
                                              MF_BYCOMMAND );
                }
            }
        }
        break;

    case WM_COMMAND :
        switch( LOWORD( wParam ) )
        {
            case IDM_LARGEICON :
            case IDM_SMALLICON :
            case IDM_LISTVIEW :
            case IDM_REPORTVIEW :
                {
                    UINT nCmd;

                    if ( (SendMessage(hToolWnd, TB_GETSTATE,
                        LOWORD(wParam), 0 ) & TBSTATE_CHECKED) == 0 )
                    {
                        for( nCmd = IDM_LARGEICON;
                            nCmd <= IDM_REPORTVIEW; nCmd++ )
                        {
                            if ( nCmd == LOWORD(wParam) )
                                SendMessage(hToolWnd, TB_SETSTATE, nCmd,
                                        TBSTATE_CHECKED |
                                        TBSTATE_ENABLED);
                            else
                                SendMessage(hToolWnd, TB_SETSTATE, nCmd,
                                        TBSTATE_ENABLED);
                        }
                    }
                }
                break;
        .
        .
        .
```

TB_GETTOOLTIPS ■ Win32s ■ Windows 95 ■ Windows NT

Description	TB_GETTOOLTIPS is a toolbar message that retrieves the handle to the tooltip control, if any, associated with the toolbar.
Parameters	
wParam	WPARAM: Set to zero.
lParam	LPARAM: Set to zero.
Returns	HWND: The handle of the tooltip control associated with the toolbar. NULL is returned if the toolbar has no tooltip control.
Include File	commctrl.h
See Also	CreateToolbarEx()
Related Messages	TB_SETTOOLTIPS

Example

This example, shown in Listing 3-22, creates a toolbar with tooltips. The example uses the TB_GETTOOLTIPS message to retrieve the handle of the tooltip control and the TTM_SETDELAYTIME message to set the reshow delay time to one second.

Listing 3-22 Using the TB_GETTOOLTIPS message

```
LRESULT CALLBACK WndProc( HWND hWnd, UINT uMsg, WPARAM wParam, LPARAM lParam )
{
static char     szTmp[80];
static LPTSTR   lpch;
static HWND     hToolWnd   = NULL;
static HWND     hStatusWnd = NULL;

    switch( uMsg )
    {
        case WM_CREATE :
                // Initialize the common control library
                // and create the status window and toolbar.
                //.........................................
                InitCommonControls();

                hStatusWnd = CreateStatusWindow(
                                WS_CHILD | WS_VISIBLE |
                                CCS_BOTTOM | SBARS_SIZEGRIP,
                                "", hWnd, 101 );

                hToolWnd = CreateToolbarEx( hWnd,
                                WS_CHILD | WS_BORDER |
                                WS_VISIBLE | TBSTYLE_TOOLTIPS,
                                102,
                                11,
                                (HINSTANCE)HINST_COMMCTRL,
                                IDB_STD_SMALL_COLOR,
                                tbButtons, 4,
                                0, 0, 100, 30, sizeof(TBBUTTON) );

                if ( hToolWnd )
                {
                    TBADDBITMAP tb;
                    HWND        hToolTip;
                    int index, stdidx;

                    // Add the system-defined view bitmaps.
                    //.....................................
                    tb.hInst = HINST_COMMCTRL;
                    tb.nID = IDB_VIEW_SMALL_COLOR;
                    stdidx = SendMessage(hToolWnd, TB_ADDBITMAP, 12, (LPARAM)&tb);

                    // Update the indices to the bitmaps.
                    //...................................
                    for (index = 4; index < 8; index++)
                        tbButtons[index].iBitmap += stdidx;

                    // Add the view buttons.
                    //......................
                    SendMessage(hToolWnd, TB_ADDBUTTONS, 4, (LONG) &tbButtons[4]);
```

```
        // Set the reshow time to 1 second for the tooltip control.
        //.........................................................
        hToolTip = (HWND)SendMessage( hToolWnd, TB_GETTOOLTIPS, 0, 0 );
        SendMessage( hToolTip, TTM_SETDELAYTIME, TTDT_RESHOW, 1000 );
    }
    break;
```

.
.
.

TB_HIDEBUTTON   ■ WIN32s   ■ WINDOWS 95   ■ WINDOWS NT

Description	TB_HIDEBUTTON is a toolbar message that hides or shows a button in a toolbar.
Parameters	
wParam	UINT: The command identifier of the button to hide or show.
lParam	BOOL: If this parameter is TRUE, the button is hidden. If it is FALSE, the button is shown.
Returns	BOOL: If successful, TRUE is returned; otherwise, FALSE is returned.
Include File	commctrl.h
See Also	CreateToolbarEx()
Related Messages	TB_ISBUTTONHIDDEN, TB_GETSTATE
Example	This example, shown in Listing 3-23, demonstrates the use of the TB_HIDEBUTTON and TB_ISBUTTONHIDDEN. When the user selects the corresponding menu item for a button, it is either hidden or shown depending on the current state of the button.

Listing 3-23 *Using the TB_HIDEBUTTON message*

```
// Toolbar buttons.
//.................
TBBUTTON tbButtons[] =
{
    { 0, IDM_TEST1, TBSTATE_ENABLED, TBSTYLE_BUTTON, 0, 0L, 0},
    { 1, IDM_TEST2, TBSTATE_ENABLED, TBSTYLE_BUTTON, 0, 0L, 0},
    { 2, IDM_TEST3, TBSTATE_ENABLED, TBSTYLE_BUTTON, 0, 0L, 0},
    { 3, IDM_TEST4, TBSTATE_ENABLED, TBSTYLE_BUTTON, 0, 0L, 0},
};

LRESULT CALLBACK WndProc( HWND hWnd, UINT uMsg, WPARAM wParam, LPARAM lParam )
{
static HWND hToolWnd   = NULL;

    switch( uMsg )
    {
        case WM_COMMAND :
            switch( LOWORD( wParam ) )
            {
                case IDM_TESTMENU1 :
```

continued on next page

continued from previous page

```
            case IDM_TESTMENU2 :
            case IDM_TESTMENU3 :
            case IDM_TESTMENU4 :
                {
                    BOOL bHidden;

                    bHidden = SendMessage( hToolWnd,
                                    TB_ISBUTTONHIDDEN,
                                    LOWORD( wParam )-IDM_TOOLBASE,
                                    0 );

                    // Hide/Show the toolbar button.
                    //..............................
                    SendMessage(hToolWnd, TB_HIDEBUTTON,
                                LOWORD( wParam )-IDM_TOOLBASE,
                                !bHidden );
                }
                break;
```

TB_INDETERMINATE   ■ WIN32S   ■ WINDOWS 95   ■ WINDOWS NT

Description	TB_INDETERMINATE is a toolbar message that sets or clears the indeterminate state of a button in a toolbar. The indeterminate state is used when the state of the button is neither checked nor unchecked. For example, the bold attribute button within a text editor may be indeterminate if the selected text contains both bold and nonbold text.
Parameters	
wParam	UINT: The command identifier of the button whose indeterminate state is to be set or cleared.
lParam	BOOL: If this parameter is TRUE, the indeterminate state is set. If it is FALSE, the state is cleared.
Returns	BOOL: If successful, TRUE is returned; otherwise, FALSE is returned.
Include File	commctrl.h
See Also	CreateToolbarEx()
Related Messages	TB_ISBUTTONINDETERMINATE, TB_GETSTATE
Example	This example, shown in Listing 3-24, demonstrates the use of the TB_INDETERMINATE and TB_ISBUTTONINDETERMINATE. When the user selects the corresponding menu item for a button, it is either set to indeterminate or normal depending on the current state of the button.

Listing 3-24 Using the TB_INDETERMINATE message

```
// Toolbar buttons.
//.................
TBBUTTON tbButtons[] =
{
```

```
     { 0, IDM_TEST1, TBSTATE_ENABLED, TBSTYLE_BUTTON, 0, 0L, 0},
     { 1, IDM_TEST2, TBSTATE_ENABLED, TBSTYLE_BUTTON, 0, 0L, 0},
     { 2, IDM_TEST3, TBSTATE_ENABLED, TBSTYLE_BUTTON, 0, 0L, 0},
     { 3, IDM_TEST4, TBSTATE_ENABLED, TBSTYLE_BUTTON, 0, 0L, 0},
};

LRESULT CALLBACK WndProc( HWND hWnd, UINT uMsg, WPARAM wParam, LPARAM lParam )
{
static HWND hToolWnd   = NULL;

   switch( uMsg )
   {
      case WM_COMMAND :
            switch( LOWORD( wParam ) )
            {
               case IDM_TESTMENU1 :
               case IDM_TESTMENU2 :
               case IDM_TESTMENU3 :
               case IDM_TESTMENU4 :
                     {
                        BOOL bIndeterminate;

                        bIndeterminate = SendMessage( hToolWnd,
                                    TB_ISBUTTONINDETERMINATE,
                                    LOWORD( wParam )-IDM_TOOLBASE,
                                    0 );

                        // Set/clear the toolbar button indeterminate.
                        //............................................
                        SendMessage(hToolWnd, TB_INDETERMINATE,
                                    LOWORD( wParam )-IDM_TOOLBASE,
                                    !bIndeterminate );
                     }
                     break;
          .
          .
          .
```

TB_INSERTBUTTON   ■ Win32s   ■ Windows 95   ■ Windows NT

Description	TB_INSERTBUTTON is a toolbar message that inserts a button in a toolbar.
Parameters	
wParam	UINT: The zero-based index of a button. The toolbar inserts the new button to the left of this button.
lParam	LPTBBUTTON: A pointer to a TBBUTTON structure that contains information about the button to insert. See the definition of the TBBUTTON structure under the CreateToolbarEx() function.
Returns	BOOL: If successful, TRUE is returned; otherwise, FALSE is returned.
Include File	commctrl.h
See Also	CreateToolbarEx()
Related Messages	TB_DELETEBUTTON, TB_ADDBUTTONS

Example
This example, shown in Listing 3-25 uses the TB_INSERTBUTTON and TB_DELETEBUTTON messages to insert and delete the corresponding button when the user selects one of the menu items.

Listing 3-25 Using the TB_INSERTBUTTON message

```
// Toolbar buttons.
//................
TBBUTTON tbButtons[] =
{
    { 0, IDM_TEST1, TBSTATE_ENABLED, TBSTYLE_BUTTON, 0, 0L, 0},
    { 1, IDM_TEST2, TBSTATE_ENABLED, TBSTYLE_BUTTON, 0, 0L, 0},
    { 2, IDM_TEST3, TBSTATE_ENABLED, TBSTYLE_BUTTON, 0, 0L, 0},
    { 3, IDM_TEST4, TBSTATE_ENABLED, TBSTYLE_BUTTON, 0, 0L, 0},
};


LRESULT CALLBACK WndProc( HWND hWnd, UINT uMsg, WPARAM wParam, LPARAM lParam )
{
static HWND hToolWnd   = NULL;

    switch( uMsg )
    {
        case WM_COMMAND :
                switch( LOWORD( wParam ) )
                {
                    case IDM_TESTMENU1 :
                    case IDM_TESTMENU2 :
                    case IDM_TESTMENU3 :
                    case IDM_TESTMENU4 :
                        {
                        int  nIdx;

                        // Check if the button already exists.
                        //...................................
                        nIdx = SendMessage( hToolWnd, TB_COMMANDTOINDEX,
                                        LOWORD( wParam )-IDM_TOOLBASE,
                                        0 );

                        // Insert the button if it does not exist;
                        // otherwise, delete the button.
                        //.......................................
                        if ( nIdx < 0 )
                        {
                            nIdx = LOWORD( wParam )-IDM_TOOLBASE-IDM_TEST1,

                            SendMessage( hToolWnd, TB_INSERTBUTTON,
                                    nIdx, (LPARAM)&tbButtons[nIdx] );

                        }
                        else
                            SendMessage( hToolWnd, TB_DELETEBUTTON,
                                    nIdx, 0 );
                        }
                        break;
                        .
                        .
                        .
```

TB_ISBUTTONCHECKED ■ WIN32s ■ WINDOWS 95 ■ WINDOWS NT

Description	TB_ISBUTTONCHECKED is a toolbar message that determines whether a button in a toolbar is checked.
Parameters	
wParam	UINT: The command identifier of the button.
lParam	LPARAM: Set to zero.
Returns	int: A nonzero value is returned if the button is checked; otherwise, zero is returned.
Include File	commctrl.h
See Also	CreateToolbarEx()
Related Messages	TB_CHECKBUTTON, TB_GETSTATE
Example	See the example for the TB_CHECKBUTTON message.

TB_ISBUTTONENABLED ■ WIN32s ■ WINDOWS 95 ■ WINDOWS NT

Description	TB_ISBUTTONENABLED is a toolbar message that determines whether a button in a toolbar is enabled.
Parameters	
wParam	UINT: The command identifier of the button.
lParam	LPARAM: Set to zero.
Returns	int: A nonzero value is returned if the button is enabled; otherwise, zero is returned.
Include File	commctrl.h
See Also	CreateToolbarEx()
Related Messages	TB_ENABLEBUTTON, TB_GETSTATE
Example	See the example for the TB_ENABLEBUTTON message.

TB_ISBUTTONHIDDEN ■ WIN32s ■ WINDOWS 95 ■ WINDOWS NT

Description	TB_ISBUTTONHIDDEN is a toolbar message that determines whether a button in a toolbar is hidden.
Parameters	
wParam	UINT: The command identifier of the button.
lParam	LPARAM: Set to zero.
Returns	int: A nonzero value is returned if the button is hidden; otherwise, zero is returned.
Include File	commctrl.h

See Also	CreateToolbarEx()
Related Messages	TB_HIDEBUTTON, TB_GETSTATE
Example	See the example for the TB_HIDEBUTTON message.

TB_ISBUTTONINDETERMINATE ■ Win32s ■ Windows 95 ■ Windows NT

Description	TB_ISBUTTONINDETERMINATE is a toolbar message that determines whether a button in a toolbar is indeterminate.
Parameters	
wParam	UINT: The command identifier of the button.
lParam	LPARAM: Set to zero.
Returns	int: A nonzero value is returned if the button is indeterminate; otherwise, zero is returned.
Include File	commctrl.h
See Also	CreateToolbarEx()
Related Messages	TB_INDETERMINATE, TB_GETSTATE
Example	See the example for the TB_INDETERMINATE message.

TB_ISBUTTONPRESSED ■ Win32s ■ Windows 95 ■ Windows NT

Description	TB_ISBUTTONPRESSED is a toolbar message that determines whether a button in a toolbar is pressed.
Parameters	
wParam	UINT: The command identifier of the button.
lParam	LPARAM: Set to zero.
Returns	int: A nonzero value is returned if the button is pressed; otherwise, zero is returned.
Include File	commctrl.h
See Also	CreateToolbarEx()
Related Messages	TB_PRESSBUTTON, TB_GETSTATE
Example	See the example for the TB_PRESSBUTTON message.

TB_PRESSBUTTON ■ Win32s ■ Windows 95 ■ Windows NT

Description	TB_PRESSBUTTON is a toolbar message that presses or releases a button in a toolbar.
Parameters	
wParam	UINT: The command identifier of the button to press or release.

lParam	BOOL: If this parameter is TRUE, the button is pressed. If it is FALSE, the button is released.
Returns	BOOL: If successful, TRUE is returned; otherwise, FALSE is returned.
Include File	commctrl.h
See Also	CreateToolbarEx()
Related Messages	TB_ISBUTTONPRESSED, TB_GETSTATE
Example	This example, shown in Listing 3-26, demonstrates the use of the TB_PRESSBUTTON and TB_ISBUTTONPRESSED messages. When the user selects the corresponding menu item for a button, it is either set to pressed or unpressed depending on the current state of the button.

Listing 3-26 Using the TB_PRESSBUTTON message

```
// Toolbar buttons.
//................
TBBUTTON tbButtons[] =
{
    { 0, IDM_TEST1, TBSTATE_ENABLED, TBSTYLE_BUTTON, 0, 0L, 0},
    { 1, IDM_TEST2, TBSTATE_ENABLED, TBSTYLE_BUTTON, 0, 0L, 0},
    { 2, IDM_TEST3, TBSTATE_ENABLED, TBSTYLE_BUTTON, 0, 0L, 0},
    { 3, IDM_TEST4, TBSTATE_ENABLED, TBSTYLE_BUTTON, 0, 0L, 0},
};

LRESULT CALLBACK WndProc( HWND hWnd, UINT uMsg, WPARAM wParam, LPARAM lParam )
{
static HWND hToolWnd   = NULL;

   switch( uMsg )
   {
      case WM_COMMAND :
             switch( LOWORD( wParam ) )
             {
                case IDM_TESTMENU1 :
                case IDM_TESTMENU2 :
                case IDM_TESTMENU3 :
                case IDM_TESTMENU4 :
                      {
                      BOOL bPressed;

                      bPressed = SendMessage( hToolWnd,
                                     TB_ISBUTTONPRESSED,
                                     LOWORD( wParam )-IDM_TOOLBASE,
                                     0 );

                      // Press/Unpress the toolbar button.
                      //...............................
                      SendMessage(hToolWnd, TB_PRESSBUTTON,
                               LOWORD( wParam )-IDM_TOOLBASE,
                               !bPressed );
                      }
                      break;
      .
      .
      .
```

TB_SAVERESTORE
■ Win32s ■ Windows 95 ■ Windows NT

Description	TB_SAVERESTORE is a toolbar message that saves or restores the state of the toolbar. The toolbar state is stored in the registry in the location defined by the provided TBSAVEPARAMS structure.
Parameters	
wParam	BOOL: If this parameter is TRUE, the information is saved. If it is FALSE, it is restored.
lParam	TBSAVEPARAMS*: A pointer to a TBSAVEPARAMS structure that specifies the registry key, subkey, and value name for the toolbar state information. See the definition of the TBSAVEPARAMS structure below.
Include File	commctrl.h
See Also	CreateToolbarEx()

TBSAVEPARAMS Definition

```
typedef struct
{
    HKEY    hkr;
    LPCTSTR pszSubKey;
    LPCTSTR pszValueName;
} TBSAVEPARAMS;
```

Members	
hkr	HKEY: A handle to the registry key. This member may be one of the predefined registry keys (HKEY_CLASSES_ROOT, HKEY_CURRENT_USER, HKEY_LOCAL_MACHINE, or HKEY_USERS) or a registry key obtained by the application.
pszSubKey	LPCTSTR: A pointer to a null-terminated string containing the subkey name.
pszValueName	LPCTSTR: A pointer to a null-terminated string containing the value name.
Example	See the example for the TB_CUSTOMIZE message.

TB_SETBITMAPSIZE
■ Win32s ■ Windows 95 ■ Windows NT

Description	TB_SETBITMAPSIZE is a toolbar message that sets the size of the bitmapped images to be added to a toolbar. This message can only be used prior to adding bitmaps to the toolbar. If an application does not explicitly set the bitmap size, the size defaults to 16 by 15 pixels.
Parameters	
wParam	WPARAM: Set to zero.
LOWORD(lParam)	WORD: The width, in pixels, of the bitmapped images.
HIWORD(lParam)	WORD: The height, in pixels, of the bitmapped images.
Returns	BOOL: If successful, TRUE is returned; otherwise, FALSE is returned.
Include File	commctrl.h

See Also	CreateToolbarEx()
Related Messages	TB_ADDBITMAP, TB_SETBUTTONSIZE
Example	See the example for the TB_SETBUTTONSIZE message.

TB_SETBUTTONSIZE   ■ Win32s   ■ Windows 95   ■ Windows NT

Description	TB_SETBUTTONSIZE is a toolbar message that sets the size of the buttons to be added to a toolbar. This message can only be used prior to adding buttons to the toolbar. If an application does not explicitly set the button size, the size defaults to 24 by 22 pixels.
Parameters	
wParam	WPARAM: Set to zero.
LOWORD(*lParam*)	WORD: The width, in pixels, of the buttons.
HIWORD(*lParam*)	WORD: The height, in pixels, of the buttons.
Returns	BOOL: If successful, TRUE is returned; otherwise, FALSE is returned.
Include File	commctrl.h
See Also	CreateToolbarEx()
Related Messages	TB_ADDBUTTONS
Example	This example, shown in Listing 3-27, demonstrates the TB_SETBUTTONSIZE and TB_SETBITMAPSIZE messages to set the bitmap and button size for a toolbar to a nonstandard size.

Listing 3-27 Using the TB_SETBUTTONSIZE message

```
// Toolbar buttons.
//................
TBBUTTON tbButtons[] =
{
    { 0, IDM_TEST1, TBSTATE_ENABLED, TBSTYLE_BUTTON, 0, 0L, 0},
    { 1, IDM_TEST2, TBSTATE_ENABLED, TBSTYLE_BUTTON, 0, 0L, 0},
    { 2, IDM_TEST3, TBSTATE_ENABLED, TBSTYLE_BUTTON, 0, 0L, 0},
    { 3, IDM_TEST4, TBSTATE_ENABLED, TBSTYLE_BUTTON, 0, 0L, 0},
};

LRESULT CALLBACK WndProc( HWND hWnd, UINT uMsg, WPARAM wParam, LPARAM lParam )
{
static HWND hToolWnd   = NULL;

   switch( uMsg )
   {
      case WM_CREATE :
              // Initialize the common control library
              // and create the toolbar.
              //.......................................
              InitCommonControls();

              hToolWnd = CreateWindowEx( 0, TOOLBARCLASSNAME, NULL,
                                WS_CHILD | WS_BORDER | WS_VISIBLE,
```

continued on next page

continued from previous page

```
                                 0, 0, 0, 0, hWnd, (HMENU)101,
                                 hInst, NULL);

        if ( hToolWnd )
        {
            HBITMAP     hBmp;
            TBADDBITMAP tb;
            int index, stdidx;

            // Set the size of the TBBUTTON structure.
            //.......................................
            SendMessage(hToolWnd, TB_BUTTONSTRUCTSIZE,
                        sizeof(TBBUTTON), 0);

            // Set the button and bitmap size.
            //...............................
            SendMessage(hToolWnd, TB_SETBUTTONSIZE, 0, MAKELPARAM(30,30 ));
            SendMessage(hToolWnd, TB_SETBITMAPSIZE, 0, MAKELPARAM(20,20 ));

            // Load bitmap to add to the toolbar.
            //..................................
            hBmp = CreateMappedBitmap( hInst, 100, 0, NULL, 0 );

            tb.hInst = NULL;
            tb.nID   = (UINT) hBmp;
            stdidx = SendMessage(hToolWnd, TB_ADDBITMAP, 4, (LPARAM)&tb);

            for (index = 0; index < 4; index++)
                tbButtons[index].iBitmap += stdidx;

            // Add the buttons to the toolbar.
            //...............................
            SendMessage(hToolWnd, TB_ADDBUTTONS, 4, (LONG) &tbButtons[0]);

            // Force the toolbar to size itself.
            //.................................
            SendMessage(hToolWnd, WM_SIZE, 0, 0 );
        }
        break;
            .
            .
            .
```

TB_SETCMDID   ■ Win32s   ■ Windows 95   ■ Windows NT

Description	TB_SETCMDID is a toolbar message that changes the command identifier of a toolbar button.
Parameters	
wParam	UINT: The zero-based index of the button whose command identifier is to be set.
lParam	UINT: The new command identifier.
Returns	BOOL: If successful, TRUE is returned; otherwise, FALSE is returned.
Include File	commctrl.h

See Also	CreateToolbarEx()
Example	This example, shown in Listing 3-28, uses the TB_SETCMDID message to change the command identifier of the second button to IDM_TEST4 when the user selects the Test! menu item.

Listing 3-28 Using the TB_SETCMDID message

```
// Toolbar buttons.
//.................
TBBUTTON tbButtons[] =
{
    { 0, IDM_TEST1, TBSTATE_ENABLED, TBSTYLE_BUTTON, 0, 0L, 0},
    { 1, IDM_TEST2, TBSTATE_ENABLED, TBSTYLE_BUTTON, 0, 0L, 0},
    { 2, IDM_TEST3, TBSTATE_ENABLED, TBSTYLE_BUTTON, 0, 0L, 0},
    { 3, IDM_TEST4, TBSTATE_ENABLED, TBSTYLE_BUTTON, 0, 0L, 0},
};


LRESULT CALLBACK WndProc( HWND hWnd, UINT uMsg, WPARAM wParam, LPARAM lParam )
{
static HWND hToolWnd   = NULL;

   switch( uMsg )
   {
      case WM_COMMAND :
              switch( LOWORD( wParam ) )
              {
                 case IDM_TEST1 :
                         MessageBox(hWnd, "Button1", lpszTitle, MB_OK);
                         break;

                 case IDM_TEST2 :
                         MessageBox(hWnd, "Button2", lpszTitle, MB_OK);
                         break;

                 case IDM_TEST3 :
                         MessageBox(hWnd, "Button3", lpszTitle, MB_OK);
                         break;

                 case IDM_TEST4 :
                         MessageBox(hWnd, "Button4", lpszTitle, MB_OK);
                         break;

                 case IDM_TEST :
                         SendMessage(hToolWnd, TB_SETCMDID, 1, IDM_TEST4);
                         break;
         .
         .
         .
```

TB_SETPARENT   ■ WIN32S   ■ WINDOWS 95   ■ WINDOWS NT

Description	TB_SETPARENT is a toolbar message that sets the parent window for a toolbar.

In the version of the Common Control Library that shipped with Windows 95, this message does not work. An application can use the SetParent() function to accomplish the desired result.

Parameters

wParam   HWND: The window handle of the new parent window.

lParam   LPARAM: Set to zero.

Include File   commctrl.h

See Also   CreateToolbarEx()

Example   This example, shown in Listing 3-29, creates a toolbar on the parent window. When the user selects the Test! menu item, a child window is created without a toolbar, and the SetParent() function is used to change the parent window of the toolbar to the new child window. The TB_SETPARENT message is also sent; however, there is no effect.

Listing 3-29 Using the TB_SETPARENT message

```
LRESULT CALLBACK WndProc( HWND hWnd, UINT uMsg, WPARAM wParam, LPARAM lParam )
{
static HWND hToolWnd   = NULL;
static HWND hChildWnd  = NULL;

   switch( uMsg )
   {
      case WM_CREATE :
              // Initialize the common control library
              // and create the status window and toolbar.
              //..........................................
              InitCommonControls();

              hToolWnd = CreateToolbarEx( hWnd,
                                 WS_CHILD | WS_BORDER | WS_VISIBLE,
                                 102,
                                 11,
                                 (HINSTANCE)HINST_COMMCTRL,
                                 IDB_STD_SMALL_COLOR,
                                 tbButtons, 4,
                                 0, 0, 100, 30, sizeof(TBBUTTON) );

              if ( hToolWnd )
              {
                 HBITMAP       hBmp;
                 TBADDBITMAP tb;
                 int index, stdidx;

                 // Add the system-defined view bitmaps.
                 //.....................................
                 tb.hInst = HINST_COMMCTRL;
                 tb.nID = IDB_VIEW_SMALL_COLOR;
                 stdidx = SendMessage( hToolWnd, TB_ADDBITMAP,
                                     12, (LPARAM)&tb );

                 // Update the indices to the bitmaps.
                 //...................................
```

```
              for (index = 4; index < 8; index++)
                 tbButtons[index].iBitmap += stdidx;

              // Add the view buttons.
              //.....................
              SendMessage( hToolWnd, TB_ADDBUTTONS, 4,
                         (LONG) &tbButtons[4] );
          }
          break;

   case WM_COMMAND :
          switch( LOWORD( wParam ) )
          {
          case IDM_TEST :
                  if ( !hChildWnd )
                  {
                      // Create child window and associate the
                      // toolbar with it.
                      //.......................................
                      hChildWnd = CreateWindow( lpszAppName,
                                     "Child Window",
                                     WS_OVERLAPPEDWINDOW,
                                     CW_USEDEFAULT, 0,
                                     CW_USEDEFAULT, 0,
                                     hWnd,
                                     NULL,
                                     hInst,
                                     NULL );

                      // This call does not work, BUG in Common Control Library!
                      //.......................................................
                      SendMessage( hToolWnd, TB_SETPARENT, (WPARAM)hChildWnd, 0 );

                      // This call does work!
                      //....................
                      SetParent( hToolWnd, hChildWnd );

                      ShowWindow( hChildWnd, SW_NORMAL );
                  }
                  break;
      .
      .
      .
```

TB_SETROWS   ■ WIN32S   ■ WINDOWS 95   ■ WINDOWS NT

Description	TB_SETROWS is a toolbar message that sets the number of rows of buttons in a toolbar. Because the system does not break up button groups when setting the number of rows, the resulting number of rows might differ from the number requested.

Parameters

LOWORD(wParam)   WORD: The number of requested rows. The minimum number of rows is one, and the maximum is equal to the number of buttons in the toolbar.

HIWORD(wParam)	BOOL: Indicates whether to create more rows than requested when the system cannot create the requested number of rows. If this parameter is TRUE, the system creates more rows. If it is FALSE, the system creates fewer rows.
lParam	LPRECT: A pointer to a RECT structure that receives the bounding rectangle of the toolbar after the rows are set.
Include File	commctrl.h
See Also	CreateToolbarEx()
Related Messages	TB_GETROWS
Example	This example, shown in Listing 3-30, uses the TB_SETROWS message to wrap the toolbar buttons as the window is sized. If the window is sized to a width that does not allow all the buttons to be displayed, two rows are created for the toolbar. If the window is resized to again allow it to display all the buttons on a single row, the number of rows is set to one.

Listing 3-30 Using the TB_SETROWS message

```
// Toolbar buttons.
//.................
TBBUTTON tbButtons[] =
{
  { STD_FILENEW,  IDM_NEW, TBSTATE_ENABLED, TBSTYLE_BUTTON, 0, 0L, 0},
  { STD_FILEOPEN, IDM_OPEN, TBSTATE_ENABLED, TBSTYLE_BUTTON, 0, 0L, 0},
  { STD_FILESAVE, IDM_SAVE, TBSTATE_ENABLED, TBSTYLE_BUTTON, 0, 0L, 0},
  { 0, 0, TBSTATE_ENABLED, TBSTYLE_SEP, 0, 0L, 0},
  { VIEW_LARGEICONS, IDM_LARGEICON, TBSTATE_ENABLED, TBSTYLE_BUTTON, 0, 0L, 0},
  { VIEW_SMALLICONS, IDM_SMALLICON, TBSTATE_ENABLED, TBSTYLE_BUTTON, 0, 0L, 0},
  { VIEW_LIST, IDM_LISTVIEW, TBSTATE_ENABLED, TBSTYLE_BUTTON, 0, 0L, 0},
  { VIEW_DETAILS, IDM_REPORTVIEW, TBSTATE_ENABLED, TBSTYLE_BUTTON, 0, 0L, 0},
};

LRESULT CALLBACK WndProc( HWND hWnd, UINT uMsg, WPARAM wParam, LPARAM lParam )
{
static HWND hToolWnd   = NULL;

   switch( uMsg )
   {
      case WM_CREATE :
              if ( !hToolWnd )
              {

                  // Initialize the common control library
                  // and create the status window and toolbar.
                  //..........................................
                  InitCommonControls();

                  hToolWnd = CreateToolbarEx( hWnd,
                                          WS_CHILD | WS_BORDER |
                                          WS_VISIBLE | TBSTYLE_WRAPABLE,
                                          102,
                                          11,
                                          (HINSTANCE)HINST_COMMCTRL,
```

```
                                        IDB_STD_SMALL_COLOR,
                                        tbButtons, 4,
                                        0, 0, 100, 30, sizeof(TBBUTTON) );

            if ( hToolWnd )
            {
                TBADDBITMAP tb;
                int index, stdidx;

                // Add the system-defined view bitmaps.
                //....................................
                tb.hInst = HINST_COMMCTRL;
                tb.nID = IDB_VIEW_SMALL_COLOR;
                stdidx = SendMessage(hToolWnd, TB_ADDBITMAP,
                                     12, (LPARAM)&tb);

                // Update the indices to the bitmaps.
                //...................................
                for (index = 4; index < 8; index++)
                    tbButtons[index].iBitmap += stdidx;

                // Add the view buttons.
                //.....................
                SendMessage(hToolWnd, TB_ADDBUTTONS, 4,
                            (LONG) &tbButtons[4]);
            }
        }
        break;

    case WM_SIZE :
        {
            RECT rect;

            // Size the toolbar and wrap the buttons if necessary.
            //....................................................
            SendMessage( hToolWnd, TB_GETITEMRECT, 7, (LPARAM)&rect );

            if ( rect.right > LOWORD(lParam) )
                SendMessage(hToolWnd, TB_SETROWS, MAKEWPARAM(2, TRUE), 0);
            else if ( SendMessage( hToolWnd, TB_GETROWS, 0, 0 ) > 1 )
                SendMessage(hToolWnd, TB_SETROWS, MAKEWPARAM(1, FALSE), 0);

            SendMessage( hToolWnd, WM_SIZE, 0, 0 );
        }
        break;
        .
        .
        .
```

TB_SETSTATE   ■ WIN32S ■ WINDOWS 95 ■ WINDOWS NT

Description   TB_SETSTATE is a toolbar message that sets the state for a button in a
                  toolbar.

Parameters

wParam   UINT: The command identifier of the button.

lParam	UINT: The button state. This can be a combination of the values listed in Table 3-11 under the TB_GETSTATE message.
Returns	BOOL: If successful, TRUE is returned; otherwise, FALSE is returned.
Include File	commctrl.h
See Also	CreateToolbarEx()
Related Messages	TB_GETSTATE
Example	See the example for the TB_GETSTATE message.

TB_SETTOOLTIPS   ■ Win32s   ■ Windows 95   ■ Windows NT

Description	TB_SETTOOLTIPS is a toolbar message that associates a tooltip control with a toolbar.
Parameters	
wParam	HWND: The handle of the tooltip control.
lParam	LPARAM: Set to zero.
Include File	commctrl.h
See Also	CreateToolbarEx()
Related Messages	TB_GETTOOLTIPS
Example	This example, shown in Listing 3-31, creates a window with a toolbar and a tooltip control. The tooltip control is created with the CreateWindowEx() function and associated with the toolbar with the TB_SETTOOLTIPS message. As the user moves the mouse over the toolbar buttons, the tooltip control is displayed as shown in Figure 3-18.

Figure 3-18 TB_SETTOOLTIPS example

Listing 3-31 Using the TB_SETTOOLTIPS message

```
// Toolbar buttons.
//................
TBBUTTON tbButtons[] =
{
  { STD_FILENEW,  IDM_NEW, TBSTATE_ENABLED, TBSTYLE_BUTTON, 0, 0L, 0},
  { STD_FILEOPEN, IDM_OPEN, TBSTATE_ENABLED, TBSTYLE_BUTTON, 0, 0L, 0},
  { STD_FILESAVE, IDM_SAVE, TBSTATE_ENABLED, TBSTYLE_BUTTON, 0, 0L, 0},
  { 0, 0, TBSTATE_ENABLED, TBSTYLE_SEP, 0, 0L, 0},
  { VIEW_LARGEICONS, IDM_LARGEICON, TBSTATE_ENABLED, TBSTYLE_BUTTON, 0, 0L, 0},
  { VIEW_SMALLICONS, IDM_SMALLICON, TBSTATE_ENABLED, TBSTYLE_BUTTON, 0, 0L, 0},
```

```
   { VIEW_LIST, IDM_LISTVIEW, TBSTATE_ENABLED, TBSTYLE_BUTTON, 0, 0L, 0},
   { VIEW_DETAILS, IDM_REPORTVIEW, TBSTATE_ENABLED, TBSTYLE_BUTTON, 0, 0L, 0},
};

LRESULT CALLBACK WndProc( HWND hWnd, UINT uMsg, WPARAM wParam, LPARAM lParam )
{
static char    szTmp[80];
static LPTSTR  lpch;
static HWND    hToolWnd  = NULL;
static HWND    hToolTip  = NULL;

   switch( uMsg )
   {
      case WM_CREATE :
             if ( !hToolWnd )
             {

                // Initialize the common control library
                // and create the status window and toolbar.
                //.........................................
                InitCommonControls();

                hToolWnd = CreateToolbarEx( hWnd,
                                    WS_CHILD | WS_BORDER |
                                    WS_VISIBLE,
                                    102,
                                    11,
                                    (HINSTANCE)HINST_COMMCTRL,
                                    IDB_STD_SMALL_COLOR,
                                    tbButtons, 4,
                                    0, 0, 100, 30, sizeof(TBBUTTON) );

                if ( hToolWnd )
                {
                    TOOLINFO    ti;
                    TBADDBITMAP tb;
                    int index, stdidx;

                    // Add the system-defined view bitmaps.
                    //....................................
                    tb.hInst = HINST_COMMCTRL;
                    tb.nID = IDB_VIEW_SMALL_COLOR;
                    stdidx = SendMessage(hToolWnd, TB_ADDBITMAP,
                                    12, (LPARAM)&tb);

                    // Update the indices to the bitmaps.
                    //....................................
                    for (index = 4; index < 8; index++)
                        tbButtons[index].iBitmap += stdidx;

                    // Add the view buttons.
                    //....................
                    SendMessage(hToolWnd, TB_ADDBUTTONS, 4,
                                (LONG) &tbButtons[4]);

                    // Create tooltip control.
                    //....................
                    hToolTip = CreateWindowEx( 0,
                                        TOOLTIPS_CLASS, NULL,
```

continued on next page

153

continued from previous page

```
                                    TTS_ALWAYSTIP,
                                    CW_USEDEFAULT,
                                    CW_USEDEFAULT,
                                    CW_USEDEFAULT,
                                    CW_USEDEFAULT,
                                    hWnd, NULL,
                                    hInst, NULL );

            // Add the tools to the tooltip control.
            //...................................
            ti.cbSize = sizeof( TOOLINFO );
            ti.hwnd   = hToolWnd;
            ti.hinst  = hInst;
            ti.uFlags = TTF_SUBCLASS;

            for( index=0; index < 8; index++ )
            {
                if ( index == 3 )
                    continue;

                SendMessage( hToolWnd, TB_GETITEMRECT,
                            index, (LPARAM)&ti.rect );

                ti.uId      = tbButtons[index].idCommand;
                ti.lpszText = (LPTSTR)tbButtons[index].idCommand;

                SendMessage( hToolTip, TTM_ADDTOOL, 0, (LPARAM)&ti );
            }

            // Set the tooltip control as
            // part of the toolbar.
            //.........................
            SendMessage( hToolWnd, TB_SETTOOLTIPS,
                        (WPARAM)hToolTip, 0 );
        }
    }
    break;
```

.
.
.

TTM_ACTIVATE   ■ Win32s   ■ Windows 95   ■ Windows NT

Description	TTM_ACTIVATE is a tooltip message that activates or deactivates a tooltip control. A tooltip normally is displayed when the mouse cursor is over a tool. When a tooltip is activated, it will show when the cursor is over the tool. When it is deactivated, the tooltip will not display even when the cursor is over the tool.
Parameters	
wParam	BOOL: If this parameter is TRUE, the tooltip control is activated. If it is FALSE, the tooltip control is deactivated.
lParam	WPARAM: Set to zero.
Include File	commctrl.h

See Also	CreateWindowEx()
Example	This example, shown in Listing 3-32, is the same as the example for the TB_SETTOOLTIPS message, except that when the user selects the Activate menu item, the tooltips are deactivated. When the user selects Activate again, they are reactivated.

Listing 3-32 Using the TTM_ACTIVATE message

```
LRESULT CALLBACK WndProc( HWND hWnd, UINT uMsg, WPARAM wParam, LPARAM lParam )
{
static HWND    hToolWnd    = NULL;
static HWND    hToolTip    = NULL;
static BOOL    bActivate   = TRUE;

   switch( uMsg )
   {
      case WM_COMMAND :
             switch( LOWORD( wParam ) )
             {
                case IDM_ACTIVATE :
                      // Activate/Deactivate the tooltip control.
                      //........................................
                      bActivate = !bActivate;
                      SendMessage( hToolTip, TTM_ACTIVATE, bActivate, 0 );
                      break;
         .
         .
         .
```

TTM_ADDTOOL ■ Win32s   ■ Windows 95   ■ Windows NT

Description	TTM_ADDTOOL is a tooltip message that registers a tool with a tooltip control.
Parameters	
wParam	WPARAM: Set to zero.
lParam	LPTOOLINFO: A pointer to a TOOLINFO structure that contains the information the tooltip control needs to display text for the tool. See the definition of the TOOLINFO structure below.
Returns	BOOL: If successful, TRUE is returned; otherwise, FALSE is returned.
Include File	commctrl.h
See Also	CreateWindowEx()
Related Messages	TTM_DELTOOL, TTN_NEEDTEXT
TOOLINFO Definition	

```
typedef struct
{
    UINT      cbSize;
    UINT      uFlags;
    HWND      hwnd;
```

continued on next page

continued from previous page

```
        UINT      uId;
        RECT      rect;
        HINSTANCE hinst;
        LPTSTR    lpszText;
} TOOLINFO, *LPTOOLINFO;
```

Members

cbSize   UINT: The size, in bytes, of the TOOLINFO structure. This member must be initialized before it is used in the TTM_ADDTOOL message.

uFlags   UINT: This member can be a combination of the values listed in Table 3-12 combined with the binary OR (|) operator.

Table 3-12 TOOLINFO *uFlags* values

Value	Meaning
TTF_CENTERTIP	Centers the tooltip window below the tool specified by the *uId* member.
TTF_IDISHWND	The *uId* member is the window handle to the tool. If this flag is not set, *uId* is the identifier of the tool.
TTF_RTLREADING	Displays text using right-to-left reading order on Hebrew or Arabic systems. This flag is only valid for Windows 95.
TTF_SUBCLASS	The tooltip control should subclass the tool's window to intercept messages, such as WM_MOUSEMOVE. If not set, you need to use the TTM_RELAYEVENT message to forward messages to the tooltip control. For a list of messages that a tooltip control processes, see the TTM_RELAYEVENT message.

hwnd   HWND: The handle of the window that contains the tool. If *lpszText* is set to the LPSTR_TEXTCALLBACK value, this member identifies the window that receives TTN_NEEDTEXT notification messages.

uId   UINT: The application-defined identifier of the tool. If *uFlags* includes the TTF_IDISHWND value, *uId* must specify the window handle to the tool.

rect   RECT: The coordinates of the bounding rectangle of the tool. The coordinates are relative to the upper left corner of the client area of the window identified by the *hwnd* member. If *uFlags* includes the TTF_IDISHWND value, this member is ignored.

hinst   HINSTANCE: The instance handle of the module that contains the string resource for the tool. If *lpszText* specifies the identifier of a string resource, this member is used.

lpszText   LPTSTR: A pointer to the buffer that contains the text for the tool, or the identifier of the string resource that contains the text. If this member is set to the LPSTR_TEXTCALLBACK value, the control sends the TTN_NEEDTEXT notification message to the owner window to retrieve the text.

Example   See the example for the TB_SETTOOLTIPS message.

TTM_DELTOOL

■ WIN32s ■ WINDOWS 95 ■ WINDOWS NT

Description   TTM_DELTOOL is a tooltip message that removes a tool from a tooltip control.

Parameters

wParam   WPARAM: Set to zero.

lParam   LPTOOLINFO: A pointer to a TOOLINFO structure. The *hwnd* and *uId* members identify the tool to remove. The *cbSize* member must also be initialized. See the definition of the TOOLINFO structure under the TTM_ADDTOOL message.

Include File   commctrl.h

See Also   CreateWindowEx()

Related Messages   TTM_ADDTOOL

Example   This example, shown in Listing 3-33, is the same as the example for the TB_SETTOOLTIPS message, except that when the user selects the Test! menu item, the File↓New toolbar button is deleted and the tool is deleted from the tooltip with the TTM_DELTOOL message.

Listing 3-33 Using the TTM_DELTOOL message

```
LRESULT CALLBACK WndProc( HWND hWnd, UINT uMsg, WPARAM wParam, LPARAM lParam )
{
static HWND    hToolWnd   = NULL;
static HWND    hToolTip   = NULL;

   switch( uMsg )
   {
      case WM_COMMAND :
            switch( LOWORD( wParam ) )
            {
               case IDM_TEST :
                     {
                        TOOLINFO ti;

                        // Delete the File/New button.
                        //............................
                        SendMessage( hToolWnd, TB_DELETEBUTTON, 0, 0 );

                        // Remove the tool from the tooltip.
                        //.................................
                        ti.cbSize = sizeof( TOOLINFO );
                        ti.hwnd   = hToolWnd;
                        ti.uId    = STD_FILENEW;
                        SendMessage( hToolTip, TTM_DELTOOL, 0, (LPARAM)&ti );
                     }
                     break;
                  .
                  .
                  .
```

157

TTM_ENUMTOOLS

■ Win32s ■ Windows 95 ■ Windows NT

Description   TTM_ENUMTOOLS is a tooltip message that retrieves the information that a tooltip control maintains about a given tool. The application can use this message to enumerate all the tools by repeatedly sending the message and incrementing the index of the tool.

Parameters

wParam   UINT: The zero-based index of the tool for which to retrieve information.

lParam   LPTOOLINFO: A pointer to a TOOLINFO structure that receives information about the tool. Before sending this message, the *cbSize* member must specify the size of the structure. See the definition of the TOOLINFO structure under the TTM_ADDTOOL message.

Returns   BOOL: If successful, TRUE is returned; otherwise, FALSE is returned.

Include File   commctrl.h

See Also   CreateWindowEx()

Related Messages   TTM_GETCURRENTTOOL

Example   This example, shown in Figure 3-19 and Listing 3-34, divides the client area into four parts that are added to a tooltip control. As the user resizes the window, the size of the sections is changed to completely fill the client area of the window. When processing the WM_SIZE message, the TTM_ENUMTOOLS message is used to enumerate the tools for the tooltip, and the TTM_SETTOOLINFO message is used to change the tool rectangle. When processing the WM_PAINT message, the TTM_ENUM-TOOLS message is used to retrieve each of the tool's rectangles. This example also uses the TTM_RELAYEVENT message to pass mouse messages on to the tooltip control.

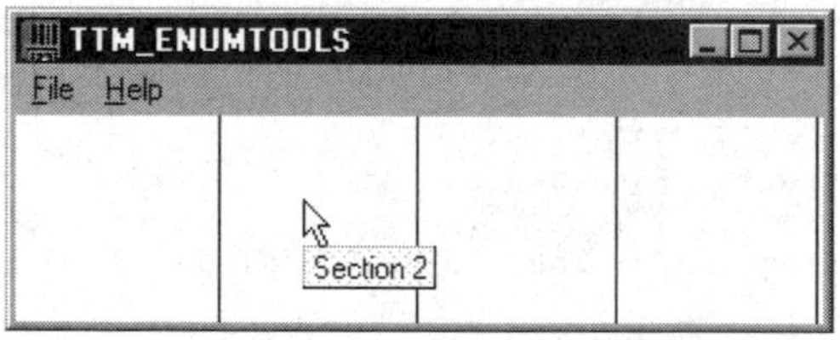

Figure 3-19 TTM_ENUMTOOLS example

Listing 3-34 Using the TTM_ENUMTOOLS message

```
LRESULT CALLBACK WndProc( HWND hWnd, UINT uMsg, WPARAM wParam, LPARAM lParam )
{
static MSG        msg;
static TOOLINFO   ti;
static int        index;
static HWND       hToolTip = NULL;
```

```
switch( uMsg )
{
    case WM_LBUTTONDOWN :
    case WM_MOUSEMOVE   :
    case WM_LBUTTONUP   :
    case WM_RBUTTONDOWN :
    case WM_MBUTTONDOWN :
    case WM_RBUTTONUP   :
    case WM_MBUTTONUP   :
            msg.hwnd    = hWnd;
            msg.message = uMsg;
            msg.wParam  = wParam;
            msg.lParam  = lParam;
            msg.time    = GetMessageTime();
            msg.pt.x    = LOWORD(GetMessagePos());
            msg.pt.y    = HIWORD(GetMessagePos());

            SendMessage( hToolTip, TTM_RELAYEVENT, 0, (LPARAM)&msg );
            break;
}

switch( uMsg )
{
    case WM_CREATE :
            {
                InitCommonControls();

                // Create tooltip control.
                //.....................
                hToolTip = CreateWindowEx( 0,
                                           TOOLTIPS_CLASS, NULL,
                                           TTS_ALWAYSTIP,
                                           CW_USEDEFAULT,
                                           CW_USEDEFAULT,
                                           CW_USEDEFAULT,
                                           CW_USEDEFAULT,
                                           hWnd, NULL,
                                           hInst, NULL );

                // Add the tools to the tooltip control.
                //......................................
                ti.cbSize = sizeof( TOOLINFO );
                ti.hwnd   = hWnd;
                ti.hinst  = NULL;

                for( index=0; index < 4; index++ )
                {
                    ti.uId      = index;
                    ti.lpszText = LPSTR_TEXTCALLBACK;

                    ti.rect.top    = 0;
                    ti.rect.bottom = 10;
                    ti.rect.left   = 10*index;
                    ti.rect.right  = 10*(index+1);

                    SendMessage( hToolTip, TTM_ADDTOOL, 0, (LPARAM)&ti );
                }
            }
            break;
```

continued on next page

continued from previous page

```
case WM_SIZE :
        {
            // Adjust the tool rectangles for the new section size.
            //.......................................
            RECT        rect;

            index = 0;

            ti.cbSize = sizeof( TOOLINFO );

            GetClientRect( hWnd, &rect );

            while ( SendMessage( hToolTip, TTM_ENUMTOOLS,
                    index, (LPARAM)&ti ) )
            {
                ti.rect.top    = 0;
                ti.rect.bottom = HIWORD( lParam );
                ti.rect.left   = (rect.right/4)*index;
                ti.rect.right  = (rect.right/4)*(index+1);

                SendMessage( hToolTip, TTM_SETTOOLINFO, index,
                            (LPARAM)&ti );

                index++;
            }
        }
        break;

case WM_PAINT  :
        {
            // Paint the vertical lines to denote the sections.
            //..............................................
            PAINTSTRUCT ps;

            index = 0;

            BeginPaint( hWnd, &ps );

            while ( SendMessage( hToolTip, TTM_ENUMTOOLS,
                    index, (LPARAM)&ti ) )
            {
                MoveToEx( ps.hdc, ti.rect.right, ti.rect.top, NULL );
                LineTo( ps.hdc, ti.rect.right, ti.rect.bottom );
                index++;
            }

            EndPaint( hWnd, &ps );
        }
        break;

case WM_NOTIFY :
        switch ( ((LPNMHDR)lParam)->code )
        {
            case TTN_NEEDTEXT :
                wsprintf( ((LPTOOLTIPTEXT)lParam)->szText,
                        "Section %d",
                        ((LPTOOLTIPTEXT)lParam)->hdr.idFrom+1 );
                break;
        }
```

```
        break;
  .
  .
  .
```

TTM_GETCURRENTTOOL
■ WIN32s ■ WINDOWS 95 ■ WINDOWS NT

Description	TTM_GETCURRENTTOOL is a tooltip message that retrieves the information that a tooltip control maintains about the current tool. The current tool is the tool for which the tooltip is currently displaying text.
Parameters	
wParam	WPARAM: Set to zero.
lParam	LPTOOLINFO: A pointer to a TOOLINFO structure that receives information about the current tool. Before sending this message, the *cbSize* member must specify the size of the structure. See the definition of the TOOLINFO structure under the TTM_ADDTOOL message.
Returns	BOOL: If successful, TRUE is returned; otherwise, FALSE is returned.
Include File	commctrl.h
See Also	CreateWindowEx()
Related Messages	TTM_ENUMTOOLS
Example	This example, shown in Listing 3-35, demonstrates how to use the TTM_GETCURRENTTOOL message when processing the TTN_SHOW notification code to retrieve the information for the tool that is currently displayed.

Listing 3-35 *Using the TTM_GETCURRENTTOOL message*

```
LRESULT CALLBACK WndProc( HWND hWnd, UINT uMsg, WPARAM wParam, LPARAM lParam )
{
static TOOLINFO ti;
static HWND     hToolTip = NULL;

   switch( uMsg )
   {
      case WM_NOTIFY :
              switch ( ((LPNMHDR)lParam)->code )
              {
                 case TTN_SHOW :
                       ti.cbSize = sizeof( TOOLINFO );
                       SendMessage( hToolTip, TTM_GETCURRENTTOOL, 0,
                                 (LPARAM)&ti );

                       // Use the tool information

                       break;

                 case TTN_NEEDTEXT :
                       wsprintf( ((LPTOOLTIPTEXT)lParam)->szText,
```

continued on next page

continued from previous page

```
                                "Section %d",
                                ((LPTOOLTIPTEXT)lParam)->hdr.idFrom+1 );
                break;
            }
            break;
        .
        .
        .
```

TTM_GETTEXT

■ WIN32S   ■ WINDOWS 95   ■ WINDOWS NT

Description	TTM_GETTEXT is a tooltip message that retrieves the text that a tooltip control maintains for a tool.
Parameters	
wParam	WPARAM: Set to zero.
lParam	LPTOOLINFO: A pointer to a TOOLINFO structure. When sending the message, the *hwnd* and *uId* members identify the tool. If the tooltip control includes the tool, the *lpszText* member receives the pointer to the string. Before sending this message, the *cbSize* member must specify the size of the structure. See the definition of the TOOLINFO structure under the TTM_ADDTOOL message.
Include File	commctrl.h
See Also	TTM_ADDTOOL
Example	This example, shown in Listing 3-36, uses the TTM_ENUMTOOLS message to enumerate the tools for a toolbar and the TTM_GETTEXT message to retrieve the button tip text when the user selects the Test! menu item. Because the tooltip text is actually a resource string identifier, the tip text is loaded with the LoadString() function. The tip text is added to the list box that is created on the client area of the window.

Listing 3-36 Using the TTM_GETTEXT message

```
LRESULT CALLBACK WndProc( HWND hWnd, UINT uMsg, WPARAM wParam, LPARAM lParam )
{
static HWND hToolWnd = NULL;
static HWND hToolTip = NULL;
static HWND hList    = NULL;

    switch( uMsg )
    {
        case WM_COMMAND :
                switch( LOWORD( wParam ) )
                {
                    case IDM_TEST :
                        {
                            TOOLINFO ti;
                            char     szTmp[64];
                            int      nIndex = 0;
```

```
        ti.cbSize = sizeof( TOOLINFO );

        while ( SendMessage( hToolTip, TTM_ENUMTOOLS,
                             nIndex, (LPARAM)&ti ) )
        {
           // Get the text for the item.
           //.......................
           SendMessage( hToolTip, TTM_GETTEXT, 0,
                        (LPARAM)&ti );

           // Load the string and add it to the list.
           //.......................................
           LoadString( ti.hinst, (UINT)ti.lpszText, szTmp,
                       sizeof( szTmp )-1 );
           SendMessage( hList, LB_INSERTSTRING,
                        (WPARAM)-1, (LPARAM)szTmp );

           nIndex++;
        }
     }
     break;
```

TTM_GETTOOLCOUNT ■ Win32s ■ Windows 95 ■ Windows NT

Description	TTM_GETTOOLCOUNT is a tooltip message that retrieves the number of tools maintained by a tooltip control.
Parameters	
wParam	WPARAM: Set to zero.
lParam	LPARAM: Set to zero.
Returns	UINT: The number of tools maintained by the tooltip control.
Include File	commctrl.h
See Also	CreateWindowEx()
Example	See the example for the TTM_UPDATETIPTEXT message.

TTM_GETTOOLINFO ■ Win32s ■ Windows 95 ■ Windows NT

Description	TTM_GETTOOLINFO is a tooltip message that retrieves the information that a tooltip control maintains about a tool.
Parameters	
wParam	WPARAM: Set to zero.
lParam	LPTOOLINFO: A pointer to a TOOLINFO structure. When sending the message, the *hwnd* and *uId* members identify the tool. If the tooltip control includes the tool, the structure receives the information about the tool. Before sending this message, the *cbSize* member must specify the size of the structure. See the definition of the TOOLINFO structure under the TTM_ADDTOOL message.

Returns	BOOL: If successful, TRUE is returned; otherwise, FALSE is returned.
Include File	commctrl.h
See Also	CreateWindowEx()
Related Messages	TTM_GETCURRENTTOOL, TTM_ENUMTOOLS, TTM_SETTOOLINFO
Example	This example, shown in Listing 3-37, demonstrates how the TTM_GETTOOLINFO message retrieves the information for a tool in a tooltip control. When the user selects a toolbar button, the tooltip information for the button is retrieved and a message box is displayed with the information.

Listing 3-37 Using the TTM_GETTOOLINFO message

```
LRESULT CALLBACK WndProc( HWND hWnd, UINT uMsg, WPARAM wParam, LPARAM lParam )
{
static HWND hToolWnd = NULL;
static HWND hToolTip = NULL;

   switch( uMsg )
   {
      case WM_COMMAND :
              switch( LOWORD( wParam ) )
              {
                 case IDM_NEW :
                 case IDM_OPEN :
                 case IDM_SAVE :
                 case IDM_LARGEICON :
                 case IDM_SMALLICON :
                 case IDM_LISTVIEW :
                 case IDM_REPORTVIEW :
                     {
                        TOOLINFO ti;
                        char     szMsg[64], szTxt[32];

                        // Retrieve the tooltip information.
                        //.................................
                        ti.cbSize = sizeof( TOOLINFO );
                        ti.hwnd   = hToolWnd;
                        ti.uId    = LOWORD( wParam );
                        SendMessage( hToolTip, TTM_GETTOOLINFO, 0,
                                 (LPARAM)&ti );

                        // Create a display string and show it.
                        //....................................
                        LoadString( ti.hinst, (UINT)ti.lpszText,
                                 szTxt, sizeof( szTxt ) );
                        wsprintf( szMsg,
                                 "Tip text: %s   rect: %d %d %d %d",
                                 szTxt,
                                 ti.rect.left, ti.rect.top,
                                 ti.rect.right, ti.rect.bottom );
```

```
              MessageBox( hWnd, szMsg, lpszTitle,
                      MB_OK | MB_ICONINFORMATION );
          }
          break;
```

.
.
.

TTM_HITTEST   ■ Win32s   ■ Windows 95   ■ Windows NT

Description	TTM_HITTEST is a tooltip message that tests a point to determine whether it is within the bounding rectangle of a specific tool. If the point is within the tool, the information for the tool is returned.
Parameters	
wParam	WPARAM: Set to zero.
lParam	LPHITTESTINFO: A pointer to a TTHITTESTINFO structure. When sending the message, the *hwnd* member must specify the handle of a tool and the *pt* member must specify the coordinates of a point. If a tool is hit, the *ti* member receives information about the tool. See the definition of the TTHITTESTINFO structure below.
Returns	BOOL: If a tool occupies the specified point, TRUE is returned; otherwise, FALSE is returned.
Include File	commctrl.h
See Also	CreateWindowEx()

TTHITTESTINFO Definition

```
typedef struct _TT_HITTESTINFO
{
    HWND     hwnd;
    POINT    pt;
    TOOLINFO ti;
} TTHITTESTINFO, *LPHITTESTINFO;
```

Members	
hwnd	HWND: The window handle of the tool or the window with the specified tool.
pt	POINT: The client coordinates of the point to test.
ti	TOOLINFO: This structure receives information about the specified tool if the point is within the tool's bounding rectangle. See the definition of the TOOLINFO structure under the TTM_ADDTOOL message.
Example	This example, shown in Listing 3-38, is the same as the example for the TTM_ENUMTOOLS message, except that when the user selects the right mouse button over a section in the client area, the TTM_HITTEST message is used to determine which section the user selected.

Listing 3-38 Using the TTM_HITTEST message

```
LRESULT CALLBACK WndProc( HWND hWnd, UINT uMsg, WPARAM wParam, LPARAM lParam )
{
static HWND hToolTip = NULL;

   switch( uMsg )
   {
      case WM_RBUTTONDOWN :
            {
               TTHITTESTINFO tthit;

               tthit.hwnd = hWnd;
               tthit.pt.x = LOWORD( lParam );
               tthit.pt.y = HIWORD( lParam );

               // Check what section was hit.
               //...........................
               if ( SendMessage( hToolTip, TTM_HITTEST, 0, (LPARAM)&tthit ) )
               {
                  char szMsg[64];

                  // Display a message about the section hit.
                  //.........................................
                  wsprintf( szMsg, "Section %d was hit.",
                              tthit.ti.uId );
                  MessageBox( hWnd, szMsg, lpszTitle,
                              MB_OK | MB_ICONINFORMATION );
               }
            }
            break;
      .
      .
      .
```

TTM_NEWTOOLRECT ■ WIN32S ■ WINDOWS 95 ■ WINDOWS NT

Description	TTM_NEWTOOLRECT is a tooltip message that sets a new bounding rectangle for a tool.
Parameters	
wParam	WPARAM: Set to zero.
lParam	LPTOOLINFO: A pointer to a TOOLINFO structure. The *hwnd* and *uId* members identify the tool, and the *rect* member specifies the new bounding rectangle. The *cbSize* member must be initialized with the size of the structure. See the definition of the TOOLINFO structure under the TTM_ADDTOOL message.
Include File	commctrl.h
See Also	CreateWindowEx()
Example	This example, shown in Listing 3-39, is the same as the example for the TTM_ENUMTOOLS message, except that the TTM_NEWTOOLRECT

message is used in place of the TTM_SETTOOLINFO message to assign the new rectangle to the tool when processing the WM_SIZE message.

Listing 3-39 Using the TTM_NEWTOOLRECT message

```
LRESULT CALLBACK WndProc( HWND hWnd, UINT uMsg, WPARAM wParam, LPARAM lParam )
{
static TOOLINFO ti;
static int      index;

static HWND hToolTip = NULL;

   switch( uMsg )
   {
      case WM_SIZE :
            {
               // Adjust the tool rectangles for the new
               // section size.
               //.....................................
               RECT      rect;

               ti.cbSize = sizeof( TOOLINFO );
               ti.hwnd   = hWnd;

               GetClientRect( hWnd, &rect );

               for( index = 0; index < 4; index++ )
               {
                  ti.uId = index;

                  ti.rect.top    = 0;
                  ti.rect.bottom = HIWORD( lParam );
                  ti.rect.left   = (rect.right/4)*index;
                  ti.rect.right  = (rect.right/4)*(index+1);

                  SendMessage( hToolTip, TTM_NEWTOOLRECT, 0, (LPARAM)&ti );
               }
            }
            break;
         .
         .
         .
```

TTM_RELAYEVENT   ■ Win32s   ■ Windows 95   ■ Windows NT

Description   TTM_RELAYEVENT is a tooltip message that passes a mouse message to a tooltip control for processing. A tooltip control only processes the following messages when passed by the TTM_RELAYEVENT message. All other messages are ignored.

WM_LBUTTONDOWN

WM_MOUSEMOVE

WM_LBUTTONUP

WM_RBUTTONDOWN

WM_MBUTTONDOWN

WM_RBUTTONUP

WM_MBUTTONUP

Parameters

wParam   WPARAM: Set to zero.

lParam   LPMSG: A pointer to an MSG structure that contains the message to relay.
See the definition of the MSG structure below.

Include File   commctrl.h

See Also   CreateWindowEx()

MSG Definition

```
typedef struct tagMSG
{
    HWND    hwnd;
    UINT    message;
    WPARAM  wParam;
    LPARAM  lParam;
    DWORD   time;
    POINT   pt;
} MSG, *LPMSG;
```

Members

hwnd   HWND: The handle of the window whose window procedure receives the
message.

message   UINT: The message number.

wParam   WPARAM: Additional information about the message. The exact meaning
depends on the value of the message member.

lParam   LPARAM: Additional information about the message. The exact meaning
depends on the value of the message member.

time   DWORD: The time at which the message was posted.

pt   POINT: The cursor position, in screen coordinates, when the message was
posted.

Example   See the example for the TTM_ENUMTOOLS message.

TTM_SETDELAYTIME   ■ Win32s   ■ Windows 95   ■ Windows NT

Description   TTM_SETDELAYTIME is a tooltip message that sets the initial, reshow,
and autopop-up durations for a tooltip control. These times determine
how quickly (and for how long) the tooltip responds to user actions.

Parameters

wParam   UINT: The duration to set. This parameter can be one of the values in
Table 3-13.

Table 3-13 TTM_SETDELAYTIME *wParam* values

Value	Meaning
TTDT_AUTOMATIC	Automatically calculates the initial, reshow, and autopop-up durations based on the value of *iDelay*.
TTDT_AUTOPOP	Sets the length of time before the tooltip window is hidden if the cursor remains stationary in the tool's bounding rectangle after the tooltip window has appeared.
TTDT_INITIAL	Sets the length of time that the cursor must remain stationary within the bounding rectangle of a tool before the tooltip window is displayed.
TTDT_RESHOW	Sets the length of the delay before subsequent tooltip windows are displayed when the cursor is moved from one tool to another.

lParam	int: The new duration time, in milliseconds.
Include File	commctrl.h
See Also	CreateWindowEx()
Example	See the example for the TB_GETTOOLTIPS message.

TTM_SETTOOLINFO   ■ Win32s   ■ Windows 95   ■ Windows NT

Description	TTM_SETTOOLINFO is a tooltip message that sets the information that a tooltip control maintains for a tool.
Parameters	
wParam	WPARAM: Set to zero.
lParam	LPTOOLINFO: A pointer to a TOOLINFO structure that contains the information to set for the tool. See the definition of the TOOLINFO structure under the TTM_ADDTOOL message.
Include File	commctrl.h
See Also	CreateWindowEx()
Related Messages	TTM_GETTOOLINFO
Example	See the example for the TTM_ENUMTOOLS message.

TTM_UPDATETIPTEXT   ■ Win32s   ■ Windows 95   ■ Windows NT

Description	TTM_UPDATETIPTEXT is a tooltip message that sets the tooltip text for a tool.
Parameters	
wParam	WPARAM: Set to zero.
lParam	LPTOOLINFO: A pointer to a TOOLINFO structure. The *hinst* and *lpszText* members specify the instance handle and the pointer to the new

text for the tool. The *hwnd* and *uId* members identify the tool to update. The *cbSize* member must be initialized with the size of the structure before sending the message. See the definition of the TOOLINFO structure under TTM_ADDTOOL message.

Include File	commctrl.h
See Also	CreateWindowEx()
Related Messages	TTM_GETTEXT
Example	In this example, shown in Listing 3-40, a tooltip control is created and tools are added to it without any tool text. When the user selects the Test! menu item, the TTM_GETTOOLCOUNT message is used to determine how many tools there are in the tooltip control, and the TTM_UPDATETIPTEXT message is used to assign tip text to each of the tools.

Listing 3-40 Using the TTM_UPDATETIPTEXT message

```
LRESULT CALLBACK WndProc( HWND hWnd, UINT uMsg, WPARAM wParam, LPARAM lParam )
{
static TOOLINFO ti;
static int      index;
static HWND     hToolTip = NULL;

   switch( uMsg )
   {
      case WM_CREATE :
            {
               InitCommonControls();

               // Create tooltip control.
               //.......................
               hToolTip = CreateWindowEx( 0,
                                          TOOLTIPS_CLASS, NULL,
                                          TTS_ALWAYSTIP,
                                          CW_USEDEFAULT,
                                          CW_USEDEFAULT,
                                          CW_USEDEFAULT,
                                          CW_USEDEFAULT,
                                          hWnd, NULL,
                                          hInst, NULL );

               // Add the tools to the tooltip control.
               //......................................
               ti.cbSize = sizeof( TOOLINFO );
               ti.hwnd   = hWnd;
               ti.hinst  = NULL;
               ti.uFlags = TTF_SUBCLASS;

               for( index=0; index < 4; index++ )
               {
                  ti.uId         = index+1;
                  ti.lpszText    = "";
                  ti.rect.top    = 0;
                  ti.rect.bottom = 10;
```

```
            ti.rect.left   = 10*index;
            ti.rect.right  = 10*(index+1);

            SendMessage( hToolTip, TTM_ADDTOOL, 0, (LPARAM)&ti );
        }
    }
    break;

case WM_COMMAND :
        switch( LOWORD( wParam ) )
        {
            case IDM_TEST :
                {
                    UINT nCount, i;

                    // Retrieve the count of the tools.
                    //.................................
                    nCount = SendMessage( hToolTip, TTM_GETTOOLCOUNT,
                                        0, 0 );

                    ti.cbSize = sizeof( TOOLINFO );
                    for( i=0; i<nCount; i++ )
                    {
                        ti.hwnd     = hWnd;
                        ti.uId      = i+1;
                        ti.hinst    = hInst;
                        ti.lpszText = (LPTSTR)i+1;

                        // Update the tip text.
                        //.....................
                        SendMessage( hToolTip, TTM_UPDATETIPTEXT,
                                    0, (LPARAM)&ti );
                    }
                }
                break;
```

.
.
.

TTM_WINDOWFROMPOINT ■ Win32s ■ Windows 95 ■ Windows NT

Description   TTM_WINDOWFROMPOINT is a tooltip message that allows a subclass procedure to cause a tooltip to display text for a window other than the one beneath the mouse cursor.

An application that subclasses a tooltip can use this message. An application cannot send this message directly to a tooltip control. A tooltip sends this message to itself before displaying the text for a window. By changing the coordinates of the point pointed to by the *lParam*, the subclass procedure can cause the tooltip to display text for a window other than the one beneath the mouse cursor.

Parameters

wParam   WPARAM: Set to zero.

lParam	LPPOINT: A pointer to a POINT structure that defines the point to be checked.
Returns	HWND: If successful, the handle of the window that contains the point is returned. If no window exists at the point, NULL is returned.
Include File	commctrl.h
See Also	CreateWindowEx()
Example	This example, shown in Listing 3-41, demonstrates how to process the TTM_WINDOWFROMPOINT message when subclassing a tooltip control. The TipProc() function is the message procedure for the subclassed tooltip control. When the TTM_WINDOWFROMPOINT message is processed, the window handle of the window in which the point resides is returned.

Listing 3-41 Using the TTM_WINDOWFROMPOINT message

```
HWND      hMainWnd;
WNDPROC OldTipProc = NULL;

LRESULT CALLBACK TipProc( HWND hWnd, UINT uMsg, WPARAM wParam, LPARAM lParam )
{
static LPPOINT  lpPoint;

   switch( uMsg )
   {
      case TTM_WINDOWFROMPOINT :
           lpPoint = (LPPOINT)lParam;

           // Modify the coordinates for the window
           // that the tooltip should be displayed for.


           // Return the window handle that
           // contains the coordinates.
           //............................
           return( (LRESULT)hMainWnd );

      default :
           return( CallWindowProc( OldTipProc, hWnd, uMsg, wParam, lParam ) );
   }

   return( 0L );
}

LRESULT CALLBACK WndProc( HWND hWnd, UINT uMsg, WPARAM wParam, LPARAM lParam )
{
static TOOLINFO ti;
static int       index;
static HWND      hToolTip = NULL;

   switch( uMsg )
   {
      case WM_CREATE :
              {
                  InitCommonControls();
```

```
                // Create tooltip control.
                //.......................
                hToolTip = CreateWindowEx( 0,
                                           TOOLTIPS_CLASS, NULL,
                                           TTS_ALWAYSTIP,
                                           CW_USEDEFAULT,
                                           CW_USEDEFAULT,
                                           CW_USEDEFAULT,
                                           CW_USEDEFAULT,
                                           hWnd, NULL,
                                           hInst, NULL );

                // Subclass the tooltip.
                //....................
                OldTipProc = (WNDPROC)SetWindowLong( hToolTip, GWL_WNDPROC,
                                              (LONG)TipProc );

                // Add the tools to the tooltip control.
                //......................................
                ti.cbSize = sizeof( TOOLINFO );
                ti.hwnd   = hWnd;
                ti.hinst  = hInst;
                ti.uFlags = TTF_SUBCLASS;

                for( index=0; index < 4; index++ )
                {
                    ti.uId        = index+1;
                    ti.lpszText   = (LPTSTR)index+1;
                    ti.rect.top    = 0;
                    ti.rect.bottom = 10;
                    ti.rect.left   = 10*index;
                    ti.rect.right  = 10*(index+1);

                    SendMessage( hToolTip, TTM_ADDTOOL, 0, (LPARAM)&ti );
                }
            }
            break;
        .
        .
        .
```

TBN_BEGINADJUST   ■ WIN32S   ■ WINDOWS 95   ■ WINDOWS NT

Description	TBN_BEGINADJUST is a toolbar notification message that notifies a toolbar's parent window that the user has begun customizing a toolbar. This message is sent in the form of a WM_NOTIFY message.
Parameters	
lParam	NMHDR*: A pointer to an NMHDR structure that contains information about the notification message. This parameter is the *lParam* of the WM_NOTIFY message. See the definition of the NMHDR structure below.
Include File	commctrl.h
Related Messages	TBN_ENDADJUST, WM_NOTIFY

NMHDR Definition

```
typedef struct tagNMHDR
{
    HWND hwndFrom;
    UINT idFrom;
    UINT code;
} NMHDR;
```

Members

hwndFrom	HWND: The window handle of the control sending the message.
idFrom	UINT: The identifier of the control sending the message.
code	UINT: The notification code. This member can be a control-specific notification code, or it can be one of the common notification values in Table 3-14.

Table 3-14 NMHDR *code* values

Value	Meaning
NM_CLICK	The user has clicked the left mouse button within the control.
NM_DBLCLK	The user has double-clicked the left mouse button within the control.
NM_KILLFOCUS	The control has lost the input focus.
NM_OUTOFMEMORY	The control could not complete an operation because there was not enough memory available.
NM_RCLICK	The user has clicked the right mouse button within the control.
NM_RDBLCLK	The user has double-clicked the right mouse button within the control.
NM_RETURN	The control has the input focus, and the user has pressed the ENTER key.
NM_SETFOCUS	The control has received the input focus.

Example	See the example for the TB_CUSTOMIZE message.

TBN_BEGINDRAG ■ WIN32s ■ WINDOWS 95 ■ WINDOWS NT

Description	TBN_BEGINDRAG is a toolbar notification message that notifies a toolbar's parent window that the user has begun dragging a button in a toolbar. This message is sent in the form of a WM_NOTIFY message.
Parameters	
lParam	TBNOTIFY*: A pointer to a TBNOTIFY structure. The *iItem* member contains the zero-based index of the button being dragged. This parameter is the *lParam* of the WM_NOTIFY message. See the definition of the TBNOTIFY structure below.
Include File	commctrl.h
Related Messages	TBN_ENDDRAG, WM_NOTIFY

TBNOTIFY Definition

```
typedef struct
{
    NMHDR    hdr;
    int      iItem;
    TBBUTTON tbButton;
    int      cchText;
    LPTSTR   pszText;
} TBNOTIFY, *LPTBNOTIFY;
```

Members

hdr	NMHDR: The notification information. See the definition of the NMHDR structure under the TBN_BEGINADJUST notification message.
iItem	int: The index of the button associated with the notification.
tbButton	TBBUTTON: A pointer to a TBBUTTON structure that contains information about the toolbar button associated with the notification. See the definition of the TBBUTTON structure under the CreateToolbarEx() function.
cchText	int: The number of characters in the button text.
pszText	LPTSTR: A pointer to a buffer that contains the button text.
Example	See the example for the TB_CUSTOMIZE message.

TBN_CUSTHELP   ■ Win32s   ■ Windows 95   ■ Windows NT

Description   TBN_CUSTHELP is a toolbar notification message that notifies a toolbar's parent window that the user has chosen the Help button in the Customize Toolbar dialog box. This message is sent in the form of a WM_NOTIFY message.

Parameters

lParam   NMHDR*: A pointer to an NMHDR structure that contains information about the notification message. This parameter is the *lParam* of the WM_NOTIFY message. See the definition of the NMHDR structure under TBN_BEGINADJUST.

Include File   commctrl.h

Related Messages   WM_NOTIFY

Example   See the example for the TB_CUSTOMIZE message.

TBN_ENDADJUST   ■ Win32s   ■ Windows 95   ■ Windows NT

Description   TBN_ENDADJUST is a toolbar notification message that notifies a toolbar's parent window that the user has stopped customizing a toolbar. This message is sent in the form of a WM_NOTIFY message.

Parameters

lParam   NMHDR*: A pointer to an NMHDR structure that contains information about the notification message. This parameter is the *lParam* of the WM_NOTIFY message. See the definition of the NMHDR structure under the TBN_BEGINADJUST message.

Include File   commctrl.h

Related Messages   TBN_BEGINADJUST, WM_NOTIFY

Example   See the example for the TB_CUSTOMIZE message.

TBN_ENDDRAG   ■ Win32s ■ Windows 95 ■ Windows NT

Description   TBN_ENDDRAG is a toolbar notification message that notifies the toolbar's parent window that the user has stopped dragging a button in a toolbar. This message is sent in the form of a WM_NOTIFY message.

Parameters

lParam   LPTBNOTIFY: A pointer to a TBNOTIFY structure. The *iItem* member contains the zero-based index of the button being dragged. This parameter is the *lParam* of the WM_NOTIFY message. See the definition of the TBNOTIFY structure under the TBN_BEGINDRAG message.

Include File   commctrl.h

Related Messages   TBN_BEGINDRAG, WM_NOTIFY

Example   See the example for the TB_CUSTOMIZE message.

TBN_GETBUTTONINFO   ■ Win32s ■ Windows 95 ■ Windows NT

Description   TBN_GETBUTTONINFO is a toolbar notification message that retrieves toolbar customization information and notifies the toolbar's parent window of any changes being made to the toolbar. This is sent in the form of a WM_NOTIFY message.

The toolbar control allocates a buffer into which the parent window must copy the text. The *cchText* member contains the length of the buffer allocated by the toolbar when TBN_GETBUTTONINFO is sent to the parent window.

Parameters

lParam   LPTBNOTIFY: A pointer to a TBNOTIFY structure. The *iItem* member specifies a zero-based index that provides a count of the buttons the Customize dialog box displays as both available and present on the toolbar. The *pszText* member specifies the address of the current button text, and *cchText* specifies its length in characters. The application should fill the structure with information about the button. This parameter is the *lParam* of the WM_NOTIFY message. See the definition of the TBNOTIFY structure under the TBN_BEGINDRAG message.

Returns	BOOL: The application should return TRUE if the button information was copied to the structure; otherwise, FALSE is returned.
Include File	commctrl.h
Related Messages	WM_NOTIFY
Example	See the example for the TB_CUSTOMIZE message.

TBN_QUERYDELETE   ■ Win32s   ■ Windows 95   ■ Windows NT

Description	TBN_QUERYDELETE is a toolbar notification message that notifies the toolbar's parent window that a button may be deleted from a toolbar while the user is customizing a toolbar. The application responds to this notification to allow or disallow the deletion of this button. This message is sent in the form of a WM_NOTIFY message.
Parameters	
lParam	LPTBNOTIFY: A pointer to a TBNOTIFY structure. The *iItem* member contains the zero-based index of the button to be deleted. This parameter is the *lParam* of the WM_NOTIFY message. See the definition of the TBNOTIFY structure under the TBN_BEGINDRAG message.
Returns	BOOL: The application returns TRUE to allow the button to be deleted. Return FALSE to prevent the button from being deleted.
Include File	commctrl.h
Related Messages	TBN_QUERYINSERT, WM_NOTIFY
Example	See the example for the TB_CUSTOMIZE message.

TBN_QUERYINSERT   ■ Win32s   ■ Windows 95   ■ Windows NT

Description	TBN_QUERYINSERT is a toolbar notification message that notifies the toolbar's parent window that a button may be inserted to the left of a given button while the user is customizing a toolbar. The application responds to allow or disallow the insertion of this button. This message is sent in the form of a WM_NOTIFY message.
Parameters	
lParam	LPTBNOTIFY: A pointer to a TBNOTIFY structure. The *iItem* member contains the zero-based index of the button to be inserted. This parameter is the *lParam* of the WM_NOTIFY message. See the definition of the TBNOTIFY structure under the TBN_BEGINDRAG message.
Returns	BOOL: The application should return TRUE to allow the button to be inserted in front of the given button. Return FALSE to prevent the button from being inserted.
Include File	commctrl.h
Related Messages	TBN_QUERYDELETE, WM_NOTIFY

Example   See the example for the TB_CUSTOMIZE message.

TBN_RESET   ■ Win32s   ■ Windows 95   ■ Windows NT

Description   TBN_RESET is a toolbar notification message that notifies the toolbar's
                      parent window that the user has reset the content of the Customize
                      Toolbar dialog box. This message is sent in the form of a WM_NOTIFY
                      message.

Parameters

lParam   NMHDR*: A pointer to an NMHDR structure that contains information
                      about the notification message. This parameter is the *lParam* of the
                      WM_NOTIFY message. See the definition of the NMHDR structure under
                      the TBN_BEGINADJUST message.

Include File   commctrl.h

Related Messages WM_NOTIFY

Example   See the example for the TB_CUSTOMIZE message.

TBN_TOOLBARCHANGE   ■ Win32s   ■ Windows 95   ■ Windows NT

Description   TBN_TOOLBARCHANGE is a toolbar notification message that notifies
                      the toolbar's parent window that the user has customized a toolbar. This
                      message is sent in the form of a WM_NOTIFY message.

Parameters

lParam   NMHDR*: A pointer to an NMHDR structure that contains information
                      about the notification message. This parameter is the *lParam* of the
                      WM_NOTIFY message. See the definition of the NMHDR structure under
                      the TBN_BEGINADJUST message.

Include File   commctrl.h

Related Messages WM_NOTIFY

Example   See the example for the TB_CUSTOMIZE message.

TTN_NEEDTEXT   ■ Win32s   ■ Windows 95   ■ Windows NT

Description   TTN_NEEDTEXT is a tooltip notification message that retrieves text for a
                      tool. This notification message is sent to the window specified in the *hwnd*
                      member of the TOOLINFO structure for the tool. This notification is sent
                      only if the LPSTR_TEXTCALLBACK value is specified when the tool is
                      added to a tooltip control. This notification message is sent in the form of
                      a WM_NOTIFY message.

                         In Windows 95, when a TTN_NEEDTEXT notification is received, the
                      application can set or clear the TTF_RTLREADING value in the *uFlags*

member of the TOOLTIPTEXT structure pointed to by *lpttt* as required. This is the only flag that can be changed during the notification callback.

Parameters

wParam   int: The identifier of the tooltip control.

lParam   LPTOOLTIPTEXT: A pointer to a TOOLTIPTEXT structure. The *hdr* member identifies the tool for which text is needed. See the definition of the TOOLTIPTEXT structure below. The receiving window can specify the string by taking one of the following actions:

- Copying the text to the buffer specified by the *szText* member.
- Copying the address of the buffer that contains the text to the *lpszText* member.
- Copying the identifier of a string resource to the *lpszText* member and copying the handle of the instance that contains the resource to the *hinst* member.

Include File commctrl.h

Related Messages WM_NOTIFY

TOOLTIPTEXT Definition

```
typedef struct
{
    NMHDR      hdr;
    LPTSTR     lpszText;
    char       szText[80];
    HINSTANCE  hinst;
    UINT       uFlags;
} TOOLTIPTEXT, *LPTOOLTIPTEXT;
```

Members

hdr   NMHDR: Required for all WM_NOTIFY messages. See the definition of the NMHDR structure under the TBN_BEGINADJUST notification.

lpszText   LPTSTR: A pointer to a string that contains or receives the text for a tool. If *hinst* specifies an instance handle, this member must be the identifier of a string resource.

szText   char[80]: A buffer that receives the tooltip text. An application can copy the text to this buffer as an alternative to specifying a string address or string resource.

hinst   HINSTANCE: The instance handle to the instance that contains a string resource to be used as the tooltip text. If *lpszText* is the pointer to the tooltip text, this member is NULL.

uFlags   UINT: A flag that indicates how to interpret the *idFrom* member of the NMHDR structure that is included in the structure. If this member is the TTF_IDISHWND value, *idFrom* is the handle of the tool. Otherwise, *idFrom* is the identifier of the tool. Windows 95 applications can set or clear the TTF_RTLREADING flag to display text on Hebrew or Arabic systems in right-to-left reading order.

Example   This example, shown in Listings 3-42 and 3-43, demonstrates how to process the TTN_NEEDTEXT, TTN_SHOW, and TTN_POP messages to show tooltip text and a more descriptive tool description on the status window. Each of the strings in the string table have descriptive text and the tip text separated by a line feed (\n) character. When the TTN_NEEDTEXT notification is received, the appropriate string is loaded and the line feed character is found, and the text that follows is returned as the tip text. When the TTN_SHOW notification is received, the appropriate string is again loaded and the status window text is set to the first portion of the string. The status window text is cleared when the TTN_POP notification is received.

Listing 3-42 String Table in NEEDTEXT.RC

```
STRINGTABLE
BEGIN
    IDM_NEW          "Create a new file.\nNew"
    IDM_OPEN         "Open an existing file.\nOpen"
    IDM_SAVE         "Save the current file.\nSave"
    IDM_LARGEICON    "View as large icons.\nLarge Icons"
    IDM_SMALLICON    "View as small icons.\nSmall Icons"
    IDM_LISTVIEW     "View as a list.\nList"
    IDM_REPORTVIEW   "View as a report.\nReport"
END
```

Listing 3-43 WndProc() in NEEDTEXT.C

```
// Toolbar buttons.
//................
TBBUTTON tbButtons[] =
{
  { STD_FILENEW,  IDM_NEW, TBSTATE_ENABLED, TBSTYLE_BUTTON, 0, 0L, 0},
  { STD_FILEOPEN, IDM_OPEN, TBSTATE_ENABLED, TBSTYLE_BUTTON, 0, 0L, 0},
  { STD_FILESAVE, IDM_SAVE, TBSTATE_ENABLED, TBSTYLE_BUTTON, 0, 0L, 0},
  { 0, 0, TBSTATE_ENABLED, TBSTYLE_SEP, 0, 0L, 0},
  { VIEW_LARGEICONS, IDM_LARGEICON, TBSTATE_ENABLED, TBSTYLE_BUTTON, 0, 0L, 0},
  { VIEW_SMALLICONS, IDM_SMALLICON, TBSTATE_ENABLED, TBSTYLE_BUTTON, 0, 0L, 0},
  { VIEW_LIST, IDM_LISTVIEW, TBSTATE_ENABLED, TBSTYLE_BUTTON, 0, 0L, 0},
  { VIEW_DETAILS, IDM_REPORTVIEW, TBSTATE_ENABLED, TBSTYLE_BUTTON, 0, 0L, 0},
};

LRESULT CALLBACK WndProc( HWND hWnd, UINT uMsg, WPARAM wParam, LPARAM lParam )
{
static char    szTmp[80];
static LPTSTR  lpch;
static HWND    hToolWnd   = NULL;
static HWND    hStatusWnd = NULL;

    switch( uMsg )
    {
      case WM_CREATE :
            if ( !hToolWnd )
            {
```

```
// Initialize the common control library
// and create the status window and toolbar.
//.............................................
InitCommonControls();

hStatusWnd = CreateStatusWindow(
                WS_CHILD | WS_VISIBLE |
                CCS_BOTTOM | SBARS_SIZEGRIP,
                "", hWnd, 101 );

hToolWnd = CreateToolbarEx( hWnd,
                           WS_CHILD | WS_BORDER |
                           WS_VISIBLE | TBSTYLE_TOOLTIPS,
                           102,
                           11,
                           (HINSTANCE)HINST_COMMCTRL,
                           IDB_STD_SMALL_COLOR,
                           tbButtons, 4,
                           0, 0, 100, 30, sizeof(TBBUTTON) );

if ( hToolWnd )
{
    TBADDBITMAP tb;
    int index, stdidx;

    // Add the system-defined view bitmaps.
    //.........................................
    tb.hInst = HINST_COMMCTRL;
    tb.nID = IDB_VIEW_SMALL_COLOR;
    stdidx = SendMessage(hToolWnd, TB_ADDBITMAP,
                         12, (LPARAM)&tb);

    // Update the indices to the bitmaps.
    //.......................................
    for (index = 4; index < 8; index++)
        tbButtons[index].iBitmap += stdidx;

    // Add the view buttons.
    //.......................
    SendMessage(hToolWnd, TB_ADDBUTTONS, 4,
                (LONG) &tbButtons[4]);
}
}
break;

case WM_NOTIFY :
    switch ( ((LPNMHDR)lParam)->code )
    {
    case TTN_NEEDTEXT :
        {
            LPTOOLTIPTEXT lptt = (LPTOOLTIPTEXT)lParam;

            LoadString( hInst, lptt->hdr.idFrom,
                        szTmp, sizeof(szTmp)-1 );

            // Find the \n character and use the
            // following string as the tooltip text.
            //.........................................
```

continued on next page

continued from previous page

```
                            if ( lpch = strchr( szTmp, '\n' ) )
                                lptt->lpszText = lpch+1;
                        }
                        break;

                case TTN_SHOW :
                        LoadString( hInst, ((LPNMHDR)lParam)->idFrom,
                                    szTmp, sizeof(szTmp)-1 );

                        // Place a NULL character at the \n character
                        // and use the first part of the string as the
                        // status window text.
                        //...........................................
                        if ( lpch = strchr( szTmp, '\n' ) )
                           *lpch = 0;

                        SendMessage( hStatusWnd, SB_SETTEXT, 0, (LPARAM)szTmp );
                        break;

                case TTN_POP :
                        SendMessage( hStatusWnd, SB_SETTEXT, 0, (LPARAM)"" );
                        break;

        }
        break;
```

TTN_POP
■ Win32s ■ Windows 95 ■ Windows NT

Description	TTN_POP is a tooltip notification message that notifies the owner window that a tooltip is about to be hidden. This notification message is sent in the form of a WM_NOTIFY message.
Parameters	
wParam	int: The identifier of the tooltip control.
lParam	NMHDR*: A pointer to an NMHDR structure that contains information about the notification message. This parameter is the *lParam* of the WM_NOTIFY message. See the definition of the NMHDR structure under the TBN_BEGINADJUST message.
Include File	commctrl.h
Related Messages	TTN_SHOW
Example	See the example for the TTN_NEEDTEXT notification message.

TTN_SHOW
■ Win32s ■ Windows 95 ■ Windows NT

Description	TTN_SHOW is a tooltip notification message that notifies the owner window that a tooltip is about to be displayed. This notification message is sent in the form of a WM_NOTIFY message.

Parameters

wParam   int: The identifier of the tooltip control.

lParam   NMHDR*: A pointer to an NMHDR structure that contains information
                 about the notification message. This parameter is the *lParam* of the
                 WM_NOTIFY message. See the definition of the NMHDR structure under
                 the TBN_BEGINADJUST message.

Include File   commctrl.h

Related Messages TTN_POP

Example   See the example for the TTN_NEEDTEXT notification message.

4

TAB CONTROLS AND PROPERTY SHEETS

4

TAB CONTROLS AND PROPERTY SHEETS

One of the main hurdles that all developers must cross when developing an application is how to arrange screens to make the most of a limited amount of space. Today's programs have many user options and settings, increasing the need to present information and choices in an organized, visually appealing way. In a character-based application, the user had to navigate through a series of different screens or pop-up screens (dialogs). This has carried through to Windows applications. In Windows, dialog boxes are a means of displaying specific information to the user that is relevant to the context in which the user is working. But what happens when the dialog box cannot be large enough to display all the information that is relevant? Applications have used different methods to cope with this information glut. A dialog box can have selections that lead to other boxes being displayed. Alternatively, the program can use a single *dynamic dialog*. Dynamic dialogs are dialogs that change the contents of the dialog based on the selection from a list of topics. Instead of cluttering up the screen with a series of boxes, the user merely selects an area of interest to change the dialog display.

Many Windows 3.x applications, such as Microsoft Word and Excel, used dynamic dialogs; however, there was no standard, and each application had a different user interface. In later versions of Microsoft Word and Excel, the dynamic dialogs were replaced by what was called a *tab dialog*. A tab dialog works in the same way as a dynamic dialog, except that the list of topics is replaced with tabs along the top of the dialog. Clicking on a tab changes the dialog *page* displayed much in the way that index tabs can be used to open different pages of a reference book. But there was still no standard for implementing the tab dialogs, and while other vendors adopted the idea, they did not maintain a consistent appearance.

With Windows 95, however, this type of dynamic dialog has been standardized in the form of two common controls known as *tab controls* and *property sheets*.

Tab Controls

Tab controls give the user an interface that resembles tab dividers in a file cabinet. Using tab controls, an application can define multiple *pages* for the same area of a window or dialog box. Each page in the display area is associated with a tab; thus the contents of the display can change for each of the tabs. The tabs in a tab control can also appear as buttons, in which case, clicking a button performs a command instead of displaying a page. Figure 4-1 shows a single-row tab control with the horizontal up-down arrow control and a multirow tab control on the client area of a window.

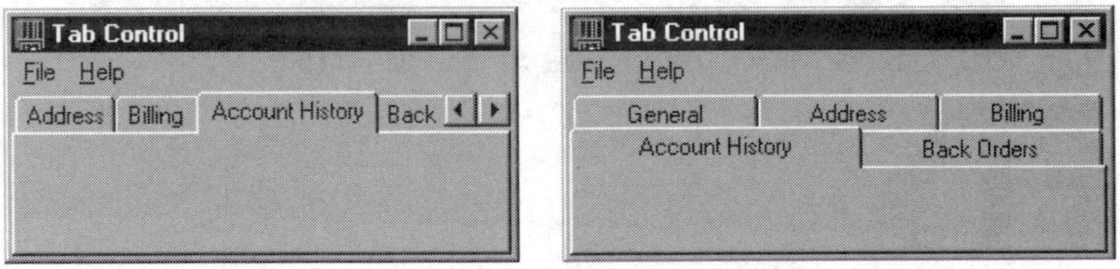

Figure 4-1 Single and multirow tab controls

Creating a Tab Control

A tab control does not have a function level API. The application uses macros that send messages to the tab control to affect the control's appearance and behavior. An application can create a tab control by using the CreateWindowEx() function and the WC_TABCONTROL class. This window class is registered when the Common Controls dynamic-link library (DLL) is loaded. The application should call the InitCommonControls() function to ensure the DLL is loaded. Tab controls are created as child windows with the WS_CHILD style. Table 4-1 lists additional window styles that are specific to a tab control.

Table 4-1 Tab control window styles

Style	Meaning
TCS_BUTTONS	Displays the tabs as push buttons.
TCS_FIXEDWIDTH	All tabs are displayed the same size.
TCS_FOCUSNEVER	The tab can never receive input focus.
TCS_FOCUSONBUTTONDOWN	The tab receives input focus when selected. This is normally specified with the TCS_BUTTONS style.
TCS_FORCEICONLEFT	The tab icon is left-justified and the tab text is centered.

Style	Meaning
TCS_FORCELABELLEFT	The tab icon and text are left-justified.
TCS_MULTILINE	The tab control will display tabs in multiple rows if the width is not sufficient to display all tabs on a single row. The default is to show an up-down control and horizontally scroll the tabs.
TCS_OWNERDRAWFIXED	The tabs in the tab control are owner drawn. The parent receives the WM_DRAWITEM message when a tab needs to be painted.
TCS_RIGHTJUSTIFY	The width of the tabs is expanded to fill the entire size of the tab control. This style cannot be used in conjunction with the TCS_FIXEDWIDTH style.
TCS_SINGLELINE	The tabs are displayed in a single row. If the width of the tabs is larger than the control, a horizontal up-down control is displayed to allow horizontal scrolling. This style is the default.
TCS_TABS	The tabs are displayed in the default style as shown in Figure 4-1.
TCS_TOOLTIPS	The tab control will create a tooltip control and display the tip text provided by the application in the TTN_NEEDTEXT notification for each tab. See Chapter 3, Toolbars and Status Windows, for more information on tooltips.

Using Tab Controls

Each tab in a tab control consists of a label, an optional icon, and optional application-defined data. When a tab control is created, it does not contain any tabs. The application must use the TabCtrl_InsertItem macro with the TC_ITEM structure to add tabs to the new tab control.

The application can associate data with each tab, such as a pointer to a structure or a window handle. By default, a tab control allocates four extra bytes per tab for application-defined data. You can increase the number of extra bytes per tab by using the TabCtrl_SetItemExtra macro. The *lParam* member of the TC_ITEM structure is the default four bytes of application-defined data. If you use more than four bytes of data, you need to define your own structure and use it instead of TC_ITEM with the TabCtrl_GetItem and TabCtrl_SetItem macros. The first member in your structure must be a TC_ITEMHEADER structure, and the remaining members are the application-defined data.

When the user selects a tab, the tab control sends its parent window the TCN_SELCHANGING notification message in the form of a WM_NOTIFY message before the selection changes. The TCN_SELCHANGE notification message is sent after the selection changes. The application can process the TCN_SELCHANGING notification to save the state of the outgoing page. The application must process the TCN_SELCHANGE notification message to display the incoming page in the display area.

Property Sheets

An application may simply need a dialog box with a tab control to allow changing of properties for an object. Instead of writing a dialog box with a tab control for this purpose, you can use the common control called a *property sheet*. A property sheet is a window that uses the tab control and does the hard work of setting up the pages and changing the contents of each page as the user selects a tab. Property sheets are used in applications to allow the user to set and view information about an object such as a cell in a spreadsheet. Figure 4-2 shows a property sheet from the Windows Explorer. Property sheets are based on dialog boxes; this section assumes you have a knowledge of dialog box templates and procedures.

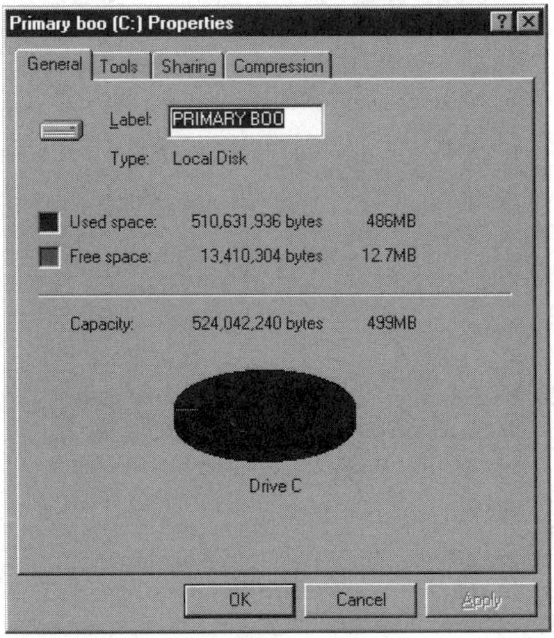

Figure 4-2 Property sheet

A property sheet and its pages are actually dialog boxes. The property sheet itself is a system-defined dialog box that can be modal or modeless. Each page is an independent application-defined dialog box with its own dialog procedure and dialog template. The property sheet sends notifications to the dialog box procedures when actions occur at the property sheet level, such as the user selecting a tab. Some of the notifications require the dialog box procedure to return either TRUE or FALSE in response to the WM_NOTIFY message. A page cannot return TRUE or FALSE the way a normal dialog box procedure can; instead, it must use the SetWindowLong() function and the DWL_MSGRESULT value to return a value.

Creating a Property Sheet

The steps used to create a property sheet are the reverse of the process for creating a tab control. You must first create one or more property pages with the CreatePropertySheetPage() function. Once all the pages that will be added initially to the property sheet are created, use the PropertySheet() function to create the property sheet. The PropertySheet() function uses the PROPSHEETHEADER structure, which contains an array of property sheet pages that were previously created.

Another option for creating a property sheet is to specify an array of PROPSHEETPAGE structures instead of creating the property sheet pages in advance. In this case, PropertySheet() creates handles for the pages before adding them to the property sheet.

The PropertySheet() function automatically sets the size and initial position of a property sheet. The position is based on the position of the owner window, and the size is based on the largest page specified in the array of pages when the property sheet is created.

A property sheet must contain at least one page and cannot contain more than the value of MAXPROPPAGES as defined in Win32. Each page is assigned a zero-based index by the property sheet according to the order in which the page is added to the property sheet. This index is used in some messages that are sent to a specific property page.

Each property sheet page has a corresponding icon and label. All property sheet pages are expected to use a nonbold font. Use the DS_3DLOOK style in the dialog template to ensure the font is not bold.

An application can add additional property sheet pages by using the PropSheet_AddPage macro. However, the size of the property sheet cannot change after it has been created, so the new page must be no larger than the largest page. The application can also remove pages with the PropSheet_RemovePage macro. Normally, the property sheet destroys all the property sheet pages; however, if a property sheet page created with the CreatePropertySheetPage() function has not been added to the property sheet, the application must use the DestroyPropertySheetPage() function to destroy the page.

Using Property Sheets

Property sheets contain OK, Cancel, Apply, and Help buttons. The Help button and the Apply button may both be hidden. The OK and Apply buttons are similar in function, with the exception that the Apply button does not destroy the property sheet after the changes are applied. When the user selects the OK or Apply button, the property sheet sends the PSN_KILLACTIVE notification to allow the current property sheet page to validate the user's changes. If the page returns TRUE, the property sheet sends the PSN_APPLY notification message to each page. Each page is responsible for applying the changes relevant to the page.

When a property sheet is initially displayed, the Apply button is disabled. When the application detects the user has made changes, it should use the PropSheet_Changed macro to notify the property sheet that changes have been made. This will cause the Apply button to be enabled. When the user chooses the Apply button, the application then uses the PropSheet_UnChanged macro to disable the Apply button. If changes that are applied cannot be undone, the application should use the PropSheet_CancelToClose macro to change the OK button to a Close button and to disable the Cancel button. This indicates to the user that the changes cannot be undone.

Property sheets can only have one active page at a time. When the user changes the selection, the property sheet sends the PSN_KILLACTIVE notification message to the page that is about to lose the activation. In response, the page can validate any changes the user has made to the page and decide whether to let the deactivation continue. If the application returns TRUE, the property sheet then sends the PSN_SETACTIVE notification message to the page that is being activated. The page should respond by initializing the contents of the controls.

Wizards

A special type of property sheet known as a *wizard* presents a series of sequential steps that lead the user through a process to an eventual end. An example for a wizard would be the steps required to set up a new printer. Figure 4-3 shows the Add Printer Wizard for Windows 95.

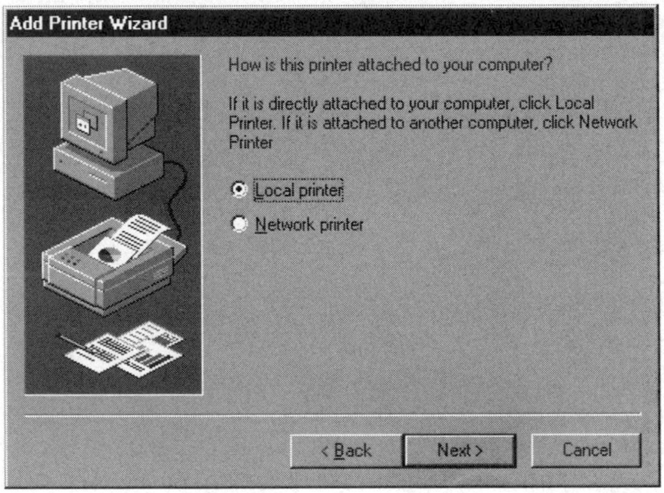

Figure 4-3 Add Printer Wizard

Wizards are basically implemented the same as property sheets, with the exception that the OK and Apply buttons are not used, and property pages (wizard pages) are only viewable in sequence and do not have tabs that allow random access as they do with property sheets.

Wizards use the Back and Next buttons to navigate between the wizard pages. Once the wizard has enough information to finish the process, the wizard can display a Finish button that allows the user to finalize the process. The Cancel button has the same function as it does on property sheets and aborts the process.

Creating a wizard is identical to creating a property sheet, except the PSH_WIZARD style is specified for the style when creating the wizard page. When creating the resources for the wizard pages, the application should use the values listed in Table 4-2 to conform to the Windows standard for wizards.

Table 4-2 Standard wizard sizes

Value	Description
WIZ_BODYCX	The width of the body of a page in a wizard property sheet. The body does not include the bitmap area.
WIZ_BODYX	The horizontal coordinate of the upper left corner of the body of a page in a wizard property sheet. Use zero for the vertical coordinate of the body of a page.
WIZ_CXBMP	The width of the bitmap area in a page of a wizard property sheet. Use WIZ_CYDLG for the height of the bitmap area.
WIZ_CXDLG	The width of a page in a wizard property sheet.
WIZ_CYDLG	The height of a page in a wizard property sheet.

The dialog box procedure for a page in a wizard receives the same notifications that a page in a property sheet does. It also receives the PSN_WIZBACK, PSN_WIZNEXT, and PSN_WIZFINISH notifications to notify the application when the user presses the Back, Next, and Finish buttons.

For an example of a wizard, see the example for the PropSheet_SetWizButtons macro later in this chapter.

Function Summary

Table 4-3 summarizes the property sheet and tab control functions and macros. The detailed function and macro descriptions follow immediately after the table.

Table 4-3 Property sheet and tab control function and macro summary

Function	Meaning
CreatePropertySheetPage	Creates a new page for an existing property sheet.
DestroyPropertySheetPage	Destroys a property sheet page.
PropertySheet	Creates a property sheet.
PropSheet_AddPage	Adds a previously created page to the end of an existing property sheet.
PropSheet_Apply	Simulates the choice of the Apply Now button by indicating that one or more pages have changed and the changes need to be validated and recorded.
PropSheet_CancelToClose	Disables the Cancel button and changes the text of the OK button to "Close".
PropSheet_Changed	Informs a property sheet that information in a page has changed.
PropSheet_GetCurrentPageHwnd	Retrieves the handle of the current property sheet.
PropSheet_GetTabControl	Retrieves the handle of the tab control of a property sheet.
PropSheet_IsDialogMessage	Passes a message to a property sheet dialog box and indicates whether the dialog box processed the message.
PropSheet_PressButton	Simulates the pressing of a property sheet button.
PropSheet_QuerySiblings	Sends the PSM_QUERYSIBLINGS message to each page in the property sheet.

continued on next page

continued from previous page

Function	Meaning
PropSheet_RebootSystem	Indicates that the system needs to be restarted before changes can take effect.
PropSheet_RemovePage	Removes a page from a property sheet.
PropSheet_RestartWindows	Indicates that Windows needs to be restarted before changes can take effect.
PropSheet_SetCurSel	Activates the specified page in a property sheet.
PropSheet_SetCurSelByID	Activates the specified page of a property sheet based on the resource identifier of the page.
PropSheet_SetFinishText	Sets the text of the Finish button in a wizard property sheet, shows and enables the button, and hides the Next and Back buttons.
PropSheet_SetTitle	Sets the title of the property sheet.
PropSheet_SetWizButtons	Enables the Back, Next, or Finish button in a wizard property sheet.
PropSheet_UnChanged	Informs a property sheet that the information in a page has reverted to the previously saved state.
TabCtrl_AdjustRect	Either calculates the tab control's display area, or calculates the window rectangle that would correspond to a display area.
TabCtrl_DeleteAllItems	Removes all items from a tab control.
TabCtrl_DeleteItem	Removes an item from a tab control.
TabCtrl_GetCurFocus	Returns the index of the tab control item with input focus.
TabCtrl_GetCurSel	Returns the currently selected tab in a tab control.
TabCtrl_GetImageList	Returns the image list associated with a tab control.
TabCtrl_GetItem	Retrieves information about a tab in a tab control.
TabCtrl_GetItemCount	Returns the number of tabs in the tab control.
TabCtrl_GetItemRect	Returns the bounding rectangle of a tab in a tab control.
TabCtrl_GetRowCount	Returns the current number of tab rows in a tab control.
TabCtrl_GetToolTips	Returns the handle of the tooltip control associated with a tab control.
TabCtrl_HitTest	Performs a hit test to determine which tab, if any, contains a specified point.
TabCtrl_InsertItem	Inserts a new tab in a tab control.
TabCtrl_RemoveImage	Removes an image from a tab control's image list.
TabCtrl_SetCurSel	Sets the current tab in a tab control.
TabCtrl_SetImageList	Assigns an image list to a tab control.
TabCtrl_SetItem	Sets the attributes for a tab.
TabCtrl_SetItemExtra	Sets the number of bytes a tab has reserved for application-defined data.
TabCtrl_SetItemSize	Sets the width and height of tabs in a fixed-width or owner-drawn tab control.
TabCtrl_SetPadding	Sets the amount of space around a tab's icon and label.
TabCtrl_SetToolTips	Assigns a tooltip control to a tab control.

Notification Message

PSN_APPLY	Indicates that the user selected the OK or Apply Now button and wants all changes to take effect.
PSN_HELP	Notifies a page that the user selected the Help button.
PSN_KILLACTIVE	Notifies a page that it is about to lose the activation either because another page is being activated or the user selected the OK button.

Notification Message	Meaning
PSN_QUERYCANCEL	Indicates that the user selected the Cancel button.
PSN_RESET	Notifies a page that the user selected the Cancel button and the property sheet is about to be destroyed.
PSN_SETACTIVE	Notifies a page that it is about to be activated.
PSN_WIZBACK	Notifies a page that the user selected the Back button in a wizard property sheet.
PSN_WIZFINISH	Notifies a page that the user selected the Finish button in a wizard property sheet.
PSN_WIZNEXT	Notifies a page that the user selected the Next button in a wizard property sheet.
TCN_KEYDOWN	Notifies the parent window of a tab control that a key was pressed.
TCN_SELCHANGE	Notifies the parent window of a tab control that the currently selected tab has changed.
TCN_SELCHANGING	Notifies the parent window of a tab control that the currently selected tab is about to change.

CREATEPROPERTYSHEETPAGE   ■ WIN32S   ■ WINDOWS 95   ■ WINDOWS NT

Description	CreatePropertySheetPage() creates a new page for a property sheet. Use the PropSheet_AddPage macro to add the new page to an existing property sheet. Use the PropertySheet() function to create a property sheet that includes the new page.
Syntax	HPROPSHEETPAGE **CreatePropertySheetPage**(LPCPROPSHEETPAGE *lppsp*)
Parameters	
lppsp	LPCPROPSHEETPAGE: A pointer to a PROPSHEETPAGE structure that defines the new page to create. See the definition of the PROPSHEETPAGE structure below.
Returns	HPROPSHEETPAGE: If successful, the handle of the new page is returned; otherwise, NULL is returned.
Include File	prsht.h
See Also	PropertySheet(), PropSheet_AddPage
Related Messages	PSM_ADDPAGE

PROPSHEETPAGE Definition

```
typedef struct _PROPSHEETPAGE
{
    DWORD     dwSize;
    DWORD     dwFlags;
    HINSTANCE hInstance;
    union
    {
        LPCTSTR        pszTemplate;
        LPCDLGTEMPLATE pResource;
    };
    union
    {
        HICON   hIcon;
        LPCTSTR pszIcon;
    };
```

continued on next page

continued from previous page

```
        LPCTSTR pszTitle;
        DLGPROC pfnDlgProc;
        LPARAM  lParam;
        LPFNPSPCALLBACK pfnCallback;
        UINT*   pcRefParent;
} PROPSHEETPAGE, *LPPROPSHEETPAGE;
typedef const PROPSHEETPAGE *LPCPROPSHEETPAGE;
```

Members

dwSize   DWORD: The size, in bytes, of the PROPSHEETPAGE structure. This size
                    includes any extra application-defined data at the end of the structure.

dwFlags   DWORD: Flags that indicate which structure members to use. This can be
                    a combination of the values in Table 4-4 combined with the binary OR (|)
                    operator.

Table 4-4 PROPSHEETPAGE *dwFlags* values

Value	Meaning
PSP_DEFAULT	Uses the default meaning for all structure members.
PSP_DLGINDIRECT	The template for the property sheet is already in memory and the *pResource* member points to the memory. The *pszTemplate* member is not used.
PSP_HASHELP	Enables the property sheet Help button when this page is active.
PSP_RTLREADING	Displays the text of *pszTitle* using right-to-left reading order on Hebrew or Arabic systems. This flag is valid only for Windows 95.
PSP_USECALLBACK	Calls the function specified by *pfnCallback* when creating or destroying the property sheet page defined by this structure.
PSP_USEHICON	Uses *hIcon* as the small icon on the tab for the page.
PSP_USEICONID	Uses *pszIcon* as the name of the icon resource to load and as the small icon on the tab for the page.
PSP_USEREFPARENT	Maintains the reference count specified by *pcRefParent* for the lifetime of the property sheet page created from this structure.
PSP_USETITLE	Uses *pszTitle* as the title of the property sheet dialog box instead of the title stored in the dialog box template.

hInstance   HINSTANCE: The instance handle from which to load the dialog box tem-
                    plate, icon, and title string resources.

pszTemplate   LPCTSTR: The dialog box template to use for the property page. This
                    member can specify either the resource identifier of the template or the
                    pointer to a string that contains the name of the template. If *dwFlags*
                    includes PSP_DLGINDIRECT, this member is ignored.

pResource   LPCDLGTEMPLATE: A pointer to a dialog box template in memory. If
                    dwFlags does not include PSP_DLGINDIRECT, this member is ignored.

hIcon	HICON: A handle to the icon to use as the small icon in the tab of the page. If *dwFlags* does not include PSP_USEHICON, this member is ignored.
pszIcon	LPCTSTR: The icon resource to use as the small icon in the tab of the page. This member can specify either the identifier of the icon resource or the pointer to the string that specifies the name of the icon resource. If *dwFlags* does not include PSP_USEICONID, this member is ignored.
pszTitle	LPCTSTR: The title of the property sheet dialog box. This title overrides the title specified in the dialog box template. This member can specify either the identifier of a string resource or the pointer to a string that contains the title. If *dwFlags* does not include PSP_USETITLE, this member is ignored.
pfnDlgProc	DLGPROC: A pointer to the dialog box procedure for the page. The dialog box procedure for a property sheet page must not call the EndDialog() function.
lParam	LPARAM: A 32-bit application-defined value.
pfnCallback	LPFNPSPCALLBACK: A pointer to an application-defined callback function that is called both when the page is created and when it is about to be destroyed. Use this function to perform cleanup operations for the page. If *dwFlags* does not include PSP_USECALLBACK, this member is ignored. For more information about the callback function, see the description of PropSheetPageProc() below.
pcRefParent	UINT*: A pointer to the reference count value. If *dwFlags* does not include the PSP_USERREFPARENT value, this member is ignored.
Callback Syntax	UINT CALLBACK **PropSheetPageProc**(HWND *hwnd*, UINT *uMsg*, PROPSHEETPAGE *ppsp*)
Callback Parameters	
hwnd	HWND: This parameter is reserved.
uMsg	UINT: The action flag. This parameter can be one of the values in Table 4-5.

Table 4-5 PropSheetPageProc() *uMsg* values

Value	Meaning
PSPCB_CREATE	A page is being created. Return a nonzero value to allow the page to be created, or zero to prevent it.
PSPCB_RELEASE	A page is being destroyed. The return value is ignored.

ppsp	PROPSHEETPAGE: A pointer to a PROPSHEETPAGE structure that contains information about the property page. See the definition of the PROPSHEETPAGE structure above.
Example	See the example for the PropertySheet() function.

DestroyPropertySheetPage ■ Win32s ■ Windows 95 ■ Windows NT

Description	DestroyPropertySheetPage() destroys a property sheet page. Applications must call this function for all pages that have not been passed to the PropertySheet() function. Pages that are passed to the PropertySheet() function are automatically destroyed when the property sheet closes.
Syntax	BOOL **DestroyPropertySheetPage**(HPROPSHEETPAGE *hPSPage*)
Parameters	
hPSPage	HPROPSHEETPAGE: The handle of the property sheet page to delete. This is the handle returned from the CreatePropertySheetPage() function.
Returns	BOOL: If successful, TRUE is returned; otherwise, FALSE is returned.
Include File	prsht.h
See Also	CreatePropertySheetPage(), PropertySheet()
Example	See the example for the PropSheet_AddPage macro.

PropertySheet ■ Win32s ■ Windows 95 ■ Windows NT

Description	PropertySheet() creates a property sheet with the pages defined in the property sheet header structure pointed to by the *lppsph* parameter. PropertySheet() creates a modal dialog by default and does not return until the user dismisses the dialog. Applications should specify the PSH_MODELESS flag to create a modeless dialog. In this case, the PropertySheet() function returns the window handle of the dialog immediately after it is created. The application's message loop should use the PropSheet_IsDialogMessage macro to pass messages to the property sheet dialog. Use the PropSheet_GetCurrentPageHwnd macro to determine when to destroy the dialog. This macro will return NULL when the user selects the OK or Cancel buttons. Use the DestroyWindow() function to destroy the dialog.
Syntax	int **PropertySheet**(LPCPROPSHEETHEADER *lppsph*)
Parameters	
lppsph	LPCPROPSHEETHEADER: A pointer to a PROPSHEETHEADER structure that defines the frame and pages of a property sheet. See the definition of the PROPSHEETHEADER structure below.
Returns	int: If successful, a positive value is returned. The return value can be one of the values in Table 4-6 or the window handle of a modeless property sheet dialog. Other positive values are also valid. If the function is not successful, -1 is returned.

Table 4-6 PropertySheet() return values

Value	Meaning
ID_PSREBOOTSYSTEM	A page sent the PSM_REBOOTSYSTEM message to the property sheet. The computer must be restarted for the user's changes to take effect.
ID_PSRESTARTWINDOWS	A page sent the PSM_RESTARTWINDOWS message to the property sheet. Windows must be restarted for the user's changes to take effect.

Include File	prsht.h
See Also	DestroyWindow(), PropSheet_IsDialogMessage, PropSheet_GetCurrentPageHwnd
Related Messages	PSM_GETCURRENTPAGEHWND, PSM_ISDIALOGMESSAGE, PSM_REBOOTSYSTEM, PSM_RESTARTWINDOWS

PROPSHEETHEADER Definition

```
typedef struct _PROPSHEETHEADER
{
    DWORD       dwSize;
    DWORD       dwFlags;
    HWND        hwndParent;
    HINSTANCE   hInstance;
    union
    {
        HICON   hIcon;
        LPCTSTR pszIcon;
    };
    LPCTSTR     pszCaption;
    UINT        nPages;
    union
    {
        UINT    nStartPage;
        LPCTSTR pStartPage;
    };
    union
    {
        LPCPROPSHEETPAGE ppsp;
        HPROPSHEETPAGE*  phpage;
    };
    PFNPROPSHEETCALLBACK pfnCallback;
} PROPSHEETHEADER, *LPPROPSHEETHEADER;
typedef const PROPSHEETHEADER* LPCPROPSHEETHEADER;
```

Members

dwSize	DWORD: The size, in bytes, of the PROPSHEETHEADER structure.
dwFlags	DWORD: A combination of the flags listed in Table 4-7 that indicates which members of the structure to use. Combine the flags with the binary OR (|) operator.

Table 4-7 PROPSHEETHEADER *dwFlags* values

Value	Meaning
PSH_DEFAULT	Uses the default meaning for all structure members.
PSH_HASHELP	Displays the property sheet Help button. The Help button is enabled only when the PSP_HASHELP flag is set in the PROPSHEETPAGE structure for the active page. If any of the initial property sheet pages set the PSP_HASHELP flag, the Help button is automatically displayed regardless of the PSH_HASHELP flag. However, PSH_HASHELP is useful when none of the initial pages set PSP_HASHELP, but pages added later might set this flag. See the definition of the PROPSHEETPAGE structure under the CreatePropertySheetPage() function.
PSH_MODELESS	Causes PropertySheet() to create the property sheet as a modeless dialog instead of the default modal dialog. When this flag is set, PropertySheet() returns immediately after the dialog is created, and the return value is the window handle of the property sheet dialog.
PSH_MULTILINETABS	Allows multiple rows of tabbed pages.
PSH_NOAPPLYNOW	Removes the Apply Now button.
PSH_PROPSHEETPAGE	Uses the *ppsp* member and ignores the *phpage* member when creating the pages for the property sheet.
PSH_PROPTITLE	Uses the "Properties for" string with the string specified by *pszCaption* in the title bar of the property sheet.
PSH_RTLREADING	Displays the title of the property sheet dialog using right-to-left reading order on Hebrew or Arabic systems. This is only valid for Windows 95.
PSH_USECALLBACK	Calls the function specified by *pfnCallback* when initializing the property sheet defined by this structure.
PSH_USEHICON	Uses *hIcon* as the small icon in the title bar of the property sheet dialog box.
PSH_USEICONID	Uses *pszIcon* as the name of the icon resource to load and as the small icon in the title bar of the property sheet dialog box.
PSH_USEPSTARTPAGE	Uses the *pStartPage* member and ignores the *nStartPage* member when displaying the initial page of the property sheet.
PSH_WIZARD	Creates a wizard property sheet. See the example for the PropSheet_SetWizButtons macro later in this chapter for an example of a wizard.

hwndParent	HWND: The window handle of the owner.
hInstance	HINSTANCE: The instance handle of the module from which to load the icon or title string resource. If *pszIcon* or *pszCaption* identifies a resource to load, this member must be specified.
hIcon	HICON: The handle of the icon to use as the small icon in the title bar of the property sheet dialog box. If *dwFlags* does not include the PSH_USEHICON value, this member is ignored.
pszIcon	LPCTSTR: The icon resource to use as the small icon in the title bar of the property sheet dialog box. This member can specify either the identifier of the icon resource or the pointer to the string that specifies the name of the

	icon resource. If *dwFlags* does not include the PSH_USEICONID value, this member is ignored.
pszCaption	LPCTSTR: The title of the property sheet dialog box. This member can specify either the identifier of a string resource or the pointer to a string that specifies the title. If *dwFlags* includes the PSH_PROPTITLE value, the string, "Properties for" is used with the title.
nPages	UINT: The number of elements in the array pointed to by the *phpage* member.
nStartPage	UINT: The zero-based index of the initial page that appears when the property sheet dialog box is created. This member is ignored if *dwFlags* includes the PSH_USEPSTARTPAGE value.
pStartPage	LPCTSTR: The name of the initial page that appears when the property sheet dialog box is created. This member can specify either the identifier of a string resource or the pointer to a string that specifies the name. This member is ignored if *dwFlags* does not include the PSH_USEPSTARTPAGE value.
ppsp	LPCPROPSHEETPAGE: A pointer to an array of PROPSHEETPAGE structures that define the pages in the property sheet. If *dwFlags* does not include the PSH_PROPSHEETPAGE value, this member is ignored. See the definition of the PROPSHEETPAGE structure under the CreatePropertySheetPage() function.
phpage	HPROPSHEETPAGE*: A pointer to an array that contains handles of property sheet pages created by previous calls to the CreatePropertySheetPage() function. If *dwFlags* includes the PSH_PROPSHEETPAGE value, this member is ignored.
pfnCallback	PFNPROPSHEETCALLBACK: A pointer to an application-defined callback function that is called when the property sheet is initialized. This function should always return zero. For more information about the callback function, see the description of PropSheetProc() below. If *dwFlags* does not include the PSP_USECALLBACK value, this member is ignored.
Callback Syntax	int CALLBACK **PropSheetProc**(HWND *hwndDlg*, UINT *uMsg*, LPARAM *lParam*)

Callback Parameters

hwndDlg	HWND: The window handle of the property sheet dialog box.
uMsg	UINT: The action flag. Only the PSCB_INITIALIZED value is defined, which indicates that the property sheet is being initialized.
lParam	LPARAM: This parameter is always zero.
Example	This example creates a property sheet dialog when the user selects the Test! menu item. The DisplayProperties() function, shown in Listings 4-1 and 4-2, creates three property pages with the CreatePropertySheetPage() function that are passed to the PropertySheet() function. Figure 4-4 shows the resulting property sheet dialog box.

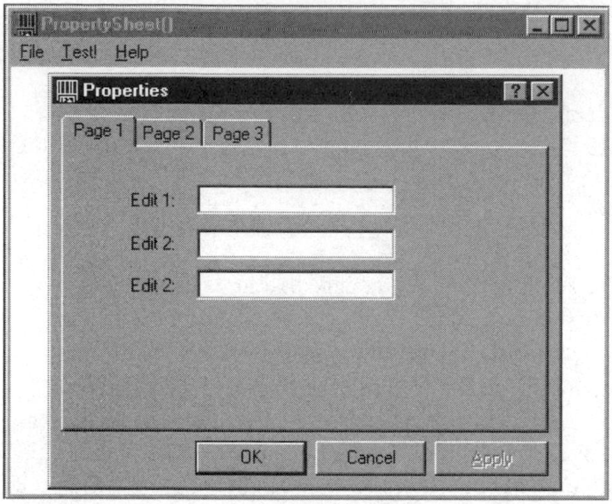

Figure 4-4 PropertySheet() example

Listing 4-1 Property Page Templates in PROPSHET.RC

```
PAGE1 DIALOG DISCARDABLE  0, 0, 186, 95
STYLE DS_MODALFRAME | WS_POPUP | WS_VISIBLE | WS_CAPTION | WS_SYSMENU
CAPTION "Page 1"
FONT 8, "MS Sans Serif"
BEGIN
    EDITTEXT        IDC_EDIT1,57,15,89,12,ES_AUTOHSCROLL
    EDITTEXT        IDC_EDIT2,57,33,89,12,ES_AUTOHSCROLL
    EDITTEXT        IDC_EDIT3,57,50,89,12,ES_AUTOHSCROLL
    LTEXT           "Edit 1:",-1,28,17,23,8
    LTEXT           "Edit 2:",-1,28,35,24,8
    LTEXT           "Edit 2:",-1,28,52,23,8
END

PAGE2 DIALOG DISCARDABLE  0, 0, 186, 95
STYLE DS_MODALFRAME | WS_POPUP | WS_VISIBLE | WS_CAPTION | WS_SYSMENU
CAPTION "Page 2"
FONT 8, "MS Sans Serif"
BEGIN
    CONTROL         "Check Box 1",IDC_CHECK1,"Button",BS_AUTOCHECKBOX |
                    WS_TABSTOP,50,32,76,10
    CONTROL         "Check Box 2",IDC_CHECK2,"Button",BS_AUTOCHECKBOX |
                    WS_TABSTOP,50,48,66,10
    GROUPBOX        "Static",-1,32,17,122,51
END

PAGE3 DIALOG DISCARDABLE  0, 0, 186, 95
STYLE DS_MODALFRAME | WS_POPUP | WS_VISIBLE | WS_CAPTION | WS_SYSMENU
CAPTION "Page 3"
FONT 8, "MS Sans Serif"
BEGIN
    CONTROL         "Radio Button 1",IDC_RADIO1,"Button",BS_AUTORADIOBUTTON |
                    WS_GROUP | WS_TABSTOP,52,25,71,10
```

```
    CONTROL         "Radio Button 2",IDC_RADIO2,"Button",BS_AUTORADIOBUTTON,
                    52,39,77,10
    CONTROL         "Radio Button 3",IDC_RADIO3,"Button",BS_AUTORADIOBUTTON,
                    52,53,70,10
    GROUPBOX        "Static",-1,41,13,105,58,WS_GROUP
END
```

Listing 4-2 WndProc() and DisplayProperties() in PROPSHET.C

```c
LRESULT CALLBACK WndProc( HWND hWnd, UINT uMsg, WPARAM wParam, LPARAM lParam )
{
    switch( uMsg )
    {
        case WM_CREATE :
                InitCommonControls();
                break;

        case WM_COMMAND :
                switch( LOWORD( wParam ) )
                {
                    case IDM_TEST :
                            DisplayProperties( hWnd );
                            break;
        .
        .
        .

}


VOID DisplayProperties( HWND hWnd )
{
    PROPSHEETPAGE    psp;
    PROPSHEETHEADER  psh;
    HPROPSHEETPAGE   hpsp[3];

    // Create the property pages.
    //..........................
    psp.dwSize    = sizeof( PROPSHEETPAGE );
    psp.dwFlags   = PSP_DEFAULT;
    psp.hInstance = hInst;

    psp.pszTemplate = "PAGE1";
    psp.pfnDlgProc  = (DLGPROC)Page1Proc;
    hpsp[0] = CreatePropertySheetPage( &psp );

    psp.pszTemplate = "PAGE2";
    psp.pfnDlgProc  = (DLGPROC)Page2Proc;
    hpsp[1] = CreatePropertySheetPage( &psp );

    psp.pszTemplate = "PAGE3";
    psp.pfnDlgProc  = (DLGPROC)Page3Proc;
    hpsp[2] = CreatePropertySheetPage( &psp );

    // Initialize the property sheet structure.
    //.........................................
    memset( &psh, 0, sizeof( PROPSHEETHEADER ) );
    psh.dwSize      = sizeof( PROPSHEETHEADER );
```

continued on next page

continued from previous page

```
    psh.dwFlags    = PSH_USEICONID;
    psh.hInstance  = hInst;
    psh.hwndParent = hWnd;
    psh.pszIcon    = "SMALL";
    psh.nPages     = 3;
    psh.phpage     = hpsp;
    psh.pszCaption = "Properties";

    // Display the property sheet.
    //........................
    PropertySheet( &psh );
}
```

PropSheet_AddPage   ■ Win32s   ■ Windows 95   ■ Windows NT

Description	PropSheet_AddPage is a macro that adds a new page to the end of an existing property sheet. The new page should not be larger than any other page in the property sheet, since the property sheet will not be resized to fit the new page.
Syntax	BOOL **PropSheet_AddPage**(HWND *hPropSheetDlg*, HPROPSHEETPAGE *hpage*)
Message Syntax	BOOL **SendMessage**(*hPropSheetDlg*, **PSM_ADDPAGE**, 0, *hPage*)
Parameters	
hPropSheetDlg	HWND: The handle of the property sheet.
hpage	HPROPSHEETPAGE: The handle of the page, created by a call to the CreatePropertySheetPage() function, to add to the property sheet.
Include File	prsht.h
See Also	CreatePropertySheetPage(), PropSheet_RemovePage
Related Messages	PSM_ADDPAGE
Example	This example, shown in Figure 4-5 and Listing 4-3, displays a property sheet modeless dialog when the user selects the Test! menu item. Once the property sheet is created, the user can add an additional page to the property sheet by selecting the Add Page! menu item. The application then uses the PropSheet_AddPage macro to add the additional page. The user can remove the added page by selecting the Remove Page! menu item, which causes the application to call the PropSheet_RemovePage macro. Note that because this is a modeless property sheet, the PropSheet_IsDialogMessage macro is used in the message loop to process the dialog messages. The PageProc() function, shown below, also must process the PSN_QUERYCANCEL and PSN_APPLY notifications; otherwise the property sheet will not be destroyed when the user selects the OK or Cancel buttons.

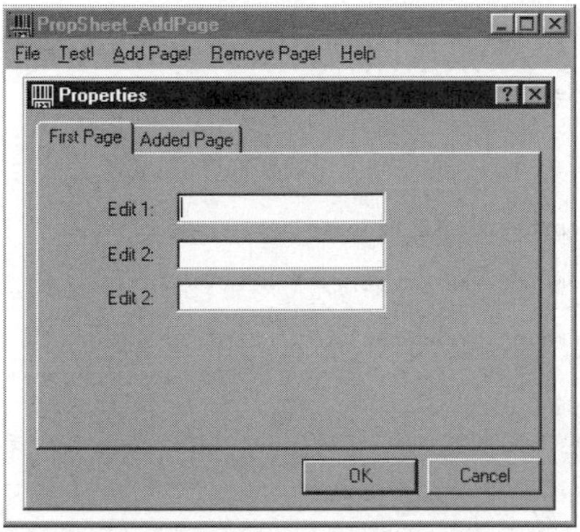

Figure 4-5 PropSheet_AddPage example

Listing 4-3 Using the Propsheet_AddPage macro

```
HWND hPropSheet = NULL;
LRESULT CALLBACK WndProc( HWND hWnd, UINT uMsg, WPARAM wParam, LPARAM lParam )
{
static HPROPSHEETPAGE hPage = NULL;

    switch( uMsg )
    {
        case WM_CREATE :
                InitCommonControls();
                break;

        case WM_COMMAND :
                switch( LOWORD( wParam ) )
                {
                    case IDM_TEST :
                            if ( !IsWindow( hPropSheet ) )
                                DisplayProperties( hWnd );
                            break;

                    case IDM_ADDPAGE :
                            if ( IsWindow( hPropSheet ) && !hPage )
                            {
                                PROPSHEETPAGE psp;

                                // Create a new page.
                                //..................
                                psp.dwSize     = sizeof( PROPSHEETPAGE );
                                psp.dwFlags    = PSP_DEFAULT;
                                psp.hInstance  = hInst;
                                psp.pszTemplate = "AddedPage";
                                psp.pfnDlgProc  = (DLGPROC)PageProc;
                                hPage = CreatePropertySheetPage( &psp );
```

continued on next page

continued from previous page

```
                                    // Add the page to the property sheet.
                                    //......................................
                                    PropSheet_AddPage( hPropSheet, hPage );
                           }
                           break;

                   case IDM_REMPAGE :
                           if ( IsWindow( hPropSheet ) && hPage )
                           {
                               // Remove the page to the property sheet.
                               //.........................................
                               PropSheet_RemovePage( hPropSheet, 1, hPage );
                               hPage = NULL;
                           }
                           break;

                   case IDM_EXIT :
                           DestroyWindow( hWnd );
                           break;
                }
                break;

        case WM_DESTROY :
                PostQuitMessage(0);

                if ( hPage )
                   DestroyPropertySheetPage( hPage );

                break;

        default :
                return( DefWindowProc( hWnd, uMsg, wParam, lParam ) );
    }

    return( 0L );
}


VOID DisplayProperties( HWND hWnd )
{
    PROPSHEETPAGE    psp;
    PROPSHEETHEADER  psh;
    HPROPSHEETPAGE   hpsp;

    // Create the property pages.
    //..........................
    psp.dwSize     = sizeof( PROPSHEETPAGE );
    psp.dwFlags    = PSP_DEFAULT;
    psp.hInstance  = hInst;
    psp.pszTemplate = "InitialPage";
    psp.pfnDlgProc  = (DLGPROC)PageProc;
    hpsp = CreatePropertySheetPage( &psp );

    // Initialize the property sheet structure.
    //.........................................
    memset( &psh, 0, sizeof( PROPSHEETHEADER ) );
    psh.dwSize     = sizeof( PROPSHEETHEADER );
    psh.dwFlags    = PSH_USEICONID | PSH_MODELESS | PSH_NOAPPLYNOW;
    psh.hInstance  = hInst;
```

```
        psh.hwndParent = hWnd;
        psh.pszIcon    = "SMALL";
        psh.nPages     = 1;
        psh.phpage     = &hpsp;
        psh.pszCaption = "Properties";

        // Create a modeless property sheet.
        //...................................
        hPropSheet = (HWND)PropertySheet( &psh );
}

LRESULT CALLBACK PageProc( HWND hDlg, UINT message,
                           WPARAM wParam, LPARAM lParam )
{
static NMHDR* nmhdr;

    switch (message)
    {
        case WM_INITDIALOG:
                return (TRUE);

        case WM_NOTIFY :
                nmhdr = (NMHDR*)lParam;
                switch( nmhdr->code )
                {
                        // The user selected the Cancel button
                        // and the properties that have been applied
                        // need to be restored.
                        //.......................................
                    case PSN_RESET :
                        // Reset data back to original state.
                        // ..................................
                        break;

                        // Cancel or Close pressed.
                        //.........................
                    case PSN_QUERYCANCEL :
                        DestroyWindow( hPropSheet );
                        break;

                        // OK Button pressed.
                        //...................
                    case PSN_APPLY :
                        DestroyWindow( hPropSheet );
                        break;

                }
                break;
    }

    return( FALSE );
}
```

PropSheet_Apply

■ Win32s ■ Windows 95 ■ Windows NT

Description PropSheet_Apply is a macro that simulates the user pressing the Apply Now button, indicating that one or more pages have changed and the changes need to be validated and recorded. The property sheet sends the

PSN_KILLACTIVE notification message to the current page. If the current page returns FALSE, the property sheet sends the PSN_APPLY notification message to all pages. See the definition of the PSN_KILLACTIVE and PSN_APPLY messages later in this chapter.

Syntax   BOOL **PropSheet_Apply**(HWND *hPropSheetDlg*)

Message Syntax   BOOL **SendMessage**(*hPropSheetDlg*, **PSM_APPLY**, 0, 0)

Parameters

hPropSheetDlg   HWND: The handle of the property sheet.

Returns   BOOL: TRUE, if all pages successfully applied the changes; otherwise, FALSE is returned.

Include File   prsht.h

Related Messages   PSM_APPLY, PSN_APPLY, PSN_KILLACTIVE

Example   This example, shown in Figure 4-6 and Listing 4-4, demonstrates how to use the Apply button on a property sheet. An additional button, Save, is added to demonstrate saving changes that cannot be canceled. As the user edits the text in the edit controls, the Save and Apply buttons are enabled. If the user selects the Save button, the OK button is changed to Close and the Cancel button is disabled. If the user selects the Apply button, the buttons remain OK and Cancel, allowing the user to select the Cancel button, which would undo the previously applied changes.

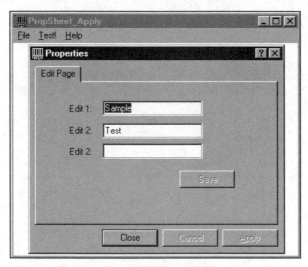

Figure 4-6 PropSheet_Apply example

Listing 4-4 Using the PropSheet_Apply macro

```
LRESULT CALLBACK PageProc( HWND hDlg, UINT message,
                           WPARAM wParam, LPARAM lParam )
{
static NMHDR* lphdr;
```

```
switch (message)
{
    case WM_INITDIALOG:
            EnableWindow( GetDlgItem( hDlg, IDC_SAVE ), FALSE );
            return (TRUE);

    case WM_COMMAND :
            switch( LOWORD( wParam ) )
            {
                case IDC_EDIT1 :
                case IDC_EDIT2 :
                case IDC_EDIT3 :
                        if ( HIWORD( wParam ) == EN_CHANGE )
                        {
                            PropSheet_Changed( GetParent( hDlg ), hDlg );
                            EnableWindow( GetDlgItem( hDlg, IDC_SAVE ), TRUE );
                        }
                        break;

                case IDC_SAVE :
                        // Permanently save the changes.

                        // Apply changes to the object.
                        //..............................
                        PropSheet_Apply( GetParent( hDlg ) );

                        // Change the OK button to Close.
                        //..............................
                        PropSheet_CancelToClose( GetParent( hDlg ) );
                        break;
            }
            break;

    case WM_NOTIFY :
            lphdr = (NMHDR*)lParam;
            if ( lphdr->code == PSN_APPLY )
            {
                // Apply changes.

                // Gray out the Apply and Save buttons.
                //.....................................
                PropSheet_UnChanged( GetParent( hDlg ), hDlg );
                EnableWindow( GetDlgItem( hDlg, IDC_SAVE ), FALSE );
            }
            break;
}

return( FALSE );
}
```

PropSheet_CancelToClose ■ Win32s ■ Windows 95 ■ Windows NT

Description   PropSheet_CancelToClose is a macro that disables the Cancel button and changes the text of the OK button to "Close". Use this macro after applying a change that cannot be canceled.

Syntax   BOOL **PropSheet_CancelToClose**(HWND *hPropSheetDlg*)

Message Syntax	BOOL **SendMessage**(*hPropSheetDlg*, **PSM_CANCELTOCLOSE**, 0, 0)
Parameters	
hPropSheetDlg	HWND: The handle of the property sheet.
Include File	prsht.h
Related Messages	PSM_CANCELTOCLOSE
Example	See the example for the PropSheet_Apply macro.

PropSheet_Changed ■ Win32s ■ Windows 95 ■ Windows NT

Description	PropSheet_Changed informs a property sheet that information in a page has changed. After this macro is called, the property sheet enables the Apply button.
Syntax	BOOL **PropSheet_Changed**(HWND *hPropSheetDlg*, HPROPSHEETPAGE *hpage*)
Message Syntax	BOOL **SendMessage**(*hPropSheetDlg*, **PSM_CHANGED**, *hpage*, 0)
Parameters	
hPropSheetDlg	HWND: The handle of the property sheet.
hpage	HPROPSHEETPAGE: The handle of the page that changed.
Include File	prsht.h
See Also	PropSheet_UnChanged
Related Messages	PSM_CHANGED
Example	See the example for the PropSheet_Apply macro.

PropSheet_GetCurrentPageHwnd ■ Win32s ■ Windows 95 ■ Windows NT

Description	PropSheet_GetCurrentPageHwnd is a macro that retrieves the handle of the current page of a property sheet. The current page is the page in the property sheet that is currently selected.
Syntax	HWND **PropSheet_GetCurrentPageHwnd**(HWND *hPropSheetDlg*)
Message Syntax	HWND **SendMessage**(*hPropSheetDlg*, **PSM_GETCURRENTPAGEHWND**, 0, 0)
Parameters	
hPropSheetDlg	HWND: The handle of the property sheet.
Returns	HWND: The handle of the current property sheet page.
Include File	prsht.h
See Also	DestroyWindow(), PropertySheet()
Related Messages	PSM_GETCURRENTPAGEHWND
Example	This example (Listing 4-5) demonstrates how to use the PropSheet_GetCurrentPageHwnd macro to retrieve the handle of the current property page so a message can be sent directly to the page.

Listing 4-5 Using the PropSheet_GetCurrentPageHwnd macro

```
LRESULT CALLBACK WndProc( HWND hWnd, UINT uMsg, WPARAM wParam, LPARAM lParam )
{
   switch( uMsg )
   {
      case WM_CREATE :
              InitCommonControls();
              DisplayProperties( hWnd );
              break;

      case WM_COMMAND :
              switch( LOWORD( wParam ) )
              {
                 case IDM_TEST :
                      if ( IsWindow( hPropSheet ) )
                      {
                         HWND hPage;

                         hPage = PropSheet_GetCurrentPageHwnd( hPropSheet );
                         SendMessage( hPage, WM_USER, 0, 0 );
                      }
                      break;
         .
         .
         .
```

PROPSHEET_GETTABCONTROL   ■ WIN32s   ■ WINDOWS 95   WINDOWS NT

Description	PropSheet_GetTabControl is a macro that retrieves the handle of the tab control to a property sheet.
Syntax	HWND **PropSheet_GetTabControl**(HWND *hPropSheetDlg*)
Message Syntax	HWND **SendMessage**(*hPropSheetDlg*, **PSM_GETTABCONTROL**, 0, 0)
Parameters	
hPropSheetDlg	HWND: The handle of the property sheet.
Returns	HWND: The handle of the tab control.
Include File	prsht.h
Related Messages	PSM_GETTABCONTROL
Example	This example (Listing 4-6) demonstrates how to use the PropSheet_GetTabControl macro to retrieve a handle to the tab control of a property sheet and assign tooltips to the tabs in the property sheet. The number of tabs is retrieved with the TabCtrl_GetItemCount macro, and each tab rectangle is retrieved with the TabCtrl_GetItemRect macro. The application adds the tools to the tooltip control, which is then associated with the tab control with the TabCtrl_SetToolTips macro.

Listing 4-6 Using the PropSheet_GetTabControl macro

```
VOID DisplayProperties( HWND hWnd )
{
```

continued on next page

continued from previous page

```
PROPSHEETPAGE     psp;
PROPSHEETHEADER   psh;
HPROPSHEETPAGE    hpsp[3];
TOOLINFO          ti;
HWND              hTabCtrl;
HWND              hToolTip;
int               nCnt, index;

psp.dwSize     = sizeof( PROPSHEETPAGE );
psp.dwFlags    = PSP_DEFAULT;
psp.hInstance  = hInst;

psp.pszTemplate = "PAGE1";
psp.pfnDlgProc  = (DLGPROC)Page1Proc;
hpsp[0] = CreatePropertySheetPage( &psp );

psp.pszTemplate = "PAGE2";
psp.pfnDlgProc  = (DLGPROC)Page2Proc;
hpsp[1] = CreatePropertySheetPage( &psp );

psp.pszTemplate = "PAGE3";
psp.pfnDlgProc  = (DLGPROC)Page3Proc;
hpsp[2] = CreatePropertySheetPage( &psp );

// Initialize the property sheet structure.
//.........................................
memset( &psh, 0, sizeof( PROPSHEETHEADER ) );
psh.dwSize     = sizeof( PROPSHEETHEADER );
psh.dwFlags    = PSH_USEICONID | PSH_MODELESS | PSH_NOAPPLYNOW;
psh.hInstance  = hInst;
psh.hwndParent = hWnd;
psh.pszIcon    = "SMALL";
psh.nPages     = 3;
psh.phpage     = hpsp;
psh.pszCaption = "Properties";

// Create a modeless property sheet.
//..................................
hPropSheet = (HWND)PropertySheet( &psh );

// Retrieve a handle to the tab control.
//......................................
hTabCtrl   = PropSheet_GetTabControl( hPropSheet );

// Create tooltip control.
//........................
hToolTip = CreateWindowEx( 0,
                           TOOLTIPS_CLASS, NULL,
                           TTS_ALWAYSTIP,
                           CW_USEDEFAULT,
                           CW_USEDEFAULT,
                           CW_USEDEFAULT,
                           CW_USEDEFAULT,
                           hWnd, NULL,
                           hInst, NULL );

// Add the tools to the tooltip control.
//.......................................
ti.cbSize = sizeof( TOOLINFO );
```

```
    ti.hwnd   = hTabCtrl;
    ti.hinst  = hInst;
    ti.uFlags = TTF_SUBCLASS;

    // Retrieve the number of tabs.
    //..........................
    nCnt = TabCtrl_GetItemCount( hTabCtrl );

    // Assign the tools to the tab control.
    //.....................................
    for( index=0; index < nCnt; index++ )
    {
        TabCtrl_GetItemRect( hTabCtrl, index, &ti.rect );

        ti.uId      = index+1;
        ti.lpszText = (LPTSTR)index+1;

        SendMessage( hToolTip, TTM_ADDTOOL, 0, (LPARAM)&ti );
    }

    // Associate the tooltip control with the tab control.
    //....................................................
    TabCtrl_SetToolTips( hTabCtrl, hToolTip );
}


LRESULT CALLBACK WndProc( HWND hWnd, UINT uMsg, WPARAM wParam, LPARAM lParam )
{
    switch( uMsg )
    {
        case WM_CREATE :
                InitCommonControls();
                break;

        case WM_COMMAND :
                switch( LOWORD( wParam ) )
                {
                    case IDM_TEST :
                            if ( !IsWindow( hPropSheet ) )
                                DisplayProperties( hWnd );
                            break;
            .
            .
            .
```

PropSheet_IsDialogMessage   ■ Win32s   ■ Windows 95   ■ Windows NT

Description	PropSheet_IsDialogMessage is a macro that passes a message to a modeless property sheet dialog box and indicates whether the dialog box processed the message. Use this function within the message loop to process the messages for the property sheet dialog before default message processing.
Syntax	BOOL **PropSheet_IsDialogMessage**(HWND *hDlg*, LPMSG *pMsg*)
Message Syntax	BOOL **SendMessage**(*hDlg*, **PSM_ISDIALOGMESSAGE**, 0, *pMsg*)

Parameters

hDlg   HWND: The handle of the property sheet.

pMsg   LPMSG: A pointer to an MSG structure that contains the message to be
                    processed by the property sheet.

Returns   BOOL: TRUE, if the message is processed; otherwise, FALSE is returned.

Include File   prsht.h

See Also   DispatchMessage(), PropertySheet(), TranslateMessage()

Related Messages PSM_ISDIALOGMESSAGE

Example   See the example for the PropSheet_AddPage macro.

PropSheet_PressButton   ■ Win32s   ■ Windows 95   ■ Windows NT

Description   PropSheet_PressButton is a macro that simulates the user pressing a prop-
                    erty sheet button.

Syntax   BOOL **PropSheet_PressButton**(HWND *hPropSheetDlg*, int *iButton*)

Message Syntax BOOL **SendMessage**(*hPropSheetDlg*, **PSM_PRESSBUTTON**, *iButton*, 0)

Parameters

hPropSheetDlg   HWND: The handle of the property sheet.

iButton   The index of the button to choose. The parameter can be one of the values
                    in Table 4-8.

Table 4-8 PropSheet_PressButton *iButton* values

Value	Meaning
PSBTN_APPLYNOW	The Apply Now button
PSBTN_BACK	The Back button
PSBTN_CANCEL	The Cancel button
PSBTN_FINISH	The Finish button
PSBTN_HELP	The Help button
PSBTN_NEXT	The Next button
PSBTN_OK	The OK button

Include File   prsht.h

Related Messages PSM_PRESSBUTTON

Example   This example (Listing 4-7) uses the PropSheet_PressButton macro to simu-
                    late the user pressing the Cancel button on a property sheet.

Listing 4-7 Using the PropSheet_PressButton macro

```
LRESULT CALLBACK WndProc( HWND hWnd, UINT uMsg, WPARAM wParam, LPARAM lParam )
{
```

```
switch( uMsg )
{
   case WM_CREATE :
            InitCommonControls();
            DisplayProperties( hWnd );
            break;

   case WM_COMMAND :
            switch( LOWORD( wParam ) )
            {
               case IDM_TEST :
                     if ( IsWindow( hPropSheet ) )
                         PropSheet_PressButton( hPropSheet, PSBTN_CANCEL );
                     break;
         .
         .
         .
```

PropSheet_QuerySiblings

■ Win32s ■ Windows 95 ■ Windows NT

Description	PropSheet_QuerySiblings is a macro that sends a PSM_QUERYSIBLINGS message to each page in the property sheet. If a page returns a nonzero value, the property sheet does not send the PSM_QUERYSIBLINGS message to subsequent pages.
	To set the return value, the dialog box procedure that receives the PSM_QUERYSIBLINGS message must use the SetWindowLong() function with the DWL_MSGRESULT value, and the dialog box procedure must return TRUE.
Syntax	int **PropSheet_QuerySiblings**(HWND *hPropSheetDlg*, WPARAM *param1*, LPARAM *param2*)
Message Syntax	int **SendMessage**(*hPropSheetDlg*, **PSM_QUERYSIBLINGS**, *param1*, *param2*)
Parameters	
hPropSheetDlg	HWND: The handle of the property sheet.
param1	WPARAM: The first application-defined parameter.
param2	LPARAM: The second application-defined parameter.
Returns	int: The nonzero value from a page in the property sheet, or zero if a page in the property sheet does not return a nonzero value.
Include File	prsht.h
Related Messages	PSM_QUERYSIBLINGS
Example	This example (Listing 4-8) uses the PropSheet_QuerySiblings macro to check the second and third pages before allowing the user to apply changes on the first page. As the user edits the first page, the sibling pages are queried to see if a check box is checked or a radio button is selected. If one is, then the Apply button is enabled.

Listing 4-8 Using the PropSheet _QuerySiblings macro

```
LRESULT CALLBACK EditProc( HWND hDlg, UINT message,
                                WPARAM wParam, LPARAM lParam )
{
    switch (message)
    {
        case WM_INITDIALOG:
                return (TRUE);

        case WM_COMMAND :
                switch( LOWORD( wParam ) )
                {
                    case IDC_EDIT1 :
                    case IDC_EDIT2 :
                    case IDC_EDIT3 :
                            if ( HIWORD( wParam ) == EN_CHANGE )
                            {
                                // Check if a button on another page is checked.
                                //...............................................
                                if ( PropSheet_QuerySiblings( GetParent( hDlg ),
                                                              0, 0 ) )
                                    PropSheet_Changed( GetParent( hDlg ), hDlg );
                            }
                            break;
                }
                break;

        case WM_NOTIFY :
                if ( ((NMHDR*)lParam)->code == PSN_APPLY )
                {
                    // Apply changes.

                    // Gray out the Apply.
                    //....................
                    PropSheet_UnChanged( GetParent( hDlg ), hDlg );
                }
                break;
    }

    return( FALSE );
}


LRESULT CALLBACK CheckProc( HWND hDlg, UINT message,
                                WPARAM wParam, LPARAM lParam )
{
    switch (message)
    {
        case WM_INITDIALOG:
                return (TRUE);

        case PSM_QUERYSIBLINGS :
                if ( IsDlgButtonChecked( hDlg, IDC_CHECK1 ) ||
                     IsDlgButtonChecked( hDlg, IDC_CHECK2 ) )
                {
                    SetWindowLong( hDlg, DWL_MSGRESULT, TRUE );
                    return( TRUE );
                }
```

```
            break;
    }

    return( FALSE );
}


LRESULT CALLBACK RadioProc( HWND hDlg, UINT message,
                            WPARAM wParam, LPARAM lParam )
{
    switch (message)
    {
        case WM_INITDIALOG:
            return (TRUE);

        case PSM_QUERYSIBLINGS :
            if ( IsDlgButtonChecked( hDlg, IDC_RADIO1 ) ||
                 IsDlgButtonChecked( hDlg, IDC_RADIO2 ) ||
                 IsDlgButtonChecked( hDlg, IDC_RADIO3 ) )
            {
                SetWindowLong( hDlg, DWL_MSGRESULT, TRUE );
                return( TRUE );
            }
            break;
    }

    return( FALSE );
}
```

PROPSHEET_REBOOTSYSTEM   ■ WIN32S   ■ WINDOWS 95   ■ WINDOWS NT

Description   PropSheet_RebootSystem indicates that the system needs to be restarted so that changes to the property sheet can take effect. An application should only use this macro in response to the PSN_APPLY or PSN_KILLACTIVE notification messages.

   This macro causes PropertySheet() to return the ID_PSREBOOTSYSTEM value if the user selects the OK button to close the property sheet. It is the application's responsibility to reboot the system, which is done by using the ExitWindowsEx() function.

Syntax   VOID **PropSheet_RebootSystem**(HWND *hPropSheetDlg*)

Message Syntax   VOID **SendMessage**(*hPropSheetDlg*, **PSM_REBOOTSYSTEM**, 0, 0)

Parameters

hPropSheetDlg   HWND: The handle of the property sheet.

Include File   prsht.h

See Also   ExitWindowsEx(), PropertySheet()

Related Messages   PSM_REBOOTSYSTEM, PSM_RESTARTWINDOWS, PSN_APPLY, PSN_KILLACTIVE

Example   This example (Listing 4-9) displays a property sheet that allows the user to select a radio button to reboot the system or to restart Windows. Depending on the radio button selected, the appropriate flag is set by using the

PropSheet_RebootSystem and PropSheet_RestartWindows macros. The return code is then checked and the appropriate action is taken.

Listing 4-9 Using the PropSheet _RebootSystem macro

```
LRESULT CALLBACK PageProc( HWND hDlg, UINT message,
                           WPARAM wParam, LPARAM lParam )
{
   switch (message)
   {
      case WM_INITDIALOG:
            return (TRUE);

      case WM_NOTIFY :
            if ( ((NMHDR*)lParam)->code == PSN_APPLY )
            {
               // Apply changes.
               if ( IsDlgButtonChecked( hDlg, IDC_REBOOT ) )
                  PropSheet_RebootSystem( GetParent( hDlg ) );

               if ( IsDlgButtonChecked( hDlg, IDC_RESTART ) )
                  PropSheet_RestartWindows( GetParent( hDlg ) );
            }
            break;
   }

   return( FALSE );
}

VOID DisplayProperties( HWND hWnd )
{
   PROPSHEETPAGE   psp;
   PROPSHEETHEADER psh;
   HPROPSHEETPAGE  hpsp;

   psp.dwSize      = sizeof( PROPSHEETPAGE );
   psp.dwFlags     = PSP_DEFAULT;
   psp.hInstance   = hInst;
   psp.pszTemplate = "RADIOPAGE";
   psp.pfnDlgProc  = (DLGPROC)PageProc;
   hpsp = CreatePropertySheetPage( &psp );

   memset( &psh, 0, sizeof( PROPSHEETHEADER ) );
   psh.dwSize      = sizeof( PROPSHEETHEADER );
   psh.dwFlags     = PSH_USEICONID | PSH_NOAPPLYNOW;
   psh.hInstance   = hInst;
   psh.hwndParent  = hWnd;
   psh.pszIcon     = "SMALL";
   psh.nPages      = 1;
   psh.phpage      = &hpsp;
   psh.pszCaption  = "Properties";

   switch( PropertySheet( &psh ) )
   {
      case ID_PSREBOOTSYSTEM :
            ExitWindowsEx( EWX_FORCE | EWX_REBOOT, 0 );
```

```
                    DestroyWindow( hWnd );
                    break;

        case ID_PSRESTARTWINDOWS :
                    ExitWindowsEx( EWX_FORCE | EW_RESTARTWINDOWS, 0 );
                    DestroyWindow( hWnd );
                    break;
    }
}
```

PropSheet_RemovePage ■ Win32s ■ Windows 95 ■ Windows NT

Description	PropSheet_RemovePage is a macro that removes a specified page from a property sheet. An application indicates the page to delete by specifying the *index* parameter, the *hpage* parameter, or both. If both parameters are specified, *hPage* takes precedence.
Syntax	VOID **PropSheet_RemovePage**(HWND *hPropSheetDlg*, int *index*, HPROPSHEETPAGE *hpage*)
Message Syntax	VOID **SendMessage**(*hPropSheetDlg*, **PSM_REMOVEPAGE**, *index*, *hpage*)
Parameters	
hPropSheetDlg	HWND: The handle of the property sheet.
index	int: The zero-based index of the page to remove.
hpage	HPROPSHEETPAGE: The handle of the page to remove.
Include File	prsht.h
Related Messages	PSM_REMOVEPAGE
Example	See the example for the PropSheet_AddPage macro.

PropSheet_RestartWindows ■ Win32s ■ Windows 95 ■ Windows NT

Description	PropSheet_RestartWindows is a macro that indicates that Windows needs to be restarted so that changes to the property sheet can take effect. An application should only use this macro in response to the PSN_APPLY or PSN_KILLACTIVE notification messages. This macro causes PropertySheet() to return the ID_PSRESTARTWINDOWS value if the user selects the OK button to close the property sheet. It is the application's responsibility to restart Windows, which can be done by using the ExitWindowsEx() function.
Syntax	VOID **PropSheet_RestartWindows**(HWND *hPropSheetDlg*)
Message Syntax	VOID **SendMessage**(*hPropSheetDlg*, **PSM_RESTARTWINDOWS**, 0, 0)
Parameters	
hPropSheetDlg	HWND: The handle of the property sheet.
Include File	prsht.h
See Also	ExitWindowsEx(), PropertySheet()

Related Messages PSM_REBOOTSYSTEM, PSM_RESTARTWINDOWS, PSN_APPLY, PSN_KILLACTIVE

Example See the example for the PropSheet_RebootSystem macro.

PropSheet_SetCurSel █ Win32s █ Windows 95 █ Windows NT

Description PropSheet_SetCurSel is a macro that activates the specified page in a property sheet. An application indicates the page to activate by specifying the *index* parameter, the *hpage* parameter, or both. If both parameters are specified, *hPage* takes precedence.

Syntax BOOL **PropSheet_SetCurSel**(HWND *hPropSheetDlg*, HPROPSHEETPAGE *hpage*, int *index*)

Message Syntax BOOL **SendMessage**(*hPropSheetDlg*, **PSM_SETCURSEL**, *index*, *hpage*)

Parameters

hPropSheetDlg HWND: The handle of the property sheet.

hpage HPROPSHEETPAGE: The handle of the page to activate.

index int: The zero-based index of the page to activate.

Returns BOOL: TRUE if successful; otherwise, FALSE is returned.

Include File prsht.h

Related Messages PSM_SETCURSEL, PSN_KILLACTIVE, PSN_SETACTIVE

Example See the example for the PropSheet_SetWizButtons macro.

PropSheet_SetCurSelByID █ Win32s █ Windows 95 █ Windows NT

Description PropSheet_SetCurSelByID is a macro that activates the specified page of a property sheet based on the resource identifier of the page.

Syntax BOOL **PropSheet_SetCurSelByID**(HWND *hPropSheetDlg*, int *id*)

Message Syntax BOOL **SendMessage**(*hPropSheetDlg*, **PSM_SETCURSELID**, 0, *id*)

Parameters

hPropSheetDlg HWND: The handle of the property sheet.

id int: The resource identifier of the page to activate.

Returns BOOL: TRUE if successful; otherwise, FALSE is returned.

Include File prsht.h

Related Message PSM_SETCURSELID, PSN_KILLACTIVE, PSN_SETACTIVE

Example See the example for the PropSheet_SetWizButtons macro.

PropSheet_SetFinishText █ Win32s █ Windows 95 █ Windows NT

Description PropSheet_SetFinishText is a macro that sets the text of the Finish button in a wizard property sheet, shows and enables the button, and hides the Next and Back buttons.

Syntax	VOID **PropSheet_SetFinishText**(HWND *hPropSheetDlg*, LPSTR *lpszText*)
Message Syntax	VOID **SendMessage**(*hPropSheetDlg*, **PSM_SETFINISHTEXT**, 0, *lpszText*)
Parameters	
hPropSheetDlg	HWND: The handle of the property sheet.
lpszText	LPSTR: A pointer to the new text for the Finish button.
Include File	prsht.h
Related Messages	PSM_SETFINISHTEXT, DM_SETDEFID
Example	See the example for the PropSheet_SetWizButtons macro.

PropSheet_SetTitle   ■ Win32s   ■ Windows 95   ■ Windows NT

Description	PropSheet_SetTitle is a macro that sets the title of the property sheet.
Syntax	VOID **PropSheet_SetTitle**(HWND *hPropSheetDlg*, DWORD *dwStyle*, LPCSTR *lpszText*)
Message Syntax	VOID **SendMessage**(*hPropSheetDlg*, **PSM_SETTITLE**, *dwStyle*, *lpszText*)
Parameters	
hPropSheetDlg	HWND: The handle of the property sheet.
dwStyle	DWORD: If *dwStyle* is PSH_PROPTITLE, the prefix "Properties for" is included with the title string; otherwise, the prefix is not used.
lpszText	LPCSTR: A pointer to a buffer containing the title string for the property sheet. If the high-order word of this parameter is NULL, the property sheet loads the string resource specified in the low-order word.
Include File	prsht.h
Related Messages	PSM_SETTITLE
Example	See the example for the PropSheet_SetWizButtons macro.

PropSheet_SetWizButtons   ■ Win32s   ■ Windows 95   ■ Windows NT

Description	PropSheet_SetWizButtons is a macro that posts the PSM_SETWIZBUTTONS message to enable the Back, Next, or Finish button in a wizard property sheet.
Syntax	VOID **PropSheet_SetWizButtons**(HWND *hPropSheetDlg*, DWORD *dwFlags*)
Message Syntax	VOID **SendMessage**(*hPropSheetDlg*, **PSM_SETWIZBUTTONS**, 0, *dwFlags*)
Parameters	
hPropSheetDlg	HWND: The handle of the property sheet.
dwFlags	DWORD: The buttons to enable in the wizard property sheet. This parameter can be a combination of the values in Table 4-9.

Table 4-9 PropSheet_SetWizButtons *dwFlags* values

Value	Meaning
PSWIZB_BACK	Back button
PSWIZB_FINISH	Finish button
PSWIZB_NEXT	Next button

Include File	prsht.h
Related Messages	PSM_SETWIZBUTTONS
Example	This example (Listing 4-10) demonstrates how to use the property sheet as a wizard. Setting up the wizard is the same as setting up a property sheet, except the user can only see one property sheet at a time. This example shows how to respond to notifications and control the navigation of the wizard.

Listing 4-10 Using the PropSheet _SetWizButtons macro

```
// Common Control Wizard Buttons.
//..............................
#define IDBACK    12323
#define IDNEXT    12324
#define IDFINISH  12325

LRESULT CALLBACK Page1Proc( HWND hDlg, UINT message,
                            WPARAM wParam, LPARAM lParam )
{
    switch (message)
    {
        case WM_INITDIALOG:
                return (TRUE);

        case WM_NOTIFY :
                switch( ((NMHDR*)lParam)->code )
                {
                    case PSN_HELP :
                        WinHelp( hDlg, "SETWIZBN.HLP", HELP_CONTEXTPOPUP, 100 );
                        break;

                    case PSN_KILLACTIVE :
                        WinHelp( hDlg, "SETWIZBN.HLP", HELP_QUIT, 0 );
                        break;

                    case PSN_SETACTIVE :
                        PropSheet_SetTitle( GetParent( hDlg ), 0, "Enter Text" );
                        PropSheet_SetWizButtons( GetParent( hDlg ),
                                                 PSWIZB_NEXT );
                        ShowWindow( GetDlgItem( GetParent( hDlg ), IDBACK ),
                                                SW_SHOW );
                        break;
```

```
                case PSN_WIZNEXT :
                    if ( SendDlgItemMessage( hDlg, IDC_EDIT1,
                                        EM_LINELENGTH, 0, 0 ) > 0 )
                    {
                        PropSheet_SetCurSel( GetParent( hDlg ), 0, 2 );
                    }
                    break;
            }
    }

    return( FALSE );
}


LRESULT CALLBACK Page2Proc( HWND hDlg, UINT message,
                        WPARAM wParam, LPARAM lParam )
{
    switch (message)
    {
        case WM_INITDIALOG:
                return (TRUE);

        case WM_NOTIFY :
                switch( ((NMHDR*)lParam)->code )
                {
                    case PSN_HELP :
                        WinHelp( hDlg, "SETWIZBN.HLP", HELP_CONTEXTPOPUP, 200 );
                        break;

                    case PSN_KILLACTIVE :
                        WinHelp( hDlg, "SETWIZBN.HLP", HELP_QUIT, 0 );
                        break;

                    case PSN_SETACTIVE :
                        PropSheet_SetTitle( GetParent( hDlg ), 0,
                                        "Check a Box" );
                        PropSheet_SetWizButtons( GetParent( hDlg ),
                                        PSWIZB_NEXT | PSWIZB_BACK );
                        break;

                    case PSN_WIZBACK :
                        if ( IsDlgButtonChecked( hDlg, IDC_CHECK1 ) ||
                             IsDlgButtonChecked( hDlg, IDC_CHECK2 ) )
                        {
                            MessageBox( hDlg,
                                        "Cannot go back because a box is checked.",
                                        lpszTitle, MB_OK | MB_ICONASTERISK );
                            return( -1 );
                        }
                        break;
                }
    }

    return( FALSE );
}


LRESULT CALLBACK Page3Proc( HWND hDlg, UINT message,
                        WPARAM wParam, LPARAM lParam )
```

continued on next page

continued from previous page

```
{
    switch (message)
    {
        case WM_INITDIALOG:
                return (TRUE);

        case WM_COMMAND :
                if ( LOWORD( wParam ) == IDC_GOBACK )
                    PropSheet_SetCurSelByID( GetParent( hDlg ), 100 );
                break;

        case WM_NOTIFY :
                switch( ((NMHDR*)lParam)->code )
                {
                    case PSN_HELP :
                        WinHelp( hDlg, "SETWIZBN.HLP", HELP_CONTEXTPOPUP, 300 );
                        break;

                    case PSN_KILLACTIVE :
                        WinHelp( hDlg, "SETWIZBN.HLP", HELP_QUIT, 0 );
                        break;

                    case PSN_SETACTIVE :
                        PropSheet_SetTitle( GetParent( hDlg ), 0,
                                            "Choose a Button and Finish" );
                        PropSheet_SetFinishText( GetParent( hDlg ),
                                                "Finish Wizard" );
                        break;

                    case PSN_WIZFINISH :
                        MessageBox( hDlg, "The wizard is finished.",
                                    lpszTitle, MB_OK | MB_ICONINFORMATION );
                        break;
                }
        }

    return( FALSE );
}


VOID DisplayWizard( HWND hWnd )
{
    PROPSHEETPAGE    psp;
    PROPSHEETHEADER  psh;
    HPROPSHEETPAGE   hpsp[3];

    psp.dwSize    = sizeof( PROPSHEETPAGE );
    psp.dwFlags   = PSP_DEFAULT | PSP_HASHELP;
    psp.hInstance = hInst;

    psp.pszTemplate = (LPCTSTR)100;
    psp.pfnDlgProc  = (DLGPROC)Page1Proc;
    hpsp[0] = CreatePropertySheetPage( &psp );

    psp.pszTemplate = (LPCTSTR)200;
    psp.pfnDlgProc  = (DLGPROC)Page2Proc;
    hpsp[1] = CreatePropertySheetPage( &psp );
```

```
        psp.pszTemplate = (LPCTSTR)300;
        psp.pfnDlgProc  = (DLGPROC)Page3Proc;
        hpsp[2] = CreatePropertySheetPage( &psp );

        memset( &psh, 0, sizeof( PROPSHEETHEADER ) );
        psh.dwSize    = sizeof( PROPSHEETHEADER );
        psh.dwFlags   = PSH_WIZARD | PSH_HASHELP;
        psh.hInstance = hInst;
        psh.hwndParent = hWnd;
        psh.nPages    = 3;
        psh.phpage    = hpsp;
        psh.pszCaption = NULL;

        PropertySheet( &psh );
}

LRESULT CALLBACK WndProc( HWND hWnd, UINT uMsg, WPARAM wParam, LPARAM lParam )
{
    switch( uMsg )
    {
        case WM_CREATE :
                InitCommonControls();
                break;

        case WM_COMMAND :
                switch( LOWORD( wParam ) )
                {
                    case IDM_TEST :
                            DisplayWizard( hWnd );
                            break;
            .
            .
            .
```

PROPSHEET_UNCHANGED   ■ WIN32S   ■ WINDOWS 95   ■ WINDOWS NT

Description	PropSheet_UnChanged is a macro that informs a property sheet that the information in a page has reverted to the previously saved state. The property sheet disables the Apply Now button if no other pages have registered changes with the property sheet.
Syntax	VOID **PropSheet_UnChanged**(HWND *hPropSheetDlg*, HWND *hwndPage*)
Message Syntax	VOID **SendMessage**(*hPropSheetDlg*, **PSM_UNCHANGED**, *hwndPage*, 0)
Parameters	
hPropSheetDlg	HWND: The handle of the property sheet.
hwndPage	HWND: The handle of the page that reverted to its previously saved state.
Include File	prsht.h
Related Messages	PSM_UNCHANGED
Example	See the example for the PropSheet_Apply macro.

TabCtrl_AdjustRect   ■ Win32s   ■ Windows 95   ■ Windows NT

Description	TabCtrl_AdjustRect is a macro that returns the tab control's display area using the given window rectangle, or returns the window rectangle that would correspond to the given display area.
Syntax	VOID **TabCtrl_AdjustRect**(HWND *hwnd*, BOOL *bLarger*, RECT* *prc*)
Message Syntax	VOID **SendMessage**(*hWnd*, **TCM_ADJUSTRECT**, *bLarger*, *prc*)
Parameters	
hwnd	HWND: The handle of the tab control.
bLarger	BOOL: The operation to perform. TRUE indicates that *prc* specifies a display rectangle and receives the corresponding window rectangle. FALSE indicates that *prc* specifies a window rectangle and receives the corresponding display area.
prc	RECT*: A pointer to a RECT structure that specifies the window rectangle and receives the calculated rectangle.
Include File	commctrl.h
Related Messages	TCM_ADJUSTRECT
Example	See the example for the TabCtrl_InsertItem macro.

TabCtrl_DeleteAllItems   ■ Win32s   ■ Windows 95   ■ Windows NT

Description	TabCtrl_DeleteAllItems is a macro that removes all items from a tab control.
Syntax	BOOL **TabCtrl_DeleteAllItems**(HWND *hwnd*)
Message Syntax	BOOL **SendMessage**(*hWnd*, **TCM_DELETEALLITEMS**, 0, 0)
Parameters	
hwnd	HWND: The handle of the tab control.
Include File	commctrl.h
Returns	BOOL: TRUE if successful; otherwise, FALSE is returned.
Related Messages	TCM_DELETEALLITEMS
Example	See the example for the TabCtrl_DeleteItem macro.

TabCtrl_DeleteItem   ■ Win32s   ■ Windows 95   ■ Windows NT

Description	TabCtrl_DeleteItem is a macro that removes an item from a tab control.
Syntax	BOOL **TabCtrl_DeleteItem**(HWND *hwnd*, int *iItem*)
Message Syntax	BOOL **SendMessage**(*hWnd*, **TCM_DELETEITEM**, *iItem*, 0)
Parameters	
hwnd	HWND: The handle of the tab control.
iItem	int: The index of the item to remove from the specified tab control.
Include File	commctrl.h

Returns	BOOL: TRUE if successful; otherwise, FALSE is returned.
Related Messages	TCM_DELETEITEM
Example	This example (Listing 4-11) demonstrates many of the tab control macros. The application starts with an empty tab control. The user can use the Edit menu to create new Circle, Rectangle, and Line tabs in the tab control. The user can also delete the current tab or all the tabs from the Edit menu. Tooltips and tab images are also demonstrated as shown in Figure 4-7.

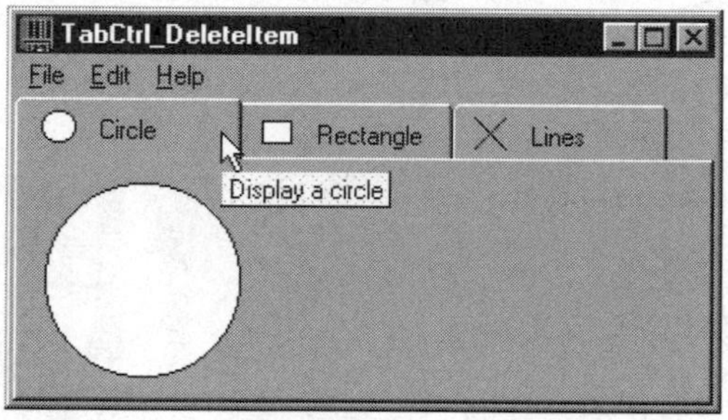

Figure 4-7 TabCtrl_DeleteItem example

Listing 4-11 Using the TabCtrl _DeleteItem macro

```
LPCTSTR szImages[]   = { "CIRCLE", "RECTANGLE", "LINES" };
LPCTSTR szMasks[]    = { "CIRCLEM", "RECTANGLEM", "LINESM" };
LPCTSTR szTips[]     = { "Display a circle", "Display a rectangle", "Display lines" };

HWND    hTab         = NULL;
FARPROC pDefStatProc = NULL;

LRESULT CALLBACK WndProc( HWND hWnd, UINT uMsg, WPARAM wParam, LPARAM lParam )
{
static RECT    rcDisp, clRect;
static TC_ITEM item;
static HWND    hStatic = NULL;

   switch( uMsg )
   {
      case WM_CREATE :
              // Initialize and create the tab control and the static control.
              //................................................................
              InitCommonControls();
              hTab = CreateWindowEx( 0, WC_TABCONTROL, "",
                                     WS_CHILD | WS_CLIPSIBLINGS |
                                     WS_VISIBLE | TCS_FIXEDWIDTH |
                                     TCS_FORCELABELLEFT | TCS_TOOLTIPS,
                                     0, 0, 10, 10, hWnd,
                                     (HMENU)101, hInst, NULL );

              hStatic = CreateWindowEx( 0, "STATIC", "", WS_CHILD | WS_VISIBLE,
                                        0, 0, 10, 10, hWnd, (HMENU)102,
                                        hInst, NULL );
```

continued on next page

continued from previous page

```
            if ( hTab )
            {
                HIMAGELIST hList;


                SendMessage( hTab, WM_SETFONT,
                            (WPARAM)GetStockObject( DEFAULT_GUI_FONT ), 0 );

                // Create an image list and associate it.
                //........................................
                hList = ImageList_Create( 16, 15, ILC_COLOR4|ILC_MASK, 3, 1 );
                TabCtrl_SetImageList( hTab, hList );

                // Set the size and spacing for the tabs.
                //........................................
                TabCtrl_SetItemSize( hTab, 100, 25 );
                TabCtrl_SetPadding( hTab, 10, 4 );

                // Change tooltip delay.
                //.......................
                SendMessage( TabCtrl_GetToolTips( hTab ),
                            TTM_SETDELAYTIME, TTDT_RESHOW, 1000 );
            }

            // Subclass the static control to perform painting.
            //.................................................
            if ( hStatic )
                pDefStatProc = (FARPROC)SetWindowLong( hStatic, GWL_WNDPROC,
                                                    (LONG)StatProc );

            break;

        case WM_SIZE :
            // Retrieve the client rect.
            //...........................
            GetClientRect( hWnd, &clRect );
            GetClientRect( hWnd, &rcDisp );

            // Calculate the tab control display area.
            //........................................
            TabCtrl_AdjustRect( hTab, FALSE, &rcDisp );

            // Size the tab control.
            //.......................
            MoveWindow( hTab, 0, 0, LOWORD(lParam), HIWORD(lParam), TRUE );
            MoveWindow( hStatic, rcDisp.left, rcDisp.top,
                            rcDisp.right-rcDisp.left,
                            rcDisp.bottom-rcDisp.top, TRUE );

            break;

        case WM_NOTIFY :
            switch( ((NMHDR*)lParam)->code )
            {
                case TCN_SELCHANGE :
                    // The user selected a different tab.
                    // Force the window to be painted.
                    //...................................
                    InvalidateRect( hTab, &rcDisp, TRUE );
                    UpdateWindow( hTab );
                    InvalidateRect( hStatic, NULL, TRUE );
                    break;
```

```
            case TTN_NEEDTEXT :
                    // Retrieve item information and set tip text.
                    //.........................................
                    item.mask = TCIF_PARAM;
                    TabCtrl_GetItem( hTab,((NMHDR*)lParam)->idFrom, &item );
                    ((LPTOOLTIPTEXT)lParam)->lpszText =
                                        (LPSTR)szTips[item.lParam-1];
                    break;
            }
            break;

    case WM_COMMAND :
            switch( LOWORD( wParam ) )
            {
            case IDM_CIRCLE :
                    item.mask = TCIF_TEXT | TCIF_PARAM | TCIF_IMAGE;
                    item.pszText = "Circle";
                    item.lParam  = 1;
                    item.iImage  = AddImage(TabCtrl_GetImageList(hTab),0);
                    TabCtrl_InsertItem( hTab, TabCtrl_GetItemCount( hTab ),
                                        &item );
                    UpdateTabWindow( hWnd, &clRect );
                    break;

            case IDM_RECTANGLE :
                    item.mask = TCIF_TEXT | TCIF_PARAM | TCIF_IMAGE;
                    item.pszText = "Rectangle";
                    item.lParam  = 2;
                    item.iImage  = AddImage(TabCtrl_GetImageList(hTab),1);
                    TabCtrl_InsertItem( hTab, TabCtrl_GetItemCount( hTab ),
                                        &item );
                    UpdateTabWindow( hWnd, &clRect );
                    break;

            case IDM_LINES :
                    item.mask = TCIF_TEXT | TCIF_PARAM | TCIF_IMAGE;
                    item.pszText = "Lines";
                    item.lParam  = 3;
                    item.iImage  = AddImage(TabCtrl_GetImageList(hTab),2);
                    TabCtrl_InsertItem( hTab, TabCtrl_GetItemCount( hTab ),
                                        &item );
                    UpdateTabWindow( hWnd, &clRect );
                    break;

            case IDM_DELETE :
                    {
                        int nSel = TabCtrl_GetCurFocus( hTab );

                        if ( nSel > -1 )
                        {
                            // Delete the tab and related image.
                            //.................................
                            TabCtrl_DeleteItem( hTab, nSel );
                            TabCtrl_RemoveImage( hTab, nSel );

                            // Set the selected tab to the next tab or
                            // the previous one if the deleted tab was the
                            // last tab in the tab control.
                            //...........................................
```

continued on next page

continued from previous page

```
                                if ( nSel > TabCtrl_GetItemCount( hTab )-1 )
                                    nSel--;

                                if ( nSel > -1 )
                                {
                                    TabCtrl_SetCurSel( hTab, nSel );

                                    InvalidateRect( hTab, &rcDisp, TRUE );
                                    UpdateWindow( hTab );
                                    InvalidateRect( hStatic, NULL, TRUE );
                                }
                                else
                                    InvalidateRect( hTab, NULL, TRUE );
                            }
                        }
                        break;

                    case IDM_DELETEALL :
                            {
                                HIMAGELIST hList;

                                TabCtrl_DeleteAllItems( hTab );

                                // Remove all images from the image list.
                                //......................................
                                hList = TabCtrl_GetImageList( hTab );
                                ImageList_Remove( hList, -1 );
                            }
                            break;

                    case IDM_EXIT :
                            DestroyWindow( hWnd );
                            break;
                }
                break;

        case WM_DESTROY :
                ImageList_Destroy( TabCtrl_GetImageList( hTab ) );

                PostQuitMessage(0);
                break;

        default :
                return( DefWindowProc( hWnd, uMsg, wParam, lParam ) );
    }

    return( FALSE );
}

LRESULT CALLBACK StatProc( HWND hWnd, UINT uMsg, WPARAM wParam, LPARAM lParam )
{
static TC_ITEM item;
static int nSel = 0;

    switch( uMsg )
    {
        case WM_PAINT :
                {
                    PAINTSTRUCT ps;
```

```
        BeginPaint( hWnd, &ps );

        // Determine which tab is displayed.
        //..................................
        nSel = TabCtrl_GetCurSel( hTab );

        if ( nSel > -1 )
        {
            item.mask = TCIF_PARAM;
            TabCtrl_GetItem( hTab, nSel, &item );

            // Paint the appropriate figure for the tab.
            //...........................................
            switch( item.lParam )
            {
                case 1 : Ellipse( ps.hdc, 10, 10, 100, 100 );
                         break;

                case 2 : Rectangle( ps.hdc, 10, 10, 100, 100 );
                         break;

                case 3 : MoveToEx( ps.hdc, 10, 10, NULL );
                         LineTo( ps.hdc, 100, 100 );
                         MoveToEx( ps.hdc, 100, 10, NULL );
                         LineTo( ps.hdc, 10, 100 );
                         break;
            }
        }
        EndPaint( hWnd, &ps );
    }
    break;

    default :
        return( (*pDefStatProc)(hWnd, uMsg, wParam, lParam) );
    }

    return( FALSE );
}

VOID UpdateTabWindow( HWND hWnd, RECT* pRect )
{
    if ( TabCtrl_GetItemCount( hTab ) == 1 )
    {
        SendMessage( hWnd, WM_SIZE, 0, MAKELPARAM(pRect->right, pRect->bottom) );
        InvalidateRect( hWnd, NULL, TRUE );
    }
}

int AddImage( HIMAGELIST hList, int nIdx )
{
    HBITMAP hBmp, hMask;

    // Load the images for the image.
    //...............................
    hBmp  = LoadBitmap( hInst, szImages[nIdx] );
    hMask = LoadBitmap( hInst, szMasks[nIdx] );

    // Add the image to the list.
    //...........................
```

continued on next page

continued from previous page

```
    nIdx = ImageList_Add( hList, hBmp, hMask );

    DeleteObject( hBmp );
    DeleteObject( hMask );

    // Return the image index.
    //......................
    return( nIdx );
}
```

TabCtrl_GetCurFocus   ■ Win32s   ■ Windows 95   ■ Windows NT

Description	TabCtrl_GetCurFocus is a macro that returns the index of the tab control item with the focus.
Syntax	int **TabCtrl_GetCurFocus**(HWND *hwnd*)
Message Syntax	int **SendMessage**(*hWnd*, **TCM_GETCURFOCUS**, 0, 0)
Parameters	
hwnd	HWND: The handle of the tab control.
Include File	commctrl.h
Returns	int: The index of the tab control item with the focus.
Related Messages	TCM_GETCURFOCUS
Example	See the example for the TabCtrl_DeleteItem macro.

TabCtrl_GetCurSel   ■ Win32s   ■ Windows 95   ■ Windows NT

Description	TabCtrl_GetCurSel is a macro that determines the currently selected tab in a tab control.
Syntax	int **TabCtrl_GetCurSel**(HWND *hwnd*)
Message Syntax	int **SendMessage**(*hWnd*, **TCM_GETCURSEL**, 0, 0)
Parameters	
hwnd	HWND: The handle of the tab control.
Include File	commctrl.h
Returns	int: The index of the selected tab, if successful; otherwise, -1 is returned if a tab is not selected.
Related Messages	TCM_GETCURSEL
Example	See the example for the TabCtrl_InsertItem macro.

TabCtrl_GetImageList   ■ Win32s   ■ Windows 95   ■ Windows NT

Description	TabCtrl_GetImageList is a macro that retrieves the image list associated with a tab control.
Syntax	HIMAGELIST **TabCtrl_GetImageList**(HWND *hwnd*)

Message Syntax	HIMAGELIST **SendMessage**(*hWnd*, **TCM_GETIMAGELIST**, 0, 0)
Parameters	
hwnd	HWND: The handle of the tab control.
Include File	commctrl.h
Returns	HIMAGELIST: The handle of the image list associated with the specified tab control.
Related Messages	TCM_GETIMAGELIST
Example	See the example for the TabCtrl_DeleteItem macro.

TabCtrl_GetItem ■ Win32s ■ Windows 95 ■ Windows NT

Description	TabCtrl_GetItem is a macro that retrieves information about a tab in a tab control.
Syntax	BOOL **TabCtrl_GetItem**(HWND *hwnd*, int *iItem*, TC_ITEM FAR * *pitem*)
Message Syntax	BOOL **SendMessage**(*hWnd*, **TCM_GETITEM**, *iItem*, *pitem*)
Parameters	
hwnd	HWND: The handle of the tab control.
iItem	int: The index of the tab.
pitem	TC_ITEM FAR *: A pointer to a TC_ITEM structure that specifies the information to retrieve and receives information about the tab. The *mask* member specifies which attributes to return. If the *mask* member specifies the TCIF_TEXT value, the *pszText* member must contain the address of the buffer that receives the item text and the *cchTextMax* member must specify the size of the buffer. See the definition of the TC_ITEM structure below.
Include File	commctrl.h
Returns	BOOL: TRUE if successful; otherwise, FALSE is returned.
Related Messages	TCM_GETITEM
TC_ITEM Definition	

```
typedef struct _TC_ITEM
{
    UINT mask;
    UINT lpReserved1;
    UINT lpReserved2;
    LPSTR pszText;
    int cchTextMax;
    int iImage;
    LPARAM lParam;
} TC_ITEM;
```

Members	
mask	UINT: A value specifying which members to retrieve or set. This value can be TCIF_ALL (meaning all members), or zero or more of the values in Table 4-10.

Table 4-10 TC_ITEM *mask* values

Value	Meaning
TCIF_IMAGE	The *iImage* member is valid.
TCIF_PARAM	The *lParam* member is valid.
TCIF_RTLREADING	In Windows 95 only, displays the text of *pszText* using right-to-left reading order on Hebrew or Arabic systems.
TCIF_TEXT	The *pszText* member is valid.

lpReserved1	UINT: This member is reserved; do not use.
lpReserved2	UINT: This member is reserved; do not use.
pszText	LPSTR: A pointer to a null-terminated string that contains the tab text if the structure contains information about a tab. If the structure is receiving information, this member specifies the address of the buffer that receives the tab text.
cchTextMax	int: The size of the buffer pointed to by the *pszText* member. If the structure is not receiving information, this member is ignored.
iImage	int: Index into the tab control's image list, or -1 if there is no image for the tab.
lParam	LPARAM: Application-defined data associated with the tab. If there are more or less than four bytes of application-defined data per tab, an application must define a structure and use it instead of the TC_ITEM structure. The first member of the application-defined structure must be a TC_ITEMHEADER structure.
Example	See the example for the TabCtrl_DeleteItem macro.

TabCtrl_GetItemCount ■ Win32s ■ Windows 95 ■ Windows NT

Description	TabCtrl_GetItemCount is a macro that retrieves the number of tabs in the tab control.
Syntax	int **TabCtrl_GetItemCount**(HWND *hwnd*)
Message Syntax	int **SendMessage**(*hWnd*, **TCM_GETITEMCOUNT**, 0, 0)
Parameters	
hwnd	HWND: The handle of the tab control.
Include File	commctrl.h
Returns	int: The number of items, if successful; otherwise, zero is returned.
Related Messages	TCM_GETITEMCOUNT
Example	See the example for the PropSheet_GetTabControl macro.

TabCtrl_GetItemRect
■ Win32s ■ Windows 95 ■ Windows NT

Description	TabCtrl_GetItemRect is a macro that retrieves the bounding rectangle for a tab in a tab control.
Syntax	BOOL **TabCtrl_GetItemRect**(HWND *hwnd*, int *iItem*, RECT FAR * *prc*)
Message Syntax	BOOL **SendMessage**(*hWnd*, **TCM_GETITEMRECT**, *iItem*, *prc*)
Parameters	
hwnd	HWND: The handle of the tab control.
iItem	int: The index of the tab.
prc	RECT FAR *: A pointer to a RECT structure that receives the bounding rectangle of the tab, in viewport coordinates. See the definition of the RECT structure in the TabCtrl_AdjustRect macro.
Include File	commctrl.h
Returns	BOOL: TRUE if successful; otherwise, FALSE is returned.
Related Messages	TCM_GETITEMRECT
Example	See the example for the PropSheet_GetTabControl macro.

TabCtrl_GetRowCount
■ Win32s ■ Windows 95 ■ Windows NT

Description	TabCtrl_GetRowCount is a macro that retrieves the current number of rows of tabs in a tab control. Only tab controls with the TCS_MULTILINE style can have multiple rows of tabs.
Syntax	int **TabCtrl_GetRowCount**(HWND *hwnd*)
Message Syntax	int **SendMessage**(*hWnd*, **TCM_GETROWCOUNT**, 0, 0)
Parameters	
hwnd	HWND: The handle of the tab control.
Include File	commctrl.h
Returns	int: The number of rows of tabs.
Related Messages	TCM_GETROWCOUNT

TabCtrl_GetToolTips
■ Win32s ■ Windows 95 ■ Windows NT

Description	TabCtrl_GetToolTips is a macro that retrieves the handle of the tooltip control associated with a tab control.
Syntax	HWND **TabCtrl_ToolTips**(HWND *hwnd*)
Message Syntax	HWND **SendMessage**(*hWnd*, **TCM_GETTOOLTIPS**, 0, 0)
Parameters	
hwnd	HWND: The handle of the tab control.
Include File	commctrl.h

Returns	HWND: The handle of the tooltip control, if successful; otherwise, NULL is returned.
Related Messages	TCM_GETTOOLTIPS, TCM_SETTOOLTIPS
Example	See the example for the TabCtrl_DeleteItem macro.

TabCtrl_HitTest ■ Win32s ■ Windows 95 ■ Windows NT

Description	TabCtrl_HitTest is a macro that determines which tab, if any, is at the specified screen position.
Syntax	int **TabCtrl_HitTest**(HWND *hwnd*, TC_HITTESTINFO FAR * *pinfo*)
Message Syntax	int **SendMessage**(*hWnd*, **TCM_HITTEST**, 0, *pinfo*)
Parameters	
hwnd	HWND: The handle of the tab control.
pinfo	TC_HITTESTINFO FAR *: A pointer to a TC_HITTESTINFO structure that specifies the screen position to test. See the definition of the TC_HITTESTINFO structure below.
Include File	commctrl.h
Returns	int: The index of the tab, or -1 if a tab is not at the specified screen position.
Related Messages	TCM_HITTEST

TC_HITTESTINFO Definition

```
typedef struct _TC_HITTESTINFO
{
    POINT pt;
    UINT  flags;
} TC_HITTESTINFO;
```

Members	
pt	POINT: The position to hit test, in client coordinates.
flags	UINT: The variable that receives the results of a hit test. The tab control sets this member to one of the values in Table 4-11.

Table 4-11 TC_HITTESTINFO *flags* values

Value	Meaning
TCHT_NOWHERE	The position is not over a tab.
TCHT_ONITEM	The position is over a tab, but not over its icon or its text. For owner-drawn tab controls, this value is specified if the position is anywhere over a tab. TCHT_ONITEM is a bitwise OR operation on TCHT_ONITEMICON and TCHT_ONITEMLABEL.
TCHT_ONITEMICON	The position is over a tab's icon.
TCHT_ONITEMLABEL	The position is over a tab's text.

TabCtrl_InsertItem

■ **Win32s**   ■ **Windows 95**   ■ **Windows NT**

Description	TabCtrl_InsertItem is a macro that inserts a new tab in a tab control.
Syntax	int **TabCtrl_InsertItem**(HWND *hwnd*, int *iItem*, const TC_ITEM* *pitem*)
Message Syntax	int **SendMessage**(*hWnd*, **TCM_INSERTITEM**, *iItem*, *pitem*)
Parameters	
hwnd	HWND: The handle of the tab control.
iItem	int: The index of the new tab.
pitem	TC_ITEM*: A pointer to a TC_ITEM structure that specifies the attributes of the tab. See the definition of the TC_ITEM structure under the TabCtrl_GetItem macro.
Include File	commctrl.h
Returns	int: The index of the new tab, if successful; otherwise, -1 is returned.
Related Messages	TCM_INSERTITEM
Example	This example, shown in Figure 4-8 and Listing 4-12, demonstrates how to create a tab control and insert items into it with the TabCtrl_InsertItem macro. The tab control is created and three tabs (Circle, Rectangle, and Lines) are added to the tab control when the example processes the WM_CREATE message. As the user selects the tabs, the graphic symbol changes.

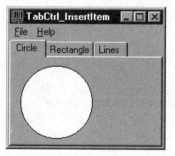

Figure 4-8 TabCtrl_InsertItem example

Listing 4-12 Using the TabCtrl_InsertItem macro

```
HWND     hTab          = NULL;
FARPROC pDefStatProc = NULL;

LRESULT CALLBACK WndProc( HWND hWnd, UINT uMsg, WPARAM wParam, LPARAM lParam )
{
static RECT   rcDisp;
static HWND    hStatic = NULL;

   switch( uMsg )
   {
```

continued on next page

continued from previous page

```
case WM_CREATE :
        // Initialize and create the tab control and the static control.
        //...........................................................
        InitCommonControls();
        hTab = CreateWindowEx( 0, WC_TABCONTROL, "",
                               WS_CHILD | WS_CLIPSIBLINGS | WS_VISIBLE,
                               0, 0, 10, 10, hWnd,
                               (HMENU)101, hInst, NULL );

        hStatic = CreateWindowEx( 0, "STATIC", "", WS_CHILD | WS_VISIBLE,
                                  0, 0, 10, 10, hWnd, (HMENU)102,
                                  hInst, NULL );

        // Add the tabs to the tab control.
        //................................
        if ( hTab )
        {
            TC_ITEM item;

            SendMessage( hTab, WM_SETFONT,
                         (WPARAM)GetStockObject( DEFAULT_GUI_FONT ), 0 );

            item.mask    = TCIF_TEXT;

            item.pszText = "Circle";
            TabCtrl_InsertItem( hTab, 0, &item );

            item.pszText = "Rectangle";
            TabCtrl_InsertItem( hTab, 1, &item );

            item.pszText = "Lines";
            TabCtrl_InsertItem( hTab, 2, &item );
        }

        // Subclass the static control to perform painting.
        //................................................
        if ( hStatic )
            pDefStatProc = (FARPROC)SetWindowLong( hStatic,
                             GWL_WNDPROC, (LONG)StatProc );
        break;

case WM_SIZE :
        // Retrieve the client rect.
        //.........................
        GetClientRect( hWnd, &rcDisp );

        // Calculate the tab control display area.
        //.......................................
        TabCtrl_AdjustRect( hTab, FALSE, &rcDisp );

        // Size the tab control.
        //.....................
        MoveWindow( hTab, 0, 0, LOWORD(lParam), HIWORD(lParam), TRUE );
        MoveWindow( hStatic, rcDisp.left, rcDisp.top,
                    rcDisp.right-rcDisp.left,
                    rcDisp.bottom-rcDisp.top, TRUE );
        break;

case WM_NOTIFY :
        switch( ((NMHDR*)lParam)->code )
```

```
              {
                 case TCN_SELCHANGE :
                         // The user selected a different tab.
                         // Force the window to be painted.
                         //......................................
                         InvalidateRect( hTab, &rcDisp, TRUE );
                         UpdateWindow( hTab );
                         InvalidateRect( hStatic, NULL, TRUE );
                         break;
              }
              break;
          .
          .
          .


LRESULT CALLBACK StatProc( HWND hWnd, UINT uMsg, WPARAM wParam, LPARAM lParam )
{
static int nSel = 0;

    switch( uMsg )
      {
        case WM_PAINT :
              {
                 PAINTSTRUCT ps;

                 BeginPaint( hWnd, &ps );

                 // Determine which tab is displayed.
                 //...................................
                 nSel = TabCtrl_GetCurSel( hTab );

                 // Paint the appropriate figure for the tab.
                 //...........................................
                 switch( nSel )
                 {
                     case 0 : Ellipse( ps.hdc, 10, 10, 100, 100 );
                              break;

                     case 1 : Rectangle( ps.hdc, 10, 10, 100, 100 );
                              break;

                     case 2 : MoveToEx( ps.hdc, 10, 10, NULL );
                              LineTo( ps.hdc, 100, 100 );
                              MoveToEx( ps.hdc, 100, 10, NULL );
                              LineTo( ps.hdc, 10, 100 );
                              break;
                 }

                 EndPaint( hWnd, &ps );
              }
              break;

        default :
              return( (*pDefStatProc)(hWnd, uMsg, wParam, lParam) );
      }

    return( FALSE );
}
```

TABCTRL_REMOVEIMAGE ■ WIN32S ■ WINDOWS 95 ■ WINDOWS NT

Description	TabCtrl_RemoveImage is a macro that removes an image from a tab control's image list.
Syntax	VOID **TabCtrl_RemoveImage**(HWND *hwnd*, int *iImage*)
Message Syntax	VOID **SendMessage**(*hWnd*, **TCM_REMOVEIMAGE**, *iImage*, 0)
Parameters	
hwnd	HWND: The handle of the tab control.
iImage	int: The index of the image to remove from the image list.
Include File	commctrl.h
Related Messages	TCM_REMOVEIMAGE
Example	See the example for the TabCtrl_DeleteItem macro.

TABCTRL_SETCURSEL ■ WIN32S ■ WINDOWS 95 ■ WINDOWS NT

Description	TabCtrl_SetCurSel is a macro that selects a tab in a tab control.
Syntax	int **TabCtrl_SetCurSel**(HWND *hwnd*, int *iItem*)
Message Syntax	int **SendMessage**(*hWnd*, **TCM_SETCURSEL**, *iItem*, 0)
Parameters	
hwnd	HWND: The handle of the tab control.
iItem	int: The index of the tab control to select.
Include File	commctrl.h
Returns	int: The index of the previously selected tab, if successful; otherwise, -1 is returned.
Related Messages	TCM_SETCURSEL, TCN_SELCHANGE, TCN_SELCHANGING
Example	See the example for the TabCtrl_DeleteItem macro.

TABCTRL_SETIMAGELIST ■ WIN32S ■ WINDOWS 95 ■ WINDOWS NT

Description	TabCtrl_SetImageList is a macro that assigns an image list to a tab control.
Syntax	HIMAGELIST **TabCtrl_SetImageList**(HWND *hwnd*, HIMAGELIST *himl*)
Message Syntax	HIMAGELIST **SendMessage**(*hWnd*, **TCM_SETIMAGELIST**, 0, *himl*)
Parameters	
hwnd	HWND: The handle of the tab control.
himl	HIMAGELIST: The handle of the image list to assign to the tab control.
Include File	commctrl.h
Returns	HIMAGELIST: The handle of the previous image list or NULL if there is not a previous list.
Related Messages	TCM_SETIMAGELIST
Example	See the example for the TabCtrl_DeleteItem macro.

TabCtrl_SetItem
■ Win32s ■ Windows 95 ■ Windows NT

Description	TabCtrl_SetItem is a macro that sets some or all of a tab's attributes.
Syntax	BOOL **TabCtrl_SetItem**(HWND *hwnd*, int *iItem*, TC_ITEM* *pitem*)
Message Syntax	BOOL **SendMessage**(*hWnd*, **TCM_SETITEM**, *iItem*, *pitem*)
Parameters	
hwnd	HWND: The handle of the tab control.
iItem	int: The index of the tab.
pitem	TC_ITEM*: A pointer to a TC_ITEM structure containing the new attributes for the specified tab. The *mask* member specifies the attributes to set. If the *mask* member specifies the LVIF_TEXT value, the *pszText* member is the address of a null-terminated string and the *cchTextMax* member is ignored. See the definition of the TC_ITEM structure in the TabCtrl_GetItem macro.
Include File	commctrl.h
Returns	BOOL: TRUE if successful; otherwise, FALSE is returned.
Related Messages	TCM_SETITEM

TabCtrl_SetItemExtra
■ Win32s ■ Windows 95 ■ Windows NT

Description	TabCtrl_SetItemExtra is a macro that sets the number of bytes per tab that are reserved for application-defined data in a tab control. Use this macro to set the size of extra data only when a tab control does not contain tabs.
Syntax	BOOL **TabCtrl_SetItemExtra**(HWND *hwnd*, int *cb*)
Message Syntax	BOOL **SendMessage**(*hWnd*, **TCM_SETITEMEXTRA**, *cb*, 0)
Parameters	
hwnd	HWND: The handle of the tab control.
cb	int: The number of extra bytes.
Include File	commctrl.h
Returns	BOOL: TRUE if successful; otherwise, FALSE is returned.
Related Messages	TCM_SETITEMEXTRA

TabCtrl_SetItemSize
■ Win32s ■ Windows 95 ■ Windows NT

Description	TabCtrl_SetItemSize is a macro that sets the width and height of tabs in a fixed-width or owner-drawn tab control.
Syntax	DWORD **TabCtrl_SetItemSize**(HWND *hwnd*, int *cx*, int *cy*)
Message Syntax	DWORD **SendMessage**(*hWnd*, **TCM_SETITEMSIZE**, 0, MAKELPARAM(*cx*, *cy*))

Parameters

cx	int: The new width, in pixels, of the tabs.
cy	int: The height, in pixels, of the tabs.
hwnd	HWND: The handle of the tab control.
Include File	commctrl.h
Returns	DWORD: The old width in the low-order word, and the height in the high-order word.
Related Messages	TCM_SETITEMSIZE
Example	See the example for the TabCtrl_DeleteItem macro.

TabCtrl_SetPadding   ■ Win32s   ■ Windows 95   ■ Windows NT

Description	TabCtrl_SetPadding is a macro that sets the amount of space around each tab's icon and label in a tab control.
Syntax	VOID **TabCtrl_SetPadding**(HWND *hwnd*, int *cx*, int *cy*)
Message Syntax	VOID **SendMessage**(*hWnd*, **TCM_SETPADDING**, 0, MAKELPARAM(*cx*, *cy*))
Parameters	
hwnd	HWND: The handle of the tab control.
cx	int: The amount of horizontal spacing, in pixels, around the icon and label.
cy	int: The amount of vertical spacing, in pixels, around the icon and label.
Include File	commctrl.h
Related Messages	TCM_SETPADDING
Example	See the example for the TabCtrl_DeleteItem macro.

TabCtrl_SetToolTips   ■ Win32s   ■ Windows 95   ■ Windows NT

Description	TabCtrl_SetToolTips is a macro that assigns a tooltip control to a tab control.
Syntax	VOID **TabCtrl_SetToolTips**(HWND *hwndTab*, HWND *hwndTT*)
Message Syntax	VOID **SendMessage**(*hWnd*, **TCM_SETTOOLTIPS**, *hwndTT*, 0)
Parameters	
hwndTab	HWND: The handle of the tab control.
hwndTT	HWND: The handle of the tooltip control.
Include File	commctrl.h
Related Messages	TCM_SETTOOLTIPS
Example	See the example for the PropSheet_GetTabControl macro.

PSN_APPLY

Description	PSN_APPLY is a notification message that indicates that the user selected the OK or Apply button and wants all changes to take effect. This notification message is sent in the form of a WM_NOTIFY message.
Parameters	
lParam	NMHDR*: A pointer to an NMHDR structure. The *hwndFrom* member, of the structure, is the handle to the property sheet. See the definition of the NMHDR structure below.
Returns	int: Return the PSNRET_INVALID_NOCHANGEPAGE value to prevent the changes from taking effect and to return the focus to the page, or the PSNRET_NOERROR value to accept the changes and allow the property sheet to be destroyed.
	To set the return value, the dialog box procedure for the page must use SetWindowLong() with the DWL_MSGRESULT value, and the dialog box procedure must return TRUE.
Include File	prsht.h
See Also	EndDialog(), SetWindowLong()
Related Messages	PSN_KILLACTIVE, WM_NOTIFY
NMHDR Definition	

```
typedef struct tagNMHDR
{
    HWND hwndFrom;
    UINT idFrom;
    UINT code;
} NMHDR;
```

Members	
hwndFrom	HWND: The handle of the control sending message.
idFrom	UINT: The identifier of the control sending message.
code	UINT: The notification code. This member can be a control-specific notification code, or it can be one of the common notification values in Table 4-12.

Table 4-12 NMHDR *code* values

Value	Meaning
NM_CLICK	The user has clicked the left mouse button within the control.
NM_DBLCLK	The user has double-clicked the left mouse button within the control.
NM_KILLFOCUS	The control has lost the input focus.
NM_OUTOFMEMORY	The control could not complete an operation because there was not enough memory available.
NM_RCLICK	The user has clicked the right mouse button within the control.
NM_RDBLCLK	The user has double-clicked the right mouse button within the control.
NM_RETURN	The control has the input focus, and the user has pressed the ENTER key.
NM_SETFOCUS	The control has received the input focus.

Example   See the example for the PropSheet_AddPage macro.

PSN_HELP   ■ Win32s   ■ Windows 95   ■ Windows NT

Description   PSN_HELP is a notification message that notifies a page that the user
                  selected the Help button. This notification message is sent in the form of a
                  WM_NOTIFY message.

Parameters

lParam   NMHDR*: A pointer to an NMHDR structure. The *hwndFrom* member, of
                  the structure, is the handle to the property sheet. See the definition of the
                  NMHDR structure under the PSN_APPLY notification message.

Include File prsht.h

Related Messages WM_NOTIFY

Example   See the example for the PropSheet_SetWizButtons macro.

PSN_KILLACTIVE   ■ Win32s   ■ Windows 95   ■ Windows NT

Description   PSN_KILLACTIVE is a notification message that notifies a page that it is
                  about to lose the activation either because another page is being activated
                  or the user selected the OK button. This notification message is sent in the
                  form of a WM_NOTIFY message.

Parameters

lParam   NMHDR*: A pointer to an NMHDR structure. The *hwndFrom* member, of
                  the structure, is the handle to the property sheet. See the definition of the
                  NMHDR structure under the PSN_APPLY notification message.

Returns   BOOL: Return TRUE to prevent the page from losing the activation; other-
                  wise, FALSE to allow it. If TRUE is returned, the dialog box procedure should
                  display a message box explaining why the page did not lose activation.

                  To set the return value, the dialog box procedure for the page must use
                  the SetWindowLong() function with the DWL_MSGRESULT value, and
                  the dialog box procedure must return TRUE.

Include File prsht.h

See Also   SetWindowLong()

Related Messages WM_NOTIFY

Example   See the example for the PropSheet_SetWizButtons macro.

PSN_QUERYCANCEL   ■ Win32s   ■ Windows 95   ■ Windows NT

Description   PSN_QUERYCANCEL is a notification message that indicates that the user
                  selected the Cancel button. This notification message is sent in the form of
                  a WM_NOTIFY message.

Parameters

lParam   NMHDR*: A pointer to an NMHDR structure. The *hwndFrom* member, of the structure, is the handle to the property sheet. See the definition of the NMHDR structure under the PSN_APPLY notification message.

Returns   BOOL: Return TRUE to prevent the cancel operation; otherwise, FALSE to allow it.

           To set the return value, the dialog box procedure for the page must use the SetWindowLong() function with the DWL_MSGRESULT value, and the dialog box procedure must return TRUE.

Include File   prsht.h

Related Messages   WM_NOTIFY

Example   See the example for the PropSheet_AddPage macro.

PSN_RESET   ■ WIN32S   ■ WINDOWS 95   ■ WINDOWS NT

Description   PSN_RESET is a notification message that notifies a page that the user selected the Cancel button and the property sheet is about to be destroyed. All changes made since the user last chose the Apply button are canceled. This notification message is sent in the form of a WM_NOTIFY message.

Parameters

lParam   NMHDR*: A pointer to an NMHDR structure. The *hwndFrom* member, of the structure, is the handle to the property sheet. See the definition of the NMHDR structure under the PSN_APPLY notification message.

Include File   prsht.h

See Also   EndDialog()

Related Messages   WM_NOTIFY

Example   See the example for the PropSheet_AddPage macro.

PSN_SETACTIVE   ■ WIN32S   ■ WINDOWS 95   ■ WINDOWS NT

Description   PSN_SETACTIVE is a notification message that notifies a page that it is about to be activated. This notification message is sent in the form of a WM_NOTIFY message.

Parameters

lParam   NMHDR*: A pointer to an NMHDR structure. The *hwndFrom* member, of the structure, is the handle to the property sheet. See the definition of the NMHDR structure under the PSN_APPLY notification message.

Returns   int: Return zero to accept the activation, -1 to activate the next or previous page (depending on whether the user selected the Next or Back button), or the resource identifier of the a specific page.

To set the return value, the dialog box procedure for the page must use the SetWindowLong() function with the DWL_MSGRESULT value, and the dialog box procedure must return TRUE.

Include File	prsht.h
See Also	SetWindowLong()
Related Messages	WM_NOTIFY
Example	See the example for the PropSheet_SetWizButtons macro.

PSN_WIZBACK   ■ Win32s   ■ Windows 95   ■ Windows NT

Description   PSN_WIZBACK is a notification message that notifies a page that the user selected the Back button in a wizard property sheet. This notification message is sent in the form of a WM_NOTIFY message.

Parameters

lParam   NMHDR*: A pointer to an NMHDR structure. The *hwndFrom* member, of the structure, is the handle to the property sheet. See the definition of the NMHDR structure under the PSN_APPLY notification message.

Returns   int: Return -1 to prevent the property sheet from advancing to the previous page.

To set the return value, the dialog box procedure for the page must use the SetWindowLong() function with the DWL_MSGRESULT value, and the dialog box procedure must return TRUE.

Include File	prsht.h
Related Messages	WM_NOTIFY
Example	See the example for the PropSheet_SetWizButtons macro.

PSN_WIZFINISH   ■ Win32s   ■ Windows 95   ■ Windows NT

Description   PSN_WIZFINISH is a notification message that notifies a page that the user selected the Finish button in a wizard property sheet. This notification message is sent in the form of a WM_NOTIFY message.

Parameters

lParam   NMHDR*: A pointer to an NMHDR structure. The *hwndFrom* member, of the structure, is the handle to the property sheet. See the definition of the NMHDR structure under the PSN_APPLY notification message.

Returns   int: Return a nonzero value to prevent the property sheet from being destroyed.

To set the return value, the dialog box procedure for the page must use the SetWindowLong() function with the DWL_MSGRESULT value, and the dialog box procedure must return TRUE.

Include File   prsht.h

Related Message	WM_NOTIFY
Example	See the example for the PropSheet_SetWizButtons macro.

PSN_WIZNEXT
■ Win32s   ■ Windows 95   ■ Windows NT

Description	PSN_WIZNEXT is a notification message that notifies a page that the user selected the Next button in a wizard property sheet. This notification message is sent in the form of a WM_NOTIFY message.
Parameters	
lParam	NMHDR*: A pointer to an NMHDR structure. The *hwndFrom* member, of the structure, is the handle to the property sheet. See the definition of the NMHDR structure under the PSN_APPLY notification message.
Returns	int: Return -1 to prevent the property sheet from advancing to the next page.
	To set the return value, the dialog box procedure for the page must use the SetWindowLong() function with the DWL_MSGRESULT value, and the dialog box procedure must return TRUE.
Include File	prsht.h
Related Messages	WM_NOTIFY
Example	See the example for the PropSheet_SetWizButtons macro.

TCN_KEYDOWN
■ Win32s   ■ Windows 95   ■ Windows NT

Description	TCN_KEYDOWN is a notification message that notifies the parent window of a tab control that a key has been pressed. This message is sent in the form of a WM_NOTIFY message.
Parameters	
lParam	TC_KEYDOWN FAR *: A pointer to a TC_KEYDOWN structure. See the definition of the TC_KEYDOWN structure below.
Include File	commctrl.h
Related Messages	WM_NOTIFY, WM_KEYDOWN

TC_KEYDOWN Definition

```
typedef struct _TC_KEYDOWN
{
    NMHDR hdr;
    WORD wVKey;
    UINT flags;
} TC_KEYDOWN;
```

Members	
hdr	NMHDR: The notification header.
wVKey	WORD: The virtual key code.
flags	UINT: The same as the *lParam* parameter of the WM_KEYDOWN message.

TCN_SELCHANGE
■ Win32s ■ Windows 95 ■ Windows NT

Description	TCN_SELCHANGE is a notification message that notifies the parent window of a tab control that the currently selected tab has changed. This message is sent in the form of a WM_NOTIFY message.
Parameters	
LOWORD(wParam)	int: The index of the tab that has changed.
lParam	HWND: The handle of the tab control.
Include File	commctrl.h
Related Messages	WM_NOTIFY
Example	See the example for the TabCtrl_InsertItem macro.

TCN_SELCHANGING
■ Win32s ■ Windows 95 ■ Windows NT

Description	TCN_SELCHANGING is a notification message that notifies the parent window of a tab control that the currently selected tab is about to change.
Parameters	
LOWORD(wParam)	int: The index of the tab that is changing.
lParam	HWND: The handle of the tab control.
Include File	commctrl.h
Returns	BOOL: TRUE to prevent the selection from changing, or FALSE to allow the selection to change.
Related Messages	WM_NOTIFY

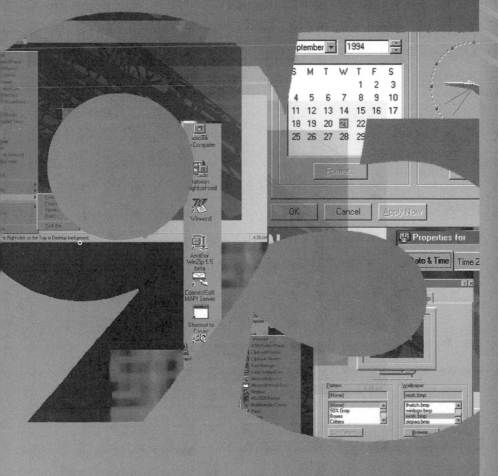

5

IMAGE LISTS

5

IMAGE LISTS

The Common Control Library is made up of several different controls that an application developer can use to enhance the user interface and to provide a uniform look and feel. Image lists, however, are not controls but rather collections of same-sized images. Image lists are used to efficiently manage large sets of icons or bitmaps such as those used with the tree view and list view controls. Image lists also facilitate drag-and-drop operations by providing a special image that represents the image that is being dragged.

Image List Types

There are two types of image lists: *masked* and *unmasked*. An unmasked image list contains one color bitmap that contains one or more images. A masked image list contains two bitmaps, the same color bitmap that the unmasked image list contains, and an identically sized monochrome bitmap that contains the corresponding masks for the color images in the first bitmap.

When an unmasked image is drawn, it is copied to the target device context with the background color of the image overlaying any existing image. When a masked image is drawn, the bits of the image are combined with the mask to produce transparent areas in the bitmap. An application should use masked images for all instances where the image has transparent areas, such as in list views and tree views. Figure 5-1 shows a color bitmap image and the monochrome mask for the image.

Using Image Lists

Before using an image list, the application must call the InitCommonControls() function to ensure that the Common Control Library is initialized. You can create an image list in many ways, the basic method being with the ImageList_Create() function. An image list can also be created with the ImageList_LoadBitmap(), ImageList_LoadImage(), and ImageList_Read() functions. For an unmasked image list, a single bitmap large enough

Figure 5-1 Image and mask

to hold the specified number of images of the given dimensions is created. The bitmap is then selected into a screen-compatible device context. A masked image list is the same, except that a second bitmap is also created and selected into a second screen-compatible device context.

An image list has an initial size that is determined at creation time. If additional images are added to the image list, thus requiring the image list to grow, the image list reallocates the bitmaps to a new, larger size determined by the number of images by which it should grow. An image list is limited to a maximum bitmap size of 32,767 by 32,767 pixels. This means that the total width of the bitmaps placed end to end cannot exceed 32K pixels. With this limit, an image list can have a maximum of 32K images of 1 pixel wide and up to 32K pixels high. Figure 5-2 shows how an image list stores 32x32 images in the image list and the size limitation.

Once an image list is no longer needed, the application must use the ImageList_Destroy() function to destroy it and free the resources.

Adding Images

An image list can contain bitmaps, icons, or cursors. Use the ImageList_Add() function to add bitmaps. This function takes two bitmap handles, the first for the image and the second for the mask. For unmasked image lists, the second bitmap handle is NULL. To add a masked bitmap without specifying a mask, use the ImageList_AddMasked() function. This function is similar to the ImageList_Add() function, except that instead of specifying a mask bitmap, you specify a color that the

Image List of 32 x 32 pixel Images

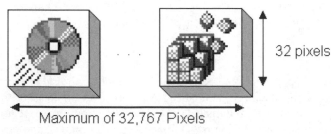

Figure 5-2 Image list diagram

system uses to generate the mask. This color effectively becomes transparent in the image.

To add icons and cursors to image lists, use the ImageList_AddIcon() function. If the image list is masked, ImageList_AddIcon() adds the mask contained in the icon or cursor.

Modifying Image Lists

Once an image list is created and images are added, the application can modify the image list by replacing images or removing images. Use the ImageList_Replace() or ImageList_ReplaceIcon() function to replace an image in an image list with a new image. The ImageList_Replace() function replaces a bitmapped image while the ImageList_ReplaceIcon() replaces an icon or cursor image.

Use the ImageList_Remove() function to remove images from an image list. You can remove a single image or clear the entire image list. The ImageList_RemoveAll macro, which is defined as the ImageList_Remove() function, is also provided to clear the image list, using the appropriate parameters to remove all the items in the image list.

The ImageList_Merge() function combines two images within an image list, storing the resulting image in a new image list. The new image is created by drawing the second image transparently over the first image.

Drawing Images

The Common Control Library provides functions for drawing the images within an image list on a device context. The two draw functions, ImageList_Draw() and ImageList_DrawEx(), draw an image on a given device context at a specified location with a specified drawing style.

A significant speed increase can be obtained if you use the ImageList_SetBkColor() function to set the background color of the image list to the same color as the destination. Setting the color eliminates the need to create transparent areas in the image and enables ImageList_Draw() and ImageList_DrawEx() to copy the image directly to the destination device context. An application can set the background color for a masked image list at any time. Setting the background color to CLR_NONE causes the images to be drawn transparently by default.

To draw the image as selected, use the ILD_BLEND25 and ILD_BLEND50 styles. These styles dither the image with the system highlight color. These styles work best with masked image lists. If the image list is not masked, the background is also dithered, which results in a nonstandard appearance for a selected image.

Every image list includes a list of up to four images to use as *overlay masks*. An overlay mask is an image drawn transparently over another image. Any image within an image list can be specified as an overlay mask. Use the ImageList_SetOverlayImage() function to specify that an image is an overlay image. To use an overlay mask, use the INDEXTOOVERLAYMASK macro with the ImageList_Draw() or ImageList_DrawEx() function. See the example for the ImageList_Replace() function later in this chapter for more information.

Dragging Images

Image lists have support for dragging an image on the screen smoothly, in color, and without cursor flicker. Both masked and unmasked images can be dragged using the provided image list functions. Begin a drag operation with the ImageList_BeginDrag() function. Move the drag image on the WM_MOUSEMOVE message with the ImageList_DragMove() function. When the user has completed the drag operation, use the ImageList_EndDrag() function.

After the ImageList_BeginDrag() function is called, use the ImageList_DragEnter() function to set the initial position of the drag image within the window and draw the image at the position. If a window handle is passed to the ImageList_DragEnter() function, the window is locked from screen updates and the drag cursor is limited to the window. If a NULL window handle is used, the desktop window is locked from updates and the drag cursor can move anywhere on the desktop. If the screen must be updated during the drag operation, such as to show a drop selection, you can temporarily hide the dragged image by using the ImageList_DragLeave() function.

The application can use the ImageList_SetDragCursorImage() function to create a new drag image by combining the current drag image with the new image (usually a mouse cursor image). The application should use the ShowCursor() function to hide the mouse cursor after calling ImageList_SetDragCursorImage(). After the drag operation is complete, use the ShowCursor() function to show the normal mouse cursor.

For a complete example of how to use the image list functions for drag-and-drop operations, see the example under the ImageList_Create() function later in this chapter.

Function Summary

Table 5-1 summarizes the image list functions and macros. The detailed function and macro descriptions follow immediately after the table.

Table 5-1 Image list function summary

Function	Meaning
ImageList_Add	Adds an image or images to an image list.
ImageList_AddIcon	Adds an icon or cursor to an image list.
ImageList_AddMasked	Adds the images from a bitmap to an image list and generates a mask from the bitmap.
ImageList_BeginDrag	Begins dragging a given image.
ImageList_Create	Creates a new image list.
ImageList_Destroy	Destroys an image list.
ImageList_DragEnter	Starts a drag operation.
ImageList_DragLeave	Ends a drag operation.
ImageList_DragMove	Moves the dragged image during a drag-and-drop operation.

Function	Meaning
ImageList_DragShowNolock	Shows or hides the image being dragged.
ImageList_Draw	Draws an image list item.
ImageList_DrawEx	Draws an image list item using a given style and color.
ImageList_EndDrag	Ends a drag operation.
ImageList_ExtractIcon	A macro that calls the ImageList_GetIcon() function.
ImageList_GetBkColor	Retrieves the background color for an image list.
ImageList_GetDragImage	Retrieves information about the drag image.
ImageList_GetIcon	Creates an icon or cursor based on an image and mask in an image list.
ImageList_GetIconSize	Retrieves the dimensions of the images in an image list.
ImageList_GetImageCount	Retrieves the number of images in an image list.
ImageList_GetImageInfo	Retrieves information about an image within an image list.
ImageList_LoadBitmap	Creates an image list from a bitmap resource.
ImageList_LoadImage	Creates an image list from a bitmap, cursor, or icon resource.
ImageList_Merge	Creates a new image by combining two existing images.
ImageList_Read	Reads the image list from a stream.
ImageList_Remove	Removes one or all images from an image list.
ImageList_RemoveAll	Removes all images from an image list.
ImageList_Replace	Replaces an image in an image list with a new image.
ImageList_ReplaceIcon	Replaces an image with an icon or cursor.
ImageList_SetBkColor	Sets the background color for an image list.
ImageList_SetDragCursorImage	Combines a given image with the current drag image to create a new drag image.
ImageList_SetIconSize	Sets the dimensions of images in an image list.
ImageList_SetOverlayImage	Adds the index of an image to the list of images to be used as overlay masks.
ImageList_Write	Writes an image list to a stream.

IMAGELIST_ADD ■ Win32s ■ Windows 95 ■ Windows NT

Description	ImageList_Add() adds an image or images to a specified image list. This function copies the bitmaps to an internal data structure so the original bitmaps are no longer needed. The application should delete the *hbmImage* and *hbmMask* bitmaps with the DeleteObject() function after ImageList_Add() returns.
Syntax	int WINAPI **ImageList_Add**(HIMAGELIST *himl*, HBITMAP *hbmImage*, HBITMAP *hbmMask*)
Parameters	
himl	HIMAGELIST: The handle of the image list.
hbmImage	HBITMAP: The handle of the bitmap that contains the image or images to add to the image list. The image size of the image list determines the number of individual images the bitmap contains.

hbmMask	HBITMAP: The handle of the bitmap that contains the mask or masks for the images. If a mask is not used with the image list, this parameter is ignored.
Returns	int: If successful, the index of the first new image is returned; otherwise, -1 is returned.
Include File	commctrl.h
See Also	ImageList_AddMasked(), ImageList_AddIcon
Example	See the example for the ImageList_Create() function.

IMAGELIST_ADDICON   ■ Win32s ■ Windows 95 ■ Windows NT

Description	ImageList_AddIcon is a macro that adds an icon or cursor to an image list. This macro calls the ImageList_ReplaceIcon() function to perform the operation.
	The icon or cursor is copied to the internal structures of the image list; therefore, the application can destroy it after the macro returns if the list was created with the CreateIcon() function. If the icon or cursor was loaded with the LoadIcon() or LoadCursor() function, the system automatically frees the resource when it is no longer needed.
Syntax	int **ImageList_AddIcon**(HIMAGELIST *himl*, HICON *hicon*)
Parameters	
himl	HIMAGELIST: The handle of the image list.
hicon	HICON: The handle of the icon or cursor containing the bitmap and mask for the new image. If *himl* identifies a masked image list, the macro copies both the image and mask bitmaps of the icon or cursor. If *himl* identifies an unmasked image list, ImageList_AddIcon copies only the image bitmap.
Returns	int: If successful, the index of the new image is returned; otherwise, -1 is returned.
Include File	commctrl.h
See Also	ImageList_ReplaceIcon(), CreateIcon(), LoadIcon()
Example	See the example for the ImageList_Create() function.

IMAGELIST_ADDMASKED   ■ Win32s ■ Windows 95 ■ Windows NT

Description	ImageList_AddMasked() adds an image or images from the specified bitmap to an image list and generates a mask from the bitmap. This function copies the bitmap to an internal data structure so the original bitmap is no longer needed. The application should delete the *hbmImage* bitmap with the DeleteObject() function after ImageList_AddMasked() returns.
Syntax	int WINAPI **ImageList_AddMasked**(HIMAGELIST *himl*, HBITMAP *hbmImage*, COLORREF *crMask*)

Parameters

himl	HIMAGELIST: The handle of the image list.
hbmImage	HBITMAP: The handle of the bitmap that contains the image or images. The image size of the image list determines the number of individual images the bitmap contains.
crMask	COLORREF: The color used when generating the mask. Each pixel of this color in the *hbmImage* bitmap is changed to black, and the corresponding bit in the mask is set to one.
Returns	int: If successful, the index of the first new image is returned; otherwise, -1 is returned.
Include File	commctrl.h
See Also	ImageList_Add()
Example	See the example for the ImageList_Create() function.

IMAGELIST_BEGINDRAG ■ Win32s ■ Windows 95 ■ Windows NT

Description	ImageList_BeginDrag() begins dragging the specified image. This function creates a temporary image list that is used for dragging. When the application receives the WM_MOUSEMOVE messages, use the ImageList_DragMove() function to move the drag image. To end the drag operation, use the ImageList_EndDrag() function.
Syntax	BOOL WINAPI **ImageList_BeginDrag**(HIMAGELIST *himlTrack*, int *iTrack*, int *dxHotspot*, int *dyHotspot*)

Parameters

himlTrack	HIMAGELIST: The handle of the image list.
iTrack	int: The index of the image to drag.
dxHotspot	int: The horizontal location of the drag position relative to the upper left corner of the image.
dyHotspot	int: The vertical location of the drag position relative to the upper left corner of the image.
Returns	BOOL: If successful, TRUE is returned; otherwise, FALSE is returned.
Include File	commctrl.h
See Also	ImageList_DragMove(), ImageList_EndDrag()
Related Messages	WM_MOUSEMOVE
Example	See the example for the ImageList_Create() function.

IMAGELIST_CREATE ■ Win32s ■ Windows 95 ■ Windows NT

Description	ImageList_Create() creates a new image list with space for *cInitial* images. If the initial number of images is used, *cGrow* additional image space is allocated.

Syntax	HIMAGELIST WINAPI **ImageList_Create**(int *cx*, int *cy*, UINT *flags* int *cInitial*, int *cGrow*)
Parameters	
cx	int: The width, in pixels, of the images.
cy	int: The height, in pixels, of the images.
flags	UINT: The type of image list to create. This parameter can be a combination of the values listed in Table 5-2.

Table 5-2 ImageList_Create() *flags* values

Value	Meaning
ILC_COLOR	Uses the default behavior if none of the other ILC_COLOR* flags is specified. Typically, the default is ILC_COLOR4; but for older display drivers, the default is ILC_COLORDDB.
ILC_COLOR4	Uses a 4-bit (16-color) device-independent bitmap (DIB) section as the bitmap for the image list.
ILC_COLOR8	Uses an 8-bit DIB section. The colors used for the color table are the same colors as the halftone palette.
ILC_COLOR16	Uses a 16-bit (32/64K color) DIB section.
ILC_COLOR24	Uses a 24-bit DIB section.
ILC_COLOR32	Uses a 32-bit DIB section.
ILC_COLORDDB	Uses a device-dependent bitmap.
ILC_MASK	Uses a mask. The image list contains two bitmaps, one of which is a monochrome bitmap used as a mask. If this value is not included, the image list contains only one bitmap.
ILC_PALETTE	Uses a color palette with the image list.

cInitial	int: The initial number of images in the image list.
cGrow	int: The number of new images allocated once the initial images are used.
Returns	HIMAGELIST: If successful, the handle of the image list is returned; otherwise, NULL is returned.
Include File	commctrl.h
See Also	ImageList_Destroy()
Example	This example (Listing 5-1) demonstrates the usage of an image list to display and move graphical objects within the client area of an application. The application creates an image list and adds two images and a cursor to it when the WM_CREATE message is processed. When the user presses the left mouse button over one of the images, the image becomes selected and the visual appearance is updated to reflect the new state. If the user continues to hold down the left mouse button and begins dragging the image, the cursor changes to a drag cursor as shown in Figure 5-3. While dragging, the drag cursor will disappear within the rectangle shown in the figure. The current drag cursor is also painted within this rectangle to demonstrate the ImageList_GetDragImage() function.

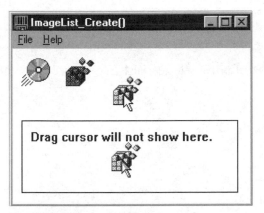

Figure 5-3 Image list drag example

Listing 5-1 Using the ImageList_Create() function

```c
#define NODRAG     0
#define POSSIBLE   1
#define DRAGGING   2

LRESULT CALLBACK WndProc( HWND hWnd, UINT uMsg, WPARAM wParam, LPARAM lParam )
{
static POINT        pt, ptWnd, movePt;
static RECT         rectangle;
static HIMAGELIST   hList      = NULL;
static int          nDragging  = NODRAG;
static int          nSel       = -1;

    switch( uMsg )
    {
        case WM_CREATE :
                InitCommonControls();

                // Create the image list.
                //......................
                hList = ImageList_Create( 32, 32, ILC_COLOR | ILC_MASK, 3, 1 );
                if ( hList )
                {
                    HBITMAP hBmp, hMask;

                    // Add masked image.
                    //..................
                    hBmp  = LoadBitmap( hInst, "BMP1" );
                    hMask = LoadBitmap( hInst, "BMP1MSK" );
                    ImageList_Add( hList, hBmp, hMask );
                    DeleteObject( hBmp );
                    DeleteObject( hMask );

                    // Add an image and build a mask.
                    //...............................
                    hBmp = LoadBitmap( hInst, "BMP2" );
```

continued on next page

continued from previous page

```
                ImageList_AddMasked( hList, hBmp, RGB( 0, 255, 0 ) );
                DeleteObject( hBmp );

                // Add an arrow cursor.
                //........................
                ImageList_AddIcon( hList, (HICON)LoadCursor(NULL,IDC_ARROW) );

                rectangle.left   = 10;
                rectangle.top    = 80;
                rectangle.right  = 250;
                rectangle.bottom = 150;
            }
            break;

    case WM_PAINT :
            {
                PAINTSTRUCT ps;

                // Paint the two images on the client area.
                //.........................................
                BeginPaint( hWnd, &ps );
                ImageList_Draw( hList, 0, ps.hdc, 10, 10,
                            ILD_NORMAL | (nSel == 0 ? ILD_SELECTED : 0));
                ImageList_Draw( hList, 1, ps.hdc, 60, 10,
                            ILD_NORMAL | (nSel == 1 ? ILD_SELECTED : 0));
                Rectangle( ps.hdc, rectangle.left, rectangle.top,
                                rectangle.right, rectangle.bottom );
                TextOut( ps.hdc, rectangle.left+10, rectangle.top+30,
                            "Drag cursor will not show here.", 31 );

                // If the image is being dragged, get the drag image
                // and display it within the rectangle on the client area.
                //.......................................................
                if ( nDragging == DRAGGING )
                {
                    HIMAGELIST hDragList = ImageList_GetDragImage( NULL, NULL );
                    int        cx,cy;

                    ImageList_GetIconSize( hDragList, &cx, &cy );
                    ImageList_Draw( hDragList, 0, ps.hdc,
                                    rectangle.left+((rectangle.right-
                                        rectangle.left-cx)/2),
                                    rectangle.top+24, ILD_NORMAL );
                }

                EndPaint( hWnd, &ps );
            }
            break;

    case WM_LBUTTONDOWN :
            {
                RECT  rect;

                rect.top    = 10;
                rect.bottom = 42;
                rect.right  = 42;
                rect.left   = 10;
```

```
            pt.x = LOWORD( lParam );
            pt.y = HIWORD( lParam );

            nSel = -1;

            // Check which image the user selected.
            //.....................................
            if ( PtInRect( &rect, pt ) )
               nSel = 0;

            rect.right = 82;
            rect.left  = 50;
            if ( PtInRect( &rect, pt ) )
               nSel = 1;

            InvalidateRect( hWnd, NULL, TRUE );

            // Calculate the offsets from the main window to the client.
            //..........................................................
            if ( nSel > -1 )
            {
               nDragging = POSSIBLE;
               SetCapture( hWnd );

               GetWindowRect( hWnd, &rect );
               ptWnd.x = rect.left;
               ptWnd.y = rect.top;

               ScreenToClient( hWnd, &ptWnd );
               ptWnd.y += GetSystemMetrics( SM_CYSIZEFRAME );
               ptWnd.x += GetSystemMetrics( SM_CXSIZEFRAME );
            }
         }
         break;

case WM_LBUTTONUP :
         // If dragging, Finish.
         //.....................
         if ( nDragging == DRAGGING )
         {
            ImageList_DragLeave( hWnd );
            ImageList_EndDrag();
            ShowCursor( TRUE );
         }

         nDragging = NODRAG;
         InvalidateRect( hWnd, &rectangle, TRUE );

         ReleaseCapture();
         break;

case WM_MOUSEMOVE :
         if ( nDragging == POSSIBLE &&
             ( abs(LOWORD( lParam ) - pt.x) > 2 ||
               abs(HIWORD( lParam ) - pt.y) > 2 ) )
         {
            nDragging = DRAGGING;
```

continued on next page

continued from previous page

```
                // Hide the mouse cursor.
                //......................
                ShowCursor( FALSE );

                // Start Dragging.
                //................
                ImageList_BeginDrag( hList, nSel, pt.x-(15+nSel*50), pt.y-15 );

                // Add the arrow to the drag cursor.
                //..................................
                ImageList_SetDragCursorImage( hList, 2, pt.x-(15+nSel*50),
                                              pt.y-15 );

                // Show the drag cursor.
                //......................
                ImageList_DragEnter( hWnd, LOWORD( lParam )-ptWnd.x,
                                     HIWORD( lParam )-ptWnd.y );
                InvalidateRect( hWnd, &rectangle, TRUE );
            }

            // If dragging, move the drag cursor.
            //..................................
            if ( nDragging == DRAGGING )
            {
                movePt.x = LOWORD( lParam );
                movePt.y = HIWORD( lParam );
                if ( PtInRect( &rectangle, movePt ) )
                    ImageList_DragShowNolock( FALSE );
                else
                    ImageList_DragShowNolock( TRUE );

                ImageList_DragMove( LOWORD( lParam )-ptWnd.x,
                                    HIWORD( lParam )-ptWnd.y );
            }
            break;

    case WM_COMMAND :
            switch( LOWORD( wParam ) )
            {
                case IDM_EXIT :
                    DestroyWindow( hWnd );
                    break;
            }
            break;

    case WM_DESTROY :
            if ( hList )
                ImageList_Destroy( hList );

            PostQuitMessage(0);
            break;

    default :
            return( DefWindowProc( hWnd, uMsg, wParam, lParam ) );
    }

    return( 0L );
}
```

IMAGELIST_DESTROY   ■ Win32s   ■ Windows 95   ■ Windows NT

Description	ImageList_Destroy() destroys the specified image list. An application should destroy an image list created with the ImageList_Create() function when it is no longer needed.
Syntax	BOOL WINAPI **ImageList_Destroy**(HIMAGELIST *himl*)
Parameters	
himl	HIMAGELIST: The handle of the image list to destroy.
Returns	BOOL: TRUE if successful; otherwise, FALSE is returned.
Include File	commctrl.h
See Also	ImageList_Create(), ImageList_LoadImage()
Example	See the example for the ImageList_Create() function.

IMAGELIST_DRAGENTER   ■ Win32s   ■ Windows 95   ■ Windows NT

Description	ImageList_DragEnter() locks updates to the given window during a drag operation and displays the drag image at the specified position within the window. The image is initially displayed at the given window coordinates. While the window is locked, no painting occurs. If the application must perform drawing during the drag operation, such as to highlight the target of the drag operation, the application can temporarily hide the dragged image and unlock the window for updates with the ImageList_DragLeave() function.
Syntax	BOOL WINAPI **ImageList_DragEnter**(HWND *hwndLock*, int *x*, int *y*)
Parameters	
hwndLock	HWND: The handle of the window that owns the drag image. If NULL is specified, the coordinates are relative to the upper left corner of the screen.
x	int: The x coordinate at which to display the drag image relative to the upper left corner of the window *hwndLock*.
y	int: The y coordinate at which to display the drag image relative to the upper left corner of the window *hwndLock*.
Returns	BOOL: If successful, TRUE is returned; otherwise, FALSE is returned.
Include File	commctrl.h
See Also	ImageList_BeginDrag(), ImageList_DragLeave()
Example	See the example for the ImageList_Create() function.

IMAGELIST_DRAGLEAVE   ■ Win32s   ■ Windows 95   ■ Windows NT

Description	ImageList_DragLeave() unlocks the specified window and hides the drag image, allowing the window to be updated. Use this function to allow

drawing in the window during a drag operation, such as highlighting the target of the drag operation.

Syntax   BOOL WINAPI **ImageList_DragLeave**(HWND *hwndLock*)

Parameters

hwndLock   HWND: The handle of the window that owns the drag image.

Returns   BOOL: If successful, TRUE is returned; otherwise, FALSE is returned.

Include File   commctrl.h

See Also   ImageList_DragEnter()

Example   See the example for the ImageList_Create() function.

IMAGELIST_DRAGMOVE ■ Win32s ■ Windows 95 ■ Windows NT

Description   ImageList_DragMove() moves the dragged image during a drag-and-drop operation. Typically, this function is called in response to a WM_MOUSEMOVE message. Use the ImageList_BeginDrag() function to begin the drag operation.

Syntax   BOOL WINAPI **ImageList_DragMove**(int *x*, int *y*)

Parameters

x   int: The new horizontal position of the image.

y   int: The new vertical position of the image.

Returns   BOOL: If successful, TRUE is returned; otherwise, FALSE is returned.

Include File   commctrl.h

See Also   ImageList_BeginDrag()

Related Messages WM_MOUSEMOVE

Example   See the example for the ImageList_Create() function.

IMAGELIST_DRAGSHOWNOLOCK ■ Win32s ■ Windows 95 ■ Windows NT

Description   ImageList_DragShowNolock() shows or hides the image being dragged.

Syntax   BOOL WINAPI **ImageList_DragShowNolock**(BOOL *bShow*)

Parameters

bShow   BOOL: Set to TRUE to show the image being dragged; set to FALSE to hide the image.

Returns   BOOL: If successful, TRUE is returned; otherwise, FALSE is returned.

Include File   commctrl.h

Example   See the example for the ImageList_Create() function.

IMAGELIST_DRAW　　　　■ Win32s　■ Windows 95　■ Windows NT

Description	ImageList_Draw() draws an image list item on a given device context using the given drawing style.
Syntax	BOOL WINAPI **ImageList_Draw**(HIMAGELIST *himl*, int *i*, HDC *hdcDst*, int *x*, int *y*, UINT *fStyle*)
Parameters	
himl	HIMAGELIST: The handle of the image list that contains the item to draw.
i	int: The index of the image in the image list to draw.
hdcDst	HDC: The destination device context.
x	int: The x coordinate at which to draw the image list item within the device context.
y	int: The y coordinate at which to draw the image list item within the device context.
fStyle	UINT: The drawing style. This parameter can be one of the values listed in Table 5-3.

Table 5-3 ImageList_Draw() *fStyle* values

Value	Meaning
ILD_BLEND	Same as ILD_BLEND50.
ILD_BLEND25	Draws the image, blending 25 percent with the system highlight color. This value has no effect if the image list does not contain a mask.
ILD_BLEND50	Draws the image, blending 50 percent with the system highlight color. This gives the image a selected appearance. This value has no effect if the image list does not contain a mask.
ILD_FOCUS	Same as ILD_BLEND25.
ILD_MASK	Draws the mask.
ILD_NORMAL	Draws the image using the background color for the image list. If the background color is the CLR_NONE value, the image is drawn transparently using the mask.
ILD_SELECTED	Same as ILD_BLEND50.
ILD_TRANSPARENT	Draws the image transparently using the mask, regardless of the background color. This value has no effect if the image list does not contain a mask.

Returns	BOOL: If successful, TRUE is returned; otherwise, FALSE is returned.
Include File	commctrl.h
See Also	ImageList_DrawEx()
Example	See the example for the ImageList_Create() function.

IMAGELIST_DRAWEX   ■ Win32s   ■ Windows 95   ■ Windows NT

Description	ImageList_DrawEx() draws an image list item on the given device context. This function uses the given drawing style and blends the image with the specified color. ImageList_DrawEx() also allows drawing a portion of the image by providing an offset within the image.
Syntax	BOOL WINAPI **ImageList_DrawEx**(HIMAGELIST *himl*, int *i*, HDC, *hdcDst*, int *x*, int *y*, int *xOffs*, int *yOffs*, COLORREF *rgbBk*, COLORREF *rgbFg*, UINT *fStyle*)
Parameters	
himl	HIMAGELIST: The handle of the image list that contains the image to draw.
i	int: The index of the image to draw.
hdcDst	HDC: The destination device context.
x	int: The x coordinate at which to draw the image list item within the device context.
y	int: The y coordinate at which to draw the image list item within the device context.
xOffs	int: The horizontal offset of the image to draw, relative to the upper left corner of the image. If *xOffs* and *yOffs* are zero, ImageList_DrawEx() draws the entire image.
yOffs	int: The vertical offset of the image to draw, relative to the upper left corner of the image. If *dx* and *dy* are zero, ImageList_DrawEx() draws the entire image.
rgbBk	COLORREF: The background color of the image. This parameter can either be an application-defined RGB value, or one of the values in Table 5-4. This parameter is used only if the image list identified by *himl* contains a mask.

Table 5-4 ImageList_DrawEx() *rgbBk* values

Value	Meaning
CLR_DEFAULT	Default background color. The image is drawn using the background color of the image list.
CLR_NONE	No background color. The image is drawn transparently.

rgbFg	COLORREF: The foreground color of the image. This parameter can either be an application-defined RGB value, or one of the values in Table 5-5. This parameter is used only if *fStyle* includes either the ILD_BLEND25 or ILD_BLEND50 value.

Table 5-5 ImageList_DrawEx() *rgbFg* values

Value	Meaning
CLR_DEFAULT	Default foreground color. The image is drawn using the system highlight color as the foreground color.
CLR_NONE	No blend color. The image is blended with the color of the destination device context.

fStyle	UINT: The drawing style. This parameter can be one or more of the values in Table 5-3.
Returns	BOOL: If successful, TRUE is returned; otherwise, FALSE is returned.
Include File	commctrl.h
See Also	ImageList_Draw()
Example	In this example, the ImageList_DrawEx() function (Listing 5-2) is used to display an image with a custom selection color and background color. When the user selects the Selected menu item, the image is drawn with a red (RGB(255, 0, 0)) selection color. The user can change the background color (which defaults to white) by selecting the Background Color menu item.

Listing 5-2 Using the ImageList_DrawEx() function

```
HIMAGELIST hList = NULL;

LRESULT CALLBACK WndProc( HWND hWnd, UINT uMsg, WPARAM wParam, LPARAM lParam )
{
static int nSel  = -1;

   switch( uMsg )
   {
      case WM_CREATE :
              InitCommonControls();

              // Create the image list.
              //......................
              hList = ImageList_Create( 32, 32, ILC_COLOR | ILC_MASK, 1, 1 );
              if ( hList )
              {
                  HBITMAP hBmp;

                  // Add an image and build a mask.
                  //...............................
                  hBmp = LoadBitmap( hInst, "BMP2" );
                  ImageList_AddMasked( hList, hBmp, RGB( 0, 255, 0 ) );
                  DeleteObject( hBmp );
              }
              break;
```

continued on next page

continued from previous page

```
        case WM_PAINT :
                {
                    PAINTSTRUCT ps;

                    // Paint the two images on the client area.
                    //.........................................
                    BeginPaint( hWnd, &ps );
                    ImageList_DrawEx( hList, 0, ps.hdc, 10, 10, 0, 0,
                                    CLR_DEFAULT, RGB( 255, 0, 0 ),
                                    ILD_NORMAL | (nSel == 0 ? ILD_BLEND25 : 0) );
                    EndPaint( hWnd, &ps );
                }
                break;

        case WM_COMMAND :
                switch( LOWORD( wParam ) )
                {
                    case IDM_SELECT :
                            nSel = (nSel == -1 ? 0 : -1);
                            InvalidateRect( hWnd, NULL, TRUE );
                            break;

                    case IDM_SETBKGRND :
                            DialogBox( hInst, "RGBDialog", hWnd,
                                        (DLGPROC)RGBDialog );
                            InvalidateRect( hWnd, NULL, TRUE );
                            break;

                    case IDM_EXIT :
                            DestroyWindow( hWnd );
                            break;
                }
                break;

        case WM_DESTROY :
                if ( hList )
                    ImageList_Destroy( hList );

                PostQuitMessage(0);
                break;

        default :
                return( DefWindowProc( hWnd, uMsg, wParam, lParam ) );
    }

    return( 0L );
}


LRESULT CALLBACK RGBDialog( HWND hDlg,
                            UINT message,
                            WPARAM wParam,
                            LPARAM lParam)
{
    switch (message)
    {
        case WM_INITDIALOG:
                {
                    COLORREF color = ImageList_GetBkColor( hList );
```

```
                    SetDlgItemInt( hDlg, IDC_RED,   GetRValue( color ), FALSE );
                    SetDlgItemInt( hDlg, IDC_GREEN, GetGValue( color ), FALSE );
                    SetDlgItemInt( hDlg, IDC_BLUE,  GetBValue( color ), FALSE );
                }
                return (TRUE);

        case WM_COMMAND:
                if ( LOWORD(wParam) == IDOK )
                {
                    ImageList_SetBkColor( hList, RGB(
                            GetDlgItemInt( hDlg, IDC_RED, NULL, FALSE ),
                            GetDlgItemInt( hDlg, IDC_GREEN, NULL, FALSE ),
                            GetDlgItemInt( hDlg, IDC_BLUE, NULL, FALSE ) ) );

                    EndDialog( hDlg, IDOK );
                    return (TRUE);
                }
                else if ( LOWORD(wParam) == IDCANCEL)
                {
                    EndDialog( hDlg, IDCANCEL );
                    return (TRUE);
                }
                break;
    }

    return (FALSE);
}
```

IMAGELIST_ENDDRAG   ■ Win32s ■ Windows 95 ■ Windows NT

Description	ImageList_EndDrag() ends a drag operation started by a call to the ImageList_BeginDrag() function.
Syntax	BOOL WINAPI **ImageList_EndDrag** (VOID)
Parameters	None.
Returns	BOOL: If successful, TRUE is returned; otherwise, FALSE is returned.
Include File	commctrl.h
See Also	ImageList_BeginDrag()
Example	See the example for the ImageList_Create() function.

IMAGELIST_EXTRACTICON   ■ Win32s ■ Windows 95 ■ Windows NT

Description	ImageList_ExtractIcon is a macro that creates an icon or cursor based on an image and mask in an image list. This macro uses the ImageList_GetIcon() function.
Syntax	HICON WINAPI **ImageList_ExtractIcon**(HINSTANCE *hi*, HIMAGELIST *himl*, int *i*)
Parameters	
hi	HINSTANCE: This parameter is ignored; set to zero.

himl	HIMAGELIST: The handle of the image list.
i	int: The index of the image.
Returns	HICON: If successful, the handle of the icon or cursor is returned; otherwise, NULL is returned.
Include File	commctrl.h
See Also	ImageList_GetIcon()
Example	This example (Listing 5-3) creates an image list with a single image. When the user selects the Test! menu item, the ImageList_ExtractIcon macro is used to set the cursor to the image. When the user selects the Test! menu item again, the cursor is restored to the arrow cursor.

Listing 5-3 Using the ImageList_ExtractIcon macro

```
LRESULT CALLBACK WndProc( HWND hWnd, UINT uMsg, WPARAM wParam, LPARAM lParam )
{
static HIMAGELIST hList = NULL;
static BOOL       bNewCursor = FALSE;

   switch( uMsg )
   {
      case WM_CREATE :
              InitCommonControls();

              // Create the image list.
              //......................
              hList = ImageList_Create( 32, 32, ILC_COLOR | ILC_MASK, 1, 1 );
              if ( hList )
              {
                  HBITMAP hBmp;

                  // Add an image and build a mask.
                  //..............................
                  hBmp = LoadBitmap( hInst, "BMP2" );
                  ImageList_AddMasked( hList, hBmp, RGB( 0, 255, 0 ) );
                  DeleteObject( hBmp );
              }
              break;

      case WM_SETCURSOR :
              if ( bNewCursor )
                SetCursor( ImageList_ExtractIcon( NULL, hList, 0 ) );
              else
                return( DefWindowProc( hWnd, uMsg, wParam, lParam ) );
              break;

      case WM_COMMAND :
              switch( LOWORD( wParam ) )
              {
                  case IDM_TEST :
                          bNewCursor = !bNewCursor;
                          break;
          .
          .
          .
```

IMAGELIST_GETBKCOLOR ■ Win32s ■ Windows 95 ■ Windows NT

Description	ImageList_GetBkColor() retrieves the current background color for an image list.
Syntax	COLORREF WINAPI **ImageList_GetBkColor**(HIMAGELIST *himl*)
Parameters	
himl	HIMAGELIST: The handle of the image list.
Returns	COLORREF: The background color for an image list.
Include File	commctrl.h
See Also	ImageList_SetBkColor()
Example	See the example for the ImageList_DrawEx() function.

IMAGELIST_GETDRAGIMAGE ■ Win32s ■ Windows 95 ■ Windows NT

Description	ImageList_GetDragImage() retrieves the temporary image list used to drag an image, the current drag position, and the offset of the drag image relative to the drag position. This temporary image list is destroyed when the ImageList_EndDrag() function is called. Use the ImageList_BeginDrag() function to begin a drag operation.
Syntax	HIMAGELIST WINAPI **ImageList_GetDragImage**(POINT* *ppt*, POINT* *pptHotspot*)
Parameters	
ppt	POINT*: A pointer to a POINT structure that receives the current x and y coordinates of the drag position. This parameter can be NULL.
pptHotspot	POINT*: A pointer to a POINT structure that receives the current x and y coordinates that indicate the offset of the drag image relative to the drag position. This parameter can be NULL.
Returns	HIMAGELIST: If successful, the handle of the image list is returned; otherwise NULL is returned.
Include File	commctrl.h
See Also	ImageList_SetDragCursorImage()
Example	See the example for the ImageList_Create() function.

IMAGELIST_GETICON ■ Win32s ■ Windows 95 ■ Windows NT

Description	ImageList_GetIcon() creates an icon or cursor based on an image and mask in an image list.
Syntax	HICON WINAPI **ImageList_GetIcon**(HIMAGELIST *himl*, int *i*, UINT *flags*)

Parameters

himl	HIMAGELIST: The handle of the image list.
i	int: The index of the image.
flags	UINT: The drawing style for the icon or cursor. This parameter can be a combination of the values in Table 5-3.
Returns	HICON: If successful, the handle of the icon or cursor is returned; otherwise, NULL is returned.
Include File	commctrl.h
See Also	ImageList_ExtractIcon, ImageList_Draw()
Example	This example (Listing 5-4) is similar to the example for the ImageList_ExtractIcon macro except that the ImageList_GetIcon() function is used to retrieve the image in a selected state.

Listing 5-4 Using the ImageList_GetIcon() function

```
LRESULT CALLBACK WndProc( HWND hWnd, UINT uMsg, WPARAM wParam, LPARAM lParam )
{
static HIMAGELIST hList = NULL;
static BOOL       bNewCursor = FALSE;

   switch( uMsg )
   {
      case WM_CREATE :
              InitCommonControls();

              // Create the image list.
              //....................
              hList = ImageList_Create( 32, 32, ILC_COLOR | ILC_MASK, 1, 1 );
              if ( hList )
              {
                  HBITMAP hBmp, hMask;

                  // Add an image and build a mask.
                  //................................
                  hBmp  = LoadBitmap( hInst, "BMP1" );
                  hMask = LoadBitmap( hInst, "BMP1MSK" );
                  ImageList_Add( hList, hBmp, hMask );
                  DeleteObject( hBmp );
                  DeleteObject( hMask );
              }
              break;

      case WM_SETCURSOR :
              if ( bNewCursor )
                SetCursor( ImageList_GetIcon( hList, 0,
                        ILD_BLEND50 | ILD_TRANSPARENT ) );
              else
                return( DefWindowProc( hWnd, uMsg, wParam, lParam ) );
              break;

      case WM_COMMAND :
              switch( LOWORD( wParam ) )
              {
```

```
case IDM_TEST :
        bNewCursor = !bNewCursor;
        break;
```

.
.
.

IMAGELIST_GETICONSIZE   ■ Win32s   ■ Windows 95   ■ Windows NT

Description	ImageList_GetIconSize() retrieves the dimensions of images in an image list. All images in an image list have the same dimensions.
Syntax	BOOL WINAPI **ImageList_GetIconSize**(HIMAGELIST *himl*, int* *cx*, int* *cy*)
Parameters	
himl	HIMAGELIST: The handle of the image list.
cx	int*: A pointer to an integer variable that receives the image width, in pixels.
cy	int*: A pointer to an integer variable that receives the image height, in pixels.
Returns	BOOL: If successful, TRUE is returned; otherwise, FALSE is returned.
Include File	commctrl.h
See Also	ImageList_SetIconSize()
Example	See the example for the ImageList_Create() function.

IMAGELIST_GETIMAGECOUNT   ■ Win32s   ■ Windows 95   ■ Windows NT

Description	ImageList_GetImageCount() retrieves the number of images in an image list.
Syntax	int WINAPI **ImageList_GetImageCount**(HIMAGELIST *himl*)
Parameters	
himl	HIMAGELIST: The handle of the image list.
Returns	int: The number of images in the image list.
Include File	commctrl.h
Example	See the example for the ImageList_GetImageInfo() function.

IMAGELIST_GETIMAGEINFO   ■ Win32s   ■ Windows 95   ■ Windows NT

Description	ImageList_GetImageInfo() retrieves information about an image in the given image list. The image list stores the images within a single bitmap. The handle of the bitmap returned contains all the images. Use the returned rectangle to retrieve the individual image.

Syntax	BOOL WINAPI **ImageList_GetImageInfo**(HIMAGELIST *himl*, int *i*, IMAGEINFO* *pImageInfo*)
Parameters	
himl	HIMAGELIST: The handle of the image list.
i	int: The index of the desired image.
pImageInfo	IMAGEINFO*: A pointer to an IMAGEINFO structure that receives information about the image. The information in this structure can be used directly to manipulate the bitmaps for the image. See the definition of IMAGEINFO below.
Returns	BOOL: If successful, TRUE is returned; otherwise, FALSE is returned.
Include File	commctrl.h

IMAGEINFO Definition

```
typedef struct _IMAGEINFO
{
    HBITMAP hbmImage;
    HBITMAP hbmMask;
    int     Unused1;
    int     Unused2;
    RECT    rcImage;
} IMAGEINFO;
```

Members

hbmImage	HBITMAP: The handle of the bitmap containing the images.
hbmMask	HBITMAP: The handle of a monochrome bitmap that contains the masks for the images. If the image list does not contain a mask, this member is NULL.
Unused1	int: This member is reserved.
Unused2	int: This member is reserved.
rcImage	RECT: The bounding rectangle of the image within the bitmap specified by *hbmImage*.
Example	This example (Listing 5-5) creates an image list with the ImageList_LoadBitmap() function. The application uses the ImageList_GetImageInfo() function to retrieve the bounding rectangle of the second image in the bitmap, which is displayed along with the two images in the image list. The number of images is also retrieved with the ImageList_GetImageCount() function.

Listing 5-5 Using the ImageList_GetImageInfo() function

```
LRESULT CALLBACK WndProc( HWND hWnd, UINT uMsg, WPARAM wParam, LPARAM lParam )
{
static HIMAGELIST hList = NULL;
static HBITMAP    hBmp  = NULL;

   switch( uMsg )
   {
```

```
    case WM_CREATE :
            InitCommonControls();

            // Load the bitmap to use for painting.
            //......................................
            hBmp  = LoadBitmap( hInst, "BMP" );

            // Create an image list from the bitmap.
            //......................................
            hList = ImageList_LoadBitmap( hInst, "BMP", 32, 1, RGB(255,0,0) );
            break;

    case WM_PAINT :
            {
                PAINTSTRUCT ps;
                IMAGEINFO   ii;
                HDC         hmemDC;
                char        szTmp[15];

                BeginPaint( hWnd, &ps );

                // Get the offset to the second image.
                //......................................
                ImageList_GetImageInfo( hList, 1, &ii );

                // Paint the image from the bitmap.
                //......................................
                hmemDC = CreateCompatibleDC( ps.hdc );
                SelectObject( hmemDC, hBmp );
                BitBlt( ps.hdc, 10, 10, 64, 32, hmemDC, ii.rcImage.left,
                        0, SRCCOPY );

                // Draw the two images in the list.
                //......................................
                ImageList_Draw( hList, 0, ps.hdc, 10, 50, ILD_NORMAL );
                ImageList_Draw( hList, 1, ps.hdc, 50, 50, ILD_NORMAL );

                // Display the number of images in the list.
                //......................................
                wsprintf( szTmp, "%d images.", ImageList_GetImageCount(hList));
                TextOut( ps.hdc, 10, 90, szTmp, strlen( szTmp ) );

                DeleteDC( hmemDC );
                EndPaint( hWnd, &ps );
            }
            break;
        .
        .
        .
```

IMAGELIST_LOADBITMAP   ■ Win32s   ■ Windows 95   ■ Windows NT

Description   ImageList_LoadBitmap is a macro that creates an image list from a bitmap resource. The ImageList_LoadBitmap macro uses the ImageList_LoadImage() function. Use the ImageList_Destroy() function to destroy the image list when it is no longer needed.

Syntax	HIMAGELIST WINAPI **ImageList_LoadBitmap**(HINSTANCE *hi*, LPCSTR *lpbmp*, int *cx*, int *cGrow*, COLORREF *crMask*)
Parameters	
hi	HINSTANCE: The instance handle of the module that contains the bitmap resource.
lpbmp	LPCSTR: The name of the bitmap resource. Use the MAKEINTRESOURCE macro to specify an integer resource identifier.
cx	int: The width of each image. The height of each image and the number of images are determined by the dimensions of the bitmap.
cGrow	int: The number of new images to allocate in the image when the initial number of images has been exceeded.
crMask	COLORREF: The color used to generate a mask. Each pixel of this color in the specified bitmap is changed to black, and the corresponding bit in the mask is set to one. If *crMask* is the CLR_NONE value, a mask is not generated.
Returns	HIMAGELIST: If successful, the handle of the image list is returned; otherwise, NULL is returned.
Include File	commctrl.h
See Also	ImageList_LoadImage(), ImageList_Destroy
Example	See the example for the ImageList_GetImageInfo() function.

IMAGELIST_LOADIMAGE   ■ Win32s   ■ Windows 95   ■ Windows NT

Description	ImageList_LoadImage() creates an image list from the specified bitmap, cursor, or icon resource. Use the ImageList_Destroy() function to destroy the image list when it is no longer needed.
Syntax	HIMAGELIST WINAPI **ImageList_LoadImage**(HINSTANCE *hi*, LPCSTR *lpbmp*, int *cx*, int *cGrow*, COLORREF *crMask*, UINT *uType*, UINT *uFlags*)
Parameters	
hi	HINSTANCE: The instance handle of the module that contains the resource. To load an OEM image, set this parameter to NULL.
lpbmp	LPCSTR: A pointer to a null-terminated string that contains the name of the image to load. If *uFlags* specifies the LR_LOADFROMFILE value, *lpbmp* must be the name of the file that contains the image. If *hi* is NULL, the low-order word of this parameter must be the identifier of the OEM image to load. The OEM image identifiers are defined in WINUSER.H. Table 5-6 contains the identifier prefixes and their meanings.

Table 5-6 ImageList_LoadImage() resource prefixes

Prefix	Meaning
OBM_	OEM bitmaps
OCR_	OEM cursors
OIC_	OEM icons

cx	int: The width of each image. The height of each image and the number of images are determined by the dimensions of the specified resource.
cGrow	int: The number of new images to allocate in the image when the initial number of images has been exceeded.
crMask	COLORREF: The color used to generate a mask. Each pixel of this color in the specified bitmap, cursor, or icon is changed to black, and the corresponding bit in the mask is set to 1. If *crMask* is the CLR_NONE value, a mask is not generated.
uType	UINT: The type of image to load. This parameter can be one of the values in Table 5-7.

Table 5-7 ImageList_LoadImage() *uType* values

Value	Meaning
IMAGE_BITMAP	Loads a bitmap.
IMAGE_CURSOR	Loads a cursor.
IMAGE_ICON	Loads an icon.

uFlags	UINT: The flags that specify how to load the image. This parameter can be a combination of the values in Table 5-8.

Table 5-8 ImageList_LoadImage() *uFlags* values

Value	Meaning
LR_DEFAULTCOLOR	Uses the color format of the display.
LR_LOADDEFAULTSIZE	Uses the width or height specified by the system metric values for cursors and icons if *cx* is set to zero. If this value is not specified and *cx* is set to zero, the function sets the size to that specified in the resource. If the resource contains multiple images, the function sets the size to that of the first image.
LR_LOADFROMFILE	Loads the image from the file specified by *lpbmp*.

continued on next page

continued from previous page

Value	Meaning
LR_LOADMAP3DCOLORS	Searches the color table for the image and replaces the following shades of gray with the corresponding three-dimensional color:

Color	RGB Values	System Color
Dk Gray	RGB(128, 128, 128)	COLOR_3DSHADOW
Gray	RGB(192, 192, 192)	COLOR_3DFACE
Lt Gray	RGB(223, 223, 223)	COLOR_3DLIGHT

Value	Meaning
LR_LOADTRANSPARENT	Retrieves the color value of the first pixel in the image and replaces the corresponding entry in the color table with the default window color (the COLOR_WINDOW display color). All pixels in the image that use that entry become the default window value color. This value applies only to images that have corresponding color tables.
LR_MONOCHROME	Loads the image in black and white.
LR_SHARED	Shares the image handle if the image is loaded multiple times. Do not use this value for images that have nontraditional sizes that might change after loading or for images that are loaded from a file.

Returns	HIMAGELIST: If successful, the handle of the image list is returned; otherwise, NULL is returned.
Include File	commctrl.h
See Also	ImageList_Create(), ImageList_Destroy()
Example	This example (Listing 5-6) demonstrates the usage of the ImageList_LoadImage() function to create an image list with an OEM bitmap of the up arrow.

Listing 5-6 Using the ImageList_LoadImage() function

```
LRESULT CALLBACK WndProc( HWND hWnd, UINT uMsg, WPARAM wParam, LPARAM lParam )
{
static HIMAGELIST hList = NULL;

   switch( uMsg )
   {
   case WM_CREATE :
           InitCommonControls();

           // Create an image list from an Image.
           //...................................
           hList = ImageList_LoadImage( NULL,
                               (LPCTSTR)MAKELONG( OBM_UPARROW, 0 ),
                               16, 1, CLR_NONE, IMAGE_BITMAP,
                               LR_DEFAULTCOLOR );
           break;

   case WM_PAINT :
           {
              PAINTSTRUCT ps;

              BeginPaint( hWnd, &ps );
```

```
            // Draw the image in the List.
            //..........................
            ImageList_Draw( hList, 0, ps.hdc, 10, 10, ILD_NORMAL );

            EndPaint( hWnd, &ps );
        }
        break;
    .
    .
    .
```

IMAGELIST_MERGE   ■ Win32s   ■ Windows 95   ■ Windows NT

Description   ImageList_Merge() creates a new image list that contains an image created
                     by combining two existing images from an image list or lists. The new
                     image consists of the second image drawn transparently over the first. The
                     mask for the new image is the result of performing a logical OR operation
                     on the masks of the two existing images.

Syntax   HIMAGELIST WINAPI **ImageList_Merge**(HIMAGELIST *himl1*, int *i1*,
                     HIMAGELIST *himl2*, int *i2*, int *xOffs*, int *yOffs*)

Parameters

himl1   HIMAGELIST: The handle of the image list that contains the first image.

i1   int: The index of the first image.

himl2   HIMAGELIST: The handle of the image list that contains the second
                     image.

i2   int: The index of the second image.

xOffs   int: The horizontal offset of the second image relative to the first image. The
                     offset controls where the second image is placed within the first image.

yOffs   int: The vertical offset of the second image relative to the first image.

Returns   HIMAGELIST: If successful, the handle of the new image list is returned;
                     otherwise, NULL is returned.

Include File   commctrl.h

Example   This example (Listing 5-7) creates an image list with two images that are
                     combined into another image list that contains a single image with the
                     ImageList_Merge() function. The application displays the image lists
                     shown in Figure 5-4.

Figure 5-4 ImageList_Merge() example

Listing 5-7 Using the ImageList_Merge() function

```c
LRESULT CALLBACK WndProc( HWND hWnd, UINT uMsg, WPARAM wParam, LPARAM lParam )
{
static HIMAGELIST hList  = NULL;
static HIMAGELIST hMerge = NULL;

   switch( uMsg )
   {
      case WM_CREATE :
              InitCommonControls();

              // Create the image list.
              //......................
              hList = ImageList_Create( 32, 32, ILC_COLOR | ILC_MASK, 1, 1 );
              if ( hList )
              {
                  HBITMAP hBmp;

                  // Add an image and build a mask.
                  //..............................
                  hBmp = LoadBitmap( hInst, "BMP2" );
                  ImageList_AddMasked( hList, hBmp, RGB( 0, 255, 0 ) );
                  DeleteObject( hBmp );

                  ImageList_AddIcon( hList, LoadCursor( NULL, IDC_ARROW ) );

                  // Build a new image list with the two images merged.
                  //...................................................
                  hMerge = ImageList_Merge( hList, 0, hList, 1, 15, 15 );
              }
              break;

      case WM_PAINT :
              {
                  PAINTSTRUCT ps;

                  // Paint the images on the client area.
                  //....................................
                  BeginPaint( hWnd, &ps );
                  ImageList_Draw( hList, 0, ps.hdc, 10, 10, ILD_NORMAL );
                  TextOut( ps.hdc, 46, 25, "+", 1 );
                  ImageList_Draw( hList, 1, ps.hdc, 60, 10, ILD_NORMAL );
                  TextOut( ps.hdc, 93, 25, "=", 1 );
                  ImageList_Draw( hMerge, 0, ps.hdc, 110, 10, ILD_NORMAL );
                  EndPaint( hWnd, &ps );
              }
              break;
              .
              .
              .
```

IMAGELIST_READ   ■ Win32s ■ Windows 95 ■ Windows NT

Description   ImageList_Read() reads an image list from a stream.

Syntax   HIMAGELIST WINAPI **ImageList_Read**(LPSTREAM *pstm*)

Parameters

pstm   LPSTREAM: A pointer to the stream.

Returns   HIMAGELIST: If successful, the image list is returned; otherwise, NULL is returned.

Include File commctrl.h

See Also   ImageList_Write()

Example   See the example for the ImageList_Write() function.

IMAGELIST_REMOVE   ■ Win32s ■ Windows 95 ■ Windows NT

Description   ImageList_Remove() removes one or all images from an image list.

Syntax   BOOL WINAPI **ImageList_Remove**(HIMAGELIST *himl*, int *i*)

Parameters

himl   HIMAGELIST: The handle of the image list.

i   int: The index of the image to remove from the image list. If set to -1, all images are removed from the list.

Returns   BOOL: If successful, TRUE is returned; otherwise, FALSE is returned.

Include File commctrl.h

See Also   ImageList_RemoveAll

Example   This example (Listing 5-8) demonstrates the dynamic usage of an image list. The user has the ability to add one of three images, shown in Figure 5-5, to the list. The user can remove the last image from the list or replace it with another image. The application uses the ImageList_Remove() function and the ImageList_ReplaceIcon() function for this feature. The user can also enlarge or reduce the image list images.

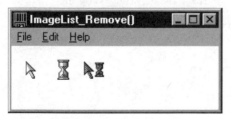

Figure 5-5 ImageList_Remove example

Listing 5-8 Using the ImageList_Remove() function

```
LRESULT CALLBACK WndProc( HWND hWnd, UINT uMsg, WPARAM wParam, LPARAM lParam )
{
static HIMAGELIST hList   = NULL;
static int        nSize   = 32;
```

continued on next page

continued from previous page

```
    switch( uMsg )
    {
        case WM_CREATE :
                InitCommonControls();

                // Create the image list.
                //......................
                hList = ImageList_Create( nSize, nSize,
                                          ILC_COLOR | ILC_MASK, 1, 1 );
                break;

        case WM_PAINT :
                {
                    PAINTSTRUCT ps;
                    int         i, nItems;

                    // Retrieve the number of images.
                    //..............................
                    nItems = ImageList_GetImageCount( hList );

                    // Paint the images on the client area.
                    //....................................
                    BeginPaint( hWnd, &ps );
                    for ( i=0; i<nItems; i++ )
                        ImageList_Draw( hList, i, ps.hdc, (i*nSize)+10, 10,
                                 (i == nItems - 1) ?
                                 ILD_SELECTED : ILD_NORMAL);
                    EndPaint( hWnd, &ps );
                }
                break;

        case WM_COMMAND :
                switch( LOWORD( wParam ) )
                {
                    case IDM_ARROW :
                    case IDM_WAITING :
                    case IDM_WORKING :
                            ImageList_AddIcon( hList, LoadCursor( NULL,
                                    LOWORD( wParam ) == IDM_ARROW ? IDC_ARROW :
                                    LOWORD( wParam ) == IDM_WAITING ? IDC_WAIT :
                                    IDC_APPSTARTING ) );
                            InvalidateRect( hWnd, NULL, TRUE );
                            break;

                    case IDM_REPARROW :
                    case IDM_REPWAITING :
                    case IDM_REPWORKING :
                            ImageList_ReplaceIcon( hList,
                                    ImageList_GetImageCount( hList )-1,
                                    LoadCursor( NULL,
                                    LOWORD( wParam ) == IDM_REPARROW ? IDC_ARROW :
                                    LOWORD( wParam ) == IDM_REPWAITING ? IDC_WAIT :
                                    IDC_APPSTARTING ) );
                            InvalidateRect( hWnd, NULL, TRUE );
                            break;

                    case IDM_REMITEM :
                            ImageList_Remove( hList,
```

```
                                  ImageList_GetImageCount( hList ) - 1 );
                        InvalidateRect( hWnd, NULL, TRUE );
                        break;

                case IDM_REMALL :
                        ImageList_RemoveAll( hList );
                        InvalidateRect( hWnd, NULL, TRUE );
                        break;

                case IDM_ENLARGE :
                        nSize += 5;
                        ImageList_SetIconSize( hList, nSize, nSize );
                        InvalidateRect( hWnd, NULL, TRUE );
                        break;

                case IDM_REDUCE :
                        nSize -= 5;
                        ImageList_SetIconSize( hList, nSize, nSize );
                        InvalidateRect( hWnd, NULL, TRUE );
                        break;

                case IDM_EXIT :
                        DestroyWindow( hWnd );
                        break;
            }
            break;

        case WM_DESTROY :
                if ( hList )
                    ImageList_Destroy( hList );

                PostQuitMessage(0);
                break;

        default :
                return( DefWindowProc( hWnd, uMsg, wParam, lParam ) );
    }

    return( 0L );
}
```

IMAGELIST_REMOVEALL   ■ Win32s ■ Windows 95 ■ Windows NT

Description	ImageList_RemoveAll is a macro that removes all images from an image list. This macro uses the ImageList_Remove() function.
Syntax	BOOL **ImageList_RemoveAll**(HIMAGELIST *himl*)
Parameters	
himl	HIMAGELIST: The handle of the image list.
Returns	BOOL: If successful, TRUE is returned; otherwise, FALSE is returned.
Include File	commctrl.h
See Also	ImageList_Remove()
Example	See the example for the ImageList_Remove() function.

IMAGELIST_REPLACE
■ Win32s ■ Windows 95 ■ Windows NT

Description	ImageList_Replace() replaces an existing image in an image list with a new image. Once the image is added to the list, the application can delete the original bitmap with the DeleteObject() function.
Syntax	BOOL WINAPI **ImageList_Replace**(HIMAGELIST *himl*, int *i*, HBITMAP *hbmImage*, HBITMAP *hbmMask*)
Parameters	
himl	HIMAGELIST: The handle of the image list.
i	int: The index of the image to replace in the image list.
hbmImage	HBITMAP: The handle of the bitmap that contains the new image.
hbmMask	HBITMAP: The handle of the bitmap that contains the mask. If a mask is not used with the image list, *hbmMask* is ignored.
Returns	BOOL: If successful, TRUE is returned; otherwise, FALSE is returned.
Include File	commctrl.h
See Also	DeleteObject()
Example	This example (Listing 5-9) creates an image list with three images, a base image and two overlay images. The example uses the ImageList_Replace() function to allow the user to replace the base image. The image is displayed on the client area of the window with one of the overlay images overlaid onto the base image. The user can select which overlay image to use from the menu.

Listing 5-9 Using the ImageList_Replace() function

```
LRESULT CALLBACK WndProc( HWND hWnd, UINT uMsg, WPARAM wParam, LPARAM lParam )
{
static HIMAGELIST hList  = NULL;
static int        nOvr   = 1;

   switch( uMsg )
   {
     case WM_CREATE :
            InitCommonControls();

            // Create an image list from an Image.
            //.................................
            hList = ImageList_Create( 32, 32, ILC_MASK, 3, 1 );
            if ( hList )
            {
               HBITMAP hBmp, hMask;
               int     nImage;

               // Add the base image.
               //...................
               hBmp  = LoadBitmap( hInst, "BMP1" );
```

```
                hMask = LoadBitmap( hInst, "BMP1MSK" );
                ImageList_Add( hList, hBmp, hMask );
                DeleteObject( hBmp );
                DeleteObject( hMask );

                // Add the overlay images.
                //......................
                nImage = ImageList_AddIcon( hList, LoadCursor(NULL,IDC_ARROW));
                if ( nImage > -1 )
                    ImageList_SetOverlayImage( hList, nImage, 1 );

                nImage = ImageList_AddIcon( hList, LoadCursor(NULL,IDC_WAIT) );
                if ( nImage > -1 )
                    ImageList_SetOverlayImage( hList, nImage, 2 );

            }
            break;

    case WM_PAINT :
            {
                PAINTSTRUCT ps;

                BeginPaint( hWnd, &ps );

                // Draw the image with the overlay image.
                //......................................
                ImageList_Draw( hList, 0, ps.hdc, 10, 10,
                                INDEXTOOVERLAYMASK( nOvr ) );

                EndPaint( hWnd, &ps );
            }
            break;

    case WM_COMMAND :
            switch( LOWORD( wParam ) )
            {
                    // Change the base image.
                    //.....................
                case IDM_IMAGE1 :
                case IDM_IMAGE2 :
                        {
                            HBITMAP hBmp, hMask;

                            hBmp  = LoadBitmap( hInst,
                                            LOWORD( wParam ) == IDM_IMAGE1 ?
                                            "BMP1" : "BMP2" );
                            hMask = LoadBitmap( hInst,
                                            LOWORD( wParam ) == IDM_IMAGE1 ?
                                            "BMP1MSK" : "BMP2MSK" );
                            ImageList_Replace( hList, 0, hBmp, hMask );
                            DeleteObject( hBmp );
                            DeleteObject( hMask );
                            InvalidateRect( hWnd, NULL, TRUE );
                        }
                        break;

                    // Set the overlay image to the arrow.
                    //...................................
```

continued on next page

continued from previous page

```
        case IDM_ARROW :
            nOvr = 1;
            InvalidateRect( hWnd, NULL, TRUE );
            break;

            // Set the overlay image to the hourglass.
            //..........................................
        case IDM_WAITING :
            nOvr = 2;
            InvalidateRect( hWnd, NULL, TRUE );
            break;
```

.
.
.

IMAGELIST_REPLACEICON   ■ Win32s ■ Windows 95 ■ Windows NT

Description	ImageList_ReplaceIcon() replaces an existing image in an image list with an icon or cursor. If the icon is created with the CreateIcon() function, it can be destroyed once it is added to the image list.
Syntax	int WINAPI **ImageList_ReplaceIcon**(HIMAGELIST *himl*, int *i*, HICON *hicon*)
Parameters	
himl	HIMAGELIST: The handle of the image list.
i	int: The index of the image to replace in the image list.
hicon	HICON: The handle of the icon or cursor containing the bitmap and mask for the new image.
Returns	int: If successful, the index of the new image is returned; otherwise, a value of -1 is returned.
Include File	commctrl.h
See Also	CreateIcon(), LoadIcon()
Example	See the example for the ImageList_Remove() function.

IMAGELIST_SETBKCOLOR   ■ Win32s ■ Windows 95 ■ Windows NT

Description	ImageList_SetBkColor() sets the background color for an image list.
Syntax	COLORREF WINAPI **ImageList_SetBkColor**(HIMAGELIST *himl*, COLORREF *clrBk*)
Parameters	
himl	HIMAGELIST: The handle of the image list.
clrBk	COLORREF: The background color to set for the image list. If *clrBk* is CLR_NONE, images are drawn transparently using the mask.
Returns	COLORREF: If successful, the previous background color of the image list is returned; otherwise, CLR_NONE is returned.

Include File	commctrl.h
See Also	ImageList_GetBkColor()
Example	See the example for the ImageList_DrawEx() function.

IMAGELIST_SETDRAGCURSORIMAGE ■ Win32s ■ Windows 95 ■ Windows NT

Description	ImageList_SetDragCursorImage() creates a new drag image by combining the specified image with the current drag image. This image is normally a mouse cursor image. The result gives the user a sense of continuity during the drag operation.
Syntax	BOOL WINAPI **ImageList_SetDragCursorImage**(HIMAGELIST *himlDrag*, int *iDrag*, int *dxHotspot*, int *dyHotspot*)
Parameters	
himlDrag	HIMAGELIST: The handle of the image list containing the new image to combine with the drag image.
iDrag	int: The index of the new image to combine with the drag image.
dxHotspot	int: The horizontal position of the hotspot within the new image.
dyHotspot	int: The vertical position of the hotspot within the new image.
Returns	BOOL: If successful, TRUE is returned; otherwise, FALSE is returned.
Include File	commctrl.h
See Also	ImageList_GetDragImage()
Example	See the example for the ImageList_Create() function.

IMAGELIST_SETICONSIZE ■ Win32s ■ Windows 95 ■ Windows NT

Description	ImageList_SetIconSize() sets the dimensions to be used for all images in an image list and removes all existing images from the list. All images within an image list must be the same size.
Syntax	BOOL WINAPI **ImageList_SetIconSize**(HIMAGELIST *himl*, int *cx*, int *cy*)
Parameters	
himl	HIMAGELIST: The handle of the image list.
cx	int: The width, in pixels, of the images in the image list.
cy	int: The height, in pixels, of the images in the image list.
Returns	BOOL: If successful, TRUE is returned; otherwise, FALSE is returned.
Include File	commctrl.h
See Also	ImageList_GetIconSize()
Example	See the example for the ImageList_Remove() function.

ImageList_SetOverlayImage ■ Win32s ■ Windows 95 ■ Windows NT

Description	ImageList_SetOverlayImage() adds the index of an image to the list of images to be used as overlay masks. A maximum of four indices can be added to the list.
	An overlay mask is an image drawn transparently over another image. Use ImageList_Draw() or ImageList_DrawEx(), with the index of the overlay mask, to draw an overlay mask over an image. Use the INDEXTOOVERLAYMASK macro to specify the overlay mask.
Syntax	BOOL WINAPI **ImageList_SetOverlayImage**(HIMAGELIST *himl*, int *iImage*, int *iOverlay*)
Parameters	
himl	HIMAGELIST: The handle of the image list.
iImage	int: The image to use as an overlay mask.
iOverlay	int: The one-based index of the overlay mask.
Returns	BOOL: If successful, TRUE is returned; otherwise, FALSE is returned.
Include File	commctrl.h
See Also	ImageList_Draw(), ImageList_DrawEx()
Example	See the example for the ImageList_Replace() function.

ImageList_Write ■ Win32s ■ Windows 95 ■ Windows NT

Description	ImageList_Write() writes an image list to a stream.
Syntax	HIMAGELIST WINAPI **ImageList_Write**(HIMAGELIST *himl*, LPSTREAM *pstm*)
Parameters	
himl	HIMAGELIST: The handle of the image list.
pstm	LPSTREAM: A pointer to the stream.
Returns	HIMAGELIST: If successful, TRUE is returned; otherwise, FALSE is returned.
Include File	commctrl.h
See Also	ImageList_Read()
Example	This example (Listing 5-10) demonstrates the usage of the ImageList_Read() and ImageList_Write() functions to load and save an image list with an OLE stream. When the user selects the Save, the image list is saved to an OLE stream and is destroyed. When the user selects the Open, the image list is opened from the stream and re-created.

Listing 5-10 Using the Imagelist_Write() function

```
LRESULT CALLBACK WndProc( HWND hWnd, UINT uMsg, WPARAM wParam, LPARAM lParam )
{
static HIMAGELIST hList  = NULL;

    switch( uMsg )
    {
        case WM_CREATE :
                InitCommonControls();

                // Create the image list.
                //......................
                hList = ImageList_LoadBitmap( hInst, "BMP", 32, 1, RGB(255,0,0) );
                break;

        case WM_PAINT :
                {
                    PAINTSTRUCT ps;

                    // Paint the images on the client area.
                    //.....................................
                    BeginPaint( hWnd, &ps );
                    if ( hList )
                    {
                        ImageList_Draw( hList, 0, ps.hdc, 10, 10, ILD_NORMAL );
                        ImageList_Draw( hList, 1, ps.hdc, 60, 10, ILD_NORMAL );
                    }
                    EndPaint( hWnd, &ps );
                }
                break;

        case WM_COMMAND :
                switch( LOWORD( wParam ) )
                {
                    case IDM_SAVE :
                            if ( hList )
                            {
                                LPSTORAGE lpst;
                                LPSTREAM  lpstr;

                                // Create the Compound document.
                                //..............................
                                if ( StgCreateDocfile( OLESTR("Image List"),
                                                STGM_READWRITE |
                                                STGM_SHARE_EXCLUSIVE |
                                                STGM_CREATE,
                                                0, &lpst ) == S_OK )
                                {
                                    // Create a stream within the document.
                                    //......................................
                                    lpst->lpVtbl->CreateStream( lpst,
                                                                OLESTR("Images"),
                                                                STGM_READWRITE |
```

continued on next page

continued from previous page

```
                                            STGM_SHARE_EXCLUSIVE |
                                            STGM_CREATE,
                                                    0, 0, &lpstr );

            // Save the image list in the document.
            //....................................
            ImageList_Write( hList, lpstr );
            ImageList_Destroy( hList );
            hList = NULL;

            InvalidateRect( hWnd, NULL, TRUE );
            UpdateWindow( hWnd );

            // Release the IStream and IStorage objects.
            //..........................................
            lpstr->lpVtbl->Release(lpstr);
            lpst->lpVtbl->Release(lpst);

            MessageBox( hWnd, "The image list is saved.",
                    lpszTitle, MB_OK | MB_ICONINFORMATION );
            }
        }
        break;

    case IDM_OPEN :
        if ( !hList )
        {
        LPSTORAGE lpst;
        LPSTREAM  lpstr;

        // Open the compound document.
        //............................
        if ( StgOpenStorage( OLESTR("Image List"), NULL,
                        STGM_READ |
                        STGM_SHARE_EXCLUSIVE,
                        NULL, 0, &lpst ) == S_OK )
            {
            // Open the stream within the document.
            //.....................................
            lpst->lpVtbl->OpenStream( lpst, OLESTR("Images"),
                                    NULL,
                                    STGM_READ |
                                    STGM_SHARE_EXCLUSIVE,
                                        0, &lpstr );

            // Read the image list from the document.
            //.......................................
            hList = ImageList_Read( lpstr );
            InvalidateRect( hWnd, NULL, TRUE );

            // Release the IStream and IStorage objects.
            //..........................................
            lpstr->lpVtbl->Release(lpstr);
            lpst->lpVtbl->Release(lpst);
            }
        }
        break;
```

6

LIST VIEW
AND DRAG LIST

6

LIST VIEW AND DRAG LIST

List boxes are used throughout Windows applications to display lists of items. The standard list box is limited in its functionality and its ability to display icons without a significant amount of custom code. In Windows 95, the Common Control Library introduces a new type of list control called a *list view*. A list view allows an application to display items in a graphical view with icons associated with each item. It also gives the application developer a list control that allows multiple-column display of data and in-place editing of the item names.

Drag-and-drop functionality is also a part of the list view control. However, when a list view is overkill for the application but drag and drop is still a required function, the *drag list* can fill that need. A drag list is the same as a normal list box, with the exception that drag-and-drop operations are supported.

Using List Views

An application can create a list view control by using the CreateWindowEx() function and specifying the WC_LISTVIEW window class. The InitCommonControls() function must be called by the application to initialize the Common Control Library prior to creating the list view control. Table 6-1 lists the list view specific window styles.

Table 6-1 List view styles

Style	Description
LVS_ALIGNLEFT	Items are left-aligned in icon and small icon view.
LVS_ALIGNTOP	Items are aligned with the top of the list view control in icon and small icon view.
LVS_AUTOARRANGE	Icons are automatically kept arranged in icon and small icon view.

continued on next page

continued from previous page

Style	Description
LVS_BUTTON	Item icons look like buttons in icon view.
LVS_EDITLABELS	Allows item text to be edited in place. The parent window must process the LVN_ENDLABELEDIT notification message.
LVS_ICON	Icon view
LVS_LIST	List view
LVS_NOCOLUMNHEADER	A column header is not displayed in report view. By default, columns have headers in report view.
LVS_NOLABELWRAP	Displays item text on a single line in icon view. By default, item text may wrap in icon view.
LVS_NOSCROLL	Disables scrolling. All items must be within the client area.
LVS_NOSORTHEADER	Specifies that column headers do not work like buttons. This style is useful if clicking a column header in report view does not carry out an action, such as sorting.
LVS_OWNERDRAWFIXED	Enables the owner window to paint items in report view. The list view control sends a WM_DRAWITEM message to paint each item; it does not send separate messages for each subitem. The *itemData* member of the DRAWITEMSTRUCT structure contains the item data for the specified list view item.
LVS_REPORT	Report view. When using this style with a list view control, the first column is always left-aligned. You cannot use LVCFMT_RIGHT to change this alignment.
LVS_SHAREIMAGELISTS	The control does not take ownership of the image lists assigned to it; that is, it does not destroy the image lists when it is destroyed. This style enables the same image lists to be used with multiple list view controls.
LVS_SHOWSELALWAYS	Always shows the selection, if any, even if the control does not have the focus.
LVS_SINGLESEL	Allows only one item at a time to be selected. By default, multiple items may be selected.
LVS_SMALLICON	Small icon view
LVS_SORTASCENDING	Sorts items based on item text in ascending order.
LVS_SORTDESCENDING	Sorts items based on item text in descending order.

Once the application creates the list view, it sends messages to the control to add, remove, arrange, and perform other manipulation procedures. All of the list view messages have corresponding macros that an application can use instead of using the messages directly. Using the macros is cleaner and sometimes easier than using the messages themselves. The list view control also notifies the parent window about events through the WM_NOTIFY message and notifications described later in this chapter.

A list view uses image lists as its source of icons for the list view items. The application creates an image list and associates it with the list view with the ListView_SetImageList macro. The application can add the images to the list before or after it is associated with the list view. Multiple image lists, one each for large icons, small icons, and state icons, may be necessary for the list view to display in all modes. To support all view modes, the minimum is the large and small icon image lists. The state image list is used for application-defined states, such as checked and cleared check boxes. Applications use bits 12 through 15 of the item's state to specify the one-based index of a state image, with zero meaning no state image. By default all associated image lists are destroyed when the list view is destroyed unless the LVS_SHAREIMAGELISTS style is used. For more about the creation and manipulation of image lists, see Chapter 5, Image Lists.

The image lists for the large and small icons can also contain overlay images that are superimposed on the item icons. A nonzero value in bits 8 through 11 of the item's state specifies the one-based index for the overlay image. Since this only allows four bits to specify the overlay image index, it must be within the first 15 images in the image list. See the ListView_GetItem macro later in this chapter for more information about item states.

Views

List view controls can display information in four different *views*. When the list view is created, the application specifies the initial view for the list view. Once the list view is created, the application can change the view by using the GetWindowLong() and SetWindowLong() functions to change the window style. Table 6-2 shows the different views, the corresponding styles, and a description of the view.

Table 6-2 View styles

View	Style	Description
Icon	LVS_ICON	The list view items appear with full-sized icons and labels below the icons. The icons can be arranged freely.
List	LVS_LIST	The list view items appear as small icons with a label to the right. The icons are arranged in columns and cannot be rearranged.
Report	LVS_REPORT	The list view items appear as small icons with a label to the right. Additional item information is displayed in separate columns. The icons cannot be arranged; however, the list view can be sorted by columns. If the LVS_NOCOLUMNHEADER window style is specified, the columns will not have headers.
Small Icon	LVS_SMALLICON	The list view items appear with a small icon with the label to the right. The icons can be arranged freely.

List Items

Every item in a list view control consists of an icon, label, current state, and an application-defined 32-bit value. An item can also have one or more associated *subitems*. Subitems only appear in the report view and are displayed in columns to the right of the item. If subitems are used, all items within a list view contain the same number of subitems even if some subitems don't contain a value.

The application adds items to a list view with the ListView_InsertItem macro and the LV_ITEM structure. If the application is adding several items, use the ListView_SetItemCount macro to allow the list view to allocate the memory in advance instead of reallocating memory for each added item. This is more efficient and results in faster insertion of the records. Item attributes, including the icon, label, state, and application-defined value, are changed with the ListView_SetItem macro. Other macros, such as the ListView_SetItemText macro, exist for changing individual item attributes.

Once an item is added to a list view, the application can associate subitems with it with the ListView_SetItem macro and the LV_ITEM structure. The *iSubItem* member is the one-based index of the subitem. The only attribute that can be set for a subitem is the item text.

Another type of item that an application can add to a list view is a *callback item*. For callback items, the application, instead of the list view, maintains the text and/or icon. When the list view requires the information that the application is maintaining, the list view control sends the LVN_GETDISPINFO notification message. If the item attributes or information that the application maintains are changed, the LVN_SET-DISPINFO notification is sent to the parent window. The *callback mask* determines which item state bits are maintained by the application. This applies to all the items in the list view, not just a single item. The callback mask is zero by default, which means the list view maintains the item states. If an application uses callback items or specifies a nonzero callback mask, it must supply list view item attributes when requested.

Using Drag Lists

Drag lists are created by creating a standard list box and then using the MakeDragList() function to "convert" (subclass) the list box into a drag list box. Drag list boxes have the same window styles and process the same messages as standard list boxes.

Before an application can use the drag list boxes, the application must use the RegisterWindowMessage() function with the DRAGLISTMSGSTRING value to register a message to be used when sending notifications to the parent window. All notification messages use the *wParam* parameter as the control identifier of the drag list box. The *lParam* parameter is the pointer to a DRAGLISTINFO structure that contains the notification code and the drag event information. See the example for the MakeDragList() function later in this chapter for more information on using drag list boxes and an example.

Function Summary

Table 6-3 summarizes the list view and drag list functions and messages. The detailed descriptions follow immediately after the table.

Table 6-3 List view and drag list function and message summary

Function	Meaning
DrawInsert	Draws the insert icon in the parent window of the specified drag list box.
LBItemFromPt	Retrieves the index of the item at the specified point in a list box.
ListView_Arrange	Arranges list view control items in icon view.
ListView_CreateDragImage	Creates a drag image list for the specified item.
ListView_DeleteAllItems	Removes all items from a list view control.
ListView_DeleteColumn	Removes a column from a list view control.
ListView_DeleteItem	Removes an item from a list view control.
ListView_EditLabel	Initiates the editing of the specified list view item's text.
ListView_EnsureVisible	Ensures that a specified list view item is at least partially visible.
ListView_FindItem	Finds the list view item with the specified characteristics.
ListView_GetBkColor	Retrieves the background color of a list view control.
ListView_GetCallbackMask	Retrieves the callback mask for a list view control.
ListView_GetColumn	Retrieves the attributes of a list view control's column.
ListView_GetColumnWidth	Retrieves the width of a column in either report or list view.
ListView_GetCountPerPage	Determines the number of items that can fit vertically in the visible area of a list view control in list or report view mode.
ListView_GetEditControl	Retrieves the handle of edit control being used to edit text in a list view item.
ListView_GetImageList	Retrieves the handle of an image list used to draw list view items.
ListView_GetISearchString	Retrieves the incremental search string of a list view control.
ListView_GetItem	Retrieves the attributes of a list view item.
ListView_GetItemCount	Retrieves the number of items in a list view control.
ListView_GetItemPosition	Determines the position of a list view item.
ListView_GetItemRect	Determines the bounding rectangle for an item.
ListView_GetItemSpacing	Retrieves the amount of spacing between items in a list view control.
ListView_GetItemState	Retrieves the state of a list view item.
ListView_GetItemText	Retrieves the text of a list view item or subitem.
ListView_GetNextItem	Searches for the specified list view item.
ListView_GetOrigin	Retrieves the current view origin of the specified list view control.
ListView_GetSelectedCount	Retrieves the number of items selected in a list view control.
ListView_GetStringWidth	Determines the width of the specified string.
ListView_GetTextBkColor	Retrieves the text background color of a list view control.
ListView_GetTextColor	Retrieves the color of the text in a list view control.
ListView_GetTopIndex	Retrieves the topmost visible item when the list view control is in list or report view.
ListView_GetViewRect	Determines the coordinates of the bounding rectangle of all items in the list view control.
ListView_HitTest	Determines which list view item is at the specified position.
ListView_InsertColumn	Inserts a new column in the specified list view control.
ListView_InsertItem	Inserts a new item in the specified list view control.
ListView_RedrawItems	Forces a list view control to redraw a specified range of items.

continued on next page

continued from previous page

Function	Meaning
ListView_Scroll	Scrolls the contents of the specified list view control.
ListView_SetBkColor	Sets the background color of the list view control.
ListView_SetCallbackMask	Sets the callback mask for a list view control.
ListView_SetColumn	Sets the attributes of a list view control.
ListView_SetColumnWidth	Changes the width of a list view control column in report or list view.
ListView_SetImageList	Assigns an image list to a list view control.
ListView_SetItem	Sets some or all of a list view item's attributes.
ListView_SetItemCount	Prepares a list view control for adding a large number of items.
ListView_SetItemPosition	Moves an item to a specified position in a list view control.
ListView_SetItemPosition32	Moves an item to a specified position, in 32-bit coordinates, in a list view control.
ListView_SetItemState	Changes the state of an item in a list view control.
ListView_SetItemText	Changes the text of a list view item or subitem.
ListView_SetTextBkColor	Sets the background color of the text in a list view control.
ListView_SetTextColor	Sets the text color of a list view control.
ListView_SortItems	Sorts the list view control items using an application-defined comparison function.
ListView_Update	Updates a list view item.
MakeDragList()	Changes the specified single-selection list box to a drag list box.
Notification Message	
DL_BEGINDRAG	The user has clicked the left mouse button on a list item in a drag list box.
DL_CANCELDRAG	The user has canceled a drag operation by clicking the right mouse button or pressing the ESC key.
DL_DRAGGING	The user has moved the mouse while dragging an item.
DL_DROPPED	The user has completed a drag operation by releasing the left mouse button.
LVN_BEGINDRAG	A drag-and-drop operation has been initiated in the list view control.
LVN_BEGINLABELEDIT	Label editing for an item has been started.
LVN_BEGINRDRAG	A drag-and-drop operation has been initiated in the list view control using the right mouse button.
LVN_COLUMNCLICK	A column in a list view control was clicked.
LVN_DELETEALLITEMS	All items in a list view control were deleted.
LVN_DELETEITEM	An item in a list view control was deleted.
LVN_ENDLABELEDIT	The label editing of an list view control item has ended.
LVN_GETDISPINFO	Requests that the parent window provide the information needed to display or sort a list view item.
LVN_INSERTITEM	A new item was inserted in the list view control.
LVN_ITEMCHANGED	A new item has changed in the list view control.
LVN_ITEMCHANGING	An item in the list view control is changing.
LVN_KEYDOWN	A key has been pressed in the list view control.
LVN_PEN	A list view control pen event has occurred.
LVN_SETDISPINFO	The information about the specified list view control item must be updated.

DRAWINSERT   ■ Win32s   ■ Windows 95   ■ Windows NT

Description	DrawInsert() draws the insert icon in the parent window of the drag list box. Use this function when drawing the insert icon during a drag operation while processing the DL_DRAGGING notification.
Syntax	void **DrawInsert**(HWND *handParent*, HWND *hLB*, int *nItem*)
Parameters	
handParent	HWND: The handle of the parent window of the drag list box.
hLB	HWND: The handle of the drag list box.
nItem	int: The list box icon item to be drawn in the parent window. This is the item returned from the LBItemFromPt() function. Use -1 to hide the insert icon when the dragging operation is complete.
Include File	commctrl.h
See Also	LBItemFromPt(), MakeDragList()
Example	See the example for the MakeDragList() function.

LBITEMFROMPT   ■ Win32s   ■ Windows 95   ■ Windows NT

Description	LBItemFromPt() retrieves the index of the list box item at the specified point in a list box. This function scrolls the list box on a timer if the bAutoScroll parameter is set to TRUE and the drag cursor is outside the client area of the list box. This provides the user a means of scrolling the list box while in a drag operation. The timer provides a delay so the list box is not scrolled too quickly.
Syntax	int **LBItemFromPt**(HWND *hLB*, POINT *pt*, BOOL *bAutoScroll*)
Parameters	
hLB	HWND: The handle of the list box to check.
pt	POINT: A pointer to a POINT structure that contains the screen coordinates to check for the item.
bAutoScroll	BOOL: The scroll flag. If set to TRUE and the point is directly above or below the list box, the function scrolls the list box one line and returns a value of -1; otherwise, the function does not scroll the list box.
Returns	int: The list box item identifier if the point is over a list item; otherwise, -1 is returned.
Include File	commctrl.h
See Also	DrawInsert(), MakeDragList()
Related Messages	DL_DRAGGING, WM_MOUSEMOVE
Example	See the example for the MakeDragList() function.

LISTVIEW_ARRANGE
■ Win32s ■ Windows 95 ■ Windows NT

Description	ListView_Arrange is a macro that arranges list view control items when the list view is in icon view.
Syntax	BOOL **ListView_Arrange**(HWND *hwnd*, UINT *code*)
Message Syntax	BOOL **SendMessage**(*hwnd*, **LVM_ARRANGE**, *code*, 0)
Parameters	
hwnd	HWND: The handle of the list view control.
code	UINT: The alignment of the items. This parameter can be one of the values in Table 6-4.

Table 6-4 ListView_Arrange *code* values

Value	Meaning
LVA_ALIGNLEFT	Aligns items along the left edge of the window.
LVA_ALIGNTOP	Aligns items along the top edge of the window.
LVA_DEFAULT	Aligns items according to the list view control's current alignment styles (the default value).
LVA_SNAPTOGRID	Snaps all icons to the nearest grid position.

Returns	BOOL: If successful, TRUE is returned; otherwise, FALSE is returned.
Include File	commctrl.h
Related Messages	LVM_ARRANGE
Example	This example (Listing 6-1) demonstrates the dynamics of a list view and how the icons can be arranged by the program or by the user. The user can select the Arrange Icons menu option to clean up the icon arrangement. The user can also use the mouse to select multiple items and drag them to a new location on the list view. The list view is created in large icon view mode and four items are added to the list view. When the user selects the Arrange Icons menu option, the icons are arranged along the top of the window. If the user selects an item or items and continues to hold down the left mouse button, the drag operation starts by the application creating a drag image, as shown in Figure 6-1. The user can move the icons to a new location by dragging the cursor to the desired location and releasing the left mouse button. Notice how the drag cursor is just the outline of the selected objects if there are multiple items selected; otherwise, the drag cursor is the actual image of the item.

Listing 6-1 Using the ListView_Arrange macro

```
LPCTSTR lpszData[4] = { "Circle", "Rectangle", "Cross", "Check" };

LRESULT CALLBACK WndProc( HWND hWnd, UINT uMsg, WPARAM wParam, LPARAM lParam )
{
```

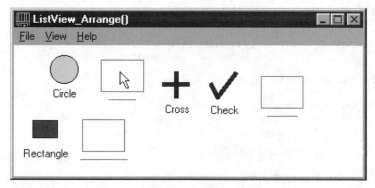

Figure 6-1 ListView_Arrange example

```
static POINT      ptHotSpot, pt;
static int        nDragItem = -1;
static HWND       hList     = NULL;
static HIMAGELIST hCursors  = NULL;
static HIMAGELIST hDragList = NULL;

  switch( uMsg )
  {
    case WM_CREATE  :
            {
              HIMAGELIST hImage;
              ICONINFO   info;

              InitCommonControls();

              hCursors = ImageList_Create( 32, 32, ILC_COLOR4 | ILC_MASK,
                                           1, 1 );
              hImage   = ImageList_Create( 32, 32, ILC_COLOR4 | ILC_MASK,
                                           4, 1 );
              hList = CreateWindowEx( 0, WC_LISTVIEW, "",
                                      WS_CHILD | WS_VISIBLE | LVS_ICON,
                                      10, 100, 100, 100,
                                      hWnd,
                                      (HMENU)1,
                                      hInst,
                                      NULL);

              if ( hList )
              {
                LV_ITEM item;
                HBITMAP hBmp;
                int     i;

                ListView_SetImageList( hList, hImage, LVSIL_NORMAL );

                item.mask = LVIF_TEXT | LVIF_IMAGE;

                for( i=0; i<4; i++ )
                {
                  hBmp = LoadBitmap( hInst, lpszData[i] );
```

continued on next page

continued from previous page

```
                                   item.pszText  = (LPTSTR)lpszData[i];
                                   item.iItem    = i;
                                   item.iSubItem = 0;
                                   item.iImage   = ImageList_AddMasked( hImage, hBmp,
                                                                        RGB( 0, 255, 0 ) );

                                   ListView_InsertItem( hList, &item );

                                   DeleteObject( hBmp );
                           }
                   }

                   ImageList_AddIcon( hCursors, LoadCursor( NULL, IDC_ARROW ) );

                   // Retrieve the hot-spot information from the cursor.
                   //.....................................................
                   GetIconInfo( LoadCursor( NULL, IDC_ARROW ), &info );
                   ptHotSpot.x = info.xHotspot;
                   ptHotSpot.y = info.yHotspot;

                   // Clean up the bitmaps from GetIconInfo().
                   //.........................................
                   DeleteObject( info.hbmMask );
                   DeleteObject( info.hbmColor );
           }
           break;

   case WM_SIZE :
           if ( hList )
               MoveWindow( hList, 0, 0, LOWORD( lParam ),
                                        HIWORD( lParam ), FALSE );
           if ( wParam == SIZE_RESTORED || wParam == SIZE_MAXIMIZED )
               ListView_RedrawItems( hList, 0,
                                     ListView_GetItemCount( hList ) );
           break;

   case WM_NOTIFY :
           if ( wParam == 1 )
           {
               NM_LISTVIEW* pNM = (NM_LISTVIEW*)lParam;

               switch ( pNM->hdr.code )
               {
                   case LVN_BEGINDRAG :
                           // Create the drag image.
                           //.......................
                           if ( ListView_GetSelectedCount( hList ) == 1 )
                               hDragList = ListView_CreateDragImage( hList,
                                                          pNM->iItem, &pt );
                           else
                               hDragList = CreateMultiDrag( hList, pNM->iItem,
                                                            &pt );

                           // Start dragging and set the drag cursor.
                           //........................................
                           ImageList_BeginDrag( hDragList, 0,
                                                pNM->ptAction.x-pt.x,
                                                pNM->ptAction.y-pt.y );
                           ImageList_SetDragCursorImage( hCursors, 0,
```

```
                              pNM->ptAction.x-pt.x-ptHotSpot.x,
                              pNM->ptAction.y-pt.y-ptHotSpot.y );
              ImageList_DragEnter( hList, pNM->ptAction.x,
                                          pNM->ptAction.y );

              // Capture the mouse and hide the normal cursor.
              //...............................................
              SetCapture( hWnd );
              ShowCursor( FALSE );

              // Save the starting drag position and item.
              //...........................................
              pt         = pNM->ptAction;
              nDragItem = pNM->iItem;
              break;
          }
      }
      break;


case WM_MOUSEMOVE :
      // Move the drag cursor if dragging.
      //..................................
      if ( hDragList )
      {
          ImageList_DragMove( LOWORD( lParam ), HIWORD( lParam ) );
      }
      break;


case WM_LBUTTONUP :
      // If dragging, drop the object in its new place.
      //...............................................
      if ( hDragList )
      {
          POINT ptPos;

          ImageList_DragLeave( hList );
          ImageList_EndDrag();
          ImageList_Destroy( hDragList );
          hDragList = NULL;
          ReleaseCapture();
          ShowCursor( TRUE );

          if ( ListView_GetSelectedCount( hList ) == 1 )
          {
              ListView_GetItemPosition( hList, nDragItem, &ptPos );
              ListView_SetItemPosition( hList, nDragItem,
                                  ptPos.x+(LOWORD( lParam )-pt.x),
                                  ptPos.y+(HIWORD( lParam )-pt.y) );
          }
          else // Dragging multiple items.
          {
              int nCur = -1;

              while ( (nCur = ListView_GetNextItem( hList, nCur,
                                      LVNI_SELECTED )) > -1 )
              {
                  ListView_GetItemPosition( hList, nCur, &ptPos );
```

continued on next page

continued from previous page

```
                    ListView_SetItemPosition( hList, nCur,
                                         ptPos.x+(LOWORD(lParam)-pt.x),
                                         ptPos.y+(HIWORD(lParam)-pt.y) );
                }
            }
        }
        break;

    case WM_COMMAND :
        switch( LOWORD( wParam ) )
        {
            case IDM_ARRANGE :
                ListView_Arrange( hList, LVA_DEFAULT );
                break;

            case IDM_EXIT :
                DestroyWindow( hWnd );
                break;
        }
        break;

    case WM_DESTROY :
        if ( ListView_GetImageList( hList, LVSIL_NORMAL ) )
            ImageList_Destroy( ListView_GetImageList( hList,
                                               LVSIL_NORMAL ) );

        PostQuitMessage(0);
        break;

    default :
        return( DefWindowProc( hWnd, uMsg, wParam, lParam ) );
    }

    return( OL );
}


HIMAGELIST CreateMultiDrag( HWND hList, int nItem, POINT* pHotPoint )
{
    HBITMAP     hBmp1, hBmp2, hTmp1, hTmp2, hImage1, hImage2;
    HIMAGELIST  hImageList;
    HPEN        hPen;
    RECT        rect, rect1, rect2, rect3, rect4;
    HDC         hMemDC1, hMemDC2;

    HDC         hDC  = GetDC( hList );
    int         i    = 0;
    int         nCur = -1;
    int         nSel = ListView_GetSelectedCount( hList );


    // Find out the size of the rect that
    // contains all items selected.
    //................................
    for ( i=0; i<nSel; i++ )
    {
        nCur = ListView_GetNextItem( hList, nCur, LVNI_SELECTED );

        ListView_GetItemRect( hList, nCur, &rect1, LVIR_LABEL );
```

```
   ListView_GetItemRect( hList, nCur, &rect2, LVIR_ICON  );
   UnionRect( &rect4, &rect1, &rect2 );

   if( i == 0 )
      rect3 = rect4;

   UnionRect( &rect, &rect3, &rect4 );
   rect3 = rect;
}

pHotPoint->x = rect.left;
pHotPoint->y = rect.top;

// Create 2 compatible bitmaps and device contexts,
// one for the drag image and one for the drag mask.
//...................................................

hBmp1   = CreateCompatibleBitmap( hDC, rect.right - rect.left,
                                       rect.bottom - rect.top );
hBmp2   = CreateCompatibleBitmap( hDC, rect.right - rect.left,
                                       rect.bottom - rect.top );
hPen    = CreatePen( PS_SOLID, 1, RGB( 128, 128, 128 ) );
hMemDC1 = CreateCompatibleDC( hDC );
hMemDC2 = CreateCompatibleDC( hDC );

// Select the empty bitmaps, brushes, and pens
// into the compatible device contexts.
//...................................................

SelectObject( hMemDC1, hBmp1 );
SelectObject( hMemDC2, hBmp2 );
SelectObject( hMemDC1, GetStockObject( BLACK_BRUSH ) );
SelectObject( hMemDC2, GetStockObject( WHITE_BRUSH ) );
SelectObject( hMemDC1, hPen );
SelectObject( hMemDC2, GetStockObject( BLACK_PEN ) );

rect3.left   -= rect.left;
rect3.right  -= rect.left;
rect3.top    -= rect.top;
rect3.bottom -= rect.top;

// Fill the entire bitmap with the
// appropriate color.
//..............................

FillRect( hMemDC1, &rect3, (HBRUSH)GetStockObject( BLACK_BRUSH ) );
FillRect( hMemDC2, &rect3, (HBRUSH)GetStockObject( WHITE_BRUSH ) );

// Draw the images on the bitmaps.
//..............................

nCur = -1;
for( i = 0; i < nSel; i++ )
{
   nCur = ListView_GetNextItem( hList, nCur, LVNI_SELECTED );

   ListView_GetItemRect( hList, nCur, &rect2, LVIR_LABEL );
   ListView_GetItemRect( hList, nCur, &rect3, LVIR_ICON  );
```

continued on next page

continued from previous page

```
      // Paint the Image.
      //.................

      Rectangle( hMemDC1, rect3.left - rect.left, rect3.top - rect.top,
                          rect3.right - rect.left, rect3.bottom - rect.top );

      MoveToEx( hMemDC1, rect2.left - rect.left,
                    (rect2.top - rect.top)+
                    ((rect2.bottom-rect.top) - (rect2.top-rect.top))/2, NULL );

      LineTo( hMemDC1, rect2.right - rect.left,
                          (rect2.top - rect.top)+
                          ((rect2.bottom-rect.top) - (rect2.top-rect.top))/2 );

      // Paint the Mask.
      //...............

      Rectangle( hMemDC2, rect3.left - rect.left, rect3.top - rect.top,
                          rect3.right - rect.left, rect3.bottom - rect.top );

      MoveToEx( hMemDC2, rect2.left - rect.left,
                    (rect2.top - rect.top)+
                    ((rect2.bottom-rect.top) - (rect2.top-rect.top))/2, NULL );

      LineTo( hMemDC2, rect2.right - rect.left,
                    (rect2.top - rect.top)+
                    ((rect2.bottom-rect.top) - (rect2.top-rect.top))/2 );
   }

   // Create temporary bitmaps and select them
   // into the device context which will then return
   // a handle to the bitmaps that we just made.
   //............................................

   hTmp1   = CreateCompatibleBitmap( hDC, 1, 1 );
   hTmp2   = CreateCompatibleBitmap( hDC, 1, 1 );
   hImage1 = (HBITMAP)SelectObject( hMemDC1, hTmp1 );
   hImage2 = (HBITMAP)SelectObject( hMemDC2, hTmp2 );

   // Create the Drag image list and add the images.
   //...............................................

   hImageList = ImageList_Create( rect.right-rect.left,
                              rect.bottom-rect.top, TRUE, 1, 1 );

   ImageList_Add( hImageList, hImage1, hImage2  );

   ReleaseDC( hList, hDC );
   DeleteDC( hMemDC1 );
   DeleteDC( hMemDC2 );

   DeleteObject( hBmp1 );
   DeleteObject( hBmp2 );
   DeleteObject( hTmp1 );
   DeleteObject( hTmp2 );
   DeleteObject( hPen );

   return( hImageList );
}
```

LISTVIEW_ CREATEDRAGIMAGE ■ Win32s ■ Windows 95 ■ Windows NT

Description	ListView_CreateDragImage is a macro that creates a drag image list for the specified list view item. Use this image list when performing drag-and-drop operations on list view items.
Syntax	HIMAGELIST **ListView_CreateDragImage**(HWND *hwnd*, int *iItem*, LPPOINT *lpptUpLeft*)
Message Syntax	HIMAGELIST **SendMessage**(*hwnd*, **LVM_CREATEDRAGIMAGE**, *iItem*, *lpptUpLeft*)
Parameters	
hwnd	HWND: The handle of the list view control.
iItem	int: The index of the item.
lpptUpLeft	LPPOINT: A pointer to a POINT structure that receives the initial location of the upper left corner of the image, in list view coordinates.
Returns	HIMAGELIST: If successful, the handle of the drag image list is returned; otherwise, NULL is returned.
Include File	commctrl.h
Related Messages	LVM_CREATEDRAGIMAGE
Example	See the example for the ListView_Arrange macro.

LISTVIEW_ DELETEALLITEMS ■ Win32s ■ Windows 95 ■ Windows NT

Description	ListView_DeleteAllItems is a macro that removes all items from a list view control.
Syntax	BOOL **ListView_DeleteAllItems**(HWND *hwnd*)
Message Syntax	BOOL **SendMessage**(*hwnd*, **LVM_DELETEALLITEMS**, 0, 0)
Parameters	
hwnd	HWND: The handle of the list view control.
Returns	BOOL: If successful, TRUE is returned; otherwise FALSE is returned.
Include File	commctrl.h
Related Messages	LVM_DELETEALLITEMS
Example	See the example for the ListView_DeleteItem macro.

LISTVIEW_ DELETECOLUMN ■ Win32s ■ Windows 95 ■ Windows NT

Description	ListView_DeleteColumn is a macro that removes a column from a list view control.
Syntax	BOOL **ListView_DeleteColumn**(HWND *hwnd*, int *iCol*)
Message Syntax	BOOL **SendMessage**(*hwnd*, **LVM_DELETECOLUMN**, *iCol*, 0)

Parameters

hwnd	HWND: The handle of the list view control.
iCol	int: The index of the column to delete from the list view control.
Returns	BOOL: If successful, TRUE is returned; otherwise FALSE is returned.
Include File	commctrl.h
Related Messages	LVM_DELETECOLUMN
Example	This example (Listing 6-2) demonstrates how to create and remove list view columns during execution. The user can add a new column or delete a column by using the New and Delete menu items. The ListView_SetColumn macro is used to allow the user to rename the columns from "Column n..." to "Field n...".

Listing 6-2 Using the ListView_DeleteColumn macro

```
// Return TRUE if a column exists.
//................................
BOOL ColumnExists( HWND hList, int nCol )
{
   LV_COLUMN lvc;

   // Retrieve the width of a column to determine if it exists.
   //...........................................................
   lvc.mask = LVCF_WIDTH;

   return( ListView_GetColumn( hList, nCol, &lvc ) );
}

// Determine the number of columns in the list view.
//..................................................
int GetNumColumns( HWND hList )
{
   int nNum = 0;

   while( ColumnExists( hList, nNum ) )
      nNum++;

   return( nNum );
}


LRESULT CALLBACK WndProc( HWND hWnd, UINT uMsg, WPARAM wParam, LPARAM lParam )
{
static HWND hList = NULL;

   switch( uMsg )
   {
      case WM_CREATE :
            {
               InitCommonControls();

               // Create the list view.
               //......................
               hList  = CreateWindowEx( 0, WC_LISTVIEW, "",
```

```
                                    WS_CHILD | WS_VISIBLE | LVS_REPORT,
                                    10, 100, 100, 100,
                                    hWnd,
                                    (HMENU)1,
                                    hInst,
                                    NULL);
            }
            break;

    case WM_SIZE :
            if ( hList )
                MoveWindow( hList,0,0, LOWORD(lParam), HIWORD(lParam), FALSE );

            if ( wParam == SIZE_RESTORED || wParam == SIZE_MAXIMIZED )
                ListView_RedrawItems( hList, 0, ListView_GetItemCount(hList) );
            break;

    case WM_COMMAND :
            switch( LOWORD( wParam ) )
            {
                case IDM_NEWCOLUMN :
                    {
                        LV_COLUMN col;
                        char      szName[40];
                        int       nNumCols = GetNumColumns( hList );

                        // Add a new column to the list view.
                        //.......................................
                        wsprintf( szName, "Column %d", nNumCols+1 );

                        col.mask     = LVCF_FMT | LVCF_SUBITEM |
                                       LVCF_WIDTH | LVCF_TEXT;
                        col.fmt      = LVCFMT_LEFT;
                        col.cx       = 100;
                        col.pszText  = szName;
                        col.iSubItem = nNumCols;

                        ListView_InsertColumn( hList, nNumCols, &col );
                    }
                    break;

                case IDM_RENCOL :
                case IDM_RENFIELD :
                    {
                        LV_COLUMN col;
                        int       nCol = 0;
                        char      szName[40];

                        while ( ColumnExists( hList, nCol ) )
                        {
                            col.mask    = LVCF_TEXT;
                            col.pszText = szName;

                            if ( LOWORD( wParam ) == IDM_RENCOL )
                                wsprintf( szName, "Column %d", nCol+1 );
                            else
                                wsprintf( szName, "Field %d", nCol+1 );

                            // Rename the column.
```

continued on next page

continued from previous page

```
                        //...................
                        ListView_SetColumn( hList, nCol, &col );

                        nCol++;
                    }
                }
                break;

    case IDM_DELETE :
                // Delete the last column from the list view.
                //...............................................
                ListView_DeleteColumn( hList, GetNumColumns(hList)-1 );
                break;
```

.
.
.

LISTVIEW_DELETEITEM   ■ Win32s ■ Windows 95 ■ Windows NT

Description	ListView_DeleteItem is a macro that removes an item from a list view control.
Syntax	BOOL **ListView_DeleteItem**(HWND *hwnd*, int *iItem*)
Message Syntax	BOOL **SendMessage**(*hwnd*, **LVM_DELETEITEM**, *iItem*, 0)
Parameters	
hwnd	HWND: The handle of the list view control.
iItem	int: The index of the list view item to delete from the list view control.
Returns	BOOL: If successful, TRUE is returned; otherwise, FALSE is returned.
Include File	commctrl.h
Related Messages	LVM_DELETEITEM
Example	This example, shown in Figure 6-2 and Listing 6-3, allows the user to add and delete items from a list view. ListView_InsertItem and ListView_DeleteItem macros are used to add and delete the list view items. The view mode can also be changed from large icon, small icon, list, and report view mode using the View menu.

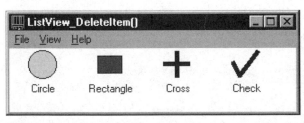

Figure 6-2 ListView_DeleteItem example

Listing 6-3 Using the ListView_DeleteItem macro

```
LPCTSTR lpszData[4]  = { "Circle", "Rectangle", "Cross", "Check" };
LPCTSTR lpszColor[4] = { "Yellow", "Red",      "Black", "Black" };

LRESULT CALLBACK WndProc( HWND hWnd, UINT uMsg, WPARAM wParam, LPARAM lParam )
{
static HWND  hList    = NULL;
static int   nCurView = IDM_VIEWLARGE;

   switch( uMsg )
   {
      case WM_CREATE  :
               {
                  HIMAGELIST hImage, hSmall;

                  InitCommonControls();

                  // Create the image lists and the list view.
                  //.....................................
                  hImage = ImageList_Create( 32, 32, ILC_COLOR4 | ILC_MASK,4,1 );
                  hSmall = ImageList_Create( 16, 16, ILC_COLOR4 | ILC_MASK,4,1 );
                  hList  = CreateWindowEx( 0, WC_LISTVIEW, "",
                                           WS_CHILD | WS_VISIBLE | LVS_ICON,
                                           10, 100, 100, 100,
                                           hWnd,
                                           (HMENU)1,
                                           hInst,
                                           NULL);

                  if ( hList && hImage && hSmall )
                  {
                     LV_COLUMN col;
                     int       i;

                     // Set the large and small image lists.
                     //.....................................
                     ListView_SetImageList( hList, hImage, LVSIL_NORMAL );
                     ListView_SetImageList( hList, hSmall, LVSIL_SMALL );

                     // Add the images to the image list.
                     //.................................
                     for( i=0; i<4; i++ )
                     {
                        ImageList_AddIcon( hImage, LoadIcon(hInst,lpszData[i]) );
                        ImageList_AddIcon( hSmall, LoadIcon(hInst,lpszData[i]) );
                     }

                     // Add the columns for the report view.
                     //.....................................
                     col.mask    = LVCF_FMT | LVCF_WIDTH |
                                   LVCF_TEXT | LVCF_SUBITEM;
                     col.fmt     = LVCFMT_LEFT;
                     col.cx      = 100;

                     col.pszText  = "Name";
                     col.iSubItem = 0;
                     ListView_InsertColumn( hList, 0, &col );
```

continued on next page

continued from previous page

```
                    col.pszText  = "Color";
                    col.iSubItem = 1;
                    ListView_InsertColumn( hList, 1, &col );
                }
            }
            break;

    case WM_SIZE :
            if ( hList )
                MoveWindow( hList, 0, 0, LOWORD( lParam ),
                                        HIWORD( lParam ), FALSE );

            if ( wParam == SIZE_RESTORED || wParam == SIZE_MAXIMIZED )
                ListView_RedrawItems( hList, 0, ListView_GetItemCount(hList) );
            break;

    case WM_INITMENU :
            CheckMenuRadioItem( (HMENU)wParam,
                            IDM_VIEWLARGE, IDM_VIEWDETAILS,
                            nCurView, MF_BYCOMMAND );

            // Enable the delete and duplicate menu commands
            // if there are any items selected in the list view.
            //..................................................
            EnableMenuItem( (HMENU)wParam, IDM_DUPLICATE, MF_BYCOMMAND |
                ListView_GetSelectedCount( hList ) ? MF_ENABLED : MF_GRAYED );

            EnableMenuItem( (HMENU)wParam, IDM_DELETE, MF_BYCOMMAND |
                ListView_GetSelectedCount( hList ) ? MF_ENABLED : MF_GRAYED );

            // Enable the clear all menu command if
            // there are any items in the list.
            //.....................................
            EnableMenuItem( (HMENU)wParam, IDM_DELETEALL, MF_BYCOMMAND |
                ListView_GetItemCount( hList ) ? MF_ENABLED : MF_GRAYED );

            break;

    case WM_COMMAND :
            switch( LOWORD( wParam ) )
            {
                case IDM_INSCIRCLE :
                case IDM_INSRECT :
                case IDM_INSCROSS :
                case IDM_INSCHECK :
                        {
                            LV_ITEM item;

                            // Insert a new item into the list view.
                            //......................................
                            item.mask     = LVIF_TEXT | LVIF_IMAGE;
                            item.pszText  = (LPTSTR)lpszData[LOWORD( wParam )-
                                                            IDM_INSCIRCLE];
                            item.iItem    = ListView_GetItemCount( hList );
                            item.iSubItem = 0;
                            item.iImage   = LOWORD( wParam )-IDM_INSCIRCLE;
                            ListView_InsertItem( hList, &item );
```

```
            item.mask     = LVIF_TEXT;
            item.pszText  = (LPTSTR)lpszColor[LOWORD( wParam )-
                                                  IDM_INSCIRCLE];
            item.iSubItem = 1;
            ListView_SetItem( hList, &item );
        }
        break;

    case IDM_DUPLICATE :
        {
            LV_ITEM item;
            char    szBuf[50];
            int     nItem = -1;

            item.mask     = LVIF_TEXT | LVIF_IMAGE | LVIF_PARAM;
            item.iSubItem = 0;

            // Duplicate all the selected items.
            //.............................
            while( (nItem = ListView_GetNextItem( hList, nItem,
                            LVNI_ALL | LVNI_SELECTED)) > -1 )
            {
                item.iItem      = nItem;
                item.pszText    = szBuf;
                item.cchTextMax = sizeof( szBuf )-1;
                ListView_GetItem( hList, &item );

                item.iItem = ListView_GetItemCount( hList );
                ListView_InsertItem( hList, &item );

                ListView_GetItemText( hList, nItem, 1, szBuf,
                                    sizeof( szBuf )-1 );
                ListView_SetItemText( hList, item.iItem, 1,
                                    szBuf );
            }

        }
        break;

    case IDM_DELETE :
        {
            int nItem = -1;

            // Delete all the selected items.
            //.............................
            while( (nItem = ListView_GetNextItem( hList, nItem,
                            LVNI_ALL | LVNI_SELECTED)) > -1 )
            {
                ListView_DeleteItem( hList, nItem );
            }

            // Make sure the icons are arranged to fill
            //  in the gaps left from the delete icons.
            //.........................................
            ListView_Arrange( hList, LVA_DEFAULT );
        }
        break;
```

continued on next page

continued from previous page

```
            case IDM_DELETEALL :
                    // Delete all the items in the list view.
                    //.......................................
                    ListView_DeleteAllItems( hList );
                    break;

            case IDM_VIEWLARGE   :
            case IDM_VIEWSMALL   :
            case IDM_VIEWLIST    :
            case IDM_VIEWDETAILS :
                    // Change the view of the list view.
                    //.................................
                    SetWindowLong( hList, GWL_STYLE, WS_CHILD | WS_VISIBLE |
                        (LOWORD( wParam ) == IDM_VIEWLARGE ? LVS_ICON :
                         LOWORD( wParam ) == IDM_VIEWSMALL ? LVS_SMALLICON :
                         LOWORD( wParam ) == IDM_VIEWLIST  ? LVS_LIST :
                         LVS_REPORT ) );

                    nCurView = LOWORD( wParam );
                    break;

            case IDM_EXIT :
                    DestroyWindow( hWnd );
                    break;
        }
        break;

    case WM_DESTROY :
            if ( ListView_GetImageList( hList, LVSIL_NORMAL ) )
                ImageList_Destroy( ListView_GetImageList(hList,LVSIL_NORMAL) );

            if ( ListView_GetImageList( hList, LVSIL_SMALL ) )
                ImageList_Destroy( ListView_GetImageList(hList,LVSIL_SMALL) );

            PostQuitMessage(0);
            break;

    default :
            return( DefWindowProc( hWnd, uMsg, wParam, lParam ) );
    }

    return( 0L );
}
```

LISTVIEW_EDITLABEL   ■ Win32s   ■ Windows 95   ■ Windows NT

Description	ListView_EditLabel is a macro that initiates the in-place editing of the specified list view item's text. The list view control must have input focus before this macro is used. Use the SetFocus() function to set the input focus.
	When the user completes the edits, the edit control is destroyed and the returned handle is no longer valid. If the application subclasses the edit control, it should not destroy it.
Syntax	HWND **ListView_EditLabel**(HWND *hwnd*, int *iItem*)

Message Syntax	HWND **SendMessage**(*hwnd*, **LVM_EDITLABEL**, *iItem*, 0)
Parameters	
hwnd	HWND: The handle of the list view control.
iItem	int: The index of the list view item to be modified. Set *iItem* to -1 to cancel editing.
Returns	HWND: If successful, the handle of the edit control used to edit the item text; otherwise, NULL is returned.
Include File	commctrl.h
Related Messages	LVM_EDITLABEL
Example	This example, shown in Figure 6-3 and Listing 6-4, demonstrates the in-place editing of a list view. If the user selects an already selected item, the edit mode is entered automatically and the LVN_BEGINLABELEDIT notification is sent. If the user selects the Rename menu item, the ListView_EditLabel macro is used to enter edit mode and the LVN_BEGINLABELEDIT notification is sent. Once the user has finished editing, it is up to the application to process the LVN_ENDLABELEDIT notification and determine if an edit has occurred. If the edit occurred, the application updates the text of the list view item.

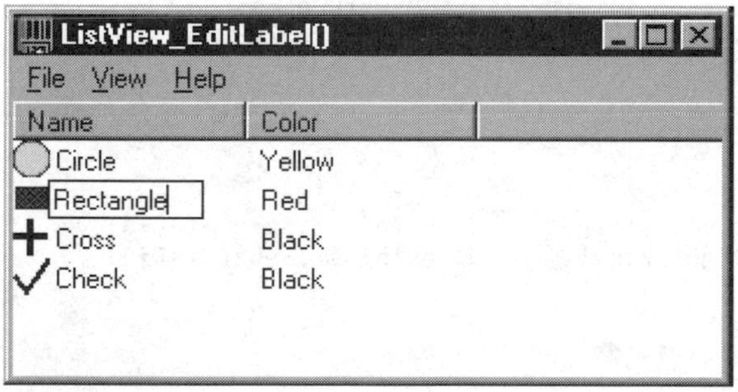

Figure 6-3 ListView_EditLabel example

Listing 6-4 Using the ListView_EditLabel macro

```
LPCTSTR lpszData[4]  = { "Circle", "Rectangle", "Cross", "Check" };
LPCTSTR lpszColor[4] = { "Yellow", "Red",       "Black", "Black" };

LRESULT CALLBACK WndProc( HWND hWnd, UINT uMsg, WPARAM wParam, LPARAM lParam )
{
static HWND  hList    = NULL;
static int   nCurView = IDM_VIEWLARGE;

   switch( uMsg )
   {
```

continued on next page

continued from previous page

```
case WM_CREATE :
        {
            HIMAGELIST hImage, hSmall;

            InitCommonControls();

            // Create the image lists and the list view.
            //........................................
            hImage = ImageList_Create( 32, 32, ILC_COLOR4 | ILC_MASK,4,1 );
            hSmall = ImageList_Create( 16, 16, ILC_COLOR4 | ILC_MASK,4,1 );
            hList  = CreateWindowEx( 0, WC_LISTVIEW, "",
                                     WS_CHILD | WS_VISIBLE |
                                     LVS_ICON | LVS_EDITLABELS,
                                     10, 100, 100, 100,
                                     hWnd,
                                     (HMENU)1,
                                     hInst,
                                     NULL);

            if ( hList && hImage && hSmall )
            {
                LV_COLUMN col;
                LV_ITEM   item;
                int       i;

                // Set the large and small image lists.
                //.....................................
                ListView_SetImageList( hList, hImage, LVSIL_NORMAL );
                ListView_SetImageList( hList, hSmall, LVSIL_SMALL );

                // Add the images to the image list.
                //..................................
                for( i=0; i<4; i++ )
                {
                    ImageList_AddIcon( hImage, LoadIcon(hInst,lpszData[i]) );
                    ImageList_AddIcon( hSmall, LoadIcon(hInst,lpszData[i]) );
                }

                // Add the columns for the report view.
                //.....................................
                col.mask    = LVCF_FMT | LVCF_WIDTH |
                              LVCF_TEXT | LVCF_SUBITEM;
                col.fmt     = LVCFMT_LEFT;
                col.cx      = 100;

                col.pszText  = "Name";
                col.iSubItem = 0;
                ListView_InsertColumn( hList, 0, &col );

                col.pszText  = "Color";
                col.iSubItem = 1;
                ListView_InsertColumn( hList, 1, &col );

                // Insert items into the list view.
                //.................................
                for( i=0; i<4; i++ )
                {
                    item.mask     = LVIF_TEXT | LVIF_IMAGE;
                    item.pszText  = (LPTSTR)lpszData[i];
```

```
                        item.iItem   = i;
                        item.iSubItem = 0;
                        item.iImage  = i;
                        ListView_InsertItem( hList, &item );

                        item.mask    = LVIF_TEXT;
                        item.pszText = (LPTSTR)lpszColor[i];
                        item.iSubItem = 1;
                        ListView_SetItem( hList, &item );
                    }
                }
            }
            break;

    case WM_SIZE :
            if ( hList )
                MoveWindow( hList,0,0, LOWORD(lParam), HIWORD(lParam), FALSE );

            if ( wParam == SIZE_RESTORED || wParam == SIZE_MAXIMIZED )
                ListView_RedrawItems( hList, 0, ListView_GetItemCount(hList) );
            break;


    case WM_INITMENU :
            CheckMenuRadioItem( (HMENU)wParam,
                    IDM_VIEWLARGE, IDM_VIEWDETAILS, nCurView, MF_BYCOMMAND );
            break;


    case WM_NOTIFY :
            if ( wParam == 1 )
            {
            LV_DISPINFO* dispInfo = (LV_DISPINFO*)lParam;

            switch( dispInfo->hdr.code )
            {
                case LVN_BEGINLABELEDIT :
                        {
                            // Limit the text length of the item.
                            //....................................
                            HWND hEdit = ListView_GetEditControl( hList );

                            if ( hEdit )
                                SendMessage( hEdit, EM_LIMITTEXT, 15, 0 );
                        }
                        break;

                case LVN_ENDLABELEDIT :
                        // If the user edited the text, update the item.
                        //.............................................
                        if ( dispInfo->item.pszText )
                        {
                            dispInfo->item.mask = LVIF_TEXT;
                            ListView_SetItem( hList, &dispInfo->item );
                        }
                        break;
                }
            }
            break;
```

continued on next page

continued from previous page

```
        case WM_COMMAND :
                switch( LOWORD( wParam ) )
                {
                case IDM_RENAME :
                        {
                            int nItem = -1;

                            nItem = ListView_GetNextItem( hList, nItem,
                                            LVNI_ALL | LVNI_SELECTED );

                            if ( nItem > -1 )
                                ListView_EditLabel( hList, nItem );
                        }
                        break;

                case IDM_VIEWLARGE   :
                case IDM_VIEWSMALL   :
                case IDM_VIEWLIST    :
                case IDM_VIEWDETAILS :
                        // Change the view of the list view.
                        //..................................
                        SetWindowLong( hList, GWL_STYLE,
                            WS_CHILD | WS_VISIBLE | LVS_EDITLABELS |
                            (LOWORD( wParam ) == IDM_VIEWLARGE ? LVS_ICON :
                             LOWORD( wParam ) == IDM_VIEWSMALL ? LVS_SMALLICON :
                             LOWORD( wParam ) == IDM_VIEWLIST  ? LVS_LIST :
                             LVS_REPORT ) );

                        nCurView = LOWORD( wParam );
                        break;
            .
            .
            .
```

LISTVIEW_ENSUREVISIBLE ■ Win32s ■ Windows 95 ■ Windows NT

Description	ListView_EnsureVisible is a macro that ensures that a specified list view item is at least partially visible. The list view is scrolled if necessary.
Syntax	BOOL **ListView_EnsureVisible**(HWND *hwnd*, int *iItem*, BOOL *bPartialOK*)
Message Syntax	BOOL **SendMessage**(*hwnd*, **LVM_ENSUREVISIBLE**, *iItem*, *bPartialOk*)
Parameters	
hwnd	HWND: The handle of the list view control.
iItem	int: The index of the list view item.
bPartialOK	BOOL: Set to TRUE if it is acceptable for the item to be partially visible.
Returns	BOOL: If successful, TRUE is returned; otherwise, FALSE is returned.
Include File	commctrl.h
Related Messages	LVM_ENSUREVISIBLE
Example	See the example for the ListView_FindItem macro.

LISTVIEW_FINDITEM ■ Win32s ■ Windows 95 ■ Windows NT

Description   ListView_FindItem is a macro that searches a list view for an item with the specified characteristics.

Syntax   int **ListView_FindItem**(HWND *hwnd*, int *iStart*, const LV_FINDINFO* *plvfi*)

Message Syntax   int **SendMessage**(*hwnd*, **LVM_FINDITEM**, *iStart*, *plvfi*)

Parameters

hwnd   HWND: The handle of the list view control.

iStart   int: The index of the item in the list where the search should begin. If set to -1, the search begins at the beginning of the list. The item at this index is excluded from the search.

plvfi   const LV_FINDINFO*: A constant pointer to an LV_FINDINFO structure that contains information about the list view item to search for. See the definition of the LV_FINDINFO structure below.

Returns   int: If an item was found that matches the search criteria, the index of the list view item is returned. If no items matched the search criteria, -1 is returned.

Include File   commctrl.h

Related Messages   LVM_FINDITEM

LV_FINDINFO Definition

```
typedef struct _LV_FINDINFO
{
    UINT    flags;
    LPCTSTR psz;
    LPARAM  lParam;
    POINT   pt;
    UINT    vkDirection;
} LV_FINDINFO;
```

Members

flags   UINT: The type of search to perform. This member can be one or more of the values in Table 6-5.

Table 6-5 LV_FINDINFO *flags* values

Value	Meaning
LVFI_NEARESTXY	Finds the item nearest the specified position in the specified direction.
LVFI_PARAM	Searches based on the *lParam* value. The *lParam* value of the matching list view item must match the *lParam* member of this structure. If this search value is specified, all other values are ignored.
LVFI_PARTIAL	Matches if the item text begins with the string pointed to by the *psz* member. This value implies use of LVFI_STRING.

continued on next page

continued from previous page

Value	Meaning
LVFI_STRING	Searches based on the item text. If no other search values are specified, the item text of the matching item must exactly match the string pointed to by the *psz* member.
LVFI_WRAP	Continues the search at the beginning of the list view if no match is found.

psz   LPCTSTR: A pointer to a null-terminated string to compare with the item text if *flags* specifies LVFI_STRING or LVFI_PARTIAL.

lParam   LPARAM: The value to compare with the *lParam* value of a list view item. This member is ignored unless the *flags* member specifies LVFI_PARAM flag.

pt   POINT: Specifies the starting position to search from. This member is ignored unless the *flags* member specifies the LVFI_NEARESTXY flag.

vkDirection   UINT: This value specifies the virtual-key code of an arrow key that represents the direction in which to search. This member is ignored unless *flags* specifies the LVFI_NEARESTXY flag.

Example   This example (Listing 6-5) uses the ListView_GetISearchString macro to demonstrate how the advanced list view searching works. Unlike a list box, a list view builds a cumulative search string as the user types. If there is a significant delay between keystrokes, the search string is reset and starts over. The current search string that the list view is maintaining is shown above the list view as shown in Figure 6-4. The user can also use the Find menu item to search for an item as demonstrated in the example with the ListView_FindItem macro.

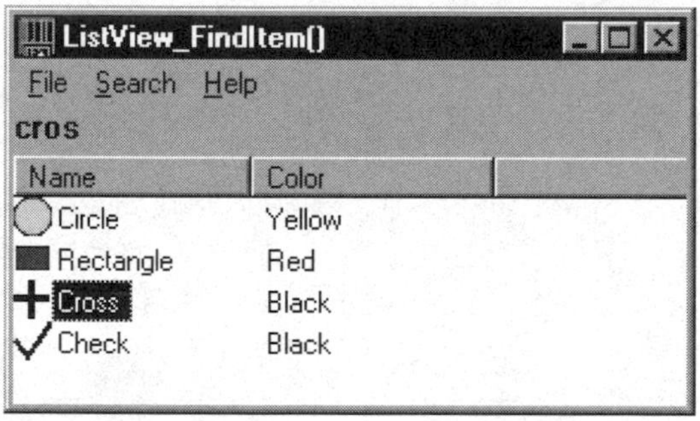

Figure 6-4 ListView_FindItem example

Listing 6-5 Using the ListView_FindItem macro

```
LPCTSTR lpszData[4] = { "Circle", "Rectangle", "Cross", "Check" };
LPCTSTR lpszColor[4] = { "Yellow", "Red",       "Black", "Black" };

LRESULT CALLBACK WndProc( HWND hWnd, UINT uMsg, WPARAM wParam, LPARAM lParam )
{
```

```
static char   szBuf[40];
static UINT   uTimerID = 0;
static HWND   hList    = NULL;
static HWND   hStatic  = NULL;

   switch( uMsg )
   {
      case WM_CREATE  :
                  {
                     HIMAGELIST hImage, hSmall;

                     InitCommonControls();

                     // Create the image lists and the list view.
                     //...........................................
                     hImage = ImageList_Create( 32, 32, ILC_COLOR4 | ILC_MASK,4,1 );
                     hSmall = ImageList_Create( 16, 16, ILC_COLOR4 | ILC_MASK,4,1 );
                     hList  = CreateWindowEx( 0, WC_LISTVIEW, "",
                                          WS_CHILD | WS_VISIBLE | LVS_REPORT |
                                          LVS_EDITLABELS | LVS_SINGLESEL,
                                          0, 20, 100, 100,
                                          hWnd,
                                          (HMENU)1,
                                          hInst,
                                          NULL);

                     hStatic = CreateWindowEx( 0, "STATIC", "",
                                          WS_CHILD | WS_VISIBLE,
                                          0, 0, 100, 20,
                                          hWnd,
                                          (HMENU)2,
                                          hInst,
                                          NULL );

                     if ( hList && hImage && hSmall )
                     {
                        LV_COLUMN col;
                        LV_ITEM   item;
                        int       i;

                        // Set the large and small image lists.
                        //.....................................
                        ListView_SetImageList( hList, hImage, LVSIL_NORMAL );
                        ListView_SetImageList( hList, hSmall, LVSIL_SMALL );

                        // Add the images to the image list.
                        //..................................
                        for( i=0; i<4; i++ )
                        {
                           ImageList_AddIcon( hImage, LoadIcon(hInst,lpszData[i]) );
                           ImageList_AddIcon( hSmall, LoadIcon(hInst,lpszData[i]) );
                        }

                        // Add the columns for the report view.
                        //.....................................
                        col.mask    = LVCF_FMT | LVCF_WIDTH |
                                      LVCF_TEXT | LVCF_SUBITEM;
                        col.fmt     = LVCFMT_LEFT;
                        col.cx      = 100;
```

continued on next page

continued from previous page

```
                col.pszText  = "Name";
                col.iSubItem = 0;
                ListView_InsertColumn( hList, 0, &col );

                col.pszText  = "Color";
                col.iSubItem = 1;
                ListView_InsertColumn( hList, 1, &col );

                // Insert items into the list view.
                //................................
                for( i=0; i<4; i++ )
                {
                    item.mask     = LVIF_TEXT | LVIF_IMAGE;
                    item.pszText  = (LPTSTR)lpszData[i];
                    item.iItem    = i;
                    item.iSubItem = 0;
                    item.iImage   = i;
                    ListView_InsertItem( hList, &item );

                    item.mask     = LVIF_TEXT;
                    item.pszText  = (LPTSTR)lpszColor[i];
                    item.iSubItem = 1;
                    ListView_SetItem( hList, &item );
                }
            }

            uTimerID = SetTimer( hWnd, 1, 500, NULL );
        }
        break;

    case WM_SIZE :
            if ( hStatic )
                MoveWindow( hStatic, 0, 0, LOWORD( lParam ), 20, FALSE );

            if ( hList )
                MoveWindow( hList, 0, 20, LOWORD( lParam ),
                                        HIWORD( lParam )-20, FALSE );

            if ( wParam == SIZE_RESTORED || wParam == SIZE_MAXIMIZED )
                ListView_RedrawItems( hList, 0, ListView_GetItemCount(hList) );
            break;


    case WM_TIMER :
            if ( wParam == uTimerID )
            {
                ListView_GetISearchString( hList, szBuf );
                SetWindowText( hStatic, szBuf );
            }
            break;

    case WM_COMMAND :
            switch( LOWORD( wParam ) )
            {
                case IDM_FIND :
                    {
                        LV_FINDINFO fi;
                        int         nItem = -1;
```

```
                        fi.flags = LVFI_STRING;
                        fi.psz   = "Rectangle";

                        nItem = ListView_FindItem( hList, -1, &fi );

                        if ( nItem > -1 &&
                           !(ListView_GetItemState( hList, nItem,
                                        LVIS_SELECTED) & LVIS_SELECTED) )
                        {
                           ListView_EnsureVisible( hList, nItem, FALSE );
                           ListView_SetItemState( hList, nItem,
                                        LVIS_SELECTED | LVIS_FOCUSED,
                                        LVIS_SELECTED | LVIS_FOCUSED);
                        }
                     }
                     break;

              case IDM_EXIT :
                     DestroyWindow( hWnd );
                     break;
           }
           break;

     case WM_DESTROY :
           KillTimer( hWnd, uTimerID );

           if ( ListView_GetImageList( hList, LVSIL_NORMAL ) )
              ImageList_Destroy( ListView_GetImageList(hList,LVSIL_NORMAL) );

           if ( ListView_GetImageList( hList, LVSIL_SMALL ) )
              ImageList_Destroy( ListView_GetImageList(hList,LVSIL_SMALL) );

           PostQuitMessage(0);
           break;

     default :
           return( DefWindowProc( hWnd, uMsg, wParam, lParam ) );
  }

  return( 0L );
}
```

LISTVIEW_GETBKCOLOR ■ Win32s ■ Windows 95 ■ Windows NT

Description	ListView_GetBkColor is a macro that retrieves the background color of the list view control.
Syntax	COLORREF **ListView_GetBkColor**(HWND *hwnd*)
Message Syntax	COLORREF **SendMessage**(*hwnd*, **LVM_GETBKCOLOR**, 0, 0)
Parameters	
hwnd	HWND: The handle of the list view control.
Returns	COLORREF: The background color of the list view control.
Include File	commctrl.h

See Also	ListView_SetBkColor
Related Messages	LVM_GETBKCOLOR
Example	This example (Listing 6-6) demonstrates how a list view's colors can be customized. When the user selects the Options... menu item, the dialog, shown in Figure 6-5, is shown and allows the user to set the RGB values for each of the list view colors.

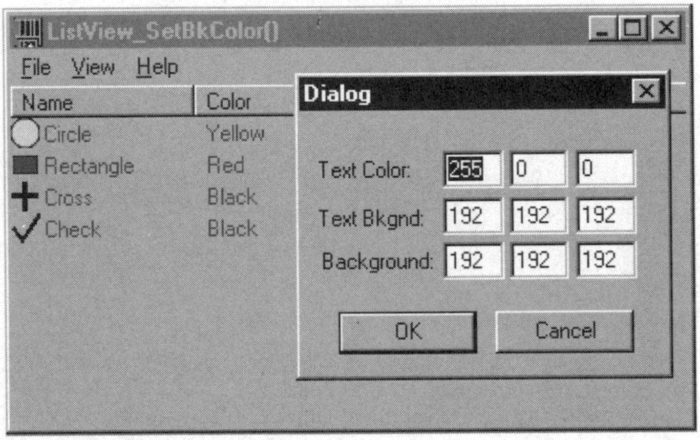

Figure 6-5 ListView Color example

Listing 6-6 Using the ListView_GetBkColor macro

```
HWND hList = NULL;

LRESULT CALLBACK OptionsDlg( HWND hDlg,
                            UINT message,
                            WPARAM wParam,
                            LPARAM lParam)
{
   switch (message)
   {
      case WM_INITDIALOG:
            {
               COLORREF cr;

               // Retrieve the list view colors.
               //...............................
               cr = ListView_GetTextColor( hList );
               SetDlgItemInt( hDlg, IDC_TR, GetRValue( cr ), FALSE );
               SetDlgItemInt( hDlg, IDC_TG, GetGValue( cr ), FALSE );
               SetDlgItemInt( hDlg, IDC_TB, GetBValue( cr ), FALSE );

               cr = ListView_GetTextBkColor( hList );
               SetDlgItemInt( hDlg, IDC_TBR, GetRValue( cr ), FALSE );
               SetDlgItemInt( hDlg, IDC_TBG, GetGValue( cr ), FALSE );
               SetDlgItemInt( hDlg, IDC_TBB, GetBValue( cr ), FALSE );
```

```
              cr = ListView_GetBkColor( hList );
              SetDlgItemInt( hDlg, IDC_BR, GetRValue( cr ), FALSE );
              SetDlgItemInt( hDlg, IDC_BG, GetGValue( cr ), FALSE );
              SetDlgItemInt( hDlg, IDC_BB, GetBValue( cr ), FALSE );
          }
          return (TRUE);

      case WM_COMMAND:
          if ( LOWORD(wParam) == IDOK )
          {
              // Update the list view colors.
              //.........................
              ListView_SetTextColor( hList,
                     RGB( GetDlgItemInt( hDlg, IDC_TR, NULL, FALSE ),
                          GetDlgItemInt( hDlg, IDC_TG, NULL, FALSE ),
                          GetDlgItemInt( hDlg, IDC_TB, NULL, FALSE ) ) );

              ListView_SetTextBkColor( hList,
                     RGB( GetDlgItemInt( hDlg, IDC_TBR, NULL, FALSE ),
                          GetDlgItemInt( hDlg, IDC_TBG, NULL, FALSE ),
                          GetDlgItemInt( hDlg, IDC_TBB, NULL, FALSE ) ) );

              ListView_SetBkColor( hList,
                     RGB( GetDlgItemInt( hDlg, IDC_BR, NULL, FALSE ),
                          GetDlgItemInt( hDlg, IDC_BG, NULL, FALSE ),
                          GetDlgItemInt( hDlg, IDC_BB, NULL, FALSE ) ) );

              ListView_RedrawItems( hList, 0, ListView_GetItemCount(hList));

              EndDialog( hDlg, IDOK );
          }
          else if ( LOWORD(wParam) == IDCANCEL )
          {
              EndDialog(hDlg, IDCANCEL);
              return (TRUE);
          }
          break;

   return (FALSE);
}
```

LISTVIEW_GETCALLBACKMASK ■ Win32s ■ Windows 95 ■ Windows NT

Description	ListView_GetCallbackMask is a macro that retrieves the callback mask for a list view control. A one bit in the callback mask means the application maintains the corresponding state bit for each list view item.
Syntax	UINT **ListView_GetCallbackMask**(HWND *hwnd*)
Message Syntax	UINT **SendMessage**(*hwnd*, **LVM_GETCALLBACKMASK**, 0, 0)
Parameters	
hwnd	HWND: The handle of the list view control.
Returns	UINT: The callback mask.
Include File	commctrl.h

See Also	ListView_SetCallbackMask
Related Messages	LVM_GETCALLBACKMASK

LISTVIEW_GETCOLUMN   ■ Win32s ■ Windows 95 ■ Windows NT

Description	ListView_GetColumn is a macro that retrieves the attributes for a list view column. Columns are visible when a list view is in report view.
Syntax	BOOL **ListView_GetColumn**(HWND *hwnd*, int *iCol*, LV_COLUMN* *pcol*)
Message Syntax	BOOL **SendMessage**(*hwnd*, **LVM_GETCOLUMN**, *iCol*, *pcol*)
Parameters	
hwnd	HWND: The handle of the list view control.
iCol	int: The index of the column.
pcol	LV_COLUMN*: A pointer to an LV_COLUMN structure that both specifies the information to retrieve and receives the information about the column. See the definition of the LV_COLUMN structure below.
	The *mask* member of the structure specifies the column attributes to retrieve. If *mask* specifies the LVCF_TEXT value, *pszText* must contain the pointer to the buffer that receives the item text, and *cchTextMax* must specify the size of the buffer.
Returns	BOOL: If successful, TRUE is returned; otherwise, FALSE is returned.
Include File	commctrl.h
Related Messages	LVM_GETCOLUMN
LV_COLUMN Definition	

```
typedef struct _LV_COLUMN
{
    UINT    mask;
    int     fmt;
    int     cx;
    LPTSTR  pszText;
    int     cchTextMax;
    int     iSubItem;
} LV_COLUMN;
```

Members	
mask	UINT: Specifies which members contain valid information. This member can be zero, or a combination of the values in Table 6-6.

Table 6-6 LV_COLUMN *mask* values

Value	Meaning
LVCF_FMT	The *fmt* member is valid.
LVCF_SUBITEM	The *iSubItem* member is valid.
LVCF_TEXT	The *pszText* member is valid.
LVCF_WIDTH	The *cx* member is valid.

fmt	int: The alignment of the column. This member can be one of the following values: LVCFMT_LEFT, LVCFMT_RIGHT, or LVCFMT_CENTER. The first column in a list view control must be left-aligned; that is, the LVCFMT_RIGHT must not be specified for the first column.
cx	int: The width of the column, in pixels.
pszText	LPTSTR: A pointer to a null-terminated string that contains the column heading if the structure contains information about a column. If the structure is receiving information about a column, this member specifies the address of the buffer that receives the column heading.
cchTextMax	int: The size of the buffer pointed to by *pszText*. If the structure is not receiving information about a column, this member is ignored.
iSubItem	int: An index of the subitem associated with a column.
Example	See the example for the ListView_DeleteColumn macro.

LISTVIEW_GETCOLUMNWIDTH   ■ Win32s   ■ Windows 95   ■ Windows NT

Description	ListView_GetColumnWidth is a macro that retrieves the width of a column in the report view of a list view control.
Syntax	int **ListView_GetColumnWidth**(HWND *hwnd*, int *iCol*)
Message Syntax	int **SendMessage**(*hwnd*, **LVM_GETCOLUMNWIDTH**, *iCol*, 0)
Parameters	
hwnd	HWND: The handle of the list view control.
iCol	int: The index of the column. This parameter is ignored in list view mode.
Returns	int: If successful, the width of the column is returned; otherwise, zero is returned.
Include File	commctrl.h
Related Messages	LVM_GETCOLUMNWIDTH
Example	This example (Listing 6-7) uses the ListView_GetColumnWidth, ListView_SetColumnWidth, and ListView_GetStringWidth macros to set the column sizes to the minimum size allowed to display the largest string added to the list view. This can be useful when the optimum column width is not known prior to loading the list view items.

Listing 6-7   Using the ListView_GetColumnWidth macro

```
LRESULT CALLBACK WndProc( HWND hWnd, UINT uMsg, WPARAM wParam, LPARAM lParam )
{
static HWND hList = NULL;

   switch( uMsg )
   {
      case WM_CREATE  :
            {
               HIMAGELIST hImage, hSmall;
```

continued on next page

continued from previous page

```
                InitCommonControls();

                // Create the image lists and the list view.
                //.........................................
                hImage = ImageList_Create( 32, 32, ILC_COLOR4 | ILC_MASK,4,1 );
                hSmall = ImageList_Create( 16, 16, ILC_COLOR4 | ILC_MASK,4,1 );
                hList  = CreateWindowEx( 0, WC_LISTVIEW, "",
                                         WS_CHILD | WS_VISIBLE | LVS_REPORT |
                                         LVS_EDITLABELS | LVS_SINGLESEL,
                                         0, 20, 100, 100,
                                         hWnd,
                                         (HMENU)1,
                                         hInst,
                                         NULL);

                if ( hList && hImage && hSmall )
                {
                    LV_COLUMN col;
                    LV_ITEM   item;
                    int       i, nWidth;

                    // Set the large and small image lists.
                    //.........................................
                    ListView_SetImageList( hList, hImage, LVSIL_NORMAL );
                    ListView_SetImageList( hList, hSmall, LVSIL_SMALL );

                    // Add the images to the image list.
                    //..................................
                    for( i=0; i<4; i++ )
                    {
                        ImageList_AddIcon( hImage, LoadIcon(hInst,lpszData[i]) );
                        ImageList_AddIcon( hSmall, LoadIcon(hInst,lpszData[i]) );
                    }

                    // Add the columns for the report view.
                    //.....................................
                    col.mask     = LVCF_FMT | LVCF_WIDTH |
                                   LVCF_TEXT | LVCF_SUBITEM;
                    col.fmt      = LVCFMT_LEFT;
                    col.cx       = 10;

                    col.pszText  = "Name";
                    col.iSubItem = 0;
                    ListView_InsertColumn( hList, 0, &col );

                    col.pszText  = "Color";
                    col.iSubItem = 1;
                    ListView_InsertColumn( hList, 1, &col );

                    // Insert items into the list view.
                    //.................................
                    for( i=0; i<4; i++ )
                    {
                        item.mask     = LVIF_TEXT | LVIF_IMAGE;
                        item.pszText  = (LPTSTR)lpszData[i];
                        item.iItem    = i;
                        item.iSubItem = 0;
                        item.iImage   = i;
                        ListView_InsertItem( hList, &item );
```

```
                    // Expand column 0 width if necessary.
                    // 20 is added to make room for the icon.
                    //.......................................
                    nWidth = ListView_GetStringWidth( hList,
                                               lpszData[i] )+20;
                    if (  nWidth > ListView_GetColumnWidth( hList, 0 ) )
                       ListView_SetColumnWidth( hList, 0, nWidth );

                    item.mask     = LVIF_TEXT;
                    item.pszText  = (LPTSTR)lpszColor[i];
                    item.iSubItem = 1;
                    ListView_SetItem( hList, &item );

                    // Expand column 1 width if necessary.
                    // 12 is added to make room for the column border.
                    //.................................................
                    nWidth = ListView_GetStringWidth( hList,
                                               lpszColor[i] )+12;
                    if (  nWidth > ListView_GetColumnWidth( hList, 1 ) )
                       ListView_SetColumnWidth( hList, 1, nWidth );

                }
            }
        }
        break;
        .
        .
        .
```

LISTVIEW_GETCOUNTPERPAGE   ■ Win32s   ■ Windows 95   ■ Windows NT

Description	ListView_GetCountPerPage is a macro that determines the number of items that will fit vertically in the visible area of a list view control in list or report view mode.
Syntax	int **ListView_GetCountPerPage**(HWND *hwnd*)
Message Syntax	int **SendMessage**(*hwnd*, **LVM_GETCOUNTPERPAGE**, 0, 0)
Parameters	
hwnd	HWND: The handle of the list view control.
Returns	int: If successful, the number of fully visible items is returned. If the current view mode is icon or small icon view, the total number of items in the list view control is returned.
Include File	commctrl.h
Related Messages	LVM_GETCOUNTPERPAGE

LISTVIEW_GETEDITCONTROL   ■ Win32s   ■ Windows 95   ■ Windows NT

Description	ListView_GetEditControl is a macro that retrieves the handle of the edit control that is editing the text of a list view item.

The edit control is not created until after the LVN_BEGINLABELEDIT notification message is sent. When the user completes or cancels editing, the edit control is destroyed and the handle is no longer valid. You can safely subclass the edit control, but you should not destroy it. To cancel editing, you can send the list view control a WM_CANCELMODE message.

The list view item being edited is the currently focused item–that is, the item in the focused state. To find an item based on its state, use the LVM_GETNEXTITEM message.

Syntax	HWND **ListView_GetEditControl**(HWND *hwnd*)
Message Syntax	HWND **SendMessage**(*hwnd*, **LVM_GETEDITCONTROL**, 0, 0)
Parameters	
hwnd	HWND: The handle of the list view control.
Returns	HWND: If successful, the handle of the edit control is returned; otherwise, NULL is returned. If a label is not being edited, NULL is returned.
Include File	commctrl.h
Related Messages	LVM_GETEDITCONTROL, LVN_BEGINLABELEDIT, WM_CANCELMODE
Example	See the example for the ListView_EditLabel macro.

LISTVIEW_GETIMAGELIST   ■ Win32s ■ Windows 95 ■ Windows NT

Description	ListView_GetImageList is a macro that retrieves the handle of an image list used for drawing list view items.
Syntax	HIMAGELIST **ListView_GetImageList**(HWND *hwnd*, int *iImageList*)
Message Syntax	HIMAGELIST **SendMessage**(*hwnd*, **LVM_GETIMAGELIST**, *iImageList*, 0)
Parameters	
hwnd	HWND: The handle of the list view control.
iImageList	int: One of the parameters in Table 6-7 indicating the type of image list to retrieve.

Table 6-7 ListView_GetImageList *iImageList* values

Value	Meaning
LVSIL_NORMAL	Image list with large icons
LVSIL_SMALL	Image list with small icons
LVSIL_STATE	Image list with state images

Returns	HIMAGELIST: The handle of the specified image list, if successful; otherwise, NULL is returned.

Include File	commctrl.h
Related Messages	LVM_GETIMAGELIST
Example	See the example for the ListView_DeleteItem macro.

LISTVIEW_GETISEARCHSTRING　　■ Win32s　■ Windows 95　■ Windows NT

Description	ListView_GetISearchString is a macro that retrieves the incremental search string typed into a list view control by the user. The system appends each character typed by the user to the search string and then uses the new string to search for the matching item. If a match is found, it is selected and scrolled into view.
Syntax	BOOL **ListView_GetISearchString**(HWND *hwnd*, LPSTR *lpsz*)
Message Syntax	BOOL **SendMessage**(*hwnd*, **LVM_GETISEARCHSTRING**, 0, *lpsz*)
Parameters	
hwnd	HWND: The handle of the list view control.
lpsz	LPSTR: A pointer to a buffer that receives the incremental search string.
Returns	BOOL: The number of characters in the incremental search string, or zero if the list view control is not in incremental search mode.
Include File	commctrl.h
Related Messages	LVM_GETISEARCHSTRING
Example	See the example for the ListView_FindItem macro.

LISTVIEW_GETITEM　　　　　　■ Win32s　■ Windows 95　■ Windows NT

Description	ListView_GetItem is a macro that retrieves the attributes of a list view item.
Syntax	BOOL **ListView_GetItem**(HWND *hwnd*, LV_ITEM* *pitem*)
Message Syntax	BOOL **SendMessage**(*hwnd*, **LVM_GETITEM**, 0, *pitem*)
Parameters	
hwnd	HWND: The handle of the list view control.
pitem	LV_ITEM*: A pointer to an LV_ITEM structure that identifies the information to retrieve and that receives information about the specified list view item.

When ListView_GetItem is sent, the *iItem* and *iSubItem* members of the LV_ITEM structure identify the item or subitem to retrieve information about and the *mask* member specifies which attributes to retrieve. If the *mask* member specifies the LVIF_TEXT value, the *pszText* member must contain the pointer to the buffer that receives the item text and the *cchTextMax* member must specify the size of the buffer. If the *mask* member specifies the LVIF_STATE value, the *stateMask* member specifies which item states are to be returned. See the definition of the LV_ITEM structure below.

Returns   BOOL: TRUE if successful; otherwise, FALSE is returned.

Include File   commctrl.h

Related Messages   LVM_GETITEM

LV_ITEM Definition

```
typedef struct _LV_ITEM
{
    UINT    mask;
    int     iItem;
    int     iSubItem;
    UINT    state;
    UINT    stateMask;
    LPTSTR  pszText;
    int     cchTextMax;
    int     iImage;
    LPARAM  lParam;
} LV_ITEM;
```

Members

mask   UINT: A set of bit flags that specify attributes of this data structure or of an operation that is using this structure.

The bit flags in Table 6-8 specify the members of the LV_ITEM structure that contain valid data or need to be filled in. One or more of these bit flags may be set.

Table 6-8 LV_ITEM *mask* values

Value	Meaning
LVIF_DI_SETITEM	This flag can only be set with the LVN_GETDISPINFO notification message. It indicates that the system should store the requested item information, and not ask for it again.
LVIF_IMAGE	The *iImage* member is valid or needs to be filled in.
LVIF_PARAM	The *lParam* member is valid or needs to be filled in.
LVIF_STATE	The *state* member is valid or needs to be filled in.
LVIF_TEXT	The *pszText* member is valid or needs to be filled in.

iItem   int: The item that this structure refers to.

iSubItem   int: The subitem that this structure refers to, or zero.

state   UINT: The current state of the item. This member can be any valid combination of state flags listed in Table 6-9.

statemask   UINT: The valid states of the item. This member can be any valid combination of state flags listed in Table 6-9.

Table 6-9 List view state values

Value	Meaning
LVIS_CUT	The item is marked for a cut-and-paste operation.
LVIS_DROPHILITED	The item is highlighted as a drag-and-drop target.
LVIS_FOCUSED	The item has the focus, so it is surrounded by a standard focus rectangle. Although more than one item may be selected, only one item can have the focus.
LVIS_OVERLAYMASK	Determines whether an item contains a overlay image index.
LVIS_SELECTED	The item is selected. The appearance of a selected item depends on whether it has the focus and on the system colors used for selection.
LVIS_STATEIMAGEMASK	Determines whether an item has an associated state image.

pszText	LPTSTR: A pointer to a null-terminated string that contains the item text if the structure specifies item attributes. If this member is the LPSTR_TEXTCALLBACK value, the item is a callback item. If the structure is receiving item attributes, this member is the pointer to the buffer that receives the item text.
cchTextMax	int: The size of the buffer pointed to by the *pszText* member if the structure is receiving item attributes. If the structure specifies item attributes, this member is ignored.
iImage	int: The index of the list view item's icon in the icon and small icon image lists. If this member is the I_IMAGECALLBACK value, the item is a callback item.
lParam	LPARAM: A 32-bit value to associate with an item.
Example	See the example for the ListView_DeleteItem macro.

LISTVIEW_GETITEMCOUNT ■ Win32s ■ Windows 95 ■ Windows NT

Description	ListView_GetItemCount is a macro that determines the number of items in a list view control.
Syntax	int **ListView_GetItemCount**(HWND *hwnd*)
Message Syntax	int **SendMessage**(*hwnd*, **LVM_GETITEMCOUNT**, 0, 0)
Parameters	
hwnd	HWND: The handle of the list view control.
Returns	int: The number of items in the specified list view control.
Include File	commctrl.h
Related Messages	LVM_GETITEMCOUNT
Example	See the example for the ListView_DeleteItem macro.

LISTVIEW_GETITEMPOSITION ■ Win32s ■ Windows 95 ■ Windows NT

Description	ListView_GetItemPosition is a macro that retrieves the position of a list view item.
Syntax	BOOL **ListView_GetItemPosition**(HWND *hwnd*, int *iItem*, POINT* *ppt*)
Message Syntax	BOOL **SendMessage**(*hwnd*, **LVM_GETITEMPOSITION**, *iItem*, *ppt*)
Parameters	
hwnd	HWND: The handle of the list view control.
iItem	int: The index of the list view item.
ppt	POINT*: A pointer to a POINT structure that receives the view coordinates of the upper left corner of the list view item.
Returns	BOOL: TRUE if successful; otherwise, FALSE is returned.
Include File	commctrl.h
Related Messages	LVM_GETITEMPOSITION
Example	See the example for the ListView_Arrange macro.

LISTVIEW_GETITEMRECT ■ Win32s ■ Windows 95 ■ Windows NT

Description	ListView_GetItemRect is a macro that retrieves the bounding rectangle for all or part of an item in the current view. This is useful when creating a drag image that represents an item.
Syntax	BOOL **ListView_GetItemRect**(HWND *hwnd*, int *iItem*, RECT* *prc*, int *code*)
Message Syntax	BOOL **SendMessage**(*hwnd*, **LVM_GETITEMRECT**, *iItem*, *prc*)
Parameters	
hwnd	HWND: The handle of the list view control.
iItem	int: The index of the list view item.
prc	RECT*: A pointer to a RECT structure that receives the bounding rectangle for the selected item. When sending the message, the *left* member of the RECT structure contains the value of the *code* parameter.
code	int: The portion of the list view item for which the bounding rectangle should be retrieved. This parameter can be one of the values in Table 6-10.

Table 6-10 ListView_GetItemRect *code* values

Value	Meaning
LVIR_BOUNDS	Returns the bounding rectangle of the entire item, including the icon and label.
LVIR_ICON	Returns the bounding rectangle of the icon or small icon.

Value	Meaning
LVIR_LABEL	Returns the bounding rectangle of the item text.
LVIR_SELECTBOUNDS	Returns the union of the LVIR_ICON and LVIR_LABEL rectangles, but excludes columns in details view.

Returns	BOOL: TRUE if successful; otherwise, FALSE is returned.
Include File	commctrl.h
Related Messages	LVM_GETITEMRECT
Example	See the example for the ListView_Arrange macro.

ListView_GetItemSpacing   ■ Win32s   ■ Windows 95   ■ Windows NT

Description	ListView_GetItemSpacing is a macro that determines the amount of spacing between items in a list view control.
Syntax	DWORD **ListView_GetItemSpacing**(HWND *hwnd*, BOOL *bSmall*)
Message Syntax	DWORD **SendMessage**(*hwnd*, **LVM_GETITEMSPACING**, *bSmall*, 0)
Parameters	
hwnd	HWND: The handle of the list view control.
bSmall	BOOL: The view mode for which to retrieve item spacing. TRUE retrieves spacing for small icon view; FALSE retrieves spacing for icon view.
Returns	DWORD: The amount of spacing between the items in the specified list view control.
Include File	commctrl.h
Related Messages	LVM_GETITEMSPACING

ListView_GetItemState   ■ Win32s   ■ Windows 95   ■ Windows NT

Description	ListView_GetItemState is a macro that retrieves the state of a list view item.
Syntax	UINT WINAPI **ListView_GetItemState**(HWND *hwnd*, int *iItem*, UINT *mask*)
Message Syntax	UINT WINAPI **SendMessage**(*hwnd*, **LVM_GETITEMSTATE**, *iItem*, *mask*)
Parameters	
hwnd	HWND: The handle of the list view control.
iItem	int: The index of the list view item.
mask	The mask that indicates which of the item's state flags to return. This can be a combination of the flags listed in Table 6-9.
Returns	UINT: The item's state flags. This can be a combination of flags listed in Table 6-9.
Include File	commctrl.h

Related Messages	LVM_GETITEMSTATE
Example	See the example for the ListView_FindItem macro.

LISTVIEW_GETITEMTEXT ■ Win32s ■ Windows 95 ■ Windows NT

Description	ListView_GetItemText is a macro that retrieves the text of a list view item or subitem.
Syntax	void WINAPI **ListView_GetItemText**(HWND *hwnd*, int *iItem*, int *iSubItem*, LPSTR *pszText*, int *cchTextMax*)
Message Syntax	void WINAPI **SendMessage**(*hwnd*, **LVM_GETITEMTEXT**, *iItem*, *pitem*)
Parameters	
hwnd	HWND: The handle of the list view control.
iItem	int: The index of the list view item.
iSubItem	int: The index of the subitem to retrieve, or zero to retrieve the label of the item.
pszText	LPSTR: A pointer to the buffer that receives the item or subitem text.
cchTextMax	int: The size of the buffer, in bytes.
pitem	LV_ITEM*: A pointer to an LV_ITEM structure. The *iSubItem* member specifies the index of a subitem, or it can be zero to get the item label. The *pszText* member points to a buffer that receives the text, and the *cchTextMax* member specifies the size of the buffer. See the definition of the LV_ITEM structure under the ListView_GetItem macro.
Include File	commctrl.h
Related Messages	LVM_GETITEMTEXT
Example	See the example for the ListView_DeleteItem macro.

LISTVIEW_GETNEXTITEM ■ Win32s ■ Windows 95 ■ Windows NT

Description	ListView_GetNextItem is a macro that searches for the list view item with the specified properties and relationship to the specified item.
Syntax	int **ListView_GetNextItem**(HWND *hwnd*, int *iStart*, UINT *flags*)
Message Syntax	int **SendMessage**(*hwnd*, **LVM_GETNEXTITEM**, *istart*, MAKELPARAM(*flags*, 0))
Parameters	
hwnd	HWND: The handle of the list view control.
iStart	int: The index of the item in the list where the search should begin, or -1 to locate the first item in the list that matches the flags. The specified item is excluded from the search.
flags	UINT: The geometric relation of the requested item to the specified item, and the state of the requested item. The geometric relation can be one of the values in Table 6-11. The state of the item can be zero, or one or more

of the values in Table 6-12. The search continues until it locates an item with all of the specified state flags.

Table 6-11 ListView_GetNextItem *flags* geometric values

Value	Meaning
LVNI_ABOVE	Searches for an item that is above the specified item.
LVNI_ALL	Searches for a subsequent item by index (the default value).
LVNI_BELOW	Searches for an item that is below the specified item.
LVNI_TOLEFT	Searches for an item to the left of the specified item.
LVNI_TORIGHT	Searches for an item to the right of the specified item.

Table 6-12 ListView_GetNextItem *flags* state values

Value	Meaning
LVNI_CUT	The item has the LVIS_CUT state flag set.
LVNI_DROPHILITED	The item has the LVIS_DROPHILITED state flag set.
LVNI_FOCUSED	The item has the LVIS_FOCUSED state flag set.
LVNI_SELECTED	The item has the LVIS_SELECTED state flag set.

Returns	int: The index of the next item, if successful; otherwise, -1 is returned.
Include File	commctrl.h
Related Messages	LVM_GETNEXTITEM
Example	See the example for the ListView_Delete macro.

LISTVIEW_GETORIGIN   ■ Win32s ■ Windows 95 ■ Windows NT

Description	ListView_GetOrigin is a macro that retrieves the current view origin of the specified list view control.
Syntax	BOOL **ListView_GetOrigin**(HWND *hwnd*, LPPOINT *lpptOrg*)
Message Syntax	BOOL **SendMessage**(*hwnd*, **LVM_GETORIGIN**, 0, *lpptOrg*)
Parameters	
hwnd	HWND: The handle of the list view control.
lpptOrg	LPPOINT: A pointer to a POINT structure that receives the view origin for the list view control. See the definition of the POINT structure in the ListView_GetItemPosition macro.
Returns	BOOL: TRUE if successful; otherwise, FALSE is returned if the list view control is in list or report view.
Include File	commctrl.h
Related Messages	LVM_GETORIGIN

LISTVIEW_GETSELECTEDCOUNT   ■ Win32s ■ Windows 95 ■ Windows NT

Description	ListView_GetSelectedCount is a macro that determines the number of items selected in a list view control.
Syntax	UINT **ListView_GetSelectedCount**(HWND *hwnd*)
Message Syntax	UINT **SendMessage**(*hwnd*, **LVM_GETSELECTEDCOUNT**, 0, 0)
Parameters	
hwnd	HWND: The handle of the list view control.
Returns	UINT: The number of items selected in the list view control.
Include File	commctrl.h
Related Messages	LVM_GETSELECTEDCOUNT
Example	See the example for the ListView_DeleteItem macro.

LISTVIEW_GETSTRINGWIDTH   ■ Win32s ■ Windows 95 ■ Windows NT

Description	ListView_GetSringWidth is a macro that determines the width of the specified string based on the current font of the list view control.
Syntax	int **ListView_GetStringWidth**(HWND *hwnd*, LPCSTR *psz*)
Message Syntax	int **SendMessage**(*hwnd*, **LVM_GETSTRINGWIDTH**, 0, *psz*)
Parameters	
hwnd	HWND: The handle of the list view control.
psz	LPCSTR: A pointer to a null-terminated string within the list view control.
Returns	int: The width of the specified string, if successful; otherwise, zero is returned.
Include File	commctrl.h
Related Messages	LVM_GETSTRINGWIDTH
Example	See the example for the ListView_GetColumnWidth macro.

LISTVIEW_GETTEXTBKCOLOR   ■ Win32s ■ Windows 95 ■ Windows NT

Description	ListView_GetTextBkColor is a macro that determines the text background color of a list view control.
Syntax	COLORREF **ListView_GetTextBkColor**(HWND *hwnd*)
Message Syntax	COLORREF **SendMessage**(*hwnd*, **LVM_GETTEXTBKCOLOR**, 0, 0)
Parameters	
hwnd	HWND: The handle of the list view control.
Returns	COLORREF: The background color of the text in the list view control.
Include File	commctrl.h
Related Messages	LVM_GETTEXTBKCOLOR
Example	See the example for the ListView_GetBkColor macro.

LISTVIEW_GETTEXTCOLOR
■ **Win32s** ■ **Windows 95** ■ **Windows NT**

Description	ListView_GetTextColor is a macro that determines the color of the text in a list view control.
Syntax	COLORREF **ListView_GetTextColor**(HWND *hwnd*)
Message Syntax	COLORREF **SendMessage**(*hwnd*, **LVM_GETTEXTCOLOR**, 0, 0)
Parameters	
hwnd	HWND: The handle of the list view control.
Returns	COLORREF: The color of the text in the list view control.
Include File	commctrl.h
Related Messages	LVM_GETTEXTCOLOR
Example	See the example for the ListView_GetBkColor macro.

LISTVIEW_GETTOPINDEX
■ **Win32s** ■ **Windows 95** ■ **Windows NT**

Description	ListView_GetTopIndex is a macro that determines the index of the topmost visible item when the list view control is in list or report view.
Syntax	int **ListView_GetTopIndex**(HWND *hwnd*)
Message Syntax	int **SendMessage**(*hwnd*, **LVM_GETTOPINDEX**, 0, 0)
Parameters	
hwnd	HWND: The handle of the list view control.
Returns	int: The index of the topmost item, if successful; otherwise, zero if the list view control is in icon or small icon view.
Include File	commctrl.h
Related Messages	LVM_GETTOPINDEX

LISTVIEW_GETVIEWRECT
■ **Win32s** ■ **Windows 95** ■ **Windows NT**

Description	ListView_GetViewRect is a macro that determines the coordinates of the bounding rectangle of all items in the list view control.
Syntax	BOOL **ListView_GetViewRect**(HWND *hwnd*, RECT* *prc*)
Message Syntax	BOOL **SendMessage**(*hwnd*, **LVM_GETVIEWRECT**, 0, *prc*)
Parameters	
hwnd	HWND: The handle of the list view control.
prc	RECT*: A pointer to a RECT structure that receives the coordinates of the visible area of the bounding rectangle. See the definition of the RECT structure under the ListView_GetItemRect macro.
Returns	BOOL: TRUE if successful; otherwise, FALSE is returned.
Include File	commctrl.h
Related Messages	LVM_GETVIEWRECT

LISTVIEW_HITTEST   ■ Win32s   ■ Windows 95   ■ Windows NT

Description	ListView_HitTest is a macro that determines which list view item is at the specified position.
Syntax	int **ListView_HitTest**(HWND *hwnd*, LV_HITTESTINFO* *pinfo*)
Message Syntax	int **SendMessage**(*hwnd*, **LVM_HITTEST**, 0, *pinfo*)
Parameters	
hwnd	HWND: The handle of the list view control.
pinfo	LV_HITTESTINFO*: A pointer to an LV_HITTESTINFO structure that both contains the position for the hit test and receives the results of the hit test. See the definition of LV_HITTESTINFO below.
Returns	int: The index of the item at the specified position, if an item exists at that position; otherwise, -1 is returned.
Include File	commctrl.h
Related Messages	LVM_HITTEST

LV_HITTESTINFO Definition

```
typedef struct _LV_HITTESTINFO
{
    POINT pt;
    UINT  flags;
    int   iItem;
} LV_HITTESTINFO;
```

Members	
pt	POINT: The position to hit test, in client coordinates.
flags	UINT: The variable that receives information about the results of a hit test. This member can be one or more of the values in Table 6-13.

Use LVHT_ABOVE, LVHT_BELOW, LVHT_TOLEFT, and LVHT_TORIGHT to determine whether to scroll the contents of a list view control. Two of these values may be combined–for example, if the position is above and to the left of the client area.

Test for the LVHT_ONITEM flag to determine whether a specified position is over a list view item. This value is a bitwise OR operation on LVHT_ONITEMICON, LVHT_ONITEMLABEL, and LVHT_ONITEMSTATEICON. |

Table 6-13 LV_HITTESTINFO *flags* values

Value	Meaning
LVHT_ABOVE	The position is above the client area of the control.
LVHT_BELOW	The position is below the client area of the control.
LVHT_NOWHERE	The position is inside the list view control's client window, but it is not over a list item.
LVHT_ONITEMICON	The position is over a list view item's icon.

Value	Meaning
LVHT_ONITEMLABEL	The position is over a list view item's text.
LVHT_ONITEMSTATEICON	The position is over the state image of a list view item.
LVHT_TOLEFT	The position is to the left of the list view control's client area.
LVHT_TORIGHT	The position is to the right of the list view control's client area.

iItem   int: The index of the matching item.

Example   This example (Listing 6-8) demonstrates the usage of the ListView_HitTest macro when displaying context menus. The application determines if an item is hit when the right mouse button is pressed, and if it was, displays a list view item menu, as shown in Figure 6-6. If no item was hit, a menu is displayed for the entire list view.

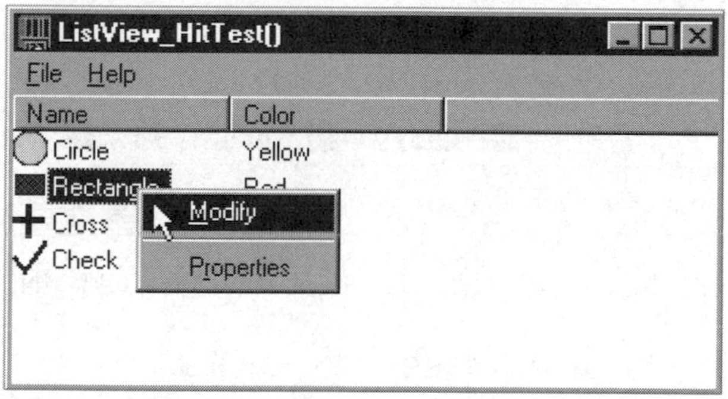

Figure 6-6 ListView_HitTest example

Listing 6-8 Using the ListView_HitTest macro

```
LRESULT CALLBACK WndProc( HWND hWnd, UINT uMsg, WPARAM wParam, LPARAM lParam )
{
static HWND  hList = NULL;

   switch( uMsg )
   {
      case WM_CONTEXTMENU :
            {
               LV_HITTESTINFO hi;
               HMENU          hMenu, hSubMenu;

               hi.pt.x = LOWORD(lParam);
               hi.pt.y = HIWORD(lParam);

               // Convert the screen coordinates to client.
               //........................................
               ScreenToClient( hList, &hi.pt );
```

continued on next page

continued from previous page

```
                    // Check if an item was hit.
                    //..........................
                    if ( ListView_HitTest( hList, &hi ) > -1 )
                       hMenu = LoadMenu( hInst, "ITEMPOPUPMENU" );
                    else
                       hMenu = LoadMenu( hInst, "POPUPMENU" );

                    // Get the submenu to display.
                    //..........................
                    hSubMenu = GetSubMenu( hMenu, 0 );

                    TrackPopupMenu( hSubMenu, TPM_LEFTALIGN |
                                 TPM_LEFTBUTTON | TPM_RIGHTBUTTON,
                                 LOWORD( lParam ), HIWORD( lParam ), 0,
                                 hWnd, NULL );

                    DestroyMenu( hMenu );
                 }
                 break;
                 .
                 .
                 .
```

LISTVIEW_INSERTCOLUMN   ■ Win32s ■ Windows 95 ■ Windows NT

Description	ListView_InsertColumn is a macro that inserts a new column in the specified list view control.
Syntax	int **ListView_InsertColumn**(HWND *hwnd*, int *iCol*, const LV_COLUMN* *pcol*)
Message Syntax	int **SendMessage**(*hwnd*, **LVM_INSERTCOLUMN**, *iCol*, *pcol*)
Parameters	
hwnd	HWND: The handle of the list view control.
iCol	int: The index of the new column to add to the specified list view control.
pcol	const LV_COLUMN*: A pointer to an LV_COLUMN structure that contains the attributes for the new column. See the definition of the LV_COLUMN structure under the ListView_GetColumn macro.
Returns	int: The index of the new column, if successful; otherwise, -1 is returned.
Include File	commctrl.h
Related Messages	LVM_INSERTCOLUMN
Example	See the example for the ListView_DeleteColumn macro.

LISTVIEW_INSERTITEM   ■ Win32s ■ Windows 95 ■ Windows NT

Description	ListView_InsertItem is a macro that inserts a new item in the specified list view control. The item is inserted in the list view prior to the item index specified in the LV_ITEM structure.
Syntax	int **ListView_InsertItem**(HWND *hwnd*, const LV_ITEM* *pitem*)

Message Syntax	int **SendMessage**(*hwnd*, **LVM_INSERTITEM**, 0, *pitem*)
Parameters	
hwnd	HWND: The handle of the list view control.
pitem	const LV_ITEM*: A pointer to an LV_ITEM structure that specifies the attributes of the new list view item. The *iItem* member of the structure specifies the index of the new item. Since this macro cannot insert subitems, the *iSubItem* member must be zero. See the definition of the LV_ITEM structure under the ListView_GetItem macro.
Returns	int: The index of the new item, if successful; otherwise, -1 is returned.
Include File	commctrl.h
Related Messages	LVM_INSERTITEM
Example	See the example for the ListView_DeleteItem macro.

LISTVIEW_REDRAWITEMS   ■ Win32s   ■ Windows 95   ■ Windows NT

Description	ListView_RedrawItems is a macro that forces a list view control to redraw the specified range of items.
	Be aware that the items are not redrawn until the list view window receives a WM_PAINT message. To have the items repainted immediately, call UpdateWindow() after using the ListView_RedrawItems macro.
Syntax	BOOL **ListView_RedrawItems**(HWND *hwnd*, int *iFirst*, int *iLast*)
Message Syntax	BOOL **SendMessage**(*hwnd*, **LVM_REDRAWITEMS**, *iFirst*, *iLast*)
Parameters	
hwnd	HWND: The handle of the list view control.
iFirst	int: The index of the first item in the list view control that should be redrawn.
iLast	int: The index of the last item of the list view control that should be redrawn.
Returns	BOOL: TRUE if successful; otherwise, FALSE is returned.
Include File	commctrl.h
See Also	UpdateWindow()
Related Messages	LVM_REDRAWITEMS
Example	This code segment shows how the ListView_RedrawItems can be used to update all the items when a window containing a list view is restored.

```
          .
          .
          .
      case WM_SIZE :
              if ( hList )
                  MoveWindow( hList, 0, 20, LOWORD( lParam ),
                                      HIWORD( lParam )-20, FALSE );
```

continued on next page

continued from previous page

```
if ( wParam == SIZE_RESTORED || wParam == SIZE_MAXIMIZED )
   ListView_RedrawItems( hList, O, ListView_GetItemCount(hList) );
break;
```

.
.
.

LISTVIEW_SCROLL   ■ Win32s ■ Windows 95 ■ Windows NT

Description	ListView_Scroll is a macro that scrolls the content of the list view control based on the specified values.
Syntax	BOOL **ListView_Scroll**(HWND *hwnd*, int *dx*, int *dy*)
Message Syntax	BOOL **SendMessage**(*hwnd*, **LVM_SCROLL**, *dx*, *dy*)
Parameters	
hwnd	HWND: The handle of the list view control.
dx	int: The amount of horizontal scrolling for the list view control. If the list view control is in icon, small icon, or report view, *dx* indicates the number of pixels to scroll. If the list view control is in list view, *dx* indicates the number of columns to scroll.
dy	int: The amount of vertical scrolling for the list view control. If the list view control is in icon, small icon, or report view, *dy* indicates the number of pixels to scroll. If the list view control is in list view, *dy* indicates the number of lines to scroll.
Returns	BOOL: TRUE if successful; otherwise; FALSE is returned.
Include File	commctrl.h
Related Messages	LVM_SCROLL

LISTVIEW_SETBKCOLOR   ■ Win32s ■ Windows 95 ■ Windows NT

Description	ListView_SetBkColor is a macro that sets the background color of the specified list view control.
Syntax	BOOL **ListView_SetBkColor**(HWND *hwnd*, COLORREF *clrBk*)
Message Syntax	BOOL **SendMessage**(*hwnd*, **LVM_SETBKCOLOR**, 0, *clrBk*)
Parameters	
hwnd	HWND: The handle of the list view control.
clrBk	COLORREF: The background color to set for the specified list view control. If *clrBk* is CLR_NONE, the list view control does not have a background color. Note that list view controls with background colors redraw themselves significantly faster than those without background colors.

Returns	BOOL: TRUE if successful; otherwise, FALSE is returned.
Include File	commctrl.h
Related Messages	LVM_SETBKCOLOR
Example	See the example for the ListView_GetBkColor macro.

LISTVIEW_SETCALLBACKMASK ■ Win32s ■ Windows 95 ■ Windows NT

Description	ListView_SetCallbackMask is a macro that sets the callback mask of the specified list view control.
Syntax	BOOL **ListView_SetCallbackMask**(HWND *hwnd*, UINT *mask*)
Message Syntax	BOOL **SendMessage**(*hwnd*, **LVM_SETCALLBACKMASK**, *mask*, 0)
Parameters	
hwnd	HWND: The handle of the list view control.
mask	UINT: The new value of the callback mask.
Returns	BOOL: TRUE if successful; otherwise, FALSE is returned.
Include File	commctrl.h
Related Messages	LVM_SETCALLBACKMASK

LISTVIEW_SETCOLUMN ■ Win32s ■ Windows 95 ■ Windows NT

Description	ListView_SetColumn is a macro that sets the column attributes for the specified list view control.
Syntax	BOOL **ListView_SetColumn**(HWND *hwnd*, int *iCol*, const LV_COLUMN* *pcol*)
Message Syntax	BOOL **SendMessage**(*hwnd*, **LVM_SETCOLUMN**, *iCol*, *pcol*)
Parameters	
hwnd	HWND: The handle of the list view control.
iCol	int: The index of the column.
pcol	const LV_COLUMN*: A pointer to an LV_COLUMN structure that contains the new column attributes. The *mask* member of the structure specifies which column attributes to set. If the *mask* member specifies the LVCF_TEXT value, the *pszText* member is the pointer to a null-terminated string and the *cchTextMax* member is ignored. See the description of the LV_COLUMN structure under the ListView_GetColumn macro.
Returns	BOOL: TRUE if successful; otherwise, FALSE is returned.
Include File	commctrl.h
Related Messages	LVM_SETCOLUMN
Example	See the example for the ListView_DeleteColumn macro.

LISTVIEW_SETCOLUMNWIDTH   ■ Win32s ■ Windows 95 ■ Windows NT

Description	ListView_SetColumnWidth is a macro that changes the width of a column in report or list view.
Syntax	BOOL **ListView_SetColumnWidth**(HWND *hwnd*, int *iCol*, int *cx*)
Message Syntax	BOOL **SendMessage**(*hwnd*, **LVM_SETCOLUMNWIDTH**, *iCol*, MAKELPARAM(*cx*, 0))
Parameters	
hwnd	HWND: The handle of the list view control.
iCol	int: The index of the column to be modified. In list view mode, *iCol* must be -1.
cx	int: The new width of the column, in list view coordinates, or one of the values in Table 6-14.

Table 6-14 ListView_SetColumnWidth *cx* values

Value	Meaning
LVSCW_AUTOSIZE	Automatically sizes the column.
LVSCW_AUTOSIZE_USEHEADER	Automatically sizes the column to fit the header text.

Returns	BOOL: TRUE if successful; otherwise, FALSE is returned.
Include File	commctrl.h
Related Messages	LVM_SETCOLUMNWIDTH
Example	See the example for the ListView_GetColumnWidth macro.

LISTVIEW_SETIMAGELIST   ■ Win32s ■ Windows 95 ■ Windows NT

Description	ListView_SetImageList is a macro that assigns an image list to a list view control.
Syntax	HIMAGELIST **ListView_SetImageList**(HWND *hwnd*, HIMAGELIST *himl*, int *iImageList*)
Message Syntax	HIMAGELIST **SendMessage**(*hwnd*, **LVM_SETIMAGELIST**, *iImageList*, *himl*)
Parameters	
hwnd	HWND: The handle of the list view control.
himl	HIMAGELIST: The handle of the image list to assign to the list view control.
iImageList	int: The type of image list specified by *himl*. This parameter can be one of the values in Table 6-15.

Table 6-15 ListView_SetImageList *ilmageList* values

Value	Meaning
LVSIL_NORMAL	Image list with large icons
LVSIL_SMALL	Image list with small icons
LVSIL_STATE	Image list with state images

Returns	HIMAGELIST: The handle of the image list that was previously associated with the specified list view control, if successful; otherwise, NULL is returned.
Include File	commctrl.h
Related Messages	LVM_SETIMAGELIST
Example	See the example for the ListView_Arrange macro.

LISTVIEW_SETITEM   ■ Win32s ■ Windows 95 ■ Windows NT

Description	ListView_SetItem is a macro that sets attributes for a list view item.
Syntax	BOOL **ListView_SetItem**(HWND *hwnd*, const LV_ITEM* *pitem*)
Message Syntax	BOOL **SendMessage**(*hwnd*, **LVM_SETITEM**, 0, *pitem*)
Parameters	
hwnd	HWND: The handle of the list view control.
pitem	const LV_ITEM*: A pointer to an LV_ITEM structure containing the new item attributes. The *iItem* and *iSubItem* members identify the item or subitem, and the *mask* member specifies which attributes to set. If the *mask* member specifies the LVIF_TEXT value, the *pszText* member is the pointer to a null-terminated string and the *cchTextMax* member is ignored. If the *mask* member specifies the LVIF_STATE value, the *stateMask* member specifies which item states to change and the *state* member contains the values for those states. See the definition of the LV_ITEM structure under the ListView_GetItem macro.
Returns	BOOL: TRUE if successful; otherwise, FALSE is returned.
Include File	commctrl.h
Related Messages	LVM_SETITEM
Example	See the example for the ListView_DeleteItem macro.

LISTVIEW_SETITEMCOUNT   ■ Win32s ■ Windows 95 ■ Windows NT

Description	ListView_SetItemCount is a macro that prepares a list view control for adding large numbers of items. Using this macro allows the list view

control to allocate its internal data structures one time rather than every time you add a new item.

Syntax	VOID **ListView_SetItemCount**(HWND *hwnd*, int *cItems*)
Message Syntax	BOOL **SendMessage**(*hwnd*, **LVM_SETITEMCOUNT**, *cItems*, 0)
Parameters	
hwnd	HWND: The handle of the list view control.
cItems	int: The number of items the list view control will contain.
Include File	commctrl.h
Related Messages	LVM_SETITEMCOUNT
Example	See the example for the ListView_SortItems macro.

LISTVIEW_SETITEMPOSITION   ■ Win32s ■ Windows 95 ■ Windows NT

Description	ListView_SetItemPosition is a macro that moves an item to a specified position in a list view control, in icon or small icon view.
Syntax	BOOL **ListView_SetItemPosition**(HWND *hwnd*, int *iItem*, int *x*, int *y*)
Message Syntax	BOOL **SendMessage**(*hwnd*, **LVM_SETITEMPOSITION**, *iItem*, MAKELPARAM(*x*, *y*))
Parameters	
hwnd	HWND: The handle of the list view control.
iItem	int: The index of the list view item.
x	int: The new horizontal position of the item's upper left corner, in view coordinates.
y	int: The new vertical position of the item's upper left corner, in view coordinates.
Returns	BOOL: TRUE if successful; otherwise, FALSE is returned.
Include File	commctrl.h
Related Messages	LVM_SETITEMPOSITION
Example	See the example for the ListView_Arrange macro.

LISTVIEW_SETITEMPOSITION32   ■ Win32s ■ Windows 95 ■ Windows NT

Description	ListView_SetItemPosition32 is a macro that moves an item to a specified position in a list view control, in icon or small icon view. Unlike the ListView_SetItemPosition, the coordinates are 32-bit numbers.
Syntax	void **ListView_SetItemPosition32**(HWND *hwnd*, int *iItem*, int *x*, int *y*)
Message Syntax	void **SendMessage**(*hwnd*, **LVM_SETITEMPOSITION32**, *iItem*, *lpptNewPos*)
Parameters	
hwnd	HWND: The handle of the list view control.

iItem	int: The index of the list view item.
x	int: The new horizontal coordinates of the specified item. For the message, this is the *x* value of the POINT structure pointed to by *lpptNewPos*.
y	int: The new vertical coordinates of the specified item. For the message, this is the *y* value of the POINT structure pointed to by *lpptNewPos*.
lpptNewPos	LPPOINT: A pointer to a POINT structure used with the LVM_SETITEMPOSITION32 message that contains the *x* and *y* values.
Include File	commctrl.h
See Also	ListView_SetItemPosition
Related Messages	LVM_SETITEMPOSITION32

LISTVIEW_SETITEMSTATE ■ Win32s ■ Windows 95 ■ Windows NT

Description	ListView_SetItemState is a macro that changes the state of an item in a list view control.
Syntax	BOOL WINAPI **ListView_SetItemState**(HWND *hwnd*, int *iItem*, UINT *state*, UINT *mask*)
Message Syntax	BOOL WINAPI **SendMessage**(*hwnd*, **LVM_SETITEMSTATE**, *iItem*, *pitem*)
Parameters	
hwnd	HWND: The handle of the list view control.
iItem	int: The index of the list view item.
state	UINT: The new state bits of the item. This can be a valid combination of flags listed in Table 6-9.
mask	UINT: A mask specifying which of the item's current state bits to change. This can be a valid combination of flags listed in Table 6-9.
pitem	LV_ITEM*: A pointer to an LV_ITEM structure. This parameter is used with the LVM_SETITEMSTATE message The *stateMask* member contains the *mask* value and the *state* member contains the new state bits from Table 6-9. See the definition of the LV_ITEM structure under the ListView_GetItem macro.
Include File	commctrl.h
Related Messages	LVM_SETITEMSTATE
Example	See the example for the ListView_FindItem macro.

LISTVIEW_SETITEMTEXT ■ Win32s ■ Windows 95 ■ Windows NT

Description	ListView_SetItemText is a macro that changes the text of a list view item or subitem.
Syntax	BOOL **ListView_SetItemText**(HWND *hwnd*, int *iItem*, int *iSubItem*, LPCSTR *pszText*)
Message Syntax	BOOL **SendMessage**(*hwnd*, **LVM_SETITEMTEXT**, *iItem*, *pitem*)

Parameters

hwnd	HWND: The handle of the list view control.
iItem	int: The index of the list view item.
iSubItem	int: The index of the subitem or zero to change the text of the item label.
pszText	LPCSTR: A pointer to a null-terminated string containing the new text for the specified item or subitem. This parameter can be NULL.
pitem	LV_ITEM*: A pointer to a LV_ITEM structure. This parameter is used with the LVM_SETITEMTEXT message The *iSubItem* member contains the index of the subitem, and the *pszText* member contains a pointer to a null-terminated string containing the new text. See the definition of the LV_ITEM structure under the ListView_GetItem macro.
Include File	commctrl.h
Related Messages	LVM_SETITEMTEXT
Example	See the example for the ListView_DeleteItem macro.

LISTVIEW_SETTEXTBKCOLOR ■ Win32s ■ Windows 95 ■ Windows NT

Description	ListView_SetTextBkColor is a macro that sets the background color of the text in a list view control.
Syntax	BOOL **ListView_SetTextBkColor**(HWND *hwnd*, COLORREF *clrText*)
Message Syntax	BOOL **SendMessage**(*hwnd*, **LVM_SETTEXTBKCOLOR**, 0, *clrText*)
Parameters	
hwnd	HWND: The handle of the list view control.
clrText	COLORREF: The new text color.
Returns	BOOL: TRUE if successful; otherwise, FALSE is returned.
Include File	commctrl.h
Related Messages	LVM_SETTEXTBKCOLOR
Example	See the example for the ListView_GetBkColor macro.

LISTVIEW_SETTEXTCOLOR ■ Win32s ■ Windows 95 ■ Windows NT

Description	ListView_SetTextColor is a macro that sets the text color of a list view control.
Syntax	BOOL **ListView_SetTextColor**(HWND *hwnd*, COLORREF *clrText*)
Message Syntax	BOOL **SendMessage**(*hwnd*, **LVM_SETTEXTCOLOR**, 0, *clrText*)
Parameters	
hwnd	HWND: The handle of the list view control.
clrText	COLORREF: The new text color.
Returns	BOOL: TRUE if successful; otherwise, FALSE is returned.
Include File	commctrl.h

Related Messages   LVM_SETTEXTCOLOR

Example   See the example for the ListView_GetBkColor macro.

LISTVIEW_SORTITEMS   ■ Win32s   ■ Windows 95   ■ Windows NT

Description	ListView_SortItems is a macro that sorts list view items using an application-defined comparison function. The index of each item in the list view control changes to reflect the new sequence.
Syntax	BOOL **ListView_SortItems**(HWND *hwnd*, PFNLVCOMPARE *pfnCompare*, LPARAM *lParamSort*)
Message Syntax	BOOL **SendMessage**(*hwnd*, **LVM_SORTITEMS**, *lParamSort*, *pfnCompare*)
Parameters	
hwnd	HWND: The handle of the list view control.
pfnCompare	PFNLVCOMPARE: A pointer to an application-defined comparison function called during the sort operation to compare the relative order of two items in the list view control. See the definition of the comparison function below.
lParamSort	LPARAM: An application-defined value that is passed to the comparison function.
Returns	BOOL: TRUE if successful; otherwise, FALSE is returned.
Include File	commctrl.h
Related Messages	LVM_SORTITEMS, LVN_COLUMNCLICK
Callback Syntax	int CALLBACK **CompareFunc**(LPARAM *lParam1*, LPARAM *lParam2*, LPARAM *lParamSort*)
Callback Parameters	
lParam1	LPARAM: The *lParam* data value of item 1.
lParam2	LPARAM: The *lParam* data value of item 2.
lParamSort	LPARAM: The *lParamSort* value used in the ListView_SortItems macro.
Callback Returns	int: Return a negative value if the first item should precede the second, a positive value if the first item should follow the second, and a zero if the two items are equivalent.
Example	This example (Listing 6-9) demonstrates a method of sorting the items in a list view control. When the example starts, 200 items are added to the list view. The ListView_SetItemCount macro is used to optimize the loading of the items. When the user selects a column button, the list is sorted in either ascending or descending order depending on the previous sort order. Notice in the callback sort function how the list view item content is retrieved to perform the comparisons. This method is not as efficient as storing all comparison information in the *lParam* value of the item, but this method can be used to perform generic sorting within a list view.

Listing 6-9 Using the ListView_SortItems macro

```
int CALLBACK pfnCompare( LPARAM lParam1, LPARAM lParam2, LPARAM lParamSort );

#define ASC   1
#define DESC  2

LPCTSTR lpszData[4]  = { "Circle", "Rectangle", "Cross", "Check" };
LPCTSTR lpszColor[4] = { "Yellow", "Red",       "Black", "Black" };

int  nSortDir[2] = {0, 0};
HWND hList       = NULL;

LRESULT CALLBACK WndProc( HWND hWnd, UINT uMsg, WPARAM wParam, LPARAM lParam )
{

    switch( uMsg )
    {
      case WM_CREATE  :
            {
                HIMAGELIST hImage, hSmall;

                InitCommonControls();

                // Create the image lists and the list view.
                //.........................................
                hImage = ImageList_Create( 32, 32, ILC_COLOR4 | ILC_MASK,4,1 );
                hSmall = ImageList_Create( 16, 16, ILC_COLOR4 | ILC_MASK,4,1 );
                hList  = CreateWindowEx( 0, WC_LISTVIEW, "",
                                         WS_CHILD | WS_VISIBLE | LVS_REPORT |
                                         LVS_EDITLABELS | LVS_SINGLESEL,
                                         0, 20, 100, 100,
                                         hWnd,
                                         (HMENU)1,
                                         hInst,
                                         NULL);

                if ( hList && hImage && hSmall )
                {
                    LV_COLUMN col;
                    LV_ITEM   item;
                    int       i;
                    char      szBuf[16];

                    // Set the large and small image lists.
                    //......................................
                    ListView_SetImageList( hList, hImage, LVSIL_NORMAL );
                    ListView_SetImageList( hList, hSmall, LVSIL_SMALL );

                    // Add the images to the image list.
                    //...................................
                    for( i=0; i<4; i++ )
                    {
                        ImageList_AddIcon( hImage, LoadIcon(hInst,lpszData[i]) );
                        ImageList_AddIcon( hSmall, LoadIcon(hInst,lpszData[i]) );
                    }

                    // Add the columns for the report view.
                    //......................................
```

```
        col.mask    = LVCF_FMT | LVCF_WIDTH |
                      LVCF_TEXT | LVCF_SUBITEM;
        col.fmt     = LVCFMT_LEFT;
        col.cx      = 100;

        col.pszText  = "Name";
        col.iSubItem = 0;
        ListView_InsertColumn( hList, 0, &col );

        col.pszText  = "Color";
        col.iSubItem = 1;
        ListView_InsertColumn( hList, 1, &col );


        // Tell the list view to expect 200 items.
        //.......................................
        ListView_SetItemCount( hList, 200 );

        // Insert items into the list view.
        //................................
        for( i=0; i<200; i++ )
        {
            wsprintf( szBuf, "Item %d", i );

            item.mask    = LVIF_TEXT | LVIF_IMAGE | LVIF_PARAM;
            item.pszText = szBuf;
            item.iItem   = i;
            item.iSubItem = 0;
            item.iImage  = i%4;
            item.lParam  = i;
            ListView_InsertItem( hList, &item );

            item.mask    = LVIF_TEXT;
            item.pszText = (LPTSTR)lpszColor[i%4];
            item.iSubItem = 1;
            ListView_SetItem( hList, &item );
        }
    }
}
break;

case WM_SIZE :
    if ( hList )
        MoveWindow( hList,0,0, LOWORD(lParam), HIWORD(lParam), FALSE );

    if ( wParam == SIZE_RESTORED || wParam == SIZE_MAXIMIZED )
        ListView_RedrawItems( hList, 0, ListView_GetItemCount(hList) );
    break;

case WM_NOTIFY :
    {
        NM_LISTVIEW* pNM = (NM_LISTVIEW*)lParam;

        // Determine if a column was clicked, then sort
        // the items in the list based on that column.
        //.............................................
        if ( pNM->hdr.code == LVN_COLUMNCLICK )
        {
            if ( nSortDir[pNM->iSubItem] == ASC )
                nSortDir[pNM->iSubItem] = DESC;
```

continued on next page

continued from previous page

```
                    else
                        nSortDir[pNM->iSubItem] = ASC;

                    ListView_SortItems( hList, pfnCompare, pNM->iSubItem );
                }
            }
            break;

        case WM_COMMAND :
            switch( LOWORD( wParam ) )
            {
                case IDM_EXIT :
                        DestroyWindow( hWnd );
                        break;
            }
            break;

        case WM_DESTROY :
            if ( hList )
            {
                if ( ListView_GetImageList( hList, LVSIL_NORMAL ) )
                    ImageList_Destroy( ListView_GetImageList( hList,
                                                    LVSIL_NORMAL ) );

                if ( ListView_GetImageList( hList, LVSIL_SMALL ) )
                    ImageList_Destroy( ListView_GetImageList( hList,
                                                    LVSIL_SMALL ) );
            }

            PostQuitMessage(0);
            break;

        default :
            return( DefWindowProc( hWnd, uMsg, wParam, lParam ) );
    }

    return( 0L );
}


int CALLBACK pfnCompare( LPARAM lParam1, LPARAM lParam2, LPARAM lParamSort )
{
static LV_FINDINFO fi;
static int        nItem1, nItem2;
static char       szBuf1[30], szBuf2[30];

    if ( lParamSort == 0 )
    {
        if ( nSortDir[0] == ASC )
            return( lParam1 < lParam2 ? -1 : lParam1 > lParam2 ? 1 : 0 );
        else
            return( lParam1 > lParam2 ? -1 : lParam1 < lParam2 ? 1 : 0 );
    }
    else
    {
        // Determine the items that we are comparing.
        //............................................
        fi.flags  = LVFI_PARAM;
        fi.lParam = lParam1;
```

```
nItem1 = ListView_FindItem( hList, -1, &fi );

fi.lParam = lParam2;
nItem2 = ListView_FindItem( hList, -1, &fi );

// Retrieve the item text so we can compare it.
//...........................................
ListView_GetItemText( hList, nItem1, 1, szBuf1, sizeof( szBuf1 ) );
ListView_GetItemText( hList, nItem2, 1, szBuf2, sizeof( szBuf2 ) );

// Return the comparison results.
//..............................
if ( nSortDir[1] == ASC )
   return( strcmp( szBuf1, szBuf2 ) );
else
   return( strcmp( szBuf1, szBuf2 ) * -1 );
   }
}
```

LISTVIEW_UPDATE ■ Win32s ■ Windows 95 ■ Windows NT

Description	ListView_Update is a macro that updates a list view item. The list view control is arranged if it has the LVS_AUTOARRANGE style. This forces any changes, such as additions or deletions of items, to become visible. Use this macro during long processes to give the list view a chance to visually update itself.
Syntax	BOOL **ListView_Update**(HWND *hwnd*, int *iItem*)
Message Syntax	BOOL **SendMessage**(*hwnd*, **LVM_UPDATE**, *iItem*, 0)
Parameters	
hwnd	HWND: The handle of the list view control.
iItem	int: The index of the list view item to update.
Returns	BOOL: TRUE if successful; otherwise, FALSE is returned.
Include File	commctrl.h
Related Messages	LVM_UPDATE

MAKEDRAGLIST ■ Win32s ■ Windows 95 ■ Windows NT

Description	MakeDragList() changes a given single-selection list box to a drag list box. In order to receive the notification messages for a drag list box, the application must use the RegisterWindowMessage() function with the DRAGLISTMSGSTRING value. All drag list notifications are received as part of the registered drag list message.
Syntax	BOOL **MakeDragList**(HWND *hLB*)
Parameters	
hLB	HWND: The handle of the single-selection list box to change.
Returns	BOOL: If successful, TRUE is returned; otherwise, FALSE is returned.

Include File   commctrl.h

Example   This example, shown in Figure 6-7 and Listing 6-10, demonstrates the usage of a drag list control. A normal list box is created and the MakeDragList() function is used to convert it to a drag list. When the user selects an item and holds down the left mouse button, the application receives drag list notifications that allow the application to respond and move an item. The drag cursor is forced to the one shown in Figure 6-7; however, an application can let the drag list use the default cursor.

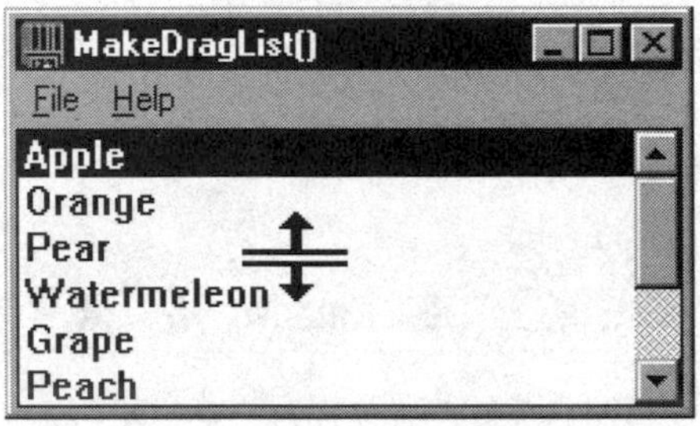

Figure 6-7 MakeDragList() example

Listing 6-10 Using the MakeDragList() function

```
LPCTSTR lpszData[8] = { "Apple", "Orange", "Pear", "Watermeleon",
                        "Grape", "Peach", "Strawberry", "Rasberry" };


LRESULT CALLBACK WndProc( HWND hWnd, UINT uMsg, WPARAM wParam, LPARAM lParam )
{
static LPDRAGLISTINFO lpdli;
static int   nItem;
static int   nItemToMove = -1;
static UINT  uDLMsg      = 0;
static HWND  hList       = NULL;

    // Handle the dragging notifications.
    //..................................
    if ( uMsg == uDLMsg )
    {
        lpdli = (LPDRAGLISTINFO)lParam;

        switch (lpdli->uNotification)
        {
            case DL_BEGINDRAG:
                    nItemToMove = LBItemFromPt(lpdli->hWnd, lpdli->ptCursor, TRUE);
                    return( TRUE );

            case DL_DRAGGING:
                    nItem = LBItemFromPt(lpdli->hWnd, lpdli->ptCursor, TRUE);
                    DrawInsert( hWnd, lpdli->hWnd, nItem);
```

Members

uNotification UINT: A notification code specifying the type of drag event. This member can be one of the values in Table 6-16.

Table 6-16 DRAGLISTINFO *uNotification* values

Value	Meaning
DL_BEGINDRAG	The user has clicked the left mouse button on a list item.
DL_CANCELDRAG	The user has canceled the drag operation by clicking the right mouse button or pressing the [ESC] key.
DL_DRAGGING	The user is currently dragging the item by moving the mouse.
DL_DROPPED	The user has released the left mouse button, completing a drag operation.

hWnd HWND: The handle of the drag list box.

ptCursor POINT: The current x and y coordinates of the mouse cursor.

Example See the example for the MakeDragList() function.

DL_CANCELDRAG ■ Win32s ■ Windows 95 ■ Windows NT

Description DL_CANCELDRAG is a notification message that indicates the user has canceled a drag operation by clicking the right mouse button or pressing the [ESC] key. A drag list box sends DL_CANCELDRAG notification via the registered drag list message.

Parameters

wParam int: The control identifier of the drag list box.

lParam LPDRAGLISTINFO: A pointer to a DRAGLISTINFO structure that contains the notification code and information about the drag operation. See the description of the DRAGLISTINFO structure under the DL_BEGINDRAG notification message.

Include File commctrl.h

Related Messages DL_BEGINDRAG, DL_DRAGGING, DL_DROPPED

Example See the example for the MakeDragList() function.

DL_DRAGGING ■ Win32s ■ Windows 95 ■ Windows NT

Description DL_DRAGGING is a notification message that indicates the user has moved the mouse during a drag operation. The DL_DRAGGING notification is also periodically sent during periods where the user does not move the mouse. This provides the application notification that a drag operation is still in progress even though the user has not moved the mouse. A drag list box sends the DL_DRAGGING notification via the registered drag list message. The application processes the DL_DRAGGING notification by determining the item under the cursor with the LBItemFromPt() function and specifying TRUE for the *bAutoScroll* parameter. This option causes the drag list box to scroll periodically if the cursor is above or below the client area of the list box. Use the DrawInsert() function to draw the insert icon.

Parameters

wParam   int: The control identifier of the drag list box.

lParam   LPDRAGLISTINFO: A pointer to a DRAGLISTINFO structure that contains the notification code and information about the drag operation. See the definition of the DRAGLISTINFO structure under the DL_BEGINDRAG message.

Returns   int: The return value determines the cursor type displayed by the drag list. One of these values can be used: DL_STOPCURSOR, DL_COPYCURSOR, or DL_MOVING. Other return values will not affect the cursor.

Include File   commctrl.h

See Also   LBItemFromPt(), DrawInsert()

Related Messages DL_BEGINDRAG, DL_CANCELDRAG, DL_DROPPED

Example   See the example for the MakeDragList() function.

DL_DROPPED   ■ Win32s ■ Windows 95 ■ Windows NT

Description   DL_DROPPED is a notification message that indicates the user has completed a drag operation by releasing the left mouse button. A drag list box sends the DL_DROPPED notification via the registered drag list message. The application should process this notification by inserting or copying the dragged list item before the list item under the cursor using standard list box messages. Use the LBItemFromPt() function to determine the item the cursor is over. If the cursor is not over an item, LBItemFromPt() returns -1.

Parameters

wParam   int: The control identifier of the drag list box.

lParam   LPDRAGLISTINFO: A pointer to a DRAGLISTINFO structure that contains the notification code and information about the drag operation. See the definition of the DRAGLISTINFO structure under the DL_BEGINDRAG message.

Include File   commctrl.h

Related Messages DL_BEGINDRAG, DL_CANCELDRAG, DL_DRAGGING

Example   See the example for the MakeDragList() function.

LVN_BEGINDRAG   ■ Win32s ■ Windows 95 ■

Description	LVN_BEGINDRAG is a notification message that notifies the parent window of a list view control of the initiation of a drag-and-drop operation. This message is sent in the form of a WM_NOTIFY message.
Parameters	
pnmv	NM_LISTVIEW*: A pointer to an NM_LISTVIEW structure that identifies the list view control item that is being dragged. The *iItem* member of the structure identifies the item; all other members of the structure are set to zero. See the definition of the NM_LISTVIEW structure below.
Include File	commctrl.h
Related Messages	WM_NOTIFY

NM_LISTVIEW Defintion

```
typedef struct tagNM_LISTVIEW
{
    NMHDR hdr;
    int   iItem;
    int   iSubItem;
    UINT  uNewState;
    UINT  uOldState;
    UINT  uChanged;
    POINT ptAction;
    LPARAM lParam;
} NM_LISTVIEW;
```

Members

hdr	NMHDR: This member is required for all WM_NOTIFY messages.
iItem	int: The list view item, or -1 if not used.
iSubItem	int: The subitem, or zero if there is no subitem.
uNewState	UINT: The new item state. This member is zero for notification messages that do not use it. This is a combination of the flags listed in Table 6-9.
uOldState	UINT: The old item state. This member is zero for notification messages that do not use it. This is a combination of the flags listed in Table 6-9.
uChanged	UINT: The item attributes that have changed. This member is zero for notifications that do not use it. Otherwise, it can have the same values as the *mask* member of the LV_ITEM structure. See the definition of the LV_ITEM structure under the ListView_GetItem macro.
ptAction	POINT: The location at which the event occurred. This member is valid only for the LVN_BEGINDRAG and LVN_BEGINRDRAG notification messages.
lParam	LPARAM: The *lParam* value associated with the list view item.
Example	See the example for the ListView_Arrange macro.

LVN_BEGINLABELEDIT ■ Win32s ■ Windows 95 ■ Windows NT

Description   LVN_BEGINLABELEDIT is a notification message that notifies the parent window of a list view control about the start of label editing for an item. This message is sent in the form of a WM_NOTIFY message.

Parameters

pdi   LV_DISPINFO*: A pointer to an LV_DISPINFO structure that contains information about the item. See the definition of the LV_DISPINFO structure below.

Returns   BOOL: FALSE to allow label editing; or TRUE to prevent it.

Include File   commctrl.h

See Also   ListView_EditLabel

Related Messages   WM_NOTIFY, LVN_ENDLABELEDIT

LV_DISPINFO Definition

```
typedef struct tagLV_DISPINFO
{
    NMHDR   hdr;
    LV_ITEM item;
} LV_DISPINFO;
```

Members

hdr   NMHDR: This member is required for all WM_NOTIFY messages.

item   LV_ITEM: The item or subitem. The structure either contains or receives information about the item. The mask member contains a set of bit flags that specify which item attributes are relevant. You can set one or more of the bit flags in Table 6-17.

Table 6-17 LV_DISPINFO *item* values

Value	Meaning
LVIF_IMAGE	The *iImage* member specifies, or is to receive, the index of the item's icon in the image list.
LVIF_STATE	The *state* member specifies, or is to receive, the state of the item.
LVIF_TEXT	The *pszText* member specifies the new item text or the address of a buffer that is to receive the item text.

Example   See the example for the ListView_EditLabel macro.

LVN_BEGINRDRAG ■ Win32s ■ Windows 95 ■ Windows NT

Description   LVN_BEGINRDRAG is a notification message that notifies the parent window of a list view control of the initiation of a drag-and-drop operation using the right mouse button. This message is sent in the form of a WM_NOTIFY message.

Parameters

pnmv   NM_LISTVIEW*: A pointer to an NM_LISTVIEW structure that identifies
                 the list view control item that is being dragged. The *iItem* member of the
                 structure identifies the item; all other members of the structure are set to
                 zero. See the definition of the NM_LISTVIEW structure under the
                 LVN_BEGINDRAG message.

Include File commctrl.h

Related Messages WM_NOTIFY

Example   This notification is identical to the LVN_BEGINDRAG message with the
                 exception that the user is using the right mouse button. Refer to the exam-
                 ple for the ListView_Arrange macro for usage of the LVN_BEGINDRAG
                 notification.

LVN_COLUMNCLICK   ■ Win32s   ■ Windows 95   ■ Windows NT

Description   LVN_COLUMNCLICK is a notification message that notifies the parent
                 window of a list view control that a column was clicked. This message is
                 sent in the form of a WM_NOTIFY message.

Parameters

pnmv   NM_LISTVIEW*: A pointer to an NM_LISTVIEW structure that identifies
                 the list view control column that was clicked. The *iSubItem* member of the
                 structure identifies the column, the *iItem* member is -1, and all other
                 members of the structure are set to zero. See the definition of the
                 NM_LISTVIEW structure under the LVN_BEGINDRAG message.

Include File commctrl.h

See Also   ListView_SortItems

Related Messages WM_NOTIFY

Example   See the example for the ListView_SortItems macro.

LVN_DELETEALLITEMS   ■ Win32s   ■ Windows 95   ■ Windows NT

Description   LVN_DELETEALLITEMS is a notification message that notifies the parent
                 window of a list view control that all items in the control were deleted.
                 This message is sent in the form of a WM_NOTIFY message.

Parameters

pnmv   NM_LISTVIEW*: A pointer to an NM_LISTVIEW structure. The *iItem*
                 member is -1, and all other members of the structure are set to zero.
                 See the definition of the NM_LISTVIEW structure under the
                 LVN_BEGINDRAG message.

Include File commctrl.h

See Also   ListView_DeleteAllItems

Related Messages WM_NOTIFY, LVN_DELETEITEM

LVN_DELETEITEM　　■ Win32s ■ Windows 95 ■ Windows NT

Description　　LVN_DELETEITEM is a notification message that notifies the parent window of a list view control that an item was deleted. This message is sent in the form of a WM_NOTIFY message.

Parameters

pnmv　　NM_LISTVIEW*: A pointer to an NM_LISTVIEW structure that identifies the list view control item that was deleted. The *iItem* member identifies the deleted item, and all other members of the structure are set to zero. See the definition of the NM_LISTVIEW structure under the LVN_BEGINDRAG message.

Include File　　commctrl.h

See Also　　ListView_DeleteItem

Related Messages　　WM_NOTIFY

LVN_ENDLABELEDIT　　■ Win32s ■ Windows 95 ■ Windows NT

Description　　LVN_ENDLABELEDIT is a notification message that notifies the parent window of a list view control about the end of label editing for an item. This message is sent in the form of a WM_NOTIFY message.

Parameters

pdi　　LV_DISPINFO*: A pointer to an LV_DISPINFO structure that identifies the item being edited. In Windows 95, the *lpszText* member is NULL if the user is canceling editing of the label. In Windows NT, the *iItem* member is -1 if the user is canceling editing of the label. See the definition of the LV_DISPINFO structure under the LVN_BEGINLABELEDIT message.

Include File　　commctrl.h

See Also　　ListView_EditLabel

Related Messages　　WM_NOTIFY, LVN_BEGINLABELEDIT

Example　　See the example for the ListView_EditLabel macro.

LVN_GETDISPINFO　　■ Win32s ■ Windows 95 ■ Windows NT

Description　　LVN_GETDISPINFO is a notification message sent to the parent window of a list view control to request the information needed to display or sort a list view item. This message is sent in the form of a WM_NOTIFY message.

Parameters

pdi　　LV_DISPINFO*: A pointer to an LV_DISPINFO structure that specifies the type of information needed and that receives the information. See the definition of the LV_DISPINFO structure under the LVN_BEGINLABELEDIT message.

Include File	commctrl.h
Related Messages	WM_NOTIFY

LVN_INSERTITEM   ■ Win32s ■ Windows 95 ■ Windows NT

Description   LVN_INSERTITEM is a notification message that notifies the parent window of a list view control that an item was inserted in the control. This message is sent in the form of a WM_NOTIFY message.

Parameters

pnmv   NM_LISTVIEW*: A pointer to an NM_LISTVIEW structure that identifies the new item added to the list view control. The *iItem* member identifies the new item, and all other members of the structure are set to zero. See the definition of the NM_LISTVIEW structure under the LVN_BEGIN-DRAG message.

Include File	commctrl.h
See Also	ListView_InsertItem
Related Messages	WM_NOTIFY

LVN_ITEMCHANGED   ■ Win32s ■ Windows 95 ■ Windows NT

Description   LVN_ITEMCHANGED is a notification message that notifies the parent window of a list view control that an item has changed. This message is sent in the form of a WM_NOTIFY message.

Parameters

pnmv   NM_LISTVIEW*: A pointer to an NM_LISTVIEW structure that identifies the item and specifies the attributes that have changed. See the definition of the NM_LISTVIEW structure under the LVN_BEGINDRAG message.

Include File	commctrl.h
Related Messages	WM_NOTIFY, LVN_ITEMCHANGING

LVN_ITEMCHANGING   ■ Win32s ■ Windows 95 ■ Windows NT

Description   LVN_ITEMCHANGING is a notification message that notifies the parent window of a list view control that an item is changing. This message is sent in the form of a WM_NOTIFY message.

Parameters

pnmv   NM_LISTVIEW*: A pointer to an NM_LISTVIEW structure that identifies the item and specifies the attributes that are changing. See the definition of the NM_LISTVIEW structure under the LVN_BEGINDRAG message.

Include File	commctrl.h
Related Messages	WM_NOTIFY, LVN_ITEMCHANGED

LVN_KEYDOWN ■ Win32s ■ Windows 95 ■ Windows NT

Description   LVN_KEYDOWN is a notification message that notifies the parent window of a list view control that a key has been pressed. This message is sent in the form of a WM_NOTIFY message.

Parameters

pnkd   LV_KEYDOWN*: A pointer to an LV_KEYDOWN structure that identifies the key that was pressed. See the definition of the LV_KEYDOWN structure below.

Include File   commctrl.h

Related Messages   WM_NOTIFY

LV_KEYDOWN Definition

```
typedef struct tagLV_KEYDOWN
{
    NMHDR hdr;
    WORD wVKey;
    UINT flags;
} LV_KEYDOWN;
```

Members

hdr   NMHDR: This member is required for all WM_NOTIFY messages.

wVKey   WORD: The virtual-key code.

flags   UINT: This member is always zero.

LVN_PEN ■ Win32s ■ Windows 95 ■ Windows NT

Description   LVN_PEN is a notification message that notifies a list view control of a pen event. The computer must have the Microsoft Windows for Pen Computing extensions installed.

Include File   commctrl.h

See Also   GetSystemMetrics()

LVN_SETDISPINFO ■ Win32s ■ Windows 95 ■ Windows NT

Description   LVN_SETDISPINFO is a notification message that notifies the parent window of a list view control that the information about the specified item needs to be updated. This message is sent in the form of a WM_NOTIFY message.

Parameters

pdi   LV_DISPINFO*: A pointer to an LV_DISPINFO structure that specifies information for the changed item. See the definition of the LV_DISPINFO structure under the LVN_BEGINLABELEDIT message.

Include File   commctrl.h

Related Messages   WM_NOTIFY

7

TREE VIEW

7

TREE VIEW

Much of the data that a user works with in applications is related to other data in a parent-child relationship, such as files and directories. A natural way of viewing parent-child data is in a hierarchical list or a tree. The Common Control Library gives the ability to easily display data in a hierachical list known as a *tree view*. The tree view control is a window that implements many of the characteristics of a list box, with the added features of an expandable/collapsible tree and graphical icons. Figure 7-1 shows how a tree view is used to display the drives and directories on a computer in the Windows Explorer.

Using Tree Views

An application can create a tree view control with the CreateWindowEx() function and the WC_TREEVIEW window class. The application must call the InitCommonControls() function prior to creating the tree view to initialize the Common Control Library and register the tree view class. The normal window styles apply to the tree view control along with the styles listed in Table 7-1.

Once a tree view is created, the application can add, remove, and manipulate items in the tree view with a series of messages. Each of the messages has one or more corresponding macros you can use instead of sending the messages directly. The macros are provided to give you an easier and cleaner method for using tree view controls. The tree view notifies the parent window about events through the WM_NOTIFY message and the special notification codes described later in this chapter. These messages notify the parent window when the user changes an item, expands the tree, starts a drag operation, presses a key, or edits an item. Two additional notifications, TVN_GETDISPINFO and TVN_SETDISPINFO, are used when the application maintains the tree view items instead of the tree view control maintaining the information.

Every item in a tree view control can have two images, nonselected and selected, associated with it. The images are drawn on the left side of the item's label. The two images allow the tree view item to display a different image when it is selected than

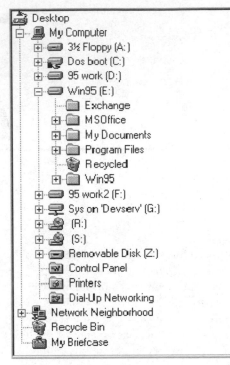

Figure 7-1 Sample tree view

Table 7-1 Tree view styles

Style	Description
TVS_DISABLEDRAGDROP	Disables drag-and-drop operations by not sending the TVN_BEGINDRAG notification.
TVS_EDITLABELS	Allows the user to edit the labels of tree view items.
TVS_HASBUTTONS	Displays plus (+) and minus (-) buttons next to parent items. The user clicks the buttons to expand or collapse a parent item's list of child items. To include buttons with items at the root of the tree view, TVS_LINESATROOT must also be specified.
TVS_HASLINES	Uses lines to show the hierarchy of items.
TVS_LINESATROOT	Uses lines to link items at the root of the tree view control. This value is ignored if TVS_HASLINES is not also specified.
TVS_SHOWSELALWAYS	Causes a selected item to remain selected when the tree view control loses focus.

when it is not selected. To use images with a tree view control, the application must create an image list with the desired images and associate it with the TreeView_SetImageList macro. The default is to use the first image in the image list for the nonselected and selected images. The application can specify a different image when the item is added by changing the image index values with the TreeView_InsertItem macro.

Parents and Children

All items in a tree view are considered *child* items, with the exception of the items at the *root* level of the tree view. The root level of a tree view is the topmost level for tree view items, and the items at this level do not have a parent. For example, the Desktop in the Windows Explorer tree view shown in Figure 7-1 is at the root level. A child item is any item that has a *parent* item. A parent item is the opposite of a child item, in that it is any item that has one or more child items. A child item can itself be a parent item if it has child items. For example, the drive icons in the Windows Explorer tree view shown in Figure 7-1 are child items of My Computer, and they are parent items for the directory folders.

An application can add both parent and child items to a tree view with the TreeView_InsertItem macro. When adding items, if the parent is TVI_ROOT, the item will be inserted at the root level. If the parent is a handle of another tree view item, the new item is inserted as a child to that item. Figure 7-1 shows how the parent and child items appear in a tree view control.

At any time the user can expand or collapse a parent item's list of child items. When the list is collapsed, the child items are hidden. When a parent item is about to be expanded or collapsed, the TVN_ITEMEXPANDING notification is sent to the parent window. If the parent window allows the item to be expanded or collapsed, the action occurs and the TVN_ITEMEXPANDED notification is sent.

Item Labels

Each item in a tree view has an item label. The item label can be managed by the tree view control or by the application. If the application manages the item label, the LPSTR_TEXTCALLBACK value is used when inserting the item, and the tree view sends a TVN_GETDISPINFO notification to retrieve the item label from the application when needed. If the tree view manages the item label, the tree view allocates sufficient memory for storing each item. This can be inefficient when the tree view manages the item labels and the tree view has many duplicate item labels.

If the tree view is created with the TVS_EDITLABELS style, the user can edit the item labels by selecting an item label that has focus. The application can also force editing of a label with the TreeView_EditLabel macro and end editing with the TreeView_EndEditLabelNow macro. When label editing begins, the tree view control sends the parent window a TVN_BEGINLABELEDIT notification. The application has the option of allowing the edit to take place or preventing it. When label editing is canceled or completed, the tree view control sends the TVN_ENDLABELEDIT message with a pointer to a TV_DISPINFO structure that contains information about the edit that occurred.

Drag and Drop

The tree view, like the list view discussed in Chapter 6, supports drag-and-drop operations. The tree view does not actually perform the drag-and-drop operation but does provide the application with the TVN_BEGINDRAG notification when one is supposed to occur. For the drag-and-drop operation to actually work, the application must process the TVN_BEGINDRAG notification by creating a drag image with the TreeView_CreateDragImage macro. The application must use the image list functions to show the drag cursor and then process the WM_LBUTTONUP message to determine when the drag-and-drop operation is completed. See the example for the TreeView_CreateDragImage macro later in this chapter for more information on drag-and-drop operations.

Function Summary

Table 7-2 summarizes the tree view functions and messages. The detailed descriptions follow immediately after the table.

Table 7-2 Tree view function and message summary

Function	Meaning
TreeView_CreateDragImage	Creates a drag image list for the specified tree view item.
TreeView_DeleteAllItems	Removes all items from the specified tree view control.
TreeView_DeleteItem	Removes the specified item from the tree view control.
TreeView_EditLabel	Edits the text of the tree view item.
TreeView_EndEditLabelNow	Terminates the editing of the tree view item label.
TreeView_EnsureVisible	Expands or scrolls the tree view control until the specified item is visible.
TreeView_Expand	Expands or collapses the list of child items.
TreeView_GetChild	Retrieves the handle of the first child item.
TreeView_GetCount	Retrieves the number of items in the tree view control.
TreeView_GetDropHilite	Retrieves the handle of the tree view item involved in a drag-and-drop operation.
TreeView_GetEditControl	Retrieves the handle of the edit control that is editing the text of the tree view control item.
TreeView_GetFirstVisible	Retrieves the handle of the first visible tree view item.
TreeView_GetImageList	Retrieves the handle of the normal or state image list associated with the control.
TreeView_GetIndent	Retrieves the amount of indentation for the child items.
TreeView_GetISearchString	Retrieves the incremental search string for the tree view control.
TreeView_GetItem	Retrieves the attributes of a tree view control.
TreeView_GetItemRect	Determines the coordinates of the bounding rectangle for the specified tree view item.
TreeView_GetNextItem	Retrieves the handle of the tree view item with the specified relationship.

Function	Meaning
TreeView_GetNextSibling	Retrieves the handle of the next sibling item.
TreeView_GetNextVisible	Retrieves the handle of the next visible item after the specified item.
TreeView_GetParent	Retrieves the parent item handle for the specified tree view item.
TreeView_GetPrevSibling	Retrieves the handle of the previous sibling item.
TreeView_GetPrevVisible	Retrieves the handle of the first visible tree view item prior to the specified item.
TreeView_GetRoot	Retrieves the handle of the first item in the tree view control.
TreeView_GetSelection	Retrieves the handle of the currently selected tree view control item.
TreeView_GetVisibleCount	Determines the number of fully visible client window items.
TreeView_HitTest	Determines the location of the specified point in relation to the client area of the tree view control.
TreeView_InsertItem	Adds a new item to the specified tree view control.
TreeView_Select	Selects and displays the specified tree view item.
TreeView_SelectDropTarget	Indicates the selected item was the target of a drag-and-drop operation.
TreeView_SelectItem	Selects the specified item.
TreeView_SelectSetFirstVisible	Scrolls the list until the specified tree view item is the first visible item.
TreeView_SetImageList	Sets the normal or state image list for a tree view control.
TreeView_SetIndent	Sets the indentation for the specified tree view control.
TreeView_SetItem	Sets the attributes of a tree view item.
TreeView_SortChildren	Sorts the child items of the specified parent item.
TreeView_SortChildrenCB	Sorts the tree view control items by using an application-defined callback function to compare the order of the items.

Notification Message

TVN_BEGINDRAG	A drag-and-drop operation was initiated using the left mouse button.
TVN_BEGINLABELEDIT	Label editing of a tree view item was initiated.
TVN_BEGINRDRAG	A drag-and-drop operation was initiated using the right mouse button.
TVN_DELETEITEM	A tree view control item was deleted.
TVN_ENDLABELEDIT	Label editing of a tree view item is complete.
TVN_GETDISPINFO	Requests information to either display or sort an item.
TVN_ITEMEXPANDED	The list of child items has either expanded or collapsed.
TVN_ITEMEXPANDING	The list of child items is going to either expand or collapse.
TVN_KEYDOWN	A key was pressed by the user and the tree view control has input focus.
TVN_SELCHANGED	The selection changed from one tree view item to another.
TVN_SELCHANGING	The selection is changing from one tree view item to another.
TVN_SETDISPINFO	Information about the specified item needs to be updated.

TreeView_CreateDragImage   ■ Win32s   ■ Windows 95   ■ Windows NT

Description   TreeView_CreateDragImage is a macro that creates a drag list image for a tree view item. This macro also creates an image list for the bitmap containing the drag list image. Use the image list functions to display the image while performing drag-and-drop operations on the item.

Syntax	HIMAGELIST **TreeView_CreateDragImage**(HWND *hwnd*, HTREEITEM *hitem*)
Message Syntax	HIMAGELIST **SendMessage**(*hwnd*, **TVM_CREATEDRAGIMAGE**, 0, *hitem*)
Parameters	
hwnd	HWND: The handle of the tree view control.
hitem	HTREEITEM: The handle of the item for which the new bitmap was created.
Returns	HIMAGELIST: If successful, the handle of the new image list that contains the drag image is returned; otherwise, NULL is returned.
Include File	commctrl.h
See Also	ImageList_BeginDrag()
Related Messages	TVM_CREATEDRAGIMAGE
Example	This example (Listing 7-1) demonstrates the drag-and-drop operation within a tree view control. The user can drag root items to reorder them within the list. The user can also drag child items to other root items. For example, the Rectangle item from one root item can be dragged to another root item, which would then have two Rectangle items. Figure 7-2 shows a drag operation with a root item "Circle 4". The list contains twenty root items, each with the same three child items. When the user drops an item, the drop target is checked to determine if it is a valid target. This could also be done during the drag operation to change the drag cursor, indicating to the user that the drop operation is not valid in the current location.

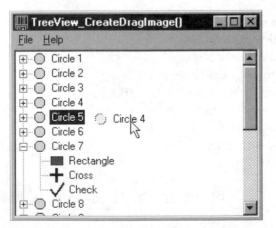

Figure 7-2 TreeView_CreateDragImage example

Listing 7-1 Using the TreeView_CreateDragImage macro

```
#define IMAGESIZE 16

LPCTSTR lpszData[4] = { "Circle", "Rectangle", "Cross", "Check" };

LRESULT CALLBACK WndProc( HWND hWnd, UINT uMsg, WPARAM wParam, LPARAM lParam )
{
static TV_HITTESTINFO  tvHitTest;
static POINT           ptHotSpot;
static HTREEITEM       hDragItem = NULL;
static HWND            hTree     = NULL;
static HIMAGELIST      hCursors  = NULL;
static HIMAGELIST      hDragList = NULL;

    switch( uMsg )
    {
        case WM_CREATE :
                {
                    HIMAGELIST hImage;
                    ICONINFO   info;

                    InitCommonControls();

                    hCursors = ImageList_Create( 32,32, ILC_COLOR4|ILC_MASK, 1,1 );
                    hImage   = ImageList_Create( IMAGESIZE, IMAGESIZE,
                                                 ILC_COLOR4 | ILC_MASK, 4, 1 );
                    hTree = CreateWindowEx( WS_EX_CLIENTEDGE, WC_TREEVIEW, "",
                                WS_CHILD | WS_BORDER | WS_VISIBLE |
                                WS_VSCROLL | TVS_HASLINES |
                                TVS_HASBUTTONS | TVS_LINESATROOT,
                                10, 100, 100, 100,
                                hWnd,
                                (HMENU)1,
                                hInst,
                                NULL);

                    if ( hTree )
                    {
                        int i;

                        // Associate the image list with the tree view.
                        //................................................
                        TreeView_SetImageList( hTree, hImage, TVSIL_NORMAL );

                        // Add the images to the tree view image list.
                        //................................................
                        for ( i=0; i<4; i++ )
                            ImageList_AddIcon( hImage, LoadIcon(hInst,lpszData[i]) );

                        AddItemsToTree( hTree );
                    }

                    // Create drag cursor icon.
                    //........................
                    ImageList_AddIcon( hCursors, LoadCursor( NULL, IDC_ARROW ) );
```

continued on next page

continued from previous page

```
                  // Retrieve the hot spot information from the cursor.
                  //....................................................
                  GetIconInfo( LoadCursor( NULL, IDC_ARROW ), &info );
                  ptHotSpot.x = info.xHotspot;
                  ptHotSpot.y = info.yHotspot;

                  // Clean up the bitmaps from GetIconInfo().
                  //........................................
                  DeleteObject( info.hbmMask );
                  DeleteObject( info.hbmColor );
            }
            break;

      case WM_SIZE :
            if ( hTree )
                MoveWindow( hTree,0,0, LOWORD(lParam), HIWORD(lParam), FALSE );
            break;


      case WM_NOTIFY :
            if ( wParam == 1 )
            {
            NM_TREEVIEW* pNM = (NM_TREEVIEW*)lParam;

            switch ( pNM->hdr.code )
            {
                case TVN_BEGINDRAG :
                      {
                          RECT rc;

                          // Create the drag image.
                          //......................
                          hDragList = TreeView_CreateDragImage( hTree,
                                            pNM->itemNew.hItem );

                          TreeView_GetItemRect( hTree, pNM->itemNew.hItem,
                                            &rc, FALSE );

                          // Start dragging and set the drag cursor.
                          //........................................
                          ImageList_BeginDrag( hDragList, 0,
                              pNM->ptDrag.x-rc.left-IMAGESIZE,
                              pNM->ptDrag.y-rc.top );
                          ImageList_SetDragCursorImage( hCursors, 0,
                              pNM->ptDrag.x-rc.left-ptHotSpot.x-IMAGESIZE,
                              pNM->ptDrag.y-rc.top-ptHotSpot.y );
                          ImageList_DragEnter( hTree, pNM->ptDrag.x,
                                                    pNM->ptDrag.y );

                          // Capture the mouse and hide the normal cursor.
                          //..............................................
                          SetCapture( hWnd );
                          ShowCursor( FALSE );

                          hDragItem = pNM->itemNew.hItem;
                      }
                      break;

            }
```

```
        }
        break;

case WM_MOUSEMOVE :
        // Move the drag cursor if dragging.
        //..............................
        if ( hDragList )
        {
            tvHitTest.pt.x = LOWORD( lParam );
            tvHitTest.pt.y = HIWORD( lParam );

            // Check to see if the item is over a tree view item,
            // if it is, then it is hilighted.
            //..................................................
            TreeView_HitTest( hTree, &tvHitTest );
            if ( tvHitTest.hItem != TreeView_GetDropHilight( hTree ) )
            {
                // Clear the drag image.
                //......................
                ImageList_DragLeave( hTree );

                // Unhilight the old item, hilight the new one.
                //..............................................
                TreeView_SelectDropTarget( hTree, NULL );
                TreeView_SelectDropTarget( hTree, tvHitTest.hItem );

                // Show the drag image.
                //.....................
                ImageList_DragEnter( hTree, LOWORD(lParam), HIWORD(lParam));
            }
            else
                ImageList_DragMove( LOWORD(lParam), HIWORD(lParam) );
        }
        break;


case WM_LBUTTONUP :
        // If dragging, drop the object in its new place.
        //...............................................
        if ( hDragList )
        {
            HTREEITEM hDropItem;

            // Stop the dragging process.
            //...........................
            ImageList_DragLeave( hTree );
            ImageList_EndDrag();
            ImageList_Destroy( hDragList );
            hDragList = NULL;
            ReleaseCapture();
            ShowCursor( TRUE );

            // Find out the item that was last hilighted.
            //...........................................
            hDropItem = TreeView_GetDropHilight( hTree );

            // Unselect the drop hilight item.
            //................................
            TreeView_SelectDropTarget( hTree, NULL );
```

continued on next page

continued from previous page

```
// Item was dropped, move the item in the tree.
//..............................................
if ( hDropItem )
{
    TV_INSERTSTRUCT tv;
    TV_ITEM         tvDropItem;
    char            szName[40];

    // Retrieve the Drag Item.
    //........................
    tv.item.hItem      = hDragItem;
    tv.item.mask       = TVIF_TEXT | TVIF_IMAGE |
                         TVIF_SELECTEDIMAGE | TVIF_PARAM;
    tv.item.pszText    = szName;
    tv.item.cchTextMax = sizeof( szName );
    TreeView_GetItem( hTree, &tv.item );

    // Retrieve the Drop Item.
    //........................
    tvDropItem.hItem      = hDropItem;
    tvDropItem.mask       = TVIF_PARAM;
    TreeView_GetItem( hTree, &tvDropItem );

    // Only let level 1 items go to level 1 and
    // level 2 items go to level 2.
    //.........................................
    if ( tv.item.lParam && tvDropItem.lParam )
    {
        tv.hParent = TreeView_GetParent( hTree, hDropItem );
        tv.hInsertAfter = hDropItem;
    }
    else if ( tv.item.lParam && !tvDropItem.lParam )
    {
        tv.hParent = hDropItem;
        tv.hInsertAfter = TVI_LAST;
    }
    else if ( !tv.item.lParam && tvDropItem.lParam )
    {
        tv.hParent = TVI_ROOT;
        tv.hInsertAfter = TreeView_GetParent( hTree, hDropItem );
    }
    else if ( !tv.item.lParam && !tvDropItem.lParam )
    {
        tv.hParent = TVI_ROOT;
        tv.hInsertAfter = hDropItem;
    }

    // Insert the dragged item into the tree
    // in the new location.
    //......................................
    tv.hParent = TreeView_InsertItem( hTree, &tv );

    // Move the children if there are any.
    //....................................
    if ( !tv.item.lParam )
    {
        tv.hInsertAfter = TVI_LAST;
        tv.item.hItem = TreeView_GetChild( hTree, hDragItem );
```

```
                while ( tv.item.hItem )
                {
                    TreeView_GetItem( hTree, &tv.item );
                    TreeView_InsertItem( hTree, &tv );
                    tv.item.hItem = TreeView_GetNextSibling( hTree,
                                                  tv.item.hItem );
                }
            }

            // Delete the original item from the tree,
            // this is because we are moving the item.
            //.....................................
            TreeView_DeleteItem( hTree, hDragItem );
        }

        // Update the tree view.
        //......................
        InvalidateRect( hTree, NULL, TRUE );

    }
    break;


case WM_COMMAND :
        switch( LOWORD( wParam ) )
        {
        case IDM_RESET :
                // Clear the tree view.
                //.....................
                TreeView_DeleteAllItems( hTree );

                // Add the items to the tree.
                //...........................
                AddItemsToTree( hTree );
                break;

        case IDM_EXIT :
                DestroyWindow( hWnd );
                break;
        }
        break;

case WM_DESTROY :
        if ( TreeView_GetImageList( hTree, TVSIL_NORMAL ) )
            ImageList_Destroy( TreeView_GetImageList(hTree,TVSIL_NORMAL) );

        PostQuitMessage(0);
        break;

default :
        return( DefWindowProc( hWnd, uMsg, wParam, lParam ) );
    }

    return( 0L );
}

VOID AddItemsToTree( HWND hTree )
{
```

continued on next page

continued from previous page

```
int              i, j;
char             szTmp[40];
TV_INSERTSTRUCT  tv;
HTREEITEM        hParent;

tv.hInsertAfter = TVI_LAST;
tv.item.mask    = TVIF_TEXT | TVIF_IMAGE |
                  TVIF_SELECTEDIMAGE | TVIF_PARAM;

// Add the items to the tree view.
//..............................
for ( i=0; i<20; i++ )
{
   wsprintf( szTmp, "%s %d", lpszData[0], i+1 );

   tv.hParent        = TVI_ROOT;
   tv.item.pszText = szTmp;
   tv.item.iImage  = 0;
   tv.item.iSelectedImage = 0;
   tv.item.lParam        = 0;

   hParent = TreeView_InsertItem( hTree, &tv );
   tv.hParent = hParent;

   // Add child items.
   //.................
   for( j=1; j<4; j++ )
   {
      tv.item.pszText = (LPTSTR)lpszData[j];
      tv.item.iImage  = j;
      tv.item.iSelectedImage = j;
      tv.item.lParam        = 1;

      TreeView_InsertItem( hTree, &tv );
   }
}
}
```

TreeView_DeleteAllItems   ■ Win32s   ■ Windows 95   ■ Windows NT

Description	TreeView_DeleteAllItems is a macro that removes all items from the tree view control. If an item in the tree view control is being modified, a TVN_ENDLABELEDIT message is sent to the parent window.
Syntax	BOOL **TreeView_DeleteAllItems**(HWND *hwnd*)
Message Syntax	BOOL **SendMessage**(*hwnd*, **TVM_DELETEITEM**, 0, TVI_ROOT)
Parameters	
hwnd	HWND: The handle of the tree view control.
Returns	BOOL: If successful, TRUE is returned; otherwise, FALSE is returned.
Include File	commctrl.h
Related Messages	TVM_DELETEITEM, TVN_DELETEITEM
Example	See the example for the TreeView_CreateDragImage macro.

TREEVIEW_DELETEITEM
■ Win32s ■ Windows 95 ■ Windows NT

Description	TreeView_DeleteItem is a macro that removes the specified item from the tree view control. If the specified item is being modified, a TVN_ENDLABELEDIT message is sent to the parent window. A TVN_DELETEITEM message is sent to the parent window when the item is deleted.
Syntax	BOOL **TreeView_DeleteItem**(HWND *hwnd*, HTREEITEM *hitem*)
Message Syntax	BOOL **SendMessage**(*hwnd*, **TVM_DELETEITEM**, 0, *hitem*)
Parameters	
hwnd	HWND: The handle of the tree view control.
hitem	HTREEITEM: The handle of the item to remove from the specified tree view control. If the value of *hitem* is TVI_ROOT, all items are removed from the tree view control. This is equivalent to the TreeView_DeleteAllItems macro.
Returns	BOOL: If successful, TRUE is returned; otherwise, FALSE is returned.
Include File	commctrl.h
See Also	TreeView_DeleteAllItems
Related Messages	TVM_DELETEITEM, TVN_DELETEITEM, TVN_ENDLABELEDIT
Example	See the example for the TreeView_CreateDragImage macro.

TREEVIEW_EDITLABEL
■ Win32s ■ Windows 95 ■ Windows NT

Description	TreeView_EditLabel is a macro that initiates the in-place editing of the text in the specified tree view item by replacing the text with a single-line edit control. The tree view control must have focus before this macro is used. Use SetFocus() to set the focus for the control. A TVN_BEGINLABELEDIT notification message is sent to the parent window of the tree view control.
	When the editing of the item is complete, the edit control is destroyed.
Syntax	HWND **TreeView_EditLabel**(HWND *hwnd*, HTREEITEM *hitem*)
Message Syntax	HWND **SendMessage**(*hwnd*, **TVM_EDITLABEL**, 0, *hitem*)
Parameters	
hwnd	HWND: The handle of the tree view control.
hitem	HTREEITEM: The handle of the item to edit.
Returns	HWND: If successful, the handle of the edit control used to modify the text of the tree view item is returned; otherwise, NULL is returned.
Include File	commctrl.h
See Also	TreeView_EndEditLabelNow, SetFocus()
Related Messages	TVM_EDITLABEL, TVN_BEGINLABELEDIT

Example

This example (Listing 7-2) demonstrates label editing of tree view items. The user can use the mouse button to select an item that has focus to start the editing process or use the Rename menu option. When the parent window is notified that an edit operation is beginning, the edit window handle is retrieved and the text length is limited. When the parent window is notified that the edit operation is complete, the *pszText* member of the TV_ITEM structure is checked to see if the edit was canceled. If the edit was not canceled, the tree view item is updated with the new label. The user can also expand or collapse a tree view item from the menu; if the user does this while in editing mode, the edit mode is canceled with the TreeVew_EndEditLabelNow macro.

Listing 7-2 Using the TreeView_EditLabel macro

```
LRESULT CALLBACK WndProc( HWND hWnd, UINT uMsg, WPARAM wParam, LPARAM lParam )
{
static HWND hTree = NULL;

   switch( uMsg )
   {
      case WM_CREATE  :
               {
               HIMAGELIST hImage;

               InitCommonControls();

               hImage   = ImageList_Create( IMAGESIZE, IMAGESIZE,
                                            ILC_COLOR4 | ILC_MASK, 4, 1 );
               hTree = CreateWindowEx( WS_EX_CLIENTEDGE, WC_TREEVIEW, "",
                                       WS_CHILD | WS_BORDER | WS_VISIBLE |
                                       WS_VSCROLL | TVS_HASLINES |
                                       TVS_HASBUTTONS | TVS_LINESATROOT |
                                       TVS_DISABLEDRAGDROP | TVS_EDITLABELS,
                                       10, 100, 100, 100,
                                       hWnd,
                                       (HMENU)1,
                                       hInst,
                                       NULL);

               if ( hTree )
               {
                  int i;

                  // Associate the image list with the tree view.
                  //...............................................
                  TreeView_SetImageList( hTree, hImage, TVSIL_NORMAL );

                  // Add the images to the tree view image list.
                  //...............................................
                  for ( i=0; i<4; i++ )
                     ImageList_AddIcon( hImage, LoadIcon(hInst,lpszData[i]) );

                  AddItemsToTree( hTree );
```

```
            }
        }
        break;

case WM_SIZE :
        if ( hTree )
            MoveWindow( hTree,0,0, LOWORD(lParam), HIWORD(lParam), FALSE );
        break;


case WM_NOTIFY :
        if ( wParam == 1 )
        {
            TV_DISPINFO* pNM = (TV_DISPINFO*)lParam;

            switch ( pNM->hdr.code )
            {
                case TVN_BEGINLABELEDIT :
                        {
                            HWND hEdit;

                            // Limit the number of characters allowed
                            // in the edit control of the tree view.
                            //........................................
                            hEdit = TreeView_GetEditControl( hTree );
                            if ( hEdit )
                                SendMessage( hEdit, EM_LIMITTEXT, 30, 0 );
                        }
                        break;

                case TVN_ENDLABELEDIT :
                        {
                            // If the text was edited, update the text.
                            //..........................................
                            if ( pNM->item.pszText )
                            {
                                pNM->item.mask = TVIF_TEXT;
                                TreeView_SetItem( hTree, &pNM->item );
                            }
                        }
                        break;
            }
        }
        break;


case WM_COMMAND :
        switch( LOWORD( wParam ) )
        {
            case IDM_RENAME :
                    {
                        HTREEITEM hItem;

                        // Rename the selected item.
                        //..........................
                        hItem = TreeView_GetSelection( hTree );
                        if ( hItem )
                            TreeView_EditLabel( hTree, hItem );
```

continued on next page

continued from previous page

```
                    }
                break;

            case IDM_COLLAPSE :
            case IDM_EXPAND :
                {
                    HTREEITEM hItem;

                    // Finish the editing, canceling changes.
                    //.....................................
                    TreeView_EndEditLabelNow( hTree, TRUE );

                    // Expand/collapse the selected item.
                    //..................................
                    hItem = TreeView_GetSelection( hTree );
                    if ( hItem )
                        TreeView_Expand( hTree, hItem,
                                        LOWORD( wParam ) == IDM_EXPAND ?
                                        TVE_EXPAND : TVE_COLLAPSE );
                }
                break;

        case IDM_EXIT :
                DestroyWindow( hWnd );
                break;
        }
    break;
        .
        .
        .
```

TreeView_EndEditLabelNow ■ Win32s ■ Windows 95 ■ Windows NT

Description	TreeView_EndEditLabelNow is a macro that terminates the editing of an item label for a tree view control. The TVN_ENDLABELEDIT notification message is sent to the parent window of the tree view control. Use this macro when the application must finish editing prematurely.
Syntax	BOOL **TreeView_EndEditLabelNow**(HWND *hwnd*, BOOL *bCancel*)
Message Syntax	BOOL **SendMessage**(*hwnd*, **TVM_ENDEDITLABELNOW**, 0, *bCancel*)
Parameters	
hwnd	HWND: The handle of the tree view control.
bCancel	BOOL: If set to TRUE, the edit process is canceled and the changes made to the tree view item label are not saved; otherwise, the label changes are saved.
Returns	BOOL: If successful, TRUE is returned; otherwise, FALSE is returned.
Include File	commctrl.h
Related Messages	TVM_ENDEDITLABELNOW
Example	See the example for the TreeView_EditLabel macro.

TreeView_EnsureVisible

Description	TreeView_EnsureVisible is a macro that ensures that the specified tree view item is visible by expanding or scrolling the tree view control. The TVN_ITEMEXPANDING and TVN_ITEMEXPANDED notification messages are sent to the parent window if the parent item was expanded.
Syntax	BOOL **TreeView_EnsureVisible**(HWND *hwnd*, HTREEITEM *hitem*)
Message Syntax	BOOL **SendMessage**(*hwnd*, **TVM_ENSUREVISIBLE**, 0, *hitem*)
Parameters	
hwnd	HWND: The handle of the tree view control.
hitem	HTREEITEM: The handle of the item.
Returns	BOOL: If the tree view control was scrolled to display the specified items, TRUE is returned; otherwise, FALSE is returned.
Include File	commctrl.h
Related Messages	TVM_ENDEDITLABELNOW
Example	This example (Listing 7-3) demonstrates the TreeView_EnsureVisible macro. The user can select a menu option, either View↓First Item or View↓Last Item, and the TreeView_EnsureVisible macro is used to scroll the tree view so the first or last item is visible. The first or last item is also selected with the TreeView_SelectItem macro.

Listing 7-3 Using the TreeView_EnsureVisible macro

```
LRESULT CALLBACK WndProc( HWND hWnd, UINT uMsg, WPARAM wParam, LPARAM lParam )
{
static HWND hTree = NULL;

   switch( uMsg )
   {
      case WM_CREATE :
            {
               HIMAGELIST hImage;

               InitCommonControls();

               hImage  = ImageList_Create( IMAGESIZE, IMAGESIZE,
                                           ILC_COLOR4 | ILC_MASK, 4, 1 );
               hTree = CreateWindowEx( WS_EX_CLIENTEDGE, WC_TREEVIEW, "",
                                       WS_CHILD | WS_BORDER | WS_VISIBLE |
                                       WS_VSCROLL | TVS_HASLINES |
                                       TVS_HASBUTTONS | TVS_LINESATROOT |
                                       TVS_DISABLEDRAGDROP,
                                       10, 100, 100, 100,
                                       hWnd,
                                       (HMENU)1,
                                       hInst,
                                       NULL);
```

continued on next page

continued from previous page

```
                    if ( hTree )
                    {
                        int i;

                        // Associate the image list with the tree view.
                        //.............................................
                        TreeView_SetImageList( hTree, hImage, TVSIL_NORMAL );

                        // Add the images to the tree view image list.
                        //..........................................
                        for ( i=0; i<4; i++ )
                            ImageList_AddIcon( hImage, LoadIcon(hInst,lpszData[i]) );

                        AddItemsToTree( hTree );
                    }
                }
                break;

        case WM_SIZE :
                if ( hTree )
                    MoveWindow( hTree,0,0, LOWORD(lParam), HIWORD(lParam), FALSE );
                break;

        case WM_COMMAND :
                switch( LOWORD( wParam ) )
                {
                    case IDM_VIEWLAST :
                    case IDM_VIEWFIRST :
                        {
                            HTREEITEM hItem;

                            // Get the first item in the tree.
                            //................................
                            hItem = TreeView_GetRoot( hTree );

                            // Find the last item if we are viewing the last.
                            //...............................................
                            if ( hItem && LOWORD( wParam ) == IDM_VIEWLAST )
                            {
                                while ( hItem )
                                {
                                    if ( TreeView_GetNextSibling( hTree, hItem ) )
                                        hItem = TreeView_GetNextSibling( hTree,
                                                                         hItem );
                                    else if ( TreeView_GetChild( hTree, hItem ) )
                                        hItem = TreeView_GetChild( hTree, hItem );
                                    else
                                        break;
                                }
                            }

                            // Select the appropriate item.
                            //.............................
                            if ( hItem )
                            {
                                TreeView_EnsureVisible( hTree, hItem );
                                TreeView_SelectItem( hTree, hItem );
```

```
            }
        }
        break;
    .
    .
    .
```

TreeView_Expand ■ Win32s ■ Windows 95 ■ Windows NT

Description	TreeView_Expand is a macro that either expands or collapses the list of child items associated with the specified parent item based on the value of the *flag* parameter.
Syntax	BOOL **TreeView_Expand**(HWND *hwnd*, HTREEITEM *hitem*, UINT *flag*)
Message Syntax	BOOL **SendMessage**(*hwnd*, **TVM_EXPAND**, *flag*, *hitem*)
Parameters	
hwnd	HWND: The handle of the tree view control.
hitem	HTREEITEM: The handle of the parent item that should be expanded or collapsed, based on the value of the *flag* parameter.
flag	UINT: The action that should be taken on the tree view control. This parameter can be one of the values in Table 7-3.

Table 7-3 TreeView_Expand *flag* values

Value	Meaning
TVE_COLLAPSE	Collapses the list.
TVE_COLLAPSERESET	Collapses the list and removes the child items. Note that TVE_COLLAPSE must also be specified.
TVE_EXPAND	Expands the list.
TVE_TOGGLE	Collapses the list if it is currently expanded or expands it if it is currently collapsed.

Returns	BOOL: If successful, TRUE is returned; otherwise, FALSE is returned.
Include File	commctrl.h
Related Messages	TVM_EXPAND
Example	See the example for the TreeView_EditLabel macro.

TreeView_GetChild ■ Win32s ■ Windows 95 ■ Windows NT

Description	TreeView_GetChild is a macro that retrieves the handle of the first child item of a parent tree view item.
Syntax	HTREEITEM **TreeView_GetChild**(HWND *hwnd*, HTREEITEM *hitem*)
Message Syntax	HTREEITEM **SendMessage**(*hwnd*, **TVM_GETNEXTITEM**, TVGN_CHILD, *hitem*)

Parameters

hwnd   HWND: The handle of the tree view control.

hitem   HTREEITEM: The handle of the parent item for which to retrieve the first
                                child item.

Returns   HTREEITEM: If successful, the handle of the first child item is returned;
                                otherwise, NULL is returned.

Include File   commctrl.h

See Also   TreeView_GetParent, TreeView_GetNextItem

Related Messages   TVM_GETITEMRECT

Example   See the example for the TreeView_CreateDragImage macro.

TREEVIEW_GETCOUNT   ■ Win32s   ■ Windows 95   ■ Windows NT

Description   TreeView_GetCount is a macro that retrieves the number of items in the
                                specified tree view control.

Syntax   UINT **TreeView_GetCount**(HWND *hwnd*)

Message Syntax   UINT **SendMessage**(*hwnd*, **TVM_GETCOUNT**, 0, 0)

Parameters

hwnd   HWND: The handle of the tree view control.

Returns   UINT: The number of items in the tree view control.

Include File   commctrl.h

Related Messages   TVM_GETCOUNT

Example   This example (Listing 7-4) demonstrates a page up and page down opera-
                                tion using the macros available for a tree view control. The user has two
                                menu options, Page Up and Page Down. When the application processes
                                the WM_INITMENU message, the status of the tree view is checked to
                                determine if the menu options should be enabled or grayed. When the
                                user selects the Page Up or Page Down, the current selection is retrieved
                                and the application determines if the tree view has to scroll to perform the
                                page up or page down. If the selection is in the middle of the viewable
                                items, the first visible or last visible item is selected. If the first or last visi-
                                ble items are already selected, then the tree view scrolls the equivalent of
                                one page of items to display a new page.

Listing 7-4 Using the TreeView_GetCount macro

```
LRESULT CALLBACK WndProc( HWND hWnd, UINT uMsg, WPARAM wParam, LPARAM lParam )
{
static HWND hTree = NULL;

   switch( uMsg )
   {
      case WM_CREATE  :
```

```
            {
                HIMAGELIST hImage;

                InitCommonControls();

                hImage   = ImageList_Create( IMAGESIZE, IMAGESIZE,
                                        ILC_COLOR4 | ILC_MASK, 4, 1 );
                hTree = CreateWindowEx( WS_EX_CLIENTEDGE, WC_TREEVIEW, "",
                                    WS_CHILD | WS_BORDER | WS_VISIBLE |
                                    WS_VSCROLL | TVS_HASLINES |
                                    TVS_HASBUTTONS | TVS_LINESATROOT |
                                    TVS_DISABLEDRAGDROP,
                                    10, 100, 100, 100,
                                    hWnd,
                                    (HMENU)1,
                                    hInst,
                                    NULL);

                if ( hTree )
                {
                    int i;

                    // Associate the image list with the tree view.
                    //..............................................
                    TreeView_SetImageList( hTree, hImage, TVSIL_NORMAL );

                    // Add the images to the tree view image list.
                    //..............................................
                    for ( i=0; i<4; i++ )
                        ImageList_AddIcon( hImage, LoadIcon(hInst,lpszData[i]) );

                    AddItemsToTree( hTree );
                }
            }
            break;

    case WM_SIZE :
            if ( hTree )
                MoveWindow( hTree,0,0, LOWORD(lParam), HIWORD(lParam), FALSE );
            break;

    case WM_INITMENU :
            // Gray out the menu options when they are not appropriate.
            //.......................................................
            if ( TreeView_GetCount( hTree ) <
                 TreeView_GetVisibleCount( hTree ) )
            {
                EnableMenuItem( (HMENU)wParam, IDM_PGUP,
                                MF_BYCOMMAND | MF_GRAYED );
                EnableMenuItem( (HMENU)wParam, IDM_PGDOWN,
                                MF_BYCOMMAND | MF_GRAYED );
            }
            else
            {
                HTREEITEM hCurItem = TreeView_GetSelection( hTree );

                EnableMenuItem( (HMENU)wParam, IDM_PGUP, MF_BYCOMMAND |
                                ( TreeView_GetPrevVisible( hTree, hCurItem ) ?
                                    MF_ENABLED : MF_GRAYED ) );
```

continued on next page

continued from previous page

```
                EnableMenuItem( (HMENU)wParam, IDM_PGDOWN, MF_BYCOMMAND |
                                ( TreeView_GetNextVisible( hTree, hCurItem ) ?
                                    MF_ENABLED : MF_GRAYED ) );
        }
        break;


    case WM_COMMAND :
        switch( LOWORD( wParam ) )
        {
        case IDM_PGUP :
        case IDM_PGDOWN :
                {
                    HTREEITEM hCurItem, hFirstVis, hNewItem;
                    int       nVisCount;

                    // Retrieve the current state of the tree view.
                    //..............................................
                    nVisCount = TreeView_GetVisibleCount( hTree );
                    hCurItem  = TreeView_GetSelection( hTree );
                    hFirstVis = TreeView_GetFirstVisible( hTree );

                    // Process the page up.
                    //.....................
                    if ( LOWORD( wParam ) == IDM_PGUP )
                    {
                        if ( hCurItem != hFirstVis )
                            hNewItem = hFirstVis;
                        else
                        {
                            int nCnt = 0;

                            hNewItem = hCurItem;
                            while ( nCnt < nVisCount &&
                                TreeView_GetPrevVisible(hTree,hNewItem) )
                            {
                                hNewItem = TreeView_GetPrevVisible( hTree,
                                                                    hNewItem );

                                nCnt++;
                            }
                        }

                        // Select the new item and
                        // make sure it is visible.
                        //.........................
                        TreeView_SelectSetFirstVisible( hTree, hNewItem );
                        TreeView_SelectItem( hTree, hNewItem );
                    }
                    // Process the Page down.
                    //.......................
                    else
                    {
                        HTREEITEM hTmp;
                        int       nCnt = 1;

                        // Find the last visible item.
                        //............................
                        hTmp = hFirstVis;
                        while( hTmp && nCnt < nVisCount &&
```

```
                         TreeView_GetNextVisible( hTree, hTmp ) )
               {
                  hTmp = TreeView_GetNextVisible( hTree, hTmp );
                  nCnt++;
               }

               // Determine the new item.
               //.......................
               if ( hTmp != hCurItem )
                  hNewItem = hTmp;
               else
               {
                  nCnt = 1;

                  hNewItem = hCurItem;

                  while ( nCnt < nVisCount &&
                      TreeView_GetNextVisible(hTree,hNewItem) )
                  {
                     hNewItem = TreeView_GetNextVisible( hTree,
                                                  hNewItem );
                     nCnt++;
                  }
               }

               // Select the new item and
               // make sure it is visible.
               //........................
               TreeView_EnsureVisible( hTree, hNewItem );
               TreeView_SelectItem( hTree, hNewItem );
            }
         }
         break;
```

TREEVIEW_GETDROPHILITE ■ Win32s ■ Windows 95 ■ Windows NT

Description	TreeView_GetDropHilite is a macro that retrieves the handle of the tree view item that is currently highlighted as the drop item. Typically in a drag-and-drop operation the item that the drag cursor is currently over is highlighted as the drop item. Use the TreeView_SelectDropTarget macro to set the current target item.
Syntax	HTREEITEM **TreeView_GetDropHilite**(HWND *hwnd*)
Message Syntax	HTREEITEM **SendMessage**(*hwnd*, **TVM_GETNEXTITEM**, TVGN_DROPHILITE, 0)
Parameters	
hwnd	HWND: The handle of the tree view control.
Returns	HTREEITEM: If successful, the handle of the drop highlighted tree view item is returned; otherwise, NULL is returned.
Include File	commctrl.h

See Also	TreeView_GetNextItem
Related Messages	TVM_GETITEMRECT
Example	See the example for the TreeView_CreateDragImage macro.

TreeView_GetEditControl ■ Win32s ■ Windows 95 ■ Windows NT

Description	TreeView_GetEditControl is a macro that retrieves the handle of the edit control that is editing the text of the tree view control item.
Syntax	HWND **TreeView_GetEditControl**(HWND *hwnd*)
Message Syntax	HWND **SendMessage**(*hwnd*, **TVM_GETEDITCONTROL**, 0, 0)
Parameters	
hwnd	HWND: The handle of the tree view control.
Returns	HWND: If successful, the handle of the edit control is returned; otherwise, NULL is returned.
Include File	commctrl.h
Related Messages	TVM_GETEDITCONTROL
Example	See the example for the TreeView_EditLabel macro.

TreeView_GetFirstVisible ■ Win32s ■ Windows 95 ■ Windows NT

Description	TreeView_GetFirstVisible is a macro that retrieves the handle of the first visible tree view item. This is the tree view item that is the topmost visible item in the tree view control.
Syntax	HTREEVIEW **TreeView_GetFirstVisible**(HWND *hwnd*)
Message Syntax	HTREEVIEW **SendMessage**(*hwnd*, **TVM_GETNEXTITEM**, TVGN_FIRSTVISIBLE, 0)
Parameters	
hwnd	HWND: The handle of the tree view control.
Returns	HTREEITEM: If successful, the handle of the first visible tree view item is returned; otherwise, NULL is returned.
Include File	commctrl.h
See Also	TreeView_GetNextItem, TreeView_SelectSetFirstVisible
Related Messages	TVM_GETITEMRECT
Example	See the example for the TreeView_GetCount macro.

TreeView_GetImageList ■ Win32s ■ Windows 95 ■ Windows NT

Description	TreeView_GetImageList is a macro that retrieves the handle of either the normal or the state image list associated with the specified tree view control.

Syntax	HIMAGELIST **TreeView_GetImageList**(HWND *hwnd*, int *nImageList*)
Message Syntax	HIMAGELIST **SendMessage**(*hwnd*, **TVM_GETIMAGELIST**, *nImageList*, 0)
Parameters	
hwnd	HWND: The handle of the image list.
nImageList	int: The type of image list to retrieve. This parameter can be one of the values in Table 7-4.

Table 7-4 TreeView_GetImageList *nImageList* values

Value	Meaning
TVSIL_NORMAL	Retrieves the normal image list, which contains the selected and unselected images for the tree view item.
TVSIL_STATE	Retrieves the state image list, which contains the images for tree view items that are in a user-defined state.

Returns	HIMAGELIST: The handle of the image list.
Include File	commctrl.h
Related Messages	TVM_GETIMAGELIST
Example	See the example for the TreeView_CreateDragImage macro.

TreeView_GetIndent   ■ Win32s   ■ Windows 95   ■ Windows NT

Description	TreeView_GetIndent is a macro that retrieves the number of pixels that the child items are indented in relation to the parent item.
Syntax	UINT **TreeView_GetIndent**(HWND *hwnd*)
Message Syntax	UINT **SendMessage**(*hwnd*, **TVM_GETINDENT**, 0, 0)
Parameters	
hwnd	HWND: The handle of the tree view control.
Returns	UINT: The number of pixels that the child items are indented in relation to the parent item.
Include File	commctrl.h
Related Messages	TVM_GETINDENT
Example	This example (Listing 7-5) allows the user to increase or decrease the indent that a child item has with respect to the parent item. As the user selects the Increase and Decrease Indent menu options, the indent is changed by a pixel using the TreeView_SetIndent macro.

Listing 7-5 Using the TreeView_GetIndent macro

```
LRESULT CALLBACK WndProc( HWND hWnd, UINT uMsg, WPARAM wParam, LPARAM lParam )
{
static HWND hTree = NULL;

    switch( uMsg )
    {
    case WM_COMMAND :
            switch( LOWORD( wParam ) )
            {
            case IDM_INCINDENT :
            case IDM_DECINDENT :
                    {
                        int nIndent;

                        // Get the first item in the tree.
                        //................................
                        nIndent = TreeView_GetIndent( hTree );

                        if ( LOWORD( wParam ) == IDM_INCINDENT )
                            nIndent++;
                        else
                            nIndent--;

                        TreeView_SetIndent( hTree, nIndent );
                    }
                    break;
```

.
.
.

TREEVIEW_GETISEARCHSTRING   ■ Win32s   ■ Windows 95   ■ Windows NT

Description	TreeView_GetISearchString is a macro that retrieves the incremental search string typed into a tree view control by the user. The system appends each character typed by the user to the search string and then uses the new string to search for the matching item. If a match is found, it is selected and scrolled into view. The search is not case sensitive.
Syntax	int **TreeView_GetISearchString**(HWND *hwnd*, LPSTR *lpsz*)
Message Syntax	int **SendMessage**(*hwnd*, **TVM_GETISEARCHSTRING**, 0, *lpsz*)
Parameters	
hwnd	HWND: The handle of the tree view control.
lpsz	LPSTR: A pointer to the buffer that receives the incremental search string.
Returns	int: The number of characters in the incremental search string, or zero if the tree view control is not in incremental search mode.
Include File	commctrl.h
Related Messages	TVM_GETISEARCHSTRING

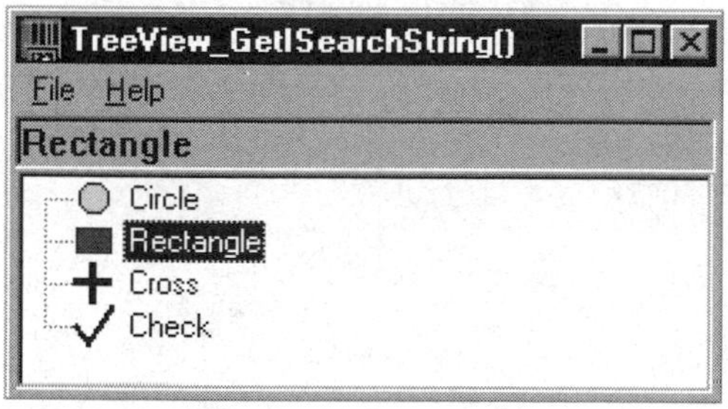

Figure 7-3 TreeView_GetISearchString example

Example

This example, shown in Figure 7-3 and Listing 7-6, demonstrates the tree view control's search capabilities. As the user types, the tree view searches for the incremental search string within the tree view's items. This example uses a timer to show the incremental search string as the user types.

Listing 7-6 Using the TreeView_GetISearchString macro

```
#define IMAGESIZE 16

LPCTSTR lpszData[4] = { "Circle", "Rectangle", "Cross", "Check" };

LRESULT CALLBACK WndProc( HWND hWnd, UINT uMsg, WPARAM wParam, LPARAM lParam )
{
static char szBuf[40];
static UINT uTimerID = 0;
static HWND hTree    = NULL;
static HWND hStatic  = NULL;

   switch( uMsg )
   {
     case WM_CREATE  :
             {
                 HIMAGELIST hImage;

                 InitCommonControls();

                 hImage = ImageList_Create( IMAGESIZE, IMAGESIZE,
                                     ILC_COLOR4 | ILC_MASK, 4, 1 );

                 hTree = CreateWindowEx( WS_EX_CLIENTEDGE, WC_TREEVIEW, "",
                                     WS_CHILD | WS_BORDER | WS_VISIBLE |
                                     WS_VSCROLL | TVS_HASLINES |
                                     TVS_HASBUTTONS | TVS_LINESATROOT |
                                     TVS_DISABLEDRAGDROP,
                                     10, 100, 100, 100,
                                     hWnd,
                                     (HMENU)1,
                                     hInst,
                                     NULL);
```

continued on next page

continued from previous page

```
                    hStatic = CreateWindowEx( WS_EX_CLIENTEDGE, "STATIC", "",
                                    WS_CHILD | WS_VISIBLE,
                                    0, 0, 100, 20,
                                    hWnd,
                                    (HMENU)2,
                                    hInst,
                                    NULL );

            if ( hTree )
            {
                int i;

                // Associate the image list with the tree view.
                //............................................
                TreeView_SetImageList( hTree, hImage, TVSIL_NORMAL );

                // Add the images to the tree view image list.
                //............................................
                for ( i=0; i<4; i++ )
                    ImageList_AddIcon( hImage, LoadIcon(hInst,lpszData[i]) );

                AddItemsToTree( hTree );
            }

            uTimerID = SetTimer( hWnd, 1, 500, NULL );
        }
        break;


    case WM_SIZE :
        if ( hStatic )
            MoveWindow( hStatic,0,0, LOWORD(lParam), 20, FALSE );

        if ( hTree )
            MoveWindow( hTree,0,20, LOWORD(lParam),
                                    HIWORD(lParam)-20, FALSE );
        break;


    case WM_TIMER :
        if ( wParam == uTimerID )
        {
            TreeView_GetISearchString( hTree, szBuf );
            SetWindowText( hStatic, szBuf );
        }
        break;


    case WM_COMMAND :
        switch( LOWORD( wParam ) )
        {
            case IDM_ABOUT :
                    DialogBox( hInst, "AboutBox", hWnd, (DLGPROC)About );
                    break;

            case IDM_EXIT :
                    DestroyWindow( hWnd );
                    break;
```

```
                }
                break;

        case WM_DESTROY :
                KillTimer( hWnd, uTimerID );

                if ( TreeView_GetImageList( hTree, TVSIL_NORMAL ) )
                    ImageList_Destroy( TreeView_GetImageList(hTree,TVSIL_NORMAL) );

                PostQuitMessage(0);
                break;

        default :
                return( DefWindowProc( hWnd, uMsg, wParam, lParam ) );
    }

    return( 0L );
}


VOID AddItemsToTree( HWND hTree )
{
    int             i;
    TV_INSERTSTRUCT tv;

    tv.hInsertAfter = TVI_LAST;
    tv.item.mask    = TVIF_TEXT | TVIF_IMAGE |
                      TVIF_SELECTEDIMAGE | TVIF_PARAM;

    // Add the items to the tree view.
    //.............................
    for ( i=0; i<4; i++ )
    {
        tv.hParent       = TVI_ROOT;
        tv.item.pszText = (LPTSTR)lpszData[i];
        tv.item.iImage  = i;
        tv.item.iSelectedImage = i;
        tv.item.lParam       = i;

        TreeView_InsertItem( hTree, &tv );
    }
}
```

TREEVIEW_GETITEM   ■ Win32s   ■ Windows 95   ■ Windows NT

Description	TreeView_GetItem is a macro that retrieves the attributes of a tree view control item.
Syntax	BOOL **TreeView_GetItem**(HWND *hwnd*, TV_ITEM * *pitem*)
Message Syntax	BOOL **SendMessage**(*hwnd*, **TVM_GETITEM**, 0, *pitem*)
Parameters	
hwnd	HWND: The handle of the tree view control.

pitem	TV_ITEM *: A pointer to a TV_ITEM structure whose *hitem* specifies the tree view item for which to retrieve information and whose *mask* member specifies the attributes to retrieve. If the value of the *mask* member is TVIF_TEXT, the *pszText* member must contain the pointer to the buffer that receives the item text, and the *cchTextMax* member must specify the size of the buffer. If the value of the *mask* member is TVIF_STATE, the *stateMask* member indicates which item states are to be returned. See the definition of the TV_ITEM structure below.
Returns	BOOL: If successful, TRUE is returned; otherwise, FALSE is returned.
Include File	commctrl.h
Related Messages	TVM_GETITEM

TV_ITEM Definition

```
typedef struct _TV_ITEM
{
    UINT        mask;
    HTREEITEM   hItem;
    UINT        state;
    UINT        stateMask;
    LPSTR       pszText;
    int         cchTextMax;
    int         iImage;
    int         iSelectedImage;
    int         cChildren;
    LPARAM      lParam;
} TV_ITEM, *LPTV_ITEM;
```

Members

mask	UINT: An array of flags that indicate which of the other structure members contain valid data or which are to be filled in. This member can be a combination of the values in Table 7-5.

Table 7-5 TreeView_GetItem TV_ITEM *mask* values

Value	Meaning
TVIF_CHILDREN	The *cChildren* member is valid.
TVIF_HANDLE	The *hItem* member is valid.
TVIF_IMAGE	The *iImage* member is valid.
TVIF_PARAM	The *lParam* member is valid.
TVIF_SELECTEDIMAGE	The *iSelectedImage* member is valid.
TVIF_STATE	The *state* and *stateMask* members are valid.
TVIF_TEXT	The *pszText* and *cchTextMax* members are valid.

hItem	HTREEITEM: The tree view control item to which this structure refers.
state	UINT: A variable specifying the current state of the tree view control item. This can be a combination of the values listed in Table 7-6.

Table 7-6 Tree view *state* values

Value	Meaning
TVIS_BOLD	The item is bold.
TVIS_CUT	The item is selected as part of a cut-and-paste operation.
TVIS_DROPHILITED	The item is selected as a drag-and-drop target.
TVIS_EXPANDED	The item's list of child items is currently expanded; that is, the child items are visible. This value applies only to parent items.
TVIS_EXPANDEDONCE	The item's list of child items has been expanded at least once. The TVN_ITEMEXPANDING and TVN_ITEMEXPANDED notification messages are not sent for parent items that have specified this value. This value applies only to parent items.
TVIS_FOCUSED	The item has the focus, so it is surrounded by a standard focus rectangle. Only one item can have the focus.
TVIS_OVERLAYMASK	The item's overlay image is included when the item is drawn. The index of the overlay image must be specified in the state member of the TV_ITEM structure by using the INDEXTOOVERLAYMASK macro. The overlay image must be added to the tree view's image list by using the ImageList_SetOverlayImage macro. This value should not be combined with any other value.
TVIS_SELECTED	The item is selected. The appearance of a selected item depends on whether it has the focus and on whether the system colors are used for selection.
TVIS_STATEIMAGEMASK	The item's state image is included when the item is drawn. The index of the state image must be specified in the state member of the TV_ITEM structure by using the INDEXTOSTATEIMAGEMASK macro. This value should not be combined with any other value.
TVIS_USERMASK	Same as TVIS_STATEIMAGEMASK.

stateMask   UINT: A variable specifying the valid states for the tree view control item. This can be a combination of one or more of the values listed in Table 7-6.

pszText   LPSTR: A pointer to a null-terminated string that contains the item text if the structure specifies item attributes. If the value of this member is LPSTR_TEXTCALLBACK, the parent window is responsible for storing the name. In this case, the tree view control sends the parent window a TVN_GETDISPINFO notification message when it needs the item text for displaying, sorting, or editing, and a TVN_SETDISPINFO notification message when the item text changes.

If the structure is receiving item attributes, *pszText* is the pointer to the buffer that receives the item text.

cchTextMax   int: The size of the buffer pointed to by the *pszText* member if the structure is receiving item attributes. If the structure specifies item attributes, this member is ignored.

iImage   int: Index of the icon image within the image list. If the value of either the *iImage* or the *iSelectedImage* member is I_IMAGECALLBACK, the parent window is responsible for storing the corresponding images. In this case, the tree view control sends the parent a TVN_GETDISPINFO notification message when it needs to display the images and a TVN_SETDISPINFO notification message when the images change.

iSelectedImage	int: Index of the selected icon image within the image list. If the value of either the *iImage* or the *iSelectedImage* member is I_IMAGECALLBACK, the parent window is responsible for storing the corresponding images. In this case, the tree view control sends the parent a TVN_GETDISPINFO notification message when it needs to display the images and a TVN_SETDISPINFO notification message when the images change.
cChildren	int: A flag indicating whether the item has associated child items. It is one if the item has one or more child items; otherwise, it is zero. If the value of *cChildren* is I_CHILDRENCALLBACK, the parent window is responsible for drawing the child items. In this case, the tree view control sends the parent a TVN_GETDISPINFO notification message when it needs to display the child items and a TVN_SETDISPINFO notification message when the attributes of a child item change.
lParam	LPARAM: A 32-bit application-defined value to associate with the item.
Example	See the example for the TreeView_CreateDragImage macro.

TreeView_GetItemRect   ■ Win32s ■ Windows 95 ■ Windows NT

Description	TreeView_GetItemRect is a macro that determines the coordinates of the bounding rectangle for the specified tree view item if the item is visible.
Syntax	BOOL **TreeView_GetItemRect**(HWND *hwnd*, HTREEITEM *hitem*, RECT * *prc*, BOOL *bItemRect*)
Message Syntax	BOOL **SendMessage**(*hwnd*, **TVM_GETITEMRECT**, *bItemRect*, *prc*)
Parameters	
hwnd	HWND: The handle of the tree view control.
hitem	HTREEITEM: The handle of the item whose bounding rectangle coordinates should be retrieved.
prc	RECT *: A pointer to a RECT structure that receives the coordinates of the bounding rectangle for the specified item relative to the upper left corner of the tree view control. See the definition of the RECT structure below.
bItemRect	BOOL: If set to TRUE, only the coordinates of the bounding rectangle for the item text are retrieved; otherwise, the coordinates for the entire line the item occupies are retrieved.
Returns	BOOL: If the item is visible and the coordinates are retrieved, TRUE is returned; otherwise, FALSE is returned and the coordinates are not retrieved.
Include File	commctrl.h

Related Messages	TVM_GETITEMRECT
Example	See the example for the TreeView_CreateDragImage macro.

TREEVIEW_GETNEXTITEM ■ Win32s ■ Windows 95 ■ Windows NT

Description	TreeView_GetNextItem is a macro that retrieves the handle of the tree view item with the indicated relationship to the specified item.
Syntax	HTREEITEM **TreeView_GetNextItem**(HWND *hwnd*, HTREEITEM *hitem*, UINT *flag*)
Message Syntax	HTREEITEM **SendMessage**(*hwnd*, **TVM_GETNEXTITEM**, *flag*, *hitem*)
Parameters	
hwnd	HWND: The handle of the tree view control.
hitem	HTREEITEM: The handle of the tree view control item.
flag	UINT: The relationship to the specified item of the item to retrieve. This parameter can be one of the values in Table 7-7.

Table 7-7 TreeView_GetNextItem *flag* values

Value	Meaning
TVGN_CARET	Retrieves the handle of the currently selected item.
TVGN_CHILD	Retrieves the handle of the first child item. The *hitem* parameter must be the handle of the parent tree view item.
TVGN_DROPHILITE	Retrieves the handle of the item that is the target of a drag-and-drop operation.
TVGN_FIRSTVISIBLE	Retrieves the handle of the first visible item.
TVGN_NEXT	Retrieves the handle of the next sibling item.
TVGN_NEXTVISIBLE	Retrieves the handle of the next visible item that follows the specified item. The specified item must be visible. Use the TVM_GETITEMRECT message to determine whether an item is visible.
TVGN_PARENT	Retrieves the handle of the parent of the specified item.
TVGN_PREVIOUS	Retrieves the handle of the previous sibling item.
TVGN_PREVIOUSVISIBLE	Retrieves the handle of the first visible item that precedes the specified item. The specified item must be visible. Use the TVM_GETITEMRECT message to determine whether an item is visible.
TVGN_ROOT	Retrieves the handle of the topmost or very first item of the tree view control.

Returns	HTREEITEM: If successful, the handle of the tree view item is returned; otherwise, NULL is returned.
Include File	commctrl.h
See Also	TreeView_GetChild, TreeView_GetDropHilite, TreeView_GetFirstVisible, TreeView_GetNextSibling, TreeView_GetNextVisible, TreeView_GetParent, TreeView_GetPrevSibling, TreeView_GetPrevVisible, TreeView_GetRoot, TreeView_GetSelection

Related Messages	TVM_GETITEMRECT
Example	See the examples for the individual related macros that correspond to the *flag* values. The usage is identical to the individual macros with the exception of the additional *flag* parameter.

TREEVIEW_GETNEXTSIBLING ■ Win32s ■ Windows 95 ■ Windows NT

Description	TreeView_GetNextSibling is a macro that retrieves the handle of the next sibling item to the specified tree view item. Sibling items are child items with the same parent item. They appear at the same level within the tree view indented under the same parent item.
Syntax	HTREEITEM **TreeView_GetNextSibling** (HWND *hwnd*, HTREEITEM *hitem*)
Message Syntax	HTREEITEM **SendMessage**(*hwnd*, **TVM_GETNEXTITEM**,TVGN_NEXT, *hitem*)
Parameters	
hwnd	HWND: The handle of the tree view control.
hitem	HTREEITEM: The handle of the tree view control item for which to retrieve the next sibling item.
Returns	HTREEITEM: If successful, the handle of the next sibling tree view item is returned; otherwise, NULL is returned.
Include File	commctrl.h
See Also	TreeView_GetPrevSibling, TreeView_GetNextItem
Related Messages	TVM_GETITEMRECT
Example	See the example for the TreeView_CreateDragImage macro.

TREEVIEW_GETNEXTVISIBLE ■ Win32s ■ Windows 95 ■ Windows NT

Description	TreeView_GetNextVisible is a macro that retrieves the handle of the next visible tree view item after the specified item. The specified item must be visible. Use the TreeView_GetItemRect macro or the TVM_GETITEMRECT message to make sure the specified item is visible before using this macro.
Syntax	HTREEITEM **TreeView_GetNextVisible**(HWND *hwnd*, HTREEITEM *hitem*)
Message Syntax	HTREEITEM **SendMessage**(*hwnd*, **TVM_GETNEXTITEM**, TVGN_NEXTVISIBLE, *hitem*)
Parameters	
hwnd	HWND: The handle of the tree view control.
hitem	HTREEITEM: The handle of the visible tree view item to use as the starting point when retrieving the next visible item.

Returns	HTREEITEM: If another visible item exists, the handle of the next visible tree view item is returned; otherwise, NULL is returned.
Include File	commctrl.h
See Also	TreeView_GetPrevVisible, TreeView_GetNextItem
Related Messages	TVM_GETITEMRECT
Example	See the example for the TreeView_GetCount macro.

TREEVIEW_GETPARENT　　　　　■ Win32s　■ Windows 95　■ Windows NT

Description	TreeView_GetParent is a macro that retrieves the handle of the parent item for the specified tree view item.
Syntax	HTREEITEM **TreeView_GetParent**(HWND *hwnd*, HTREEITEM *hitem*)
Message Syntax	HTREEITEM **SendMessage**(*hwnd*, **TVM_GETNEXTITEM**, TVGN_PARENT, *hitem*)
Parameters	
hwnd	HWND: The handle of the tree view control.
hitem	HTREEITEM: The handle of the tree view item for which to retrieve the parent item.
Returns	HTREEITEM: If the item has a parent, the handle of the parent tree view item is returned; otherwise, NULL is returned.
Include File	commctrl.h
See Also	TreeView_GetChild, TreeView_GetNextItem
Related Messages	TVM_GETITEMRECT
Example	See the example for the TreeView_CreateDragImage macro.

TREEVIEW_GETPREVSIBLING　　　■ Win32s　■ Windows 95　■ Windows NT

Description	TreeView_GetPrevSibling is a macro that retrieves the handle of the previous sibling item relative to the specified tree view item. Sibling items are child items with the same parent item. They appear at the same level within the tree view indented under the same parent item.
Syntax	HTREEITEM **TreeView_GetPrevSibling**(HWND *hwnd*, HTREEITEM *hitem*)
Message Syntax	HTREEITEM **SendMessage**(*hwnd*, **TVM_GETNEXTITEM**, TVGN_PREVIOUS, *hitem*)
Parameters	
hwnd	HWND: The handle of the tree view control.
hitem	HTREEITEM: The handle of the tree view control item for which to retrieve the previous sibling.

Returns	HTREEITEM: If a previous sibling exists, the handle of the previous sibling tree view item is returned; otherwise, NULL is returned.
Include File	commctrl.h
See Also	TreeView_GetNextSibling, TreeView_GetNextItem
Related Messages	TVM_GETITEMRECT
Example	See the example for the TreeView_CreateDragImage macro. Although this macro is not used in this example, the usage is identical to the TreeView_GetNextSibling macro.

TREEVIEW_GETPREVVISIBLE   ■ Win32s ■ Windows 95 ■ Windows NT

Description	TreeView_GetPrevVisible is a macro that retrieves the handle of the first visible tree view item that precedes the specified item. The specified item must be visible. Use either the TreeView_GetItemRect macro or the TVM_GETITEMRECT message to verify that the item is visible prior to using the TreeView_GetPrevVisible macro.
Syntax	HTREEITEM **TreeView_GetPrevVisible**(HWND *hwnd*, HTREEITEM *hitem*)
Message Syntax	HTREEITEM **SendMessage**(*hwnd*, **TVM_GETNEXTITEM**, TVGN_FIRSTVISIBLE, *hitem*)
Parameters	
hwnd	HWND: The handle of the tree view control.
hitem	HTREEITEM: The handle of the visible tree view item to use as the starting point when retrieving the previous visible item.
Returns	HTREEITEM: If a visible item exists previous to the given item, the handle of the previous tree view item is returned; otherwise, NULL is returned.
Include File	commctrl.h
See Also	TreeView_GetNextVisible, TreeView_GetNextItem
Related Messages	TVM_GETITEMRECT
Example	See the example for the TreeView_GetCount macro.

TREEVIEW_GETROOT   ■ Win32s ■ Windows 95 ■ Windows NT

Description	TreeView_GetRoot is a macro that retrieves the handle of the first or top item in the specified tree view control. This is the first item in the tree view.
Syntax	HTREEITEM **TreeView_GetRoot**(HWND *hwnd*)
Message Syntax	HTREEITEM **SendMessage**(*hwnd*, **TVM_GETNEXTITEM**, TVGN_ROOT, 0)
Parameters	
hwnd	HWND: The handle of the tree view control.

Returns	HTREEITEM: If successful, the handle of the first tree view item is returned; otherwise, NULL is returned.
Include File	commctrl.h
See Also	TreeView_GetNextItem
Related Messages	TVM_GETITEMRECT
Example	See the example for the TreeView_EnsureVisible macro.

TREEVIEW_GETSELECTION ■ Win32s ■ Windows 95 ■ Windows NT

Description	TreeView_GetSelection is a macro that retrieves the handle of the item that is currently selected in the specified tree view control.
Syntax	HTREEITEM **TreeView_GetSelection**(HWND *hwnd*)
Message Syntax	HTREEITEM **SendMessage**(*hwnd*, **TVM_GETNEXTITEM**, TVGN_CARET, 0)
Parameters	
hwnd	HWND: The handle of the tree view control.
Returns	HTREEITEM: If a tree view item is selected, the handle of the selected tree view item is returned; otherwise, NULL is returned.
Include File	commctrl.h
See Also	TreeView_GetNextItem, TreeView_SelectItem
Related Messages	TVM_GETITEMRECT
Example	See the example for the TreeView_EditLabel macro.

TREEVIEW_GETVISIBLECOUNT ■ Win32s ■ Windows 95 ■ Windows NT

Description	TreeView_GetVisibleCount is a macro that determines the number of fully visible items in the client window of the specified tree view control.
Syntax	UINT **TreeView_GetVisibleCount**(HWND *hwnd*)
Message Syntax	UINT **SendMessage**(*hwnd*, **TVM_GETVISIBLECOUNT**, 0,0)
Parameters	
hwnd	HWND: The handle of the tree view control.
Returns	UINT: The number of items fully visible in the client window is returned.
Include File	commctrl.h
Related Messages	TVM_GETVISIBLECOUNT
Example	See the example for the TreeView_GetCount macro.

TREEVIEW_HITTEST ■ Win32s ■ Windows 95 ■ Windows NT

Description	TreeView_HitTest is a macro that determines which tree view item is at the specified location.
Syntax	HTREEITEM **TreeView_HitTest**(HWND *hwnd*, LPTV_HITTESTINFO *lpht*)

Message Syntax	HTREEITEM **SendMessage**(*hwnd*, **TVM_HITTEST**, *hwnd*, *lpht*)
Parameters	
hwnd	HWND: The handle of the tree view control.
lpht	LPTV_HITTESTINFO: A pointer to a TV_HITTESTINFO structure whose *pt* member specifies the coordinates of the point to test. When the macro is finished, the *hitem* member contains the handle of the item at the specified point, or NULL if there is not a tree view item at that point. The *flags* member indicates the location of the specified point. See the description of the TV_HITTESTINFO structure.
Returns	HTREEITEM: The handle of the tree view item at the specified point is returned; otherwise, NULL is returned if a tree view item does not exist at that point.
Include File	commctrl.h
Related Messages	TVM_HITTEST
Example	See the example for the TreeView_CreateDragImage macro.

TreeView_InsertItem ■ Win32s ■ Windows 95 ■ Windows NT

Description	TreeView_InsertItem is a macro that adds a new item to the specified tree view control. The location of the new item is determined by the *hInsertAfter* member of the TV_INSERTSTRUCT structure passed to the macro. If the label of the tree view control item is being edited, the operation is canceled and the parent window receives the TVN_ENDLABELEDIT notification message.
Syntax	HTREEITEM **TreeView_InsertItem**(HWND *hwnd*, LPTV_INSERTSTRUCT *lpis*)
Message Syntax	HTREEITEM **SendMessage**(*hwnd*, **TVM_INSERTITEM**, 0, *lpis*)
Parameters	
hwnd	HWND: The handle of the tree view control.
lpis	LPTV_INSERTSTRUCT: A pointer to a TV_INSERTSTRUCT structure that contains the attributes of the new item to add to the specified tree view control. See the definition of the TV_INSERTSTRUCT structure below.
Returns	HTREEITEM: If successful, the handle of the new tree view item is returned; otherwise, NULL is returned.
Include File	commctrl.h
Related Messages	TVM_GETITEMRECT, TVM_INSERTITEM, TVN_ENDLABELEDIT

TV_INSERTSTRUCT Definition

```
typedef struct _TV_INSERTSTRUCT
{
  HTREEITEM hParent;
  HTREEITEM hInsertAfter;
  TV_ITEM   item;
} TV_INSERTSTRUCT, *LPTV_INSERTSTRUCT;
```

Members

hParent   HTREEITEM: The handle of the parent item. If the value of *hParent* is either TVI_ROOT or NULL, the new item is inserted at the root of the tree view control.

hInsertAfter   HTREEITEM: If *hInsertAfter* is the handle of an item, the new item should be inserted after the specified item; otherwise, it should be inserted based on one of the values in Table 7-8.

Table 7-8 TreeView_InsertItem TV_INSERTSTRUCT *hInsertAfter* values

Value	Meaning
TVI_FIRST	Inserts the item at the beginning of the list.
TVI_LAST	Inserts the item at the end of the list.
TVI_SORT	Inserts the item into the list in alphabetical order.

item   TV_ITEM: A TV_ITEM structure containing information about the item to add. See the definition of the TV_ITEM structure under the TreeView_GetItem macro.

Example   See the example for the TreeView_CreateDragImage macro.

TreeView_Select   ■ Win32s ■ Windows 95 ■ Windows NT

Description   TreeView_Select is a macro that selects the specified tree view item and makes sure the item is visible by using the display option specified by the *flag* parameter.

Syntax   BOOL **TreeView_Select**(HWND *hwnd*, HTREEITEM *hitem*, int *flag*)

Message Syntax BOOL **SendMessage**(*hwnd*, **TVM_SELECTITEM**, *flag*, *hitem*)

Parameters

hwnd   HWND: The handle of the tree view control.

hitem   HTREEITEM: The handle of the tree view control item. If *hitem* is NULL, the selection is removed from the currently selected item.

flag   int: The type of display option to use when selecting the specified item. This parameter can be one of the values in Table 7-9.

Table 7-9 TreeView_Select *flag* values

Value	Meaning
TVGN_CARET	Sets the selection to the specified item.
TVGN_DROPHILITE	Redraws the specified tree view item in the style used to indicate the target of a drag-and-drop operation.
TVGN_FIRSTVISIBLE	Scrolls the tree view vertically so that the specified item is the first visible item in the list.

Returns	BOOL: If successful, TRUE is returned; otherwise, FALSE is returned.
Include File	commctrl.h
See Also	TreeView_SelectDropTarget, TreeView_SelectItem, TreeView_SelectSetFirstVisible
Related Messages	TVM_SELECTITEM
Example	See the individual related macros for the appropriate *flag* values. The usage of the individual related macros is identical except for the additional *flag* parameter.

TreeView_SelectDropTarget   ■ Win32s ■ Windows 95 ■ Windows NT

Description	TreeView_SelectDropTarget is a macro that redraws the specified tree view item to indicate that it was the target of a drag-and-drop operation. This macro is the same as TreeView_Select with the TVGN_DROPHILITE flag.
Syntax	BOOL **TreeView_SelectDropTarget**(HWND *hwnd*, HTREEITEM *hitem*)
Message Syntax	BOOL **SendMessage**(*hwnd*, **TVM_SELECTITEM**, TVGN_DROPHILITE, *hitem*)
Parameters	
hwnd	HWND: The handle of the tree view control.
hitem	HTREEITEM: The handle of the tree view control item. If *hitem* is NULL, the selection is removed from the currently selected item.
Returns	BOOL: If successful, TRUE is returned; otherwise, FALSE is returned.
Include File	commctrl.h
See Also	TreeView_Select
Related Messages	TVM_SELECTITEM
Example	See the example for the TreeView_CreateDragImage macro.

TreeView_SelectItem   ■ Win32s ■ Windows 95 ■ Windows NT

Description	TreeView_SelectItem is a macro that selects the specified tree view item. This macro is the same as TreeView_Select with the TVGN_CARET flag.
Syntax	BOOL **TreeView_SelectItem**(HWND *hwnd*, HTREEITEM *hitem*)

Message Syntax	BOOL **SendMessage**(*hwnd*, **TVM_SELECTITEM**, TVGN_CARET, *hitem*)
Parameters	
hwnd	HWND: The handle of the tree view control.
hitem	HTREEITEM: The handle of the tree view control item. If *hitem* is NULL, the selection is removed from the currently selected item.
Returns	BOOL: If successful, TRUE is returned; otherwise, FALSE is returned.
Include File	commctrl.h
See Also	TreeView_Select
Related Messages	TVM_SELECTITEM
Example	See the example for the TreeView_EnsureVisible macro.

TREEVIEW_SELECTSETFIRSTVISIBLE ■ Win32s ■ Windows 95 ■ Windows NT

Description	TreeView_SelectSetFirstVisible is a macro that scrolls the list until the specified tree view item is the first visible item.
Syntax	BOOL **TreeView_SelectSetFirstVisible**(HWND *hwnd*, HTREEITEM *hitem*)
Message Syntax	BOOL **SendMessage**(*hwnd*, **TVM_SELECTITEM**, TVGN_FIRSTVISI-BLE, *hitem*)
Parameters	
hwnd	HWND: The handle of the tree view control.
hitem	HTREEITEM: The handle of the tree view control item. If *hitem* is NULL, the selection is removed from the currently selected item.
Returns	BOOL: If successful, TRUE is returned; otherwise, FALSE is returned.
Include File	commctrl.h
See Also	TreeView_Select
Related Messages	TVM_SELECTITEM
Example	See the example for the TreeView_GetCount macro.

TREEVIEW_SETIMAGELIST ■ Win32s ■ Windows 95 ■ Windows NT

Description	TreeView_SetImageList is a macro that sets the normal or the state image list for the specified tree view control and then redraws the control using the new images.
Syntax	HIMAGELIST **TreeView_SetImageList**(HWND *hwnd*, HIMAGELIST *himl*, int *nImageList*)
Message Syntax	HIMAGELIST **SendMessage**(*hwnd*, **TVM_GETIMAGELIST**, *nImageList*, *himl*)
Parameters	
hwnd	HWND: The handle of the tree view control.

himl	HIMAGELIST: The handle of the image list.
nImageList	int: The type of image list to set. This parameter can be one of the values in Table 7-4.
Returns	HIMAGELIST: The handle of the previous image list is returned, if one exists; otherwise, NULL is returned.
Include File	commctrl.h
Related Messages	TVM_SETIMAGELIST
Example	See the example for the TreeView_CreateDragImage macro.

TREEVIEW_SETINDENT ■ Win32s ■ Windows 95 ■ Windows NT

Description	TreeView_SetIndent is a macro that sets the number of pixels that the tree view control is indented and redraws the control to reflect the new indentation width.
Syntax	BOOL **TreeView_SetIndent**(HWND *hwnd*, int *indent*)
Message Syntax	BOOL **SendMessage**(*hwnd*, **TVM_SETINDENT**, *indent*, 0)
Parameters	
hwnd	HWND: The handle of the tree view control.
indent	int: The number of pixels to indent the tree view control. If the value of *indent* is less than the system-defined minimum width, the new width of the control is the system-defined value.
Include File	commctrl.h
Related Messages	TVM_SETINDENT
Example	See the example for the TreeView_GetIndent macro.

TREEVIEW_SETITEM ■ Win32s ■ Windows 95 ■ Windows NT

Description	TreeView_SetItem is a macro that sets the attributes for the specified tree view item.
Syntax	BOOL **TreeView_SetItem**(HWND *hwnd*, TV_ITEM * *pitem*)
Message Syntax	BOOL **SendMessage**(*hwnd*, **TVM_SETITEM**, 0, *pitem*)
Parameters	
hwnd	HWND: The handle of the tree view control.
pitem	TV_ITEM *: A pointer to a TV_ITEM structure that contains the new attributes for the tree view item. The *hitem* member of the structure identifies the item whose attributes should be set, and the *mask* member identifies the attributes to set for the item. If the value of the *mask* member is TVIF_TEXT, the *pszText* member is a pointer to a null-terminated string and the *cchTextMax* member is ignored. If the value of the *mask* member is TVIF_STATE, the *stateMask* member identifies the item's states to change

and the *state* member contains the new state values. See the definition of the TV_ITEM structure under the TreeView_GetItem macro.

Returns	BOOL: If successful, zero is returned; otherwise, -1 is returned.
Include File	commctrl.h
Related Messages	TVM_SETITEM
Example	See the example for the TreeView_EditLabel macro.

TreeView_SortChildren   ■ Win32s   ■ Windows 95   ■ Windows NT

Description	TreeView_SortChildren is a macro that sorts the child items of the specified parent item in the tree view control. The sort is ascending and alphabetic. If the application requires a different sort, use the TreeView_SortChildrenCB macro.
Syntax	BOOL **TreeView_SortChildren**(HWND *hwnd*, HTREEITEM *hitem*, int *nRecurse*)
Message Syntax	BOOL **SendMessage**(*hwnd*, **TVM_SORTCHILDREN**, *nRecurse*, *hitem*)
Parameters	
hwnd	HWND: The handle of the tree view control.
hitem	HTREEITEM: The handle of the parent item of child items to be sorted. Set to NULL to sort the top-level tree view items.
nRecurse	int: This parameter is reserved for future use and must be zero.
Returns	BOOL: If successful, TRUE is returned; otherwise, FALSE is returned.
Include File	commctrl.h
Related Messages	TVM_SORTCHILDREN
Example	This example (Listing 7-7) demonstrates both methods of sorting tree view items. The first method sorts by the item label in an ascending order based on alphanumeric precedence. When the user selects the Sort Alpha menu option, the TreeView_SortChildren macro is used to perform an alphanumeric sort. The second sort method sorts the items based on the numeric order in which the items were added to the list. The *lParam* value of each item is set to the integer order in which the item was added to the list. When the user selects the Sort Numeric menu option, the TreeView_SortChildrenCB macro is used to sort the items. The SortCompare() function compares the two *lParam* values and returns the appropriate value.

Listing 7-7 Using the TreeView_SortChildren macro

```
#define IMAGESIZE 16

LPCTSTR lpszData[4] = { "Circle", "Rectangle", "Cross", "Check" };

LRESULT CALLBACK WndProc( HWND hWnd, UINT uMsg, WPARAM wParam, LPARAM lParam )
```

continued on next page

continued from previous page

```
{
static HWND hTree = NULL;

    switch( uMsg )
    {
        case WM_CREATE   :
                {
                    HIMAGELIST hImage;

                    InitCommonControls();

                    hImage = ImageList_Create( IMAGESIZE, IMAGESIZE,
                                            ILC_COLOR4 | ILC_MASK, 4, 1 );

                    hTree = CreateWindowEx( WS_EX_CLIENTEDGE, WC_TREEVIEW, "",
                                            WS_CHILD | WS_BORDER | WS_VISIBLE |
                                            WS_VSCROLL | TVS_HASLINES |
                                            TVS_HASBUTTONS | TVS_LINESATROOT |
                                            TVS_DISABLEDRAGDROP,
                                            10, 100, 100, 100,
                                            hWnd,
                                            (HMENU)1,
                                            hInst,
                                            NULL);

                    if ( hTree )
                    {
                        int i;

                        // Associate the image list with the tree view.
                        //...............................................
                        TreeView_SetImageList( hTree, hImage, TVSIL_NORMAL );

                        // Add the images to the tree view image list.
                        //...............................................
                        for ( i=0; i<4; i++ )
                            ImageList_AddIcon( hImage, LoadIcon(hInst,lpszData[i]) );

                        AddItemsToTree( hTree );
                    }
                }
                break;

        case WM_SIZE :
                if ( hTree )
                    MoveWindow( hTree,0,0, LOWORD(lParam), HIWORD(lParam), FALSE );
                break;

        case WM_COMMAND :
                switch( LOWORD( wParam ) )
                {
                    case IDM_SORTALPHA :
                            TreeView_SortChildren( hTree, NULL, 0 );
                            break;

                    case IDM_SORTNUMERIC :
```

```
                        {
                            TV_SORTCB tvs;

                            tvs.hParent      = NULL;
                            tvs.lpfnCompare  = SortCompare;
                            tvs.lParam       = 0;

                            TreeView_SortChildrenCB( hTree, &tvs, 0 );
                        }
                        break;

                    case IDM_EXIT :
                            DestroyWindow( hWnd );
                            break;
                }
                break;

         .
         .
         .

int CALLBACK SortCompare( LPARAM lParam1, LPARAM lParam2, LPARAM lParamSort )
{
    if ( lParam1 < lParam2 )
        return( -1 );

    if ( lParam1 > lParam2 )
        return( 1 );

    return( 0 );
}


VOID AddItemsToTree( HWND hTree )
{
    char              szBuf[40];
    int               i;
    TV_INSERTSTRUCT tv;

    tv.hInsertAfter = TVI_LAST;
    tv.item.mask    = TVIF_TEXT | TVIF_IMAGE |
                      TVIF_SELECTEDIMAGE | TVIF_PARAM;

    // Add the items to the tree view.
    //...............................
    for ( i=0; i<4; i++ )
    {
        wsprintf( szBuf, "%s [%d]", lpszData[i], i+1 );

        tv.hParent        = TVI_ROOT;
        tv.item.pszText = szBuf;
        tv.item.iImage  = i;
        tv.item.iSelectedImage = i;
        tv.item.lParam         = i+1;

        TreeView_InsertItem( hTree, &tv );
    }
}
```

TREEVIEW_SORTCHILDRENCB ■ Win32s ■ Windows 95 ■ Windows NT

Description	TreeView_SortChildrenCB is a macro that sorts the tree view control items by using an application-defined callback function to compare the relative order of two items.
Syntax	BOOL **TreeView_SortChildrenCB**(HWND *hwnd*, LPTV_SORTCB *psort*, int *nRecurse*)
Message Syntax	BOOL **SendMessage**(*hwnd*, **TVM_SORTCHILDRENCB**, *nRecurse*, *psort*)

Parameters

hwnd	HWND: The handle of the tree view control.
psort	LPTV_SORTCB: A pointer to a TV_SORTCB structure whose *lpfnCompare* member is a pointer to the application-defined callback function that compares the relative order of two items during the sort operation. See the definition of the TV_SORTCB structure below.
nRecurse	int: This parameter is reserved for future use and must be zero.
Returns	BOOL: If successful, TRUE is returned; otherwise, FALSE is returned.
Include File	commctrl.h
Related Messages	TVM_SORTCHILDREN

TV_SORTCB Definition

```
typedef struct _TV_SORTCB
{
    HTREEITEM     hParent;
    PFNTVCOMPARE  lpfnCompare;
    LPARAM        lParam;
} TV_SORTCB, *LPTV_SORTCB;
```

Members

hParent	HTREEITEM: The handle to the parent item.
lpfnCompare	PFNTVCOMPARE: A pointer to an application-defined callback function, called during a sort operation to compare the relative order of two list items. See the definition of the callback function below.
lParam	LPARAM: An application-defined 32-bit value.
Callback Syntax	int CALLBACK **CompareFunc**(LPARAM *lParam1*, LPARAM *lParam2*, LPARAM *lParamSort*)

Callback Parameters

lParam1	LPARAM: The *lParam* value of the first item to compare.
lParam2	LPARAM: The *lParam* value of the second item to compare.
lParamSort	LPARAM: The *lParam* value used with the TreeView_SortChildrenCB macro in the TV_SORTCB structure.
Callback Returns	int: A negative value if the first item should precede the second, a positive value if the first item should follow the second, or zero if the two items are equal.
Example	See the example for the TreeView_SortChildren macro.

TVN_BEGINDRAG

■ Win32s ■ Windows 95 ■ Windows NT

Description
TVN_BEGINDRAG is a notification message that notifies the parent window of a tree view control that the left mouse button initiated a drag-and-drop operation. This notification message is sent in the form of a WM_NOTIFY message. This message is not sent if the tree view control has the TVS_DISABLEDRAGDROP style.

Parameters

lParam
NM_TREEVIEW *: A pointer to an NM_TREEVIEW structure whose *itemNew* member is a TV_ITEM structure containing information about the item being dragged in the *hItem*, *state*, and *lParam* members. The *ptDrag* member specifies the current screen coordinates of the mouse. See the definition of the NM_TREEVIEW structure below. See the definition of the TV_ITEM structure under the TreeView_GetItem macro.

Include File
commctrl.h

Related Messages
WM_NOTIFY

NM_TREEVIEW Definition

```
typedef struct _NM_TREEVIEW
{
    NMHDR      hdr;
    UINT       action;
    TV_ITEM    itemOld;
    TV_ITEM    itemNew;
    POINT      ptDrag;
} NM_TREEVIEW;
typedef NM_TREEVIEW *LPNM_TREEVIEW;
```

Members

hdr
NMHDR: This member is required for all WM_NOTIFY messages.

action
UINT: The notification-specific action flag.

itemOld
TV_ITEM: The address of a TV_ITEM structure containing information about the old item state. This member is zero for notification messages that do not use it.

itemNew
TV_ITEM: The address of TV_ITEM structures that contain information about the new item state. This member is zero for notification messages that do not use it.

ptDrag
POINT: The client coordinates of the mouse when the event occurred that is responsible for the notification message.

Example
See the example for the TreeView_CreateDragImage macro.

TVN_BEGINLABELEDIT

■ Win32s ■ Windows 95 ■ Windows NT

Description
TVN_BEGINLABELEDIT is a notification message that notifies the parent window of a tree view control of the initiation of label editing for an item. This notification message is sent in the form of a WM_NOTIFY message.

Parameters

lParam   TV_DISPINFO *: A pointer to a TV_DISPINFO structure whose *item*
                    member is a TV_ITEM structure containing information about the item
                    being edited in the *hItem*, *state*, *lParam*, and *pszText* members. See the
                    definition of the TV_DISPINFO structure below. See the definition of
                    the TV_ITEM structure under the TreeView_GetItem macro.

Returns   BOOL: TRUE is returned to cancel label editing.

Include File   commctrl.h

Related Messages WM_NOTIFY

TV_DISPINFO Definition

```
typedef struct _TV_DISPINFO
{
    NMHDR   hdr;
    TV_ITEM item;
} TV_DISPINFO;
```

Members

hdr   NMHDR: This member is required for all WM_NOTIFY messages.

item   TV_ITEM: A TV_ITEM structure that identifies and contains information
                    about the specified tree view item.

Example   See the example for the TreeView_EditLabel macro.

TVN_BEGINRDRAG   ■ Win32s   ■ Windows 95   ■ Windows NT

Description   TVN_BEGINRDRAG is a notification message that notifies the parent
                    window of a tree view control that the right mouse button initiated a drag-
                    and-drop operation. This notification message is sent in the form of a
                    WM_NOTIFY message.

Parameters

lParam   NM_TREEVIEW *: A pointer to an NM_TREEVIEW structure whose
                    itemNew member is a TV_ITEM structure containing information in the
                    hItem, *state*, and *lParam* members about the item to be dragged. The
                    ptDrag member specifies the current screen coordinates of the mouse.
                    See the definition of the NM_TREEVIEW structure under the
                    TVN_BEGINDRAG message. See the definition of the TV_ITEM
                    structure under the TreeView_GetItem macro.

Include File   commctrl.h

Related Messages WM_NOTIFY

Example   See the example for the TreeView_CreateDragImage macro. The usage
                    of this notification is identical to the TVN_BEGINDRAG notification
                    message.

TVN_DELETEITEM ■ Win32s ■ Windows 95 ■ Windows NT

Description   TVN_DELETEITEM is a notification message that notifies the parent window of a tree view control when an item is deleted. This notification message is sent in the form of a WM_NOTIFY message.

Parameters

lParam   NM_TREEVIEW *: A pointer to an NM_TREEVIEW structure whose *itemOld* member is a TV_ITEM structure containing information about the deleted item in the *hItem* and *lParam* members. See the definition of the NM_TREEVIEW structure under the TVN_BEGINDRAG message. See the definition of the TV_ITEM structure under the TreeView_GetItem macro.

Include File   commctrl.h

Related Messages   WM_NOTIFY

TVN_ENDLABELEDIT ■ Win32s ■ Windows 95 ■ Windows NT

Description   TVN_ENDLABELEDIT is a notification message that notifies the parent window of a tree view control that label editing for an item has ended. This notification message is sent in the form of a WM_NOTIFY message.

Parameters

lParam   TV_DISPINFO *: A pointer to a TV_DISPINFO structure whose *item* member is a TV_ITEM structure containing information about the edited item in the *hItem*, *lParam*, and *pszText* members. If label editing was canceled, the *pszText* member is zero. See the definition of the TV_DISPINFO structure under the TVN_BEGINLABELEDIT message. See the definition of the TV_ITEM structure under the TreeView_GetItem macro.

Include File   commctrl.h

Related Messages   WM_NOTIFY

Example   See the example for the TreeView_EditLabel macro.

TVN_GETDISPINFO ■ Win32s ■ Windows 95 ■ Windows NT

Description   TVN_GETDISPINFO is a notification message that requests the necessary information from the parent window of a tree view control to either display or sort an item. This notification message is sent in the form of a WM_NOTIFY message.

Parameters

lParam   TV_DISPINFO *: A pointer to a TV_DISPINFO structure whose *item* member is a TV_ITEM structure containing the required information in

the *hItem*, *lParam*, and *pszText* members. See the definition of the
TV_DISPINFO structure under the TVN_BEGINLABELEDIT message. See
the definition of the TV_ITEM structure under the TreeView_GetItem
macro.

Include File   commctrl.h
Related Messages   WM_NOTIFY

TVN_ITEMEXPANDED ■ Win32s ■ Windows 95 ■ Windows NT

Description   TVN_ITEMEXPANDED is a notification message that notifies the parent
window of a tree view control that the list of child items has either
expanded or collapsed. This notification message is sent in the form of a
WM_NOTIFY message.

Parameters

lParam   NM TREEVIEW *: A pointer to an NM_TREEVIEW structure whose
itemNew member is a TV_ITEM structure containing information about the
parent item in the *hItem*, *state*, and *lParam* members. The *action* member
indicates whether the list expanded or collapsed. See the definition of the
NM_TREEVIEW structure under the TVN_BEGINDRAG message. See the
definition of the TV_ITEM structure under the TreeView_GetItem macro.

Include File   commctrl.h
Related Messages   WM_NOTIFY

TVN_ITEMEXPANDING ■ Win32s ■ Windows 95 ■ Windows NT

Description   TVN_ITEMEXPANDING is a notification message that notifies the parent
window of a tree view control that the list of child items is either going to
expand or collapse. This notification message is sent in the form of a
WM_NOTIFY message.

Parameters

lParam   NM TREEVIEW *: A pointer to an NM_TREEVIEW structure whose
itemNew member is a TV_ITEM structure containing information about
the parent item in the *hItem*, *state*, and *lParam* members. The *action*
member indicates whether the list is expanding or collapsing. See the
definition of the NM_TREEVIEW structure under the TVN_BEGINDRAG
message. See the definition of the TV_ITEM structure under the
TreeView_GetItem macro.

Returns   BOOL: TRUE to prevent the list from expanding or collapsing.
Include File   commctrl.h
Related Messages   WM_NOTIFY

TVN_KEYDOWN ■ Win32s ■ Windows 95 ■ Windows NT

Description   TVN_KEYDOWN is a notification message that notifies the parent window of a tree view control that a key was pressed and the tree view control has the input focus. This notification message is sent in the form of a WM_NOTIFY message.

Parameters

lParam   TV_KEYDOWN *: A pointer to a TV_KEYDOWN structure whose *wVKey* member specifies the virtual-key code of the key that was pressed by the user. See the definition of the TV_KEYDOWN structure below.

Include File   commctrl.h

Related Messages   WM_NOTIFY

TV_KEYDOWN Definition

```
typedef struct _TV_KEYDOWN
{
    NMHDR hdr;
    WORD  wVKey;
    UINT  flags;
} TV_KEYDOWN;
```

Members

hdr   NMHDR: This member is required for all WM_NOTIFY messages.

wVKey   WORD: The virtual-key code.

flags   UINT: This member is always zero.

TVN_SELCHANGED ■ Win32s ■ Windows 95 ■ Windows NT

Description   TVN_SELCHANGED is a notification message that notifies the parent window of a tree view control that the selection has changed from one item to another. This notification message is sent in the form of a WM_NOTIFY message.

Parameters

lParam   NM_TREEVIEW *: A pointer to an NM_TREEVIEW structure whose *itemOld* and *itemNew* members are TV_ITEM structures containing information about the previously selected item and the newly selected items in the *hItem*, *state*, and *lParam* members. The *stateMask* members in the TV_ITEM structures specified by *itemOld* and *itemNew* are undefined on input. See the definition of the NM_TREEVIEW structure under the TVN_BEGINDRAG message. See the definition of the TV_ITEM structure under the TreeView_GetItem macro.

Include File   commctrl.h

Related Messages   WM_NOTIFY

TVN_SELCHANGING   ■ Win32s   ■ Windows 95   ■ Windows NT

Description   TVN_SELCHANGING is a notification message that notifies the parent window of a tree view control when the selection is changing from one item to another. This notification message is sent in the form of a WM_NOTIFY message.

Parameters

lParam   NM_TREEVIEW *: A pointer to an NM_TREEVIEW structure whose *itemOld* and *itemNew* members contain information about the currently selected item and the newly selected item. See the definition of the NM_TREEVIEW structure under the TVN_BEGINDRAG message. See the definition of the TV_ITEM structure under the TreeView_GetItem macro.

Returns   BOOL: TRUE to prevent the selection from changing.

Include File   commctrl.h

Related Messages   WM_NOTIFY

TVN_SETDISPINFO   ■ Win32s   ■ Windows 95   ■ Windows NT

Description   TVN_SETDISPINFO is a notification message that indicates that the parent window of a tree view control needs to update the information about the specified item. This notification message is sent in the form of a WM_NOTIFY message and is sent when the user finishes editing the label of an item whose text is set to LPSTR_TEXTCALLBACK.

Parameters

lParam   TV_DISPINFO *: A pointer to a TV_DISPINFO structure whose *item* member is a TV_ITEM structure containing information about the item in the *hItem* and *lParam* members. See the definition of the TV_DISPINFO structure under the TVN_BEGINLABELEDIT message. See the definition of the TV_ITEM structure under the TreeView_GetItem macro.

Include File   commctrl.h

Related Messages   WM_NOTIFY

8

RICH-TEXT EDIT CONTROLS

8

RICH-TEXT EDIT CONTROLS

The standard edit control is a good control for data entry applications that don't require special fonts or formatting. The standard edit control does allow multiple-line entry for memo fields and also supports a single font for the edit control, but what does the application developer do when the edit control requires multiple fonts within a single edit control? The answer has typically been to subclass the edit control to perform custom painting. Now there is a better solution, the *rich-text edit control*.

The rich-text edit control is basically the same as a multiline edit control; however, text can be assigned character and paragraph formatting. The rich-text edit control can also include embedded OLE objects. The editing features have been enhanced with drag-and-drop text movement.

This chapter uses a single example application, shown in Figure 8-1, to demonstrate the more common features of a rich edit control by implementing a simple rich-text editor.

Creating a Rich-Text Control

An application can create a rich-text edit control directly or indirectly. The application can create the control directly with the CreateWindowEx() function specifying the RichEdit window class. The other way to create a rich-text edit control is to include the control within a dialog template. Before an application can do any work with rich-text edit controls, the RICHED32.DLL library must be loaded with the LoadLibrary() function.

Rich edit controls support most window styles used with standard edit controls as well as the additional styles listed in Table 8-1, which are specific to rich-text edit controls.

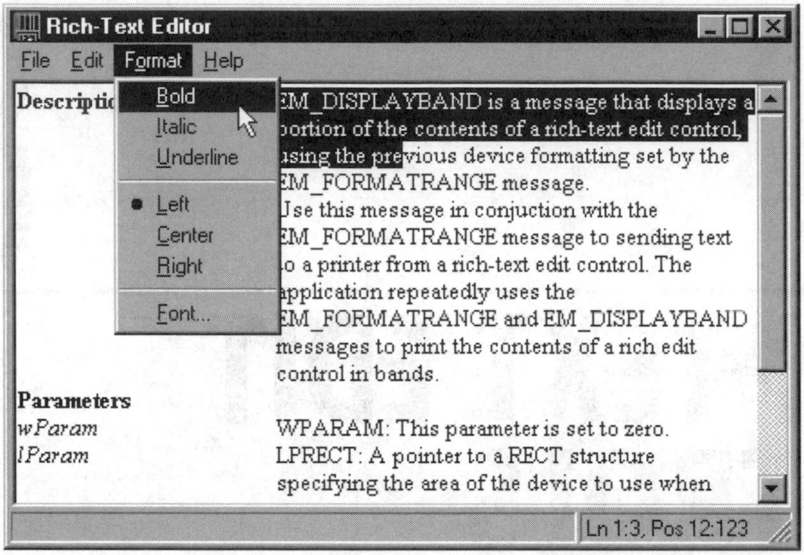

Figure 8-1 Rich-Text editor example

Table 8-1 Rich-text edit control styles

Style	Meaning
ES_DISABLENOSCROLL	Disables scroll bars when they are not needed. The default is to hide them.
ES_EX_NOCALLOLEINIT	Prevents the control from calling the OleInitialize() function when created. This style only has meaning in dialog templates. The CreateWindowEx() function does not accept this style.
ES_NOIME	Disables the input method editor (IME) operation. Available for Asian languages only.
ES_SAVESEL	Preserves the selection when the control loses the focus. By default, the entire contents of the control are selected when it regains the focus.
ES_SELFIME	Directs the rich edit control to allow the application to handle all IME operations. Available for Asian languages only.
ES_SUNKEN	Displays the control with a sunken border style so that the rich edit control appears recessed into its parent window. Applications developed for Windows 95 should use WS_EX_CLIENTEDGE instead of ES_SUNKEN.
ES_VERTICAL	Draws text and objects in a vertical direction. Available for Asian languages only.

Rich edit controls do not support the ES_LOWERCASE, ES_PASSWORD, ES_OEMCONVERT, and ES_UPPERCASE styles because they have no meaning in a rich-text edit control that is designed for WYSIWYG (What You See Is What You Get) editing. If the application requires multiline editing, the ES_MULTILINE style must be specified.

Using Rich-Text Edit Controls

Rich edit controls support almost all of the messages and notification messages used with standard multiline edit controls. This allows rich edit controls to easily replace the standard edit control within an application. Additional messages and notifications, described in this chapter, enable applications to access the functionality unique to rich edit controls. These messages perform operations such as formatting text, printing, and saving. Table 8-2 lists the standard edit control messages that are not supported with rich edit controls.

Table 8-2 Unsupported edit control messages

Message	Meaning
EM_FMTLINES	Not supported.
EM_GETHANDLE	Rich edit controls do not store text as a simple array of characters.
EM_GETMARGINS	Not supported.
EM_GETPASSWORDCHAR	The ES_PASSWORD style is not supported.
EM_SETHANDLE	Rich edit controls do not store text as a simple array of characters.
EM_SETMARGINS	Not supported.
EM_SETPASSWORDCHAR	The ES_PASSWORD style is not supported.
EM_SETRECTNP	Not supported.
EM_SETTABSTOPS	The EM_SETPARAFORMAT message is used instead.
WM_CTLCOLOR	The EM_SETBKGNDCOLOR message is used instead.
WM_GETFONT	The EM_GETCHARFORMAT message is used instead.

A rich edit control does not directly give the user the control over the formatting of the text within the control. However, the programming interface for a rich edit control provides the application with the tools needed to control the formatting, and the application provides the user interface to format the text. The EM_SETPARAFORMAT and EM_SETCHARFORMAT messages provide the formatting for rich edit controls. Paragraph formatting attributes include alignment, tabs, indents, and numbering. Character formatting includes typeface, size, color, and effects.

Some messages such as EM_GETSEL and EM_SETSEL have equivalent rich edit control messages, EM_EXGETSEL and EM_EXSETSEL. Both sets of messages work with rich edit controls; however, the EM_GETSEL and EM_SETSEL messages use two 16-bit indexes packed into a single 32-bit value. This imposes a limit of 64K characters within the edit control. By default, the rich edit control does not allow more than 32K characters, so this limitation is not an issue. However, the application can extend the maximum number of characters with the EM_EXLIMITTEXT message, and for selections that extend beyond the first 64K of text, the EM_GETSEL message now returns -1. It is good practice to use the rich edit control messages when there are equivalent messages to ensure that limits are not exceeded.

Printing

Printing the contents of a rich-text edit control is a simple process when using the provided messages. The application can render the contents of a rich edit control for a specific device such as a printer.

Before the text of a rich edit control can be displayed or printed for a device, the EM_FORMATRANGE message must be used to format a part of the rich edit control's contents for a specific device.

After the text is formatted for an output device, the application sends the EM_DISPLAYBAND message to send the output to the target device context. By repeatedly using the EM_FORMATRANGE and EM_DISPLAYBAND messages, an application can print the entire contents of the rich edit control. See the code segment under the EM_DISPLAYBAND message later in this chapter for an example.

Stream I/O

An application can use streams when transferring data into or out of a rich edit control. There are two messages, EM_STREAMIN and EM_STREAMOUT, that give applications the ability to easily read and save the contents of a rich edit control from and to a file or other stream device.

To read data into a rich edit control, use the EM_STREAMIN message. The control repeatedly calls an application-defined callback function to retrieve the contents of the stream into the edit control. Each time the callback function is called, a block of data is read into the buffer.

The process of saving data to a stream is similar to reading. The application uses the EM_STREAMOUT message, which causes the rich edit control to repeatedly call an application-defined callback function with small blocks of data to save to the stream.

For an example of how to read and save rich edit control contents to an RTF format file, see the examples under the EM_STREAMIN and EM_STREAMOUT messages later in this chapter.

Message Summary

Table 8-3 summarizes the rich-text edit control messages. The detailed descriptions follow immediately after the table.

Table 8-3 Rich-text edit fields message summary

Message	Meaning
EM_CANPASTE	Determines if a rich-text edit control can paste a specified clipboard format.
EM_DISPLAYBAND	Displays a portion of the contents of a rich-text edit control.
EM_EXGETSEL	Determines the coordinates of a rich-text edit control selection.
EM_EXLIMITTEXT	Specifies the text limit for the rich-text edit control.

Message	Meaning
EM_EXLINEFROMCHAR	Determines the location of the specified character in the rich-text edit control.
EM_EXSETSEL	Selects a range of characters in the rich-text edit control.
EM_FINDTEXT	Locates the specified text within the rich-text edit control.
EM_FINDTEXTEX	Locates the specified text within the rich-text edit control and the character range in which the text was found.
EM_FINDWORDBREAK	Retrieves the desired word-break information about the specified character position in the rich-text edit control.
EM_FORMATRANGE	Formats a range of text in a rich-text edit control.
EM_GETCHARFORMAT	Determines the current character formatting of the rich-text edit control.
EM_GETEVENTMASK	Retrieves the event mask for a rich-text edit control.
EM_GETIMECOLOR	Retrieves the IME composition color for Asian-language versions of Windows 95.
EM_GETIMEOPTIONS	Retrieves the IME options for Asian-language versions of Windows 95.
EM_GETOLEINTERFACE	Retrieves the IRichEditOle object of a rich-text edit control.
EM_GETOPTIONS	Retrieves the rich-text edit control options.
EM_GETPARAFORMAT	Retrieves the paragraph formatting of the current selection.
EM_GETPUNCTUATION	Determines the current punctuation characters of the rich-text edit control.
EM_GETSELTEXT	Retrieves the currently selected text of a rich-text edit control.
EM_GETTEXTRANGE	Retrieves the specified range of characters from a rich-text edit control.
EM_GETWORDBREAKPROCEX	Retrieves the address of the currently registered extended word-break procedure.
EM_GETWORDWRAPMODE	Retrieves the current word wrapping and breaking options for Asian-language versions of Windows 95.
EM_HIDESELECTION	Either hides or shows the selection in the rich-text edit control.
EM_PASTESPECIAL	Pastes the specified clipboard format in the rich-text edit control.
EM_REQUESTRESIZE	Instructs a rich-text edit control to send an EN_REQUESTRESIZE notification message to the parent window.
EM_SELECTIONTYPE	Determines the selection type of the rich-text edit control.
EM_SETBKGNDCOLOR	Sets the background color of the rich-text edit control.
EM_SETCHARFORMAT	Sets the character formatting for the rich-text edit control.
EM_SETEVENTMASK	Sets the event mask for the rich-text edit control.
EM_SETIMECOLOR	Sets the IME composition color for Asian-language versions of Windows 95.
EM_SETIMEOPTIONS	Sets the IME options for Asian-language versions of Windows 95.
EM_SETOLEINTERFACE	Gives the rich-text edit control an IRichEditOleCallback object to use to obtain OLE-related resources and information from the client.
EM_SETOPTIONS	Sets the options for a rich-text edit control.
EM_SETPARAFORMAT	Sets the paragraph formatting for the current selection in the rich-text edit control.
EM_SETPUNCTUATION	Sets the punctuation characters for the rich-text edit control in Asian-language versions of Windows 95.
EM_SETTARGETDEVICE	Sets the target device and line width of the WYSIWYG formatting in the rich-text edit control.

continued on next page

continued from previous page

Message	Meaning
EM_SETWORDBREAKPROCEX	Sets the extended word-break procedure for the rich-text edit control.
EM_SETWORDWRAPMODE	Sets the word wrapping and breaking options for the rich-edit control in Asian-language versions of Windows 95.
EM_STREAMIN	Replaces the contents of the rich-text edit control with the specified data stream.
EM_STREAMOUT	Writes the contents of the rich-text edit control to the specified data stream.

Notification Message	
EN_CORRECTTEXT	A SYV_CORRECT gesture has occurred.
EN_DROPFILES	User is attempting to drop files into a control.
EN_IMECHANGE	The IME conversion status has changed in an Asian-language version of Windows 95.
EN_MSGFILTER	A keyboard or mouse event exists in the rich-text edit control.
EN_OLEOPFAILED	The user action on the OLE object has failed.
EN_PROTECTED	The user is performing an action that will change a protected range of text.
EN_REQUESTRESIZE	The rich-text edit control's contents are either smaller or larger than the control's window.
EN_SAVECLIPBOARD	Indicates the clipboard contains information and it is closing.
EN_SELCHANGE	The current selection in the rich-text edit control has changed.
EN_STOPNOUNDO	An action occurred for which the control cannot maintain the undo state.

EM_CANPASTE ■ Win32s ■ Windows 95 ■ Windows NT

Description	EM_CANPASTE is a message that determines whether a rich-text edit control can paste a specified clipboard format.
Parameters	
wParam	UINT: A value identifying the clipboard format to try, or zero to try any format currently on the clipboard. This value can be any of the defined CF_ clipboard formats or a registered clipboard format.
lParam	LPARAM: Set to zero.
Returns	int: A nonzero value is returned if the clipboard format can be pasted; otherwise zero is returned.
Include File	richedit.h

EM_DISPLAYBAND ■ Win32s ■ Windows 95 ■ Windows NT

Description	EM_DISPLAYBAND is a message that displays a portion of the contents of a rich-text edit control, using the previous device formatting set by the EM_FORMATRANGE message.

Use this message in conjunction with the EM_FORMATRANGE message to send text to a printer from a rich-text edit control. The application repeatedly uses the EM_FORMATRANGE and EM_DISPLAYBAND messages to print the contents of a rich edit control in bands. |

Parameters

wParam	WPARAM: This parameter is set to zero.
lParam	LPRECT: A pointer to a RECT structure specifying the area of the device to use when displaying. See the definition of the RECT structure below.
Returns	BOOL: If successful, TRUE is returned; otherwise FALSE is returned.
Include File	richedit.h
Related Messages	EM_FORMATRANGE

RECT Definition

```
typedef struct _RECT
{
    LONG left;
    LONG top;
    LONG right;
    LONG bottom;
} RECT;
```

Members

left	LONG: The x-coordinate of the upper-left corner of the rectangle.
top	LONG: The y-coordinate of the upper-left corner of the rectangle.
right	LONG: The x-coordinate of the lower-right corner of the rectangle.
bottom	LONG: The y-coordinate of the lower-right corner of the rectangle.

Example   This code segment (Listing 8-1) demonstrates printing the contents of a rich edit control. This function expects a PRINTDLG structure to be filled in by a previous call to the PrintDlg() function. All the print options are taken into account in this code, such as printing ranges, the selected text, and the entire document. Also, multiple copies and collated copies are supported. The EM_FORMATRANGE message is used to prepare a page for printing, and the EM_DISPLAYBAND message actually sends the page to the printer.

Listing 8-1 Using the EM_DISPLAYBAND message

```
VOID PrintDocument( PRINTDLG* ppd )
{
    FORMATRANGE fr;
    DOCINFO     di;
    UINT        nPage, i, j, nCollateCopies;
    LONG        lTextLength;
    char        szTitle[MAX_PATH];
    LPTSTR      szName;
    RECT        rcTmp;

    SetCursor( LoadCursor( NULL, IDC_WAIT ) );

    // Clear the abort flag before setting
    // abort proc or calling StartDoc.
    //................................
    bAbort = FALSE;
```

continued on next page

continued from previous page

```
// Define the abort function.
//..........................
SetAbortProc( ppd->hDC, AbortProc );

// Start the printing process.
//..........................
memset( &di, 0, sizeof( DOCINFO ) );

di.cbSize = sizeof(DOCINFO);
szName = szFileName;
if ( !GetFileTitle( szName, szTitle, sizeof(szTitle) ) )
  di.lpszDocName = szTitle;
else
  di.lpszDocName = szName;

di.lpszOutput = ( (ppd->Flags & PD_PRINTTOFILE) ? "FILE: " : NULL );

try
{
   if ( StartDoc( ppd->hDC, &di ) < 0)
   {
      szName = "An error occured while trying to print.";
      RaiseException( 1, 0, 0, NULL );
   }

   // Create the modeless Abort dialog box.
   //......................................
   hDlgAbort = CreateDialog( hInst, "AbortDlg",
                             hMainWnd, AbortDlg );

   if ( !hDlgAbort )
   {
      szName = "The abort dialog count not be created.";
      RaiseException( 2, 0, 0, NULL );
   }
}
except ( EXCEPTION_EXECUTE_HANDLER )
{
   SetCursor( LoadCursor( NULL, IDC_ARROW ) );

   MessageBox( hMainWnd,
               szName,
               lpszTitle,
               MB_OK | MB_ICONHAND );

   DeleteDC( ppd->hDC );
   return;
}

// Show Abort dialog.
//...................
ShowWindow( hDlgAbort, SW_NORMAL );
UpdateWindow( hDlgAbort );

// Disable the main window
// to prevent the user from accessing a
// menu option while printing.
//...........................
EnableWindow( hMainWnd, FALSE );
SetCursor( LoadCursor( NULL, IDC_ARROW ) );
```

```
// Find out real size of document in characters.
//...............................................
lTextLength = SendMessage( hEdit,
                             WM_GETTEXTLENGTH, 0, 0 );

// Render to the same DC as the measure DC.
//.......................................
fr.hdc = ppd->hDC;
fr.hdcTarget = ppd->hDC;

// Set page rect to phys page size in twips
//.......................................
fr.rcPage.left   = 0;
fr.rcPage.top    = 0;
fr.rcPage.right  = MulDiv(
                       GetDeviceCaps( ppd->hDC, PHYSICALWIDTH ),
                       1440,
                       GetDeviceCaps( ppd->hDC, LOGPIXELSX ) );

fr.rcPage.bottom = MulDiv(
                       GetDeviceCaps( ppd->hDC, PHYSICALHEIGHT ),
                       1440,
                       GetDeviceCaps( ppd->hDC, LOGPIXELSY ) );

// Set up 3/4" horizontal and 1" vertical margins,
// with a minimum of 1" printable space in each direction.
//.......................................................
fr.rc = fr.rcPage; // initially, the full page

if ( fr.rcPage.right > (2*3*1440/4 + 1440) )
{
   fr.rc.left = 3*1440/4;
   fr.rc.right -= 3*1440/4;
}
if ( fr.rcPage.bottom > 3*1440 )
{
   fr.rc.top = 1440;
   fr.rc.bottom -= 1440;
}

// Keep a copy of the page size.
//............................
rcTmp = fr.rc;

if ( ppd->Flags & PD_COLLATE )
{
   nCollateCopies = ppd->nCopies;
   ppd->nCopies = 1;
}
else
   nCollateCopies = 1;

for ( i=0; i < nCollateCopies && !bAbort; i++ )
{
   nPage = 1;

   // Set range for the entire document (default)
   //...........................................
   fr.chrg.cpMin = 0;
   fr.chrg.cpMax = lTextLength;
```

continued on next page

continued from previous page

```
    // Are we only printing the current selection?
    //..........................................
    if ( ppd->Flags & PD_SELECTION )
    {
        SendMessage( hEdit, EM_EXGETSEL, 0, (LPARAM)&fr.chrg );
        if ( fr.chrg.cpMax >= fr.chrg.cpMin )
            lTextLength = fr.chrg.cpMax;
    }

    // Perform the actual printing.
    //............................
    do
    {
        // Format as much as will fit on a page. The return value
        // is the index of the first character on the next page.
        //.........................................................
        fr.chrg.cpMin = SendMessage( hEdit,
                                     EM_FORMATRANGE,
                                     FALSE,
                                     (LPARAM)&fr);

        // Print the page if supposed to.
        //...............................
        if ( !( (ppd->Flags & PD_PAGENUMS) && nPage < ppd->nFromPage ) )
        {
            for ( j=0; j < ppd->nCopies && !bAbort; j++ )
            {
                StartPage( ppd->hDC );
                SendMessage( hEdit,
                             EM_DISPLAYBAND,
                             0,
                             (LPARAM)&fr.rc);
                EndPage( ppd->hDC );
            }
        }

        // EM_FORMATRANGE modifies fr.rc.bottom, reset here.
        //..................................................
        fr.rc = rcTmp;

        nPage++;

        // Are we done?
        //.............
        if ( (ppd->Flags & PD_PAGENUMS) && nPage > ppd->nToPage )
            break;
    }
    while ( fr.chrg.cpMin < lTextLength && !bAbort );
}

// Restore the RTF Edit controls position.
//........................................
SendMessage( hEdit, EM_FORMATRANGE, TRUE, (LPARAM)NULL );

if ( !bAbort )
    EndDoc( ppd->hDC );

// Clean up.
//..........
EnableWindow( hMainWnd, TRUE );
```

```
    DestroyWindow( hDlgAbort );
    DeleteDC( ppd->hDC );
}
```

EM_EXGETSEL
■ Win32s ■ Windows 95 ■ Windows NT

Description	EM_EXGETSEL is a message that determines the starting and ending character positions of the selection in a rich-text edit control.
Parameters	
wParam	WPARAM: Set to zero.
lParam	CHARRANGE*: A pointer to a CHARRANGE structure that receives the coordinates of the selection. See the definition of the CHARRANGE structure below.
Include File	richedit.h
Related Messages	EM_EXSETSEL, EM_GETSEL

CHARRANGE Definition

```
typedef struct _charrange
{
    LONG cpMin;
    LONG cpMax;
} CHARRANGE;
```

Members	
cpMin	LONG: The index of the first character position in the selection.
cpMax	LONG: The index of the last character position in the selection.
Example	This code segment (Listing 8-2) enables and disables edit menu items for the rich-text editor example. This function is called on the WM_INIT-MENUPOPUP message and receives the handle to the pop-up menu. The Paste menu item is enabled if text or RTF text is on the clipboard. The EM_EXGETSEL message is used to determine if a range of text is selected to enable or disable the Cut, Copy, and Delete menu items. If the edit control has a text length, the Select All menu item is enabled.

Listing 8-2 Using the EM_EXGETSEL message

```
VOID HandleEditMenu( HMENU hMenu )
{
    CHARRANGE cr;
    UINT      uEnable;

    // Set the Paste menu item.
    //........................
    if ( OpenClipboard( hMainWnd ) )
    {
        // Check to see if one of these formats is available.
        //..................................................
        if ( IsClipboardFormatAvailable( CF_TEXT ) ||
             IsClipboardFormatAvailable( nRTF ) )
            EnableMenuItem( hMenu, IDM_PASTE, MF_BYCOMMAND | MF_ENABLED );
```

continued on next page

continued from previous page

```
    else
        EnableMenuItem( hMenu, IDM_PASTE, MF_BYCOMMAND | MF_GRAYED );

    CloseClipboard();
}

// Set the Cut/Copy/Delete menu items.
//.............................
SendMessage( hEdit, EM_EXGETSEL, 0, (LPARAM)&cr );
uEnable = cr.cpMin != cr.cpMax ? MF_ENABLED : MF_GRAYED;

EnableMenuItem( hMenu, IDM_CUT, MF_BYCOMMAND | uEnable );
EnableMenuItem( hMenu, IDM_COPY, MF_BYCOMMAND | uEnable );
EnableMenuItem( hMenu, IDM_DELETE, MF_BYCOMMAND | uEnable );

// Set the Select All menu item.
//.............................
if ( SendMessage( hEdit, WM_GETTEXTLENGTH, 0, 0 ) )
    EnableMenuItem( hMenu, IDM_SELECTALL, MF_BYCOMMAND | MF_ENABLED );
else
    EnableMenuItem( hMenu, IDM_SELECTALL, MF_BYCOMMAND | MF_GRAYED );
}
```

EM_EXLIMITTEXT   ■ Win32s ■ Windows 95 ■ Windows NT

Description	EM_EXLIMITTEXT is a message that specifies the maximum number of characters for the text in a rich-text edit control. An OLE object counts as a single character. Rich-text edit controls are not limited by a 32K limitation; however, the default maximum is 32K.
Parameters	
wParam	WPARAM: Set to zero.
lParam	DWORD: The maximum amount of text in the rich-text edit control, or zero to set the limit at the default maximum of 32K.
Include File	richedit.h
Example	See the example for the EM_SETEVENTMASK message.

EM_EXLINEFROMCHAR   ■ Win32s ■ Windows 95 ■ Windows NT

Description	EM_EXLINEFROMCHAR is a message that determines the line number on which a given character in a rich-text edit control resides.
Parameters	
wParam	WPARAM: Set to zero.
lParam	LPARAM: The zero-based index of the character.
Returns	int: The zero-based index of the line where the character is located in the rich-text edit control is returned.
Include File	richedit.h

Example   This function is called when the EN_SELCHANGE notification is received. The lines for the beginning and ending of the current selection are retrieved with the EM_LINEFROMCHAR message and displayed on the status bar.

```
VOID HandleSelChange( CHARRANGE* cr )
{
    static char szTmp[32];
    int nLineMin, nLineMax;

    // Retrieve the line number of the positions.
    //.........................................
    nLineMin = SendMessage( hEdit, EM_LINEFROMCHAR,
                            cr->cpMin, 0 );
    nLineMax = SendMessage( hEdit, EM_LINEFROMCHAR,
                            cr->cpMax, 0 );

    // Display the line pos.
    //......................
    if ( cr->cpMin != cr->cpMax )
    {
        if ( nLineMin != nLineMax )
            wsprintf( szTmp, "Ln %d:%d, Pos %d:%d",
                    nLineMin+1, nLineMax+1,
                    cr->cpMin+1,
                    cr->cpMax+1 );
        else
            wsprintf( szTmp, "Ln %d, Pos %d:%d",
                    nLineMin+1, cr->cpMin+1,
                    cr->cpMax+1 );
    }
    else
        wsprintf( szTmp, "Ln %d, Pos %d",
                nLineMin+1, cr->cpMin+1 );

    SendMessage( hStatusWnd, SB_SETTEXT, 1, (LPARAM)szTmp );
}
```

EM_EXSETSEL   ■ Win32s ■ Windows 95 ■ Windows NT

Description	EM_EXSETSEL is a message that selects a range of characters in a rich-text edit control.
Parameters	
wParam	WPARAM: Set to zero.
lParam	CHARRANGE *: A pointer to a CHARRANGE structure that contains the zero-based index of the characters. See the definition of the CHARRANGE structure under the EM_EXGETSEL message.
Returns	int: The zero-based index of the coordinates is returned.
Include File	richedit.h
Related Messages	EM_EXGETSEL, EM_SETSEL
Example	See the example for the EM_FINDWORDBREAK message.

EM_FINDTEXT
■ Win32s ■ Windows 95 ■ Windows NT

Description EM_FINDTEXT is a message that searches for a given text string within a rich-text edit control.

Parameters

wParam UINT: Zero or more of the values in Table 8-4 specifying how to match the specified string text.

Table 8-4 EM_FINDTEXT *wParam* values

Value	Meaning
FR_MATCHCASE	Match the case of the specified text.
FR_WHOLEWORD	Match the exact text in the rich-text edit control.

lParam FINDTEXT *: A pointer to a FINDTEXT structure containing information about both the range in the rich-text edit control to search and the string to find. See the definition of the FINDTEXT structure below.

Returns int: If a match is found, the zero-based character position of the next match is returned; otherwise, -1 is returned if there are no matches in the rich-text edit control.

Include File richedit.h

FINDTEXT Definition

```
typedef struct _findtext
{
    CHARRANGE chrg;
    LPSTR     lpstrText;
} FINDTEXT;
```

Members

chrg CHARRANGE: A CHARRANGE structure specifying the range of the rich-text edit control to search. See the definition of the CHARRANGE structure under the EM_EXGETSEL message.

lpstrText LPSTR: The null-terminated string to find.

Example See the example for the EM_FINDTEXTEX message, which has similar functionality.

EM_FINDTEXTEX
■ Win32s ■ Windows 95 ■ Windows NT

Description EM_FINDTEXTEX is a message that searches for a given text string within a rich-text edit control. The difference between this message and EM_FINDTEXT is that this message also retrieves the character range the text was located within.

Parameters

wParam	UINT: Zero or more of the values in Table 8-4 specifying how to match the specified string text.
lParam	FINDTEXTEX *: A pointer to a FINDTEXTEX structure containing information about both the range in the rich-text edit control to search and the string to find. See the definition of the FINDTEXTEX structure below.
Returns	int: If a match is found, the zero-based character position of the next match is returned; otherwise, -1 is returned if there are no matches in the rich-text edit control.
Include File	richedit.h

FINDTEXTEX Definition

```
typedef struct _findtextex
{
    CHARRANGE chrg;
    LPSTR     lpstrText;
    CHARRANGE chrgText;
}  FINDTEXT;
```

Members

chrg	CHARRANGE: A CHARRANGE structure specifying the range to search for the specified text. See the definition of the CHARRANGE structure under the EM_EXGETSEL message.
lpstrText	LPSTR: The null-terminated string to find in the rich-text edit control.
chrgText	CHARRANGE: A CHARRANGE structure that receives the range where the text was located. See the definition of the CHARRANGE structure under the EM_EXGETSEL message.
Example	This code segment (Listing 8-3) shows how to respond to the Edit/Find menu item. A Find common dialog is created when the user selects the Edit/Find menu item. Notifications for the Find dialog are sent via a registered message and passed on to the HandleFindMsg() function shown in the example. See Chapter 2 for more information on the Find common dialog.

Listing 8-3 Using the EM_FINDTEXTEX message

```
LRESULT CALLBACK WndProc( HWND hWnd, UINT uMsg, WPARAM wParam, LPARAM lParam )
{
static RECT strect;
static UINT nFindMsg = 0;

   if ( uMsg == nFindMsg )
   {
      HandleFindMsg( (FINDREPLACE*)lParam );
      return( 0 );
   }

   switch( uMsg )
   {
      case WM_CREATE :
              InitCommonControls();
```

continued on next page

continued from previous page

```
              szFindWhat[O] = '';
              nFindMsg = RegisterWindowMessage( "commdlg_FindReplace" );
        .
        .
        .


    case WM_COMMAND :
            switch( LOWORD( wParam ) )
            {
                case IDM_FIND :
                    if ( !hFindWnd )
                    {
                        fr.lStructSize   = sizeof( FINDREPLACE );
                        fr.hwndOwner     = hWnd;
                        fr.lpstrFindWhat = szFindWhat;
                        fr.Flags         = FR_NOUPDOWN;
                        fr.wFindWhatLen  = sizeof( szFindWhat );

                        hFindWnd = FindText( &fr );

                        CommDlgExtendedError();
                    }
                    else
                        SetFocus( hFindWnd );
                    break;
        .
        .
        .


VOID HandleFindMsg( FINDREPLACE* pFR )
{
    if ( pFR->Flags & FR_FINDNEXT )
    {
        FINDTEXTEX ft;
        LONG       lPos;
        UINT       uFlags = pFR->Flags;

        // Retrieve current position.
        //...........................
        SendMessage( hEdit, EM_EXGETSEL, 0, (LPARAM)&ft.chrg );

        // Increment the position by 1 to skip where we are.
        //..................................................
        ft.chrg.cpMin++;

        // Search to the end of the text.
        //...............................
        ft.chrg.cpMax = -1;

        ft.lpstrText = pFR->lpstrFindWhat;

        lPos = SendMessage( hEdit, EM_FINDTEXTEX, uFlags, (LPARAM)&ft );

        if ( lPos > -1 )
            SendMessage( hEdit, EM_EXSETSEL, 0, (LPARAM)&ft.chrgText );
        else
            MessageBox( hMainWnd, "Text not found.", "Find",
                        MB_OK | MB_ICONINFORMATION );
    }
}
```

```
    // The user closed the Find dialog.
    //................................
    if ( pFR->Flags & FR_DIALOGTERM )
        hFindWnd = NULL;
}
```

EM_FINDWORDBREAK   ■ Win32s ■ Windows 95 ■ Windows NT

Description   EM_FINDWORDBREAK is a message that retrieves the desired word-
                        break information about the specified character position in the rich-text
                        information. The information retrieved is based on the action flag value of
                        the wParam parameter.

Parameters

wParam   UINT: The action to take with the specified character position. This para-
                        meter can be one of the values in Table 8-5.

Table 8-5 EM_FINDWORDBREAK *wParam* values

Value	Meaning
WB_CLASSIFY	Returns the character class and word-break flags of the character at the specified position.
WB_ISDELIMITER	Returns TRUE if the character at the specified position is a delimiter; otherwise FALSE.
WB_LEFT	Finds the nearest character before the specified position that begins a word.
WB_LEFTBREAK	Finds the next word end before the specified position.
WB_MOVEWORDLEFT	Finds the next character that begins a word before the specified position. This value is used during CTRL+← key processing.
WB_MOVEWORDRIGHT	Finds the next character that begins a word after the specified position. This value is used during CTRL+→ key processing.
WB_RIGHT	Finds the next character that begins a word after the specified position.
WB_RIGHTBREAK	Finds the next end-of-word delimiter after the specified position.

lParam   DWORD: The zero-based character position to start from.

Returns   int: The character index of the word break is returned, unless *wParam* is
                        the WB_CLASSIFY or WB_ISDELIMITER value.

Include File   richedit.h

Example   This code segment (Listing 8-4) from the rich-text editor example searches
                        for the next word in response the Next Word menu item. The starting and
                        ending positions of the next word are retrieved with the EM_FINDWORD-
                        BREAK message, and the word is selected with the EM_EXSETSEL message.

Listing 8-4 Using the EM_FINDWORDBREAK message

```
LRESULT CALLBACK WndProc( HWND hWnd, UINT uMsg, WPARAM wParam, LPARAM lParam )
{
    switch( uMsg )
```

continued on next page

continued from previous page

```
{
    case WM_COMMAND :
            switch( LOWORD( wParam ) )
            {
                case IDM_NEXTWORD :
                    {
                        CHARRANGE cr;

                        SendMessage( hEdit, EM_EXGETSEL, 0, (LPARAM)&cr );

                        // Retrieve the position of the next word.
                        //......................................
                        cr.cpMin = SendMessage( hEdit, EM_FINDWORDBREAK,
                                                WB_RIGHT, cr.cpMax );

                        cr.cpMax = SendMessage( hEdit, EM_FINDWORDBREAK,
                                                WB_RIGHTBREAK, cr.cpMin );

                        SendMessage( hEdit, EM_EXSETSEL, 0, (LPARAM)&cr );
                    }
                    break;
        .
        .
        .
```

EM_FORMATRANGE ■ Win32s ■ Windows 95 ■ Windows NT

Description   EM_FORMATRANGE is a message that formats a range of text in a rich-text edit control for a specific device. This message is normally used with the EM_DISPLAYBAND message.

It is very important to free cached information after the last time you use this message.

Parameters

wParam   BOOL: If *wParam* is a nonzero value, the text is rendered; otherwise, the text is just measured.

lParam   FORMATRANGE *: A pointer to a FORMATRANGE structure containing information about the output device, or NULL to free information cached by the control. See the definition of the FORMATRANGE structure below.

Returns   int: The index, plus one, of the last character that fits in the region is returned.

Include File   richedit.h

Related Messages   EM_DISPLAYBAND

FORMATRANGE Definition

```
typedef struct _formatrange
{
    HDC         hdc;
    HDC         hdcTarget;
    RECT        rc;
    RECT        rcPage;
    CHARRANGE   chrg;
} FORMATRANGE;
```

Members

hdc	HDC: The device to render to.
hdcTarget	HDC: The target device to format for.
rc	RECT: A RECT structure specifying the area to render to. See the definition of the RECT structure under the EM_DISPLAYBAND message.
rcPage	RECT: A RECT structure specifying the entire area of the rendering device. See the definition of the RECT structure under the EM_DISPLAYBAND message.
chrg	CHARRANGE: A CHARRANGE structure specifying the range of text to format. See the definition of the CHARRANGE structure under the EM_EXGETSEL message.
Example	See the example for the EM_DISPLAYBAND message.

EM_GETCHARFORMAT ■ Win32s ■ Windows 95 ■ Windows NT

Description	EM_GETCHARFORMAT is a message that retrieves the current character formatting in a rich-text edit control.
Parameters	
wParam	BOOL: If the value of *wParam* is zero, the default formatting of the character is returned; otherwise, the current selection's formatting is returned.
lParam	CHARFORMAT *: A pointer to a CHARFORMAT structure to receive the information specified by *wParam*. If the formatting of the current selection is being retrieved, the structure receives the attributes of the first character, and the *dwMask* member specifies which attributes are consistent throughout the entire selection. See the definition of the CHARFORMAT structure below.
Returns	DWORD: The value of the *dwMask* member of the CHARFORMAT structure.
Include File	richedit.h

CHARFORMAT Definition

```
typedef struct _charformat
{
    UINT     cbSize;
    DWORD    dwMask;
    DWORD    dwEffects;
    LONG     yHeight;
    LONG     yOffset;
    COLORREF crTextColor;
    BYTE     bCharSet;
    BYTE     bPitchAndFamily;
    TCHAR    szFaceName[LF_FACESIZE];
}   CHARFORMAT;
```

Members

cbSize	UINT: The size of the structure. This member must be set to the size of the structure before using it in a message to a rich-text edit control.

dwMask	DWORD: The valid information or attributes to set. This member can be zero or more of values in Table 8-6.

Table 8-6 CHARFORMAT *dwMask* values

Value	Meaning
CFM_BOLD	The CFE_BOLD value of the *dwEffects* member is valid.
CFM_COLOR	The *crTextColor* member and the CFE_AUTOCOLOR value of the *dwEffects* member are valid.
CFM_FACE	The *szFaceName* member is valid.
CFM_ITALIC	The CFE_ITALIC value of the *dwEffects* member is valid.
CFM_OFFSET	The *yOffset* member is valid.
CFM_PROTECTED	The CFE_PROTECTED value of the *dwEffects* member is valid.
CFM_SIZE	The *yHeight* member is valid.
CFM_STRIKEOUT	The CFE_STRIKEOUT value of the *dwEffects* member is valid.
CFM_UNDERLINE	The CFE_UNDERLINE value of the *dwEffects* member is valid.

dwEffects	DWORD: The character effects. This member can be a combination of the values in Table 8-7.

Table 8-7 CHARFORMAT *dwEffects* values

Value	Meaning
CFE_AUTOCOLOR	The text color is the return value of GetSysColor(COLOR_WINDOWTEXT).
CFE_BOLD	Characters are bold.
CFE_ITALIC	Characters are italic.
CFE_STRIKEOUT	Characters are struck out.
CFE_UNDERLINE	Characters are underlined.
CFE_PROTECTED	Characters are protected; an attempt to modify them will cause an EN_PROTECTED notification message.

yHeight	LONG: The character height.
yOffset	LONG: The character offset from the baseline. If this member is positive, the character is a superscript; if it is negative, the character is a subscript.
crTextColor	COLORREF: The text color. This member is ignored if the CFE_AUTOCOLOR character effect is specified as a value for the *dwEffects* member.
bCharSet	BYTE: The character set. This can be one of the following values: ANSI_CHARSET DEFAULT_CHARSET SYMBOL_CHARSET SHIFTJIS_CHARSET GB2312_CHARSET

	HANGEUL_CHARSET
	CHINESEBIG5_CHARSET
	OEM_CHARSET
	These values are also valid in Windows 95:
	JOHAB_CHARSET
	HEBREW_CHARSET
	ARABIC_CHARSET
	GREEK_CHARSET
	TURKISH_CHARSET
	THAI_CHARSET
	EASTEUROPE_CHARSET
	RUSSIAN_CHARSET
	MAC_CHARSET
	BALTIC_CHARSET
bPitchAndFamily	BYTE: The font family and pitch. The two low-order bits can be one of the following values specifying the pitch of the font:
	DEFAULT_PITCH
	FIXED_PITCH
	VARIABLE_PITCH
	Bits 4 through 7 of the *bPitchAndFamily* member specify the font family and can be one of the following values:
	FF_DECORATIVE
	FF_DONTCARE
	FF_MODERN
	FF_ROMAN
	FF_SCRIPT
	FF_SWISS
szFaceName	TCHAR: A null-terminated character array specifying the font face name.
Example	This code segment (Listing 8-5) is a function from the rich-text editor example that handles the WM_INITMENUPOPUP message for the Format pop-up menu. The EM_GETCHARFORMAT message is used to determine the formatting of the current selection, and the EM_GETPARAFORMAT message is used to determine the alignment of the current selection. The menu items are updated according to the current settings.

Listing 8-5 Using the EM_GETCHARFORMAT message

```
VOID HandleFormatMenu( HMENU hMenu )
{
    CHARFORMAT cf;
    PARAFORMAT pf;

    cf.cbSize = sizeof( CHARFORMAT );
    SendMessage( hEdit, EM_GETCHARFORMAT, TRUE, (LPARAM)&cf );
```

continued on next page

continued from previous page

```
    // Set the Bold/Italic/Underline menu items
    //........................................
    if ( cf.dwMask & CFM_BOLD )
        CheckMenuItem( hMenu, IDM_BOLD, MF_BYCOMMAND |
                        (cf.dwEffects & CFE_BOLD) ?
                        MF_CHECKED : MF_UNCHECKED );

    if ( cf.dwMask & CFM_ITALIC )
        CheckMenuItem( hMenu, IDM_ITALIC, MF_BYCOMMAND |
                        (cf.dwEffects & CFE_ITALIC) ?
                        MF_CHECKED : MF_UNCHECKED );

    if ( cf.dwMask & CFM_UNDERLINE )
        CheckMenuItem( hMenu, IDM_UNDERLINE, MF_BYCOMMAND |
                        (cf.dwEffects & CFE_UNDERLINE) ?
                        MF_CHECKED : MF_UNCHECKED );

    pf.cbSize = sizeof( PARAFORMAT );
    SendMessage( hEdit, EM_GETPARAFORMAT, TRUE, (LPARAM)&pf );

    if ( pf.dwMask & PFM_ALIGNMENT )
        CheckMenuRadioItem( hMenu, IDM_ALIGNLEFT, IDM_ALIGNRIGHT,
                    pf.wAlignment == PFA_LEFT ? IDM_ALIGNLEFT :
                    pf.wAlignment == PFA_CENTER ? IDM_ALIGNCENTER :
                    IDM_ALIGNRIGHT,  MF_BYCOMMAND );
}
```

EM_GETEVENTMASK   ■ Win32s   ■ Windows 95   ■ Windows NT

Description	EM_GETEVENTMASK is a message that retrieves the event mask for a rich-text edit control. The event mask specifies which notification messages the control sends to its parent window.
Parameters	This message does not use *wParam* or *lParam*.
Returns	DWORD: The event mask for the rich edit control. This can be any combination of the flags listed in Table 8-8. Use the binary AND (&) operator to determine which flags are set.

Table 8-8 Rich edit control event mask flags

Value	Meaning
ENM_CHANGE	Sends EN_CHANGE notifications.
ENM_CORRECTTEXT	Sends EN_CORRECTTEXT notifications.
ENM_DROPFILES	Sends EN_DROPFILES notifications.
ENM_KEYEVENTS	Sends EN_MSGFILTER notifications for keyboard events.
ENM_MOUSEEVENTS	Sends EN_MSGFILTER notifications for mouse events.
ENM_PROTECTED	Sends EN_PROTECTED notifications.
ENM_RESIZEREQUEST	Sends EN_REQUESTRESIZE notifications.
ENM_SCROLL	Sends EN_HSCROLL notifications.
ENM_SELCHANGE	Sends EN_SELCHANGE notifications.
ENM_UPDATE	Sends EN_UPDATE notifications.

Include File	richedit.h
Example	See the example for the EM_SETEVENTMASK message.

EM_GETIMECOLOR ■ Win32s ■ Windows 95 ■ Windows NT

Description	EM_GETIMECOLOR is a message used in Asian-language versions of Windows 95 to retrieve the IME composition color.
Parameters	
wParam	WPARAM: This parameter is set to zero.
lParam	COMPCOLOR *: The address of a four-element array of COMPCOLOR structures that receives the IME composition color. See the definition of the COMPCOLOR structure below.
Returns	int: If successful, a nonzero value is returned; otherwise, zero is returned.
Include File	richedit.h

COMPCOLOR Definition

```
typedef struct _compcolor
{
    COLORREF crText;
    COLORREF crBackground;
    DWORD    dwEffects;
} COMPCOLOR;
```

Members	
crText	COLORREF: The color of the text in the string.
crBackground	COLORREF: The background color.
dwEffects	DWORD: The character formatting effects. This member can be combination of the values in Table 8-7.

EM_GETIMEOPTIONS ■ Win32s ■ Windows 95 ■ Windows NT

Description	EM_GETIMEOPTIONS is a message that is used in Asian-language versions of Windows 95 to retrieve the current IME options.
Parameters	This message does not use *wParam* or *lParam*.
Returns	int: One of the IME option flags in Table 8-9 is returned.

Table 8-9 EM_GETIMEOPTIONS return values

Value	Meaning
IMF_CLOSESTATUSWINDOW	Closes the IME status window when the control receives the input focus.
IMF_FORCEACTIVE	Activates the IME when the control receives the input focus.
IMF_FORCEDISABLE	Disables the IME when the control receives the input focus.
IMF_FORCEENABLE	Enables the IME when the control receives the input focus.
IMF_FORCEINACTIVE	Inactivates the IME when the control receives the input focus.
IMF_FORCENONE	Disables IME handling.
IMF_FORCEREMEMBER	Restores the previous IME status when the control receives the input focus.

Include File	richedit.h
Related Messages	EM_SETIMEOPTIONS

EM_GETOLEINTERFACE　　■ Win32s　■ Windows 95　■ Windows NT

Description	EM_GETOLEINTERFACE is a message that retrieves an IRichEditOle interface object that a client can use to access the OLE functionality of a rich-text edit control.
Parameters	
wParam	WPARAM: This parameter is set to zero.
lParam	LPVOID *: The address where the control stores a pointer to the IRichEditOle object. The rich-text edit control calls AddRef() for the object before returning, so the calling application must call Release() when it is done with the object.
Returns	int: If successful, a nonzero value is returned; otherwise, zero is returned.
Include File	richedit.h
Related Messages	EM_SETOLEINTERFACE

EM_GETOPTIONS　　■ Win32s　■ Windows 95　■ Windows NT

Description	EM_GETOPTIONS is a message the retrieves the rich-text edit control options.
Parameters	This message does not use wParam or lParam.
Returns	UINT: The current option values for the rich-text edit control. This parameter can be a combination of the values in Table 8-10.

Table 8-10 EM_GETOPTIONS return values

Value	Meaning
ECO_AUTOHSCROLL	Automatically scrolls the text of the control right 10 characters.
ECO_AUTOVSCROLL	Automatically scrolls the text of the control vertically.
ECO_AUTOWORDSELECTION	Automatic selection of word on double-click.
ECO_NOHIDESEL	The selected text maintains the inverted font (that indicates a selection) even when the control does not have the focus.
ECO_READONLY	Text cannot be typed or edited in the rich-text edit control.
ECO_SAVESEL	Preserves the selection when the rich-text edit control loses focus.
ECO_SELECTIONBAR	Same as ES_SELECTIONBAR style, which is the same as the WS_MAXIMIZE style.
ECO_VERTICAL	Draws text and objects in a vertical direction. This value is only available in Asian-language versions of Windows 95.
ECO_WANTRETURN	A carriage return should be inserted when the ENTER key is pressed as text is entered into the control.

Include File	richedit.h
Related Messages	EM_SETOPTIONS

EM_GETPARAFORMAT ■ Win32s ■ Windows 95 ■ Windows NT

Description	EM_GETPARAFORMAT is a message that retrieves the paragraph formatting of the current selection in a rich edit control.
Parameters	
wParam	WPARAM: This parameter is set to zero.
lParam	PARAFORMAT *: A pointer to a PARAFORMAT structure that receives the paragraph formatting attributes of the current selection. If more than one paragraph is selected, the structure receives the attributes of the first paragraph, and the *dwMask* member of the PARAFORMAT structure specifies which attributes are consistent throughout the entire selection. See the definition of the PARAFORMAT structure below.
Returns	DWORD: The value of the *dwMask* member of the PARAFORMAT structure is returned.
Include File	richedit.h

PARAFORMAT Definition

```
typedef struct _paraformat
{
    UINT  cbSize;
    DWORD dwMask;
    WORD  wNumbering;
    WORD  wReserved;
    LONG  dxStartIndent;
    LONG  dxRightIndent;
    LONG  dxOffset;
    WORD  wAlignment;
    SHORT cTabCount;
    LONG  rgxTabs[MAX_TAB_STOPS];
} PARAFORMAT;
```

Members	
cbSize	UINT: The size in bytes of this structure. This member must be filled before the structure is passed to the rich-text edit control.
dwMask	DWORD: This parameter can be zero or a combination of the values in Table 8-11, indicating the members of the structure containing valid information or attributes to set. If both the PFM_STARTINDENT and the PFM_OFFSETINDENT values are specified, the PFM_STARTINDENT value takes precedence.

Table 8-11 EM_GETPARAFORMAT PARAFORMAT *dwMask* values

Value	Meaning
PFM_ALIGNMENT	The *wAlignment* member is valid.
PFM_NUMBERING	The *wNumbering* member is valid.

continued on next page

continued from previous page

Value	Meaning
PFM_OFFSET	The *dxOffset* member is valid.
PFM_OFFSETINDENT	The *dxStartIndent* member is valid and specifies a relative value.
PFM_RIGHTINDENT	The *dxRightIndent* member is valid.
PFM_STARTINDENT	The *dxStartIndent* member is valid.
PFM_TABSTOPS	The *cTabStobs* and *rgxTabStops* members are valid.

wNumbering	WORD: This member can be zero or PFN_BULLET to specify the numbering option for the paragraph.
wReserved	WORD: Reserved.
dxStartIndent	LONG: Indentation of the first line in the paragraph. If the paragraph formatting is being set and the PFM_OFFSETINDENT value is specified for the *dwMask* member, this member is treated as a relative value that is added to the starting indentation of each affected paragraph.
dxRightIndent	LONG: The size of the right indentation, relative to the right margin.
dxOffset	LONG: Indentation of the second line and subsequent lines, relative to the starting indentation. The first line is indented if this member is negative, or outdented if this member is positive.
wAlignment	WORD:One of the values in Table 8-12 specifying the paragraph alignment.

Table 8-12 EM_GETPARAFORMAT PARAFORMAT *wAlignment* values

Value	Meaning
PFA_CENTER	Paragraphs are centered.
PFA_LEFT	Paragraphs are aligned with the left margin.
PFA_RIGHT	Paragraphs are aligned with the right margin.

cTabCount	SHORT: The number of tab stops.
rgxTabs	LONG: An array of absolute tab stop positions.
Example	See the example for the EM_GETCHARFORMAT message.

EM_GETPUNCTUATION ■ Win32s ■ Windows 95 ■ Windows NT

Description	EM_GETPUNCTUATION is a message that is available in Asian-language versions of Windows 95 to retrieve the punctuation characters of the rich-text edit control.

Parameters

wParam   UINT: One of the values in Table 8-13 that specifies the punctuation that
                            the message is looking for.

Table 8-13 EM_GETPUNCTUATION *wParam* values

Value	Meaning
PC_DELIMITER	Delimiter
PC_FOLLOWING	Following punctuation characters
PC_LEADING	Leading punctuation characters

lParam   PUNCTUATION *: The address of the PUNCTUATION structure that
                            receives the punctuation characters for the rich-text edit control. See the
                            definition of the PUNCTUATION structure below.

Returns   int: If successful, a nonzero value is returned; otherwise, zero is returned.

Include File   richedit.h

PUNCTUATION Definition

```
typedef struct _punctuation
{
    UINT   iSize;
    LPSTR  szPunctuation;
} PUNCTUATION;
```

Members

iSize   UINT: The size in bytes of the buffer pointed to by the *szPunctuation*
                            member.

szPunctuation   LPSTR: The address of the buffer containing the punctuation characters.

EM_GETSELTEXT   ■ Win32s ■ Windows 95 ■ Windows NT

Description   EM_GETSELTEXT is a message that retrieves the text that is currently
                            selected in a rich-text edit control.

Parameters

wParam   WPARAM: This parameter is set to zero.

lParam   LPSTR: A pointer to a buffer that receives the selected text of the rich-text
                            edit control. The calling application must ensure that the buffer is large
                            enough to hold the selected text.

Returns   int: The number of characters copied to the buffer, not including the
                            terminating null character, is returned.

Include File   richedit.h

EM_GETTEXTRANGE ■ Win32s ■ Windows 95 ■ Windows NT

Description   EM_GETTEXTRANGE is a message that retrieves a specified range of characters from a rich-text edit control.

Parameters

wParam   WPARAM: This parameter is set to zero.

lParam   TEXTRANGE *: A pointer to a TEXTRANGE structure specifying the range of characters to retrieve and the buffer to receive a copy of the characters. See the definition of the TEXTRANGE structure below.

Returns   int: The number of characters copied to the buffer, not including the terminating null character, is returned.

Include File   richedit.h

TEXTRANGE Definition

```
typedef struct _textrange
{
    CHARRANGE chrg;
    LPSTR     lpstrText;
} TEXTRANGE;
```

Members

chrg   CHARRANGE: A CHARRANGE structure that specifies the range of characters to retrieve from the rich-text edit control. See the definition of the CHARRANGE structure under the EM_EXGETSEL message.

lpstrText   LPSTR: The buffer to receive the text.

EM_GETWORDBREAKPROCEX ■ Win32s ■ Windows 95 ■ Windows NT

Description   EM_GETWORDBREAKPROCEX is a message that retrieves the address of the currently registered word-break procedure used to break a line of text in the rich-text edit control.

Parameters   This message does not use *wParam* or *lParam*.

Returns   EDITWORDBREAKPROC: The address of the current word-break procedure.

Include File   richedit.h

Related Messages   EM_SETWORDBREAKPROCEX

EM_GETWORDWRAPMODE ■ Win32s ■ Windows 95 ■ Windows NT

Description   EM_GETWORDWRAPMODE is a message available in Asian-language versions of Windows 95 to retrieve the current word wrapping and breaking options for the rich-edit control.

Parameters   This message does not use *wParam* or *lParam*.

Returns	UINT: The current word wrapping and breaking options are returned. This can be one or more of the values listed in Table 8-18.
Include File	richedit.h

EM_HIDESELECTION   ■ Win32s   ■ Windows 95   ■ Windows NT

Description	EM_HIDESELECTION is a message the either hides or shows the selection in a rich-text edit control.
Parameters	
wParam	BOOL: If the value of the *wParam* parameter is zero, the selection is shown; otherwise, the selection is hidden.
lParam	BOOL: If the value of the *lParam* parameter is nonzero and the control has the focus, the selection is hidden or shown as appropriate and the ES_NOHIDESEL style of the control is changed; otherwise, if the value is zero, the selection is temporarily hidden or shown.
Include File	richedit.h

EM_PASTESPECIAL   ■ Win32s   ■ Windows 95   ■ Windows NT

Description	EM_PASTESPECIAL is a message that pastes the specified clipboard format in a rich-text edit control.
Parameters	
wParam	UINT: The clipboard format to paste in the rich-text edit control. This can be one of the CF_ clipboard formats or a format registered by the application with the RegisterClipboardFormat() function.
lParam	LPARAM: This parameter is set to zero.
Include File	richedit.h
See Also	SetClipboardData()
Example	This function from the rich-text editor example pastes the contents of the clipboard into the rich edit control. The RTF clipboard format is favored over the standard CF_TEXT format. The EM_PASTESPECIAL message is used to perform the paste (Listing 8-6).

Listing 8-6 Using the EM_PASTESPECIAL message

```
VOID PasteClipboard()
{
   if ( OpenClipboard( hMainWnd ) )
   {
      // Check if the clipboard format is RTF.
      //.....................................
      BOOL bRTF = IsClipboardFormatAvailable( nRTF );

      CloseClipboard();
```

continued on next page

continued from previous page

```
    // Paste the clipboard contents into the
    // rich-text edit control.
    // The RTF format is preferred.
    //.....................................
    SendMessage( hEdit, EM_PASTESPECIAL,
                 bRTF ? nRTF : CF_TEXT, 0 );
  }
  SetFocus( hEdit );
}
```

EM_REQUESTRESIZE ■ Win32s ■ Windows 95 ■ Windows NT

Description EM_REQUESTRESIZE is a message that causes a rich-text edit control to send an EN_REQUESTRESIZE notification message to notify the parent window that the contents of the control are larger or smaller than the window size.

Parameters This message does not use *wParam* or *lParam*.

Include File richedit.h

Related Messages EN_REQUESTRESIZE

EM_SELECTIONTYPE ■ Win32s ■ Windows 95 ■ Windows NT

Description EM_SELECTIONTYPE is a message that determines the selection type of a rich-text edit control.

Parameters This message does not use *wParam* or *lParam*.

Returns int: The return value is one or more of the values in Table 8-14.

Table 8-14 EM_SELECTIONTYPE return values

Value	Meaning
SEL_EMPTY	The selection is empty.
SEL_MULTICHAR	Contains more than one character of text.
SEL_MULTIOBJECT	Contains more than one OLE object.
SEL_OBJECT	Contain at least one OLE object.
SEL_TEXT	Contents of the selection is text.

Include File richedit.h

EM_SETBKGNDCOLOR ■ Win32s ■ Windows 95 ■ Windows NT

Description EM_SETBKGNDCOLOR is a message that sets the background color for a rich-text edit control.

Parameters

wParam	BOOL: If the value of *wParam* is nonzero, the background is set to the window background system color; otherwise, if the value of *wParam* is zero, the background is set to the color specified by the *lParam* parameter.
lParam	COLORREF: A COLORREF value specifying the background color for the rich-text edit control if the value of the *wParam* parameter is zero.
Returns	COLORRFF: The old background color of the rich-text edit control.
Include File	richedit.h

EM_SETCHARFORMAT   ■ Win32s   ■ Windows 95   ■ Windows NT

Description	EM_SETCHARFORMAT is a message that sets the character formatting in a rich-text edit control.

Parameters

wParam	UINT: Zero or more of the values in Table 8-15 specifying the portion of the rich-text edit control to which the character formatting should be applied.

Table 8-15 EM_SETCHARFORMAT *wParam* values

Value	Meaning
SCF_SELECTION	Apply the formatting to the current selection, or set the default formatting if the selection is empty.
SCF_WORD	Apply the formatting to the selected word or words. If the selection is empty but the insertion point is inside a word, the formatting is applied to the word. Use this value in conjunction with the SCF_SELECTION value.

lParam	CHARFORMAT *: A pointer to a CHARFORMAT structure specifying the character formatting to use with the rich-text edit control. See the definition of the CHARFORMAT structure under the EM_GETCHARFORMAT message.
Returns	int: If successful, a nonzero value is returned; otherwise, zero is returned.
Include File	richedit.h
Example	This function from the rich-text editor example changes the character format for the current selection. The format that is selected (Bold, Italic, Underline) is toggled from its current state and changed with the EM_SETCHARFORMAT message (Listing 8-7).

Listing 8-7 Using the EM_SETCHARFORMAT message

```
VOID ChangeCharFormat( UINT uCmd )
{
    CHARFORMAT cf;
```

continued on next page

continued from previous page

```
// Retrieve the current setting.
//.............................
cf.cbSize = sizeof( CHARFORMAT );
SendMessage( hEdit, EM_GETCHARFORMAT, TRUE, (LPARAM)&cf );

// Toggle the appropriate format.
//..............................
switch( uCmd )
{
    case IDM_BOLD :
            cf.dwMask = CFM_BOLD;
            cf.dwEffects ^= CFE_BOLD;
            break;

    case IDM_ITALIC :
            cf.dwMask = CFM_ITALIC;
            cf.dwEffects ^= CFE_ITALIC;
            break;

    case IDM_UNDERLINE :
            cf.dwMask = CFM_UNDERLINE;
            cf.dwEffects ^= CFE_UNDERLINE;
            break;
}

// Make the change in the RTF edit control.
//..........................................
SendMessage( hEdit, EM_SETCHARFORMAT, SCF_SELECTION, (LPARAM)&cf );
SetFocus( hEdit );
}
```

EM_SETEVENTMASK   ■ Win32s ■ Windows 95 ■ Windows NT

Description	EM_SETEVENTMASK is a message that sets the event mask for a rich-text edit control specifying the notification messages sent to the parent window.
Parameters	
wParam	WPARAM: This parameter is set to zero.
lParam	DWORD: The new event mask for the rich edit control.
Returns	DWORD: The previous event mask.
Include File	richedit.h
Example	This code segment (Listing 8-8) from the rich-text editor example shows the creation of the rich edit control and initialization. The EM_GETEVENTMASK and EM_SETEVENTMASK messages are used to retrieve the current settings and add the EN_SELCHANGE notification.

Listing 8-8 Using the EM_SETEVENTMASK message

```
#define MAXFILESIZE  0x000FFFFF

LRESULT CALLBACK WndProc( HWND hWnd, UINT uMsg, WPARAM wParam, LPARAM lParam )
{
static RECT strect;
```

```
switch( uMsg )
{
   case WM_CREATE :
          InitCommonControls();

          hRtfLib = LoadLibrary( "RICHED32.DLL" );
          hEdit   = CreateWindowEx( WS_EX_CLIENTEDGE,
                                    "RICHEDIT",
                                    "",
                                    WS_CHILD | WS_VISIBLE |
                                    WS_BORDER | ES_MULTILINE |
                                    WS_VSCROLL | WS_HSCROLL |
                                    ES_AUTOVSCROLL,
                                    0, 0,
                                    0, 0,
                                    hWnd,
                                    (HMENU)1,
                                    hInst,
                                    NULL );

          hStatusWnd = CreateStatusWindow(
                            WS_CHILD | WS_VISIBLE |
                            CCS_BOTTOM | SBARS_SIZEGRIP,
                            "", hWnd, 101 );

          // Register the RTF clipboard format.
          //...................................
          nRTF = RegisterClipboardFormat( CF_RTF );

          // Set the default Font.
          //......................
          if ( hEdit )
          {
              CHARFORMAT cf;
              DWORD      dwEvent;

              cf.cbSize = sizeof( CHARFORMAT );
              cf.dwMask = CFM_FACE | CFM_BOLD | CFM_UNDERLINE |
                          CFM_ITALIC | CFM_COLOR;
              cf.dwEffects = CFE_AUTOCOLOR;
              strcpy( cf.szFaceName, "Arial" );

              SendMessage( hEdit, EM_SETCHARFORMAT,
                           SCF_SELECTION, (LPARAM)&cf );
              SetFocus( hEdit );

              // Set the event mask to return EN_SELCHANGE.
              //...........................................
              dwEvent = SendMessage( hEdit, EM_GETEVENTMASK, 0, 0 );
              dwEvent |= ENM_SELCHANGE;
              SendMessage( hEdit, EM_SETEVENTMASK, 0, dwEvent );

              // Set the maximum number of characters.
              //......................................
              SendMessage( hEdit, EM_EXLIMITTEXT, 0, MAXFILESIZE );
          }
```

continued on next page

continued from previous page

```
              // Retrieve the status window size.
              //.................................
              if ( hStatusWnd )
                GetClientRect( hStatusWnd, &strect );

          break;

      case WM_NOTIFY :
              switch( ((NMHDR*)lParam)->code )
              {
                  case EN_SELCHANGE :
                      HandleSelChange( &((SELCHANGE*)lParam)->chrg );
                      break;

                  case EN_SAVECLIPBOARD :
                      if ( MessageBox( hWnd,
                                       "Data is on the clipboard."
                                       "Do you want to make it available?",
                                       lpszTitle,
                                       MB_YESNO | MB_ICONQUESTION ) == IDNO )
                      {
                          return( TRUE );
                      }
                      break;

                  case EN_STOPNOUNDO :
                      if ( MessageBox( hWnd,
                                       "This operation is too big to be undone."
                                       "Do you want to continue without undo?",
                                       lpszTitle,
                                       MB_YESNO | MB_ICONQUESTION ) == IDNO )
                      {
                          return( TRUE );
                      }
                      break;
              }
          break;
              .
              .
              .
```

EM_SETIMECOLOR ■ Win32s ■ Windows 95 ■ Windows NT

Description	EM_SETIMECOLOR is a message that is available in Asian-language versions of Windows 95 to set the IME composition color.
Parameters	
wParam	WPARAM: This parameter is set to zero.
lParam	COMPCOLOR *: The address of a four-element array of COMPCOLOR structures that receives the IME composition color. See the definition of the COMPCOLOR structure under the EM_GETIMECOLOR message.
Returns	int: If successful, a nonzero value is returned; otherwise, zero is returned.
Include File	richedit.h
Related Messages	EM_GETIMECOLOR

EM_SETIMEOPTIONS ■ Win32s ■ Windows 95 ■ Windows NT

Description	EM_SETIMEOPTIONS is a message that is available in Asian-language versions of Windows 95 to set the IME options for the rich-text edit control.
Parameters	
wParam	WPARAM: This parameter is set to zero.
lParam	int: A combination of the values in Table 8-16 specifying the IME options for the rich-text edit control.
Returns	int: If successful, a nonzero value is returned; otherwise, zero is returned.
Include File	richedit.h
Related Messages	EM_GETIMEOPTIONS

EM_SETOLEINTERFACE ■ Win32s ■ Windows 95 ■ Windows NT

Description	EM_SETOLEINTERFACE is a message that provides the rich-text edit control with an IRichEditOleCallback object to use to obtain OLE-related resources and information from the client.
Parameters	
wParam	WPARAM: This parameter is set to zero.
lParam	LPARAM: A pointer to an IRichEditOleCallback object. The control calls AddRef() for the object before returning.
Returns	int: A nonzero value if successful; otherwise, zero is returned.
Include File	richedit.h
Related Messages	EM_GETOLEINTERFACE

EM_SETOPTIONS ■ Win32s ■ Windows 95 ■ Windows NT

Description	EM_SETOPTIONS is a message that sets the options for a rich-text edit control.
Parameters	
wParam	UINT: A combination of the values in Table 8-16 specifying the operation.

Table 8-16 EM_SETOPTIONS *wParam* values

Value	Meaning
ECOOP_AND	Retains only those current options that are also specified by *lParam*.
ECOOP_OR	Combines the specified options with the current options.
ECOOP_SET	Sets the options to those specified by *lParam*.
ECOOP_XOR	Retains only those current options that are not specified by *lParam*.

lParam	UINT: A combination of the values in Table 8-17 specifying the rich edit control options.

Table 8-17 EM_SETOPTIONS *lParam* values

Value	Meaning
ECO_AUTOHSCROLL	Automatically scrolls text horizontally, if necessary.
ECO_AUTOVSCROLL	Automatically scrolls text vertically, if necessary.
ECO_AUTOWORDSELECTION	Automatic selection of word when the mouse is double-clicked.
ECO_NOHIDESEL	The selected text is not hidden when the edit control loses the keyboard focus.
ECO_READONLY	The edit control is read-only.
ECO_SAVESEL	Preserves the selection when the control loses the focus. By default, the entire contents of the control are selected when it regains the focus.
ECO_WANTRETURN	Inserts a carriage return when the ENTER key is pressed in the edit control.

Returns	UINT: The current option of the edit control.
Include File	richedit.h

EM_SETPARAFORMAT ■ Win32s ■ Windows 95 ■ Windows NT

Description	EM_SETPARAFORMAT is a message that sets the paragraph formatting for the current selection in a rich-text edit control.
Parameters	
wParam	WPARAM: This parameter is set to zero.
lParam	PARAFORMAT *: A pointer to a PARAFORMAT structure specifying the new paragraph formatting attributes for the current selection of the rich-text edit control. See the definition of the PARAFORMAT structure under the EM_GETPARAFORMAT message.
Returns	int: If successful, a nonzero value is returned; otherwise, zero is returned.
Include File	richedit.h
See Also	PARAFORMAT
Related Messages	EM_GETPARAFORMAT
Example	This function from the rich-text editor example changes the paragraph alignment when the user selects Left, Center, or Right from the menu. The EM_SETPARAFORMAT message is used to update the paragraph alignment for the current selection (Listing 8-9).

Listing 8-9 Using the EM_SETPARAFORMAT message

```
VOID ChangeAlignment( UINT uCmd )
{
    PARAFORMAT pf;
```

```
    pf.cbSize = sizeof( PARAFORMAT );
    pf.dwMask = PFM_ALIGNMENT;

    switch( uCmd )
    {
        case IDM_ALIGNLEFT   : pf.wAlignment = PFA_LEFT;   break;
        case IDM_ALIGNCENTER : pf.wAlignment = PFA_CENTER; break;
        case IDM_ALIGNRIGHT  : pf.wAlignment = PFA_RIGHT;  break;
    }

    SendMessage( hEdit, EM_SETPARAFORMAT, 0, (LPARAM)&pf );
    SetFocus( hEdit );
}
```

EM_SETPUNCTUATION ■ Win32s ■ Windows 95 ■ Windows NT

Description   EM_SETPUNCTUATION is a message that is available in Asian-language versions of Windows 95 to set the punctuation characters of the rich-text edit control.

Parameters

wParam   UINT: One of the values in Table 8-13 that specifies the punctuation to set for the rich-text edit control.

lParam   PUNCTUATION *: The address of the PUNCTUATION structure that receives the punctuation characters for the rich-text edit control. See the definition of the PUNCTUATION structure under the EM_GETPUNCTUATION message.

Returns   int: If successful, a nonzero value is returned; otherwise, zero is returned.

Include File   richedit.h

Related Messages   EM_GETPUNCTUATION

EM_SETTARGETDEVICE ■ Win32s ■ Windows 95 ■ Windows NT

Description   EM_SETTARGETDEVICE is a message that establishes the target device and line width for WYSIWYG formatting in a rich-text edit control.

Parameters

wParam   HDC: The handle of the device context for the target device. Usually a printer device context.

lParam   int: The line width to use for the WYSIWYG formatting.

Returns   int: If successful, a nonzero value is returned; otherwise zero is returned.

Include File   richedit.h

EM_SETWORDBREAKPROCEX ■ Win32s ■ Windows 95 ■ Windows NT

Description   EM_SETWORDBREAKPROCEX is a message that sets the extended word-break procedure for the rich-text edit control.

Parameters

wParam	WPARAM: Set to zero.
lParam	EDITWORDBREAKPROC: The address of the EditWordBreakProcEx() or NULL to use the default procedure for the rich-text edit control. See the definition of the callback procedure below.
Returns	EDITWORDBREAKPROC: The address of the previous word-break procedure is returned.
Include File	richedit.h
Related Messages	EM_GETWORDBREAKPROCEX
Callback Syntax	LONG **EditWordBreakProcEx(** char* *pchText*, LONG *cchText*, BYTE *bCharSet*, INT *code*)
pchText	char*: A pointer to the text at the current position. If the *code* parameter indicates movement to the left, the text is in the elements *pchText*[-1] through *pchText*[-*cchText*], and *pchText*[0] is undefined. For all other actions, the text is in the elements *pchText*[0] through *pchText*[*cchText* -1].
cchText	LONG: The number of characters in the buffer for the direction indicated by the code parameter.
bCharSet	BYTE: The character set of the text.
code	INT: The action to take. This can be one of the values listed in Table 8-5 under the EM_FINDWORDBREAK message.

EM_SETWORDWRAPMODE   ■ Win32s   ■ Windows 95   ■ Windows NT

Description	EM_SETWORDWRAPMODE is a message that is available in Asian-language versions of Windows 95 to set the word wrapping and breaking options.
Parameters	
wParam	UINT: One of the values in Table 8-18 specifying the options for the control.

Table 8-18 EM_SETWORDWRAPMODE *wParam* values

Value	Meaning
WBF_CUSTOM	Sets application-defined punctuation table.
WBF_LEVEL1	Sets level 1 punctuation table as default.
WBF_LEVEL2	Sets level 2 punctuation table as default.
WBF_OVERFLOW	Recognizes overflow punctuation. This is not currently supported by Windows 95.
WBF_WORDBREAK	Enables English word-breaking operation.
WBF_WORDWRAP	Enables Asian-specific word-wrap operation, such as Kinsoku in Japanese.

Returns	UINT: The current word wrapping and breaking options of the rich-text edit control are returned.
Include File	richedit.h
Related Messages	EM_GETWORDWRAPMODE

EM_STREAMIN ■ Win32s ■ Windows 95 ■ Windows NT

Description EM_STREAMIN is a message that replaces the contents of a rich-text edit control with the specified data stream.

Parameters

wParam UINT: One of the data formats in Table 8-19, optionally combined with the SFF_SELECTION flag. If the SFF_SELECTION flag is specified, the stream replaces the contents of the current selection; otherwise, the stream replaces the entire contents of the control.

Table 8-19 EM_STREAMIN *wParam* values

Value	Meaning
SF_TEXT	Text
SF_RTF	Rich-text format

lParam EDITSTREAM *: A pointer to an EDITSTREAM structure that specifies the data stream to read into the control. The control reads the data by repeatedly calling the function specified by the *pfnCallback* member of the EDITSTREAM structure. See the definition of the EDITSTREAM structure below.

Returns int: The number of characters read into the control is returned.

Include File richedit.h

Related Messages EM_STREAMOUT

EDITSTREAM Definition

```
typedef struct _editstream
{
    DWORD              dwCookie;
    DWORD              dwError;
    EDITSTREAMCALLBACK pfnCallback;
}  EDITSTREAM;
```

Members

dwCookie DWORD: Application-defined value that is passed to the callback function.

dwError DWORD: Error encountered while streaming. If an error was not encountered, this member is zero.

pfnCallback	EDITSTREAMCALLBACK: The address of an application-defined function that the control calls to transfer data. See the definition of the callback function below.
Callback Syntax	DWORD CALLBACK **EditStreamCallback**(DWORD *dwCookie*, LPBYTE *pbBuff*, LONG *cb*, LONG* *pcb*)

Callback Parameters

dwCookie	DWORD: The value of the *dwCookie* member of the EDITSTREAM structure.
pbBuff	LPBYTE: A pointer to the buffer to read from or write to depending on the direction.
cb	LONG: The count of bytes to read or write.
pcb	LONG*: A pointer to a variable that receives the number of bytes actually read or written. When reading data and the end-of-file (EOF) is reached, this value should be set to zero.
Callback Returns	DWORD: If data is being read, the return value should be zero unless an error occurs. The return value is placed in the *dwError* member of the EDITSTREAM structure. If data is being written, the return value is a nonzero value to continue to transferring data. Return zero to abort the save.
Example	This code segment from the rich-text editor example (Listing 8-10) demonstrates how to open an existing rich-text file and read it into the rich edit control. The Open common dialog box is used to retrieve the file name and the EM_STREAMIN message is used to read the contents of the file into the editor.

Listing 8-10 Using the EM_STREAMIN message

```
DWORD CALLBACK ReadProc( DWORD dwCookie, LPBYTE pbBuff,
                         LONG cb, LONG* pcb )
{
   // Read the data from the file.
   //........................
   ReadFile( (HANDLE)dwCookie,
          pbBuff, cb,
          pcb,
          NULL );

   return( FALSE );
}


VOID Open()
{
   OPENFILENAME ofn;

   memset( &ofn, 0, sizeof( OPENFILENAME ) );

   // Fill OPENFILENAME structure.
   //...........................
```

```
ofn.lStructSize = sizeof( OPENFILENAME );
ofn.hwndOwner   = hMainWnd;
ofn.lpstrFilter = "Rich-Text File (*.RTF)*.RTF";
ofn.lpstrFile   = szFileName;
ofn.nMaxFile    = MAX_PATH;
ofn.Flags       = OFN_FILEMUSTEXIST | OFN_HIDEREADONLY;
ofn.lpstrDefExt = "RTF";

// Get a filename and save the file.
//.................................
if ( GetOpenFileName( &ofn ) )
{
    EDITSTREAM es;
    HANDLE     hFile;

    // Open the file.
    //..............
    hFile = CreateFile( szFileName, GENERIC_READ, 0, NULL,
                        OPEN_EXISTING,
                        FILE_ATTRIBUTE_NORMAL,
                        NULL );

    if ( hFile )
    {
        // Fill the EDITSTREAM structure.
        //..............................
        es.dwCookie = (DWORD)hFile;
        es.dwError  = 0;
        es.pfnCallback = ReadProc;

        // Read the data from the file.
        //............................
        SendMessage( hEdit, EM_STREAMIN, SF_RTF, (LPARAM)&es );

        // Clear the modify flag.
        //......................
        SendMessage( hEdit, EM_SETMODIFY, 0, 0 );
    }

    CloseHandle( hFile );
}
}
```

EM_STREAMOUT ■ Win32s ■ Windows 95 ■ Windows NT

Description   EM_STREAMOUT is a message that writes the contents of a rich-text edit control to the specified data stream.

Parameters

wParam   UINT: A value specifying one of the data formats in Table 8-20, optionally combined with the SFF_SELECTION flag. If the SFF_SELECTION flag is specified, only the contents of the current selection are written out; otherwise, the entire contents of the control are written out.

Table 8-20 EM_STREAMOUT *wParam* values

Value	Meaning
SF_RTF	Rich-text format (RTF)
SF_RTFNOOBJS	RTF with spaces in place of OLE objects
SF_TEXT	Text with spaces in place of OLE objects
SF_TEXTIZED	Text with a text representation of OLE objects

lParam	EDITSTREAM *: A pointer to an EDITSTREAM structure that contains information about the data stream. The control writes out the data by repeatedly calling the function specified by the *pfnCallback* member of the EDITSTREAM structure. See the definition of the EDITSTREAM structure under the EM_STREAMIN message.
Returns	int: The number of characters written to the data stream is returned.
Include File	richedit.h
Related Messages	EM_STREAMIN
Example	This code segment (Listing 8-11) from the rich-text editor example shows how to save the contents of a rich edit control to an RTF format file. The EM_STREAMOUT message calls the SaveProc() function repeatedly until the entire contents of the edit control are saved to the file. If a file name is not assigned for the current document, the Save As common dialog is displayed to assign a file name to the document before saving.

Listing 8-11 Using the EM_STREAMOUT message

```
DWORD CALLBACK SaveProc( DWORD dwCookie, LPBYTE pbBuff,
                         LONG cb, LONG* pcb )
{
   // Write the data to the file.
   //...........................
   if ( WriteFile( (HANDLE)dwCookie,
                   pbBuff, cb,
                   pcb,
                   NULL ) )
   {
      return( TRUE );
   }

   return( FALSE );
}

VOID Save()
{
   // If there is no filename,
   // go to save as.
   //........................
   if ( !szFileName[0] )
      SaveAs();
   else
   {
```

```
        EDITSTREAM es;
        HANDLE    hFile;

        // Create a new file, always.
        //........................
        hFile = CreateFile( szFileName, GENERIC_WRITE, 0, NULL,
                            CREATE_ALWAYS,
                            FILE_ATTRIBUTE_NORMAL |
                            FILE_FLAG_WRITE_THROUGH,
                            NULL );

        // Fill the EDITSTREAM structure.
        //..............................
        es.dwCookie = (DWORD)hFile;
        es.dwError  = 0;
        es.pfnCallback = SaveProc;

        // Save the data to the file.
        //..........................
        SendMessage( hEdit, EM_STREAMOUT, SF_RTF, (LPARAM)&es );

        // Clear the modify flag.
        //......................
        SendMessage( hEdit, EM_SETMODIFY, 0, 0 );

        CloseHandle( hFile );
    }
}


VOID SaveAs()
{
    OPENFILENAME ofn;

    memset( &ofn, 0, sizeof( OPENFILENAME ) );

    // Fill OPENFILENAME structure.
    //............................
    ofn.lStructSize = sizeof( OPENFILENAME );
    ofn.hwndOwner   = hMainWnd;
    ofn.lpstrFilter = "Rich-Text File (*.RTF)*.RTF";
    ofn.lpstrFile   = szFileName;
    ofn.nMaxFile    = MAX_PATH;
    ofn.Flags       = OFN_PATHMUSTEXIST | OFN_HIDEREADONLY;
    ofn.lpstrDefExt = "RTF";

    // Get a filename and save the file.
    //.................................
    if ( GetSaveFileName( &ofn ) )
        Save();
}
```

EN_CORRECTTEXT ■ Win32s ■ Windows 95 ■ Windows NT

Description   EN_CORRECTTEXT is a notification message that is sent if pen capabilities are available to notify the parent window of a rich-text edit control that a SYV_CORRECT gesture occurred. A rich-text edit control sends this notification message in the form of a WM_NOTIFY message.

Parameters

wParam   UINT: The identifier of the rich-text edit control.

lParam   ENCORRECTTEXT *: A pointer to an ENCORRECTTEXT structure speci-
                  fying the selection to be corrected. See the definition of the
                  ENCORRECTTEXT structure below.

Returns   int: Zero is returned to ignore the action; otherwise, a nonzero value is
                  returned to process it.

Include File   richedit.h

Related Messages WM_NOTIFY

ENCORRECTTEXT Definition

```
typedef struct _encorrecttext
{
    NMHDR     nmhdr;
    CHARRANGE chrg;
    WORD      seltyp;
} ENCORRECTTEXT;
```

Members

nmhdr   NMHDR: An NMHDR structure that contains information about the notifi-
                  cation header. See the definition of the NMHDR structure below.

chrg   CHARRANGE: A CHARRANGE structure that specifies information about
                  the current selection. See the definition of the CHARRANGE structure
                  under the EM_EXGETSEL message.

seltyp   WORD: One of the values in Table 8-21 specifying the contents of the new
                  selection, or SEL_EMPTY if the selection is empty.

Table 8-21 EN_CORRECTTEXT ENCORRECTTEXT *seltyp* values

Value	Meaning
SEL_MULTICHAR	Contains more than one character of text.
SEL_MULTIOBJECT	Contains more than one OLE object.
SEL_OBJECT	Contains at least one OLE object.
SEL_TEXT	Contains text.

NMHDR Definition

```
typedef struct tagNMHDR
{
    HWND hwndFrom;
    UINT idFrom;
    UINT code;
} NMHDR;
```

Members

hwndFrom   HWND: The handle to the control sending the message.

idFrom   UINT: The identifier of the control sending the message.

code   UINT: A control-specific notification code, or one of the common notification values in Table 8-22.

Table 8-22 EN_CORRECTTEXT NMHDR *code* values

Value	Meaning
NM_CLICK	The user has clicked the left mouse button within the control.
NM_DBLCLK	The user has double-clicked the left mouse button within the control.
NM_KILLFOCUS	The control has lost the input focus.
NM_OUTOFMEMORY	The control could not complete an operation because there was not enough memory available.
NM_RCLICK	The user has clicked the right mouse button within the control.
NM_RDBLCLK	The user has double-clicked the right mouse button within the control.
NM_RETURN	The control has the input focus, and the user has pressed the ⟨ENTER⟩ key.
NM_SETFOCUS	The control has received the input focus.

EN_DROPFILES   ■ Win32s   ■ Windows 95   ■ Windows NT

Description   EN_DROPFILES is a notification message that notifies the parent window of a rich-text edit control that the user is attempting to drop files into the control. The control sends this notification message in the form of a WM_NOTIFY message when it receives the WM_DROPFILES message.

Parameters

wParam   UINT: The identifier of the rich-text edit control.

lParam   ENDROPFILES *: A pointer to an ENDROPFILES structure containing information about the dropped files. See the definition of the ENDROPFILES structure below.

Returns   int: A nonzero value is returned to allow the drop operation; otherwise, zero is returned to ignore the drop.

Include File   richedit.h

Related Messages   WM_DROPFILES, WM_NOTIFY

ENDROPFILES Definition

```
typedef struct _endropfiles
{
    NMHDR   nmhdr;
    HANDLE  hDrop;
    LONG    cp;
    BOOL    fProtected;
} ENDROPFILES;
```

Members

nmhdr   NMHDR: An NMHDR structure that contains information about the notification header. See definition of the NMHDR structure under EN_CORRECTTEXT message.

hDrop   HANDLE: The handle of the dropped files list.

cp   LONG: The character position at which the dropped files would be inserted.

fProtected   BOOL: TRUE indicates the specified position is protected, and FALSE indicates the position is not protected.

EN_IMECHANGE   ■ Win32s ■ Windows 95 ■ Windows NT

Description   EN_IMECHANGE is a notification message that is available for Asian-language versions of Windows 95 to notify the parent window of a rich-text edit control that the IME conversion status has changed.

Parameters

wParam   UINT: The rich-text edit control.

lParam   LPARAM: This parameter is set to zero.

Returns   int: A value of zero is returned.

Include File   richedit.h

EN_MSGFILTER   ■ Win32s ■ Windows 95 ■ Windows NT

Description   EN_MSGFILTER is a notification message that notifies the parent window of a rich-text edit control that a keyboard or mouse event is in the control. A rich edit control sends this notification message in the form of a WM_NOTIFY message.

Parameters

wParam   UINT: The rich-text edit control.

lParam   MSGFILTER: A pointer to an MSGFILTER structure containing information about the keyboard or mouse message. If the parent window modifies this structure and returns a nonzero value, the modified message is processed instead of the original one. See the definition of the MSGFILTER structure below.

Returns   int: A nonzero value is returned if the control should process the event; otherwise, zero is returned if the control should ignore the event.

Include File   richedit.h

Related Messages WM_NOTIFY

MSGFILTER Definition

```
typedef struct _msgfilter
{
    NMHDR   nmhdr;
    UINT    msg;
    WPARAM  wParam;
    LPARAM  lParam;
}  MSGFILTER;
```

Members

nmhdr	NMHDR: An NMHDR structure that contains information about the notification header. See the definition of the NMHDR structure under the EN_CORRECTTEXT structure.
msg	UINT: The keyboard or mouse message identifier.
wParam	WPARAM: The *wParam* parameter of the message.
lParam	LPARAM: The *lParam* parameter of the message.

EN_OLEOPFAILED ■ Win32s ■ Windows 95 ■ Windows NT

Description   EN_OLEOPFAILED is a notification message that notifies the parent window of a rich-text edit control that a user action on an OLE object failed.

Parameters

wParam	UINT: The rich-text edit control.
lParam	ENOLEOPFAILED *: A pointer to an ENOLEOPFAILED structure that contains information about the action that failed. See the definition of the ENOLEOPFAILED structure below.

Returns   int: A value of zero is returned.

Include File   richedit.h

ENOLEOPFAILED Definition

```
typedef struct _enoleopfailed
{
    NMHDR    nmhdr;
    LONG     iob;
    LONG     lOper;
    HRESULT hr;
} ENOLEOPFAILED;
```

Members

nmhdr	NMHDR: An NMHDR structure that contains information about the notification header. See the definition of the NMHDR structure under the EN_CORRECTTEXT message.
iob	LONG: The index of the object.
lOper	LONG: The OLE operation that failed.
hr	HRESULT: The error code returned should be the object of the operation.

EN_PROTECTED ■ Win32s ■ Windows 95 ■ Windows NT

Description   EN_PROTECTED is a notification message that notifies the parent window of a rich-text edit control that the user is performing an action that will change a protected range of text. A rich-text edit control sends this notification message in the form of a WM_NOTIFY message.

Parameters

wParam   UINT: The identifier of the rich edit control.

lParam   ENPROTECTED *: A pointer to an ENPROTECTED structure containing information about the message that is responsible for sending the notification message. See the definition of the ENPROTECTED structure below.

Returns   int: A zero is returned to allow the operation to be performed; otherwise, a nonzero value is returned to prevent it.

Include File richedit.h

Related Messages WM_NOTIFY

ENPROTECTED Definition

```
typedef struct _enprotected
{
    NMHDR     nmhdr;
    UINT      msg;
    WPARAM    wParam;
    LPARAM    lParam;
    CHARRANGE chrg;
} ENPROTECTED;
```

Members

nmhdr   NMHDR: An NMHDR structure that contains information about the notification header. See the definition of the NMHDR structure under the EN_CORRECTTEXT message.

msg   UINT: The message that triggered the notification.

wParam   WPARAM: The *wParam* parameter of the message.

lParam   LPARAM: The *lParam* parameter of the message.

chrg   CHARRANGE: A CHARRANGE structure that contains information about the current selection. See the definition of the CHARRANGE structure under the EM_EXGETSEL message.

EN_REQUESTRESIZE   ■ Win32s ■ Windows 95 ■ Windows NT

Description   EN_REQUESTRESIZE is a notification message that notifies the parent window of a rich-text edit control that the control contents are either smaller or larger than the control's window size. A rich edit control sends this notification message in the form of a WM_NOTIFY message.

Parameters

wParam   UINT: The identifier of the rich edit control.

lParam   REQRESIZE *: A pointer to a REQRESIZE structure that contains the requested size of the rich-text edit control. See the definition of the REQRESIZE structure below.

Include File richedit.h

Related Messages WM_NOTIFY

REQRESIZE Definition

```
typedef struct _reqresize
{
  NMHDR nmhdr;
  RECT  rc;
} REQRESIZE;
```

Members

nmhdr　　　　　NMHDR: An NMHDR structure that contains information about the notification header. See the definition of the NMHDR structure under the EN_CORRECTTEXT message.

rc　　　　　　RECT: A RECT structure that contains information about the requested new size of the control. See the definition of the RECT structure under the EM_DISPLAYBAND message.

EN_SAVECLIPBOARD　　　■ Win32s　■ Windows 95　■ Windows NT

Description　　　EN_SAVECLIPBOARD is a notification message that notifies the parent window of a rich-text edit control that the clipboard contains information and it is closing.

Parameters

wParam　　　　UINT: The rich-text edit control.

lParam　　　　ENSAVECLIPBOARD *: A pointer to an ENSAVECLIPBOARD structure that contains information about the contents of the clipboard. See the definition of the ENSAVECLIPBOARD structure below.

Returns　　　　int: If the clipboard information should be made available to other applications, zero is returned; otherwise, a nonzero value is returned to indicate the clipboard information should not be saved.

Include File　　richedit.h

ENSAVECLIPBOARD Definition

```
typedef struct _ensaveclipboard
{
    NMHDR nmhdr;
    LONG  cObjectCount;
    LONG  cch;
} ENSAVECLIPBOARD;
```

Members

nmhdr　　　　　NMHDR: An NMHDR structure that contains information about the notification header. See the definition of the NMHDR structure under the EN_CORRECTTEXT message.

cObjectCount　　LONG: The number of objects in the clipboard.

cch　　　　　　LONG: The number of characters in the clipboard.

Example　　　　See the example for the EM_SETEVENTMASK message.

EN_SELCHANGE ■ Win32s ■ Windows 95 ■ Windows NT

Description   EN_SELCHANGE is a notification message that notifies the parent window of a rich-text edit control that the current selection has changed. A rich-text edit control sends this notification message in the form of a WM_NOTIFY message.

Parameters

wParam   UINT: The identifier of the rich-text edit control.

lParam   SELCHANGE*: A pointer to a SELCHANGE structure that contains information about the new selection. See the definition of the SELCHANGE structure below.

Include File   richedit.h

Related Messages   WM_NOTIFY

SELCHANGE Definition

```
typedef struct _selchange
{
    NMHDR      nmhdr;
    CHARRANGE  chrg;
    WORD       seltyp;
} SELCHANGE;
```

Members

nmhdr   NMHDR: An NMHDR structure that contains information about the notification header. See the definition of the NMHDR structure under the EN_CORRECTTEXT message.

chrg   CHARRANGE: A CHARRANGE structure that contains the range of the new selection. See the definition of the CHARRANGE structure under the EM_EXGETSEL message.

seltyp   WORD: A value from Table 8-23 that specifies the contents of the new selection.

Table 8-23 EN_SELCHANGE SELCHANGE *seltyp* values

Value	Meaning
SEL_EMPTY	The selection is empty.
SEL_MULTICHAR	Contains more than one character of text.
SEL_MULTIOBJECT	Contains more than one OLE object.
SEL_OBJECT	Contains at least one OLE object.
SEL_TEXT	Contains text.

Example   See the example for the EM_SETEVENTMASK message.

EN_STOPNOUNDO
■ Win32s   ■ Windows 95   ■ Windows NT

Description	EN_STOPNOUNDO is a notification message that notifies the parent window of a rich-text edit control that an action occurred for which the control cannot allocate enough memory to maintain the undo state. A rich-text edit control sends this notification message in the form of a WM_NOTIFY message.
Parameters	
wParam	UINT: The identifier of the rich edit control.
lParam	NMHDR *: A pointer to an NMHDR structure that contains information about the message. See the definition of the NMHDR structure under the EN_CORRECTTEXT message.
Returns	int: A value of zero is returned to continue the action; otherwise, a nonzero value is returned to stop it.
Include File	richedit.h
Related Messages	WM_NOTIFY
Example	See the example for the EM_SETEVENTMASK message.

9

MISCELLANEOUS CONTROLS

9

MISCELLANEOUS CONTROLS

The Common Control Library contains many small controls, such as the trackbar and progress controls, that can give an application a more user friendly interface. Because these controls are in the Common Control Library, they are used throughout Windows 95 and in third party applications designed for Windows 95. Thus, if you use these controls as appropriate, they will add to the uniform look and feel of your application. This chapter covers the lesser-known but useful common controls that are available with the Common Control Library. These include the trackbar, progress, header, up-down, animation, and hot-key controls.

Trackbar Control

The trackbar control, shown in Figure 9-1, is a control that allows the user to select a value within a defined range by sliding a *thumb* or *slider* to a location on a line. The thumb or slider is the position indicator that shows the current value of the trackbar. The trackbar is similar to the scroll bar that Windows 3.x applications have traditionally used in situations where the user can select a value from a range. Windows 95 applications should use the trackbar. Not only does it provide the same functionality that the scroll bar provides, it provides additional functionality with the addition of selection ranges.

Figure 9-1 Trackbar controls

Trackbars are useful when you want the user to select a value within a defined range of values. For example, an application can use a trackbar to allow the user to set the repeat rate of the keyboard or the priority of a background printing process. A trackbar that allows selection ranges allows the user to select a range of values within the defined minimum and maximum range of the trackbar. For example, the selection range could represent the starting and ending points within an AVI file that you want to cut if the trackbar represents the total length of the AVI file.

The slider in a trackbar moves in application-defined increments. For example, if the trackbar has a range of five, the slider can occupy six positions. The extra position is the first position, which is followed by the five additional positions. Each position is typically identified by a tick mark; however, the trackbar control allows the application to define the frequency of the tick marks or the actual position of each tick mark.

Creating a Trackbar

An application creates a trackbar control by using the CreateWindowEx() function, specifying the TRACKBAR_CLASS window class. To ensure that the Common Control Library is initialized, the application should call the InitCommonControls() function prior to creating a trackbar. Once the trackbar is created, use the trackbar messages described in this chapter to change or retrieve its properties. These changes include setting the range of the trackbar, the position of the slider, drawing tick marks, and setting the selection range. Table 9-1 lists the specific trackbar styles you can use when creating a trackbar control. These styles are in addition to the standard window styles. Typically, the WS_CHILD and WS_VISIBLE styles are defined.

Table 9-1 Trackbar control styles

Style	Meaning
TBS_AUTOTICKS	Specifies that tick marks are automatically drawn for each increment in the range of values.
TBS_BOTH	Specifies that tick marks be displayed on both sides of the trackbar.
TBS_BOTTOM	Specifies that tick marks be displayed on the bottom of the trackbar (default for horizontal trackbars).
TBS_ENABLESELRANGE	Creates a trackbar that can display a selection range.
TBS_FIXEDLENGTH	Creates a trackbar for which the length of the slider remains the same. By default the length of the slider changes as the selection range changes.
TBS_HORZ	Creates a horizontal trackbar control (default).
TBS_LEFT	Specifies that tick marks be displayed on the left side of the trackbar (vertical trackbars only).
TBS_NOTHUMB	Creates a trackbar that does not include a slider.
TBS_NOTICKS	Creates a trackbar that does not include tick marks.
TBS_RIGHT	Specifies that tick marks be displayed on the right side of the trackbar (default for vertical trackbars).
TBS_TOP	Specifies that tick marks be displayed on the top of the trackbar (horizontal trackbars only).
TBS_VERT	Creates a vertical trackbar control.

Trackbar Notifications

A trackbar control notifies an application of events (normally, the user moving the slider) by sending WM_HSCROLL messages to the parent window of the trackbar control. The processing of this message is very similar to that of a standard horizontal scroll bar. The low-order word of the *wParam* parameter of the WM_HSCROLL contains the notification code, and the high-order word specifies the position of the slider.

The primary difference between notifications sent by scroll bars and trackbars is the notification messages used. Scroll bars send the SB_ notification messages such as SB_LINEDOWN and SB_LINEUP, while trackbars send TB_ notification codes. Table 9-2 lists the trackbar notification messages and the reasons they are sent.

Table 9-2 Trackbar notification messages

Message	Meaning
TB_BOTTOM	The VK_END key was pressed.
TB_ENDTRACK	The user released a key that sent a relevant virtual-key code, such as VK_LEFT, and a WM_KEYUP message was received.
TB_LINEDOWN	The VK_RIGHT or VK_DOWN key was pressed.
TB_LINEUP	The VK_LEFT or VK_UP key was pressed.
TB_PAGEDOWN	The user clicked the channel below or to the right of the slider. The VK_NEXT key code is processed.
TB_PAGEUP	The user clicked the channel above or to the left of the slider. The VK_PRIOR key code is processed.
TB_THUMBPOSITION	This message is sent when the WM_LBUTTONUP message is received following a TB_THUMBTRACK notification message.
TB_THUMBTRACK	The user dragged the slider.
TB_TOP	The VK_HOME key was pressed.

Progress Control

The progress bar is a window that an application can use to display the progress of a long operation. The rectangular area of the progress bar is gradually filled, from left to right, with the system highlight color as an operation progresses. Figure 9-2 shows a progress bar used in the ScanDisk program that comes with Windows 95.

An application can create a progress bar by using the CreateWindowEx() function with the PROGRESS_CLASS window class. To ensure that the Common Control Library is initialized and the PROGRESS_CLASS window class is registered, the application should call the InitCommonControls() function prior to creating a progress bar. Use the standard window styles when creating the progress bar. Typically the WS_CHILD and WS_VISIBLE styles are specified.

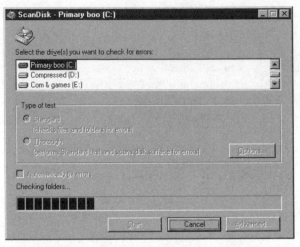

Figure 9-2 Progress bar in ScanDisk

Progress bars have a possible range of 0 to 65,535 (64K), or any minimum and maximum values within this range. The range represents the entire duration of the operation, while the current position represents the progress the application has made toward the completion of the entire task. For example, if the application is processing 100 records, the range would be 0 to 100. As the application processes the records, the position would be the record number the application last processed. The progress bar provides several messages, described in this chapter, that you can use to set the range and position of the progress bar.

Header Control

The header control is widely seen throughout Windows 95, typically in conjunction with list view controls. This is because the header control is a building block for the list view control. By itself, the header control only provides the actual header of the list view with the titles within the columns. The header control also allows the user to resize the columns by dragging the column separators. Figure 9-4, in the example under the Header_InsertItem macro, shows a header control used on top of the client area of a window. When using a header control, it is up to the application to display the data within the columns using standard painting methods.

Creating Header Controls

Creating a header control is the same as creating most of the common controls: use the CreateWindowEx() function with the WC_HEADER window class. This class is registered when the Common Control Library is initialized. To ensure the library is initialized before creating the header control, call the InitCommonControls() function.

In addition to the standard window styles, the header control has two unique styles, HDS_BUTTONS and HDS_HORZ. The HDS_BUTTONS style creates a header control in which the columns in the control look and behave like push buttons. This is useful if an application carries out a task when the user clicks an item in the header control. For example, the application could sort the list based on the column that is selected. The HDS_HORZ style creates a header control that is oriented horizontally. This is the normal orientation as it appears within the list view control.

Once the header control is created, the application can send messages to the header control directly or via defined macros. The header control, in return, sends notification messages to its parent window to notify the application of events that occur, such as dragging and selecting a column. These messages and macros are covered later in this chapter.

Header Control Items

When a header control is first created, it does not include any columns. The application must add the items (columns) with the Header_InsertItem macro. Each item in the header control can have a string, a bitmapped image, and an application-defined 32-bit value associated with it. The string and bitmap are displayed within the header control. If an item includes both a string and a bitmap, the image is displayed above the string. If the string and image overlap, the string overwrites the bitmap in the overlapping areas.

When the application inserts an item with the Header_InsertItem macro, the index of the newly added item is returned. The application can use this index to reference the item with other macros. For example, you can change the properties of a column with the Header_SetItem macro.

Owner-Drawn Header Controls

Individual items within the header control can be defined as owner drawn. This allows the application to have more control over the appearance of the header item. To insert an owner-drawn item, use the Header_InsertItem macro with the HDF_OWNERDRAW value specified within the HD_ITEM structure.

When the header control must draw an owner-drawn item, it sends the WM_DRAWITEM message to the parent window. The *wParam* parameter of the message is the child window identifier of the header control, and the *lParam* parameter is a pointer to a DRAWITEMSTRUCT structure. Table 9-3 shows the members of DRAWITEMSTRUCT and the values they contain for owner-drawn header items.

Table 9-3 DRAWITEMSTRUCT owner-drawn member values

Member	Value
CtlType	ODT_HEADER owner-drawn control type.
CtlID	The child-window identifier of the header control.
itemID	The index of the item to be drawn.
itemAction	ODA_DRAWENTIRE drawing-action flag.

continued on next page

continued from previous page

Member	Value
itemState	ODS_SELECTED drawing-action flag if the cursor is on the item and the mouse button is down. Otherwise, this member is zero.
hwndItem	The window handle of the header control.
hDC	The handle of the device context of the header control.
rcItem	Coordinates of the header item to be drawn. The coordinates are relative to the upper left corner of the header control.
itemData	The application-defined 32-bit value associated with the item.

Up-Down Control

The up-down control is a pair of arrow buttons that the user can select to increment or decrement a value. The action and appearance of an up-down control is similar to a scroll bar without a slider. The *auto buddy* is a unique feature of an up-down control that makes it useful by allowing a user to increment or decrement the value within an edit control. The auto buddy feature automatically combines the up-down control with an edit control and acts upon the contents of the edit control. This edit control is known as the *buddy window*. Figure 9-3 under the CreateUpDownControl() function shows an edit control as a buddy window with an up-down control.

The most common use for an up-down control is in conjunction with an edit control, which creates the look of a single control as seen in Figure 9-3. Another use for an up-down control is without a buddy window. In this case, the control works as a simplified scroll bar. For example, a tab control that does not support multiple rows of tabs uses a horizontal up-down control to scroll through the tabs.

An application can create an up-down control in two ways. The first is to use the CreateUpDownControl() function. The second is to use the CreateWindowEx() function with the UPDOWN_CLASS window class. The second method also requires the application to call the InitCommonControls() function to initialize the Common Control Library.

If the application uses the CreateUpDownControl(), the range and buddy window for the up-down control are set with one function call. When using the CreateWindowEx() function, the application must use the messages provided to set the range and the buddy window.

For more information on the up-down control and how to use it, see the example under the CreateUpDownControl() function later in this chapter.

Animation Control

The animation control is a window that plays silent audio video interleaved (AVI) clips. In order to work with this control, the AVI clips must not have sound. The animation control creates an additional thread that continues to execute while the application performs an operation. A common use for an animation control is to indicate system activity during a long operation where the end of the operation is unknown. For example, the Find dialog box of the Windows Explorer displays a moving magnifying class as the system searches for a file. Another example is the copy progress dialog of the Windows Explorer, which displays a paper flying from one folder to another. Since the capabilities of an animation control are severely limited and subject to change, use the multimedia playback and recording capabilities of the MCIWnd control if you need more advanced features.

An animation control can display an AVI clip that is either uncompressed or compressed using run-length encoding (RLE). The AVI clip can be added to your application as an AVI resource, or it can be in an .AVI file.

An application can create an animation control with the Animate_Create macro. This macro uses the CreateWindow() function with the ANIMATE_CLASS window class. Animate_Create also sets the width and height of the control to zero. You can use the SetWindowPos() function to set the position and size of the control.

Once the animation control is created, the application uses macros that send messages to the control to open, play, stop, and close an AVI clip. These macros and corresponding messages are covered later in this chapter.

Hot-Key Control

Hot-key controls are windows that enable the user to enter a combination of keystrokes to be used as a *hot key*. A hot key is a key combination that the user can press to perform an action. For example, the user can create a hot key that activates a window. The hot-key control displays the user's choice for a hot key and ensures that the user selects a valid key combination.

A hot-key control appears to the user to be a normal edit control; however, when the input focus is placed in the control, all key combinations pressed are translated into the character representations of a hot key. For example, if CTRL-K is pressed, "Ctrl + K" is displayed in the hot-key control.

After the user has selected a key combination, the application retrieves the key combination from the hot-key control with the HKM_GETHOTKEY message and uses it to set up a hot key in the system.

An application can create a hot-key control by using the CreateWindowEx() function with the HOTKEY_CLASS window class. Once the hot-key control is created, the application generally sets some rules about invalid hot-key combinations with the HKM_SETRULES message.

See the example under the HKM_GETHOTKEY message for more information on how to use hot-key controls.

Function Summary

Table 9-4 summarizes the miscellaneous control macros and messages. The detailed descriptions follow immediately after the table.

Table 9-4 Miscellaneous controls function and message summary

Function	Meaning
Animate_Create	Creates an animation control.
Animate_Close	Closes an open AVI clip.
Animate_Open	Opens a silent AVI clip and displays the first frame in the control.
Animate_Play	Plays an open AVI clip.
Animate_Seek	Seeks to a specific frame within the AVI clip.
Animate_Stop	Stops playing the AVI clip.
CreateUpDownControl	Creates an up-down control.
Header_DeleteItem	Deletes an item from a header control.
Header_GetItem	Retrieves information about an item in the header control.
Header_GetItemCount	Determines the number of items in the header control.
Header_InsertItem	Inserts a new item in the header control.
Header_Layout	Determines the dimensions for a new header control for the specified rectangle.
Header_SetItem	Sets the attributes of an item in the header control.

Message	
HDM_HITTEST	Determines which header control item is located at the specified point.
HKM_GETHOTKEY	Determines the virtual-key code and modifier flags for a hot key.
HKM_SETHOTKEY	Sets the hot-key combination for the hot-key control.
HKM_SETRULES	Specifies the invalid key combinations and default modifier combination for a hot-key control.
PBM_DELTAPOS	Advances the progress bar by the specified increment and then redraws the progress bar to reflect the new position.
PBM_SETPOS	Sets the position of the progress bar and then redraws the bar to reflect the new position.
PBM_SETRANGE	Sets the minimum and maximum values of the progress bar and redraws the bar to reflect the new values.
PBM_SETSTEP	Sets the increment value for the progress bar.
PBM_STEPIT	Advances the current position of the progress bar and redraws the bar to reflect the setting.
TBM_CLEARSEL	Clears the current selection in a trackbar.
TBM_CLEARTICS	Removes the current tick marks from the trackbar.
TBM_GETCHANNELRECT	Determines the size and position of the bounding rectangle for the channel of a trackbar.
TBM_GETLINESIZE	Retrieves the size of the line for a trackbar.
TBM_GETNUMTICS	Determines the number of tick marks on the trackbar.
TBM_GETPAGESIZE	Determines the size of the page for the trackbar.
TBM_GETPOS	Determines the current position of the slider on the trackbar.
TBM_GETPTICS	Retrieves the pointer to the array that contains the positions of the tick marks for the trackbar.
TBM_GETRANGEMAX	Determines the maximum position of the slider in the trackbar.
TBM_GETRANGEMIN	Determines the minimum position of the slider in the trackbar.
TBM_GETSELEND	Determines the ending position of the current selection in the trackbar.
TBM_GETSELSTART	Determines the starting position of the current selection in the trackbar.

Message	Meaning
TBM_GETTHUMBLENGTH	Determines the length of the trackbar slider.
TBM_GETTHUMBRECT	Determines the size and position of the bounding rectangle for the trackbar slider.
TBM_GETTIC	Determines the position of the specified tick mark in the trackbar.
TBM_GETTICPOS	Determines the position of the specified tick mark in client coordinates.
TBM_SETLINESIZE	Sets the size of the line for the trackbar.
TBM_SETPAGESIZE	Sets the page size for the trackbar.
TBM_SFTPOS	Sets the position of the slider in the trackbar.
TBM_SETRANGE	Sets the range of the slider in the trackbar.
TBM_SETRANGEMAX	Sets the maximum position of the slider for the trackbar.
TBM_SETRANGEMIN	Sets the minimum position of the slider for the trackbar.
TBM_SETSEL	Sets the starting and ending positions for the current selection in the trackbar.
TBM_SETSELEND	Sets the ending position for the selection in the trackbar.
TBM_SETSELSTART	Sets the starting position for the selection in the trackbar.
TBM_SETTHUMBLENGTH	Sets the slider length in the trackbar.
TBM_SETTIC	Sets the position of a tick mark in the trackbar.
TBM_SETTICFREQ	Sets the interval frequency for the tick marks in the trackbar.
UDM_GETACCEL	Determines the acceleration information for the up-down control.
UDM_GETBASE	Determines the radix base for the up-down control.
UDM_GETBUDDY	Retrieves the handle of the current buddy window for the up-down control.
UDM_GETPOS	Determines the current position of the up-down control.
UDM_GETRANGE	Determines the minimum and maximum range values for the up-down control.
UDM_SETACCEL	Sets the acceleration information for the up-down control.
UDM_SETBASE	Sets the radix base for the up-down control.
UDM_SETBUDDY	Sets the buddy window for the up-down control.
UDM_SETPOS	Sets the current position of the up-down control.
UDM_SETRANGE	Sets the minimum and maximum range values of the up-down control.
Notification Message	
ACN_START	The AVI clip has started playing.
ACN_STOP	The AVI clip has stopped playing.
HDN_BEGINTRACK	A divider in the header control is being dragged.
HDN_DIVIDERDBLCLICK	The divider area of the control was double-clicked with the mouse.
HDN_ENDTRACK	The dragging of the divider is finished.
HDN_ITEMCHANGED	The attributes of an item in the header control have changed.
HDN_ITEMCHANGING	The attributes of an item in the header control are changing.
HDN_ITEMCLICK	The header control item was clicked with the mouse.
HDN_ITEMDBLCLICK	The header control was double-clicked with the mouse.
HDN_TRACK	The divider of the header control is being dragged by the user.
UDN_DELTAPOS	The position in the up-down control is going to change.

ANIMATE_CREATE

Description	Animate_Create is a macro that creates an animation control by calling the CreateWindow() function with the ANIMATE_CLASS class. If the ACS_CENTER style is specified, the width and height of the control are set to zero; otherwise, the control sets the width and height based on the dimensions of a frame in the AVI clip. Use AVI clips that do not include audio tracks, as this control does not support AVI clips with audio tracks.
Syntax	HWND **Animate_Create**(HWND *hwndP*, UINT *id*, DWORD *dwStyle*, HINSTANCE *hInstance*)
Parameters	
hwndP	HWND: The handle of the parent window.
id	UINT: The identifier of the animation control.
dwStyle	DWORD: The window style of the animation control. This can be one or more of the standard window styles. Additionally, an application can specify one of the animation control window styles listed in Table 9-5.

Table 9-5 Animate_Create *dwStyle* values

Value	Meaning
ACS_AUTOPLAY	Plays the animation as soon as the animation clip is opened.
ACS_CENTER	Centers the animation in the animation window.
ACS_TRANSPARENT	Draws a transparent background for the animation rather than the background specified for the animation clip.

hInstance	HINSTANCE: The instance handle of the module that is creating the animation control.
Returns	HWND: If successful, the handle of the animation control is returned; otherwise, NULL is returned.
Include File	commctrl.h
See Also	CreateWindow()
Example	This example (Listing 9-1) demonstrates how to use the animation control as a basic AVI file player. When the application starts, an animation control is created as a child window on the client area of the application with the Animate_Create macro. When the user selects the Open menu item, an AVI file TEST.AVI is opened. The user has the ability to play the AVI file and control the progress with menu items provided. The menu items provide the following functions: Play, Stop, Go To End, and Close.

Listing 9-1 Using the Animate_Create macro

```
LRESULT CALLBACK WndProc( HWND hWnd, UINT uMsg, WPARAM wParam, LPARAM lParam )
{
static HWND hAnimate = NULL;

   switch( uMsg )
   {
      case WM_CREATE :
              InitCommonControls();

              // Create the animate control.
              //............................
              hAnimate = Animate_Create( hWnd, 1,
                                         WS_CHILD | WS_BORDER |
                                         WS_VISIBLE, hInst );
              break;


      case WM_COMMAND :
              switch( LOWORD( wParam ) )
              {
                  case IDM_OPEN :
                          // Use common dialog to retrieve file name.
                          // In this example, we use TEST.AVI.
                          //.........................................
                          Animate_Open( hAnimate, "TEST.AVI" );
                          break;

                  case IDM_CLOSE :
                          Animate_Close( hAnimate );
                          InvalidateRect( hAnimate, NULL, TRUE );
                          break;

                  case IDM_PLAY :
                          Animate_Play( hAnimate, 0, (WORD)-1, -1 );
                          break;

                  case IDM_STOP :
                          Animate_Stop( hAnimate );
                          break;

                  case IDM_SEEKEND :
                          Animate_Seek( hAnimate, (WORD)-1 );
                          break;
         .
         .
         .
```

ANIMATE_CLOSE   ■ WIN32S   ■ WINDOWS 95   ■ WINDOWS NT

Description	Animate_Close is a macro that closes an open AVI clip.
Syntax	BOOL **Animate_Close**(HWND *hwnd*)
Message Syntax	BOOL **SendMessage**(*hwnd*, **ACM_OPEN**, 0, 0)

Parameters

hwnd   HWND: The handle of the animation control.

Returns   BOOL: FALSE is always returned.

Include File   commctrl.h

See Also   Animate_Open

Related Messages   ACM_OPEN

Example   See the example for the Animate_Create macro.

ANIMATE_OPEN   ■ WIN32S   ■ WINDOWS 95   ■ WINDOWS NT

Description   Animate_Open is a macro that opens a *silent* AVI clip and displays the first
                         frame in the animation control. Silent AVI clips do not contain audio
                         tracks.

Syntax   BOOL **Animate_Open**(HWND *hwnd*, LPSTR *lpszName*)

Message Syntax   BOOL **SendMessage**(*hwnd*, **ACM_OPEN**, 0, *lpszName*)

Parameters

hwnd   HWND: The handle of the animation control.

lpszName   LPSTR: A pointer to a buffer containing either the path of the AVI file or
                         the name of the AVI resource. The AVI file or resource must not contain
                         audio. This parameter can also specify a resource identifier in the low-
                         order word and zero in the high-order word of an AVI resource. Use the
                         MAKEINTRESOURCE macro to create this value.

Returns   BOOL: If successful, TRUE is returned; otherwise, FALSE is returned.

Include File   commctrl.h

See Also   Animate_Close

Related Messages   ACM_OPEN

Example   See the example for the Animate_Create macro.

ANIMATE_PLAY   ■ WIN32S   ■ WINDOWS 95   ■ WINDOWS NT

Description   Animate_Play is a macro that plays an open AVI clip in the background as
                         a thread executes.

Syntax   BOOL **Animate_Play**(HWND *hwndAnim*, WORD *wFrom*, WORD *wTo*,
                         UINT *cRepeat*)

Message Syntax   BOOL **SendMessage**(*hwndAnim*, **ACM_PLAY**, *cRepeat*,
                         MAKELPARAM(*wFrom*, *wTo*))

Parameters

hwndAnim   HWND: The handle of the animation control where the AVI clip should
                         play.

wFrom	WORD: The zero-based index of the frame where playing begins. A value of zero starts with the first frame in the AVI clip. The value of this parameter must be less than 65,536.
wTo	WORD: The zero-based index of the frame where playing ends. A value of -1 ends with the last frame in the AVI clip. The value of this parameter must be less than 65,536.
cRepeat	UINT: The number of times to replay the AVI clip in the animation control. A value of -1 replays the AVI clip indefinitely.
Returns	BOOL: If the operation succeeds, TRUE is returned; otherwise, FALSE is returned.
Include File	commctrl.h
See Also	Animate_Stop, Animate_Seek
Related Messages	ACM_PLAY
Example	See the example for the Animate_Create macro.

ANIMATE_SEEK   ■ WIN32S   ■ WINDOWS 95   ■ WINDOWS NT

Description	Animate_Seek is a macro that seeks to a specific frame within the AVI clip.
Syntax	BOOL **Animate_Seek**(HWND *hwndAnim*, WORD *wFrame*)
Message Syntax	BOOL **SendMessage**(*hwndAnim*, **ACM_PLAY**, 1, MAKELPARAM(*wFrame, wFrame*))
Parameters	
hwndAnim	HWND: The handle of the animation control.
wFrame	WORD: The zero-based index of the AVI frame to display. Use -1 to seek to the end of the AVI clip.
Returns	BOOL: If successful, TRUE is returned; otherwise, FALSE is returned.
Include File	commctrl.h
See Also	Animate_Play
Related Messages	ACM_PLAY
Example	See the example for the Animate_Create macro.

ANIMATE_STOP   ■ WIN32S   ■ WINDOWS 95   ■ WINDOWS NT

Description	Animate_Stop is a macro that stops playing the AVI clip in the specified animation control.
Syntax	BOOL **Animate_Stop**(HWND *hwnd*)
Message Syntax	BOOL **SendMessage**(*hwnd*, **ACM_STOP**, 0, 0)
Parameters	
hwnd	HWND: The handle of the animation control.

Returns	BOOL: If successful, TRUE is returned; otherwise, FALSE is returned.
Include File	commctrl.h
See Also	Animate_Play
Related Messages	ACM_STOP
Example	See the example for the Animate_Create macro.

CreateUpDownControl ■ Win32s ■ Windows 95 ■ Windows NT

Description   CreateUpDownControl() creates an up-down control. Use up-down controls to provide a method of incrementing and decrementing values within edit controls with the mouse cursor.

Syntax   HWND **CreateUpDownControl**(DWORD *dwStyle*, int *x*, int *y*, int *cx*, int *cy*, HWND *hParent*, int *nID*, HINSTANCE *hInst*, HWND *hBuddy*, int *nUpper*, int *nLower*, int *nPos*)

Parameters

dwStyle   DWORD: The window style for the up-down control. Use zero or more of the up-down control styles in Table 9-6 combined with the WS_CHILD, WS_BORDER, and WS_VISIBLE styles.

Table 9-6 CreateUpDownControl() *dwStyle* **values**

Value	Meaning
UDS_ALIGNLEFT	Positions the up-down control next to the left edge of the buddy window.
UDS_ALIGNRIGHT	Positions the up-down control next to the right edge of the buddy window.
UDS_ARROWKEYS	The up-down control increments and decrements the position when the up arrow and down arrow keys are pressed.
UDS_AUTOBUDDY	Automatically selects the previous window in the Z order as the up-down control's buddy window.
UDS_HORZ	The up-down control's arrows point left and right instead of up and down.
UDS_NOTHOUSANDS	Does not insert a thousands separator between every three decimal digits.
UDS_SETBUDDYINT	The up-down control sets the decimal or hexadecimal text of the buddy window (using the WM_SETTEXT message) when the position changes.
UDS_WRAP	The position wraps if it is incremented or decremented beyond the ending or beginning of the control's range.

x   int: The horizontal coordinate, in client coordinates, of the upper left corner of the up-down control.

y   int: The vertical coordinate, in client coordinates, of the upper left corner of the up-down control.

cx   int: The width, in pixels, of the up-down control.

cy   int: The height, in pixels, of the up-down control.

hParent	HWND: The window handle of the parent window.
nID	int: The identifier of the up-down control.
hInst	HINSTANCE: The instance handle of the application creating the up-down control.
hBuddy	HWND: The window handle of the buddy window associated with the up-down control. If the value of *hBuddy* is NULL, the up-down control does not have an associated buddy window unless the UDS_AUTOBUDDY style is specified.
nUpper	int: The upper range of the up-down control.
nLower	int: The lower range of the up-down control.
nPos	int: The starting position of the up-down control.
Returns	HWND: If the function succeeds, the window handle of the up-down control is returned; otherwise, NULL is returned.
Include File	commctrl.h
Example	This example (Listing 9-2) demonstrates the functionality of the up-down control. When the application starts, an edit control and an associated up-down control are created. The user can change the options for the up-down control by selecting the Options menu item. Figure 9-3 shows the options dialog and the up-down control. For the purpose of demonstrating the UDN_DELTAPOS notification, the number 10 is eliminated when the user scrolls through the values. The WM_VSCROLL message is also processed to demonstrate the custom display of the value in the edit control.

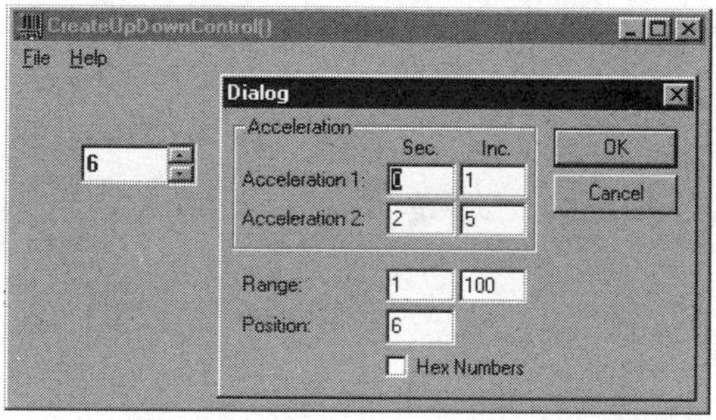

Figure 9-3 CreateUpDownControl() example

Listing 9-2 Using the CreateUpDownControl() function

```
LRESULT CALLBACK WndProc( HWND hWnd, UINT uMsg, WPARAM wParam, LPARAM lParam )
{
static HWND hEdit    = NULL;
static HWND hUpDown  = NULL;

   switch( uMsg )
   {
```

continued on next page

continued from previous page

```
     case WM_CREATE :
             // Create the edit control.
             //.......................
             hEdit = CreateWindowEx( WS_EX_CLIENTEDGE, "EDIT", "",
                                     WS_CHILD | WS_BORDER | WS_VISIBLE,
                                     40, 40, 70, 25, hWnd,
                                     (HMENU)IDC_EDIT, hInst, NULL );

             // Create the up-down control.
             //...........................
             hUpDown = CreateUpDownControl( WS_CHILD | WS_BORDER |
                                            WS_VISIBLE |
                                            UDS_ALIGNRIGHT,
                                            0, 0, 18, 25, hWnd, IDC_UPDOWN,
                                            hInst, NULL,
                                            100, 1, 1 );

             // The buddy window could have been specified with the
             // CreateUpDownControl() function. However, for this
             // example, we will use the UDM_SETBUDDY message.
             //....................................................
             SendMessage( hUpDown, UDM_SETBUDDY, (WPARAM)hEdit, 0 );

             // Initialize the edit control to the beginning value.
             //....................................................
             SendMessage( hEdit, WM_SETTEXT, 0, (LPARAM)"1" );
             break;

     case WM_VSCROLL :
             if ( (HWND)lParam == hUpDown )
             {
                 HWND   hBuddyWnd;
                 TCHAR  szTmp[10];

                 // Retrieve the buddy window. This is useful if we
                 // are not sure which buddy window the scroll is for.
                 //...................................................
                 hBuddyWnd = (HWND)SendMessage( hUpDown, UDM_GETBUDDY, 0, 0 );

                 // Find out the base of the up-down control and
                 // format the string for the buddy window.
                 //............................................
                 if ( SendMessage( hUpDown, UDM_GETBASE, 0, 0 ) == 10 )
                     wsprintf( szTmp, "%d", HIWORD( wParam ) );
                 else
                     wsprintf( szTmp, "%X", HIWORD( wParam ) );

                 // Set the new value into the edit control
                 // and make it the selected text.
                 //........................................
                 SendMessage( hBuddyWnd, WM_SETTEXT, 0, (LPARAM)szTmp );
                 SendMessage( hBuddyWnd, EM_SETSEL, 0, -1 );
             }
             break;

     case WM_NOTIFY :
             {
                 NM_UPDOWN* ud = (NM_UPDOWN*)lParam;
```

```
                    if ( ud->hdr.code == UDN_DELTAPOS )
                    {
                        // Disallow the value of 10 by modifying
                        // the iDelta value to skip over it.
                        //.....................................
                        if ( (ud->iPos + ud->iDelta) == 10 )
                        {
                            if ( ud->iDelta > 0 )
                                ud->iDelta++;
                            else
                                ud->iDelta--;
                        }
                    }
                }
                break;

        case WM_COMMAND :
                switch( LOWORD( wParam ) )
                {
                    case IDM_OPTIONS :
                            DialogBox( hInst, "OptionsDlg", hWnd,
                                       (DLGPROC)Options );
                            break;

                    case IDM_EXIT :
                            DestroyWindow( hWnd );
                            break;
                }
                break;

        case WM_DESTROY :
                PostQuitMessage(0);
                break;

        default :
                return( DefWindowProc( hWnd, uMsg, wParam, lParam ) );
    }

    return( 0L );
}


LRESULT CALLBACK Options( HWND hDlg,
                          UINT message,
                          WPARAM wParam,
                          LPARAM lParam)
{
    switch (message)
    {
        case WM_INITDIALOG:
                {
                    HWND    hUpDown;
                    UDACCEL accel[2];
                    DWORD   dwRange;
                    DWORD   dwPos;
                    DWORD   dwBase;
                    int     nNumAccel;
```

continued on next page

continued from previous page

```
                // Retrieve the up-down control.
                //................................
                hUpDown = GetDlgItem( GetParent( hDlg ), IDC_UPDOWN );

                // Retrieve the acceleration information.
                //.......................................
                nNumAccel = SendMessage( hUpDown, UDM_GETACCEL,
                                         2, (LPARAM)accel );

                // Retrieve the range.
                //....................
                dwRange = SendMessage( hUpDown, UDM_GETRANGE, 0, 0 );

                // Retrieve the current position.
                //...............................
                dwPos = SendMessage( hUpDown, UDM_GETPOS, 0, 0 );

                // Retrieve the current base.
                //...........................
                dwBase = SendMessage( hUpDown, UDM_GETBASE, 0, 0 );

                // Initialize the dialog controls.
                //................................
                SetDlgItemInt( hDlg, IDC_RANGE1, HIWORD( dwRange ), FALSE );
                SetDlgItemInt( hDlg, IDC_RANGE2, LOWORD( dwRange ), FALSE );
                SetDlgItemInt( hDlg, IDC_POS,    LOWORD( dwPos ), FALSE );

                SetDlgItemInt( hDlg, IDC_SEC1, accel[0].nSec, FALSE );
                SetDlgItemInt( hDlg, IDC_INC1, accel[0].nInc, FALSE );
                if ( nNumAccel > 1 )
                {
                    SetDlgItemInt( hDlg, IDC_SEC2, accel[1].nSec, FALSE );
                    SetDlgItemInt( hDlg, IDC_INC2, accel[1].nInc, FALSE );
                }

                CheckDlgButton( hDlg, IDC_HEX,
                            dwBase == 16 ? BST_CHECKED : BST_UNCHECKED );
            }
            return (TRUE);

        case WM_COMMAND:
            switch( LOWORD( wParam ) )
            {
            case IDOK :
                    {
                        HWND    hUpDown;
                        UDACCEL accel[2];
                        DWORD   dwRange;
                        DWORD   dwPos;
                        DWORD   dwBase;
                        int     nNumAccel;

                        // Retrieve the up-down control.
                        //................................
                        hUpDown = GetDlgItem( GetParent( hDlg ),
                                              IDC_UPDOWN );

                        // Retrieve the information from the dialog.
                        //.........................................
```

```
                    dwRange = MAKELONG(
                            (WORD)GetDlgItemInt( hDlg, IDC_RANGE2,
                                                NULL, FALSE ),
                            (WORD)GetDlgItemInt( hDlg, IDC_RANGE1,
                                                NULL, FALSE ) );

                    dwPos = GetDlgItemInt( hDlg, IDC_POS, NULL, FALSE );

                    accel[0].nSec = GetDlgItemInt( hDlg, IDC_SEC1,
                                                NULL, FALSE );
                    accel[0].nInc = GetDlgItemInt( hDlg, IDC_INC1,
                                                NULL, FALSE );
                    accel[1].nSec = GetDlgItemInt( hDlg, IDC_SEC2,
                                                NULL, FALSE );
                    accel[1].nInc = GetDlgItemInt( hDlg, IDC_INC2,
                                                NULL, FALSE );

                    nNumAccel = 1;
                    if ( accel[1].nInc ) nNumAccel++;

                    if ( IsDlgButtonChecked( hDlg, IDC_HEX ) )
                       dwBase = 16;
                    else
                       dwBase = 10;

                    // Set the attributes for the up-down control.
                    //....................................................
                    SendMessage( hUpDown, UDM_SETACCEL, nNumAccel,
                                               (LPARAM)accel );
                    SendMessage( hUpDown, UDM_SETBASE, dwBase, 0 );
                    SendMessage( hUpDown, UDM_SETPOS, 0,
                               MAKELONG( (WORD)dwPos, 0 ) );
                    SendMessage( hUpDown, UDM_SETRANGE, 0, dwRange );

                    EndDialog( hDlg, IDOK );
                 }
                 break;

          case IDCANCEL :
                 EndDialog( hDlg, IDCANCEL );
                 break;
        }
        break;
   }

   return (FALSE);
}
```

HEADER_DELETEITEM　　　　　■ WIN32S　■ WINDOWS 95　■ WINDOWS NT

Description	Header_DeleteItem is a macro that deletes an item from a header control.
Syntax	BOOL **Header_DeleteItem**(HWND *hwndHD*, int *index*)
Message Syntax	BOOL **SendMessage**(*hwndHD*, **HDM_DELETEITEM**, *index*, 0)
Parameters	
hwndHD	HWND: The handle of the header control.
index	int: The index of the item to delete.

Returns	BOOL: If the operation succeeds, TRUE is returned; otherwise, FALSE is returned.
Include File	commctrl.h
Related Messages	HDM_DELETEITEM
Example	This example (Listing 9-3) demonstrates the Header_DeleteItem macro by allowing the user to add and delete columns from a header control by selecting the Insert and Delete menu items.

Listing 9-3 Using the Header_DeleteItem macro

```
LRESULT CALLBACK WndProc( HWND hWnd, UINT uMsg, WPARAM wParam, LPARAM lParam )
{
static HD_LAYOUT hl;
static WINDOWPOS wp;
static RECT      rc;
static HWND      hHeader = NULL;

    switch( uMsg )
    {
      case WM_CREATE :
              InitCommonControls();

              // Create the header control.
              //........................
              hHeader = CreateWindowEx( 0, WC_HEADER, "",
                                        WS_CHILD | WS_VISIBLE |
                                        HDS_BUTTONS,
                                        0, 0, 10, 10, hWnd,
                                        (HMENU)1, hInst, NULL );

              // Initialize the HD_LAYOUT members.
              //.................................
              hl.pwpos = &wp;
              hl.prc   = &rc;
              break;

      case WM_SIZE :
              rc.top    = 0;
              rc.left   = 0;
              rc.right  = LOWORD( lParam );
              rc.bottom = HIWORD( lParam );

              Header_Layout( hHeader, &hl );
              SetWindowPos( hHeader, hWnd, wp.x, wp.y, wp.cx, wp.cy, wp.flags );
              break;

      case WM_COMMAND :
              switch( LOWORD( wParam ) )
              {
                case IDM_INSERT :
                    {
                        char    szTitle[32];
                        HD_ITEM hi;
                        int     i;
```

```
                    SendMessage( hHeader, WM_SETFONT,
                        (WPARAM)GetStockObject( DEFAULT_GUI_FONT ), 0 );

                    wsprintf( szTitle, "Column %d",
                                Header_GetItemCount( hHeader )+1 );

                    hi.mask    = HDI_FORMAT | HDI_TEXT | HDI_WIDTH;
                    hi.pszText = (LPTSTR)szTitle;
                    hi.fmt     = HDF_STRING;
                    hi.cxy     = 100;

                    Header_InsertItem( hHeader,
                                        Header_GetItemCount( hHeader ),
                                        (LPARAM)&hi );
                }
                break;

        case IDM_DELETE :
                Header_DeleteItem( hHeader,
                                Header_GetItemCount( hHeader )-1 );
                break;
    .
    .
    .
```

HEADER_GETITEM   ■ WIN32S   ■ WINDOWS 95   ■ WINDOWS NT

Description	Header_GetItem is a macro that retrieves information about an item in a header control.
Syntax	BOOL **Header_GetItem**(HWND *hwndHD*, int *index*, HD_ITEM * *phdi*)
Message Syntax	BOOL **SendMessage**(*hwndHD*, **HDM_GETITEM**, *index*, *phdi*)
Parameters	
hwndHD	HWND: The handle of the header control.
index	int: The index of the item for which to retrieve the information.
phdi	HD_ITEM *: A pointer to an HD_ITEM structure whose *mask* member specifies the type of information to retrieve about the item. See the definition of the HD_ITEM structure below.
Returns	BOOL: If the operation is successful, TRUE is returned; otherwise, FALSE is returned.
Include File	commctrl.h
Related Messages	HDM_GETITEM
HD_ITEM Definition	

```
        typedef struct _HD_ITEM
        {
            UINT    mask;
            int     cxy;
            LPSTR   pszText;
            HBITMAP hbm;
            int     cchTextMax;
            int     fmt;
            LPARAM  lParam;
        } HD_ITEM;
```

Members

mask   UINT: A combination of the values in Table 9-7 indicating the valid struc-
                                ture members.

Table 9-7 Header_GetItem HD_ITEM *mask* values

Value	Meaning
HDI_BITMAP	The *hbm* member is valid.
HDI_FORMAT	The *fmt* member is valid.
HDI_HEIGHT	The *cxy* member is valid and specifies the height of the item.
HDI_LPARAM	The *lParam* member is valid.
HDI_TEXT	The *pszText* and *cchTextMax* members are valid.
HDI_WIDTH	The *cxy* member is valid and specifies the width of the item.

cxy   int: The width or height of the item depending on the value of the *mask*
                                member.
pszText   LPSTR: The address of the item string.
hbm   HBITMAP: The handle of the item bitmap.
cchTextMax   int: The length of the item string, in characters.
fmt   int: One of the values of Table 9-8 combined with a value of Table 9-9,
                                indicating the format of the item.

Table 9-8 Header_GetItem HD_ITEM *fmt* initial values

Value	Meaning
HDF_CENTER	Centers the contents of the item.
HDF_LEFT	Left-aligns the contents of the item.
HDF_RIGHT	Right-aligns the contents of the item.
HDF_RTLREADING	Displays text using right-to-left reading order on Hebrew and Arabic versions of Windows 95.

Table 9-9 Header_GetItem HD_ITEM *fmt* values

Value	Meaning
HDF_BITMAP	The item displays a bitmap.
HDF_OWNERDRAW	The owner window of the header control draws the item.
HDF_STRING	The item displays a string.

lParam   LPARAM: An application-defined value associated with the item.
Example   See the example for the Header_InsertItem macro.

HEADER_GETITEMCOUNT ■ WIN32S ■ WINDOWS 95 ■ WINDOWS NT

Description	Header_GetItemCount is a macro that returns the number of items in a header control.
Syntax	BOOL **Header_GetItemCount**(HWND *hwndHD*)
Message Syntax	BOOL **SendMessage**(*hwndHD*, **HDM_GETITEMCOUNT**, 0, 0)
Parameters	
hwndHD	HWND: The handle of the header control.
Returns	BOOL: If successful, the number of items in the header control is returned; otherwise, -1 is returned.
Include File	commctrl.h
Related Messages	HDM_GETITEMCOUNT
Example	See the example for the Header_DeleteItem macro.

HEADER_INSERTITEM ■ WIN32S ■ WINDOWS 95 ■ WINDOWS NT

Description	Header_InsertItem is a macro that inserts a new item into a header control.
Syntax	BOOL **Header_InsertItem**(HWND *hwndHD*, int *index*, const HD_ITEM * *phdi*)
Message Syntax	BOOL **SendMessage**(*hwndHD*, **HDM_INSERTITEM**, *index*, *phdi*)
Parameters	
hwndHD	HWND: The handle of the header control.
index	int: The index of the item after which the new item is to be inserted. If the value of *index* is greater than or equal to the number of items in the header control, the new item is inserted at the end of the control. If the value of *index* is zero, the new item is inserted at the beginning of the header control.
phdi	const HD_ITEM *: A pointer to an HD_ITEM structure containing information about the new item. See the definition of the HD_ITEM structure under the Header_GetItem macro.
Returns	BOOL: If successful, TRUE is returned; otherwise, FALSE is returned.
Include File	commctrl.h
Related Messages	HDM_INSERTITEM
Example	This example, shown in Figure 9-4 and Listing 9-4, demonstrates the usage of the header control to organize the client area of a window into columns. The column drag functionality is implemented in this example as a demonstration of how this could be accomplished in a manner that is consistent with the list view control. Three columns are created in the header when the application starts. The user can change the size and alignment of the second and third columns. If the user tries to change the first column, the HDN_ITEMCHANGING notification is processed, returning TRUE, which disallows any changes.

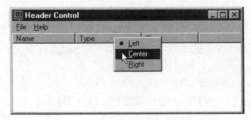

Figure 9-4 Header control example

Listing 9-4 Using the Header_InsertItem macro

```
LPCTSTR pszTitles[] = { "Name", "Type", "Size" };

LRESULT CALLBACK WndProc( HWND hWnd, UINT uMsg, WPARAM wParam, LPARAM lParam )
{
static HD_LAYOUT hl;
static WINDOWPOS wp;
static RECT     rc;
static HDC      hdc;
static int      nCurItem;
static HWND     hHeader = NULL;

    switch( uMsg )
    {
        case WM_CREATE :
                InitCommonControls();

                // Create the header control.
                //..........................
                hHeader = CreateWindowEx( 0, WC_HEADER, "",
                                          WS_CHILD | WS_VISIBLE |
                                          HDS_BUTTONS,
                                          0, 0, 10, 10, hWnd,
                                          (HMENU)1, hInst, NULL );

                // Initialize the HD_LAYOUT members.
                //..................................
                hl.pwpos = &wp;
                hl.prc   = &rc;

                if ( hHeader )
                {
                    HD_ITEM hi;
                    int     i;

                    SendMessage( hHeader, WM_SETFONT,
                                (WPARAM)GetStockObject( DEFAULT_GUI_FONT ), 0 );

                    for( i=0; i<3; i++ )
                    {
                        hi.mask    = HDI_FORMAT | HDI_TEXT | HDI_WIDTH;
                        hi.pszText = (LPTSTR)pszTitles[i];
                        hi.fmt     = HDF_STRING;
                        hi.cxy     = 100;
```

```
                    Header_InsertItem( hHeader, i, (LPARAM)&hi );
                }
            }
            break;

case WM_SIZE :
            rc.top    = 0;
            rc.left   = 0;
            rc.right  = LOWORD( lParam );
            rc.bottom = HIWORD( lParam );

            Header_Layout( hHeader, &hl );
            SetWindowPos( hHeader, hWnd, wp.x, wp.y, wp.cx, wp.cy, wp.flags );
            break;

case WM_CONTEXTMENU :
        {
            HD_HITTESTINFO hi;

            hi.pt.x = LOWORD( lParam );
            hi.pt.y = HIWORD( lParam );

            // Convert the coordinates to client.
            //..................................
            ScreenToClient( hHeader, &hi.pt );

            // Test for a hit.
            //................
            SendMessage( hHeader, HDM_HITTEST, 0, (LPARAM)&hi );

            // If a hit occurred, display menu.
            //................................
            if ( hi.flags & HHT_ONHEADER )
            {
                HD_ITEM hdi;
                HMENU   hMenu = CreatePopupMenu();

                // Retrieve the current format.
                //............................
                hdi.mask = HDI_FORMAT;
                Header_GetItem( hHeader, hi.iItem, &hdi );

                nCurItem = hi.iItem;

                // Build the menu and display it.
                //..............................
                AppendMenu( hMenu, MF_STRING, IDM_LEFT, "&Left" );
                AppendMenu( hMenu, MF_STRING, IDM_CENTER, "&Center" );
                AppendMenu( hMenu, MF_STRING, IDM_RIGHT, "&Right" );

                CheckMenuRadioItem( hMenu, IDM_LEFT, IDM_RIGHT,
                    (hdi.fmt & HDF_JUSTIFYMASK) == HDF_LEFT ? IDM_LEFT :
                    (hdi.fmt & HDF_JUSTIFYMASK) == HDF_CENTER ? IDM_CENTER :
                     IDM_RIGHT, MF_BYCOMMAND );

                TrackPopupMenu( hMenu, TPM_LEFTALIGN | TPM_LEFTBUTTON |
                                    TPM_RIGHTBUTTON,
                                    LOWORD( lParam ), HIWORD( lParam ),
                                    0, hWnd, NULL );
```

continued on next page

continued from previous page

```
                    DestroyMenu( hMenu );
                }
            }
            break;

    case WM_NOTIFY :
            {
                int         x;
                HD_NOTIFY* pHN = (HD_NOTIFY*)lParam;

                switch( pHN->hdr.code )
                {
                    case HDN_BEGINTRACK :
                            // Only allow Left Mouse Drag.
                            //............................
                            if ( pHN->iButton != 0 )
                                return( TRUE );

                            // Get the column offset.
                            //.......................
                            x = GetColumnOffs( hHeader, pHN->iItem ) +
                                    pHN->pitem->cxy;

                            GetClientRect( hWnd, &rc );

                            // Fix up rect for the invert.
                            //............................
                            rc.left   = x;
                            rc.top    = wp.cy;
                            rc.right  = x+1;

                            // Get the window DC and invert the rect.
                            //.......................................
                            hdc = GetDC( hWnd );
                            InvertRect( hdc, &rc );

                            break;

                    case HDN_TRACK :
                            // Turn off the invert on the old rect.
                            //.....................................
                            InvertRect( hdc, &rc );

                            // Get the column offset.
                            //.......................
                            x = GetColumnOffs( hHeader, pHN->iItem ) +
                                    pHN->pitem->cxy;

                            GetClientRect( hWnd, &rc );

                            // Invert the new rect.
                            //.....................
                            rc.left   = x;
                            rc.top    = wp.cy;
                            rc.right  = x+1;
                            InvertRect( hdc, &rc );
                            break;

                    case HDN_ENDTRACK :
```

```
                    // Turn off the invert and release the DC.
                    //..........................................
                    InvertRect( hdc, &rc );
                    ReleaseDC( hWnd, hdc );
                    break;

                case HDN_ITEMCHANGING :
                    // Do not allow the first column to be changed.
                    //..............................................
                    if ( pHN->iItem == 0 )
                        return( TRUE );

                    break;

                case HDN_ITEMCHANGED :
                    // Update the contents of the window to reflect
                    // the new column alignment.
                    //..............................................
                    break;

                case HDN_ITEMCLICK :
                    // Sort the column's contents
                    //............................
                    break;
            }
        }
        break;

case WM_COMMAND :
        switch( LOWORD( wParam ) )
        {
            case IDM_LEFT :
            case IDM_RIGHT :
            case IDM_CENTER :
                    {
                        HD_ITEM hdi;

                        // Update the alignment of the column.
                        //.....................................
                        hdi.mask = HDI_FORMAT;
                        hdi.fmt  = HDF_STRING +
                            ( LOWORD( wParam ) == IDM_LEFT ? HDF_LEFT :
                              LOWORD( wParam ) == IDM_CENTER ? HDF_CENTER :
                              HDF_RIGHT );

                        Header_SetItem( hHeader, nCurItem, &hdi );
                    }
                    break;

            case IDM_EXIT :
                    DestroyWindow( hWnd );
                    break;
        }
        break;

case WM_DESTROY :
        PostQuitMessage(0);
        break;
```

continued on next page

continued from previous page

```
        default :
              return( DefWindowProc( hWnd, uMsg, wParam, lParam ) );
    }

    return( OL );
}


int GetColumnOffs( HWND hHeader, int nColNum )
{
    HD_ITEM hi;
    int     i;
    int     x = 0;

    hi.mask = HDI_WIDTH;

    // Calculate the column position.
    //..............................
    for( i=0; i<nColNum; i++ )
    {
        Header_GetItem( hHeader, i, &hi );
        x += hi.cxy;
    }

    return( x );
}
```

HEADER_LAYOUT   ■ WIN32S   ■ WINDOWS 95   ■ WINDOWS NT

Description	Header_Layout is a macro that determines the dimensions (size and position) for a new header control within the specified rectangle.
Syntax	BOOL **Header_Layout**(HWND *hwndHD*, HD_LAYOUT * *playout*)
Message Syntax	BOOL **SendMessage**(*hwndHD*, **HDM_LAYOUT**, 0, *playout*)
Parameters	
hwndHD	HWND: The handle of the header control.
playout	HD_LAYOUT *: A pointer to an HD_LAYOUT structure that contains the coordinates of the rectangle and receives the coordinates for the new header control. See the definition of the HD_LAYOUT structure below.
Returns	BOOL: If successful, TRUE is returned; otherwise, FALSE is returned.
Include File	commctrl.h
Related Messages	HDM_INSERTITEM

HD_LAYOUT Definition

```
typedef struct _HD_LAYOUT
{
    RECT*      prc;
    WINDOWPOS* pwpos;
} HD_LAYOUT;
```

Members

prc	RECT *: The address of a RECT structure that contains the coordinates of a rectangle that the header control is to occupy.
pwpos	WINDOWPOS *: The address of a WINDOWPOS structure that receives information about the appropriate size and position of the header control. See the definition of the WINDOWPOS structure below.

WINDOWPOS Definition

```
typedef struct _WINDOWPOS
{
    HWND hwnd;
    HWND hwndInsertAfter;
    int  x;
    int  y;
    int  cx;
    int  cy;
    UINT flags;
} WINDOWPOS;
```

Members

hwnd	HWND: The handle of the window.
hwndInsertAfter	HWND: The position of the window that precedes the window identified by *hwnd* in Z order (front-to-back position). This member can be the handle of the window or one of the values in Table 9-10.

Table 9-10 Header_Layout WINDOWPOS *hwndInsertAfter* values

Value	Meaning
HWND_BOTTOM	Places the window at the bottom of the Z order. If the *hwnd* parameter identifies a topmost window, the window loses its topmost status and is placed at the bottom of all other windows.
HWND_NOTOPMOST	Places the window above all non-topmost windows (that is, behind all topmost windows). This flag has no effect if the window is already a non-topmost window.
HWND_TOP	Places the window at the top of the Z order.
HWND_TOPMOST	Places the window above all non-topmost windows. The window maintains its topmost position even when it is deactivated.

x	int: The position of the left edge of the window.
y	int: The position of the top edge of the window.
cx	int: The window width, in pixels.
cy	int: The window height, in pixels.
flags	UINT: One of the values in Table 9-11 indicating the position of the window.

Table 9-11 WINDOWPOS *flags* values

Value	Meaning
SWP_DRAWFRAME	Draws a frame (defined in the window's class description) around the window. The window receives a WM_NCCALCSIZE message.
SWP_HIDEWINDOW	Hides the window.
SWP_NOACTIVATE	Does not activate the window.
SWP_NOCOPYBITS	Discards the entire contents of the client area. If this flag is not specified, the valid contents of the client area are saved and copied back into the client area after the window has been sized or repositioned.
SWP_NOMOVE	Retains the current position (ignores the *x* and *y* parameters).
SWP_NOOWNERZORDER	Does not change the owner window's position in the Z order.
SWP_NOREDRAW	Does not redraw changes.
SWP_NOREPOSITION	Does not change the owner window's position in the Z order.
SWP_NOSIZE	Retains the current size (ignores the *cx* and *cy* parameters).
SWP_NOZORDER	Retains the current Z order (ignores the *hwndInsertAfter* member).
SWP_SHOWWINDOW	Displays the window.

Example   See the example for the Header_InsertItem macro.

HEADER_SETITEM   ■ WIN32s   ■ WINDOWS 95   ■ WINDOWS NT

Description   Header_SetItem is a macro that sets the attributes of an item in the header control. The HDN_ITEMCHANGING message is sent to the parent window before any attributes are changed for the specified item. An HDN_ITEMCHANGED message is sent after the changes are made to the item.

Syntax   BOOL **Header_SetItem**(HWND *hwndHD*, int *index*, const HD_ITEM * *phdi*)

Message Syntax   BOOL **SendMessage**(*hwndHD*, **HDM_SETITEM**, *index*, *phdi*)

Parameters

hwndHD   HWND: The handle of the header control.

index   int: The index of the item in the header control whose attributes should be changed.

phdi   const HD_ITEM *: A pointer to an HD_ITEM structure containing information about the attributes to set for the item. See the definition of the HD_ITEM structure under the Header_GetItem macro.

Returns   BOOL: If successful, TRUE is returned; otherwise, FALSE is returned.

Include File   commctrl.h

Related Messages   HDN_ITEMCHANGED, HDN_ITEMCHANGING

Example   See the example for the Header_InsertItem macro.

HDM_HITTEST   ■ Win32s   ■ Windows 95   ■ Windows NT

Description   HDM_HITTEST is a message that tests a point to determine which header item is located at the specified point.

Parameters

wParam   WPARAM: This parameter is set to zero.

lParam   HD_HITTESTINFO *: A pointer to an HD_HITTESTINFO structure that contains the position to test and receives information about the results of the test. See the definition of the HD_HITTESTINFO structure below.

Returns   int: If successful, the index of the item at the specified position is returned; otherwise, -1 is returned.

Include File   commctrl.h

HD_HITTESTINFO Definition

```
typedef struct _HD_HITTESTINFO
{
    POINT pt;
    UINT  flags;
    int   iItem;
} HD_HITTESTINFO;
```

Members

pt   POINT: The points in the header control to test, in client coordinates.

flags   UINT: The results of a hit test. This member can be one or more of the values in Table 9-12.

Table 9-12 HDM_HITTEST HD_HITTESTINFO *flags* values

Value	Meaning
HHT_NOWHERE	The point is inside the bounding rectangle of the header control but is not over a header item.
HHT_ONDIVIDER	The point is on the divider between two header items.
HHT_ONDIVOPEN	The point is on the divider of an item that has a width of zero. Dragging the divider reveals the item instead of resizing the item to the left of the divider.
HHT_ONHEADER	The point is inside the bounding rectangle of the header control.
HHT_TOLEFT	The point is to the left of the bounding rectangle of the header control.
HHT_TORIGHT	The point is to the right of the bounding rectangle of the header control.

iItem   int: The index of the header control item at a point.

Example   See the example for the Header_InsertItem macro.

HKM_GETHOTKEY

■ WIN32S   ■ WINDOWS 95   ■ WINDOWS NT

Description   HKM_GETHOTKEY is a message that retrieves the virtual-key code and the modifier flags for the hot key in a hot-key control. The return value of HKM_GETHOTKEY can be used by the *wParam* parameter of the WM_SETHOTKEY message.

Parameters   This message does not use *wParam* or *lParam*.

Returns   DWORD: The virtual-key code is returned in the low-order byte and the modifier flags are returned in the high-order byte. The modifier flags can be a combination of the values in Table 9-13.

Table 9-13 HKM_GETHOTKEY modifier flags

Value	Meaning
HOTKEYF_ALT	ALT key
HOTKEYF_CONTROL	CTRL key
HOTKEYF_EXT	Extended key
HOTKEYF_SHIFT	SHIFT key

Include File   commctrl.h

See Also   RegisterHotKey()

Related Messages   WM_SETHOTKEY, WM_HOTKEY

Example   This example, shown in Figure 9-5 and Listing 9-5, creates a hot-key control on the client area of the window. The hot key that is specified in the control is registered as the hot key for the window when the user selects the Set Hot-Key! menu item. Once a hot key is registered and the user presses the key combination, the window is activated.

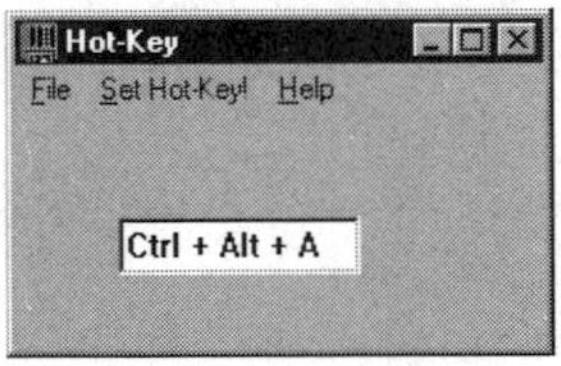

Figure 9-5 Hot-key example

Listing 9-5 Using the HKM_GETHOTKEY message

```
LRESULT CALLBACK WndProc( HWND hWnd, UINT uMsg, WPARAM wParam, LPARAM lParam )
{
static HWND hHotKey = NULL;

   switch( uMsg )
```

```
{
    case WM_CREATE :
            InitCommonControls();

            // Create the edit control.
            //..........................
            hHotKey = CreateWindowEx( WS_EX_CLIENTEDGE, HOTKEY_CLASS, "",
                                      WS_CHILD | WS_BORDER | WS_VISIBLE,
                                      40, 40, 100, 25, hWnd,
                                      (HMENU)1, hInst, NULL );

            // Make ALT the default modifier.
            //...............................
            SendMessage( hHotKey, HKM_SETRULES,
                         (WPARAM) HKCOMB_NONE | HKCOMB_S,
                         MAKELPARAM( HOTKEYF_ALT, 0) );

            // Set CTRL + ALT + A as the default
            // hot key for this window.
            //...................................
            SendMessage( hHotKey, HKM_SETHOTKEY,
                         MAKEWORD( 0x41,
                         HOTKEYF_CONTROL | HOTKEYF_ALT), 0);

            // Associate the hot key with the window.
            //.......................................
            SendMessage( hWnd, WM_SETHOTKEY,
                         MAKEWORD( 0x41,
                         HOTKEYF_CONTROL | HOTKEYF_ALT), 0 );
            break;


    case WM_COMMAND :
            switch( LOWORD( wParam ) )
            {
                case IDM_SETHOTKEY :
                        {
                                WORD wHotkey;
                                UINT iSetResult;

                                // Retrieve the hot key.
                                //......................
                                wHotkey = (WORD)SendMessage( hHotKey,
                                            HKM_GETHOTKEY, 0, 0 );

                                // Associate the hot
                                // key with the window.
                                //.....................
                                iSetResult = SendMessage( hWnd,
                                            WM_SETHOTKEY, wHotkey, 0 );

                                switch ( iSetResult )
                                {
                                    case 2 :
                                        MessageBox( hWnd,
                                            "Hot key previously assigned",
                                            lpszTitle, MB_OK );
                                        break;
```

continued on next page

continued from previous page

```
                              case 1 : // Successful
                                break;

                              case 0 :
                                  MessageBox( hWnd,
                                          "Invalid window for hot key",
                                          "Error", MB_OK );
                                break;

                              case -1 :
                                  MessageBox( hWnd, "Invalid hot key",
                                          "Error", MB_OK);
                                break;

                              default:
                                  MessageBox( hWnd,
                                          "Unknown error",
                                          "Error", MB_OK);
                                break;
                          }
                      }
                      break;
        .
        .
        .
```

HKM_SETHOTKEY ■ Win32s ■ Windows 95 ■ Windows NT

Description	HKM_SETHOTKEY is a message that sets the hot-key combination for a hot-key control.
Parameters	
LOWORD(wParam)	WORD: The virtual-key code of the hot key.
HIWORD(wParam)	WORD: The modifier flags of the hot key. This parameter can be a combination of the values in Table 9-13.
lParam	LPARAM: This parameter is set to zero.
Include File	commctrl.h
Related Messages	HKM_GETHOTKEY
Example	See the example for the HKM_GETHOTKEY message.

HKM_SETRULES ■ Win32s ■ Windows 95 ■ Windows NT

Description	HKM_SETRULES is a message that specifies the invalid key combinations and the default modifier combination for a hot-key control.
Parameters	
wParam	WPARAM: An array of the values in Table 9-14 specifying the invalid key combinations for the hot-key control.

Table 9-14 HKM_SETRULES *wParam* values

Value	Meaning
HKCOMB_A	ALT
HKCOMB_C	CTRL
HKCOMB_CA	CTRL + ALT
HKCOMB_NONE	Unmodified keys
HKCOMB_S	SHIFT
HKCOMB_SA	SHIFT + ALT
HKCOMB_SC	SHIFT + CTRL
HKCOMB_SCA	SHIFT + CTRL + ALT

LOWORD(lParam)	WORD: An array of the values in Table 9-13 specifying the key combination to use when the user enters an invalid combination.
HIWORD(lParam)	WORD: This parameter is set to zero.
Include File	commctrl.h
Related Messages	HKM_GETHOTKEY
Example	See the example for the HKM_GETHOTKEY message.

PBM_DELTAPOS   ■ Win32s   ■ Windows 95   ■ Windows NT

Description	PBM_DELTAPOS is a message that advances the current position of a progress bar by a given increment and redraws the bar to reflect the new position.
Parameters	
wParam	WPARAM: The amount to advance the current position of the progress bar.
lParam	LPARAM: This parameter is set to zero.
Returns	int: The previous position of the progress bar is returned.
Include File	commctrl.h
Related Messages	PBM_STEPIT
Example	This example, shown in Figure 9-6 and Listing 9-6, shows how to create and use a progress bar as a feedback mechanism while performing long processes. Two methods of incrementing the progress bar are demonstrated. The first one increments the progress bar by an increasing number for each iteration of the process. This is common in processes that have variable length subprocess times. The second method sets the step value and steps the progress bar for each iteration. This method is used for processes that have equal subprocesses.

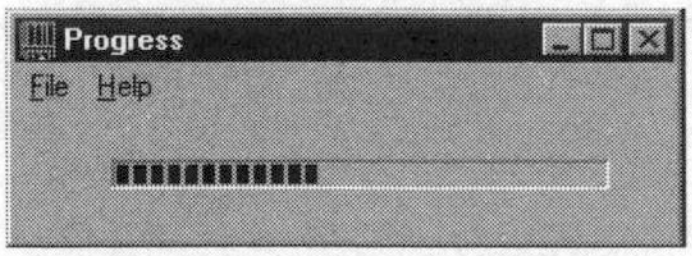

Figure 9-6 Progress example

Listing 9-6 Using the PBM_DELTAPOS message

```
LRESULT CALLBACK WndProc( HWND hWnd, UINT uMsg, WPARAM wParam, LPARAM lParam )
{
static HWND hProgress = NULL;

    switch( uMsg )
    {
    case WM_CREATE :
            InitCommonControls();

            // Create the edit control.
            //.........................
            hProgress = CreateWindowEx( 0, PROGRESS_CLASS, "",
                                        WS_CHILD | WS_VISIBLE,
                                        40, 20, 200, 12, hWnd,
                                        (HMENU)1, hInst, NULL );

            break;


    case WM_COMMAND :
            switch( LOWORD( wParam ) )
            {
            case IDM_TEST1 :
                    {
                        int i = 0;

                        // Reset the Progress bar.
                        //.......................
                        SendMessage( hProgress, PBM_SETPOS, 0, 0 );

                        // Make sure the range is set.
                        //...........................
                        SendMessage( hProgress, PBM_SETRANGE,
                                    0, MAKELPARAM(0,20) );

                        while( i<20 )
                        {
                            // Add delay to simulate a process.
                            //.................................
                            Sleep( 500 );


                            // Increment the position.
                            //.......................
                            i = SendMessage( hProgress,
                                            PBM_DELTAPOS, i+1, 0 );
                        }
                    }
                    break;
```

```
case IDM_TEST2 :
    {
        int i = 0;

        // Reset the Progress bar.
        //........................
        SendMessage( hProgress, PBM_SETPOS, 0, 0 );

        // Make sure the range is set.
        //...........................
        SendMessage( hProgress, PBM_SETRANGE,
                    0, MAKELPARAM(0,20) );

        // Set the step value to 2.
        //........................
        SendMessage( hProgress, PBM_SETSTEP, 2, 0 );

        while( i<18 )
        {
            // Add delay to simulate a process.
            //................................
            Sleep( 500 );


            // Step the position.
            //..................
            i = SendMessage( hProgress,
                        PBM_STEPIT, 0, 0 );
        }
    }
    break;
```

.
.
.

PBM_SETPOS   ■ WIN32s ■ WINDOWS 95 ■ WINDOWS NT

Description   PBM_SETPOS is a message that sets the current position for a progress bar and redraws the bar to reflect the new position.

Parameters

wParam   WPARAM: The new position of the progress bar.

lParam   LPARAM: This parameter is set to zero.

Returns   int: The previous position of the progress bar is returned.

Include File   commctrl.h

Example   See the example for the PBM_DELTAPOS message.

PBM_SETRANGE   ■ WIN32s ■ WINDOWS 95 ■ WINDOWS NT

Description   PBM_SETRANGE is a message that sets the minimum and maximum values for a progress bar and redraws the bar to reflect the new range.

Parameters

wParam   WPARAM: This parameter is set to zero.

LOWORD(lParam)   WORD: The minimum range value for the progress bar. The default value is zero.

HIWORD(lParam)   WORD: The maximum range value for the progress bar. The default value is 100.

Returns   DWORD: If successful, the previous minimum range value is returned in the low-order word and the previous maximum value is returned in the high-order word; otherwise zero is returned.

Include File   commctrl.h

Example   See the example for the PBM_DELTAPOS message.

PBM_SETSTEP   ■ Win32s   ■ Windows 95   ■ Windows NT

Description   PBM_SETSTEP is a message that sets the amount used to increment the progress bar when a PBM_STEPIT message is received.

Parameters

wParam   WPARAM: The new increment value for the progress bar. The default increment value is 10.

lParam   LPARAM: This parameter is set to zero.

Returns   int: The previous step increment value is returned.

Include File   commctrl.h

Related Messages   PBM_STEPIT

Example   See the example for the PBM_DELTAPOS message.

PBM_STEPIT   ■ Win32s   ■ Windows 95   ■ Windows NT

Description   PBM_STEPIT is a message that advances the current position of a progress bar by the step increment and redraws the bar to reflect the new position. The PBM_SETSTEP message is used to set the step increment for the progress bar. If the position of the progress bar exceeds the maximum range, the progress indicator of the progress bar starts over again from the minimum (beginning) range position.

Parameters   This message does not use wParam or lParam.

Returns   int: The previous position of the progress bar is returned.

Include File   commctrl.h

Related Messages   PBM_SETSTEP, PBM_DELTAPOS

Example   See the example for the PBM_DELTAPOS message.

TBM_CLEARSEL
■ WIN32S   ■ WINDOWS 95   ■ WINDOWS NT

Description	TBM_CLEARSEL is a message that clears the current selection in a track-bar. The selection is the portion of the trackbar that is selected to denote a range within the range of the trackbar.
Parameters	
wParam	BOOL: If the value of this parameter is TRUE, the trackbar is redrawn after the selection is cleared.
lParam	LPARAM: This parameter is set to zero.
Include File	commctrl.h
Related Messages	TBM_SETSEL
Example	See the example for the TBM_SETRANGE message.

TBM_CLEARTICS
■ WIN32S   ■ WINDOWS 95   ■ WINDOWS NT

Description	TBM_CLEARTICS is a message that removes the current tick marks from the trackbar.
Parameters	
wParam	BOOL: If the value of this parameter is TRUE, the trackbar is redrawn after the tick marks are cleared.
lParam	LPARAM: This parameter is set to zero.
Include File	commctrl.h
Related Messages	TBM_SETTIC, TBM_SETTICFREQ
Example	See the example for the TBM_SETRANGE message.

TBM_GETCHANNELRECT
■ WIN32S   ■ WINDOWS 95   ■ WINDOWS NT

Description	TBM_GETCHANNELRECT is a message that determines the size and position of the bounding rectangle for the channel of a trackbar. The channel is the area over which the slider moves and which contains the highlight when a range is selected.
Parameters	
wParam	WPARAM: This parameter is set to zero.
lParam	LPRECT: A pointer to a RECT structure that contains the size and position of the channel's bounding rectangle when the function returns.
Include File	commctrl.h

TBM_GETLINESIZE   ■ Win32s   ■ Windows 95   ■ Windows NT

Description	TBM_GETLINESIZE is a message that retrieves the size of the line for a trackbar. The default line size is 1. The line size affects how much the slider moves for the TB_LINEUP and TB_LINEDOWN notification messages.
Parameters	This message does not use *wParam* or *lParam*.
Returns	int: If successful, the 32-bit value that specifies the size of a line for the trackbar is returned.
Include File	commctrl.h
Related Messages	TBM_SETLINESIZE, WM_HSCROLL, TB_LINEDOWN, TB_LINEUP
Example	See the example for the TBM_SETRANGE message.

TBM_GETNUMTICS   ■ Win32s   ■ Windows 95   ■ Windows NT

Description	TBM_GETNUMTICS determines the number of tick marks currently on the trackbar.
Parameters	This message does not use *wParam* or *lParam*.
Returns	int: If successful, the number of tick marks on the trackbar is returned.
Include File	commctrl.h
Example	See the example for the TBM_SETRANGE message.

TBM_GETPAGESIZE   ■ Win32s   ■ Windows 95   ■ Windows NT

Description	TBM_GETPAGESIZE is a message that determines the size of the page for a trackbar. The page size affects how much the slider moves for the TB_PAGEUP and TB_PAGEDOWN notification messages.
Parameters	This message does not use *wParam* or *lParam*.
Returns	int: If successful, the 32-bit value that specifies the size of a page for the trackbar is returned.
Include File	commctrl.h
Related Messages	TBM_SETPAGESIZE, WM_HSCROLL, TB_LINEDOWN, TB_LINEUP
Example	See the example for the TBM_SETRANGE message.

TBM_GETPOS   ■ Win32s   ■ Windows 95   ■ Windows NT

Description	TBM_GETPOS is a message that retrieves the current position of the slider on the trackbar control.
Parameters	This message does not use *wParam* or *lParam*.
Returns	int: If successful, the 32-bit value that indicates the current position of the slider is returned.

Include File	commctrl.h
Related Messages	TBM_SETPOS
Example	See the example for the TBM_SETRANGE message.

TBM_GETPTICS   ■ Win32s   ■ Windows 95   ■ Windows NT

Description	TBM_GETPTICS is a message that retrieves the pointer to an array that contains the positions of tick marks for the trackbar.
Parameters	This message does not use *wParam* or *lParam*.
Returns	LPLONG: If successful, the pointer to an array that contains the tick mark positions is returned.
Related Messages	TBM_SETTIC, TBM_SETTICFREQ
Include File	commctrl.h

TBM_GETRANGEMAX   ■ Win32s   ■ Windows 95   ■ Windows NT

Description	TBM_GETRANGEMAX is a message that retrieves the maximum position for the slider in the trackbar.
Parameters	This message does not use *wParam* or *lParam*.
Returns	int: If successful, the 32-bit value that specifies the maximum position of the slider is returned.
Include File	commctrl.h
Related Messages	TBM_GETRANGEMIN, TBM_SETRANGEMAX, TBM_SETRANGE
Example	See the example for the TBM_SETRANGE message.

TBM_GETRANGEMIN   ■ Win32s   ■ Windows 95   ■ Windows NT

Description	TBM_GETRANGEMIN is a message that retrieves the minimum position of the slider in the trackbar.
Parameters	This message does not use *wParam* or *lParam*.
Returns	int: If successful, the 32-bit value that specifies the minimum position of the slider is returned.
Include File	commctrl.h
Related Messages	TBM_GETRANGEMAX, TBM_SETRANGEMIN, TBM_SETRANGE
Example	See the example for the TBM_SETRANGE message.

TBM_GETSELEND   ■ Win32s   ■ Windows 95   ■ Windows NT

Description	TBM_GETSELEND is a message that retrieves the ending position of the current selection in the trackbar.

Parameters	This message does not use *wParam* or *lParam*.
Returns	int: If successful, the 32-bit value that specifies the ending position of the current selection is returned.
Include File	commctrl.h
Related Messages	TBM_GETSELSTART, TBM_SETSELEND
Example	See the example for the TBM_SETRANGE message.

TBM_GETSELSTART ■ Win32s ■ Windows 95 ■ Windows NT

Description	TBM_GETSELSTART is a message that retrieves the starting position of the current selection in the trackbar.
Parameters	This message does not use *wParam* or *lParam*.
Returns	int: If successful, the 32-bit value that specifies the starting position of the current selection is returned.
Include File	commctrl.h
Related Messages	TBM_GETSELEND, TBM_SETSELSTART
Example	See the example for the TBM_SETRANGE message.

TBM_GETTHUMBLENGTH ■ Win32s ■ Windows 95 ■ Windows NT

Description	TBM_GETTHUMBLENGTH is a message that retrieves the length of the slider in the trackbar.
Parameters	This message does not use *wParam* or *lParam*.
Returns	int: If successful, the length, in pixels, of the slider is returned.
Include File	commctrl.h
Related Messages	TBM_SETTHUMBLENGTH, TBM_GETTHUMBRECT
Example	See the example for the TBM_SETRANGE message.

TBM_GETTHUMBRECT ■ Win32s ■ Windows 95 ■ Windows NT

Description	TBM_GETTHUMBRECT is a message that retrieves the size and position of the bounding rectangle for the slider in the trackbar.
Parameters	
wParam	WPARAM: This parameter is set to zero.
lParam	LPRECT: A pointer to a RECT structure that receives the bounding rectangle for the slider when the function returns.
Include File	commctrl.h

TBM_GETTIC   ■ Win32s   ■ Windows 95   ■ Windows NT

Description	TBM_GETTIC is a message that determines the position of the specified tick mark in the trackbar.
Parameters	
wParam	WORD: The zero-based index of the tick mark.
lParam	LPARAM: This parameter is set to zero.
Returns	int: If the value of *wParam* specifies a valid tick mark, the position of the tick mark is returned; otherwise, a value of -1 is returned.
Include File	commctrl.h
Related Messages	TBM_GETTICPOS, TBM_SETTIC

TBM_GETTICPOS   ■ Win32s   ■ Windows 95   ■ Windows NT

Description	TBM_GETTICPOS is a message that determines the current position of the specified tick mark in a trackbar, in client coordinates.
Parameters	
wParam	WORD: The zero-based index of the tick mark.
lParam	LPARAM: This parameter is set to zero.
Returns	int: If the value specified in *wParam* is a valid tick mark, the position, in client coordinates, of the specified tick mark is returned; otherwise, a value of -1 is returned.
Include File	commctrl.h
Related Messages	TBM_GETTIC, TBM_SETTIC

TBM_SETLINESIZE   ■ Win32s   ■ Windows 95   ■ Windows NT

Description	TBM_SETLINESIZE is a message that sets the size of the line for a trackbar. The line size affects how much the slider moves for the TB_LINEUP and TB_LINEDOWN notification messages.
Parameters	
wParam	WPARAM: This parameter is set to zero.
lParam	LONG: The new line size for the trackbar.
Returns	int: If successful, the 32-bit value specifying the previous line size is returned.
Include File	commctrl.h
Related Messages	TBM_GETLINESIZE, WM_HSCROLL, TB_LINEDOWN, TB_LINEUP
Example	See the example for the TBM_SETRANGE message.

TBM_SETPAGESIZE ■ Win32s ■ Windows 95 ■ Windows NT

Description   TBM_SETPAGESIZE is a message that sets the size of the page for a track-
                     bar. The page size affects how much the slider moves for the TB_PAGEUP
                     and TB_PAGEDOWN notification messages.

Parameters

wParam   WPARAM: This parameter is set to zero.

lParam   LONG: The new page size of the trackbar.

Returns   int: If successful, the 32-bit value specifying the previous page size is
                     returned.

Include File   commctrl.h

Related Messages TBM_GETPAGESIZE, WM_HSCROLL, TB_LINEDOWN, TB_LINEUP

Example   See the example for the TBM_SETRANGE message.

TBM_SETPOS ■ Win32s ■ Windows 95 ■ Windows NT

Description   TBM_SETPOS is a message that sets the current position of the slider in a
                     trackbar control.

Parameters

wParam   BOOL: If *wParam* is TRUE, the slider is set at the position specified by the
                     lParam parameter; otherwise, the message ensures that the current posi-
                     tion is within the current minimum and maximum positions, but it does
                     not move the slider.

lParam   LONG: The new position of the slider.

Returns   BOOL: If *wParam* is not set to TRUE, the return value indicates if the
                     position is within the range of the trackbar.

Include File   commctrl.h

Related Messages TBM_GETPOS

Example   See the example for the TBM_SETRANGE message.

TBM_SETRANGE ■ Win32s ■ Windows 95 ■ Windows NT

Description   TBM_SETRANGE is a message that sets the minimum and maximum
                     positions for the slider in a trackbar control. If the range is greater than
                     64K, use the TBM_SETRANGEMIN and TBM_SETRANGEMAX messages.

Parameters

wParam   BOOL: If *wParam* is TRUE, the slider is redrawn after the range is set.

LOWORD(lParam)   WORD: The minimum position for the slider.

HIWORD(lParam)   WORD: The maximum position for the slider.

Include File   commctrl.h

Related Messages   TBM_SETRANGEMAX, TBM_SETRANGEMIN, TBM_GETRANGEMAX, TBM_GETRANGEMIN

Example   This example (Listing 9-7) creates a trackbar on the client area of the application window and allows the user to change many of the characteristics for the trackbar. When the user selects the Properties menu item, a properties dialog is displayed to allow the user to change the attributes for the trackbar. Figure 9-7 shows the properties dialog and the resulting trackbar control.

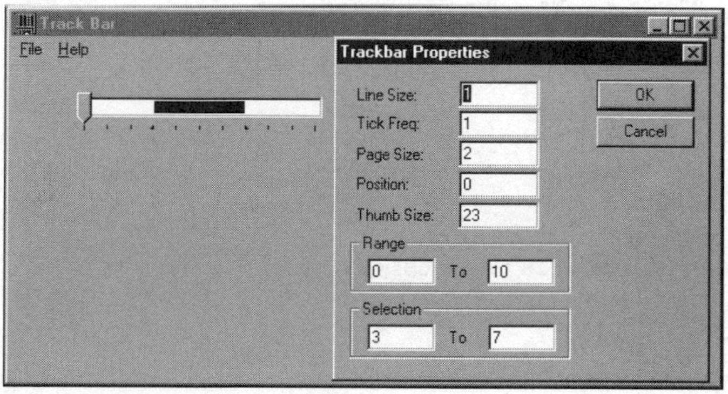

Figure 9-7 Trackbar example

Listing 9-7 Using the TBM_SETRANGE message

```
LRESULT CALLBACK WndProc( HWND hWnd, UINT uMsg, WPARAM wParam, LPARAM lParam )
{
static HWND hTrack = NULL;

   switch( uMsg )
   {
      case WM_CREATE :
            InitCommonControls();

            // Create the edit control.
            //........................
            hTrack = CreateWindowEx( 0, TRACKBAR_CLASS, "",
                                 WS_CHILD | WS_VISIBLE |
                                 TBS_ENABLESELRANGE | TBS_AUTOTICKS,
                                 40, 20, 200, 30, hWnd,
                                 (HMENU)IDC_TRACKBAR, hInst, NULL );

            if ( hTrack )
               SendMessage( hTrack, TBM_SETRANGE, TRUE, MAKELPARAM(0,10) );

            break;

      case WM_COMMAND :
            switch( LOWORD( wParam ) )
            {
               case IDM_PROPERTIES :
```

continued on next page

continued from previous page

```
                        DialogBox( hInst, "OptionsDlg", hWnd,(DLGPROC)Options );
                        break;

                case IDM_RESET :
                        SendMessage( hTrack, TBM_SETRANGE, TRUE,
                                            MAKELPARAM(0,10) );
                        SendMessage( hTrack, TBM_CLEARSEL, TRUE, 0 );
                        SendMessage( hTrack, TBM_CLEARTICS, TRUE, 0 );
                        break;

                case IDM_EXIT :
                        DestroyWindow( hWnd );
                        break;
            }
            break;

    case WM_DESTROY :
            PostQuitMessage(0);
            break;

    default :
            return( DefWindowProc( hWnd, uMsg, wParam, lParam ) );
    }

    return( 0L );
}


LRESULT CALLBACK Options( HWND hDlg,
                          UINT message,
                          WPARAM wParam,
                          LPARAM lParam)
{
    switch (message)
    {
        case WM_INITDIALOG:
                {
                    HWND    hTrack;
                    DWORD   dwLineSize;
                    DWORD   dwNumTics;
                    DWORD   dwPageSize;
                    DWORD   dwPos;
                    DWORD   dwThSize;
                    DWORD   dwMaxRange;
                    DWORD   dwMinRange;
                    DWORD   dwSelStart;
                    DWORD   dwSelEnd;

                    // Retrieve the trackbar handle.
                    //................................
                    hTrack = GetDlgItem( GetParent( hDlg ), IDC_TRACKBAR );

                    // Retrieve the information from the trackbar.
                    //...........................................
                    dwLineSize = SendMessage( hTrack, TBM_GETLINESIZE, 0, 0 );
                    dwNumTics  = SendMessage( hTrack, TBM_GETNUMTICS, 0, 0 );
                    dwPageSize = SendMessage( hTrack, TBM_GETPAGESIZE, 0, 0 );
                    dwPos      = SendMessage( hTrack, TBM_GETPOS, 0, 0 );
                    dwMinRange = SendMessage( hTrack, TBM_GETRANGEMIN, 0, 0 );
```

```
                dwMaxRange = SendMessage( hTrack, TBM_GETRANGEMAX, 0, 0 );
                dwSelStart = SendMessage( hTrack, TBM_GETSELSTART, 0, 0 );
                dwSelEnd   = SendMessage( hTrack, TBM_GETSELEND, 0, 0 );
                dwThSize   = SendMessage( hTrack, TBM_GETTHUMBLENGTH, 0, 0 );

                // Initialize the dialog controls with the values.
                //.................................................
                SetDlgItemInt( hDlg, IDC_LINESIZE, dwLineSize, FALSE );
                SetDlgItemInt( hDlg, IDC_TICKFREQ,
                               (dwMaxRange-dwMinRange)/(dwNumTics-1), FALSE );
                SetDlgItemInt( hDlg, IDC_PAGESIZE, dwPageSize, FALSE );
                SetDlgItemInt( hDlg, IDC_POS, dwPos, FALSE );
                SetDlgItemInt( hDlg, IDC_THUMBSIZE, dwThSize, FALSE );
                SetDlgItemInt( hDlg, IDC_RANGE1, dwMinRange, FALSE );
                SetDlgItemInt( hDlg, IDC_RANGE2, dwMaxRange, FALSE );
                SetDlgItemInt( hDlg, IDC_SEL1, dwSelStart, FALSE );
                SetDlgItemInt( hDlg, IDC_SEL2, dwSelEnd, FALSE );
            }
            return (TRUE);

    case WM_COMMAND:
            if ( LOWORD(wParam) == IDOK )
            {
                HWND    hTrack;
                DWORD   dwLineSize;
                DWORD   dwNumTics;
                DWORD   dwPageSize;
                DWORD   dwPos;
                DWORD   dwThSize;
                DWORD   dwMaxRange;
                DWORD   dwMinRange;
                DWORD   dwSelStart;
                DWORD   dwSelEnd;

                // Retrieve the trackbar handle.
                //.............................
                hTrack = GetDlgItem( GetParent( hDlg ), IDC_TRACKBAR );

                // Retrieve the new settings from the dialog.
                //...........................................
                dwLineSize = GetDlgItemInt( hDlg, IDC_LINESIZE, NULL, FALSE );
                dwNumTics  = GetDlgItemInt( hDlg, IDC_TICKFREQ, NULL, FALSE );
                dwPageSize = GetDlgItemInt( hDlg, IDC_PAGESIZE, NULL, FALSE );
                dwPos      = GetDlgItemInt( hDlg, IDC_POS, NULL, FALSE );
                dwThSize   = GetDlgItemInt( hDlg, IDC_THUMBSIZE, NULL,FALSE );
                dwMinRange = GetDlgItemInt( hDlg, IDC_RANGE1, NULL, FALSE );
                dwMaxRange = GetDlgItemInt( hDlg, IDC_RANGE2, NULL, FALSE );
                dwSelStart = GetDlgItemInt( hDlg, IDC_SEL1, NULL, FALSE );
                dwSelEnd   = GetDlgItemInt( hDlg, IDC_SEL2, NULL, FALSE );

                // Set the new attributes of the trackbar control.
                //................................................
                SendMessage( hTrack, TBM_SETLINESIZE, 0, dwLineSize );
                SendMessage( hTrack, TBM_SETTICFREQ, dwNumTics, 0 );
                SendMessage( hTrack, TBM_SETPAGESIZE, 0, dwPageSize );
                SendMessage( hTrack, TBM_SETPOS, TRUE, dwPos );
                SendMessage( hTrack, TBM_SETRANGEMIN, TRUE, dwMinRange );
                SendMessage( hTrack, TBM_SETRANGEMAX, TRUE, dwMaxRange );
                SendMessage( hTrack, TBM_SETSELSTART, TRUE, dwSelStart );
```

continued on next page

continued from previous page

```
                    SendMessage( hTrack, TBM_SETSELEND, TRUE, dwSelEnd );
                    SendMessage( hTrack, TBM_SETTHUMBLENGTH, dwThSize, 0 );

                    EndDialog( hDlg, IDOK );
            }
            else if ( LOWORD(wParam) == IDCANCEL )
                    EndDialog( hDlg, IDCANCEL );
            break;
    }

    return (FALSE);
}
```

TBM_SETRANGEMAX ■ Win32s ■ Windows 95 ■ Windows NT

Description	TBM_SETRANGEMAX is a message that sets the maximum position for the slider in a trackbar control. Use this message to set the range when it is greater than 64K.
Parameters	
wParam	WPARAM: If *wParam* is TRUE, the slider is redrawn after the range is set.
lParam	LPARAM: The maximum position for the slider.
Include File	commctrl.h
Related Messages	TBM_GETRANGEMAX, TBM_SETRANGE, TBM_SETRANGEMIN
Example	See the example for the TBM_SETRANGE message.

TBM_SETRANGEMIN ■ Win32s ■ Windows 95 ■ Windows NT

Description	TBM_SETRANGEMIN is a message that sets the minimum position for the slider in a trackbar. Use this message to set the range when it is greater than 64K.
Parameters	
wParam	WPARAM: If *wParam* is TRUE, the slider is redrawn after the range is set.
lParam	LPARAM: The minimum position for the slider.
Include File	commctrl.h
Related Messages	TBM_GETRANGEMIN, TBM_SETRANGE, TBM_SETRANGEMAX
Example	See the example for the TBM_SETRANGE message.

TBM_SETSEL ■ Win32s ■ Windows 95 ■ Windows NT

Description	TBM_SETSEL is a message that sets the starting and ending positions for the current selection in the trackbar. Use this message when the selection range falls within the 64K limit. Otherwise, use the TBM_SETSELEND and TBM_SETSELSTART messages.

Parameters

wParam	WPARAM: If *wParam* is TRUE, the slider is redrawn after the selection is set.
LOWORD(*lParam*)	WORD: The starting position for the slider.
HIWORD(*lParam*)	WORD: The ending position for the slider.
Include File	commctrl.h
Related Messages	TBM_SETSELEND, TBM_SETSELSTART

TBM_SETSELEND   ■ Win32s   ■ Windows 95   ■ Windows NT

Description	TBM_SETSELEND is a message that sets the ending position of the current selection in the trackbar. Use this message instead of the TBM_SETSEL message if the range is greater than 64K.

Parameters

wParam	WPARAM: If *wParam* is TRUE, the slider is redrawn after the selection is set.
lParam	LONG: The ending position of the selection.
Include File	commctrl.h
Related Messages	TBM_GETSELEND, TBM_SETSELSTART, TBM_SETSEL
Example	See the example for the TBM_SETRANGE message.

TBM_SETSELSTART   ■ Win32s   ■ Windows 95   ■ Windows NT

Description	TBM_SETSELSTART is a message that sets the starting position of the current selection in the trackbar. Use this message instead of the TBM_SETSEL message if the range is greater than 64K.

Parameters

wParam	WPARAM: If *wParam* is TRUE, the slider is redrawn after the selection is set.
lParam	LONG: The starting position of the selection.
Include File	commctrl.h
Related Messages	TBM_GETSELSTART, TBM_SETSELEND, TBM_SETSEL
Example	See the example for the TBM_SETRANGE message.

TBM_SETTHUMBLENGTH   ■ Win32s   ■ Windows 95   ■ Windows NT

Description	TBM_SETTHUMBLENGTH is a message that sets the length of the slider in a trackbar control.

Parameters

wParam	UINT: The length, in pixels, of the slider.
lParam	LPARAM: This parameter is set to zero.
Include File	commctrl.h

Related Messages	TBM_GETTHUMBLENGTH
Example	See the example for the TBM_SETRANGE message.

TBM_SETTIC ■ Win32s ■ Windows 95 ■ Windows NT

Description	TBM_SETTIC is a message that sets the position of a tick mark in the trackbar. This message should not be used to create the first or last tick mark in a trackbar; these are created by the trackbar.
Parameters	
wParam	WPARAM: This parameter is set to zero.
lParam	LONG: The position of the tick mark. This must be a positive value.
Returns	BOOL: If the tick mark is set in the trackbar, TRUE is returned; otherwise, FALSE is returned.
Related Messages	TBM_GETTIC
Include File	commctrl.h

TBM_SETTICFREQ ■ Win32s ■ Windows 95 ■ Windows NT

Description	TBM_SETTICFREQ is a message that sets the interval frequency for tick marks in the trackbar. This message can only be used with trackbars that have a TBS_AUTOTICKS style.
Parameters	
wParam	WPARAM: The frequency of the tick marks in the trackbar. The default frequency is 1. If *wParam* is set to 2, a tick mark displays for every other increment in the trackbar.
lParam	LONG: This parameter is set to zero.
Include File	commctrl.h
Example	See the example for the TBM_SETRANGE message.

UDM_GETACCEL ■ Win32s ■ Windows 95 ■ Windows NT

Description	UDM_GETACCEL is a message that retrieves the acceleration information for an up-down control.
Parameters	
wParam	WPARAM: The number of elements in the array specified by the *lParam* parameter.
lParam	LPUDACCEL: The address of an array of UDACCEL structures that receives acceleration information. See the definition of the UDACCEL structure below.
Returns	int: The number of accelerator structures retrieved is returned.
Include File	commctrl.h

Related Messages UDM_SETACCEL

UDACCEL Definition

```
typedef struct
{
    UINT nSec;
    UINT nInc;
} UDACCEL, *LPUDACCEL;
```

Members

nSec UINT: The amount of elapsed time, in seconds, before the position change increment specified by the *nInc* member is used.

nInc UINT: The position change increment to use after the time specified by the *nSec* member elapses.

Example See the example for the CreateUpDownControl() function.

UDM_GETBASE ■ Win32s ■ Windows 95 ■ Windows NT

Description UDM_GETBASE retrieves the current radix base for the up-down control. The valid radix base values are 10 and 16.

Parameters This message does not use *wParam* or *lParam*.

Returns int: The current base value of the up-down control is returned.

Include File commctrl.h

Related Messages UDM_SETBASE

Example See the example for the CreateUpDownControl() function.

UDM_GETBUDDY ■ Win32s ■ Windows 95 ■ Windows NT

Description UDM_GETBUDDY is a message that retrieves the handle of the current buddy window for the up-down control.

Parameters This message does not use *wParam* or *lParam*.

Returns HWND: The handle of the current buddy window is returned.

Include File commctrl.h

Related Messages UDM_SETBUDDY

Example See the example for the CreateUpDownControl() function.

UDM_GETPOS ■ Win32s ■ Windows 95 ■ Windows NT

Description UDM_GETPOS is a message that determines the current position of the up-down control.

Parameters This message does not use *wParam* or *lParam*.

Returns DWORD: The current position of the up-down control is returned in the low-order word. If an error occurred, a nonzero value is returned in the high-order word. An error is returned if there is not a buddy window, or if the caption of the buddy window specifies a value that is invalid or out of range.

Include File	commctrl.h
Related Messages	UDM_SETPOS
Example	See the example for the CreateUpDownControl() function.

UDM_GETRANGE ■ Win32s ■ Windows 95 ■ Windows NT

Description	UDM_GETRANGE is a message that determines the minimum and maximum range values for the up-down control.
Parameters	This message does not use *wParam* or *lParam*.
Returns	DWORD: A 32-bit value that contains the minimum and maximum range values of the up-down control is returned. The low-order word is the maximum position for the control, and the high-order word is the minimum position.
Include File	commctrl.h
Related Messages	UDM_SETRANGE
Example	See the example for the CreateUpDownControl() function.

UDM_SETACCEL ■ Win32s ■ Windows 95 ■ Windows NT

Description	UDM_SETACCEL is a message that sets the acceleration information for the up-down control.
Parameters	
wParam	WPARAM: The number of UDACCEL structures specified by the *lParam* parameter.
lParam	LPUDACCEL: The address of an array of UDACCEL structures that contains acceleration information. See the definition of the UDACCEL structure under the UDM_GETACCEL message.
Returns	BOOL: If successful, TRUE is returned; otherwise, FALSE is returned.
Include File	commctrl.h
Related Messages	UDM_GETACCEL
Example	See the example for the CreateUpDownControl() function.

UDM_SETBASE ■ Win32s ■ Windows 95 ■ Windows NT

Description	UDM_SETBASE is a message that sets the radix base for an up-down control. A radix value of 10 displays the numbers in decimal digits; these numbers are signed. A radix value of 16 displays the numbers in hexadecimal digits; these numbers are unsigned.

Parameters

wParam	WPARAM: The new base value for the control. A value of 10 specifies decimal numbers, and a value of 16 specifies hexadecimal numbers.
lParam	LPARAM: This parameter is set to zero.
Returns	int: If successful, the previous base value is returned; otherwise, zero is returned.
Include File	commctrl.h
Related Messages	UDM_GETBASE
Example	See the example for the CreateUpDownControl() function.

UDM_SETBUDDY   ■ Win32s ■ Windows 95 ■ Windows NT

Description	UDM_SETBUDDY is a message that sets the buddy window for the up-down control.

Parameters

wParam	HWND: The window handle of the new buddy window.
lParam	LPARAM: This parameter is set to zero.
Returns	HWND: The handle of the previous buddy window is returned.
Include File	commctrl.h
Related Messages	UDM_GETBUDDY
Example	See the example for the CreateUpDownControl() function.

UDM_SETPOS   ■ Win32s ■ Windows 95 ■ Windows NT

Description	UDM_SETPOS is a message that sets the current position of the up-down control.

Parameters

wParam	WPARAM: This parameter is set to zero.
LOWORD(*lParam*)	short: The new position for the up-down control. The new position value must be within the upper and lower range limits for the up-down control.
HIWORD(*lParam*)	short: This parameter is set to zero.
Returns	short: The previous position of the up-down control is returned.
Include File	commctrl.h
Related Messages	UDM_GETPOS
Example	See the example for the CreateUpDownControl() function.

UDM_SETRANGE   ■ Win32s   ■ Windows 95   ■ Windows NT

Description   UDM_SETRANGE is a message that sets the minimum and maximum range values of the up-down control. The maximum value can be less than the minimum value.

Parameters

wParam   WPARAM: This parameter is set to zero.

LOWORD(lParam)   short: The maximum position of the up-down control. This value cannot be greater than the UD_MAXVAL value of the control, and the difference between maximum and minimum cannot exceed UD_MAXVAL.

HIWORD(lParam)   short: The minimum position of the up-down control. This value cannot be less than the UD_MINVAL value of the control, and the difference between maximum and minimum cannot exceed UD_MAXVAL.

Include File   commctrl.h

Related Messages UDM_GETRANGE

Example   See the example for the CreateUpDownControl() function.

ACN_START   ■ Win32s   ■ Windows 95   ■ Windows NT

Description   ACN_START is a notification message that notifies the parent window of an animation control that the AVI clip has started playing. This notification message is sent in the form of a WM_COMMAND message. The high word of the *wParam* is the notification code.

Include File   commctrl.h

Related Messages ACN_STOP, WM_COMMAND

ACN_STOP   ■ Win32s   ■ Windows 95   ■ Windows NT

Description   ACN_STOP is a notification message that notifies the parent window of an animation control that the AVI clip has stopped playing. This notification message is sent in the form of a WM_COMMAND message.

Include File   commctrl.h

Related Messages ACN_START, WM_COMMAND

HDN_BEGINTRACK   ■ Win32s   ■ Windows 95   ■ Windows NT

Description   HDN_BEGINTRACK is a notification message that notifies the parent window of a header control that the user has begun dragging a divider in the control. The divider is dragged by pressing the left mouse button while the mouse cursor is on a divider in the header control. This notification message is sent in the form of a WM_NOTIFY message.

Parameters

lParam   HD_NOTIFY *: A pointer to an HD_NOTIFY structure that contains information about the header control and the item whose divider is to be dragged. See the definition of the HD_NOTIFY structure below.

Returns   BOOL: FALSE is returned to allow tracking of the divider; otherwise, TRUE is returned to prevent tracking.

Include File   commctrl.h

Related Messages   WM_NOTIFY, HDN_ENDTRACK, HDN_TRACK

HD_NOTIFY Definition

```
typedef struct _HD_NOTIFY
{
    NMHDR     hdr;
    int       iItem;
    int       iButton;
    HD_ITEM*  pitem;
} HD_NOTIFY;
```

Members

hdr   NMHDR: An NMHDR structure that contains information about the header control. This member is required for all WM_NOTIFY messages. See the definition of the NMHDR structure below.

iItem   int: The index of the item associated with the notification message.

iButton   int: The index of the mouse button involved in generating the notification message. This member can be one of the values in Table 9-15.

Table 9-15 HDN_BEGINTRACK HD_NOTIFY *iButton* values

Value	Meaning
0	Left button
1	Right button
2	Middle button

pitem   HD_ITEM *: The address of an HD_ITEM structure that contains information about the header item associated with the notification message. See the definition of the HD_ITEM structure under the Header_GetItem macro.

NMHDR Definition

```
typedef struct tagNMHDR
{
    HWND hwndFrom;
    UINT idFrom;
    UINT code;
} NMHDR;
```

Members

hwndFrom	HWND: The handle of the control sending the message.
idFrom	UINT: The identifier of the control sending the message.
code	UINT: A control-specific notification code, or one of the common notification values in Table 9-16.

Table 9-16 HDN_BEGINTRACK NMHDR *code* values

Value	Meaning
NM_CLICK	The user has clicked the left mouse button within the control.
NM_DBLCLK	The user has double-clicked the left mouse button within the control.
NM_KILLFOCUS	The control has lost the input focus.
NM_OUTOFMEMORY	The control could not complete an operation because there was not enough memory available.
NM_RCLICK	The user has clicked the right mouse button within the control.
NM_RDBLCLK	The user has double-clicked the right mouse button within the control.
NM_RETURN	The control has the input focus, and the user has pressed the ENTER key.
NM_SETFOCUS	The control has received the input focus.

Example   See the example for the Header_InsertItem macro.

HDN_DIVIDERDBLCLICK   ■ Win32s ■ Windows 95 ■ Windows NT

Description   HDN_DIVIDERDBLCLICK is a notification message that notifies the parent window of a header control that the user double-clicked the divider area of the control. This notification message is sent in the form of a WM_NOTIFY message.

Parameters

lParam   HD_NOTIFY *: A pointer to an HD_NOTIFY structure that contains information about the header control and the item whose divider was double-clicked. See the definition of the HD_NOTIFY structure under the HDN_BEGINTRACK message.

Include File   commctrl.h

Related Messages   WM_NOTIFY, HDN_ITEMDBLCLICK

HDN_ENDTRACK   ■ Win32s ■ Windows 95 ■ Windows NT

Description   HDN_ENDTRACK is a notification message that notifies the parent window of a header control that the user has finished dragging a divider. This notification message is sent in the form of a WM_NOTIFY message.

Parameters

lParam HD_NOTIFY *: A pointer to an HD_NOTIFY structure containing information about the header control and the item whose divider was dragged. See the definition of the HD_NOTIFY structure under the HDN_BEGINTRACK message.

Include File commctrl.h

Related Messages WM_NOTIFY, HDN_BEGINTRACK, HDN_TRACK

Example See the example for the Header_InsertItem macro.

HDN_ITEMCHANGED ■ Win32s ■ Windows 95 ■ Windows NT

Description HDN_ITEMCHANGED is a notification message that notifies the parent window of a header control that the attributes of an item in the control have changed. This notification message is sent in the form of a WM_NOTIFY message.

Parameters

lParam HD_NOTIFY *: A pointer to an HD_NOTIFY structure that contains information about the header control, including the attributes that have changed. See the definition of the HD_NOTIFY structure under the HDN_BEGINTRACK message.

Include File commctrl.h

Related Messages WM_NOTIFY

Example See the example for the Header_InsertItem macro.

HDN_ITEMCHANGING ■ Win32s ■ Windows 95 ■ Windows NT

Description HDN_ITEMCHANGING is a notification message that notifies the parent window of a header control that the attributes are changing for an item in the control. This notification message is sent in the form of a WM_NOTIFY message.

Parameters

lParam HD_NOTIFY *: A pointer to an HD_NOTIFY structure that contains information about the header control and the header item attributes that are about to change. See the definition of the HD_NOTIFY structure under the HDN_BEGINTRACK message.

Returns BOOL: FALSE is returned to allow the changes to occur; otherwise, TRUE is returned to prevent them.

Include File commctrl.h

Related Messages WM_NOTIFY

Example See the example for the Header_InsertItem macro.

HDN_ITEMCLICK ■ Win32s ■ Windows 95 ■ Windows NT

Description   HDN_ITEMCLICK is a notification message that notifies the parent window of a header control that the user clicked an item in the control. This notification message is sent in the form of a WM_NOTIFY message after the left mouse button is released.

Parameters

lParam   HD_NOTIFY *: A pointer to an HD_NOTIFY structure that identifies the header control and specifies the index of the header item that was clicked and the mouse button used to click the item. The *pitem* member of the structure is set to NULL. See the definition of the HD_NOTIFY structure under the HDN_BEGINTRACK message.

Include File   commctrl.h

Related Messages WM_NOTIFY

Example   See the example for the Header_InsertItem macro.

HDN_ITEMDBLCLICK ■ Win32s ■ Windows 95 ■ Windows NT

Description   HDN_ITEMDBLCLICK is a notification message that notifies the parent window of a header control that the user double-clicked the control. This notification message is sent in the form of a WM_NOTIFY message by header controls with the HDS_BUTTONS style. If the header control has the HDS_DIVIDERTRACK style, this message is not sent when the user double-clicks the divider.

Parameters

lParam   NMHDR *: A pointer to an NMHDR structure that contains the handle and identifier of the header control and the HDN_ITEMDBLCLICK notification code. See the definition of the NMHDR structure under the HDN_BEGINTRACK message.

Include File   commctrl.h

Related Messages WM_NOTIFY

HDN_TRACK ■ Win32s ■ Windows 95 ■ Windows NT

Description   HDN_TRACK is a notification message that notifies the parent window of a header control that the user is dragging a divider in the header control. This notification message is sent in the form of a WM_NOTIFY message.

Parameters

lParam   HD_NOTIFY *: A pointer to an HD_NOTIFY structure that contains information about the header control and the item whose divider is being dragged. See the definition of the HD_NOTIFY structure under the HDN_BEGINTRACK message.

Returns	BOOL: FALSE is returned to continue tracking the divider; otherwise, TRUE is returned to end the tracking.
Include File	commctrl.h
Related Messages	WM_NOTIFY, HDN_BEGINTRACK, HDN_ENDTRACK
Example	See the example for the Header_InsertItem macro.

UDN_DELTAPOS   ■ Win32s   ■ Windows 95   ■ Windows NT

Description	UDN_DELTAPOS is a notification message that is sent to the parent window of an up-down control when the position of the control is going to change. This occurs when the user presses either the up or down arrow of the control .This message is sent in the form of a WM_NOTIFY message, before the WM_VSCROLL message that actually changes the control's position, allowing you to examine, allow, modify, or disallow the change.
Parameters	
lParam	NM_UPDOWN*: A pointer to an NM_UPDOWN structure that contains information about the position change. The *iPos* member of this structure contains the current position of the control. The *iDelta* member of the structure is a positive value if the user has clicked on the up button and a negative value if the user has clicked on the down button. See the definition of the NM_UPDOWN structure below.
Returns	BOOL: TRUE is returned to prevent the change in the control's position; otherwise, FALSE is returned to allow the change.
Include File	commctrl.h
Related Messages	WM_COMMAND, WM_VSCROLL

NM_UPDOWN Definition

```
typedef struct _NM_UPDOWN
{
    NMHDR hdr;
    int   iPos;
    int   iDelta;
} NM_UPDOWNW;
```

Members	
hdr	NMHDR: The notification message header structure. This is required for all WM_NOTIFY messages.
iPos	int: A signed integer value that is the current position of the up-down control.
iDelta	int: A signed integer value that is the change in the position of the up-down control. The number will be positive or negative depending on the direction of change. The new position is calculated by adding the *iPos* and *iDelta* members.
Example	See the example for the CreateUpDownControl() function.

PART II

DYNAMIC DATA EXCHANGE

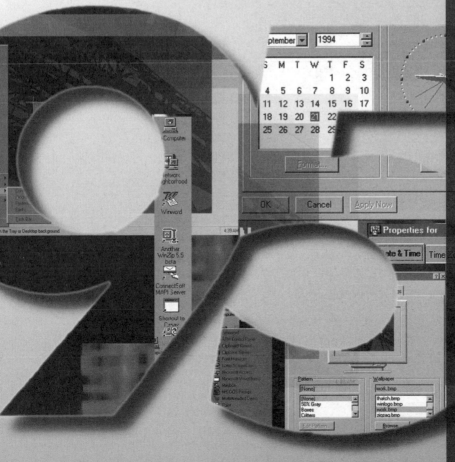

10

DYNAMIC DATA EXCHANGE MANAGEMENT LIBRARY

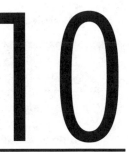

DYNAMIC DATA EXCHANGE MANAGEMENT LIBRARY

Dynamic data exchange (DDE) is the process of exchanging data between two running applications. Many applications use disk files to share data, which could be called "static" data exchange. DDE skips the process of writing and reading data from files by sending data directly to another application, using shared memory blocks. DDE can also send commands to other applications, thus allowing one application to control another application.

Dynamic data exchange has been available since Windows 2.0. However, it was not widely used and was complex to implement. In Windows 3.1, the Dynamic Data Exchange Management Library (DDEML) was introduced, which made implementing DDE easier. The advent of OLE 2 has taken some of the interest away from DDE and DDEML. However, there are instances where DDE is still useful, such as sending commands to other applications, and real-time data exchange such as is used with stock quotes.

DDE Basics

Dynamic data exchange is typically used to share data between applications in a real-time mode. For example, a communications program can continually send data to another program such as a stock market program. DDE can also send command strings to other programs, allowing one program to control many others.

An application can connect to several DDE servers, and each DDE server can have several connections. With a number of applications communicating with other applications, it is important to determine where a block of data came from. Each separate link between two programs is called a DDE *conversation*. As with human conversations, applications can be both senders and receivers of data. In any one data transfer, the sender is known as the *server*, and the receiver of the data is known as the *client*. Most sophisticated DDE applications such as Microsoft Excel can act as a server or a client, depending on which way data is flowing.

In order for DDE to work properly, the operating system must be able to control both the client and the server applications. Windows is able to control the client and server applications via the *DDE callback function*. The DDE callback function is a special function the application registers with the DDEML as part of preparing to communicate using DDE. The callback function works in the same manner as WndProc(), except that only DDE transactions are passed to the function.

Transactions and Callback Functions

DDE transactions are similar to Windows messages. Transactions, such as XTYP_CONNECT, have unique integer ID numbers that are defined in the DDEML.H header file. The transactions are processed only by an application's DDE callback function and not the WndProc() function. Also, transactions have more associated data than standard Windows messages.

The logic in the DDE callback function tracks what is happening with a DDE conversation. Transactions can be processed or ignored, leaving any default processing to the DDEML. Listing 10-1 shows a small DDE callback function that processes the XTYP_CONNECT transaction.

Listing 10-1 DDE callback function

```
HDDEDATA CALLBACK DdemlCallback( UINT     uType,
                                 UINT     uFmt,
                                 HCONV    hconv,
                                 HSZ      hsz1,
                                 HSZ      hsz2,
                                 HDDEDATA hdata,
                                 DWORD    dwData1,
                                 DWORD    dwData2 )
{
   switch( uType )
   {
      case XTYP_CONNECT :
```

```
        // Check if the service is the one supported.
        //...........................................
        if ( DdeCmpStringHandles( hsz2, hszService ) )
            break; // Service is not supported.

        // Check if the topic is one of the three supported.
        //..................................................
        if ( DdeCmpStringHandles( hsz1, hszTopic1 ) &&
             DdeCmpStringHandles( hsz1, hszTopic2 ) &&
             DdeCmpStringHandles( hsz1, hszTopic3 ) )
        {
            break; // Topic is not supported.
        }

        // Allow the conversation.
        //........................
        return( (HDDEDATA)TRUE );
    }

    return( NULL );
}
```

String Handles

Although any one application will have only one DDE callback function, it can partici-
pate in more than one DDE conversation at one time. For example, the same
communications program might be supplying one type of data to Excel and another
type of data to Word for Windows. To keep this straight, each conversation is tagged
with special ID numbers known as *string handles*. String handles are created using the
DdeCreateStringHandle() function. Given a character string, DdeCreateStringHandle()
creates a unique ID number. If two applications pass the same character string to
DdeCreateStringHandle(), both will end up with the same unique ID number.

DDE conversations use a combination of three string handles. These are known as
the *item*, *topic*, and *service*. This allows applications to share a range of different types
of data. Each individual item is a specific data item or command, while the collection
of all the types of data and commands the two applications share makes up a single
topic. The entire group of topics makes up a service.

Synchronous and Asynchronous Links

There are two basic ways to transfer data between applications, *synchronous* and *asynchronous links*. A synchronous link is one that waits for data to be returned from the
server. In this way, the client is synchronized with the server. This type of link is the
easiest to use; however, the disadvantage is that the client application cannot continue
to run and process messages while the server processes the request. Use synchronous
links for small, fast transactions where the server responds quickly.

Asynchronous links are more complicated. The client application continues to
operate and process messages after the client requests data via an asynchronous link.
Once the server gets the data prepared, the server sends the data to the client. The
client application's DDE callback function receives an XTYP_XACT_COMPLETE

transaction, which passes the handle to the data block prepared by the server as a parameter.

Cold, Hot, and Warm DDE Links

When a client requests data when it requires the data, the link is known as a *cold* link. In a cold link there are no background DDE transactions keeping the DDE connection active. Cold links are ideal when the client is completely in control of the data exchange.

There are some situations where the client application may not know when to request data from the server. For example, if the server is a communications program that receives updates periodically from a modem connection, it is the server that will know when new data is available. In these situations it is best to let the server take the initiative in starting data exchange. If the server is in control, the DDE link is said to be either a *warm* or *hot* DDE exchange, because the server keeps the DDE linkage active by periodically letting the client know that new data is available.

The difference between a warm and hot DDE link is subtle. In both cases the server initiates the transfer of data. For example, a modem program (the server) might initiate transfer of the latest stock quotes to a spreadsheet (the client). If the client wants to process the transmitted data every time it is available, a hot link is used. The server transfers the data block, and the client processes it. See the example under the DdeEnableCallback() function later in this chapter for an example of a hot DDE link.

There may be situations where the client application is busy with other duties, and some of the server's data is best ignored. In these cases a warm DDE link is more appropriate. In a warm link, the server only alerts the client each time new data is available. The client has the option of requesting that the actual data be sent, or can decline to receive this data.

Using DDE

In order to get a general idea of the sequence of events that make up a DDE conversation, Table 10-1 outlines the steps involved in establishing a DDE conversation for both the client and server. In this case, the client is attempting to get a single block of data from the server. Technically, Table 10-1 outlines a synchronous cold DDE link, which is the simplest method for transferring data via DDE.

Table 10-1 Outline of a DDE conversation

Step	Client Activities	Server Activities
1.	Calls DdeInitialize() to start a DDE session. This loads DDEML.DLL into memory (if not already loaded), and passes the address of the client's DDE callback to the DLL.	Calls DdeInitialize() to start a DDE session. This loads DDEML.DLL into memory (if not already loaded), and passes the address of the server's DDE callback function to the DLL.

Step	Client Activities	Server Activities
2.	Calls DdeConnect() to attempt to start a DDE conversation based on specific service and topic names.	The server's DDE callback function processes an XTYP_CONNECT transaction. The server checks to see if the service and topic names match data that the server supports, and returns TRUE if there is a match.
3.	Calls DdeClientTransaction() to send an XTYP_REQUEST transaction to the server with a specific item name for the requested data.	The server's DDE callback function processes an XTYP_REQUEST transaction. If the topic and item names match data that the server supports, the server creates a memory block using DdeCreateDataHandle(), copies the requested data to the block, and returns the handle of the block.
4.	DdeClientTransaction() returns the data handle for the global memory block from the server as its returned value. The client uses DdeAccessData() to read the data, and does whatever actions are appropriate with the data.	(Server idle)
5.	Steps 3 and 4 can be repeated as often as desired by the client to request different data items.	The server's DDE callback function passively waits for transactions to process, but does not initiate any activities.
6.	The client calls DdeDisconnect() to end the DDE conversation.	The server's DDE callback function will receive an XTYP_DISCONNECT transaction. This notifies the server that the DDE conversation is terminated.
7.	The client calls DdeUninitialize(), notifying DDEML.DLL that the client is no longer an active DDEML application.	The server calls DdeUninitialize(), notifying DDEML.DLL that the server is no longer an active DDEML application.

See the examples for the DDEML functions later in this chapter for demonstrations of these steps in DDE conversations.

Function Summary

Table 10-2 summarizes the DDEML functions. The detailed function descriptions follow immediately after the table.

Table 10-2 DDEML function summary

Function	Meaning
DdeAbandonTransaction	Abandons an asynchronous transaction and releases associated resources.
DdeAccessData	Provides access to the data of a DDE object.
DdeAddData	Adds data to a DDE object.

continued on next page

continued from previous page

Function	Meaning
DdeClientTransaction	Begins a data transaction between a client and a server.
DdeCmpStringHandles	Compares the values of two string handles.
DdeConnect	Establishes a conversation with a server application.
DdeConnectList	Establishes a conversation with all server applications that support a specific service name and topic name pair.
DdeCreateDataHandle	Creates a DDE object and fills the object with data from a buffer.
DdeCreateStringHandle	Creates a handle that identifies a string.
DdeDisconnect	Terminates a DDE conversation.
DdeDisconnectList	Destroys a conversation list terminating all conversations associated with the list.
DdeEnableCallback	Enables or disables transactions for a conversation or all conversations established by the calling application.
DdeFreeDataHandle	Frees a DDE object and deletes the associated data handle.
DdeFreeStringHandle	Frees a string handle.
DdeGetData	Copies data from a DDE object to a local buffer.
DdeGetLastError	Returns the most recent error value.
DdeInitialize	Registers an application with the Dynamic Data Exchange Management Library.
DdeKeepStringHandle	Increments the usage count associated with a string handle.
DdeNameService	Registers or unregisters the service names a DDE server supports.
DdePostAdvise	Sends an XTYP_ADVREQ transaction to each client application with an active advise loop on a topic and an item.
DdeQueryConvInfo	Queries information about a DDE transaction and the conversation in which the transaction takes place.
DdeQueryNextServer	Queries the next conversation handle in a conversation list.
DdeQueryString	Copies the text associated with a string handle into a buffer.
DdeReconnect	Attempts to reestablish a conversation with a service that has terminated a conversation.
DdeSetUserHandle	Associates an application-defined 32-bit value with a conversation handle or transaction identifier.
DdeUnaccessData	Unaccesses a DDE object.
DdeUninitialize	Frees all DDEML resources associated with the calling application.

DdeAbandonTransaction　　■ Win32s　■ Windows 95　■ Windows NT

Description　　DdeAbandonTransaction() abandons the specified asynchronous transaction and releases all resources associated with the transaction. Only client applications should call this function. Once an application has called this function, all results of transactions the server processes are discarded. DdeAbandonTransaction() has no effect on synchronous transactions.

Syntax　　BOOL **DdeAbandonTransaction**(DWORD *idInst*, HCONV *hConv*, DWORD *idTransaction*)

Parameters

idInst   DWORD: The application instance identifier obtained from the DdeInitialize() function.

hConv   HCONV: The conversation identifier in which the transaction was initiated. If this parameter is 0L, the *idTransaction* parameter is ignored.

idTransaction   DWORD: The transaction identifier to abandon. If this parameter is 0L, all active transactions in the specified conversation are abandoned.

Returns   BOOL: If successful, TRUE is returned; otherwise, FALSE is returned. Use the DdeGetLastError() function to retrieve the error value, which may be one of the following:

    DMLERR_DLL_NOT_INITIALIZED
    DMLERR_INVALIDPARAMETER
    DMLERR_NO_ERROR
    DMLERR_UNFOUND_QUEUE_ID

Include File   ddeml.h

See Also   DdeClientTransaction(), DdeInitialize(), DdeQueryConvInfo()

Example   This example (Listing 10-2) demonstrates how an application can abandon long DDE transactions using the DdeAbandonTransaction() function. This example connects to a DDEML server and executes a long command in asynchronous mode. If the user selects the Abort! command from the menu, the transaction is abandoned.

Listing 10-2 Using the DdeAbandonTransaction() function

```
DWORD ddeInst    = 0;
HSZ    hszTopic   = NULL;
HSZ    hszService = NULL;
HCONV hConv      = NULL;
DWORD dwTranID;

LRESULT CALLBACK WndProc( HWND hWnd, UINT uMsg, WPARAM wParam, LPARAM lParam )
{
   switch( uMsg )
   {
   case WM_CREATE :
           // Initialize DDEML.
           //.................
           if ( DdeInitialize( &ddeInst, DdemlCallback,
               APPCMD_CLIENTONLY, 0 ) != DMLERR_NO_ERROR )
           {
               MessageBox( hWnd, "Could not initialize DDEML.",
                           NULL, MB_OK | MB_ICONSTOP );
               return( -1 );
           }

           // Allocate strings.
           //.................
           hszService = DdeCreateStringHandle( ddeInst,"Server",CP_WINANSI );
```

continued on next page

continued from previous page

```
            hszTopic   = DdeCreateStringHandle( ddeInst,"Msg",CP_WINANSI );
            break;

    case WM_COMMAND :
            switch( LOWORD( wParam ) )
            {
               case IDM_TEST :
                       // Connect to server.
                       //...................
                       hConv = DdeConnect( ddeInst, hszService,
                                            hszTopic, NULL );
                       if ( hConv )
                       {
                           // Execute a DDE transaction on the
                           // DDEML server in asynchronous mode.
                           //....................................
                           HDDEDATA hRet = DdeClientTransaction(
                                              "This is a sample message",
                                              25, hConv, 0L, 0, XTYP_EXECUTE,
                                              TIMEOUT_ASYNC,
                                              &dwTranID );

                           if ( !hRet )
                           {
                               DdeDisconnect( hConv );
                               hConv = NULL;
                           }
                       }
                       break;

               case IDM_ABORT :
                       // If the conversation is active, abort the transaction.
                       //......................................................
                       if ( hConv )
                       {
                           DdeAbandonTransaction( ddeInst, hConv, dwTranID );
                           DdeDisconnect( hConv );
                           hConv = NULL;
                       }
                       break;

               case IDM_ABOUT :
                       DialogBox( hInst, "AboutBox", hWnd, (DLGPROC)About );
                       break;

               case IDM_EXIT :
                       DestroyWindow( hWnd );
                       break;
            }
            break;

    case WM_DESTROY :
            if ( hConv )
               DdeDisconnect( hConv );

            DdeFreeStringHandle( ddeInst, hszService );
            DdeFreeStringHandle( ddeInst, hszTopic );
            DdeUninitialize( ddeInst );
            PostQuitMessage(0);
            break;
```

```
        default :
                return( DefWindowProc( hWnd, uMsg, wParam, lParam ) );
    }

    return( 0L );
}
```

DdeAccessData   ■ Win32s ■ Windows 95 ■ Windows NT

Description	DdeAccessData() provides access to the data in a dynamic data exchange (DDE) object. An application must call the DdeUnaccessData() function when it has finished accessing the data in the object. If the *hData* parameter has been used in a DDEML function, the pointer should only be used for read-only access.
Syntax	LPBYTE **DdeAccessData**(HDDEDATA *hData*, LPDWORD *pcbDataSize*)
Parameters	
hData	HDDEDATA: The handle of the DDE object to access.
pcbDataSize	LPDWORD: A pointer to a variable that receives the size, in bytes, of the DDE object identified by the *hData* parameter. If this parameter is NULL, no size information is returned.

Returns	LPBYTE: If successful, a pointer to the first byte of data in the DDE object. If the function fails, the return value is NULL. Use the DdeGetLastError() function to retrieve the error value, which may be one of the following:
	  DMLERR_DLL_NOT_INITIALIZED
	  DMLERR_INVALIDPARAMETER
	  DMLERR_NO_ERROR

Include File	ddeml.h
See Also	DdeAddData(), DdeCreateDataHandle(), DdeFreeDataHandle(), DdeUnaccessData()
Example	This example (Listing 10-3) shows the callback function from a DDEML server. The DdeAccessData() function is used in the XTYP_EXECUTE transaction to access the command string that was sent to the server from the client. The DdeUnaccessData() function is used afterwards to release the data.

Listing 10-3 Using the DdeAccessData() Function

```
HDDEDATA CALLBACK DdemlCallback( UINT     uType,
                                 UINT     uFmt,
                                 HCONV    hconv,
                                 HSZ      hsz1,
                                 HSZ      hsz2,
                                 HDDEDATA hdata,
                                 DWORD    dwData1,
                                 DWORD    dwData2 )
{
static LPBYTE lpMsg = NULL;
```

continued on next page

continued from previous page

```
    switch( uType )
    {
        case XTYP_EXECUTE :
                // Check if this is the appropriate topic.
                //............................................
                if ( !DdeCmpStringHandles( hsz1, hszTopic2 ) )
                {
                    if ( lpMsg )
                        return( (HDDEDATA)DDE_FBUSY );

                    // Get a pointer to the command string.
                    //....................................
                    lpMsg = DdeAccessData( hdata, NULL );

                    MessageBox( NULL, lpMsg, "DDE Message", MB_OK );

                    // Unaccess the data.
                    //...................
                    DdeUnaccessData( hdata );
                    lpMsg = NULL;

                    return( (HDDEDATA)DDE_FACK );
                }
                return( (HDDEDATA)DDE_FNOTPROCESSED );

            .
            .
            .
    }

    return( NULL );
}
```

DdeAddData   ■ Win32s ■ Windows 95 ■ Windows NT

Description	DdeAddData() adds data to a dynamic data exchange (DDE) object. This is normally how a DDE server provides data to a client. Applications can write to any location in the data object. If data already exists at the location, it is overwritten. The contents of the object that have not been written to are undefined. If the amount of data originally allocated is not sufficient to hold the new data, DdeAddData() reallocates a global memory object of the appropriate size. Once a data handle has been used in a DDEML function or returned by a DDE callback function, use read-only access.
Syntax	HDDEDATA **DdeAddData**(HDDEDATA *hData*, LPBYTE *pSrc*, DWORD *cb*, DWORD *cbOff*)
Parameters	
hData	HDDEDATA: The handle of the DDE object.
pSrc	LPBYTE: A pointer to a buffer containing the data to add to the DDE object.
cb	DWORD: The length, in bytes, of the data to be added to the DDE object.

Figure 10-1 DdeAddData() example

cbOff	DWORD: The offset, in bytes, from the beginning of the DDE object. The additional data is copied to the object beginning at this offset.
Returns	HDDEDATA: If the function succeeds, the new handle of the DDE object is returned. If the function fails, zero is returned. Use the DdeGetLastError() function to retrieve the error value, which may be one of the following: DMLERR_DLL_NOT_INITIALIZED DMLERR_INVALIDPARAMETER DMLERR_MEMORY_ERROR DMLERR_NO_ERROR
Include File	ddeml.h
See Also	DdeAccessData(), DdeCreateDataHandle(), DdeUnaccessData()
Example	This example, shown in Listings 10-4 and 10-5, requests data from a DDE server on the Data topic and displays the retrieved data in a message boas shown in Figure 10-1. When the server callback receives the XTYP_REQUEST transaction, it allocates a DDE data object with the DdeCreateDataHandle() function. The server then places data in the DDE data object using the DdeAddData() function and returns the handle to the DDE client.

When the client receives the handle of the DDE data object, the data is copied with the DdeGetData() function and the object is freed with the DdeFreeDataHandle() function. The data that was returned is then displayed in a message box.

Listing 10-4 DDE client WndProc()

```
DWORD  ddeInst     = 0;
HSZ    hszTopic    = NULL;
HSZ    hszService  = NULL;
HCONV  hConv       = NULL;
```

continued on next page

continued from previous page

```
LRESULT CALLBACK WndProc( HWND hWnd, UINT uMsg, WPARAM wParam, LPARAM lParam )
{
    switch( uMsg )
    {
    case WM_CREATE :
            // Initialize DDEML.
            //..................
            if ( DdeInitialize( &ddeInst, DdemlCallback,
                APPCMD_CLIENTONLY, 0 ) != DMLERR_NO_ERROR )
            {
                MessageBox( hWnd, "Could not initialize DDEML.",
                            NULL, MB_OK | MB_ICONSTOP );
                return( -1 );
            }

            // Allocate strings.
            //..................
            hszService = DdeCreateStringHandle( ddeInst,"Server",CP_WINANSI );
            hszTopic   = DdeCreateStringHandle( ddeInst,"Data",CP_WINANSI );

            // Connect to server.
            //..................
            hConv = DdeConnect( ddeInst, hszService,
                            hszTopic, NULL );

            if ( DdeGetLastError( ddeInst ) != DMLERR_NO_ERROR )
                MessageBox( hWnd, "Could not connect to server.",
                            NULL, MB_OK | MB_ICONSTOP );


            break;

    case WM_COMMAND :
            switch( LOWORD( wParam ) )
            {
            case IDM_TEST :
                    if ( hConv )
                    {
                        // Execute a request from the
                        // DDEML server in synchronous mode.
                        //...................................
                        HDDEDATA hRet = DdeClientTransaction(
                                            NULL,
                                            0, hConv, hszTopic, CF_TEXT,
                                            XTYP_REQUEST,
                                            30000,
                                            NULL );

                    if ( !hRet &&
                        DdeGetLastError( ddeInst ) != DMLERR_NO_ERROR )
                    {
                        MessageBox( hWnd, "An error occured.",
                                    lpszAppName, MB_OK | MB_ICONASTERISK );
                    }
                    else if ( hRet )
                    {
                        char szBuf[51];

                        DdeGetData( hRet, szBuf, sizeof( szBuf ), 0 );
```

```
                              DdeFreeDataHandle( hRet );

                              MessageBox( hWnd, szBuf, "Data",
                                          MB_OK | MB_ICONINFORMATION );
                     }
                  }
                  break;
      .
      .
      .
```

Listing 10-5 DDE server callback

```
HDDEDATA CALLBACK DdemlCallback( UINT      uType,
                                 UINT      uFmt,
                                 HCONV     hconv,
                                 HSZ       hsz1,
                                 HSZ       hsz2,
                                 HDDEDATA  hdata,
                                 DWORD     dwData1,
                                 DWORD     dwData2 )
{
static LPBYTE lpMsg = NULL;

   switch( uType )
   {
      case XTYP_CONNECT :
           if ( DdeCmpStringHandles( hsz2, hszService ) )
              break;

           if ( DdeCmpStringHandles( hsz1, hszTopic1 ) &&
                DdeCmpStringHandles( hsz1, hszTopic2 )  )
           {
              break;
           }

           // Allow the conversation.
           //.......................
           return( (HDDEDATA)TRUE );


      case XTYP_REQUEST :
           // Check if the topic is correct.
           //...............................
           if ( !DdeCmpStringHandles( hsz1, hszTopic1 ) )
           {
              // Allocate a DDE object.
              //......................
              HDDEDATA hData = DdeCreateDataHandle( ddeInst, NULL, 50, 0,
                                                    hszTopic2, CF_TEXT, 0 );
              // Place data in the DDE object.
              //..............................
              if ( hData )
              {
                 SHORT i, offs;
                 char  szTmp[3];

                 hData = DdeAddData( hData, "Data: ", 6, 0 );
```

continued on next page

continued from previous page

```
                    offs = 6;

                    for( i=0; i<10; i++ )
                    {
                        itoa( i, szTmp, 10 );
                        hData = DdeAddData( hData, szTmp, strlen( szTmp ), offs );
                        offs += strlen( szTmp );
                    }
                    szTmp[0] = 0;
                    hData = DdeAddData( hData, szTmp, 1, offs );

                    // Return the DDE object.
                    //......................
                    return( hData );
                }
                return( NULL );
            }
            return( NULL );
```

DDECLIENTTRANSACTION   ■ Win32s   ■ Windows 95   ■ Windows NT

Description   DdeClientTransaction() begins a data transaction between a client and a
                        server. Only a DDE client application can call this function, and the appli-
                        cation can use it only after establishing a conversation with the server.

                        When an application has finished using the data handle returned by
                        DdeClientTransaction(), the application should free the handle by calling
                        the DdeFreeDataHandle() function.

                        Synchronous transactions do not return until the transaction either
                        completes successfully or fails. Asynchronous transactions return after the
                        transaction starts. Once the transaction is finished, the server sends the
                        XTYP_XACT_COMPLETE transaction to the client.

Syntax   HDDEDATA **DdeClientTransaction**(LPBYTE *pData*, DWORD *cbData*,
                        HCONV *hConv*, HSZ *hszItem*, UINT *wFmt*, UINT *wType*, DWORD
                        dwTimeout, LPDWORD *pdwResult*)

Parameters

pData   LPBYTE: A pointer to the beginning of the client data that is passed to the
                        server. Optionally, an application can specify a data handle (HDDEDATA),
                        created by a previous call to DdeCreateDataHandle(), to pass to the server,
                        in which case the *cbData* parameter should be set to 0xFFFFFFFF. This
                        parameter is required only if the *wType* parameter is XTYP_EXECUTE or
                        XTYP_POKE. Otherwise, this parameter should be NULL.

cbData   DWORD: The length, in bytes, of the data pointed to by the *pData* para-
                        meter. A value of 0xFFFFFFFF indicates that *pData* is a data handle that
                        identifies the data being sent.

hConv	HCONV: The handle of the conversation in which the transaction is to take place.
hszItem	HSZ: The handle of the data item for which data is being exchanged during the transaction. This handle must have been created by a previous call to the DdeCreateStringHandle() function. If the *wType* parameter is XTYP_EXECUTE, this parameter is ignored and should be set to 0L.
wFmt	UINT: The standard clipboard format or a valid registered clipboard format in which the data item is being submitted or requested. If the transaction specified by the *wType* parameter does not pass data or is XTYP_EXECUTE, this parameter should be set to zero.
wType	UINT: The transaction type. This parameter can be one of the types listed in Table 10-3.

Table 10-3 DdeClientTransaction() *wType* values

Value	Meaning
XTYP_ADVSTART	Begins an advise loop. Any number of distinct advise loops can exist within a conversation. An application can alter the advise loop type by combining the XTYP_ADVSTART transaction type with the binary OR (I) operator with one or more of the flags in the following list.
Flag	
XTYPF_ACKREQ	Instructs the server to wait until the client acknowledges that it received the previous data item before sending the next data item.
XTYPF_NODATA	Instructs the server to notify the client of any data changes without actually sending the data.
XTYP_ADVSTOP	Ends an advise loop.
XTYP_EXECUTE	Begins an execute transaction.
XTYP_POKE	Begins a poke transaction.
XTYP_REQUEST	Begins a request transaction.

dwTimeout	DWORD: The maximum length of time, in milliseconds, that the client will wait for a response from the server application in a synchronous transaction. For asynchronous transactions, set this parameter to TIMEOUT_ASYNC.
pdwResult	LPDWORD: A pointer to a DWORD variable that receives the result of the transaction. If the application does not require the result, this parameter can be set to NULL. For synchronous transactions, the low-order word of this variable contains any applicable DDE_ flags resulting from the transaction. This provides support for applications dependent on DDE_APPSTATUS bits. However, it is recommended that applications no longer use these bits because they may not be supported in future versions of DDEML. For asynchronous transactions, this variable receives a unique transaction identifier for use with the DdeAbandonTransaction() function and the XTYP_XACT_COMPLETE transaction.

Returns	HDDEDATA: If the function is successful, synchronous transactions return a data handle that identifies the data if the client expects data from the server; otherwise, a nonzero value is returned. Asynchronous transactions also return a nonzero value if the function is successful. If the function is not successful, zero is returned.

Use the DdeGetLastError() function to retrieve the error value, which may be one of the following:

DMLERR_ADVACKTIMEOUT
DMLERR_BUSY
DMLERR_DATAACKTIMEOUT
DMLERR_DLL_NOT_INITIALIZED
DMLERR_EXECACKTIMEOUT
DMLERR_INVALIDPARAMETER
DMLERR_MEMORY_ERROR
DMLERR_NO_CONV_ESTABLISHED
DMLERR_NO_ERROR
DMLERR_NOTPROCESSED
DMLERR_POKEACKTIMEOUT
DMLERR_POSTMSG_FAILED
DMLERR_REENTRANCY
DMLERR_SERVER_DIED
DMLERR_UNADVACKTIMEOUT

Include File	ddeml.h
See Also	DdeAbandonTransaction(), DdeAccessData(), DdeConnect(), DdeConnectList(), DdeCreateDataHandle(), DdeCreateStringHandle(), DdeFreeDataHandle()
Example	This example (Listing 10-6) connects to a DDEML server using the Msg topic. When the user selects the Test! menu item, a synchronous DDE transaction is executed using the DdeClientTransaction() function. After the transaction returns, the return value is checked and any error code is retrieved with the DdeGetLastError() function and displayed in a message box.

Lilsting 10-6 Using the DdeClientTransaction() function

```
DWORD ddeInst     = 0;
HSZ    hszTopic    = NULL;
HSZ    hszService  = NULL;
HCONV  hConv       = NULL;

LRESULT CALLBACK WndProc( HWND hWnd, UINT uMsg, WPARAM wParam, LPARAM lParam )
{
   switch( uMsg )
   {
      case WM_CREATE :
              // Initialize DDEML.
              //.................
```

```
        if ( DdeInitialize( &ddeInst, DdemlCallback,
            APPCMD_CLIENTONLY, 0 ) != DMLERR_NO_ERROR )
        {
            MessageBox( hWnd, "Could not initialize DDEML.",
                        NULL, MB_OK | MB_ICONSTOP );
            return( -1 );
        }

        // Allocate strings.
        //..................
        hszService = DdeCreateStringHandle( ddeInst,"Server",CP_WINANSI );
        hszTopic   = DdeCreateStringHandle( ddeInst,"Msg",CP_WINANSI );

        // Connect to server.
        //...................
        hConv = DdeConnect( ddeInst, hszService,
                            hszTopic, NULL );

        if ( DdeGetLastError( ddeInst ) != DMLERR_NO_ERROR )
            MessageBox( hWnd, "Could not connect to server.",
                        NULL, MB_OK | MB_ICONSTOP );


        break;

case WM_COMMAND :
        switch( LOWORD( wParam ) )
        {
            case IDM_TEST :
                    if ( hConv )
                    {
                        // Execute DDE transaction on the
                        // DDEML server in asynchronous mode.
                        //...................................
                        HDDEDATA hRet = DdeClientTransaction(
                                        "This is a sample message",
                                        37, hConv, 0L, 0,
                                        XTYP_EXECUTE,
                                        30000,
                                        NULL );

                        // If an error occured, check for the
                        // errors in which we are interested.
                        //...................................
                        if ( !hRet )
                        {
                            UINT    uError  = DdeGetLastError( ddeInst );
                            LPTSTR  lpError = NULL;

                            switch( uError )
                            {
                                case DMLERR_BUSY :
                                    lpError = "The server is busy.";
                                    break;

                                case DMLERR_EXECACKTIMEOUT    :
                                    lpError = "The transaction timed out.";
                                    break;
```

continued on next page

continued from previous page

```
                            case DMLERR_NOTPROCESSED :
                                    lpError = "The transaction was not"\
                                              "processed.";
                                    break;

                            case DMLERR_REENTRANCY :
                                    lpError = "Still waiting for a response"\
                                              "from server.";
                                    break;

                            default :
                                    lpError = "An error occured."; break;
                    }

                            MessageBox( hWnd, lpError, lpszAppName,
                                        MB_OK | MB_ICONASTERISK );
                    }
                }
                break;

        case IDM_ABOUT :
                DialogBox( hInst, "AboutBox", hWnd, (DLGPROC)About );
                break;

        case IDM_EXIT :
                DestroyWindow( hWnd );
                break;
        }
        break;

    case WM_DESTROY :
            if ( hConv )
                DdeDisconnect( hConv );

            DdeFreeStringHandle( ddeInst, hszService );
            DdeFreeStringHandle( ddeInst, hszTopic );
            DdeUninitialize( ddeInst );
            PostQuitMessage(0);
            break;

    default :
            return( DefWindowProc( hWnd, uMsg, wParam, lParam ) );
    }

    return( OL );
}
```

DdeCmpStringHandles
■ Win32s ■ Windows 95 ■ Windows NT

Description	DdeCmpStringHandles() compares the values of two string handles. This is a case insensitive comparison. Applications that require a case sensitive comparison should compare the string handles directly.
Syntax	int **DdeCmpStringHandles**(HSZ *hsz1*, HSZ *hsz2*)

Parameters

hsz1	HSZ: Identifies the first string.
hsz2	HSZ: Identifies the second string.
Returns	int: The return value can be one of the values in Table 10-4.

Table 10-4 DdeCmpStringHandles() return values

Value	Meaning
-1	The value of *hsz1* is either 0 or less than the value of *hsz2*.
0	The values of *hsz1* and *hsz2* are equal (both can be 0).
1	The value of *hsz2* is either 0 or less than the value of *hsz1*.

Include File	ddeml.h
See Also	DdeAccessData(), DdeCreateStringHandle(), DdeFreeStringHandle()
Example	This example (Listing 10-7) demonstrates how a DDE server callback checks the service and topic names with the DdeCmpStringHandles() function.

Listing 10-7 Using the DdeCmpStringHandles() function

```
DWORD  ddeInst     = 0;
HSZ    hszService  = NULL;
HSZ    hszTopic1   = NULL;
HSZ    hszTopic2   = NULL;

HDDEDATA CALLBACK DdemlCallback( UINT     uType,
                                 UINT     uFmt,
                                 HCONV    hconv,
                                 HSZ      hsz1,
                                 HSZ      hsz2,
                                 HDDEDATA hdata,
                                 DWORD    dwData1,
                                 DWORD    dwData2 )
{
static LPBYTE lpMsg = NULL;

   switch( uType )
   {
      case XTYP_CONNECT :
             // Make sure that the service is one we support.
             //............................................
             if ( DdeCmpStringHandles( hsz2, hszService ) )
                break;

             // Make sure the topic is one that we support.
             //............................................
             if ( DdeCmpStringHandles( hsz1, hszTopic1 ) &&
                  DdeCmpStringHandles( hsz1, hszTopic2 )  )
```

continued on next page

continued from previous page

```
                {
                    break;
                }

                // Allow the conversation.
                //........................
                return( (HDDEDATA)TRUE );

        case XTYP_EXECUTE :
                if ( lpMsg )
                    return( (HDDEDATA)DDE_FBUSY );

                // Check if this the "Msg" Topic.
                //..............................
                if ( !DdeCmpStringHandles( hsz1, hszTopic2 ) )
                {
                    lpMsg = DdeAccessData( hdata, NULL );
                    MessageBox( NULL, lpMsg, "DDE Message", MB_OK );

                    DdeUnaccessData( hdata );
                    lpMsg = NULL;

                    return( (HDDEDATA)DDE_FACK );
                }
                return( (HDDEDATA)DDE_FNOTPROCESSED );
        }

    return( NULL );
}


LRESULT CALLBACK WndProc( HWND hWnd, UINT uMsg, WPARAM wParam, LPARAM lParam )
{
    switch( uMsg )
    {
        case WM_CREATE :
                // Initialize DDEML.
                //..................
                if ( DdeInitialize( &ddeInst, DdemlCallback,
                    APPCLASS_STANDARD, 0 ) != DMLERR_NO_ERROR )
                {
                    MessageBox( hWnd, "Could not initialize DDEML.",
                                NULL, MB_OK | MB_ICONSTOP );
                    return( -1 );
                }

                // Allocate strings.
                //..................
                hszService = DdeCreateStringHandle( ddeInst,"Server",CP_WINANSI );
                hszTopic1  = DdeCreateStringHandle( ddeInst,"Long",CP_WINANSI );
                hszTopic2  = DdeCreateStringHandle( ddeInst,"Msg",CP_WINANSI );

                DdeNameService( ddeInst, hszService, 0L, DNS_REGISTER );
                break;
            .
            .
            .
```

DDECONNECT

■ Win32s ■ Windows 95 ■ Windows NT

Description	DdeConnect() establishes a conversation with a server application that supports the specified service name and topic name pair. If more than one such server exists, only one is selected by the system.
Syntax	HCONV **DdeConnect**(DWORD *idInst*, HSZ *hszService*, HSZ *hszTopic*, PCONVCONTEXT *pCC*)
Parameters	
idInst	DWORD: The application instance identifier obtained by a previous call to the DdeInitialize() function.
hszService	HSZ: The handle of the string that specifies the service name of the server application with which a conversation is to be established. If this parameter is 0L, a conversation is established with any available server.
hszTopic	HSZ: The handle of the string that specifies name of the topic on which a conversation is to be established. If this parameter is 0L, a conversation on any topic supported by the selected server is established.
pCC	PCONVCONTEXT: A pointer to a CONVCONTEXT structure that contains conversation context information. If this parameter is NULL, the server receives the default CONVCONTEXT structure during the XTYP_CONNECT or XTYP_WILDCONNECT transaction. See the definition of the CONVCONTEXT structure below.
Returns	HCONV: If successful, the handle of the established conversation is returned; otherwise, 0L is returned. Use the DdeGetLastError() function to retrieve the error value, which may be one of the following: DMLERR_DLL_NOT_INITIALIZED DMLERR_INVALIDPARAMETER DMLERR_NO_CONV_ESTABLISHED DMLERR_NO_ERROR
Include File	ddeml.h
See Also	DdeConnectList(), DdeCreateStringHandle(), DdeDisconnect(), DdeDisconnectList(), DdeInitialize()

CONVCONTEXT Definition

```
typedef struct tagCONVCONTEXT
{
    UINT  cb;
    UINT  wFlags;
    UINT  wCountryID;
    int   iCodePage;
    DWORD dwLangID;
    DWORD dwSecurity;
    SECURITY_QUALITY_OF_SERVICE qos;
} CONVCONTEXT;
```

Members

cb	UINT: The size of the structure, in bytes.

wFlags	UINT: The conversation context flags. Currently, there are no flags defined.
wCountryID	UINT: The country-code identifier for topic name and item name strings.
iCodePage	int: The code page for topic name and item name strings. Nonmultilingual clients should set this member to CP_WINANSI. Unicode clients should set this value to CP_WINUNICODE.
dwLangID	DWORD: The language identifier for topic name and item name strings.
dwSecurity	DWORD: A private (application-defined) security code.
qos	SECURITY_QUALITY_OF_SERVICE (Windows NT only): The quality of service a DDE client wants from the system during a given conversation. The quality of service level specified lasts for the duration of the conversation. It cannot be changed once the conversation is started.
Example	This example (Listing 10-8) shows how a DDEML client connects to a DDE server with the Server service name and the Msg topic name using the DdeConnect() function.

Listing 10-8 Using the DdeConnect() function

```
DWORD ddeInst     = 0;
HSZ   hszTopic    = NULL;
HSZ   hszService  = NULL;
HCONV hConv       = NULL;

LRESULT CALLBACK WndProc( HWND hWnd, UINT uMsg, WPARAM wParam, LPARAM lParam )
{
   switch( uMsg )
   {
      case WM_CREATE :
            // Initialize DDEML.
            //..................
            if ( DdeInitialize( &ddeInst, DdemlCallback,
                APPCMD_CLIENTONLY, 0 ) != DMLERR_NO_ERROR )
            {
               MessageBox( hWnd, "Could not initialize DDEML.",
                           NULL, MB_OK | MB_ICONSTOP );
               return( -1 );
            }

            // Allocate strings.
            //..................
            hszService = DdeCreateStringHandle( ddeInst,"Server",CP_WINANSI );
            hszTopic   = DdeCreateStringHandle( ddeInst,"Msg",CP_WINANSI );

            // Connect to server.
            //...................
            hConv = DdeConnect( ddeInst, hszService,
                            hszTopic, NULL );

            if ( DdeGetLastError( ddeInst ) != DMLERR_NO_ERROR )
               MessageBox( hWnd, "Could not connect to server.",
                           NULL, MB_OK | MB_ICONSTOP );
```

```
    break;
```
.
.
.

DdeConnectList   ■ Win32s   ■ Windows 95   ■ Windows NT

Description   DdeConnectList() establishes a conversation with all server applications that support the specified service name and topic name pair.

An application can also use this function to obtain a list of conversation handles by passing the function an existing conversation handle. In this case, DDEML removes the handles of any terminated conversations from the conversation list and returns a conversation list that contains the handles of all currently established conversations that support the specified service name and topic name.

It is the application's responsibility to free the conversation list handle returned by DdeConnectList() with the DdeDisconnectList() function.

Syntax   HCONVLIST **DdeConnectList**(DWORD *idInst*, HSZ *hszService*, HSZ *hszTopic*, HCONVLIST *hConvList*, PCONVCONTEXT *pCC*)

Parameters

idInst   DWORD: The application instance identifier obtained by a previous call to the DdeInitialize() function.

hszService   HSZ: A handle to the string that specifies the service name of the server application with which a conversation is to be established. If this parameter is 0L, the system attempts to establish conversations with all available servers that support the specified topic name.

hszTopic   HSZ: A handle to the string that specifies the name of the topic on which a conversation is to be established. If this parameter is 0L, the system will attempt to establish conversations on all topics supported by the selected server (or servers).

hConvList   HCONVLIST: The conversation list to be enumerated. This parameter should be 0L if a new conversation list is to be established.

pCC   PCONVCONTEXT: A pointer to a CONVCONTEXT structure that contains conversation-context information. If this parameter is NULL, the server receives the default CONVCONTEXT structure during the XTYP_CONNECT or XTYP_WILDCONNECT transaction. See the definition of the CONVCONTEXT structure under the DdeConnect() function.

Returns   HCONVLIST: If successful, the handle of a new conversation list is returned; otherwise, 0L is returned. The handle of the old conversation list is no longer valid. Use the DdeGetLastError() function to retrieve the error value, which may be one of the following:

    DMLERR_DLL_NOT_INITIALIZED
    DMLERR_INVALID_PARAMETER

DMLERR_NO_CONV_ESTABLISHED
DMLERR_NO_ERROR
DMLERR_SYS_ERROR

Include File   ddeml.h

See Also   DdeConnect(), DdeCreateStringHandle(), DdeDisconnect(), DdeDisconnectList(), DdeInitialize(), DdeQueryNextServer()

Example   This example, shown in Figure 10-2 and Listing 10-9, establishes a DDE connection with all running applications that are either a DDEML application that supports the XTYP_WILDCONNECT transaction or a non-DDEML application that supports the System topic. The names of the services that support this type of connection are displayed on the window in a list box when the user selects the Test! menu item. The DDE links are established with the DdeConnectList() function.

The name of each service is extracted using the DdeQueryConvInfo() function for each conversation. DdeQueryNextServer() does the work of moving from one conversation to the next in the list of conversations. DdeQueryString() is used to retrieve the service name from the string handle in the CONVINFO structure. The DdeDisconnectList() function disconnects all the conversations in the list.

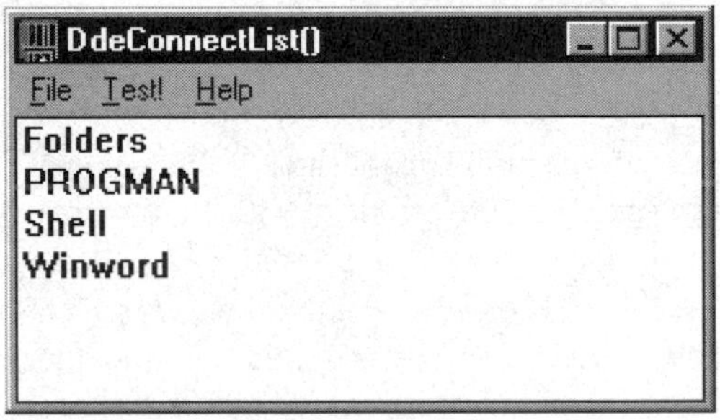

Figure 10-2 DdeConnectList() example

Listing 10-9 Using the DdeConnectList() function

```
LRESULT CALLBACK WndProc( HWND hWnd, UINT uMsg, WPARAM wParam, LPARAM lParam )
{
static DWORD     ddeInst    = 0;
static HSZ       hszTopic   = NULL;
static HCONVLIST hConvList  = NULL;
static HWND      hList      = NULL;

   switch( uMsg )
   {
      case WM_CREATE :
              // Initialize DDEML.
              //................
```

```
        if ( DdeInitialize( &ddeInst, DdemlCallback,
            APPCMD_CLIENTONLY, 0 ) != DMLERR_NO_ERROR )
        {
            MessageBox( hWnd, "Could not initialize DDEML.",
                        NULL, MB_OK | MB_ICONSTOP );
            return( -1 );
        }

        // Allocate strings.
        //.................
        hszTopic = DdeCreateStringHandle( ddeInst,"System",CP_WINANSI );

        hList = CreateWindow( "LISTBOX", "",
                              WS_CHILD | LBS_STANDARD |
                              WS_VISIBLE | LBS_NOINTEGRALHEIGHT,
                              0, 0,
                              0, 0,
                              hWnd,
                              (HMENU)101,
                              hInst,
                              NULL
                            );
        break;

case WM_SIZE :
        MoveWindow( hList, 0, 0,
                    LOWORD( lParam ),
                    HIWORD( lParam ), TRUE );
        break;

case WM_COMMAND :
        switch( LOWORD( wParam ) )
        {
            case IDM_TEST :
                // Connect to all servers that support "System".
                //...............................................
                hConvList = DdeConnectList( ddeInst, NULL,
                                            hszTopic, NULL, NULL );

                if ( DdeGetLastError( ddeInst ) != DMLERR_NO_ERROR )
                {
                    MessageBox( hWnd, "Could not connect to servers.",
                                NULL, MB_OK | MB_ICONSTOP );
                }
                else
                {
                    CONVINFO ConvInfo;
                    char     szService[31];
                    HCONV    hConv = NULL;

                    ConvInfo.cb = sizeof( CONVINFO );
                    SendMessage( hList, LB_RESETCONTENT, 0, 0 );

                    // Find out all the servers we connected to
                    // and display them in the list box.
                    //........................................
                    while( hConv = DdeQueryNextServer(hConvList, hConv) )
                    {
                        DdeQueryConvInfo( hConv, QID_SYNC, &ConvInfo );
```

continued on next page

continued from previous page

```
                              DdeQueryString( ddeInst, ConvInfo.hszSvcPartner,
                                      szService, 30, CP_WINANSI );

                              SendMessage( hList, LB_ADDSTRING, 0,
                                      (LPARAM)szService );
                      }

                      // Disconnect from all servers.
                      //............................
                      DdeDisconnectList( hConvList );
                  }
                  break;

            case IDM_ABOUT :
                  DialogBox( hInst, "AboutBox", hWnd, (DLGPROC)About );
                  break;

            case IDM_EXIT :
                  DestroyWindow( hWnd );
                  break;
        }
        break;

    case WM_DESTROY :
            DdeFreeStringHandle( ddeInst, hszTopic );
            DdeUninitialize( ddeInst );
            PostQuitMessage(0);
            break;

    default :
            return( DefWindowProc( hWnd, uMsg, wParam, lParam ) );
    }

    return( 0L );
}


HDDEDATA CALLBACK DdemlCallback( UINT     uType,
                                 UINT     uFmt,
                                 HCONV    hconv,
                                 HSZ      hsz1,
                                 HSZ      hsz2,
                                 HDDEDATA hdata,
                                 DWORD    dwData1,
                                 DWORD    dwData2 )
{
    return( NULL );
}
```

DdeCreateDataHandle   ■ Win32s   ■ Windows 95   ■ Windows NT

Description   DdeCreateDataHandle() creates a dynamic data exchange (DDE) object
and fills the object with data from the buffer pointed to by the *pSrc*
parameter. Use this function during transactions that involve passing data
to the partner application.

Syntax	HDDEDATA **DdeCreateDataHandle**(DWORD *idInst*, LPBYTE *pSrc*, DWORD *cb*, DWORD *cbOff*, HSZ *hszItem*, UINT *wFmt*, UINT *afCmd*)
Parameters	
idInst	DWORD: The application instance identifier returned from the DdeInitialize() function.
pSrc	LPBYTE: A pointer to a buffer that contains data to be copied to the DDE object. If this parameter is NULL, no data is copied to the object.
cb	DWORD: The amount of memory, in bytes, to allocate for the DDE object. If this parameter is zero, the *pSrc* parameter is ignored.
cbOff	DWORD: The offset, in bytes, from the beginning of the buffer pointed to by the *pSrc* parameter. The data beginning at this offset is copied to the DDE object.
hszItem	HSZ: A handle to the string that specifies the data item corresponding to the DDE object. If the data handle is to be used in an XTYP_EXECUTE transaction, this parameter must be 0L.
wFmt	UINT: The standard clipboard format or valid registered format of the data.
afCmd	UINT: The creation flags. This parameter can be HDATA_APPOWNED, which specifies that the server application calling the DdeCreateDataHandle() function owns the data handle. This flag enables the application to share the data handle with other DDEML applications rather than creating a separate handle to pass to each application. If this flag is specified, the application must eventually free the shared memory object associated with the handle by using the DdeFreeDataHandle() function. If this flag is not specified, the handle becomes invalid in the application that created the handle after the data handle is returned by the application's DDE callback function or is used as a parameter in another DDEML function.

Returns	HDDEDATA: If successful, a valid data handle is returned; otherwise 0L is returned. Use the DdeGetLastError() function to retrieve the error value, which may be one of the following:
	    DMLERR_DLL_NOT_INITIALIZED
	    DMLERR_INVALIDPARAMETER
	    DMLERR_MEMORY_ERROR
	    DMLERR_NO_ERROR

Include File	ddeml.h
See Also	DdeAccessData(), DdeCreateStringHandle(), DdeFreeDataHandle(), DdeGetData(), DdeInitialize()
Example	See example for the DdeAddData() function.

DdeCreateStringHandle   ■ Win32s   ■ Windows 95   ■ Windows NT

Description	DdeCreateStringHandle() creates a handle that identifies a string. A dynamic data exchange (DDE) client or server application can pass the string handle as a parameter to other DDEML functions.
Syntax	HSZ **DdeCreateStringHandle**(DWORD *idInst*, LPTSTR *psz*, int *iCodePage*)
Parameters	
idInst	DWORD: The application instance identifier returned from the DdeInitialize() function.
psz	LPTSTR: A pointer to a buffer that contains the null-terminated string for which a handle is to be created. This string may be of any length.
iCodePage	int: The code page used to render the string. This value should be either CP_WINANSI (the default code page) or CP_WINUNICODE, depending on whether the ANSI or Unicode version of DdeInitialize() was called by the client application.
Returns	HSZ: If successful, a valid string handle is returned; otherwise, 0L is returned. Use the DdeGetLastError() function to retrieve the error value, which may be one of the following:
	DMLERR_INVALIDPARAMETER
	DMLERR_NO_ERROR
	DMLERR_SYS_ERROR
Include File	ddeml.h
See Also	DdeAccessData(), DdeCmpStringHandles(), DdeFreeStringHandle(), DdeInitialize(), DdeKeepStringHandle(), DdeQueryString()
Example	See example for the DdeDisconnect() function.

DdeDisconnect   ■ Win32s   ■ Windows 95   ■ Windows NT

Description	DdeDisconnect() terminates a conversation started by either the DdeConnect() or DdeConnectList() function and invalidates the conversation handle.
Syntax	BOOL **DdeDisconnect**(HCONV *hConv*)
Parameters	
hConv	HCONV: The active conversation to be terminated.
Returns	BOOL: If successful, TRUE is returned; otherwise, FALSE is returned. Use the DdeGetLastError() function to retrieve the error value, which may be one of the following:
	DMLERR_DLL_NOT_INITIALIZED
	DMLERR_NO_CONV_ESTABLISHED
	DMLERR_NO_ERROR
Include File	ddeml.h

See Also   DdeConnect(), DdeConnectList(), DdeDisconnectList()

Example   This example (Listing 10-10) shows how to disconnect from a DDE server
                  using the DdeDisconnect() function before a client application terminates.

Listing 10-10 Using the DdeDisconnect() function

```
DWORD ddeInst    = 0;
HSZ   hszTopic   = NULL;
HSZ   hszService = NULL;
HCONV hConv      = NULL;

LRESULT CALLBACK WndProc( HWND hWnd, UINT uMsg, WPARAM wParam, LPARAM lParam )
{
    switch( uMsg )
    {
        case WM_CREATE :
                // Initialize DDEML.
                //...................
                if ( DdeInitialize( &ddeInst, DdemlCallback,
                        APPCMD_CLIENTONLY, 0 ) != DMLERR_NO_ERROR )
                {
                    MessageBox( hWnd, "Could not initialize DDEML.",
                                NULL, MB_OK | MB_ICONSTOP );
                    return( -1 );
                }

                // Allocate strings.
                //..................
                hszService = DdeCreateStringHandle( ddeInst,"Server",CP_WINANSI );
                hszTopic   = DdeCreateStringHandle( ddeInst,"Data",CP_WINANSI );

                // Connect to server.
                //...................
                hConv = DdeConnect( ddeInst, hszService,
                                    hszTopic, NULL );

                if ( DdeGetLastError( ddeInst ) != DMLERR_NO_ERROR )
                    MessageBox( hWnd, "Could not connect to server.",
                                NULL, MB_OK | MB_ICONSTOP );


                break;

            .
            .
            .

    case WM_DESTROY :
                // If a conversation was established,
                // disconnect from the server.
                //...................................
                if ( hConv )
                    DdeDisconnect( hConv );

                DdeFreeStringHandle( ddeInst, hszService );
                DdeFreeStringHandle( ddeInst, hszTopic );
```

continued on next page

continued from previous page

```
            DdeUninitialize( ddeInst );
            PostQuitMessage(0);
            break;

    default :
            return( DefWindowProc( hWnd, uMsg, wParam, lParam ) );
    }

    return( 0L );
}
```

DdeDisconnectList   ■ Win32s ■ Windows 95 ■ Windows NT

Description	DdeDisconnectList() destroys the specified conversation list and terminates all conversations associated with the list. Applications can use the DdeDisconnect() function to disconnect individual conversations.
Syntax	BOOL **DdeDisconnectList**(HCONVLIST *hConvList*)
Parameters	
hConvList	HCONVLIST: The handle of the conversation list. This handle must have been created by a previous call to the DdeConnectList() function.
Returns	BOOL: If successful, TRUE is returned; otherwise, FALSE is returned. Use the DdeGetLastError() function to retrieve the error value, which may be one of the following:
	DMLERR_DLL_NOT_INITIALIZED
	DMLERR_INVALIDPARAMETER
	DMLERR_NO_ERROR
Include File	ddeml.h
See Also	DdeConnect(), DdeConnectList(), DdeDisconnect()
Example	See the example for the DdeConnectList() function.

DdeEnableCallback   ■ Win32s ■ Windows 95 ■ Windows NT

Description	DdeEnableCallback() enables or disables transactions for a specific conversation or for all conversations currently established by the calling application. When an application disables transactions for a conversation, all the transactions are held in a queue associated with the application. The application should reenable transactions as soon as possible to avoid losing transactions.
	An application can disable transactions for a specific conversation by returning the CBR_BLOCK return code from the DDE callback function. To reenable the conversation, use the DdeEnableCallback() function. Once the transactions are re-enabled, the operating system generates the same transaction that was in process when the conversation was disabled.

An application typically disables a conversation when it is temporarily unable to process DDE requests. This may occur when an application is processing a previous DDE request that takes an extended period of time.

Syntax   BOOL **DdeEnableCallback**(DWORD *idInst*, HCONV *hConv*, UINT *wCmd*)

Parameters

idInst   DWORD: The application instance identifier returned from the DdeInitialize() function.

hConv   HCONV: The handle of the conversation to enable or disable. If this parameter is NULL, the function affects all conversations.

wCmd   UINT: The function code. This parameter can be one of the values in Table 10-5.

Table 10-5 DdeEnableCallback() *wCmd* values

Value	Meaning
EC_DISABLE	Disables all blockable transactions for a conversation. A server application can disable the following transactions:
	XTYP_ADVSTART
	XTYP_ADVSTOP
	XTYP_EXECUTE
	XTYP_POKEXTYP_REQUEST
	A client application can disable the following transactions:
	XTYP_ADVDATA
	XTYP_XACT_COMPLETE
EC_ENABLEALL	Enables all transactions for a conversation.
EC_ENABLEONE	Enables one transaction for a conversation.
EC_QUERYWAITING	Determines whether any transactions are in the queue for a conversation.

Returns   BOOL: If successful, TRUE is returned; otherwise, FALSE is returned. Use the DdeGetLastError() function to retrieve the error value, which may be one of the following:

DMLERR_DLL_NOT_INITIALIZED
DMLERR_INVALIDPARAMETER
DMLERR_NO_ERROR

Include File   ddeml.h

See Also   DdeConnect(), DdeConnectList(), DdeDisconnect(), DdeInitialize()

Example   This example, in Listings 10-11 and 10-12, shows how a "hot" DDE advise loop works for a client and server application. The client connects to the server using the Time topic when the client starts. When the user selects the Test! menu item, the client requests an advise loop on the TimeItem data item. The server callback then receives the XTYP_ADVSTART transaction, where it starts a timer. The server's TimeProc() function receives notification when the timer expires, and DdePostAdvise() is called to post an advise transaction to the server's callback function. The server then receives the XTYP_ADVREQ transaction, where it retrieves the current time and returns it in a DDE data object. The client receives this object in the XTYP_ADVDATA transaction, where it places it in the list boon the client area of the window, as shown in Figure 10-3. When the client application terminates, the advise loop is terminated and the server receives the XTYP_ADVSTOP transaction, where it kills the timer.

If the user selects the Disable! menu item on the server before selecting the Test! menu item on the client, the server calls the DdeEnableCallback() function to disable processing of the advise loop until the user selects the Enable! menu item.

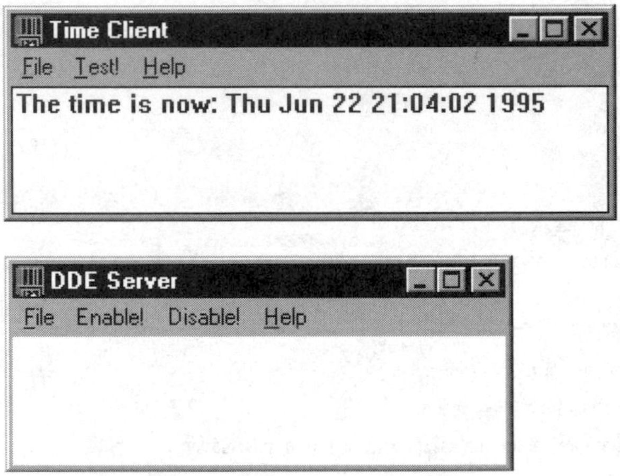

Time Client
File Test! Help

The time is now: Thu Jun 22 21:04:02 1995

DDE Server
File Enable! Disable! Help

Figure 10-3 EnableCallback() example

Listing 10-11 TIMECLI.C WndProc() and DdemlCallback()

```
DWORD     ddeInst     = 0;
HSZ       hszService  = NULL;
HSZ       hszTopic    = NULL;
HSZ       hszItem     = NULL;
HCONV     hConv       = NULL;

LRESULT CALLBACK WndProc( HWND hWnd, UINT uMsg, WPARAM wParam, LPARAM lParam )
{
static BOOL bAdv   = FALSE;
static HWND hList  = NULL;

    switch( uMsg )
    {
```

```
case WM_CREATE :
        // Initialize DDEML.
        //..................
        if ( DdeInitialize( &ddeInst, DdemlCallback,
             APPCMD_CLIENTONLY, 0 ) != DMLERR_NO_ERROR )
        {
            MessageBox( hWnd, "Could not initialize DDEML.",
                        NULL, MB_OK | MB_ICONSTOP );
            return( -1 );
        }

        // Allocate strings.
        //..................
        hszService = DdeCreateStringHandle( ddeInst,"Server",CP_WINANSI );
        hszTopic = DdeCreateStringHandle( ddeInst,"Time",CP_WINANSI );
        hszItem = DdeCreateStringHandle( ddeInst,"TimeItem",CP_WINANSI );

        hList = CreateWindow( "LISTBOX", "",
                              WS_CHILD | LBS_STANDARD |
                              WS_VISIBLE | LBS_NOINTEGRALHEIGHT,
                              0, 0,
                              0, 0,
                              hWnd,
                              (HMENU)101,
                              hInst,
                              NULL
                            );

        // Connect to server.
        //...................
        hConv = DdeConnect( ddeInst, hszService, hszTopic, NULL );

        if ( DdeGetLastError( ddeInst ) != DMLERR_NO_ERROR )
        {
            MessageBox( hWnd, "Could not connect to server.",
                        NULL, MB_OK | MB_ICONSTOP );
        }
        else
            // Store the handle of the list box
            // in the conversation user data.
            //..................................
            DdeSetUserHandle( hConv, QID_SYNC, (DWORD)hList );
        break;

case WM_SIZE :
        MoveWindow( hList, 0, 0,
                    LOWORD( lParam ),
                    HIWORD( lParam ), TRUE );
        break;

case WM_COMMAND :
        switch( LOWORD( wParam ) )
        {
            case IDM_TEST :
                if ( hConv && !bAdv )
                {
                    // Start the advise loop.
                    //......................
                    DdeClientTransaction( NULL, 0, hConv, hszItem,
```

continued on next page

continued from previous page

```
                                              CF_TEXT, XTYP_ADVSTART,
                                              2000,  NULL );

                    bAdv = DdeGetLastError( ddeInst ) == DMLERR_NO_ERROR;
                }
                break;

            case IDM_ABOUT :
                DialogBox( hInst, "AboutBox", hWnd, (DLGPROC)About );
                break;

            case IDM_EXIT :
                DestroyWindow( hWnd );
                break;
        }
        break;

    case WM_DESTROY :
        if ( hConv )
        {
            // End the advise loop if it exists.
            //.................................
            if ( bAdv )
                DdeClientTransaction( NULL, 0, hConv, hszItem,
                                      CF_TEXT, XTYP_ADVSTOP,
                                      2000,  NULL );
            DdeDisconnect( hConv );
        }

        DdeFreeStringHandle( ddeInst, hszService );
        DdeFreeStringHandle( ddeInst, hszTopic );
        DdeFreeStringHandle( ddeInst, hszItem );

        DdeUninitialize( ddeInst );
        PostQuitMessage(0);
        break;

    default :
        return( DefWindowProc( hWnd, uMsg, wParam, lParam ) );
    }

    return( 0L );
}


HDDEDATA CALLBACK DdemlCallback( UINT     uType,
                                 UINT     uFmt,
                                 HCONV    hconv,
                                 HSZ      hsz1,
                                 HSZ      hsz2,
                                 HDDEDATA hdata,
                                 DWORD    dwData1,
                                 DWORD    dwData2 )
{
static char     szTime[128];
static CONVINFO convInfo;

    switch( uType )
    {
```

```
        case XTYP_ADVDATA :
                // Get the data and display it in the list.
                //.......................................
                DdeGetData( hdata, szTime, sizeof( szTime ), 0 );
                szTime[strlen(szTime)-2] = 0;

                // Retrieve the conversation info
                // to get the handle of the list box.
                //....................................
                convInfo.cb = sizeof( CONVINFO );
                DdeQueryConvInfo( hConv, QID_SYNC, &convInfo );

                SendMessage((HWND)convInfo.hUser, LB_RESETCONTENT, 0, 0);
                SendMessage((HWND)convInfo.hUser, LB_ADDSTRING, 0, (LPARAM)szTime);
                break;
    }

    return( NULL );
}
```

Listing 10-12 SERVER.C WndProc(), TimeProc(), and DdemlCallback()

```
DWORD ddeInst    = 0;
HSZ   hszService = NULL;
HSZ   hszTopic1  = NULL;
HSZ   hszTopic2  = NULL;
HSZ   hszTopic3  = NULL;
HSZ   hszItem    = NULL;

LRESULT CALLBACK WndProc( HWND hWnd, UINT uMsg, WPARAM wParam, LPARAM lParam )
{
    switch( uMsg )
    {
    case WM_CREATE :
            // Initialize DDEML.
            //..................
            if ( DdeInitialize( &ddeInst, DdemlCallback,
                APPCLASS_STANDARD, 0 ) != DMLERR_NO_ERROR )
            {
                MessageBox( hWnd, "Could not initialize DDEML.",
                            NULL, MB_OK | MB_ICONSTOP );
                return( -1 );
            }

            // Allocate strings.
            //..................
            hszService = DdeCreateStringHandle( ddeInst,"Server",CP_WINANSI );
            hszTopic1  = DdeCreateStringHandle( ddeInst,"Data",CP_WINANSI );
            hszTopic2  = DdeCreateStringHandle( ddeInst,"Msg",CP_WINANSI );
            hszTopic3  = DdeCreateStringHandle( ddeInst,"Time",CP_WINANSI );
            hszItem    = DdeCreateStringHandle( ddeInst,"TimeItem",CP_WINANSI );

            DdeNameService( ddeInst, hszService, 0L, DNS_REGISTER );
            break;

    case WM_COMMAND :
            switch( LOWORD( wParam ) )
```

continued on next page

continued from previous page

```
                {
                    case IDM_ENABLE :
                            DdeEnableCallback( ddeInst, NULL, EC_ENABLEONE );
                            break;

                    case IDM_DISABLE :
                            DdeEnableCallback( ddeInst, NULL, EC_DISABLE );
                            break;

                    case IDM_ABOUT :
                            DialogBox( hInst, "AboutBox", hWnd, (DLGPROC)About );
                            break;

                    case IDM_EXIT :
                            DestroyWindow( hWnd );
                            break;
                }
                break;

        case WM_DESTROY :
                DdeNameService( ddeInst, hszService, OL, DNS_UNREGISTER );

                DdeFreeStringHandle( ddeInst, hszService );
                DdeFreeStringHandle( ddeInst, hszTopic1 );
                DdeFreeStringHandle( ddeInst, hszTopic2 );
                DdeFreeStringHandle( ddeInst, hszTopic3 );
                DdeFreeStringHandle( ddeInst, hszItem );

                DdeUninitialize( ddeInst );
                PostQuitMessage(O);
                break;

        default :
                return( DefWindowProc( hWnd, uMsg, wParam, lParam ) );
    }

    return( OL );
}


VOID CALLBACK TimeProc( HWND   hwnd,
                        UINT   uMsg,
                        UINT   idEvent,
                        DWORD  dwTime )
{
    // Timer message received, post advise.
    //.....................................
    DdePostAdvise( ddeInst, hszTopic3, hszItem );
}


HDDEDATA CALLBACK DdemlCallback( UINT     uType,
                                 UINT     uFmt,
                                 HCONV    hconv,
                                 HSZ      hsz1,
                                 HSZ      hsz2,
                                 HDDEDATA hdata,
                                 DWORD    dwData1,
                                 DWORD    dwData2 )
```

```
{
static UINT uTimerID = 0;

   switch( uType )
   {
      case XTYP_CONNECT :
            if ( DdeCmpStringHandles( hsz2, hszService ) )
               break;

            if ( DdeCmpStringHandles( hsz1, hszTopic1 ) &&
                 DdeCmpStringHandles( hsz1, hszTopic2 ) &&
                 DdeCmpStringHandles( hsz1, hszTopic3 ) )
            {
               break;
            }

            // Allow the conversation.
            //........................
            return( (HDDEDATA)TRUE );

      case XTYP_ADVSTART :
            // Start the advise loop if the
            // topic and data item are valid.
            //...............................
            if ( DdeCmpStringHandles( hsz1, hszTopic3 ) == 0 &&
                 DdeCmpStringHandles( hsz2, hszItem   ) == 0 )
            {
               uTimerID = SetTimer( NULL, 0, 1000, (TIMERPROC)TimeProc );
               return( (HDDEDATA)TRUE );
            }

            return( FALSE );

      case XTYP_ADVREQ :
            // Update the time data and return it to the client.
            //..................................................
            if ( DdeCmpStringHandles( hsz1, hszTopic3 ) == 0 &&
                 DdeCmpStringHandles( hsz2, hszItem   ) == 0 )
            {
               time_t  ltime;
               char    szBuf[128];
               HDDEDATA hDdeData;

               HSZ     hszDataName = DdeCreateStringHandle( ddeInst,
                                          "Hour", CP_WINANSI );
               time( &ltime );
               wsprintf( szBuf, "The time is now: %s ",
                             (LPTSTR)ctime(&ltime) );

               hDdeData = DdeCreateDataHandle( ddeInst, szBuf,
                                   strlen( szBuf )+1, 0,
                                   hszDataName, CF_TEXT, 0 );

               DdeFreeStringHandle( ddeInst, hszDataName );
               return( hDdeData );
            }
            return( NULL );
```

continued on next page

continued from previous page

```
    case XTYP_ADVSTOP :
            KillTimer( NULL, uTimerID );
            break;

    }

    return( NULL );
}
```

DdeFreeDataHandle ■ Win32s ■ Windows 95 ■ Windows NT

Description   DdeFreeDataHandle() frees a dynamic data exchange (DDE) object created
with the DdeCreateDataHandle() function and deletes the data handle
associated with the object. Applications should delete a data handle in the
following instances:

■ If the DDE object was created with the DdeCreateDataHandle() function and not used in a DDEML function.

■ If the DDE object was created with the HDATA_APPOWNED flag in
the DdeCreateDataHandle() function.

■ To free a data handle returned from a call to the
DdeClientTransaction() function.

The system automatically frees an unowned object when its handle is
returned by a DDE callback function or is used as a parameter in a
DDEML function.

Syntax   BOOL **DdeFreeDataHandle**(HDDEDATA *hData*)

Parameters

hData   HDDEDATA: The handle of the DDE object to be freed.

Returns   BOOL: If successful, TRUE is returned; otherwise, FALSE is returned. Use
the DdeGetLastError() function to retrieve the error value, which may be
one of the following:

DMLERR_INVALIDPARAMETER
DMLERR_NO_ERROR

Include File   ddeml.h

See Also   DdeAccessData(), DdeCreateDataHandle(), DdeClientTransaction()

Example   See example for the DdeAddData() function.

DdeFreeStringHandle ■ Win32s ■ Windows 95 ■ Windows NT

Description   DdeFreeStringHandle() frees a string handle in the calling application. An
application should free only string handles that it created with the
DdeCreateStringHandle() function. String handles passed to the application's DDE callback function or in the CONVINFO structure should not be
deleted.

Syntax	BOOL **DdeFreeStringHandle**(DWORD *idInst*, HSZ *hsz*)
Parameters	
idInst	DWORD: The application instance identifier returned from the DdeInitialize() function.
hsz	HSZ: The string handle to be freed. This handle must have been created by a previous call to the DdeCreateStringHandle() function.
Returns	BOOL: If successful, TRUE is returned; otherwise, FALSE is returned.
Include File	ddeml.h
See Also	DdeCmpStringHandles(), DdeCreateStringHandle(), DdeInitialize(), DdeKeepStringHandle(), DdeQueryConvInfo(), DdeQueryString()
Example	See the example for the DdeUninitialize() function.

DdeGetData
■ Win32s ■ Windows 95 ■ Windows NT

Description	DdeGetData() copies data from a dynamic data exchange (DDE) object to a local buffer.
Syntax	DWORD **DdeGetData**(HDDEDATA *hData*, LPBYTE *pDst*, DWORD *cbMax*, DWORD *cbOff*)
Parameters	
hData	HDDEDATA: The DDE object that contains the data to be copied.
pDst	LPBYTE: A pointer to the buffer that receives the data. If this parameter is NULL, the function returns the amount of data, in bytes, that would be copied to the buffer.
cbMax	DWORD: The maximum amount of data, in bytes, to copy to the buffer pointed to by the *pDst* parameter.
cbOff	DWORD: An offset within the DDE object where the copy starts.
Returns	DWORD: If *pDst* is not NULL and the function is successful, the number of bytes copied is returned. If *pDst* is NULL, the size, in bytes, of the DDE object is returned. Use the DdeGetLastError() function to retrieve the error value, which may be one of the following: DMLERR_DLL_NOT_INITIALIZED DMLERR_INVALIDPARAMETER DMLERR_NO_ERROR
Include File	ddeml.h
See Also	DdeAccessData(), DdeCreateDataHandle(), DdeFreeDataHandle()
Example	See example for the DdeAddData() function.

DdeGetLastError

■ Win32s   ■ Windows 95   ■ Windows NT

Description	DdeGetLastError() returns the most recent error value set by the failure of a Dynamic Data Exchange Management Library (DDEML) function and resets the error value to DMLERR_NO_ERROR.
Syntax	UINT **DdeGetLastError**(DWORD *idInst*)
Parameters	
idInst	DWORD: The application instance identifier returned from the DdeInitialize() function.
Returns	UINT: The error value. Table 10-6 lists the possible DDEML errors.

Table 10-6 DdeGetLastError( ) return values

Value	Meaning
DMLERR_ADVACKTIMEOUT	A request for a synchronous advise transaction has timed out.
DMLERR_BUSY	The response to the transaction caused the DDE_FBUSY flag to be set.
DMLERR_DATAACKTIMEOUT	A request for a synchronous data transaction has timed out.
DMLERR_DLL_NOT_INITIALIZED	A DDEML function was called without first calling the DdeInitialize() function, or an invalid instance identifier was passed to a DDEML function.
DMLERR_DLL_USAGE	An application initialized as APPCLASS_MONITOR has attempted to perform a dynamic data exchange (DDE) transaction, or an application initialized as APPCMD_CLIENTONLY has attempted to perform server transactions.
DMLERR_EXECACKTIMEOUT	A request for a synchronous execute transaction has timed out.
DMLERR_INVALIDPARAMETER	A parameter failed to be validated by the DDEML. The following is a list of some of the possible causes.
	■ The application used a data handle initialized with a different item name handle than was required by the transaction.
	■ The application used a data handle that was initialized with a different clipboard data format than was required by the transaction.
	■ The application used a client-side conversation handle with a server-side function or vice versa.
	■ The application used a freed data handle or string handle. This can happen when more than one instance of the application used the same object.
DMLERR_LOW_MEMORY	A DDEML application has created a prolonged race condition (in which the server application outruns the client), causing large amounts of memory to be consumed.
DMLERR_MEMORY_ERROR	A memory allocation has failed.
DMLERR_NO_CONV_ESTABLISHED	A client's attempt to establish a conversation has failed.
DMLERR_NOTPROCESSED	A transaction has failed.
DMLERR_POKEACKTIMEOUT	A request for a synchronous poke transaction has timed out.
DMLERR_POSTMSG_FAILED	An internal call to the PostMessage() function has failed.

Value	Meaning
DMLERR_REENTRANCY	An application instance with a synchronous transaction already in progress attempted to initiate another synchronous transaction, or the DdeEnableCallback() function was called from within a DDEML callback function.
DMLERR_SERVER_DIED	A server-side transaction was attempted on a conversation terminated by the client, or the server terminated before completing a transaction.
DMLERR_SYS_ERROR	An internal error has occurred in the DDEML.
DMLERR_UNADVACKTIMEOUT	A request to end an advise transaction has timed out.
DMLERR_UNFOUND_QUEUE_ID	An invalid transaction identifier was passed to a DDEML function. Once the application has returned from an XTYP_XACT_COMPLETE callback, the transaction identifier for that callback function is no longer valid.

Include File	ddeml.h
See Also	DdeEnableCallback(), DdeInitialize()
Example	See example for the DdeClientTransaction() function.

DdeInitialize

■ Win32s ■ Windows 95 ■ Windows NT

Description DdeInitialize() registers an application with the Dynamic Data Exchange Management Library (DDEML). An application must call this function before calling any other DDEML function.

Syntax UINT **DdeInitialize**(LPDWORD *pidInst*, PFNCALLBACK *pfnCallback*, DWORD *afCmd*, DWORD *ulRes*)

Parameters

pidInst LPDWORD: A pointer to a DWORD variable that receives the application instance identifier. At initialization, the value of the variable should be set to zero. If the function succeeds, the value will be the instance identifier for the application. This value should be passed as the *idInst* parameter in all other DDEML functions that require it. If an application uses multiple instances of the DDEML dynamic-link library (DLL), the application should provide a different callback function for each instance. If the value of the variable is a nonzero value at initialization, reinitialization of the DDEML is implied. In this case, *pidInst* must point to a valid application-instance identifier.

pfnCallback PFNCALLBACK: A pointer to the application-defined dynamic data exchange (DDE) callback function. This function processes DDE transactions sent by the system. See the description of the callback function below.

afCmd DWORD: Specifies a set of APPCMD_, CBF_, and MF_ flags from Table 10-7 combined using the binary OR (|) operator. Using these flags enhances the performance of a DDE application by eliminating unnecessary calls to the callback function.

The APPCMD_ flags provide special instructions to DdeInitialize(). The CBF_ flags are filters that prevent specific types of transactions from being processed by the callback function. The MF_ flags specify the types of DDE activity that a DDE monitoring application monitors.

Table 10-7 DdeInitialize() *afCmd* values

Value	Meaning
APPCLASS_MONITOR	Allows the application to monitor DDE activity in the system. This flag is for use by DDE monitoring applications.
APPCLASS_STANDARD	Registers the application as a standard DDEML application.
APPCMD_CLIENTONLY	Prevents the application from becoming a server in a DDE conversation. The application can only be a client. This flag reduces consumption of resources by the DDEML.
APPCMD_FILTERINITS	Prevents the DDEML from sending XTYP_CONNECT and XTYP_WILDCONNECT transactions to the application until the application has created its string handles and registered its service names or has turned off filtering by a subsequent call to the DdeNameService() or DdeInitialize() function. This flag is always in effect when an application calls DdeInitialize() for the first time, regardless of whether the application specifies the flag. On subsequent calls to DdeInitialize(), not specifying this flag turns off the application's service name filters, but specifying it turns on the application's service name filters.
CBF_FAIL_ADVISES	Prevents the callback function from receiving XTYP_ADVSTART and XTYP_ADVSTOP transactions. The system returns DDE_FNOTPROCESSED to each client that sends an XTYP_ADVSTART or XTYP_ADVSTOP transaction to the server.
CBF_FAIL_ALLSVRXACTIONS	Prevents the callback function from receiving server transactions. The system returns DDE_FNOTPROCESSED to each client that sends a transaction to this application. This flag is equivalent to combining all CBF_FAIL_ flags.
CBF_FAIL_CONNECTIONS	Prevents the callback function from receiving XTYP_CONNECT and XTYP_WILDCONNECT transactions.
CBF_FAIL_EXECUTES	Prevents the callback function from receiving XTYP_EXECUTE transactions. The system returns DDE_FNOTPROCESSED to a client that sends an XTYP_EXECUTE transaction to the server.
CBF_FAIL_POKES	Prevents the callback function from receiving XTYP_POKE transactions. The system returns DDE_FNOTPROCESSED to a client that sends an XTYP_POKE transaction to the server.
CBF_FAIL_REQUESTS	Prevents the callback function from receiving XTYP_REQUEST transactions. The system returns DDE_FNOTPROCESSED to a client that sends an XTYP_REQUEST transaction to the server.
CBF_FAIL_SELFCONNECTIONS	Prevents the callback function from receiving XTYP_CONNECT transactions from the application's own instance. This flag prevents an application from establishing a DDE conversation with its own instance. An application should use this flag if it needs to communicate with other instances of itself but not with itself.
CBF_SKIP_ALLNOTIFICATIONS	Prevents the callback function from receiving any notifications. This flag is equivalent to combining all CBF_SKIP_ flags.

Value	Meaning
CBF_SKIP_CONNECT_CONFIRMS	Prevents the callback function from receiving XTYP_CONNECT_CONFIRM notifications.
CBF_SKIP_DISCONNECTS	Prevents the callback function from receiving XTYP_DISCONNECT notifications.
CBF_SKIP_REGISTRATIONS	Prevents the callback function from receiving XTYP_REGISTER notifications.
CBF_SKIP_UNREGISTRATIONS	Prevents the callback function from receiving XTYP_UNREGISTER notifications.
MF_CALLBACKS	Notifies the callback function whenever a transaction is sent to any DDE callback function in the system.
MF_CONV	Notifies the callback function whenever a conversation is established or terminated.
MF_ERRORS	Notifies the callback function whenever a DDE error occurs.
MF_HSZ_INFO	Notifies the callback function whenever a DDE application creates, frees, or increments the usage count of a string handle or whenever a string handle is freed as a result of a call to the DdeUninitialize() function.
MF_LINKS	Notifies the callback function whenever an advise loop is started or ended.
MF_POSTMSGS	Notifies the callback function whenever the system or an application posts a DDE message.
MF_SENDMSGS	Notifies the callback function whenever the system or an application sends a DDE message.

ulRes	DWORD: This parameter is reserved and must be set to zero.
Returns	UINT: If successful, DMLERR_NO_ERROR is returned; otherwise, one of the following values is returned:
	DMLERR_DLL_USAGE
	DMLERR_INVALIDPARAMETER
	DMLERR_SYS_ERROR
Include File	ddeml.h
See Also	DdeClientTransaction(), DdeConnect(), DdeCreateDataHandle(), DdeEnableCallback(), DdeNameService(), DdePostAdvise(), DdeUninitialize()
Example	This example (Listing 10-13) demonstrates a simple DDEML server application without any functionality implemented. The example shows how to use the DdeInitialize() function to initialize DDEML and register the application's callback function. The callback function shows the XTYP_CONNECT transaction, which is processed when a DDEML client requests a conversation.

Listing 10-13 Using the DdeInitialize() function

```
DWORD ddeInst     = 0;
HSZ   hszService = NULL;
HSZ   hszTopic1  = NULL;
HSZ   hszTopic2  = NULL;

LRESULT CALLBACK WndProc( HWND hWnd, UINT uMsg, WPARAM wParam, LPARAM lParam )
{
   switch( uMsg )
```

continued on next page

continued from previous page

```
    {
        case WM_CREATE :
                // Initialize DDEML.
                //..................
                if ( DdeInitialize( &ddeInst, DdemlCallback,
                     APPCLASS_STANDARD, 0 ) != DMLERR_NO_ERROR )
                {
                    MessageBox( hWnd, "Could not initialize DDEML.",
                                NULL, MB_OK | MB_ICONSTOP );
                    return( -1 );
                }

                // Allocate strings.
                //..................
                hszService = DdeCreateStringHandle( ddeInst,"Server",CP_WINANSI );
                hszTopic1  = DdeCreateStringHandle( ddeInst,"Long",CP_WINANSI );
                hszTopic2  = DdeCreateStringHandle( ddeInst,"Msg",CP_WINANSI );

                // Register service name.
                //......................
                DdeNameService( ddeInst, hszService, 0L, DNS_REGISTER );
                break;

            .
            .
            .

        case WM_DESTROY :
                // Free any strings that have been allocated.
                //...........................................
                DdeFreeStringHandle( ddeInst, hszService );
                DdeFreeStringHandle( ddeInst, hszTopic1 );
                DdeFreeStringHandle( ddeInst, hszTopic2 );

                // Uninitialize DDEML.
                //....................
                DdeUninitialize( ddeInst );

                PostQuitMessage(0);
                break;

        default :
                return( DefWindowProc( hWnd, uMsg, wParam, lParam ) );
    }

    return( 0L );
}


HDDEDATA CALLBACK DdemlCallback( UINT       uType,
                                 UINT       uFmt,
                                 HCONV      hconv,
                                 HSZ        hsz1,
                                 HSZ        hsz2,
                                 HDDEDATA   hdata,
                                 DWORD      dwData1,
                                 DWORD      dwData2 )
{
static LPBYTE lpMsg = NULL;
```

```
switch( uType )
{
   case XTYP_CONNECT :
          if ( DdeCmpStringHandles( hsz2, hszService ) )
             break;

          if ( DdeCmpStringHandles( hsz1, hszTopic1 ) &&
               DdeCmpStringHandles( hsz1, hszTopic2 )  )
          {
             break;
          }

          // Allow the conversation.
          //......................
          return( (HDDEDATA)TRUE );

          .
          .
          .

}

   return( NULL );
}
```

Callback Syntax   HDDEDATA CALLBACK **DdeCallback**(UINT *uType*, UINT *uFmt*, HCONV *hconv*, HSZ *hsz1*, HSZ *hsz2*, HDDEDATA *hdata*, DWORD *dwData1*, DWORD *dwData2*)

Callback Parameters

uType   UINT: The current transaction type. This parameter consists of a combination of transaction class flags and transaction type flags. Table 10-8 describes each type of transaction and lists the transaction types in each class. For detailed information on specific transaction types, see the transaction type descriptions below.

Table 10-8 DdeCallback() *uType* values

Value	Meaning
XCLASS_BOOL	A DDE callback function should return TRUE or FALSE when it finishes processing a transaction that belongs to this class. The XCLASS_BOOL transaction class consists of the following types: XTYP_ADVSTART XTYP_CONNECT
XCLASS_DATA	A DDE callback function should return a DDE handle, the CBR_BLOCK return code, or NULL when it finishes processing a transaction that belongs to this class. The XCLASS_DATA transaction class consists of the following types: XTYP_ADVREQ XTYP_REQUEST XTYP_WILDCONNECT

continued on next page

continued from previous page

Value	Meaning
XCLASS_FLAGS	A DDE callback function should return DDE_FACK, DDE_FBUSY, or DDE_FNOTPROCESSED when it finishes processing a transaction that belongs to this class. The XCLASS_FLAGS transaction class consists of the following types: XTYP_ADVDATA XTYP_EXECUTE XTYP_POKE
XCLASS_NOTIFICATION	The transaction types that belong to this class are for notification purposes only. The return value from the callback function is ignored. The XCLASS_NOTIFICATION transaction class consists of the following types: XTYP_ADVSTOP XTYP_CONNECT_CONFIRM XTYP_DISCONNECT XTYP_ERROR XTYP_MONITOR XTYP_REGISTER XTYP_UNREGISTER XTYP_XACT_COMPLETE

uFmt	UINT: The data format. This can be one of the standard clipboard formats or an application-defined format.
hconv	HCONV: The handle of the conversation associated with the current transaction.
hsz1	HSZ: A handle to a string. The meaning of this parameter depends on the type of the transaction. See the description of the transaction type below.
hsz2	HSZ: A handle to a string. The meaning of this parameter depends on the type of the transaction. See the description of the transaction type below.
hdata	HDDEDATA: A handle to a DDE data object. The meaning of this parameter depends on the type of the transaction. See the description of the transaction type below.
dwData1	DWORD: Transaction-specific data. See the description of the transaction type below.
dwData2	DWORD: Transaction-specific data. See the description of the transaction type below.
Callback Returns	HDDEDATA: The return value depends on the transaction class. See the description below for each transaction class in Table 10-7 for return value information.

XTYP_ADVDATA

Description

A client callback function receives the XTYP_ADVDATA transaction after establishing an advise loop with a server to indicate that the value of the data item has changed.

An application must not free the data handle obtained during this transaction. If the application must process the data after the callback function returns, copy the data associated with the data handle. An application can use the DdeGetData() function to copy the data.

Parameters

uFmt   UINT: The format of the data sent from the server.

hconv   HCONV: The handle of the conversation.

hsz1   HSZ: The topic name.

hsz2   HSZ: The item name.

hdata   HDDEDATA: A handle to the data associated with the topic name and item name pair. This parameter is NULL if the client specified the XTYPF_NODATA flag when it requested the advise loop.

dwData1   DWORD: Not used.

dwData2   DWORD: Not used.

Returns   HDDEDATA: Return DDE_FACK if the callback function processes this transaction, DDE_FBUSY if it is too busy to process this transaction, or DDE_FNOTPROCESSED if it rejects this transaction.

XTYP_ADVREQ

Description

The system sends the XTYP_ADVREQ transaction to a server after the server calls the DdePostAdvise() function. This transaction informs the server that an advise transaction is outstanding on the specified topic name and item name pair, and that data corresponding to the topic name and item name pair has changed.

Parameters

uFmt   UINT: The format in which the data should be submitted to the client.

hconv   HCONV: The handle of the conversation.

hsz1   HSZ: The topic name.

hsz2   HSZ: The item name that has changed.

hdata   HDDEDATA: Not used.

dwData1   DWORD: The low-order word is the number of XTYP_ADVREQ transactions that remain to be processed on the same topic, item, and format name used with the DdePostAdvise() function. The high-order word is not used.

The number of transactions is zero if the current XTYP_ADVREQ transaction is the last one. A server can use this number to determine whether to create an HDATA_APPOWNED data handle for the advise data.

If DDEML issued the XTYP_ADVREQ transaction because of a late DDE_ACK message from a client being outrun by the server, the number is set to CADV_LATEACK.

dwData2	DWORD: Not used.
Returns	HDDEDATA: The server should use the DdeCreateDataHandle() function to create a data handle that identifies the changed data and return the resulting handle. The server should return NULL if it is unable to complete the transaction.

XTYP_ADVSTART

Description	A server callback function receives this transaction when a client specifies XTYP_ADVSTART in the DdeClientTransaction() function to establish an advise loop with the server.
Parameters	
uFmt	UINT: The data format requested by the client.
hconv	HCONV: The handle of the conversation.
hsz1	HSZ: The topic name.
hsz2	HSZ: The item name.
hdata	HDDEDATA: Not used.
dwData1	DWORD: Not used.
dwData2	DWORD: Not used.
Returns	HDDEDATA: Return TRUE to allow an advise loop on the specified topic name and item name pair, or FALSE to deny the advise loop. If TRUE is returned, any subsequent calls to the DdePostAdvise() function by the server on the same topic name and item name pair causes the system to send XTYP_ADVREQ transactions to the server.

XTYP_ADVSTOP

Description	A server callback function receives the XTYP_ADVSTOP transaction when a client specifies XTYP_ADVSTOP in the DdeClientTransaction() function to end an advise loop with a server.
Parameters	
uFmt	UINT: The data format associated with the advise loop being ended.
hconv	HCONV: The handle of the conversation.
hsz1	HSZ: The topic name.
hsz2	HSZ: The item name.
hdata	HDDEDATA: Not used.
dwData1	DWORD: Not used.

dwData2	DWORD: Not used.
Returns	HDDEDATA: Return value is ignored.

XTYP_CONNECT

Description   A server callback function receives the XTYP_CONNECT transaction when a client uses the DdeConnect() function with a service name that the server supports and a topic name that is not NULL.

Parameters

uFmt	UINT: Not used.
hconv	HCONV: Not used.
hsz1	HSZ: The topic name.
hsz2	HSZ: The service name.
hdata	HDDEDATA: Not used.
dwData1	DWORD: A pointer to a CONVCONTEXT structure that contains context information for the conversation. If the client is not a DDEML application, this parameter is 0.
dwData2	DWORD: Specifies whether the client is the same application instance as the server. If the parameter is 1, the client is the same instance. If the parameter is 0, the client is a different instance.
Returns	HDDEDATA: Return TRUE to allow the client to establish a conversation on the specified service name and topic name pair. Return FALSE to deny the conversation.
	If the callback function returns TRUE and a conversation is successfully established, the system passes the conversation handle to the server by issuing an XTYP_CONNECT_CONFIRM transaction to the server's callback function (unless the server specified the CBF_SKIP_CONNECT_CONFIRMS flag in the DdeInitialize() function).

XTYP_CONNECT_CONFIRM

Description   A server callback function receives the XTYP_CONNECT_CONFIRM transaction to confirm that a conversation has been established with a client and to provide the server with the conversation handle. The system sends this transaction as a result of a previous XTYP_CONNECT or XTYP_WILDCONNECT transaction.

Parameters

uFmt	UINT: Not used.
hconv	HCONV: The handle of the new conversation.
hsz1	HSZ: The topic name on which the conversation has been established.
hsz2	HSZ: The service name on which the conversation has been established.
hdata	HDDEDATA: Not used.
dwData1	DWORD: Not used.

dwData2	DWORD: Specifies whether the client is the same application instance as the server. If the parameter is 1, the client is the same instance. If the parameter is 0, the client is a different instance.
Returns	HDDEDATA: Return value is ignored.

XTYP_DISCONNECT

Description	An application's callback function receives the XTYP_DISCONNECT transaction when the application's partner in a conversation uses the DdeDisconnect() function to terminate the conversation. The application can obtain the status of the terminated conversation by calling the DdeQueryConvInfo() function while processing this transaction. After the callback function returns, the conversation handle becomes invalid.
Parameters	
uFmt	UINT: Not used.
hconv	HCONV: Identifies that the conversation was terminated.
hsz1	HSZ: Not used.
hsz2	HSZ: Not used.
hdata	HDDEDATA: Not used.
dwData1	DWORD: Not used.
dwData2	DWORD: Specifies whether the partners in the conversation are the same application instance. If this parameter is 1, the partners are the same instance. If this parameter is 0, the partners are different instances.
Returns	HDDEDATA: Return value is ignored.

XTYP_ERROR

Description	A callback function receives the XTYP_ERROR transaction when a critical error occurs.
Parameters	
uFmt	UINT: Not used.
hconv	HCONV: The handle of the conversation associated with the error. This parameter is NULL if the error is not associated with a conversation.
hsz1	HSZ: Not used.
hsz2	HSZ: Not used.
hdata	HDDEDATA: Not used.
dwData1	DWORD: The low-order word contains the error code. Currently, only the DMLERR_LOW_MEMORY error code is supported. This error indicates that memory is low; advise, poke, or execute data may be lost, or the system may fail.
dwData2	DWORD: Not used.
Returns	HDDEDATA: Return value is ignored.

XTYP_EXECUTE

Description   A server callback function receives the XTYP_EXECUTE transaction when a client specifies XTYP_EXECUTE in the DdeClientTransaction() function. A client uses this transaction to send a command string to the server. Most applications expect a server application to perform an XTYP_EXECUTE transaction synchronously; therefore, a server should attempt to completely process the transaction in the callback function or return CBR_BLOCK.

An application must free the data handle obtained during this transaction. If the application requires the command string associated with the data handle, it must copy the string if processing of the string occurs after the callback function returns.

Parameters

uFmt   UINT: Not used.

hconv   HCONV: The handle of the conversation.

hsz1   HSZ: The topic name.

hsz2   HSZ: Not used.

hdata   HDDEDATA: The command string.

dwData1   DWORD: Not used.

dwData2   DWORD: Not used.

Returns   HDDEDATA: A server callback function should return DDE_FACK if it processes this transaction, DDE_FBUSY if it is too busy to process this transaction, or DDE_FNOTPROCESSED if it rejects this transaction.

XTYP_MONITOR

Description   The callback function of a DDE debugging application receives the XTYP_MONITOR transaction whenever a DDE event occurs in the system. To receive this transaction, an application must specify the APPCLASS_MONITOR flag in the DdeInitialize() function.

Parameters

uFmt   UINT: Not used.

hconv   HCONV: Not used.

hsz1   HSZ: Not used.

hsz2   HSZ: Not used.

hdata   HDDEDATA: The handle of the DDE object that contains information about the DDE event. The application should use the DdeAccessData() function to obtain a pointer to the object.

dwData1   DWORD: Not used.

dwData2   DWORD: The DDE event. This parameter may be one of the values listed in Table 10-9.

Table 10-9 XTYP_MONITOR *dwData2* values

Value	Meaning
MF_CALLBACKS	The system sent a transaction to a DDE callback function. The DDE object contains a MONCBSTRUCT structure that provides information about the transaction. See the definition of the MONCBSTRUCT structure below.
MF_CONV	A DDE conversation was established or terminated. The DDE object contains a MONCONVSTRUCT structure that provides information about the conversation. See the definition of the MONCONVSTRUCT structure below.
MF_ERRORS	A DDE error occurred. The DDE object contains a MONERRSTRUCT structure that provides information about the error. See the definition of the MONERRSTRUCT structure below.
MF_HSZ_INFO	A DDE application created, freed, or incremented the usage count of a string handle, or a string handle was freed as a result of a call to the DdeUninitialize() function. The DDE object contains a MONHSZSTRUCT structure that provides information about the string handle. See the definition of the MONHSZSTRUCT structure below.
MF_LINKS	A DDE application started or stopped an advise loop. The DDE object contains a MONLINKSTRUCT structure that provides information about the advise loop. See the definition of the MONLINKSTRUCT structure below.
MF_POSTMSGS	The system or an application posted a DDE message. The DDE object contains a MONMSGSTRUCT structure that provides information about the message. See the definition of the MONMSGSTRUCT structure below.
MF_SENDMSGS	The system or an application sent a DDE message. The DDE object contains a MONMSGSTRUCT structure that provides information about the message. See the definition of the MONMSGSTRUCT structure below.

Returns   HDDEDATA: If the callback function processes this transaction, it should return zero.

MONCBSTRUCT Definition

```
typedef struct tagMONCBSTRUCT
{
    UINT    cb;
    DWORD   dwTime;
    HANDLE  hTask;
    DWORD   dwRet;
    UINT    wType;
    UINT    wFmt;
    HCONV   hConv;
    HSZ     hsz1;
    HSZ     hsz2;
    HDDEDATA hData;
    DWORD    dwData1;
    DWORD    dwData2;
    CONVCONTEXT cc;
    DWORD   cbData;
    DWORD   Data[8];
} MONCBSTRUCT;
```

cb	UINT: The size, in bytes, of the structure.
dwTime	DWORD: The Windows time that the transaction occurred. Windows time is the number of milliseconds that have elapsed since the system was booted.
hTask	HANDLE: The task (application instance) containing the DDE callback function that received the transaction.
dwRet	DWORD: The value returned by the DDE callback function that processed the transaction.
wType	UINT: The transaction type.
wFmt	UINT: The format of the data exchanged (if any) during the transaction.
hConv	HCONV: The conversation in which the transaction took place.
hsz1	HSZ: Identifies a string.
hsz2	HSZ: Identifies a string.
hData	HDDEDATA: Identifies the data exchanged (if any) during the transaction.
dwData1	DWORD: Additional data.
dwData2	DWORD: Additional data.
cc	CONVCONTEXT: Specifies a CONVCONTEXT structure containing language information used to share data in different languages. See the definition of the CONVCONTEXT structure under the DdeConnect() function.
cbData	DWORD: The size, in bytes, of the data being passed with the transaction. This value may be more than 32 bytes.
Data	DWORD[8]: Contains the first 32 bytes of data being passed with the transaction.

MONCONVSTRUCT Definition

```
typedef struct tagMONCONVSTRUCT
{
    UINT   cb;
    BOOL   fConnect;
    DWORD  dwTime;
    HANDLE hTask;
    HSZ    hszSvc;
    HSZ    hszTopic;
    HCONV  hConvClient;
    HCONV  hConvServer;
} MONCONVSTRUCT;
```

cb	UINT: The size, in bytes, of the structure.
fConnect	BOOL: TRUE if the conversation is currently established; otherwise, set to FALSE.
dwTime	DWORD: The Windows time at which the conversation was established or terminated. Windows time is the number of milliseconds that have elapsed since the system was booted.

hTask	HANDLE: The task (application instance) that is a partner in the conversation.
hszSvc	HSZ: The service name on which the conversation is established.
hszTopic	HSZ: The topic name on which the conversation is established.
hConvClient	HCONV: The client conversation.
hConvServer	HCONV: The server conversation.

MONERRSTRUCT Definition

```
typedef struct tagMONERRSTRUCT
{
    UINT    cb;
    UINT    wLastError;
    DWORD   dwTime;
    HANDLE  hTask;
} MONERRSTRUCT;
```

cb	UINT: The size, in bytes, of the structure.
wLastError	UINT: The current error.
dwTime	DWORD: The Windows time that the error occurred. Windows time is the number of milliseconds that have elapsed since the system was booted.
hTask	HANDLE: The task (application instance) that called the DDE function that caused the error.

MONHSZSTRUCT Definition

```
typedef struct tagMONHSZSTRUCT
{
    UINT    cb;
    BOOL    fsAction;
    DWORD   dwTime;
    HSZ     hsz;
    HANDLE  hTask;
    TCHAR   str[1];
} MONHSZSTRUCT;
```

cb	UINT: The size, in bytes, of the structure.
fsAction	BOOL: The action being performed on the string identified by the *hsz* member.

Table 10-10 MONHSZSTRUCT fsAction Values

Value	Meaning
MH_CLEANUP	An application is freeing its DDE resources, causing the system to delete string handles the application had created. This occurs when the application calls the DdeUninitialize() function.
MH_CREATE	An application is creating a string handle. This occurs when the application calls the DdeCreateStringHandle() function.

Value	Meaning
MH_DELETE	An application is deleting a string handle. This occurs when the application calls the DdeFreeStringHandle( ) function.
MH_KEEP	An application is increasing the usage count of a string handle. This occurs when the application calls the DdeKeepStringHandle( ) function.

dwTime	DWORD: The Windows time when the action specified by the fsAction member takes place. Windows time is the number of milliseconds that have elapsed since the system was booted.
hsz	HSZ: The string on which the action is occurring. Because string handles are local to the process, this member is a global atom.
hTask	HANDLE: The task (application instance) performing the action on the string handle.
str	TCHAR[1]: A pointer to the string identified by the *hsz* member.

MONLINKSTRUCT Definition

NOTE   The MONLINKSTRUCT structure contains HSZ and HCONV values. Because the string handles are local to the process, they contain global atoms. Also, the HCONV values do not contain the same values as would be seen by the applications engaging in the conversation. Instead, they contain unique global values that identify the conversation.

```
typedef struct tagMONLINKSTRUCT
{
    UINT   cb;
    DWORD  dwTime;
    HANDLE hTask;
    BOOL   fEstablished;
    BOOL   fNoData;
    HSZ    hszSvc;
    HSZ    hszTopic;
    HSZ    hszItem;
    UINT   wFmt;
    BOOL   fServer;
    HCONV  hConvServer;
    HCONV  hConvClient;
} MONLINKSTRUCT;
```

cb	UINT: The size, in bytes, of the structure.
dwTime	DWORD: The Windows time when the advise loop was started or ended. Windows time is the number of milliseconds that have elapsed since the system was booted.
hTask	HANDLE: The task (application instance) that is a partner in the advise loop.

fEstablished	BOOL: TRUE if an advise loop was established; otherwise, FALSE.
fNoData	BOOL: TRUE if the XTYPF_NODATA flag is set for the advise loop; otherwise, FALSE.
hszSvc	HSZ: The service name of the server in the advise loop.
hszTopic	HSZ: The topic name on which the advise loop is established.
hszItem	HSZ: The item name that is the subject of the advise loop.
wFmt	UINT: The format of the data exchanged (if any) during the advise loop.
fServer	BOOL: TRUE if the notification came from the server; otherwise, FALSE.
hConvServer	HCONV: The server conversation.
hConvClient	HCONV: The client conversation.

MONMSGSTRUCT Definition

```
typedef struct tagMONMSGSTRUCT
{
    UINT   cb;
    HWND   hwndTo;
    DWORD  dwTime;
    HANDLE hTask;
    UINT   wMsg;
    WPARAM wParam;
    LPARAM lParam;
    DDEML_MSG_HOOK_DATA dmhd;
} MONMSGSTRUCT;
```

cb	UINT: The size, in bytes, of the structure.
hwndTo	HWND: The window handle that receives the DDE message.
dwTime	DWORD: The Windows time at which the message was sent or posted. Windows time is the number of milliseconds that have elapsed since the system was booted.
hTask	HANDLE: The task (application instance) containing the window that receives the DDE message.
wMsg	UINT: The identifier of the DDE message.
wParam	WPARAM: The wParam parameter of the DDE message.
lParam	LPARAM: The lParam parameter of the DDE message.
dmhd	DDEML_MSG_HOOK_DATA: A DDEML_MSG_HOOK_DATA structure that contains additional information about the DDE message. See the definition of the DDEML_MSG_HOOK_DATA structure below.

DDEML_MSG_HOOK_DATA Definition

```
typedef struct tagDDEML_MSG_HOOK_DATA
{
    UINT  uiLo;
    UINT  uiHi;
    DWORD cbData;
    DWORD Data[8];
} DDEML_MSG_HOOK_DATA;
```

uiLo	UINT: The unpacked low-order word of the *lParam* parameter associated with the DDE message.
uiHi	UINT: The unpacked high-order word of the *lParam* parameter associated with the DDE message.
cbData	DWORD: The size, in bytes, of data being passed with the message. This value can be greater than 32.
Data	DWORD[8]: Contains the first 32 bytes of data being passed with the message.

XTYP_POKE

Description	A server callback function receives the XTYP_POKE transaction when a client specifies XTYP_POKE in the DdeClientTransaction() function. A client uses this transaction to send unsolicited data to the server.

Parameters

uFmt	UINT: The format of the data sent from the server.
hconv	HCONV: The handle of the conversation.
hsz1	HSZ: The topic name.
hsz2	HSZ: The item name.
hdata	HDDEDATA: The handle of the data that the client is sending to the server.
dwData1	DWORD: Not used.
dwData2	DWORD: Not used.
Returns	HDDEDATA: Return the DDE_FACK flag if the server processes this transaction, the DDE_FBUSY flag if it is too busy to process this transaction, or the DDE_FNOTPROCESSED flag if it rejects this transaction.

XTYP_REGISTER

Description	A callback function receives the XTYP_REGISTER transaction type whenever a DDEML server application uses the DdeNameService() function to register a service name, or whenever a non-DDEML application that supports the System topic is started.

Parameters

uFmt	UINT: Not used.
hconv	HCONV: Not used.
hsz1	HSZ: The base service name being registered.
hsz2	HSZ: The instance-specific service name being registered.
hdata	HDDEDATA: Not used.
dwData1	DWORD: Not used.
dwData2	DWORD: Not used.
Returns	HDDEDATA: Return value is ignored.

XTYP_REQUEST

Description	A server callback function receives the XTYP_REQUEST transaction when a client specifies XTYP_REQUEST in the DdeClientTransaction() function. A client uses this transaction to request data from a server.
	If responding to this transaction requires lengthy processing, the server can return the CBR_BLOCK return code to suspend future transactions on the current conversation and then process the transaction asynchronously. When the server has finished and the data is ready to pass to the client, the server can call the DdeEnableCallback() function to resume the conversation.

Parameters

uFmt	UINT: The format in which the server should submit data to the client.
hconv	HCONV: The handle of the conversation.
hsz1	HSZ: The topic name.
hsz2	HSZ: The item name.
hdata	HDDEDATA: Not used.
dwData1	DWORD: Not used.
dwData2	DWORD: Not used.
Returns	HDDEDATA: The server should use the DdeCreateDataHandle() function to create a data handle that identifies the data and then return the handle. The server should return NULL if it is unable to complete the transaction. If the server returns NULL, the client will receive a DDE_FNOT-PROCESSED flag.

XTYP_UNREGISTER

Description	A callback function receives the XTYP_UNREGISTER transaction whenever a DDEML server application uses the DdeNameService() function to unregister a service name, or whenever a non-DDEML application that supports the System topic is terminated.

Parameters

uFmt	UINT: Not used.
hconv	HCONV: Not used.
hsz1	HSZ: The base service name being unregistered.
hsz2	HSZ: The instance-specific service name being unregistered.
hdata	HDDEDATA: Not used.
dwData1	DWORD: Not used.
dwData2	DWORD: Not used.
Returns	HDDEDATA: Return value is ignored.

XTYP_WILDCONNECT

Description A server callback function receives the XTYP_WILDCONNECT transaction when a client specifies a NULL service name, a NULL topic name, or both in a call to the DdeConnect() or DdeConnectList() function. A client application can use this transaction to establish a conversation on each of a server's service-topic name pairs that match the specified service name or topic name.

Parameters

uFmt UINT: Not used.

hconv HCONV: Not used.

hsz1 HSZ: The topic name. If this parameter is NULL, the client is requesting a conversation on all topic names that the server supports.

hsz2 HSZ: The service name. If this parameter is NULL, the client is requesting a conversation on all service names that the server supports.

hdata HDDEDATA: Not used.

dwData1 DWORD: A pointer to a CONVCONTEXT structure that contains context information for the conversation. If the client is not a DDEML application, this parameter is set to zero. See the definition of the CONVCONTEXT structure under the DdeConnect() function.

dwData2 DWORD: Specifies whether the client is the same application instance as the server. If the parameter is 1, the client is the same instance. If the parameter is 0, the client is a different instance.

Returns HDDEDATA: The server should return a data handle that identifies an array of HSZPAIR structures which is defined below. The array should contain one structure for each service name and topic name pair that matches the pair requested by the client. The array must be terminated by a NULL string handle. The system sends the XTYP_CONNECT_CONFIRM transaction to the server to confirm each conversation and to pass the conversation handles to the server. The server will not receive these confirmations if it specified the CBF_SKIP_CONNECT_CONFIRMS flag in the DdeInitialize() function.

The server should return NULL to refuse the XTYP_WILDCONNECT transaction.

HSZPAIR Definition

```
typedef struct tagHSZPAIR
{
    HSZ hszSvc;
    HSZ hszTopic;
} HSZPAIR;
```

hszSvc HSZ: Identifies the service name.

hszTopic HSZ: Identifies the topic name.

XTYP_XACT_COMPLETE

Description	A client callback function receives the XTYP_XACT_COMPLETE transaction when an asynchronous transaction, initiated by a call to the DdeClientTransaction() function, has completed.
Parameters	
uFmt	UINT: The format of the data associated with the completed transaction (if applicable) or NULL if no data was exchanged during the transaction.
hconv	HCONV: The handle of the conversation.
hsz1	HSZ: The topic name involved in the completed transaction.
hsz2	HSZ: The item name involved in the completed transaction.
hdata	HDDEDATA: The handle of the data involved in the completed transaction, if applicable. If the transaction was successful but involved no data, this parameter is TRUE. This parameter is NULL if the transaction was unsuccessful.
dwData1	DWORD: The transaction identifier of the completed transaction.
dwData2	DWORD: The low-word contains any applicable DDE_ status flags. This parameter provides support for applications dependent on DDE_APPSTATUS bits. It is recommended that applications no longer use these flags because future versions of DDEML may not support them.
Returns	HDDEDATA: Return value is ignored.

DdeKeepStringHandle ■ Win32s ■ Windows 95 ■ Windows NT

Description	DdeKeepStringHandle() increments the usage count associated with the specified handle. This function enables an application to save a string handle passed to the application's callback function. Otherwise, a string handle passed to the callback function is deleted when the callback function returns. This function should also be used to keep a copy of a string handle referenced by the CONVINFO structure returned by the DdeQueryConvInfo() function.
Syntax	BOOL **DdeKeepStringHandle**(DWORD *idInst*, HSZ *hsz*)
Parameters	
idInst	DWORD: The application instance identifier returned from the DdeInitialize() function.
hsz	HSZ: The string handle to be saved.
Returns	BOOL: If successful, TRUE is returned; otherwise, FALSE is returned.
Include File	ddeml.h
See Also	DdeCreateStringHandle(), DdeFreeStringHandle(), DdeInitialize(), DdeQueryConvInfo(), DdeQueryString()

Example   This example (Listing 10-14) demonstrates using the
DdeKeepStringHandle() function to retain two string handles so that they
can be processed later by the application. When the application receives
the XTYP_REGISTER transaction, the two string handles passed to the
callback function are saved and the WM_USER message is sent to the
WndProc() function. Once the WndProc() function receives the
WM_USER message, it invalidates the window, which causes a
WM_PAINT to occur. The strings are accessed and displayed, as shown in
Figure 10-4, when the WM_PAINT message is received.

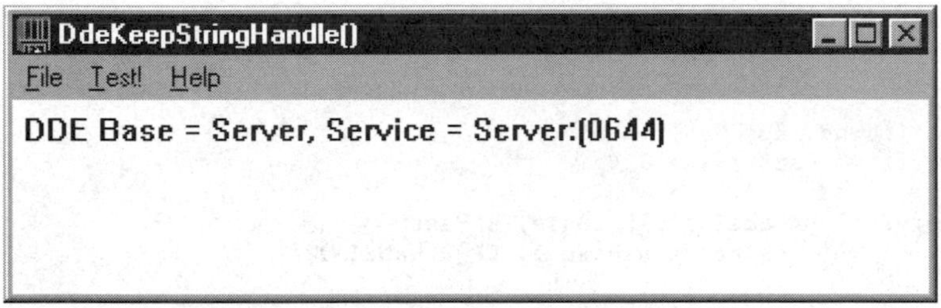

Figure 10-4 DdeKeepStringHandle() example

Listing 10-14 Using the DdeKeepStringHandle() function

```
HWND   hWindow    = NULL;
DWORD  ddeInst    = 0;
HSZ    hszBase    = NULL;
HSZ    hszService = NULL;

LRESULT CALLBACK WndProc( HWND hWnd, UINT uMsg, WPARAM wParam, LPARAM lParam )
{
static char        szBuf[128];
static char        szBase[40];
static char        szService[40];
static PAINTSTRUCT ps;

   switch( uMsg )
   {
   case WM_CREATE :
           // Initialize DDEML.
           //.................
           if ( DdeInitialize( &ddeInst, DdemlCallback,
               APPCMD_CLIENTONLY, 0 ) != DMLERR_NO_ERROR )
           {
               MessageBox( hWnd, "Could not initialize DDEML.",
                           NULL, MB_OK | MB_ICONSTOP );
               return( -1 );
           }
           hWindow = hWnd;
           break;
```

continued on next page

continued from previous page

```
        case WM_COMMAND :
                switch( LOWORD( wParam ) )
                {
                    case IDM_ABOUT :
                            DialogBox( hInst, "AboutBox", hWnd, (DLGPROC)About );
                            break;

                    case IDM_EXIT :
                            DestroyWindow( hWnd );
                            break;
                }
                break;

        case WM_USER :
                InvalidateRect( hWnd, NULL, TRUE );
                break;

        case WM_PAINT :
                BeginPaint( hWnd, &ps );
                if ( hszBase && hszService )
                {
                    DdeQueryString( ddeInst, hszBase, szBase,
                                sizeof( szBase ), CP_WINANSI );

                    DdeQueryString( ddeInst, hszService, szService,
                                sizeof( szService ), CP_WINANSI );

                    wsprintf( szBuf, "DDE Base = %s, Service = %s",
                                (LPTSTR)szBase, (LPTSTR)szService );

                    TextOut( ps.hdc, 5, 5, szBuf, strlen( szBuf ) );

                    // Free the string handles.
                    //........................
                    DdeFreeStringHandle( ddeInst, hszBase );
                    DdeFreeStringHandle( ddeInst, hszService );

                    hszBase    = NULL;
                    hszService = NULL;
                }
                EndPaint( hWnd, &ps );
                break;

        case WM_DESTROY :
                DdeUninitialize( ddeInst );
                PostQuitMessage(0);
                break;

        default :
                return( DefWindowProc( hWnd, uMsg, wParam, lParam ) );
    }

    return( 0L );
}
```

```
HDDEDATA CALLBACK DdemlCallback( UINT      uType,
                                 UINT      uFmt,
                                 HCONV     hconv,
                                 HSZ       hsz1,
                                 HSZ       hsz2,
                                 HDDEDATA  hdata,
                                 DWORD     dwData1,
                                 DWORD     dwData2 )
{
   switch( uType )
   {
           // A new service has been registered.
           //................................
      case XTYP_REGISTER :
           DdeKeepStringHandle( ddeInst, hsz1 );
           DdeKeepStringHandle( ddeInst, hsz2 );
           hszBase    = hsz1;
           hszService = hsz2;
           SendMessage( hWindow, WM_USER, 0, 0 );
           break;
   }

   return( NULL );
}
```

DDENAMESERVICE   ■ Win32s ■ Windows 95 ■ Windows NT

Description	DdeNameService() registers or unregisters the service names a DDE server supports. This function causes the system to send XTYP_REGISTER or XTYP_UNREGISTER transactions to other running DDEML client applications.
	A DDE server application should use this function to register each service name that it supports and to unregister names it previously registered but no longer supports. Before terminating, a server should also use this function to unregister its service names.
Syntax	HDDEDATA **DdeNameService**(DWORD *idInst*, HSZ *hsz1*, HSZ *hsz2*, UINT *afCmd*)
Parameters	
idInst	DWORD: The application instance identifier returned from the DdeInitialize() function.
hsz1	HSZ: The string that specifies the base service name (without instance-specific information) the server is registering or unregistering. Set this parameter to NULL to unregister all of the service names.
hsz2	HSZ: Reserved; should be set to NULL.
afCmd	UINT: The service name flags. This parameter can be one of the values listed in Table 10-11.

Table 10-11 DdeNameService() *afCmd* values

Value	Meaning
DNS_FILTEROFF	Turns off service name initiation filtering. If this flag is specified, the server receives an XTYP_CONNECT transaction whenever another DDE application calls the DdeConnect() function, regardless of the service name.
DNS_FILTERON	Turns on service name initiation filtering. The filter prevents a server from receiving XTYP_CONNECT transactions for service names it has not registered. This filter is on by default. If a server application does not register any service names and this filter is set, the application cannot receive XTYP_WILDCONNECT transactions.
DNS_REGISTER	Registers the service name.
DNS_UNREGISTER	Unregisters the service name. If the *hsz1* parameter is 0L, all service names registered by the server are unregistered.

Returns   HDDEDATA: If successful, a nonzero value is returned; otherwise, 0L is returned. This value is not a true HDDEDATA value, it is a Boolean indicator of a successful operation. To allow for future expansion, the function is typed as HDDEDATA.

Use the DdeGetLastError() function to retrieve the error value, which may be one of the following:

DMLERR_DLL_NOT_INITIALIZED
DMLERR_DLL_USAGE
DMLERR_INVALIDPARAMETER
DMLERR_NO_ERROR

Include File   ddeml.h

See Also   DdeConnect(), DdeConnectList(), DdeInitialize()

Example   This example (Listing 10-15) shows how a DDEML server initializes and registers its service name with the DdeNameService() function. When the server is about to terminate, the service name is unregistered again using the DdeNameService() function.

Listing 10-15 Using the DdeNameService() function

```
DWORD ddeInst    = 0;
HSZ   hszService = NULL;
HSZ   hszTopic1  = NULL;
HSZ   hszTopic2  = NULL;

LRESULT CALLBACK WndProc( HWND hWnd, UINT uMsg, WPARAM wParam, LPARAM lParam )
{
   switch( uMsg )
   {
     case WM_CREATE :
            // Initialize DDEML.
```

```
            //..................
            if ( DdeInitialize( &ddeInst, DdemlCallback,
                APPCLASS_STANDARD, 0 ) != DMLERR_NO_ERROR )
            {
                MessageBox( hWnd, "Could not initialize DDEML.",
                            NULL, MB_OK | MB_ICONSTOP );
                return( -1 );
            }

            // Allocate strings.
            //.................
            hszService = DdeCreateStringHandle( ddeInst,"Server",CP_WINANSI );
            hszTopic1  = DdeCreateStringHandle( ddeInst,"Data",CP_WINANSI );
            hszTopic2  = DdeCreateStringHandle( ddeInst,"Msg",CP_WINANSI );

            // Let all clients know about the server.
            //........................................
            DdeNameService( ddeInst, hszService, 0L, DNS_REGISTER );
            break;
        .
        .
        .
case WM_DESTROY :
            // Unregister the service name.
            //............................
            DdeNameService( ddeInst, hszService, 0L, DNS_UNREGISTER );

            DdeFreeStringHandle( ddeInst, hszService );
            DdeFreeStringHandle( ddeInst, hszTopic1 );
            DdeFreeStringHandle( ddeInst, hszTopic2 );

            DdeUninitialize( ddeInst );
            PostQuitMessage(0);
            break;

    default :
            return( DefWindowProc( hWnd, uMsg, wParam, lParam ) );
    }

    return( 0L );
}
```

DdePostAdvise
■ Win32s ■ Windows 95 ■ Windows NT

Description	DdePostAdvise() causes the system to send an XTYP_ADVREQ transaction to the calling (server) application's DDE callback function for each client with an active advise loop on a topic and an item. Server applications should use this function whenever the data associated with the topic name or item name pair changes.
Syntax	BOOL **DdePostAdvise**(DWORD *idInst*, HSZ *hszTopic*, HSZ *hszItem*)
Parameters	
idInst	DWORD: The application instance identifier returned from the DdeInitialize() function.

hszTopic	HSZ: A handle to a string that specifies the topic name. Set this parameter to NULL to send notifications for all topics with active advise loops.
hszItem	HSZ: A handle to a string that specifies the item name. Set this parameter to NULL to send notifications for all items with active advise loops.
Returns	BOOL: If successful, TRUE is returned; otherwise, FALSE is returned. Use the DdeGetLastError() function to retrieve the error value, which may be one of the following:
	DMLERR_DLL_NOT_INITIALIZED
	DMLERR_DLL_USAGE
	DMLERR_NO_ERROR
Include File	ddeml.h
See Also	DdeInitialize()
Example	See the example for the DdeEnableCallback() function.

DdeQueryConvInfo ■ Win32s ■ Windows 95 ■ Windows NT

Description	DdeQueryConvInfo() retrieves information about a dynamic data exchange (DDE) transaction and about the conversation in which the transaction takes place. An application should not free string handles referenced by the CONVINFO structure returned. If the application must use a string in the structure, use the DdeKeepStringHandle() function.
Syntax	UINT **DdeQueryConvInfo**(HCONV *hConv*, DWORD *idTransaction*, PCONVINFO *pConvInfo*)
Parameters	
hConv	HCONV: The handle of the conversation.
idTransaction	DWORD: The transaction. For asynchronous transactions, this parameter should be a transaction identifier returned by the DdeClientTransaction() function. For synchronous transactions, this parameter should be QID_SYNC.
pConvInfo	PCONVINFO: A pointer to a CONVINFO structure that receives information about the transaction and conversation. The *cb* member of the CONVINFO structure must specify the length of the buffer allocated for the structure. See the definition of the CONVINFO structure below.
Returns	UINT: If successful, the number of bytes copied to the buffer pointed to by the *pConvInfo* parameter. If the function fails, FALSE is returned. Use the DdeGetLastError() function to retrieve the error value, which may be one of the following:
	DMLERR_DLL_NOT_INITIALIZED
	DMLERR_NO_CONV_ESTABLISHED
	DMLERR_NO_ERROR
	DMLERR_UNFOUND_QUEUE_ID
Include File	ddeml.h

See Also   DdeClientTransaction(), DdeConnect(), DdeConnectList(), DdeKeepStringHandle(), DdeQueryNextServer()

CONVINFO Definition

```
typedef struct tagCONVINFO
{
    DWORD       cb;
    DWORD       hUser;
    HCONV       hConvPartner;
    HSZ         hszSvcPartner;
    HSZ         hszServiceReq;
    HSZ         hszTopic;
    HSZ         hszItem;
    UINT        wFmt;
    UINT        wType;
    UINT        wStatus;
    UINT        wConvst;
    UINT        wLastError;
    HCONVLIST   hConvList;
    CONVCONTEXT ConvCtxt;
    HWND        hwnd;
    HWND        hwndPartner;
} CONVINFO;
```

Members

cb   DWORD: The size, in bytes, of the structure.

hUser   DWORD: Application-defined data.

hConvPartner   HCONV: The conversation handle of the partner application in the DDE conversation. This member is zero if the partner has not registered itself (using the DdeInitialize() function) to make DDEML function calls. An application should not use this member with any DDEML function except DdeQueryConvInfo().

hszSvcPartner   HSZ: The service name of the partner application.

hszServiceReq   HSZ: The service name of the server application that was requested for connection.

hszTopic   HSZ: The name of the requested topic.

hszItem   HSZ: The name of the requested item. This member is transaction specific.

wFmt   UINT: The format of the data being exchanged. This member is transaction specific.

wType   UINT: The type of the current transaction. This member is transaction specific; it can be one of the values listed in Table 10-12.

Table 10-12 CONVINFO *wType* values

Value	Meaning
XTYP_ADVDATA	Informs a client that advise data from a server has arrived.
XTYP_ADVREQ	Requests a server to send updated data to the client during an advise loop.
XTYP_ADVSTART	Requests a server to begin an advise loop with a client.

continued on next page

continued from previous page

Value	Meaning
XTYP_ADVSTOP	Notifies a server that an advise loop is stopping.
XTYP_CONNECT	Requests a server to establish a conversation with a client.
XTYP_CONNECT_CONFIRM	Notifies a server that a conversation with a client has been established.
XTYP_DISCONNECT	Notifies a server that a conversation has terminated.
XTYP_EXECUTE	Requests a server to execute a command sent by a client.
XTYP_MONITOR	Notifies an application registered as APPCMD_MONITOR that DDE data is being transmitted.
XTYP_POKE	Requests a server to accept unsolicited data from a client.
XTYP_REGISTER	Notifies other DDEML applications that a server has registered a service name.
XTYP_REQUEST	Requests a server to send data to a client.
XTYP_UNREGISTER	Notifies other DDEML applications that a server has unregistered a service name.
XTYP_WILDCONNECT	Requests a server to establish multiple conversations with the same client.
XTYP_XACT_COMPLETE	Notifies a client that an asynchronous data transaction has been completed.

wStatus   UINT: The status of the current conversation. This member can be a combination of the values listed in Table 10-13 combined with the binary OR (|) operator.

Table 10-13 CONVINFO *wStatus* values

Value	Meaning
ST_ADVISE	One or more links are in progress.
ST_BLOCKED	The conversation is blocked.
ST_BLOCKNEXT	The conversation will block after calling the next callback.
ST_CLIENT	The conversation handle passed to the DdeQueryConvInfo() function is a client-side handle.
ST_CONNECTED	The conversation is connected.
ST_INLIST	The conversation is a member of a conversation list.
ST_ISLOCAL	Both sides of the conversation are using the DDEML.
ST_ISSELF	Both sides of the conversation are using the same instance of the DDEML.
ST_TERMINATED	The conversation has been terminated by the partner.

wConvst   UINT: The conversation state. This member can be one of the values in Table 10-14.

Table 10-14 CONVINFO *wConvst* values

Value	Meaning
XST_ADVACKRCVD	The advise transaction has just been completed.
XST_ADVDATAACKRCVD	The advise data transaction has just been completed.

Value	Meaning
XST_ADVDATASENT	Advise data has been sent and is awaiting an acknowledgment.
XST_ADVSENT	An advise transaction is awaiting an acknowledgment.
XST_CONNECTED	The conversation has no active transactions.
XST_DATARCVD	The requested data has just been received.
XST_EXECACKRCVD	An execute transaction has just been completed.
XST_EXECSENT	An execute transaction is awaiting an acknowledgment.
XST_INCOMPLETE	The last transaction failed.
XST_INIT1	Mid-initiate state 1.
XST_INIT2	Mid-initiate state 2.
XST_NULL	Preinitiate state.
XST_POKEACKRCVD	A poke transaction has just been completed.
XST_POKESENT	A poke transaction is awaiting an acknowledgment.
XST_REQSENT	A request transaction is awaiting an acknowledgment.
XST_UNADVACKRCVD	An unadvise transaction has just been completed.
XST_UNADVSENT	An unadvise transaction is awaiting an acknowledgment.

wLastError	UINT: The error value associated with the last transaction.
hConvList	HCONVLIST: The conversation list if the handle of the current conversation is in a conversation list. This member is NULL if the conversation is not in a conversation list.
ConvCtxt	CONVCONTEXT: The conversation context. See the definition of the CONVCONTEXT structure under the DdeConnect() function.
hwnd	HWND: The handle of the window of the calling application involved in the conversation.
hwndPartner	HWND: The handle of the window of the partner application involved in the current conversation.
Example	See the example for the DdeConnectList() function.

DdeQueryNextServer ■ Win32s ■ Windows 95 ■ Windows NT

Description	DdeQueryNextServer() retrieves the next conversation handle in a conversation list.
Syntax	HCONV **DdeQueryNextServer**(HCONVLIST *hConvList*, HCONV *hConvPrev*)
Parameters	
hConvList	HCONVLIST: The handle of the conversation list.
hConvPrev	HCONV: The handle of the conversation previously returned by this function. Set this parameter to NULL to return the first conversation handle in the list.

Returns	HCONV: If successful, the next conversation handle in the list is returned; otherwise, NULL is returned.
Include File	ddeml.h
See Also	DdeConnectList(), DdeDisconnectList()
Example	See the example for the DdeConnectList() function.

DdeQueryString   ■ Win32s ■ Windows 95 ■ Windows NT

Description	DdeQueryString() copies text associated with a string handle into a buffer.
Syntax	DWORD **DdeQueryString**(DWORD *idInst*, HSZ *hsz*, LPTSTR *psz*, DWORD *cchMax*, int *iCodePage*)
Parameters	
idInst	DWORD: The application instance identifier returned from the DdeInitialize() function.
hsz	HSZ: The handle of the string to copy.
psz	LPTSTR: A pointer to a buffer that receives the string. Set this parameter to NULL to return the length of the string.
cchMax	DWORD: The length, in characters, of the buffer pointed to by the *psz* parameter. If the string is longer than (*cchMax* -1), it will be truncated. If the *psz* parameter is set to NULL, this parameter is ignored.
iCodePage	int: The code page used to render the string. This value should be either CP_WINANSI or CP_WINUNICODE.
Returns	DWORD: If the function is successful and the *psz* parameter is not NULL, the number of bytes copied to the buffer is returned; otherwise, the length of the string is returned. If an error occurs, 0L is returned.
Include File	ddeml.h
See Also	DdeCmpStringHandles(), DdeCreateStringHandle(), DdeFreeStringHandle(), DdeInitialize()
Example	See the example for the DdeConnectList() function.

DdeReconnect   ■ Win32s ■ Windows 95 ■ Windows NT

Description	DdeReconnect() allows a client DDEML application to attempt to reestablish a conversation with a service that has terminated a conversation with the client. When the conversation is reestablished, the DDEML attempts to reestablish any preexisting advise loops.
Syntax	HCONV **DdeReconnect**(HCONV *hConv*)
Parameters	
hConv	HCONV: The handle of the conversation to be reestablished. A client must have retrieved the conversation handle with the DdeConnect() function or from an XTYP_DISCONNECT transaction.

Returns	HCONV: If successful, the reestablished conversation handle is returned; otherwise, 0L is returned. Use the DdeGetLastError() function to retrieve the error value, which may be one of the following:

> DMLERR_DLL_NOT_INITIALIZED
> DMLERR_INVALIDPARAMETER
> DMLERR_NO_CONV_ESTABLISHED
> DMLERR_NO_ERROR

Include File	ddeml.h
See Also	DdeConnect(), DdeDisconnect()
Example	This example (Listing 10-16) shows the entry that could be added to a DDEML client's callback function to attempt a reconnect when a server disconnects. If the client does not want to allow disconnects, the DdeReconnect() function is called with the current conversation handle to attempt a reconnect. If the reconnect is successful, a new conversation handle is returned.

Listing 10-16 Using the DdeReconnect() function

```
HDDEDATA CALLBACK DdemlCallback( UINT      uType,
                                 UINT      uFmt,
                                 HCONV     hconv,
                                 HSZ       hsz1,
                                 HSZ       hsz2,
                                 HDDEDATA  hdata,
                                 DWORD     dwData1,
                                 DWORD     dwData2 )
{
    switch( uType )
    {
        case XTYP_DISCONNECT :
                if ( !bAllowDisconnect )
                {
                    if ( hThisConv = DdeReconnect( hConv ) )
                        // Reconnected...
                    else
                        // Could not reconnect...
                }
                break;
            .
            .
            .
```

DdeSetUserHandle

■ Win32s ■ Windows 95 ■ Windows NT

Description	DdeSetUserHandle() associates an application-defined 32-bit value with a conversation handle or a transaction identifier. This is useful for simplifying the processing of asynchronous transactions. Use the DdeQueryConvInfo() function to retrieve this value from a conversation.
Syntax	BOOL **DdeSetUserHandle**(HCONV *hConv*, DWORD *id*, DWORD *hUser*)

Parameters

hConv	HCONV: The handle of the conversation.
id	DWORD: The transaction identifier to associate with the value specified by the *hUser* parameter. An application should set this parameter to QID_SYNC to associate *hUser* with the conversation identified by the *hConv* parameter.
hUser	DWORD: The value to associate with the conversation handle.
Returns	BOOL: If successful, TRUE is returned; otherwise, FALSE is returned. Use the DdeGetLastError() function to retrieve the error value, which may be one of the following:

        DMLERR_DLL_NOT_INITIALIZED
        DMLERR_INVALIDPARAMETER
        DMLERR_NO_ERROR
        DMLERR_UNFOUND_QUEUE_ID

Include File	ddeml.h
See Also	DdeQueryConvInfo()
Example	See the example for the DdeEnableCallback() function.

DdeUnaccessData   ■ Win32s   ■ Windows 95   ■ Windows NT

Description	DdeUnaccessData() unaccesses a dynamic data exchange (DDE) object. An application must call this function after it has finished accessing the object.
Syntax	BOOL **DdeUnaccessData**(HDDEDATA *hData*)
Parameters	
hData	HDDEDATA: The handle of the DDE object.
Returns	BOOL: If successful, TRUE is returned; otherwise, FALSE is returned. Use the DdeGetLastError() function to retrieve the error value, which may be one of the following:

        DMLERR_DLL_NOT_INITIALIZED
        DMLERR_INVALIDPARAMETER
        DMLERR_NO_ERROR

Include File	ddeml.h
See Also	DdeAccessData(), DdeAddData(), DdeCreateDataHandle(), DdeFreeDataHandle()
Example	See the example for the DdeAccessData() function.

DdeUninitialize   ■ Win32s   ■ Windows 95   ■ Windows NT

Description	DdeUninitialize() frees all DDEML resources associated with the calling application. This function will terminate all open conversations for the application.

Syntax	BOOL **DdeUninitialize**(DWORD *idInst*)
Parameters	
idInst	DWORD: The application instance identifier returned from the DdeInitialize() function.
Returns	BOOL: If successful, TRUE is returned; otherwise, FALSE is returned.
Include File	ddeml.h
See Also	DdeDisconnect(), DdeDisconnectList(), DdeInitialize()
Example	This example (Listing 10-17) demonstrates how to use the DdeUninitialize() and DdeFreeStringHandle() functions as a DDEML application exits to free memory associated with it.

Listing 10-17 Using the DdeUninitialize() and DdeFreeStringHandle() functions

```
DWORD ddeInst     = 0;
HSZ   hszService = NULL;
HSZ   hszTopic1  = NULL;
HSZ   hszTopic2  = NULL;

LRESULT CALLBACK WndProc( HWND hWnd, UINT uMsg, WPARAM wParam, LPARAM lParam )
{
   switch( uMsg )
   {
      case WM_CREATE :
              // Initialize DDEML.
              //...................
              if ( DdeInitialize( &ddeInst, DdemlCallback,
                  APPCLASS_STANDARD, 0 ) != DMLERR_NO_ERROR )
              {
                 MessageBox( hWnd, "Could not initialize DDEML.",
                             NULL, MB_OK | MB_ICONSTOP );
                 return( -1 );
              }

              // Allocate strings.
              //...................
              hszService = DdeCreateStringHandle( ddeInst,"Server",CP_WINANSI );
              hszTopic1  = DdeCreateStringHandle( ddeInst,"Long",CP_WINANSI );
              hszTopic2  = DdeCreateStringHandle( ddeInst,"Msg",CP_WINANSI );

              // Register service name.
              //.......................
              DdeNameService( ddeInst, hszService, OL, DNS_REGISTER );
              break;

              .
              .
              .

      case WM_DESTROY :
              // Free any strings that have been allocated.
              //...........................................
              DdeFreeStringHandle( ddeInst, hszService );
              DdeFreeStringHandle( ddeInst, hszTopic1 );
```

continued on next page

continued from previous page

```
            DdeFreeStringHandle( ddeInst, hszTopic2 );

            // Uninitialize DDEML.
            //....................
            DdeUninitialize( ddeInst );

            PostQuitMessage(0);
            break;

    default :
            return( DefWindowProc( hWnd, uMsg, wParam, lParam ) );
    }

    return( 0L );
}
```

MESSAGES AND MACROS

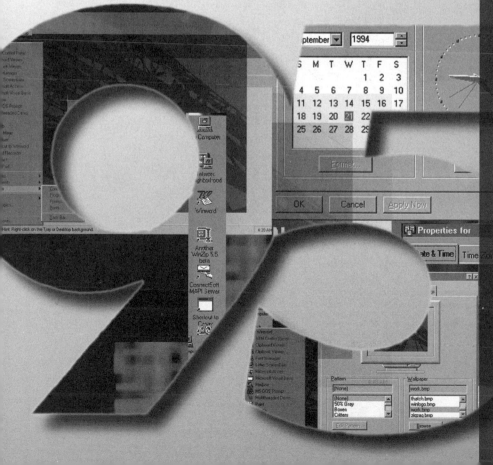

11

MESSAGES

MESSAGES

Windows is an event-oriented operating system. Events in Windows are identified by messages that an application receives when something relevant to the application occurs. An application receives and sends thousands of messages during execution. Every action the user takes triggers a message of some sort. For example, when the mouse is moved, the WM_MOUSEMOVE message is sent to the application's window that the mouse cursor is currently over. Other messages are generated by the system to send data or retrieve data from other applications or other parts of the same application.

This chapter provides a detailed description of the messages that a Windows application can expect to receive and send during execution. Some of the messages are very specific to an API, such as the multimedia messages. Others are general to all Windows applications and can be sent or received by any application.

Because of space limitations, this chapter does not include examples for each message; however, most of these messages are used in the examples provided in other chapters of this book and the other two books, *Windows 95 WIN 32 Programming API Bible*, and *Windows 95 Multimedia & ODBC API Bible*.

Message Summary

Table 11-1 summarizes the different message types that exist in the Win32 API and other supporting APIs, such as multimedia and the common controls. Message descriptions, in alphabetical order, follow immediately after the table.

Table 11-1 Message type summary

Message Prefix	Meaning
ACM_	Animation control message
ACN_	Animation control notification message
BM_	Button message
BN_	Button notification message

continued on next page

continued from previous page

Message Prefix	Meaning
CB_	Combo box message
CBN_	Combo box notification message
CDM_	Common dialog box message
CDN_	Common dialog box notification message
CPL_	Control Panel message
DBT_	Device message
DL_	Drag list message
DM_	Dialog box message
EM_	Edit control message
EN_	Edit control notification message
HDM_	Header control message
HDN_	Header control notification message
HKM_	Hot-key control message
ICM_	Video compression message
LB_	List box message
LBN_	List box notification message
LVM_	List view control message
LVN_	List view control notification message
MCIWNDM_	MCI window message
MIM_	MIDI input device callback message
MM_	Multimedia message
MMIOM_	Multimedia I/O message
MOM_	MIDI output device callback message
NM_	Notification message
PBM_	Progress bar message
PSM_	Property sheet message
PSN_	Property sheet notification message
SB_	Status window message
SBM_	Scroll bar message
STM_	Static control message
STN_	Static control notification message
TB_	Toolbar message
TBM_	Trackbar message
TBN_	Toolbar notification message
TCM_	Tab control message
TCN_	Tab control notification message
TTM_	Tooltip control message
TTN_	Tooltip control notification message

Message Prefix	Meaning
TVM_	Tree view message
TVN_	Tree view notification message
UDM_	Up-down control messages
UDN_	Up-down control notification message
WIM_	Waveform audio input message
WM_	All other Windows messages
WOM_	Waveform audio output message

ACM_OPEN
■ Win32s ■ Windows 95 ■ Windows NT

Description   ACM_OPEN is a message that opens an AVI clip and displays its first frame in an animation control. For more information, refer to the Animate_Open macro in Chapter 9, Miscellaneous Controls.

ACM_PLAY
■ Win32s ■ Windows 95 ■ Windows NT

Description   ACM_PLAY is a message that plays an open AVI clip. For more information, refer to the Animate_Play macro in Chapter 9, Miscellaneous Controls.

ACM_STOP
■ Win32s ■ Windows 95 ■ Windows NT

Description   ACM_STOP is a message that stops the playing of an AVI clip in an animation control. For more information, refer to the Animate_Stop macro in Chapter 9, Miscellaneous Controls.

ACN_START
■ Win32s ■ Windows 95 ■ Windows NT

Description   ACN_START is a notification message that notifies the parent window of an animation control that the associated AVI clip has started playing. For more information, refer to the ACN_START notification message in Chapter 9, Miscellaneous Controls.

ACN_STOP
■ Win32s ■ Windows 95 ■ Windows NT

Description   ACN_STOP is a notification message that notifies the parent window of an animation control that the associated AVI clip has stopped playing. For more information, refer to the ACN_STOP notification message in Chapter 9, Miscellaneous Controls.

BM_CLICK

Win32s ■ Windows 95 ■ Windows NT

Description	BM_CLICK is a message that simulates the action of a user clicking a button. When the message is sent, the button receives a WM_LBUTTONDOWN and a WM_LBUTTONUP message, and the parent window of the button receives a BN_CLICKED notification message.
Parameters	This message does not use *wParam* or *lParam*; therefore, both must be set to zero.
Include File	winuser.h
Related Messages	BN_CLICKED, WM_LBUTTONDOWN, WM_LBUTTONUP

BM_GETCHECK

■ Win32s ■ Windows 95 ■ Windows NT

Description	BM_GETCHECK is a message that retrieves the check state of a radio button or check box. Figure 11-1 shows the Attributes check boxes of the properties dialog for the Windows Explorer.
Parameters	This message does not use *wParam* or *lParam*; therefore, both must be set to zero.
Returns	int: A value in Table 11-2 is returned if the button is created with the BS_AUTOCHECKBOX, BS_AUTORADIOBUTTON, BS_AUTO3STATE, BS_CHECKBOX, BS_RADIOBUTTON, or BS_3STATE style; otherwise, if the button has any other style, the return value is zero.

Table 11-2 BM_GETCHECK button values

Value	Meaning
0	Button is unchecked.
1	Button is checked.
2	Button is grayed, indicating an indeterminate state (this value applies only if the button has either the BS_3STATE or BS_AUTO3STATE style).
BST_CHECKED	In Windows 95 only the button is checked.
BST_INDETERMINATE	In Windows 95 only the button is grayed, indicating an indeterminate state (this value applies only if the button has the BS_3STATE or BS_AUTO3STATE style).
BST_UNCHECKED	In Windows 95 only the button is unchecked.

Include File	winuser.h
Related Messages	BM_GETSTATE, BM_SETCHECK

Figure 11-1 Check Boxes

BM_GETIMAGE

Win32s ■ Windows 95   Windows NT

Description	BM_GETIMAGE is a message that retrieves the handle of the icon or bitmap image associated with the button.
Parameters	This message does not use *wParam* or *lParam*; therefore, both must be set to zero.
Returns	HBITMAP: If an image exists for the button, the handle is returned; otherwise, NULL is returned.
Include File	winuser.h
Related Messages	BM_SETIMAGE

BM_GETSTATE

■ Win32s ■ Windows 95 ■ Windows NT

Description	BM_GETSTATE is a message that determines the state of a button or check box.
Parameters	This message does not use *wParam* or *lParam*; therefore, both must be set to zero.
Returns	int: The current state of the button or check box is returned. This can be a combination of one or more flags listed in Table 11-3. Use the binary AND (&) operator to determine which flags are set.

Table 11-3 BM_GETSTATE values

Value	Meaning
BST_CHECKED	Indicates that the button is checked.
BST_FOCUS	Indicates that the button has the keyboard focus.
BST_INDETERMINATE	Indicates that the button is grayed because the state of the button is indeterminate. This value applies only if the button has the BS_3STATE or BS_AUTO3STATE style.
BST_PUSHED	Indicates that the button is highlighted as if the user had pushed it.
BST_UNCHECKED	Indicates that the button is unchecked.

Include File	winuser.h
Related Messages	BM_GETCHECK, BM_SETSTATE

BM_SETCHECK

■ Win32s ■ Windows 95 ■ Windows NT

Description	BM_SETCHECK is a message that sets the check state of a radio button or check box.
Parameters	
wParam	WPARAM: One of the values in Table 11-2 indicating the check state of the radio button or check box.

lParam	LPARAM: Set to zero.
Returns	int: Zero is always returned.
Include File	winuser.h
Related Messages	BM_GETCHECK, BM_GETSTATE, BM_SETSTATE

BM_SETIMAGE   Win32s ■ Windows 95   Windows NT

Description	BM_SETIMAGE is a message that associates a new icon or bitmap image with the button.
Parameters	
wParam	WPARAM: Set to zero.
lParam	HANDLE: The image to associate with the button.
Returns	HBITMAP: If an image was associated with the button, the handle of the image is returned; otherwise, NULL is returned.
Include File	winuser.h
Related Messages	BM_GETIMAGE

BM_SETSTATE   ■ Win32s ■ Windows 95 ■ Windows NT

Description	BM_SETSTATE is a message that changes the highlight state of a button. Highlighting does not affect the check state of the button. The button is automatically highlighted when the user positions the cursor over the button and presses and holds the left mouse button. When the mouse button is released, the highlighting is removed.
Parameters	
wParam	WPARAM: TRUE highlights the button, and FALSE removes any highlighting.
lParam	LPARAM: Set to zero.
Returns	int: Zero is always returned.
Include File	winuser.h
Related Messages	BM_GETSTATE, BM_SETCHECK

BM_SETSTYLE   ■ Win32s ■ Windows 95 ■ Windows NT

Description	BM_SETSTYLE is a message that changes the style of a button.
Parameters	
wParam	WPARAM: One of the button styles in Table 11-4.

Table 11-4 BM_SETSTYLE *wParam* values

Value	Meaning
BS_3STATE	Creates a button with the characteristics of a check box, except that the box can also be grayed as well as checked or unchecked. Use the grayed state to show that the state of the check box is not determined.
BS_AUTO3STATE	Creates a button with the characteristics of a three-state check box, except that the box changes its state when the user selects it. The state cycles through checked, grayed, and unchecked.
BS_AUTOCHECKBOX	Creates a button with the characteristics of a check box, except that the check state automatically toggles between checked and unchecked each time the user selects the check box.
BS_AUTORADIOBUTTON	Creates a button with the characteristics of a radio button, except that when the user selects it, Windows automatically sets the button's check state to checked and automatically sets the check state for all other buttons in the same group to unchecked.
BS_BITMAP	In Windows 95, specifies that the button displays a bitmap.
BS_BOTTOM	In Windows 95, places text at the bottom of the button rectangle.
BS_CENTER	In Windows 95, centers text horizontally in the button rectangle.
BS_CHECKBOX	Creates a small, empty check box with text. By default, the text displays to the right of the check box. To display the text to the left of the check box, combine this flag with the BS_LEFTTEXT style (or in Windows 95, with the equivalent BS_RIGHTBUTTON style).
BS_DEFPUSHBUTTON	Creates a push button that behaves like a BS_PUSHBUTTON style button, but also has a heavy black border. If the button is in a dialog box, the user can select the button by pressing the (ENTER) key, even when the button does not have the input focus. This style is useful for enabling the user to quickly select the most likely option.
BS_GROUPBOX	Creates a rectangle in which other controls can be grouped. Any text associated with this style is displayed in the rectangle's upper left corner.
BS_ICON	In Windows 95, specifies that the button displays an icon.
BS_LEFT	In Windows 95, left-justifies the text in the button rectangle. However, if the button is a check box or radio button that does not have the BS_RIGHTBUTTON style, the text is left-justified on the right side of the check box or radio button.
BS_LEFTTEXT	Places text on the left side of the radio button or check box when combined with a radio button or check box style. Same as the Windows 95 BS_RIGHTBUTTON style.
BS_MULTILINE	In Windows 95, wraps the button text to multiple lines if the text string is too long to fit on a single line in the button rectangle.
BS_NOTIFY	In Windows 95, sends the parent window notification messages in addition to BN_CLICKED and BN_DBLCLK, which a button sends regardless of whether it has this style.
BS_OWNERDRAW	Creates an owner-drawn button. The owner window receives a WM_MEASUREITEM message when the button is created and a WM_DRAWITEM message when a visual aspect of the button has changed. Do not combine the BS_OWNERDRAW style with any other button styles.
BS_PUSHBUTTON	Creates a push button that posts a WM_COMMAND message to the owner window when the user selects the button.

continued on next page

continued from previous page

Value	Meaning
BS_PUSHLIKE	In Windows 95, makes a button (such as a check box, three-state check box, or radio button) look and act like a push button. The button looks raised when it isn't pushed or checked, and sunken when it is pushed or checked.
BS_RADIOBUTTON	Creates a small circle with text. By default, the text is displayed to the right of the circle. To display the text to the left of the circle, combine this flag with the BS_LEFTTEXT style (or in Windows 95, with the equivalent BS_RIGHTBUTTON style). Use radio buttons for groups of related but mutually exclusive choices.
BS_RIGHT	In Windows 95, right-justifies text in the button rectangle. However, if the button is a check box or radio button that does not have the BS_RIGHTBUTTON style, the text is right-justified on the right side of the check box or radio button.
BS_RIGHTBUTTON	In Windows 95, positions a radio button's circle or a check box's square on the right side of the button rectangle. Same as the BS_LEFTTEXT style.
BS_TEXT	In Windows 95, specifies that the button displays text.
BS_TOP	In Windows 95, places text at the top of the button rectangle.
BS_VCENTER	In Windows 95, places text in the middle (vertically) of the button rectangle.

LOWORD(lParam)	WORD: TRUE redraws the button; a value of FALSE does not redraw the button.
HIWORD(lParam)	WORD: Set to zero.
Returns	int: Zero is always returned.
Include File	winuser.h
Related Messages	WM_COMMAND, WM_DRAWITEM, WM_MEASUREITEM

BN_CLICKED ■ Win32s ■ Windows 95 ■ Windows NT

Description	BN_CLICKED is a notification message that notifies the parent window that the user clicked a mouse button. The parent window receives this notification message through the WM_COMMAND message. This message is not sent by a disabled button.
Parameters	
LOWORD(wParam)	int: The button identifier.
lParam	HWND: The window handle of the button control.
Include File	winuser.h
Related Messages	WM_COMMAND

BN_KILLFOCUS Win32s ■ Windows 95 Windows NT

Description	BN_KILLFOCUS is a notification message that is sent to the parent window when a button loses the keyboard focus. The button must have the

BS_NOTIFY style to send this notification message. The parent window receives this notification message through the WM_COMMAND message.

Parameters   This message does not use *wParam* or *lParam*; therefore, both must be set to zero.

Include File   winuser.h

Related Messages BN_SETFOCUS, WM_COMMAND

BN_SETFOCUS   Win32s ■ Windows 95   Windows NT

Description   BN_SETFOCUS is a notification message that is sent to the parent window when a button receives the keyboard focus. The button must have the BS_NOTIFY style to send this notification message. The parent window receives this notification message through the WM_COMMAND message.

Parameters   This message does not use *wParam* or *lParam*; therefore, both must be set to zero.

Include File   winuser.h

Related Messages BN_KILLFOCUS, WM_COMMAND

CB_ADDSTRING   ■ Win32s ■ Windows 95 ■ Windows NT

Description   CB_ADDSTRING is a message that adds a string to the list box of a combo box. If the combo box does not have the CBS_SORT style, the string is added to the end of the list. Otherwise, the string is inserted into the list, and the list is sorted.

Parameters

wParam   WPARAM: Set to zero.

lParam   LPCTSTR: A pointer to the null-terminated string to add to the list box. If the combo box is created without the CBS_HASSTRINGS style, the value is stored as item data rather than a pointer to a string. The item data can be retrieved or modified by sending either the CB_GETITEMDATA or the CB_SETITEMDATA message.

Returns   int: If successful, the zero-based index of the string in the list box of the combo box is returned; otherwise, CB_ERR is returned if an error occurred. If insufficient space is available to store the new string, CB_ERRSPACE is returned.

Include File   winuser.h

Related Messages CB_DIR, CB_INSERTSTRING, WM_COMPAREITEM

CB_DELETESTRING   ■ Win32s ■ Windows 95 ■ Windows NT

Description   CB_DELETESTRING is a message that deletes a string in the list box of a combo box. If the combo box was not created using the CBS_HASSTRINGS style, Windows sends a WM_DELETEITEM message to the owner of the combo box so the application can free any additional data associated with the item.

Parameters

wParam WPARAM: The zero-based index of the string to delete from the list box of the combo box.

lParam LPARAM: Set to zero.

Returns int: A count of the strings remaining in the list box is returned. If *wParam* specifies an index value greater than the number of strings in the list, CB_ERR is returned.

Include File winuser.h

Related Messages CB_RESETCONTENT, WM_DELETEITEM

CB_DIR   ■ Win32s ■ Windows 95 ■ Windows NT

Description CB_DIR is a message that adds a list of file names to the list box of a combo box. (See Figure 11-2.)

Parameters

wParam UINT: A combination of the values in Table 11-5 indicating the attributes of the files to be added to the list box.

Table 11-5 CB_DIR *wParam* values

Value	Meaning
DDL_ARCHIVE	Archived files.
DDL_DIRECTORY	Subdirectories. Subdirectory names are enclosed in square brackets ([ ]).
DDL_DRIVES	Drives. Drives are listed in the form [-x-], where x is the drive letter.
DDL_EXCLUSIVE	Only files with the specified attributes. By default, read-write files are listed even if DDL_READWRITE is not specified.
DDL_HIDDEN	Hidden files.
DDL_READONLY	Read-only files.
DDL_READWRITE	Read-write files with no additional attributes.
DDL_SYSTEM	System files.

lParam LPCTSTR: A pointer to the null-terminated string specifying the file name to add to the list. If the file name contains any wildcards (for example, *.*) all files that match the string and have the attributes specified by *wParam* are added to the list.

Returns int: If successful, the zero-based index of the last file name added to the list is returned. If an error occurs, the CB_ERR value is returned. If insufficient space is available to store the new strings, CB_ERRSPACE is returned.

Include File	winuser.h
See Also	DlgDirList(), DlgDirListComboBox()
Related Messages	CB_ADDSTRING, CB_INSERTSTRING

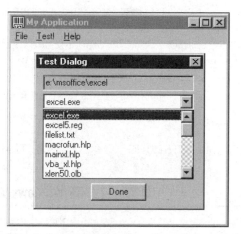

Figure 11-2 DlgDirListComboBox() Example

CB_FINDSTRING   ■ Win32s ■ Windows 95 ■ Windows NT

Description	CB_FINDSTRING is a message that searches the list box of a combo box for an item beginning with the characters in a specified string.
Parameters	
wParam	WPARAM: The zero-based index of the item preceding the first item to be searched. When the search reaches the bottom of the list box, it continues from the top of the list box back to the item specified by *wParam*. If *wParam* is -1, the entire list box is searched from the beginning.
lParam	LPCSTR: A pointer to the null-terminated string that contains the prefix to search for. The search is not case sensitive, so this string can contain any combination of uppercase and lowercase letters.
Returns	int: The zero-based index of the matching item is returned if the search is successful; otherwise, CB_ERR is returned.
Include File	winuser.h
Related Messages	CB_FINDSTRINGEXACT, CB_SELECTSTRING, CB_SETCURSEL, WM_COMPAREITEM

CB_FINDSTRINGEXACT   ■ Win32s ■ Windows 95 ■ Windows NT

Description	CB_FINDSTRINGEXACT is a message that finds the first list box string in a combo box that matches the string specified by *lParam*.

Parameters

wParam	WPARAM: The zero-based index of the item preceding the first item to be searched. When the search reaches the bottom of the list box, it continues from the top of the list box back to the item specified by *wParam*. If *wParam* is -1, the entire list box is searched from the beginning.
lParam	LPCSTR: A pointer to the null-terminated string for which to search. This string must match all the characters exactly without regard to case. Since the search is not case sensitive, the string can contain any combination of uppercase and lowercase letters.
Returns	int: The zero-based index of the matching item is returned if the search is successful; otherwise, CB_ERR is returned.
Include File	winuser.h
Related Messages	CB_FINDSTRING, CB_SELECTSTRING, WM_COMPAREITEM

CB_GETCOUNT ■ Win32s ■ Windows 95 ■ Windows NT

Description	CB_GETCOUNT is a message that retrieves the number of items in the list box of a combo box. Since the index of the list box is zero-based, the value returned is one greater than the index value of the last item.
Parameters	This message does not use *wParam* or *lParam*; therefore, both must be set to zero.
Returns	int: If successful, the number of items in the list box is returned; otherwise, CB_ERR is returned.
Include File	winuser.h

CB_GETCURSEL ■ Win32s ■ Windows 95 ■ Windows NT

Description	CB_GETCURSEL is a message that retrieves the index of the currently selected item, if any, in the list box of a combo box.
Parameters	This message does not use *wParam* or *lParam*; therefore, both must be set to zero.
Returns	int: If an item is selected, the zero-based index of the currently selected item is returned; otherwise, CB_ERR is returned.
Include File	winuser.h
Related Messages	CB_SELECTSTRING, CB_SETCURSEL

CB_GETDROPPEDCONTROLRECT ■ Win32s ■ Windows 95 ■ Windows NT

Description	CB_GETDROPPEDCONTROLRECT is a message that retrieves the screen coordinates of the drop-down list box of a combo box.

Parameters

wParam   WPARAM: Set to zero.

lParam   RECT *: A pointer to the RECT structure that is to receive the screen coordinates.

Returns   int: CB_OKAY is always returned.

Include File   winuser.h

CB_GETDROPPEDSTATE   ■ Win32s ■ Windows 95 ■ Windows NT

Description   CB_GETDROPPEDSTATE is a message that determines whether the list box of a combo box is dropped down.

Parameters   This message does not use *wParam* or *lParam*; therefore, both must be set to zero.

Returns   BOOL: If the list box is visible, TRUE is returned; otherwise, FALSE is returned.

Include File   winuser.h

Related Messages CB_SHOWDROPDOWN

CB_GETDROPPEDWIDTH   Win32s ■ Windows 95 Windows NT

Description   CB_GETDROPPEDWIDTH is a message that retrieves the minimum allowable width, in pixels, of the list box of a combo box with either the CBS_DROPDOWN or CBS_DROPDOWNLIST style. The default minimum width of the drop-down list box is zero. The width of the list box is either the minimum allowable width or the combo box width, whichever is larger.

Parameters   This message does not use *wParam* or *lParam*; therefore, both must be set to zero.

Returns   int: If successful, the width, in pixels, of the list box is returned; otherwise, CB_ERR is returned.

Include File   winuser.h

Related Messages CB_SETDROPPEDWIDTH

CB_GETEDITSEL   ■ Win32s ■ Windows 95 ■ Windows NT

Description   CB_GETEDITSEL is a message that determines the starting and ending character positions of the current selection in the edit control of a combo box.

Parameters

wParam   LPDWORD: A pointer to a 32-bit value that receives the starting position of the selection. This parameter can be set to NULL.

lParam	LPDWORD: A pointer to a 32-bit value that receives the ending position of the selection. This parameter can be set to NULL.
Returns	DWORD: A zero-based 32-bit value is returned with the starting position of the selection in the low-order word and with the ending position of the first character after the last selected character in the high-order word.
Include File	winuser.h
Related Messages	CB_SETEDITSEL

CB_GETEXTENDEDUI ■ Win32s ■ Windows 95 ■ Windows NT

Description	CB_GETEXTENDEDUI is a message that determines whether a combo box has the default user interface or the extended user interface. By default, the F4 key either opens or closes the list, and the down arrow key changes the current selection. In a combo box with the extended user interface, the F4 key is disabled, and pressing the down arrow key opens the drop-down list.
Parameters	This message does not use *wParam* or *lParam*; therefore, both must be set to zero.
Returns	BOOL: TRUE is returned if the combo box has the extended user interface; otherwise, FALSE is returned.
Include File	winuser.h
Related Messages	CB_SETEXTENDEDUI

CB_GETHORIZONTALEXTENT Win32s ■ Windows 95 Windows NT

Description	CB_GETHORIZONTALEXTENT is a message that retrieves from a combo box the width, in pixels, that the list box can be scrolled horizontally. This message is only applicable if the list box has a horizontal scroll bar.
Parameters	This message does not use *wParam* or *lParam*; therefore, both must be set to zero.
Returns	int: The scrollable width of the combo box, in pixels, is returned.
Include File	winuser.h
Related Messages	CB_SETHORIZONTALEXTENT

CB_GETITEMDATA ■ Win32s ■ Windows 95 ■ Windows NT

Description	CB_GETITEMDATA is a message that retrieves the application-supplied 32-bit value associated with the specified item in the combo box.
Parameters	
wParam	WPARAM: The zero-based index of the item.
lParam	LPARAM: Set to zero.

Returns	int: If successful, the 32-bit value associated with the item is returned; otherwise, CB_ERR is returned. If the item is in an owner-drawn combo box created without the CBS_HASSTRINGS style, the return value is the 32-bit value in the *lParam* parameter of either the CB_ADDSTRING or CB_INSERTSTRING message that added the item to the combo box. If the CBS_HASSTRINGS style was not used, the return value is the *lParam* of a CB_SETITEMDATA message.
Include File	winuser.h
Related Messages	CB_ADDSTRING, CB_INSERTSTRING, CB_SETITEMDATA

CB_GETITEMHEIGHT
■ Win32s ■ Windows 95 ■ Windows NT

Description	CB_GETITEMHEIGHT is a message that determines the height of list items or the selection field in a combo box.
Parameters	
wParam	WPARAM: The value of *wParam* is either -1 to retrieve the height of the selection field, or zero to retrieve the height of list items in the combo box. If the combo box has the CBS_OWNERDRAWVARIABLE style, *wParam* is the zero-based index of a specific list item.
lParam	LPARAM: Set to zero.
Returns	int: If the combo box has the CBS_OWNERDRAWVARIABLE style, the height of the item specified by *wParam* is returned; otherwise, if *wParam* is -1, the return value is the height of the selection field. CB_ERR is returned if an error occurs.
Include File	winuser.h
Related Messages	CB_SETITEMHEIGHT, WM_MEASUREITEM

CB_GETLBTEXT
■ Win32s ■ Windows 95 ■ Windows NT

Description	CB_GETLBTEXT is a message that retrieves a string from the list of a combo box. The buffer pointed to by the *lParam* parameter must have sufficient space for the string and a terminating null character. Send a CB_GETLBTEXTLEN message prior to the CB_GETLBTEXT message to retrieve the length, in bytes, of the combo box string. If the combo box is created without the CBS_ HASSTRINGS style, the buffer pointed to by *lParam* receives the 32-bit value associated with the item.
Parameters	
wParam	WPARAM: The zero-based index of the string to retrieve from the combo box.
lParam	LPARAM: A pointer to the buffer that receives the string.

Returns	int: If successful, the length of the string, in bytes, excluding the terminating null character, is returned; otherwise, CB_ERR is returned if the index parameter does not specify a valid index.
Include File	winuser.h
Related Messages	CB_GETLBTEXTLEN

CB_GETLBTEXTLEN   ■ Win32s ■ Windows 95 ■ Windows NT

Description	CB_GETLBTEXTLEN is a message that retrieves the length, in characters, of a string in the list of a combo box.
Parameters	
wParam	WPARAM: The zero-based index of the string.
lParam	LPARAM: Set to zero.
Returns	int: If successful, the length of the string, in characters, excluding the terminating null character, is returned; otherwise, CB_ERR is returned if the index parameter does not specify a valid index. Under certain mixtures of ANSI and Unicode, the return value may be larger than the actual length of the string. The return value will always be at least as large as the actual length of the string, so you can always use the value to guide in buffer allocation.
Include File	winuser.h
See Also	GetWindowText()
Related Messages	CB_GETLBTEXT, LB_GETTEXT, WM_GETTEXT

CB_GETLOCALE   Win32s ■ Windows 95 ■ Windows NT

Description	CB_GETLOCALE is a message that retrieves the current locale of the combo box. The locale is used to determine the correct sorting order of displayed text for combo boxes with the CBS_SORT style and text added by using the CB_ADDSTRING message.
Parameters	This message does not use *wParam* or *lParam*; therefore, both must be set to zero.
Returns	DWORD: A 32-bit value specifying the current locale of the combo box is returned. The high word of the return value contains the country code and the low-order word contains the language identifier.
Include File	winuser.h
Related Messages	CB_ADDSTRING, CB_SETLOCALE

CB_GETTOPINDEX   Win32s ■ Windows 95   Windows NT

Description	CB_GETTOPINDEX is a message that retrieves the zero-based index of the first visible item in the list box portion of a combo box. Initially the item

with an index value of zero is at the top of the list box, but if the list box contents have been scrolled, an item with a different index value may be at the top of the list.

Parameters   This message does not use *wParam* or *lParam*; therefore, both must be set to zero.

Returns   int: If successful, the index of the first visible item in the list box of the combo box is returned; otherwise, CB_ERR is returned.

Include File   winuser.h

Related Messages   CB_SETTOPINDEX

CB_INITSTORAGE   Win32s ■ Windows 95   Windows NT

Description   CB_INITSTORAGE is a message that preallocates the memory needed to store a large number of items added to the list box portion of a combo box. The values for *wParam* and *lParam* can be estimates, although if it is overestimated, extra memory is allocated, and if it is underestimated, normal allocation is used for items that exceed the preallocated amount.

Parameters

wParam   int: The number of items to add to the list box.

lParam   DWORD: The amount of memory to allocate for item strings, in bytes.

Returns   int: if successful, the maximum number of items that the memory object can store is returned; otherwise, CB_ERR is returned.

Include File   winuser.h

Related Messages   CB_ADDSTRING, CB_DIR, CB_INSERTSTRING

CB_INSERTSTRING   ■ Win32s ■ Windows 95 ■ Windows NT

Description   CB_INSERTSTRING is a message that inserts a string into the list box of a combo box. Unlike the CB_ADDSTRING message, the CB_INSERTSTRING message does not cause a list with the CBS_SORT style to be sorted.

Parameters

wParam   WPARAM: The zero-based index of the position at which to insert the string. If *wParam* is -1, the string is added to the end of the list.

lParam   LPCTSTR: A pointer to the null-terminated string to be inserted in the list. If the combo box is created without the CBS_HASSTRINGS style, the value of *lParam* is stored rather than the string it points to.

Returns   int: If successful, the index of the position where the string was inserted in the combo box is returned; otherwise, CB_ERR is returned. If there is insufficient space available to store the new string, CB_ERRSPACE is returned.

Include File   winuser.h

Related Messages   CB_ADDSTRING, CB_DIR

CB_LIMITTEXT

■ Win32s ■ Windows 95 ■ Windows NT

Description	CB_LIMITTEXT is a message that limits the length of the text the user may type into the edit control of a combo box. This message does not affect text already in the edit control, that is, text copied to the control when a string in the list box is selected. The default limit to the text a user can enter in the edit control is 30,000 characters.
Parameters	
wParam	WPARAM: The maximum number of characters the user can enter. If *wParam* is zero, the text length is set to 0x7FFFFFFE characters.
lParam	LPARAM: Set to zero.
Returns	BOOL: TRUE is always returned.
Include File	winuser.h

CB_RESETCONTENT

■ Win32s ■ Windows 95 ■ Windows NT

Description	CB_RESETCONTENT is a message that removes all items from the list box and edit control of a combo box. If the combo box is created without the CBS_HASSTRINGS style, the owner of the combo box receives a WM_DELETEITEM message for each item in the combo box.
Parameters	This message does not use *wParam* or *lParam*; therefore, both must be set to zero.
Returns	int: CB_OKAY is always returned.
Include File	winuser.h
Related Messages	CB_DELETESTRING, WM_DELETEITEM

CB_SELECTSTRING

■ Win32s ■ Windows 95 ■ Windows NT

Description	CB_SELECTSTRING is a message that searches the list of a combo box for an item that begins with the characters in a specified string. If a matching item is found, it is selected and copied to the edit control.
Parameters	
wParam	WPARAM: The zero-based index of the item preceding the first item in the list to search. When the search reaches the end of the list, it continues from the top of the list back to the item specified by *wParam*. If *wParam* is -1, the entire list is searched from the beginning.
lParam	LPCSTR: A pointer to the null-terminated string that contains the prefix to search for. The search is not case sensitive, so this string can contain any combination of uppercase and lowercase letters.
Returns	int: If successful, the index of the selected item is returned; otherwise, CB_ERR is returned and the current selection is not changed.

Include File	winuser.h
Related Messages	CB_FINDSTRING, CB_FINDSTRINGEXACT, CB_SETCURSEL, WM_COMPAREITEM

CB_SETCURSEL ■ Win32s ■ Windows 95 ■ Windows NT

Description CB_SETCURSEL is a message that selects a string in the list of a combo box. If necessary, the list scrolls the string into view. The text in the edit control of the combo box changes to reflect the new selection, and any previous selection in the list is removed.

Parameters

wParam WPARAM: The zero-based index of the string to select. If *wParam* is -1, any current selection in the list is removed and the edit control is cleared.

lParam LPARAM: Set to zero.

Returns int: If successful, the index of the item selected is returned; otherwise, if *wParam* is either greater than the number of items in the list or set to -1, CB_ERR is returned and the selection is cleared.

Include File winuser.h

Related Messages CB_FINDSTRING, CB_GETCURSEL, CB_SELECTSTRING

CB_SETDROPPEDWIDTH Win32s ■ Windows 95 Windows NT

Description CB_SETDROPPEDWIDTH is a message that sets the maximum allowable width, in pixels, of the list box of a combo box with the CBS_DROPDOWN or CBS_DROPDOWNLIST style.

Parameters

wParam WPARAM: The width of the list box, in pixels.

lParam LPARAM: Set to zero.

Returns int: If successful, the new width of the list box is returned; otherwise, CB_ERR is returned.

Include File winuser.h

Related Messages CB_GETDROPPEDWIDTH

CB_SETEDITSEL ■ Win32s ■ Windows 95 ■ Windows NT

Description CB_SETEDITSEL is a message that selects characters in the edit control of a combo box.

Parameters

wParam WPARAM: Set to zero.

LOWORD(lParam) LPARAM: The starting character position. If this parameter is set to -1, the selection, if any, is removed.

HIWORD(lParam)	LPARAM: The ending character position. If this parameter is set to -1, all text from the starting position to the last character in the edit control is selected.
Returns	BOOL: If successful, TRUE is returned. If the message is sent to a combo box with the CBS_DROPDOWNLIST style, CB_ERR is returned.
Include File	winuser.h
Related Messages	CB_GETEDITSEL

CB_SETEXTENDEDUI ■ Win32s ■ Windows 95 ■ Windows NT

Description	CB_SETEXTENDEDUI is a message that selects either the default user interface or the extended user interface for a combo box that has the CBS_DROPDOWN or CBS_DROPDOWNLIST style. By default, the F4 key opens or closes the list and the down arrow key changes the current selection. In the extended user interface, the F4 key is disabled and the down arrow key opens the drop-down list.
Parameters	
wParam	BOOL: TRUE selects the extended user interface; FALSE selects the standard user interface.
lParam	LPARAM: Set to zero.
Returns	int: If successful, CB_OKAY is returned; otherwise, CB_ERR is returned.
Include File	winuser.h
Related Messages	CB_GETEXTENDEDUI

CB_SETHORIZONTALEXTENT Win32s ■ Windows 95 Windows NT

Description	CB_SETHORIZONTALEXTENT is a message that sets the width, in pixels, that a list box can be scrolled horizontally. If the width of the list box is smaller than this value, the horizontal scroll bar horizontally scrolls items in the list box. If the width of the list box is equal to or greater than this value, the horizontal scroll bar is hidden or, if the combo box has the CBS_DISABLENOSCROLL style, disabled.
Parameters	
wParam	WPARAM: The scrollable width of the list box, in pixels.
lParam	LPARAM: Set to zero.
Include File	winuser.h
Related Messages	CB_GETHORIZONTALEXTENT

CB_SETITEMDATA ■ Win32s ■ Windows 95 ■ Windows NT

Description	CB_SETITEMDATA is a message that sets the 32-bit value associated with the specified item in a combo box.

Parameters

wParam	WPARAM: The zero-based index of the item.
lParam	DWORD: The new value to be associated with the item.
Returns	int: CB_ERR is returned if an error occurs.
Include File	winuser.h
Related Messages	CB_ADDSTRING, CB_GETITEMDATA, CB_INSERTSTRING

CB_SETITEMHEIGHT   ■ Win32s ■ Windows 95 ■ Windows NT

Description   CB_SETITEMHEIGHT is a message that sets the height of either the list items or the selection field in a combo box. The selection field height in a combo box is set independently of the height of the list items. An application must ensure that the height of the selection field is not smaller than the height of a particular list item.

Parameters

wParam   WPARAM: The component of the combo box for which to set the height. *wParam* must be -1 to set the height of the selection field. It must be zero to set the height of list items, unless the combo box has the CBS_OWNERDRAWVARIABLE style. In that case, *wParam* is the zero-based index of a specific list item.

lParam   int: The height, in pixels, of the combo box component identified by index.

Returns   int: CB_ERR is returned if the index is invalid.

Include File   winuser.h

Related Messages   CB_GETITEMHEIGHT, WM_MEASUREITEM

CB_SETLOCALE   Win32s ■ Windows 95 ■ Windows NT

Description   CB_SETLOCALE is a message that sets the current locale of the combo box. If the combo box has the CBS_SORT style and strings are added using CB_ADDSTRING, the locale of a combo box affects how list items are sorted.

Parameters

wParam   WORD: The locale identifier for the combo box to use for sorting when adding text.

lParam   LPARAM: Set to zero.

Returns   WORD: If successful, the previous locale identifier is returned; otherwise, if *wParam* specifies a locale not installed on the system, CB_ERR is returned and the current combo box locale is not changed.

Include File   winuser.h

Related Messages   CB_ADDSTRING, CB_GETLOCALE

CB_SETTOPINDEX

Win32s ■ Windows 95   Windows NT

Description   CB_SETTOPINDEX is a message that ensures that a particular item is visible in the list box of a combo box. The system scrolls the list box contents until either the specified item appears at the top of the list box or the maximum scroll range has been reached.

Parameters

wParam   WPARAM: The zero-based index of the list item.

lParam   LPARAM: Set to zero.

Returns   int: If successful, zero is returned; otherwise, CB_ERR is returned.

Include File   winuser.h

Related Messages   CB_GETTOPINDEX

CB_SHOWDROPDOWN

■ Win32s ■ Windows 95 ■ Windows NT

Description   CB_SHOWDROPDOWN is a message that either shows or hides the list box of a combo box that has the CBS_DROPDOWN or CBS_DROPDOWNLIST style. This message has no effect on a combo box created with the CBS_SIMPLE style.

Parameters

wParam   BOOL: TRUE shows the list box; FALSE hides it.

lParam   LPARAM: Set to zero.

Returns   BOOL: TRUE is always returned.

Include File   winuser.h

Related Messages   CB_GETDROPPEDSTATE

CBN_CLOSEUP

■ Win32s ■ Windows 95 ■ Windows NT

Description   CBN_CLOSEUP is a notification message that is sent when the list box of a combo box has been closed. The parent window receives this notification message through the WM_COMMAND message. CBN_CLOSEUP is not sent to a combo box with the CBS_SIMPLE style.

Parameters

LOWORD(wParam)   int: The combo box identifier.

lParam   HWND: The handle of the combo box.

Include File   winuser.h

Related Messages   CBN_DROPDOWN, CBN_SELCHANGE, WM_COMMAND

CBN_DBLCLK
■ Win32s ■ Windows 95 ■ Windows NT

Description   CBN_DBLCLK is a notification message that is sent when the user double-clicks a string in the list box of a combo box. The parent window of the combo box receives this notification message through the WM_COMMAND message. This notification message only occurs for a combo box with the CBS_SIMPLE style. In a combo box with the CBS_DROPDOWN or CBS_DROPDOWNLIST style, a double-click cannot occur, because a single click closes the list box.

Parameters

LOWORD(wParam)   int: The combo box identifier.

lParam   HWND: The handle of the combo box.

Include File   winuser.h

Related Messages   CBN_SELCHANGE, WM_COMMAND

CBN_DROPDOWN
■ Win32s ■ Windows 95 ■ Windows NT

Description   CBN_DROPDOWN is a notification message that is sent when the list box of a combo box is about to be made visible. The parent window of the combo box receives this notification message through the WM_COMMAND message. This notification message can occur only for a combo box with the CBS_DROPDOWN or CBS_DROPDOWNLIST style.

Parameters

LOWORD(wParam)   int: The combo box identifier.

lParam   HWND: The handle of the combo box.

Include File   winuser.h

Related Messages   CBN_CLOSEUP, WM_COMMAND

CBN_EDITCHANGE
■ Win32s ■ Windows 95 ■ Windows NT

Description   CBN_EDITCHANGE is a notification message that is sent after the user has taken an action that may have altered the text in the edit control portion of a combo box. The parent window of the combo box receives this notification message through the WM_COMMAND message after Windows updates the screen. If the combo box has the CBS_DROPDOWNLIST style, this notification message does not occur.

Parameters

LOWORD(wParam)   int: The combo box identifier.

lParam   HWND: The handle of the combo box.

Include File   winuser.h

Related Messages   CBN_EDITUPDATE, WM_COMMAND

CBN_EDITUPDATE ■ Win32s ■ Windows 95 ■ Windows NT

Description	CBN_EDITUPDATE is a notification message that is sent when the edit control portion of a combo box is about to display altered text. This notification message is sent after the control has formatted the text, but before it displays the text. The parent window of the combo box receives this notification message through the WM_COMMAND message. If the combo box has the CBS_DROPDOWNLIST style, this notification message does not occur.

Parameters

LOWORD(wParam)	int: The combo box identifier.
lParam	HWND: The handle of the combo box.
Include File	winuser.h
Related Messages	CBN_EDITCHANGE, WM_COMMAND

CBN_ERRSPACE ■ Win32s ■ Windows 95 ■ Windows NT

Description	CBN_ERRSPACE is a notification message that is sent when a combo box cannot allocate enough memory to meet a specific request. The parent window of the combo box receives this notification message through the WM_COMMAND message.

Parameters

LOWORD(wParam)	int: The combo box identifier.
lParam	HWND: The handle of the combo box.
Include File	winuser.h
Related Messages	WM_COMMAND

CBN_KILLFOCUS ■ Win32s ■ Windows 95 ■ Windows NT

Description	CBN_KILLFOCUS is a notification message that is sent when a combo box loses the keyboard focus. The parent window of the combo box receives this notification message through the WM_COMMAND message.

Parameters

LOWORD(wParam)	int: The combo box identifier.
lParam	HWND: The handle of the combo box.
Include File	winuser.h
Related Messages	CBN_SETFOCUS, WM_COMMAND

CBN_SELCHANGE ■ Win32s ■ Windows 95 ■ Windows NT

Description   CBN_SELCHANGE is a notification message that is sent when the selection in the list box of a combo box is about to be changed as a result of the user either clicking in the list box or changing the selection by using the arrow keys. The parent window of the combo box receives this message through the WM_COMMAND message.

Parameters

LOWORD(wParam)   int: The combo box identifier.

lParam   HWND: The handle of the combo box.

Include File   winuser.h

Related Messages   CBN_DBLCLK, WM_COMMAND

CBN_SELENDCANCEL Win32s ■ Windows 95 ■ Windows NT

Description   CBN_SELENDCANCEL is a notification message that is sent when the user selects an item, but then selects another control or closes the dialog box. This notification message indicates that the user's initial selection should be ignored. The parent window of the combo box receives this notification message through the WM_COMMAND message. In a combo box with either the CBS_SIMPLE style or the WS_EX_NOPARENTNOTIFY style, the CBN_SELENDCANCEL notification message is not sent.

Parameters

LOWORD(wParam)   int: The combo box identifier.

lParam   HWND: The handle of the combo box.

Include File   winuser.h

Related Messages   CBN_SELCHANGE, CBN_SELENDOK, WM_COMMAND

CBN_SELENDOK Win32s ■ Windows 95 ■ Windows NT

Description   CBN_SELENDOK is a notification message that is sent when the user selects a list item, or selects an item and then closes the list. This notification message indicates that the user's selection should be processed. The parent window of the combo box receives this notification message through the WM_COMMAND message. In a combo box with the CBS_SIMPLE style, the CBN_SELENDOK notification message is sent immediately before every CBN_SELCHANGE notification message. If the combo box has the WS_EX_NOPARENTNOTIFY extended window style, the CBN_SELENDOK notification message is not sent.

Parameters

LOWORD(wParam)   int: The combo box identifier.

lParam	HWND: The handle of the combo box.
Include File	winuser.h
Related Messages	CBN_SELCHANGE, CBN_SELENDCANCEL, WM_COMMAND

CBN_SETFOCUS ■ Win32s ■ Windows 95 ■ Windows NT

Description   CBN_SETFOCUS is a notification message that is sent when a combo box receives the keyboard focus. The parent window of the combo box receives this notification message through the WM_COMMAND message.

Parameters

LOWORD(wParam)	int: The combo box identifier.
lParam	HWND: The handle of the combo box.
Include File	winuser.h
Related Messages	CBN_KILLFOCUS, WM_COMMAND

CDM_GETFILEPATH ■ Win32s ■ Windows 95 ■ Windows NT

Description   CDM_GETFILEPATH is a message that retrieves the path and file name of the selected file in either the common Open or Save As dialog box. The common dialog box must have been created with the OFN_EXPLORER flag; otherwise, the message fails.

Parameters

wParam	WPARAM: The size, in bytes, of the buffer.
lParam	LPTSTR: The address of the buffer that receives the file name and path.
Include File	commdlg.h
Returns	int: If successful, the number of bytes copied to the buffer specified by *lParam*, including the terminating NULL character, is returned. If the buffer is too small to contain the file name and path, the required buffer size is returned. If the message fails, zero is returned.

CDM_GETFOLDERIDLIST ■ Win32s ■ Windows 95 ■ Windows NT

Description   CDM_GETFOLDERIDLIST is a message that retrieves the address of the item identifier list corresponding to the folder that either the common Open or Save As dialog box currently has open.

Parameters

wParam	WPARAM: The size, in bytes, of the buffer.
lParam	LPVOID: The address of the buffer that receives the list of item identifiers.

Returns   int: If successful, the number of bytes copied to the buffer specified by *lParam* is returned. If the buffer is too small to contain the list, the required buffer size is returned. If the message fails, zero is returned.

Include File   commdlg.h

CDM_GETFOLDERPATH   ■ Win32s ■ Windows 95 ■ Windows NT

Description   CDM_GETFOLDERPATH is a message that retrieves the path and name of the currently open folder or directory for either the common Open or Save As dialog box. The common dialog box must have been created with the OFN_EXPLORER flag; otherwise, the message fails.

Parameters

wParam   WPARAM: The size, in bytes, of the buffer.

lParam   LPTSTR: The address of the buffer that receives the path and name.

Returns   int: If successful, the number of bytes copied to the buffer specified by *lParam*, including the terminating NULL character, is returned. If the buffer is too small to contain the path and name, the required buffer size is returned. If the message fails, zero is returned.

Include File   commdlg.h

CDM_GETSPEC   ■ Win32s ■ Windows 95 ■ Windows NT

Description   CDM_GETSPEC is a message that retrieves the file name of the currently selected file in either the common Open or Save As dialog box. The common dialog box must have been created with the OFN_EXPLORER flag; otherwise, the message fails.

Parameters

wParam   WPARAM: The size, in bytes, of the buffer.

lParam   LPTSTR: The address of the buffer that receives file name.

Returns   int: If successful, the number of bytes copied to the buffer specified by *lParam*, including the terminating NULL character, is returned. If the buffer is too small to contain the path and name, the required buffer size is returned. If the message fails, zero is returned.

Include File   commdlg.h

CDM_HIDECONTROL   ■ Win32s ■ Windows 95 ■ Windows NT

Description   CDM_HIDECONTROL is a message that hides the specified control.

Parameters

wParam   WPARAM: The identifier of the control to hide.

lParam   LPARAM: Set to zero.

Include File   commdlg.h

CDM_SETCONTROLTEXT ■ Win32s ■ Windows 95 ■ Windows NT

Description CDM_SETCONTROLTEXT is a message that sets the text for the specified control.

Parameters

wParam WPARAM: The identifier of the control.

lParam LPARAM: The address of the null-terminating string specifying the new text for the control.

Include File commdlg.h

CDM_SETDEFEXT ■ Win32s ■ Windows 95 ■ Windows NT

Description CDM_SETDEFEXT is a message that sets the default file name extension for the dialog box.

Parameters

wParam WPARAM: Set to zero.

lParam LPARAM: The address of the new file name extension. The extension must not include the dot (.).

Include File commdlg.h

CDN_FILEOK ■ Win32s ■ Windows 95 ■ Windows NT

Description CDN_FILEOK is a notification message that is sent when either the Open or Save As dialog box is about to close. This notification message is sent as a WM_NOTIFY message to the hook function for the dialog box. CDN_FILEOK is only sent if the dialog box was created using the OFN_EXPLORER value.

Parameters

wParam WPARAM: Set to zero.

lParam LPOFNOTIFY: The address of the OFNOTIFY structure that contains the file information. The structure includes the address of an OPENFILENAME structure whose *lpstrFile* member specifies the address of the selected file name.

Returns int: A nonzero value is returned to prevent the dialog box from closing.

Include File commdlg.h

See Also SetWindowLong()

CDN_FOLDERCHANGE ■ Win32s ■ Windows 95 ■ Windows NT

Description CDN_FOLDERCHANGE is a notification message that is sent when a new folder is opened in either the Open or Save As dialog box. This notification message is sent as a WM_NOTIFY message to the hook function for the dialog box. CDN_FOLDERCHANGE is only sent if the dialog box was created using the OFN_EXPLORER value.

Parameters

wParam   WPARAM: Set to zero.

lParam   LPOFNOTIFY: The address of an OFNOTIFY structure that contains the file information.

Returns   The return value is ignored.

Include File   commdlg.h

Related Messages WM_NOTIFY

CDN_HELP   ■ Win32s ■ Windows 95 ■ Windows NT

Description   CDN_HELP is a notification message that is sent when the user clicks the Help button in either the Open or Save As dialog box. This notification message is sent as a WM_NOTIFY message to the hook function for the dialog box. CDN_HELP is only sent if the dialog box was created using the OFN_EXPLORER value.

Parameters

wParam   WPARAM: Set to zero.

lParam   LPOFNOTIFY: The address of an OFNOTIFY structure that contains file information.

Returns   The return value is ignored.

Include File   commdlg.h

Related Messages WM_NOTIFY

CDN_INITDONE   ■ Win32s ■ Windows 95 ■ Windows NT

Description   CDN_INITDONE is a notification message that is sent when the system has finished arranging controls in either the Open or Save As dialog box to make room for the controls of the child dialog box. This notification message is sent as a WM_NOTIFY message to the hook function for the dialog box. CDN_INITDONE is only sent if the dialog box was created using the OFN_EXPLORER value.

Parameters

wParam   WPARAM: Set to zero.

lParam   LPOFNOTIFY: The address of an OFNOTIFY structure that contains file information.

Returns   The return value is ignored.

Include File   commdlg.h

Related Messages WM_NOTIFY

CDN_SELCHANGE
■ Win32s ■ Windows 95 ■ Windows NT

Description CDN_SELCHANGE is a notification message that is sent when the user selects a new file or folder in the file list of either the common Open or Save As dialog box. This notification message is sent as a WM_NOTIFY message to the hook function for the dialog box. CDN_SELCHANGE is only sent if the dialog box was created using the OFN_EXPLORER value.

Parameters

wParam WPARAM: Set to zero.

lParam LPOFNOTIFY: The address of an OFNOTIFY structure that contains file information.

Returns The return value is ignored.

Include File commdlg.h

Related Messages WM_NOTIFY

CDN_SHAREVIOLATION
■ Win32s ■ Windows 95 ■ Windows NT

Description CDN_SHAREVIOLATION is a notification message that is sent when either the Open or Save As dialog box encounters a sharing violation on the file about to be returned. This notification message is sent as a WM_NOTIFY message to the hook function for the dialog box. Use SetWindowLong() with the DWL_MSGRESULT value to return a result from the hook function. CND_SHAREVIOLATION is only sent if the dialog box was created using the OFN_EXPLORER value.

Parameters

wParam WPARAM: Set to zero.

lParam LPOFNOTIFY: The address of the OFNOTIFY structure that contains the file information. The *pszFile* member of the structure points to the name of the file that had the sharing violation.

Returns int: One of the values in Table 11-6 indicating the action performed.

Table 11-6 CDN_SHAREVIOLATION return values

Value	Meaning
OFN_SHAREFALLTHROUGH	The file name is returned by the dialog box even though there is a share violation.
OFN_SHARENOWARN	No further action.
OFN_SHAREWARN	The user receives the standard warning message for this error.

Include File commdlg.h

See Also SetWindowLong()

Related Messages WM_NOTIFY

CDN_TYPECHANGE
■ Win32s ■ Windows 95 ■ Windows NT

Description	CDN_TYPECHANGE is a notification message that is sent when the user selects a new file type from the list of file types in either the Open or Save As dialog box. This notification is sent as a WM_NOTIFY message to the hook function for the dialog box. CDN_TYPECHANGE is sent only if the dialog box was created using the OFN_EXPLORER value.
Parameters	
wParam	WPARAM: Set to zero.
lParam	LPOFNOTIFY: The address of an OFNOTIFY structure that contains the file information.
Returns	The return value is ignored.
Include File	commdlg.h
Related Messages	WM_NOTIFY

CPL_DBLCLK
Win32s ■ Windows 95 ■ Windows NT

Description	CPL_DBLCLK is a message that is sent to a Control Panel application when the user double-clicks the icon of a dialog box supported by the application. In response to this message, a Control Panel application must display the corresponding dialog box.
Parameters	
lParam1	UINT: The dialog box number. This number must be in the range zero through one less than the value returned in response to CPL_GETCOUNT.
lParam2	LONG: The value that the Control Panel application loaded into the *lData* member of either the CPLINFO or NEWCPLINFO structure for the dialog box. The application loads the *lData* member in response to the CPL_NEWINQUIRE message.
Returns	int: If a Control Panel application processes this message successfully, zero is returned; otherwise, a nonzero value is returned.
Include File	cpl.h
Related Messages	CPL_GETCOUNT, CPL_NEWINQUIRE, CPL_SELECT

CPL_EXIT
Win32s ■ Windows 95 ■ Windows NT

Description	CPL_EXIT is a message that is sent to a Control Panel application before the controlling application releases the DLL containing the application. CPL_EXIT is sent after the last CPL_STOP message is sent. In response to this message, a Control Panel application must free any memory that it has allocated and perform global-level cleanup.

Parameters	This message does not use *wParam* or *lParam*; therefore, both must be set to zero.
Returns	int: If a Control Panel application processes this message successfully, zero is returned.
Include File	cpl.h
Related Messages	CPL_STOP

CPL_GETCOUNT ■ Win32s ■ Windows 95 ■ Windows NT

Description	CPL_GETCOUNT is a message that is sent to a Control Panel application to retrieve the number of dialog boxes supported by the application. This message is sent immediately after the CPL_INIT message.
Parameters	This message does not use *wParam* or *lParam*; therefore, both must be set to zero.
Returns	int: The number of dialog boxes supported by the Control Panel application is returned.
Include File	cpl.h
Related Messages	CPL_INIT

CPL_INIT ■ Win32s ■ Windows 95 ■ Windows NT

Description	CPL_INIT is a message that is sent to a Control Panel application to prompt it to perform global initialization, especially memory allocation.
Parameters	This message does not use *wParam* or *lParam*; therefore, both must be set to zero.
Returns	int: If initialization succeeds, a Control Panel application returns a nonzero value; otherwise, it returns zero. If the application returns zero, the controlling application ends communication and releases the DLL containing the Control Panel application.
Include File	cpl.h
See Also	FreeLibrary()

CPL_NEWINQUIRE ■ Win32s ■ Windows 95 ■ Windows NT

Description	CPL_NEWINQUIRE is a message that is sent to a Control Panel application to request information about a dialog box that the application supports. This message is sent once for each dialog box supported by the application, immediately after the CPL_GETCOUNT message. Upon receiving this message, the application can initialize the dialog box. If the application must allocate memory, it should do so in response to CPL_INIT.

Parameters

lParam1	UINT: The dialog box number. This number must be in the range zero through one less than the value returned in response to the CPL_GETCOUNT message.
lParam2	LPNEWCPLINFO: The address of a NEWCPLINFO structure. The Control Panel application should fill this structure with information about the dialog box.
Returns	int: If a Control Panel application processes this message successfully, zero is returned.
Include File	cpl.h
Related Messages	CPL_GETCOUNT, CPL_INIT

CPL_SELECT   Win32s ■ Windows 95 ■ Windows NT

Description	CPL_SELECT is a message that is sent to a Control Panel application when the user selects the icon of a dialog box supported by the application.

Parameters

lParam1	UINT: The dialog box number.
lParam2	LONG: The value that the Control Panel application loaded into the *lData* member of either the CPLINFO or NEWCPLINFO structure for the dialog box. The application loads the *lData* member in response to the CPL_NEWINQUIRE message.
Returns	int: If a Control Panel application processes this message successfully, zero is returned.
Include File	cpl.h
Related Messages	CPL_DBLCLK, CPL_NEWINQUIRE

CPL_STOP   Win32s ■ Windows 95 ■ Windows NT

Description	CPL_STOP is a message that is sent once for each dialog box when the application controlling the Control Panel application closes. In response to this message, a Control Panel application must perform a cleanup for the specified dialog box.

Parameters

lParam1	UINT: The dialog box number.
lParam2	LONG: The value that the Control Panel application loaded into the *lData* member of either the CPLINFO or NEWCPLINFO structure for the dialog box. The application loads the *lData* member in response to the CPL_NEWINQUIRE message.
Returns	int: If a Control Panel application processes this message successfully, zero is returned.

Include File	cpl.h
Related Messages	CPL_EXIT, CPL_GETCOUNT, CPL_NEWINQUIRE

DBT_CONFIGCHANGED   Win32s ■ Windows 95   Windows NT

Description   DBT_CONFIGCHANGED is a message that indicates that the current configuration has changed, due to either a dock or undock of a device. An application or driver that stores data in the registry under the HKEY_CURRENT_CONFIG key should update the data.

Parameters

wParam   WPARAM: Set to zero.

lParam   DWORD: A pointer to a DEV_BROADCAST_HDR structure identifying the device.

Returns   BOOL: Return TRUE.

Include File   dbt.h

DBT_DEVICEARRIVAL   Win32s ■ Windows 95   Windows NT

Description   DBT_DEVICEARRIVAL is a message that is sent when a device has been inserted and is now available.

Parameters

wParam   WPARAM: Set to zero.

lParam   DWORD: A pointer to a DEV_BROADCAST_HDR structure identifying the device inserted.

Returns   BOOL: Return TRUE.

Include File   dbt.h

DBT_DEVICEQUERYREMOVE   Win32s ■ Windows 95   Windows NT

Description   DBT_DEVICEQUERYREMOVE is a message that is sent to request permission to remove a device. Any application can deny this request and cancel the removal.

Parameters

wParam   WPARAM: Set to zero.

lParam   DWORD: A pointer to a DEV_BROADCAST_HDR structure identifying the device to remove.

Returns   BOOL: TRUE is returned to grant permission; otherwise, FALSE is returned.

Include File   dbt.h

DBT_DEVICEQUERYREMOVEFAILED

Win32s ■ Windows 95   Windows NT

Description	DBT_DEVICEQUERYREMOVEFAILED is a message that is sent when a request to remove a device has been canceled.
Parameters	
wParam	WPARAM: Set to zero.
lParam	DWORD: A pointer to a DEV_BROADCAST_HDR structure identifying the device.
Returns	BOOL: TRUE is returned.
Include File	dbt.h

DBT_DEVICEREMOVECOMPLETE

Win32s ■ Windows 95   Windows NT

Description	DBT_DEVICEREMOVECOMPLETE is a message that is sent when a device has been removed. The operating system may send DBT_DEVICEREMOVECOMPLETE without previously sending corresponding DBT_DEVICEQUERYREMOVE and DBT_DEVICEREMOVEPENDING messages.
Parameters	
wParam	WPARAM: Set to zero.
lParam	DWORD: A pointer to a DEV_BROADCAST_HDR structure identifying the device removed.
Returns	BOOL: TRUE is returned.
Include File	dbt.h
Related Messages	DBT_DEVICEQUERYREMOVE, DBT_DEVICEREMOVEPENDING

DBT_DEVICEREMOVEPENDING

Win32s ■ Windows 95   Windows NT

Description	DBT_DEVICEREMOVEPENDING is a message that is sent to inform applications and drivers that the device is about to be removed.
Parameters	
wParam	WPARAM: Set to zero.
lParam	DWORD: A pointer to a DEV_BROADCAST_HDR structure identifying the device to remove.
Returns	BOOL: TRUE is returned.
Include File	dbt.h
Related Messages	DBT_DEVICEQUERYREMOVE, DBT_DEVICEREMOVECOMPLETE

DBT_DEVICETYPESPECIFIC
Win32s ■ Windows 95   Windows NT

Description	DBT_DEVICETYPESPECIFIC is a message that is sent when a device-specific event occurs.
Parameters	
wParam	WPARAM: Set to zero.
lParam	DWORD: A pointer to a DEV_BROADCAST_HDR structure identifying the device. This parameter may be set to zero.
Returns	BOOL: TRUE is returned.
Include File	dbt.h

DBT_USERDEFINED
Win32s ■ Windows 95   Windows NT

Description	DBT_USERDEFINED is a message that identifies a user-defined system message. DBT_USERDEFINED is sent as the *wParam* of WM_DEVICECHANGE.
Parameters	
wParam	WPARAM: Set to zero.
lParam	DWORD: The address of the user-defined data. The data must be in the format specified by the _DEV_BROADCAST_USERDEFINED structure. This parameter may be set to zero.
Include File	dbt.h
Related Messages	WM_DEVICECHANGE

DL_BEGINDRAG
■ Win32s ■ Windows 95 ■ Windows NT

Description	DL_BEGINDRAG is a notification message that notifies the parent window of a drag list box when the user clicked the left mouse button on a list item. For more information, refer to the DL_BEGINDRAG message in Chapter 6, List View and Drag List.

DL_CANCELDRAG
■ Win32s ■ Windows 95 ■ Windows NT

Description	DL_CANCELDRAG is a notification message that notifies the parent window that the user canceled a drag operation by clicking the right mouse button or pressing the (ESC) key. For more information, refer to the DL_CANCELDRAG message in Chapter 6, List View and Drag List.

DL_DRAGGING
■ Win32s ■ Windows 95 ■ Windows NT

Description	DL_DRAGGING is a notification message that notifies the parent window that the user moved the mouse while dragging an item. For more

information, refer to the DL_DRAGGING message in Chapter 6, List View and Drag List.

DL_DROPPED   ■ Win32s ■ Windows 95 ■ Windows NT

Description   DL_DROPPED is a notification message that notifies the parent window that the user completed a drag operation by releasing the left mouse button. For more information, refer to the DL_DROPPED message in Chapter 6, List View and Drag List.

DM_GETDEFID   ■ Win32s ■ Windows 95 ■ Windows NT

Description   DM_GETDEFID is a message that retrieves the identifier of the default push button control for a dialog box.

Parameters   This message does not use *wParam* or *lParam*; therefore, both must be set to zero.

Returns   DWORD: If a default push button exists, the high-order word of the return value contains the value DC_HASDEFID, and the low-order word contains the control identifier; otherwise, zero is returned.

Include File   winuser.h

See Also   DefDlgProc()

Related Messages   DM_SETDEFID

DM_REPOSITION   Win32s ■ Windows 95   Windows NT

Description   DM_REPOSITION is a message that repositions a top-level dialog box so that it fits within the desktop area. An application can send this message to a dialog box after resizing it to ensure that the entire dialog box remains visible.

Parameters   This message does not use *wParam* or *lParam*; therefore, both must be set to zero.

Include File   winuser.h

DM_SETDEFID   ■ Win32s ■ Windows 95 ■ Windows NT

Description   DM_SETDEFID is a message that changes the default push button of the dialog. This can result in two push buttons appearing as the default push button. Windows may not remove the default button border from the original push button. In these cases, the application should send a BM_SETSTYLE message to change the first original button's style to not include the default button border style.

Parameters

wParam   WPARAM: The identifier of the push button that becomes the default push button.

Include File   winuser.h

See Also   BM_SETSTYLE

EM_CANPASTE   ■ Win32s ■ Windows 95 ■ Windows NT

Description   EM_CANPASTE is a message that determines whether a rich-text edit control can paste a specified clipboard format. For more information, refer to the EM_CANPASTE message in Chapter 8, Rich-Text Edit Controls.

EM_CANUNDO   ■ Win32s ■ Windows 95 ■ Windows NT

Description   EM_CANUNDO is a message that determines whether an edit control can process the EM_UNDO message by undoing the operation.

Parameters   This message does not use *wParam* or *lParam*; therefore, both must be set to zero.

Returns   BOOL: If the edit control can correctly process the EM_UNDO message, TRUE is returned; otherwise, FALSE is returned.

Include File   winuser.h

Related Messages   EM_UNDO

EM_CHARFROMPOS   Win32s ■ Windows 95 Windows NT

Description   EM_CHARFROMPOS is a message that retrieves the zero-based character index and zero-based line index of the character nearest the specified point in an edit control.

Parameters

wParam   WPARAM: Set to zero.

LOWORD(lParam)   LPARAM: The x coordinate of a point relative to the upper left corner of the client area.

HIWORD(lParam)   LPARAM: The y coordinate of a point relative to the upper left corner of the client area.

Returns   DWORD: The return value contains the character index in the low-order word and the line index in the high-order word. For single-line edit controls, the line index is always 0. The last character in the edit control is returned if the given point is beyond the last character in the control. The return value is -1 if the specified point is outside the client area of the edit control.

Include File   winuser.h

Related Messages   EM_POSFROMCHAR

EM_DISPLAYBAND ■ Win32s ■ Windows 95 ■ Windows NT

Description   EM_DISPLAYBAND is a message that displays a portion of the contents of a rich-text edit control. For more information, refer to the EM_DISPLAYBAND message in Chapter 8, Rich-Text Edit Controls.

EM_EMPTYUNDOBUFFER ■ Win32s ■ Windows 95 ■ Windows NT

Description   EM_EMPTYUNDOBUFFER is a message that resets the undo flag of an edit control. The undo flag is set anytime an operation within the edit control can be undone. The undo flag is automatically reset when the edit control receives either a WM_SETTEXT or EM_SETHANDLE message.

Parameters   This message does not use *wParam* or *lParam*; therefore, both must be set to zero.

Include File   winuser.h

Related Messages   EM_CANUNDO, EM_SETHANDLE, EM_UNDO, WM_SETTEXT

EM_EXGETSEL ■ Win32s ■ Windows 95 ■ Windows NT

Description   EM_EXGETSEL is a message that determines the coordinates of a rich edit control selection. For more information, refer to the EM_EXGETSEL message in Chapter 8, Rich-Text Edit Controls.

EM_EXLIMITTEXT ■ Win32s ■ Windows 95 ■ Windows NT

Description   EM_EXLIMITTEXT is a message that specifies the text limit for the rich-text edit control. For more information, refer to the EM_EXLIMITTEXT message in Chapter 8, Rich-Text Edit Controls.

EM_EXLINEFROMCHAR ■ Win32s ■ Windows 95 ■ Windows NT

Description   EM_EXLINEFROMCHAR is a message that determines which line contains the specified character in the rich-text edit control. For more information, refer to the EM_EXLINEFROMCHAR message in Chapter 8, Rich-Text Edit Controls.

EM_EXSETSEL ■ Win32s ■ Windows 95 ■ Windows NT

Description   EM_EXSETSEL is a message that selects a range of characters in a rich-text edit control. For more information, refer to the EM_EXSETSEL message in Chapter 8, Rich-Text Edit Controls.

EM_FINDTEXT ■ Win32s ■ Windows 95 ■ Windows NT

Description EM_FINDTEXT is a message that locates the specified text within a rich-text edit control. For more information, refer to the EM_FINDTEXT message in Chapter 8, Rich-Text Edit Controls.

EM_FINDTEXTEX ■ Win32s ■ Windows 95 ■ Windows NT

Description EM_FINDTEXTEX is a message that locates the specified text within a rich-text edit control. For more information, refer to the EM_FINDTEXTEX message in Chapter 8, Rich-Text Edit Controls.

EM_FINDWORDBREAK ■ Win32s ■ Windows 95 ■ Windows NT

Description EM_FINDWORDBREAK is a message that retrieves the desired word-break information about the specified character position in the rich-text edit control. For more information, refer to the EM_FINDWORDBREAK message in Chapter 8, Rich-Text Edit Controls.

EM_FMTLINES ■ Win32s ■ Windows 95 ■ Windows NT

Description EM_FMTLINES is a message that sets the inclusion flag of soft line-break characters to either on or off within a multiline edit control. A soft line break consists of two carriage returns and a linefeed and is inserted at the end of a line that is broken because of word wrapping. EM_FMTLINES affects only the buffer returned by the EM_GETHANDLE message and the text returned by WM_GETTEXT. It has no effect on the display of the text within the edit control.

Parameters

wParam BOOL: TRUE inserts soft line-break characters; otherwise FALSE removes them.

lParam LPARAM: Set to zero.

Returns BOOL: TRUE is returned if soft line-break characters are inserted; otherwise, FALSE is returned indicating they were removed.

Include File winuser.h

Related Messages EM_GETHANDLE, WM_GETTEXT

EM_FORMATRANGE ■ Win32s ■ Windows 95 ■ Windows NT

Description EM_FORMATRANGE is a message that formats a range of text in a rich-text edit control. For more information, refer to the EM_FORMATRANGE message in Chapter 8, Rich-Text Edit Controls.

EM_GETCHARFORMAT
■ Win32s ■ Windows 95 ■ Windows NT

Description EM_GETCHARFORMAT is a message that determines the current character formatting in a rich-text edit control. For more information, refer to the EM_GETCHARFORMAT message in Chapter 8, Rich-Text Edit Controls.

EM_GETEVENTMASK
■ Win32s ■ Windows 95 ■ Windows NT

Description EM_GETEVENTMASK is a message that retrieves the event mask for a rich-text edit control. For more information, refer to the EM_GETEVENTMASK message in Chapter 8, Rich-Text Edit Controls.

EM_GETFIRSTVISIBLELINE
■ Win32s ■ Windows 95 ■ Windows NT

Description EM_GETFIRSTVISIBLELINE is a message that determines the uppermost visible line in an edit control.

Parameters This message does not use *wParam* or *lParam*; therefore, both must be set to zero.

Returns int: In a multiline edit control, the zero-based index of the uppermost visible line is returned. For single-line edit controls, the zero-based index of the first visible character is returned.

Include File winuser.h

EM_GETHANDLE
■ Win32s ■ Windows 95 ■ Windows NT

Description EM_GETHANDLE is a message that retrieves the handle of the memory currently allocated for the text of a multiline edit control.

Parameters This message does not use *wParam* or *lParam*; therefore, both must be set to zero.

Returns HLOCAL: If successful, the memory handle of the buffer containing the content of the edit control is returned; otherwise, zero is returned.

Include File winuser.h

Related Messages EM_SETLIMITTEXT

EM_GETIMECOLOR
Win32s ■ Windows 95 Windows NT

Description EM_GETIMECOLOR is a message that retrieves the IME composition color in Asian-language versions of Windows 95. For more information, refer to the EM_GETIMECOLOR message in Chapter 8, Rich-Text Edit Controls.

EM_GETIMEOPTIONS

Win32s ■ Windows 95   Windows NT

Description   EM_GETIMEOPTIONS is a message that retrieves the IME options for Asian-language versions of Windows 95. For more information, refer to the EM_GETIMEOPTIONS message in Chapter 8, Rich-Text Edit Controls.

EM_GETLIMITTEXT

Win32s ■ Windows 95   Windows NT

Description   EM_GETLIMITTEXT is a message that retrieves the current text limit, in characters, for an edit control.

Parameters   This message does not use *wParam* or *lParam*; therefore, both must be set to zero.

Returns   int: The text limit.

Include File   winuser.h

Related Messages   EM_SETLIMITTEXT

EM_GETLINE

■ Win32s ■ Windows 95 ■ Windows NT

Description   EM_GETLINE is a message that copies a line of text from an edit control and places it in a specified buffer. The copied line does not contain a terminating null character.

Parameters

wParam   WPARAM: The zero-based index of the line to retrieve from a multiline edit control. A value of zero specifies the topmost line. This parameter is ignored by a single-line edit control.

lParam   LPCSTR: A pointer to the buffer that receives a copy of the line. The first word of the buffer specifies the maximum number of characters that can be copied to the buffer.

Returns   int: If successful, the number of characters copied is returned; otherwise, zero is returned if the line number specified by the line parameter is greater than the number of lines in the edit control.

Include File   winuser.h

Related Messages   EM_LINELENGTH, WM_GETTEXT

EM_GETLINECOUNT

■ Win32s ■ Windows 95 ■ Windows NT

Description   EM_GETLINECOUNT is a message that retrieves the number of lines in a multiline edit control.

Parameters   This message does not use *wParam* or *lParam*; therefore, both must be set to zero.

Returns	int: If the control contains text, the number of lines is returned; otherwise, 1 is returned.
Include File	winuser.h
Related Messages	EM_GETLINE, EM_LINELENGTH

EM_GETMARGINS
Win32s ■ Windows 95 Windows NT

Description	EM_GETMARGINS is a message that retrieves the widths of the left and right margins for an edit control.
Parameters	This message does not use *wParam* or *lParam*; therefore, both must be set to zero.
Returns	DWORD: The return value contains the width of the left margin in the low-order word, and the width of the right margin in the high-order word.
Include File	winuser.h
Related Messages	EM_SETMARGINS

EM_GETMODIFY
■ Win32s ■ Windows 95 ■ Windows NT

Description	EM_GETMODIFY is a message that determines whether the content of an edit control has been modified. This is determined by checking the internal flag maintained by the system for the edit control. The EM_SETMODIFY message can be used to clear the flag.
Parameters	This message does not use *wParam* or *lParam*; therefore, both must be set to zero.
Returns	BOOL: TRUE, if the content of the edit control has been modified; otherwise, FALSE is returned.
Include File	winuser.h
Related Messages	EM_SETMODIFY

EM_GETOLEINTERFACE
Win32s ■ Windows 95 ■ Windows NT

Description	EM_GETOLEINTERFACE is a message that retrieves the IRichEditOle object of a rich-text edit control. For more information, refer to the EM_GETOLEINTERFACE message in Chapter 8, Rich-Text Edit Controls.

EM_GETOPTIONS
■ Win32s ■ Windows 95 ■ Windows NT

Description	EM_GETOPTIONS is a message that retrieves the rich-text edit control options. For more information, refer to the EM_GETOPTIONS message in Chapter 8, Rich-Text Edit Controls.

EM_GETPARAFORMAT ■ Win32s ■ Windows 95 ■ Windows NT

Description   EM_GETPARAFORMAT is a message that retrieves the paragraph formatting of the current selection in a rich-text edit control. For more information, refer to the EM_GETPARAFORMAT message in Chapter 8, Rich-Text Edit Controls.

EM_GETPASSWORDCHAR Win32s ■ Windows 95 ■ Windows NT

Description   EM_GETPASSWORDCHAR is a message that retrieves the password character displayed in an edit control when the user enters text. If the edit control is created with the ES_PASSWORD style, the default password character is set to an asterisk (*).

Parameters   This message does not use *wParam* or *lParam*; therefore, both must be set to zero.

Returns   CHAR: The character to be displayed in place of the character typed by the user is returned. If a password character does not exist, NULL is returned.

Include File   winuser.h

Related Messages   EM_SETPASSWORDCHAR

EM_GETPUNCTUATION Win32s ■ Windows 95 Windows NT

Description   EM_GETPUNCTUATION is a message that is available in Asian-language versions of Windows 95 to retrieve the punctuation characters of the rich-text edit control. For more information, refer to the EM_GETPUNCTUATION message in Chapter 8, Rich-Text Edit Controls.

EM_GETRECT ■ Win32s ■ Windows 95 ■ Windows NT

Description   EM_GETRECT is a message that retrieves the formatting rectangle of an edit control. The formatting rectangle is the limiting rectangle of the text. The limiting rectangle is independent of the size of the edit-control window.

Parameters

wParam   WPARAM: Set to zero.

lParam   LPRECT: A pointer to the RECT structure that receives the formatting rectangle.

Include File   winuser.h

Related Messages   EM_SETRECT, EM_SETRECTNP

EM_GETSEL
■ Win32s ■ Windows 95 ■ Windows NT

Description   EM_GETSEL is a message that gets the starting and ending character positions of the current selection in an edit control.

Parameters

wParam   LPDWORD: A pointer to a 32-bit value that receives the starting position of the selection. This parameter can be NULL.

lParam   LPDWORD: A pointer to a 32-bit value that receives the position of the first nonselected character after the end of the selection. This parameter can be NULL.

Returns   DWORD: A zero-based 32-bit value with the starting position of the selection in the low-order word and the position of the first character after the last selected character in the high-order word is returned.

Include File   winuser.h

Related Messages   EM_SETSEL

EM_GETSELTEXT
■ Win32s ■ Windows 95 ■ Windows NT

Description   EM_GETSELTEXT is a message that retrieves the currently selected text in a rich-text edit control. For more information, refer to the EM_GETSELTEXT message in Chapter 8, Rich-Text Edit Controls.

EM_GETTEXTRANGE
■ Win32s ■ Windows 95 ■ Windows NT

Description   EM_GETTEXTRANGE is a message that retrieves a specified range of characters from a rich-text edit control. For more information, refer to the EM_GETTEXTRANGE message in Chapter 8, Rich-Text Edit Controls.

EM_GETTHUMB
Win32s ■ Windows 95 ■ Windows NT

Description   EM_GETTHUMB is a message that retrieves the position of the scroll box (thumb) in a multiline edit control.

Parameters   This message does not use *wParam* or *lParam*; therefore, both must be set to zero.

Returns   int: The position, in scroll units, of the scroll box is returned.

Include File   winuser.h

EM_GETWORDBREAKPROC
■ Win32s ■ Windows 95 ■ Windows NT

Description   EM_GETWORDBREAKPROC is a message that retrieves the address of the current word wrap function from an edit control.

Parameters	This message does not use *wParam* or *lParam*; therefore, both must be set to zero.
Returns	EDITWORDBREAKPROC: If successful, the address of the application-defined word wrap function is returned; otherwise, if a word wrap function does not exist, NULL is returned.
Include File	winuser.h
See Also	EditWordBreakProc()
Related Messages	EM_FMTLINES, EM_SETWORDBREAKPROC

EM_GETWORDBREAKPROCEX ■ Win32s ■ Windows 95 ■ Windows NT

Description EM_GETWORDBREAKPROCEX is a message that retrieves the address of the currently registered extended word-break procedure for the rich-text edit control. For more information, refer to the EM_GETWORDBREAKPROCEX message in Chapter 8, Rich-Text Edit Controls.

EM_GETWORDWRAPMODE Win32s ■ Windows 95 Windows NT

Description EM_GETWORDWRAPMODE is a message that retrieves the current word wrapping and breaking options for Asian-language versions of Windows 95. For more information, refer to the EM_GETWORDWRAPMODE message in Chapter 8, Rich-Text Edit Controls.

EM_HIDESELECTION ■ Win32s ■ Windows 95 ■ Windows NT

Description EM_HIDESELECTION is a message that either hides or shows the selection in a rich-text edit control. For more information, refer to the EM_HIDESELECTION message in Chapter 8, Rich-Text Edit Controls.

EM_LINEFROMCHAR ■ Win32s ■ Windows 95 ■ Windows NT

Description EM_LINEFROMCHAR is a message that retrieves the index of the line that contains the specified character index in a multiline edit control.

Parameters

wParam WPARAM: The index of the character contained in the line whose number is to be retrieved. If *wParam* is -1, either the line number of the current line is retrieved, or, if there is a selection, the line number of the line containing the beginning of the selection is retrieved.

lParam LPARAM: Set to zero.

Returns int: The zero-based line number of the line containing the character index specified by *wParam* is returned.

Include File   winuser.h
Related Messages   EM_LINEINDEX

EM_LINEINDEX   ■ Win32s ■ Windows 95 ■ Windows NT

Description   EM_LINEINDEX is a message that retrieves the character index of a line in a multiline edit control.

Parameters

wParam   WPARAM: The zero-based line number. A value of -1 specifies the current line number.

lParam   LPARAM: Set to zero.

Returns   int: The return value is the character index of the line specified by *wParam*, or -1 if the specified line number is greater than the number of lines in the edit control.

Include File   winuser.h
Related Messages EM_LINEFROMCHAR

EM_LINELENGTH   ■ Win32s ■ Windows 95 ■ Windows NT

Description   EM_LINELENGTH is a message that retrieves the length of a line, in characters, in an edit control.

Parameters

wParam   WPARAM: The character index of a character in the line whose length is to be retrieved when EM_LINELENGTH is sent to a multiline edit control. If *wParam* is -1, the message returns the number of unselected characters on lines containing selected characters.

lParam   LPARAM: Set to zero.

Returns   int: The return value is the length, in characters, of the line specified by *wParam* when an EM_LINELENGTH message is sent to a multiline edit control.

Include File   winuser.h
Related Messages EM_LINEINDEX

EM_LINESCROLL   ■ Win32s ■ Windows 95 ■ Windows NT

Description   EM_LINESCROLL is a message that scrolls the text vertically or horizontally in a multiline edit control.

Parameters

wParam   WPARAM: The number of characters to scroll horizontally.

lParam   LPARAM: The number of lines to scroll vertically.

Returns	BOOL: TRUE is returned if the message is sent to a multiline edit control; otherwise, FALSE is returned if the message is sent to a single-line edit control.
Include File	winuser.h

EM_PASTESPECIAL ■ Win32s ■ Windows 95 ■ Windows NT

Description	EM_PASTESPECIAL is a message that pastes a specific clipboard format in a rich-text edit control. For more information, refer to the EM_PASTESPECIAL message in Chapter 8, Rich-Text Edit Controls.

EM_POSFROMCHAR Win32s ■ Windows 95 Windows NT

Description	EM_POSFROMCHAR is a message that retrieves the coordinates of the specified character in an edit control. The coordinates are relative to the upper left corner of the edit control's client area. For a single-line edit control, the y coordinate is always zero. A returned coordinate can be negative if the character has been scrolled outside the edit control's client area. The coordinates are truncated to integer values.
Parameters	
wParam	WPARAM: The zero-based index of the character.
lParam	LPARAM: Set to zero.
Returns	DWORD: The coordinates, relative to the edit control, of the upper left corner of the character are returned. If *wParam* is greater than the index of the last character in the control, the return value specifies the coordinates of the position just past the last character in the control. The x coordinate is in the low-order word and the y coordinate is in the high-order word.
Include File	winuser.h
Related Messages	EM_CHARFROMPOS

EM_REPLACESEL ■ Win32s ■ Windows 95 ■ Windows NT

Description	EM_REPLACESEL is a message that replaces the current selection in an edit control with the specified text. If there is not a current selection, the replacement text is inserted at the current location of the caret. Use EM_REPLACESEL to replace only a portion of the text in an edit control. To replace all of the text, use WM_SETTEXT.
Parameters	
wParam	BOOL: TRUE indicates that the replacement operation can be undone; otherwise, FALSE indicates the operation cannot be undone.
lParam	LPCTSTR: A pointer to a null-terminated string containing the replacement text.

Include File	winuser.h
Related Messages	WM_SETTEXT

EM_REQUESTRESIZE ■ Win32s ■ Windows 95 ■ Windows NT

Description   EM_REQUESTRESIZE is a message that instructs a rich-text edit control to send an EN_REQUESTRESIZE notification message to the parent window. For more information, refer to the EM_REQUESTRESIZE message in Chapter 8, Rich-Text Edit Controls.

EM_SCROLL ■ Win32s ■ Windows 95 ■ Windows NT

Description   EM_SCROLL is a message that scrolls the text vertically in a multiline edit control. This message is equivalent to sending a WM_VSCROLL message to the edit control.

Parameters

wParam   int: One or more of the values in Table 11-7 indicating the action that the scroll bar should take.

Table 11-7 EM_SCROLL *wParam* values

Value	Meaning
SB_LINEDOWN	Scroll down one line.
SB_LINEUP	Scroll up one line.
SB_PAGEDOWN	Scroll down one page.
SB_PAGEUP	Scroll up one page.

lParam   LPARAM: Set to zero.

Returns   DWORD: If the message is successful, the high-order word of the return value is TRUE, and the low-order word is the number of lines that the command scrolls. The number returned may not be the same as the actual number of lines scrolled if the scrolling moves to the beginning or the end of the text. If *wParam* specifies an invalid value, the return value is FALSE.

Include File   winuser.h

Related Messages   EM_LINESCROLL, EM_SCROLLCARET, WM_VSCROLL

EM_SCROLLCARET ■ Win32s ■ Windows 95 ■ Windows NT

Description   EM_SCROLLCARET is a message that scrolls the caret into view in an edit control.

Parameters	This message does not use *wParam* or *lParam*; therefore, both must be set to zero.
Returns	int: A nonzero value if the message is sent to an edit control.
Include File	winuser.h
Related Messages	EM_SETSEL

EM_SELECTIONTYPE   ■ Win32s ■ Windows 95 ■ Windows NT

Description   EM_SELECTIONTYPE is a message that determines the selection type for a rich-text edit control. For more information, refer to the EM_SELEC-TIONTYPE message in Chapter 8, Rich-Text Edit Controls.

EM_SETBKGNDCOLOR   ■ Win32s ■ Windows 95 ■ Windows NT

Description   EM_SETBKGNDCOLOR is a message that sets the background color for a rich-text edit control. For more information, refer to the EM_SETBKGND-COLOR message in Chapter 8, Rich-Text Edit Controls.

EM_SETCHARFORMAT   ■ Win32s ■ Windows 95 ■ Windows NT

Description   EM_SETCHARFORMAT is a message that sets character formatting in a rich-text edit control. For more information, refer to the EM_SETCHAR-FORMAT message in Chapter 8, Rich-Text Edit Controls.

EM_SETEVENTMASK   ■ Win32s ■ Windows 95 ■ Windows NT

Description   EM_SETEVENTMASK is a message that sets the event mask for the rich-text edit control. For more information, refer to the EM_SETEVENTMASK message in Chapter 8, Rich-Text Edit Controls.

EM_SETHANDLE   Win32s   Windows 95 ■ Windows NT

Description   EM_SETHANDLE is a message that sets the handle of the memory buffer that the multiline edit control will use to store the currently displayed text. Before an application sets a new memory handle, it should send an EM_GETHANDLE message to retrieve the handle of the current memory buffer to free. An edit control automatically either reallocates the buffer whenever it needs additional space for text, or it removes enough text so that additional space is no longer needed. An application can only send this message to a multiline edit control in a dialog box if it created the dialog box with the DS_LOCALEDIT style flag set.

Parameters

wParam   HLOCAL: The handle of the memory buffer the edit control uses to store the currently displayed text. If necessary, the edit control reallocates this memory.

lParam   Set to zero.

Include File   winuser.h

Related Messages   EM_CANUNDO, EM_GETHANDLE, EM_GETMODIFY

EM_SETIMECOLOR
Win32s ■ Windows 95   Windows NT

Description   EM_SETIMECOLOR is a message that sets the IME composition color for Asian-language versions of Windows 95. For more information, refer to the EM_SETIMECOLOR message in Chapter 8, Rich-Text Edit Controls.

EM_SETIMEOPTIONS
Win32s ■ Windows 95   Windows NT

Description   EM_SETIMEOPTIONS is a message that sets the IME options for Asian-language versions of Windows 95. For more information, refer to the EM_SETIMEOPTIONS message in Chapter 8, Rich-Text Edit Controls.

EM_SETLIMITTEXT
Win32s ■ Windows 95 ■ Windows NT

Description   EM_SETLIMITTEXT is a message that sets the maximum amount of text that an edit control can contain.

Parameters

wParam   WPARAM: The new text limit, in bytes. If *wParam* is 0, the maximum text limit is 32,766 bytes for a single-line edit control, and 65,535 bytes for a multiline edit control.

lParam   LPARAM: Set to zero.

Include File   winuser.h

Related Messages   EM_GETLIMITTEXT

EM_SETMARGINS
Win32s ■ Windows 95   Windows NT

Description   EM_SETMARGINS is a message that sets the widths of the left and right margins for an edit control and then redraws the control in pixels to reflect the new margins.

Parameters

wParam   WPARAM: One or more of the values in Table 11-8 indicating which margins to set for the edit control.

Table 11-8 EM_SETMARGINS *wParam* values

Value	Meaning
EC_LEFTMARGIN	Sets the left margin.
EC_RIGHTMARGIN	Sets the right margin.
EC_USEFONTINFO	Uses the information about the current font of the edit control to set the margins. For a single-line edit control, sets margins to the average width of characters in the font. For a multiline edit control, sets the right margin to the A width of the font (the distance added to the current position before drawing a character), and the left margin to the C width (the distance added to the current position to provide white space to the right of a character).

LOWORD(lParam)	LPARAM: The width of the left margin, in pixels. This value is ignored if *wParam* does not include EC_LEFTMARGIN or if EC_USEFONTINFO is specified.
HIWORD(lParam)	LPARAM: The width of the right margin, in pixels. This value is ignored if *wParam* does not include EC_RIGHTMARGIN or if EC_USEFONTINFO is specified.
Include File	winuser.h
Related Messages	EM_GETMARGINS

EM_SETMODIFY   ■ Win32s ■ Windows 95 ■ Windows NT

Description	EM_SETMODIFY is a message that either sets or clears the modification flag for an edit control. The flag is automatically set when the user changes the text. EM_GETMODIFY can also be sent to retrieve the value of the modification flag.
Parameters	
wParam	UINT: TRUE indicates that the text in the edit control has been modified, and FALSE indicates that it has not been modified.
lParam	LPARAM: Set to zero.
Include File	winuser.h
Related Messages	EM_GETMODIFY

EM_SETOLEINTERFACE   ■ Win32s ■ Windows 95 ■ Windows NT

Description	EM_SETOLEINTERFACE is a message that gives the rich-text edit control an IRichEditOleCallback object to use to obtain OLE-related resources and information from the client. For more information, refer to the EM_SETOLEINTERFACE message in Chapter 8, Rich-Text Edit Controls.

EM_SETOPTIONS
■ Win32s ■ Windows 95 ■ Windows NT

Description
EM_SETOPTIONS is a message that sets the options for a rich-text edit control. For more information, refer to the EM_SETOPTIONS message in Chapter 8, Rich-Text Edit Controls.

EM_SETPARAFORMAT
■ Win32s ■ Windows 95 ■ Windows NT

Description
EM_SETPARAFORMAT is a message that sets the paragraph formatting for the current selection in a rich-text edit control. For more information, refer to the EM_SETPARAFORMAT message in Chapter 8, Rich-Text Edit Controls.

EM_SETPASSWORDCHAR
■ Win32s ■ Windows 95 ■ Windows NT

Description
EM_SETPASSWORDCHAR is a message that either sets or removes the password character for a single-line edit control when the user types text. When a password character is set, that character displays in place of each character the user types. When EM_SETPASSWORDCHAR is received by an edit control, all the visible characters in the control are redrawn using the character specified by *wParam*. If the edit control is created with the ES_PASSWORD style, the default password character is set to an asterisk (*). This style is removed if EM_SETPASSWORDCHAR is sent with *wParam* set to zero.

Parameters

wParam
UINT: The character to be displayed in place of the character typed by the user. If *wParam* is zero, the characters typed by the user display on the screen.

lParam
LPARAM: Set to zero.

Include File
winuser.h

Related Messages
EM_GETPASSWORDCHAR

EM_SETPUNCTUATION
Win32s ■ Windows 95 Windows NT

Description
EM_GETPUNCTUATION is a message that sets the punctuation characters for the rich-text edit control in Asian-language versions of Windows 95. For more information, refer to the EM_SETPUNCTUATION message in Chapter 8, Rich-Text Edit Controls.

EM_SETREADONLY   ■ Win32s ■ Windows 95 ■ Windows NT

Description   EM_SETREADONLY is a message that either sets or removes the read-only style (ES_READONLY) of an edit control. When an edit control has the ES_READONLY style, the user cannot change the text within the edit control. To determine whether an edit control has the ES_READONLY style, use GetWindowLong() with the GWL_STYLE flag.

Parameters

wParam   BOOL: TRUE sets the ES_READONLY style; FALSE removes the ES_READONLY style.

lParam   LPARAM: Set to zero.

Returns   int: If the operation succeeds, a nonzero value is returned; otherwise, zero is returned.

Include File   winuser.h

See Also   GetWindowLong()

EM_SETRECT   ■ Win32s ■ Windows 95 ■ Windows NT

Description   EM_SETRECT is a message that sets the formatting rectangle of the text in a multiline edit control, and then redraws the text of the control. The formatting rectangle is independent of the size of the edit control window. When the edit control is first created, the formatting rectangle is the same as the client area of the edit control window. By using EM_SETRECT, an application can make the formatting rectangle larger or smaller than the edit control window.

Parameters

wParam   WPARAM: Set to zero.

lParam   LPRECT: A pointer to a RECT structure that specifies the new dimensions of the rectangle.

Include File   winuser.h

Related Messages EM_GETRECT, EM_SETRECTNP

EM_SETRECTNP   ■ Win32s ■ Windows 95 ■ Windows NT

Description   EM_SETRECTNP is a message that sets the formatting rectangle of the text in a multiline edit control, but it does not redraw the text of the control. The formatting rectangle is independent of the size of the edit control window. When the edit control is first created, the formatting rectangle is the same as the client area of the edit control window. By using EM_SETRECTNP, an application can make the formatting rectangle larger or smaller than the edit control window.

Parameters

wParam	WPARAM: Set to zero.
lParam	LPRECT: A pointer to a RECT structure that specifies the new dimensions of the rectangle.
Include File	winuser.h
Related Messages	EM_SETRECT

EM_SETSEL   ■ Win32s ■ Windows 95 ■ Windows NT

Description   EM_SETSEL is a message that selects a range of characters in an edit control. If *wParam* is 0 and *lParam* is -1, all the text in the edit control is selected. If *wParam* is -1, any current selection is removed.

Parameters

wParam	int: The starting character position of the selection.
lParam	int: The ending character position of the selection.
Include File	winuser.h
Related Messages	EM_GETSEL, EM_REPLACESEL, EM_SCROLLCARET

EM_SETTABSTOPS   ■ Win32s ■ Windows 95 ■ Windows NT

Description   EM_SETTABSTOPS is a message that sets the tab stops in a multiline edit control. When text is copied to the control, any tab character in the text causes spaces to be generated up to the next tab stop.

Parameters

wParam	WPARAM: If *wParam* is zero, *lParam* is ignored and default tab stops are set at every 32 dialog box units. If *wParam* is 1, tab stops are set at distances specified by *lParam*. If *wParam* is greater than 1, *lParam* points to an array of tab stops.
lParam	LPDWORD: A pointer to an array of unsigned integers specifying the tab stops, in dialog units. If *wParam* is 1, *lParam* points to an unsigned integer containing the distance between all tab stops, in dialog box units.
Returns	BOOL: TRUE is returned if all the tabs are set; otherwise, FALSE is returned.
Include File	winuser.h
See Also	GetDialogBaseUnits(), InvalidateRect()

EM_SETTARGETDEVICE   ■ Win32s ■ Windows 95 ■ Windows NT

Description   EM_SETTARGETDEVICE is a message that sets the target device and line width of the WYSIWYG formatting in the rich-text edit control. For more information, refer to the EM_SETTARGETDEVICE message in Chapter 8, Rich-Text Edit Controls.

EM_SETWORDBREAKPROC ■ Win32s ■ Windows 95 ■ Windows NT

Description   EM_SETWORDBREAKPROC is a message that is sent to an edit control to replace the default word wrap function with an application-defined word wrap function.

Parameters

wParam   WPARAM: Set to zero.

lParam   EDITWORDBREAKPROC: The address of the application-defined word wrap function.

Include File   winuser.h

See Also   EditWordBreakProc()

Related Messages   EM_FMTLINES, EM_GETWORDBREAKPROC

EM_SETWORDBREAKPROCEX ■ Win32s ■ Windows 95 ■ Windows NT

Description   EM_SETWORDBREAKPROCEX is a message that sets the extended word-break procedure for the rich-text edit control. For more information, refer to the EM_SETWORDBREAKPROCEX message in Chapter 8, Rich-Text Edit Controls.

EM_SETWORDWRAPMODE Win32s ■ Windows 95 Windows NT

Description   EM_SETWORDWRAPMODE is a message that sets the word wrapping and breaking options for the rich-text edit control in Asian-language versions of Windows 95. For more information, refer to the EM_SETWORDWRAPMODE message in Chapter 8, Rich-Text Edit Controls.

EM_STREAMIN ■ Win32s ■ Windows 95 ■ Windows NT

Description   EM_STREAMIN is a message that replaces the contents of a rich-text edit control with the specified data stream. For more information, refer to the EM_STREAMIN message in Chapter 8, Rich-Text Edit Controls.

EM_STREAMOUT ■ Win32s ■ Windows 95 ■ Windows NT

Description   EM_STREAMOUT is a message that writes the contents of a rich-text edit control to the specified data stream. For more information, refer to the EM_STREAMOUT message in Chapter 8, Rich-Text Edit Controls.

EM_UNDO

■ Win32s ■ Windows 95 ■ Windows NT

Description	EM_UNDO is a message that undoes the last edit control operation. An undo operation can also be undone.
Parameters	This message does not use *wParam* or *lParam*; therefore, both must be set to zero.
Returns	BOOL: TRUE is returned for a single-line edit control. For a multiline edit control, TRUE is returned if the undo operation is successful; otherwise, FALSE is returned.
Include File	winuser.h
Related Messages	EM_CANUNDO

EN_CHANGE

■ Win32s ■ Windows 95 ■ Windows NT

Description	EN_CHANGE is a notification message that is sent when the user has taken an action that may have altered text in an edit control. Unlike EN_UPDATE, this notification message is sent after Windows updates the screen. The parent window of the edit control receives this notification message through WM_COMMAND.
Parameters	
wParam	int: The edit control identifier.
lParam	HWND: The handle of the edit control.
Include File	winuser.h
Related Messages	EN_UPDATE, WM_COMMAND

EN_CORRECTTEXT

■ Win32s ■ Windows 95 ■ Windows NT

Description	EN_CORRECTTEXT is a notification message that notifies the parent window of a rich-text edit control that a SYV_CORRECT gesture has occurred. For more information, refer to the EN_CORRECTTEXT notification message in Chapter 8, Rich-Text Edit Controls.

EN_DROPFILES

■ Win32s ■ Windows 95 ■ Windows NT

Description	EN_DROPFILES is a notification message that notifies the parent window of a rich-text edit control that the user is attempting to drop files into the control. For more information, refer to the EN_DROPFILES notification message in Chapter 8, Rich-Text Edit Controls.

EN_ERRSPACE
■ Win32s ■ Windows 95 ■ Windows NT

Description   EN_ERRSPACE is a notification message that is sent when an edit control cannot allocate enough memory to meet a specific request. The parent window of the edit control receives this notification message through the WM_COMMAND message.

Parameters

LOWORD(wParam)   int: The identifier of the edit control.

lParam   HWND: The handle of the edit control.

Include File   winuser.h

Related Messages   WM_COMMAND

EN_HSCROLL
■ Win32s ■ Windows 95 ■ Windows NT

Description   EN_HSCROLL is a notification message that is sent when the user clicks an edit control's horizontal scroll bar. The parent window of the edit control receives this notification message through the WM_COMMAND message before the screen is updated.

Parameters

LOWORD(wParam)   int: The identifier of the edit control.

lParam   HWND: The handle of the edit control.

Include File   winuser.h

Related Messages   EN_VSCROLL, WM_COMMAND

EN_IMECHANGE
Win32s ■ Windows 95   Windows NT

Description   EN_IMECHANGE is a notification message that notifies the parent window of a rich-text edit control that the IME conversion status has changed in an Asian-language version of Windows 95. For more information, refer to the EN_IMECHANGE notification message in Chapter 8, Rich-Text Edit Controls.

EN_KILLFOCUS
■ Win32s ■ Windows 95 ■ Windows NT

Description   EN_KILLFOCUS is a notification message that is sent when an edit control loses the keyboard focus. The parent window of the edit control receives this notification message through the WM_COMMAND message.

Parameters

LOWORD(wParam)   int: The identifier of the edit control.

HIWORD(wParam)   HIWORD: The notification code.

lParam   HWND: The handle of the edit control.

Include File	winuser.h
Related Messages	EN_SETFOCUS, WM_COMMAND

EN_MAXTEXT   ■ Win32s ■ Windows 95 ■ Windows NT

Description   EN_MAXTEXT is a notification message that is sent when the current text insertion has exceeded the specified number of characters for the edit control and has been truncated. This message is also sent when an edit control does not have the ES_AUTOHSCROLL style, and the number of characters to be inserted would exceed the width of the edit control, or when an edit control does not have the ES_AUTOVSCROLL style, and the total number of lines resulting from a text insertion would exceed the height of the edit control. The parent window of the edit control receives this notification message through the WM_COMMAND message.

Parameters

LOWORD(wParam)	int: The identifier of the edit control.
lParam	HWND: The handle of the edit control.
Include File	winuser.h
Related Messages	WM_COMMAND

EN_MSGFILTER   ■ Win32s ■ Windows 95 ■ Windows NT

Description   EN_MSGFILTER is a notification message that notifies the parent window that a keyboard or mouse event exists in the rich-text edit control. For more information, refer to the EN_MSGFILTER notification message in Chapter 8, Rich-Text Edit Controls.

EN_OLEOPFAILED   ■ Win32s ■ Windows 95 ■ Windows NT

Description   EN_OLEOPFAILED is a notification message that notifies the parent window of a rich-text edit control that the user action on the OLE object has failed. For more information, refer to the EN_OLEOPFAILED notification message in Chapter 8, Rich-Text Edit Controls.

EN_PROTECTED   ■ Win32s ■ Windows 95 ■ Windows NT

Description   EN_PROTECTED is a notification message that notifies the parent window of a rich-text edit control that the user is taking an action that would change a protected range of text. For more information, refer to the EN_PROTECTED notification message in Chapter 8, Rich-Text Edit Controls.

EN_REQUESTRESIZE
■ Win32s ■ Windows 95 ■ Windows NT

Description   EN_REQUESTRESIZE is a notification message that notifies the parent window that the rich-text edit control's contents are either smaller or larger than the control's window. For more information, refer to the EN_REQUESTRESIZE notification message in Chapter 8, Rich-Text Edit Controls.

EN_SAVECLIPBOARD
■ Win32s ■ Windows 95 ■ Windows NT

Description   EN_SAVECLIPBOARD is a notification message that notifies the parent window of a rich-text edit control that the clipboard contains information and it is closing. For more information, refer to the EN_SAVECLIPBOARD notification message in Chapter 8, Rich-Text Edit Controls.

EN_SELCHANGE
■ Win32s ■ Windows 95 ■ Windows NT

Description   EN_SELCHANGE is a notification message that notifies the parent window that the current selection in the rich-text edit control has changed. For more information, refer to the EN_SELCHANGE notification message in Chapter 8, Rich-Text Edit Controls.

EN_SETFOCUS
■ Win32s ■ Windows 95 ■ Windows NT

Description   EN_SETFOCUS is a notification message that is sent when an edit control receives the keyboard focus. The parent window of the edit control receives this notification message through the WM_COMMAND message.

Parameters
LOWORD(wParam)   int: The identifier of the edit control.
HIWORD(wParam)   WPARAM: The notification code.
lParam   HWND: The handle of the edit control.
Include File   winuser.h
Related Messages   EN_KILLFOCUS, WM_COMMAND

EN_STOPNOUNDO
■ Win32s ■ Windows 95 ■ Windows NT

Description   EN_STOPNOUNDO is a notification message that notifies the parent window that an action occurred for which the rich-text edit control cannot maintain the undo state. For more information, refer to the EN_STOPNOUNDO notification message in Chapter 8, Rich-Text Edit Controls.

EN_UPDATE
■ Win32s ■ Windows 95 ■ Windows NT

Description EN_UPDATE is a notification message that is sent when an edit control is about to display altered text. This notification message is sent after the control has formatted the text, but before it displays the text; making it possible to resize the edit control window. The parent window of the edit control receives this notification message through the WM_COMMAND message.

Parameters

LOWORD(wParam) int: The identifier of the edit control.

lParam HWND: The handle of the edit control.

Include File winuser.h

Related Messages EN_CHANGE, WM_COMMAND

EN_VSCROLL
■ Win32s ■ Windows 95 ■ Windows NT

Description EN_VSCROLL is a notification message that is sent when the user clicks an edit control's vertical scroll bar. The parent window of the edit control receives this notification message through the WM_COMMAND message before the screen is updated.

Parameters

LOWORD(wParam) int: The identifier of the edit control.

lParam HWND: The handle of the edit control.

Include File winuser.h

Related Messages EN_HSCROLL, WM_COMMAND

HDM_DELETEITEM
■ Win32s ■ Windows 95 ■ Windows NT

Description HDM_DELETEITEM is a message that deletes an item from a header control. For more information, refer to the Header_DeleteItem macro in Chapter 9, Miscellaneous Controls.

HDM_GETITEM
■ Win32s ■ Windows 95 ■ Windows NT

Description HDM_GETITEM is a message that retrieves information about an item in a header control. For more information, refer to the Header_GetItem macro in Chapter 9, Miscellaneous Controls.

HDM_GETITEMCOUNT ■ Win32s ■ Windows 95 ■ Windows NT

Description   HDM_GETITEMCOUNT is a message that determines the number of items in a header control. For more information, refer to the Header_GetItemCount macro in Chapter 9, Miscellaneous Controls.

HDM_HITTEST ■ Win32s ■ Windows 95 ■ Windows NT

Description   HDM_HITTEST is a message that determines which header control item is located at the specified point. For more information, refer to the HDM_HITTEST message in Chapter 9, Miscellaneous Controls.

HDM_INSERTITEM ■ Win32s ■ Windows 95 ■ Windows NT

Description   HDM_INSERTITEM is a message that inserts a new item into a header control. For more information, refer to the Header_InsertItem macro in Chapter 9, Miscellaneous Controls.

HDM_LAYOUT ■ Win32s ■ Windows 95 ■ Windows NT

Description   HDM_LAYOUT is a message that determines the dimensions for a new header control for the specified rectangle. For more information, refer to the Header_Layout macro in Chapter 9, Miscellaneous Controls.

HDM_SETITEM ■ Win32s ■ Windows 95 ■ Windows NT

Description   HDM_SETITEM is a message that sets the attributes of the specified item in a header control. For more information, refer to the Header_SetItem macro in Chapter 9, Miscellaneous Controls.

HDN_BEGINTRACK ■ Win32s ■ Windows 95 ■ Windows NT

Description   HDN_BEGINTRACK is a notification message that notifies the parent window that a divider in the header control is being dragged. For more information, refer to the HDN_BEGINTRACK notification message in Chapter 9, Miscellaneous Controls. (See Figure 11-3.)

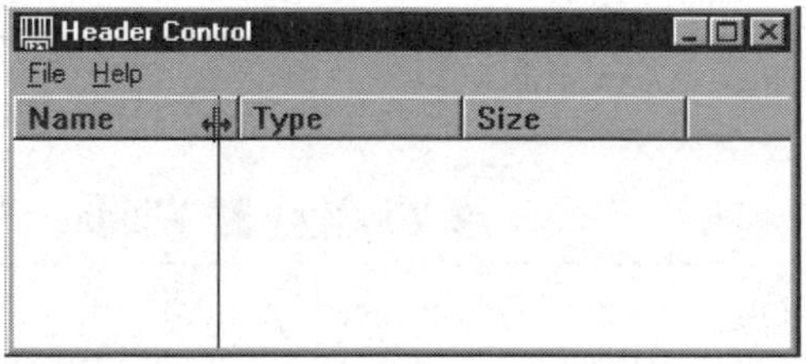

Figure 11-3 HDN_BEGINTRACK Example

HDN_DIVIDERDBLCLICK   ■ Win32s ■ Windows 95 ■ Windows NT

Description   HDN_DIVIDERDBLCLICK is a notification message that notifies the parent window of a header control that the divider area of the control was double-clicked with the mouse. For more information, refer to the HDN_DIVIDERDBLCLICK notification message in Chapter 9, Miscellaneous Controls.

HDN_ENDTRACK   ■ Win32s ■ Windows 95 ■ Windows NT

Description   HDN_ENDTRACK is a notification message that notifies the parent window of a header control that the dragging of the divider is finished. For more information, refer to the HDN_ENDTRACK notification message in Chapter 9, Miscellaneous Controls.

HDN_ITEMCHANGED   ■ Win32s ■ Windows 95 ■ Windows NT

Description   HDN_ITEMCHANGED is a notification message that notifies the parent window that the attributes of an item in the header control have changed. For more information, refer to the HDN_ITEMCHANGED notification message in Chapter 9, Miscellaneous Controls.

HDN_ITEMCHANGING   ■ Win32s ■ Windows 95 ■ Windows NT

Description   HDN_ITEMCHANGING is a notification message that notifies the parent window that the attributes of an item in the header control are about to change. For more information, refer to the HDN_ITEMCHANGING notification message in Chapter 9, Miscellaneous Controls.

HDN_ITEMCLICK   ■ Win32s ■ Windows 95 ■ Windows NT

Description   HDN_ITEMCLICK is a notification message that notifies the parent window that the header control item was clicked with the mouse. For more information, refer to the HDN_ITEMCLICK notification message in Chapter 9, Miscellaneous Controls.

HDN_ITEMDBLCLICK ■ Win32s ■ Windows 95 ■ Windows NT

Description   HDN_ITEMDBLCLICK is a notification message that notifies the parent window that the header control was double-clicked with the mouse. For more information, refer to the HDN_ITEMDBLCLICK notification message in Chapter 9, Miscellaneous Controls.

HDN_TRACK ■ Win32s ■ Windows 95 ■ Windows NT

Description   HDN_TRACK is a notification message that notifies the parent window that the divider of the header control is being dragged by the user. For more information, refer to the HDN_TRACK notification message in Chapter 9, Miscellaneous Controls.

HKM_GETHOTKEY ■ Win32s ■ Windows 95 ■ Windows NT

Description   HKM_GETHOTKEY is a message that determines the virtual-key code and modifier flags for a hot key. For more information, refer to the HKM_GETHOTKEY message in Chapter 9, Miscellaneous Controls.

HKM_SETHOTKEY ■ Win32s ■ Windows 95 ■ Windows NT

Description   HKM_SETHOTKEY is a message that sets the hot-key combination for the hot-key control. For more information, refer to the HKM_SETHOTKEY message in Chapter 9, Miscellaneous Controls.

HKM_SETRULES ■ Win32s ■ Windows 95 ■ Windows NT

Description   HKM_SETRULES is a message that defines the invalid combinations and the default modifier combination for a hot-key control. For more information, refer to the HKM_SETRULES message in Chapter 9, Miscellaneous Controls.

ICM_ABOUT ■ Win32s ■ Windows 95 ■ Windows NT

Description   ICM_ABOUT is a message that either notifies a video compression driver to display its About dialog box, or queries a video compression driver to determine if it has an About dialog box.

Parameters

wParam	UINT: The handle of the parent window of the displayed dialog box. A value of -1 in *wParam* determines if a driver has an About dialog box.
lParam	LPARAM: Set to zero.
Returns	int: if the driver supports this message, ICERR_OK is returned; otherwise, ICERR_UNSUPPORTED is returned.
Include File	vfw.h

ICM_COMPRESS
■ Win32s ■ Windows 95 ■ Windows NT

Description	ICM_COMPRESS is a message that notifies a video compression driver to compress a frame of data into an application-defined buffer. The driver should allocate the necessary tables and memory for compressing the data formats.

Parameters

wParam	LPVOID: The address of an ICCOMPRESS structure. The following members of the structure specify the compression parameters: *lpbiInput*, *lpInput*, *lpbiOutput*, *lpOutput*, *lpbiPrev*, *lpPrev*, *lpckid*, *lpdwFlags*, *dwFrameSize*, and *dwQuality*.
lParam	ICCOMPRESS: The size, in bytes, of the ICCOMPRESS structure.
Returns	int: If successful, ICERR_OK is returned; otherwise, an error is returned.
Include File	vfw.h

ICM_COMPRESS_BEGIN
■ Win32s ■ Windows 95 ■ Windows NT

Description	ICM_COMPRESS_BEGIN is a message that notifies a video compression driver to prepare to compress data.

Parameters

wParam	LPVOID: The address of a BITMAPINFO structure containing the input format.
lParam	LPVOID: The address of a BITMAPINFO structure containing the output format.
Returns	int: If the specified compression is supported, ICERR_OK is returned; otherwise, ICERR_BADFORMAT is returned if the input or output format is not supported.
Include File	vfw.h

ICM_COMPRESS_END
■ Win32s ■ Windows 95 ■ Windows NT

Description	ICM_COMPRESS_END is a message that notifies a video compression driver to end compression and free resources allocated for compression.

Parameters	This message does not use *wParam* or *lParam*; therefore, both must be set to zero.
Returns	int: If the driver is successful, ICERR_OK is returned; otherwise, an error is returned.
Include File	vfw.h

ICM_COMPRESS_FRAMES_INFO ■ Win32s ■ Windows 95 ■ Windows NT

Description	ICM_COMPRESS_FRAMES_INFO is a message that notifies a compression driver to set the parameters for the pending compression.
Parameters	
wParam	LPVOID: The address of an ICCOMPRESSFRAMES structure. The *GetData* and *PutData* members of this structure are not used with this message.
lParam	ICCOMPRESSFRAMES: The size, in bytes, of the ICCOMPRESSFRAMES structure.
Returns	int: If the driver is successful, ICERR_OK is returned; otherwise, an error is returned.
Include File	vfw.h

ICM_COMPRESS_GET_FORMAT ■ Win32s ■ Windows 95 ■ Windows NT

Description	ICM_COMPRESS_GET_FORMAT is a message that requests the output format of the compressed data from a video compression driver.
Parameters	
wParam	LPVOID: The address of a BITMAPINFO structure containing the input format.
lParam	LPVOID: The address of a BITMAPINFO structure to contain the output format. A value of zero requests only the size of the output format. If *lParam* is a nonzero value, the driver should fill the BITMAPINFO structure with the default output format corresponding to the input format specified for *wParam*.
Returns	int: If the driver is successful, ICERR_OK is returned; otherwise, an error is returned.
Include File	vfw.h

ICM_COMPRESS_GET_SIZE ■ Win32s ■ Windows 95 ■ Windows NT

Description	ICM_COMPRESS_GET_SIZE is a message that requests that the video compression driver supply the maximum size of one frame of data when compressed into the specified output format.

Parameters

wParam	LPVOID: The address of a BITMAPINFO structure containing the input format.
lParam	LPVOID: The address of a BITMAPINFO structure containing the output format.
Returns	int: The maximum number of bytes a single compressed frame can occupy is returned.
Include File	vfw.h

ICM_COMPRESS_QUERY ■ Win32s ■ Windows 95 ■ Windows NT

Description   ICM_COMPRESS_QUERY is a message that queries a video compression driver to determine if it supports a specific input format or if it can compress a specific input format to a specific output format.

Parameters

wParam	LPVOID: The address of a BITMAPINFO structure containing the input format.
lParam	LPVOID: The address of a BITMAPINFO structure containing the output format. A zero indicates any output format is acceptable.
Returns	int: If the specified compression is supported, ICERR_OK is returned; otherwise, ICERR_BADFORMAT is returned.
Include File	vfw.h

ICM_CONFIGURE ■ Win32s ■ Windows 95 ■ Windows NT

Description   ICM_CONFIGURE is a message that either notifies a video compression driver to display its configuration dialog box or queries a video compression driver to determine if it has a configuration dialog box.

Parameters

wParam	UINT: The handle of the parent window of the displayed dialog box.
lParam	LPARAM: Set to zero.
Returns	int: If the driver supports this message, ICERR_OK is returned; otherwise, ICERR_UNSUPPORTED is returned.
Include File	vfw.h
Related Messages	ICM_GETSTATE, ICM_SETSTATE

ICM_DECOMPRESS ■ Win32s ■ Windows 95 ■ Windows NT

Description   ICM_DECOMPRESS is a message that notifies a video decompression driver to decompress a frame of data into an application-defined buffer. Send the ICM_DRAW message to decompress data directly to the screen.

Parameters

wParam   LPVOID: The address of an ICDECOMPRESS structure.

lParam   ICDECOMPRESS: The size, in bytes, of the ICDECOMPRESS structure.

Returns   int: If the driver is successful, ICERR_OK is returned; otherwise an error is returned. An error is also returned if ICM_DECOMPRESS is received prior to the ICM_DECOMPRESS_BEGIN message.

Include File   vfw.h

Related Messages ICM_DRAW, ICM_DECOMPRESS_BEGIN

ICM_DECOMPRESS_BEGIN   ■ Win32s ■ Windows 95 ■ Windows NT

Description   ICM_DECOMPRESS_BEGIN is a message that notifies a video decompression driver to prepare to decompress data. When the driver receives this message, it should allocate the necessary buffers and perform any other time-consuming operations so that it can process ICM_DECOMPRESS messages efficiently. Send the ICM_DRAW message to decompress data directly to the screen. ICM_DECOMPRESS_BEGIN and ICM_DECOMPRESS_END do not nest. If your driver receives ICM_DECOMPRESS_BEGIN before decompression is stopped with ICM_DECOMPRESS_END, it should restart decompression with new parameters.

Parameters

wParam   LPVOID: The address of a BITMAPINFO structure containing the input format.

lParam   LPVOID: The address of a BITMAPINFO structure containing the output format.

Returns   int: If the specified decompression is supported, ICERR_OK is returned; otherwise ICERR_BADFORMAT is returned.

Include File   vfw.h

Related Messages ICM_DECOMPRESS, ICM_DECOMPRESS_END

ICM_DECOMPRESS_END   ■ Win32s ■ Windows 95 ■ Windows NT

Description   ICM_DECOMPRESS_END is a message that notifies a video decompression driver to end decompression and free resources allocated for decompression. The driver should free any resources allocated for ICM_DECOMPRESS_BEGIN. ICM_DECOMPRESS_BEGIN and ICM_DECOMPRESS_END do not nest. If your driver receives ICM_DECOMPRESS_BEGIN before decompression is stopped with ICM_DECOMPRESS_END, it should restart decompression with new parameters.

Parameters	This message does not use *wParam* or *lParam*; therefore, both must be set to zero.
Returns	int: If the driver is successful, ICERR_OK is returned; otherwise, an error is returned.
Include File	vfw.h
Related Messages	ICM_DECOMPRESS_BEGIN

ICM_DECOMPRESS_GET_FORMAT ■ Win32s ■ Windows 95 ■ Windows NT

Description ICM_DECOMPRESS_GET_FORMAT is a message that requests the output format of the decompressed data from a video decompression driver. If *wParam* is a nonzero value, the driver should fill the BITMAPINFO structure with the default output format corresponding to the input format specified for *wParam*. If the compressor can produce several formats, the default format should be the one that preserves the greatest amount of information.

Parameters

wParam LPVOID: The address of a BITMAPINFO structure containing the input format.

lParam LPVOID: The address of a BITMAPINFO structure to contain the output format. Zero requests only the size of the output format.

Returns int: If the driver is successful, ICERR_OK is returned; otherwise, an error is returned.

Include File vfw.h

ICM_DECOMPRESS_GET_PALETTE ■ Win32s ■ Windows 95 ■ Windows NT

Description ICM_DECOMPRESS_GET_PALETTE is a message that requests that the video decompression driver supply the color table of the output BITMAPINFOHEADER structure. The driver should support this message only if it uses a palette other than the one specified in the input format. If *lParam* is a nonzero value, the driver sets the *biClrUsed* member of the BITMAPINFOHEADER structure to the number of colors in the color table and fills the *bmiColors* members of BITMAPINFO with the actual colors.

Parameters

wParam LPVOID: The address of a BITMAPINFOHEADER structure containing the input format.

lParam LPVOID: The address of a BITMAPINFOHEADER structure to contain the color table. The space reserved for the color table is always at least 256 colors. Specify zero for this parameter to return only the size of the color table.

Returns	int: If the driver is successful, ICERR_OK is returned; otherwise, an error is returned.
Include File	vfw.h

ICM_DECOMPRESS_QUERY   ■ Win32s   ■ Windows 95   ■ Windows NT

Description	ICM_DECOMPRESS_QUERY is a message that queries a video decompression driver to determine if it supports a specific input format or if it can decompress a specific input format to a specific output format.
Parameters	
wParam	LPVOID: The address of a BITMAPINFO structure containing the input format.
lParam	LPVOID: The address of a BITMAPINFO structure containing the output format. Specify zero for lParam to indicate that any output format is acceptable.
Returns	int: If the specified decompression is supported, ICERR_OK is returned; otherwise ICERR_BADFORMAT is returned.
Include File	vfw.h

ICM_DECOMPRESS_SET_PALETTE   ■ Win32s   ■ Windows 95   ■ Windows NT

Description	ICM_DECOMPRESS_SET_PALETTE is a message that specifies a palette for a video decompression driver to use if it is decompressing to a format that uses a palette. This message is used primarily when a driver decompresses images to the screen and another application that uses a palette is in the foreground, forcing the decompression driver to adapt to a foreign set of colors.
Parameters	
wParam	LPVOID: The address of a BITMAPINFOHEADER structure whose color table contains the colors that should be used if possible. Specify zero to use the default set of output colors.
lParam	LPARAM: Set to zero.
Returns	int: ICERR_OK is returned if the decompression driver can precisely decompress images to the suggested palette using the set of colors as they are arranged in the palette; otherwise, ICERR_UNSUPPORTED is returned.
Include File	vfw.h
Related Messages	ICM_DECOMPRESS_GET_FORMAT, ICM_DECOMPRESS_GET_PALLETE

ICM_DECOMPRESSEX   ■ Win32s   ■ Windows 95   ■ Windows NT

Description	ICM_DECOMPRESSEX is a message that notifies a video compression driver to decompress a frame of data directly to the screen, decompress to an

upside-down DIB, or decompress images described with source and destination rectangles. Send ICM_DRAW to decompress the data directly to the screen.

Parameters

wParam   LPVOID: The address of an ICDECOMPRESSEX structure.

lParam   ICDECOMPRESSEX: The size, in bytes, of the ICDECOMPRESSEX structure.

Returns   int: ICERR_OK if the driver is successful; otherwise an error is returned. An error is returned if this message is received before ICM_DECOMPRESSEX_BEGIN.

Include File vfw.h

Related Messages ICM_DECOMPRESSEX_BEGIN, ICM_DRAW

ICM_DECOMPRESSEX_BEGIN   ■ Win32s ■ Windows 95 ■ Windows NT

Description   ICM_DECOMPRESSEX_BEGIN is a message that notifies a video compression driver to prepare to decompress data. When the driver receives this message, it should allocate the necessary buffers and perform any time-consuming operations so that it can process ICM_DECOMPRESSEX messages efficiently. Send ICM_DRAW_BEGIN to decompress data directly to the screen. ICM_DECOMPRESSEX_BEGIN and ICM_DECOMPRESSEX_END do not nest. If the driver receives ICM_DECOMPRESSEX_BEGIN before decompression is stopped with ICM_DECOMPRESSEX_END, it should restart decompression with new parameters.

Parameters

wParam   LPVOID: The address of an ICDECOMPRESSEX structure containing the input and output formats.

lParam   ICDECOMPRESSEX: The size, in bytes, of the ICDECOMPRESSEX structure.

Returns   int: If the specified decompression is supported, ICERR_OK is returned; otherwise ICERR_BADFORMAT is returned.

Include File vfw.h

Related Messages ICM_DECOMPRESS, ICM_DECOMPRESSEX_END, ICM_DRAW_BEGIN

ICM_DECOMPRESSEX_END   ■ Win32s ■ Windows 95 ■ Windows NT

Description   ICM_DECOMPRESSEX_END is a message that notifies a video decompression driver to end decompression and free resources allocated for decompression. ICM_DECOMPRESSEX_BEGIN and ICM_DECOMPRESSEX_END do not nest. If the driver receives ICM_DECOMPRESSEX_BEGIN before decompression is stopped with ICM_DECOMPRESSEX_END, it should restart decompression with new parameters.

Parameters   This message does not use *wParam* or *lParam*; therefore, both must be set to zero.

Returns   int: If successful, ICERR_OK is returned; otherwise, an error is returned.

Include File   vfw.h

Related Messages   ICM_DECOMPRESS_BEGIN

ICM_DECOMPRESSEX_QUERY   ■ Win32s ■ Windows 95 ■ Windows NT

Description   ICM_DECOMPRESSEX_QUERY is a message that queries a video compression driver to determine if it supports a specific input format or if it can decompress a specific input format to a specific output format.

Parameters

wParam   LPVOID: The address of an ICDECOMPRESSEX structure containing the input format.

lParam   ICDECOMPRESSEX: The size, in bytes, of the ICDECOMPRESSEX structure.

Returns   int: If the specified decompression is supported, ICERR_OK is returned; otherwise, ICERR_BADFORMAT is returned.

Include File   vfw.h

Related Messages   ICM_DECOMPRESSEX

ICM_DRAW   ■ Win32s ■ Windows 95 ■ Windows NT

Description   ICM_DRAW is a message that notifies a rendering driver to decompress a frame of data and draw it to the screen. Send ICM_DECOMPRESS to decompress the data into a buffer.

Parameters

wParam   LPVOID: The address of an ICDRAW structure.

lParam   ICDRAW: The size, in bytes, of the ICDRAW structure.

Returns   int: If successful, ICERR_OK is returned; otherwise, an error is returned.

Include File   vfw.h

Related Messages   ICM_DECOMPRESS

ICM_DRAW_BEGIN   ■ Win32s ■ Windows 95 ■ Windows NT

Description   ICM_DRAW_BEGIN is a message that notifies a rendering driver to prepare to draw data. Send ICM_DECOMPRESS_BEGIN to decompress data into a buffer. ICM_DRAW_BEGIN and ICM_DRAW_END do not nest. If the driver receives ICM_DRAW_BEGIN before decompression is stopped with ICM_DRAW_END, it should restart decompression with new parameters.

Parameters

wParam   LPVOID: The address of an ICDRAWBEGIN structure containing the input format.

lParam   ICDRAW: The size, in bytes, of the ICDRAWBEGIN structure.

Returns   int: ICERR_OK is returned if the driver supports drawing the data to the screen in the specified manner and format; otherwise, an error code in Table 11-9 is returned.

Table 11-9 ICM_DRAW_BEGIN return values

Value	Description
ICERR_BADFORMAT	Input or output format is not supported.
ICERR_NOTSUPPORTED	Driver does not draw directly to the screen or does not support this message.

Include File   vfw.h
Related Messages   ICM_DECOMPRESS_BEGIN, ICM_DRAW_END

ICM_DRAW_CHANGEPALETTE   ■ Win32s ■ Windows 95 ■ Windows NT

Description   ICM_DRAW_CHANGEPALETTE is a message that notifies a rendering driver that the movie palette is changing.

Parameters

wParam   LPVOID: The address of a BITMAPINFO structure containing the new format and optional color table.

lParam   LPARAM: Set to zero.

Returns   int: If successful, ICERR_OK is returned; otherwise, FALSE is returned.

Include File   vfw.h

ICM_DRAW_END   ■ Win32s ■ Windows 95 ■ Windows NT

Description   ICM_DRAW_END is a message that notifies a rendering driver to decompress the current image to the screen and to release resources allocated for decompression and drawing. ICM_DRAW_BEGIN and ICM_DRAW_END do not nest. If the driver receives ICM_DRAW_BEGIN before decompression is stopped with ICM_DRAW_END, it should restart decompression with new parameters.

Parameters	This message does not use *wParam* or *lParam*; therefore, both must be set to zero.
Returns	int: If successful, ICERR_OK is returned; otherwise, FALSE is returned.
Include File	vfw.h
Related Messages	ICM_DRAW_BEGIN

ICM_DRAW_FLUSH ■ Win32s ■ Windows 95 ■ Windows NT

Description	ICM_DRAW_FLUSH is a message that notifies a rendering driver to render the contents of any image buffers that are waiting to be drawn. This message is used only by hardware that performs its own asynchronous decompression, timing, and drawing.
Parameters	This message does not use *wParam* or *lParam*; therefore, both must be set to zero.
Returns	int: If successful, ICERR_OK is returned; otherwise, FALSE is returned.
Include File	vfw.h

ICM_DRAW_GET_PALETTE ■ Win32s ■ Windows 95 ■ Windows NT

Description	ICM_DRAW_GET_PALETTE is a message that requests a rendering driver to return a palette.
Parameters	This message does not use *wParam* or *lParam*; therefore, both must be set to zero.
Returns	HPALETTE: If successful, the handle of the palette being used is returned; otherwise, either NULL is returned, if the driver doesn't have a handle to return, or ICERR_UNSUPPORTED is returned if the driver doesn't support palettes.
Include File	vfw.h

ICM_DRAW_GETTIME ■ Win32s ■ Windows 95 ■ Windows NT

Description	ICM_DRAW_GETTIME is a message that requests a rendering driver that controls the timing of drawing frames to return the current value of its internal clock. This message is generally supported by hardware that performs its own asynchronous decompression, timing, and drawing. The message can also be sent if the hardware is being used as the synchronization master.
Parameters	
wParam	LPVOID: The address to contain the current time.
lParam	LPARAM: Set to zero.
Returns	int: If successful, ICERR_OK is returned; otherwise an error is returned.
Include File	vfw.h

ICM_DRAW_QUERY
■ Win32s ■ Windows 95 ■ Windows NT

Description	ICM_DRAW_QUERY is a message that queries a rendering driver to determine if it can render data in a specific format.
Parameters	
wParam	LPVOID: The address of a BITMAPINFO structure containing the input format.
lParam	LPARAM: Set to zero.
Returns	int: If the driver can render data in the specified format, ICERR_OK is returned; otherwise, ICERR_BADFORMAT is returned.
Include File	vfw.h

ICM_DRAW_REALIZE
■ Win32s ■ Windows 95 ■ Windows NT

Description	ICM_DRAW_REALIZE is a message that notifies a rendering driver to realize its drawing palette while drawing.
Parameters	
wParam	HDC: The handle of the DC used to realize the palette.
lParam	BOOL: TRUE realizes the palette as a background task; FALSE realizes the palette in the foreground.
Returns	int: If the drawing palette is realized, ICERR_OK is returned; otherwise, ICERR_UNSUPPORTED is returned.
Include File	vfw.h

ICM_DRAW_RENDERBUFFER
■ Win32s ■ Windows 95 ■ Windows NT

Description	ICM_DRAW_RENDERBUFFER is a message that notifies a rendering driver to draw the frames that have been passed to it. Use this message with hardware that performs its own asynchronous decompression, timing, and drawing.
Parameters	This message does not use *wParam* or *lParam*; therefore, both must be set to zero.
Include File	vfw.h

ICM_DRAW_SETTIME
■ Win32s ■ Windows 95 ■ Windows NT

Description	ICM_DRAW_SETTIME is a message that provides synchronization information (the sample number of the frame to draw) to a rendering driver that handles the timing of drawing frames.
Parameters	
wParam	DWORD: The sample number of the frame to render.

lParam	LPARAM: Set to zero.
Returns	int: If successful, ICERR_OK is returned; otherwise, an error is returned.
Include File	vfw.h

ICM_DRAW_START ■ Win32s ■ Windows 95 ■ Windows NT

Description	ICM_DRAW_START is a message that notifies a rendering driver to start its internal clock for the timing of drawing frames. This message is used by hardware that performs its own asynchronous decompression, timing, and drawing.
Parameters	This message does not use *wParam* or *lParam*; therefore, both must be set to zero.
Include File	vfw.h
Related Messages	ICM_DRAW_BEGIN, ICM_DRAW_STOP

ICM_DRAW_START_PLAY ■ Win32s ■ Windows 95 ■ Windows NT

Description	ICM_DRAW_START_PLAY is a message that provides the start and end times of a play operation to a rendering driver. The units for *wParam* and *lParam* are specified with ICM_DRAW_BEGIN. For video data this is normally a frame number. If the end time is less than the start time, the playback direction is reversed.
Parameters	
wParam	DWORD: The start time.
lParam	DWORD: The end time.
Include File	vfw.h
Related Messages	ICM_DRAW_BEGIN

ICM_DRAW_STOP ■ Win32s ■ Windows 95 ■ Windows NT

Description	ICM_DRAW_STOP is a message that notifies a rendering driver to stop its internal clock for the timing of drawing frames. This message is used by hardware that performs its own asynchronous decompression, timing, and drawing.
Parameters	This message does not use *wParam* or *lParam*; therefore, both must be set to zero.
Include File	vfw.h

ICM_DRAW_STOP_PLAY ■ Win32s ■ Windows 95 ■ Windows NT

| **Description** | ICM_DRAW_STOP_PLAY is a message that notifies a rendering driver when a play operation is complete. |

Parameters	This message does not use *wParam* or *lParam*; therefore, both must be set to zero.
Include File	vfw.h
Related Messages	ICM_DRAW_STOP

ICM_DRAW_SUGGESTFORMAT ■ Win32s ■ Windows 95 ■ Windows NT

Description	ICM_DRAW_SUGGESTFORMAT is a message that queries a rendering driver to suggest a decompressed format that it can draw.
Parameters	
wParam	LPVOID: The address of an ICDRAWSUGGEST structure.
lParam	ICDRAWSUGGEST: The size, in bytes, of the ICDRAWSUGGEST structure.
Returns	int: If successful, ICERR_OK is returned. If the *lpbiSuggest* member of the ICDRAWSUGGEST structure is NULL, this message returns the amount of memory required to contain the suggested format.
Include File	vfw.h

ICM_DRAW_WINDOW ■ Win32s ■ Windows 95 ■ Windows NT

Description	ICM_DRAW_WINDOW is a message that notifies a rendering driver that the window specified by ICM_DRAW_BEGIN needs to be redrawn because the window has either moved or become temporarily obscured. This message is supported by hardware that performs its own asynchronous decompression, timing, and drawing.
Parameters	
wParam	LPVOID: The address of the destination rectangle in screen coordinates. If this parameter points to an empty rectangle, drawing should be turned off.
lParam	LPARAM: Set to zero.
Returns	int: ICERR_OK if successful; otherwise an error is returned.
Include File	vfw.h
Related Messages	ICM_DRAW_BEGIN

ICM_GET ■ Win32s ■ Windows 95 ■ Windows NT

Description	ICM_GET is a message that retrieves an application-defined double word from a video compression driver.
Parameters	
wParam	LPVOID: The address of a block of memory to be filled. Specify NULL to determine the amount of memory required by the state information.

lParam	DWORD: The size, in bytes, of the block of memory.
Returns	int: The amount of memory, in bytes, required to store the information is returned.
Include File	vfw.h

ICM_GETBUFFERSWANTED　　■ Win32s ■ Windows 95 ■ Windows NT

Description	ICM_GETBUFFERSWANTED is a message that queries a driver for the number of buffers to allocate. This message is used by drivers that use hardware to render data and want to ensure a minimal time lag caused by waiting for buffers to arrive.
Parameters	
wParam	LPVOID: The address to contain the number of samples the driver needs to efficiently render the data.
lParam	LPARAM: Set to zero.
Returns	int: If successful, ICERR_OK is returned; otherwise, ICERR_UNSUPPORTED is returned.
Include File	vfw.h

ICM_GETDEFAULTKEYFRAMERATE　　■ Win32s ■ Windows 95 ■ Windows NT

Description	ICM_GETDEFAULTKEYFRAMERATE is a message that queries a video compression driver for its default (or preferred) key-frame spacing.
Parameters	
wParam	LPVOID: The address to contain the preferred key-frame spacing.
lParam	LPARAM: Set to zero.
Returns	int: If successful, ICERR_OK is returned; otherwise, ICERR_UNSUPPORTED is returned.
Include File	vfw.h

ICM_GETDEFAULTQUALITY　　■ Win32s ■ Windows 95 ■ Windows NT

Description	ICM_GETDEFAULTQUALITY is a message that queries a video compression driver to provide its default quality setting.
Parameters	
wParam	LPVOID: The address to contain the default quality value. Quality values range from 0 to 10,000.
lParam	LPARAM: Set to zero.
Returns	int: If successful, ICERR_OK is returned; otherwise, ICERR_UNSUPPORTED is returned.
Include File	vfw.h

ICM_GETINFO
■ Win32s ■ Windows 95 ■ Windows NT

Description	ICM_GETINFO is a message that queries a video compression driver to return a description of itself in an ICINFO structure. This message is used to display a list of the installed compressors.
Parameters	
wParam	LPVOID: The address of an ICINFO structure to contain information.
lParam	ICINFO: The size, in bytes, of the ICINFO structure.
Returns	int: The size, in bytes, of the ICINFO structure is returned; otherwise, zero is returned if an error occurs.
Include File	vfw.h

ICM_GETQUALITY
■ Win32s ■ Windows 95 ■ Windows NT

Description	ICM_GETQUALITY is a message that queries a video compression driver to return its current quality setting.
Parameters	
wParam	LPVOID: The address to contain the current quality value. Quality values range from 0 to 10,000.
lParam	LPARAM: Set to zero.
Returns	int: If successful, ICERR_OK is returned; otherwise, ICERR_UNSUPPORTED is returned.
Include File	vfw.h

ICM_GETSTATE
■ Win32s ■ Windows 95 ■ Windows NT

Description	ICM_GETSTATE is a message that queries a video compression driver to return its current configuration in a block of memory or to determine the amount of memory required to retrieve the configuration information.
Parameters	
wParam	LPVOID: The address of a block of memory to contain the current configuration information. Specify NULL for *wParam* to determine the amount of memory required for the configuration information.
lParam	DWORD: The size, in bytes, of the block of memory.
Returns	int: The amount of memory, in bytes, required by the state information is returned.
Include File	vfw.h

ICM_SET_STATUS_PROC ■ Win32s ■ Windows 95 ■ Windows NT

Description   ICM_SET_STATUS_PROC is a message that provides a status callback function with the status of a lengthy operation. This message should be supported if either the compression or decompression takes more than one-tenth of a second.

Parameters

wParam   LPVOID: The address of an ICSETSTATUSPROC structure.

lParam   ICSETSTATUSPROC: The size, in bytes, of the ICSETSTATUSPROC structure.

Returns   int: If successful, ICERR_OK is returned; otherwise, an error is returned.

Include File   vfw.h

ICM_SETQUALITY ■ Win32s ■ Windows 95 ■ Windows NT

Description   ICM_SETQUALITY is a message that provides a video compression driver with a quality level to use during compression.

Parameters

wParam   LPVOID: The new quality value. Quality values range from 0 to 10,000.

lParam   LPARAM: Set to zero.

Returns   int: If successful, ICERR_OK is returned; otherwise, ICERR_UNSUPPORTED is returned.

Include File   vfw.h

ICM_SETSTATE ■ Win32s ■ Windows 95 ■ Windows NT

Description   ICM_SETSTATE is a message that notifies a video compression driver to set the state of the compressor.

Parameters

wParam   LPVOID: The address of a block of memory containing configuration data. Specify NULL for *wParam* to reset the compressor to its default state.

lParam   DWORD: The size, in bytes, of the block of memory.

Returns   int: If successful, the number of bytes used by the compressor is returned; otherwise zero is returned.

Include File   vfw.h

Related Messages   ICM_CONFIGURE

LB_ADDFILE

Description	LB_ADDFILE is a message that adds the specified file name to a list box containing a directory listing. The list box must have been filled by DlgDirList().
Parameters	
wParam	WPARAM: Set to zero.
lParam	LPCTSTR: A pointer to the name of the file to add to the list box.
Returns	int: If successful, the zero-based index of the file that was added is returned; otherwise, LB_ERR is returned if an error occurs.
Include File	winuser.h
See Also	DlgDirList()
Related Messages	LB_ADDSTRING

LB_ADDSTRING

Description	LB_ADDSTRING is a message that adds a string to a list box. If the list box does not have the LBS_SORT style, the string is added to the end of the list; otherwise, the string is inserted into the list and the list is sorted.
Parameters	
wParam	WPARAM: Set to zero.
lParam	LPCTSTR: A pointer to the null-terminated string that is to be added. If the list box is created with an owner-drawn style but without the LBS_HASSTRINGS style, the value of *lParam* is stored as item data instead of a pointer to a string. You can send LB_GETITEMDATA and LB_SETITEMDATA to retrieve or modify the item data.
Returns	int: If successful, the zero-based index of the string in the list box is returned; otherwise, if an error occurs, LB_ERR is returned, or if there is insufficient space to store the new string, LB_ERRSPACE returned.
Include File	winuser.h
Related Messages	LB_DELETESTRING, LB_INSERTSTRING, LB_SELECTSTRING, WM_COMPAREITEM

LB_DELETESTRING

Description	LB_DELETESTRING is a message that deletes a string in a list box.
Parameters	
wParam	WPARAM: The zero-based index of the string to be deleted. In Windows 95, the *wParam* is limited to 16-bit values for list box messages; therefore, list boxes cannot contain more than 32,767 items, although the total size in bytes of the items in a list box is limited only by available memory.

lParam	LPARAM: Set to zero.
Returns	int: If successful, a count of the strings remaining in the list is returned; otherwise, LB_ERR is returned if *wParam* is larger than the number of items in the list.
Include File	winuser.h
Related Messages	LB_ADDSTRING, LB_INSERTSTRING, WM_DELETEITEM

LB_DIR   ■ Win32s ■ Windows 95 ■ Windows NT

Description	LB_DIR is a message that adds a list of file names to a list box.
Parameters	
wParam	UINT: The attributes of the files to be added to the list box. This parameter can be a combination of the values in Table 11-5.
lParam	LPCTSTR: A pointer to the null-terminated string identifying the file name to add to the list. If the string contains wildcard values (for example, *.*), all files that match the wildcards and have the attributes specified by *wParam* are added to the list.
Returns	int: If successful, the zero-based index of the last file name added to the list is returned; otherwise, if an error occurs, LB_ERR is returned. If there is insufficient space to store the new strings, LB_ERRSPACE is returned.
Include File	winuser.h
See Also	DlgDirList()

LB_FINDSTRING   ■ Win32s ■ Windows 95 ■ Windows NT

Description	LB_FINDSTRING is a message that locates the first string in a list box containing the specified prefix.
Parameters	
wParam	WPARAM: The zero-based index of the item before the first item to be searched. When the search reaches the bottom of the list box, it continues from the top of the list box back to the item specified by *wParam*. If *wParam* is -1, the entire list box is searched from the beginning. In Windows 95, the *wParam* is limited to 16-bit values for list box messages; therefore, list boxes cannot contain more than 32,767 items, although the total size in bytes of the items in a list box is limited only by available memory.
lParam	LPCTSTR: A pointer to the null-terminated string that contains the prefix to search for. Since the search is case independent, the string can contain any combination of uppercase and lowercase letters.
Returns	int: If successful, the index of the matching item is returned; otherwise, LB_ERR is returned if the search was unsuccessful. If a list box is created

with an owner-drawn style but without the LBS_HASSTRINGS style, this message returns the index of the item with a long value matching the value supplied by *lParam*.

Include File   winuser.h

Related Messages   LB_ADDSTRING, LB_INSERTSTRING, LB_SELECTSTRING

LB_FINDSTRINGEXACT   ■ Win32s ■ Windows 95 ■ Windows NT

Description   LB_FINDSTRINGEXACT is a message that locates the first list box string that exactly matches the string identified by *lParam*. This search is not case sensitive.

Parameters

wParam   WPARAM: The zero-based index of the item before the first item to be searched. When the search reaches the bottom of the list box, it continues from the top of the list box back to the item specified by *wParam*. If *wParam* is -1, the entire list box is searched from the beginning. In Windows 95, the *wParam* is limited to 16-bit values for list box messages; therefore, list boxes cannot contain more than 32,767 items, although the total size in bytes of the items in a list box is limited only by available memory.

lParam   LPARAM: A pointer to the null-terminated string to search for. This string can contain a complete file name, including the extension. The search is not case sensitive, so this string can contain any combination of uppercase and lowercase letters.

Returns   int: If successful, the zero-based index of the matching item is returned; otherwise, LB_ERR is returned if the search was unsuccessful.

Include File   winuser.h

Related Messages   LB_FINDSTRING, LB_SELECTSTRING, WM_COMPAREITEM

LB_GETANCHORINDEX   Win32s ■ Windows 95   Windows NT

Description   LB_GETANCHORINDEX is a message that retrieves the index of the item where a multiple selection starts. A multiple selection spans all items from the anchor item to the caret item.

Parameters   This message does not use *wParam* or *lParam*; therefore, both must be set to zero.

Returns   int: The index of the anchor item is returned.

Include File   winuser.h

Related Messages   LB_SETANCHORINDEX

LB_GETCARETINDEX
■ Win32s ■ Windows 95 ■ Windows NT

Description	LB_GETCARETINDEX is a message that determines the index of the item that has the focus rectangle in a multiple-selection list box. The item may or may not be selected.
Parameters	This message does not use *wParam* or *lParam*; therefore, both must be set to zero.
Returns	int: The zero-based index of the list box item that has the focus rectangle is returned. If the list box is a single-selection list box, the return value is the zero-based index of the item that is selected.
Include File	winuser.h
Related Messages	LB_SETCARETINDEX

LB_GETCOUNT
■ Win32s ■ Windows 95 ■ Windows NT

Description	LB_GETCOUNT is a message that retrieves the number of items in a list box. The returned value is one greater than the zero-based index value of the last item in the list box.
Parameters	This message does not use *wParam* or *lParam*; therefore, both must be set to zero.
Returns	int: If successful, the number of items in the list box is returned; otherwise, LB_ERR is returned if an error occurs.
Include File	winuser.h
Related Messages	LB_SETCOUNT

LB_GETCURSEL
■ Win32s ■ Windows 95 ■ Windows NT

Description	LB_GETCURSEL is a message that retrieves the index of the currently selected item in a single-selection list box. For a multiple-selection list box, the message retrieves the index of the first selected item.
Parameters	This message does not use *wParam* or *lParam*; therefore, both must be set to zero.
Returns	int: The zero-based index of the currently selected item or of the base item in a multiple selection is returned; if there is no selection, LB_ERR is returned.
Include File	winuser.h
Related Messages	LB_GETCARETINDEX, LB_SETCURSEL

LB_GETHORIZONTALEXTENT
■ Win32s ■ Windows 95 ■ Windows NT

Description	LB_GETHORIZONTALEXTENT is a message that retrieves the scrollable width, in pixels, of a list box, if the list box has a horizontal scroll bar.

Parameters	This message does not use *wParam* or *lParam*; therefore, both must be set to zero.
Returns	int: The scrollable width, in pixels, of the list box is returned.
Include File	winuser.h
Related Messages	LB_SETHORIZONTALEXTENT

LB_GETITEMDATA ■ Win32s ■ Windows 95 ■ Windows NT

Description	LB_GETITEMDATA is a message that retrieves the application-defined 32-bit value associated with the specified list box item.
Parameters	
wParam	WPARAM: The index of the item. In Windows 95, the *wParam* is limited to 16-bit values for list box messages; therefore, list boxes cannot contain more than 32,767 items, although the total size in bytes of the items in a list box is limited only by available memory.
lParam	LPARAM: Set to zero.
Returns	int: If successful, the 32-bit value associated with the item is returned; otherwise, LB_ERR is returned if an error occurs. If the item is in an owner-drawn list box and was created without the LBS_HASSTRINGS style, the *lParam* of the LB_ADDSTRING or LB_INSERTSTRING message that added the item to the list box is returned; otherwise, the *lParam* of an LB_SETITEMDATA message is returned.
Include File	winuser.h
Related Messages	LB_ADDSTRING, LB_INSERTSTRING, LB_SETITEMDATA

LB_GETITEMHEIGHT ■ Win32s ■ Windows 95 ■ Windows NT

Description	LB_GETITEMHEIGHT is a message that retrieves the height of items in a list box.
Parameters	
wParam	WPARAM: The zero-based index of the list box item. This parameter is only used if the list box has the LBS_OWNERDRAWVARIABLE style; otherwise, it must be zero. In Windows 95, the *wParam* is limited to 16-bit values for list box messages; therefore, list boxes cannot contain more than 32,767 items, although the total size in bytes of the items in a list box is limited only by available memory.
lParam	LPARAM: Set to zero.
Returns	int: If successful, the height, in pixels, of each item in the list box is returned. The height of the item specified by *wParam* is returned if the list box has the LBS_OWNERDRAWVARIABLE style. LB_ERR is returned if an error occurs.

Include File	winuser.h
Related Messages	LB_SETITEMHEIGHT

LB_GETITEMRECT ■ Win32s ■ Windows 95 ■ Windows NT

Description LB_GETITEMRECT is a message that retrieves the dimensions of the rectangle that bounds a list box item as it is currently displayed in the list box.

Parameters

wParam WPARAM: The zero-based index of the item. In Windows 95, the *wParam* is limited to 16-bit values for list box messages; therefore, list boxes cannot contain more than 32,767 items, although the total size in bytes of the items in a list box is limited only by available memory.

lParam RECT*: A pointer to a RECT structure that will receive the client coordinates for the item in the list box.

Returns int: If an error occurs, LB_ERR is returned.

Include File winuser.h

LB_GETLOCALE Win32s ■ Windows 95 ■ Windows NT

Description LB_GETLOCALE is a message that retrieves the current locale of the list box. Use the retrieved locale to determine the correct sorting order of displayed text (for list boxes with the LBS_SORT style) and of text added by the LB_ADDSTRING message.

Parameters This message does not use *wParam* or *lParam*; therefore, both must be set to zero.

Returns DWORD: A 32-bit value that specifies the current locale of the list box. The high-order word contains the country code and the low-order word contains the language identifier.

Include File winuser.h

Related Messages LB_ADDSTRING, LB_SETLOCALE

LB_GETSEL ■ Win32s ■ Windows 95 ■ Windows NT

Description LB_GETSEL is a message that retrieves the selection state of an item.

Parameters

wParam WPARAM: The zero-based index of the item. In Windows 95, the *wParam* is limited to 16-bit values for list box messages; therefore, list boxes cannot contain more than 32,767 items, although the total size in bytes of the items in a list box is limited only by available memory.

lParam LPARAM: Set to zero.

Returns   int: If an item is selected, a value greater than zero is returned; otherwise, zero is returned. If an error occurs, LB_ERR is returned.

Include File   winuser.h

Related Messages   LB_SETSEL

LB_GETSELCOUNT ■ Win32s ■ Windows 95 ■ Windows NT

Description   LB_GETSELCOUNT is a message that retrieves the total number of selected items in a multiple-selection list box.

Parameters   This message does not use *wParam* or *lParam*; therefore, both must be set to zero.

Returns   int: If successful, the count of selected items in the list box is returned. If the list box is a single-selection list box, LB_ERR is returned.

Include File   winuser.h

Related Messages   LB_SETSEL

LB_GETSELITEMS ■ Win32s ■ Windows 95 ■ Windows NT

Description   LB_GETSELITEMS is a message that fills a buffer with an array of integers that specify the item numbers of selected items in a multiple-selection list box.

Parameters

wParam   WPARAM: The maximum number of selected items whose item numbers are to be placed in the buffer. In Windows 95, the *wParam* is limited to 16-bit values for list box messages; therefore, list boxes cannot contain more than 32,767 items, although the total size in bytes of the items in a list box is limited only by available memory.

lParam   LPINT: A pointer to a buffer large enough for the number of integers specified by *wParam*.

Returns   int: If successful, the number of items placed in the buffer is returned. If the list box is a single-selection list box, LB_ERR is returned.

Include File   winuser.h

Related Messages   LB_GETSELCOUNT

LB_GETTEXT ■ Win32s ■ Windows 95 ■ Windows NT

Description   LB_GETTEXT is a message that retrieves a string from a list box.

Parameters

wParam   WPARAM: The zero-based index of the string to retrieve. In Windows 95, the *wParam* is limited to 16-bit values for list box messages; therefore, list boxes cannot contain more than 32,767 items, although the total size in bytes of the items in a list box is limited only by available memory.

lParam	LPCTSTR: A pointer to the buffer that will receive the string. The buffer must have sufficient space for the string and a terminating null character. LB_GETTEXTLEN can be sent prior to LB_GETTEXT to retrieve the length, in characters, of the string.
Returns	int: If successful, the length of the string, in characters, excluding the terminating null character is returned. If *wParam* does not specify a valid index, LB_ERR is returned.
Include File	winuser.h
Related Messages	LB_GETTEXTLEN

LB_GETTEXTLEN   ■ Win32s   ■ Windows 95   ■ Windows NT

Description	LB_GETTEXTLEN is a message that retrieves the length of a string in a list box.
Parameters	
wParam	WPARAM: The zero-based index of the string. In Windows 95, the *wParam* is limited to 16-bit values for list box messages; therefore, list boxes cannot contain more than 32,767 items, although the total size in bytes of the items in a list box is limited only by available memory.
lParam	LPARAM: Set to zero.
Returns	int: A value at least as large as the actual length of the text.
Include File	winuser.h
See Also	GetWindowText()
Related Messages	CB_GETLBTEXT, LB_GETTEXT, WM_GETTEXT

LB_GETTOPINDEX   ■ Win32s   ■ Windows 95   ■ Windows NT

Description	LB_GETTOPINDEX is a message that retrieves the index of the first visible item in a list box. Initially the item of the list box has an index value of 0, but if the list box contents have been scrolled, another item may be at the top.
Parameters	This message does not use *wParam* or *lParam*; therefore, both must be set to zero.
Returns	int: The index of the first visible item in the list box is returned.
Include File	winuser.h
Related Messages	LB_SETTOPINDEX

LB_INITSTORAGE
Win32s ■ Windows 95   Windows NT

Description   LB_INITSTORAGE is a message that allocates memory for storing list box items. This message is sent prior to adding a large number of items to a list box to preallocate the necessary memory. If you overestimate, some extra memory is allocated; if you underestimate, the normal allocation is used for items that exceed the preallocated amount.

Parameters

wParam   int: The number of items to add. In Windows 95, the *wParam* is limited to 16-bit values for list box messages; therefore, list boxes cannot contain more than 32,767 items, although the total size in bytes of the items in a list box is limited only by available memory.

lParam   DWORD: The amount of memory, in bytes, to allocate for item strings.

Returns   int: If successful, the maximum number of items that the memory object can store before another memory reallocation is needed is returned; otherwise, LB_ERRSPACE is returned if not enough memory is available.

Include File   winuser.h

Related Messages   LB_ADDFILE, LB_ADDSTRING, LB_DIR, LB_INSERTSTRING

LB_INSERTSTRING
■ Win32s ■ Windows 95 ■ Windows NT

Description   LB_INSERTSTRING is a message that inserts a string into a list box. Unlike LB_ADDSTRING, LB_INSERTSTRING does not cause a list with the LBS_SORT style to be sorted.

Parameters

wParam   WPARAM: The zero-based index of the position at which to insert the string. If *wParam* is -1, the string is added to the end of the list. In Windows 95, the *wParam* is limited to 16-bit values for list box messages; therefore, list boxes cannot contain more than 32,767 items, although the total size in bytes of the items in a list box is limited only by available memory.

lParam   LPCTSTR: A pointer to the null-terminated string to be inserted.

Returns   int: If successful, the index of the position at which the string was inserted is returned; otherwise, if an error occurs, LB_ERR is returned. If there is insufficient space to store the new string, LB_ERRSPACE is returned.

Include File   winuser.h

Related Messages   LB_ADDSTRING, LB_SELECTSTRING

LB_ITEMFROMPOINT

Win32s ■ Windows 95   Windows NT

Description	LB_ITEMFROMPOINT is a message that retrieves the zero-based index of the item nearest the specified point in a list box.
Parameters	
wParam	WPARAM: Set to zero.
LOWORD(lParam)	WORD: The x coordinate of a point, relative to the upper left corner of the client area of the list box.
HIWORD(lParam)	WORD: The y coordinate of a point, relative to the upper left corner of the client area of the list box.
Returns	DWORD: The index of the nearest item in the low-order word is returned. The high-order word is zero if the specified point is in the client area of the list box, or 1 if it is outside the client area.
Include File	winuser.h

LB_RESETCONTENT

■ Win32s ■ Windows 95 ■ Windows NT

Description	LB_RESETCONTENT is a message that removes all items from a list box.
Parameters	This message does not use *wParam* or *lParam*; therefore, both must be set to zero.
Include File	winuser.h
Related Messages	WM_DELETEITEM

LB_SELECTSTRING

■ Win32s ■ Windows 95 ■ Windows NT

Description	LB_SELECTSTRING is a message that searches a list box for an item that begins with the characters in a specified string. If a matching item is found, the item is selected. Do not use this message with a list box that has the LBS_MULTIPLESEL style.
Parameters	
wParam	WPARAM: The zero-based index of the item before the first item to be searched. When the search reaches the bottom of the list box, it continues from the top of the list box back to the item specified by *wParam*. If *wParam* is -1, the entire list box is searched from the beginning. In Windows 95, the *wParam* is limited to 16-bit values for list box messages; therefore, list boxes cannot contain more than 32,767 items, although the total size in bytes of the items in a list box is limited only by available memory.
lParam	LPCTSTR: A pointer to the null-terminated string that contains the prefix to search for. Since the search is case independent, this string can contain any combination of uppercase and lowercase letters.

Returns	If the search is successful, the index of the selected item is returned; otherwise, LB_ERR is returned and the current selection is not changed. If you create the list box with an owner-drawn style but without the LBS_HASSTRINGS style, this message returns the index of the item whose long value matches the value *lParam*.
Include File	winuser.h
Related Messages	LB_ADDSTRING, LB_FINDSTRING, LB_INSERTSTRING

LB_SELITEMRANGE ■ Win32s ■ Windows 95 ■ Windows NT

Description	LB_SELITEMRANGE is a message that selects one or more consecutive items in a multiple-selection list box. This message can select a range only within the first 65,536 items. For list boxes with more items, use the LB_SELITEMRANGEEX message.
Parameters	
wParam	WPARAM: Specifies how to set the selection. If *wParam* is TRUE, the string is selected and highlighted; if *wParam* is zero, the highlight is removed and the string is no longer selected.
LOWORD(lParam)	WORD: The zero-based index of the first item to select.
HIWORD(lParam)	WORD: The zero-based index of the last item to select.
Returns	int: If an error occurs, LB_ERR is returned.
Include File	winuser.h
Related Messages	LB_SELITEMRANGEEX, LB_SETSEL

LB_SELITEMRANGEEX ■ Win32s ■ Windows 95 ■ Windows NT

Description	LB_SELITEMRANGEEX is a message that selects one or more consecutive items in a multiple-selection list box. If the value of *wParam* is less than *lParam*, the specified range of items is selected. If *wParam* is greater than *lParam*, the selection is removed from the specified range of items. Use this message for list boxes that have more than 65,536 items.
Parameters	
wParam	WPARAM: The zero-based index of the first item to select. In Windows 95, the *wParam* is limited to 16-bit values for list box messages; therefore, list boxes cannot contain more than 32,767 items, although the total size in bytes of the items in a list box is limited only by available memory.
lParam	LPARAM: The zero-based index of the last item to select.
Returns	int: If an error occurs, LB_ERR is returned.
Include File	winuser.h
Related Messages	LB_SELITEMRANGE, LB_SETSEL

LB_SETANCHORINDEX

Win32s ■ Windows 95   Windows NT

Description	LB_SETANCHORINDEX is a message that sets the anchor item (the item from which a multiple selection starts). A multiple selection spans all items from the anchor item to the caret item.
Parameters	
wParam	WPARAM: The index of the new anchor item. In Windows 95, the *wParam* is limited to 16-bit values for list box messages; therefore, list boxes cannot contain more than 32,767 items, although the total size in bytes of the items in a list box is limited only by available memory.
lParam	LPARAM: Set to zero.
Returns	int: If the message succeeds, zero is returned; otherwise, LB_ERR is returned.
Include File	winuser.h
Related Messages	LB_GETANCHORINDEX

LB_SETCARETINDEX

■ Win32s ■ Windows 95 ■ Windows NT

Description	LB_SETCARETINDEX is a message that sets the focus rectangle to the item at the specified index in a multiple-selection list box. If the item is not visible, it is scrolled into view.
Parameters	
wParam	WPARAM: The zero-based index of the list box item that is to receive the focus rectangle. In Windows 95, the *wParam* is limited to 16-bit values for list box messages; therefore, list boxes cannot contain more than 32,767 items, although the total size in bytes of the items in a list box is limited only by available memory.
LOWORD(lParam)	WORD: If this value is FALSE, the item is scrolled until it is fully visible; if it is TRUE, the item is scrolled until it is at least partially visible.
HIWORD(lParam)	WORD: Set to zero.
Returns	int: If an error occurs, LB_ERR is returned.
Include File	winuser.h
Related Messages	LB_GETCARETINDEX

LB_SETCOLUMNWIDTH

■ Win32s ■ Windows 95 ■ Windows NT

Description	LB_SETCOLUMNWIDTH is a message that is sent to a multiple-column list box (created with the LBS_MULTICOLUMN style) to set the width, in pixels, of all columns in the list box.
Parameters	
wParam	WPARAM: The width, in pixels, of all columns.

lParam	LPARAM: Set to zero.
Include File	winuser.h
Related Messages	LB_SETTABSTOPS

LB_SETCOUNT   Win32s ■ Windows 95 ■ Windows NT

Description	LB_SETCOUNT is a message that sets the count of items in a list box created with the LBS_NODATA style and not created with the LBS_HASSTRINGS style.
Parameters	
wParam	int: The new count of items in the list box. In Windows 95, the *wParam* is limited to 16-bit values for list box messages; therefore, list boxes cannot contain more than 32,767 items, although the total size in bytes of the items in a list box is limited only by available memory.
lParam	LPARAM: Set to zero.
Returns	int: If an error occurs, LB_ERR is returned. If there is insufficient memory to store the items, LB_ERRSPACE is returned.
Include File	winuser.h
Related Messages	LB_GETCOUNT

LB_SETCURSEL   ■ Win32s ■ Windows 95 ■ Windows NT

Description	LB_SETCURSEL is a message that selects a string in a single-selection list box and scrolls it into view, if necessary. When the new string is selected, the list box removes the highlight from the previously selected string. (See Figure 11-4.)
Parameters	
wParam	WPARAM: The zero-based index of the string that is selected. If *wParam* is -1, the list box is set to have no selection. In Windows 95, the *wParam* is limited to 16-bit values for list box messages; therefore, list boxes cannot contain more than 32,767 items, although the total size in bytes of the items in a list box is limited only by available memory.
lParam	LPARAM: Set to zero.

Figure 11-4 Single-Selection List Box

Returns	int: If an error occurs, LB_ERR is returned. If the value of *wParam* is -1, LB_ERR is returned even though an error did not occur.
Include File	winuser.h
Related Messages	LB_GETCURSEL

LB_SETHORIZONTALEXTENT   ■ Win32s   ■ Windows 95   ■ Windows NT

| Description | LB_SETHORIZONTALEXTENT is a message that sets the scrollable width, in pixels, of a list box. If the width of the list box is smaller than this value, the horizontal scroll bar displays to provide scrolling of the items in the list box. If the width of the list box is equal to or greater than this value, the horizontal scroll bar is hidden. |

Parameters

wParam	WPARAM: The number of pixels by which the list box can be scrolled. In Windows 95, *wParam* is limited to 16-bit values for list box messages.
lParam	LPARAM: Set to zero.
Include File	winuser.h
Related Messages	LB_GETHORIZONTALEXTENT

LB_SETITEMDATA   ■ Win32s   ■ Windows 95   ■ Windows NT

| Description | LB_SETITEMDATA is a message that sets a 32-bit value associated with the specified item in a list box. |

Parameters

wParam	WPARAM: The zero-based index of the item. In Windows 95, the *wParam* is limited to 16-bit values for list box messages; therefore, list boxes cannot contain more than 32,767 items, although the total size in bytes of the items in a list box is limited only by available memory.
lParam	LPARAM: The 32-bit value to be associated with the item.
Returns	int: If an error occurs, LB_ERR is returned.
Include File	winuser.h
Related Messages	LB_ADDSTRING, LB_GETITEMDATA, LB_INSERTSTRING

LB_SETITEMHEIGHT   ■ Win32s   ■ Windows 95   ■ Windows NT

| Description | LB_SETITEMHEIGHT is a message that sets the height, in pixels, of items in a list box. If the list box has the LBS_OWNERDRAWVARIABLE style, this message sets the height of the item specified by *wParam*. Otherwise, LB_SETITEMHEIGHT sets the height of all items in the list box. |

Parameters

wParam	WPARAM: The zero-based index of the item in the list box. Use *wParam* only if the list box has the LBS_OWNERDRAWVARIABLE style; otherwise, set it to zero. In Windows 95, the *wParam* is limited to 16-bit values for list box messages; therefore, list boxes cannot contain more than 32,767 items, although the total size in bytes of the items in a list box is limited only by available memory.
LOWORD(lParam)	WORD: The height, in pixels, of the item.
HIWORD(lParam)	WORD: Set to zero.
Returns	int: If the index or height is invalid, LB_ERR is returned.
Include File	winuser.h
Related Messages	LB_GETITEMHEIGHT

LB_SETLOCALE   Win32s ■ Windows 95 ■ Windows NT

Description	LB_SETLOCALE is a message that sets the current locale of the list box. Use the locale to determine the correct sorting order of displayed text (for list boxes with the LBS_SORT style) and of text added by the LB_ADDSTRING message.

Parameters

wParam	WPARAM: The locale identifier that the list box will use for sorting when adding text.
lParam	LPARAM: Set to zero.
Returns	DWORD: The previous locale identifier is returned. If *wParam* specifies a locale that is not installed on the system, LB_ERR is returned and the current list box locale is not changed.
Include File	winuser.h
Related Messages	LB_ADDSTRING, LB_GETLOCALE

LB_SETSEL   ■ Win32s ■ Windows 95 ■ Windows NT

Description	LB_SETSEL is a message that selects a string in a multiple-selection list box.

Parameters

wParam	BOOL: If *wParam* is TRUE, the string is selected and highlighted; if *wParam* is FALSE, the highlight is removed and the string is no longer selected.
lParam	UINT: The zero-based index of the string to set. If the value of *lParam* is -1, the selection is added to or removed from all strings, depending on the value of *wParam*.

Returns	int: If an error occurs, LB_ERR is returned.
Include File	winuser.h
Related Messages	LB_GETSEL, LB_SELITEMRANGE

LB_SETTABSTOPS   ■ Win32s ■ Windows 95 ■ Windows NT

Description	LB_SETTABSTOPS is a message that sets the tab-stop positions in a list box. To respond to this message, the list box must have been created with the LBS_USETABSTOPS style. If the value of *wParam* is 0 and *lParam* is NULL, the default tab stop is two dialog box units. If the value of *wParam* is 1, the list box will have tab stops separated by the distance specified by *lParam*. If *lParam* points to more than a single value, a tab stop will be set for each value in *lParam*, up to the number specified by *wParam*.
Parameters	
wParam	WPARAM: The number of tab stops in the list box.
lParam	LPINT: A pointer to the first member of an array of integers containing the tab stops, in dialog box units. The tab stops must be sorted in ascending order; backward tabs are not allowed.
Returns	BOOL: If all of the specified tabs are set, TRUE is returned; otherwise, FALSE is returned.
Include File	winuser.h
See Also	GetDialogBaseUnits()

LB_SETTOPINDEX   ■ Win32s ■ Windows 95 ■ Windows NT

Description	LB_SETTOPINDEX is a message that ensures that a particular item in a list box is visible.
Parameters	
wParam	WPARAM: The zero-based index of the item in the list box. In Windows 95, the *wParam* is limited to 16-bit values for list box messages; therefore, list boxes cannot contain more than 32,767 items, although the total size in bytes of the items in a list box is limited only by available memory.
lParam	LPARAM: Set to zero.
Returns	int: If an error occurs, LB_ERR is returned.
Include File	winuser.h
Related Messages	LB_GETTOPINDEX

LBN_DBLCLK   ■ Win32s ■ Windows 95 ■ Windows NT

Description	LBN_DBLCLK is a notification message that is sent when the user double-clicks a string in a list box. The parent window of the list box receives this

notification message through the WM_COMMAND message. Only a list
box with the LBS_NOTIFY style sends this notification message.

Parameters

LOWORD(wParam)   int: The identifier of the list box.

lParam   HWND: The handle of the list box.

Include File   winuser.h

Related Messages   LBN_SELCHANGE, WM_COMMAND

LBN_ERRSPACE   ■ Win32s ■ Windows 95 ■ Windows NT

Description   LBN_ERRSPACE is a notification message that is sent when a list box
cannot allocate enough memory to meet a specific request. The parent
window of the list box receives this notification message through the
WM_COMMAND message.

Parameters

LOWORD(wParam)   int: The identifier of the list box.

lParam   HWND: The handle of the list box.

Include File   winuser.h

Related Messages   WM_COMMAND

LBN_KILLFOCUS   ■ Win32s ■ Windows 95 ■ Windows NT

Description   LBN_KILLFOCUS is a notification message that is sent when a list box
loses the keyboard focus. The parent window of the list box receives this
notification message through the WM_COMMAND message.

Parameters

LOWORD(wParam)   int: The identifier of the list box.

lParam   HWND: The handle of the list box.

Include File   winuser.h

Related Messages   LBN_SETFOCUS, WM_COMMAND

LBN_SELCANCEL   ■ Win32s ■ Windows 95 ■ Windows NT

Description   LBN_SELCANCEL is a notification message that is sent when the user
cancels the selection in a list box. The parent window of the list box
receives this notification message through the WM_COMMAND message.
This notification message applies only to list boxes with the LBS_NOTIFY
style.

Parameters

LOWORD(wParam)   int: The identifier of the list box.

lParam	HWND: The handle of the list box.
Include File	winuser.h
Related Messages	LB_SETCURSEL, LBN_DBLCLK, LBN_SELCHANGE, WM_COMMAND

LBN_SELCHANGE ■ Win32s ■ Windows 95 ■ Windows NT

Description	LBN_SELCHANGE is a notification message that is sent when the selection in a list box is about to change. The parent window of the list box receives this notification message through the WM_COMMAND message. LBN_SELCHANGE is not sent if the LB_SETCURSEL message changes the selection. This notification message applies only to a list box with the LBS_NOTIFY style. For a multiple-selection list box, LBN_SELCHANGE is sent whenever the user presses an arrow key, even if the selection does not change.

Parameters

LOWORD(wParam)	int: The identifier of the list box.
lParam	HWND: The handle of the list box.
Include File	winuser.h
Related Messages	LB_SETCURSEL, LBN_DBLCLK, LBN_SELCANCEL, WM_COMMAND

LBN_SETFOCUS ■ Win32s ■ Windows 95 ■ Windows NT

Description	LBN_SETFOCUS is a notification message that is sent when a list box receives the keyboard focus. The parent window of the list box receives this notification message through the WM_COMMAND message.

Parameters

LOWORD(wParam)	int: The identifier of the list box.
lParam	HWND: The handle of the list box.
Include File	winuser.h
Related Messages	LBN_KILLFOCUS, WM_COMMAND

LVM_ARRANGE ■ Win32s ■ Windows 95 ■ Windows NT

Description	LVM_ARRANGE is a message that arranges items in icon view. For more information, refer to the ListView_Arrange macro in Chapter 6, List View and Drag List.

LVM_CREATEDRAGIMAGE ■ Win32s ■ Windows 95 ■ Windows NT

Description	LVM_CREATEDRAGIMAGE is a message that creates a drag image list for the specified item. For more information, refer to the

ListView_CreateDragImage macro in Chapter 6, List View and Drag List. (See Figure 11-5.)

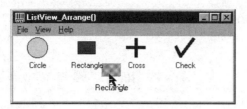

Figure 11-5 LVM_CREATEDRAGIMAGE message

LVM_DELETEALLITEMS ■ Win32s ■ Windows 95 ■ Windows NT

Description   LVM_DELETEALLITEMS is a message that removes all items from a list view control. For more information, refer to the ListView_DeleteAllItems macro in Chapter 6, List View and Drag List.

LVM_DELETECOLUMN ■ Win32s ■ Windows 95 ■ Windows NT

Description   LVM_DELETECOLUMN is a message that removes a column from a list view control. For more information, refer to the ListView_DeleteColumn macro in Chapter 6, List View and Drag List.

LVM_DELETEITEM ■ Win32s ■ Windows 95 ■ Windows NT

Description   LVM_DELETEITEM is a message that removes an item from a list view control. For more information, refer to the ListView_DeleteItem macro in Chapter 6, List View and Drag List.

LVM_EDITLABEL ■ Win32s ■ Windows 95 ■ Windows NT

Description   LVM_EDITLABEL is a message that begins in-place editing of the specified list view item's text. The message implicitly selects and focuses the specified item. For more information, refer to the ListView_EditLabel macro in Chapter 6, List View and Drag List.

LVM_ENSUREVISIBLE ■ Win32s ■ Windows 95 ■ Windows NT

Description   LVM_ENSUREVISIBLE is a message that ensures that a specified list view item is at least partially visible. For more information, refer to the ListView_EnsureVisible macro in Chapter 6, List View and Drag List.

LVM_FINDITEM
■ Win32s ■ Windows 95 ■ Windows NT

Description   LVM_FINDITEM is a message that searches for a list view item with the specified characteristics. For more information, refer to the ListView_FindItem macro in Chapter 6, List View and Drag List.

LVM_GETBKCOLOR
■ Win32s ■ Windows 95 ■ Windows NT

Description   LVM_GETBKCOLOR is a message that retrieves the background color of a list view control. For more information, refer to the ListView_GetBkColor macro in Chapter 6, List View and Drag List.

LVM_GETCALLBACKMASK
■ Win32s ■ Windows 95 ■ Windows NT

Description   LVM_GETCALLBACKMASK is a message that retrieves the callback mask for a list view control. For more information, refer to the ListView_GetCallbackMask macro in Chapter 6, List View and Drag List.

LVM_GETCOLUMN
■ Win32s ■ Windows 95 ■ Windows NT

Description   LVM_GETCOLUMN is a message that retrieves the attributes of a list view control's column. For more information, refer to the ListView_GetColumn macro in Chapter 6, List View and Drag List.

LVM_GETCOLUMNWIDTH
■ Win32s ■ Windows 95 ■ Windows NT

Description   LVM_GETCOLUMNWIDTH is a message that retrieves the width of a column in report or list view. For more information, refer to the ListView_GetColumnWidth macro in Chapter 6, List View and Drag List.

LVM_GETCOUNTPERPAGE
■ Win32s ■ Windows 95 ■ Windows NT

Description   LVM_GETCOUNTPERPAGE is a message that calculates the number of items that can fit vertically in the visible area of a list view control when in list or report view. For more information, refer to the ListView_GetCountPerPage macro in Chapter 6, List View and Drag List.

LVM_GETEDITCONTROL
■ Win32s ■ Windows 95 ■ Windows NT

Description   LVM_GETEDITCONTROL is a message that retrieves the handle of the edit control that is editing a list view item's text. For more information, refer to the ListView_GetEditControl macro in Chapter 6, List View and Drag List.

LVM_GETIMAGELIST   ■ Win32s   ■ Windows 95   ■ Windows NT

Description   LVM_GETIMAGELIST is a message that retrieves the handle to an image list used for drawing list view items. For more information, refer to the ListView_GetImageList macro in Chapter 6, List View and Drag List.

LVM_GETISEARCHSTRING   ■ Win32s   ■ Windows 95   ■ Windows NT

Description   LVM_GETISEARCHSTRING is a message that retrieves the incremental search string of a list view control. For more information, refer to the ListView_GetISearchString macro in Chapter 6, List View and Drag List.

LVM_GETITEM   ■ Win32s   ■ Windows 95   ■ Windows NT

Description   LVM_GETITEM is a message that retrieves some or all of a list view item's attributes. For more information, refer to the ListView_GetItem macro in Chapter 6, List View and Drag List.

LVM_GETITEMCOUNT   ■ Win32s   ■ Windows 95   ■ Windows NT

Description   LVM_GETITEMCOUNT is a message that retrieves the number of items in a list view control. For more information, refer to the ListView_GetItemCount macro in Chapter 6, List View and Drag List.

LVM_GETITEMPOSITION   ■ Win32s   ■ Windows 95   ■ Windows NT

Description   LVM_GETITEMPOSITION is a message that retrieves the position of a list view item. For more information, refer to the ListView_GetItemPosition macro in Chapter 6, List View and Drag List.

LVM_GETITEMRECT   ■ Win32s   ■ Windows 95   ■ Windows NT

Description   LVM_GETITEMRECT is a message that retrieves the bounding rectangle for all or part of an item in the current view. For more information, refer to the ListView_GetItemRect macro in Chapter 6, List View and Drag List.

LVM_GETITEMSPACING   ■ Win32s   ■ Windows 95   ■ Windows NT

Description   LVM_GETITEMSPACING is a message that determines the spacing between items in a list view control. For more information, refer to the ListView_GetItemSpacing macro in Chapter 6, List View and Drag List.

LVM_GETITEMSTATE ■ Win32s ■ Windows 95 ■ Windows NT

Description   LVM_GETITEMSTATE is a message that retrieves the state of a list view item. For more information, refer to the ListView_GetItemState macro in Chapter 6, List View and Drag List.

LVM_GETITEMTEXT ■ Win32s ■ Windows 95 ■ Windows NT

Description   LVM_GETITEMTEXT is a message that retrieves the text of a list view item or subitem. For more information, refer to the ListView_GetItemText macro in Chapter 6, List View and Drag List.

LVM_GETNEXTITEM ■ Win32s ■ Windows 95 ■ Windows NT

Description   LVM_GETNEXTITEM is a message that searches for the list view item with the specified properties. For more information, refer to the ListView_GetNextItem macro in Chapter 6, List View and Drag List.

LVM_GETORIGIN ■ Win32s ■ Windows 95 ■ Windows NT

Description   LVM_GETORIGIN is a message that retrieves the current view origin for a list view control. For more information, refer to the ListView_GetOrigin macro in Chapter 6, List View and Drag List.

LVM_GETSELECTEDCOUNT ■ Win32s ■ Windows 95 ■ Windows NT

Description   LVM_GETSELECTEDCOUNT is a message that determines the number of selected items in a list view control. For more information, refer to the ListView_GetSelectedCount macro in Chapter 6, List View and Drag List.

LVM_GETSTRINGWIDTH ■ Win32s ■ Windows 95 ■ Windows NT

Description   LVM_GETSTRINGWIDTH is a message that determines the width of the specified string. For more information, refer to the ListView_GetStringWidth macro in Chapter 6, List View and Drag List.

LVM_GETTEXTBKCOLOR ■ Win32s ■ Windows 95 ■ Windows NT

Description   LVM_GETTEXTBKCOLOR is a message that retrieves the text background color of a list view control. For more information, refer to the ListView_GetTextBkColor macro in Chapter 6, List View and Drag List.

LVM_GETTEXTCOLOR
■ Win32s ■ Windows 95 ■ Windows NT

Description LVM_GETTEXTCOLOR is a message that retrieves the text color of a list view control. For more information, refer to the ListView_GetTextColor macro in Chapter 6, List View and Drag List.

LVM_GETTOPINDEX
■ Win32s ■ Windows 95 ■ Windows NT

Description LVM_GETTOPINDEX is a message that retrieves the index of the topmost visible item when the list view control is in list or report view. For more information, refer to the ListView_GetTopIndex macro in Chapter 6, List View and Drag List.

LVM_GETVIEWRECT
■ Win32s ■ Windows 95 ■ Windows NT

Description LVM_GETVIEWRECT is a message that determines the bounding rectangle of all items in the list view control. For more information, refer to the ListView_GetViewRect macro in Chapter 6, List View and Drag List.

LVM_HITTEST
■ Win32s ■ Windows 95 ■ Windows NT

Description LVM_HITTEST is a message that determines which list view item is at the specified position. For more information, refer to the ListView_HitTest macro in Chapter 6, List View and Drag List.

LVM_INSERTCOLUMN
■ Win32s ■ Windows 95 ■ Windows NT

Description LVM_INSERTCOLUMN is a message that inserts a new column in a list view control. For more information, refer to the ListView_InsertColumn macro in Chapter 6, List View and Drag List.

LVM_INSERTITEM
■ Win32s ■ Windows 95 ■ Windows NT

Description LVM_INSERTITEM is a message that inserts a new item in a list view control. For more information, refer to the ListView_InsertItem macro in Chapter 6, List View and Drag List.

LVM_REDRAWITEMS
■ Win32s ■ Windows 95 ■ Windows NT

Description LVM_REDRAWITEMS is a message that forces a list view control to redraw a range of items. For more information, refer to the ListView_RedrawItems macro in Chapter 6, List View and Drag List.

LVM_SCROLL ■ Win32s ■ Windows 95 ■ Windows NT

Description   LVM_SCROLL is a message that scrolls the content of a list view control. For more information, refer to the ListView_Scroll macro in Chapter 6, List View and Drag List.

LVM_SETBKCOLOR ■ Win32s ■ Windows 95 ■ Windows NT

Description   LVM_SETBKCOLOR is a message that sets the background color of a list view control. For more information, refer to the ListView_SetBkColor macro in Chapter 6, List View and Drag List.

LVM_SETCALLBACKMASK ■ Win32s ■ Windows 95 ■ Windows NT

Description   LVM_SETCALLBACKMASK is a message that sets the callback mask for a list view control. For more information, refer to the ListView_SetCallbackMask macro in Chapter 6, List View and Drag List.

LVM_SETCOLUMN ■ Win32s ■ Windows 95 ■ Windows NT

Description   LVM_SETCOLUMN is a message that sets the attributes of a list view column. For more information, refer to the ListView_SetColumn macro in Chapter 6, List View and Drag List.

LVM_SETCOLUMNWIDTH ■ Win32s ■ Windows 95 ■ Windows NT

Description   LVM_SETCOLUMNWIDTH is a message that changes the width of a column in report or list view. For more information, refer to the ListView_SetColumnWidth macro in Chapter 6, List View and Drag List.

LVM_SETIMAGELIST ■ Win32s ■ Windows 95 ■ Windows NT

Description   LVM_SETIMAGELIST is a message that assigns an image list to a list view control. For more information, refer to the ListView_SetImageList macro in Chapter 6, List View and Drag List.

LVM_SETITEM ■ Win32s ■ Windows 95 ■ Windows NT

Description   LVM_SETITEM is a message that sets some or all of the attributes for a list view item. For more information, refer to the ListView_SetItem macro in Chapter 6, List View and Drag List.

LVM_SETITEMCOUNT
■ Win32s ■ Windows 95 ■ Windows NT

Description   LVM_SETITEMCOUNT is a message that prepares a list view control for adding a large number of items. For more information, refer to the ListView_SetItemCount macro in Chapter 6, List View and Drag List.

LVM_SETITEMPOSITION
■ Win32s ■ Windows 95 ■ Windows NT

Description   LVM_SETITEMPOSITION is a message that moves an item to a specified position in a list view control. For more information, refer to the ListView_SetItemPosition macro in Chapter 6, List View and Drag List.

LVM_SETITEMPOSITION32
■ Win32s ■ Windows 95 ■ Windows NT

Description   LVM_SETITEMPOSITION32 is a message that moves an item to a specified position in a list view control. For more information, refer to the ListView_SetItemPosition32 macro in Chapter 6, List View and Drag List.

LVM_SETITEMSTATE
■ Win32s ■ Windows 95 ■ Windows NT

Description   LVM_SETITEMSTATE is a message that changes the state of an item in a list view control. For more information, refer to the ListView_SetItemState macro in Chapter 6, List View and Drag List.

LVM_SETITEMTEXT
■ Win32s ■ Windows 95 ■ Windows NT

Description   LVM_SETITEMTEXT is a message that changes the text of a list view item or subitem. For more information, refer to the ListView_SetItemText macro in Chapter 6, List View and Drag List.

LVM_SETTEXTBKCOLOR
■ Win32s ■ Windows 95 ■ Windows NT

Description   LVM_SETTEXTBKCOLOR is a message that sets the background color of text in a list view control. For more information, refer to the ListView_SetTextBkColor macro in Chapter 6, List View and Drag List.

LVM_SETTEXTCOLOR
■ Win32s ■ Windows 95 ■ Windows NT

Description   LVM_SETTEXTCOLOR is a message that sets the text color of a list view control. For more information, refer to the ListView_SetTextColor macro in Chapter 6, List View and Drag List.

LVM_SORTITEMS
■ Win32s ■ Windows 95 ■ Windows NT

Description   LVM_SORTITEMS is a message that sorts the list view control items using an application-defined comparison function. For more information, refer to the ListView_SortItems macro in Chapter 6, List View and Drag List.

LVM_UPDATE
■ Win32s ■ Windows 95 ■ Windows NT

Description   LVM_UPDATE is a message that updates a list view item. For more information, refer to the ListView_Update macro in Chapter 6, List View and Drag List.

LVN_BEGINDRAG
■ Win32s ■ Windows 95 ■ Windows NT

Description   LVN_BEGINDRAG is a notification message that notifies the parent window that a drag-and-drop operation has been initiated in the list view control. For more information, refer to the LVN_BEGINDRAG notification message in Chapter 6, List View and Drag List.

LVN_BEGINLABELEDIT
■ Win32s ■ Windows 95 ■ Windows NT

Description   LVN_BEGINLABELEDIT is a notification message that notifies the parent window of the list view control that label editing is starting for an item. For more information, refer to the LVN_BEGINLABELEDIT notification message in Chapter 6, List View and Drag List.

LVN_BEGINRDRAG
■ Win32s ■ Windows 95 ■ Windows NT

Description   LVN_BEGINRDRAG is a notification message that notifies the parent window that a drag-and-drop operation has been initiated in the list view control using the right mouse button. For more information, refer to the LVN_BEGINRDRAG notification message in Chapter 6, List View and Drag List.

LVN_COLUMNCLICK
■ Win32s ■ Windows 95 ■ Windows NT

Description   LVN_COLUMNCLICK is a notification message that notifies the parent window of a list view control that a column was clicked. For more information, refer to the LVN_COLUMNCLICK notification message in Chapter 6, List View and Drag List.

LVN_DELETEALLITEMS ■ Win32s ■ Windows 95 ■ Windows NT

Description LVN_DELETEALLITEMS is a notification message that notifies the parent window that all items in the list view control were deleted. For more information, refer to the LVN_DELETEALLITEMS notification message in Chapter 6, List View and Drag List.

LVN_DELETEITEM ■ Win32s ■ Windows 95 ■ Windows NT

Description LVN_DELETEITEM is a notification message that notifies the parent window that a list view control item was deleted. For more information, refer to the LVN_DELETEITEM notification message in Chapter 6, List View and Drag List.

LVN_ENDLABELEDIT ■ Win32s ■ Windows 95 ■ Windows NT

Description LVN_ENDLABELEDIT is a notification message that notifies the parent window that the label editing of a list view control item has ended. For more information, refer to the LVN_ENDLABELEDIT notification message in Chapter 6, List View and Drag List.

LVN_GETDISPINFO ■ Win32s ■ Windows 95 ■ Windows NT

Description LVN_GETDISPINFO is a notification message that requests that the parent window provide the information needed to display or sort a list view control item. For more information, refer to the LVN_GETDISPINFO notification message in Chapter 6, List View and Drag List.

LVN_INSERTITEM ■ Win32s ■ Windows 95 ■ Windows NT

Description LVN_INSERTITEM is a notification message that notifies the parent window that a new item was inserted in the list view control. For more information, refer to the LVN_INSERTITEM notification message in Chapter 6, List View and Drag List.

LVN_ITEMCHANGED ■ Win32s ■ Windows 95 ■ Windows NT

Description LVN_ITEMCHANGED is a notification message that notifies the parent window that an item has changed in the list view control. For more information, refer to the LVN_ITEMCHANGED notification message in Chapter 6, List View and Drag List.

LVN_ITEMCHANGING ■ Win32s ■ Windows 95 ■ Windows NT

Description   LVN_ITEMCHANGING is a notification message that notifies the parent window that an item in the list view control is changing. For more information, refer to the LVN_ITEMCHANGING notification message in Chapter 6, List View and Drag List.

LVN_KEYDOWN ■ Win32s ■ Windows 95 ■ Windows NT

Description   LVN_KEYDOWN is a notification message that notifies the parent window that a key has been pressed in the list view control. For more information, refer to the LVN_KEYDOWN notification message in Chapter 6, List View and Drag List.

LVN_PEN Win32s ■ Windows 95 Windows NT

Description   LVN_PEN is a notification message that notifies the parent window that a list view control pen event has occurred. For more information, refer to the LVN_PEN notification message in Chapter 6, List View and Drag List.

LVN_SETDISPINFO ■ Win32s ■ Windows 95 ■ Windows NT

Description   LVN_SETDISPINFO is a notification message that notifies the parent window that the information about the specified list view control item must be updated. For more information, refer to the LVN_SETDISPINFO notification message in Chapter 6, List View and Drag List.

MCIWNDM_CAN_CONFIG ■ Win32s ■ Windows 95 ■ Windows NT

Description   MCIWNDM_CAN_CONFIG is a message that determines if an MCI device can display a configuration dialog box.

Parameters   This message does not use *wParam* or *lParam*; therefore, both must be set to zero.

Returns   BOOL: If the device supports configuration, TRUE is returned; otherwise, FALSE is returned.

Include File   vfw.h

See Also   MCIWndCanConfig

MCIWNDM_CAN_EJECT ■ Win32s ■ Windows 95 ■ Windows NT

Description   MCIWNDM_CAN_EJECT is a message that determines if an MCI device can eject its media.

Parameters	This message does not use *wParam* or *lParam*; therefore, both must be set to zero.
Returns	BOOL: If the device can eject its media, TRUE is returned; otherwise, FALSE is returned.
Include File	vfw.h
See Also	MCIWndCanEject

MCIWNDM_CAN_PLAY ■ Win32s ■ Windows 95 ■ Windows NT

Description	MCIWNDM_CAN_PLAY is a message that determines if an MCI device can play a data file or contents of some other kind.
Parameters	This message does not use *wParam* or *lParam*; therefore, both must be set to zero.
Returns	BOOL: If the device supports playing the data, TRUE is returned; otherwise, FALSE is returned.
Include File	vfw.h
See Also	MCIWndCanPlay

MCIWNDM_CAN_RECORD ■ Win32s ■ Windows 95 ■ Windows NT

Description	MCIWNDM_CAN_RECORD is a message that determines if an MCI device supports recording.
Parameters	This message does not use *wParam* or *lParam*; therefore, both must be set to zero.
Returns	BOOL: If the device supports recording, TRUE is returned; otherwise, FALSE is returned.
Include File	vfw.h
See Also	MCIWndCanRecord

MCIWNDM_CAN_SAVE ■ Win32s ■ Windows 95 ■ Windows NT

Description	MCIWNDM_CAN_SAVE is a message that determines if an MCI device can save data.
Parameters	This message does not use *wParam* or *lParam*; therefore, both must be set to zero.
Returns	BOOL: If the device supports saving data, TRUE is returned; otherwise, FALSE is returned.
Include File	vfw.h
See Also	MCIWndCanSave

MCIWNDM_CAN_WINDOW   ■ Win32s ■ Windows 95 ■ Windows NT

Description	MCIWNDM_CAN_WINDOW is a message that determines if an MCI device supports window-oriented MCI commands.
Parameters	This message does not use *wParam* or *lParam*; therefore, both must be set to zero.
Returns	BOOL: If the device supports window-oriented MCI commands, TRUE is returned; otherwise, FALSE is returned.
Include File	vfw.h
See Also	MCIWndCanWindow

MCIWNDM_CHANGESTYLES   ■ Win32s ■ Windows 95 ■ Windows NT

Description	MCIWNDM_CHANGESTYLES is a message that changes the styles used by the MCIWnd window.
Parameters	
wParam	UINT: The mask that identifies the styles that can change. This mask is the bitwise OR operator of all styles that will be permitted to change.
lParam	LONG: The new style settings for the window. Specify zero for *lParam* to turn off all styles identified in the mask.
Returns	int: Zero is returned.
Include File	vfw.h
See Also	MCIWndChangeStyles

MCIWNDM_EJECT   ■ Win32s ■ Windows 95 ■ Windows NT

Description	MCIWNDM_EJECT is a message that sends a command to an MCI device to eject its media.
Parameters	This message does not use *wParam* or *lParam*; therefore, both must be set to zero.
Returns	int: If successful, zero is returned; otherwise, an error is returned.
Include File	vfw.h
See Also	MCIWndEject

MCIWNDM_GET_DEST   ■ Win32s ■ Windows 95 ■ Windows NT

Description	MCIWNDM_GET_DEST is a message that retrieves the coordinates of the destination rectangle used for zooming or stretching the images of an AVI file during playback.

Parameters

wParam	WPARAM: Set to zero.
lParam	LPRECT: The address of a RECT structure to return the coordinates of the destination rectangle.

Returns   int: If successful, zero is returned; otherwise, an error is returned.

Include File vfw.h

See Also   MCIWndGetDest

MCIWNDM_GET_SOURCE   ■ Win32s ■ Windows 95 ■ Windows NT

Description   MCIWNDM_GET_SOURCE is a message that retrieves the coordinates of the source rectangle used to crop the images of an AVI file during playback.

Parameters

wParam	WPARAM: Set to zero.
lParam	LPRECT: The address of a RECT structure to contain the coordinates of the source rectangle.

Returns   int: If successful, zero is returned; otherwise, an error is returned.

Include File vfw.h

See Also   MCIWndGetSource

MCIWNDM_GETACTIVETIMER   ■ Win32s ■ Windows 95 ■ Windows NT

Description   MCIWNDM_GETACTIVETIMER is a message that retrieves the update period used when the MCIWnd window is the active window.

Parameters   This message does not use *wParam* or *lParam*; therefore, both must be set to zero.

Returns   int: The update period in milliseconds is returned. The default value is 500 milliseconds.

Include File vfw.h

See Also   MCIWndGetActiveTimer

MCIWNDM_GETALIAS   ■ Win32s ■ Windows 95 ■ Windows NT

Description   MCIWNDM_GETALIAS is a message that retrieves the alias used to open an MCI device or file with mciSendString().

Parameters   This message does not use *wParam* or *lParam*; therefore, both must be set to zero.

Returns   hwnd: The handle of the device alias is returned.

Include File vfw.h

See Also   mciSendString(), MCIWndGetAlias

MCIWNDM_GETDEVICE ■ Win32s ■ Windows 95 ■ Windows NT

Description	MCIWNDM_GETDEVICE is a message that retrieves the name of the currently open MCI device.
Parameters	
wParam	UINT: The size, in bytes, of the buffer.
lParam	LPVOID: The address of an application-defined buffer to return the device name.
Returns	int: If successful, zero is returned; otherwise, an error is returned.
Include File	vfw.h
See Also	MCIWndGetDevice

MCIWNDM_GETDEVICEID ■ Win32s ■ Windows 95 ■ Windows NT

Description	MCIWNDM_GETDEVICEID is a message that retrieves the identifier of the currently open MCI device to use with mciSendCommand().
Parameters	This message does not use *wParam* or *lParam*; therefore, both must be set to zero.
Returns	UINT: The device identifier is returned.
Include File	vfw.h
See Also	mciSendCommand(), MCIWndGetDeviceID

MCIWNDM_GETEND ■ Win32s ■ Windows 95 ■ Windows NT

Description	MCIWNDM_GETEND is a message that retrieves the location of the end of the content for an MCI device or file.
Parameters	This message does not use *wParam* or *lParam*; therefore, both must be set to zero.
Returns	LONG: The location in the current time format is returned.
Include File	vfw.h
See Also	MCIWndGetEnd

MCIWNDM_GETERROR ■ Win32s ■ Windows 95 ■ Windows NT

Description	MCIWNDM_GETERROR is a message that retrieves the last MCI error encountered.
Parameters	
wParam	UINT: The size, in bytes, of the error buffer.
lParam	LPVOID: The address of an application-defined buffer used to return the error string.

Returns	int: The integer error value is returned.
Include File	vfw.h
See Also	MCIWndGetError

MCIWNDM_GETFILENAME ■ Win32s ■ Windows 95 ■ Windows NT

Description	MCIWNDM_GETFILENAME is a message that retrieves the file name currently used by an MCI device.
Parameters	
wParam	UINT: The size, in bytes, of the buffer.
lParam	LPVOID: The address of an application-defined buffer to return the file name.
Returns	int: If successful, zero is returned; otherwise, a value of 1 is returned.
Include File	vfw.h
See Also	MCIWndGetFileName

MCIWNDM_GETINACTIVETIMER ■ Win32s ■ Windows 95 ■ Windows NT

Description	MCIWNDM_GETINACTIVETIMER is a message that retrieves the update period used when the MCIWnd window is the inactive window.
Parameters	This message does not use *wParam* or *lParam*; therefore, both must be set to zero.
Returns	int: The update period, in milliseconds, is returned. The default value is 2000 milliseconds.
Include File	vfw.h
See Also	MCIWndGetInactiveTimer

MCIWNDM_GETLENGTH ■ Win32s ■ Windows 95 ■ Windows NT

Description	MCIWNDM_GETLENGTH is a message that retrieves the length of the content or file currently used by an MCI device.
Parameters	This message does not use *wParam* or *lParam*; therefore, both must be set to zero.
Returns	int: The length of the content or file is returned. The units for the length depend on the current time format.
Include File	vfw.h
See Also	MCIWndGetLength

MCIWNDM_GETMODE   ■ Win32s   ■ Windows 95   ■ Windows NT

Description	MCIWNDM_GETMODE is a message that retrieves the current operating mode of an MCI device.
Parameters	
wParam	UINT: The size, in bytes, of the buffer used to return the mode.
lParam	LPSTR: The address of the application-defined buffer used to return the mode.
Returns	LONG: One of the values in Table 11-10 indicating the mode of the MCI device is returned.
Include File	vfw.h
See Also	MCIWndGetMode

Table 11-10 MCIWNDM_GETMODE return values

Value	Meaning
MCI_MODE_NOT_READY	Not ready
MCI_MODE_OPEN	Open
MCI_MODE_PAUSE	Paused
MCI_MODE_PLAY	Playing
MCI_MODE_RECORD	Recording
MCI_MODE_SEEK	Seeking
MCI_MODE_STOP	Stopped

MCIWNDM_GETPALETTE   ■ Win32s   ■ Windows 95   ■ Windows NT

Description	MCIWNDM_GETPALETTE is a message that retrieves the handle of the palette used by an MCI device.
Parameters	This message does not use *wParam* or *lParam*; therefore, both must be set to zero.
Returns	HPALETTE: If successful, the handle of the palette is returned.
Include File	vfw.h
See Also	MCIWndGetPalette

MCIWNDM_GETPOSITION   ■ Win32s   ■ Windows 95   ■ Windows NT

Description	MCIWNDM_GETPOSITION is a message that retrieves the current position within the content of the MCI device.

Parameters	This message does not use *wParam* or *lParam*; therefore, both must be set to zero.
Returns	int: The current position is returned. The units for the position value depend on the current time format.
Include File	vfw.h
See Also	MCIWndGetPosition

MCIWNDM_GETREPEAT   ■ Win32s ■ Windows 95 ■ Windows NT

Description	MCIWNDM_GETREPEAT is a message that determines if continuous playback has been activated.
Parameters	This message does not use *wParam* or *lParam*; therefore, both must be set to zero.
Returns	BOOL: If continuous playback is activated, TRUE is returned; otherwise, FALSE is returned.
Include File	vfw.h
See Also	MCIWndGetRepeat

MCIWNDM_GETSPEED   ■ Win32s ■ Windows 95 ■ Windows NT

Description	MCIWNDM_GETSPEED is a message that retrieves the playback speed of an MCI device.
Parameters	This message does not use *wParam* or *lParam*; therefore, both must be set to zero.
Returns	int: If successful; the playback speed is returned. The value for normal speed is 1000. Larger values indicate faster speeds.
Include File	vfw.h
See Also	MCIWndGetSpeed

MCIWNDM_GETSTART   ■ Win32s ■ Windows 95 ■ Windows NT

Description	MCIWNDM_GETSTART is a message that retrieves the location of the beginning of the content of an MCI device or file.
Parameters	This message does not use *wParam* or *lParam*; therefore, both must be set to zero.
Returns	int: The location of the beginning of the content in the current time format is returned.
Include File	vfw.h
See Also	MCIWndGetStart

MCIWNDM_GETSTYLES ■ Win32s ■ Windows 95 ■ Windows NT

Description	MCIWNDM_GETSTYLES is a message that retrieves the flags specifying the current MCIWnd window styles used by a window.
Parameters	This message does not use *wParam* or *lParam*; therefore, both must be set to zero.
Returns	int: A value representing the current styles of the MCIWnd window is returned. The return value is the bitwise OR operator of the MCIWnd window styles.
Include File	vfw.h
See Also	MCIWndGetStyles

MCIWNDM_GETTIMEFORMAT ■ Win32s ■ Windows 95 ■ Windows NT

Description	MCIWNDM_GETTIMEFORMAT is a message that retrieves the current time format of an MCI device as both a numerical value and a string.
Parameters	
wParam	UINT: The size of the buffer to contain the time format.
lParam	LPSTR: The address of a buffer to contain the null-terminated string form of the time format.
Returns	int: An integer value corresponding to the MCI constant defining the time format is returned.
Include File	vfw.h
See Also	MCIWndGetTimeFormat

MCIWNDM_GETVOLUME ■ Win32s ■ Windows 95 ■ Windows NT

Description	MCIWNDM_GETVOLUME is a message that retrieves the current volume setting of an MCI device.
Parameters	This message does not use *wParam* or *lParam*; therefore, both must be set to zero.
Returns	int: The current volume setting of the MCI device is returned. The default value is 1000. Higher values indicate louder volumes.
Include File	vfw.h
See Also	MCIWndGetVolume

MCIWNDM_GETZOOM ■ Win32s ■ Windows 95 ■ Windows NT

Description	MCIWNDM_GETZOOM is a message that retrieves the current zoom value used by an MCI device.

Parameters	This message does not use *wParam* or *lParam*; therefore, both must be set to zero.
Returns	UINT: The most recent zoom value used with the MCIWndSetZoom macro is returned. A return value of 100 indicates the image is not zoomed, 200 indicates the image is twice its original size, and 50 indicates the image is half its original size.
Include File	vfw.h
See Also	MCIWndGetZoom

MCIWNDM_NEW   ■ Win32s ■ Windows 95 ■ Windows NT

Description	MCIWNDM_NEW is a message that creates a new file for the current MCI device.
Parameters	
wParam	WPARAM: Set to zero.
lParam	LPVOID: The address of a buffer containing the name of the MCI device that will use the new file.
Returns	int: If successful, zero is returned; otherwise, an error is returned.
Include File	vfw.h
See Also	MCIWndNew

MCIWNDM_NOTIFYERROR   ■ Win32s ■ Windows 95 ■ Windows NT

Description	MCIWND_NOTIFYERROR is a notification message that notifies the parent window of an application that an MCI error has occurred. MCI error notification is enabled by specifying the MCIWNDF_NOTIFYERROR window style.
Parameters	
wParam	HWND: The handle of the MCIWnd window.
lParam	LONG: The numerical code for the MCI error.
Include File	vfw.h

MCIWNDM_NOTIFYMEDIA   ■ Win32s ■ Windows 95 ■ Windows NT

Description	MCIWNDM_NOTIFYMEDIA is a notification message that notifies the parent window of an application that the media has changed. MCI error notification is enabled by specifying the MCIWNDF_NOTIFYMEDIA window style.
Parameters	
wParam	HWND: The handle of the MCIWnd window.

lParam	LPSTR: The address of a null-terminated string containing the new file name. If the media is closing, it specifies a null string.
Include File	vfw.h

MCIWNDM_NOTIFYMODE ■ Win32s ■ Windows 95 ■ Windows NT

Description	MCIWNDM_NOTIFYMODE is a notification message that notifies the parent window of an application that the operating mode of the MCI device has changed. MCI error notification is enabled by specifying the MCIWNDF_NOTIFYMODE window style.
Parameters	
wParam	HWND: The handle of the MCIWnd window.
lParam	LONG: An integer corresponding to the MCI operating mode.
Include File	vfw.h

MCIWNDM_NOTIFYPOS ■ Win32s ■ Windows 95 ■ Windows NT

Description	MCIWNDM_NOTIFYPOS is a notification message that notifies the parent window of an application that the window position has changed. MCI error notification is enabled by specifying the MCIWNDF_NOTIFYPOS window style.
Parameters	
wParam	HWND: The handle of the MCIWnd window.
lParam	LONG: The new window position.
Include File	vfw.h

MCIWNDM_NOTIFYSIZE ■ Win32s ■ Windows 95 ■ Windows NT

Description	MCIWNDM_NOTIFYSIZE is a notification message that notifies the parent window of an application that the window size has changed. MCI error notification is enabled by specifying the MCIWNDF_NOTIFYSIZE window style.
Parameters	
wParam	HWND: The handle of the MCIWnd window.
lParam	LPARAM: Set to zero.
Include File	vfw.h

MCIWNDM_OPEN ■ Win32s ■ Windows 95 ■ Windows NT

Description	MCIWNDM_OPEN is a message that opens an MCI device and associates it with an MCIWnd window.

Parameters

wParam   UINT: The flags associated with the device or file to open. The
MCIWNDOPENF_NEW flag specifies a new file is to be created with
the name specified by *lParam*.

lParam   LPVOID: The address of a null-terminated string identifying the file name
or MCI device name to open. Specify -1 for *lParam* to display the Open
dialog box.

Returns   int: If successful, zero is returned; otherwise, an error is returned.

Include File   vfw.h

See Also   MCIWndOpen

MCIWNDM_OPENINTERFACE   ■ Win32s   ■ Windows 95   ■ Windows NT

Description   MCIWNDM_OPENINTERFACE is a message that attaches the data stream
or file associated with the specified interface to an MCIWnd window.

Parameters

wParam   WPARAM: Set to zero.

lParam   LPUNKNOWN: The address of an IAVI interface that points to either a file
or a data stream in a file.

Returns   int: If successful, zero is returned; otherwise, an error is returned.

Include File   vfw.h

See Also   MCIWndOpenInterface

MCIWNDM_PLAYFROM   ■ Win32s   ■ Windows 95   ■ Windows NT

Description   MCIWNDM_PLAYFROM is a message that plays the content of an MCI
device from the specified location to the end of the content or until another
command stops the playback.

Parameters

wParam   WPARAM: Set to zero.

lParam   LONG: The starting location in the content. The units for the starting location depend on the current time format.

Returns   int: If successful, zero is returned; otherwise, an error is returned.

Include File   vfw.h

See Also   MCIWndPlayFrom

MCIWNDM_PLAYREVERSE   ■ Win32s   ■ Windows 95   ■ Windows NT

Description   MCIWNDM_PLAYREVERSE is a message that plays the current content in
the reverse direction, beginning at the current position and ending at the
beginning of the content or when another command stops playback.

Parameters	This message does not use *wParam* or *lParam*; therefore, both must be set to zero.
Returns	int: If successful, zero is returned; otherwise, an error is returned.
Include File	vfw.h
See Also	MCIWndPlayReverse

MCIWNDM_PLAYTO ■ Win32s ■ Windows 95 ■ Windows NT

Description	MCIWNDM_PLAYTO is a message that plays the content of an MCI device from the current position to the specified ending location or until another command stops the playback. If the specified ending location is beyond the end of the content, playback stops at the end of the content.
Parameters	
wParam	WPARAM: Set to zero.
lParam	LONG: The ending location in the content. The units for the ending location depend on the current time format.
Returns	int: If successful, zero is returned; otherwise, an error is returned.
Include File	vfw.h
See Also	MCIWndPlayTo

MCIWNDM_PUT_DEST ■ Win32s ■ Windows 95 ■ Windows NT

Description	MCIWNDM_PUT_DEST is a message that redefines the coordinates of the destination rectangle used for zooming or stretching the images of an AVI file during playback.
Parameters	
wParam	WPARAM: Set to zero.
lParam	LPRECT: The address of a RECT structure containing the coordinates of the destination rectangle.
Returns	int: If successful, zero is returned; otherwise, an error is returned.
Include File	vfw.h
See Also	MCIWndPutDest

MCIWNDM_PUT_SOURCE ■ Win32s ■ Windows 95 ■ Windows NT

Description	MCIWNDM_PUT_SOURCE is a message that redefines the coordinates of the source rectangle used for cropping the images of an AVI file during playback.
Parameters	
wParam	WPARAM: Set to zero.

lParam	LPARAM: The address of a RECT structure containing the coordinates of the source rectangle.
Returns	int: If successful, zero is returned; otherwise, an error is returned.
Include File	vfw.h
See Also	MCIWndPutSource

MCIWNDM_REALIZE   ■ Win32s ■ Windows 95 ■ Windows NT

Description	MCIWNDM_REALIZE is a message that realizes the palette currently used by the MCI device in an MCIWnd window. MCIWNDM_REALIZE uses the palette of the MCI device and calls RealizePalette().
Parameters	
wParam	BOOL: The background flag. TRUE indicates that the window is a background application.
lParam	LPARAM: Set to zero.
Returns	int: If successful, zero is returned; otherwise, an error is returned.
Include File	vfw.h
See Also	MCIWndRealize, RealizePalette()

MCIWNDM_RETURNSTRING   ■ Win32s ■ Windows 95 ■ Windows NT

Description	MCIWNDM_RETURNSTRING is a message that retrieves the reply to the most recent MCI string command sent to an MCI device. Information in the reply is supplied as a null-terminated string. The string is terminated if it is longer than the buffer specified by *wParam*.
Parameters	
wParam	UINT: The size of the buffer to contain the null-terminated string.
lParam	LPVOID: The address of an application-defined buffer to contain the null-terminated string.
Returns	int: An integer that corresponds to the most recent MCI string command is returned.
Include File	vfw.h
See Also	MCIWndReturnString

MCIWNDM_SENDSTRING   ■ Win32s ■ Windows 95 ■ Windows NT

Description	MCIWNDM_SENDSTRING is a message that sends an MCI command in string form to the device associated with the MCIWnd window.
Parameters	
wParam	WPARAM: Set to zero.

lParam	LPSTR: The string command to send to the MCI device.
Returns	int: If successful, zero is returned; otherwise, an error is returned.
Include File	vfw.h
See Also	MCIWndSendString

MCIWNDM_SETACTIVETIMER ■ Win32s ■ Windows 95 ■ Windows NT

Description	MCIWNDM_SETACTIVETIMER is a message that sets the update period used by MCIWnd to update the trackbar in the MCIWnd window, update position information displayed in the window title bar, and send notification messages to the parent window when the MCIWnd window is active.
Parameters	
wParam	UINT: The update period, in milliseconds, for the MCIWnd window trackbar. The default is 500 milliseconds.
lParam	LPARAM: Set to zero.
Include File	vfw.h
See Also	MCIWndSetActiveTimer

MCIWNDM_SETINACTIVETIMER ■ Win32s ■ Windows 95 ■ Windows NT

Description	MCIWNDM_SETINACTIVETIMER is a message that sets the update period used by MCIWnd to update the trackbar in the MCIWnd window, update position information displayed in the window title bar, and send notification messages to the parent window when the MCIWnd window is inactive.
Parameters	
wParam	UINT: The update period, in milliseconds, for the MCIWnd window trackbar. The default is 500 milliseconds.
lParam	LPARAM: Set to zero.
Include File	vfw.h
See Also	MCIWndSetInactiveTimer

MCIWNDM_SETOWNER ■ Win32s ■ Windows 95 ■ Windows NT

Description	MCIWNDM_SETOWNER is a message that sets the window to receive notification messages associated with the MCIWnd window.
Parameters	
wParam	WPARAM: The handle of the window to receive the notification messages.
lParam	LPARAM: Set to zero.
Returns	int: Zero is returned.

Include File	vfw.h
See Also	MCIWndSetOwner

MCIWNDM_SETPALETTE   ■ Win32s ■ Windows 95 ■ Windows NT

Description	MCIWNDM_SETPALETTE is a message that sends a palette handle to the MCI device associated with the MCIWnd window.
Parameters	
wParam	HPALETTE. The palette handle.
lParam	LPARAM: Set to zero.
Returns	int: If successful, zero is returned; otherwise, an error is returned.
Include File	vfw.h
See Also	MCIWndSetPalette

MCIWNDM_SETREPEAT   ■ Win32s ■ Windows 95 ■ Windows NT

Description	MCIWNDM_SETREPEAT is a message that sets the repeat flag associated with continuous playback. This message works in conjunction with the MCI_PLAY command to provide a continuous playback loop. Currently, MCIAVI is the only device that supports continuous playback.
Parameters	
wParam	WPARAM: Set to zero.
lParam	BOOL: The new state of the repeat flag. TRUE turns on continuous playback.
Returns	int: Zero is returned.
Include File	vfw.h
See Also	MCIWndSetRepeat

MCIWNDM_SETSPEED   ■ Win32s ■ Windows 95 ■ Windows NT

Description	MCIWNDM_SETSPEED is a message that sets the playback speed of an MCI device.
Parameters	
wParam	WPARAM: Set to zero.
lParam	UINT: The playback speed of the MCI device. Specify 1000 for normal speed, larger values for faster speeds, and smaller values for slower speeds.
Returns	int: If successful, zero is returned; otherwise, an error is returned.
Include File	vfw.h
See Also	MCIWndSetSpeed

MCIWNDM_SETTIMEFORMAT ■ Win32s ■ Windows 95 ■ Windows NT

Description	MCIWNDM_SETTIMEFORMAT is a message that sets the time format of an MCI device.
Parameters	
wParam	WPARAM: Set to zero.
lParam	LPSTR: The address of a buffer containing the null-terminated string indicating the time format. Specify "frames" to set the time format to frames, or "ms" to set the time format to milliseconds.
Returns	int: If successful, zero is returned; otherwise, an error is returned.
Include File	vfw.h
See Also	MCIWndChangeStyles, MCIWndSetTimeFormat

MCIWNDM_SETTIMERS ■ Win32s ■ Windows 95 ■ Windows NT

Description	MCIWNDM_SETTIMERS is a message that sets the update periods used by MCIWnd to update the trackbar in the MCIWnd window, update the position information displayed in the window title bar, and send notification messages to the parent window.
Parameters	
wParam	UINT: The update period used by MCIWnd when it is the active window. The default value is 500 milliseconds. The storage for this value is limited to 16 bits.
lParam	UINT: The update period used by MCIWnd when it is the inactive window. The default value is 2000 milliseconds. The storage for this value is limited to 16 bits.
Include File	vfw.h
See Also	MCIWndSetTimers

MCIWNDM_SETVOLUME ■ Win32s ■ Windows 95 ■ Windows NT

Description	MCIWNDM_SETVOLUME is a message that sets the volume level for an MCI device.
Parameters	
wParam	WPARAM: Set to zero.
lParam	UINT: The new volume level for an MCI device. Specify 1000 for normal volume level. Specify a higher value for a louder volume or a lower value for a quieter volume.
Returns	int: If successful, zero is returned; otherwise, an error is returned.
Include File	vfw.h
See Also	MCIWndSetVolume

MCIWNDM_SETZOOM ■ Win32s ■ Windows 95 ■ Windows NT

Description MCIWNDM_SETZOOM is a message that resizes a video image according to a zoom factor.

Parameters

wParam WPARAM: Set to zero.

lParam UINT: The zoom factor to use in displaying a video image. This value is expressed as a percentage of the original image. Specify 100 to display the image at its authored size, 200 to display the image at twice its normal size, or 50 to display the image at half its normal size.

Include File vfw.h

See Also MCIWndSetZoom

MCIWNDM_VALIDATEMEDIA ■ Win32s ■ Windows 95 ■ Windows NT

Description MCIWNDM_VALIDATEMEDIA is a message that updates the starting and ending locations of the content, the current position in the content, and the trackbar according to the current time format.

Parameters This message does not use *wParam* or *lParam*; therefore, both must be set to zero.

Include File vfw.h

See Also MCIWndValidateMedia

MIM_CLOSE ■ Win32s ■ Windows 95 ■ Windows NT

Description MIM_CLOSE is a message that is sent to a MIDI input callback function when a MIDI input device is closed.

Parameters This message does not use *dwParam1* or *dwParam2*; therefore, both must be set to zero.

Include File mmsystem.h

MIM_DATA ■ Win32s ■ Windows 95 ■ Windows NT

Description MIM_DATA is a message that is sent to a MIDI input callback function when a MIDI message is received by a MIDI input device. This message is not sent when a MIDI system-exclusive message is received.

Parameters

LOWORD(dwParam1) DWORD: The first part of the MIDI message received by the MIDI input device. The low-order byte contains the MIDI status. The high-order byte contains the first byte of the MIDI data, when needed.

HIWORD(dwParam1)   DWORD: The second part of the MIDI message received by the MIDI input device. The low-order byte contains the second byte of the MIDI data, when needed. The high-order byte is not used.

dwParam2   DWORD: The time that the message was received by the input device driver. The time stamp is specified in milliseconds, and it is set at zero when midiInStart() is called.

Include File   mmsystem.h

See Also   midiInStart()

MIM_ERROR   ■ Win32s ■ Windows 95 ■ Windows NT

Description   MIM_ERROR is a message that is sent to a MIDI input callback function when an invalid MIDI message is received.

Parameters

dwParam1   DWORD: The invalid MIDI message that was received. The message is packed into a double-word value with the first byte of the message in the low-order byte.

dwParam2   DWORD: The time that the message was received by the input device driver. The time stamp is specified in milliseconds, and is set at zero when midiInStart() is called.

Include File   mmsystem.h

See Also   midiInStart()

MIM_LONGDATA   ■ Win32s ■ Windows 95 ■ Windows NT

Description   MIM_LONGDATA is a message that is sent to a MIDI input callback function when a system-exclusive buffer has been filled with data and is being returned to the application. To determine the number of bytes recorded into the returned buffer, use the *dwBytesRecorded* member of the MIDIHDR structure specified by *dwParam1*.

Parameters

dwParam1   DWORD: The address of a MIDIHDR structure identifying the input buffer.

dwParam2   DWORD: The time that the message was received by the input device driver. The time stamp is specified in milliseconds, and is set at zero when midiInStart() is called.

Include File   mmsystem.h

See Also   midiInStart()

MIM_LONGERROR
■ Win32s ■ Windows 95 ■ Windows NT

Description	MIM_LONGERROR is a message that is sent to a MIDI input callback function when an invalid or incomplete MIDI system-exclusive message is received. To determine the number of bytes recorded into the returned buffer, use the *dwBytesRecorded* member of the MIDIHDR structure specified by *dwParam1*.
Parameters	
dwParam1	DWORD: The address of a MIDIHDR structure identifying the buffer containing the invalid message.
dwParam2	DWORD: The time that the message was received by the input device driver. The time stamp is specified in milliseconds, and is set at zero when midiInStart() is called.
Include File	mmsystem.h
See Also	midiInStart()

MIM_MOREDATA
■ Win32s ■ Windows 95 ■ Windows NT

Description	MIM_MOREDATA is a message that is sent to a MIDI input callback function when a MIDI message is received by a MIDI input device but the application is not processing MIM_DATA messages fast enough to keep up with the input device driver. The callback function receives this message only when the application specifies MIDI_IO_STATUS in the call to midiInOpen(). This message is not sent when a MIDI system-exclusive message is received.
Parameters	
LOWORD(dwParam1)	DWORD: The first part of the MIDI message that was received by the MIDI input device. The low-order byte contains the MIDI status value. The high-order byte contains the first byte of the MIDI data, when needed.
HIWORD(dwParam1)	DWORD: The second part of the MIDI message that was received by the MIDI input device. The low-order byte contains the second byte of the MIDI data, when needed. The high-order byte is not used.
dwParam2	DWORD: The time that the message was received by the input device driver. The time stamp is specified in milliseconds, and is set at zero when midiInStart() is called.
Include File	mmsystem.h
See Also	midiOpen()

MIM_OPEN

■ Win32s ■ Windows 95 ■ Windows NT

Description	MIM_OPEN is a message that is sent to a MIDI input callback function when a MIDI input device is opened.
Parameters	This message does not use *dwParam1* or *dwParam2*; therefore, both must be set to zero.
Include File	mmsystem.h

MM_ACM_FILTERCHOOSE

■ Win32s ■ Windows 95 ■ Windows NT

Description	MM_ACM_FILTERCHOOSE is a message that notifies acmFilterChoose() before adding an element to one of the three drop-down list boxes. This message allows an application to further customize the selections available through the user interface.
Parameters	
wParam	WPARAM: The drop-down list box being initialized and a verify or add operation value from Table 11-11.

Table 11-11 MM_ACM_FILTERCHOOSE *wParam* values

Value	Meaning
FILTERCHOOSE_CUSTOM_VERIFY	*lParam* is a pointer to a WAVEFILTER structure to be added to the custom Name drop-down list box.
FILTERCHOOSE_FILTER_ADD	*lParam* is a pointer to a buffer that will accept a WAVEFILTER structure to be added to the Filter drop-down list box. The application must copy the filter structure to be added into this buffer.
FILTERCHOOSE_FILTER_VERIFY	*lParam* is a pointer to a WAVEFILTER structure to be added to the Filter drop-down list box.
FILTERCHOOSE_FILTERTAG_ADD	*lParam* is a pointer to a DWORD that will accept a waveform-audio filter tag to be added to the Filter Tag drop-down list box.
FILTERCHOOSE_FILTERTAG_VERIFY	*lParam* is a waveform-audio filter tag to be listed in the Filter Tag drop-down list box.

lParam	LONG: The value defined by the list box value specified by *wParam*; refer to Table 11-11.
Returns	BOOL: If the application handles this message, TRUE is returned; otherwise, FALSE is returned.
Include File	mmsystem.h
See Also	acmMetrics(), SetWindowLong()

MM_ACM_FORMATCHOOSE   ■ Win32s ■ Windows 95 ■ Windows NT

Description   MM_ACM_FORMATCHOOSE is a message that notifies acmFormatChoose() before adding an element to one of the three drop-down list boxes. This message allows an application to further customize the selections available through the user interface.

Parameters

wParam   WPARAM: The drop-down list box being initialized and a verify or add operation value from Table 11-12.

Table 11-12 MM_ACM_FORMATCHOOSE *wParam* values

Value	Meaning
FORMATCHOOSE_CUSTOM_VERIFY	*lParam* is a pointer to a WAVEFORMATEX structure to be added to the custom Name drop-down list box.
FORMATCHOOSE_FORMAT_ADD	*lParam* is a pointer to a buffer that will accept a WAVEFORMATEX structure to be added to the Format drop-down list box. The application must copy the format structure to be added into this buffer.
FORMATCHOOSE_FORMAT_VERIFY	*lParam* is a pointer to a WAVEFORMATEX structure to be added to the Format drop-down list box.
FORMATCHOOSE_FORMATTAG_ADD	*lParam* is a pointer to a variable that will accept a waveform-audio format tag to be added to the Format Tag drop-down list box.
FORMATCHOOSE_FORMATTAG_VERIFY	*lParam* is a waveform-audio format tag to be listed in the Format Tag drop-down list box.

lParam   LONG: The value defined by the list box value specified by *wParam*; refer to Table 11-12.

Returns   BOOL: If the application handles this message, TRUE is returned; otherwise, FALSE is returned.

Include File   mmsystem.h

See Also   acmFormatChoose(), SetWindowLong()

MM_JOY1BUTTONDOWN   ■ Win32s ■ Windows 95 ■ Windows NT

Description   MM_JOY1BUTTONDOWN is a message that notifies the window that has captured joystick JOYSTICKID1 that a joystick button was pressed.

Parameters

wParam   WPARAM: The button that has changed state and the buttons that are pressed. This parameter can be one of the values in Table 11-13 and one of the values in Table 11-14.

Table 11-13 MM_JOY1BUTTONDOWN *wParam* button change values

Value	Meaning
JOY_BUTTON1CHG	First joystick button has changed state.
JOY_BUTTON2CHG	Second joystick button has changed state.
JOY_BUTTON3CHG	Third joystick button has changed state.
JOY_BUTTON4CHG	Fourth joystick button has changed state.

Table 11-14 MM_JOY1BUTTONDOWN *wParam* button pressed values

Value	Meaning
JOY_BUTTON1	First joystick button is pressed.
JOY_BUTTON2	Second joystick button is pressed.
JOY_BUTTON3	Third joystick button is pressed.
JOY_BUTTON4	Fourth joystick button is pressed.

LOWORD(lParam)	WORD: The x coordinate of the joystick relative to the upper left corner of the client area.
HIWORD(lParam)	WORD: The y coordinate of the joystick relative to the upper left corner of the client area.
Include File	mmsystem.h

MM_JOY1BUTTONUP   ■ Win32s ■ Windows 95 ■ Windows NT

Description	MM_JOY1BUTTONUP is a message that notifies the window that has captured joystick JOYSTICKID1 that a joystick button has been released.
Parameters	
wParam	WPARAM: The button that has changed state and the buttons that are pressed. This parameter can be one of the values in Table 11-13 and one of the values in Table 11-14.
LOWORD(lParam)	WORD: The x coordinate of the joystick relative to the upper left corner of the client area.
HIWORD(lParam)	WORD: The y coordinate of the joystick relative to the upper left corner of the client area.
Include File	mmsystem.h

MM_JOY1MOVE   ■ Win32s ■ Windows 95 ■ Windows NT

Description	MM_JOY1MOVE is a message that notifies the window that has captured joystick JOYSTICKID1 that the joystick position has changed.

Parameters

wParam	WPARAM: The buttons that are pressed on the joystick. This parameter can be one or more of the values in Table 11-14.
LOWORD(lParam)	WORD: The x coordinate of the joystick relative to the upper left corner of the client area.
HIWORD(lParam)	WORD: The y coordinate of the joystick relative to the upper left corner of the client area.
Include File	mmsystem.h

MM_JOY1ZMOVE ■ Win32s ■ Windows 95 ■ Windows NT

Description MM_JOY1ZMOVE is a message that notifies the window that has captured joystick JOYSTICKID1 that the joystick position on the z axis has changed.

Parameters

wParam	WPARAM: The buttons that are pressed on the joystick. This parameter can be one or more of the values in Table 11-14.
LOWORD(lParam)	WORD: The z coordinate of the joystick relative to the upper left corner of the client area.
Include File	mmsystem.h

MM_JOY2BUTTONDOWN ■ Win32s ■ Windows 95 ■ Windows NT

Description MM_JOY2BUTTONDOWN is a message that notifies the window that has captured joystick JOYSTICKID2 that a joystick button has been pressed.

Parameters

wParam	WPARAM: The button that has changed state and the buttons that are pressed. This parameter can be one of the values in Table 11-13 and one of the values in Table 11-14.
LOWORD(lParam)	WORD: The x coordinate of the joystick relative to the upper left corner of the client area.
HIWORD(lParam)	WORD: The y coordinate of the joystick relative to the upper left corner of the client area.
Include File	mmsystem.h

MM_JOY2BUTTONUP ■ Win32s ■ Windows 95 ■ Windows NT

Description MM_JOY2BUTTONUP is a message that notifies the window that has captured joystick JOYSTICKID2 that a joystick button has been released.

Parameters

wParam	WPARAM: The button that has changed state and the buttons that are pressed. This parameter can be one of the values in Table 11-13 and one of the values in Table 11-14.
LOWORD(lParam)	WORD: The x coordinate of the joystick relative to the upper left corner of the client area.
HIWORD(lParam)	WORD: The y coordinate of the joystick relative to the upper left corner of the client area.
Include File	mmsystem.h

MM_JOY2MOVE   ■ Win32s ■ Windows 95 ■ Windows NT

Description   MM_JOY2MOVE is a message that notifies the window that has captured joystick JOYSTICKID2 that the joystick position has changed.

Parameters

wParam	WPARAM: The buttons that are pressed on the joystick. This parameter can be one or more of the values in Table 11-14.
LOWORD(lParam)	WORD: The x coordinate of the joystick relative to the upper left corner of the client area.
HIWORD(lParam)	WORD: The y coordinate of the joystick relative to the upper left corner of the client area.
Include File	mmsystem.h

MM_JOY2ZMOVE   ■ Win32s ■ Windows 95 ■ Windows NT

Description   MM_JOY2ZMOVE is a message that notifies the window that has captured joystick JOYSTICKID2 that the joystick position on the z axis has changed.

Parameters

wParam	WPARAM: The buttons that are pressed on the joystick. This parameter can be one or more of the values in Table 11-14.
LOWORD(lParam)	WORD: The z coordinate of the joystick relative to the upper left corner of the client area.
Include File	mmsystem.h

MM_MCINOTIFY   ■ Win32s ■ Windows 95 ■ Windows NT

Description   MM_MCINOTIFY is a message that notifies an application that an MCI device has completed an operation. MCI devices send this message only when the MCI_NOTIFY flag is used.

Parameters

wParam WPARAM: A value in Table 11-15 indicating the reason for the notification.

Table 11-15 MM_MCINOTIFY *wParam* values

Value	Meaning
MCI_NOTIFY_ABORTED	The device received a command that prevented the current conditions for initiating the callback function from being met. If a new command interrupts the current command and it also requests notification, the device sends this message only and not MCI_NOTIFY_SUPERSEDED.
MCI_NOTIFY_FAILURE	A device error occurred while the device was executing the command.
MCI_NOTIFY_SUCCESSFUL	The conditions initiating the callback function have been met.
MCI_NOTIFY_SUPERSEDED	The device received another command with the "notify" flag set, and the current conditions for initiating the callback function have been superseded.

lParam LONG: The identifier of the device initiating the callback function.

Returns int: If successful, zero is returned; otherwise, an error is returned.

Include File mmsystem.h

See Also mciSendCommand(), mciSendString()

MM_MCISIGNAL ■ Win32s ■ Windows 95 ■ Windows NT

Description MM_MCISIGNAL is a message that is sent to a window to notify an application that an MCI device has reached a position defined in a previous signal (MCI_SIGNAL) command.

Parameters

wParam WPARAM: The identifier of the device initiating the signal message.

lParam LONG: The value passed in the *dwUserParam* member of the MCI_DGV_SIGNAL_PARAMS structure when the signal command has defined either mciSendCommand() or mciSendString(). Alternatively, it might contain the position value.

Returns int: If successful, zero is returned; otherwise, an error is returned.

Include File mmsystem.h

See Also mciSendCommand(), mciSendString()

MM_MIM_CLOSE ■ Win32s ■ Windows 95 ■ Windows NT

Description MM_MIM_CLOSE is a message that is sent to a window when a MIDI input device is closed. The device handle is no longer valid after this message has been sent.

Parameters

wParam	WPARAM: The handle of the MIDI input device that was closed.
lParam	LPARAM: Set to zero.
Include File	mmsystem.h

MM_MIM_DATA ■ Win32s ■ Windows 95 ■ Windows NT

Description	MM_MIM_DATA is a message that is sent to a window when a complete MIDI message is received by a MIDI input device. This message is not sent when a MIDI system-exclusive message is received.

Parameters

wParam	WPARAM: The handle of the MIDI input device that received the MIDI message.
LOWORD(*lParam*)	DWORD: The first part of the MIDI message received by the MIDI input device. The low-order byte contains the MIDI status. The high-order byte contains the first byte of the MIDI data, when needed.
HIWORD(*lParam*)	DWORD: The second part of the MIDI message received by the MIDI input device. The low-order byte contains the second byte of the MIDI data, when needed. The high-order byte is not used.
Include File	mmsystem.h

MM_MIM_ERROR ■ Win32s ■ Windows 95 ■ Windows NT

Description	MM_MIM_ERROR is a message that is sent to a window when an invalid MIDI message is received.

Parameters

wParam	WPARAM: The handle of the MIDI input device that received the invalid message.
lParam	DWORD: The invalid MIDI message received by the MIDI input device. The message is packed into a double-word value with the first byte of the message in the low-order byte.
Include File	mmsystem.h

MM_MIM_LONGDATA ■ Win32s ■ Windows 95 ■ Windows NT

Description	MM_MIM_LONGDATA is a message that is sent to a window when either a complete MIDI system-exclusive message is received or when a buffer has been filled with system-exclusive data. To determine the number of bytes recorded into the returned buffer, use the *dwBytesRecorded* member of the MIDIHDR structure pointed to by *lParam*.

Parameters

wParam	WPARAM: The handle of the MIDI input device that received the data.
lParam	LPARAM: The address of a MIDIHDR structure identifying the buffer.
Include File	mmsystem.h

MM_MIM_LONGERROR   ■ Win32s ■ Windows 95 ■ Windows NT

Description   MM_MIM_LONGERROR is a message that is sent to a window when an invalid or incomplete MIDI system-exclusive message is received. To determine the number of bytes recorded into the returned buffer, use the *dwBytesRecorded* member of the MIDIHDR structure specified by *lParam*.

Parameters

wParam	WPARAM: The handle of the MIDI input device that received the invalid message.
lParam	LPARAM: The address of a MIDIHDR structure identifying the buffer containing the invalid message.
Include File	mmsystem.h

MM_MIM_MOREDATA   ■ Win32s ■ Windows 95 ■ Windows NT

Description   MM_MIM_MOREDATA is a message that is sent to a callback window when a MIDI message is received by a MIDI input device but the application is not processing MIM_DATA messages fast enough to keep up with the input device driver. The window receives this message only when the application specifies MIDI_IO_STATUS in the call to midiInOpen().This message is not sent when a MIDI system-exclusive message is received.

Parameters

wParam	WPARAM: The handle of the MIDI input device that received the MIDI message.
LOWORD(*lParam*)	DWORD: The first part of the MIDI message received by the MIDI input device. The low-order byte contains the MIDI status. The high-order byte contains the first byte of the MIDI data, when needed.
HIWORD(*lParam*)	DWORD: The second part of the MIDI message received by the MIDI input device. The low-order byte contains the second byte of the MIDI data, when needed. The high-order byte is not used.
Include File	mmsystem.h
See Also	PostMessage()
Related Messages	MIM_MOREDATA

MM_MIM_OPEN
■ Win32s ■ Windows 95 ■ Windows NT

Description   MM_MIM_OPEN is a message that is sent to a window when a MIDI input device is opened.

Parameters

wParam   WPARAM: The handle of the opened MIDI input device.

lParam   LPARAM: Set to zero.

Include File   mmsystem.h

MM_MIXM_CONTROL_CHANGE
■ Win32s ■ Windows 95 ■ Windows NT

Description   MM_MIXM_CONTROL_CHANGE is a message that is sent by a mixer device to notify an application that the state of a control associated with an audio line has changed. The application should refresh its display and cached values for the specified control. An application must open a mixer device and specify a callback window to receive the MM_MIXM_CONTROL_CHANGE message.

Parameters

wParam   WPARAM: The handle of the mixer device that sent the notification message.

lParam   LPARAM: The control identifier for the mixer control that has changed state. This identifier is the same value as the *dwControlID* member of the MIXERCONTROL structure returned by mixerGetLineControls().

Include File   mmsystem.h

See Also   mixerGetLineControls()

MM_MIXM_LINE_CHANGE
■ Win32s ■ Windows 95 ■ Windows NT

Description   MM_MIXM_LINE_CHANGE is a message that is sent by a mixer device to notify an application that the state of an audio line on the specified device has changed. The application should refresh its display and cached values for the specified audio line. An application must open a mixer device and specify a callback window to receive the MM_MIXM_LINE_CHANGE message.

Parameters

wParam   WPARAM: The handle of the mixer device that sent the notification message.

lParam   LPARAM: The line identifier for the audio line that has changed state. This identifier is the same value as the *dwLineID* member of the MIXERLINE structure returned by mixerGetLineInfo().

Include File   mmsystem.h

See Also   mixerGetLineInfo()

MM_MOM_CLOSE
■ Win32s ■ Windows 95 ■ Windows NT

Description	MM_MOM_CLOSE is a message that is sent to a window when a MIDI output device is closed. The device handle, specified by *wParam*, is no longer valid after this message has been sent.
Parameters	
wParam	WPARAM: The handle of the closed MIDI output device.
lParam	LPARAM: Set to zero.
Include File	mmsystem.h

MM_MOM_DONE
■ Win32s ■ Windows 95 ■ Windows NT

Description	MM_MOM_DONE is a message that is sent to a window when the specified MIDI system-exclusive or stream buffer has been played and is being returned to the application.
Parameters	
wParam	WPARAM: The handle of the MIDI output device that played the buffer.
lParam	LPARAM: The address of a MIDIHDR structure identifying the buffer.
Include File	mmsystem.h

MM_MOM_OPEN
■ Win32s ■ Windows 95 ■ Windows NT

Description	MM_MOM_OPEN is a message that is sent to a window when a MIDI output device is opened.
Parameters	
wParam	WPARAM: The handle of the opened MIDI output device.
lParam	LPARAM: Set to zero.
Include File	mmsystem.h

MM_MOM_POSITIONCB
■ Win32s ■ Windows 95 ■ Windows NT

Description	MM_MOM_POSITIONCB is a message that is sent to a window when a MEVT_F_CALLBACK event is reached in the MIDI output stream. The playback of the stream buffer continues while the callback function is executing.
Parameters	
wParam	WPARAM: The address of a MIDIHDR structure that identifies the event that caused the callback. The *dwOffset* member of the structure gives the offset of the event.
lParam	LPARAM: Set to zero.
Include File	mmsystem.h

MM_WIM_CLOSE   ■ Win32s ■ Windows 95 ■ Windows NT

Description	MM_WIM_CLOSE is a message that is sent to a window when a waveform-audio input device is closed. The device handle is no longer valid after this message has been sent.
Parameters	
wParam	WPARAM: The handle of the waveform-audio input device that was closed.
lParam	LPARAM: Set to zero.
Include File	mmsystem.h

MM_WIM_DATA   ■ Win32s ■ Windows 95 ■ Windows NT

Description	MM_WIM_DATA is a message that is sent to a window when waveform-audio data is present in the input buffer and the buffer is being returned to the application. The message can be sent either when the buffer is full or after waveInReset() is called. Use the *dwBytesRecorded* member of the WAVEHDR structure specified by *lParam* to determine the number of bytes recorded into the returned buffer.
Parameters	
wParam	WPARAM: The handle of the waveform-audio input device that received the data.
lParam	LONG: The address of a WAVEHDR structure that identifies the buffer containing the data.
Include File	mmsystem.h

MM_WIM_OPEN   ■ Win32s ■ Windows 95 ■ Windows NT

Description	MM_WIM_OPEN is a message that is sent to a window when a waveform-audio input device is opened.
Parameters	
wParam	WPARAM: The handle of the opened input device.
lParam	LPARAM: Set to zero.
Include File	mmsystem.h

MM_WOM_CLOSE   ■ Win32s ■ Windows 95 ■ Windows NT

Description	MM_WOM_CLOSE is a message that is sent to a window when a waveform-audio output device is closed. The device handle is no longer valid after this message has been sent.

Parameters

wParam   WPARAM: The handle of the closed waveform-audio output device.

lParam   LPARAM: Set to zero.

Include File   mmsystem.h

MM_WOM_DONE   ■ Win32s ■ Windows 95 ■ Windows NT

Description   MM_WOM_DONE is a message that is sent to a window when the given output buffer is being returned to the application. Output buffers are returned to the application when they have been played, or as the result of a call to waveOutReset().

Parameters

wParam   WPARAM: The handle of the waveform-audio output device that played the buffer.

lParam   LONG: The address of a WAVEHDR structure identifying the output buffer being returned.

Include File   mmsystem.h

MM_WOM_OPEN   ■ Win32s ■ Windows 95 ■ Windows NT

Description   MM_WOM_OPEN is a message that is sent to a window when the given waveform-audio output device is opened.

Parameters

wParam   WPARAM: The handle of the opened waveform-audio output device.

lParam   LPARAM: Set to zero.

Include File   mmsystem.h

MMIOM_CLOSE   ■ Win32s ■ Windows 95 ■ Windows NT

Description   MMIOM_CLOSE is a message that is sent to an I/O procedure by mmioClose() to request that a file be closed.

Parameters

lParam1   LPARAM: The flags in the *wFlag* parameter of mmioClose().

lParam2   LPARAM: Set to zero.

Returns   int: If the file is successfully closed, zero is returned; otherwise, an error is returned.

Include File   mmsystem.h

See Also   mmioClose()

MMIOM_OPEN
■ Win32s ■ Windows 95 ■ Windows NT

Description	MMIOM_OPEN is a message that is sent to an I/O procedure by mmioOpen() to request that a file be opened or deleted.
Parameters	
lParam1	LPARAM: A null-terminated string containing the name of the file to open.
lParam2	LPARAM: Set to zero.
Returns	int: Returns MMSYSERR_NOERROR if successful; otherwise one of the error values in Table 11-16 is returned.
Include File	mmsystem.h
See Also	mmioOpen()

Table 11-16 MMIOM_OPEN return values

Value	Meaning
MMIOM_CANNOTOPEN	The file could not be opened.
MMIOM_OUTOFMEMORY	Not enough memory to perform the operation.

MMIOM_READ
■ Win32s ■ Windows 95 ■ Windows NT

Description	MMIOM_READ is a message that is sent to an I/O procedure by mmioRead() to request that a specified number of bytes be read from an open file. The I/O procedure is responsible for updating the *lDiskOffset* member of the MMIOINFO structure to reflect the new file position after the read operation.
Parameters	
lParam1	LPARAM: The address of the buffer to be filled with data read from the file.
lParam2	LPARAM: The number of bytes to read from the open file.
Returns	int: The number of bytes actually read from the file is returned. If additional bytes cannot be read, a value of zero is returned. If there is an error, -1 is returned.
Include File	mmsystem.h
See Also	mmioRead()

MMIOM_RENAME
■ Win32s ■ Windows 95 ■ Windows NT

Description	MMIOM_RENAME is a message that is sent to an I/O procedure by mmioRename() to request that the specified file be renamed.

Parameters

lParam1   LPARAM: The address of a string containing the file name of the file to rename.

lParam2   LPARAM: The address of a string containing the new file name.

Returns   int: If the file is renamed successfully, zero is returned; otherwise, if the specified file is not found, MMIOERR_FILENOTFOUND is returned.

Include File   mmsystem.h

See Also   mmioRename()

MMIOM_SEEK   ■ Win32s ■ Windows 95 ■ Windows NT

Description   MMIOM_SEEK is a message that is sent to an I/O procedure by mmioSeek() to request that the current file position be moved. The I/O procedure is responsible for maintaining the current file position in the *lDiskOffset* member of the MMIOINFO structure.

Parameters

lParam1   LPARAM: The new file position. The meaning of *lParam1* is based on the flag specified in *lParam2*.

lParam2   LPARAM: A flag specifying how the file position is changed. The values in Table 11-17 are defined for *lParam2*.

Returns   int: If successful, the new file position is returned; otherwise, a value of -1 is returned.

Include File   mmsystem.h

See Also   mmioSeek()

Table 11-17 MMIOM_SEEK *lParam2* values

Value	Meaning
SEEK_CUR	Move the file position to be *lParam1* bytes from the current position. *lParam1* can be a positive or negative value.
SEEK_END	Move the file position to be *lParam1* bytes from the end of the file.
SEEK_SET	Move the file position to be *lParam1* bytes from the beginning of the file.

MMIOM_WRITE   ■ Win32s ■ Windows 95 ■ Windows NT

Description   MMIOM_WRITE is a message that is sent to an I/O procedure by mmioWrite() to request that data be written to an open file. The I/O procedure is responsible for updating the *lDiskOffset* member of the MMIOINFO structure to reflect the new file position after the write operation.

Parameters

lParam1	LPARAM: The address of a buffer containing the data to write to the file.
lParam2	LPARAM: The number of bytes to write to the open file.
Returns	int: If successful, the number of bytes actually written to the open file is returned; otherwise, a value of -1 is returned.
Include File	mmsystem.h
See Also	mmioWrite()

MMIOM_WRITEFLUSH ■ Win32s ■ Windows 95 ■ Windows NT

Description	MMIOM_WRITEFLUSH is a message that is sent to an I/O procedure by mmioWrite() to request that data be written to an open file and that any internal buffers used by the I/O procedure be flushed to disk. The I/O procedure is responsible for updating the *lDiskOffset* member of the MMIOINFO structure to reflect the new file position after the write operation.

Parameters

lParam1	LPARAM: The address of a buffer containing the data to write to the open file.
lParam2	LPARAM: The number of bytes to write to the open file.
Returns	int: If successful, the number of bytes actually written to the open file is returned; otherwise, a value of -1 is returned.
Include File	mmsystem.h
See Also	mmioWrite()
Related Messages	MMIOM_WRITE

MOM_CLOSE ■ Win32s ■ Windows 95 ■ Windows NT

Description	MOM_CLOSE is a message that is sent to a MIDI output callback function when a MIDI output device is closed. The device handle is no longer valid after this message has been sent.
Parameters	This message does not use *dwParam1* or *dwParam2*, therefore, both must be set to zero.
Include File	mmsystem.h

MOM_DONE ■ Win32s ■ Windows 95 ■ Windows NT

Description	MOM_DONE is a message that is sent to a MIDI output callback function when the specified system-exclusive or stream buffer has been played and is being returned to the application.

Parameters

dwParam1   DWORD: The address of a MIDIHDR structure identifying the buffer.

dwParam2   DWORD: Set to zero.

Include File   mmsystem.h

MOM_OPEN   ■ Win32s ■ Windows 95 ■ Windows NT

Description   MOM_OPEN is a message that is sent to a MIDI output callback function when a MIDI output device is opened.

Parameters   This message does not use *dwParam1* or *dwParam2*; therefore, both must be set to zero.

Include File   mmsystem.h

MOM_POSITIONCB   ■ Win32s ■ Windows 95 ■ Windows NT

Description   MOM_POSITIONCB is sent to a window when a MEVT_F_CALLBACK event is reached in the MIDI output stream.

Parameters

dwParam1   DWORD: The handle of the MIDI output device.

dwParam2   DWORD: The address of a MIDIHDR structure that identifies the event that caused the callback function. The *dwOffset* member, of the MIDIHDR structure, provides the offset of the event.

Include File   mmsystem.h

NM_CLICK   Win32s ■ Windows 95 ■ Windows NT

Description   NM_CLICK is a notification message that notifies the parent window of a control that the user has clicked the left mouse button within the control. NM_CLICK is sent in the form of a WM_NOTIFY message.

Parameters

wParam   WPARAM: Set to zero.

lParam   NMHDR *: A pointer to the NMHDR structure that contains information about the control.

Include File   winuser.h

Related Messages WM_NOTIFY

NM_DBLCLK   Win32s ■ Windows 95 ■ Windows NT

Description   NM_DBLCLK is a notification message that notifies the parent window of a control that the user has double-clicked the left mouse button within the control. NM_DBLCLK is sent in the form of a WM_NOTIFY message.

Parameters

wParam　　　　　　WPARAM: Set to zero.

lParam　　　　　　NMHDR *: A pointer to the NMHDR structure that contains information
　　　　　　　　　　about the control.

Include File　　　winuser.h

Related Messages　WM_NOTIFY

NM_KILLFOCUS ■ Win32s ■ Windows 95 ■ Windows NT

Description　　　NM_KILLFOCUS is a notification message that notifies the parent window
　　　　　　　　　　of a control that the control has lost the input focus. NM_KILLFOCUS is
　　　　　　　　　　sent in the form of a WM_NOTIFY message.

Parameters

wParam　　　　　　WPARAM: Set to zero.

lParam　　　　　　NMHDR *: A pointer to the NMHDR structure that contains information
　　　　　　　　　　about the control.

Include File　　　winuser.h

Related Messages　WM_NOTIFY

NM_OUTOFMEMORY Win32s ■ Windows 95 ■ Windows NT

Description　　　NM_OUTOFMEMORY is a notification message that notifies the parent
　　　　　　　　　　window of a control that the control could not complete an operation
　　　　　　　　　　because there was not enough memory available. NM_OUTOFMEMORY
　　　　　　　　　　is sent in the form of a WM_NOTIFY message.

Parameters

wParam　　　　　　WPARAM: Set to zero.

lParam　　　　　　NMHDR *: A pointer to the NMHDR structure that contains information
　　　　　　　　　　about the control.

Include File　　　winuser.h

Related Messages　WM_NOTIFY

NM_RCLICK ■ Win32s ■ Windows 95 ■ Windows NT

Description　　　NM_RCLICK is a notification message that notifies the parent window of a
　　　　　　　　　　control that the user has clicked the right mouse button within the
　　　　　　　　　　control. NM_RCLICK is sent in the form of a WM_NOTIFY message.

Parameters

wParam　　　　　　WPARAM: Set to zero.

lParam   NMHDR *: A pointer to the NMHDR structure that contains information
                           about the control.

Include File   winuser.h

Related Messages   WM_NOTIFY

NM_RDBLCLK   Win32s ■ Windows 95 ■ Windows NT

Description   NM_RDBLCLK is a notification message that notifies the parent window of
                           a control that the user has double-clicked the right mouse button within
                           the control. NM_RDBLCLK is sent in the form of a WM_NOTIFY
                           message.

Parameters

wParam   WPARAM: Set to zero.

lParam   NMHDR *: A pointer to the NMHDR structure that contains information
                           about the control.

Include File   winuser.h

Related Messages   WM_NOTIFY

NM_RETURN   Win32s ■ Windows 95 ■ Windows NT

Description   NM_RETURN is a notification message that notifies the parent window of
                           a control that the control has the input focus and that the user has pressed
                           the (ENTER) key. NM_RETURN is sent in the form of a WM_NOTIFY
                           message.

Parameters

wParam   WPARAM: Set to zero.

lParam   NMHDR *: A pointer to the NMHDR structure that contains information
                           about the control.

Include File   winuser.h

Related Messages   WM_NOTIFY

NM_SETFOCUS   Win32s ■ Windows 95 ■ Windows NT

Description   NM_SETFOCUS is a notification message that notifies the parent window
                           of a control that the control has received the input focus. NM_SETFOCUS
                           is sent in the form of a WM_NOTIFY message.

Parameters

wParam   WPARAM: Set to zero.

lParam   NMHDR *: A pointer to the NMHDR structure that contains information
                           about the control.

Include File   winuser.h
Related Messages WM_NOTIFY

PBM_DELTAPOS   ■ Win32s ■ Windows 95 ■ Windows NT

Description   PBM_DELTAPOS is a message that advances the current position of a progress bar by a specified increment and redraws the bar to reflect the new position. For more information, refer to the PBM_DELTAPOS message in Chapter 9, Miscellaneous Controls.

PBM_SETPOS   ■ Win32s ■ Windows 95 ■ Windows NT

Description   PBM_SETPOS is a message that sets the current position for a progress bar and redraws the bar to reflect the new position. For more information, refer to the PBM_SETPOS message in Chapter 9, Miscellaneous Controls. (See Figure 11-6.)

Figure 11-6 Progress Control

PBM_SETRANGE   ■ Win32s ■ Windows 95 ■ Windows NT

Description   PBM_SETRANGE is a message that sets the minimum and maximum values for a progress bar and redraws the bar to reflect the new range. For more information, refer to the PBM_SETRANGE message in Chapter 9, Miscellaneous Controls.

PBM_SETSTEP   ■ Win32s ■ Windows 95 ■ Windows NT

Description   PBM_SETSTEP is a message that specifies the amount used to increment the progress bar when a PBM_STEPIT message is received. For more information, refer to the PBM_SETSTEP message in Chapter 9, Miscellaneous Controls.

PBM_STEPIT   ■ Win32s ■ Windows 95 ■ Windows NT

Description   PBM_STEPIT is a message that advances the current position for a progress bar by the step increment and redraws the bar to reflect the new position. An application sets the step increment by sending the PBM_SETSTEP message. For more information, refer to the PBM_STEPIT message in Chapter 9, Miscellaneous Controls.

PSM_ADDPAGE
■ Win32s ■ Windows 95 ■ Windows NT

Description   PSM_ADDPAGE is a message that adds a new page to the end of an existing property sheet. For more information, refer to the PropSheet_AddPage macro in Chapter 4, Tab Controls and Property Sheets.

PSM_APPLY
■ Win32s ■ Windows 95 ■ Windows NT

Description   PSM_APPLY is a message that simulates the choice of the Apply Now button by indicating that one or more pages have changed and the changes need to be validated and recorded. For more information, refer to the PropSheet_Apply macro in Chapter 4, Tab Controls and Property Sheets.

PSM_CANCELTOCLOSE
■ Win32s ■ Windows 95 ■ Windows NT

Description   PSM_CANCELTOCLOSE is a message that disables the Cancel button and changes the text of the OK button to "Close". For more information, refer to the PropSheet_CancelToClose macro in Chapter 4, Tab Controls and Property Sheets.

PSM_CHANGED
■ Win32s ■ Windows 95 ■ Windows NT

Description   PSM_CHANGED is a message that informs a property sheet that information in a page has changed. For more information, refer to the PropSheet_Changed macro in Chapter 4, Tab Controls and Property Sheets.

PSM_GETCURRENTPAGEHWND
■ Win32s ■ Windows 95 ■ Windows NT

Description   PSM_GETCURRENTPAGEHWND is a message that retrieves the handle of the window of the current property sheet page. For more information, refer to the PropSheet_GetCurrentPageHwnd macro in Chapter 4, Tab Controls and Property Sheets.

PSM_GETTABCONTROL
■ Win32s ■ Windows 95 ■ Windows NT

Description   PSM_GETTABCONTROL is a message that retrieves the handle to the tab control of a property sheet. For more information, refer to the PropSheet_GetTabControl macro in Chapter 4, Tab Controls and Property Sheets.

PSM_ISDIALOGMESSAGE ■ Win32s ■ Windows 95 ■ Windows NT

Description   PSM_ISDIALOGMESSAGE is a message that passes a message to the property sheet dialog box and determines if the box processes the message. For more information, refer to the PropSheet_IsDialogMessage macro in Chapter 4, Tab Controls and Property Sheets.

PSM_PRESSBUTTON ■ Win32s ■ Windows 95 ■ Windows NT

Description   PSM_PRESSBUTTON is a message that simulates the choice of a property sheet button. For more information, refer to the PropSheet_PressButton macro in Chapter 4, Tab Controls and Property Sheets.

PSM_QUERYSIBLINGS ■ Win32s ■ Windows 95 ■ Windows NT

Description   PSM_QUERYSIBLINGS is a message that is sent to each page in the property sheet. For more information, refer to the PropSheet_QuerySiblings macro in Chapter 4, Tab Controls and Property Sheets.

PSM_REBOOTSYSTEM ■ Win32s ■ Windows 95 ■ Windows NT

Description   PSM_REBOOTSYSTEM is a message that indicates that the system needs to be restarted for the changes to take effect. For more information, refer to the PropSheet_RebootSystem macro in Chapter 4, Tab Controls and Property Sheets.

PSM_REMOVEPAGE ■ Win32s ■ Windows 95 ■ Windows NT

Description   PSM_REMOVEPAGE is a message that removes a page from a property sheet. For more information, refer to the PropSheet_RemovePage macro in Chapter 4, Tab Controls and Property Sheets.

PSM_RESTARTWINDOWS ■ Win32s ■ Windows 95 ■ Windows NT

Description   PSM_RESTARTWINDOWS is a message that indicates that Windows needs to be restarted before the changes will take effect. For more information, refer to the PropSheet_RestartWindows macro in Chapter 4, Tab Controls and Property Sheets.

PSM_SETCURSEL

■ Win32s ■ Windows 95 ■ Windows NT

Description   PSM_SETCURSEL is a message that activates the given page in a property sheet. For more information, refer to the PropSheet_SetCurSel macro in Chapter 4, Tab Controls and Property Sheets.

PSM_SETCURSELID

■ Win32s ■ Windows 95 ■ Windows NT

Description   PSM_SETCURSELID is a message that activates the given page in a property sheet based on the resource identifier of the page. For more information, refer to the PropSheet_SetCurSelByID macro in Chapter 4, Tab Controls and Property Sheets.

PSM_SETFINISHTEXT

■ Win32s ■ Windows 95 ■ Windows NT

Description   PSM_SETFINISHTEXT is a message that sets the text of the Finish button in a wizard property sheet, shows and enables the button, and hides the Next and Back buttons. For more information, refer to the PropSheet_SetFinishText macro in Chapter 4, Tab Controls and Property Sheets.

PSM_SETTITLE

■ Win32s ■ Windows 95 ■ Windows NT

Description   PSM_SETTITLE is a message that sets the title of a property sheet. For more information, refer to the PropSheet_SetTitle macro in Chapter 4, Tab Controls and Property Sheets.

PSM_SETWIZBUTTONS

■ Win32s ■ Windows 95 ■ Windows NT

Description   PSM_SETWIZBUTTONS is a message that enables the Back, Next, or Finish button in a wizard property sheet. For more information, refer to the PropSheet_SetWizButtons macro in Chapter 4, Tab Controls and Property Sheets.

PSM_UNCHANGED

■ Win32s ■ Windows 95 ■ Windows NT

Description   PSM_UNCHANGED is a message that informs a property sheet that information in a page has reverted to the previously saved state. For more information, refer to the PropSheet_Unchanged macro in Chapter 4, Tab Controls and Property Sheets.

PSN_APPLY ■ Win32s ■ Windows 95 ■ Windows NT

Description   PSN_APPLY is a notification message that indicates that the user chose the OK or Apply Now button and wants all changes to take effect. For more information, refer to the PSN_APPLY notification message in Chapter 4, Tab Controls and Property Sheets.

PSN_HELP ■ Win32s ■ Windows 95 ■ Windows NT

Description   PSN_HELP is a notification message that notifies a page that the user has chosen the Help button. For more information, refer to the PSN_HELP notification message in Chapter 4, Tab Controls and Property Sheets.

PSN_KILLACTIVE ■ Win32s ■ Windows 95 ■ Windows NT

Description   PSN_KILLACTIVE is a notification message that notifies a page that it is about to lose the activation either because another page is being activated or the user has chosen the OK button. For more information, refer to the PSN_KILLACTIVE notification message in Chapter 4, Tab Controls and Property Sheets.

PSN_QUERYCANCEL ■ Win32s ■ Windows 95 ■ Windows NT

Description   PSN_QUERYCANCEL is a notification message that indicates that the user chose the Cancel button. For more information, refer to the PSN_QUERYCANCEL notification message in Chapter 4, Tab Controls and Property Sheets.

PSN_RESET ■ Win32s ■ Windows 95 ■ Windows NT

Description   PSN_RESET is a notification message that notifies a page that the user has chosen the Cancel button, and the property sheet is about to be destroyed. For more information, refer to the PSN_RESET notification message in Chapter 4, Tab Controls and Property Sheets.

PSN_SETACTIVE ■ Win32s ■ Windows 95 ■ Windows NT

Description   PSN_SETACTIVE is a notification message that notifies a page that it is about to be activated. For more information, refer to the PSN_SETACTIVE notification message in Chapter 4, Tab Controls and Property Sheets.

PSN_WIZBACK
■ Win32s ■ Windows 95 ■ Windows NT

Description   PSN_WIZBACK is a notification message that notifies a page that the user
has chosen the Back button in a wizard property sheet. For more informa-
tion, refer to the PSN_WIZBACK notification message in Chapter 4, Tab
Controls and Property Sheets.

PSN_WIZFINISH
■ Win32s ■ Windows 95 ■ Windows NT

Description   PSN_WIZFINISH is a notification message that notifies a page that the
user has chosen the Finish button in a wizard property sheet. For more
information, refer to the PSN_WIZFINISH notification message in Chapter
4, Tab Controls and Property Sheets.

PSN_WIZNEXT
■ Win32s ■ Windows 95 ■ Windows NT

Description   PSN_WIZNEXT is a notification message that notifies a page that the user
has chosen the Next button in a wizard property sheet. For more
information, refer to the PSN_WIZNEXT notification message in Chapter
4, Tab Controls and Property Sheets.

SB_GETBORDERS
■ Win32s ■ Windows 95 ■ Windows NT

Description   SB_GETBORDERS is a message that retrieves the current widths of the
horizontal and vertical borders of a status window. For more information,
refer to the SB_GETBORDERS message in Chapter 3, Toolbars and Status
Windows.

SB_GETPARTS
■ Win32s ■ Windows 95 ■ Windows NT

Description   SB_GETPARTS is a message that retrieves a count of the current parts in a
status window. For more information, refer to the SB_GETPARTS message
in Chapter 3, Toolbars and Status Windows.

SB_GETRECT
■ Win32s ■ Windows 95 ■ Windows NT

Description   SB_GETRECT is a message that retrieves the bounding rectangle of a part
in a status window. For more information, refer to the SB_GETRECT
message in Chapter 3, Toolbars and Status Windows.

SB_GETTEXT
■ Win32s ■ Windows 95 ■ Windows NT

Description
SB_GETTEXT is a message that retrieves the text from the specified part of a status window. For more information, refer to the SB_GETTEXT message in Chapter 3, Toolbars and Status Windows.

SB_GETTEXTLENGTH
■ Win32s ■ Windows 95 ■ Windows NT

Description
SB_GETTEXTLENGTH is a message that retrieves the length, in characters, of the text from the specified part of a status window. For more information, refer to the SB_GETTEXTLENGTH message in Chapter 3, Toolbars and Status Windows.

SB_SETMINHEIGHT
■ Win32s ■ Windows 95 ■ Windows NT

Description
SB_SETMINHEIGHT is a message that sets the minimum height of the drawing area in a status window. For more information, refer to the SB_SETMINHEIGHT message in Chapter 3, Toolbars and Status Windows.

SB_SETPARTS
■ Win32s ■ Windows 95 ■ Windows NT

Description
SB_SETPARTS is a message that sets the number of parts in a status window and the coordinate of the right edge of each part. For more information, refer to the SB_SETPARTS message in Chapter 3, Toolbars and Status Windows.

SB_SETTEXT
■ Win32s ■ Windows 95 ■ Windows NT

Description
SB_SETTEXT is a message that sets the text in the specified part of a status window. For more information, refer to the SB_SETTEXT message in Chapter 3, Toolbars and Status Windows.

SB_SIMPLE
■ Win32s ■ Windows 95 ■ Windows NT

Description
SB_SIMPLE is a message that specifies whether a status window displays simple text or displays all window parts set by a previous SB_SETPARTS message. For more information, refer to the SB_SIMPLE message in Chapter 3, Toolbars and Status Windows.

SBM_ENABLE_ARROWS
■ Win32s ■ Windows 95 ■ Windows NT

Description   SBM_ENABLE_ARROWS is a message that either enables or disables one or both arrows of a scroll bar control.

Parameters

wParam   WPARAM: One of the values in Table 11-18, indicating whether the scroll bar arrows are enabled or disabled, and identifying the arrows that are either enabled or disabled.

Table 11-18 SBM_ENABLE_ARROWS *wParam* values

Value	Meaning
ESB_DISABLE_BOTH	Disables both arrows on a scroll bar.
ESB_DISABLE_DOWN	Disables the down arrow on a vertical scroll bar.
ESB_DISABLE_LEFT	Disables the left arrow on a horizontal scroll bar.
ESB_DISABLE_LTUP	Disables the left arrow on a horizontal scroll bar or the up arrow on a vertical scroll bar.
ESB_DISABLE_RTDN	Disables the right arrow on a horizontal scroll bar or the down arrow on a vertical scroll bar.
ESB_DISABLE_UP	Disables the up arrow on a vertical scroll bar.
ESB_ENABLE_BOTH	Enables both arrows on a scroll bar.

lParam   LPARAM: Set to zero.

Returns   BOOL: If the message succeeds, TRUE is returned; otherwise, FALSE is returned.

Include File   winuser.h

SBM_GETPOS
Win32s ■ Windows 95 ■ Windows NT

Description   SBM_GETPOS is a message that retrieves the current position of the scroll box of a scroll bar control. The current position is a relative value that is based upon the current scrolling range. For example, if the scrolling range is 0 through 100 and the scroll box is in the middle of the bar, the current position is 50.

Parameters   This message does not use *wParam* or *lParam*; therefore, both must be set to zero.

Returns   int: If the message succeeds, the current position of the scroll box in the scroll bar is returned.

Include File   winuser.h

Related Messages   SBM_GETRANGE, SBM_SETPOS, SBM_SETRANGE, SBM_SETRANGEREDRAW

SBM_GETRANGE   Win32s ■ Windows 95 ■ Windows NT

Description	SBM_GETRANGE is a message that is sent to a scroll bar control to retrieve the minimum and maximum position values for the control.
Parameters	
wParam	LPINT: A pointer to a value that receives the minimum scrolling position.
lParam	LPINT: A pointer to a value that receives the maximum scrolling position.
Include File	winuser.h
Related Messages	SBM_GETPOS, SBM_SETPOS, SBM_SETRANGE, SBM_SETRANGEREDRAW

SBM_GETSCROLLINFO   Win32s ■ Windows 95 ■ Windows NT

Description	SBM_GETSCROLLINFO is a message that retrieves the parameters of a scroll bar.
Parameters	
wParam	WPARAM: Set to zero.
lParam	LPSCROLLINFO: A pointer to a SCROLLINFO structure whose *fMask* member specifies the scroll bar parameters to be retrieved by SBM_GETSCROLLINFO. Before returning, the message copies the specified parameters to the appropriate members of the structure.
Returns	BOOL: If the message retrieved the scroll bar parameters, TRUE is returned; otherwise, FALSE is returned.
Related Messages	SBM_SETSCROLLINFO

SBM_SETPOS   Win32s ■ Windows 95 ■ Windows NT

Description	SBM_SETPOS is a message that is sent to a scroll bar control to set the position of the scroll box and, if requested, redraw the scroll bar to reflect the new position of the scroll box.
Parameters	
wParam	WPARAM: The new position of the scroll box. It must be within the scrolling range.
lParam	BOOL: TRUE indicates that the scroll bar should be redrawn to reflect the new position of the scroll box; FALSE indicates that the scroll bar should not be redrawn.
Returns	int: If the position of the scroll box changed, the previous position of the scroll box is returned; otherwise, zero is returned.
Include File	winuser.h
Related Messages	SBM_GETPOS, SBM_GETRANGE, SBM_SETRANGE, SBM_SETRANGEREDRAW

SBM_SETRANGE
Win32s ■ Windows 95 ■ Windows NT

Description   SBM_SETRANGE is a message that is sent to a scroll bar control to set the minimum and maximum position values for the control. If the minimum and maximum values are equal, the scroll bar control is hidden.

Parameters

wParam   WPARAM: The minimum scrolling position of the scroll bar control.

lParam   LPARAM: The maximum scrolling position of the scroll bar control.

Returns   int: If the position of the scroll box changed, the previous position of the scroll box is returned; otherwise, zero is returned.

Include File   winuser.h

Related Messages   SBM_GETPOS, SBM_GETRANGE, SBM_SETPOS, SBM_SETRANGEREDRAW

SBM_SETRANGEREDRAW
Win32s ■ Windows 95 ■ Windows NT

Description   SBM_SETRANGEREDRAW is a message that is sent to a scroll bar control to set the minimum and maximum position values and to redraw the control. If the minimum and maximum values are equal, the scroll bar control is hidden.

Parameters

wParam   WPARAM: The minimum scrolling position of the scroll bar control.

lParam   LPARAM: The maximum scrolling position of the scroll bar control.

Returns   int: If the position of the scroll box changed, the previous position of the scroll box is returned; otherwise, zero is returned.

Include File   winuser.h

Related Messages   SBM_GETPOS, SBM_GETRANGE, SBM_SETPOS, SBM_SETRANGE

SBM_SETSCROLLINFO
■ Win32s ■ Windows 95 ■ Windows NT

Description   SBM_SETSCROLLINFO is a message that sets the parameters of a scroll bar.

Parameters

wParam   WPARAM: TRUE indicates that the scroll bar is redrawn to reflect the new scroll box position; FALSE indicates that the scroll bar is not redrawn.

lParam   LPSCROLLINFO: A pointer to a SCROLLINFO structure whose *fMask* member specifies the scroll bar parameters to be set by SBM_SETSCROLLINFO.

Returns   int: The current position of the scroll box is returned.

Include File   winuser.h

Related Messages   SBM_GETSCROLLINFO

STM_GETICON ■ Win32s ■ Windows 95 ■ Windows NT

Description	STM_GETICON is a message that retrieves the handle of the icon associated with a static control that has the SS_ICON style.
Parameters	This message does not use *wParam* or *lParam*; therefore, both must be set to zero.
Returns	int: If successful, the handle of the icon is returned; otherwise, NULL is returned if either the static control does not have an associated icon or if an error occurred.
Include File	winuser.h
Related Messages	STM_SETICON

STM_GETIMAGE Win32s ■ Windows 95 ■ Windows NT

Description	STM_GETIMAGE is a message that retrieves the handle of the image associated with a static control.
Parameters	
wParam	WPARAM: One or more of the values in Table 11-19 indicating the type of image to retrieve.

Table 11-19 STM_GETIMAGE *wParam* values

Value	Meaning
IMAGE_BITMAP	Retrieve a bitmap.
IMAGE_CURSOR	Retrieve a cursor.
IMAGE_ENHMETAFILE	Retrieve an enhanced metafile.
IMAGE_ICON	Retrieve an icon.

lParam	LPARAM: Set to zero.
Returns	HANDLE: If successful, the handle of the image is returned; otherwise, NULL is returned.
Include File	winuser.h
Related Messages	STM_SETIMAGE

STM_SETICON ■ Win32s ■ Windows 95 ■ Windows NT

Description	STM_SETICON is a message that associates an icon with an icon control.
Parameters	
wParam	HICON: The handle of the icon to associate with the icon control.
lParam	LPARAM: Set to zero.

Returns	HICON: If successful, the handle of the icon previously associated with the icon control is returned; otherwise, zero is returned if an error occurs.
Include File	winuser.h
See Also	LoadIcon()
Related Messages	STM_GETICON

STM_SETIMAGE   Win32s ■ Windows 95 ■ Windows NT

Description	STM_SETIMAGE is a message that associates a new icon or bitmap image with a static control.
Parameters	
wParam	WPARAM: One or more of the values in Table 11-19 indicating the type of image to retrieve.
lParam	HANDLE: The image to associate with the static control.
Returns	HANDLE: If successful, the handle of the image previously associated with the static control is returned; otherwise, NULL is returned.
Include File	winuser.h
Related Messages	STM_GETIMAGE

STN_CLICKED   Win32s ■ Windows 95   Windows NT

Description	STN_CLICKED is a notification message that is sent when the user clicks a static control that has the SS_NOTIFY style. The parent window of the control receives this notification message through the WM_COMMAND message.
Parameters	
LOWORD(wParam)	int: The identifier of the static control.
LOWORD(lParam)	HWND: The handle of the static control.
Include File	winuser.h
Related Messages	STN_DBLCLK, WM_COMMAND

STN_DBLCLK   Win32s ■ Windows 95   Windows NT

Description	STN_DBLCLK is a notification message that is sent when the user double-clicks a static control that has the SS_NOTIFY style. The parent window of the control receives this notification message through the WM_COMMAND message.
Parameters	
LOWORD(wParam)	int: The identifier of the static control.
LOWORD(lParam)	HWND: The handle of the static control.

Include File   winuser.h
Related Messages   STN_CLICKED, WM_COMMAND

STN_DISABLE   Win32s ■ Windows 95   Windows NT

Description   STN_DISABLE is a notification message that is sent when a static control is disabled. The static control must have the SS_NOTIFY style to receive this notification message. The parent window of the control receives this notification message through the WM_COMMAND message.

Parameters

LOWORD(wParam) int: The identifier of the static control.

LOWORD(lParam) HWND: The handle of the static control.

Include File   winuser.h

Related Messages   STN_ENABLE, WM_COMMAND

STN_ENABLE   Win32s ■ Windows 95   Windows NT

Description   STN_ENABLE is a notification message that is sent when a static control is enabled. The static control must have the SS_NOTIFY style to receive this notification message. The parent window of the control receives this notification message through the WM_COMMAND message.

Parameters

LOWORD(wParam) int: The identifier of the static control.

LOWORD(lParam) HWND: The handle of the static control.

Include File   winuser.h

Related Messages   STN_DISABLE, WM_COMMAND

TB_ADDBITMAP   ■ Win32s ■ Windows 95 ■ Windows NT

Description   TB_ADDBITMAP is a message that adds one or more images to the list of button images available for a toolbar. For more information, refer to the TB_ADDBITMAP message in Chapter 3, Toolbars and Status Windows.

TB_ADDBUTTONS   ■ Win32s ■ Windows 95 ■ Windows NT

Description   TB_ADDBUTTONS is a message that adds one or more buttons to a toolbar. For more information, refer to the TB_ADDBUTTONS message in Chapter 3, Toolbars and Status Windows.

TB_ADDSTRING ■ Win32s ■ Windows 95 ■ Windows NT

Description TB_ADDSTRING is a message that adds a new string to the list of strings available for a toolbar. For more information, refer to the TB_ADDSTRING message in Chapter 3, Toolbars and Status Windows. (See Figure 11-7.)

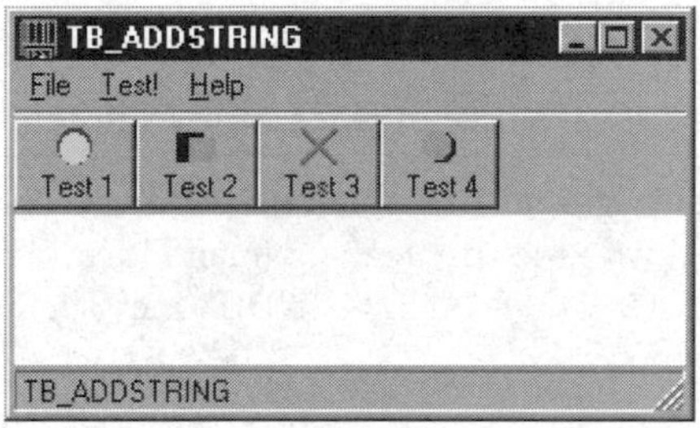

Figure 11-7 TB_ADDSTRING message

TB_AUTOSIZE ■ Win32s ■ Windows 95 ■ Windows NT

Description TB_AUTOSIZE is a message that causes a toolbar to be resized. For more information, refer to the TB_AUTOSIZE message in Chapter 3, Toolbars and Status Windows.

TB_BUTTONCOUNT ■ Win32s ■ Windows 95 ■ Windows NT

Description TB_BUTTONCOUNT is a message that determines the number of the buttons currently in the toolbar. For more information, refer to the TB_BUTTONCOUNT message in Chapter 3, Toolbars and Status Windows.

TB_BUTTONSTRUCTSIZE ■ Win32s ■ Windows 95 ■ Windows NT

Description TB_BUTTONSTRUCTSIZE is a message that specifies the size of the TBBUTTON structure. For more information, refer to the TB_BUTTONSTRUCTSIZE message in Chapter 3, Toolbars and Status Windows.

TB_CHANGEBITMAP ■ Win32s ■ Windows 95 ■ Windows NT

Description TB_CHANGEBITMAP is a message that changes the bitmap for a button in a toolbar. For more information, refer to the TB_CHANGEBITMAP message in Chapter 3, Toolbars and Status Windows.

TB_CHECKBUTTON   ■ Win32s ■ Windows 95 ■ Windows NT

Description   TB_CHECKBUTTON is a message that either checks or unchecks a given button in a toolbar. For more information, refer to the TB_CHECKBUTTON message in Chapter 3, Toolbars and Status Windows.

TB_COMMANDTOINDEX   ■ Win32s ■ Windows 95 ■ Windows NT

Description   TB_COMMANDTOINDEX is a message that retrieves the zero-based index for the button associated with the specified command identifier. For more information, refer to the TB_COMMANDTOINDEX message in Chapter 3, Toolbars and Status Windows.

TB_CUSTOMIZE   ■ Win32s ■ Windows 95 ■ Windows NT

Description   TB_CUSTOMIZE is a message that displays the Customize Toolbar dialog box. For more information, refer to the TB_CUSTOMIZE message in Chapter 3, Toolbars and Status Windows.

TB_DELETEBUTTON   ■ Win32s ■ Windows 95 ■ Windows NT

Description   TB_DELETEBUTTON is a message that deletes a button from a toolbar. For more information, refer to the TB_DELETEBUTTON message in Chapter 3, Toolbars and Status Windows.

TB_ENABLEBUTTON   ■ Win32s ■ Windows 95 ■ Windows NT

Description   TB_ENABLEBUTTON is a message that enables or disables the specified button in a toolbar. For more information, refer to the TB_ENABLEBUTTON message in Chapter 3, Toolbars and Status Windows.

TB_GETBITMAP   ■ Win32s ■ Windows 95 ■ Windows NT

Description   TB_GETBITMAP is a message that retrieves the index of the bitmap associated with a button in a toolbar. For more information, refer to the TB_GETBITMAP message in Chapter 3, Toolbars and Status Windows.

TB_GETBITMAPFLAGS ■ Win32s ■ Windows 95 ■ Windows NT

Description TB_GETBITMAPFLAGS is a message that retrieves the bitmap flags. For more information, refer to the TB_GETBITMAPFLAGS message in Chapter 3, Toolbars and Status Windows.

TB_GETBUTTON ■ Win32s ■ Windows 95 ■ Windows NT

Description TB_GETBUTTON is a message that retrieves information about the specified button in a toolbar. For more information, refer to the TB_GETBUTTON message in Chapter 3, Toolbars and Status Windows.

TB_GETBUTTONTEXT ■ Win32s ■ Windows 95 ■ Windows NT

Description TB_GETBUTTONTEXT is a message that retrieves the text of a button in a toolbar. For more information, refer to the TB_GETBUTTONTEXT message in Chapter 3, Toolbars and Status Windows.

TB_GETITEMRECT ■ Win32s ■ Windows 95 ■ Windows NT

Description TB_GETITEMRECT is a message that retrieves the bounding rectangle of a button in a toolbar. For more information, refer to the TB_GETITEMRECT message in Chapter 3, Toolbars and Status Windows.

TB_GETROWS ■ Win32s ■ Windows 95 ■ Windows NT

Description TB_GETROWS is a message that retrieves the number of rows of buttons in a toolbar. For more information, refer to the TB_GETROWS message in Chapter 3, Toolbars and Status Windows.

TB_GETSTATE ■ Win32s ■ Windows 95 ■ Windows NT

Description TB_GETSTATE is a message that retrieves information about the state of the specified button in a toolbar. For more information, refer to the TB_GETSTATE message in Chapter 3, Toolbars and Status Windows.

TB_GETTOOLTIPS ■ Win32s ■ Windows 95 ■ Windows NT

Description TB_GETTOOLTIPS is a message that retrieves the handle to the tooltip control associated with the toolbar. For more information, refer to the TB_GETTOOLTIPS message in Chapter 3, Toolbars and Status Windows.

TB_HIDEBUTTON
■ Win32s ■ Windows 95 ■ Windows NT

Description   TB_HIDEBUTTON is a message that either hides or shows the specified button in a toolbar. For more information, refer to the TB_HIDEBUTTON message in Chapter 3, Toolbars and Status Windows.

TB_INDETERMINATE
■ Win32s ■ Windows 95 ■ Windows NT

Description   TB_INDETERMINATE is a message that either sets or clears the indeterminate state of the specified button in a toolbar. For more information, refer to the TB_INDETERMINATE message in Chapter 3, Toolbars and Status Windows.

TB_INSERTBUTTON
■ Win32s ■ Windows 95 ■ Windows NT

Description   TB_INSERTBUTTON is a message that inserts a button in a toolbar. For more information, refer to the TB_INSERTBUTTON message in Chapter 3, Toolbars and Status Windows.

TB_ISBUTTONCHECKED
■ Win32s ■ Windows 95 ■ Windows NT

Description   TB_ISBUTTONCHECKED is a message that determines whether the specified button in a toolbar is checked. For more information, refer to the TB_ISBUTTONCHECKED message in Chapter 3, Toolbars and Status Windows.

TB_ISBUTTONENABLED
■ Win32s ■ Windows 95 ■ Windows NT

Description   TB_ISBUTTONENABLED is a message that determines whether the specified button in a toolbar is enabled. For more information, refer to the TB_ISBUTTONENABLED message in Chapter 3, Toolbars and Status Windows.

TB_ISBUTTONHIDDEN
■ Win32s ■ Windows 95 ■ Windows NT

Description   TB_ISBUTTONHIDDEN is a message that determines whether the specified button in a toolbar is hidden. For more information, refer to the TB_ISBUTTONHIDDEN message in Chapter 3, Toolbars and Status Windows.

TB_ISBUTTONINDETERMINATE ■ Win32s ■ Windows 95 ■ Windows NT

Description TB_ISBUTTONINDETERMINATE is a message that determines whether the specified button in a toolbar is indeterminate. For more information, refer to the TB_ISBUTTONINDETERMINATE message in Chapter 3, Toolbars and Status Windows.

TB_ISBUTTONPRESSED ■ Win32s ■ Windows 95 ■ Windows NT

Description TB_ISBUTTONPRESSED is a message that determines whether the specified button in a toolbar is pressed. For more information, refer to the TB_ISBUTTONPRESSED message in Chapter 3, Toolbars and Status Windows.

TB_PRESSBUTTON ■ Win32s ■ Windows 95 ■ Windows NT

Description TB_PRESSBUTTON is a message that either presses or releases the specified button in a toolbar. For more information, refer to the TB_PRESSBUTTON message in Chapter 3, Toolbars and Status Windows.

TB_SAVERESTORE ■ Win32s ■ Windows 95 ■ Windows NT

Description TB_SAVERESTORE is a message that either saves or restores the state of the toolbar. For more information, refer to the TB_SAVERESTORE message in Chapter 3, Toolbars and Status Windows.

TB_SETBITMAPSIZE ■ Win32s ■ Windows 95 ■ Windows NT

Description TB_SETBITMAPSIZE is a message that sets the size of the bitmapped images to be added to a toolbar. For more information, refer to the TB_SETBITMAPSIZE message in Chapter 3, Toolbars and Status Windows.

TB_SETBUTTONSIZE ■ Win32s ■ Windows 95 ■ Windows NT

Description TB_SETBUTTONSIZE is a message that sets the size of the buttons to be added to a toolbar. For more information, refer to the TB_SETBUTTONSIZE message in Chapter 3, Toolbars and Status Windows.

TB_SETCMDID ■ Win32s ■ Windows 95 ■ Windows NT

Description   TB_SETCMDID is a message that sets the command identifier of a toolbar button. For more information, refer to the TB_SETCMDID message in Chapter 3, Toolbars and Status Windows.

TB_SETPARENT ■ Win32s ■ Windows 95 ■ Windows NT

Description   TB_SETPARENT is a message that sets the parent window for a toolbar. For more information, refer to the TB_SETPARENT message in Chapter 3, Toolbars and Status Windows.

TB_SETROWS ■ Win32s ■ Windows 95 ■ Windows NT

Description   TB_SETROWS is a message that sets the number of rows of buttons in a toolbar. For more information, refer to the TB_SETROWS message in Chapter 3, Toolbars and Status Windows.

TB_SETSTATE ■ Win32s ■ Windows 95 ■ Windows NT

Description   TB_SETSTATE is a message that sets the state for the specified button in a toolbar. For more information, refer to the TB_SETSTATE message in Chapter 3, Toolbars and Status Windows.

TB_SETTOOLTIPS ■ Win32s ■ Windows 95 ■ Windows NT

Description   TB_SETTOOLTIPS is a message that associates a tooltip control with a toolbar. For more information, refer to the TB_SETTOOLTIPS message in Chapter 3, Toolbars and Status Windows.

TBM_CLEARSEL ■ Win32s ■ Windows 95 ■ Windows NT

Description   TBM_CLEARSEL is a message that clears the current selection in a trackbar. For more information, refer to the TBM_CLEARSEL message in Chapter 9, Miscellaneous Controls.

TBM_CLEARTICS ■ Win32s ■ Windows 95 ■ Windows NT

Description   TBM_CLEARTICS is a message that removes the current tick marks from a trackbar. For more information, refer to the TBM_CLEARTICS message in Chapter 9, Miscellaneous Controls.

TBM_GETCHANNELRECT ■ Win32s ■ Windows 95 ■ Windows NT

Description   TBM_GETCHANNELRECT is a message that determines the size and position of the bounding rectangle for the channel of a trackbar. For more information, refer to the TBM_GETCHANNELRECT message in Chapter 9, Miscellaneous Controls.

TBM_GETLINESIZE ■ Win32s ■ Windows 95 ■ Windows NT

Description   TBM_GETLINESIZE is a message that retrieves the size of the line for a trackbar. For more information, refer to the TBM_GETLINESIZE message in Chapter 9, Miscellaneous Controls.

TBM_GETNUMTICS ■ Win32s ■ Windows 95 ■ Windows NT

Description   TBM_GETNUMTICS is a message that retrieves the number of tick marks in a trackbar. For more information, refer to the TBM_GETNUMTICS message in Chapter 9, Miscellaneous Controls.

TBM_GETPAGESIZE ■ Win32s ■ Windows 95 ■ Windows NT

Description   TBM_GETPAGESIZE is a message that retrieves the size of the page for a trackbar. The page size affects how much the slider moves for the TB_PAGEUP and TB_PAGEDOWN notification messages. For more information, refer to the TBM_GETPAGESIZE message in Chapter 9, Miscellaneous Controls.

TBM_GETPOS ■ Win32s ■ Windows 95 ■ Windows NT

Description   TBM_GETPOS is a message that retrieves the current position of the slider in a trackbar. For more information, refer to the TBM_GETPOS message in Chapter 9, Miscellaneous Controls.

TBM_GETPTICS ■ Win32s ■ Windows 95 ■ Windows NT

Description   TBM_GETPTICS is a message that retrieves the pointer to the array that contains the positions of tick marks for a trackbar. For more information, refer to the TBM_GETPTICS message in Chapter 9, Miscellaneous Controls.

TBM_GETRANGEMAX ■ Win32s ■ Windows 95 ■ Windows NT

Description   TBM_GETRANGEMAX is a message that retrieves the maximum position
for the slider in a trackbar. For more information, refer to the
TBM_GETRANGEMAX message in Chapter 9, Miscellaneous Controls.

TBM_GETRANGEMIN ■ Win32s ■ Windows 95 ■ Windows NT

Description   TBM_GETRANGEMIN is a message that retrieves the minimum position
for the slider in a trackbar. For more information, refer to the
TBM_GETRANGEMIN message in Chapter 9, Miscellaneous Controls.

TBM_GETSELEND ■ Win32s ■ Windows 95 ■ Windows NT

Description   TBM_GETSELEND is a message that retrieves the ending position of the
current selection in a trackbar. For more information, refer to the
TBM_GETSELEND message in Chapter 9, Miscellaneous Controls.

TBM_GETSELSTART ■ Win32s ■ Windows 95 ■ Windows NT

Description   TBM_GETSELSTART is a message that retrieves the starting position of the
current selection in a trackbar. For more information, refer to the
TBM_GETSELSTART message in Chapter 9, Miscellaneous Controls.

TBM_GETTHUMBLENGTH ■ Win32s ■ Windows 95 ■ Windows NT

Description   TBM_GETTHUMBLENGTH is a message that retrieves the length of
the slider in a trackbar. For more information, refer to the
TBM_GETTHUMBLENGTH message in Chapter 9, Miscellaneous
Controls.

TBM_GETTHUMBRECT ■ Win32s ■ Windows 95 ■ Windows NT

Description   TBM_GETTHUMBRECT is a message that retrieves the size and position
of the bounding rectangle for the slider in a trackbar. For more information, refer to the TBM_GETTHUMBRECT message in Chapter 9,
Miscellaneous Controls.

TBM_GETTIC ■ Win32s ■ Windows 95 ■ Windows NT

Description   TBM_GETTIC is a message that retrieves the relative position of a tick
mark in a trackbar. For more information, refer to the TBM_GETTIC
message in Chapter 9, Miscellaneous Controls.

TBM_GETTICPOS
■ Win32s ■ Windows 95 ■ Windows NT

Description   TBM_GETTICPOS is a message that retrieves the current physical position of a tick mark in a trackbar. For more information, refer to the TBM_GETTICPOS message in Chapter 9, Miscellaneous Controls.

TBM_SETLINESIZE
■ Win32s ■ Windows 95 ■ Windows NT

Description   TBM_SETLINESIZE is a message that sets the size of the line for a trackbar. For more information, refer to the TBM_SETLINESIZE message in Chapter 9, Miscellaneous Controls.

TBM_SETPAGESIZE
■ Win32s ■ Windows 95 ■ Windows NT

Description   TBM_SETPAGESIZE is a message that sets the size of the page for a trackbar. For more information, refer to the TBM_SETPAGESIZE message in Chapter 9, Miscellaneous Controls.

TBM_SETPOS
■ Win32s ■ Windows 95 ■ Windows NT

Description   TBM_SETPOS is a message that sets the current position of the slider in a trackbar. For more information, refer to the TBM_SETPOS message in Chapter 9, Miscellaneous Controls.

TBM_SETRANGE
■ Win32s ■ Windows 95 ■ Windows NT

Description   TBM_SETRANGE is a message that sets the minimum and maximum positions for the slider in a trackbar. For more information, refer to the TBM_SETRANGE message in Chapter 9, Miscellaneous Controls. (See Figure 11-8.)

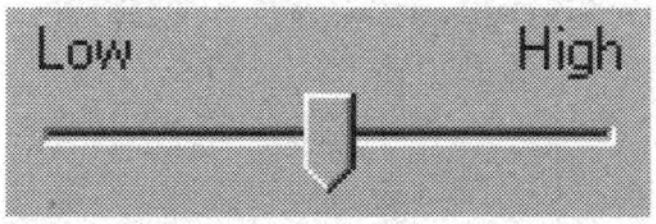

Figure 11-8 Slider Control

TBM_SETRANGEMAX
■ Win32s ■ Windows 95 ■ Windows NT

Description   TBM_SETRANGEMAX is a message that sets the maximum position for the slider in a trackbar. For more information, refer to the TBM_SETRANGEMAX message in Chapter 9, Miscellaneous Controls.

TBM_SETRANGEMIN ■ Win32s ■ Windows 95 ■ Windows NT

Description   TBM_SETRANGEMIN is a message that sets the minimum position for the slider in a trackbar. For more information, refer to the TBM_SETRANGEMIN message in Chapter 9, Miscellaneous Controls.

TBM_SETSEL ■ Win32s ■ Windows 95 ■ Windows NT

Description   TBM_SETSEL is a message that sets the starting and ending positions for the current selection in a trackbar. For more information, refer to the TBM_SETSEL message in Chapter 9, Miscellaneous Controls.

TBM_SETSELEND ■ Win32s ■ Windows 95 ■ Windows NT

Description   TBM_SETSELEND is a message that sets the ending position of the current selection in a trackbar. For more information, refer to the TBM_SETSELEND message in Chapter 9, Miscellaneous Controls.

TBM_SETSELSTART ■ Win32s ■ Windows 95 ■ Windows NT

Description   TBM_SETSELSTART is a message that sets the starting position of the current selection in a trackbar. For more information, refer to the TBM_SETSELSTART message in Chapter 9, Miscellaneous Controls.

TBM_SETTHUMBLENGTH ■ Win32s ■ Windows 95 ■ Windows NT

Description   TBM_SETTHUMBLENGTH is a message that sets the length of the slider in a trackbar. For more information, refer to the TBM_SETTHUMBLENGTH message in Chapter 9, Miscellaneous Controls.

TBM_SETTIC ■ Win32s ■ Windows 95 ■ Windows NT

Description   TBM_SETTIC is a message that sets the position of a tick mark in a trackbar. For more information, refer to the TBM_SETTIC message in Chapter 9, Miscellaneous Controls.

TBM_SETTICFREQ ■ Win32s ■ Windows 95 ■ Windows NT

Description   TBM_SETTICFREQ is a message that sets the interval frequency for tick marks in a trackbar. For more information, refer to the TBM_SETTICFREQ message in Chapter 9, Miscellaneous Controls.

TBN_BEGINADJUST   ■ Win32s   ■ Windows 95   ■ Windows NT

Description   TBN_BEGINADJUST is a notification message that notifies the parent window that the user has begun customizing a toolbar. For more information, refer to the TBN_BEGINADJUST notification message in Chapter 3, Toolbars and Status Windows.

TBN_BEGINDRAG   ■ Win32s   ■ Windows 95   ■ Windows NT

Description   TBN_BEGINDRAG is a notification message that notifies the parent window that the user has begun dragging a button in a toolbar. For more information, refer to the TBN_BEGINDRAG notification message in Chapter 3, Toolbars and Status Windows.

TBN_CUSTHELP   ■ Win32s   ■ Windows 95   ■ Windows NT

Description   TBN_CUSTHELP is a notification message that notifies the parent window that the user has chosen the Help button in the Customize Toolbar dialog box. For more information, refer to the TBN_CUSTHELP notification message in Chapter 3, Toolbars and Status Windows.

TBN_ENDADJUST   ■ Win32s   ■ Windows 95   ■ Windows NT

Description   TBN_ENDADJUST is a notification message that notifies the parent window that the user has stopped customizing a toolbar. For more information, refer to the TBN_ENDADJUST notification message in Chapter 3, Toolbars and Status Windows.

TBN_ENDDRAG   ■ Win32s   ■ Windows 95   ■ Windows NT

Description   TBN_ENDDRAG is a notification message that notifies the parent window that the user has stopped dragging a button in a toolbar. For more information, refer to the TBN_ENDDRAG notification message in Chapter 3, Toolbars and Status Windows.

TBN_GETBUTTONINFO   ■ Win32s   ■ Windows 95   ■ Windows NT

Description   TBN_GETBUTTONINFO is a notification message that notifies the parent window of modifications made to the toolbar. For more information, refer to the TBN_GETBUTTONINFO notification message in Chapter 3, Toolbars and Status Windows.

TBN_QUERYDELETE ■ Win32s ■ Windows 95 ■ Windows NT

Description   TBN_QUERYDELETE is a notification message that queries the toolbar's parent window to determine if a button may be deleted from a toolbar while the user is customizing a toolbar. For more information, refer to the TBN_QUERYDELETE notification message in Chapter 3, Toolbars and Status Windows.

TBN_QUERYINSERT ■ Win32s ■ Windows 95 ■ Windows NT

Description   TBN_QUERYINSERT is a notification message that queries the toolbar's parent window to determine if a button may be inserted to the left of the specified button while the user is customizing a toolbar. For more information, refer to the TBN_QUERYINSERT notification message in Chapter 3, Toolbars and Status Windows.

TBN_RESET ■ Win32s ■ Windows 95 ■ Windows NT

Description   TBN_RESET is a notification message that notifies the parent window that the user has reset the content of the Customize Toolbar dialog box. For more information, refer to the TBN_RESET notification message in Chapter 3, Toolbars and Status Windows.

TBN_TOOLBARCHANGE ■ Win32s ■ Windows 95 ■ Windows NT

Description   TBN_TOOLBARCHANGE is a notification message that notifies the parent window that the user has customized a toolbar. For more information, refer to the TBN_TOOLBARCHANGE notification message in Chapter 3, Toolbars and Status Windows.

TCM_ADJUSTRECT ■ Win32s ■ Windows 95 ■ Windows NT

Description   TCM_ADJUSTRECT is a message that either calculates the tab control's display area, or calculates the window rectangle that would correspond to a display area. For more information, refer to the TabCtrl_AdjustRect macro in Chapter 4, Tab Controls and Property Sheets.

TCM_DELETEALLITEMS ■ Win32s ■ Windows 95 ■ Windows NT

Description   TCM_DELETEALLITEMS is a message that removes all items from a tab control. For more information, refer to the TabCtrl_DeleteAllItems macro in Chapter 4, Tab Controls and Property Sheets.

TCM_DELETEITEM
■ Win32s ■ Windows 95 ■ Windows NT

Description   TCM_DELETEITEM is a message that removes an item from a tab control. For more information, refer to the TabCtrl_DeleteItem macro in Chapter 4, Tab Controls and Property Sheets.

TCM_GETCURFOCUS
■ Win32s ■ Windows 95 ■ Windows NT

Description   TCM_GETCURFOCUS is a message that returns the index of the item that has the focus in a tab control. For more information, refer to the TabCtrl_GetCurFocus macro in Chapter 4, Tab Controls and Property Sheets.

TCM_GETCURSEL
■ Win32s ■ Windows 95 ■ Windows NT

Description   TCM_GETCURSEL is a message that determines the currently selected tab in a tab control. For more information, refer to the TabCtrl_GetCurSel macro in Chapter 4, Tab Controls and Property Sheets.

TCM_GETIMAGELIST
■ Win32s ■ Windows 95 ■ Windows NT

Description   TCM_GETIMAGELIST is a message that retrieves the image list associated with a tab control. For more information, refer to the TabCtrl_GetImageList macro in Chapter 4, Tab Controls and Property Sheets.

TCM_GETITEM
■ Win32s ■ Windows 95 ■ Windows NT

Description   TCM_GETITEM is a message that retrieves information about a tab in a tab control. For more information, refer to the TabCtrl_GetItem macro in Chapter 4, Tab Controls and Property Sheets.

TCM_GETITEMCOUNT
■ Win32s ■ Windows 95 ■ Windows NT

Description   TCM_GETITEMCOUNT is a message that retrieves the number of tabs in the tab control. For more information, refer to the TabCtrl_GetItemCount macro in Chapter 4, Tab Controls and Property Sheets.

TCM_GETITEMRECT
■ Win32s ■ Windows 95 ■ Windows NT

Description   TCM_GETITEMRECT is a message that retrieves the bounding rectangle for a tab in a tab control. For more information, refer to the

TabCtrl_GetItemRect macro in Chapter 4, Tab Controls and Property Sheets.

TCM_GETROWCOUNT ■ Win32s ■ Windows 95 ■ Windows NT

Description TCM_GETROWCOUNT is a message that retrieves the current number of rows of tabs in a tab control. For more information, refer to the TabCtrl_GetRowCount macro in Chapter 4, Tab Controls and Property Sheets.

TCM_GETTOOLTIPS ■ Win32s ■ Windows 95 ■ Windows NT

Description TCM_GETTOOLTIPS is a message that retrieves the handle to the tooltip control associated with a tab control. For more information, refer to the TabCtrl_GetToolTips macro in Chapter 4, Tab Controls and Property Sheets.

TCM_HITTEST ■ Win32s ■ Windows 95 ■ Windows NT

Description TCM_HITTEST is a message that determines which tab is located at a specified screen position. For more information, refer to the TabCtrl_HitTest macro in Chapter 4, Tab Controls and Property Sheets.

TCM_INSERTITEM ■ Win32s ■ Windows 95 ■ Windows NT

Description TCM_INSERTITEM is a message that inserts a new tab in a tab control. For more information, refer to the TabCtrl_InsertItem macro in Chapter 4, Tab Controls and Property Sheets.

TCM_REMOVEIMAGE ■ Win32s ■ Windows 95 ■ Windows NT

Description TCM_REMOVEIMAGE is a message that removes an image from a tab control's image list. For more information, refer to the TabCtrl_RemoveImage macro in Chapter 4, Tab Controls and Property Sheets.

TCM_SETCURSEL ■ Win32s ■ Windows 95 ■ Windows NT

Description TCM_SETCURSEL is a message that selects a tab in a tab control. For more information, refer to the TabCtrl_SetCurSel macro in Chapter 4, Tab Controls and Property Sheets.

TCM_SETIMAGELIST   ■ Win32s ■ Windows 95 ■ Windows NT

Description   TCM_SETIMAGELIST is a message that assigns an image list to a tab control. For more information, refer to the TabCtrl_SetImageList macro in Chapter 4, Tab Controls and Property Sheets.

TCM_SETITEM   ■ Win32s ■ Windows 95 ■ Windows NT

Description   TCM_SETITEM is a message that sets some or all of a tab's attributes. For more information, refer to the TabCtrl_SetItem macro in Chapter 4, Tab Controls and Property Sheets.

TCM_SETITEMEXTRA   ■ Win32s ■ Windows 95 ■ Windows NT

Description   TCM_SETITEMEXTRA is a message that sets the number of bytes per tab reserved for application-defined data in a tab control. For more information, refer to the TabCtrl_SetItemExtra macro in Chapter 4, Tab Controls and Property Sheets.

TCM_SETITEMSIZE   ■ Win32s ■ Windows 95 ■ Windows NT

Description   TCM_SETITEMSIZE is a message that sets the width and height of tabs in a fixed-width or owner-drawn tab control. For more information, refer to the TabCtrl_SetItemSize macro in Chapter 4, Tab Controls and Property Sheets.

TCM_SETPADDING   ■ Win32s ■ Windows 95 ■ Windows NT

Description   TCM_SETPADDING is a message that sets the amount of padding around each tab's icon and label in a tab control. For more information, refer to the TabCtrl_SetPadding macro in Chapter 4, Tab Controls and Property Sheets.

TCM_SETTOOLTIPS   ■ Win32s ■ Windows 95 ■ Windows NT

Description   TCM_SETTOOLTIPS is a message that assigns a tooltip control to a tab control. For more information, refer to the TabCtrl_SetToolTips macro in Chapter 4, Tab Controls and Property Sheets.

TCN_KEYDOWN ■ Win32s ■ Windows 95 ■ Windows NT

Description   TCN_KEYDOWN is a notification message that notifies a tab control's parent window that a key has been pressed. For more information, refer to the TCN_KEYDOWN notification message in Chapter 4, Tab Controls and Property Sheets.

TCN_SELCHANGE ■ Win32s ■ Windows 95 ■ Windows NT

Description   TCN_SELCHANGE is a notification message that notifies a tab control's parent window that the currently selected tab has changed. For more information, refer to the TCN_SELCHANGE notification message in Chapter 4, Tab Controls and Property Sheets.

TCN_SELCHANGING ■ Win32s ■ Windows 95 ■ Windows NT

Description   TCN_SELCHANGING is a notification message that notifies a tab control's parent window that the currently selected tab is about to change. For more information, refer to the TCN_SELCHANGING notification message in Chapter 4, Tab Controls and Property Sheets.

TTM_ACTIVATE ■ Win32s ■ Windows 95 ■ Windows NT

Description   TTM_ACTIVATE is a message that either activates or deactivates a tooltip control. For more information, refer to the TTM_ACTIVATE message in Chapter 3, Toolbars and Status Windows.

TTM_ADDTOOL ■ Win32s ■ Windows 95 ■ Windows NT

Description   TTM_ADDTOOL is a message that registers a tool with a tooltip control. For more information, refer to the TTM_ADDTOOL message in Chapter 3, Toolbars and Status Windows.

TTM_DELTOOL ■ Win32s ■ Windows 95 ■ Windows NT

Description   TTM_DELTOOL is a message that removes a tool from a tooltip control. For more information, refer to the TTM_DELTOOL message in Chapter 3, Toolbars and Status Windows.

TTM_ENUMTOOLS
■ Win32s ■ Windows 95 ■ Windows NT

Description   TTM_ENUMTOOLS is a message that retrieves the information that a tooltip control maintains about a specific tool. For more information, refer to the TTM_ENUMTOOLS message in Chapter 3, Toolbars and Status Windows.

TTM_GETCURRENTTOOL
■ Win32s ■ Windows 95 ■ Windows NT

Description   TTM_GETCURRENTTOOL is a message that retrieves the information that a tooltip control maintains about the current tool. For more information, refer to the TTM_GETCURRENTTOOL message in Chapter 3, Toolbars and Status Windows.

TTM_GETTEXT
■ Win32s ■ Windows 95 ■ Windows NT

Description   TTM_GETTEXT is a message that retrieves the text that a tooltip control maintains for a tool. For more information, refer to the TTM_GETTEXT message in Chapter 3, Toolbars and Status Windows.

TTM_GETTOOLCOUNT
■ Win32s ■ Windows 95 ■ Windows NT

Description   TTM_GETTOOLCOUNT is a message that retrieves a count of the tools maintained by a tooltip control. For more information, refer to the TTM_GETTOOLCOUNT message in Chapter 3, Toolbars and Status Windows.

TTM_GETTOOLINFO
■ Win32s ■ Windows 95 ■ Windows NT

Description   TTM_GETTOOLINFO is a message that retrieves the information that a tooltip control maintains about a tool. For more information, refer to the TTM_GETTOOLINFO message in Chapter 3, Toolbars and Status Windows.

TTM_HITTEST
■ Win32s ■ Windows 95 ■ Windows NT

Description   TTM_HITTEST is a message that performs a hit test on a tool. For more information, refer to the TTM_HITTEST message in Chapter 3, Toolbars and Status Windows.

TTM_NEWTOOLRECT ■ Win32s ■ Windows 95 ■ Windows NT

Description   TTM_NEWTOOLRECT is a message that sets a new bounding rectangle for a tool. For more information, refer to the TTM_NEWTOOLRECT message in Chapter 3, Toolbars and Status Windows.

TTM_RELAYEVENT ■ Win32s ■ Windows 95 ■ Windows NT

Description   TTM_RELAYEVENT is a message that passes a mouse message to a tooltip control for processing. For more information, refer to the TTM_RELAYEVENT message in Chapter 3, Toolbars and Status Windows.

TTM_SETDELAYTIME ■ Win32s ■ Windows 95 ■ Windows NT

Description   TTM_SETDELAYTIME is a message that sets the initial, reshow, and autopop-up durations for a tooltip control. For more information, refer to the TTM_SETDELAYTIME message in Chapter 3, Toolbars and Status Windows.

TTM_SETTOOLINFO ■ Win32s ■ Windows 95 ■ Windows NT

Description   TTM_SETTOOLINFO is a message that sets the information that a control maintains for a tool. For more information, refer to the TTM_SETTOOLINFO message in Chapter 3, Toolbars and Status Windows.

TTM_UPDATETIPTEXT ■ Win32s ■ Windows 95 ■ Windows NT

Description   TTM_UPDATETIPTEXT is a message that sets the tooltip text for a tool. For more information, refer to the TTM_UPDATETIPTEXT message in Chapter 3, Toolbars and Status Windows.

TTM_WINDOWFROMPOINT ■ Win32s ■ Windows 95 ■ Windows NT

Description   TTM_WINDOWFROMPOINT is a message that allows a subclass procedure to cause a tooltip to display text for a window other than the one beneath the mouse cursor. For more information, refer to the TTM_WINDOWFROMPOINT message in Chapter 3, Toolbars and Status Windows.

TTN_NEEDTEXT

■ Win32s ■ Windows 95 ■ Windows NT

Description   TTN_NEEDTEXT is a notification message that retrieves text for a tool. For more information, refer to the TTN_NEEDTEXT notification message in Chapter 3, Toolbars and Status Windows.

TTN_POP

■ Win32s ■ Windows 95 ■ Windows NT

Description   TTN_POP is a notification message that notifies the owner window that a tooltip is about to be hidden. For more information, refer to the TTN_POP notification message in Chapter 3, Toolbars and Status Windows.

TTN_SHOW

■ Win32s ■ Windows 95 ■ Windows NT

Description   TTN_SHOW is a notification message that notifies the owner window that a tooltip is about to be displayed. For more information, refer to the TTN_SHOW notification message in Chapter 3, Toolbars and Status Windows.

TVM_CREATEDRAGIMAGE

■ Win32s ■ Windows 95 ■ Windows NT

Description   TVM_CREATEDRAGIMAGE is a message that creates a dragging bitmap for the specified item in a tree view control, creates an image list for the bitmap, and adds the bitmap to the image list. For more information, refer to the TreeView_CreateDragImage macro in Chapter 7, Tree View.

TVM_DELETEITEM

■ Win32s ■ Windows 95 ■ Windows NT

Description   TVM_DELETEITEM is a message that removes an item from a tree view control. For more information, refer to the TreeView_DeleteItem macro in Chapter 7, Tree View.

TVM_EDITLABEL

■ Win32s ■ Windows 95 ■ Windows NT

Description   TVM_EDITLABEL is a message that begins in-place editing of the specified item's text, replacing the text of the item with a single-line edit control containing the text. For more information, refer to the TreeView_EditLabel macro in Chapter 7, Tree View.

TVM_ENDEDITLABELNOW   ■ Win32s ■ Windows 95 ■ Windows NT

Description   TVM_ENDEDITLABELNOW is a message that ends the editing of a tree view item's label. For more information, refer to the TreeView_EndEditLabelNow macro in Chapter 7, Tree View.

TVM_ENSUREVISIBLE   ■ Win32s ■ Windows 95 ■ Windows NT

Description   TVM_ENSUREVISIBLE is a message that ensures that a tree view item is visible by expanding the parent item or scrolling the tree view control, if necessary. For more information, refer to the TreeView_EnsureVisible macro in Chapter 7, Tree View.

TVM_EXPAND   ■ Win32s ■ Windows 95 ■ Windows NT

Description   TVM_EXPAND is a message that expands or collapses the list of child items associated with the specified parent item. For more information, refer to the TreeView_Expand macro in Chapter 7, Tree View. (See Figure 11-9.)

Figure 11-9 TreeView in Windows Explorer

TVM_GETCOUNT   ■ Win32s ■ Windows 95 ■ Windows NT

Description   TVM_GETCOUNT is a message that retrieves a count of the items in a tree view control. For more information, refer to the TreeView_GetCount macro in Chapter 7, Tree View.

TVM_GETEDITCONTROL ■ Win32s ■ Windows 95 ■ Windows NT

Description   TVM_GETEDITCONTROL is a message that retrieves the handle to the edit control being used to edit a tree view item's text. For more information, refer to the TreeView_GetEditControl macro in Chapter 7, Tree View.

TVM_GETIMAGELIST ■ Win32s ■ Windows 95 ■ Windows NT

Description   TVM_GETIMAGELIST is a message that retrieves the handle to the normal or state image list associated with a tree view control. For more information, refer to the TreeView_GetImageList macro in Chapter 7, Tree View.

TVM_GETINDENT ■ Win32s ■ Windows 95 ■ Windows NT

Description   TVM_GETINDENT is a message that retrieves the amount, in pixels, that child items are indented relative to their parent items. For more information, refer to the TreeView_GetIndent macro in Chapter 7, Tree View.

TVM_GETISEARCHSTRING ■ Win32s ■ Windows 95 ■ Windows NT

Description   TVM_GETISEARCHSTRING is a message that retrieves the incremental search string for a tree view control. For more information, refer to the TreeView_GetISearchString macro in Chapter 7, Tree View.

TVM_GETITEM ■ Win32s ■ Windows 95 ■ Windows NT

Description   TVM_GETITEM is a message that retrieves some or all of a tree view item's attributes. For more information, refer to the TreeView_GetItem macro in Chapter 7, Tree View.

TVM_GETITEMRECT ■ Win32s ■ Windows 95 ■ Windows NT

Description   TVM_GETITEMRECT is a message that retrieves the bounding rectangle for a tree view item and indicates whether the item is visible. For more information, refer to the TreeView_GetItemRect macro in Chapter 7, Tree View.

TVM_GETNEXTITEM ■ Win32s ■ Windows 95 ■ Windows NT

Description   TVM_GETNEXTITEM is a message that retrieves the tree view item that bears the specified relationship to a specified item. For more information, refer to the TreeView_GetNextItem macro in Chapter 7, Tree View.

TVM_GETVISIBLECOUNT ■ Win32s ■ Windows 95 ■ Windows NT

Description   TVM_GETVISIBLECOUNT is a message that obtains the number of items that are fully visible in the client window of a tree view control. For more information, refer to the TreeView_GetVisibleCount macro in Chapter 7, Tree View.

TVM_HITTEST ■ Win32s ■ Windows 95 ■ Windows NT

Description   TVM_HITTEST is a message that determines the location of the specified point relative to the client area of a tree view control. For more information, refer to the TreeView_HitTest macro in Chapter 7, Tree View.

TVM_INSERTITEM ■ Win32s ■ Windows 95 ■ Windows NT

Description   TVM_INSERTITEM is a message that inserts a new item in a tree view control. For more information, refer to the TreeView_InsertItem macro in Chapter 7, Tree View.

TVM_SELECTITEM ■ Win32s ■ Windows 95 ■ Windows NT

Description   TVM_SELECTITEM is a message that selects the specified tree view item, scrolls the item into view, or redraws the item in the style used to indicate the target of a drag-and-drop operation. For more information, refer to the TreeView_SelectItem macro in Chapter 7, Tree View.

TVM_SETIMAGELIST ■ Win32s ■ Windows 95 ■ Windows NT

Description   TVM_SETIMAGELIST is a message that sets the normal or state image list for a tree view control and redraws the control using the new images. For more information, refer to the TreeView_SetImageList macro in Chapter 7, Tree View.

TVM_SETINDENT ■ Win32s ■ Windows 95 ■ Windows NT

Description   TVM_SETINDENT is a message that sets the width of indentation for a tree view control and redraws the control to reflect the new width. For more information, refer to the TreeView_SetIndent macro in Chapter 7, Tree View.

TVM_SETITEM
■ Win32s ■ Windows 95 ■ Windows NT

Description   TVM_SETITEM is a message that sets some or all of a tree view item's attributes. For more information, refer to the TreeView_SetItem macro in Chapter 7, Tree View.

TVM_SORTCHILDREN
■ Win32s ■ Windows 95 ■ Windows NT

Description   TVM_SORTCHILDREN is a message that sorts the child items of the specified parent item in a tree view control. For more information, refer to the TreeView_SortChildren macro in Chapter 7, Tree View.

TVM_SORTCHILDRENCB
■ Win32s ■ Windows 95 ■ Windows NT

Description   TVM_SORTCHILDRENCB is a message that sorts tree view items using an application-defined callback function that compares the items. For more information, refer to the TreeView_SortChildrenCB macro in Chapter 7, Tree View.

TVN_BEGINDRAG
■ Win32s ■ Windows 95 ■ Windows NT

Description   TVN_BEGINDRAG is a notification message that notifies a tree view control's parent window that a drag-and-drop operation involving the left mouse button is being initiated. For more information, refer to the TVN_BEGINDRAG notification message in Chapter 7, Tree View.

TVN_BEGINLABELEDIT
■ Win32s ■ Windows 95 ■ Windows NT

Description   TVN_BEGINLABELEDIT is a notification message that notifies a tree view control's parent window about the start of label editing for an item. For more information, refer to the TVN_BEGINLABELEDIT notification message in Chapter 7, Tree View.

TVN_BEGINRDRAG
■ Win32s ■ Windows 95 ■ Windows NT

Description   TVN_BEGINRDRAG is a notification message that notifies a tree view control's parent window about the initiation of a drag-and-drop operation involving the right mouse button. For more information, refer to the TVN_BEGINRDRAG notification message in Chapter 7, Tree View.

TVN_DELETEITEM
■ Win32s ■ Windows 95 ■ Windows NT

Description   TVN_DELETEITEM is a notification message that notifies a tree view control's parent window that an item has been deleted. For more information, refer to the TVN_DELETEITEM notification message in Chapter 7, Tree View.

TVN_ENDLABELEDIT
■ Win32s ■ Windows 95 ■ Windows NT

Description   TVN_ENDLABELEDIT is a notification message that notifies a tree view control's parent window about the end of label editing for an item. For more information, refer to the TVN_ENDLABELEDIT notification message in Chapter 7, Tree View.

TVN_GETDISPINFO
■ Win32s ■ Windows 95 ■ Windows NT

Description   TVN_GETDISPINFO is a notification message that requests that a tree view control's parent window provide information needed to display or sort an item. For more information, refer to the TVN_GETDISPINFO notification message in Chapter 7, Tree View.

TVN_ITEMEXPANDED
■ Win32s ■ Windows 95 ■ Windows NT

Description   TVN_ITEMEXPANDED is a notification message that notifies a tree view control's parent window that a parent item's list of child items has expanded or collapsed. For more information, refer to the TVN_ITEMEXPANDED notification message in Chapter 7, Tree View.

TVN_ITEMEXPANDING
■ Win32s ■ Windows 95 ■ Windows NT

Description   TVN_ITEMEXPANDING is a notification message that notifies a tree view control's parent window that a parent item's list of child items is about to expand or collapse. For more information, refer to the TVN_ITEMEXPANDING notification message in Chapter 7, Tree View.

TVN_KEYDOWN
■ Win32s ■ Windows 95 ■ Windows NT

Description   TVN_KEYDOWN is a notification message that notifies a tree view control's parent window that the user pressed a key and the tree view control has the input focus. For more information, refer to the TVN_KEYDOWN notification message in Chapter 7, Tree View.

TVN_SELCHANGED
■ Win32s   ■ Windows 95   ■ Windows NT

Description   TVN_SELCHANGED is a notification message that notifies a tree view control's parent window that the selection has changed from one item to another. For more information, refer to the TVN_SELCHANGED notification message in Chapter 7, Tree View.

TVN_SELCHANGING
■ Win32s   ■ Windows 95   ■ Windows NT

Description   TVN_SELCHANGING is a notification message that notifies a tree view control's parent window that the selection is about to change from one item to another. For more information, refer to the TVN_SELCHANGING notification message in Chapter 7, Tree View.

TVN_SETDISPINFO
■ Win32s   ■ Windows 95   ■ Windows NT

Description   TVN_SETDISPINFO is a notification message that notifies a tree view control's parent window that it must update the information it maintains about an item. For more information, refer to the TVN_SETDISPINFO notification message in Chapter 7, Tree View.

UDM_GETACCEL
■ Win32s   ■ Windows 95   ■ Windows NT

Description   UDM_GETACCEL is a message that retrieves acceleration information for an up-down control. For more information, refer to the UDM_GETACCEL message in Chapter 9, Miscellaneous Controls.

UDM_GETBASE
■ Win32s   ■ Windows 95   ■ Windows NT

Description   UDM_GETBASE is a message that determines the radix base for the up-down control. For more information, refer to the UDM_GETBASE message in Chapter 9, Miscellaneous Controls.

UDM_GETBUDDY
■ Win32s   ■ Windows 95   ■ Windows NT

Description   UDM_GETBUDDY is a message that retrieves the handle of the current buddy window for the up-down control. For more information, refer to the UDM_GETBUDDY message in Chapter 9, Miscellaneous Controls.

UDM_GETPOS
■ Win32s ■ Windows 95 ■ Windows NT

Description   UDM_GETPOS is a message that retrieves the current position of an up-down control. For more information, refer to the UDM_GETPOS message in Chapter 9, Miscellaneous Controls.

UDM_GETRANGE
■ Win32s ■ Windows 95 ■ Windows NT

Description   UDM_GETRANGE is a message that determines the minimum and maximum range values for the up-down control. For more information, refer to the UDM_GETRANGE message in Chapter 9, Miscellaneous Controls.

UDM_SETACCEL
■ Win32s ■ Windows 95 ■ Windows NT

Description   UDM_SETACCEL is a message that sets the acceleration for an up-down control. For more information, refer to the UDM_SETACCEL message in Chapter 9, Miscellaneous Controls.

UDM_SETBASE
■ Win32s ■ Windows 95 ■ Windows NT

Description   UDM_SETBASE is a message that sets the radix base for the up-down control. For more information, refer to the UDM_SETBASE message in Chapter 9, Miscellaneous Controls.

UDM_SETBUDDY
■ Win32s ■ Windows 95 ■ Windows NT

Description   UDM_SETBUDDY is a message that sets the buddy window for an up-down control. For more information, refer to the UDM_SETBUDDY message in Chapter 9, Miscellaneous Controls.

UDM_SETPOS
■ Win32s ■ Windows 95 ■ Windows NT

Description   UDM_SETPOS is a message that sets the current position for an up-down control. For more information, refer to the UDM_SETPOS message in Chapter 9, Miscellaneous Controls.

UDM_SETRANGE
■ Win32s ■ Windows 95 ■ Windows NT

Description   UDM_SETRANGE is a message that sets the minimum and maximum range values of the up-down control. For more information, refer to the UDM_SETRANGE message in Chapter 9, Miscellaneous Controls.

UDN_DELTAPOS
■ Win32s ■ Windows 95 ■ Windows NT

Description UDN_DELTAPOS is a notification message that notifies the parent window that the position in the up-down control is going to change. For more information, refer to the UDN_DELTAPOS notification message in Chapter 9, Miscellaneous Controls.

WIM_CLOSE
■ Win32s ■ Windows 95 ■ Windows NT

Description WIM_CLOSE is a message that is sent to the given waveform-audio input callback function when a waveform-audio input device is closed. The device handle is no longer valid after this message has been sent.

Parameters This message does not use *dwParam1* or *dwParam2*; therefore, both must be set to zero.

Include File mmsystem.h

WIM_DATA
■ Win32s ■ Windows 95 ■ Windows NT

Description WIM_DATA is a message that is sent to the given waveform-audio input callback function when waveform-audio data is present in the input buffer and the buffer is being returned to the application. The message is sent when the buffer is full or after waveInReset() is called.

Parameters

dwParam1 DWORD: The address of a WAVEHDR structure that identifies the buffer containing the data.

dwParam2 DWORD: Set to zero.

Include File mmsystem.h

WIM_OPEN
■ Win32s ■ Windows 95 ■ Windows NT

Description WIM_OPEN is a message that is sent to a waveform-audio input callback function when a waveform-audio input device is opened.

Parameters This message does not use *dwParam1* or *dwParam2*; therefore, both must be set to zero.

Include File mmsystem.h

WM_ACTIVATE
■ Win32s ■ Windows 95 ■ Windows NT

Description WM_ACTIVATE is a message that is sent when a window is either being activated or deactivated. This message is sent first to the window procedure of the top-level window being deactivated. Then the WM_ACTIVATE

message is sent to the window procedure of the top-level window being
activated. If the window is activated by a mouse click, it also receives a
WM_MOUSEACTIVATE message.

Parameters

LOWORD(wParam)   WORD: One of more of the values in Table 11-20 indicating whether the
window is being activated or deactivated.

Table 11-20 WM_ACTIVATE *LOWORD(lParam)* values

Value	Meaning
WA_ACTIVE	Activated by some method other than a mouse click (for example, by a call to the SetActiveWindow() function or by use of the keyboard interface to select the window).
WA_CLICKACTIVE	Activated by a mouse click.
WA_INACTIVE	Deactivated.

HIWORD(wParam)   BOOL: The minimized state of the window being activated or deactivated.
A nonzero value indicates the window is minimized.

lParam   HWND: The window being activated or deactivated, depending on the
value of *LOWORD(wParam)*. If the value of *LOWORD(wParam)* is
WA_INACTIVE, *lParam* is the handle of the window being activated. If the
value of *LOWORD(wParam)* is WA_ACTIVE or WA_CLICKACTIVE,
lParam is the handle of the window being deactivated. The value of *lParam*
can be NULL.

Returns   int: An application should return zero if it processes this message.

Include File   winuser.h

See Also   DefWindowProc(), SetActiveWindow()

Related Messages   WM_MOUSEACTIVATE, WM_NCACTIVATE

WM_ACTIVATEAPP   ■ Win32s ■ Windows 95 ■ Windows NT

Description   WM_ACTIVATEAPP is a message that is sent when a window belonging to
a different application than the active window is about to be activated. The
message is sent to the application whose window is being activated and to
the application whose window is being deactivated.

Parameters

wParam   BOOL: TRUE if the window is being activated; FALSE if the window is
being deactivated.

lParam   DWORD: Specifies a thread identifier. If *wParam* is TRUE, *lParam* identifies the thread that owns the window being deactivated. If *wParam* is
FALSE, *lParam* identifies the thread that owns the window being activated.

Returns	int: An application should return zero if it processes this message.
Include File	winuser.h
Related Messages	WM_ACTIVATE

WM_ASKCBFORMATNAME ■ Win32s ■ Windows 95 ■ Windows NT

Description	WM_ASKCBFORMATNAME is a message that is sent to the clipboard owner by a clipboard viewer window to request the name of a CF_OWNERDISPLAY clipboard format.
Parameters	
wParam	DWORD: The size, in characters, of the buffer pointed to by *lParam*.
lParam	LPSTR: A pointer to the buffer that receives the clipboard format name.
Returns	int: An application should return zero if it processes this message.
Include File	winuser.h

WM_CANCELJOURNAL Win32s ■ Windows 95 ■ Windows NT

Description	WM_CANCELJOURNAL is a message that is posted to an application when a user cancels the journaling activities of an application. The message is posted with a NULL window handle. When an application sees WM_CANCELJOURNAL, it assumes that the user has intentionally canceled the journal record or playback mode, and the system has already unhooked any journal record or playback hook procedures.
Parameters	This message does not use *wParam* or *lParam*; therefore, both must be set to zero.
Include File	winuser.h
See Also	JournalPlaybackProc(), JournalRecordProc(), GetMsgProc(), SetWindowsHookEx()

WM_CANCELMODE ■ Win32s ■ Windows 95 ■ Windows NT

Description	WM_CANCELMODE is a message that is sent to the focus window when a dialog box or message box is displayed; this enables the focus window to cancel modes, such as mouse capture.
Parameters	This message does not use *wParam* or *lParam*; therefore, both must be set to zero.
Returns	int: An application should return zero if it processes this message.
Include File	winuser.h
See Also	DefWindowProc(), ReleaseCapture()

WM_CAP_ABORT ■ Win32s ■ Windows 95 ■ Windows NT

Description	WM_CAP_ABORT is a message that terminates the video capture operation. In the case of step capture, the image data collected up to the point of the WM_CAP_ABORT message is retained in the capture file, but audio is not captured.
Parameters	This message does not use *wParam* or *lParam*; therefore, both must be set to zero.
Returns	BOOL: If successful, TRUE is returned; otherwise, FALSE is returned.
Include File	vfw.h
Related Messages	WM_CAP_STOP

WM_CAP_DLG_VIDEOCOMPRESSION

■ Win32s ■ Windows 95 ■ Windows NT

Description	WM_CAP_DLG_VIDEOCOMPRESSION is a message that displays a dialog box in which the user can select a compressor to use during the capture process. The list of available compressors can vary with the video format selected in the capture driver's Video Format dialog box. This message is most useful in the step capture operation to combine capture and compression in a single operation.
Parameters	This message does not use *wParam* or *lParam*; therefore, both must be set to zero.
Returns	BOOL: If successful, TRUE is returned; otherwise, FALSE is returned.
Include File	vfw.h

WM_CAP_DLG_VIDEODISPLAY ■ Win32s ■ Windows 95 ■ Windows NT

Description	WM_CAP_DLG_VIDEODISPLAY is a message that displays a dialog box used to set or adjust the video output. This dialog box can contain controls that affect the hue, contrast, and brightness of the displayed image, as well as key color alignment. Applications can determine if the capture driver supports this message by checking the *fHasDlgVideoDisplay* member of the CAPDRIVERCAPS structure.
Parameters	This message does not use *wParam* or *lParam*; therefore, both must be set to zero.
Returns	BOOL: If successful, TRUE is returned; otherwise, FALSE is returned.
Include File	vfw.h

WM_CAP_DLG_VIDEOFORMAT ■ Win32s ■ Windows 95 ■ Windows NT

Description WM_CAP_DLG_VIDEOFORMAT is a message that displays a dialog box used to select the video format for a video capture operation. The Video Format dialog box can be used to select image dimensions, bit depth, and hardware compression options. Applications can determine if the capture driver supports this message by checking the *fHasDlgVideoFormat* member of the CAPDRIVERCAPS structure.

Parameters This message does not use *wParam* or *lParam*; therefore, both must be set to zero.

Returns BOOL: If successful, TRUE is returned; otherwise, FALSE is returned.

Include File vfw.h

WM_CAP_DLG_VIDEOSOURCE ■ Win32s ■ Windows 95 ■ Windows NT

Description WM_CAP_DLG_VIDEOSOURCE is a message that displays a dialog box used to control the video source for a video capture operation. The Video Source dialog box can contain controls that select input sources, alter the hue, contrast, and brightness of the image, and modify the video quality before digitizing the images into the frame buffer. Applications can determine if the video capture driver supports this message by checking the *fHasDlgVideoSource* member of the CAPDRIVERCAPS structure.

Parameters This message does not use *wParam* or *lParam*; therefore, both must be set to zero.

Returns BOOL: If successful, TRUE is returned; otherwise, FALSE is returned.

Include File vfw.h

WM_CAP_DRIVER_CONNECT ■ Win32s ■ Windows 95 ■ Windows NT

Description WM_CAP_DRIVER_CONNECT is a message that connects a video capture window to a capture driver. Connecting a capture driver to a capture window automatically disconnects any previously connected capture driver.

Parameters

wParam WPARAM: The index of the capture driver. The index value can range from 0 to 9.

lParam LONG: Set to zero.

Returns BOOL: If successful, TRUE is returned; otherwise, FALSE is returned.

Include File vfw.h

WM_CAP_DRIVER_DISCONNECT ■ Win32s ■ Windows 95 ■ Windows NT

Description	WM_CAP_DRIVER_DISCONNECT is a message that disconnects a video capture driver from a capture window.
Parameters	This message does not use *wParam* or *lParam*; therefore, both must be set to zero.
Returns	BOOL: If successful, TRUE is returned; otherwise, FALSE is returned.
Include File	vfw.h

WM_CAP_DRIVER_GET_CAPS ■ Win32s ■ Windows 95 ■ Windows NT

Description	WM_CAP_DRIVER_GET_CAPS is a message that returns the hardware capabilities of the video capture driver currently connected to a capture window.
Parameters	
wParam	WPARAM: The size, in bytes, of the CAPDRIVERCAPS structure pointed to by *lParam*.
lParam	LPCAPDRIVERCAPS: The address of the CAPDRIVERCAPS structure to receive the hardware capabilities.
Returns	BOOL: If successful, TRUE is returned; otherwise, FALSE is returned.
Include File	vfw.h

WM_CAP_DRIVER_GET_NAME ■ Win32s ■ Windows 95 ■ Windows NT

Description	WM_CAP_DRIVER_GET_NAME is a message that returns the name of the video capture driver connected to the capture window.
Parameters	
wParam	WPARAM: The size, in bytes, of the buffer referenced by *lParam*.
lParam	LPSTR: The address of an application-defined buffer used to return the device name as a null-terminated string.
Returns	BOOL: If successful, TRUE is returned; otherwise, FALSE is returned.
Include File	vfw.h

WM_CAP_EDIT_COPY ■ Win32s ■ Windows 95 ■ Windows NT

Description	WM_CAP_EDIT_COPY is a message that copies the contents of the video frame buffer and associated palette to the clipboard.
Parameters	This message does not use *wParam* or *lParam*; therefore, both must be set to zero.
Returns	BOOL: If successful, TRUE is returned; otherwise, FALSE is returned.
Include File	vfw.h

WM_CAP_FILE_ALLOCATE   ■ Win32s ■ Windows 95 ■ Windows NT

Description	WM_CAP_FILE_ALLOCATE is a message that creates a video capture file of a specified size.
Parameters	
wParam	WPARAM: Set to zero.
lParam	DWORD: The size, in bytes, to create the capture file.
Returns	BOOL: If successful, TRUE is returned; otherwise, FALSE is returned.
Include File	vfw.h

WM_CAP_FILE_GET_CAPTURE_FILE
   ■ Win32s ■ Windows 95 ■ Windows NT

Description	WM_CAP_FILE_GET_CAPTURE_FILE is a message that returns the name of the current video capture file. The default capture file name is C:\CAPTURE.AVI.
Parameters	
wParam	WPARAM: The size, in bytes, of the buffer pointed to by *lParam*.
lParam	LPSTR: The address of the application-defined buffer that returns the name of the capture file as a null-terminated string.
Returns	BOOL: If successful, TRUE is returned; otherwise, FALSE is returned.
Include File	vfw.h

WM_CAP_FILE_SAVEAS   ■ Win32s ■ Windows 95 ■ Windows NT

Description	WM_CAP_FILE_SAVEAS is a message that copies the contents of the video capture file to another file.
Parameters	
wParam	WPARAM: Set to zero.
lParam	LPSTR: The address of the null-terminated string containing the name of the destination file that receives a copy of the capture file.
Returns	BOOL: If successful, TRUE is returned; otherwise, FALSE is returned.
Include File	vfw.h

WM_CAP_FILE_SAVEDIB   ■ Win32s ■ Windows 95 ■ Windows NT

Description	WM_CAP_FILE_SAVEDIB is a message that copies the current video frame to a DIB file. If the capture driver supplies frames in a compressed format, WM_CAP_FILE_SAVEDIB attempts to decompress the frame before writing the file.

Parameters

wParam	WPARAM: Set to zero.
lParam	LPSTR: The address of the null-terminated string containing the name of the destination DIB file.

Returns   BOOL: If successful, TRUE is returned; otherwise, FALSE is returned.

Include File   vfw.h

WM_CAP_FILE_SET_CAPTURE_FILE

■ Win32s   ■ Windows 95   ■ Windows NT

Description   WM_CAP_FILE_SET_CAPTURE_FILE is a message that identifies the file to use for video capture. This message stores the file name in an internal structure and does not create, allocate, or open the file. The default capture file name is C:\CAPTURE.AVI.

Parameters

wParam	WPARAM: Set to zero.
lParam	LPSTR: The address of the null-terminated string containing the name of the capture file to use for video capture.

Returns   BOOL: If successful, TRUE is returned; otherwise, FALSE is returned.

Include File   vfw.h

WM_CAP_FILE_SET_INFOCHUNK

■ Win32s   ■ Windows 95   ■ Windows NT

Description   WM_CAP_FILE_SET_INFOCHUNK is a message that sets and clears information chunks. The information chunks can be inserted into an AVI file during the capture process to embed text strings or custom data. Once an information chunk is set, it continues to be added to subsequent capture files until either the entry is cleared or all information chunk entries are cleared. To clear a single entry, specify the information chunk in the *fccInfoID* member and NULL in the *lpData* member of the CAPINFOCHUNK structure. To clear all entries, specify NULL in *fccInfoID*.

Parameters

wParam	WPARAM: Set to zero.
lParam	LPINFOCHUNK: The address of a CAPINFOCHUNK structure defining the information chunk to be created or deleted.

Returns   BOOL: If successful, TRUE is returned; otherwise, FALSE is returned.

Include File   vfw.h

WM_CAP_GET_AUDIOFORMAT   ■ Win32s   ■ Windows 95   ■ Windows NT

Description   WM_CAP_GET_AUDIO_FORMAT is a message that obtains the audio format or the size of the audio format. Because compressed audio formats vary in size requirements, applications must first retrieve the size, then allocate memory, and finally request the audio format data.

Parameters

wParam   WPARAM: The size, in bytes, of the WAVEFORMATEX structure pointed to by *lParam*.

lParam   LPWAVEFORMATEX: The address of a WAVEFORMATEX structure, or a value of NULL.

Returns   int: If successful, the size, in bytes, of the audio format is returned; otherwise, the size of the WAVEFORMATEX structure is returned if *lParam* is NULL.

Include File   vfw.h

WM_CAP_GET_MCI_DEVICE   ■ Win32s   ■ Windows 95   ■ Windows NT

Description   WM_CAP_GET_MCI_DEVICE is a message that retrieves the name of an MCI device previously set with WM_CAP_SET_MCI_DEVICE.

Parameters

wParam   WPARAM: The length, in bytes, of the null-terminated string pointed to by *lParam*.

lParam   LPSTR: The address of a null-terminated string that contains the MCI device name.

Returns   BOOL: If successful, TRUE is returned; otherwise, FALSE is returned.

Include File   vfw.h

WM_CAP_GET_SEQUENCE_SETUP   ■ Win32s   ■ Windows 95   ■ Windows NT

Description   WM_CAP_GET_SEQUENCE_SETUP is a message that retrieves the current settings of the streaming capture parameters.

Parameters

wParam   WPARAM: The size, in bytes, of the CAPTUREPARMS structure pointed to by *lParam*.

lParam   LPCAPTUREPARMS: The address of a CAPTUREPARMS structure.

Returns   BOOL: If successful, TRUE is returned; otherwise, FALSE is returned.

Include File   vfw.h

WM_CAP_GET_STATUS   ■ Win32s   ■ Windows 95   ■ Windows NT

Description	WM_CAP_GET_STATUS is a message that retrieves the status of the video capture window.
Parameters	
wParam	WPARAM: The size, in bytes, of the CAPSTATUS structure pointed to by *lParam*.
lParam	LPCAPSTATUS: The address of a CAPSTATUS structure.
Returns	BOOL: If successful, TRUE is returned; otherwise, FALSE is returned.
Include File	vfw.h

WM_CAP_GET_USER_DATA   ■ Win32s   ■ Windows 95   ■ Windows NT

Description	WM_CAP_GET_USER_DATA is a message that retrieves a LONG data value associated with a capture window.
Parameters	This message does not use *wParam* or *lParam*; therefore, both must be set to zero.
Returns	LONG: A value previously saved using WM_CAP_SET_USER_DATA is returned.
Include File	vfw.h

WM_CAP_GET_VIDEOFORMAT   ■ Win32s   ■ Windows 95   ■ Windows NT

Description	WM_CAP_GET_VIDEOFORMAT is a message that retrieves a copy of the video format in use or the size required for the video format.
Parameters	
wParam	WPARAM: The size, in bytes, of the BITMAPINFO structure pointed to by *lParam*.
lParam	LPVOID: The address of a BITMAPINFO structure. If *lParam* is zero, the number of bytes needed by BITMAPINFO is retrieved.
Returns	int: If successful, the size, in bytes, of the video format is returned; otherwise, zero is returned if the capture window is not connected to a capture driver. For video formats that require a palette, the current palette is also returned.
Include File	vfw.h

WM_CAP_GRAB_FRAME   ■ Win32s   ■ Windows 95   ■ Windows NT

Description	WM_CAP_GRAB_FRAME is a message that retrieves and displays a single frame from the capture driver. After the capture, the overlay and preview options are disabled.

Parameters   This message does not use *wParam* or *lParam*; therefore, both must be set to zero.

Returns   BOOL: If successful, TRUE is returned; otherwise, FALSE is returned.

Include File   vfw.h

WM_CAP_GRAB_FRAME_NOSTOP

■ Win32s ■ Windows 95 ■ Windows NT

Description   WM_CAP_GRAB_FRAME_NOSTOP is a message that fills the frame buffer with a single uncompressed frame from the capture device and then displays it. Unlike WM_CAP_GRAB_FRAME, the state of overlay or preview is not altered by this message.

Parameters   This message does not use *wParam* or *lParam*; therefore, both must be set to zero.

Returns   BOOL: If successful, TRUE is returned; otherwise, FALSE is returned.

Include File   vfw.h

WM_CAP_PAL_AUTOCREATE

■ Win32s ■ Windows 95 ■ Windows NT

Description   WM_CAP_PAL_AUTOCREATE is a message that requests that the capture driver sample video frames and automatically create a new palette.

Parameters

wParam   WPARAM: The number of frames to be sampled by the capture driver.

lParam   DWORD: The number of colors in the new palette. The maximum value is 256.

Returns   BOOL: If successful, TRUE is returned; otherwise, FALSE is returned.

Include File   vfw.h

WM_CAP_PAL_MANUALCREATE

■ Win32s ■ Windows 95 ■ Windows NT

Description   WM_CAP_PAL_MANUALCREATE is a message that requests that the capture driver manually sample video frames and create a new palette.

Parameters

wParam   WPARAM: The palette histogram flag. Set *wParam* to TRUE for each frame included in creating the optimal palette. Set *wParam* to FALSE, after the last frame has been collected, to calculate the optimal palette and send it to the capture driver.

lParam   DWORD: The number of colors in the new palette. The maximum value is 256.

Returns   BOOL: If successful, TRUE is returned; otherwise, FALSE is returned.

Include File   vfw.h

WM_CAP_PAL_OPEN   ■ Win32s   ■ Windows 95   ■ Windows NT

Description   WM_CAP_PAL_OPEN is a message that loads a new palette from a palette file and passes it to a capture driver. Palette files typically use the file name extension .PAL. A capture driver uses a palette when required by the specified digitized image format.

Parameters

wParam   WPARAM: Set to zero.

lParam   LPSTR: The address of a null-terminated string containing the file name.

Returns   BOOL: If successful, TRUE is returned; otherwise, FALSE is returned.

Include File   vfw.h

WM_CAP_PAL_PASTE   ■ Win32s   ■ Windows 95   ■ Windows NT

Description   WM_CAP_PAL_PASTE is a message that copies the palette from the clipboard and passes it to a capture driver.

Parameters   This message does not use *wParam* or *lParam*; therefore, both must be set to zero.

Returns   BOOL: If successful, TRUE is returned; otherwise, FALSE is returned.

Include File   vfw.h

WM_CAP_PAL_SAVE   ■ Win32s   ■ Windows 95   ■ Windows NT

Description   WM_CAP_PAL_SAVE is a message that saves the current palette to a palette file. Palette files typically use the file name extension .PAL.

Parameters

wParam   WPARAM: Set to zero.

lParam   LPSTR: The address of a null-terminated string containing the palette file name.

Returns   BOOL: If successful, TRUE is returned; otherwise, FALSE is returned.

Include File   vfw.h

WM_CAP_SEQUENCE   ■ Win32s   ■ Windows 95   ■ Windows NT

Description   WM_CAP_SEQUENCE is a message that initiates streaming video and audio capture to a file.

Parameters   This message does not use *wParam* or *lParam*; therefore, both must be set to zero.

Returns   BOOL: If successful, TRUE is returned; otherwise, FALSE is returned.

Include File   vfw.h

WM_CAP_SEQUENCE_NOFILE   ■ Win32s ■ Windows 95 ■ Windows NT

Description   WM_CAP_SEQUENCE_NOFILE is a message that initiates streaming video capture without writing data to a file.

Parameters   This message does not use *wParam* or *lParam*; therefore, both must be set to zero.

Returns   BOOL: If successful, TRUE is returned; otherwise, FALSE is returned.

Include File   vfw.h

WM_CAP_SET_AUDIOFORMAT   ■ Win32s ■ Windows 95 ■ Windows NT

Description   WM_CAP_SET_AUDIOFORMAT is a message that sets the audio format to be used when performing streaming or step capture.

Parameters

wParam   WPARAM: The size, in bytes, of the structure pointed to by *lParam*.

lParam   LPWAVEFORMATEX: The address of a WAVEFORMATEX or PCMWAVEFORMAT structure that defines the audio format.

Returns   BOOL: If successful, TRUE is returned; otherwise, FALSE is returned.

Include File   vfw.h

WM_CAP_SET_CALLBACK_CAPCONTROL

■ Win32s ■ Windows 95 ■ Windows NT

Description   WM_CAP_SET_CALLBACK_CAPCONTROL is a message that sets a callback function in the application, giving it precise recording control.

Parameters

wParam   WPARAM: Set to zero.

lParam   LPVOID: The address of the callback function. A NULL value disables a previously installed callback function.

Returns   BOOL: If successful, TRUE is returned; otherwise, FALSE is returned.

Include File   vfw.h

WM_CAP_SET_CALLBACK_ERROR

■ Win32s ■ Windows 95 ■ Windows NT

Description   WM_CAP_SET_CALLBACK_ERROR is a message that sets an error callback function in the client application. AVICap calls this procedure when errors occur.

Parameters

wParam	WPARAM: Set to zero.
lParam	LPVOID: The address of the callback function. A NULL value disables a previously installed callback function.
Returns	BOOL: If successful, TRUE is returned; otherwise, FALSE is returned.
Include File	vfw.h

WM_CAP_SET_CALLBACK_FRAME

■ **Win32s** ■ **Windows 95** ■ **Windows NT**

Description	WM_CAP_SET_CALLBACK_FRAME is a message that sets a preview callback function in the application. AVICap calls this procedure when the capture window captures preview frames. This callback function is not used during streaming video capture.

Parameters

wParam	WPARAM: Set to zero.
lParam	LPVOID: The address of the callback function. A NULL value disables a previously installed callback function.
Returns	BOOL: If successful, TRUE is returned; otherwise, FALSE is returned.
Include File	vfw.h

WM_CAP_SET_CALLBACK_STATUS

■ **Win32s** ■ **Windows 95** ■ **Windows NT**

Description	WM_CAP_SET_CALLBACK_STATUS is a message that sets a status callback function in the application. AVICap calls this procedure whenever the capture window status changes.

Parameters

wParam	WPARAM: Set to zero.
lParam	LPVOID: The address of the callback function. A NULL value disables a previously installed callback function.
Returns	BOOL: If successful, TRUE is returned; otherwise, FALSE is returned.
Include File	vfw.h

WM_CAP_SET_CALLBACK_VIDEOSTREAM

■ **Win32s** ■ **Windows 95** ■ **Windows NT**

Description	WM_CAP_SET_CALLBACK_VIDEOSTREAM is a message that sets a callback function in the application. AVICap calls this procedure during streaming capture when a video buffer is filled.

Parameters

wParam	WPARAM: Set to zero.
lParam	LPVOID: The address of the callback function. A NULL value disables a previously installed callback function.
Returns	BOOL: If successful, TRUE is returned; otherwise, FALSE is returned.
Include File	vfw.h

WM_CAP_SET_CALLBACK_WAVESTREAM

■ **Win32s** ■ **Windows 95** ■ **Windows NT**

Description WM_CAP_SET_CALLBACK_WAVESTREAM is a message that sets a callback function in the application. AVICap calls this procedure during streaming capture when a new audio buffer becomes available.

Parameters

wParam	WPARAM: Set to zero.
lParam	LPVOID: The address of the callback function. A NULL value disables a previously installed callback function.
Returns	BOOL: If successful, TRUE is returned; otherwise, FALSE is returned.
Include File	vfw.h

WM_CAP_SET_CALLBACK_YIELD

■ **Win32s** ■ **Windows 95** ■ **Windows NT**

Description WM_CAP_SET_CALLBACK_YIELD is a message that sets a callback function in the application. AVICap calls this procedure when the capture window yields during streaming capture. Applications can optionally set a yield callback function. The yield callback function is called at least once for each video frame captured during streaming capture.

Parameters

wParam	WPARAM: Set to zero.
lParam	LPVOID: The address of the callback function. A NULL value disables a previously installed callback function.
Returns	BOOL: If successful, TRUE is returned; otherwise, FALSE is returned.
Include File	vfw.h

WM_CAP_SET_MCI_DEVICE

■ **Win32s** ■ **Windows 95** ■ **Windows NT**

Description WM_CAP_SET_MCI_DEVICE is a message that specifies the name of the MCI video device to be used to capture data.

Parameters

wParam	WPARAM: Set to zero.
lParam	LPSTR: The address of a null-terminated string containing the name of the device. The default name is NULL.
Returns	BOOL: If successful, TRUE is returned; otherwise, FALSE is returned.
Include File	vfw.h

WM_CAP_SET_OVERLAY   ■ Win32s ■ Windows 95 ■ Windows NT

Description   WM_CAP_SET_OVERLAY is a message that enables or disables overlay mode. In overlay mode, video is displayed using hardware overlay. Using an overlay does not require CPU resources. Enabling overlay mode automatically disables preview mode.

Parameters

wParam	BOOL: The overlay flag. TRUE enables overlay mode, and FALSE disables it.
lParam	LONG: Set to zero.
Returns	BOOL: If successful, TRUE is returned; otherwise, FALSE is returned.
Include File	vfw.h

WM_CAP_SET_PREVIEW   ■ Win32s ■ Windows 95 ■ Windows NT

Description   WM_CAP_SET_PREVIEW is a message that enables or disables preview mode. In preview mode, frames are transferred from the capture hardware to system memory and then displayed in the capture window using GDI functions. The preview mode uses substantial CPU resources. Applications can disable the preview mode or lower the preview rate when another application has the focus. Enabling preview mode automatically disables overlay mode.

Parameters

wParam	BOOL: The preview flag. TRUE enables preview mode, and FALSE disables it.
lParam	LONG: Set to zero.
Returns	BOOL: If successful, TRUE is returned; otherwise, FALSE is returned.
Include File	vfw.h

WM_CAP_SET_PREVIEWRATE   ■ Win32s ■ Windows 95 ■ Windows NT

Description   WM_CAP_SET_PREVIEWRATE is a message that sets the frame display rate in preview mode. The preview mode uses substantial CPU resources.

Parameters

wParam	WPARAM: The rate, in milliseconds, at which new frames are captured and displayed in preview mode.
lParam	LONG: Set to zero.
Returns	BOOL: If successful, TRUE is returned; otherwise, FALSE is returned.
Include File	vfw.h

WM_CAP_SET_SCALE   ■ Win32s   ■ Windows 95   ■ Windows NT

Description   WM_CAP_SET_SCALE is a message that enables or disables scaling of the preview video images. If scaling is enabled, the captured video frame is stretched to the dimensions of the capture window. Scaling preview images controls the immediate presentation of captured frames within the capture window. It has no effect on the size of the frames saved to file. Scaling has no effect when using overlay to display video in the frame buffer.

Parameters

wParam	BOOL: The preview scaling flag. TRUE stretches the preview frames to the size of the capture window, and FALSE displays them in the original size.
lParam	LONG: Set to zero.
Returns	BOOL: If successful, TRUE is returned; otherwise, FALSE is returned.
Include File	vfw.h

WM_CAP_SET_SCROLL   ■ Win32s   ■ Windows 95   ■ Windows NT

Description   WM_CAP_SET_SCROLL is a message that defines the portion of the video frame to display in the capture window. This message sets the upper left corner of the client area of the capture window to the coordinates of a specified pixel within the video frame. The scroll position affects the image in both preview and overlay modes.

Parameters

wParam	WPARAM: Set to zero.
lParam	LPPOINT: The address of the portion of the video frame to contain the desired scroll position.
Returns	BOOL: If successful, TRUE is returned; otherwise, FALSE is returned.
Include File	vfw.h

WM_CAP_SET_SEQUENCE_SETUP   ■ Win32s   ■ Windows 95   ■ Windows NT

Description   WM_CAP_SET_SEQUENCE_SETUP is a message that sets the configuration parameters used with streaming capture.

Parameters

wParam	WPARAM: The size, in bytes, of the CAPTUREPARMS structure pointed to by *lParam*.
lParam	LPCAPTUREPARMS: The address of a CAPTUREPARMS structure.
Returns	BOOL: If successful, TRUE is returned; otherwise, FALSE is returned.
Include File	vfw.h

WM_CAP_SET_USER_DATA ■ Win32s ■ Windows 95 ■ Windows NT

Description   WM_CAP_SET_USER_DATA is a message that associates a LONG data value with a video capture window.

Parameters

wParam	WPARAM: Set to zero.
lParam	LPARAM: The data value to be associated with a capture window.
Returns	BOOL: If successful, TRUE is returned; otherwise, FALSE is returned.
Include File	vfw.h

WM_CAP_SET_VIDEOFORMAT ■ Win32s ■ Windows 95 ■ Windows NT

Description   WM_CAP_SET_VIDEOFORMAT is a message that sets the format of the captured video data.

Parameters

wParam	WPARAM: The size, in bytes, of the BITMAPINFO structure pointed to by *lParam*.
lParam	LPVOID: The address of a BITMAPINFO structure.
Returns	BOOL: If successful, TRUE is returned; otherwise, FALSE is returned.
Include File	vfw.h

WM_CAP_SINGLE_FRAME ■ Win32s ■ Windows 95 ■ Windows NT

Description   WM_CAP_SINGLE_FRAME is a message that appends a single frame to a video capture file opened using WM_CAP_SINGLE_FRAME_OPEN.

Parameters   This message does not use *wParam* or *lParam*; therefore, both must be set to zero.

Returns   BOOL: If successful, TRUE is returned; otherwise, FALSE is returned.

Include File   vfw.h

Related Messages   WM_CAP_SINGLE_FRAME_OPEN

WM_CAP_SINGLE_FRAME_CLOSE

■ Win32s   ■ Windows 95   ■ Windows NT

Description	WM_CAP_SINGLE_FRAME_CLOSE is a message that closes the video capture file opened using WM_CAP_SINGLE_FRAME_OPEN.
Parameters	This message does not use *wParam* or *lParam*; therefore, both must be set to zero.
Returns	BOOL: If successful, TRUE is returned; otherwise, FALSE is returned.
Include File	vfw.h

WM_CAP_SINGLE_FRAME_OPEN

■ Win32s   ■ Windows 95   ■ Windows NT

Description	WM_CAP_SINGLE_FRAME_OPEN is a message that opens the video capture file for single-frame capturing. Any previous information in the capture file is overwritten.
Parameters	This message does not use *wParam* or *lParam*; therefore, both must be set to zero.
Returns	BOOL: If successful, TRUE is returned; otherwise, FALSE is returned.
Include File	vfw.h

WM_CAP_STOP

■ Win32s   ■ Windows 95   ■ Windows NT

Description	WM_CAP_STOP is a message that stops the video capture operation. In step frame capture, the image data that was collected before this message was sent is retained in the capture file. An equivalent duration of audio data is also retained in the capture file if audio capture was enabled.
Parameters	This message does not use *wParam* or *lParam*; therefore, both must be set to zero.
Returns	BOOL: If successful, TRUE is returned; otherwise, FALSE is returned.
Include File	vfw.h
Related Messages	WM_CAP_ABORT

WM_CAPTURECHANGED

■ Win32s   ■ Windows 95   ■ Windows NT

Description	WM_CAPTURECHANGED is a message that is sent to the window that is losing the mouse capture. A window receives this message even if it calls ReleaseCapture(). When it receives this message, a window should redraw itself, if necessary, to reflect the new mouse-capture state.

Parameters

wParam	WPARAM: Set to zero.
lParam	HWND: The window that is gaining the mouse capture.
Returns	int: An application should return zero if it processes this message.
Include File	winuser.h
See Also	ReleaseCapture(), SetCapture()

WM_CHANGECBCHAIN   ■ Win32s   ■ Windows 95   ■ Windows NT

Description   WM_CHANGECBCHAIN is a message that is sent to the first window in the clipboard viewer chain when a window is being removed from the chain. When a clipboard viewer window receives the WM_CHANGECBCHAIN message, it should call SendMessage() to pass the message to the next window in the chain, unless the next window is the window being removed. In this case, the clipboard viewer should save the handle specified by *lParam* as the next window in the chain.

Parameters

wParam	HWND: The window being removed from the clipboard viewer chain.
lParam	HWND: The next window in the chain following the window being removed, identified by *wParam*. This parameter has a value of NULL if the window identified by *wParam* is the last window in the chain.
Returns	int: An application should return zero if it processes this message.
Include File	winuser.h
See Also	SendMessage(), SetClipboardViewer()

WM_CHAR   ■ Win32s   ■ Windows 95   ■ Windows NT

Description   WM_CHAR is a message that is posted to the window with the keyboard focus when a WM_KEYDOWN message is translated by TranslateMessage(). WM_CHAR contains the character code of the key that was pressed.

Parameters

wParam	TCHAR: The character code of the key that was pressed.
lParam	LPARAM: The repeat count, scan code, extended-key flag, context code, previous key-state flag, and transition-state flag, as shown in Table 11-21.

Table 11-21 WM_CHAR *lParam* values

Value	Meaning
0–15	The repeat count. Indicates the number of times the keystroke is repeated as a result of the user holding down the key.
16–23	The scan code. Depends on the original equipment manufacturer (OEM).
24	Specifies whether the key is an extended key, such as the right-hand ALT and CTRL keys that appear on an enhanced 101- or 102-key keyboard. The value is 1 if it is an extended key; otherwise, it is 0.
25–28	Reserved value; do not use.
29	The context code. The value is 1 if the ALT key is held down while the key is pressed; otherwise, the value is 0.
30	The previous key state. The value is 1 if the key is down before the message is sent, or it is 0 if the key is up.
31	The transition state. The value is 1 if the key is being released, or it is 0 if the key is being pressed.

Returns	int: An application should return zero if it processes this message.
Include File	winuser.h
See Also	TranslateMessage()
Related Messages	WM_KEYDOWN

WM_CHARTOITEM　　　　■ Win32s　■ Windows 95　■ Windows NT

Description	WM_CHARTOITEM is a message that is sent by a list box with the LBS_WANTKEYBOARDINPUT style to its owner in response to a WM_CHAR message. Only owner-drawn list boxes that do not have the LBS_HASSTRINGS style can receive this message.
Parameters	
LOWORD(wParam)	WORD: The value of the key the user pressed.
HIWORD(wParam)	WORD: The current position of the caret.
lParam	LPARAM: The list box.
Returns	int: A value indicating the action that the application performed in response to the message is returned. A value of -1 or -2 indicates that the application handled all aspects of selecting the item and requires no further action by the list box. A value of 0 or greater specifies the zero-based index of an item in the list box and indicates that the list box should perform the default action for the keystroke on the given item.
Include File	winuser.h
See Also	DefWindowProc()
Related Messages	WM_CHAR, WM_VKEYTOITEM

WM_CHILDACTIVE
■ Win32s ■ Windows 95 ■ Windows NT

Description	WM_CHILDACTIVATE is a message that is sent to a multiple document interface (MDI) child window when the user clicks the window's title bar or when the window is activated, moved, or sized.
Parameters	This message does not use *wParam* or *lParam*; therefore, both must be set to zero.
Returns	int: If an application processes this message, it should return zero.
Include File	winuser.h
See Also	MoveWindow(), SetWindowPos()

WM_CHOOSEFONT_GETLOGFONT
■ Win32s ■ Windows 95 ■ Windows NT

Description	WM_CHOOSEFONT_GETLOGFONT is a message that is sent to the Font dialog box created by ChooseFont() to retrieve the current LOGFONT structure.
Parameters	
wParam	WPARAM: Set to zero.
lParam	LPARAM: A pointer to a LOGFONT structure that receives information about the current logical font.
Include File	commdlg.h
See Also	ChooseFont()
Related Messages	WM_GETFONT

WM_CHOOSEFONT_SETFLAGS
■ Win32s ■ Windows 95 ■ Windows NT

Description	WM_CHOOSEFONT_SETFLAGS is a message that is sent to the Font dialog box created by ChooseFont() to set the display options for the dialog box.
Parameters	
wParam	WPARAM: Set to zero.
lParam	LPARAM: A pointer to a CHOOSEFONT structure whose *Flags* member contains the new dialog box settings.
Include File	commdlg.h
See Also	ChooseFont()
Related Messages	WM_GETFONT

WM_CHOOSEFONT_SETLOGFONT

■ Win32s   ■ Windows 95   ■ Windows NT

Description	WM_CHOOSEFONT_SETLOGFONT is a message that is sent to the Font dialog box created by ChooseFont() to set the current logical font information.
Parameters	
wParam	WPARAM: Set to zero.
lParam	LPARAM: A pointer to a LOGFONT structure that contains information about the current logical font.
Include File	commdlg.h
See Also	ChooseFont()
Related Messages	WM_GETFONT

WM_CLEAR

■ Win32s   ■ Windows 95   ■ Windows NT

Description	WM_CLEAR is a message that is sent to an edit control or combo box to delete the current selection from the edit control. The deletion can be undone by sending the edit control an EM_UNDO message. This message has no effect when sent to a combo box with the CBS_DROPDOWNLIST style.
Parameters	This message does not use *wParam* or *lParam*; therefore, both must be set to zero.
Include File	winuser.h
Related Messages	EM_UNDO, WM_COPY, WM_CUT, WM_PASTE

WM_CLOSE

■ Win32s   ■ Windows 95   ■ Windows NT

Description	WM_CLOSE is a message that indicates that a window or an application should terminate.
Parameters	This message does not use *wParam* or *lParam*; therefore, both must be set to zero.
Returns	int: If an application processes this message, it should return zero.
Include File	winuser.h
See Also	DefWindowProc(), DestroyWindow()

WM_COMMAND

■ Win32s   ■ Windows 95   ■ Windows NT

Description	WM_COMMAND is a message that is sent when the user selects a command item from a menu, when a control sends a notification message to

its parent window, or when an accelerator keystroke is translated. Accelerator keystrokes that select items from the System menu are translated into WM_SYSCOMMAND messages.

Parameters

LOWORD(wParam) WORD: The identifier of the menu item, control, or accelerator.

HIWORD(wParam) WORD: The notification code if the message is from a control. If the message is from an accelerator, this parameter is 1. If the message is from a menu, this parameter is 0.

lParam HWND: If the message is from a control, the handle of the control sending the message; otherwise, this parameter is NULL.

Returns int: An application should return zero if it processes this message.

Include File winuser.h

Related Messages WM_SYSCOMMAND

WM_COMPACTING ■ Win32s ■ Windows 95 ■ Windows NT

Description WM_COMPACTING is a message that is sent to all top-level windows when Windows detects that during a 30- to 60-second interval more than 12.5 percent of system time is spent compacting memory. This indicates that system memory is low.

Parameters

wParam WPARAM: The ratio of central processing unit (CPU) time currently spent by Windows compacting memory to CPU time currently spent by Windows performing other operations. For example, 0x8000 represents 50 percent of CPU time spent compacting memory.

lParam LPARAM: Set to zero.

Returns int: An application should return zero if it processes this message.

Include File winuser.h

WM_COMPAREITEM ■ Win32s ■ Windows 95 ■ Windows NT

Description WM_COMPAREITEM is a message that is sent to determine the relative position of a new item in the sorted list of either an owner-drawn combo box or list box. Whenever the application adds a new item, Windows sends this message to the owner of either a combo box or a list box created with the CBS_SORT or LBS_SORT style.

Parameters

wParam WPARAM: The identifier of the control that sent the WM_COMPAREITEM message.

lParam	LPCOMPAREITEMSTRUCT: A pointer to a COMPAREITEMSTRUCT structure that contains the identifiers and application-supplied data for two items in the combo or list box.
Returns	int: A value from Table 11-22, indicating the relative position of the two items.

Table 11-22 WM_COMPAREITEM return values

Value	Meaning
-1	Item 1 precedes item 2 in the sorted order.
0	Items 1 and 2 are equivalent in the sorted order.
1	Item 1 follows item 2 in the sorted order.

Include File	winuser.h

WM_CONTEXTMENU ■ Win32s ■ Windows 95 ■ Windows NT

Description	WM_CONTEXTMENU is a message that notifies a window that the user clicked the right mouse button in the window.
Parameters	
wParam	HWND: The handle of the window in which the user right-clicked the mouse. This can be a child window of the window receiving the message.
LOWORD(*lParam*)	WORD: The horizontal position of the cursor, in screen coordinates, at the time of the mouse click.
HIWORD(*lParam*)	WORD: The vertical position of the cursor, in screen coordinates, at the time of the mouse click.
Include File	winuser.h
See Also	DefWindowProc(), TrackPopupMenu(), TrackPopupMenuEx()
Related Messages	WM_NCRBUTTONUP, WM_RBUTTONUP

WM_COPY ■ Win32s ■ Windows 95 ■ Windows NT

Description	WM_COPY is a message that is sent to either an edit control or combo box to copy the current selection to the clipboard in CF_TEXT format. When sent to a combo box, the WM_COPY message is handled by its edit control. This message has no effect when sent to a combo box with the CBS_DROPDOWNLIST style.
Parameters	This message does not use *wParam* or *lParam*; therefore, both must be set to zero.
Include File	winuser.h
Related Messages	WM_CLEAR, WM_CUT, WM_PASTE

WM_COPYDATA
■ Win32s ■ Windows 95 ■ Windows NT

Description   WM_COPYDATA is a message that is sent when an application passes data to another application. An application must use SendMessage() to send this message. The data being passed must not contain pointers or other references to objects that are not accessible to the application receiving the data. While this message is being sent, the referenced data must not be changed by another thread of the sending process.

Parameters

wParam   HWND: The window passing the data.

lParam   PSCOPYDATASTRUCT: A pointer to a COPYDATASTRUCT structure that contains the data to be passed.

Returns   BOOL: If processed by the receiving application, TRUE is returned; otherwise, FALSE is returned.

Include File   winuser.h

See Also   SendMessage()

WM_CPL_LAUNCH
■ Win32s ■ Windows 95 ■ Windows NT

Description   WM_CPL_LAUNCH is a message that is sent to Windows Control Panel to request that a Control Panel application be started.

Parameters

wParam   HWND: The handle of the window sending the message. The WM_CPL_LAUNCHED message is sent to the window identified by *wParam*.

lParam   LPSTR: A far pointer to a string containing the name of the Control Panel application to open.

Returns   BOOL: If the application starts, TRUE is returned; otherwise, FALSE is returned.

Include File   cpl.h

Related Messages WM_CPL_LAUNCHED

WM_CPL_LAUNCHED
■ Win32s ■ Windows 95 ■ Windows NT

Description   WM_CPL_LAUNCHED is a message that is sent when a Control Panel application, started by the WM_CPL_LAUNCH message, has started. The WM_CPL_LAUNCHED message is sent to the window identified by the *wParam* parameter of the WM_CPL_LAUNCH message that started the application.

Parameters

wParam   BOOL: If the application was started, TRUE is returned; otherwise, this parameter is FALSE.

lParam	LPARAM: Set to zero.
Include File	cpl.h
Related Messages	WM_CPL_LAUNCH

WM_CREATE   ■ Win32s   ■ Windows 95   ■ Windows NT

Description	WM_CREATE is a message that is sent when an application calls either CreateWindowEx() or CreateWindow() and requests to create a new a window. The window procedure of the new window receives this message after the window is created, but before the window becomes visible. WM_CREATE is sent before CreateWindowEx() or CreateWindow() returns.
Parameters	
wParam	WPARAM: Set to zero.
lParam	LPCREATESTRUCT: A pointer to a CREATESTRUCT structure that contains information about the window being created. The members of CREATESTRUCT are identical to the parameters of CreateWindowEx().
Returns	int: If an application processes this message, it returns 0 to continue creation of the window. If the application returns -1, the window is destroyed and either CreateWindowEx() or CreateWindow() returns a NULL handle.
Include File	winuser.h
See Also	CreateWindow(), CreateWindowEx()
Related Messages	WM_NCCREATE

WM_CTLCOLORBTN   ■ Win32s   ■ Windows 95   ■ Windows NT

Description	WM_CTLCOLORBTN is a message that is sent to the parent window of a button when the button is about to be drawn. By responding to this message, the parent window can set a button's text and background colors.
Parameters	
wParam	HDC: The display context for the button.
lParam	HWND: The button identifier.
Returns	HBRUSH: If an application processes this message, the handle of a brush is returned. Windows uses the brush to paint the background of the button.
Include File	winuser.h
See Also	DefWindowProc(), RealizePalette(), SelectPalette()
Related Messages	WM_CTLCOLORDLG, WM_CTLCOLOREDIT, WM_CTLCOLORLISTBOX, WM_CTLCOLORMSGBOX, WM_CTLCOLORSCROLLBAR, WM_CTLCOLORSTATIC

WM_CTLCOLORDLG
■ Win32s ■ Windows 95 ■ Windows NT

Description   WM_CTLCOLORDLG is a message that is sent to a dialog box before Windows draws the dialog box. By responding to this message, the dialog box can set its text and background colors by using the given display device context handle.

Parameters

wParam   HDC: The device context for the dialog box.

lParam   HWND: The dialog box identifier.

Returns   HBRUSH: If an application processes this message, the handle of a brush is returned. Windows uses the brush to paint the background of the dialog box.

Include File   winuser.h

See Also   DefWindowProc(), RealizePalette(), SelectPalette()

Related Messages   WM_CTLCOLORBTN, WM_CTLCOLOREDIT, WM_CTLCOLORLISTBOX, WM_CTLCOLORMSGBOX, WM_CTLCOLORSCROLLBAR, WM_CTLCOLORSTATIC

WM_CTLCOLOREDIT
■ Win32s ■ Windows 95 ■ Windows NT

Description   WM_CTLCOLOREDIT is a message that is sent to the parent window of an edit control when the control is about to be drawn. By responding to this message, the parent window can use the given device context handle to set the text and background colors of the edit control.

Parameters

wParam   HDC: The device context for the edit control window.

lParam   HWND: The edit control identifier.

Returns   HBRUSH: If an application processes this message, the handle of a brush is returned. Windows uses the brush to paint the background of the edit control.

Include File   winuser.h

See Also   DefWindowProc(), RealizePalette(), SelectPalette()

Related Messages   WM_CTLCOLORBTN, WM_CTLCOLORDLG, WM_CTLCOLORLISTBOX, WM_CTLCOLORMSGBOX, WM_CTLCOLORSCROLLBAR, WM_CTLCOLORSTATIC

WM_CTLCOLORLISTBOX
■ Win32s ■ Windows 95 ■ Windows NT

Description   WM_CTLCOLORLISTBOX is a message that is sent to the parent window of a list box before Windows draws the list box. By responding to this message, the parent window can set the text and background colors of the list box by using the given display device context handle.

Parameters	
wParam	HDC: The device context for the list box.
lParam	HWND: The list box identifier.
Returns	HBRUSH: If an application processes this message, the handle of a brush is returned. Windows uses the brush to paint the background of the list box.
Include File	winuser.h
See Also	DefWindowProc(), RealizePalette(), SelectPalette()
Related Messages	WM_CTLCOLORBTN, WM_CTLCOLORDLG, WM_CTLCOLOREDIT, WM_CTLCOLORMSGBOX, WM_CTLCOLORSCROLLBAR, WM_CTLCOLORSTATIC

WM_CTLCOLORMSGBOX   ■ Win32s   ■ Windows 95   ■ Windows NT

Description	WM_CTLCOLORMSGBOX is a message that is sent to the owner window of a message box before Windows draws the message box. By responding to this message, the owner window can set the text and background colors of the message box by using the given display device context handle.
Parameters	
wParam	HDC: The device context for the message box.
lParam	HWND: The message box identifier.
Returns	HBRUSH: If an application processes this message, the handle of a brush is returned. Windows uses the brush to paint the background of the message box.
Include File	winuser.h
See Also	DefWindowProc(), RealizePalette(), SelectPalette()
Related Messages	WM_CTLCOLORBTN, WM_CTLCOLORDLG, WM_CTLCOLOREDIT, WM_CTLCOLORLISTBOX, WM_CTLCOLORSCROLLBAR, WM_CTLCOLORSTATIC

WM_CTLCOLORSCROLLBAR   ■ Win32s   ■ Windows 95   ■ Windows NT

Description	WM_CTLCOLORSCROLLBAR is a message that is sent to the parent window of a scroll bar control when the control is about to be drawn. By responding to this message, the parent window can use the given display context handle to set the background color of the scroll bar control.
Parameters	
wParam	HDC: The device context for the scroll bar control.
lParam	HWND: The scroll bar control identifier.

Returns	HBRUSH: If an application processes this message, the handle of a brush is returned. Windows uses the brush to paint the background of the scroll bar control.
Include File	winuser.h
See Also	DefWindowProc(), RealizePalette(), SelectPalette()
Related Messages	WM_CTLCOLORBTN, WM_CTLCOLORDLG, WM_CTLCOLOREDIT, WM_CTLCOLORLISTBOX, WM_CTLCOLORMSGBOX, WM_CTLCOLORSTATIC

WM_CTLCOLORSTATIC   ■ Win32s ■ Windows 95 ■ Windows NT

Description	WM_CTLCOLORSTATIC is a message that is sent to the parent window of a static control when the control is about to be drawn. By responding to this message, the parent window can use the given device context handle to set the text and background colors of the static control.
Parameters	
wParam	HDC: The device context for the static control window.
lParam	HWND: The static control window identifier.
Returns	HBRUSH: If an application processes this message, the handle of a brush is returned. Windows uses the brush to paint the background of the static control window and the background of the button.
Include File	winuser.h
See Also	DefWindowProc(), RealizePalette(), SelectPalette()
Related Messages	WM_CTLCOLORBTN, WM_CTLCOLORDLG, WM_CTLCOLOREDIT, WM_CTLCOLORLISTBOX, WM_CTLCOLORMSGBOX, WM_CTLCOLORSCROLLBAR

WM_CUT   ■ Win32s ■ Windows 95 ■ Windows NT

Description	WM_CUT is a message that is sent to either an edit control or combo box to delete the current selection and copy the deleted text to the clipboard in CF_TEXT format. The deletion performed by WM_CUT can be undone by sending the edit control an EM_UNDO message. This message has no effect when sent to a combo box with the CBS_DROPDOWNLIST style.
Parameters	This message does not use wParam or lParam; therefore, both must be set to zero.
Include File	winuser.h
Related Messages	WM_CLEAR, WM_COPY, WM_PASTE

WM_DEADCHAR
■ Win32s ■ Windows 95 ■ Windows NT

Description	WM_DEADCHAR is a message that is posted to the window with the keyboard focus when a WM_KEYUP message is translated by TranslateMessage(). WM_DEADCHAR specifies a character code generated by a dead key. A dead key generates a character, such as the umlaut (double dot), that is combined with another character to form a composite character. For example, the umlaut-O character (Ö) is generated by typing the dead key for the umlaut character, and then typing the O key.
Parameters	
wParam	TCHAR: The character code generated by the dead key.
lParam	LPARAM: The repeat count, scan code, extended-key flag, context code, previous key-state flag, and transition-state flag as detailed in Table 11-21.
Returns	int: An application should return zero if it processes this message.
Include File	winuser.h
See Also	TranslateMessage()
Related Messages	WM_KEYDOWN, WM_KEYUP, WM_SYSDEADCHAR

WM_DELETEITEM
■ Win32s ■ Windows 95 ■ Windows NT

Description	WM_DELETEITEM is a message that is sent to the owner of either an owner-drawn list box or combo box when the list box or combo box is either destroyed or when items are removed by the LB_DELETESTRING, LB_RESETCONTENT, CB_DELETESTRING, or CB_RESETCONTENT message.
Parameters	
wParam	WPARAM: The identifier of the control that sent the WM_DELETEITEM message.
lParam	LPDELETEITEMSTRUCT: A pointer to a DELETEITEMSTRUCT structure that contains information about the item deleted from a list box.
Returns	BOOL: An application should return TRUE if it processes this message.
Include File	winuser.h
Related Messages	CB_DELETESTRING, CB_RESETCONTENT, LB_DELETESTRING, LB_RESETCONTENT

WM_DESTROY
■ Win32s ■ Windows 95 ■ Windows NT

Description	WM_DESTROY is a message that is sent to the window procedure of a window that is being destroyed after the window is removed from the screen. This message is sent first to the window being destroyed and then to the child windows as they are destroyed.

Parameters	This message does not use *wParam* or *lParam*; therefore, both must be set to zero.
Returns	int: An application should return zero if it processes this message.
Include File	winuser.h
See Also	ChangeClipboardChain(), DestroyWindow(), PostQuitMessage(), SetClipboardViewer()
Related Messages	WM_CLOSE

WM_DESTROYCLIPBOARD ■ Win32s ■ Windows 95 ■ Windows NT

Description	WM_DESTROYCLIPBOARD is a message that is sent to the clipboard owner when a call to EmptyClipboard() empties the clipboard.
Parameters	This message does not use *wParam* or *lParam*; therefore, both must be set to zero.
Returns	int: An application should return zero if it processes this message.
Include File	winuser.h
See Also	EmptyClipboard()

WM_DEVICECHANGE Win32s ■ Windows 95 Windows NT

Description	WM_DEVICECHANGE notifies an application or device driver of a change in the hardware configuration of a device or the computer. DBT_DEVICEREMOVEPENDING is normally sent for devices with software-controllable features, such as ejection and locking, to provide the applications and device drivers the opportunity to terminate the use of the device gracefully.
Parameters	
wParam	UINT: One or more of the values in Table 11-23 indicating the type of hardware event.

Table 11-23 WM_DEVICECHANGE *wParam* values

Value	Meaning
DBT_CONFIGCHANGED	Current configuration has changed.
DBT_DEVICEARRIVAL	A device has been inserted and is now available.
DBT_DEVICEQUERYREMOVE	Permission to remove a device is requested. Any application can deny this request and cancel the removal.
DBT_DEVICEQUERYREMOVEFAILED	Request to remove a device has been canceled.
DBT_DEVICEREMOVECOMPLETE	Device has been removed.
DBT_DEVICEREMOVEPENDING	Device is about to be removed. Cannot be denied.
DBT_DEVICETYPESPECIFIC	Device-specific event.
DBT_DEVNODES_CHANGED	Device node has changed.

lParam	DWORD: The address of a structure that contains event-specific data. The meaning of the data is based on the specific event.
Returns	BOOL: To complete the requested action, TRUE is returned; otherwise, FALSE is returned.
Include File	winuser.h
Related Messages	DBT_CONFIGCHANGED, DBT_DEVICEARRIVAL, DBT_DEVICEQUERYREMOVE, DBT_DEVICEQUERYREMOVEFAILED, DBT_DEVICEREMOVECOMPLETE, DBT_DEVICEREMOVEPENDING, DBT_DEVICETYPESPECIFIC

WM_DEVMODECHANGE ■ Win32s ■ Windows 95 ■ Windows NT

Description	WM_DEVMODECHANGE is a message that is sent to all top-level windows whenever the user changes device-mode settings.
Parameters	
wParam	WPARAM: Set to zero.
lParam	LPCTSTR: A pointer to the device name specified in the WIN.INI file.
Returns	int: An application should return zero if it processes this message.
Include File	winuser.h
Related Messages	WM_SETTINGCHANGE

WM_DISPLAYCHANGE Win32s ■ Windows 95 Windows NT

Description	WM_DISPLAYCHANGE is a message that is sent to all windows when the display resolution has changed.
Parameters	
wParam	WPARAM: The new image depth of the display in bits per pixel.
LOWORD(lParam)	WORD: The new horizontal resolution of the screen.
HIWORD(lParam)	WORD: The new vertical resolution of the screen.
Include File	winuser.h

WM_DRAWCLIPBOARD ■ Win32s ■ Windows 95 ■ Windows NT

Description	WM_DRAWCLIPBOARD is a message that is sent to the first window in the clipboard viewer chain when the content of the clipboard changes. This enables a clipboard viewer window to display the new content of the clipboard. Each window that receives the WM_DRAWCLIPBOARD message must call SendMessage() to pass the message on to the next window in the clipboard viewer chain.

Parameters	This message does not use *wParam* or *lParam*; therefore, both must be set to zero.
Include File	winuser.h
See Also	SendMessage(), SetClipboardViewer()
Related Messages	WM_CHANGECBCHAIN

WM_DRAWITEM ■ Win32s ■ Windows 95 ■ Windows NT

Description	WM_DRAWITEM is a message that is sent to the owner window of an owner-drawn button, combo box, list box, or menu when a visual aspect of the button, combo box, list box, or menu has changed.
Parameters	
wParam	UINT: The identifier of the control that sent the WM_DRAWITEM message. If sent by a message, *wParam* is zero.
lParam	LPDRAWITEMSTRUCT: A pointer to a DRAWITEMSTRUCT structure containing information about the item to be drawn and the type of drawing required.
Returns	BOOL: An application should return TRUE if it processes this message.
Include File	winuser.h
See Also	DefWindowProc()

WM_DROPFILES ■ Win32s ■ Windows 95 ■ Windows NT

Description	WM_DROPFILES is a message that is sent when the user releases the left mouse button while the cursor is in the window of an application that has registered itself as a recipient of dropped files.
Parameters	
wParam	HANDLE: The internal structure describing the dropped files. This is used by DragFinish(), DragQueryFile(), and DragQueryPoint() to retrieve information about the dropped files.
lParam	LPARAM: Set to zero.
Returns	int: An application should return zero if it processes this message.
Include File	winuser.h
See Also	DragAcceptFiles(), DragFinish(), DragQueryFile(), DragQueryPoint()

WM_ENABLE ■ Win32s ■ Windows 95 ■ Windows NT

Description	WM_ENABLE is a message that is sent when an application changes the enabled state of a window. It is sent to the window whose enabled state is changing before EnableWindow() returns, but after the enabled state (WS_DISABLED style bit) of the window has changed.

Parameters

wParam   BOOL: TRUE if the window has been enabled, or FALSE if the window has been disabled.

lParam   LPARAM: Set to zero.

Returns   int: An application should return zero if it processes this message.

Include File   winuser.h

See Also   EnableWindow()

WM_ENDSESSION ■ Win32s ■ Windows 95 ■ Windows NT

Description   WM_ENDSESSION is a message that notifies an application that the Windows session is ending. It is sent after Windows processes the results of the WM_QUERYENDSESSION message. If *wParam* is TRUE, the Windows session can end any time after all applications have returned from processing this message. Therefore, an application should perform all tasks required for termination before returning from this message.

Parameters

wParam   BOOL: TRUE if the session is ending; otherwise, *wParam* is FALSE.

lParam   BOOL: This parameter is only available for Windows 95. TRUE if the user is logging off the system, or FALSE if the user is shutting down the system.

Returns   int: An application should return zero if it processes this message.

Include File   winuser.h

See Also   DestroyWindow(), PostQuitMessage()

Related Messages WM_QUERYENDSESSION

WM_ENTERIDLE ■ Win32s ■ Windows 95 ■ Windows NT

Description   WM_ENTERIDLE is a message that is sent to the owner window of a modal dialog box or menu that is entering an idle state. A modal dialog box or menu enters an idle state when no messages are waiting in its queue after it has processed one or more previous messages.

Parameters

wParam   WPARAM: One of the values in Table 11-24 indicating whether the message is the result of a dialog box or a menu being displayed.

Table 11-24 WM_ENTERIDLE *wParam* values

Value	Meaning
MSGF_DIALOGBOX	The system is idle because a dialog box is displayed.
MSGF_MENU	The system is idle because a menu is displayed.

lParam	HWND: The handle of the dialog box or owner window.
Returns	int: An application should return zero if it processes this message.
Include File	winuser.h
See Also	DefWindowProc()

WM_ENTERMENULOOP

Win32s ■ Windows 95 ■ Windows NT

Description	WM_ENTERMENULOOP is a message that informs an application's main window procedure that a menu modal loop has been entered.
Parameters	
wParam	BOOL: TRUE if the menu is a pop-up; otherwise, wParam is FALSE.
lParam	LPARAM: Set to zero.
Returns	int: An application should return zero if it processes this message.
Include File	winuser.h
See Also	DefWindowProc()
Related Messages	WM_EXITMENULOOP

WM_ENTERSIZEMOVE

Win32s ■ Windows 95 ■ Windows NT

Description	WM_ENTERSIZEMOVE is a message that is sent once to a window when it enters the moving or sizing mode. The window enters the moving or sizing mode when the user clicks the window's title bar or sizing border, or when the window passes the WM_SYSCOMMAND message to DefWindowProc() and the wParam parameter of the message specifies the SC_MOVE or SC_SIZE value. Windows sends the WM_ENTERSIZEMOVE message regardless of whether the dragging of full windows is enabled.
Parameters	This message does not use wParam or lParam; therefore, both must be set to zero.
Returns	int: An application should return zero if it processes this message.
Include File	winuser.h
See Also	DefWindowProc()
Related Messages	WM_EXITSIZEMOVE, WM_SYSCOMMAND

WM_ERASEBKGND

■ Win32s ■ Windows 95 ■ Windows NT

Description	WM_ERASEBKGND is a message that is sent when the window background must be erased. The message is sent to prepare an invalidated portion of a window for painting.
Parameters	
wParam	HDC: The handle of the device context.

lParam	LPARAM: Set to zero.
Returns	int: A nonzero value if the background is erased; otherwise, zero is returned.
Include File	winuser.h
See Also	BeginPaint(), DefWindowProc()
Related Messages	WM_ICONERASEBKGND

WM_EXITMENULOOP
Win32s ■ Windows 95 ■ Windows NT

Description	WM_EXITMENULOOP is a message that informs an application's main window procedure that a menu modal loop has been exited.
Parameters	
wParam	BOOL: TRUE indicates that a pop-up menu is involved; FALSE indicates it is not a pop-up menu.
lParam	LPARAM: Set to zero.
Returns	int: An application should return zero if it processes this message.
Include File	winuser.h
Related Messages	WM_ENTERMENULOOP

WM_EXITSIZEMOVE
Win32s ■ Windows 95 ■ Windows NT

Description	WM_EXITSIZEMOVE is a message that is sent once to a window after it has exited the moving or sizing mode.
Parameters	This message does not use *wParam* or *lParam*; therefore, both must be set to zero.
Returns	int: An application should return zero if it processes this message.
Include File	winuser.h
Related Messages	WM_ENTERSIZEMOVE

WM_FONTCHANGE
■ Win32s ■ Windows 95 ■ Windows NT

Description	WM_FONTCHANGE is a message that is sent to all top-level windows in the system after changing the pool of font resources.
Parameters	This message does not use *wParam* or *lParam*; therefore, both must be set to zero.
Include File	winuser.h
See Also	AddFontResource(), RemoveFontResource(), SendMessage()

WM_GETDLGCODE

■ Win32s   ■ Windows 95   ■ Windows NT

Description	WM_GETDLGCODE is a message that is sent to the dialog box procedure associated with a control. Normally, Windows handles all arrow-key and TAB-key input to the control. By responding to the WM_GETDLGCODE message, an application can take control of a particular type of input and process the input itself.
Parameters	This message does not use *wParam* or *lParam*; therefore, both must be set to zero.
Returns	int: One or more of the values in Table 11-25, indicating which type of input the application processes.

Table 11-25 WM_GETDLGCODE return values

Value	Meaning
DLGC_BUTTON	Button
DLGC_DEFPUSHBUTTON	Default push button
DLGC_HASSETSEL	EM_SETSEL messages
DLGC_RADIOBUTTON	Radio button
DLGC_STATIC	Static control
DLGC_UNDEFPUSHBUTTON	Nondefault push button
DLGC_WANTALLKEYS	All keyboard input
DLGC_WANTARROWS	Direction keys
DLGC_WANTCHARS	WM_CHAR messages
DLGC_WANTMESSAGE	All keyboard input (the application passes this message on to a control)
DLGC_WANTTAB	TAB key

Include File	winuser.h
See Also	DefWindowProc()
Related Messages	EM_SETSEL, WM_CHAR

WM_GETFONT

■ Win32s   ■ Windows 95   ■ Windows NT

Description	WM_GETFONT is a message that retrieves the font with which the control is currently drawing its text.
Parameters	This message does not use *wParam* or *lParam*; therefore, both must be set to zero.
Returns	HFONT: The handle of the font used by the control is returned, or NULL if the control is using the system font.
Include File	winuser.h
Related Messages	WM_SETFONT

WM_GETHOTKEY

Description	WM_GETHOTKEY is a message that determines the hot key associated with a window.
Parameters	This message does not use *wParam* or *lParam*; therefore, both must be set to zero.
Returns	DWORD: The virtual-key code and modifiers for the hot key, or NULL if no hot key is associated with the window. The virtual-key code is in the low byte of the return value and the modifiers are in the high byte. The modifiers can be a combination of the flags in Table 11-26.

Table 11-26 WM_GETHOTKEY values

Value	Meaning
HOTKEYF_ALT	ALT key
HOTKEYF_CONTROL	CTRL key
HOTKEYF_EXT	Extended key
HOTKEYF_SHIFT	SHIFT key

Include File	winuser.h
See Also	RegisterHotKey()
Related Messages	WM_SETHOTKEY

WM_GETICON

Description	WM_GETICON is a message that is sent to a window to retrieve the handle of the big or small icon associated with a window. Windows retrieves the big icon when drawing a minimized window, and retrieves the small icon when drawing a title bar.
Parameters	
wParam	BOOL: TRUE retrieves the big icon associated with the window; FALSE retrieves the small icon.
lParam	LPARAM: Set to zero.
Returns	HICON: The handle of the big or small icon, based on the value of *wParam*.
Include File	winuser.h
See Also	DefWindowProc()
Related Messages	WM_SETICON

WM_GETMINMAXINFO   ■ Win32s ■ Windows 95 ■ Windows NT

Description	WM_GETMINMAXINFO is a message that is sent to a window when the size or position of the window is about to change. An application can use this message to override the window's default maximized size and position, or its default minimum or maximum tracking size.
Parameters	
wParam	WPARAM: Set to zero.
lParam	LPARAM: A pointer to a MINMAXINFO structure that contains the default maximized position and dimensions, and the default minimum and maximum tracking sizes. An application can override the defaults by setting the members of this structure.
Returns	int: An application should return zero if it processes this message.
Include File	winuser.h
See Also	MoveWindow(), SetWindowPos()

WM_GETTEXT   ■ Win32s ■ Windows 95 ■ Windows NT

Description	WM_GETTEXT is a message that copies the text that corresponds to a window into a buffer provided by the caller.
Parameters	
wParam	WPARAM: The maximum number of characters to be copied, including the terminating null character.
lParam	LPARAM: A pointer to the buffer that receives the text.
Returns	int: The number of characters copied.
Include File	winuser.h
See Also	DefWindowProc(), GetWindowText(), GetWindowTextLength()
Related Messages	LB_GETTEXT, WM_GETTEXTLENGTH, WM_SETTEXT

WM_GETTEXTLENGTH   ■ Win32s ■ Windows 95 ■ Windows NT

Description	WM_GETTEXTLENGTH is a message that determines the length, in characters, of the text associated with a window. The length does not include the terminating null character.
Parameters	This message does not use *wParam* or *lParam*; therefore, both must be set to zero.
Returns	int: The length, in characters, of the text.
Include File	winuser.h
See Also	DefWindowProc(), GetWindowText(), GetWindowTextLength()
Related Messages	CB_GETLBTEXT, LB_GETTEXT, LB_GETTEXTLEN, WM_GETTEXT

WM_HELP

Description	WM_HELP is a message that indicates that the user pressed the F1 key. If a menu is active when F1 is pressed, WM_HELP is sent to the window associated with the menu; otherwise, WM_HELP is sent to the window that has the keyboard focus. If a window does not have the keyboard focus, WM_HELP is sent to the currently active window.
Parameters	
wParam	WPARAM: Set to zero.
lParam	LPHELPINFO: A pointer to a HELPINFO structure containing information about the menu item, dialog box, or window for which help was requested.
Returns	BOOL: TRUE is returned.
Include File	winuser.h
See Also	DefWindowProc()

WM_HOTKEY

Description	WM_HOTKEY is a message that is posted when the user presses a hot key registered by RegisterHotKey(). The message is placed at the top of the message queue associated with the thread that registered the hot key.
Parameters	
wParam	int: The identifier of the hot key that generated the message. If WM_HOTKEY was generated by a system-defined hot key, *wParam* will be one of the values in Table 11-27.

Table 11-27 WM_HOTKEY *wParam* values

Value	Meaning
IDHOT_SNAPDESKTOP	The "snap desktop" hot key was pressed.
IDHOT_SNAPWINDOW	The "snap window" hot key was pressed.

LOWORD(lParam)   UINT: A combination of the values in Table 11-28 indicating the keys that were pressed in combination with the key specified by *HIWORD(lParam)* to generate the WM_HOTKEY message.

Table 11-28 WM_HOTKEY *LOWORD(lParam)* values

Value	Meaning
MOD_ALT	Either ALT key was held down.
MOD_CONTROL	Either CTRL key was held down.

continued on next page

continued from previous page

Value	Meaning
MOD_SHIFT	Either ⌷SHIFT⌷ key was held down.
MOD_WIN	Either Windows key was held down. These keys appear on the Microsoft Natural Keyboard and are labeled with the Microsoft Windows logo.

HIWORD(lParam)	UINT: The virtual-key code of the hot key.
Include File	winuser.h
See Also	RegisterHotKey()
Related Messages	WM_GETHOTKEY, WM_SETHOTKEY

WM_HSCROLL   ■ Win32s   ■ Windows 95   ■ Windows NT

Description	WM_HSCROLL is a message that is sent to a window when a scroll event occurs in the window's standard horizontal scroll bar. This message is also sent to the owner of a horizontal scroll bar control when a scroll event occurs in the control.
Parameters	
LOWORD(wParam)	int: One of the values in Table 11-29 indicating the type of scrolling requested by the user.

Table 11-29 WM_HSCROLL *LOWORD(wParam)* values

Value	Meaning
SB_BOTTOM	Scrolls to the lower right.
SB_ENDSCROLL	Ends the scroll.
SB_LINELEFT	Scrolls left by one unit.
SB_LINERIGHT	Scrolls right by one unit.
SB_PAGELEFT	Scrolls left by the width of the window.
SB_PAGERIGHT	Scrolls right by the width of the window.
SB_THUMBPOSITION	Scrolls to the absolute position of the scroll bar. The current position is specified by *HIWORD(wParam)*.
SB_THUMBTRACK	Drags scroll box to the specified position. The current position is specified by *HIWORD(wParam)*.
SB_TOP	Scrolls to the upper left.

HIWORD(wParam)	short int: The current thumb position of the scroll bar in the window. This parameter is used only when *LOWORD(wParam)* is SB_THUMBPOSITION or SB_THUMBTRACK.
lParam	LPARAM: The control if WM_HSCROLL is sent by a scroll bar control. If WM_HSCROLL is sent by a window's standard scroll bar, *lParam* is not used.

Returns	int: An application should return zero if it processes this message.
Include File	winuser.h
See Also	GetScrollPos(), GetScrollRange(), SetScrollPos(), SetScrollRange()
Related Messages	WM_VSCROLL

WM_HSCROLLCLIPBOARD   ■ Win32s ■ Windows 95 ■ Windows NT

Description   WM_HSCROLLCLIPBOARD is a message that is sent to the clipboard owner by a clipboard viewer window. This occurs when the clipboard contains data in the CF_OWNERDISPLAY format and an event occurs in the clipboard viewer's horizontal scroll bar. The owner should scroll the clipboard image and update the scroll bar values.

Parameters

wParam   HWND: The handle of the clipboard viewer window.

LOWORD(lParam)   int: One of the values in Table 11-30 indicating the type of scroll bar event to occur.

Table 11-30 WM_HSCROLLCLIPBOARD *LOWORD(lParam)* values

Value	Meaning
SB_BOTTOM	Scroll to lower right.
SB_ENDSCROLL	Ends the scroll.
SB_LINEDOWN	Scroll one line down.
SB_LINEUP	Scroll one line up.
SB_PAGEDOWN	Scroll one page down.
SB_PAGEUP	Scroll one page up.
SB_THUMBPOSITION	Scroll to absolute position of the scroll bar. The current position is specified by *HIWORD(lParam)*.
SB_TOP	Scroll to upper left.

HIWORD(lParam)	int: The current position of the scroll box. This parameter is used only if *LOWORD(lParam)* is SB_THUMBPOSITION.
Returns	int: An application should return zero if it processes this message.
Include File	winuser.h
See Also	ScrollWindow()

WM_ICONERASEBKGND   ■ Win32s ■ Windows 95 ■ Windows NT

Description   WM_ICONERASEBKGND is a message that is sent to a minimized window when the background of the icon must be filled before painting the icon. A window receives this message only if a class icon is defined for the window; otherwise, WM_ERASEBKGND is sent.

Parameters	
wParam	HDC: The device context of the icon.
lParam	LPARAM: Set to zero.
Returns	int: An application should return a nonzero value if it processes this message.
Include File	winuser.h
See Also	DefWindowProc()
Related Messages	WM_ERASEBKGND

WM_IME_CHAR   Win32s ■ Windows 95   Windows NT

Description	WM_IME_CHAR is a message that is sent to an application when the IME gets a character of the conversion result. Unlike WM_CHAR, this message can include double-byte as well as single-byte character values. If WM_IME_CHAR contains a double-byte character, DefWindowProc() converts it into two WM_CHAR messages, each containing one byte of the double-byte character.
Parameters	
LOBYTE(wParam)	TCHAR: The single-byte character of the conversion result.
HIBYTE(wParam)	TCHAR: The double-byte character of the conversion result.
lParam	LPARAM: The repeat count, scan code, extended-key flag, context code, previous key-state flag, and transition-state flag, as outlined in Table 11-31.

Table 11-31 WM_IME_CHAR *lParam* values

Value	Meaning
0–15	The repeat count; since the first and second bytes are continuous, this is always 1.
16–23	The scan code for completing an FE character.
24–28	Not used.
29	The context code.
31	The conversion state.

Include File	imm.h
See Also	DefWindowProc()
Related Messages	WM_CHAR

WM_IME_COMPOSITION

Description　WM_IME_COMPOSITION is a message that is sent to an application when the IME changes composition status as a result of a keystroke. An application should process this message if it displays composition characters; otherwise, it should send the message to the IME window.

Parameters

wParam　WORD: The DBCS character representing the latest change to the composition string.

lParam　BOOL: One or more of the values in Table 11-32 indicating how the composition string or character changed.

Table 11-32 WM_IME_COMPOSITION *lParam* values

Value	Meaning
CS_INSERTCHAR	The given composition character should be inserted at the current insertion point. An application should display the composition character if it processes this message.
CS_NOMOVECARET	The application must not move the caret position as a result of processing the message.
GCR_ERRORSTR	Retrieves or updates the error string.
GCR_INFOSTR	Retrieves or updates the information string.
GCS_COMPATTR	Retrieves or updates the attribute of the composition string.
GCS_COMPCLAUSE	Retrieves or updates clause information of the composition string.
GCS_COMPREADATTR	Retrieves or updates the attributes of the reading string of the current composition.
GCS_COMPREADCLAUSE	Retrieves or updates the clause information of the reading string of the composition string.
GCS_COMPREADSTR	Retrieves or updates the reading string of the current composition.
GCS_COMPSTR	Retrieves or updates the current composition string.
GCS_RESULTCLAUSE	Retrieves or updates clause information of the result string.
GCS_RESULTREADCLAUSE	Retrieves or updates clause information of the reading string.
GCS_RESULTREADSTR	Retrieves or updates the reading string.
GCS_RESULTSTR	Retrieves or updates the string of the composition result.
GCS_SETCURSORPOS	Retrieves or updates the cursor position.
GCS_TYPINGINFO	Retrieves or updates the typing information of the reading string.

Include File　imm.h

See Also　DefWindowProc(), ImmGetCompositionString()

WM_IME_COMPOSITIONFULL

Description　WM_IME_COMPOSITIONFULL is a notification message that is sent to an application when the IME window finds no space to extend the area for the composition window.

Parameters	This message does not use *wParam* or *lParam*; therefore, both must be set to zero.
Include File	imm.h
See Also	SendMessage()

WM_IME_CONTROL
Win32s ■ Windows 95 Windows NT

Description WM_IME_CONTROL is a message that directs the IME window to carry out the requested command. An application uses this message to control the IME window created by the application.

Parameters

wParam DWORD: One of the values in Table 11-33 indicating the command value for the IME window.

Table 11-33 WM_IME_CONTROL *wParam* values

Value	Meaning
IMC_CLOSESTATUSWINDOW	Hides the status window. The *lParam* parameter is set to zero. Returns zero if successful; otherwise a nonzero value is returned.
IMC_GETCANDIDATEPOS	Gets the position of the candidate window. The *lParam* parameter is a pointer to the CANDIDATEFORM structure that receives the position of the candidate window. Returns zero if successful; otherwise, a nonzero value is returned.
IMC_GETCOMPOSITIONFONT	Retrieves the logical font used to display intermediate characters in the composition window. The *lParam* parameter is a pointer to the LOGFONT structure that receives information about the logical font. Returns zero if successful; otherwise a nonzero value is returned.
IMC_GETCOMPOSITIONWINDOW	Determines the position of the composition window. The *lParam* parameter is a pointer to the COMPOSITIONFORM structure that receives the position of the composition window. Returns zero if successful; otherwise, a nonzero value is returned.
IMC_GETCONVERSIONMODE	Obtains the current conversion mode of an IME window. The *lParam* parameter is set to zero. Returns a value indicating the current conversion mode.
IMC_GETOPENSTATUS	Determines whether the IME is open. The *lParam* parameter is set to zero. Returns a nonzero value if the current IME is open; otherwise, zero is returned.
IMC_GETSENTENCEMODE	Obtains the current sentence mode of an IME window. The *lParam* parameter is set to zero. Returns a value indicating the current sentence mode.
IMC_GETSTATUSWINDOWPOS	Obtains the position of the status window. The *lParam* parameter is set to zero. Returns a POINTS structure that contains the x and y coordinates of the status window position.
IMC_OPENSTATUSWINDOW	Shows the status window. The *lParam* parameter is set to zero. Returns zero if successful; otherwise, a nonzero value is returned.
IMC_SETCANDIDATEPOS	Sets the position of the candidate window. The *lParam* parameter is a pointer to the CANDIDATE structure that contains the x and y coordinates of the candidate window. Returns zero if successful; otherwise, a nonzero value is returned.

Value	Meaning
IMC_SETCOMPOSITIONFONT	Specifies the logical font to use to display intermediate characters in the composition window. The *lParam* parameter is a pointer to the LOGFONT structure that contains information about the logical font. Returns zero if successful; otherwise, a nonzero value is returned.
IMC_SETCOMPOSITIONWINDOW	Sets the style of the composition window. The *lParam* parameter is a pointer to the COMPOSITIONFORM structure that contains the style information. Returns zero if successful; otherwise, a nonzero value is returned.
IMC_SETCONVERSIONMODE	Sets the current conversion mode of the IME window. The *lParam* parameter specifies the conversion mode. Returns zero if successful; otherwise a nonzero value is returned.
IMC_SETOPENSTATUS	Opens or closes the current IME. The *lParam* parameter is TRUE to open the IME, or FALSE to close the IME. Returns zero if successful; otherwise a nonzero value is returned.
IMC_SETSENTENCEMODE	Sets the current sentence mode of the IME window. The *lParam* parameter specifies the sentence mode. Returns zero if successful; otherwise, a nonzero value is returned.
IMC_SETSTATUSWINDOWPOS	Sets the position of the status window. The *lParam* parameter is a pointer to a POINTS structure that contains the x and y coordinates of the position of the status window. Returns zero if successful; otherwise a nonzero value is returned.

lParam	DWORD: A command-specific value, based on the value of *wParam*. Refer to Table 11-33 for more information.
Returns	A command-specific value, based on the value of *wParam*. Refer to Table 11-33 for more information.
Include File	imm.h

WM_IME_ENDCOMPOSITION   Win32s ■ Windows 95   Windows NT

Description	WM_IME_ENDCOMPOSITION is a message that is sent to an application when the IME ends composition. An application should process this message if it displays composition characters itself.
Parameters	This message does not use *wParam* or *lParam*; therefore, both must be set to zero.
Include File	imm.h
See Also	DefWindowProc()

WM_IME_NOTIFY   Win32s ■ Windows 95   Windows NT

Description	WM_IME_NOTIFY is sent to an application to notify it of changes to the IME window. An application processes this message if it is responsible for managing the IME window.
Parameters	
wParam	DWORD: One of the values in Table 11-34 indicating the command value for the IME window.

Table 11-34 WM_IME_NOTIFY *wParam* values

Value	Meaning
IMN_CHANGECANDIDATE	Indicates that an IME is about to change the contents of the candidate window. The *lParam* parameter indicates the candidate list flag. Bit 0 is the first list, bit 1 the second, etc.; a value of 1 for a specific bit indicates that the corresponding candidate window is changing. No value is returned.
IMN_CLOSECANDIDATE	Indicates that an IME is about to close a candidate window. The *lParam* parameter indicates the candidate list flag. Bit 0 is the first list, bit 1 the second, etc.; a value of 1 for a specific bit indicates that the corresponding candidate window is closing. No value is returned.
IMN_CLOSESTATUSWINDOW	Indicates that an IME is about to close the status window. The *lParam* parameter is not used and a value is not returned.
IMN_GUIDELINE	Indicates that an IME is about to show an error message or other information. The *lParam* parameter is not used and a value is not returned.
IMN_OPENCANDIDATE	Indicates that an IME is about to open the candidate window. The *lParam* parameter indicates the candidate list flag. Bit 0 is the first list, bit 1 the second, etc.; a value of 1 for a specific bit indicates that the corresponding candidate window is opening. No value is returned.
IMN_OPENSTATUSWINDOW	Indicates that an IME is about to create the status window. The *lParam* parameter is not used and a value is not returned.
IMN_PRIVATE	A private notification message.
IMN_SETCANDIDATEPOS	Indicates that the IME is about to move the candidate window. The *lParam* parameter indicates the candidate list flag. Bit 0 is the first list, bit 1 the second, etc.; a value of 1 for a specific bit indicates that the corresponding candidate window is moving. No value is returned.
IMN_SETCOMPOSITIONFONT	Indicates that the font of the input context is being updated. The *lParam* parameter is not used and a value is not returned.
IMN_SETCOMPOSITIONWINDOW	Indicates that the style or position of the composition window is being updated. The *lParam* parameter is not used and a value is not returned.
IMN_SETCONVERSIONMODE	Indicates that the conversion mode of the input context is being updated. The *lParam* parameter is not used and a value is not returned.
IMN_SETOPENSTATUS	Indicates that the open status of the input context is being updated. The *lParam* parameter is not used and a value is not returned.
IMN_SETSENTENCEMODE	Indicates that the sentence mode of the input context is being updated. The *lParam* parameter is not used and a value is not returned.
IMN_SETSTATUSWINDOWPOS	Indicates that the status window position in the input context is being updated. The *lParam* parameter is not used and a value is not returned.

lParam	DWORD: A command-specific value, based on the value of *wParam*. Refer to Table 11-34 for more information.
Returns	A command-specific value, based on the value of *wParam*. Refer to Table 11-34 for more information.
Include File	imm.h

WM_IME_SELECT

Win32s ■ Windows 95   Windows NT

Description	WM_IME_SELECT is a message that is sent to an application when the system is about to change the current IME. An application that has created an IME window should pass this message to that window so that it can retrieve the keyboard layout handle for the newly selected IME.
Parameters	
wParam	BOOL: TRUE if the specified IME is selected; FALSE if the specified IME is no longer selected.
lParam	HANDLE: The handle of the keyboard layout associated with the specified IME.
Include File	imm.h
See Also	DefWindowProc()

WM_IME_SETCONTEXT

Win32s ■ Windows 95   Windows NT

Description	WM_IME_SETCONTEXT is a message that is sent to an application when a window is activated. If the application has created an IME window, it should call ImmIsUIMessage(); otherwise, it should pass this message to DefWindowProc().
Parameters	
wParam	BOOL: TRUE if the input context is active; otherwise, FALSE, indicating the context is inactive.
lParam	DWORD: A combination of the values in Table 11-35 indicating the displayed windows.

Table 11-35 WM_IME_SETCONTEXT *lParam* values

Value	Meaning
ISC_SHOWUICANDIDATEWINDOW	Shows the candidate window of Index 0 by UI window.
ISC_SHOWUICANDIDATEWINDOW << 1	Shows the candidate window of Index 1 by UI window.
ISC_SHOWUICANDIDATEWINDOW << 2	Shows the candidate window of Index 2 by UI window.
ISC_SHOWUICANDIDATEWINDOW << 3	Shows the candidate window of Index 3 by UI window.
ISC_SHOWUICOMPOSITIONWINDOW	Shows the composition window by UI window.
ISC_SHOWUIGUIDWINDOW	Shows the guide window by UI window.
ISC_SHOWUISOFTKBD	Shows the soft keyboard by UI window.

Returns	int: An application should return zero if it processes this message.
Include File	imm.h
See Also	DefWindowProc(), ImmIsUIMessage()

WM_IME_STARTCOMPOSITION

Win32s ■ Windows 95   Windows NT

Description	WM_IME_STARTCOMPOSITION is a message that is sent immediately before the IME generates a composition string as a result of a keystroke. The message is a notification to an IME window to open its composition window. An application should process this message if it displays composition characters.
Parameters	This message does not use *wParam* or *lParam*; therefore, both must be set to zero.
Include File	imm.h
See Also	DefWindowProc()

WM_INITDIALOG

■ Win32s   ■ Windows 95   ■ Windows NT

Description   WM_INITDIALOG is a message that is sent to the dialog box procedure immediately before a dialog box is displayed. Normally, dialog box procedures use WM_INITDIALOG to initialize controls and perform any other initialization tasks that affect the appearance of the dialog box.

Parameters

wParam   HWND: The handle of the control that receives the default keyboard focus. This parameter is only assigned if the dialog procedure returns TRUE.

lParam   LPARAM: Additional initialization data that is passed in a call to CreateDialogIndirectParam(), CreateDialogParam(), DialogBoxIndirectParam(), or DialogBoxParam() to create the dialog box. If another dialog box creation function is used, *lParam* is zero.

Returns   BOOL: To set keyboard focus to the control specified by *wParam*, TRUE is returned; otherwise, FALSE is returned to prevent setting the keyboard focus.

Include File   winuser.h

See Also   CreateDialogIndirectParam(), CreateDialogParam(), DialogBoxIndirectParam(), DialogBoxParam(), SetFocus()

WM_INITMENU

■ Win32s   ■ Windows 95   ■ Windows NT

Description   WM_INITMENU is a message that is sent when a menu is about to become active, due to the user selecting an item on the menu bar or pressing a menu key. This message allows the application to modify the menu before it is displayed.

Parameters

wParam   HMENU: The handle of the menu that is going to be initialized.

lParam	LPARAM: Set to zero.
Returns	int: An application should return zero if it processes this message.
Include File	winuser.h
Related Messages	WM_INITMENUPOPUP

WM_INITMENUPOPUP ■ Win32s ■ Windows 95 ■ Windows NT

Description	WM_INITMENUPOPUP is a message that is sent when a pop-up menu is about to become active. This allows an application to modify the pop-up menu before it is displayed, without changing the entire menu.
Parameters	
wParam	HMENU: The handle of the pop-up menu.
LOWORD(lParam)	UINT: The zero-based relative position of the menu item that invokes the specified pop-up menu.
HIWORD(lParam)	BOOL: TRUE if the pop-up menu is a System menu (Control menu); otherwise, this parameter is FALSE.
Returns	int: An application should return zero if it processes this message.
Include File	winuser.h
Related Messages	WM_INITMENU

WM_INPUTLANGCHANGE Win32s ■ Windows 95 Windows NT

Description	WM_INPUTLANGCHANGE is a message that is sent to the topmost affected window after a task's locale has been changed. An application should make any application-specific settings and then allow DefWindowProc() to pass the message on to any children.
Parameters	
wParam	WPARAM: The character set of the new keyboard layout.
lParam	HKL: The new keyboard layout identifier.
Returns	int: An application should return a nonzero value if it processes this message.
Include File	winuser.h
See Also	DefWindowProc()
Related Messages	WM_INPUTLANGCHANGEREQUEST

WM_INPUTLANGCHANGEREQUEST

Win32s ■ Windows 95 Windows NT

Description	WM_INPUTLANGCHANGEREQUEST is a message that is sent when the user selects an input language, either with an input language change hot

key or from the system languages menu. An application can accept the change by passing the message to DefWindowProc() or prevent the change by returning immediately.

Parameters	
wParam	BOOL: TRUE if the handle of the keyboard layout can be used with the system character set; otherwise this parameter is FALSE.
lParam	HKL: The keyboard layout to switch to.
Returns	int: An application should return a nonzero value if it processes this message; otherwise, zero is returned to reject the change.
Include File	winuser.h
See Also	DefWindowProc()
Related Messages	WM_INPUTLANGCHANGE

WM_KEYDOWN ■ Win32s ■ Windows 95 ■ Windows NT

Description	WM_KEYDOWN is a message that is posted to the window with the keyboard focus when a nonsystem key is pressed. A nonsystem key is a key that is pressed when the ⟨ALT⟩ key is not pressed. Because of the autorepeat feature, more than one WM_KEYDOWN message can be posted before a WM_KEYUP message is posted. The previous key state value (bit 30) of *lParam* indicates whether the WM_KEYDOWN message is the first down transition or a repeated down transition.
Parameters	
wParam	int: The virtual-key code of the nonsystem key.
lParam	LPARAM: The repeat count, scan code, extended-key flag, context code, previous key-state flag, and transition-state flag, as shown in the Table 11-36.

Table 11-36 WM_KEYDOWN *lParam* values

Value	Meaning
0–15	The repeat count. The value is the number of times the keystroke is repeated as a result of the user holding down the key.
16–23	The scan code. The value depends on the original equipment manufacturer (OEM).
24	Specifies whether the key is an extended key, such as the right-hand ⟨ALT⟩ and ⟨CTRL⟩ keys that appear on an enhanced 101- or 102-key keyboard. The value is 1 if it is an extended key; otherwise, it is 0.
25–28	Reserved; do not use.
29	The context code. The value is always 0 for WM_KEYDOWN.
30	The previous key state. The value is 1 if the key is down before the message is sent, or it is 0 if the key is up.
31	The transition state. The value is always 0 for WM_KEYDOWN.

Returns	int: An application should return zero if it processes this message.
Include File	winuser.h
See Also	DefWindowProc()
Related Messages	WM_CHAR, WM_KEYUP, WM_SYSCOMMAND

WM_KEYUP ■ Win32s ■ Windows 95 ■ Windows NT

Description	WM_KEYUP is a message that is posted to the window with the keyboard focus when a nonsystem key is released. A nonsystem key is a key that is pressed when the [ALT] key is not pressed, or a keyboard key that is pressed when a window has the keyboard focus.
Parameters	
wParam	int: The virtual-key code of the nonsystem key.
lParam	LPARAM: The repeat count, scan code, extended-key flag, context code, previous key-state flag, and transition-state flag, as shown in the Table 11-37.

Table 11-37 WM_KEYUP *lParam* values

Value	Meaning
0–15	The repeat count. The value is the number of times the keystroke is repeated as a result of the user holding down the key. The repeat count is always 1 for WM_KEYUP.
16–23	The scan code. The value depends on the original equipment manufacturer (OEM).
24	Specifies whether the key is an extended key, such as the right-hand [ALT] and [CTRL] keys that appear on an enhanced 101- or 102-key keyboard. The value is 1 if it is an extended key; otherwise, it is 0.
25–28	Reserved; do not use.
29	The context code. The value is always 0 for WM_KEYUP.
30	The previous key state. The value is always 1 for WM_KEYUP.
31	The transition state. The value is always 1 for WM_KEYUP.

Returns	int: An application should return zero if it processes this message.
Include File	winuser.h
See Also	DefWindowProc()
Related Messages	WM_KEYDOWN, WM_SYSCOMMAND

WM_KILLFOCUS ■ Win32s ■ Windows 95 ■ Windows NT

Description	WM_KILLFOCUS is a message that is sent to a window immediately before it loses the keyboard focus. If an application is displaying a caret, the caret should be destroyed at this point.

Parameters

wParam	HWND: The handle of the window that receives the keyboard focus. The value of this parameter may be NULL.
lParam	LPARAM: Set to zero.
Returns	int: An application should return zero if it processes this message.
Include File	winuser.h
See Also	SetFocus()
Related Messages	WM_SETFOCUS

WM_LBUTTONDBLCLK ■ Win32s   ■ Windows 95   ■ Windows NT

Description	WM_LBUTTONDBLCLK is a message that is posted when the user double-clicks the left mouse button while the cursor is in the client area of a window. If the mouse is not captured, the message is posted to the window beneath the cursor; otherwise, the message is posted to the window that has captured the mouse.

Parameters

wParam	WPARAM: A combination of the values in Table 11-38 indicating which virtual keys are down.

Table 11-38 WM_LBUTTONDBLCLK *wParam* values

Value	Meaning
MK_CONTROL	The CTRL key is down.
MK_LBUTTON	The left mouse button is down.
MK_MBUTTON	The middle mouse button is down.
MK_RBUTTON	The right mouse button is down.
MK_SHIFT	The SHIFT key is down.

LOWORD(lParam)	WORD: The x coordinate of the cursor relative to the upper left corner of the client area.
HIWORD(lParam)	WORD: The y coordinate of the cursor relative to the upper left corner of the client area.
Returns	int: An application should return zero if it processes this message.
Include File	winuser.h
See Also	GetCapture(), GetDoubleClickTime(), SetCapture(), SetDoubleClickTime()
Related Messages	WM_LBUTTONDOWN, WM_LBUTTONUP

WM_LBUTTONDOWN
■ Win32s ■ Windows 95 ■ Windows NT

Description	WM_LBUTTONDOWN is a message that is posted when the user presses the left mouse button while the cursor is in the client area of a window. If the mouse is not captured, the message is posted to the window beneath the cursor; otherwise, the message is posted to the window that has captured the mouse.
Parameters	
wParam	WPARAM: Indicates which virtual keys are down. This parameter can be any combination of the values in Table 11-38.
LOWORD(lParam)	WORD: The x coordinate of the cursor relative to the upper left corner of the client area.
HIWORD(lParam)	WORD: The y coordinate of the cursor relative to the upper left corner of the client area.
Returns	int: An application should return zero if it processes this message.
Include File	winuser.h
See Also	GetCapture(), SetCapture()
Related Messages	WM_LBUTTONDBLCLK, WM_LBUTTONUP

WM_LBUTTONUP
■ Win32s ■ Windows 95 ■ Windows NT

Description	WM_LBUTTONUP is a message that is posted when the user releases the left mouse button while the cursor is in the client area of a window. If the mouse is not captured, the message is posted to the window beneath the cursor; otherwise, the message is posted to the window that has captured the mouse.
Parameters	
wParam	WPARAM: Indicates which virtual keys are down. This parameter can be any combination of the values in Table 11-38.
LOWORD(lParam)	WORD: The x coordinate of the cursor relative to the upper left corner of the client area.
HIWORD(lParam)	WORD: The y coordinate of the cursor relative to the upper left corner of the client area.
Returns	int: An application should return zero if it processes this message.
Include File	winuser.h
See Also	GetCapture(), SetCapture()
Related Messages	WM_LBUTTONDBLCLK, WM_LBUTTONDOWN

WM_MBUTTONDBLCLK   ■ Win32s   ■ Windows 95   ■ Windows NT

Description WM_MBUTTONDBLCLK is a message that is posted when the user double-clicks the middle mouse button while the cursor is in the client area of a window. If the mouse is not captured, the message is posted to the window beneath the cursor; otherwise, the message is posted to the window that has captured the mouse.

Parameters

wParam WPARAM: Indicates which virtual keys are down. This parameter can be any combination of the values in Table 11-38.

LOWORD(lParam) WORD: The x coordinate of the cursor relative to the upper left corner of the client area.

HIWORD(lParam) WORD: The y coordinate of the cursor relative to the upper left corner of the client area.

Returns int: An application should return zero if it processes this message.

Include File winuser.h

See Also GetCapture(), GetDoubleClickTime(),SetCapture(), SetDoubleClickTime()

Related Messages WM_MBUTTONDOWN, WM_MBUTTONUP

WM_MBUTTONDOWN   ■ Win32s   ■ Windows 95   ■ Windows NT

Description WM_MBUTTONDOWN is a message that is posted when the user presses the middle mouse button while the cursor is in the client area of a window. If the mouse is not captured, the message is posted to the window beneath the cursor; otherwise, the message is posted to the window that has captured the mouse.

Parameters

wParam WPARAM: Indicates which virtual keys are down. This parameter can be any combination of the values in Table 11-38.

LOWORD(lParam) WORD: The x coordinate of the cursor relative to the upper left corner of the client area.

HIWORD(lParam) WORD: The y coordinate of the cursor relative to the upper left corner of the client area.

Returns int: An application should return zero if it processes this message.

Include File winuser.h

See Also GetCapture(), SetCapture()

Related Messages WM_MBUTTONDBLCLK, WM_MBUTTONUP

WM_MBUTTONUP   ■ Win32s   ■ Windows 95   ■ Windows NT

Description	WM_MBUTTONUP is a message that is posted when the user releases the middle mouse button while the cursor is in the client area of the window. If the mouse is not captured, the message is posted to the window beneath the cursor; otherwise, the message is posted to the window that captured the mouse.

Parameters

wParam	WPARAM: Indicates which virtual keys are down. This parameter can be any combination of the values in Table 11-38.
LOWORD(lParam)	WORD: The x coordinate of the cursor relative to the upper left corner of the client area.
HIWORD(lParam)	WORD: The y coordinate of the cursor relative to the upper left corner of the client area.
Returns	int: An application should return zero if it processes this message.
Include File	winuser.h
See Also	GetCapture(), SetCapture()
Related Messages	WM_MBUTTONDBLCLK, WM_MBUTTONDOWN

WM_MDIACTIVATE   ■ Win32s   ■ Windows 95   ■ Windows NT

Description	WM_MDIACTIVATE is a message that is sent to an MDI client window to instruct the client window to activate a different MDI child window. The client window processes this message and sends it to both the child window being deactivated and to the child window being activated.

Parameters Sent to MDI Client Window

wParam	HWND: The child window to be activated.
lParam	LPARAM: Set to zero.

Parameters Sent to MDI Child Window

wParam	HWND: The child window to be deactivated.
lParam	HWND: The child window to be activated.
Returns	int: If the message is sent to the MDI client window, zero is returned. An MDI window returns zero if it processes the message.
Include File	winuser.h
Related Messages	WM_MDIGETACTIVE, WM_MDINEXT, WM_NCACTIVATE

WM_MDICASCADE   ■ Win32s   ■ Windows 95   ■ Windows NT

Description	WM_MDICASCADE is a message that is sent to an MDI client window to arrange all its child windows in a cascade format.

Parameters

wParam	UINT: A cascade flag. The only flag currently available, MDITILE_SKIPDISABLED, prevents a disabled MDI child window from being cascaded.
lParam	LPARAM: Set to zero.
Returns	BOOL: If successful, TRUE is returned; otherwise, FALSE is returned.
Include File	winuser.h
Related Messages	WM_MDIICONARRANGE, WM_MDITILE

WM_MDICREATE ■ Win32s ■ Windows 95 ■ Windows NT

Description	WM_MDICREATE is a message that is sent to an MDI client window to create an MDI child window.

Parameters

wParam	WPARAM: Set to zero.
lParam	LPMDICREATESTRUCT: A pointer to an MDICREATESTRUCT structure containing information used to create the MDI window.
Returns	HWND: If successful, the handle of the new child window is returned; otherwise, a NULL value is returned.
Include File	winuser.h
See Also	CreateMDIWindow()
Related Messages	WM_CREATE, WM_MDIDESTROY

WM_MDIDESTROY ■ Win32s ■ Windows 95 ■ Windows NT

Description	WM_MDIDESTROY is a message that is sent to an MDI client window to close an MDI child window. WM_MDIDESTROY removes the title of the MDI child window from the MDI frame window and deactivates the child window. An application should use this message to close all MDI child windows.

Parameters

wParam	HWND: The handle of the MDI child window to close.
lParam	LPARAM: Set to zero.
Returns	int: Zero is always returned.
Include File	winuser.h
Related Messages	WM_MDICREATE

WM_MDIGETACTIVE
■ Win32s ■ Windows 95 ■ Windows NT

Description
WM_MDIGETACTIVE is a message that is sent to an MDI client window to retrieve the handle of the active MDI child window.

Parameters

wParam
WPARAM: Set to zero.

lParam
LPBOOL: An optional pointer to a maximized state flag variable. If *lParam* is a non-NULL value, it points to a BOOL variable that indicates the maximized state of the MDI child window. If the BOOL variable is TRUE, it indicates that the window is maximized; otherwise, FALSE indicates it is not maximized. If *lParam* is NULL, it is ignored.

Returns
HWND: The handle of active MDI child window is returned.

Include File
winuser.h

WM_MDIICONARRANGE
■ Win32s ■ Windows 95 ■ Windows NT

Description
WM_MDIICONARRANGE is a message that is sent to an MDI client window to arrange all minimized MDI child windows. It does not affect child windows that are not minimized.

Parameters
This message does not use *wParam* or *lParam*; therefore, both must be set to zero.

Include File
winuser.h

Related Messages
WM_MDICASCADE, WM_MDITILE

WM_MDIMAXIMIZE
■ Win32s ■ Windows 95 ■ Windows NT

Description
WM_MDIMAXIMIZE is a message that is sent to an MDI client window to maximize an MDI child window. Windows resizes the child window to make its client area fill the client window. Windows places the child window's System menu icon in the rightmost position of the frame window's menu bar, and places the child window's restore icon in the leftmost position. Windows also appends the title bar text of the child window to that of the frame window.

Parameters

wParam
HWND: The handle of the MDI child window to maximize.

lParam
LPARAM: Set to zero.

Returns
int: Zero is always returned.

Include File
winuser.h

Related Messages
WM_MDIRESTORE

WM_MDINEXT ■ Win32s ■ Windows 95 ■ Windows NT

Description	WM_MDINEXT is a message that is sent to an MDI client window to activate either the next or previous child window.
Parameters	
wParam	HWND: The current MDI child window. The child window that is immediately before or after the given child window is activated, based on the value of *lParam*. If *wParam* is NULL, child window that is immediately before or after the currently active child window is activated.
lParam	LPARAM: If *lParam* is zero, the next MDI window is activated and the child window identified by *wParam* is placed behind all other child windows. If *lParam* is a nonzero value, the previous child window is activated and placed in front of the child window identified by *wParam*.
Returns	int: Zero is always returned.
Include File	winuser.h
Related Messages	WM_MDIACTIVATE, WM_MDIGETACTIVE

WM_MDIREFRESHMENU ■ Win32s ■ Windows 95 ■ Windows NT

Description	WM_MDIREFRESHMENU is a message that is sent to an MDI client window to refresh the Window menu of the MDI frame window.
Parameters	This message does not use *wParam* or *lParam*; therefore, both must be set to zero.
Returns	HMENU: If successful, the handle of the frame window menu is returned; otherwise, NULL is returned.
Include File	winuser.h
See Also	DrawMenuBar()
Related Messages	WM_MDISETMENU

WM_MDIRESTORE ■ Win32s ■ Windows 95 ■ Windows NT

Description	WM_MDIRESTORE is a message that is sent to an MDI client window to restore an MDI child window from maximized or minimized size.
Parameters	
wParam	HWND: The handle of the MDI child window to restore.
lParam	LPARAM: Set to zero.
Returns	int: Zero is always returned.
Include File	winuser.h
Related Messages	WM_MDIMAXIMIZE

WM_MDISETMENU

■ Win32s ■ Windows 95 ■ Windows NT

Description	WM_MDISETMENU is a message that is sent to an MDI client window to replace the entire menu of an MDI frame window, to replace the Window menu of the frame window, or both.
Parameters	
wParam	HMENU: The new frame window menu. If *wParam* is NULL, the frame window menu is not changed.
lParam	HMENU: The new Window menu. If *lParam* is NULL, the Window menu is not changed.
Returns	HMENU: If successful, the handle of the old frame window is returned; otherwise, zero is returned.
Include File	winuser.h
See Also	DrawMenuBar()
Related Messages	WM_MDIREFRESHMENU

WM_MDITILE

■ Win32s ■ Windows 95 ■ Windows NT

Description	WM_MDITILE is a message that is sent to an MDI client window to arrange all of its MDI child windows in a tile format.
Parameters	
wParam	UINT: One of the values in Table 11-39 indicating how to tile the MDI child windows.

Table 11-39 WM_MDITILE *wParam* values

Value	Meaning
MDITILE_HORIZONTAL	Tiles MDI child windows so that they are wide rather than tall.
MDITILE_SKIPDISABLED	Prevents disabled MDI child windows from being tiled.
MDITILE_VERTICAL	Tiles MDI child windows so that they are tall rather than wide.

lParam	LPARAM: Set to zero.
Returns	BOOL: If successful, TRUE is returned; otherwise, FALSE is returned.
Include File	winuser.h
Related Messages	WM_MDICASCADE, WM_MDIICONARRANGE

WM_MEASUREITEM

■ Win32s ■ Windows 95 ■ Windows NT

Description	WM_MEASUREITEM is a message that is sent to the owner window of an owner-drawn button, combo box, list box, or menu item when the control or menu is created to obtain the dimensions.

Parameters

wParam	UINT: The value from the *CtlID* member of the MEASUREITEMSTRUCT structure pointed to by *lParam*. This value identifies the control that sent WM_MEASUREITEM. If *wParam* is zero, the message was sent by a menu. If it is a nonzero value, the message was sent by a combo box or by a list box. If it is nonzero value, and the value of the *itemID* member of the MEASUREITEMSTRUCT pointed to by *lParam* is (UINT) -1, the message was sent by a combo edit field.
lParam	LPMEASUREITEMSTRUCT: A pointer to a MEASUREITEMSTRUCT structure that contains the dimensions of the owner-drawn control or menu item.
Returns	BOOL: An application should return TRUE if it processes this message.
Include File	winuser.h
Related Messages	WM_INITDIALOG

WM_MENUCHAR ■ Win32s ■ Windows 95 ■ Windows NT

Description	WM_MENUCHAR is a message that is sent when a menu is active and the user presses a key that does not correspond to any mnemonic or accelerator key. This message is sent to the window that owns the menu.

Parameters

LOWORD(wParam)	char: The ASCII character that corresponds to the key pressed by the user.
HIWORD(wParam)	UINT: One of the values in Table 11-40 indicating the active menu type.

Table 11-40 WM_MENUCHAR *HIWORD(wParam)* values

Value	Meaning
MF_POPUP	Pop-up menu
MF_SYSMENU	System menu

lParam	HMENU: The handle of the active menu.
Returns	DWORD: One of the values in Table 11-41 is returned in the high-order word value.

Table 11-41 WM_MENUCHAR return values

Value	Meaning
0	Discard the character the user pressed and create a short beep on the system speaker. The low-order word value is ignored.
1	Close the active menu. The low-order word value is ignored.

Value	Meaning
2	The low-order word of the return value specifies the zero-based relative position of a menu item. This item is selected by Windows.

Include File   winuser.h

WM_MENUSELECT   ■ Win32s   ■ Windows 95   ■ Windows NT

Description   WM_MENUSELECT is a message that is sent to a menu's owner window when the user selects a menu item.

Parameters

LOWORD(wParam)   UINT: If the user selected a command item, *LOWORD(wParam)* identifies the menu item. If the selected item invokes a pop-up menu, *LOWORD(wParam)* contains the menu index of the pop-up menu in the main menu, and *lParam* contains the handle of the main menu; use GetSubMenu() to get the menu handle of the pop-up menu.

HIWORD(wParam)   UINT: A combination of the values in Table 11-42 indicating the status of the menu item. If *HIWORD(wParam)* contains 0xFFFF and *lParam* contains NULL, Windows has closed the menu because the user pressed the ESC key or clicked outside the menu.

Table 11-42 WM_MENUSELECT *HIWORD(wParam)* values

Value	Meaning
MF_BITMAP	Item displays a bitmap.
MF_CHECKED	Item is checked.
MF_DISABLED	Item is disabled.
MF_GRAYED	Item is grayed.
MF_HILITE	Item is highlighted.
MF_MOUSESELECT	Item is selected with the mouse.
MF_OWNERDRAW	Item is an owner-drawn item.
MF_POPUP	Item invokes a pop-up menu.
MF_SYSMENU	Item is contained in the System menu and *lParam* identifies the System menu associated with the message.

lParam   HMENU: The handle of the selected menu.
Returns   int: An application should return zero if it processes this message.
Include File   winuser.h
See Also   GetSubMenu()

WM_MOUSEACTIVATE　　■ Win32s　■ Windows 95　■ Windows NT

Description　　WM_MOUSEACTIVATE is a message that is sent when the cursor is in an inactive window and the user presses a mouse button. The parent window receives this message only if the child window passes it to DefWindowProc().

Parameters

wParam　　HWND: The handle of the top-level parent window of the window to activate.

LOWORD(lParam)　　int: The hit-test value returned by DefWindowProc() as a result of processing the WM_NCHITTEST message.

HIWORD(lParam)　　UINT: The identifier of the mouse message generated when the user pressed a mouse button. The mouse message is either discarded or posted to the window, depending on the message return value.

Returns　　int: One of the values in Table 11-43, indicating whether the window should be activated and if the identifier of the mouse message should be discarded.

Table 11-43　WM_MOUSEACTIVATE return values

Value	Meaning
MA_ACTIVATE	Activates the window and does not discard the mouse message.
MA_ACTIVATEANDEAT	Activates the window and discards the mouse message.
MA_NOACTIVATE	Does not activate the window and does not discard the mouse message.
MA_NOACTIVATEANDEAT	Does not activate the window, but discards the mouse message.

Include File　　winuser.h

See Also　　DefWindowProc()

Related Messages　　WM_NCHITTEST

WM_MOUSEMOVE　　■ Win32s　■ Windows 95　■ Windows NT

Description　　WM_MOUSEMOVE is a message that is posted to a window when the cursor moves. If the mouse is not captured, the message is posted to the window that contains the cursor; otherwise, the message is posted to the window that captured the mouse.

Parameters

wParam　　WPARAM: Any combination of the values in Table 11-38 indicating which virtual keys are down.

LOWORD(lParam)　　WORD: The x coordinate of the cursor relative to the upper left corner of the client area.

HIWORD(lParam)   WORD: The y coordinate of the cursor relative to the upper left corner of
                  the client area.
Include File winuser.h
See Also   GetCapture(), SetCapture()

WM_MOVE   ■ Win32s   ■ Windows 95   ■ Windows NT

Description   WM_MOVE is a message that is sent after a window has been moved.
Parameters
wParam   WPARAM: Set to zero.
LOWORD(lParam)   WORD: The x coordinate of the upper left corner of the client area of the
                  window. This parameter is in screen coordinates for overlapped and
                  pop-up windows, and parent-child coordinates for child windows.
HIWORD(lParam)   WORD: The y coordinate of the upper left corner of the client area of the
                  window. This parameter is in screen coordinates for overlapped and pop-
                  up windows, and parent-child coordinates for child windows.
Returns   int: An application should return zero if it processes this message.
Include File winuser.h

WM_MOVING   Win32s   ■ Windows 95   Windows NT

Description   WM_MOVING is a message that is sent to a window that the user is moving.
                  By processing this message, an application can monitor the size and position
                  of the drag rectangle and, if needed, change its size or position.

Parameters
wParam   WPARAM: A combination of the values in Table 11-44 specifying the edge
                  of the window being moved.

Table 11-44 WM_MOVING *wParam* values

Value	Meaning
WMSZ_BOTTOM	Bottom edge
WMSZ_BOTTOMLEFT	Bottom left corner
WMSZ_BOTTOMRIGHT	Bottom right corner
WMSZ_LEFT	Left edge
WMSZ_RIGHT	Right edge
WMSZ_TOP	Top edge
WMSZ_TOPLEFT	Top left corner
WMSZ_TOPRIGHT	Top right corner

lParam	LPRECT: The address of a RECT structure with the screen coordinates of the drag rectangle. To change the size or position of the drag rectangle, an application must change the members of the RECT structure.
Returns	BOOL: An application should return TRUE if it processes this message.
Include File	winuser.h
Related Messages	WM_MOVE, WM_SIZING

WM_NCACTIVATE ■ Win32s ■ Windows 95 ■ Windows NT

Description	WM_NCACTIVATE is a message that is sent to a window when its non-client area needs to be changed to indicate an active or inactive state.
Parameters	
wParam	BOOL: TRUE indicates that an active title bar or icon should be drawn; FALSE indicates that an inactive title bar or icon should be drawn.
lParam	LPARAM: Set to zero.
Returns	BOOL: If *wParam* is FALSE, indicating Windows should proceed with default processing, TRUE is returned; otherwise, if *wParam* is TRUE, the value returned is ignored.
Include File	winuser.h
See Also	DefWindowProc()

WM_NCCALCSIZE ■ Win32s ■ Windows 95 ■ Windows NT

Description	WM_NCCALCSIZE is a message that is sent when the size and position of a window's client area must be calculated. By processing this message, an application can control the content of the window's client area when the size or position of the window changes.
Parameters	
wParam	BOOL: TRUE specifies that the application should indicate the part of the client area that contains valid information so the system can copy the information to the specified area in the new client area. Also, TRUE indicates that the data type of *lParam* is LPNCCALCSIZE_PARAMS. FALSE indicates that the application does not need to indicate the valid part of the client area and that the data type of *lParam* is LPRECT.
lParam	LPNCCALCSIZE_PARAMS: If *wParam* is TRUE, a pointer to an NCCALCSIZE_PARAMS structure containing information that an application can use to calculate the new size and position of the client rectangle. LPRECT: If *wParam* is FALSE, a pointer to a RECT structure containing the new coordinates of the window that has moved or been resized.
Returns	int: An application should return zero if *wParam* is FALSE. If *wParam* is TRUE, the application either returns zero or a combination of the values in Table 11-45.

Table 11-45 WM_NCCALCSIZE return values

Value	Meaning
WVR_ALIGNBOTTOM, WVR_ALIGNLEFT, WVR_ALIGNRIGHT, WVR_ALIGNTOP	These values, used in combination, specify that the client area of the window is to be preserved and aligned appropriately relative to the new position of the window.
WVR_HREDRAW, WVR_VREDRAW	These values, used in combination with any other values, cause the window to be completely redrawn if the client rectangle changes size horizontally or vertically.
WVR_REDRAW	This value causes the entire window to be redrawn. It is a combination of WVR_HREDRAW and WVR_VREDRAW values.
WVR_VALIDRECTS	This value indicates that, upon return from WM_NCCALCSIZE, the rectangles specified by the *rgrc[1]* and *rgrc[2]* members of the NCCALCSIZE_PARAMS structure contain valid source and destination area rectangles, respectively. Windows combines these rectangles to calculate the area of the window to be preserved. Windows copies any part of the window image that is within the source rectangle and clips the image to the destination rectangle. Both rectangles are in parent-relative or screen-relative coordinates. This return value allows an application to implement more elaborate client-area preservation strategies, such as centering or preserving a subset of the client area.

Include File	winuser.h
See Also	DefWindowProc(), MoveWindow(), SetWindowPos()

WM_NCCREATE ■ Win32s ■ Windows 95 ■ Windows NT

Description	WM_NCCREATE is a message that is sent when a window is initially created prior to the WM_CREATE message.
Parameters	
wParam	WPARAM: Set to zero.
lParam	LPCREATESTRUCT: A pointer to the CREATESTRUCT structure of the window.
Returns	BOOL: TRUE is returned to continue the window creation; otherwise FALSE is returned and CreateWindow() or CreateWindowEx() returns a NULL handle.
Include File	winuser.h
See Also	CreateWindow(), CreateWindowEx(), DefWindowProc()

WM_NCDESTROY ■ Win32s ■ Windows 95 ■ Windows NT

Description	WM_NCDESTROY is a message that informs a window that its nonclient area is being destroyed. DestroyWindow() sends WM_NCDESTROY to the window following the WM_DESTROY message. WM_DESTROY is used to free the allocated memory object associated with the window.

Parameters	This message does not use *wParam* or *lParam*; therefore, both must be set to zero.
Returns	int: If an application processes this message, it should return zero.
Include File	winuser.h
See Also	DestroyWindow()
Related Messages	WM_DESTROY, WM_NCCREATE

WM_NCHITTEST ■ Win32s ■ Windows 95 ■ Windows NT

Description	WM_NCHITTEST is a message that is sent to a window when the cursor moves, or when a mouse button is pressed or released. If the mouse is not captured, the message is sent to the window beneath the cursor; otherwise, the message is posted to the window that captured the mouse.
Parameters	
wParam	WPARAM: Set to zero.
LOWORD(lParam)	WORD: The x coordinate of the cursor relative to the upper left corner of the screen.
HIWORD(lParam)	WORD: The y coordinate of the cursor relative to the upper left corner of the screen.
Returns	int: One of the values in Table 11-46 is returned by DefWindowProc(), indicating the position of the cursor hotspot.

Table 11-46 WM_NCHITTEST return values

Value	Meaning
HTBORDER	The hotspot is located in the border of a window that does not have a sizing border.
HTBOTTOM	The hotspot is located in the lower horizontal border of a window.
HTBOTTOMLEFT	The hotspot is located in the lower left corner of a window border.
HTBOTTOMRIGHT	The hotspot is located in the lower right corner of a window border.
HTCAPTION	The hotspot is located in a title bar.
HTCLIENT	The hotspot is located in a client area.
HTERROR	The hotspot is located on the screen background or on a dividing line between windows (same as HTNOWHERE, except that DefWindowProc() produces a system beep to indicate an error).
HTGROWBOX	The hotspot is located in a size box (same as HTSIZE).
HTHSCROLL	The hotspot is located in a horizontal scroll bar.
HTLEFT	The hotspot is located in the left border of a window.
HTMENU	The hotspot is located in a menu.
HTNOWHERE	The hotspot is located on the screen background or on a dividing line between windows.
HTREDUCE	The hotspot is located in a Minimize button.
HTRIGHT	The hotspot is located in the right border of a window.

Value	Meaning
HTSIZE	The hotspot is located in a size box (same as HTGROWBOX).
HTSYSMENU	The hotspot is located in a System menu or in a Close button in a child window.
HTTOP	The hotspot is located in the upper horizontal border of a window.
HTTOPLEFT	The hotspot is located in the upper left corner of a window border.
HTTOPRIGHT	The hotspot is located in the upper right corner of a window border.
HTTRANSPARENT	The hotspot is located in a window currently covered by another window.
HTVSCROLL	The hotspot is located in the vertical scroll bar.
HTZOOM	The hotspot is located in a Maximize button.

Include File	winuser.h
See Also	DefWindowProc(), GetCapture()

WM_NCLBUTTONDBLCLK   ■ Win32s   ■ Windows 95   ■ Windows NT

Description   WM_NCLBUTTONDBLCLK is a message that is posted when the user double-clicks the left mouse button while the cursor is within the non-client area of a window. This message is posted to the window that contains the cursor. If a window has captured the mouse, this message is not posted.

Parameters

wParam   int: The hit-test value returned by DefWindowProc() as a result of processing the WM_NCHITTEST message.

lParam   MAKEPOINTS: A pointer to a points structure containing the x and y coordinates of the cursor relative to the upper left corner of the screen.

Returns   int: An application should return zero if it processes this message.

Include File   winuser.h

See Also   DefWindowProc()

Related Messages   WM_NCHITTEST, WM_NCLBUTTONDOWN, WM_NCLBUTTONUP, WM_SYSCOMMAND

WM_NCLBUTTONDOWN   ■ Win32s   ■ Windows 95   ■ Windows NT

Description   WM_NCLBUTTONDOWN is a message that is posted when the user presses the left mouse button while the cursor is within the nonclient area of a window. This message is posted to the window that contains the cursor. If a window captured the mouse, this message is not posted.

Parameters

wParam   int: The hit-test value returned by DefWindowProc() as a result of processing the WM_NCHITTEST message.

lParam	MAKEPOINTS: A pointer to a points structure containing the x and y coordinates of the cursor relative to the upper left corner of the screen.
Returns	int: An application should return zero if it processes this message.
Include File	winuser.h
See Also	DefWindowProc()
Related Messages	WM_NCHITTEST, WM_NCLBUTTONDBLCLK, WM_NCLBUTTONUP, WM_SYSCOMMAND

WM_NCLBUTTONUP   ■ Win32s   ■ Windows 95   ■ Windows NT

Description	WM_NCLBUTTONUP is a message that is posted when the user releases the left mouse button while the cursor is within the nonclient area of a window. This message is posted to the window that contains the cursor. If a window captured the mouse, this message is not posted.
Parameters	
wParam	int: The hit-test value returned by DefWindowProc() as a result of processing the WM_NCHITTEST message.
lParam	MAKEPOINTS: A pointer to a points structure containing the x and y coordinates of the cursor relative to the upper left corner of the screen.
Returns	int: An application should return zero if it processes this message.
Include File	winuser.h
See Also	DefWindowProc()
Related Messages	WM_NCHITTEST, WM_NCLBUTTONDBLCLK, WM_NCLBUTTONDOWN, WM_SYSCOMMAND

WM_NCMBUTTONDBLCLK   ■ Win32s   ■ Windows 95   ■ Windows NT

Description	WM_NCMBUTTONDBLCLK is a message that is posted when the user double-clicks the middle mouse button while the cursor is within the nonclient area of a window. This message is posted to the window that contains the cursor. If a window captured the mouse, this message is not posted.
Parameters	
wParam	int: The hit-test value returned by DefWindowProc() as a result of processing the WM_NCHITTEST message.
lParam	MAKEPOINTS: A pointer to a points structure containing the x and y coordinates of the cursor relative to the upper left corner of the screen.
Returns	int: An application should return zero if it processes this message.
Include File	winuser.h
See Also	DefWindowProc(),

Related Messages   WM_NCHITTEST, WM_NCMBUTTONDOWN, WM_NCMBUTTONUP,
WM_SYSCOMMAND

WM_NCMBUTTONDOWN ■ Win32s ■ Windows 95 ■ Windows NT

Description	WM_NCMBUTTONDOWN is a message that is posted when the user presses the middle mouse button while the cursor is within the nonclient area of a window. This message is posted to the window that contains the cursor. If a window captured the mouse, this message is not posted.
Parameters	
wParam	int: The hit-test value returned by DefWindowProc() as a result of processing the WM_NCHITTEST message.
lParam	MAKEPOINTS: A pointer to a points structure containing the x and y coordinates of the cursor relative to the upper left corner of the screen.
Returns	int: An application should return zero if it processes this message.
Include File	winuser.h
See Also	DefWindowProc()
Related Messages	WM_NCHITTEST, WM_NCMBUTTONDBLCLK, WM_NCMBUTTONUP, WM_SYSCOMMAND

WM_NCMBUTTONUP ■ Win32s ■ Windows 95 ■ Windows NT

Description	WM_NCMBUTTONUP is a message that is posted when the user releases the middle mouse button while the cursor is within the nonclient area of a window. This message is posted to the window that contains the cursor. If a window captured the mouse, this message is not posted.
Parameters	
wParam	int: The hit-test value returned by DefWindowProc() as a result of processing the WM_NCHITTEST message.
lParam	MAKEPOINTS: A pointer to a points structure containing the x and y coordinates of the cursor relative to the upper left corner of the screen.
Returns	int: An application should return zero if it processes this message.
Include File	winuser.h
See Also	DefWindowProc()
Related Messages	WM_NCHITTEST, WM_NCMBUTTONDBLCLK, WM_NCMBUTTONDOWN, WM_SYSCOMMAND

WM_NCMOUSEMOVE ■ Win32s ■ Windows 95 ■ Windows NT

Description	WM_NCMOUSEMOVE is a message that is posted to a window when the cursor is moved within the nonclient area of the window. This message is

posted to the window that contains the cursor. If a window captured the mouse, this message is not posted.

Parameters

wParam   int: The hit-test value returned by DefWindowProc() as a result of processing the WM_NCHITTEST message.

lParam   MAKEPOINTS: A pointer to a points structure containing the x and y coordinates of the cursor relative to the upper left corner of the screen.

Returns   int: An application should return zero if it processes this message.

Include File   winuser.h

See Also   DefWindowProc()

Related Messages WM_NCHITTEST, WM_SYSCOMMAND

WM_NCPAINT ■ Win32s ■ Windows 95 ■ Windows NT

Description   WM_NCPAINT is a message that is sent to a window when its frame must be painted. DefWindowProc() paints the window frame. An application can intercept WM_NCPAINT and paint its own custom window frame.

Parameters

wParam   HRGN: The update region of the window. This region is clipped to the window frame.

lParam   LPARAM: Set to zero.

Returns   int: An application should return zero if it processes this message.

Include File   winuser.h

See Also   DefWindowProc(), GetWindowDC()

Related Messages WM_PAINT

WM_NCRBUTTONDBLCLK ■ Win32s ■ Windows 95 ■ Windows NT

Description   WM_NCRBUTTONDBLCLK is a message that is posted when the user double-clicks the right mouse button while the cursor is within the nonclient area of a window. This message is posted to the window that contains the cursor. If a window captured the mouse, this message is not posted.

Parameters

wParam   int: The hit-test value returned by DefWindowProc() as a result of processing the WM_NCHITTEST message.

lParam   MAKEPOINTS: A pointer to a points structure containing the x and y coordinates of the cursor relative to the upper left corner of the screen.

Returns   int: An application should return zero if it processes this message.

Include File	winuser.h
See Also	DefWindowProc()
Related Messages	WM_NCHITTEST, WM_NCRBUTTONDOWN, WM_NCRBUTTONUP, WM_SYSCOMMAND

WM_NCRBUTTONDOWN   ■ Win32s   ■ Windows 95   ■ Windows NT

Description	WM_NCRBUTTONDOWN is a message that is posted when the user presses the right mouse button while the cursor is within the nonclient area of a window. This message is posted to the window that contains the cursor. If a window captured the mouse, this message is not posted.
Parameters	
wParam	int: The hit-test value returned by DefWindowProc() as a result of processing the WM_NCHITTEST message.
lParam	MAKEPOINTS: A pointer to a points structure containing the x and y coordinates of the cursor relative to the upper left corner of the screen.
Returns	int: An application should return zero if it processes this message.
Include File	winuser.h
See Also	DefWindowProc()
Related Messages	WM_NCHITTEST, WM_NCRBUTTONDBLCLK, WM_NCRBUTTONUP, WM_SYSCOMMAND

WM_NCRBUTTONUP   ■ Win32s   ■ Windows 95   ■ Windows NT

Description	WM_NCRBUTTONUP is a message that is posted when the user releases the right mouse button while the cursor is within the nonclient area of a window. This message is posted to the window that contains the cursor. If a window captured the mouse, this message is not posted.
Parameters	
wParam	int: The hit-test value returned by DefWindowProc() as a result of processing the WM_NCHITTEST message.
lParam	MAKEPOINTS: A pointer to a points structure containing the x and y coordinates of the cursor relative to the upper left corner of the screen.
Returns	int: An application should return zero if it processes this message.
Include File	winuser.h
See Also	DefWindowProc()
Related Messages	WM_NCHITTEST, WM_NCRBUTTONDBLCLK, WM_NCRBUTTONDOWN, WM_SYSCOMMAND

WM_NEXTDLGCTL
■ Win32s   ■ Windows 95   ■ Windows NT

Description	WM_NEXTDLGCTL is a message that is sent to a dialog box procedure to set the keyboard focus to a different control in the dialog box. Do not use SendMessage() to send WM_NEXTDLGCTL if your application will concurrently process other messages that set the focus. UsePostMessage() instead.
Parameters	
wParam	WPARAM: If *lParam* is TRUE, *wParam* identifies the control that receives the focus. If *lParam* is FALSE, *wParam* is a flag that indicates whether the next or previous control with the WS_TABSTOP style receives the focus. If *wParam* is zero, the next control receives the focus; otherwise, the previous control with the WS_TABSTOP style receives the focus.
LOWORD(*lParam*)	BOOL: A flag that indicates how *wParam* is used. TRUE indicates that *wParam* is the handle of the control that receives the focus; otherwise, FALSE indicates that *wParam* is a flag that indicates whether the next or previous control with the WS_TABSTOP style receives the focus.
Returns	int: An application should return zero if it processes this message.
Include File	winuser.h
See Also	PostMessage(), SendMessage(), SetFocus()

WM_NOTIFY
Win32s   ■ Windows 95   ■ Windows NT

Description	WM_NOTIFY is a message that informs the parent window of a control that an event has occurred in the control or that the control requires some kind of information.
Parameters	
wParam	int: The control sending the message.
lParam	LPNMHDR: A pointer to an NMHDR structure containing the notification code and additional information.
Returns	The value returned is ignored, except for notification codes that specify otherwise.
Include File	winuser.h

WM_NOTIFYFORMAT
Win32s   ■ Windows 95   ■ Windows NT

Description	WM_NOTIFYFORMAT is a message that is used by common controls, custom controls, and their parent windows to determine whether the control should use ANSI or Unicode structures in the WM_NOTIFY notification messages that the control uses to communicate with its parent window. WM_NOTIFYFORMAT messages are sent from a control to its parent window, and from the parent window to the control.

Parameters

wParam	HWND: The handle of the window sending WM_NOTIFYFORMAT. If *lParam* is NF_QUERY, *wParam* is the handle of a control. If *lParam* is NF_REQUERY, *wParam* is the handle of the parent window of a control.
lParam	LPARAM: A value from Table 11-47 that specifies the purpose of WM_NOTIFYFORMAT.

Table 11-47 WM_NOTIFYFORMAT *lParam* values

Value	Meaning
NF_QUERY	A query to determine whether ANSI or Unicode structures should be used in WM_NOTIFY messages. This command is sent from a control to its parent window. This command is sent during the creation of a control, and in response to an NF_REQUERY command.
NF_REQUERY	A request that a control send an NF_QUERY form of WM_NOTIFYFORMAT to its parent window. This command is sent from a control's parent window to the control. The parent window is asking the control to requery it about the type of structures to use in WM_NOTIFY messages.

Returns   int: If *lParam* is NF_REQUERY, the result of the requery operation is returned; otherwise, one of the values in Table 11-48 is returned.

Table 11-48 WM_NOTIFYFORMAT return values

Value	Meaning
0	An error occurred.
NFR_ANSI	ANSI structures should be used in WM_NOTIFY messages sent by the control.
NFR_UNICODE	Unicode structures should be used in WM_NOTIFY messages sent by the control.

Include File	winuser.h
See Also	DefDlgProc(), DefWindowProc()
Related Messages	WM_NOTIFY

WM_PAINT   ■ Win32s ■ Windows 95 ■ Windows NT

Description   WM_PAINT is a message that is sent when Windows or another application makes a request to paint a portion of an application's window. The message is sent when UpdateWindow() or RedrawWindow() is called, or by DispatchMessage() when the application obtains a WM_PAINT message using GetMessage() or PeekMessage().

Parameters

wParam	HDC: Enables drawing in a device context other than the default device context. If this parameter is NULL, use the default device context. This

parameter is only used by some common controls; other windows can ignore it.

lParam   LPARAM: Set to zero.

Include File   winuser.h

See Also   BeginPaint(), DefWindowProc(), DispatchMessage(), EndPaint(), GetMessage(), GetUpdateRect(), PeekMessage(), RedrawWindow(), UpdateWindow()

Related Messages WM_ERASEBKGND, WM_NCPAINT

WM_PAINTCLIPBOARD   ■ Win32s ■ Windows 95 ■ Windows NT

Description   WM_PAINTCLIPBOARD is a message that is sent to the clipboard owner by a clipboard viewer window when the clipboard contains data in the CF_OWNERDISPLAY format and the clipboard viewer's client area needs repainting. To determine whether the entire client area or just a portion of it needs repainting, the clipboard owner must compare the dimensions of the drawing area given in the *rcpaint* member of PAINTSTRUCT to the dimensions given in the most recent WM_SIZECLIPBOARD message.

Parameters

wParam   HWND: The handle of the clipboard viewer window.

lParam   HGLOBAL: The handle of a global DDESHARE object containing a PAINTSTRUCT structure that defines the part of the client area to paint.

Returns   int: An application should return zero if it processes this message.

Include File   winuser.h

See Also   GlobalLock(), GlobalUnlock()

Related Messages WM_SIZECLIPBOARD

WM_PAINTICON   ■ Win32s ■ Windows 95 ■ Windows NT

Description   WM_PAINTICON is a message that is sent to a minimized window when the icon is to be painted, but only if the application is written for Windows 3.x. A window receives this message only if a class icon is defined for the window; otherwise, WM_PAINT is sent. DefWindowProc() draws the class icon. For compatibility with Windows 3.x, *wParam* is TRUE. However, this value has no significance.

Parameters   This message does not use *wParam* or *lParam*; therefore, both must be set to zero.

Returns   int: An application should return zero if it processes this message.

Include File   winuser.h

See Also   DefWindowProc()

Related Messages WM_ICONERASEBKGND, WM_PAINT

WM_PALETTECHANGED ■ Win32s ■ Windows 95 ■ Windows NT

Description   WM_PALETTECHANGED is a message that is sent to all top-level and overlapped windows after the window with the keyboard focus has realized its logical palette, thereby changing the system palette. This message enables a window that uses a color palette but does not have the keyboard focus to realize its logical palette and update its client area.

Parameters

wParam   HWND: The handle of the window that caused the system palette to change.

lParam   LPARAM: Set to zero.

Include File   winuser.h

Related Messages   WM_PALETTEISCHANGING, WM_QUERYNEWPALETTE

WM_PALETTEISCHANGING ■ Win32s ■ Windows 95 ■ Windows NT

Description   WM_PALETTEISCHANGING is a message that informs applications that an application is going to realize its logical palette.

Parameters

wParam   HWND: The handle of the window that is realizing its logical palette.

lParam   LPARAM: Set to zero.

Returns   int: An application should return zero if it processes this message.

Include File   winuser.h

Related Messages   WM_PALETTECHANGED, WM_QUERYNEWPALETTE

WM_PARENTNOTIFY ■ Win32s ■ Windows 95 ■ Windows NT

Description   WM_PARENTNOTIFY is a message that is sent to the parent of a child window when the child window is created or destroyed, or when the user clicks a mouse button while the cursor is over the child window. When the child window is being created, the system sends WM_PARENTNOTIFY just before CreateWindow() or CreateWindowEx(), which creates the window, returns. When the child window is being destroyed, Windows sends the message before any processing to destroy the window occurs.

Parameters

LOWORD(wParam)   WORD: The event for which the parent is being notified. One of the values in Table 11-49 indicating why the parent was notified.

Table 11-49 WM_PARENTNOTIFY *LOWORD(wParam)* values

Value	Meaning
WM_CREATE	The child window is being created.
WM_DESTROY	The child window is being destroyed.
WM_LBUTTONDOWN	The user has placed the cursor over the child window and has clicked the left mouse button.
WM_MBUTTONDOWN	The user has placed the cursor over the child window and has clicked the middle mouse button.
WM_RBUTTONDOWN	The user has placed the cursor over the child window and has clicked the right mouse button.

HIWORD(wParam)	WORD: If *LOWORD(wParam)* is WM_CREATE or WM_DESTROY, *HIWORD(wParam)* specifies the identifier of the child window; otherwise, it is undefined.
lParam	LPARAM: The handle of the child window, if *LOWORD(wParam)* is WM_CREATE or WM_DESTROY; otherwise, *lParam* contains the x coordinate of the cursor in the low order word and the y coordinate in the high-order word.
Returns	int: An application should return zero if it processes this message.
Include File	winuser.h
See Also	CreateWindow(), CreateWindowEx()
Related Messages	WM_CREATE, WM_DESTROY, WM_LBUTTONDOWN, WM_MBUTTONDOWN, WM_RBUTTONDOWN

WM_PASTE   ■ Win32s   ■ Windows 95   ■ Windows NT

Description	WM_PASTE is a message that is sent to an edit control or combo box to copy the current content of the clipboard to the edit control at the current caret position. Data is inserted only if the clipboard contains data in CF_TEXT format. This message has no effect when sent to a combo box with the CBS_DROPDOWNLIST style.
Parameters	This message does not use *wParam* or *lParam*; therefore, both must be set to zero.
Include File	winuser.h
Related Messages	WM_CLEAR, WM_COPY, WM_CUT

WM_POWERBROADCAST   Win32s   ■ Windows 95   Windows NT

Description	WM_POWERBROADCAST is a message that is sent to an application to notify it of power-management events.
Parameters	
wParam	DWORD: Event notification message. One of the values in Table 11-50 indicating the type of power-management event that occurred.

Table 11-50 WM_POWERBROADCAST *wParam* values

Value	Meaning
PBT_APMBATTERYLOW	The battery power is low.
PBT_APMOEMEVENT	An OEM-defined event has occurred.
PBT_APMPOWERSTATUSCHANGED	The power status has changed. The *lParam* parameter is set to zero.
PBT_APMQUERYSTANDBY	A request for permission to place system in standby mode. The *lParam* parameter indicates the action flags. If bit zero has a value of 1, the installable driver can prompt the user for directions on preparing for the change to standby; otherwise, the driver must prepare without user interaction. (All other bit values are reserved.)
PBT_APMQUERYSTANDBYFAILED	The standby request was denied. The *lParam* parameter is set to zero.
PBT_APMQUERYSUSPEND	Requests for permission to suspend the computer. The *lParam* parameter indicates the action flags. If bit zero has a value of 1, the application can prompt the user for directions on preparing for the suspension; otherwise, the application must prepare without user interaction. (All other bit values are reserved.)
PBT_APMQUERYSUSPENDFAILED	Suspension request was denied. The *lParam* parameter is set to zero.
PBT_APMRESUMECRITICAL	System operation is resuming after a critical suspension caused by a failing battery. The *lParam* parameter is set to zero.
PBT_APMRESUMESTANDBY	System operation is resuming after being in standby mode. The *lParam* parameter is set to zero.
PBT_APMRESUMESUSPEND	System operation is resuming after being suspended. The *lParam* parameter is set to zero.
PBT_APMSTANDBY	System is changing to standby mode. The *lParam* parameter is set to zero.
PBT_APMSUSPEND	System is suspending operation. The *lParam* parameter is set to zero.

lParam	DWORD: Function-specific data, based on the value of *wParam*. Refer to Table 11-50 for more information.
Returns	BOOL: If successful, TRUE is returned; otherwise, FALSE is returned.
Include File	winuser.h

WM_PRINT
Win32s ■ Windows 95   Windows NT

Description	WM_PRINT is a message that is sent to a window to request that it draw itself in the specified device context, most commonly in a printer device context.
Parameters	
wParam	HDC: The device context to draw the window in.
lParam	LPARAM: One or more of the values in Table 11-51 indicating the drawing options.

Table 11-51 WM_PRINT *lParam* values

Value	Meaning
PRF_CHECKVISIBLE	Draw the window only if it is visible.
PRF_CHILDREN	Draw all visible children windows.
PRF_CLIENT	Draw the client area of the window.
PRF_ERASEBKGND	Erase the background before drawing the window.
PRF_NONCLIENT	Draw the nonclient area of the window.
PRF_OWNED	Draw all owned windows.

Include File	winuser.h
See Also	DefWindowProc()
Related Messages	WM_ERASEBKGND, WM_PRINTCLIENT

WM_PRINTCLIENT   Win32s ■ Windows 95   Windows NT

Description	WM_PRINTCLIENT is a message that is sent to a window to request that it draw its client area in the specified device context, most commonly in a printer device context.
wParam	HDC: The device context to draw the window in.
lParam	LPARAM: One or more of the values in Table 11-51 indicating the drawing options.
Include File	winuser.h
See Also	BeginPaint(), EndPaint()
Related Messages	WM_PAINT

WM_PSD_ENVSTAMPRECT   ■ Win32s ■ Windows 95   ■ Windows NT

Description	WM_PSD_ENVSTAMPRECT is a message that informs a hook function of the coordinates of the envelope-stamp rectangle in the sample page of the Page Setup dialog box. Before drawing in the envelope-stamp rectangle, the system passes this message to the hook function specified in the *lpfnPagePaintHook* member of the PAGESETUPDLG structure used to create the dialog box.
Parameters	
wParam	HDC: The handle of the device context for the sample page.
lParam	LPRECT: A pointer to a RECT structure containing the coordinates, in pixels, of the envelope-stamp rectangle.
Returns	BOOL: A hook procedure should return TRUE to prevent the system from drawing the envelope-stamp rectangle; otherwise, it should return FALSE.
Include File	commdlg.h

WM_PSD_FULLPAGERECT ■ Win32s ■ Windows 95 ■ Windows NT

Description   WM_PSD_FULLPAGERECT is a message that informs a hook function of the coordinates of the sample page rectangle in the Page Setup dialog box. Before drawing in the sample page rectangle, the system sends this message to the hook function specified in the *lpfnPagePaintHook* member of the PAGESETUPDLG structure used to create the dialog box.

Parameters

wParam   HDC: The handle of the device context for the sample page.

lParam   LPRECT: A pointer to a RECT structure containing the coordinates, in pixels, of the sample page.

Returns   BOOL: A hook procedure should return TRUE to prevent the system from drawing in the sample page rectangle; otherwise, it should return FALSE. If it returns TRUE, the hook procedure does not receive any additional messages until the next time the system needs to redraw the sample page.

Include File   commdlg.h

WM_PSD_GREEKTEXTRECT ■ Win32s ■ Windows 95 ■ Windows NT

Description   WM_PSD_GREEKTEXTRECT is a message that informs a hook function of the coordinates of the greek-text rectangle in the sample page of the Page Setup dialog box. The system fills the greek-text rectangle with random characters to demonstrate how text is to be formatted on a printed page. Before drawing the greek text, the system passes this message to the hook function specified in the *lpfnPagePaintHook* member of the PAGESETUPDLG structure used to create the dialog box.

Parameters

wParam   HDC: The handle of the device context for the sample page.

lParam   LPRECT: A pointer to a RECT structure containing the coordinates, in pixels, of the greek-text rectangle.

Returns   BOOL: A hook function should return TRUE to prevent the system from drawing in the greek-text rectangle; otherwise, it should return FALSE.

Include File   commdlg.h

WM_PSD_MARGINRECT ■ Win32s ■ Windows 95 ■ Windows NT

Description   WM_PSD_MARGINRECT is a message that informs a hook function of the coordinates of the margin rectangle in the sample page of the Page Setup dialog box. Before drawing the margin rectangle, the system passes this message to the hook function specified in the *lpfnPagePaintHook* member of the PAGESETUPDLG structure used to create the dialog box.

Parameters

wParam	HDC: The handle of the device context for the sample page.
lParam	LPRECT: A pointer to a RECT structure containing the coordinates, in pixels, of the margin rectangle.
Returns	BOOL: A hook function should return TRUE to prevent the system from drawing the margin rectangle; otherwise, is should return FALSE.
Include File	commdlg.h

WM_PSD_MINMARGINRECT   ■ Win32s   ■ Windows 95   ■ Windows NT

Description	WM_PSD_MINMARGINRECT is a message that informs a hook function of the coordinates of the minimum margin rectangle of the sample page in the Page Setup dialog box. The system passes this message to the hook function specified in the *lpfnPagePaintHook* member of the PAGESETUPDLG structure used to create the dialog box.

Parameters

wParam	HDC: The handle of the device context for the sample page.
lParam	LPRECT: A pointer to a RECT structure containing the coordinates, in pixels, of the minimum margin rectangle.
Returns	BOOL: A hook function should return TRUE to prevent the system from any further drawing in the sample page rectangle; otherwise, it should return FALSE. If it returns TRUE, the hook function does not receive any additional messages until the next time the system needs to redraw the sample page.
Include File	commdlg.h

WM_PSD_PAGESETUPDLG   ■ Win32s   ■ Windows 95   ■ Windows NT

Description	WM_PSD_PAGESETUPDLG is a message that is sent when the system is about to draw the contents of the sample page in the Page Setup dialog box. The system sends this message to the hook function specified in the *lpfnPagePaintHook* member of the PAGESETUPDLG structure used to create the dialog box. The hook function can use this message to carry out initialization tasks related to drawing the contents of the sample page.

Parameters

LOWORD(wParam)	WORD: One of the values in Table 11-52 indicating the paper size.

Table 11-52 WM_PSD_PAGESETUPDLG *LOWORD(wParam)* values

Value	Meaning
DMPAPER_10X14	10 by 14 inch sheet
DMPAPER_11X17	11 by 17 inch sheet

Value	Meaning
DMPAPER_A3	A3 sheet, 297 by 420 millimeters
DMPAPER_A4	A4 Sheet, 210 by 297 millimeters
DMPAPER_A4SMALL	A4 small sheet, 210 by 297 millimeters
DMPAPER_A5	A5 sheet, 148 by 210 millimeters
DMPAPER_B4	B4 sheet, 250 by 354 millimeters
DMPAPER_B5	B5 sheet, 182 by 257 millimeters
DMPAPER_CSHEET	C sheet, 17 by 22 inches
DMPAPER_DSHEET	D sheet, 22 by 34 inches
DMPAPER_ENV_9	#9 envelope, 3 7/8 by 8 7/8 inches
DMPAPER_ENV_10	#10 envelope, 4 1/8 by 9 1/2 inches
DMPAPER_ENV_11	#11 envelope, 4 1/2 by 10 3/8 inches
DMPAPER_ENV_12	#12 envelope, 4 3/4 by 11 inches
DMPAPER_ENV_14	#14 envelope, 5 by 11 1/2 inches
DMPAPER_ENV_B4	B4 envelope, 250 by 353 millimeters
DMPAPER_ENV_B5	B5 envelope, 176 by 250 millimeters
DMPAPER_ENV_B6	B6 envelope, 176 by 125 millimeters
DMPAPER_ENV_C3	C3 envelope, 324 by 458 millimeters
DMPAPER_ENV_C4	C4 envelope, 229 by 324 millimeters
DMPAPER_ENV_C5	C5 envelope, 162 by 229 millimeters
DMPAPER_ENV_C6	C6 envelope, 114 by 162 millimeters
DMPAPER_ENV_C65	C65 envelope, 114 by 229 millimeters
DMPAPER_ENV_DL	DL envelope, 110 by 220 millimeters
DMPAPER_ENV_ITALY	Italy envelope, 110 by 230 millimeters
DMPAPER_ENV_MONARCH	Monarch envelope, 3 7/8 by 7 1/2 inches
DMPAPER_ENV_PERSONAL	6 3/4 envelope, 3 5/8 by 6 1/2 inches
DMPAPER_ESHEET	E sheet, 34 by 44 inches
DMPAPER_EXECUTIVE	Executive, 7 1/4 by 10 1/2 inches
DMPAPER_FANFOLD_LGL_GERMAN	German legal fanfold, 8 1/2 by 13 inches
DMPAPER_FANFOLD_STD_GERMAN	German standard fanfold, 8 1/2 by 12 inches
DMPAPER_FANFOLD_US	U.S. standard fanfold, 14 7/8 by 11 inches
DMPAPER_FOLIO	Folio, 8 1/2 by 13 inches
DMPAPER_LEDGER	Ledger, 17 by 11 inches
DMPAPER_LEGAL	Legal, 8 1/2 by 14 inches
DMPAPER_LETTER	Letter, 8 1/2 by 11 inches
DMPAPER_LETTERSMALL	Letter, small, 8 1/2 by 11 inches
DMPAPER_NOTE	Note, 8 1/2 by 11 inches
DMPAPER_QUARTO	Quarto, 215 by 275 millimeters
DMPAPER_STATEMENT	Statement, 5 1/2 by 8 1/2 inches
DMPAPER_TABLOID	Tabloid, 11 by 17 inches

HIWORD(wParam)   WORD: One of the values in Table 11-53 indicating the orientation of the paper or envelope, and whether the printer is a dot matrix or HPPCL (Hewlett-Packard Printer Control Language) device.

Table 11-53 WM_PSD_PAGESETUPDLG *HIWORD(wParam)* values

Value	Meaning
0x0001	Paper in landscape mode (dot matrix)
0x0003	Paper in landscape mode (HPPCL)
0x0005	Paper in portrait mode (dot matrix)
0x0007	Paper in portrait mode (HPPCL)
0x000b	Envelope in landscape mode (HPPCL)
0x000d	Envelope in portrait mode (dot matrix)
0x0019	Envelope in landscape mode (dot matrix)
0x001f	Envelope in portrait mode (HPPCL)

lParam   LPPAGESETUPDLG: A pointer to a PAGESETUPDLG structure that contains information used to initialize the Page Setup dialog box.

Returns   BOOL: A hook function should return TRUE to prevent the system from drawing in the sample page rectangle; otherwise, it should return FALSE. If it returns TRUE, the hook function does not receive any additional messages until the next time the system needs to redraw the sample page.

Include File   commdlg.h

WM_PSD_YAFULLPAGERECT   ■ Win32s   ■ Windows 95   ■ Windows NT

Description   WM_PSD_YAFULLPAGERECT is a message that informs a hook function of the coordinates of the sample page rectangle in the Page Setup dialog box. The system sends this message to the hook function specified in the *lpfnPagePaintHook* member of the PAGESETUPDLG structure used to create the dialog box.

Parameters

wParam   HDC: The handle of the device context for the sample page.

lParam   LPRECT: A pointer to a RECT structure that contains the coordinates, in pixels, of the sample page.

Returns   BOOL: A hook function should return TRUE to prevent the system from drawing in the return address rectangle of the sample page. It should return FALSE to allow the system to draw in the return address rectangle. If the paper type is not an envelope, the return value does not have an effect.

Include File   commdlg.h

WM_QUERYDRAGICON
■ Win32s ■ Windows 95 ■ Windows NT

Description	WM_QUERYDRAGICON is a message that is sent to a minimized window to indicate that the window is about to be dragged by the user but there is no icon defined for its class. An application can return the handle of an icon or cursor. The system displays this cursor or icon while the user drags the icon.
Parameters	This message does not use *wParam* or *lParam*; therefore, both must be set to zero.
Returns	HICON: The handle of a cursor or icon that Windows is to display while the user drags the icon is returned. The cursor or icon must be compatible with the display driver's resolution. If the application returns NULL, the system displays the default cursor.
Include File	winuser.h
See Also	DefWindowProc(), LoadCursor(), LoadIcon()

WM_QUERYENDSESSION
Win32s ■ Windows 95 ■ Windows NT

Description	WM_QUERYENDSESSION is sent when the user chooses to end the Windows session or when an application calls ExitWindows(). If an application returns zero, the Windows session is not ended and the system stops sending WM_QUERYENDSESSION. After processing this message, Windows sends WM_ENDSESSION with the *wParam* parameter set to the results of the WM_QUERYENDSESSION message.
Parameters	
wParam	UINT: The source of the request to end the Windows session. This parameter is zero if the request occurred because the user clicked the Logoff or Shutdown button in the Shut Down Windows dialog box. This parameter is nonzero if the user clicked the End Task button in the Task List dialog box.
lParam	BOOL: This parameter is used only in Windows 95. TRUE indicates that the user is logging off; FALSE indicates that the user is shutting down the system.
Returns	BOOL: If an application can terminate conveniently, TRUE is returned; otherwise, FALSE is returned.
Include File	winuser.h
See Also	DefWindowProc(), ExitWindows()
Related Messages	WM_ENDSESSION

WM_QUERYNEWPALETTE   ■ Win32s   ■ Windows 95   ■ Windows NT

Description	WM_QUERYNEWPALETTE is a message that informs a window that it is about to receive the keyboard focus, giving the window the opportunity to realize its logical palette when it receives the focus.
Parameters	This message does not use *wParam* or *lParam*; therefore, both must be set to zero.
Returns	BOOL: If the window realizes its logical palette, TRUE is returned; otherwise, FALSE is returned.
Include File	winuser.h
Related Messages	WM_PALETTECHANGED, WM_PALETTEISCHANGING

WM_QUERYOPEN   ■ Win32s   ■ Windows 95   ■ Windows NT

Description	WM_QUERYOPEN is a message that is sent to an icon when the user requests that the window be restored to its previous size and position.
Parameters	This message does not use *wParam* or *lParam*; therefore, both must be set to zero.
Returns	BOOL: If the icon can be opened, TRUE is returned; otherwise, FALSE is returned to prevent the icon from being opened.
Include File	winuser.h
See Also	DefWindowProc()

WM_QUEUESYNC   ■ Win32s   ■ Windows 95   ■ Windows NT

Description	WM_QUEUESYNC is a message that is sent by a computer-based training (CBT) application to separate user-input messages from other messages sent through the WH_JOURNALPLAYBACK hook procedure.
Parameters	This message does not use *wParam* or *lParam*; therefore, both must be set to zero.
Returns	int: A CBT application should return zero if it processes this message.
Include File	winuser.h

WM_QUIT   ■ Win32s   ■ Windows 95   ■ Windows NT

Description	WM_QUIT is a message that indicates a request to terminate an application and is generated when the application calls PostQuitMessage(). It causes GetMessage() to return zero.
Parameters	
wParam	int: The exit code given to PostQuitMessage().

lParam	LPARAM: Set to zero.
Include File	winuser.h
See Also	GetMessage(), PostQuitMessage()

WM_RASDIALEVENT   Win32s ■ Windows 95 ■ Windows NT

Description	WM_RASDIALEVENT is a message that is sent to a window procedure when a change of state event occurs during a remote access service (RAS) connection process, and a window has been specified to handle notifications of such events by using the *notifier* parameter of RasDial().
Parameters	
wParam	RASCONNSTATE: A RASCONNSTATE enumerator value indicating the state the RasDial remote access connection process is about to enter. The parameter has the same value as the *rasconnstate* parameter of RasDialFunc() and RasDialFunc1().
lParam	DWORD: A nonzero value indicating the error that has occurred, or zero if an error has not occurred. This parameter has the same value as the *dwError* parameter of RasDialFunc() and RasDialFunc1().
Returns	BOOL: An application should return TRUE if it processes this message.
Include File	ras.h
See Also	RasDial(), RasDialFunc(), RasDialFunc1()

WM_RBUTTONDBLCLK   ■ Win32s ■ Windows 95 ■ Windows NT

Description	WM_RBUTTONDBLCLK is a message that is posted when the user double-clicks the right mouse button while the cursor is in the client area of a window. If the mouse is not captured, the message is posted to the window beneath the cursor; otherwise, the message is posted to the window that captured the mouse.
Parameters	
wParam	WPARAM: This parameter can be any combination of the values in Table 11-38 indicating which virtual keys are down.
LOWORD(lParam)	WORD: The x coordinate of the cursor relative to the upper left corner of the client area.
HIWORD(lParam)	WORD: The y coordinate of the cursor relative to the upper left corner of the client area.
Returns	int: An application should return zero if it processes this message.
Include File	winuser.h
See Also	GetCapture(), GetDoubleClickTime(), SetCapture(), SetDoubleClickTime()
Related Messages	WM_RBUTTONDOWN, WM_RBUTTONUP

WM_RBUTTONDOWN ■ Win32s ■ Windows 95 ■ Windows NT

Description	WM_RBUTTONDOWN is a message that is posted when the user presses the right mouse button while the cursor is in the client area of a window. If the mouse is not captured, the message is posted to the window beneath the cursor; otherwise, the message is posted to the window that captured the mouse.
Parameter	
wParam	WPARAM: This parameter can be any combination of the values in Table 11-38 indicating which virtual keys are down.
LOWORD(lParam)	WORD: The x coordinate of the cursor relative to the upper left corner of the client area.
HIWORD(lParam)	WORD: The y coordinate of the cursor relative to the upper left corner of the client area.
Returns	int: An application should return zero if it processes this message.
Include File	winuser.h
See Also	GetCapture(), SetCapture()
Related Messages	WM_RBUTTONDBLCLK, WM_RBUTTONUP

WM_RBUTTONUP ■ Win32s ■ Windows 95 ■ Windows NT

Description	WM_RBUTTONUP is a message that is posted when the user releases the right mouse button while the cursor is in the client area of a window. If the mouse is not captured, the message is posted to the window beneath the cursor; otherwise, the message is posted to the window that captured the mouse.
Parameter	
wParam	WPARAM: This parameter can be any combination of the values in Table 11-38 indicating which virtual keys are down.
LOWORD(lParam)	WORD: The x coordinate of the cursor relative to the upper left corner of the client area.
HIWORD(lParam)	WORD: The y coordinate of the cursor relative to the upper left corner of the client area.
Returns	int: An application should return zero if it processes this message.
Include File	winuser.h
See Also	GetCapture(), SetCapture()
Related Messages	WM_RBUTTONDBLCLK, WM_RBUTTONDOWN

WM_RENDERALLFORMATS ■ Win32s ■ Windows 95 ■ Windows NT

Description	WM_RENDERALLFORMATS is a message that is sent to the clipboard owner before it is destroyed, if the clipboard owner has delayed rendering one or more clipboard formats. For the content of the clipboard to remain available to other applications, the clipboard owner must render data in all the formats it is capable of generating, and place the data on the clipboard by calling SetClipboardData().
Parameters	This message does not use *wParam* or *lParam*; therefore, both must be set to zero.
Returns	int: An application should return zero if it processes this message.
Include File	winuser.h
See Also	SetClipboardData()
Related Messages	WM_RENDERFORMAT

WM_RENDERFORMAT ■ Win32s ■ Windows 95 ■ Windows NT

Description	WM_RENDERFORMAT is a message that is sent to the clipboard owner if it has delayed rendering a specific clipboard format and if an application has requested data in that format. The clipboard owner must render data in the specified format and place it on the clipboard by calling SetClipboardData().
Parameters	
wParam	UINT: The clipboard format to be rendered.
lParam	LPARAM: Set to zero.
Returns	int: An application should return zero if it processes this message.
Include File	winuser.h
See Also	SetClipboardData()
Related Messages	WM_RENDERALLFORMATS

WM_SETCURSOR ■ Win32s ■ Windows 95 ■ Windows NT

Description	WM_SETCURSOR is a message that is sent to a window if the mouse causes the cursor to move within a window and mouse input is not captured.
Parameters	
wParam	HWND: The handle of the window containing the cursor.
LOWORD(lParam)	WORD: The hit-test code.
HIWORD(lParam)	WORD: The identifier of the mouse message. This parameter is zero when the window enters menu mode.

Include File	winuser.h
See Also	DefWindowProc(), MessageBeep()

WM_SETFOCUS   ■ Win32s   ■ Windows 95   ■ Windows NT

Description	WM_SETFOCUS is a message that is sent to a window after it has gained the keyboard focus.
Parameters	
wParam	HWND: The handle of the window that lost keyboard focus. This parameter may be NULL.
lParam	LPARAM: Set to zero.
Returns	int: An application should return zero if it processes this message.
Include File	winuser.h
See Also	SetFocus()
Related Messages	WM_KILLFOCUS

WM_SETFONT   ■ Win32s   ■ Windows 95   ■ Windows NT

Description	WM_SETFONT is a message that specifies the font that a control is to use when drawing text. The size of the control does not change as a result of receiving this message. To avoid clipping text that does not fit within the boundaries of the control, the application should correct the size of the control window before it sets the font.
Parameters	
wParam	WPARAM: The handle of the font to use when drawing text. If *wParam* is NULL, the system font is used to draw text.
LOWORD(lParam)	WORD: TRUE causes the control to redraw itself immediately after setting the new text font.
HIWORD(lParam)	WORD: Set to zero.
Include File	winuser.h
See Also	CreateDialogIndirect(), CreateDialogIndirectParam(), DeleteObject(), DialogBoxIndirect(), DialogBoxIndirectParam()
Related Messages	WM_INITDIALOG

WM_SETHOTKEY   Win32s   ■ Windows 95   ■ Windows NT

Description	WM_SETHOTKEY is a message that is sent to a window to associate a hot key with the window. When the user presses the hot key, the system activates the window. A window can only have one hot key. If the window already has a hot key associated with it, the new hot key replaces the old

one. If more than one window has the same hot key, the window that is activated by the hot key is random.

Parameters

LOWORD(wParam) WORD: The virtual-key code of the hot key. Set this parameter to NULL to remove the hot key associated with a window.

HIWORD(wParam) WORD: A combination of the values in Table 11-54 indicating the hot key.

Table 11-54 WM_SETHOTKEY *HIWORD(wParam)* values

Value	Meaning
HOTKEYF_ALT	ALT key
HOTKEYF_CONTROL	CTRL key
HOTKEYF_EXT	Extended key
HOTKEYF_SHIFT	SHIFT key

lParam LPARAM: Set to zero.

Returns int: One of the values in Table 11-55 is returned.

Table 11-55 WM_SETHOTKEY return values

Value	Meaning
-1	The function is unsuccessful and the hot key is invalid.
0	The function is unsuccessful and the window is invalid.
1	The function is successful, and no other window has the same hot key.
2	The function is successful, but another window already has the same hot key.

Include File winuser.h

See Also RegisterHotKey()

Related Messages WM_GETHOTKEY, WM_SYSCOMMAND

WM_SETICON

Win32s ■ Windows 95   Windows NT

Description WM_SETICON is a message that associates a new big or small icon with a window. Windows draws the big icon when the window is minimized, and the small icon is in the window's title bar.

Parameters

wParam BOOL: TRUE sets the big icon; FALSE sets the small icon.

lParam HICON: The handle of the big or small icon, based on the value of *wParam*. If *lParam* is NULL, the icon indicated by *wParam* is removed.

Returns	HICON: The handle of the previous big or small icon, based on the value of *wParam*, is returned. A NULL value is returned if the window did not have a previous icon of the type indicated by *wParam*.
Include File	winuser.h
See Also	DefWindowProc()
Related Messages	WM_GETICON

WM_SETREDRAW ■ Win32s ■ Windows 95 ■ Windows NT

Description	WM_SETREDRAW is a message that is sent to a window to allow changes in that window to be redrawn or to prevent changes in that window from being redrawn.
Parameters	
wParam	WPARAM: TRUE sets the redraw flag; FALSE clears the flag.
lParam	LPARAM: Set to zero.
Returns	int: An application should return zero if it processes this message.
Include File	winuser.h
See Also	InvalidateRect()

WM_SETTEXT ■ Win32s ■ Windows 95 ■ Windows NT

Description	WM_SETTEXT is a message that sets the text of a window. For an edit control, the text is the contents of the edit control. For a combo box, the text is the contents of the edit control portion of the combo box. For a button, the text is the button name. For other windows, the text is the window title.
Parameters	
wParam	WPARAM: Set to zero.
lParam	LPCTSTR: A pointer to a null-terminated string that is the window text.
Returns	BOOL: If the text is set in the window, TRUE is returned; otherwise, FALSE for an edit control, LB_ERRSPACE for a list box, or CB_ERRSPACE for a combo box, indicating there is insufficient space to set text, is returned. CB_ERR is returned if the message is sent to a combo box without an edit control.
Include File	winuser.h
See Also	DefWindowProc()
Related Messages	CB_SELECTSTRING, WM_GETTEXT

WM_SETTINGCHANGE

Win32s ■ Windows 95   Windows NT

Description	WM_SETTINGCHANGE is a message that is sent to all windows when an application uses SystemParametersInfo() to change a systemwide setting.
Parameters	
wParam	WPARAM: The systemwide parameter that changed.
lParam	LPCTSTR: A pointer to a buffer that contains the string "WindowMetrics" if *wParam* specifies SPI_SETANIMATION, SPI_SETNONCLIENTMETRICS, SPI_SETICONMETRICS, or SPI_SETMINIMIZEDMETRICS; otherwise, *lParam* is NULL.
Returns	int: An application should return zero if it processes this message.
Include File	winuser.h
See Also	SystemParametersInfo()

WM_SHOWWINDOW

■ Win32s   ■ Windows 95   ■ Windows NT

Description	WM_SHOWWINDOW is a message that is sent to a window when the window is about to be hidden or shown. If a window has the WS_VISIBLE style when it is created, the window receives this message after it is created, but before it is displayed. A window also receives this message when its visibility state is changed by ShowWindow() or ShowOwnedPopups(). WM_SHOWWINDOW is not sent when a top-level, overlapped window is created with the WS_MAXIMIZE or WS_MINIMIZE style, or when the SW_SHOWNORMAL flag is specified in the call to ShowWindow().
Parameters	
wParam	BOOL: TRUE indicates the window is being shown; FALSE indicates the window is being hidden.
lParam	int: The status of the window being shown. This parameter is zero if WM_SHOWWINDOW is sent due to a call to ShowWindow(); otherwise *lParam* is one of the values in Table 11-56.

Table 11-56 WM_SHOWWINDOW *lParam* values

Value	Meaning
SW_OTHERUNZOOM	Window is being uncovered because a maximized window was restored or minimized.
SW_OTHERZOOM	Window is being covered by another window that has been maximized.
SW_PARENTCLOSING	Window's owner window is being minimized.
SW_PARENTOPENING	Window's owner window is being restored.

Returns	int: An application should return zero if it processes this message.

| Include File | winuser.h |
| See Also | DefWindowProc(), ShowOwnedPopups(), ShowWindow() |

WM_SIZE   ■ Win32s ■ Windows 95 ■ Windows NT

Description WM_SIZE is a message that is sent to a window after its size has changed.

Parameters

wParam WPARAM: One of the values in Table 11-57 indicating the type of resizing for the window.

Table 11-57 WM_SIZE *wParam* values

Value	Meaning
SIZE_MAXHIDE	Message is sent to all pop-up windows when some other window is maximized.
SIZE_MAXIMIZED	Window has been maximized.
SIZE_MAXSHOW	Message is sent to all pop-up windows when another window has been restored to its former size.
SIZE_MINIMIZED	Window has been minimized.
SIZE_RESTORED	Window has been resized, but neither the SIZE_MINIMIZED nor the SIZE_MAXIMIZED value applies.

LOWORD(lParam)	WORD: The new width of the client area.
HIWORD(lParam)	WORD: The new height of the client area.
Returns	int: An application should return zero if it processes this message.
Include File	winuser.h
See Also	MoveWindow(), SetScrollPos()

WM_SIZECLIPBOARD   ■ Win32s ■ Windows 95 ■ Windows NT

Description WM_SIZECLIPBOARD is a message that is sent to the clipboard owner by a clipboard viewer window when the clipboard contains data in the CF_OWNERDISPLAY format and the clipboard viewer's client area has changed size.

Parameters

wParam HWND: The handle of the clipboard viewer window.

lParam HGLOBAL: The handle of a global memory object that contains a RECT structure. The structure contains the new dimensions of the clipboard viewer's client area.

Include File winuser.h

See Also GlobalLock(), GlobalUnlock()

WM_SIZING   Win32s   ■ Windows 95   Windows NT

Description   WM_SIZING is a message that is sent to a window that the user is resizing. By processing this message, an application can monitor the size and position of the drag rectangle and, if needed, change its size or position.

Parameters

wParam   WPARAM: A combination of the values in Table 11-44 indicating the edge of the window being sized.

lParam   LPRECT: The address of a RECT structure with the screen coordinates of the drag rectangle. To change the size or position of the drag rectangle, an application must change the members of this structure.

Returns   BOOL: An application should return TRUE if it processes this message.

Include File   winuser.h

Related Messages   WM_MOVING, WM_SIZE

WM_SPOOLERSTATUS   ■ Win32s   ■ Windows 95   ■ Windows NT

Description   WM_SPOOLERSTATUS is a message that is sent from Windows Print Manager whenever a job is added to or removed from the Print Manager queue.

Parameters

wParam   WPARAM: The PR_JOBSTATUS flag.

LOWORD(lParam)   WORD: The number of jobs remaining in the Print Manager queue.

Returns   int: An application should return zero if it processes this message.

Include File   winuser.h

WM_STYLECHANGED   Win32s   ■ Windows 95   ■ Windows NT

Description   WM_STYLECHANGED is a message that is sent to a window after SetWindowLong() has changed one or more of the window's styles.

Parameters

wParam   WPARAM: A combination of the values in Table 11-58 indicating whether the window's extended or nonextended styles have changed.

Table 11-58 WM_STYLECHANGED *wParam* values

Value	Meaning
GWL_EXSTYLE	The window's extended styles have changed.
GWL_STYLE	The window's nonextended styles have changed.

lParam	LPSTYLESTRUCT: A pointer to a STYLESTRUCT structure that contains the new styles for the window. An application can examine the styles, but cannot change them.
Returns	int: An application should return zero if it processes this message.
Include File	winuser.h
See Also	SetWindowLong()
Related Messages	WM_STYLECHANGING

WM_STYLECHANGING   Win32s ■ Windows 95 ■ Windows NT

Description	WM_STYLECHANGING is a message that is sent to a window when SetWindowLong() is about to change one or more of the window's styles.
Parameters	
wParam	WPARAM: A combination of the values in Table 11-58 indicating whether the window's extended or nonextended styles have changed.
lParam	LPSTYLESTRUCT: A pointer to a STYLESTRUCT structure that contains the proposed new styles for the window. An application can examine the styles and, if necessary, change them.
Returns	int: An application should return zero if it processes this message.
Include File	winuser.h
Related Messages	WM_STYLECHANGED

WM_SYSCHAR   ■ Win32s ■ Windows 95 ■ Windows NT

Description	WM_SYSCHAR is a message that is posted to the window with the keyboard focus when a WM_SYSKEYDOWN message is translated by TranslateMessage(). It specifies the character code of a character key that is pressed while the ALT key is down.
Parameters	
wParam	TCHAR: The character code of the System menu key.
lParam	LPARAM: The repeat count, scan code, extended-key flag, context code, previous key-state flag, and transition-state flag, as shown in Table 11-21.
Returns	int: An application should return zero if it processes this message.
Include File	winuser.h
See Also	TranslateAccelerator(),TranslateMessage()
Related Messages	WM_SYSKEYDOWN

WM_SYSCOLORCHANGE   ■ Win32s ■ Windows 95 ■ Windows NT

Description	WM_SYSCOLORCHANGE is a message that is sent to all top-level windows when a change is made to a system color setting. Windows sends a WM_PAINT message to any window that is affected by a system color change.

Parameters This message does not use *wParam* or *lParam*; therefore, both must be set to zero.

Include File winuser.h

Related Messages WM_PAINT

WM_SYSCOMMAND ■ Win32s ■ Windows 95 ■ Windows NT

Description WM_SYSCOMMAND is a message that is sent to a window when the user chooses a command from the System menu or when the user chooses either the Maximize or Minimize button.

Parameters

wParam WPARAM: One of the values in Table 11-59 indicating the type of system command selected by the user.

Table 11-59 WM_SYSCOMMAND *wParam* values

Value	Meaning
SC_CLOSE	Closes the window.
SC_CONTEXTHELP	Changes the cursor to a question mark with a pointer. If the user then clicks a control in the dialog box, the control receives a WM_HELP message.
SC_DEFAULT	Selects the default item; the user double-clicked the System menu.
SC_HOTKEY	Activates the window associated with the application-specified hot key. *LOWORD(lParam)* identifies the window to activate.
SC_HSCROLL	Scrolls horizontally.
SC_ICON	Minimizes the window.
SC_KEYMENU	Retrieves the System menu as a result of a keystroke.
SC_MAXIMIZE	Maximizes the window.
SC_MINIMIZE	Minimizes the window.
SC_MONITORPOWER	In Windows 95 only, sets the state of the display. This command supports devices, such as battery-powered personal computers, that have power-saving features.
SC_MOUSEMENU	Retrieves the System menu as a result of a mouse click.
SC_MOVE	Moves the window.
SC_NEXTWINDOW	Moves to the next window.
SC_PREVWINDOW	Moves to the previous window.
SC_RESTORE	Restores the window to its normal position and size.
SC_SCREENSAVE	Executes the screen saver application specified in the [boot] section of the SYSTEM.INI file.
SC_SIZE	Sizes the window.
SC_TASKLIST	Executes or activates Windows Task Manager.
SC_VSCROLL	Scrolls vertically.
SC_ZOOM	Maximizes the window.

LOWORD(lParam)	WORD: The horizontal position of the cursor, in screen coordinates, if the System menu command is selected with a mouse; otherwise, *LOWORD(lParam)* is not used.
HIWORD(lParam)	WORD: The vertical position of the cursor, in screen coordinates, if the System menu command is selected with a mouse. This parameter is -1 if the command is chosen using a system accelerator, or zero if selected using a mnemonic.
Returns	int: An application should return zero if it processes this message.
Include File	winuser.h
See Also	AppendMenu(), DefWindowProc(), GetSystemMenu(), InsertMenu(), ModifyMenu()
Related Messages	WM_COMMAND

WM_SYSDEADCHAR ■ Win32s ■ Windows 95 ■ Windows NT

Description	WM_SYSDEADCHAR is a message that is sent to the window with the keyboard focus when a WM_SYSKEYDOWN message is translated by TranslateMessage(). WM_SYSDEADCHAR specifies the character code of a system dead key that is pressed while holding down the [ALT] key.
Parameters	
wParam	TCHAR: The character code generated by the dead key that is pressed while holding down the [ALT] key.
lParam	LPARAM: The repeat count, scan code, extended-key flag, context code, previous key-state flag, and transition-state flag, as shown in Table 11-21.
Returns	int: An application should return zero if it processes this message.
Include File	winuser.h
See Also	TranslateMessage()
Related Messages	WM_DEADCHAR, WM_SYSKEYDOWN

WM_SYSKEYDOWN ■ Win32s ■ Windows 95 ■ Windows NT

Description	WM_SYSKEYDOWN is a message that is posted to the window with the keyboard focus when the user holds down the [ALT] key and then presses another key. It also occurs when currently there is no window with keyboard focus; in this case, WM_SYSKEYDOWN is sent to the active window. The window that receives the message can distinguish between these two contexts by checking the context code in *lParam*.
Parameters	
wParam	int: The virtual-key code of the key being pressed.
lParam	LPARAM: The repeat count, scan code, extended-key flag, context code, previous key-state flag, and transition-state flag, as shown in Table 11-21.

Returns	int: An application should return zero if it processes this message.
Include File	winuser.h
See Also	DefWindowProc(), TranslateAccelerator()
Related Messages	WM_SYSCOMMAND, WM_SYSKEYUP

WM_SYSKEYUP   ■ Win32s   ■ Windows 95   ■ Windows NT

Description   WM_SYSKEYUP is a message that is posted to the window with the keyboard focus when the user releases a key that was pressed while the ⟨ALT⟩ key was held down. It also occurs when currently there is no window with the keyboard focus; in this case, WM_SYSKEYUP is sent to the active window. The window that receives the message can distinguish between these two contexts by checking the context code in *lParam*.

Parameters

wParam   int: The virtual-key code of the key being released.

lParam   LPARAM: The repeat count, scan code, extended-key flag, context code, previous key-state flag, and transition-state flag, as shown in Table 11-21.

Returns	int: An application should return zero if it processes this message.
Include File	winuser.h
See Also	DefWindowProc(), TranslateAccelerator()
Related Messages	WM_SYSCOMMAND, WM_SYSKEYDOWN

WM_TCARD   ■ Win32s   ■ Windows 95   ■ Windows NT

Description   WM_TCARD is a message that is sent to an application that has initiated a training card with Windows Help. The message informs the application when the user clicks an authorable button. An application initiates a training card by specifying the HELP_TCARD command in a call to WinHelp().

Parameters

wParam   WPARAM: One of the values in Table 11-60 indicating the action taken by the user.

Table 11-60 WM_TCARD *wParam* values

Value	Meaning
HELP_TCARD_DATA	The user clicked an authorable button. *lParam* contains a long integer specified by the Help author.
HELP_TCARD_NEXT	The user clicked an authorable Next button.
HELP_TCARD_OTHER_CALLER	Another application has requested training cards.
IDABORT	The user clicked an authorable Abort button.

continued on next page

continued from previous page

Value	Meaning
IDCANCEL	The user clicked an authorable Cancel button.
IDCLOSE	The user closed the training card.
IDHELP	The user clicked an authorable Windows Help button.
IDIGNORE	The user clicked an authorable Ignore button.
IDNO	The user clicked an authorable No button.
IDOK	The user clicked an authorable OK button.
IDRETRY	The user clicked an authorable Retry button.
IDYES	The user clicked an authorable Yes button.

lParam	LPARAM: If *wParam* specifies HELP_TCARD_DATA, *lParam* is a long integer specified by the Help author; otherwise, *lParam* is zero.
Returns	int: The return value is ignored; however, the application should return zero.
Include File	winuser.h
See Also	Winhelp()

WM_TIMECHANGE
■ Win32s ■ Windows 95 ■ Windows NT

Description	WM_TIMECHANGE is a message that is sent to all top-level windows after changing the system time. To send the WM_TIMECHANGE message to all top-level windows, an application can use SendMessage() with the *hwnd* parameter set to HWND_TOPMOST.
Parameters	This message does not use *wParam* or *lParam*; therefore, both must be set to zero.
Returns	int: An application should return zero if it processes this message.
Include File	winuser.h
See Also	SendMessage()

WM_TIMER
■ Win32s ■ Windows 95 ■ Windows NT

Description	WM_TIMER is a message that is posted to the installing thread's message queue or sent to the appropriate TimerProc() callback function after each interval specified by SetTimer() when installing a timer.
Parameters	
wParam	WPARAM: The timer identifier.
lParam	TIMEPROC *: A pointer to an application-defined callback function that was passed to SetTimer() when the timer was installed. If *lParam* is not NULL, Windows passes WM_TIMER to the specified callback function rather than posting the message to the thread's message queue.

Returns	int: An application should return zero if it processes this message.
Include File	winuser.h
See Also	DispatchMessage(), SetTimer(), TimerProc()

WM_UNDO　　　　　　　　■ Win32s　■ Windows 95　■ Windows NT

Description	WM_UNDO is a message that is sent to an edit control to undo the last operation. When this message is sent to an edit control, the previously deleted text is restored or the previously added text is deleted.
Parameters	This message does not use *wParam* or *lParam*; therefore, both must be set to zero.
Returns	BOOL: If successful, TRUE is returned; otherwise, FALSE is returned.
Include File	winuser.h
Related Messages	WM_CLEAR, WM_COPY, WM_CUT, WM_PASTE

WM_USER　　　　　　　　■ Win32s　■ Windows 95　■ Windows NT

| Description | WM_USER is a message that is used by applications to help define private messages. WM_USER uses the ranges in Table 11-61 to distinguish between message values that are reserved for use by Windows and values that can be used by an application to send messages within a private window class. |

Table 11-61　WM_USER ranges

Value	Meaning
0 through WM_USER -1	Messages reserved for use by Windows.
WM_USER through 0x7FFF	Integer messages for use by private window classes.
0x8000 through 0xBFFF	Messages reserved for future use by Windows.
0xC000 through 0xFFFF	String messages for use by applications.
Greater than 0xFFFF	Reserved by Windows for future use.

Parameters	This message does not use *wParam* or *lParam*; therefore, both must be set to zero.
Include File	winuser.h
See Also	RegisterWindowMessage()

WM_USERCHANGED　　　　　Win32s　■ Windows 95　　Windows NT

| Description | WM_USERCHANGED is a message that is sent to all windows after the user has logged on or off. When the user logs on or off, the system updates |

the user-specific settings. The system sends this message immediately after updating the settings.

Parameters	This message does not use *wParam* or *lParam*; therefore, both must be set to zero.
Returns	int: An application should return zero if it processes this message.
Include File	winuser.h

WM_VKEYTOITEM ■ Win32s ■ Windows 95 ■ Windows NT

Description	WM_VKEYTOITEM is a message that is sent by a list box with the LBS_WANTKEYBOARDINPUT style to its owner in response to a WM_KEYDOWN message. This message indicates the key pressed by the user and the location of the cursor when it was pressed.
Parameters	
LOWORD(wParam)	WORD: The virtual-key code of the key the user pressed.
HIWORD(wParam)	WORD: The current position of the caret.
lParam	LPARAM: The handle of the list box.
Returns	int: A value that specifies the action the application performed in response to the message is returned. A value of -2 indicates that the application handled all aspects of selecting the item and requires no further action by the list box. A value of -1 indicates that the list box should perform the default action in response to the keystroke. A value of 0 or greater specifies the index of an item in the list box and indicates that the list box should perform the default action for the keystroke on the given item.
Include File	winuser.h
See Also	DefWindowProc()
Related Messages	WM_CHARTOITEM, WM_KEYDOWN

WM_VSCROLL ■ Win32s ■ Windows 95 ■ Windows NT

Description	WM_VSCROLL is a message that is sent to a window when a scroll event occurs in the window's standard vertical scroll bar. This message is also sent to the owner of a vertical scroll bar control when a scroll event occurs in the control.
Parameters	
LOWORD(wParam)	int: One of the values in Table 11-30 indicating the scrolling request.
HIWORD(wParam)	short int: The current position of the scroll box if *LOWORD(wParam)* is SB_THUMBPOSITION or SB_THUMBTRACK; otherwise, *HIWORD(wParam)* is not used.
lParam	HWND: The handle of the control if WM_VSCROLL is sent by a scroll bar control. If WM_VSCROLL is sent by a window's standard scroll bar, *lParam* is not used.

Returns	int: An application should return zero if it processes this message.
Include File	winuser.h
See Also	GetScrollPos(), GetScrollRange(), SetScrollPos(), SetScrollRange()
Related Messages	WM_HSCROLL

WM_VSCROLLCLIPBOARD　　■ Win32s　■ Windows 95　■ Windows NT

Description	WM_VSCROLLCLIPBOARD is a message that is sent to the clipboard owner by a clipboard viewer window when the clipboard contains data in the CF_OWNERDISPLAY format and an event occurs in the clipboard viewer's vertical scroll bar. The owner should scroll the clipboard image and update the scroll bar values.
Parameters	
wParam	HWND: The handle of the clipboard viewer window.
LOWORD(*lParam*)	int: One of the values in Table 11-30 indicating the scroll bar event.
HIWORD(*lParam*)	int: The current position of the scroll box if LOWORD(*lParam*) is SB_THUMBPOSITION; otherwise, HIWORD(*lParam*) is not used.
Returns	int: An application should return zero if it processes this message.
Include File	winuser.h
See Also	ScrollWindow()

WM_WINDOWPOSCHANGED　　■ Win32s　■ Windows 95　■ Windows NT

Description	WM_WINDOWPOSCHANGED is a message that is sent to a window whose size, position, or place in the Z order has changed as a result of a call to SetWindowPos() or another window-management function.
Parameters	
wParam	WPARAM: Set to zero.
lParam	LPWINDOWPOS: A pointer to a WINDOWPOS structure that contains information about the window's new size and position.
Returns	int: An application should return zero if it processes this message.
Include File	winuser.h
See Also	DefWindowProc(), EndDeferWindowPos(), SetWindowPos()
Related Messages	WM_MOVE, WM_SIZE, WM_WINDOWPOSCHANGING

WM_WINDOWPOSCHANGING　　■ Win32s　■ Windows 95　■ Windows NT

| Description | WM_WINDOWPOSCHANGING is a message that is sent to a window whose size, position, or place in the Z order is about to change as a result of a call to SetWindowPos() or another window-management function. |

Parameters

wParam	WPARAM: Set to zero.
lParam	LPWINDOWPOS: A pointer to a WINDOWPOS structure that contains information about the window's new size and position.
Returns	int: An application should return zero if it processes this message.
Include File	winuser.h
See Also	DefWindowProc(), EndDeferWindowPos(), SetWindowPos()
Related Messages	WM_GETMINMAXINFO, WM_MOVE, WM_SIZE, WM_WINDOWPOSCHANGED

WOM_CLOSE ■ Win32s ■ Windows 95 ■ Windows NT

Description	WOM_CLOSE is a message that is sent to a waveform-audio output callback function when a waveform-audio output device is closed. The device handle is no longer valid after this message has been sent.
Parameters	This message does not use *dwParam1* or *dwParam2*; therefore both must be set to zero.
Include File	mmsystem.h

WOM_DONE ■ Win32s ■ Windows 95 ■ Windows NT

Description	WOM_DONE is a message that is sent to a waveform-audio output callback function when the given output buffer is being returned to the application. Buffers are returned to the application when they have been played, or as the result of a call to waveOutReset().
Parameters	
dwParam1	DWORD: The address of a WAVEHDR structure identifying the buffer.
dwParam2	DWORD: Set to zero.
Include File	mmsystem.h

WOM_OPEN ■ Win32s ■ Windows 95 ■ Windows NT

Description	WOM_OPEN is a message that is sent to a waveform-audio output callback function when a waveform-audio output device is opened.
Parameters	This message does not use *dwParam1* or *dwParam2*; therefore, both must be set to zero.
Include File	mmsystem.h

12

MACROS

12

MACROS

The Win32 API provides a selection of macros to help facilitate common conversions and utility activities. Macros appear to be the same as functions, but in reality they are identifiers that are replaced with code during compilation. For example, the HIWORD macro takes a 32-bit parameter in the same manner as a function. However, when the source code is compiled, HIWORD is replaced with its defined value. Listing 12-1 shows the conversion that takes place during compilation.

Listing 12-1 Macro example

```
WORD  wVal;
DWORD dwVal = 39289382;

// This line uses the HIWORD macro.
//..................................
wVal = HIWORD( dwVal );

// This line shows what HIWORD equates to.
//.........................................
wVal = (WORD)((dwVal >> 16) & 0xFFFF);
```

From this example, it is clear that macros simplify your code and increase its readability. Macros do not increase the overhead during runtime, because the macro is replaced with the appropriate code at compile time. In the above example, both lines of code are identical after the application is compiled.

This chapter provides descriptions of the common utility macros available in the Win32 API.

Macro Summary

Table 12-1 summarizes the common macros used in the Win32 API. The detailed macro descriptions follow after the table.

Table 12-1 Win32 API macros summary

Macro	Meaning
CMYK	Creates a CMYK color value by combining the specified values of cyan, magenta, yellow, and black.
FORWARD_WM_NOTIFY	Sends or posts a WM_NOTIFY message.
GetBValue	Retrieves the blue intensity value of a 32-bit RGB value.
GetCValue	Retrieves the cyan intensity value from a CMYK value.
GetGValue	Retrieves the green intensity value of a 32-bit RGB value.
GetKValue	Retrieves the black intensity value from a CMYK value.
GetMValue	Retrieves the magenta intensity value from a CMYK value.
GetRValue	Retrieves the red intensity value of a 32-bit RGB value.
GetYValue	Retrieves the yellow intensity value from a CMYK value.
HANDLE_WM_NOTIFY	Calls a function that processes the WM_NOTIFY message.
HIBYTE	Retrieves the high-order byte of a 16-bit value.
HIWORD	Retrieves the high-order word of a 32-bit value.
INDEXTOOVERLAYMASK	Prepares the index of an overlay mask to be used by ImageList_Draw().
INDEXTOSTATEIMAGEMASK	Prepares the index of a state image so that it can be used by a tree view or list view control to retrieve the state image.
LANGIDFROMLCID	Retrieves a language identifier from a locale identifier.
LOBYTE	Retrieves the low-order byte of a 16-bit value.
LOWORD	Retrieves the low-order word of a 32-bit value.
MAKEINTATOM	Creates an integer atom that represents a character string of decimal digits.
MAKEINTRESOURCE	Converts an integer value to a resource type compatible with Win32 resource-management functions.
MAKELANGID	Creates a language identifier.
MAKELCID	Creates a locale identifier from a language identifier.
MAKELONG	Concatenates two 16-bit values to create an unsigned 32-bit value.
MAKELPARAM	Concatenates two 16-bit values to create an unsigned 32-bit value to be used as the *lParam* parameter in a message.
MAKELRESULT	Concatenates two 16-bit values to create an unsigned 32-bit value to be used as the return value from a window procedure.
MAKEPOINTS	Converts a value containing the x and y coordinates of a point into a POINTS structure.
MAKEROP4	Creates a quaternary raster operation code for use with MaskBlt().
MAKEWORD	Concatenates two unsigned character values to create an unsigned 16-bit integer.
MAKEWPARAM	Concatenates two 16-bit values to create an unsigned 32-bit value to be used as the *wParam* parameter in a message.
max	Compares two values and returns the larger value.
MCI_HMS_HOUR	Retrieves the hours component from an HMS value.
MCI_HMS_MINUTE	Retrieves the minutes component from an HMS value.
MCI_HMS_SECOND	Retrieves the seconds component from an HMS value.

Macro	Meaning
MCI_MAKE_HMS	Creates an HMS time value from the specified hours, minutes, and seconds values.
MCI_MAKE_MSF	Creates an MSF time value from the specified minutes, seconds, and frames values.
MCI_MAKE_TMSF	Creates a TMSF time value from the specified tracks, minutes, seconds, and frames values.
MCI_MSF_FRAME	Retrieves the frames component from an MSF value.
MCI_MSF_MINUTE	Retrieves the minutes component from an MSF value.
MCI_MSF_SECOND	Retrieves the seconds component from an MSF value.
MCI_TMSF_FRAME	Retrieves the frames component from a TMSF value.
MCI_TMSF_MINUTE	Retrieves the minutes component from a TMSF value.
MCI_TMSF_SECOND	Retrieves the seconds component from a TMSF value.
MCI_TMSF_TRACK	Retrieves the tracks component from a TMSF value.
MEVT_EVENTPARM	Retrieves the event parameters or length from the *dwEvent* member of a MIDIEVENT structure.
MEVT_EVENTTYPE	Retrieves the event type from the *dwEvent* member of a MIDIEVENT structure.
min	Compares two values and returns the smaller value.
PALETTEINDEX	Specifies the 32-bit COLORREF value of the color associated with the specified index.
PALETTERGB	Creates an RGB specifier from the relative intensities values of red, green, and blue.
POINTSTOPOINT	Copies the contents of a POINTS structure into a POINT structure.
POINTTOPOINTS	Converts a POINT structure to a POINTS structure.
PRIMARYLANGID	Extracts the primary language identifier from a language identifier.
RGB	Selects an RGB color based on the supplied arguments and the color capabilities of the output device.
SORTIDFROMLCID	Retrieves a sort identifier from a locale identifier.
SUBLANGID	Extracts the sublanguage identifier from a language identifier.
TEXT	Identifies a string as Unicode when the UNICODE compile flag is used or as an ANSI string when Unicode is not defined.

CMYK

Win32s ■ **Windows 95** **Windows NT**

Description	CMYK is a macro that creates a CMYK color value by combining the specified values of cyan, magenta, yellow, and black.
Syntax	COLORREF **CMYK**(BYTE *c*, BYTE *m*, BYTE *y*, BYTE *k*)
Parameters	
c	BYTE: The intensity of the color cyan.
m	BYTE: The intensity of the color magenta.
y	BYTE: The intensity of the color yellow.
k	BYTE: The intensity of the color black.
Include File	wingdi.h
See Also	GetCValue, GetMValue, GetKValue, GetYValue

FORWARD_WM_NOTIFY
Win32s ■ Windows 95 ■ Windows NT

Description	FORWARD_WM_NOTIFY is a macro that sends or posts a WM_NOTIFY message.
Syntax	VOID **FORWARD_WM_NOTIFY**(HWND *hwnd*, UINT *idfrom*, LPNMHDR *pnmhdr*, VOID * *fn*)
Parameters	
hwnd	HWND: The window handle of the window that receives the WM_NOTIFY message.
idFrom	UINT: The control identifier sending the message.
pnmhdr	LPNMHDR: A pointer to an NMHDR structure that contains the notification code and additional information for the WM_NOTIFY message. For some notification messages, *pnmhdr* points to a larger structure with the NMHDR structure as its first member. Refer to the definition of the NMHDR structure below.
fn	VOID *: The function that sends or posts the WM_NOTIFY message. This parameter can be either the SendMessage() or PostMessage() function.
Returns	LRESULT/BOOL: A value based on the *fn* parameter is returned. The return type is LRESULT if *fn* is set to the SendMessage() function. The return type is BOOL if *fn* is set to the PostMessage() function.

NMHDR Definition

```
typedef struct tagNMHDR
{
    HWND hwndFrom;
    UINT idFrom;
    UINT code;
} NMHDR;
```

Members	
hwndFrom	HWND: The handle of the control sending message.
idFrom	UINT: The identifier of control sending message.
code	UINT: The notification code. This is a control-specific notification code.

Include File	commctrl.h
See Also	SendMessage(), PostMessage(), HANDLE_WM_NOTIFY
Related Messages	WM_NOTIFY

GetBValue
Win32s ■ Windows 95   Windows NT

Description	GetBValue is a macro that retrieves the blue intensity value of a 32-bit RGB (red, green, and blue) value.
Syntax	BYTE **GetBValue**(COLORREF *rgb*)

Parameters	
rgb	COLORREF: An RGB color value.
Returns	BYTE: The blue intensity value of the specified RGB value is returned.
Include File	wingdi.h
See Also	GetGValue, GetRValue, PALETTEINDEX, PALETTERGB, RGB

GetCValue

Description	GetCValue is a macro that retrieves the cyan intensity value from a CMYK (cyan, magenta, yellow, and black) value.
Syntax	BYTE **GetCValue**(COLORREF *cmyk*)
Parameters	
cmyk	COLORREF: A CMYK color value.
Returns	BYTE: The cyan intensity value of the specified CMYK value is returned.
Include File	wingdi.h
See Also	CMYK, GetKValue, GetMValue, GetYValue

GetGValue

Description	GetGValue is a macro that retrieves the green intensity value of a 32-bit RGB (red, green, and blue) value.
Syntax	BYTE **GetGValue**(COLORREF *rgb*)
Parameters	
rgb	COLORREF: An RGB color value.
Returns	BYTE: The green intensity value of the specified RGB value is returned.
Include File	wingdi.h
See Also	GetBValue, GetRValue, PALETTEINDEX, PALETTERGB, RGB

GetKValue

Description	GetKValue is a macro that retrieves the black intensity value from a CMYK (cyan, magenta, yellow, and black) value.
Syntax	BYTE **GetKValue**(COLORREF *cmyk*)
Parameters	
cmyk	COLORREF: A CMYK color value.
Returns	BYTE: The black intensity value of the specified CMYK value is returned.
Include File	wingdi.h
See Also	CMYK, GetCValue, GetMValue, GetYValue

GetMValue

Description	GetMValue is a macro that retrieves the magenta intensity value from a CMYK (cyan, magenta, yellow, and black) value.
Syntax	BYTE **GetMValue**(COLORREF *cmyk*)
Parameters	
cmyk	COLORREF: A CMYK color value.
Returns	BYTE: The magenta intensity value of the given specified value is returned.
Include File	wingdi.h
See Also	CMYK, GetCValue, GetKValue, GetYValue

GetRValue

Description	GetRValue is a macro that retrieves the red intensity value of a 32-bit RGB (red, green, and blue) value.
Syntax	BYTE **GetRValue**(COLORREF *rgb*)
Parameters	
rgb	COLORREF: An RGB color value.
Returns	BYTE: The red intensity value of the specified RGB value is returned.
Include File	wingdi.h
See Also	GetBValue, GetGValue, PALETTEINDEX, PALETTERGB, RGB

GetYValue

Description	GetYValue is a macro that retrieves the yellow intensity value from a CMYK (cyan, magenta, yellow, and black) value.
Syntax	BYTE **GetYValue**(COLORREF *cmyk*)
Parameters	
cmyk	COLORREF: A CMYK color value.
Returns	BYTE: The yellow intensity value of the specified CMYK value is returned.
Include File	wingdi.h
See Also	CMYK, GetCValue, GetKValue, GetMValue

HANDLE_WM_NOTIFY

Description	HANDLE_WM_NOTIFY is a macro that calls a function to process the WM_NOTIFY message.
Syntax	LRESULT **HANDLE_WM_NOTIFY**(HWND *hwnd*, WPARAM *wParam*, LPNMHDR *lParam*, VOID * *fn*)

Parameters

hwnd HWND: The window handle of the window that received the WM_NOTIFY message.

wParam WPARAM: The first parameter of the WM_NOTIFY message. This parameter identifies the control sending the message.

lParam LPNMHDR: The second parameter of the WM_NOTIFY message. This is a pointer to an NMHDR structure that contains the notification code and additional information about the message. See the definition of the NMHDR structure under the FORWARD_WM_NOTIFY macro.

fn VOID *: A pointer to the function that processes the WM_NOTIFY message. The function must have the following form:

Function(HWND *hwnd*, WPARAM *wParam*, LPNMHDR *lpnmhdr*)

Returns LRESULT: The value returned from the application-supplied function.

Include File commctrl.h

See Also FORWARD_WM_NOTIFY

Related Messages WM_NOTIFY

HIBYTE
■ **Win32s** ■ **Windows 95** ■ **Windows NT**

Description HIBYTE is a macro that retrieves the high-order byte from a 16-bit value.

Syntax BYTE **HIBYTE**(WORD *wValue*)

Parameters

wValue WORD: The 16-bit value from which to retrieve the high-order byte.

Returns BYTE: The high-order byte is returned.

Include File windef.h

See Also HIWORD, LOBYTE

HIWORD
■ **Win32s** ■ **Windows 95** ■ **Windows NT**

Description HIWORD is a macro that retrieves the high-order word from a 32-bit value.

Syntax WORD **HIWORD**(DWORD *dwValue*)

Parameters

dwValue DWORD: The 32-bit value from which to retrieve the high-order word.

Returns WORD: The high-order word is returned.

Include File windef.h

See Also HIBYTE, LOWORD

INDEXTOOVERLAYMASK
Win32s ■ Windows 95 ■ Windows NT

Description	INDEXTOOVERLAYMASK is a macro that prepares the index of an overlay mask so that ImageList_Draw() can use it. For more information on image lists, refer to Chapter 5, Image Lists.
Syntax	UINT **INDEXTOOVERLAYMASK**(UINT *uIndex*)
Parameters	
uIndex	UINT: The index of the overlay mask.
Include File	commctrl.h
See Also	ImageList_Draw()

INDEXTOSTATEIMAGEMASK
Win32s ■ Windows 95 ■ Windows NT

Description	INDEXTOSTATEIMAGEMASK is a macro that prepares the index of a state image so that a tree view control or list view control can use it to retrieve the state image for an item. For more information on list views refer to Chapter 6, List View and Drag List. For more information on tree views, refer to Chapter 7, Tree View.
Syntax	UINT **INDEXTOSTATEIMAGEMASK**(UINT *uIndex*)
Parameters	
uIndex	UINT: The index of the state image of an item.
Include File	commctrl.h

LANGIDFROMLCID
■ Win32s ■ Windows 95 ■ Windows NT

Description	LANGIDFROMLCID is a macro that retrieves a language identifier from a locale identifier.
Syntax	WORD **LANGIDFROMLCID**(LCID *lcid*)
Parameters	
lcid	LCID: The locale identifier.
Returns	WORD: The language identifier is returned.
Include File	winnt.h
See Also	MAKELANGID, MAKELCID, PRIMARYLANGID, SUBLANGID

LOBYTE
■ Win32s ■ Windows 95 ■ Windows NT

Description	LOBYTE is a macro that retrieves the low-order byte from a 16-bit value.
Syntax	BYTE **LOBYTE**(WORD *wValue*)
Parameters	
wValue	WORD: The 16-bit value from which to retrieve the low-order byte.

Returns	BYTE: the low-order byte of the value is returned.	
Include File	windef.h	
See Also	HIBYTE, LOWORD	

LOWORD ■ Win32s ■ Windows 95 ■ Windows NT

Description	LOWORD is a macro that retrieves the low-order word from a 32-bit value.
Syntax	WORD **LOWORD**(DWORD *dwValue*)
Parameters	
dwValue	DWORD: The 32-bit value from which to retrieve the low-order word.
Returns	WORD: The low-order word of the value is returned.
Include File	windef.h
See Also	HIWORD, LOBYTE

MAKEINTATOM ■ Win32s ■ Windows 95 ■ Windows NT

Description	MAKEINTATOM is a macro that creates an integer atom that represents a character string of decimal digits. Use the AddAtom() or GlobalAddAtom() functions to add integer atoms created by the MAKEINTATOM macro.
Syntax	LPTSTR **MAKEINTATOM**(WORD *wInteger*)
Parameters	
wInteger	WORD: The numeric value to be converted into an integer atom.
Returns	LPTSTR: A pointer to the atom created for the integer value is returned. Be aware that this value can only be used as a string pointer when it is passed to atom-management functions that require an LPTSTR argument.
Include File	winbase.h
See Also	AddAtom(), DeleteAtom(), GetAtomName(), GlobalAddAtom(), GlobalDeleteAtom(), GlobalGetAtomName()

MAKEINTRESOURCE ■ Win32s ■ Windows 95 ■ Windows NT

Description	MAKEINTRESOURCE is a macro that converts an integer value to a resource type compatible with Win32 resource-management functions. This macro is used in place of a string containing the name of the resource.
Syntax	LPTSTR **MAKEINTRESOURCE**(WORD *wInteger*)
Parameters	
wInteger	WORD: The integer value to be converted.

| Returns | LPTSTR: The specified value is returned in the low-order word and zero is returned in the high-order word. This value should only be passed to Win32 resource-management functions. |
| Include File | winuser.h |

MAKELANGID ■ Win32s ■ Windows 95 ■ Windows NT

| Description | MAKELANGID is a macro that creates a language identifier from a primary language identifier and a sublanguage identifier. |
| Syntax | WORD **MAKELANGID**(USHORT *usPrimaryLanguage*, USHORT *usSubLanguage*) |

Parameters

| *usPrimaryLanguage* | USHORT: Either a user-defined primary language value in the range 0x0200 to 0x03FF, or one of the values in Table 12-2. |

Table 12-2 MAKELANGID *usPrimaryLanguage* values

Value	Meaning
LANG_AFRIKAANS	Only available in Windows 95. Afrikaans.
LANG_ALBANIAN	Only available in Windows 95. Albanian.
LANG_ARABIC	Only available in Windows 95. Arabic.
LANG_BASQUE	Only available in Windows 95. Basque.
LANG_BULGARIAN	Bulgarian.
LANG_BYELORUSSIAN	Only available in Windows 95. Byelorussian.
LANG_CATALAN	Only available in Windows 95. Catalan.
LANG_CHINESE	Chinese.
LANG_CROATIAN	Croatian.
LANG_CZECH	Czech.
LANG_DANISH	Danish.
LANG_DUTCH	Dutch.
LANG_ENGLISH	English.
LANG_ESTONIAN	Only available in Windows 95. Estonian.
LANG_FINNISH	Finnish.
LANG_FRENCH	French.
LANG_GERMAN	German.
LANG_GREEK	Greek.
LANG_HEBREW	Only available in Windows 95. Hebrew.
LANG_HUNGARIAN	Hungarian.
LANG_ICELANDIC	Icelandic.
LANG_INDONESIAN	Only available in Windows 95. Indonesian.
LANG_ITALIAN	Italian.

Value	Meaning
LANG_JAPANESE	Japanese.
LANG_KOREAN	Korean.
LANG_LATVIAN	Only available in Windows 95. Latvian.
LANG_LITHUANIAN	Only available in Windows 95. Lithuanian.
LANG_NEUTRAL	Neutral.
LANG_NORWEGIAN	Norwegian.
LANG_POLISH	Polish.
LANG_PORTUGUESE	Portuguese.
LANG_ROMANIAN	Romanian.
LANG_RUSSIAN	Russian.
LANG_SLOVAK	Slovak.
LANG_SLOVENIAN	Slovenian.
LANG_SORBIAN	Only available in Windows 95. Sorbian.
LANG_SPANISH	Spanish.
LANG_SWEDISH	Swedish.
LANG_TURKISH	Turkish.
LANG_THAI	Only available in Windows 95. Thai.
LANG_UKRAINIAN	Only available in Windows 95. Ukrainian.

usSubLanguage   USHORT: Either a user-defined sublanguage value in the range 0x20 to 0x3F, or one of the values in Table 12-3.

Table 12-3 MAKELANGID *usSubLanguage* values

Value	Meaning
SUBLANG_CHINESE_HONGKONG	Chinese spoken in Hong Kong.
SUBLANG_CHINESE_SIMPLIFIED	Simplified Chinese.
SUBLANG_CHINESE_SINGAPORE	Chinese spoken in Singapore.
SUBLANG_CHINESE_TRADITIONAL	Traditional Chinese.
SUBLANG_DEFAULT	Combined with LANG_NEUTRAL specifies a user default language.
SUBLANG_DUTCH	Dutch.
SUBLANG_DUTCH_BELGIAN	Dutch spoken in Belgium.
SUBLANG_ENGLISH_AUS	English spoken in Australia.
SUBLANG_ENGLISH_CAN	English spoken in Canada.
SUBLANG_ENGLISH_EIRE	English spoken in Ireland.
SUBLANG_ENGLISH_NZ	English spoken in New Zealand.
SUBLANG_ENGLISH_UK	English spoken in the United Kingdom.
SUBLANG_ENGLISH_US	English spoken in the United States of America.
SUBLANG_FRENCH	French.

continued on next page

continued from previous page

Value	Meaning
SUBLANG_FRENCH_BELGIAN	French spoken in Belgium.
SUBLANG_FRENCH_CANADIAN	French spoken in Canada.
SUBLANG_FRENCH_SWISS	French spoken in Switzerland.
SUBLANG_GERMAN	German.
SUBLANG_GERMAN_AUSTRIAN	German spoken in Austria.
SUBLANG_GERMAN_SWISS	German spoken in Switzerland.
SUBLANG_ITALIAN	Italian.
SUBLANG_ITALIAN_SWISS	Italian spoken in Switzerland.
SUBLANG_NEUTRAL	Combined with LANG_NEUTRAL specifies language neutral.
SUBLANG_NORWEGIAN_BOKMAL	Literary form of Norwegian based on gradual reform of written Danish.
SUBLANG_NORWEGIAN_NYNORSK	Literary form of Norwegian based on spoken dialects of Norway.
SUBLANG_PORTUGUESE	Portuguese.
SUBLANG_PORTUGUESE_BRAZILIAN	Portuguese spoken in Brazil.
SUBLANG_SPANISH	Spanish.
SUBLANG_SPANISH_MEXICAN	Spanish spoken in Mexico.
SUBLANG_SPANISH_MODERN	Modern Spanish.
SUBLANG_SYS_DEFAULT	Combined with LANG_NEUTRAL specifies system default language.

Returns	WORD: A language identifier that can be used with the FindResouceEx() and EnumResLangProc() functions is returned.
Include File	winnt.h
See Also	EnumResLangProc(), FindResourceEx(), LANGIDFROMLCID, MAKELCID, PRIMARYLANGID, SUBLANGID

MAKELCID ■ Win32s ■ Windows 95 ■ Windows NT

Description	MAKELCID is a macro that creates a locale identifier from a language identifier.
Syntax	DWORD **MAKELCID**(WORD *wLanguageID*, WORD *wSortID*)
Parameters	
wLanguageID	WORD: The language identifier. This value is a combination of the primary language and sublanguage identifiers and is usually created using the MAKELANGID macro.
wSortID	WORD: The sort identifier. Use SORT_DEFAULT as the value for this parameter.
Returns	DWORD: The locale identifier is returned.
Include File	winnt.h
See Also	LANGIDFROMLCID, MAKELANGID, SORTIDFROMLCID

MAKELONG ■ Win32s ■ Windows 95 ■ Windows NT

Description	MAKELONG is a macro that creates an unsigned 32-bit value by concatenating two specified 16-bit values.
Syntax	DWORD **MAKELONG**(WORD *wLow*, WORD *wHigh*)
Parameters	
wLow	WORD: The low-order word of the new 32-bit value.
wHigh	WORD: The high-order word of the new 32-bit value.
Returns	DWORD: An unsigned 32-bit value is returned.
Include File	windef.h
See Also	MAKELPARAM

MAKELPARAM ■ Win32s ■ Windows 95 ■ Windows NT

Description	MAKELPARAM is a macro that concatenates two 16-bit values to create an unsigned 32-bit value to be used as the *lParam* parameter in a message.
Syntax	LPARAM **MAKELPARAM**(WORD *wLow*, WORD *wHigh*)
Parameters	
wLow	WORD: The low-order word of the new 32-bit value.
wHigh	WORD: The high-order word of the new 32-bit value.
Returns	LPARAM: An unsigned 32-bit value is returned.
Include File	winuser.h
See Also	MAKELONG, MAKELRESULT, MAKEWPARAM

MAKELRESULT ■ Win32s ■ Windows 95 ■ Windows NT

Description	MAKELRESULT is a macro that concatenates two 16-bit values to create an unsigned 32-bit value for use as a return value from a window procedure.
Syntax	LRESULT **MAKELRESULT**(WORD *wLow*, WORD *wHigh*)
Parameters	
wLow	WORD: The low-order word of the 32-bit value.
wHigh	WORD: The high-order word of the 32-bit value.
Returns	LRESULT: An unsigned 32-bit value is returned.
Include File	winuser.h
See Also	MAKELONG, MAKELPARAM, MAKEWPARAM

MAKEPOINTS   ■ Win32s   ■ Windows 95   ■ Windows NT

Description	MAKEPOINTS is a macro that converts a value that contains the x and y coordinates of a point in the low-order and high-order words into a POINTS structure.
Syntax	POINTS **MAKEPOINTS**(DWORD *dwValue*)

Parameters

dwValue	DWORD: The coordinates of a point. The x coordinate is in the low-order word, and the y coordinate is in the high-order word.
Returns	POINTS: A POINTS structure containing the x and y coordinates of a point is returned. See the definition of the POINTS structure below.

POINTS Definition

```
typedef struct tagPOINTS
{
    SHORT x;
    SHORT y;
} POINTS;
```

Members

x	SHORT: The x coordinate of the point.
y	SHORT: The y coordinate of the point.
Include File	wingdi.h
See Also	GetMessagePos()

MAKEROP4   ■ Win32s   ■ Windows 95   ■ Windows NT

Description	MAKEROP4 is a macro that creates a quaternary raster operation code for use with MaskBlt(). The macro takes two ternary raster operation codes as input, one for the foreground and one for the background, and packs their Boolean operation indexes into the high-order word of a 32-bit value. The low-order word of this value will be ignored.
Syntax	DWORD **MAKEROP4**(DWORD *fore*, DWORD *back*)

Parameters

fore	DWORD: A foreground ternary raster operation code.
back	DWORD: A background ternary raster operation code.
Returns	DWORD: A quaternary raster operation code for use with MaskBlt() is returned.
Include File	wingdi.h
See Also	MaskBlt()

MAKEWORD
■ Win32s ■ Windows 95 ■ Windows NT

Description	MAKEWORD is a macro that creates an unsigned 16-bit integer by concatenating two unsigned byte values.
Syntax	WORD **MAKEWORD**(BYTE *bLow*, BYTE *bHigh*)
Parameters	
bLow	BYTE: The low-order byte of the new 16-bit value.
bHigh	BYTE: The high-order byte of the new 16-bit value.
Returns	WORD: An unsigned 16-bit integer value is returned.
Include File	windef.h

MAKEWPARAM
■ Win32s ■ Windows 95 ■ Windows NT

Description	MAKEWPARAM is a macro that concatentates two 16-bit values to create an unsigned 32-bit value to be used as the *wParam* parameter in a message.
Syntax	WPARAM **MAKEWPARAM**(WORD *wLow*, WORD *wHigh*)
Parameters	
wLow	WORD: The low-order word of the new 32-bit value.
wHigh	WORD: The high-order word of the new 32-bit value.
Returns	WPARAM: An unsigned 32-bit value is returned.
Include File	winuser.h
See Also	MAKELONG, MAKELPARAM, MAKELRESULT

MAX
Win32s ■ Windows 95 ■ Windows NT

Description	max is a macro that compares two values and returns the larger value. The data type can be any numeric data type, signed or unsigned. The data type of the arguments and the return value is the same.
Syntax	**max**(*value1*, *value2*)
Parameters	
value1	The first of the two values to be compared.
value2	The second of the two value to be compared.
Returns	The largest of the two specified values is returned.
Include File	windef.h
See Also	min

MCI_HMS_HOUR
■ Win32s ■ Windows 95 ■ Windows NT

Description	MCI_HMS_HOUR is a macro that retrieves the hours component from a parameter containing hours/minutes/seconds (HMS) information.
Syntax	BYTE **MCI_HMS_HOUR**(DWORD *dwHMS*)
Parameters	
dwHMS	DWORD: The time in HMS format. The least significant byte contains the hours, the next least significant byte contains the minutes, and the next least significant byte contains the seconds. The most significant byte is not used.
Returns	BYTE: The hours component of the value specified by *dwHMS* is returned.
Include File	mmsystem.h
See Also	MCI_HMS_MINUTE, MCI_HMS_SECOND, MCI_MAKE_HMS

MCI_HMS_MINUTE
■ Win32s ■ Windows 95 ■ Windows NT

Description	MCI_HMS_MINUTE is a macro that retrieves the minutes component from a parameter containing hours/minutes/seconds (HMS) information.
Syntax	BYTE **MCI_HMS_MINUTE**(DWORD *dwHMS*)
Parameters	
dwHMS	DWORD: The time in HMS format. The least significant byte contains the hours, the next least significant byte contains the minutes, and the next least significant byte contains the seconds. The most significant byte is not used.
Returns	BYTE: The minutes component of the value specified by *dwHMS* is returned.
Include File	mmsystem.h
See Also	MCI_HMS_HOUR, MCI_HMS_SECOND, MCI_MAKE_HMS

MCI_HMS_SECOND
■ Win32s ■ Windows 95 ■ Windows NT

Description	MCI_HMS_SECOND is a macro that retrieves the seconds component from a parameter containing hours/minutes/seconds (HMS) information.
Syntax	BYTE **MCI_HMS_SECOND**(DWORD *dwHMS*)
Parameters	
dwHMS	DWORD: The time in HMS format. The least significant byte contains the hours, the next least significant byte contains the minutes, and the next least significant byte contains the seconds. The most significant byte is not used.
Returns	BYTE: The seconds component of the value specified by *dwHMS* is returned.
Include File	mmsystem.h
See Also	MCI_HMS_MINUTE, MCI_HMS_HOUR, MCI_MAKE_HMS

MCI_MAKE_HMS   ■ Win32s   ■ Windows 95   ■ Windows NT

Description	MCI_MAKE_HMS is a macro that creates a time value in a packed hours/minutes/seconds (HMS) format from the specified hours, minutes, and seconds values.
Syntax	DWORD **MCI_MAKE_HMS**(BYTE *hours*, BYTE *minutes*, BYTE *seconds*)
Parameters	
hours	BYTE: The number of hours.
minutes	BYTE: The number of minutes.
seconds	BYTE: The number of seconds.
Returns	DWORD: The time is returned in HMS format. The least significant byte contains the hours, the next least significant byte contains minutes, and the next least significant byte contains the seconds. The most significant byte is not used.
Include File	mmsystem.h
See Also	MCI_HMS_HOUR, MCI_HMS_MINUTE, MCI_HMS_SECOND

MCI_MAKE_MSF   ■ Win32s   ■ Windows 95   ■ Windows NT

Description	MCI_MAKE_MSF is a macro that creates a time value in a packed minutes/seconds/frames (MSF) format from the specified minutes, seconds, and frames values.
Syntax	DWORD **MCI_MAKE_MSF**(BYTE *minutes*, BYTE *seconds*, BYTE *frames*)
Parameters	
minutes	BYTE: The number of minutes.
seconds	BYTE: The number of seconds.
frames	BYTE: The number of frames.
Returns	DWORD: The time is returned in MSF format. The least significant byte contains the minutes, the next least significant byte contains seconds, and the next least significant byte contains the frames. The most significant byte is not used.
Include File	mmsystem.h
See Also	MCI_MAKE_HMS, MCI_MAKE_TMSF, MCI_MSF_FRAME

MCI_MAKE_TMSF   ■ Win32s   ■ Windows 95   ■ Windows NT

Description	MCI_MAKE_TMSF is a macro that creates a time value in a packed tracks/minutes/seconds/frames (TMSF) format from the specified tracks, minutes, seconds, and frames values.
Syntax	DWORD **MCI_MAKE_TMSF**(BYTE *tracks*, BYTE *minutes*, BYTE *seconds*, BYTE *frames*)

Parameters

tracks	BYTE: The number of tracks.
minutes	BYTE: The number of minutes.
seconds	BYTE: The number of seconds.
frames	BYTE: The number of frames.
Returns	DWORD: The time is returned in TMSF format. The least significant byte contains the tracks, the next least significant byte contains minutes, the next least significant byte contains the seconds, and the most significant byte contains the frames.
Include File	mmsystem.h
See Also	MCI_MAKE_HMS, MCI_MAKE_MSF, MCI_TMSF_FRAME, MCI_TMSF_MINUTE, MCI_TMSF_SECOND, MCI_TMSF_TRACK

MCI_MSF_FRAME   ■ Win32s   ■ Windows 95   ■ Windows NT

Description	MCI_MSF_FRAME is a macro that retrieves the frames component from a parameter containing minutes/seconds/frames (MSF) information.
Syntax	BYTE **MCI_MSF_FRAME**(DWORD *dwMSF*)
Parameters	
dwMSF	DWORD: The time in MSF format. The least significant byte contains the minutes, the next least significant byte contains the seconds, and the next least significant byte contains the frames. The most significant byte is not used.
Returns	BYTE: The frames component of the value specified by *dwMSF* is returned.
Include File	mmsystem.h
See Also	MCI_MAKE_MSF, MCI_MSF_MINUTE, MCI_MSF_SECOND

MCI_MSF_MINUTE   ■ Win32s   ■ Windows 95   ■ Windows NT

Description	MCI_MSF_MINUTE is a macro that retrieves the minutes component from a parameter containing minutes/seconds/frames (MSF) information.
Syntax	BYTE **MCI_MSF_MINUTE**(DWORD *dwMSF*)
Parameters	
dwMSF	DWORD: The time in MSF format. The least significant byte contains the minutes, the next least significant byte contains the seconds, and the next least significant byte contains the frames. The most significant byte is not used.
Returns	BYTE: The minutes component of the value specified by *dwMSF* is returned.
Include File	mmsystem.h
See Also	MCI_MAKE_MSF, MCI_MSF_FRAME, MCI_MSF_SECOND

MCI_MSF_SECOND
■ Win32s ■ Windows 95 ■ Windows NT

Description	MCI_MSF_SECOND is a macro that retrieves the seconds component from a parameter containing minutes/seconds/frames (MSF) information.
Syntax	BYTE **MCI_MSF_SECOND**(DWORD *dwMSF*)
Parameters	
dwMSF	DWORD: The time in MSF format. The least significant byte contains the minutes, the next least significant byte contains the seconds, and the next least significant byte contains the frames. The most significant byte is not used.
Returns	BYTE: The seconds component of the value specified by *dwMSF* is returned.
Include File	mmsystem.h
See Also	MCI_MAKE_MSF, MCI_MSF_FRAME, MCI_MSF_MINUTE

MCI_TMSF_FRAME
■ Win32s ■ Windows 95 ■ Windows NT

Description	MCI_TMSF_FRAME is a macro that retrieves the frames component from a parameter containing tracks/minutes/seconds/frames (TMSF) information.
Syntax	BYTE **MCI_TMSF_FRAME**(DWORD *dwTMSF*)
Parameters	
dwTMSF	DWORD: The time in TMSF format. The least significant byte contains the tracks, the next least significant byte contains the minutes, the next least significant byte contains the seconds, and the most significant byte contains the frames.
Returns	BYTE: The frames component of the value specified by *dwTMSF* is returned.
Include File	mmsystem.h
See Also	MCI_MAKE_TMSF, MCI_TMSF_MINUTE, MCI_TMSF_SECOND, MCI_TMSF_TRACK

MCI_TMSF_MINUTE
■ Win32s ■ Windows 95 ■ Windows NT

Description	MCI_TMSF_MINUTE is a macro that retrieves the minutes component from a parameter containing tracks/minutes/seconds/frames (TMSF) information.
Syntax	BYTE **MCI_TMSF_MINUTE**(DWORD *dwTMSF*)
Parameters	
dwTMSF	DWORD: The time in TMSF format. The least significant byte contains the tracks, the next least significant byte contains the minutes, the next least

significant byte contains the seconds, and the most significant byte contains the frames.

Returns   BYTE: The minutes component of the value specified by *dwTMSF* is returned.

Include File   mmsystem.h

See Also   MCI_MAKE_TMSF, MCI_TMSF_FRAME, MCI_TMSF_SECOND, MCI_TMSF_TRACK

MCI_TMSF_SECOND   ■ Win32s   ■ Windows 95   ■ Windows NT

Description   MCI_TMSF_SECOND is a macro that retrieves the seconds component from a parameter containing tracks/minutes/seconds/frames (TMSF) information.

Syntax   BYTE **MCI_TMSF_SECOND**(DWORD *dwTMSF*)

Parameters

dwTMSF   DWORD: The time in TMSF format. The least significant byte contains the tracks, the next least significant byte contains the minutes, the next least significant byte contains the seconds, and the most significant byte contains the frames.

Returns   BYTE: The seconds component of the value specified by *dwTMSF* is returned.

Include File   mmsystem.h

See Also   MCI_MAKE_TMSF, MCI_TMSF_MINUTE, MCI_TMSF_FRAME, MCI_TMSF_TRACK

MCI_TMSF_TRACK   ■ Win32s   ■ Windows 95   ■ Windows NT

Description   MCI_TMSF_TRACK is a macro that retrieves the tracks component from a parameter containing tracks/minutes/seconds/frames (TMSF) information.

Syntax   BYTE **MCI_TMSF_TRACK**(DWORD *dwTMSF*)

Parameters

dwTMSF   DWORD: The time in TMSF format. The least significant byte contains the tracks, the next least significant byte contains the minutes, the next least significant byte contains the seconds, and the most significant byte contains the frames.

Returns   BYTE: The tracks component of the value specified by *dwTMSF* is returned.

Include File   mmsystem.h

See Also   MCI_MAKE_TMSF, MCI_TMSF_MINUTE, MCI_TMSF_SECOND, MCI_TMSF_FRAME

MEVT_EVENTPARM ■ Win32s ■ Windows 95 ■ Windows NT

Description	MEVT_EVENTPARM is a macro that retrieves the event parameters or length from the value specified in the *dwEvent* member of a MIDIEVENT structure.
Syntax	DWORD **MEVT_EVENTPARM**(DWORD *dwEvent*)
Parameters	
dwEvent	DWORD: The code for the MIDI event and the event parameters or length as specified in the *dwEvent* member of the MIDIEVENT structure. See the definition of the MIDIEVENT structure below.
Returns	DWORD: The event parameters or length of the MIDI event is returned.
Include File	mmsystem.h
See Also	MEVT_EVENTTYPE

MIDIEVENT Definition

```
typedef struct
{
    DWORD dwDeltaTime;
    DWORD dwStreamID;
    DWORD dwEvent;
    DWORD dwParms[];
} MIDIEVENT;
```

Members

dwDeltaTime	DWORD: The time, in MIDI ticks, between the previous event and the current event. The length of a tick is defined by the time format and possibly the tempo associated with the stream.
dwEvent	DWORD: The event code and event parameters or length. Use the MEVT_EVENTTYPE and MEVT_EVENTPARM macros to parse this information.

> The high byte of this member contains one or more of the flags listed in Table 12-4 and an event code from Table 12-5.
>
> Either MEVT_F_LONG or MEVT_F_SHORT flag must be specified, but MEVT_F_CALLBACK flag is optional.

Table 12-4 MIDIEVENT Flags

Value	Meaning
MEVT_F_CALLBACK	The system generates a callback when the event is about to be executed.
MEVT_F_LONG	The event is a long event. The low 24-bits of *dwEvent* contains the length of the event parameters.
MEVT_F_SHORT	The event is a short event. The event parameters are contained in the low 24-bits of *dwEvent*.
MEVT_COMMENT	(Long event) This event is intended to store commentary information about the stream. The event data will be ignored.

continued on next page

continued from previous page

Value	Meaning
MEVT_LONGMSG	(Long event) The event data is assumed to be system-exclusive data and is transmitted verbatim. The running status will be cleared when the event is executed and running status from any previous events will not be applied to any channel events in the event data.
MEVT_NOP	(Short event) This event does nothing and is simply a placeholder.
MEVT_SHORTMSG	(Short event) The low 24-bits of the *dwEvent* is a MIDI short message.
MEVT_TEMPO	(Short event) The low 24-bits of the *dwEvent* contains the new tempo in microseconds per quarter note.
MEVT_VERSION	(Long event) The event data must contain a MIDISTRMBUFFVER structure which is defined below.

dwParms DWORD: Parameters for the event, if *dwEvent* specifies the MEVT_F_LONG flag and the length of the buffer. This parameter data must be padded with zeros so that an integral number of double-word values are stored or double-word aligned. For example, if the event is five bytes long, three pad bytes must follow the data for a total of eight bytes. In this case, the low 24 bits of *dwEvent* would contain the value 5.

MIDISTRMBUFFVER Definition

```
typedef struct
{
    DWORD dwVersion;
    DWORD dwMid;
    DWORD dwOEMVersion;
} MIDISTRMBUFFVER;
```

Members

dwVersion DWORD: The version of the stream. The high-word contains the major version, and the low-word contains the minor version.

dwMid DWORD: The manufacturer identifier.

dwOEMVersion DWORD: The OEM version of the stream. Original equipment manufacturers can use this field to version-stamp any custom events they have specified. If a custom event is specified, it must be the first event sent after the stream is opened.

MEVT_EVENTTYPE ■ Win32s ■ Windows 95 ■ Windows NT

Description MEVT_EVENTTYPE is a macro that retrieves the event type from the value specified in the *dwEvent* member of a MIDIEVENT structure.

Syntax DWORD **MEVT_EVENTTYPE**(DWORD *dwEvent*)

Parameters

dwEvent DWORD: The code for the MIDI event and the event parameters or length as specified in the *dwEvent* member of the MIDIEVENT structure. See the definition of the MIDIEVENT structure under the MEVT_EVENTPARM macro.

Returns	DWORD: The event type of the MIDI event is returned.
Include File	mmsystem.h
See Also	MEVT_EVENTPARM

MIN   ■ Win32s   ■ Windows 95   ■ Windows NT

Description	min is a macro that compares two values and returns the smaller value. The data type can be any numeric data type, signed or unsigned. The data type of the arguments and the return value is the same.
Syntax	**min**(*value1*, *value2*)
Parameters	
value1	The first of the two values to be compared.
value2	The second of the two values to be compared.
Returns	The smallest of the two specified values is returned.
Include File	windef.h
See Also	max

PALETTEINDEX   ■ Win32s   ■ Windows 95   ■ Windows NT

Description	PALETTEINDEX is a macro that accepts an index to a logical-color palette entry and returns a palette-entry specifier consisting of a 32-bit COLORREF value that identifies the color associated with the specified index. An application using a logical-color palette can pass this specifier, instead of an explicit red, green, blue (RGB) value, to GDI functions that expect a color.
Syntax	COLORREF **PALETTEINDEX**(WORD *wPaletteIndex*)
Parameters	
wPaletteIndex	WORD: The index of the palette entry containing the color to be used for a graphics operation.
Returns	COLORREF: A logical-palette index specifier is returned.
Include File	wingdi.h
See Also	COLORREF, PALETTERGB, RGB

PALETTERGB   ■ Win32s   ■ Windows 95   ■ Windows NT

Description	PALETTERGB is a macro that accepts the relative intensities values of red, green, and blue and returns a palette-relative red, green, blue (RGB) specifier consisting of 2 in the high-order byte and an RGB value in the three low-order bytes. An application using a color palette can pass this specifier, instead of an explicit RGB value, to functions that expect a color.

Syntax	COLORREF **PALETTERGB**(BYTE *bRed*, BYTE *bGreen*, BYTE *bBlue*)
Parameters	
bRed	BYTE: The intensity of the red color field.
bGreen	BYTE: The intensity of the green color field.
bBlue	BYTE: The intensity of the blue color field.
Returns	COLORREF: A palette-relative RGB specifier is returned.
Include File	wingdi.h
See Also	PALETTEINDEX, RGB

POINTSTOPOINT ■ Win32s ■ Windows 95 ■ Windows NT

Description	POINTSTOPOINT is a macro that copies the contents of a POINTS structure into a POINT structure.
Syntax	**POINTSTOPOINT**(POINT *pt*, POINTS *pts*)
Parameters	
pt	POINT: The POINT structure that receives the contents of the specified POINTS structure. See the definition of the POINT structure below.
pts	POINTS: The POINTS structure to copy. See the definition of the POINTS structure under the MAKEPOINTS macro.
POINT Definition	

```
typedef struct tagPOINT
  {
      LONG x;
      LONG y;
  } POINT;
```

Members	
x	LONG: The x coordinate of the point.
y	LONG: The y coordinate of the point.
Include File	winuser.h
See Also	MAKEPOINTS, POINTTOPOINTS

POINTTOPOINTS ■ Win32s ■ Windows 95 ■ Windows

Description	POINTTOPOINTS is a macro that converts a POINT structure to a POINTS structure.
Syntax	POINTS **POINTTOPOINTS**(POINT *pt*)
Parameters	
pt	POINT: The POINT structure to convert. See the definition of the POINT structure under the POINTSTOPOINT macro.
Returns	POINTS: A POINTS structure is returned. See the definition of the POINTS structure under the MAKEPOINTS macro.

| Include File | winuser.h |
| See Also | MAKEPOINTS, POINTSTOPOINT |

PRIMARYLANGID   ■ Win32s   ■ Windows 95   ■ Windows NT

Description	PRIMARYLANGID is a macro that extracts a primary language identifier from a language identifier.
Syntax	WORD **PRIMARYLANGID**(WORD *lgid*)
Parameters	
lgid	WORD: This value is a combination of a primary language identifier and a sublanguage identifier that is usually created using the MAKELANGID macro.
Returns	WORD: A value from Table 12-2 indicating the primary language identifier is returned.
Include File	winnt.h
See Also	LANGIDFROMLCID, MAKELANGID, SUBLANGID

RGB   ■ Win32s   ■ Windows 95   ■ Windows NT

Description	RGB is a macro that selects a red, green, blue (RGB) color based on the arguments supplied and the color capabilities of the output device. The intensity of each argument is in the range of 0 through 255. If all three intensities are zero, the result is black. If all three intensities are 255, the result is white.
Syntax	COLORREF **RGB** (BYTE *bRed*, BYTE *bGreen*, BYTE *bBlue*)
Parameters	
bRed	BYTE: The intensity of the red color.
bGreen	BYTE: The intensity of the green color.
bBlue	BYTE: The intensity of the blue color.
Returns	COLORREF: The resultant RGB color based on the values of *bRed*, *bGreen*, and *bBlue* is returned.
Include File	wingdi.h
See Also	PALETTEINDEX, PALETTERGB

SORTIDFROMLCID   ■ Win32s   ■ Windows 95   ■ Windows NT

| Description | SORTIDFROMLCID is a macro that retrieves a sort identifier from a locale identifier. |
| Syntax | WORD **SORTIDFROMLCID**(LCID *lcid*) |

Parameters

lcid　　　　　　　　　LCID: The locale identifier. This parameter may have been created using the MAKELCID macro.

Returns　　　　　　WORD: One of the sort identifiers in Table 12-6 is returned.

Table 12-5 SORTIDFROMLCID return values

Value	Meaning
SORT_CHINESE_BIG5	Chinese BIG5 order
SORT_CHINESE_UNICODE	Chinese Unicode order
SORT_DEFAULT	The default sort identifier
SORT_JAPANESE_UNICODE	Japanese Unicode order
SORT_JAPANESE_XJIS	Japanese XJIS order
SORT_KOREAN_KSC	Korean KSC order
SORT_KOREAN_UNICODE	Korean Unicode order

Include File　　　　winnt.h

See Also　　　　　　MAKELANGID, MAKELCID, PRIMARYLANGID, SUBLANGID

SUBLANGID ■ Win32s ■ Windows 95 ■ Windows NT

Description　　　　SUBLANGID is a macro that extracts a sublanguage identifier from a language identifier.

Syntax　　　　　　WORD **SUBLANGID**(WORD *lgid*)

Parameters

lgid　　　　　　　　WORD: This value is a combination of a primary language identifier and a sublanguage identifier that is usually created using the MAKELANGID macro.

Returns　　　　　　WORD: A value in Table 12-3 indicating the sublanguage identifier is returned.

Include File　　　　winnt.h

See Also　　　　　　LANGIDFROMLCID, MAKELANGID, PRIMARYLANGID

TEXT ■ Win32s ■ Windows 95 ■ Windows NT

Description　　　　TEXT is a macro that identifies a string as Unicode when the UNICODE compile flag is used or as an ANSI string when Unicode is not defined.

Syntax　　　　　　**TEXT**(LPTSTR *string*)

Parameters

string　　　　　　　LPTSTR: The string to be interpreted as either Unicode or ANSI.

Include File　　　　winnt.h

A

APPENDIX

Companion Volumes

This book's two companion volumes, *Windows 95 Win32 Programming API Bible* and *Windows 95 Multimedia and ODBC API Bible,* complete the comprehensive programmer's reference. These thorough compendiums cover all Win32 APIs common to Windows 95 and Windows NT. Descriptions, summaries, example programs, and a CD with all the source code demonstrate the proper variables and syntax. To give you a better idea of the companion books' contents, here are their Tables of Contents:

Windows 95 Win32 Programming API Bible (Book 1)

Windows 95 Multimedia and ODBC API Bible (Book 3)

Part I: Open Database Connectivity (ODBC)

Part II: Telephony API

Part III: Common Messaging Calls (CMC)

Part IV: Multimedia

INDEX

messages *(continued)*
 trackbar control, 479
 tree view, 415-420, 799-801. *See* TVN *under* messages
 up-down control, 535, 803. *See* UDN *under* messages
 wizard, 193, 246-247, 769. *See* PSN_WIZ *under* messages

O

OLE, 446, 457, 469, 661, 670, 677
orientation, 886
overlay images, 295
overlay masks, 253, 288, 916
owner-drawn header control, 481-482
owner-drawn parts, 79
owner-drawn tabs, 189

P

page, dialog, 187-188
page orientation, 886
page setup, 54-58
page size, 884-886
paper size, 884-885
parent-child, tree view, 369, 371
parts, owner-drawn, 79
parts, status window, 79, 95-97, 102-103, 769-770
print, page setup, 54-58
print, printer setup, 58-67
progress bar, 5, 11, 479-480
 messages, 511-514, 764. *See* PBM *under* messages
progress control. *See* progress bar
property sheet, 5, 8-9, 188-193
 functions, 195-225
 messages, 193, 243-247, 765-769. *See* PSM *and* PSN *under* messages
 pages, 190-192
 wizard. *See* wizard

R

raster operation macro, 922
registered messages, 17-18
RGB value macros, 912-914, 931-933
rich-text edit control, 6, 10-11, 423-426
 messages, 425-473, 656-679. *See* EM *and* EN *under* messages
 styles, 423-424
right-to-left reading order, 91, 98, 104, 156, 178-179, 196, 200, 234, 498

S

scroll bar messages, 771-773. *See* SBM *under* messages
scroll box. *See* slider
size grip, 79, 84
slider, 477-479, 516-525, 663, 771-772, 783-786
static control messages, 774-776. *See* STM *and* STN *under* messages
status bar. *See* status window
status text, 90-92, 98-100, 103-104
status window, 5, 7, 73, 78-80, 83-85
 help, 92-95
 messages, 95-106, 769-770. *See* SB *under* messages
 parts, 79, 95-97, 102-103, 769-770
 simple mode, 80, 104-106, 770
 size, 79, 100-102
 style, SBARS_SIZEGRIP, 79, 84
structures
 CHARFORMAT, 441-443
 CHARRANGE, 433
 CHOOSECOLOR, 19-22
 CHOOSEFONT, 24-28
 COLORMAP, 83
 COMPCOLOR, 445
 CONVCONTEXT, 561-562
 CONVINFO, 607-609
 DDEML_MSG_HOOK_DATA, 596
 DEVMODE, 56, 60
 DEVNAMES, 56, 60, 63-64
 DRAGLISTINFO, 358-359

Books have a substantial influence on the destruction of the forests of the Earth. For example, it takes 17 trees to produce one ton of paper. A first printing of 30,000 copies of a typical 480-page book consumes 108,000 pounds of paper, which will require 918 trees!

Waite Group Press™ is against the clear-cutting of forests and supports reforestation of the Pacific Northwest of the United States and Canada, where most of this paper comes from. As a publisher with several hundred thousand books sold each year, we feel an obligation to give back to the planet. We will therefore support organizations that seek to preserve the forests of planet Earth.

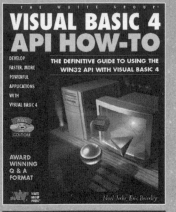

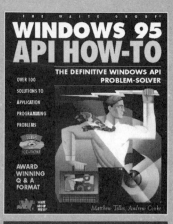
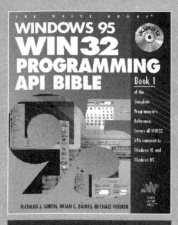

This is a legal agreement between you, the end user and purchaser, and The Waite Group®, Inc., and the authors of the programs contained in the disk. By opening the sealed disk package, you are agreeing to be bound by the terms of this Agreement. If you do not agree with the terms of this Agreement, promptly return the unopened disk package and the accompanying items (including the related book and other written material) to the place you obtained them for a refund.

SOFTWARE LICENSE

1. The Waite Group, Inc. grants you the right to use one copy of the enclosed software programs (the programs) on a single computer system (whether a single CPU, part of a licensed network, or a terminal connected to a single CPU). Each concurrent user of the program must have exclusive use of the related Waite Group, Inc. written materials.

2. The program, including the copyrights in each program, is owned by the respective author and the copyright in the entire work is owned by The Waite Group, Inc. and they are therefore protected under the copyright laws of the United States and other nations, under international treaties. You may make only one copy of the disk containing the programs exclusively for backup or archival purposes, or you may transfer the programs to one hard disk drive, using the original for backup or archival purposes. You may make no other copies of the programs, and you may make no copies of all or any part of the related Waite Group, Inc. written materials.

3. You may not rent or lease the programs, but you may transfer ownership of the programs and related written materials (including any and all updates and earlier versions) if you keep no copies of either, and if you make sure the transferee agrees to the terms of this license.

4. You may not decompile, reverse engineer, disassemble, copy, create a derivative work, or otherwise use the programs except as stated in this Agreement.

GOVERNING LAW

This Agreement is governed by the laws of the State of California.

LIMITED WARRANTY

The following warranties shall be effective for 90 days from the date of purchase: (i) The Waite Group, Inc. warrants the enclosed disk to be free of defects in materials and workmanship under normal use; and (ii) The Waite Group, Inc. warrants that the programs, unless modified by the purchaser, will substantially perform the functions described in the documentation provided by The Waite Group, Inc. when operated on the designated hardware and operating system. The Waite Group, Inc. does not warrant that the programs will meet purchaser's requirements or that operation of a program will be uninterrupted or error-free. The program warranty does not cover any program that has been altered or changed in any way by anyone other than The Waite Group, Inc. The Waite Group, Inc. is not responsible for problems caused by changes in the operating characteristics of computer hardware or computer operating systems that are made after the release of the programs, nor for problems in the interaction of the programs with each other or other software.

THESE WARRANTIES ARE EXCLUSIVE AND IN LIEU OF ALL OTHER WARRANTIES OF MERCHANTABILITY OR FITNESS FOR A PARTICULAR PURPOSE OR OF ANY OTHER WARRANTY, WHETHER EXPRESS OR IMPLIED.

EXCLUSIVE REMEDY

The Waite Group, Inc. will replace any defective disk without charge if the defective disk is returned to The Waite Group, Inc. within 90 days from date of purchase.

This is Purchaser's sole and exclusive remedy for any breach of warranty or claim for contract, tort, or damages.

LIMITATION OF LIABILITY

THE WAITE GROUP, INC. AND THE AUTHORS OF THE PROGRAMS SHALL NOT IN ANY CASE BE LIABLE FOR SPECIAL, INCIDENTAL, CONSEQUENTIAL, INDIRECT, OR OTHER SIMILAR DAMAGES ARISING FROM ANY BREACH OF THESE WARRANTIES EVEN IF THE WAITE GROUP, INC. OR ITS AGENT HAS BEEN ADVISED OF THE POSSIBILITY OF SUCH DAMAGES.

THE LIABILITY FOR DAMAGES OF THE WAITE GROUP, INC. AND THE AUTHORS OF THE PROGRAMS UNDER THIS AGREEMENT SHALL IN NO EVENT EXCEED THE PURCHASE PRICE PAID.

COMPLETE AGREEMENT

This Agreement constitutes the complete agreement between The Waite Group, Inc. and the authors of the programs, and you, the purchaser.

Some states do not allow the exclusion or limitation of implied warranties or liability for incidental or consequential damages, so the above exclusions or limitations may not apply to you. This limited warranty gives you specific legal rights; you may have others, which vary from state to state.